Material Life in America, 1600–1860

Material Life in America, 1600–1860

edited by Robert Blair St. George

Northeastern University Press   Boston

The illustrations on the cover are used courtesy of Cary
Carson and Chinh Hoang; the National Gallery of Art; The
Metropolitan Museum of Art, Harris Brisbane Dick Fund;
and the Lowell Historical Society.

Northeastern University Press

Library of Congress Cataloging in Publication Data

Material life in America, 1600–1860.

   Bibliography: p.
   Includes index.
   1. Material culture—United States. 2. United States—
Social life and customs—Colonial period, ca. 1600–1775.
3. United States—Social life and customs—1783–1865.
I. St. George, Robert Blair.
E161.M36   1987   973.2   87-16197
ISBN 1-55553-019-2 (alk. paper)
ISBN 1-55553-020-6 (pbk. : alk. paper)

Designed by David Ford.
Composed in Trump Medieval by Graphic Composition,
Athens, Georgia. Printed and bound by Murray Printing
Co., Westford, Massachusetts.
The paper is Glatfelter Offset, an acid-free sheet.

MANUFACTURED IN THE UNITED STATES OF AMERICA
93 92 91 90 89   5 4 3 2

"The mere smell of cooking can evoke a whole civilisation."

—FERNAND BRAUDEL

Contents

Contents

Contents

Acknowledgments

As this collection turned from my imagination into tangible pages filled with printed words and images, I have been the grateful recipient of good counsel and helpful assistance from many friends and colleagues. First and foremost, I am indebted to David D. Hall, who first suggested this project to me and encouraged its pursuit. Pondering the complexities of material culture and its relationship to other fields of social and intellectual history is a pursuit that David and I occasionally share, and this collection of essays is stronger for advice he at times unknowingly gave. Other colleagues at Boston University were generous in conversation, lending me their time and ideas while this volume took shape. Richard M. Candee and Thomas F. Glick offered observations and suggestions about America's technological history, and a few chats with Patricia Hills supported my interest in trying to link aesthetic dimensions of the landscape to shifting power relations in society at large. I am indebted also to James A. Henretta and J. Ritchie Garrison, whose constructive comments helped bring the goals of this volume into clearer focus. Alice Gray Read offered her insightful criticism during the volume's planning stages, and her wonderful sense of humor at key points during its completion.

I feel especially fortunate to have been able to work with the staff of the Northeastern University Press. Deborah Kops, Bill Frohlich, and Ann Twombly offered their constant support and constructive criticism. For assistance with old and new illustrations, I am indebted to: Bernard L. Herman of the University of Delaware; Deborah Dependahl Waters at the Museum of the City of New York; Bernard C. Reilly, Pat Dempsey, and Ford Peatross at the Library of Congress; Pat Malone and Ruth Macaulay at the Slater Mill Historic Site; Marcy Karp at the Metropolitan Museum of Art; Lacy Dicks at the Valentine Museum; Susan Mosely at the Georgia Department of Archives and History; Barbara Isaac at the Peabody Museum's Photographic Archives; John Hench and Audrey T. Zook at the American Antiquarian Society; Carl Lounsbury and Graham Hood at The Colonial Williamsburg Foundation; Kathryn Haywood at the University of North Carolina Press; Len Tucker and Ross Urquhart at the Massachusetts Historical Society; Cindy Stone at Old South Meeting House, Inc.; Mary Lou Neighbour and John Williams at Hagley Museum/Eleutherian Mills; Martha Mayo at the Lydon Library, University of Lowell; Lawrence Gross at the Museum of American Textile History; Cammie Naylor at The New-York Historical Society; Ken Finkel at the Library Company of Philadelphia; Emery Channing at Penn Center, St. Helena Island, S.C.; Robert F. Trent at The Connecticut Historical Society; Philip Zea at Historic Deerfield, Inc.; and the staffs of the Institute of Early American History and Culture, the Wadsworth Atheneum, The Historical Society of Pennsylvania, Panopticon, Inc., and Yale University Art Gallery.

No collection of essays can exist without the generosity of its contributing authors. Part of the pleasure of assembling this collection was getting to know better scholars whose work I have long admired and found useful in teaching. To those individuals who have generously lent their efforts to this volume—a task which for some meant rereading work already a decade or more old—I am very grateful.

Robert Blair St. George
Ipswich, Massachusetts

The editor and Northeastern University Press are indebted to the publications in which the essays in this collection first appeared. In most instances, the articles in this volume appear as they were originally published. Some, however, have had subsequent revisions added by the author(s) or editor, or have been slightly abridged. The essay by John L. Brooke appears in English for the first time in this volume.

Thomas Bender, "The 'Rural' Cemetery Movement: Urban Travail and the Appeal of Nature," *New England Quarterly* 47 (1974): 196–211. Reprinted by permission of the editor of the *New England Quarterly*.

Betsy Blackmar, "Re-walking the 'Walking City': Housing and Property Relations in New York City, 1780–1840," *Radical History Review* 21 (Fall 1979): 131–48. Reprinted by permission of the editors of *Radical History Review.* Copyright © 1979 by MARHO, the Radical Historians' Organization.

Cary Carson, Norman F. Barka, William M. Kelso, Garry Wheeler Stone, and Dell Upton, "Impermanent Architecture in the Southern American Colonies," *Winterthur Portfolio* 16, no. 2/3 (1981): 135–78. Reprinted by permission of The University of Chicago Press.

Clifford E. Clark, Jr., "Domestic Architecture as an Index to Social History: The Romantic Revival and the Cult of Domesticity in America, 1840–1870," *Journal of Interdisciplinary History* 7, no. 1 (1976): 33–56. Reprinted by permission of the editors of the *Journal of Interdisciplinary History* and the MIT Press, Cambridge, Massachusetts. Copyright © 1976 by The Massachusetts Institute of Technology and the editors of the *Journal of Interdisciplinary History.*

Susan G. Davis, "The Career of Colonel Pluck: Folk Drama and Popular Protest in Early Nineteenth-Century Philadelphia," *Pennsylvania Magazine of History and Biography* 109, no. 2 (1985): 179–202. Reprinted by permission of the editor of the *Pennsylvania Magazine of History and Biography* and The Historical Society of Pennsylvania, Philadelphia.

Robert J. Dinkin, "Seating the Meeting House in Early Massachusetts," *New England Quarterly* 43 (1970): 450–64. Reprinted by permission of the editor of the *New England Quarterly.*

Henry Glassie, "Meaningful Things and Appropriate Myths: The Artifact's Place in American Studies," *Prospects* 3 (1977): 1–49. Reprinted by permission of the editor of *Prospects* and the Syndics of Cambridge University Press, New York.

Robert A. Gross, "Culture and Cultivation: Agriculture and Society in Thoreau's Concord," *Journal of American History* 69, no. 1 (1982): 42–61. Reprinted by permission of the Organization of American Historians, Bloomington, Indiana, and the editor of the *Journal of American History.*

Sam B. Hilliard, "Hog Meat and Cornpone: Food Habits in the Antebellum South," *Proceedings of the American Philosophical Society* 113, no. 1 (1969): 1–13. Reprinted by permission of the American Philosophical Society, Philadelphia, Pennsylvania; and, in extending this essay for the present volume, Southern Illinois University Press for permission to reprint: Sam Bowers Hilliard, *Hog Meat and Hoecake: Food Supply in the Old South, 1840–1860* (Carbondale: Southern Illinois University Press, 1972), 56–69.

Rhys Isaac, "Ethnographic Method in History: An Action Approach," *Historical Methods* 13, no. 1 (1980): 43–61.

By permission of the editor of *Historical Methods.* Copyright © 1980 by *Historical Methods,* a publication of the Helen Dwight Read Educational Fund.

Gary Kulik, "Pawtucket Village and the Strike of 1824: The Origins of Class Conflict in Rhode Island," *Radical History Review* 17 (Spring 1978): 5–35. Reprinted by permission of the editors of *Radical History Review.* Copyright © 1978 by MARHO, the Radical Historians' Organization.

Russell R. Menard, Lois Green Carr, and Lorena S. Walsh, "A Small Planter's Profits: The Cole Estate and the Growth of the Early Chesapeake Economy," *William and Mary Quarterly,* 3d ser., 40 (1983): 171–96.

James H. Merrell, "The Indians' New World: The Catawba Experience," *William and Mary Quarterly,* 3d ser., 41 (1984): 537–65.

Philip D. Morgan, "Work and Culture: The Task System and the World of Lowcountry Blacks, 1700–1880," *William and Mary Quarterly,* 3d ser., 39 (1982): 563–99.

Jules David Prown, "Mind in Matter: An Introduction to Material Culture Theory and Method," *Winterthur Portfolio* 17, no. 1 (1982): 1–19. Reprinted by permission of The University of Chicago Press.

A. G. Roeber, "Authority, Law, and Custom: The Rituals of Court Day in Tidewater Virginia, 1720–1750," *William and Mary Quarterly,* 3d ser., 37 (1980): 29–53.

Rodris Roth, "Tea-Drinking in 18th-Century America: Its Etiquette and Equipage," *Contributions from the Museum of History and Technology, United States National Museum Bulletin* 225, paper no. 14 (Washington, D.C.: Smithsonian Institution, 1961): 61–91. Reprinted by permission of the Smithsonian Institution Press.

Robert Blair St. George, "Artifacts of Regional Consciousness in the Connecticut River Valley, 1700–1780," in *The Great River: Art and Society of the Connecticut Valley, 1635–1820,* eds. William N. Hosley, Jr., and Gerald W. R. Ward (Hartford: Wadsworth Atheneum, 1985), pp. 29–40. Reprinted by permission of the Wadsworth Atheneum, Hartford, Connecticut.

Marylynn Salmon, "Women and Property in South Carolina: The Evidence from Marriage Settlements, 1730–1830," *William and Mary Quarterly,* 3d ser., 39 (1982): 655–85.

Billy G. Smith, "The Material Lives of Laboring Philadelphians, 1750–1800," *William and Mary Quarterly,* 3d ser., 38 (1981): 163–202.

Kevin M. Sweeney, "Furniture and the Domestic Environment in Wethersfield, Connecticut, 1639–1800," *Connecticut Antiquarian* 36, no. 2 (1984): 10–39. Reprinted by permission of Antiquarian and Landmarks Society, Incorporated, Hartford, Connecticut.

Dell Upton, "White and Black Landscapes of Eighteenth-Century Virginia," *Places* 2, no. 2 (1985): 59–72. Reprinted by permission of the editors of *Places* and the MIT Press, Cambridge, Massachusetts. Copyright © 1985 by The Massachusetts Institute of Technology and the editors of *Places.*

Melvin Wade, "'Shining in Borrowed Plumage': Affirmation of Community in the Black Coronation Festivals of New England (c. 1750–c. 1850)," *Western Folklore* 40, no. 3 (1981): 211–31. Reprinted by permission of the editor of *Western Folklore.*

Joseph S. Wood, "Village and Community in Early Colonial New England," *Journal of Historical Geography* 8, no. 4 (1982): 333–46. Reprinted by permission of the editor of the *Journal of Historical Geography* and Academic Press, Inc. (London), Ltd., Sidcup, Kent, England. Copyright © 1982 by Academic Press, Inc. (London), Ltd., and the editors of the *Journal of Historical Geography.*

Material Life in America,
1600–1860

Introduction

ROBERT BLAIR ST. GEORGE

When I was eight years old, my mother gave me a book entitled *Fair Is Our Land,* a magnificent collection of photographs and etchings of the American landscape edited by Samuel Chamberlain. Childhood nights disappeared as I immersed myself in seemingly unending panoramas of Iowa cornfields, rocky Maine fishing villages, and log cabins perched in the Appalachian foothills. Seen with adult eyes, the images remain masterful evocations of place and human feeling: Farm Security Administration photographs taken by Marion Post Wolcott, Ewing Galloway, and Frances Benjamin Johnston, drypoints and lithographs by Stow Wengenroth, Childe Hassam, and Chamberlain himself.[1] Arrow-straight rows left by a combine cutting its way through miles of Kansas wheat, the bucolic order of a sleepy New England town common, the puzzling, earthen geometry of the deserted Anasazi village at Mesa Verde—these vistas suggest that the silent drama of America's material environment captured a complicated fusion of hope and labor, of aspiration and tragedy, in the lives of people whose actions seldom ripple history's surface. Yet troubling questions immediately appear. What was the confrontation between American Indians and the expansionist policies of European empires really like? How did the "consumer revolution" actually affect the daily lives and fashions of eighteenth-century Philadelphians? Why did Thoreau warn his acquisitive neighbors that they might soon feel themselves possessed by their own property? How, in fact, does language shape our understanding of objects? These worries converge in a single, more simple concern. How fair, after all, *was* our land?

The twenty-five essays in this volume explore these and other issues by focusing on material life in America between the initial years of European settlement and the Civil War. What is *material life*? It is a term with a complex intellectual genealogy that means, in general terms, a history more about daily routine than about exceptional deeds, more about common houses, fences, and fields than about country estates and Copley portraits, and as much about the lives of poor men and women as about their rich neighbors. The study of American material life is grounded in the concrete, interwoven reality of men's and women's environmental, economic, and cultural circumstances. As it was first conceived by the French historian Fernand Braudel, its meaning was clear. Material life is the bedrock stratum of economic life, the basis of all power derived from the elaboration and acceleration of commodity exchange. At issue in the study of material life, he maintained, "is growth in the economy of the *ancien régime.*"[2] Yet in America, "material life" remains a metaphor, its meaning imprecise. It is often used as a synonym of "material culture" and, more recently, of "material history." To clarify the utility of material life as a paradigm for American cultural studies we need to reassess carefully the place of material life in Braudel's thought.

Braudel imagined the progress of the economic growth that transformed social life in Western Europe—no less in Paris or London than in their Atlantic colonies—in three interlocking planes: "material life," "market economy," and "capitalism." Of these, material life is the most basic, enduring, and universal. In opening his *Capitalism and Material Life, 1400–1800,* Braudel defined his approach in a way that seems consistent with the broader aims of this volume:

Braudel's def. of material life

The expression material life will . . . denote repeated actions, empirical processes, old methods and solutions handed down from time immemorial, like money or the separation of town and country. It is an elementary life but is neither entirely passive nor, above all, completely static. It has moments of acceleration and occasionally of surprise: new plants become acclimatised, techniques improve and spread, changes occur in processes employed by blacksmiths, weavers, and, still more, by miners and shipbuilders. These changes take place slowly but steadily. Money and towns play a continually increasing part and some innovations are of decisive importance.[3]

Material life, in other words, spans an impressive range of social relations and owes its being to the force of "traditional" knowledge realized through familiar rhythms of work and leisure. So conceived, it emerges as a cycle of routine that "predominates at the level of everyday life." But precisely because it is so familiar, we commonly fail to recognize its power or feel its presence. Material life is an "enormous mass of history barely conscious of itself" that can provide the alert historian with a concrete index to "the life that man throughout the course of his previous history has made a part of his very being, has in some way absorbed into his entrails, turning the experiments and exhilarating experiences of the past into everyday, banal necessities."[4] Material life devours novelty and reproduces it as domesticated commonality. Material life is a totalizing force.

Yet material life cannot be studied in romantic isolation. Its meaning can be examined only in the context of the two systems of exchange relations to which it is historically connected: the market economy and capitalism. In Braudel's works, the three are described as interdependent parts of an overall *structure*. If material life is the base of all economic life, then the next level—the market economy—represented in his view a level of everyday existence that takes in a wider geographic sphere and demands some attention to calculation in regulating nearby trade networks. The market economy is distinct from material life not only because it covers more territory but because "it is born of trade, transport, differentiated market structures, and of contact between already industrialized countries and those still primitive or underdeveloped, between rich and poor, creditors and borrowers, monetary and pre-monetary economies." It is, Braudel admitted, "already almost a system in itself."[5] Capitalism, the third and highest level, involves long-distance trade and extensive calculation among merchants able to control the flow of currency, the availability of credit, and the function of markets. Unlike the muscle and human tissue that bind together material life and the market economy, capitalism is a "mechanism, which encroaches on all forms of life, whether economic or material, however little they lend themselves to its manoeuvres."[6] Braudel conceived these three levels in Marxist terms—a material "base" that in turn supported "superstructures" of greater and greater economic and, finally, cultural complexity.

The metaphor that Braudel used to describe his economic edifice will seem comforting and familiar to students of American material culture who use this book: a house. At its foundation lay the constant, enduring tension between poverty and luxury that enlivened social life and sparked change. Its ground floor was material life, the level affected most directly by what was happening immediately beneath it. Up in the first story was the market economy. Capitalism occupied the chambers in the second story, that heady realm of mobility and adaptability where, once the attainment of superfluity had been won through struggles taking place in the floors below, spiritual life, art, and genteel learning could flourish. In the penthouse, the house's ultimate "superstructure" (the word is Braudel's) were the great European market fairs of the sixteenth and seventeenth centuries, where exchange in both commodities and identity merged in carnivalesque rituals of social inversion. At this height, the market became theater.[7]

The house is a useful vernacular metaphor in other ways. As one rises in the house from foundation to penthouse, rates of change in historical time alter dramatically. While the foundation is by definition constant, the ground floor of material life is slow to change. It is the *longue durée* of French historical time, its structural relations inflexible, almost immovable. The pace of first-floor activity quickens as traders ply their wares with known customers in face-to-face encounters. Values here are readily apparent; exchanges are transparent in that personal relations are known and their outcomes predictable. Capitalism's second story is an arena of rapid change, constant transformation, fluidity, adaptability, and illusion. Yet as one climbs the narrow stairs in this house, other qualities emerge as well. Material life is the terrain, Braudel claimed, of "the *unconscious daily round*."[8] It follows that the market economy, with its reliance on face-to-face encounters and personal relations, is a realm where economic self-awareness is constantly emerging, where its subtle contours are shaped and tested by common transactions. Capitalism, in its emphasis on planning, detailed advanced calculations, and risk-taking, makes one acutely aware of the limits of economic activity it constantly seeks to extend. If Marx built the first metaphorical house that Braudel has guided us through, then surely Freud made some major restorations, adding layers extending from the immovable, unconscious depths to the heights of conscious awareness framed by limitation and expansion.

Still other metaphoric structures support this intellectual mansion. Material life persists longest and is most visible among the poor on the world's "periphery," while capitalism is most vibrant at the "core" of large, populated towns—Amsterdam, Paris, London—where wealth concentrates amid the bustle of dockworkers, carters, warehouse hands, and confident merchants. Moving from the outside in, each ring has a qualitatively different concept of history. The "vast and structural history" of material life yields to an inner series of "conjunctures" and "economic crises" in the market economy, while a history celebrating "great actors and great events" dominates the central, collective mythology of capitalism.[9]

Ground floors, upper chambers, and garrets are fragments of a playful language that gives shape to complex ideas. It was through such language that Braudel both exposed the limits of his own economic edifice and suggested paths for future research. He was always unsure of his terminology; the three levels of economic life he outlined were problematic, their boundaries fluid, their definitions unresolved. They were, after all, intended to make sense of global change. Looking back in the mid-1970s, Braudel worried about the difficulty of finding a discourse that could convey at once the structural complexity and ethnographic detail he imagined. "Material life," he felt, was evocative yet imprecise because its meanings extended wildly in all directions. "Capitalism" was even more problematic. On one hand, he advocated its ahistorical use to describe economic relations in the sixteenth and seventeenth centuries. He felt that while this was tantamount to letting the "wolf into the sheepfold," it was nonetheless permissible because "there is no adequate substitute for this word, and that fact alone is symptomatic." On the other hand, like material life, its reality as an economic system was by no means linked to any one set of relations. We say "capitalism," Braudel admitted, "but what capitalism? Capitalism is protean, a hydra with a hundred heads."[10] We, too, need to be mindful of the language we use. When we use the term *material life* in this volume, it implies at once not only long-term processes of work and domestic life but also the way those processes are conditioned at

higher levels by the market economy and capitalism. Law, ritual protests, institutional structure, and arguments about the moral reformation of tradition interact at all levels.

If we examine Braudel's language more closely, difficulties arise less over his stratigraphy of exchange relations than in his particularly difficult conception of how "primitive" society, "culture," and "civilization" are related. Writing from Paris, Braudel was sure of civilization. It was all around him in the markets, the restaurants, the opera. Civilization was the aesthetic region where cuisine merged into art, where costume swept the eye and mind away in a rush of seductive style. It was, more profoundly, "a category of history, consequently a necessary classification" of economic activity that had only emerged in Europe with the dramatic expansion of capitalism in the late fifteenth century. Civilization is the linkage through long-distance, moneyed exchange of two or more different "cultures," which Braudel equated at one point with "individual civilizations." But if a culture is a discrete civilization, it is one "that has not yet achieved maturity, its greatest potential, nor consolidated its growth." A culture is an "immature" civilization, a "semi-civilisation" often characterized by an observably low population density.[11]

Below and beyond the level of culture are "primitive" peoples who live in widely dispersed, erratic settlements on marginal wastelands devoid of productive agriculture. We commonly encounter and classify these primitive societies through the eyes of civilized Western observers. Primitives, familiar to us through the writings of explorers, merchant princes, and nineteenth-century anthropologists, are the "food gatherers, hunters, fishermen—they attract our attention from the four corners of the world . . . the situation is the same everywhere, whether it concerns Eskimos in the Great North, Negritos in the Philippines, or pygmies in the African forests: primitive populations who have somehow to take what they need to survive from the wild flora and fauna surrounding them."[12] To reverse the process, society's first achievement is to attain "culture" from the depths of primitivism and then to progress in linear fashion to the level of civilization. At the same time, the abstract, adaptive relations of capitalism emerge.

Something in this model of reality is unsettling. It is one thing to conceive of economic life as a series of dynamic, interlocking layers in which material life stands for long-term rhythms of small-scale production and capitalism, the pinnacle of freedom and flexibility. It is quite another to suggest that it follows that civilization and capitalism provide an accurate barometer of cultural complexity on a world scale. Perhaps this ethnocentric view is itself borne of the highly "civilized" time and place in which Braudel himself was writing. In 1949 he finished his monumental study *The Mediterranean and the Mediterranean World in the Age of Philip II* (not translated into English until 1972). During the next year or two he conceived the massive, three-volume exploration, *Civilization and Capitalism, 15th–18th Centuries*, the remarkable completion of which would occupy the rest of his career.[13] He was then forty-eight years old. Marxism and existentialism were in the Parisian air. At night the cafés crackled with conversation and argument. The plays of Jean-Paul Sartre, three years his senior, were attracting notice among the literary cognoscenti.

At the same time, Claude Lévi-Strauss was busy building a structural anthropology that bore some resemblance to Braudel's historical edifice. Like the historian, Lévi-Strauss was influenced in his youth by both Marx and Freud. Yet for the anthropologist, the notion that some cultures were, on the basis of economic development, more advanced than others—that some were primitive, others civilized—made no theoretical sense. Based on the systematic, exhaustive study of totemic structure, of myth, and of material culture, Lévi-Strauss boldly argued that the so-called primitive mind was no more or less complex than that of the most sophisticated Parisian intellectual. Braudel might insist that "elaborate cooking" and extensive geographic knowledge are common to every "mature civilization," but Lévi-Strauss could counter that Indians of the upper Amazon basin had different names for every plant in the bush, every tree in the forest. Braudel might point to the elliptical eloquence of Voltaire, but Lévi-Strauss could reply by demonstrating the amazing symbolic complexity of so-called primitive myths. He could also balk at Braudel's econocentric statement that the Yoruba of Nigeria, the Ashanti of Ghana, the Aztecs of Mexico, and the Incas of Peru were "immature" civilizations before the arrival of European invaders in the seventeenth century. It is difficult to confront the complex mythologies and intricate artworks of these peoples and agree with Braudel that they were,

in his terms, mere "cultures" and not civilizations in their own right.[14] Or, once having seen things from Lévi-Strauss's view, it becomes almost awkward to imagine that printing presses, gunpowder, or ocean navigation techniques were anything except means of extending the real and symbolic boundaries of Western empires.

When viewed in the light of the pressure Lévi-Strauss was exerting on prevailing anthropological paradigms, Braudel's historical model seems ambiguously formed from an old-fashioned anthropology and a hesitancy to complicate theories of economic causation by acknowledging what he knew to be true: that exchange relations are simultaneously instrumental and symbolic and that economic history demands the study of *mentalité.* Although a theoretical concern for "transformation" appears at many points in his writing, Braudel seems to have relied in practice on principles of classification drawn from Marcel Mauss and Emile Durkheim and an idea of linear cultural evolution that is strangely reminiscent of E. B. Tylor's *Primitive Culture.* With such a linear concept of culture and civilization in mind, it is logical for ethnographers to study isolated pockets of rural "peasant culture" for clues to what civilized people were formerly like. Here Braudel's work may reveal the continuing influence of an approach that Marc Bloch built into the *Annales* "paradigm" in the late 1920s: the belief that an authentic history could only be gleaned from field and archival study of French peasants, among whom folk customs survived that demonstrated what Parisians were once like but had now moved comfortably beyond.[15]

Braudel's apparent lack of attention to symbolic thought derives from a belief that the essential conditions of human life and culture have their formative bases in economic life. Differences in building materials, for example, he argued, are "linked only to cost" or regional availability and not to man's will to control the chaotic forms of nature through aesthetic acts. The arrangement of table-settings is readily subsumed to differences in wealth, as if an ability to afford elaborate dining objects de facto informed aspiring consumers of their proper symbolic usage. Even money, that most powerful of human symbolic constructs, is subsumed under the general category of "the history of technology" and not the history of art.[16]

Yet as a historian who read ethnographic literature

avidly and even tried to embrace its terms, Braudel realized that "primitive" societies could at times seem identical to civilizations. And on one crucial matter, Lévi-Strauss was right. In reviewing the different moneys used by different cultures, Braudel turned to the functions of wampum among American Indians; its complex nature led him to an epiphany. "It must really be concluded," he reports, "that in every case primitive money was genuine money and had the appearance and properties of money."[17] Here, with the very medium of exchange that supposedly set market economies and capitalism above the waist-deep routines of material life and cultures and civilizations apart from primitive wanderers without agriculture, we find inconsistency. For wampum, as currency, was also a barter commodity and part of a symbolic costume system related to gradations in rank in coastal Algonquian society. The truth is inescapable. Primitive societies were as closely knit by intersections of art, money, barter, reciprocity, credit, and debt as were their "civilized" capitalist counterparts.

If Braudel's concept of material life does not fully account for symbolic communication and the life of the mind, he was certainly aware of its growing importance. The omission of such evidence in *Capitalism and Material Life, 1400–1800* was due no doubt to an original plan that his own work would be complemented by Lucien Febvre's projected (but, alas, never completed) companion volume, *Western Thought and Belief, 1400–1800*. And certainly Braudel's commitment to the study of *mentalité* emerges from the pages of *Annales: Economies, Sociétés, Civilisations*, over whose editorial policy he exerted a sustained influence from 1949 until his death in 1985.[18] It emerges as well in scattered allusions to the power of belief and thought in his own writing. Civilizations are more than just elaborate machines driven by the energies of capitalism. They are "strange collections" not only of commodities but also of "symbols, illusions, phantasms, and intellectual models." Changes in cooking and eating represent a "new code of behavior." "Costume is a language," and maize was so significant in Yoruban diet that a "cycle of legends" developed around it. Braudel admits the singular power of the material environment to shape our memories, the stuff of history itself. "A bend in a path or a street can take anyone back to the past," he maintained. "Even in highly developed countries, the residual presence of the old material past makes itself felt."[19]

Conversely, spiritual beliefs and morals shape the landscapes and buildings we inhabit at every level. House plans may vary but almost always encode ideas about appropriate family government and social segregation. Churches do not take shape randomly but must conform to rigid demands of liturgy. Recognizing this interpenetration of economy and belief, we can question the utility of base-superstructure models derived from the artificial isolation of economic life from other forms of symbolic exchange. Are not beliefs emergent as part of economic life, as part of a dual reality whose segments are contexts for each other in the human psyche? Is not exchange itself an artistic form, a fluid medium shaped by an aesthetic as powerful as that which imprints this painting, that sculpture, on our consciousness? Is not "capitalism" protean precisely because it simultaneously invokes forms of economic relations *and* structures of attitude and belief?

Even if Braudel and Febvre had both completed their volumes, that they were conceived as separate texts implies that a false sense of disjunction between material life (the way we live?) and symbolic life (the way we think?) would have remained, reminding us of our own cultural need to imagine the body and mind as unhinged through time. The concept of material life that unifies the essays in this volume seeks to reconnect exchange and belief, sign and structure. Yet how, indeed, should "symbolic texts"—the structures of knowledge, the elusive forms of popular culture—be linked to the hard indices of wealth, the probate records, and tax lists that inform our image of social life? How, in other words, should we link intellectual history and the history of material life?

That problem—one many of the essays in this book raise implicitly—is complicated for two reasons. First, ideas do not change predictably or correlate neatly with divisions in social structure. In colonial America, supposedly "elite" ministers knew the latest local legends and "remarkables," while shoemakers and maidservants read detailed commentaries on the Bible and questioned minute variations in church doctrine. Second, the rarely synchronous chronologies of change in material life and intellectual life lead scholars to separate the meanings of the physical environment from those in the world of ideas. The inspiring pronouncements of eighteenth-century political philosophers may strike similar chords in our own thought, but if we were forced to eat their food, sleep in their beds, take their medicines, or travel on their roads we would recoil in horror. As do we, past Americans were able to live in two (or more) different worlds at the same time—the worlds of "vernacular" and "high-style" culture, oral traditions and written rules, verbal symbols and material metaphors. Their lived reality accommodated these and other divisions; it is the historian's challenge to overcome its apparent contradictions. How can these tears in historical fabric be mended? Can history become authentic to experience? Can the wholeness of material life be restored?

The essays in this volume argue that it can. The concept of material life as the ground floor of a new architecture of history, a new way to think about economic and social life, provides the armature on which this collection is formed. The authors of these essays survey a variety of historical landscapes, situations, events, and people typically overlooked in general views of the American past. The volume attempts to find common approaches, themes, and arguments that together discover coherence beneath seemingly disparate essays. Its overall purpose, then, is to define some of the goals and methods of studying material life in America between 1600 and 1860.

This study places three demands on its readers. The first is that he or she be open to and optimistic about the challenge of doing interdisciplinary research with a dazzling array of historical evidence. Houses, furniture, teacups, probate inventories, diaries, account books, newspaper advertisements, and tax lists may all warrant investigation in the course of a single topic. As part of this challenge, the study of material life urges that social historians, economic historians, and students of material culture learn one another's methods and theories (implicit or explicit) in order to define common issues and perfect new approaches. This alone is an ambitious agenda. As many of us know, the fields of American history and material culture are often kept strangely apart. They are regularly segregated, appearing in different journals intended for varied audiences. And with the notable exception of a handful of graduate programs, they are segregated within the academy, presented in different courses by different teachers in different departments. What should be a common pursuit is divided into two camps: "document people," full of exciting stories about tax lists, probate inventories, and neurotic tidbits from aristocratic diaries, and "object people," with their odd concern for house carpentry, lateral dovetails, and folk pottery.

One place this bifurcation emerges is in the schism between university professors and museum professionals, a division of labor this volume implicitly challenges. The separation is due in part to the different types of artifacts these groups feel comfortable using. On their side, many social historians assume the evidential priority of the written word. To them, research based on physical artifacts is perhaps a passing fad. As one historian recently put it, "Studies of 'material culture' have gained at least a margin of legitimacy among historians . . .[but] such work has developed as a side stream—adjacent to, but rarely intersecting with, the main currents of scholarship." Historians, too, often feel that the sensual presence of artifacts—their immediacy, their visceral quality—disrupts or interferes with the metaphoric play that literary artifacts allow.[20] Objects, in other words, seem to obstruct the imaginative process on which the historian relies. Yet courageous scholars like W. G. Hoskins and Rhys Isaac have demonstrated that objects like barns and courthouses can actively assist in imaginatively reconstructing a more inclusive view of past life than documents alone can afford.[21] If our goal is to encounter and make sense of an alien mind—whether that of seventeenth-century New England Puritans or nineteenth-century Southern yeomen—then complex material objects, whether plows or paintings, tools or art, are crucial. These "things" are whole texts, each one an objectification of thought, a concrete enactment of morality, an eloquent essay in the difficult reconciliation of ethics, aesthetics, and economics.[22] The essays in this volume demonstrate that artifacts and documents can be brought together and that their combined weight can help to define what the "main currents" in American history—by no means a static body of traditional beliefs sustaining an isolated tribe—should be.

The fusion of artifacts and history depends on field research and, to an equal degree, on museum research. Museum curators are indispensable participants in the classification and interpretation of American material life because their intimate and intensive knowledge of objects allows them to make

Introduction

the leaps of imagination necessary to penetrate the minds of dead creators. Intuitively, they learn to reason from within the maker's culture and not from some external, omniscient viewpoint. Given this special skill and genuine insight, it is not surprising that America's leading anthropologists—Franz Boas, Margaret Mead, and Robert Lowie among them—had museum experience. Indeed, no finer summary of the importance of museum work to history and anthropology exists than that offered by another former "museum person"—Lévi-Strauss:

> The museographer enters into close contact with the objects: A spirit of humility is inculcated in him by all the small tasks (unpacking, cleaning, maintenance, etc.) he has to perform. He develops a keen sense of the concrete through the classification, identification, and analysis of the objects in the various collections. He establishes indirect contact with the native environment by means of tools and comes to know this environment and the ways in which to handle it correctly: Texture, form, and, in many cases, smell, repeatedly experienced, make him instinctively familiar with distant forms of life and activities. Finally, he acquires for the various externalizations of human genius that respect which cannot fail to be inspired in him by the constant appeals to his taste, intellect, and knowledge made by apparently insignificant objects.[23]

Nor was it mere coincidence that Boas was trained initially as a geographer, able to see the physical relationships of the landscape as intellectually significant. Direct, unmediated encounters with artifacts form the backbone of material culture study. Call it what you may—"fieldwork" for the folklorist, anthropologist, and archaeologist, "connoisseurship" for the art historian—the deep respect for human dignity one learns when holding the creation of an alien mind in one's hands can be acquired only through everyday contact and systematic contemplation.

Many of the contributors to this volume—whether art historians, folklorists, archaeologists, social historians, or geographers—currently work or have worked in or with museums, and their close contact with objects informs their interpretive writing. Jules D. Prown, Henry Glassie, Cary Carson, Rodris Roth, Robert Blair St. George, Kevin M. Sweeney, Dell Upton, Lorena S. Walsh, Garry Wheeler Stone, William

Kelso, and Gary Kulik have taken advantage of the persective on past life that museum experience provides. The point of reconciliation between documents and objects on which the essayists in this volume agree is alarmingly simple: words and things—language and the objects of language—should properly be conceived of as interdependent signs in a single, unified, symbolic discourse. In seeking the elusive connections between related yet apparently disparate kinds of language, students of American material life have much to learn from folklorists, whose disciplinary emphasis on achieving "ethnographies of communication" has been advancing steadily over the past two decades.[24]

A second demand the study of material life makes is that we recall once again the common interest that unites all students of the American past: intellectual historians, literary historians, and students of the landscape converge in their desire to reconstruct the totality of past cultures. But carelessness often intervenes. The tendency to fragment the culture concept that gave unity to the American Studies movement by reifying "culture" as modes of transmission must be avoided. The invention of terms like "material culture," "oral culture," and "print culture" and such categories as "architectural history," "political history," and "the history of the book" reminds us how easily conceptual tools can be used to carve out academic territories at the expense of theoretical precision. The study of material life reminds us that culture does not reside in books, in buildings, or in political parties. Culture exists in the human mind, a bundle of values in tension, interlocking and closed in transformation but open to perception and novelty, internalizing contexts and suiting performance to situation. Culture as lived cannot be reduced to its artifacts. All sherds—ceramic, literary, and religious—are only remnants, pieces of torn cloth, broken vessels, mere shadows of whole culture. They can only be given new life when they are interpreted as related parts of a larger puzzle. Read socially, artifacts are the glue that held American culture together.

A final task that students of material life must undertake lies in recognizing the basic unity of the typically opposed, pure concepts of economy and art. Here Braudel has given us a clue in his lucid characterization of money—as opposed to barter—as a medium through which exchange is accelerated, its force intensified. So, too, do art and myth—as opposed to other artifacts and stories—accelerate the exchange of ideas and intensify the contemplation of values. Used to thinking economically, mechanically, we accept the accelerating force of money but question its extension to the function of art. Yet the same idea has long been concealed in the literature of art history, awaiting rediscovery; Henry Focillon claimed as early as 1931 that folk art "represents . . . a movement of exchange."[25] Both money and art, like twin poles of consciousness, make us think more intensively about relative values.

Money and art are the two faces of material life and capitalism, but they work in interdependent opposition. Money, as a kind of instrumental power, intensifies exchange as it moves through the hands of merchant-middlemen to restrict public access to a fixed scarcity of needed resources. As cash and commodities circulate, money substitutes one experience for another. Its goal is the centralization and conservation of value through private accumulation. Art, however, as a type of metaphoric power, accelerates exchange as it translates one experience into another or causes one experience to merge affectively into another. This process has many qualities, from symbol—the flower that reminds us of the Virgin Mary's purity—to phenomenological presence—in church, the faithful communicant who actually believes that the body and blood of Christ exist transubstantiated in the bread and wine of the Holy Eucharist. The goal of art is the diffusion and exhaustion of value through public gift. The fusion of economy and art, instrument and affecting presence, can only be realized when we realize their virtual contiguity; as two ways in which exchange is intensified, they complete one another. "Everything," Braudel believed, "is connected."[26]

Once we admit the two ideal faces of human exchange, the inverse forces that drive people apart or pull them together, we can see that art and economy almost never appear as ideals. Rather they work and combine in differing degrees in all forms and together define a nexus of values that shape a culture's dominant structure of feeling. Hence all economy is partly artful; Western coins are even adorned with small bas-relief sculptures signed by individual artists. Contemporary advertisements praise the "art of business," and young painters find a creative outlet in Madison Avenue offices. All art is in part economic, suspended in a marketplace that constantly tries to subvert its value as gift through commodification; museums have "official" reproduction wares for sale in shopping malls. A simple conclusion is unavoidable: born of economy and art, the built landscape is inherently political and ethical. In much the same way that artifacts are uneven mixtures of tool and art, the social exchanges that define material life are at once economic and affective.

Like literature, material culture is rife with metaphors of dominance, deference, and mystery. Apparently simple material forms—land, houses, chests, and chairs—provide another axis along which power relations are established, maintained, and sometimes upset. Material life makes the experience of ideology a constant process that is both intellectual *and* sensual. Material life argues that the routines and processes that shaped daily life in America derived much of their affective force from the built, cultural landscape—from artifacts like city and town plans, houses, household furniture, and agricultural tools to parades, labor strikes, and festivals—and from the complex fashion systems that framed the design, exchange, and use of these expressive forms. Material life, in other words, is the intentional convergence of economy and art on social history.

As they work to close the gap between history and folklore, between written texts and material culture, the essays that follow explore the social history of property acquisition and distribution, and the power derived from the accumulation of material possessions. They seek to discover the logic of how property and its symbolic functions actively shaped and transformed social relations—how neighbors got along, how men and women sought to protect their rights, how slavery could be subverted by the emergence of hidden trade networks. They also demonstrate the benefits that result when scholars from complementary traditions focus on related sets of historical and cultural issues—issues like settlement process, cultural confrontation, technological innovation, deference, emergent class consciousness, and the ritual display of social authority.

The essays on **Method and Meaning** by Jules Prown, Rhys Isaac, and Henry Glassie that begin the volume set high standards for the disciplined use of artifacts and theory in cultural history. Prown, an art historian, offers a rigorous method, a starting place, for students interested in learning to decode the landscape. Historian Rhys Isaac offers a model for the study of "ethnographic history" and gives detailed examples of how specific occasions or events might be read as social dramas for their symbolic meanings. Drawing on his background in fieldwork and his training in literature and folklore, Henry Glassie outlines a series of issues that must be addressed in order to keep people—their complex ideas, their idiosyncratic lives—as the focus of responsibly engaged social history. Taken together, these essays define the intellectual challenges of those that follow: to help us learn to sense and comprehend the world from the point of view of those who created it and felt its living structures of power, desire, and mystery; to be able to see that specific artifacts, customs, and occasions were structurally linked to one another; and to explore the rules that set limits on but still allowed for innovative action.

In order to concentrate on human issues, the sections that follow concentrate on specific thematic issues within an overall chronological framework. In their essays on **New World Cultures,** James Merrell, Cary Carson et al., Joseph S. Wood, and Melvin Wade examine different aspects of the interactions of Indian, English, and African cultures in America during the seventeenth and eighteenth centuries. Their discussions on trade, war, the timing of architectural improvement, the symbolic meaning of town plans, and ritual inversions in race relations make clear one point: the processes of settlement, territorial expansion, and enslavement that marked the colonial and early national experiences were not accompanied by any linear sense of acculturation. From the start of European colonization, American material life was defined by the remarkable cultural diversity of its participants: Indian peoples, English, Africans of many nations, Swedes, French, Scots, Germans, Portuguese, Irish, Spaniards, and Welsh. Peoples and traditions influenced one another, and from its earliest beginnings American culture was complex, contradictory, and prone to creolization as well as confrontation.

If American material life grew more stable over the course of the first century of settlement, it did so as household economies assumed a central role in **The Production and Control of Property.** Although the texture and exact seasonal schedule of household production changed depending on geographic location and labor supply, certain similarities bound them in common routines. As Russell Menard, Lois

Green Carr, and Lorena S. Walsh demonstrate, families had to struggle to break even if they hoped to survive. In New England this meant smaller farms and family labor. In the labor-intensive, market-oriented economy of the South, as Philip D. Morgan points out, it meant slavery—the organization of which depended at least in part on the crop being produced. In Philadelphia, as in other coastal ports like New York and Boston, working people had to bear the brunt of economic depression and foreign competition while still managing to live with a minimum of resources. As Billy Smith makes clear, shoemakers, tailors, and laborers faced a constant struggle to conserve and protect limited earnings. Marylynn Salmon extends our understanding of the internal order of households by pointing to marriage as a precarious joining of property in which women commonly found themselves economically and legally subordinate to their husbands. By appealing to equity law, women in South Carolina and elsewhere devised a strategy for preserving some autonomy. Sam B. Hilliard broadens our view of household production by pointing to cultural and racial inequalities in food preparation, consumption, and nutrition in the antebellum South. What seems to us a "traditional" foodways system has specific historical origins in the extensive husbandry practices of Southern planters.

As some households triumphed and others failed, America became a series of **Landscapes of Social Distance.** The importance of the essays by Robert Blair St. George, Dell Upton, Betsy Blackmar, and Gary Kulik in this section lies in their attention to the ways in which the built landscape enacted deeper patterns of authority. Whether in the Connecticut River Valley or in Virginia, wealthy farmers drew on a repertoire of Anglo-American architectural forms to create dramatic mansions that demanded limited access, ritualized entrance, and coercive hospitality. Like the English gentry houses they selectively imitated, they were intended to make visitors feel in awe, in debt, and in grateful submission. In New York City, the appearance of similar country estates was accompanied by an active real estate market that saw more and more land falling into fewer and fewer hands. Working people fell on hard times as renters, migrants, and tenement dwellers. By the early nineteenth century, New York's street plan already marked out a topography of wealth and poverty, of privilege and stigma. But the engines of structural change in American society at the turn of the nineteenth century were driven by country people as often as they were by urbanites. As industrial capitalism transformed America's rural hinterlands, farm people turned first to the regularity of seasonal outwork and then to full-time factory labor. Yet, as Gary Kulik demonstrates, as country folk opted increasingly to work in the mills, the rights they had in their own labor became uncertain. By the 1820s, labor actions were common, and in Pawtucket, Rhode Island, angry textile workers—men and women alike—went on strike. These essays argue that the built environment was never morally neutral but rather was a tangible, visible witness to a constant struggle to mold the appearance of things for social and political ends.

Throughout the colonial and early national periods, people created and used specific types of **Ritual Space** in order to reveal to themselves periodically the inner structure of their own lives. In a series of topical essays, Robert J. Dinkin, A. G. Roeber, Rodris Roth, John Brooke, and Susan G. Davis examine the meaning of five major types of public space from a variety of places and periods: meetinghouses in early New England, eighteenth-century Virginia courthouses, tea-drinking in eighteenth-century American domestic buildings, burial grounds and church polity in Massachusetts between 1730 and 1790, and Philadelphia street parades in the early nineteenth century. Individually, each essay is a model in the detailed ethnographic study of environment and social structure. As a group, they demonstrate the remarkable extent to which people relied on the landscape as a means of realizing legitimacy and power in the maintenance and constant reshaping of local societies.

Reshaping American society by purposefully **Reforming the Environment** is a topic the final three essays address. Thomas Bender charts the close relationship between nineteenth-century urbanism and a simultaneous antiurban rural cemetery reform movement. By the outbreak of the Civil War, the American landscape was already deeply divided by divergent views about nature, work, and the need to flee the pressures of urban life. Robert A. Gross examines the agricultural economy of Concord, Massachusetts, in the years between 1800 and 1860 and encounters the farmers that Thoreau knew embracing an expanding "scientific" approach to profit-oriented agri-

culture. Finally, Clifford E. Clark, Jr., examines life on the home front in mid-nineteenth-century America, where once again we discover people trying to puzzle through their lives amid a new plethora of advice manuals, domestic furniture fashions, and the ambiguous messages of the domesticity movement. By 1860, America was a moral paradox. It nurtured a nostalgic belief in the possibility of consensus as it bewailed the disappearing "traditions" and "folk customs" of Yankees, Dutchmen, and Quakers while at the same supporting industrial enterprises that sanctioned new transformations of inequality.

As a fusion of economy and art, material life confronts us with basic processes of American life, work, and thought. It draws our attention anew to artifacts, whole, intentional, surviving from the past to invade our present sensibilities, ideal building blocks for a *new* "new history." In his essay, Henry Glassie rightly argues that artifacts are vital to social history because they force us "to enroll in reality's school"; they help us to transcend the limits of our own experience by expanding into an alien consciousness. Braudel admitted that he turned to the study of material life for a similar reason—"because it tied me down to realities at a time when philosophy, social science and mathematicization [were] dehumanizing history." Finally, he came to regard material life as a "return to mother earth."[27]

Looking back through *Fair Is Our Land* now, once again I come across my favorite picture: a photograph by Minor White of Oregon's Grande Ronde Valley. In the background, a house, barn, and small sheds are silhouetted against foggy hills; they impose human scale on a dimensionless landscape. The foreground is an essay in the dusty, cracked, relentless logic of farming. No land escapes artifice, not one inch of soil is left unsculpted by the plow. Like the places and people you will discover in the essays that follow, this is terrain where human ideas are emergent in material life. Here, even metaphors seem real. The mind of America *is* cut into its earth.

Notes

1. Samuel Chamberlain, ed., *Fair is Our Land* (Chicago, 1942).

2. Fernand Braudel, *Capitalism and Material Life, 1400–*

1800, trans. Miriam Kochan (New York, 1975), 439.

3. Braudel, *Capitalism and Material Life*, xii.

4. Braudel, *Capitalism and Material Life*, ix; see also Braudel, *Afterthoughts on Material Civilization and Capitalism*, trans. Patricia M. Ranum (Baltimore, 1977), 7.

5. Braudel, *Capitalism and Material Life*, xii–xiii.

6. Braudel, *Capitalism and Material Life*, xiii.

7. Braudel, *Capitalism and Material Life*, ix, xii, 201, 443, esp. 445: "I did think that it was not possible to achieve an understanding of the whole if the foundation of the house were not explored first." See also Braudel, *Afterthoughts*, 25. On the theatricality of market fairs, see Jean-Christophe Agnew, *Worlds Apart: The Market and the Theatre in Anglo-American Thought, 1550–1750* (New York, 1986), 149–94.

8. Braudel, *Capitalism and Material Life*, 445 (italics added).

9. Braudel, *Capitalism and Material Life*, 233; Braudel, *Afterthoughts*, 5.

10. Braudel, *Afterthoughts*, 7, 45; Braudel, *Capitalism and Material Life*, 440.

11. Braudel, *Capitalism and Material Life*, 63, 66, 108, 443.

12. Braudel, *Capitalism and Material Life*, 30, 118–19.

13. Originally published in Paris in 1979, the three volumes of *Civilization and Capitalism* were translated by Sian Reynolds and printed in English as: *The Structures of Everyday Life: The Limits of the Possible* (New York, 1985); *The Wheels of Commerce* (New York, 1985); and *The Perspective of the World* (New York, 1985).

14. Braudel, *Capitalism and Material Life*, 63; see Claude Lévi-Strauss, *Tristes Tropiques: An Anthropological Study of Primitive Societies in Brazil*, trans. John Russell (New York, 1970); Lévi-Strauss, *The Savage Mind* (Chicago, 1966); Lévi-Strauss, *Totemism* (Boston, 1963); and Lévi-Strauss, "History and Anthropology," and "The Structural Study of Myth," in *Structural Anthropology*, trans. Claire Jacobson and Brooke Grundfest Schoepf (New York, 1963), 1–30, 206–31. For a detailed analysis of Braudel's understanding of the anthropological concept of "structure," see Samuel Kinser, "Annaliste Paradigm? The Geohistorical Structure of Fernand Braudel," *American Historical Review* 86 (1981):71–75.

15. See Marcel Mauss and Emile Durkheim, *On Primitive Classification*, trans. Rodney Needham (Chicago, 1963), 3–9; E. B. Tylor, *Primitive Culture* (London, 1871); and Bryce Lyon, "Foreword," in Marc Bloch, *French Rural History: An Essay on Its Basic Characteristics*, trans. Janet Sondheimer (Berkeley, Calif., 1966), xi. See also Claude Lévi-Strauss, *Introduction to the Work of Marcel Mauss*, trans. Felicity Baker (London, 1987).

16. Braudel, *Capitalism and Material Life*, 195–97, 364.

17. Braudel, *Capitalism and Material Life*, xiii, 333.

18. Braudel, *Capitalism and Material Life*, 133; for Braudel's importance to the so-called "*Annales* paradigm," see his "Foreword" in Traian Stoianovich, *French Historical Method: The Annales Paradigm* (Ithaca, N.Y., 1976), 13–17. Examples of *Annales* scholarship exploring *mentalité* done in the Braudel era may be consulted in Robert Forster and Orest Ranum, eds., *Ritual, Religion, and the Sacred: Selections from Annales: Economies, Sociétés, Civilisations*, vol. 7, trans. Elborg Forster and Patricia M. Ranum (Baltimore, 1982).

19. Braudel, *Capitalism and Material Life*, 32, 66, 113, 139, 235–36, 243, 441; for an example of the merging of form and spirit in an early American context, see John Archer, "Puritan Town Planning in New Haven," *Journal of the Society of Architectural Historians* 34, no. 2 (1975): 140–49.

20. John Demos, "Words and Things: A Review and Discussion of 'New England Begins'," *William and Mary Quarterly*, 3d ser., 40 (1983): 584–85.

21. See, for example, W. G. Hoskins, *The Making of the English Landscape* (Harmondsworth, 1955); Hoskins, *The Midland Peasant: The Economic and Social History of a Leicestershire Village* (London, 1957); Hoskins, *Old Devon* (London, 1966); and Rhys Isaac, *The Transformation of Virginia, 1740 to 1790* (Chapel Hill, N.C., 1982).

22. Henry Glassie, "Folkloristic Study of the American Artifact: Objects and Objectives," in *Handbook of American Folklore*, ed. Richard M. Dorson (Bloomington, Ind., 1983), 336–37.

23. Lévi-Strauss, "The Place of Anthropology in the Social Sciences and the Problems Raised in Teaching It," in *Structural Anthropology*, trans. Claire Jacobson and Brooke Grundfest Schoepf (New York, 1963), p. 375. Lévi-Strauss elsewhere in the same essay (p. 335) likens museum work to some aspects of ethnography: ". . . in the case of material objects, which . . . may be regarded as an extension of field work."

24. For the classic statement, see Dell Hymes, "Directions in (Ethno-) Linguistic Theory," in A. Rodney Kimball and Roy G. D'Andrade, eds., "Transcultural Studies in Cognition," *American Anthropologist* 66, no. 3, 2 (1964): 6–56, and Hymes, "Introduction: Toward Ethnographies of Communication," in John J. Gumperz and Dell Hymes, eds., "The Ethnography of Communication," *American Anthropologist* 66, no. 6 (1964): 1–34. See also Hymes, *Foundations in Sociolinguistics: An Ethnographic Approach* (Philadelphia, 1974).

25. Braudel, *Afterthoughts*, 15; Henri Focillon, "Introduction" in *Art Populaire* (Paris, 1931), reprinted and trans. Robert F. Trent, in Trent, *Hearts and Crowns: Folk Chairs of the Connecticut Coast, 1720–1840, as Viewed in the Light of Henri Focillon's Introduction to* Art Populaire (New Haven, Conn., 1977), 19.

26. On the relationship of metaphor to phenomenological presence in "art," see Robert Plant Armstrong's trilogy of works: *The Affecting Presence: An Essay in Humanistic Anthropology* (Urbana, Ill., 1971); *Wellspring: On the Myth and Source of Culture* (Berkeley, Calif., 1975); and *The Powers of Presence: Consciousness, Myth, and Affecting Presence* (Philadelphia, 1981); Braudel, *Capitalism and Material Life*, 236.

27. Braudel, *Capitalism and Material Life*, 444–45.

Part One: Method and Meaning

Mind in Matter: An Introduction to Material Culture Theory and Method

JULES DAVID PROWN

An important foundation for the interpretive study of material life lies in the accurate description of artifacts and landscapes. At some point in their work, all students of human behavior past or present confront the duality of form and content, the dialectic of context and performance, and the need to build useful typologies of symbolic action. Yet because scholars from so many different disciplines and fields are involved in the study of material life, the quality of informed description varies widely. More dangerous is an unacknowledged belief that the "mere description" of cultural texts is somehow an objective process immune from the intrusions of theory. Adequate description and insightful interpretation demand the recognition and control of subjectivity and a disciplined approach to systematic observation.

To this end, Jules David Prown in this essay sketches the particular discipline of artifact study in five broad strokes. First, he offers a definition of "material culture" that asserts the utility of using objects as direct evidence of underlying cultural beliefs; artifacts, he argues, are complex representations of latent values, sensual enactments of deeper cognitive structures breaking above the surface of felt reality. The very term "material culture" is wonderfully paradoxical, deriving both ambiguity and power from the simultaneous invocation of the concrete and the abstract. Next, he forwards a tentative classification system to aid in organizing data for future study. Third, as a historian of art, he attempts to persuade historians to recognize in the study of material culture—especially its aesthetic dimension—an untapped cache of documentation, arguing that objects are more broadly representative of social life than are written documents and that they constitute a unique body of surviving historical actions whose veracity is guaranteed. He also stresses that artifacts, as whole symbolic statements, can

help us transcend ethnocentrism as we make "affective contact" with the sensibilities of people in the past. He reiterates the key theoretical underpinnings that should guide any study of material culture: that objects are enactments of mind; that because they are signs whose meanings are arbitrarily determined, their surface significance can shift with changing patterns of use and valuation; and that all artifacts are intentional, cultural, and not the result of historical accident. Finally, he outlines a method of observation that, once mastered, should allow interested students to learn the language of artifacts.

In this final section, Prown draws heavily upon established analytical traditions in the history of art— the field of his own training and research. But as he lays out the steps of description, deduction, and speculation, Prown not only demonstrates the continuing centrality of art historical approaches to the study of objects. He also raises the thorny issue of how "vernacular" objects relate to "high style" masterpieces, and he challenges students of material life to respond by generating a paradigm able to bridge all artifacts as it interprets the physical contours, the sensual textures, of mentalité *manifest in tangible forms.*

Although art museums, historical societies, museums of history and technology, historic houses, open-air museums, and museums of ethnography, science, and even natural history have long collected, studied, and exhibited the material of what has come to be called *material culture,* no comprehensive academic philosophy or discipline for the investigation of material culture has as yet been developed. Recently, however, there has been increased scholarly interest in the subject, as witnessed by the establishment of a periodical, *Winterthur Portfolio*, devoted specifically to material culture; graduate programs that emphasize material culture at the University of Delaware, the University of Notre Dame, and Boston University; an experimental Center for American Art and Material Culture at Yale University; and a substantial amount of innovative scholarship, especially in such academic areas as folk life and cultural geography (a selective material culture bibliography is appended below). These developments and activities have been spontaneous and largely uncoordinated responses to a perceived scholarly need and opportunity. This essay attempts to define material culture and considers the nature of the discipline. It makes no claim to be either the first or the last word on material culture, but it does seek to illuminate the subject and to provide a basis for further discussion. It also proposes a particular methodology based on the proposition that artifacts are primary data for the study of material culture, and, therefore, that they can be used actively as evidence rather than passively as illustrations.[1]

What is Material Culture?

Material culture is the study through artifacts of the beliefs—values, ideas, attitudes, and assumptions—of a particular community or society at a given time. The term *material culture* is also frequently used to refer to artifacts themselves, to the body of material available for such study. I shall restrict the term to mean the study and refer to the evidence simply as *material* or *artifacts*.

Material culture is singular as a mode of cultural investigation in its use of objects as primary data, but in its scholarly purposes it can be considered a branch of cultural history or cultural anthropology. It is a means rather than an end, a discipline rather than a field. In this, material culture differs from art history, for example, which is both a discipline (a mode of investigation) in its study of history through art and a field (a subject of investigation) in its study of the history of art itself. Material culture is comparable to art history as a discipline in its study of culture through artifacts. As such, it provides a scholarly approach to artifacts that can be used by investigators in a variety of fields. But the material of material culture is too diverse to constitute a single field. In practice it consists of subfields investigated

by specialists—cultural geographers or historians of art, architecture, decorative arts, science, and technology.

Material culture as a study is based upon the obvious fact that the existence of a man-made object is concrete evidence of the presence of a human intelligence operating at the time of fabrication. The underlying premise is that objects made or modified by man reflect, consciously or unconsciously, directly or indirectly, the beliefs of the individuals who made, commissioned, purchased, or used them and, by extension, the beliefs of the larger society to which they belonged. The term *material culture* thus refers quite directly and efficiently, if not elegantly, both to the subject matter of the study, *material*, and to its purpose, the understanding of *culture*.

Despite its concision and aptness, the term *material culture* seems unsatisfactory, indeed, self-contradictory. *Material* is a word we associate with base and pragmatic things; *culture* is a word we associate with lofty, intellectual, abstract things. Our unease with this apparent disjunction is not superficial; it derives from a fundamental human perception of the universe as divided between earth and sky. That empirically observed opposition of lower and higher provides a powerful and pervasive metaphor for the distinctions we make between such elemental polarities as material and spiritual, concrete and abstract, finite and infinite, real and ideal. In its theological formulation this metaphor invariably locates heaven upward, above the earth, accessible not to the body but only to the mind or spirit (with mortification of the flesh [material] one way to achieve spiritual ends), and places hell in the bowels of the earth, down deep in the midst of matter. Material things are heir to all sorts of ills—they break, get dirty, smell, wear out; abstract ideas remain pristine, free from such worldly debilities.

The Western conception of history is that it has been characterized by man's increasing understanding and mastery of the physical environment, by the progressive triumph of mind over matter. The evidence of human history seems to confirm our sense that abstract, intellectual, spiritual elements are superior to material and physical things. This has led inevitably to a hierarchical ordering that informs our apprehension and judgment of human activities and experiences.[2] This unconscious ordering makes us uncomfortable with the terminological coupling of base *material* and lofty *culture*. Nevertheless, the term *material culture*, if not ideal, has the advantage of being concise, accurate, and in general use.

Material

The word *material* in material culture refers to a broad, but not unrestricted, range of objects. It embraces the class of objects known as artifacts—objects made by people or modified by people. It excludes natural objects. Thus, the study of material culture might include a hammer, a plow, a microscope, a house, a painting, a city. It would exclude trees, rocks, fossils, skeletons. Two general observations should be made here. First, natural objects are occasionally encountered in a pattern that indicates human activity—a stone wall or a row of trees in an otherwise random forest, a concentration of chicken bones in a pit or a pile of oyster shells, topiary or a clipped poodle, a tattooed body or a prepared meal. In the broadest sense these natural materials are artifacts—objects modified by men and women—and are of cultural interest. Second, works of art constitute a large and special category within artifacts because their inevitable aesthetic and occasional ethical or spiritual (iconic) dimensions make them direct and often overt or intentional expressions of cultural belief. The self-consciously expressive character of this material, however, raises problems as well as opportunities; in some ways artifacts that express culture unconsciously are more useful as objective cultural indexes.[3] For the moment, however, let it simply be borne in mind that all tangible works of art are part of material culture, but not all the material of material culture is art.

The range of objects that fall within the compass of material culture is so broad as to make some system of classification desirable. Sorting by physical materials does not work because of the multiplicity of substances used, even at times in a single artifact. The same is true of methods of fabrication. The most promising mode of classification is by function. The following list is arranged in a sequence of categories that progresses from the more decorative (or aesthetic) to the more utilitarian.

1. Art (paintings, drawings, prints, sculpture, photography)
2. Diversions (books, toys, games, meals, theatrical performances)
3. Adornment (jewelry, clothing, hairstyles, cosmetics, tattooing, other alterations of the body)
4. Modifications of the landscape (architecture, town planning, agriculture, mining)
5. Applied arts (furniture, furnishings, receptacles)
6. Devices (machines, vehicles, scientific instruments, musical instruments, implements)

These categories are broad; they undoubtedly require modification and refining; the list is intended simply to define the terrain and suggest the outlines of a system. Many objects straddle categories, but taxonomic shortcomings do not cause analytical problems. Classification for purposes of manageability and discussion does not affect the actual process of material culture analysis described below, which applies to all artifacts. Although the range of categories suggests the potential applicability of a variety of specialized techniques and methodologies, no systematic attempt is made in this general essay to correlate categories of objects with particular analytical methods or with the production of particular kinds of cultural data. However, further consideration is given to these categories in the final section.

Why Material Culture?

Why should one bother to investigate material objects in the quest for culture, for a society's systems of belief? Surely people in all societies express and have expressed their beliefs more explicitly and openly in their words and deeds than in the things they have made. Are there aspects of mind to be discovered in objects that differ from, complement, supplement, or contradict what can be learned from more traditional literary and behavioral sources?

Inherent and Attached Value

The most obvious cultural belief associated with material objects has to do with *value*. There are different kinds of value. One, intrinsic in the fabric of an object itself, is established by the rarity of the materials used. Such value will inhere in the object for as long as the material continues to be valuable. With gold or silver or precious stones, this kind of value is persistent. More transient or variable are those values that have been attached by the people who originally made or used the object, by us today, or by people at any intervening moment. A value that accrues from utility will inhere as long as an object continues to be useful and can return when an obsolete object again becomes useful (wood stoves in an oil shortage). In addition to material and utilitarian values, certain objects have aesthetic value (art), some possess spiritual value (icons, cult objects), and some express attitudes toward other human beings (a fortress, a love seat) or toward the world (using materials in their natural condition as opposed to reshaping them).

Obviously, then, objects do embody and reflect cultural beliefs. But, although such embodiments of value differ in form from verbal and behavioral modes of cultural expression, they do not necessarily differ in character or content. In the following regards, however, objects do constitute distinctive cultural expressions.

Surviving Historical Events

Objects created in the past are the only historical occurrences that continue to exist in the present. They provide an opportunity by which "we encounter the past at first hand; we have direct sensory experience of surviving historical events."[4] Artifacts may not be important historical events, but they are, to the extent that they can be experienced and interpreted as evidence, significant.

More Representative

Henry Glassie has observed that only a small percentage of the world's population is and has been literate and that the people who write literature or keep diaries are atypical. Objects are used by a much broader cross section of the population and are therefore potentially a more wide-ranging, representative source of information than words.[5] They offer the possibility of a way to understand the mind of the great majority of nonliterate people, past and present, who remain otherwise inaccessible except through impersonal records and the distorting view of a contemporary literary elite. This promise perhaps explains why many of the leading early proponents, indeed pioneers, of material culture have come from the field of folklore and folk life and have studied vernacular objects. Such study has required a considerable amount of scholarly innovation. Vernacular

objects pose interpretive difficulties because our scholarly traditions and experience, especially in regard to art, architecture, and the decorative arts, have focused on high-style objects.

The theoretical democratic advantage of artifacts in general, and vernacular material in particular, is partially offset by the skewed nature of what in fact survives from an earlier culture. Foremost in this is the destructive, or the preservative, effect of particular environments on particular materials. Materials from the deeper recesses of time are often buried, and recovered archaeologically. Of the material heritage of such cultures, glass and ceramics survive in relatively good condition, metal in poor to fair condition, wood in the form of voids (postholes), and clothing not at all (except for metallic threads, buttons, and an odd clasp or hook).

Inherent and attached value, discussed above, is another major element in what survives. A significant aspect of this is taste or, more specifically, changes in taste over the years. A "degree-of-sophistication" scale, ranging from vernacular at one end to high style at the other, comes into play. The calibrations on this scale have obvious implications of social class. High-style objects, sometimes of precious materials and fabricated with technical skill that elicits admiration, tend to be preserved; ruder objects, which for economic reasons sometimes have much less invested in them in terms of the quality of the material or the craftsmanship, simply may not last as long or, if they do, tend eventually to be discarded as junk. Objects with iconic or associational value are preserved, but when they lose that association (religious paintings in a secular society, photographs of unknown ancestors), they become disposable.

Even allowing for the distortions of survival, it remains true that objects can make accessible aspects, especially nonelite aspects, of a culture that are not always present or detectable in other modes of cultural expression.

Veracity

Certain fundamental beliefs in any society are so generally accepted that they never need to be articulated (see *Cultural Perspective*, below). These basic cultural assumptions, the detection of which is essential for cultural understanding, are consequently not perceivable in *what* a society expresses. They can, however, be detected in the *way* in which a society expresses itself, in the configuration or form of things, in *style*.[6] Stylistic evidence can be found in all modes of cultural expression, whether verbal, behavioral, or material. But a society puts a considerable amount of cultural spin on what it consciously says and does. Cultural expression is less self-conscious, and therefore potentially more truthful, in what a society produces, especially such mundane, utilitarian objects as domestic buildings, furniture, or pots.

Cultural Perspective

Perhaps the most difficult problem to recognize and surmount in cultural studies is that of cultural stance or cultural perspective. The evidence we study is the product of a particular cultural environment. We, the interpreters, are products of a different cultural environment. We are pervaded by the beliefs of our own social groups—nation, locality, class, religion, politics, occupation, gender, age, race, ethnicity—beliefs in the form of assumptions that we make unconsciously. These are biases that we take for granted; we accept them as mindlessly as we accept the tug of gravity. Is it possible to step outside of one's own cultural givens and interpret evidence objectively in terms of the beliefs of the individuals and the society that produced that evidence? If not, if we are irredeemably biased by our own unconscious beliefs, if we are hopelessly culture bound, than the entire enterprise of cultural interpretation should be avoided since our interpretations will inevitably be distorted. It is possible to argue, as Arnold Hauser does in response to the contention of Karl Marx that we see all things from the perspective of our social interest and our view is therefore inevitably distorted, that once we become aware of the problem we can struggle against subjectivity, against individual and class interests, and can move toward greater objectivity.[7] Awareness of the problem of one's own cultural bias is a large step in the direction of neutralizing the problem, but material culture offers a scholarly approach that is more specific and trustworthy than simple awareness. The study of systems of belief through an analysis of artifacts offers opportunities to circumvent the investigator's own cultural perspective. By undertaking cultural interpretation through artifacts, we can engage the other

culture in the first instance not with our minds, the seat of our cultural biases, but with our senses. "This affective mode of apprehension through the senses that allows us to put ourselves, figuratively speaking, inside the skins of individuals who commissioned, made, used, or enjoyed these objects, to see with their eyes and touch with their hands, to identify with them empathetically, is clearly a different way of engaging the past than abstractly through the written word. Instead of our minds making intellectual contact with minds of the past, our senses make affective contact with senses of the past."[8]

The methodology of material culture, with its affective approach that aspires to the objectivity of scientific method, affords a procedure for overcoming the distortions of our particular cultural stance, and, of almost equal importance, it makes visible the otherwise invisible, unconscious biases of our own cultural perspective. Awareness of what one normally takes for granted occurs only in the forced confrontation with another norm. For example, we become particularly aware of gravity as gravity when it is not there, as in our observation of astronauts working in a spacecraft. When we identify with another culture through the affective, sensory apprehension of its artifacts, we have an opportunity to accept the other culture as the norm and become aware of the differentness, the special qualities, of our own culture. The culture being studied provides a platform, a new cultural stance, for a perspective on our culture. This can be of interest for its own sake, but specifically and practically in terms of the study of material culture, increasing awareness of the biases of one's own cultural perspective helps achieve objectivity in subsequent investigations.

The fact is that cultural perspective is only a problem or liability to the extent that one is unaware of or unable to adjust for it. Indeed, it is our quarry, the cultural patterns of belief, of mind, that we seek.

Final Note

A disclaimer should be entered regarding the completeness of what can be learned from material culture. In certain instances—prehistoric or preliterate societies, for example—artifacts constitute the only surviving evidence, so there is little choice but to use them as best one can to determine cultural values as well as historical facts. But it would be a delusion to assume we acquire complete access to the belief systems of a culture through its material survivals. Cultural expression is not limited to things. But the techniques of material culture should be part of the tool kit of the well-equipped cultural scholar. The obverse of this disclaimer is the argument advanced here: although the study of artifacts is only one route to the understanding of culture, it is a special, important, and qualitatively different route. An investigation that ignores material culture will be impoverished.

Theoretical Background

Culture and Society

The definition given at the beginning stated that the study of material culture can be considered a methodological branch of cultural history or cultural anthropology. Material culture is the object-based aspect of the study of culture. As with cultural history and cultural anthropology, the study of material culture touches on the allied concerns of social history and social anthropology. A society, a group of interdependent persons forming a single community, has a culture, a set of beliefs. Social history and social anthropology study the relationships between individuals or groups of individuals in a society, especially the patterns and details of the daily existence of large subgroups as defined by class, race, religion, place of residence, wealth, and so forth. Cultural history and cultural anthropology study the peculiar achievements, especially intellectual, that characterize a society, such as art, science, technology, religion. Obviously there are significant areas of overlap. Society and culture are inextricably intertwined, and their study cannot and should not be isolated except for analytical purposes.

Cultural history and cultural anthropology, with their sister subjects of social history and social anthropology, thus constitute a field-of-interest umbrella that arches over the study of material culture.[9] The theoretical underpinnings of the study will be noted in the sections that follow but are not explored extensively in view of their complexity and the introductory nature of this essay.

Structuralism and Semiotics

The fundamental purpose of the study of material culture is the quest for cultural belief systems, the patterns of belief of a particular group of people in a certain time and place. The methodology is to some extent *structuralist* in its premise that the configurations or properties of an artifact correspond to patterns in the mind of the individual producer or producers and of the society of which he, she, or they were a part.

Modern linguistic theory has made us aware of the significance of language as the manifestation of the human capacity, indeed compulsion, to impose structure on the world and our experience of it. This structuring, apparent in language, is the only reality humans know. Their reality is relative, endlessly changing, true only for the moment; it is the empirical shadow of a hypothetical underlying permanent universe, a world of ideas, a unified field. The reality humans experience is created by humans, and language, the naming of that reality, is a manifestation and measure of the current structure of reality in any given place and time. It is therefore significant cultural evidence as the reflection of human mental structuring. But language is not solely human. Animals communicate by arrangements of sounds and, in the case of dolphins, for example, may have languages. Perhaps more special to humans than language is the capacity to make implements and, more special yet, objects for aesthetic gratification. There is a language of form as there is a language of words; a naming through making as there is a naming through saying. That humans express their human need to structure their world through forms as well as through language is a basic premise of the structuralist approach to material culture.[10]

The methodology of material culture is also concerned with *semiotics* in its conviction that artifacts transmit signals that elucidate mental patterns or structures. Complementing the structuralist premise and semiotic promise of the interpretation of artifacts is the knowledge that artifacts serve as cultural releasers. Perceivers in other societies who have a different mix of cultural values, some in concert and some at variance with those of the producing society, respond positively to certain artifacts or aspects of artifacts while neglecting others. This is why an object or an entire category of objects falls in and out of fashion. The object stays relatively the same, but people change and cultural values change. From the time it is created, an artifact can arouse different patterns of response according to the belief systems of the perceivers' cultural matrices. The sequence of synchronic patterns that could be triggered by an artifact resembles the sequence of frames in a motion picture; in theory, if we could retrieve all the patterns, we would have a film of history. In practice, only a few patterns are accessible, primarily those of the original fabricator and the modern perceiver. Artifacts, then, can yield evidence of the patterns of mind of the society that fabricated them, of our society as we interpret our responses (and nonresponses), and of any other society intervening in time or removed in space for which there are recorded responses.

Determinism

The fundamental attitude underlying the study of material culture is, as with most contemporary scholarship, a pervasive *determinism*. This statement may seem to belabor the obvious, but a strict determinism not only underlies the other theoretical aspects of the study of material culture but also dictates the methodological procedures outlined below whereby, through a variety of techniques, an object is unpacked. The basic premise is that every effect observable in or induced by the object has a cause. Therefore, the way to understand the cause (some aspect of culture) is the careful and imaginative study of the effect (the object). In theory, if we could perceive all of the effects, we could understand all of the causes; an entire cultural universe is in the object waiting to be discovered. The theoretical approach here is modified, however, by the conviction that in practice omniperception leading to omniscience is not a possibility. External information—that is, evidence drawn from outside of the object, including information regarding the maker's purpose or intent—plays an essential role in the process. Such an approach is inclusive, not exclusive.

Although the fundamental concern of material culture is with the artifact as the embodiment of mental structures or patterns of belief, it is also of interest that the fabrication of the object is a manifestation of behavior, of human acts. As noted above in the discussion of culture and society, belief and behavior are inextricably intertwined. The material culturalist is, therefore, necessarily interested in the motive forces that condition behavior, specifically the making, the distribution, and the use of artifacts. There is an underlying assumption that every living being acts so as to gratify his or her self-interest as he or she determines that interest to be at any given moment. This is an inevitable by-product of the fundamental concern with cause and effect. Thus, such issues as availability of materials, demands of patronage, channels of distribution, promotion, available technology, and means of exchange, which require the investigation of external evidence, are pertinent.

Methodology

How does one extract information about culture, about mind, from mute objects? We have been taught to retrieve information in abstract form, words and numbers, but most of us are functionally illiterate when it comes to interpreting information encoded in objects. Several academic disciplines, notably art history and archaeology, routinely work with artifacts as evidence and over the years have built up a considerable amount of theoretical and methodological expertise. Work in these fields is often directed inward, toward the accumulation and explication of information required by the discipline itself. In the history of art this takes the form of resolving questions of stylistic and iconographic influence, of dating and authorship, of quality and authenticity. In archaeology it is the basic task of assembling, sorting, dating, and quantifying the assembled data. But art history and archaeology also have fundamental concerns with the cultures that produced the objects, and the methodologies of these two fields, to the extent that they provide means for the interpretation of culture, are essential to material culture. At present they are the two disciplines most directly relevant to the actual work of investigating material culture. But, as they are usually defined, they are not adequate to the total task. The exploration of patterns of belief and behavior, in an intellectual borderland where the interests of humanities and social sciences merge, requires an openness to other methodologies, including those of cultural and social history, cultural and social anthropology, psychohistory, sociology, cultural geography, folklore and folk life, and linguistics. But the approach to material culture set forth below dictates that these broader concerns and methodologies *not* be brought into play until the evidence of the artifact itself has been plumbed as objectively as possible. Therefore the first steps are most closely related to the basic descriptive techniques of art history and archaeology, and in this there is more overlap with the natural than with the social sciences. The initial descriptive steps in the approach to objects resembles fieldwork in such a science as geology, and description can also involve the use of scientific equipment.

The method of object analysis proposed below progresses through three stages. To keep the distorting biases of the investigator's cultural perspective in check, these stages must be undertaken in sequence and kept as discrete as possible. The analysis proceeds from *description*, recording the internal evidence of the object itself; to *deduction*, interpreting the interaction between the object and the perceiver; to *speculation*, framing hypotheses and questions that lead out from the object to external evidence for testing and resolution.[11]

Description

Description is restricted to what can be observed in the object itself, that is, to internal evidence. In practice, it is desirable to begin with the largest, most comprehensive observations and progress systematically to more particular details. The terminology should be as accurate as possible; technical terms are fine as long as they can be understood. The analyst must, however, continually guard against the intrusion of either subjective assumptions or conclusions derived from other experience.

This is a synchronic exercise; the physical object is read at a particular moment. The object is almost certainly not identical to what it was when it was fabricated; time, weather, usage will all have taken their toll. At this stage no consideration is given to condition or to other diachronic technological, iconographic, or stylistic influences.

Substantial Analysis

Description begins with substantial analysis, an account of the physical dimensions, material, and articulation of the object. To determine physical dimensions, the object is measured and perhaps weighed. The degree of precision depends on the interests of the investigator. If he or she will be considering a series of objects, a certain amount of precision is desirable, given the possible subsequent significance of and need for quantification. However, it is not desirable to carry decimals to the point of losing an immediate sense of dimension in a welter of numbers; real significance may lie in general measure, as with Glassie's discovery of the modal importance of spans and cubits in the vernacular architecture of Virginia.[12] Next comes a description of the materials—what they are, how extensively they are used, and the pattern of their distribution throughout the object. Finally, the ways in which the materials are put together in the fabrication of the object, the articulation, should be noted. For example, with fabrics one would look at the weave; with metals, the welding, soldering, riveting; with wood, the dovetails, dowels, miter joints, mortise-and-tenon joints, glue.

Substantial analysis is a descriptive physical inventory of the object. It is achieved with the assistance of whatever technical apparatus is appropriate and available. Simple tape measures and scales, ultraviolet lamps and infrared photographs, or complex electron microscopes and X-ray defraction machines are all basically enhancements of one's ability to perceive and take the measure of the physical properties and dimensions of the object.[13]

Content

The next step in description is analysis of content. The investigator is concerned simply with subject matter. This is usually a factor only with works of art or other decorated objects. The procedure is iconography in its simplest sense, a reading of overt representations. In the case of a painting, this may simply be what is represented, as if the work were a window on the world (or on some kind of world). Content may include decorative designs or motifs, inscriptions, coats of arms, or diagrams, engraved or embossed on metal, carved or painted on wood or stone, woven in textiles, molded or etched in glass.

Formal Analysis

Finally, and very important, is analysis of the object's form or configuration, its visual character. It is useful to begin by describing the two-dimensional organization—lines and areas—either on the surface of a flat object or in elevations or sections through a solid object.[14] Next comes the three dimensional organization of forms in space, whether actual in a three-dimensional object or represented in a pictorial object. Subsequently, such other formal elements as color, light, and texture should be analyzed with, as in the case of the initial description of materials, an account of their nature, extent, and pattern of distribution (rhythm) in each case. Determination of the degree of detail must be left to the discretion of the investigator; too much can be almost as bad as too little, the forest can be lost for the trees.

Deduction

The second stage of analysis moves from the object itself to the relationship between the object and the perceiver. It involves the empathetic linking of the material (actual) or represented world of the object with the perceiver's world of existence and experience. To put it another way, the analyst contemplates what it would be like to use or interact with the object or, in the case of a representational object, to be transported empathetically into the depicted world. If conditions permit, he or she handles, lifts, uses, walks through, or experiments physically with the object. The paramount criterion for deductions drawn from this interaction is that they must meet the test of reasonableness and common sense; that is, most people, on the basis of their knowledge of the physical world and the evidence of their own life experience, should find the deductions to be unstrained interpretations of the evidence elicited by the description. If these deductions are not readily acceptable as reasonable, they must be considered hypothetical and deferred to the next stage.

Although the analyst in the deductive stage moves away from a concern solely with the internal evidence of the object and injects him or herself into the investigation, the process remains synchronic. Just as the object is only what it is at the moment of investigation, and as such may be more or less different than what it was when it was made, so too the analyst is what he or she is at the moment of investigation. Ten years hence he or she might respond differently to the object because of different interests and a different mix of life experiences near the surface of con-

scious awareness. The particular encounter between an object with its history and an individual with his or her history shapes the deductions. Neither is what they were nor what they may become. Yet the event does not occur within a vacuum. The object is at least in some ways what it was or bears some recognizable relationship to what it was; the same, although less germane, is true of the investigator. The object may not testify with complete accuracy about its culture, but it can divulge something. It is the analyst's task to find out what it can tell and, perhaps, to deduce what it can no longer tell.

Sensory Engagement

The first step in deduction is sensory experience of the object. If possible, one touches it to feel its texture and lifts it to know its heft. Where appropriate, consideration should be given to the physical adjustments a user would have to make to its size, weight, configuration, and texture. The experience of architecture or a townscape would involve sensory perceptions while moving through it. If the object is not accessible, then these things must be done imaginatively and empathetically. In the case of a picture, the engagement is necessarily empathetic; the analyst projects him or herself into the represented world (or, in Alois Riegl's sense, considers that the pictorial space continues into the viewer's world of existence) and records what he or she would see, hear, smell, taste, and feel.[15]

Intellectual Engagement

The second step is intellectual apprehension of the object. With a tool or implement this is a consideration of what it does and how it does it, and in such cases may need to precede or accompany the sensory engagement. The degree of understanding at this stage (before the admission of external evidence) depends on the complexity of the object and the analyst's prior knowledge and experience. It is unnecessary to ignore what one knows and feign innocence for the appearance of objectivity, but it is desirable to test one's external knowledge to see if it can be deduced from the object itself and, if it cannot, to set that knowledge aside until the next stage.

In the case of a pictorial object, a number of questions may be addressed to and answered by the object itself, especially if it is representational. What is the time of day? What is the season of the year? What is the effect on what is depicted of such natural forces as heat and cold or the pull of gravity? In the relation between the depicted world and our world, where are we positioned, what might we be doing, and what role, if any, might we play? How would we enter pictorial space? What transpired before the depicted moment? What may happen next?

Emotional Response

Finally, there is the matter of the viewer's emotional response to the object. Reactions vary in kind, intensity, and specificity, but it is not uncommon to discover that what one considered a subjective response is in fact widely shared. A particular object may trigger joy, fright, awe, perturbation, revulsion, indifference, curiosity, or other responses that can be quite subtly distinguished. These subjective reactions, difficult but by no means impossible to articulate, tend to be significant to the extent that they are generally shared. They point the way to specific insights when the analyst identifies the elements noted in the descriptive stage that have precipitated them.

I have stressed the importance of attempting to maintain rigorous discreteness and sequence in the stages of object analysis. In fact, this is difficult if not impossible to achieve. Deductions almost invariably creep into the initial description. These slips, usually unnoted by the investigator, are undesirable since they undercut objectivity. But in practice, while striving to achieve objectivity and to maintain the scientific method as an ideal, the investigator should not be so rigorous and doctrinaire in the application of methodological rigor as to inhibit the process. Vigilance, not martial law, is the appropriate attitude. Often an individual's subjective assumptions are not recognized as such until considerably later. In fact, it is instructive in regard to understanding one's own cultural biases, one's own cultural perspective, to mark those assumptions that remain undetected the longest in the descriptive stage. These are often the most deeply rooted cultural assumptions.

Speculation

Having progressed from the object itself in description to the interaction between object and perceiver

in deduction, the analysis now moves completely to the mind of the perceiver, to *speculation*. There are few rules or proscriptions at this stage. What is desired is as much creative imagining as possible, the free association of ideas and perceptions tempered only, and then not too quickly, by the analyst's common sense and judgment as to what is even vaguely plausible.

Theories and Hypotheses

The first step in speculation is to review the information developed in the descriptive and deductive stages and to formulate hypotheses. This is the time of summing up what has been learned from the internal evidence of the object itself, turning those data over in one's mind, developing theories that might explain the various effects observed and felt. Speculation takes place in the mind of the investigator, and his or her cultural stance now becomes a major factor. However, since the objective and deductive evidence is already in hand, this cultural bias has little distorting effect. Indeed, it is an asset rather than a liability; it fuels the creative work that now must take place. Because of cultural perspective, it is impossible to respond to and interpret the object in exactly the same way as did the fabricating society, or any other society that may have been exposed to and reacted to the object during its history and peregrinations. Where there is a common response, it provides an affective insight into the cultural values of another society. Where there is divergence, the distinctive cultural perspective of our society can illuminate unseen and even unconscious aspects of the other culture. There was gravity before Newton; there was economic determinism before Marx; there was sex before Freud. We are free to use the insights afforded by our cultural and historical perspective, as long as we do not make the mistake of assigning intentionality or even awareness to the fabricating culture. Our cultural distance from the culture of the object precludes affective experience of those beliefs that are at variance with our own belief systems, but the process now begun can lead to the recovery of some of those beliefs. That is a goal of the exercise.

Program of Research

The second step in the speculative stage is developing a program for validation, that is, a plan for scholarly investigation of questions posed by the material evidence. This shifts the inquiry from analysis of internal evidence to the search for and investigation of external evidence. Now the methodologies and techniques of various disciplines can be brought into play according to the nature of the questions raised and the skills and inclinations of the scholar.

The object is not abandoned after the preliminary analysis—description, deduction, speculation—is complete and the investigation has moved to external evidence. There should be continual shunting back and forth between the outside evidence and the artifact as research suggests to the investigator the need for more descriptive information or indicates other hypotheses that need to be tested effectively.

Investigation of External Evidence

Allied Disciplines

Pursuing a program of research in material culture based on questions and hypotheses arising from artifact analysis involves the techniques and approaches of any of a dozen or more subjects or disciplines divided between the humanities and the social sciences.[16] The following can or do use artifacts evidentially: archaeology, cultural geography, folklore and folk life, history of art, social and cultural anthropology, and social and cultural history. Several others that do not to any substantial degree are linguistics, psychohistory, and psychology. Since the study of material culture as a distinct discipline (rather than as a part of art history or archaeology) is relatively recent and the theoretical substructure is still being formulated, the list of allied disciplines is probably incomplete.

The different relationships the allied disciplines bear to material culture need clarification. In regard to the three disciplines that do not use objects, the relationship is one-sided; material culture does not contribute significantly to, but profits from, techniques and insights of linguistics, psychohistory, and psychology.[17] Conversely, one subject area that does use artifacts, folklore and folk life, profits from, but does not make a readily definable or distinctive

methodological contribution to, material culture. Folklore and folk life seems out of place on the list since it refers to a broad area of investigation; as a field rather than a discipline, it is the opposite of material culture, which is a discipline and not a field. In addition to employing most of the other disciplinary approaches listed here, studies in folklore and folk life have made especially effective use of material evidence, inasmuch as material culture is particularly useful for any investigation of nonliterate or quasiliterate societies or segments of societies.

The relationship of material culture to other disciplines that use artifacts is one of common or parallel interests rather than one of interdependence. As noted above, social and cultural history, social and cultural anthropology, and, it might be added, sociology can view material culture as simply a methodological sub-branch to be utilized when appropriate.

Cultural geography has an especially close connection with material culture. The explanation may be that, since cultural geography deals directly with the shaping influence of the human mind on the physical environment, it is essentially material culture writ large. As with material culture, its primary evidence exists in the form of both artifacts and pictorial representatives. Cultural geography may be defined as an important branch of material culture (as with art, all cultural geography is material culture, but not all material culture is cultural geography); in time the two subjects may turn out to be aspects of a single discipline. For the moment the study of each is in its infancy, and their precise relationship remains to be determined.

Art History and Archaeology

I turn now to the two areas of scholarship that have had the longest working experience with material culture—art history and archaeology. The initial step in the analytical process, the physical description of objects (including the use of technical apparatus), is common to both these fields. Moreover the most obvious methodological steps away from the internal evidence and into external evidence also spring from, although they are not limited to, these fields.

Quantitative Analysis

Quantitative analysis, more common to archaeology than to art history, is most frequently the extension of descriptive physical analysis to other objects in order to determine the distribution, in time and in space, of certain forms, materials, or modes of construction. Quantitative study can also use the original object and others like it for considering such abstract questions as the relationship of objects to patrons or users vis-à-vis class, religion, politics, age, wealth, sex, place of residence, profession, and so on. For example, a student in my material culture seminar, Rachel Feldberg, investigated one mid-eighteenth-century Connecticut desk-and-bookcase. She began by noting the number of apertures, then she considered how the openings might have been used by the original owner and hypothesized that they were for sorting and storing papers. Given the desk-and-bookcase's functional associations with reading and writing, its division into upper case and lower case (as in typefaces), and the possible use of the lower section as a press (as in "linen press"), her thoughts turned to printing. She speculated that if envisioned in a horizontal plane, this particular desk-and-bookcase had the same number of openings as did a printer's tray. This suggested alphabetization, with the usual conflation of certain letters (p/q, x/y/z), and the use of the apertures for systematic filing. A quantitative survey of similar desk-and-bookcases would help to confirm or negate her hypothesis.[18] The development of computer technology makes possible a range and variety of quantitative research previously unmanageable.

Stylistic Analysis

The other two aspects of the descriptive stage, stylistic analysis and iconography, also lend themselves to broader diachronic and geographic consideration. The search for stylistic influences or sources is a basic art historical procedure. Within the broader framework of material culture, tracing stylistic influence has considerable potential. For example, New England in the sixteenth century had few if any gravestones. With the beginning of European settlement in the seventeenth century, gravestones appeared in the coastal towns; subsequently their use spread up the river valleys and across the countryside. Since gravestones are often inscribed with considerable data regarding the deceased, a corpus of subject information can be assembled about age, sex, religion, profession, and residence. Gravestones also have a formal design component. Analysis of the evolution and spread of gravestones styles in New England, previously a stylistic tabula rasa, might lead to a significant study of the dispersion of style, of how formal information is disseminated in a given culture.[19] Like radioactive isotopes injected into the bloodstread of a cancer patient, the gravestones would make visible the culture and its pattern of diffusion.

Iconology

Iconography is also a basic art historical procedure for the investigation of art influencing art. There is a gain in research potential when iconography moves to iconology and studies are made of the intellectual matrix—the web of myth, religion, historical circumstance—that spawned the legends and imbue the iconographic elements with their intellectual and symbolic power. The study of iconology leads ineluctably to the study of semiotics; all objects, not only works of art with highly developed narrative, imagic, metaphoric, and symbolic content, are the transmitters of signs and signals, whether consciously or subconsciously sent or received. And the interpretation of cultural signals transmitted by artifacts is what material culture is all about.

Another student in my seminar, Kimberly Rorschach, investigated an eighteenth-century Connecticut tall clock. Traditional research into external evidence, which is part of any investigation into material culture, led to estate inventories in an attempt to determine the normal placement of such clocks and to prove patterns of distribution by economic status. Similarly, clockmakers' account books were consulted for information about shop practices. But the deductive and speculative stages of object analysis framed qualitatively different questions and hypotheses. The tall clock stands slim and erect, slightly larger than human scale. It has human characteristics, yet it is both less and more than human. It has a face behind which a surrogate brain ticks relentlessly. It is not capable of independent life, yet once wound its mechanism ticks on and its hands move without rest. The human occupants of a house are mortal, with an allotted span of time to use or waste while the clock measures its irretrievable passage. Could the clock have played a metaphorical role as the unblinking toller of time who watches the inhabitants of the house, the agent of some extrahuman, divine power? A student in another course, Joel Pfister, analyzed a Victorian coal-fired parlor stove, a very different object. A useful black imp who ate coal voraciously and had to be emptied (its fecal ashes a material by-product in contrast to the abstract output of the clock), who would inflict a nasty burn on the unwary and could, if untended, destroy the house, the stove was not a celestial watcher but an iron Caliban that itself needed to be watched. How does one explore the mental landscape, the beliefs, to validate or deny such speculations? Sermons, private diaries, poetry, and fiction are among the sources for the investigator seeking not only facts but also the hints or suggestions of belief. Even if such hypotheses or speculations remain unproved, they are not necessarily invalid.

Observations on the Categories of Artifacts

Although all human creations are, in theory, useful evidence of cultural mind, in practice different categories of material yield different kinds of information in response to different investigative techniques. Some categories are responsive to familiar scholarly methodologies; some seem obdurate and mute. This final section reviews the categories of the material of material culture and considers their evidential promise.

Art

The fine arts in general have two advantages as material for the study of material culture. One, already discussed, is the applicability of the experience and methodologies of an existing discipline, the history of art. The other is that objects of art possess considerable underlying theoretical complexity (as opposed to technical or mechanical complexity), embodying by definition aesthetic and even ethical decision making.[20] On the other hand, as noted in the discussion of veracity, the self-consciousness of artistic expression makes art less neutral as cultural evidence than are mundane artifacts. Moreover, there is a special problem connected with the consideration

of works of art as cultural evidence, what might be called the aesthetic dilemma.

Hauser has argued that there is no relationship between an object's aesthetic value and its cultural significance. Each is judged by different criteria, and each set of standards is perfectly valid as long as the two are not confused. It is self-deluding to consider an object aesthetically better because it has cultural potency or to elevate an object as a cultural document because it accords with our sense of aesthetic quality. The aesthetic dilemma arises when an analytical approach breaks down the complexity of a work of art into simple categories and in so doing destroys the aesthetic experience irretrievably.[21] The question is whether the analytical procedures of material culture wreak this kind of aesthetic damage.

The initial steps of the methodology proposed here are completely descriptive and do not compromise the aesthetic response. Close examination of the object accords with accepted procedures for aesthetic evaluation. And the second stage of deductive and interpretative analysis involves objective procedures that only enhance and magnify familiarity, understanding, and aesthetic appreciation. Danger lies in the third stage—speculation. The aesthetic dilemma does not in fact arise from analysis; it arises from speculation. The aesthetic experience of a work of art (or music or literature) can be affected, even permanently altered, by external associations—a distasteful experience at the time of perception, the intrusion of a parody, an unsolicited, uncongenial interpretation. Speculation, especially by an "expert," can color, perhaps permanently, the perception of others. Regardless of the validity of the interpretation, the state of mind of the listener or reader is altered, innocence is lost, what has been said cannot be unsaid, the aesthetic experience is irredeemably changed.

Students of material culture who have applied the analytical techniques, including speculation, have in fact found their aesthetic pleasure in the object enhanced, not compromised. But aesthetic damage is done not to the interpreter, for whom the speculations are arrived at freely, but to his or her audience. This, however, is one of the pitfalls in the play of ideas, especially in the area of aesthetic criticism. Speculation is essential to a democracy of ideas, and the danger of restricting ideas or associations is much more serious than the occasional aesthetic damage caused by their expression. Imaginative critical interpretation may change an object irretrievably, but our ideas and our perceptions are continually being altered by new ideas and perceptions. That is life. The "aesthetic dilemma" turns out on close inspection to be less a real problem and more in the order of normal intellectual growing pains.

Diversions

In attempting to classify artifacts, I initially established a miscellaneous category for such things as books, toys and games, prepared meals, and the accoutrements of theatrical performance that did not fit into the other obvious categories. These objects share the quality of giving pleasure, or entertainment, to the mind and body, and the category has an affinity with, although separate from, art. This is a category in the process of definition, and further discussion of it must be deferred.

Adornment

Adornment, especially clothing, has, like the applied arts, the advantage of touching on a wide range of quotidian functions and of embodying a relatively uncomplicated partnership of function and style that permits the isolation and study of style. The potency of this material as cultural evidence can be tested by the simple act of criticizing someone's clothes; the reaction is much more intense than that aroused by comparable criticism of a house, a car, or a television set. Criticism of clothing is taken more personally, suggesting a high correlation between clothing and personal identity and values. Although personal adornment promises to be a particularly rich vein for material culture studies, to date little significant work has been done with it.

Modifications of the Landscape

The most essential quality of an object for the study of material culture, after survival, is authenticity. The optimum object is the gravestone because it is geographically rooted and attended by a great deal of primary data; we are quite secure in attaching it to a particular cultural complex. There has been little or no faking of gravestones and only a limited amount of recarving or relocating. Although an individual gravestone can be considered as sculpture, gravestones and graveyards (or cemeteries) belong fundamentally to a broader category, modifications of the natural landscape. Architecture, town planning, and indeed all aspects of the human-shaped landscape (cultural geography) share with gravestones the same quality of rootedness that ties artifacts to a particular fabricating culture. Although lacking the inscribed data of grave markers, architecture has much greater complexity. Having been built for human occupancy, it responds in very direct ways to people's needs. Glassie has observed that historically oriented folklorists have concentrated on architecture because the material survives, it is geographically sited, and it is complex. It is both a work of art and a tool for living, combining aesthetic with utilitarian drives at a variety of conceptual levels.[22] Town and city planning, that is, architecture on a larger scale, share these qualities. In the case of less complex alterations in the physical landscape a distinction must be made between conscious shaping, as in plowing or the construction of a stone wall, and simple behavioral consequences, such as accumulations of animal bones indicative of eating habits.

Applied Arts

Applied arts (furniture, furnishings, receptacles), like architecture, are a partnership of art and craft, of aesthetic appeal and utility.[23] They lack the rootedness of architecture and, except in the case of material retrieved archaeologically, present greater hazard in associating objects with their originating culture. Applied arts, however, have an advantage in their simplicity of function that makes it easier to isolate that potent cultural indicator, style. As discussed above in *Cultural Perspective*, the fundamental values of a society are often unexpressed because they are taken for granted.[24] As a result, they are manifest in style rather than in content. Stylistic expression can be affected by functional utility or conscious purposefulness. The configuration of a tool or machine is almost completely dictated by its use; the configuration of a story or a play or a painting may be similarly conditioned by its content or message. In architecture and the applied arts form and function are partners. Where the function is simple and constant, as with teapots or chairs, it can be factored out. The remaining variable is style, bespeaking cultural values and attitudes in itself and in its variations across time, space, class, and so forth.

There is, of course, significant cultural evidence in the utilitarian aspect of artifacts. Both architecture and the applied arts, by their use in a wide range of daily activities, especially domestic, are bearers of information about numerous, sometimes quite private, reaches of human experience. Another student in my material culture course, Barbara Mount, studied a seventeenth-century Boston trencher salt. We take salt for granted because our contemporary (largely processed) diet more than satisfies our requirements. Yet the physiological need for salt is fundamental; if deprived of it we, like all animals, would have severe physical and mental problems. Early economies developed a salt trade. Salt containers historically occupied a place of honor at the dinner table, and it mattered who was seated above or below the salt. Salt appears frequently in biblical imagery, representing desiccation and purity. People dream of salt. Human life emerged from brackish pools, the saline content of which is encoded in the human bloodstream. Salt has ritual functions associated with baptism; salt water is put on the infant's lips in Catholic baptismal rites; the forms of early trencher salts derive from medieval and renaissance baptismal fonts. Many body fluids are salty—blood, urine, tears—and in some cultures are associated with fertility rites. These scattered observations suggest the multiple possibilities for cultural investigation that can arise from one simple applied arts object.

Devices

Devices—implements, tools, utensils, appliances, machines, vehicles, instruments—constitute the most problematic and, to date, a relatively unproductive range of artifacts for the study of material culture. Much of the scholarship on devices has been taxonomic, recording functional details and mechanical variations. Little writing has been culturally interpretive except on the automobile, a machine with powerful personal stylistic overtones.[25] Theoretical writing that relates devices to culture has dealt with the stylistic modification of machine forms to make them culturally acceptable and pervasive images of technology in the popular mind.[26] But there has been little cultural analysis of the devices themselves, and no theoretical literature has as yet established a tech-

nological or scientific counterpart to the link between art and beliefs.[27] Certain devices have particular promise for cultural interpretation. For example, clocks and watches, linked with a significant aspect of everyday human experience—time—surely have cultural significance. Ocular devices—telescopes, microscopes, eyeglasses—also readily suggest themselves as extensions of the fundamental human activity of seeing. Although there may be cultural potency in a wide range of device materials, a question persists. Does the fact that they have been less successfully interpreted as cultural evidence than have other categories of artifacts simply reflect the present state of scholarship and scholarly interest, or are there fundamental differences in the nature of certain artifacts that affect their value as cultural evidence? We will consider one aspect of this question in the conclusion.

Conclusion

We have discussed the categories of the materials of material culture in a sequence moving from the more aesthetic to the more utilitarian with, given the broad scope of the categories, considerable overlap. Does the position of a general category or a specific artifact on such an aesthetic/utility scale provide any index of evidential promise?

The cultural interpretation of artifacts is still too young as a scholarly enterprise to permit final or fixed generalizations regarding the comparative potential of artifacts as evidence. But the weight of scholarly evidence, if one simply compares the body of cultural interpretation in the literature of art history, architectural history, and the history of the applied arts with the literature of the history of science and technology, suggests that it is the aesthetic or artistic dimensions of objects, to whatever extent and in whatever form they are present, that open the way to cultural understanding. The straightforward statements of fact in purely utilitarian objects provide only limited cultural insights. The fundamental reason why the cultural interpretation of works of art has been more fruitful than that of devices is the disparate character of the material itself. Art objects are the products of the needs of belief; devices are the products of physical necessity. Inasmuch as material culture is fundamentally a quest for mind, for belief, works of art are more direct sources of cultural evidence than are devices. Although devices clearly express human attitudes and values in regard to achieving control over the physical environment, the correspondence between the device and the need that brought it into existence is so direct that there seems little need for further investigation. And yet, such devices as clocks and telescopes have clear cultural significance. Moreover, devices respond as well as do the other categories of artifacts to the analytical procedures outlined earlier in this essay. Those procedures, especially in the descriptive stage, are largely derived from the practice of art history, and when artifacts are subjected to that analysis, they are analyzed as if they were works of art. Where devices respond to this mode of analysis—as, for example, in the perceptions of my colleague Margaretta Lovell regarding sewing machines, buttons and switches, calculators and buses—they do so not in terms of what they do, but rather in the way they are formed and the way in which they operate, that is, their *style*. If the cultural significance of a device is perceivable in its style rather than its function, then there is reason to conclude that, for purposes of material culture analysis, the aesthetic aspects of artifacts are more significant than the utilitarian. Why this should be the case is explained by Jan Mukařovský.[28] Mukařovský observes that all products of creative human activity reveal intention. In the case of implements (he speaks specifically of implements, but his argument holds for all devices), that intention, purpose, or aim is directed externally, outside of the implement itself. An art object, on the other hand, is self-referential; it is an aim, an intention in itself. People are users of implements—they apply them externally; people are perceivers of art—they refer it to themselves. Virtually all objects have an artistic dimension; only with devices do we encounter a class of objects that approaches the purely utilitarian. Even there, most devices incorporate some decorative or aesthetic elements, and every device can be contemplated as an art object, a piece of abstract sculpture, completely apart from the utilitarian considerations.

It is characteristic of an implement that a change or modification affecting the way it accomplishes its task does not alter its essential nature as a particular type of implement. But a change, even a minor change, in any of the properties of a work of art transforms it into a different work of art. Mukařovský's example is a hammer. Viewed as an implement, a hammer that has its grip thickened or its peen flattened is still a hammer; but the hammer as an art object, an organization of certain shapes and colors and textures, becomes a different object if the organization of design elements is altered, if the plain wooden handle is painted red or the cleft in the claws is narrowed. The explanation for this, and here we enter the realm of semiotics, derives from Mukařovský's premise that every product of human activity has an organizing principle and a unifying intention. Different observers may interpret that intention in different ways, but the artist(s) had a single purpose in mind. It may be unrealistic and unrealizable, indeed quixotic, for a maker to intend that his or her purpose be understood by all perceivers equally—in the same way and in the same degree as he or she understands it. Nevertheless, any fabricator must have that purpose, even unconsciously, in order to make. Therefore, objects are signs that convey meaning, a mode of communication, a form of language. The object may, like words, communicate a specific meaning outside of itself. This is the case with a content-filled art object such as a magazine illustration, or with an implement, a device. Such objects relate to externals. But a work of art that is self-referential, that is, an artistic sign in and of itself rather than a communicative sign relating to some outside function, establishes understanding among people "that does not pertain to *things*, even when they are represented in the work, but to a certain *attitude* toward *things*, a certain attitude on the part of man toward the entire reality that surrounds him, not only to that reality which is directly represented in the given case."[29] The art object is self-sufficient and when apprehended evokes in the perceiver a certain attitude toward reality that resonates with the maker's attitude toward reality. Because we cannot really experience a reality other than the one into which we are locked in time and space, we can make only limited use of an artifact as an informational sign, as a referent outside of itself, as an implement. We are dependent upon the degree of identity between its original world and ours. We may still be able to use the hammer as a hammer, but we may not be able to cure illness with a shaman's rattle. We can, however, use the work of art as an autonomous artistic sign, as an affective link with the culture that called it into being, because of our shared physiological experience as perceivers and our sensory overlap with the maker and the original perceivers. This is the gift and the promise of material culture. Artifacts are disappointing as communicators of historical fact; they tell us something, but facts are transmitted better by verbal documents. Artifacts are, however, excellent and special indexes of culture, concretions of the realities of belief of other people in other times and places, ready and able to be reexperienced and interpreted today.

Notes

1. There are material culture studies that do not require object analysis, in part because they address questions posed by the very existence of artifacts that lead directly to the consideration of external evidence. This is particularly true of socioeconomic studies that deal with artifacts abstractly, often statistically, to address issues of class, patronage, patterns of usage, levels of technology, availability of materials, means of distribution, and so on.

2. For example, poetry, because more abstract, is considered loftier than prose, chess than wrestling, and the practice of law than collecting garbage. In the world of scholarship the more abstract subjects—mathematics, philosophy, literature—are more highly regarded than such concrete and practical subjects as engineering. Such ordering takes place even within the material realm of artifacts, where all things are not equal. Higher value has been attached to works of art than to utilitarian craft objects since the Renaissance, when a distinction was made between the arts, which require intellectual activity and creative imagination in their making, and the crafts, which require greater physical exertion and mechanical ingenuity. Even in a specific art such as painting, there has long been an ordering of genres, ranging from history painting, which springs from the painter's imagination, at the top of the scale, to still-life painting, the replication of worldly objects, at the bottom. In architecture, the mental activity of design has been considered an appropriate pursuit for gentlemen (for example, Thomas Jefferson), while the actual physical labor of building has been carried out by laborers of the lower classes. In sculpture in the nineteenth century, the realization of the form indwelling in the marble was the work of the artist; hacking out replications was the work of stonemasons.

3. See the section on veracity, below.

4. Jules David Prown, "Style as Evidence," *Winterthur Portfolio* 15, no. 3 (Autumn 1980): 208. Peter Gay has observed that "the most undramatic work of art presents precisely the same causal puzzles as the eruption of a war, the making of a treaty, or the rise of a class" (*Art and Act: On Causes in History—Manet, Gropius, Mondrian* [New York, 1976], 3).

5. Henry Glassie, "Meaningful Things and Appropriate Myths: The Artifact's Place in American Studies," reprinted in this volume.

6. For an extended discussion of this issue, see Prown, "Style as Evidence," esp. 197–200.

7. Arnold Hauser, "Sociology of Art," in *Marxism and Art: Writings in Aesthetics and Criticism*, ed. Berel Lang and Forrest Williams (New York, 1972), 272.

8. Prown, "Style as Evidence," 208.

9. The location of material culture within the broader confines of cultural and social history and anthropology does not, however, preclude the use in the study of material culture of investigative techniques normally associated with other fields and disciplines. These techniques will be discussed later.

10. A measure of the potency of the language of form is the role that matter—and human experience of the physical world—plays in language. This is obviously true with poetic imagery and metaphor, where concretions vivify abstractions, and in the imagery of vernacular expressions, which articulate and expose human perceptions of the realities of existence.

11. The issue of sequence undoubtedly needs further study. I am aware that the insistence upon strict adherence to a particular series of steps seems rigid and arbitrary, an uncalled-for fettering of the investigator. Yet, I have come to appreciate the virtues of sequence empirically on the basis of considerable classroom experience with artifact analysis. It simply works better. The closer the sequence suggested below is followed, especially in regard to the major stages, and the greater the care taken with each analytical step before proceeding, the more penetrating, complex, and satisfying the final interpretation. Obviously, the procedure is time-consuming, and there is a natural impatience to move along. My experience has been, however, that this should be resisted until the analysis is exhausted and the obvious next question requires advancing to the next step.

12. Henry Glassie, *Folk Housing in Middle Virginia: A Structural Analysis of Historic Artifacts* (Knoxville, Tenn., 1975), 22–26.

13. The procedures outlined here for collecting internal evidence have other significant applications. Physical analysis, including the use of scientific apparatus, can provide crucial information in regard to authenticity. Other procedures noted below, notably formal analysis, can also be exceedingly useful in determining authenticity. These applications of the methodology can take place at any time, but it is preferable for the issue of authenticity to be resolved before the analysis proceeds beyond *description*. If a material culture investigator is to arrive at cultural conclusions on the basis of material evidence, the specimen being studied *must* be an authentic product of the culture in question. The investigator must determine what aspects of the objects, if any, are not authentic products of the presumed culture. A fake may be a useful artifact in relation to the culture that produced the fake, but it is deceptive in relation to the feigned culture.

14. The procedures of formal analysis summarized briefly here will be familiar to any art historian. They are not, however, arcane, and investigators need not be specially trained. Formal analysis is a matter of articulating and re-

cording what one sees, preferably in a systematic sequence as suggested here.

15. See Sheldon Nodelman, "Structural Analysis in Art and Anthropology," in *Structuralism*, ed. Jacques Ehrmann (Garden City, N.Y., 1970), 87. This splendid article sets forth succinctly the basis for contemporary structural analysis in the early art historical work of the German School of *Strukturforschung*, especially as initiated by Riegl and developed by Guido von Kaschnitz-Weinberg, and the *anthropologie structurale* of Claude Lévi-Strauss.

16. There is some question in academic circles whether social and cultural history belong to the humanities or to the social sciences. This perhaps suggests the lessening utility of a distinction between the study of human beliefs, values, and history on the one hand and the study of human behavior on the other, and the need for a new term to encompass those disciplines that study the interaction of human belief and behavior, whether historical or contemporary.

17. Inasmuch as the essential purpose of material culture is the quest for mind, psychohistory holds particular promise, but as yet the methodologies of this equally new (and more controversial) approach are as rudimentary as those of material culture.

18. This example is simplified for illustrative purposes and should not be interpreted as reductive either of the possibilities for quantification studies or of the scope of Feldberg's inquiry. Most quantitative studies would deal with a much larger number of variables, as indeed would Feldberg's study of desk-and-bookcases if actually undertaken. Also, her investigation into external evidence led to various other issues not apposite here, such as the use of letters of credit, which might be filed in the bookcase, in the eighteenth century; the velocity of correspondence of a New England businessman; locks and safekeeping; and the issue of reconciling gentlemanliness and commerce.

19. See James Deetz, *In Small Things Forgotten: The Archaeology of Early American Life* (Garden City, N.Y., 1977), 64–90.

20. "The more complex an object is, the more decisions its design required, the more a particular mind in operation can be discovered behind it" (Glassie, "Folkloristic Study of the American Artifact: Objects and Objectives," in *Handbook of American Folklore*, ed. Richard M. Dorson with Inta Gale Carpenter [Bloomington, Ind., 1983], 377).

21. Hauser, "Sociology of Art," 274–76.

22. Glassie, "Folkloristic Study," 377.

23. The English usage of the term *applied arts* is preferable to the American *decorative arts* for material culture purposes. The term is intended to describe objects whose essential character is that they combine aesthetic and utilitarian roles. Since the noun *arts* common to both terms takes care of the aesthetic aspect, it seems sensible to have the descriptor emphasize utility, that is, *applied* rather than *decorative*.

24. See also Prown, "Style as Evidence," 69–71.

25. For example, Roland Barthes, "The New Citroën," in *Mythologies*, trans. Annette Lavers (1972; reprint ed., New York, 1978), 88–90.

26. John Kasson, *Civilizing the Machine: Technology and Republican Values in America, 1776–1900* (New York, 1976), and Leo Marx, *The Machine in the Garden: Technology and the Pastoral Ideal in America* (New York, 1964).

27. Perhaps this will be achieved in time. Glassie speaks of the importance of banjos as well as banjo playing for folklorists ("Folkloristic Study," 380), but it remains to be seen whether this assertion will be validated. Glassie had discussed banjos briefly earlier in *Pattern in the Material Folk Culture of the Eastern United States* (Philadelphia: 1968), 22–24, but did not follow through to any cultural interpretations there.

28. Margaretta Lovell and I cotaught a course in material culture. Jan Mukařovský, "The Essence of the Visual Arts," in *Semiotics of Art: Prague School Contributions*, ed. Ladislav Matejka and Irwin R. Titunik (Cambridge, Mass., 1977), 229–44, and Mukařovský, *Structure, Sign, and Function: Selected Essays*, trans. and eds. John Burbank and Peter Steiner (New Haven, Conn., 1978), 220–35.

29. Mukařovský, "Visual Arts," 237, and *Structure, Sign, and Function*, 228.

Selected Bibliography

For more specific and comprehensive material culture bibliographies, see the works of Simon J. Bronner, Henry Glassie, and Thomas J. Schlereth listed below.

GENERAL WORKS

Braudel, Fernand. *Afterthoughts on Material Civilization and Capitalism.* Trans. Patricia M. Ranum. Baltimore and London, 1977.

Braudel, Fernand. *Capitalism and Material Life, 1400–1800.* Trans. Miriam Kochan. New York, 1975.

Bronner, Simon J. *Bibliography of American Folk and Vernacular Art.* Bloomington, Ind., 1980.

Bronner, Simon J. "Concepts in the Study of Material Aspects of American Folk Culture." *Folklore Forum* 12 (1979): 133–72.

Bronner, Simon J. "From Neglect to Concept: An Introduction to the Study of Material Aspects of American Folk Culture." *Folklore Forum* 12 (1979): 117–32.

Bronner, Simon J. "Researching Material Culture: A Selected Bibliography." *Middle Atlantic Folklife Association Newsletter* (October 1981): 5–12.

Chavis, John. "The Artifact and the Study of History." *Curator* 7 (1977): 156–62.

Ferguson, E. "The Mind's Eye: Nonverbal Thought in Technology." *Science* 197 (1977): 827–36.

Fleming, E. McClung. "Artifact Study: A Proposed Model." *Winterthur Portfolio* 9 (1973): 153–73.

Foucault, Michel. *The Order of Things.* New York, 1973.

Giedion, Siegfried. *Mechanization Takes Command.* New York, 1948.

Glassie, Henry. "Folkloristic Study of the American Artifact: Objects and Objectives." In *Handbook of American Folklore,* ed. Richard M. Dorson, with Inta Gale Carpenter, 376–83. Bloomington, Ind., 1983.

Glassie, Henry. "Meaningful Things and Appropriate Myths: The Artifact's Place in American Studies." *Prospects* 3 (1977): 1–49. (Also, rpt. in this volume.)

Glassie, Henry. *Pattern in the Material Folk Culture of the Eastern United States.* Philadelphia, 1968.

Hindle, Brooke. "How Much Is a Piece of the True Cross Worth?" In *Material Culture and the Study of American Life,* ed. Ian M. G. Quimby, 5–20. New York, 1978.

Jones, Michael Owen. *The Hand Made Object and Its Maker.* Berkeley and Los Angeles, 1975.

Kouwenhoven, John. *The Arts in Modern American Civilization.* New York, 1948; reprint ed., 1967.

Mayo, Edith. "Introduction: Focus on Material Culture." *Journal of American Culture* 3 (1980): 595–604.

Place, Linna Funk, et al. "The Object as Subject: The Role of Museums and Material Culture Collections in American Studies." *American Quarterly* 26 (1974): 281–94.

Quimby, Ian M. G., ed. *Material Culture and the Study of American Life.* New York, 1978.

Schlereth, Thomas J. *Artifacts and the American Past.* Nashville, Tenn., 1980.

Schlereth, Thomas J. "Material Culture Studies in America: Notes toward a Historical Perspective." *Material History Bulletin* 8 (1979): 89–98.

Skramstad, Harold. "American Things: A Neglected Material Culture." *American Studies International* 10 (1972): 11–22.

Smith, Cyril Stanley. *Structure and Spirit: Selected Essays on Science, Art, and History.* Cambridge, Mass., 1981.

Weitzman, David. *Underfoot: An Everyday Guide to Exploring the American Past.* New York, 1976.

Winner, Langdon. "Do Artifacts Have Politics?" *Daedalus* 109 (1980): 121–36.

THEORETICAL WORKS

Structuralism and Semiotics

Barthes, Roland. *Camera Lucida: Reflections on Photography.* New York, 1981.

Barthes, Roland. *Elements of Semiology.* New York, 1977.

Barthes, Roland. *Mythologies.* Trans. Annette Lavers. New York, 1972.

Blair, John G. "Structuralism and the Humanities." *American Quarterly* 30 (1978): 261–81.

Coward, Rosalind, and John Ellis. *Language and Materialism: Developments in Semiology and the Theory of the Subject.* London and Boston, 1977.

Ehrmann, Jacques, ed. *Structuralism.* Garden City, N.Y., 1970.

Gardner, Howard. *The Quest for Mind: Piaget, Lévi-Strauss, and the Structuralist Movement.* New York, 1973.

Glassie, Henry. "Structure and Function, Folklore and the Artifact." *Semiotica* 7 (1973): 313–51.

Hawkes, Terence. *Structuralism and Semiotics.* Berkeley and Los Angeles, 1977.

Kurzweil, Edith. *The Age of Structuralism: Lévi-Strauss to Foucault.* New York, 1977.

Laferrière, Daniel. "Making Room for Semiotics." *Academe* 65 (1979): 434–40.

Lévi-Strauss, Claude. *Structural Anthropology.* Trans. Claire Jacobson and Brooke Grundfest Schoepf. New York, 1967.

Martinet, Andre. "Structure and Language." In *Structuralism,* ed. Jacques Ehrmann, 1–9. Garden City, N.Y., 1970.

Matejka, Ladislav, and Irwin R. Titunik, eds. *Semiotics of Art: Prague School Contributions.* Cambridge, Mass., 1977.

Michaelson, Annette. "Art and the Structuralist Perspective." In *On the Future of Art,* ed. Edward F. Fry, 37–59. New York, 1970.

Mukařovský, Jan. *Structure, Sign, and Function: Selected Essays.* Trans. and ed. John Burbank and Peter Steiner. New Haven, Conn., 1978.

Nodelman, Sheldon. "Structural Analysis in Art and Anthropology." In *Structuralism,* ed. Jacques Ehrmann, 79–93. Garden City, N.Y., 1970.

Piaget, Jean. *Structuralism.* Trans. Chaninah Maschler. New York: Basic Books, 1970.

Trachtenberg, Alan. *Brooklyn Bridge: Fact and Symbol.* 2d ed. Chicago and London, 1979.

Marxism

Antal, Frederick, "Remarks on the Method of Art History." In *Marxism and Art,* ed. Berel Lang and Forrest Williams, 256–68. New York, 1972.

Arvon, Henry. *Marxist Esthetics.* Ithaca, N.Y., 1973.

Barbaro, Umberto. "Materialism and Art." In *Marxism and Art,* ed. Berel Lang and Forrest Williams, 161–76. New York, 1972.

Benjamin, Walter. "The Work of Art in the Age of Mechanical Reproduction." In *Marxism and Art,* ed. Berel Lang and Forrest Williams, 281–300. New York, 1972.

Fischer, Ernst. *The Necessity of Art: A Marxist Approach.* Harmondsworth, Middlesex, and New York, 1978.

Gombrich, E. H. "The Social History of Art." In *Medita-*

tions on a Hobby Horse: And Other Essays on the Theory of Art, 86–94. 3d ed. London and New York, 1978.

Hadjinicolaou, Nicos. Art History and Class Struggle. London, 1978.

Hauser, Arnold. "Sociology of Art." In Marxism and Art, ed. Berel Lang and Forrest Williams, 269–80. New York, 1972.

Laing, Dave. The Marxist Theory of Art: An Introductory Survey. Hassocks, Sussex; Atlantic Highlands, N.J., 1978.

Lang, Berel, and Forrest Williams, eds. Marxism and Art. New York, 1972.

Marcuse, Herbert. The Aesthetic Dimension: Toward a Critique of Marxist Aesthetic. Boston, 1978.

Solomon, Maynard, ed. Marxism and Art: Essays Classic and Contemporary. Detroit, Mich., 1979.

Formalism

Fisher, J. L. "Art Styles as Cultural Cognitive Maps." American Anthropologist 63, no. 1 (1961): 71–93.

Gombrich, E. H. "Visual Metaphors of Value in Art." In Meditations on a Hobby Horse: And Other Essays on the Theory of Art, 12–29. 3d ed. London and New York, 1978.

Lakoff, George, and Mark Johnson. Metaphors We Live By. Chicago and London, 1980.

Lang, Berel, ed. The Concept of Style. Philadelphia, 1979.

Prown, Jules David. "Style as Evidence." Winterthur Portfolio 15, no. 3 (1980): 197–210.

Schapiro, Meyer. "Style." In Anthropology Today, ed. Sol Tax, 287–312. Chicago, 1961. Also in Aesthetics Today, ed. Morris Philipson, 81–113. Chicago, 1961.

CULTURAL STUDIES

Anthropology

Deetz, James. In Small Things Forgotten: The Archaeology of Early American Life. Garden City, N.Y., 1977.

Dolgin, Janet L., David S. Kemnitzer, and David M. Schneider, eds. Symbolic Anthropology: A Reader in the Study of Symbols and Meanings. New York, 1977.

Firth, Raymond. Symbols: Public and Private. Ithaca, N.Y., 1973.

Geertz, Clifford. The Interpretation of Cultures: Selected Essays. New York, 1973.

Greenhalgh, Michael, and Vincent Megaw, eds. Art in Society: Studies in Style, Culture, and Aesthetics. New York, 1978.

Harris, Marvin. Cultural Materialism: A Struggle for a Science of Culture. New York, 1979.

Layton, Robert. The Anthropology of Art. New York, 1981.

Otten, Charlotte M., ed. Anthropology and Art: Readings in Cross-Cultural Aesthetics. Garden City, N.Y., 1971.

Geography

Hart, John Fraser. The Look of the Land. Englewood Cliffs, N.J., 1975.

Hoskins, W. G. The Making of the English Landscape. Harmondsworth, Middlesex, and Baltimore, 1970.

Lewis, Peirce. "Common Houses, Cultural Spoor." Landscape 19 (1975): 1–22.

Meinig, D. W., ed. The Interpretation of Ordinary Landscapes: Geographical Essays. New York and Oxford, 1979.

Zelinsky, Wilbur. The Cultural Geography of the United States. Englewood Cliffs, N.J., 1973.

History (Includes *Archaeology, Architecture, Art*)

Alpers, Svetlana. "Is Art History?" Daedalus 1 (1977): 1–13.

Ariès, Philippe. "Pictures of the Family." In Centuries of Childhood: A Social History of Family Life, trans. Robert Baldick, 339–64. New York, 1962.

Ariès, Philippe. Western Attitudes toward Death from the Middle Ages to the Present. Trans. Patricia M. Ranum. Baltimore and London, 1974.

Carson, Cary. "Doing History with Material Culture." In Material Culture and the Study of American Life, ed. Ian M. G. Quimby, 41–64. New York, 1978.

Glassie, Henry. "Archaeology and Folklore: Common Anxieties, Common Hopes." In Historical Archaeology and the Importance of Material Things, ed. Leland G. Ferguson, 23–35. Columbia, S.C., 1977.

Glassie, Henry. Folk Housing in Middle Virginia: A Structural Analysis of Historic Artifacts. Knoxville, Tenn., 1975.

Gombrich, E. H. Art History and the Social Sciences. Oxford, 1975.

Hume, Ivor Noël. "Material Culture with the Dirt on It: A Virginia Perspective." In Material Culture and the Study of American Life, ed. Ian M. G. Quimby, 21–40. New York, 1978.

Kasson, John. Civilizing the Machine: Technology and Republican Values in America, 1776–1900. New York, 1976.

Nygren, Edward. "Edward Winslow's Sugar Boxes." Yale University Art Gallery Bulletin 33 (1971): 39–52.

Paulson, Ronald. "Card Games and Hoyle's Whist." In Popular and Polite Art in the Age of Hogarth and Fielding, 85–102. Notre Dame, Ind., 1979.

Powell, Sumner C. Puritan Village: The Formation of a New England Town. Middletown, Conn., 1963.

Rapoport, Amos. House Form and Culture. Englewood Cliffs, N.J., 1969.

St. George, Robert Blair. The Wrought Covenant: Source Material for the Study of Craftsmen and Community in Southeastern New England, 1620–1700. Brockton, Mass., 1979.

Turnbaugh, Sarah P. "Ideo-Cultural Variations and Change in the Massachusetts Bay Colony." *Conference on Historical Site Archaeology Papers* 10 (1975): 169–235.

Wilderson, Paul. "Archaeology and the American Historian." *American Quarterly* 27 (1975): 115–33.

Psychohistory and Psychology

Abell, Walter. *The Collective Dream in Art: A Psycho-Historical Theory of Culture Based on Relations between the Arts, Psychology, and the Social Sciences.* Cambridge, Mass., 1957.

Arnheim, Rudolf. *Toward a Psychology of Art: Collected Essays.* Berkeley and Los Angeles, 1966.

Brobeck, Stephen. "Images of the Family." *Journal of Psychohistory* 5 (1977): 81–106.

Freud, Sigmund. *Leonardo da Vinci and a Memory of His Childhood.* Ed. J. Strachey. New York, 1964.

Gay, Peter. *Art and Act: On Causes in History—Manet, Gropius, Mondrian.* New York and London, 1976.

Gombrich, E. H. "Psycho-Analysis and the History of Art." In *Meditations on a Hobby Horse: And Other Essays on the Theory of Art,* 30–44. 3d ed. London and New York, 1978.

Gombrich, E. H. *The Sense of Order: A Study in the Psychology of Decorative Art.* Ithaca, 1979.

Hugel, J. C. *The Psychology of Clothes.* London, 1930.

Rose, Gilbert J. *The Power of Form: A Psychoanalytic Approach to Aesthetic Form.* New York, 1980.

Stannard, David. *Shrinking History: On Freud and the Failure of Psychohistory.* New York and Oxford, 1980.

Vygotsky, Lev Semenovich. *The Psychology of Art.* Cambridge, Mass., and London, 1974.

QUANTIFICATION

Garvan, Anthony N. B. "Historical Depth in Comparative Culture Study." *American Quarterly* 14 (1962): 260–74.

Hewitt, Benjamin, Patricia E. Kane, and Gerald W. R. Ward. *The Work of Many Hands: Card Tables in Federal America.* New Haven, 1982.

Montgomery, Charles F. *American Furniture: The Federal Period.* New York, 1966.

Prown, Jules David. "The Art Historian and the Computer: An Analysis of Copley's Patronage, 1753–1774." *Smithsonian Journal of History* 1 (1966): 17–30.

Prown, Jules David. *John Singleton Copley,* 2 vols. Cambridge, Mass., 1966, 1:97–199.

Ethnographic Method in History: An Action Approach

RHYS ISAAC

Potential linkages between history and anthropology abound, promising innovations in the way we think about past people, their work, their emotions, and their use of language and art in order to communicate with friends and neighbors, subjects, superiors, and peers. While these two disciplines have always existed in a state of productive tension, recent historians of material life have found in the work of field ethnographers and sociologists fresh approaches to the study of ritual performance and symbolic interaction. In this exciting essay on the framing of symbolic action in eighteenth-century Virginia, Rhys Isaac draws upon the work of anthropologist Clifford Geertz and sociologist Erving Goffman in order to develop a method that discovers the rich, ambiguous meanings of face-to-face communication in colonial American society.

In Isaac's view, the systematic study of "historical ethnography" allows us to see society as dynamic, as a process of symbol-making that is constantly transforming itself. Two major frameworks support Isaac's method. First, building on the work of Kenneth Burke, he maintains that people of all cultures in all periods are skilled in the use of metaphor. We think and act in metaphor, know ourselves and others through metaphor, and conceive of values in terms of metaphors. People, in sum, are metaphoric creatures. Yet the social use of metaphor is not constant through time; profound historical discontinuities typically consist of metaphoric shifts, moments when systems of collective epistemology—myth—are redefined. On the ground, in houses, factories, and fields, communication weaves both mundane and poetic metaphor into seamless, Geertzian "webs of significance" in which we intentionally suspend ourselves. The second pole of Isaac's method follows logically from the first: the creation of these webs is the essential cultural "act," one fragment of the human tendency to think of social life as a form of theater. His eighteenth-century Virginia plantation owners and their slaves were historical "actors" playing "roles." The landscape of supporting artifacts—houses, courthouses, churches—provided the necessary "stage settings" that in part defined the meaning of dramatic dances, legal proceedings, and sermons. These events can be interpreted as a series of bounded "scenarios" that bring into clear focus processes of social exchange that are in reality encountered as continuous.

Although such anthropological and textual models are useful in the analysis of both elaborated and restricted dramas in the past, they seem to suggest that a concern for ritual and metaphor demands that we overlook time's presence. Isaac avoids this pitfall. He reinserts linear chronology by pointing to three dimensions of social process: economic exchange, social intercourse, and the exercise of power and authority. In some ways, these topics are the traditional domain of social historians, but Isaac enlivens them by again alerting us to their symbolic qualities; he notes, for example, that exchange—which is, after all, what communication is in one sense about—and the exercise of power have expressive as well as instrumental dimensions. His method of historical ethnography raises new questions about how art and architecture functioned in Virginia society and how contemporary ideas of beauty and pleasure themselves may have been shaped in relation to prevailing ideology.

Anthropologists cross frontiers to explore societies other than their own. Social historians cross timespans to study earlier eras. Whether one moves away from oneself in cultural space or historic time, one does not go far before one is in a world where the taken-for-granted must cease to be so. Forms of translation become necessary. Methods must be found of reaching an understanding of the meanings that the inhabitants of other worlds have given to their own familiar ways. Social historians have therefore been drawn to anthropology as a source of inspiration in their endeavors to enter into past cultural systems. Attempts to open interdisciplinary approaches have, however, tended to take the form of raids in which particular cultural configurations, described in anthropologists' enthnographic reports from around the world, are seized on—a kinship support-group here, or a patriarch-dominated extended household there. The strained nature of such eclectic comparisons rightly produces uneasiness in those who offer them and has aroused scepticism concerning the possibilities of fruitful interchange between the disciplines.

Meanwhile, at a different level, anthropological conceptions of culture have been slowly gaining ground in the formulation of approaches to social history. Quite recently, and especially through the writings of Clifford Geertz, some historians have discovered alluring similarities between their own aspirations and those of some anthropologists—similarities that extend both to the thrust of inquiry and to a shared preference for close concern with actual, identifiable people and situations. The historian's notorious obsession with the seemingly intractable particularities of nonrecurrent, unique events and contexts has stood as a barrier to interchanges with aggressively generalizing, nomothetic social sciences. But ethnographers, it becomes clear, also have a primary concern with subjects of inquiry—cultural systems—that are unique and nonrecurrent in their complex configuration. Both anthropological and historical ethnography need a stock of general concepts by which the particular patterns of the societies which they study may be analyzed and made intelligible to the observer.[1] This essay will, therefore, take the form of a systematic laying out of a series of such concepts, beginning with fundamentals. The first and most important of these is the obvious, but little regarded, fact that *a society is not primarily a material entity*. It is rather to be understood *as a dynamic product of* the activities of its members—a product profoundly shaped by the *images* the participants have of their own and others' performances. A search for ways of interpreting social action-processes will be the principal purpose of this study.

The direct observation and interrogation methods of anthropology cannot be applied to social worlds long vanished, but there is an approach by which the historian can approximate, albeit fragmentarily, the notebook of the field ethnographer. A large proportion of the entries in such books consists of accounts of the doings of particular people in particular circumstances. Often the recorded actions may be noted as having a patterned recurrence. Not infrequently the entries relate to doings having peculiar features of a nonrecurrent kind. Both varieties of record are important to the ethnographer. Everywhere in the documents available to the social historian there can be discovered traces—occasionally vivid glimpses—of *people doing things*. The searching out of the meanings such actions contained and conveyed for the participants lies at the heart of the enterprise of ethnographic history. Action statements must be interpreted or translated into words the historians and their readers can understand.

"Translation" is the fundamental task of ethnographers, and in its inherent perplexities lies their greatest challenge. A culture may be thought of as a total language, or system of communication. More than just words, it comprises also gesture, demeanor, dress, architecture, and all the codes by which those who share in it convey significance to each other. Sentences in a given language cannot be translated unless, as we say, we "know" the language. On the other hand, if we ask *how* we get to "know" the language, we see that it can only be by repeated exercise in the handling of particular words and sentences, until we have learned and internalized both their meaning and the syntax by which they are strung together into intelligible statements. Much the same is true for the process of mastering the paralinguistic forms of expression—deportment, costume, buildings, and so on—that have already been noted as making up the total communications repertoire of a society. Action-statements (with or without a verbal component) cannot be comprehended and translated by ethnographers unless they have some understanding of the culture, but such grasp can only be effectively acquired by close attention to particular action-statements. This is all the more true of the processes by which, in the way of empirical research, existing understanding is refined into ever more discriminating appreciation of the subtle nuances to which cultural forms, like languages, are finely tuned. All the examples (except the first) in this method paper are drawn from a single regional culture, to the study of which the writer (who will act as the readers' "guide") has given the best part of ten years. Yet the intention is not to direct attention to particular findings about that culture but, step by step, to review *ways of examining action-statements wherever found. We must learn, by elucidating contexts, structures, and meanings, to undertake the reconstruction of the participants' worlds as they saw them*. The importance of the distinction between observers' perspectives (for example, our own as twentieth-century social scientists) and participants' categories (for example, those of the past peoples we study) should be borne in mind throughout the reading of this essay.[2]

Homo sum. The search for the understanding of others—be it persons of different time or place, or merely of different identity to the self—lies at the heart of the whole humanistic enterprise and is not a pursuit in which anthropology serves as the only guide. The concepts—and the artistry—of all who have found ways to enter powerfully into the lives and imaginative universes of others, whether as novelists, dramatists, painters, literary critics, or social scientists, must be employed wherever they promise to be serviceable in the quest.

The *primary sources for the method to be expounded here are records of human encounters.* For clarity and ease of reference the depictions of action that are collected for the readers' consideration as materials for close analysis will be labeled and numbered: *Scenario 1, Scenario 2*, and so on. These will be subdivided (a), (b), (c), and so on, for every significant shift in the time or place of action of which the reader is to take special note.

Concerted Ritual

A start may be made with a set-piece in which very explicit social relationships were expressed in a highly elaborated pattern of action. The time is March 1762, the place, Boston. The selectmen were reporting on one of their annual formal exercises of public authority made during the previous summer. Their report has the quality of a *tableau vivant*:

Scenario 1

(a)

Pursuant to a Vote of the Town of Boston at their Annual Meeting the 10th of March 1761, desiring the Selectmen to visit the several Publick Schools in the Town, and to invite such Gentlemen to accompany them therein As they should think proper, and to Report thereon

(b)

We the Subscribers accordingly attended that service on Wednesday the first Day of July last, accompanied by the following Gentlemen——Viz[t].

His Excell[ency] the Governor
The Hon[ble]. Samuel Wells Esq.   ⎫
The Hon[ble]. Andrew Oliver Esq.   ⎪ [Members of
The Hon[ble]. James Bowdoin Esq.   ⎬ His Majesty's
The Hon[ble]. Thomas Hancock Esq.   ⎭ Council]
The Hon[ble]. James Otis Esq. [Speaker of the House]
The Representatives of the Town
The Overseers of the Poor—
   Joshua Winslow Esq.
   [plus 8 other esquires]
   Rev[d]. M[r]. Hooper
   M[r]. David Jeffries
   [plus 7 other Misters, a Dr., and a Capt.]
   Rev[d]. Alexander Cummings
   Rev[d]. Samuel Checkley Esq.
   Rev[d]. Samuel Cooper
   Rev[d]. Andrew Elliot
   Rev[d]. Ebenezer Pemberton
   D[r]. Charles Chancey
   D[r]. Joseph Sewall

And found the South Grammar School had 117 Scholars, the North Grammar School 57 Scholars, the South Writing School 234 Scholars, the North Writing School 157 Scholars, the Writing School in Queen Street 249 Scholars all in very good order—
   Thomas Cushing   ⎫
   [plus 6 others] ⎬ Selectmen of Boston
                    ⎭

(c)

Voted, that this Report be accepted, and that the Gentlemen the Selectmen be desired to visit the Publick Schools the Year ensuing, and that they desire such Gentlemen to accompany them as they shall think convenient, and that they Report thereon.[3]

With the vote for a repeated inspection the next year a complete ritual cycle is encapsulated in this document. Simple but powerful statements about the forms of society and of authority within it were being made in this report and even more strikingly in the enactment to which it related. To begin with, a characteristic legitimization by equating a part with the whole may be noted. A number of people gathered together in a certain form, upon an occasion, were identified with "the Town of Boston," so that their "Vote" (or that of a part of them) conferred dignity and authority upon a yet smaller part (the Selectmen) who were empowered to act formally for the whole. (The word *authority* incorporates explicit reference to this *metonymic* process.) The enactment authorized by "the Town" was itself a powerful statement of the order in which named persons stood in the ranks of society and, more generally, of the hierarchy of offices that conferred worth upon their holders. More generally still the whole performance was a spelling out of the fact that society was indeed a ranked structure of many fine gradations from the very top down, with a sharp line implicitly drawn between those who were "Gentlemen" and those who were not. The entire, formalized visitation was an action statement of the dignity of learning—that it should be honored by the attentions of so many important gentlemen for a day. The taken-for-granted association between learning and the character of a gentleman was also rendered clearly in the action. There was no suggestion of educational professionalism or inappropriateness for gentlemen at large to perform the function of school inspection; on the contrary, the assumption that, as gentlemen, they had such a capacity was integral to the whole performance. Closely associated with the relationship between learning and gentility was the precedence accorded to the select Latin grammar schools, where instruction was given in those classical branches of learning that more particularly distinguished the gentry from others.

The *tableau vivant* format, which encompasses secular and sacred ritual, constitutes a kind of action-cosmology. Very explicit, high-order "statements" are forcefully presented about the nature of the social universe—that is, about the way in which the enactors intend that it should be ultimately grasped. The understanding of such complex configurations by those for whom they are intended depends, however, upon the incorporation of elements made intelligible in the course of experience in the everyday world.

Dramatic Interaction and Structures of Everyday Life

From elaborately orchestrated rituals we turn for the remainder of this methodological study to the recalcitrant complexities of mundane social dramas where, in place of concerted declarations concerning the nature of things, we will typically find the confusion of competing and conflicting definitions of what the actual situation was. The initial difficulties, as will certainly appear, are great, but it is to be hoped that the proportional greatness of the rewards will equally clearly be demonstrated.

Some basic concepts for the analysis of mundane social action will be illustrated in the course of a step-by-step explication of a complicated sequence involving a gentleman plantation-owner and his slaves. This is an episode that is, as far as the writer's knowledge extends, unmatched as a source of insights into the interconnection of slaves on an eighteenth-century Virginia plantation with each other, as well as with their master, his family, and his neighbors. It is further suited to present purposes in that it contains within itself most of the information needed to interpret and elucidate the patterns of relationship that it brings into view. (In a few places, vital information drawn from other parts of the diarist's extensive records is supplied in square brackets.)

The long passage that follows contains a multitude of scenarios: some of these will later be extracted, numbered, and subjected to close scrutiny. The time of this extended dramatic sequence was the cold, wet spring of 1766; the place was Sabine Hall, the seat of Col. Landon Carter in Richmond County on the northern shore of the Rappahannock River. Action extended also to the colonel's outlying Mangorike quarter and its fields.

March 4th being Tuesday, the serch warrant I obtained from Williamson Ball, a Justice being yesterday executed at the house of Robert Smith Junr., and there being found there 80½[lbs] of wool, washed and unwashed [and] also a cart rope that had been stolen, that warrant was . . . returned and enquired into before the Justice, who ordered a Called Court on that day week.

12. Wednesday. This day all the evidence attended the called Court, but no Court held. At night found that my ox carter, Simon, was run away, and examined Billy the foreman, who said he [Simon] complained of the belly ake and went away, the overseer being an [evi]dence at Court.

Extremely wet all through the month but very few drye days, but no Snow to speak of. [April too was cold and wet with occasional hard frosts.]

APRIL
23. Wednesday. Began yesterday to cart out my cow yard dung which I fear will be a long and troublesome job. . . . Oxen brake but badly—out of 8 taken up to break to the draft 1 broke its neck, 2 more so sullen that nothing can do them therefore turned out again. The fellow to the broken neck oxen also turned out as much hurt by his fellow. Two only work [tolerably?] The other still very sullen.

24. Thursday. Simon [the ox carter], one of the outlaws, came home. He ran away the 12th of March and by being out and doing mischief was outlawed in all the Churches 2 several Sundays; and, on the 10th of this month, having a great suspicion that he was entertained at my home quarter where his Aunt and Sisterinlaw lives, Mr[s] Carter's favourite maid, I had him R[*illegible*] watched by Talbot and Tom with guns loaded with small shot; and Toney withdrew. Just at dark according to my suspicion they came along my lane [and] over the lucern field talking loudly, as if secure they should be concealed, when Talbot, commanding them to stand, upon their running, shot Simon in the right leg, foot, and ham. He got away and Simon has stayed out ever since then, so that he has been now shot to this day 14 days. . . . It seems that Simon the runaway was shot at only about 11 days agoe. And he did not come in himself, for Mangorike Will [alias Billy the foreman?], seeing a smoke yesterday amongst some cedars by the side of the corn field when he was working, at night went to see what it was, and was long hunting for it as smoke is but rarely seen in the night. At last he got to some burnt coals and saw no one there. But, creeping through the cedars, he came to a fire burning and Simon lying by it, who instantly started up to run away, but Billy was too swift, and after a small struggle made him surrender, and brought him in to Tom and Nassau, who concealed this from me, in order to make as if the fellow came in himself.

Willy says he was not lame last night although he has now strummed it on account of his leg being shot. I shall punish him accordingly.

*   *   *

25. Friday. . . . My man Bart came in this day. He has been gone ever since New Years day. His reason is only that I had ordered him a whipping for saying he then brought in two load of wood when he was coming with his first load only. This he still insists on was the truth. Although the whole plantation asserts the contrary, and the boy with him. He is the most incorrigeable villain I believe alive, and has deserved hanging; which I will get done if his mate in roguery can be tempted to turn evidence against him.

Bart broke open the house in which he was tyed and locked up, he got out before 2 o'clock but not discovered till night. Talbot is a rogue. He was put in charge of him. I do imagine the gardiner's boy Sam, a rogue I have suspected to have maintained Bart and Simon all the while they have been out. . . . I sent this boy with a letter to the Island ferry at breakfast, but he never returned although he was seen coming back about 12, and was seen at night by Hart George at night pretending to be looking for his cattle. I kept this fellow up two nights about these fellows before. And have given Rit the Miller a light whipping as having fed them by the hands of Gardiner Sam.

*   *   *

27. Sunday. Yesterday my son [who constantly finds fault with my management] brought a story from Lansdown old Tom, that Johnny my gardiner, had harboured Bart and Simon all the while they were out, sometimes in his inner room and sometimes in my kitchen vault. Tom had this from Adam, his wife's grandson: that they were placed in the vault in particular the day my militia were hunting for them.

This Simon owned, and the boy Adam repeated it to me, but Tom of Lansdown said that George belonging to Capn. Beale saw them in my quarter when he came from setting my weir. It seemed to me so plausible that I sent Johnny [to] Goal and locked his son in Law Postilion Tom up. Note: every body denied they had ever seen them, and, in particular Mrs Carter's wench Betty, wife to

Sawney, brother of Simon, denied that she had ever seen them; as she did to me with great impudence some days ago. However Capn. Beale's George this day came to me and before Mrs Carter [in whom I see all the ill-treatment my son gives and has given me], told the story, and in Simon's hearing, that, coming from the weir he went into Frank's room and then into Sawney's room, when Simon came in to them. So that favourites and all are liars and villains.

These rogues could not have been so entertained without some advantage to those who harboured them; from whence I may conclude the making away of my wool, wheat etc., and the death of my horses. I never rightly saw into the assertion that negroes are honest only from a religious principle. Johnny is the most constant churchgoer I have; but he is a drunkard, a thief, and a rogue. They are only [honest] through sobriety, and but few of them.[4]

Seen as a whole, this affair of the runaways has the character of being a series of dramatic events meshed together like the figured knots in a lacework ribbon. Human lives generally have this dual character of significant encounters stranded together by continuing relationships. The patterns of such events initiate, reshape, or, more often, repeat and confirm continuing relationships from the threads of which they are woven. This depiction of life experience (and by extension, ongoing social life) as dramatic-encounter knots suspended in webs of continuing relationships is one to be held in mind as a visual model for the action approach to social organization. In the ensuing analytic reconstruction of a portion of the fabric of a single eighteenth-century plantation society, the attempt must be made, by close study of some nodal events, to reach an understanding of how the meshes of continuing threads spread out and, by attention to patterns of the converging strands, to interpret more surely the interlocking that occurred in the knots of drama.

Time and place are the dimensions within which drama occurs; persons are its "elements." The formal procedure for mounting a study of this kind must consist, in the first place, of atomizing these basic constituents and ordering the discrete items for analysis. A series of note cards separately registering each encounter of which we have direct or indirect intelli-gence must be prepared and filed by date and time of day (known or inferred). Likewise another series, to be filed by person, must note for each person in the affair, separately, each action or particular fact. (Places and actions in this case can be subsumed within the entries in these two series.) The "time-file" will identify for us, in sequence, each drama, great or small, and its actors. Out of the person file may be drawn diagrams of the patterns of known relationships surrounding each of the participants. These may seem dreary mechanical steps, but they are not, if the ethnographic investigator brings to life each encounter as it is reconstructed in its place in the dramatic sequence. Each scene must be played as it were through the talking picture projector of the mind. In preparing the person file there should be satisfying "clicks" in the mind as the collation of data on individuals makes possible the recognition of patterns of structured relationship.

The capture of Simon was clearly the key episode in the tangled ribbon of events and disclosures recorded in the long diary excerpt.

Scenario 2

Mangorike Will [alias Willy, alias Billy], seeing a smoke . . . amongst some cedars by the side of the corn field when he was working, at night went to see what it was, and was long hunting for it. . . . At last he got to some burnt coals and saw no one there. But, creeping through the cedars, he came to a fire burning and Simon lying by it, who instantly started up to run away, but Billy was too swift, and after a small struggle made him surrender, and brought him in to Tom and Nassau. . . .

The taking of a captive by a captor constitutes a hostile act. It establishes a relationship that may be treated as the central *structure* of this drama—although we do not have, as yet, sufficient knowledge to determine whether this relationship was newly created by the action or whether existing strands in the lacework ribbon were being multiplied. Mangorike Will had evidently gone beyond the minimal course of duty and had run considerable risks of injury in order to return Simon to servitude. The first identified *structure*, then, may be expressed in the formulaic mode:

Mangorike Willy [MW] *v.* Simon the Ox-carter [S].

In the conclusion to this continuous sequence, Tom and Nassau were enlisted as associates in Will's undertaking, thus making a more complex structure of apparent alliance against Simon. Perhaps the captor's transfer of his captive to them was an expression of plantation as functional hierarchy, they being personal attendants of the master. More probably it had to do with residence patterns, another potential source of structured relationships. It was doubtless late at night when Will came to the Hall. The master was probably not accessible, and Will was away from his own home quarter. At this stage the *structures* of alliance and adversary relationships appeared as:

$$MW + Tom + Nassau \; v. \; S$$

In the sequel can be seen a realignment of some of the structures:

Scenario 3

Tom and Nassau . . . concealed this [the fact of Simon's capture] from me, in order to make as if the fellow came in himself. . . . he has now strummed it [i.e., played the part of being lame and in pain] on account of his leg being shot.

Tom and Nassau, coopted as Will's agents in delivering Simon to the master, had formed a conspiracy with Simon and had cut Will out. The lineup was now:

$$Tom + Nassau + S \; v. \; Landon \; Carter \; [LC] + MW$$

The next encounter further complicated the structures connecting the actors, as well as reinforcing and making more explicit some of the antagonistic relationships already expressed in the previous two enactments:

Scenario 4

[Willy has come to me and tells] that Simon the runaway was shot at only about 11 days agoe [not 14 as on first report]. And he did not come in himself. . . . Willy [further] says he [Simon] was not lame last night. . . . I shall punish him accordingly.

Mangorike Willy now had not only engaged in acts hostile to Simon but had also entered into a league with the master, reinforced the hostility between himself and his captive (who would be punished "ac-cordingly"), and engaged in antagonistic action against Tom and Nassau, whose deception he had uncovered. Crucial parts of this last scenario (shown in brackets) are arrived at by inference of a kind that the historian, concerned to reconstruct interaction sequences for ethnographic observation, must frequently employ. The logic of the situation, indicated by the diarist's changed information, requires us to postulate an interview between Landon Carter and Mangorike Will. The unquestioning tone of the colonel's initial entry of misinformation suggests that he did not go out making inquiries but that the interaction took place on Willy's initiative. This deduction has important implications for the framework of relationship structures being delineated. A system is revealed in which an alliance was offered on the one hand while a conspiracy was exposed on the other.

$$MW + LC \; v. \; S + T + N$$

This process of scenario analysis may be applied to all the encounters of which the extended sequence contains traces. The action-structures may be identified, and the relationships between interactors that they project may be plotted. If this is done for each person who appeared in the sequence, there can be established (as far as the episode extends) a pattern of the relationships at the center of which that person stood. Taking the runaway ox-carter as an example, the pattern may be rendered verbally or diagrammatically. Simon had a trio of known kinfolk—brother, sister-in-law, and aunt—who lived at Carter's "home quarter." Betty, his sister-in-law, was a favorite of the colonel's detested daughter-in-law. The kin group showed marked solidarity and worked together under pressure with the master's slave assistants and others resident at the home quarter. (Note: Talbot, who shot Simon in an ambush, evidently was not as deep in this as the others, although the shot was directed very low and he later was suspected of giving help to Simon's accomplice, Bart.) Robert Smith, Jr., a neighboring small planter, must be included in the supportive configuration. If Landon Carter's suspicions were well founded, Smith was the channel through which were supplied the payments (in the form of liquor) that helped cement the alliance. All this may also be represented graphically, with supportiveness and hostility measured to right and left of a zero axis respectively, and estimated social status on the vertical scale (fig. 1).

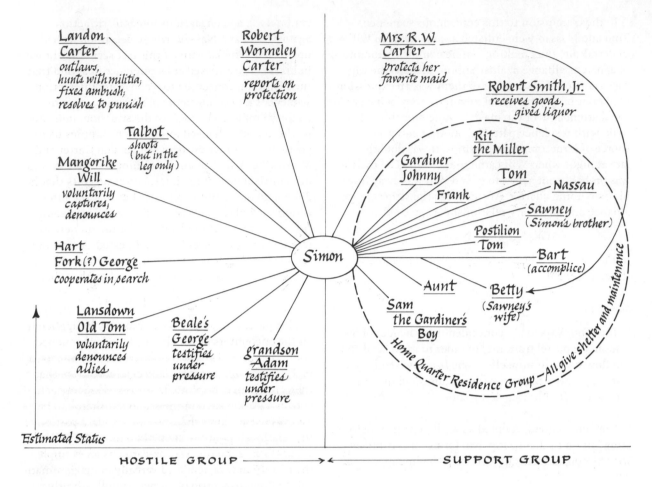

Fig. 1. The social relationships of Simon the ox-carter: enemies and allies. (Drawing by Richard J. Stinely, courtesy of the University of North Carolina Press.)

A map-diagram of this kind derives complexity from the conjunction of numbers of such elementary action-structures as were dissected out in the analyses of scenarios 2–4. The juxtaposition enables the diagram to reveal—or at least to suggest—larger patterns. Two kinds of Anglo-Virginian involvement on the side of an Afro-Virginian conspiracy show up in the diagram: the receiver-of-plundered-goods and supplier-of-liquor; and the lady protectress and her favorite maid, the latter perhaps an indication that female alliances against the dominating males might at times transcend the lines of rank and race. The most notable pattern, however, is that all Simon's supporters seem to belong to the home quarter residence group and that the antagonistic witnesses all are identified as belonging to settlements at other quarters. From Mangorike, the Fork, and Lansdown came the three who took action or volunteered information against members of the home quarter confederacy. Beale's George, who had spread accounts of the goings-on and who confirmed such accounts to the outraged Landon Carter, was from another plantation altogether.

Dramatic Interaction and the Dynamics of Everyday Life

Diagrams of the kind just considered have a great weakness in relation to the action-perspective with which we are concerned. They collapse onto the flatness of a page the time dimension that is so vital a part of the fullness of human interactions and continuing relationships. We need to look for concepts that fasten our attention explicitly on the dynamic character of social structure.

Exchange

Consider once again scenario 4, in which Willy had come to the master to tell *his* story. To make the interaction fully available for ethnographic interpretation, we must clearly go beyond anatomizing skeletal "structures." We must run it through the talking-picture projector of the mind. We become concerned not just with noting the fact that Willy's approach constituted an offer of cooperative alliance against Simon, Tom, and Nassau nor even just with the main content of what he had to tell—his account of the capture on the night of April 23. We must locate Willy's narration of his actions in the context of the developing structure of the continuing drama. If the rest of scenario 2 is carefully examined with an eye to a reconstruction of the encounter between the slave and the master (scenario 4), it will be seen that Willy's manner of speaking (if not his actual words) are very close behind the diarist's résumé of what he had been told. We can *see* Willy telling emphatically how he carefully noted the location of the smoke as he kept to his labors in the cornfield, how he thoroughly searched the dark woods (now bereft of the tell-tale smoke place marker), and how he continued his search even after he had found a cold fire. We must imagine him coming to the climax of his narration as he related how stealthily he crept through the cedars, how swiftly he sprang on the escaping Simon, and how "small" a struggle the runaway (who was not *really* lame) was able to maintain against this determined attack.

As captor, Willy had incurred or intensified the ill will of Simon and his faction. As informer, he had extended the direct impact of his antagonism by exposing the conspiracy to deceive. Willy's actions have to be understood as exchange. He was offering information and collaboration to the master in expectation of good will. He was offsetting with the benevolence of the master the malevolence of those whom he had offended. This example is very open and obvious, but it serves nevertheless to draw our attention to a constant *accounting process*—most of it far

more subtle and elusive than this—that runs through nearly all significant interaction. The gratifications exchanged in social transactions are not, of course, exclusively or even primarily material. Respect, approval, thanks, kindness, and companionship are some of the most valuable considerations sought after, while scorn, deferential self-effacement, malice, and hostility are among the prices dearly paid.[5]

The Significant Other

Mangorike Willy was engaged in *social trading* with Landon Carter on decidedly uneven terms. This was not merely an anomaly arising out of the extreme character of slave-master relationships. While exchange of gratifications is a vital part of social intercourse—and hence of social structure in its dynamic aspect—it does not usually, in its most important manifestations, take the form of equal bargains. Even within peer groups there are almost always leaders for whose approval and favors the rest must compete, with obvious consequences to the nature and extent of the gratifications exchanged.

The term *significant others* will be introduced here to designate those whose responses in the interaction process are of particular importance for those to whom they stand in this relationship. Feedback from the significant others—whether they be acknowledged superiors, equals, or inferiors—typically plays a vital part in the maintenance of the *identity* of every social person.[6] The most important exchanges and valued gratifications are likely to be involved in social transactions with the significant others. For this reason the most painstaking interaction performances are certain to be addressed to those who stand in this relationship to the actor. Mangorike Willy's emphatic narrative of his forceful capture of Simon was clearly an elaborate performance offered to a figure who loomed large in his social landscape.

Power and Authority

One who stands in the significant-other relationship to considerable numbers of persons is thereby endowed with *social power* and enters into transactions on markedly advantageous terms. Typically the inequalities of interactional exchanges in such cases are formalized into modes of *deference* on one side and *condescension* on the other. Where inequalities are extreme, explicit self-abasement on one side and marks of disdain on the other may be ritualized. Such ritualization of mutual postures makes them readily available at least for partial internalization by the interactors as inherent to the order of things. Where this is the case the social power of the dominant significant other becomes formalized as *social authority*.

The case of a master and his slaves is extreme, but the actions here analyzed reveal that even there, for authority to be effective as social *power*—or *control*—meaningful exchanges must be constantly performed. The master's disposition of material and social resources, extending even to the domicile of the slaves, rendered him inevitably a dominant significant other in their landscape, yet he needed to give protection, subsistence, and appropriate signs of acknowledgment as valued returns to these subordinates, from whose respectful demeanor and cooperation alone could arise any satisfying, identity-confirming sense of masterfulness. It was Landon Carter's ineptitude in managing exchanges by which he might have maximized control that is clearly revealed in the extended extract. His use of his diary as an outlet for his frustration and overflowing passion supplies us with these records for ethnographic analysis.[7]

Action-Meaning

Action in the social world is patterned by culture. Generalized concepts of hostility and support, deference and scorn, or the exchange of favors serve to identify very basic social-dramatic structures, but they are profoundly misleading if they do not draw us on to seek an understanding of the forms of action that are seen as hostile, the ways support is shaped by expectations, the manner in which anger and affection are expressed and controlled in the society being studied. The valuations of benefits in interaction exchanges are not fixed according to some universal scale of just prices but are determined by the culturally relative meanings with which participants imbue both actions and objects. The interest in exploring human activity ultimately consists in entering into those meanings—into the imaginative universes of other persons and cultures. It is for this reason that formal analysis of very basic action-structures, of the kind dissected in the preceding pages, is not incorpo-

rated in completed reports of findings. It can be subsumed implicitly in narrative or be incorporated in commentary on specific cultural features or both. The storyteller's art, informed now by ethnographic perspectives, must come into its own again in social history.

Participant's Perceptions

How did the actors themselves perceive the dramas thus far analyzed only in a social-science observer's perspective? They certainly would not have been content to interpret their own and other's actions and intentions in terms of such elemental structures as the "hostility" between Mangorike Willy and Simon or the "exchange" offered in Willy's approach to Landon Carter.

What, we must ask, did Willy see himself to be about, down among the cedars on the night of April 23? The entire record conveys strong impressions of an ethos of close neighborhood, in which the maneuvers of every person were known to a great many others—or could be guessed. It is tolerably certain, then, that Willy had at least a shrewd idea that it was the smoke of a runaway's fire that he saw. Would he have gone alone had he expected both the marauders to be there? Had he word then that there would only be one, and that it would be Simon? Willy may have been the same person as Billy the foreman and thus have had a grudge arising from (or intensified by) the circumstances of Simon's departure. He may have suffered for having been deceived and taken advantage of by the ox-carter who "complained of the belly ake and went away."[8] Beyond personal motivation, however, a more telling question for the ethnographer is how Willy's actions vis-à-vis Simon appeared to fellow members of their social world. The master's matter-of-fact acceptance of it appears on the diary page. The resentment of Simon and his supporters has been assumed in the analysis so far, but taking that as a relationship structure does not tell us the meaning the victims assigned to the action. Did they see it as treason by one of their own kind? *We* are impelled to this view, but there are reasons for concluding that *they* were not. Four years later Simon himself was selected by the master to lie in wait and catch another runaway who was being given shelter by a sibling. The residence pattern perhaps supplies a key. Informers and victims were consistently from different quarters, and it may be that membership of different settlements was a basis of accepted factional divisions, with life perceived as a struggle in which the power of the master was a taken-for-granted weapon in the hands of whichever side could use it to gain advantage. All this is reasoning to the limit from a scattering of clues, but if we are to get anywhere in our search for indications of the worlds of obscure men like Simon and Willy, we must assume the searching keenness of Sherlock Holmes rather than the stolidity of Dr. Watson.

Continuing the inquiry, we may ask what Simon the ox-carter was doing on his own, making a fire within sight of the field in the daytime. Was he preparing to make contact? To negotiate a return-to-work settlement? We do know that the time would have been right for that, since that very day Landon Carter was taking note of how "troublesome" the task of carting out the dung was likely to be, given the poor conditions of the draft oxen. If the runaway ox-handler (and trainer?) can be assumed to have been attached to the beasts his patient skill had transformed into working teams, then it can be supposed that he was doubly concerned to seize this moment to be reinstated by the master so that he could return to lead his creatures before any more injuries occurred. By such reasoning we may have gained insight simultaneously into the meaning of Simon's movements on the twenty-third and into one of his self-defining identifications. In this we may have gained a fleeting glimpse of Simon's world of meanings—perhaps even to know something of him that is not entirely from the outside.

Metaphor and Definition of the Situation

We can see further and a little more surely into actors' meanings by examining a different sequence of encounters that were acted out a day-and-a-half after Simon's capture.

Scenario 5

(a)

25. *Friday* . . . My man Bart came in this day. He has been gone ever since New Years day. His reason is only that I had ordered him a whipping for saying he then brought in two load of wood. . . .
This he still insists on was the truth. Although the whole plantation asserts the contrary, and the boy with him. He is the most incorrigeable villain I believe alive, and has deserved hanging; which I will get done if his mate in roguery can be tempted to turn evidence against him.

(b)

Bart broke open the house in which he was tyed and locked up, he got out before 2 o'clock but not discovered till night. Talbot is a rogue. He was put in charge of him. I do imagine the gardiner's boy Sam, a rogue I have suspected to have maintained Bart and Simon all the while they have been out.

The action-structure of this encounter centered on a proferred exchange that was at first accepted but that shortly after met with violent hostility in return. Bart's initial "gift" (or presentation) lay in artfully assigning to his master, Col. Landon Carter, the estimable role of fair judge in appeal. We can readily see how the primary form and meaning of the encounter were shaped by this opening move. Bart evidently "came in" of his own accord, went directly before the master, and initiated a rehearing of charges made against him nearly five months before. He insisted that the defense he then offered "was the truth." Wherever this approach actually took place, Bart's opening, by casting Landon Carter as judge and himself as appellant against wrongful conviction and unjust sentence, traced in the circle of the developing interaction a metaphor of the courtroom. The master could have instantly disallowed the judicial metaphor by ordering the runaway seized and whipped. Indeed, had he done so he would only have been carrying out his own earlier orders. Landon Carter's immediate response, however, further filled out the proposed metaphor by calling witnesses (or by recalling their former testimony). A retrial appeared to be granted. Clearly Bart's intention was that his innocence should be formally established by the process, the sentence against him quashed, and these circumstances allowed in extenuation of his four-and-a-half-month withdrawal of labor and obedience.[9]

Despite the fact, however, that the master's initial response implied acceptance of Bart's definition as a point of departure for proceedings, things did not turn out as the returned runaway had designed; such is the nature of dramatic, as opposed to routine, interaction. Bart was apparently isolated by Landon Carter's lineup of witnesses, who testified against him—whether under duress we cannot tell. Furthermore, the master was judge in his own cause—such is the nature of slavery—and so the encounter was terminated when Landon Carter, angered at the slave's refusal to yield to his overbearing insistence, gave Bart as prisoner into Talbot's charge, to be "tyed and locked up," himself turning to enter a vengeful judgment in his diary-cum-court-record.

The master's anger is ethnographically instructive in a number of ways. We may see in it the manner in which power and meaning, structure and statement, jangle together in the clashes of dramatic interaction. Bart's *definition of the situation* constituted a power-play, creating the action-structures we have seen. He might, of course, have opened with a feigned or real confession, with contrition, and with a plea for mercy. Yet even under pressure the slave refused to switch to such a groveling line, though the master evidently urged it upon him by the way he handled the citation of the witnesses. In his course of action Bart was not only adhering to his own initial definition (a man on trial *may* persist in asserting his innocence) but also was laying claim to an independent social personality, itself a form of power. It was this last that particularly evoked the master's wrath, in turn revealing clearly how *he* had come to redefine the situation. The sequel showed that he was right to feel threatened. His will in the matter and his animosity to the prisoner were clear to all, yet although the fact that Bart "broke open the house in which he was tyed and locked up" was known "before 2 o'clock," it was "not discovered [that is, reported to the master] till night." We must assume that Bart's escape was connived at, if not actively assisted, by those who knew when it occurred. Landon Carter, then, had overbid his hand in this power play. The runaway had come in freely and proferred his master a worthy role as judge with the opportunity to make a dignified retreat. Bart had, however, received in return a forced demonstration of his social isolation: rough treatment and dark threats of worse to come. Yet Bart was indeed a "person"—not isolated but rather endowed with evident social power. He had no need to submit to the crushing of his social personality; he could not so easily be held a prisoner in the close little world of Sabine Hall when it became clear this his offer of terms was not to be accepted. Bart

was able to step once more outside the metaphoric framework of "plantation law," which he himself had evoked, and resume the life of an outlaw, freebooting in the woods. In Bart's powers as a person (including his ability to open granaries and stores to supply extras to a needy people) lay the roots of Landon Carter's humiliation. The gossip that Lansdown old Tom brought out of how the outlaws had been concealed in the colonel's kitchen vault while his militia (that is, poorer neighbors called from their crops) were out hunting for them, must have been for Bart's faction an epic of the master's shaming, and so of the hero's triumph.

Judges and Fathers

The master's imprudent anger is significant in another way. Taken in conjunction with a great deal we know about the self-defeating anger to which Landon Carter was prone (with his close kin as well as with his slaves), it suggests that the meaning of the encounter with Bart is not adequately rendered if it is taken simply as a retrial upon appeal followed by judicial confirmation of sentence, imprisonment, and escape. The strong emotion evident in the master's entry concerning the hearing was properly incompatible with the role of stern judge implicit in the definition of the situation as he first accepted it. Tracing the course of the encounter, we see how rapidly Landon Carter was moved implicitly to redefine the action. In place of the courthouse metaphor with which Bart had opened, he began passionately to act out another, that of the outraged "father" whose will *must* prevail in the settlement of disputes within his household. (His outrage against Simon, in scenario 4, seemed likewise to be less at the six-week "strike" than at the employment of deceptions—pretended voluntary return and shammed lameness—to evade an abject submission.)

One of the dominant metaphors of the culture in which Landon Carter had his entire being, and Bart an extensive part of his, was patriarchalism—the image of stern fatherhood. In the context of the plantation community, often referred to by the patriarchs as "my family," the metaphor found some of its most powerful expressions, but it was a pervasive mode of construing social authority in the North as well as the South, on the eastern as well as the western side of the Atlantic. Let us, therefore, before leaving the now almost familiar context of Sabine Hall, take a close look at a further enactment, featuring largely the two-sided metaphor of stern judge-father/father-judge. This figure had it in his power to punish or pardon and typically was less concerned with good or consistent outward performance than with inward dispositions of the soul—that is, with wills broken into submission.

Scenario 6

(a)

[Nassau was Landon Carter's surgeon. He had been sent to attend to an overseer who feared he was dying. Nassau was also a chronic alcoholic. He had previously, at church, arranged with a slave from another plantation to supply him with liquor.] Yet Nassau went to this man [his supplier], whose name he says he does not know, and there took such a dose that just held him to get to the overseer; and what he did then God only Knows; but I do hope he [God] was graciously Pleased to prevent the drun[k]ard's doing wrong and [to] bless my endeavours in this humane way with Success. But what should I not do to Mr. Nassau? Nobody could find him; at last Tom Parker on horseback found him at sunset a Sleep on the ground dead drunk; as soon as he was got home I offered to give him a box on the ear—and he fairly forced himself against me. However I tumbled him into the Sellar and there had him tied Neck and heels all night and

(b)

this morning had him stripped and tied up to a limb and, with a number of switches Presented to his eyes and a fellow with an uplifted arm, He encreased his crying Petitions to be forgiven but this once, and desired the man to bear witness that he called upon God to record his solemn Vow that he never more would touch liquor. I expostulated with him on his and his father's blasphemy of denying the wholy word of God in bolding [i.e., boldly] asserting that there was neither a hell nor a devil, and asked him if he did not dread to hear how he had set the word of God at nought who promised everlasting happiness to those who loved him and obeyed his words[,] and eternal torments

[to those] who set his goodness at nought and despised his holy word. After all I forgave this creature out of humanity, religion, and every virtuous duty with hopes, though I hardly dare mention it, that I shall by it save one soul more Alive.[10]

On this occasion, for Landon Carter, the image of a merciful father, though initially eclipsed by that of a wrathful one, finally shone forth radiant. Thus he was left with the prayerful hope that his clement example might lead the soul of his servant into dependent gratitude towards his God. The resistance of the recurrently repentant but incurably alcoholic slave to the doctrine of hellfire—and perhaps an ambivalence toward the alternately harsh and merciful God—is finely caught in the master's excruciating reminder, even as the victim offered expiatory oaths, that he—*and his father*—had blasphemously set the word of God (with *its* promises of forgiveness) at nought.

The reference to Nassau's father reminds us forcibly of the constrictive closeness of this little world of generational, ongoing, face-to-face interaction. Therein we see clearly the social context of the comprehensive metaphor of fatherhood, encompassing as it did all order and rebellion, crime and punishment, suffering and relief. The close intimacy of extended household relationships was projected by the metaphor of the Father-Creator into the cosmic order. A meaningful social history of Anglo-America might be written in terms of the rise on one hand of impersonal contexts of interaction (including "the media") and the declining relevance and pervasiveness of the patriarchal metaphor for authority on the other.[11]

Cultural Frameworks

Most of the steps that have been spelled out so far have been concerned with the ethnography of a single episode, with a close look at some of the knots of interaction and strands of continuing relationship that worked into the extended lacework of social life on one plantation. No apology is offered for this narrow focus. Clearly, empirical ethnography must begin with tracing the strands through closely observed nodal actions. Historians are unable, in the manner of field anthropologists, to generate their own documents by looking about them, notebook in hand. They are restricted to the "notebook" entries that past record systems and the hazards of survival have left them and so must make a virtue of their necessity by scrutinizing those "notes" that do survive.

In life, the encounters, which are the units of study in action-oriented ethnography, do not occur—as they may do on a page—isolated from context. The participants must act within particular frames of reference by means of which they can orient themselves to each other in order to share, exchange, or even contest meanings. It is necessary to consider now some systematic approaches to the generally available public symbols and shared meanings through which actors relate to and communicate with each other. The action approach must explicitly take into account some of the ways in which culture is composed of interlocking sets of paradigms, or metaphors, that shape participants' perceptions by linking diverse forms of action into more or less coherent chains of experience.

Interchangeable Metaphors

The course of the interaction in scenario 5 flowed from Bart's definition of the situation through an appeal for justice to a "judge," who proceeded to become an angry patriarch. The ordeal of Nassau (scenario 6b) owed its development to Landon Carter's redefinition of himself from stern "judge" to forgiving "father." The identification of these pairs of alternatives in each case need not pose a dilemma in the interpretation of the scenes nor suggest a confusion that renders analysis in terms of metaphoric definitions of the situations inappropriate. On the contrary, these two cases serve as homely paradigms of important cultural means by which encounters can be linked to each other to form patterns that are intelligible in the first instance to the participants and, after careful "reading," to the ethnographer.

The sequences of metaphoric definition and redefinition noted above did not disturb the coherence of the encounter events because the two metaphors of authority involved—the judge and the patriarch—were in marked degree interchangeable. They stood as two sides of the same coin: either can be presented uppermost; the other is known to be present simultaneously. This reading of the situation can be reinforced, first, by taking note of the colonel's angrily stated program for vengeance upon the recalcitrant Bart and, second, by an extract from a court record.

When Landon Carter blustered to his diary that he would get Bart hanged, "if his mate in roguery can be tempted to turn evidence against him," he made it clear how closely present were the forms of judicial action, both to himself and, undoubtedly, to Bart, present not merely as metaphor but as institutionalized social constraint. There were limits to the kinds of reprisals that could be taken against the slave without a form of judicial process involving the testimony of witnesses. Landon Carter, himself the presiding judge in his county, had deeply internalized the role and its legal constraints.

In the following extract, drawn from an earlier period, another example may be seen of the metaphor of the "patriarch" vis-à-vis a "family member" from whom a child's submission was expected. In this case, however, the *actual* context was the courthouse. Real judges there assumed the paternal role so that the example also serves to indicate the broad extension of the stern fatherhood metaphor beyond the social context of the slave plantation.

Scenario 7

> At a Court Contd. and held for Richmond County [Va.] the Ninth day of March 1715—
> John Tarpley   Edward Barrow ⎤ Gent.
> William Robinson William Fantleroy ⎦ Justices
> The Court takeing into Consideration the Order passed on Wednesday last against William Leach, upon William Leach's appearing in Court and with humble Submission on his Knees acknowledging his offence and begging the Court's pardon, have Ordered that the ffine of ffifty Shillings Currant Money imposed on him by the sd. Order be remitted.[12]

The complementary relationship between the judicial and the patriarchal metaphors appears even more clearly when the above is considered in the context from which it was drawn. The records reveal how continuously the court rituals, supported by seating arrangements and insignia, proclaimed the fact that the justices sat as commissioned agents of a Father King. The figurative presence of this being, and of a Father God above him, makes it clear that the patriarchal metaphor was inclusive and that the judicial mode was one expression of the attributes of fatherhood in their fullest extension.

The Content of Metaphors

The task of the ethnographer begins rather than ends with the identification and labeling of the metaphors that inform interaction encounters and link them together in a patterned system of socially established meanings, or *typifications*. Neither fatherhood nor the judicial role are universals whose meaning is the same, regardless of time and place. Both have vastly different connotations in our world to those discernible in the foregoing encounters. Metaphors, then, may be likened to containers to be handled according to their *actual content*. The contents of metaphors of the kind here considered are, of course, closely related to forms of action. In the actual behavior of fathers and judges in a given society will be established *particular* meanings of the paternal and judicial metaphors in *its* culture. Metaphoric meanings conversely enter into and shape forms of action. Clearly we here contemplate a form of circular relationship familiar in the riddle about the chicken and egg. In the terminology of social theory, such a system in which the reciprocal relationship between "phases" (or *moments*) of this kind means that they are each simultaneously producer and product, cause and effect, is designated as a *dialectic*.[13]

Sources of Metaphors

The metaphors considered in this review of method have been those created by the association of images of one form of social action with another. Cases illustrating how readily such association may be reciprocal have been analyzed. Action-contexts are not, however, the only sources of metaphors that, by entering into fundamental perceptions of reality, have powerful formative influence on behavior. The human body, for example, is a ready source of the most pervasive metaphors for society.[14] Constant usage dulls our awareness that phrases such as "head" of a household, "member" of society are figures of speech with the body as referent. The content and operation of these metaphors depends, of course, on the ways in which the body itself is understood and experienced. Landon Carter's diary makes it clear that he—in common with his contemporaries—had perceptions of the body's functioning quite different from our own. For progress to be made in historical ethnography we shall have to break down the artificial compartments that separate such important modes of perception as those usually considered under the heading "medical history" and seek to discover the manner in which anatomical and physiological metaphors entered into past peoples' ways of understanding their world.

The Communication of Power and Authority: A Theater Model

In the preceding sections, consideration of action-structures and action-meaning has brought to light on the one hand issues of *exchange and power* and on the other modes of *definition* and *understanding*. The preceding examples (scenarios 2–7) could be expressed in reduced form as a simple structural opposition between master and slaves (or between judges and accused). In furtherance of systematic inquiry into the cultural frameworks with which actual complex interactions take place, questions must be asked about the overall ways in which ultimate significance comes to be established. Of particular interest in this connection are the ways in which demands and expectations are transmitted to be received as obligation. These are the essential processes by which *power* is defined, *communicated*, and internalized as *authority*.

Dramaturgy

The intent of social interaction is typically both *expressive* and *instrumental*. The successful externalization of actors' inner states so as to orient others to themselves and make them "understand" contains inherent satisfactions, as has already been implied under the structural heading of exchange. Interaction, however, frequently embodies purposes beyond the immediate gratifications arising from successful communication. In proportion as that is so, the actions may be defined as instrumental. The "power" of persons, for many purposes, is indicated by the extent to which they can make those with whom they engage serve in the achievement of ends beyond the encounter transaction itself. Historians, perhaps from a traditional concern with causation, have been largely preoccupied with instrumental action, the ulterior motive. Long neglect of expressive action must be redressed in ethnographic history, but the latter is no less concerned with instrumental power and the social means by which the actions of some are directed by others.

The whole congeries of social-dramatic devices by means of which interaction communication—expression, direction, and, ultimately, coercion—may be carried through is conveniently designated by the term *dramaturgy*. It will readily be seen that each culture and subculture has its own distinctive dramaturgical kit, consisting of settings, props, costumes, roles, script formulas, and, as elusive as they are important, styles of action and gesture. The word *role* has become so much a commonplace not only of sociological but also of everyday discourse that its origin as a striking metaphor drawn from the theater has been obscured. Its vitality and utility will be greatly enhanced if we constantly remind ourselves of its original reference and employ it explicitly in the context of dramaturgical analysis.

The theater model serves to emphasize the formalities that govern so much of social life. The shared meanings with which settings, costumes, roles, and styles are invested serve at once as limiting constraints on the actors and as channels through which effective—indeed, powerful and coercive—communication can be directed. Relating this model to earlier discussion of definitions of the situation and encompassing metaphors, it can be seen that the former approximate actor-initiated stage directions for any particular scene, while the latter constitute the overall theatrical conventions of a particular culture. The great metaphors enter into the creation and interpretation of settings; they are a major source of available roles, governing also the actors' selection among them and their styles of self-presentation. Above all, it is through the great metaphors that the very perception of what constitutes significant action, or drama, is determined.

Settings

The illustration of method in the analysis of the communication of meaning and power through the particular dramaturgical "kit" of a past regional culture can best begin with one of the most concrete and determinative of the items involved: physical setting.

Willy's capture of Simon in the woods has been ob-

served; Bart's appeal to Landon Carter for justice has been analyzed. It is true that Simon's campfire amongst the cedars effectively defined, especially at night, a social space in that wild surround and that this setting was integral to the shape of the action, but so tenuous a demarcation hardly lends itself to formal analysis. The contrary is true of the returned runaway's calculated play for reinstatement. Whether it took place in the central hallway of the master's great house, at one of the grand portals, or in the courtyard, this enactment was integrated with a highly formal setting.

Architecture provides a potent medium for elaborately coded nonverbal statement. Such encompassing messages stood in reciprocal relationship to much of Anglo-American, and even Afro-American, significant action. Considering Bart's appeal, rejection, and abortive punishment in the context of the high-order statements of dignity and authority made by its setting must serve briefly to illustrate the importance of architectural interpretation for the ethnographic historian. Sabine Hall was a gentleman's seat built on a pattern that had become standard in eighteenth-century Virginia (and elsewhere in Anglo-America). The pattern, or theme with minor variations, was a colonial adaptation of English classical design. Andrea Palladio's *Four Books of Architecture* had appeared in English editions three times in the decades before Sabine Hall was built, as though to make altogether verbally explicit the meaning of the form of country-house architecture that had become universal in the Anglophone world by that time. Figure 2 shows a sketch reproduction of Sabine Hall approximately as it stood, with its elaborate, tight symmetries, in 1766. The lengthy caption beneath contains the essence of the social symbolism expounded in Palladio's formulations about domestic architecture:

> Palladio, First Book, c I: An edifice may be esteemed commodious, when every part or member stands in its due place and fit situation, neither above nor below its dignity and use. . . .
>
> Beauty will result from the form and correspondence of the whole, with respect to the several parts, of the parts with regard to each other, and again to the whole; that the structure may appear *an entire and compleat body*, wherein each member agrees with the other.[15]

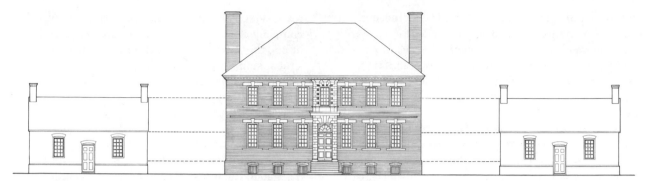

Fig. 2. Sabine Hall, home of Landon Carter, Richmond County, Virginia, ca. 1740; this reconstruction shows it as it was about 1766. In fine neo-Palladian fashion, it was "An edifice . . . [with] every part . . . in its due place and fit situation, neither above nor below its dignity" (Isaac Ware, trans., *The Four Books of Andrea Palladio's Architecture* . . . [London, 1738], i). (Drawing by Benjamin Hellier, courtesy of the University of North Carolina Press.)

For Palladio and his followers the house was informed by the metaphor of the body, conventionally conceived as a hierarchy of parts extending upward from the lowest parts, concerned with the elimination of waste, to the head. The elevated grand portal and the stately reception rooms of the *piano nobile* not only provided, therefore, a fine setting for the master's displays of high social worth but also literally figured the social hierarchy of which he was the patriarchal head. In a close, face-to-face society in which the gentry had extensive control of access to scarce resources and filled most of the significant symbolic roles, one might bargain over the terms of domination as Bart did, but one could not argue with the basic statements embodied in the great buildings.

Role Definition

The great house was essential in sustaining the master's part in social drama. It stood in a dialectic relationship to him, for it took its meaning from his social existence and, in turn, contributed powerfully to the shaping of his patterns of behavior. Brief consideration of some basic modes of role definition, of expressive style, and of social characterization must be entered upon.

Such polarities as light and dark, high and low, right and left, male and female enter profoundly into the socialization process by which culture is both maintained and transmitted. As with all else in human perception, these oppositions are internalized with culturally assigned content and meaning.[16] Two brief examples must serve to open for us this infinitely complex process, the first a routine, weekly enactment observed by a New Jersey Presbyterian tutor, newly arrived in Landon Carter's neighborhood in the fall of 1773. He was describing the manner of church attendance there:

Scenario 8

I observe it is a general custom on Sundays here, with Gentlemen to invite one another home to dine, after Church, and to consult about, determine their common business, either before or after Service—It is not the Custom for Gentlemen to go into Church til Service is beginning, when they enter in a Body, in the same manner as they come out. . . . They stay also after the Service is over, usually as long, sometimes longer than the Parson was preaching—Almost every Lady wears a red cloak, and when they ride out they tye a white handkerchief over their Head and face.[17]

No obvious metaphor was here stated in action, and yet a dramatic pattern is evident: important sets of social oppositions were reinforced, boundaries demarcated. The contrasts that the forms of action highlighted may be listed in ascending order of clarity and emphasis. First, there was the line drawn by status: the socially inferior slaves, servants, overseers, and tenants were not part of the company that defined its superiority by coming in only as the service was beginning. Second, there was a clear age distinction: only grown persons would be included in the select company. Third, and most definitive, there was the ever-recurrent division of the sexes. It was the gentle*men*, and not females of any description, who entered the church dramatically and took possession of it by pressing through to its "highest" seats at the front.

An oppositional structure of conventional sex roles is one of the most basic items in the dramaturgical kit of every culture. The identification of this item—as with the labeling of metaphors—is only a beginning. Each culture endows the contrasting roles with a degree of intensity and a specific content of its own, deriving from the whole a complex of action-forms and meanings. In the above case, the public performance of the most prestigious male role, that of the gentleman, provides a clue. Closer examination will show that the role of gentleman derived much of its content from the great patriarchal metaphor. Those who proudly played the male part of gentleman by their entrance into the church were supremely those who played the patriarchal part in the churchyard, before and after, when they issued invitations to dine. A man could not be a gentleman in the fullest sense of the word in this society unless he was the independent head of his own household having slaves, certainly, and a wife and children, ideally, to reflect in their degrees the greatness of the master. The way in which sex-role oppositions underpinned the maintenance of social personality in this mode is subtly reinforced by the note on the riding-out attire of the ladies. In contrast to the bold-faced gentlemen, these females protected, by means of the kerchief, delicate complexions from a climate considered ferocious.

Further illustration of these themes may be sought from a traveler's account of a wedding at a Palladian great house. The place is Blandfield, the seat of Landon Carter's son-in-law, Robert Beverley. The time is December 1785:

Scenario 9

We arrived at Mr Beverley's at one o'clock. . . . About two the company became very much crowded. We were now shown into the drawing room and there had the pleasure of seeing Miss Beverley and Mr Randolph joined together in holy matrimony. The ceremony was really affecting and awful. The sweet bride could not help shedding tears, which affected her mother and the whole company. After the ceremony of saluting [the bride], the ladies retired. At four we joined them to a most sumptuous dinner that would have done honor to any nobleman's house in England. We were about a hundred in company. . . . After dinner we danced cotillions, minuets, Virginia and Scotch reels, country dances, jigs, etc. till ten o'clock. . . . After supper, which was as elegant as the dinner . . . we continued dancing. [The next day] Our dinner was to the full as elegant as yesterday and the company rather larger. Mr Beverley has everything within himself—no markets to go to here.

At five . . . began dancing again. . . . We were all exceedingly happy in each other's company, the ladies being perfectly free and easy and at the same time elegant in their manners. They would grace any country whatsoever. The manner in which this affair has been managed does honor to Mr Beverley.[18]

Weddings, of course, explicitly ritualize the differentiation of the sexes. This case clearly depicts sets of stylized sex roles, with the women shedding tears and enabling the "whole company," including the men, to show tender emotions by way of identification with them. The ceremony and accompanying festivities, however, constituted overall a strong statement of the male role of the patriarch-provider who gave his daughter in marriage and, by supplying the means, created the occasion for the celebration. The feasting and the music manifested the master's capacity to extend his munificence widely. The elaborate sequences of dance forms, the signs of shared happiness, and the combination of "ease" with "elegance" all served to affirm his greatness in a refined mode and celebrated the fact that the persons in his connection were worthy of the hospitality afforded and could add luster to his "house." On both sides of the exchanges between host and guests, performance in a "high" style was of great importance, being most richly coded in the "statements" of the dance, which, in the dominant cultural tradition of Blandfield, offered courtly representations of polite social intercourse between males and females. The cultural provincialism of this and other parts of America at the time meant that the known derivation of these dance forms from the fashionable circles of the English metropolis contributed strongly to their appreciation as high style. The same considerations invited—almost compelled—the explicit comparisons made by this diarist-traveler.

The effect striven for in all the display, ritual, and stylized interaction apparent here was to create and sustain for the man who contrived the occasion a certain clear social identity or personality. Such a culturally meaningful identity—in this case that of the great gentleman—can conveniently be designated by the Latin word *persona* which though ancestor to our word *person* directly refers to the conventionalized masks connoting familiar roles and role-types on the Roman stage. The concept has value in the application of the theater model to ethnographic history since it directs attention to the manner in which a past cultural system defines both what a person is and what kinds of persons there are in the society, as well as what different *personae* an individual might, on different occasions, present to the world.[19]

Milieux

The renditions of exalted style so evident in the festivities at Blandfield, and so important in contributing to the received *personae* of Robert Beverley, cannot be socially understood in isolation. These performances were *high* precisely in contrast, as all were aware, to *lower* styles found elsewhere or in the same place on other occasions. The issue of cultural diversification—actual or incipient *pluralism*—must at last be dealt with explicitly.

The authors of the classic anthropological ethnographies did not face this problem in acute form. The societies studied by these pioneers all had indeed at least a radical division into male and female subcultures, but, by contrast with urbanized, class-divided western society, they seemed "simple" and were designated as such. By and large they could be treated as the repositories of single, rather than multiple, cultural systems. It seems, however, that the use of writing in a society both indicates a fairly high degree of specialized division of labor and reinforces such divisions by the uneven development of literacy skills. Thus, historians working from written records invariably face actual or incipient cultural pluralism as a fact of the social worlds they study.

Extending the application of the theater model, it may be seen that every social system will contain congeries of action settings with overlapping casts,

styles, and conventions. Such clusters, based on shared stagecraft, may be designated *milieux*. In this context the term must operate as the dramaturgical transportation of the concept of *subculture*—itself a term that, in the ethnographic perspective, subsumes the phenomenon that is commonly designated by the word *class*. The resonances of meaning sounded by the word *milieu* should render it particularly useful as an aid in the analysis of such small-community social systems as made up nearly all of early America. The term suggests habitual associations, specialized styles of communication, and shared understandings, without having the connotations of self-contained exclusiveness that are strong for such terms as *subculture* and *class*, connotations that are inappropriate to the face-to-face intimacy of interaction extending from top to bottom in premodern agrarian societies.

Dancing, which has been seen to feature so largely at the grand wedding, provides us with a little paradigm of distinct but intercommunicating milieux. At Blandfield, performances were evidently confined to elegant measures in the European tradition, cotillions and minuets predominating, and forms of country dance (*contre dans*) that had been stylized into a courtly mold, much as the peasant village had been transformed into the Petit Trianon. Yet this was not the only mode known to—nor even practiced by—the Virginia gentry, as may be seen in the following vivid glimpses drawn from the journal of an English traveler visiting on the Potomac in 1774:

Scenario 10

[Sunday, May 29, 1774]
Mr. Bayley and I went to see a Negro Ball. Sundays . . . they generally meet together and amuse themselves with Dancing to the Banjo. This musical instrument . . . is made of a Gourd . . . with only four strings and played with the fingers. . . . Some of them sing to it. . . . In their songs they generally relate the usage they have received from their Masters and Mistresses in a very satirical stile and manner. . . . Their Dancing is most violent exercise, but so irregular and grotesque I cannot describe it.

Soon after, the same traveler attended two celebrations held among poor white farm folk on the Maryland side of the Potomac but still within the Chesapeake cultural region:

Scenario 11

(a)

I went ashore to what they call a reaping frolic. This is a Harvest Feast. The people very merry, Dancing without either Shoes or Stockings and the Girls without stays.

(b)

These Barbecues are Hogs, roasted whole. This was under a large Tree. A great number of young people met together with a Fiddle and Banjo played by two Negroes, with Plenty of Toddy, which both Men and Women seem to be very fond of. I believe they have danced and drunk till there are few sober people amongst them.

Later he went to a Twelfth Night ball conducted by the gentlemen and ladies of Alexandria, on the Virginia side of the river:

Scenario 12

Betwixt the Country dances [i.e., *contre danses*] they have what I call everlasting jigs. A couple gets up and begins to dance a jig (to some Negro tune) others comes and cuts them out, and these dances always last as long as the Fiddler can play. This is sociable, but I think it looks more like a Bacchanalian dance than one in a polite assembly.[20]

The complexes of traditions, performances, and sex roles, of which intimations are given in these and other accounts, cannot be treated here. The present concern is with the spectrum of performance styles clearly apparent and with the possibilities for social statement that such a system establishes. That the spectrum is, in fact, a circle, cannot be inferred only from the recorded inclusion of "Negro" measures in gentry dancing but also from the assurance we may have that, unobserved (or uncomprehended) by our English traveler, the Blacks would extend their satires to incorporate parodies of the courtly forms. Such systems not only are found in the potent action statements of the dance, but they are common in speech, where the words *accent* or *tone* are applied (*register*

in the sociolinguist's term), and in writing, where they are comprehended under the heading *style*— which in turn supplies our metaphor for all coded patterns of action.[21]

Conclusion

Interaction supplies the threads of which social fabric is woven. The quality and patterning of such threads in a society, or milieu, will largely determine the texture of the lives of its members. The preceding sections have set forth some steps of a method designed to develop comprehension of the spinning and weaving of the patterned, textured fabrics of past societies as they may be discovered fragmentarily in documents remaining for the historian. Since attention has necessarily been fixed on forms of action, the structural model of threads and lacework has needed to be complemented by another more dynamic one—the theater—to which processes of communication are central. Accordingly, the aim of ethnographic history is formulated as a reaching out to understand life as it was experienced by actors on past stages, each playing his or her own part and responding to the parts of others according to their conceptions of the nature of the play.

The step-by-step approach adopted, with commentary on the modes of reading the documents at each stage, has intentionally stressed the need for systematic analysis rather than intuition. The objective of the endeavor—the understanding and depiction of life itself—is, however, very close to the quest of the artist. It should not, therefore, be surprising that devices developed in forms of art and concepts arising in the discourse concerning art, such as *metaphor*, *dramaturgy*, and *milieu*, have been found serviceable for incorporation in the models proposed for use in ethnographic analysis.

Systematic method is essential for science, demanding first that the investigators review their evidence, assumptions, and processes of inference. The method delineated above will have served its turn if it helps the reader (as the setting out has the writer) to sharpen awareness of procedures and to heighten sensitivity to modes of social communication in their proper time-and-place contexts. If, however, ethnographic history is not just to be information stored in an investigator's head (or note cards), it must, itself, aim at effective *performance*. The final statements should not be primarily records of researchers' endeavors but *persuasive reconstructions of the experiences of past actors.* Let it be through narrative skills traditional among historians or newer forms developed by scenario writers, but art that conceals art must make its contribution to the performances in which ethnographic historians evoke ways of life in vanished worlds.

Notes

1. For highly instructive uses by historians of the culture concept, although not of direct anthropological inspiration, see Bernard Bailyn, *The Origins of American Politics* (New York, 1968), 3–58, and Jack P. Greene, "Search for Identity: An Interpretation of Selected Patterns of Social Response in Eighteenth-Century America," *Journal of Social History* 3 (1969–70): 189–220. Clifford Geertz's works on the nature of culture and the reading of ethnographic "texts" have assumed such importance for social historians that they are taken as at once the departure point and the destination of this paper, the aim of which is to spell out step-by-step method approaches to the kinds of insights with which Geertz dazzles his readers. See suggestions on further reading, below, for references to crucial writings by Geertz, Peter Berger and Thomas Luckmann, Erving Goffman, and others on culture, meaning systems, and interaction processes.

2. The relationship between "experience-far" (observers') and "experience-near" (participants') categories is explored in Geertz, "On the Nature of Anthropological Understanding," *American Scientist* 63 (1975): 47–48.

3. *Reports of the Record Commissioners of the City of Boston* (Boston, 1876–1909), 16:78.

4. Jack P. Greene, ed., *The Diary of Colonel Landon Carter of Sabine Hall, 1752–1778* (Charlottesville, Va., 1965), 286–92. On the colonel's relationship with his son and daughter-in-law and his performance as father and grandfather, see 310, 314. In a few places I have departed from the editor's reading of the manuscript as the requirements of sense have given cause.

5. The striking of bargains implicit in much of social life is given extended theoretical treatment in Peter Blau, *Exchange and Power in Social Life* (New York, 1964).

6. See Peter Berger and Thomas Luckmann, *The Social Construction of Reality: A Treatise in the Sociology of Knowledge* (New York, 1967), 149–52.

7. Landon Carter's ineptitude has been sensitively analyzed and contrasted with the successful authority styles of other gentlemen planters in Gerald W. Mullin, *Flight and Rebellion: Slave Resistance in Eighteenth-Century Virginia* (New York, 1972). Mullin develops and applies a concept of role performance that deserves the closet attention of ethnographic historians (19–33, 63–72).

8. The diary refers interchangeably to Mangorike Will, Willy, and Billy. There are also references to "Billy the foreman" and to "Billy" unqualified. That Mangorike Will was a slave trusted with responsibility is made clear by a later entry that he will be put in charge of a quarter in place of an unsatisfactory overseer, who is to be dismissed. Greene, ed., *Diary of Landon Carter*, 168, 308, 483, 551, 742, 773, 1141.

9. On definition-of-the-situation, see Goffman, *The Presentation of Self in Everyday Life* (New York, 1956), 15–27 and passim. On metaphor, the literature is more diffuse. (See references listed in further reading, below.) Metaphors are the predominant form of "model" in systems of everyday of commonsense knowledge. Models as used in social science are usually elaborate metaphors. In the latter case, however, it is essential that the comparison necessarily present in the metaphor be scrutinized and controlled as precisely as possible. I have throughout reserved the term *metaphor* for the constructs in the minds of past actors and the term *model* for those to be employed by the investigating historian.

10. Greene, ed., *Diary of Landon Carter*, 940–41.

11. Two recent works deserve particular mention for their treatment of Anglo-American perceptions of fatherhood and social-cultural system. The power of the metaphor in religious feeling and the formation of personalities is finely treated in Philip J. Greven, Jr., *The Protestant Temperament: Patterns of Child-Rearing, Religious Experience, and the Self in Early America* (New York, 1978). The pervasiveness of the metaphor as a mediator of social relations is a central theme in Eugene D. Genovese, *Roll, Jordan, Roll: The World the Slaves Made* (New York, 1974). Ultimately this is a speculative model eclectically compiled from diverse regions and epochs, but the subtlety with which it explores structured ambiguities and contested meanings in situations and encounters involving slaves and masters provides a wealth of further instruction for those who have attended to the interactions of Simon and Bart with Landon Carter.

12. Richmond Co., Va., "Criminal Trials, 1710–1754." Microfilm record kindly made available by the Virginia State Library, Richmond.

13. This crucial concept is defined extensively in use in Berger and Luckmann, *Social Construction of Reality*, 61, 173–74, and passim.

14. For a sustained theoretical discussion of the use of the human body as a cosmological reference system, see Mary Douglas, *Natural Symbols: Explorations in Cosmology* (2d rev. ed., New York, 1973). This work is highly suggestive in its discussion of relationships between forms of social communication, intensities of concern for boundary maintenance, and modes of viewing the world.

15. Isaac Ware, trans., *The Four Books of Andrea Palladio's Architecture . . .* ([London, 1738], facsimile rpt., intro. Adolf K. Placzek [New York, 1965]), i. Palladio's architectural conceptions included complex mathematical harmonies as well as the organic metaphor emphasized here. See James S. Ackerman, *Palladio* (Harmondsworth, Middlesex,

1966), 160–85. Sabine Hall has been extensively altered since 1768.

16. A convenient set of illustrations of both settings and roles highly structured by paired oppositions may be found in Douglas, ed., *Rules and Meanings: The Anthropology of Everyday Knowledge: Selected Readings* (Harmondsworth, Middlesex, 1973), esp. J. C. Faris, "'Occasions' and 'non-occasions'" (45–59); P. Bourdieu, "The Berber House" (98–110); and R. Hertz, "The Hands" (118–24). With the subject of oppositional pairs, the "structuralist" system of Claude Lévi-Strauss is squinted at. This author deems it prudent not to take a position here with regard to the intense controversies surrounding this theorist.

17. Hunter D. Farish, ed., *Journal and Letters of Philip Vickers Fithian, 1773–1774: A Plantation Tutor of the Old Dominion* (Charlottesville, Va., 1968), 29.

18. Louis B. Wright and Marion Tinling, eds., *Quebec to Carolina in 1785–1786: Being the Travel Diary and Observations of Robert Hunter, Jr., A Young Merchant of London* (San Marino, Calif., 1943), 206–8.

19. Geertz, "On the Nature of Anthropological Understanding," is largely directed to the elucidation of different cultural modes of defining what *persons* are. For an exquisite elaboration of one particular mode, see his "Person, Time, and Conduct in Bali," in Geertz, *The Interpretation of Cultures: Selected Essays* (New York, 1973), 360–411.

20. *The Journal of Nicholas Cresswell, 1774–1777* (London, 1925), 18, 26, 30, 52–53.

21. The subject of different codes in use in society is here opened, although it cannot be dealt with. Useful readings are Douglas, *Natural Symbols*, 41–51, and Basil Bernstein, *Class, Codes, and Control*, vol. 1: *Theoretical Studies towards a Sociology of Language*, (London, 1971). On "registers," see R. Hasan, "Codes, Register, and Social Dialect" in Bernstein, *Class, Codes, and Control*, vol. 2: *Applied Studies towards a Sociology of Language* (London, 1973), 253–92.

For Further Reading

The following suggestions, like the methodological statement they follow, are not intended to point out the one true way to approach ethnography. The methods and concepts that can usefully be employed in that enterprise are as many and various as the answers to the question: *How may human social life be described?*

Readers taking the tour to which this essay is a guide should attempt as much exploring on their own as possible. They would do well to begin by asking themselves which are the most powerful statements they can recall in which they have found life observed, represented, and rendered intelligible. *Voila l'ethnographie!* Many modes of perception involved in the practice of this science can most usefully be developed by inquiring about the ways in which such memorable descriptive-interpretive successes were attained. How was the overall pattern of the particular situation or slice of life comprehended? By what selection of data, or focus on chosen parts, was the whole evoked? How were meanings, projected by participants in action, caught and represented?

Great novel writing abounds in examples of ways in which the reporting of strategic particular facts conjures up whole milieux. Such intermediate forms as memoirs may also furnish edifying ethnographic riches. For example, a close scrutiny of Flora Thompson's English village childhood recollections, *Lark Rise to Candleford* (reprint ed., New York, 1974), is rewarding if questions are brought to it about the contexts and meanings conveyed by the information included. Why does the pig in the yard, with which the description begins, tell so much? Elizabeth Bohannan's *Return to Laughter* (New York, 1964) will actually take the sympathetic reader through the perplexities of discovering the meanings behind the unfamiliar everyday routines of an alien culture as well as revealing limits to what ultimately can be understood and accepted. But if the search is for accounts of ways of being—for explorations of cultural systems that fix attention on day-to-day patterns of action—then seekers would be unwise, in the current world, to confine their survey to the written word. We live in the time of the ethnographic movie (one has only to think of *American Graffiti* or even *Nashville*) in which the intelligible presentation of a subculture has far more to do with the sustaining of interest than does any overarching dramatic plot.

Those seeking to develop their ethnographic sensitivity in order to apply it to the past may be disappointed when they survey historiography for intimations of real social life. Even writers justly renowned for their evocation of ethos, such as Perry Miller, will too often be found on scrutiny to have allowed their attention to be held and stopped by the words on the pages of their documents. The thrust of ethnographic history must be to press past writing to the social situations from which it arose. Readers are again urged to search their own memories for specimens of historical writing that achieve edifying success in this endeavor. Two examples only will therefore be preferred here. In *The Armada* (Boston, 1959), Garrett Mattingly shows astonishing virtuosity at subsuming ethnographic information in what appears to be conventional historical narrative. (Note especially the deft analysis, with no Goffman-apparatus showing, of the competing definitions-of-the-situation at play in the opening account of the execution of Mary Queen of Scots, pp. 1–5. The culturally determined possibilities of architecture as a mode of personal expression have rarely been revealed with such insight as appears in his sketch of the Escorial palace, pp. 71–75.) More self-consciously an "ethnographic" analysis of action forms is E. P. Thompson's "The Moral Economy of the English Crowd in the Eighteenth Century," *Past and Present* 50 (1972): 76–136. Of particular relevance also to the reader of this methodological statement are its author's essays in ethnographic history. See Rhys Isaac, "Evangelical Revolt: The Nature of the Baptists' Challenge to the Traditional Order in Virginia, 1765–1775," *William and Mary Quarterly*, 3d ser., 31 (1974): 345–68; "Dramatizing the Ideology of Revolution: Popular Mobilization in Virginia, 1774 to 1776," *William and Mary Quarterly*, 3d ser., 33 (1976): 357–85; and "Preachers and Patriots: Popular Culture and the Revolution in Virginia," in Alfred F. Young, ed., *The American Revolution: Explorations in the History of American Radicalism* (De Kalb, Ill., 1976), 125–56.

The study of examples is instructive, but a mastery of ethnographic approaches must derive ultimately from developed social theory. Lingering beliefs must be dispelled that, outside of "hard" quantification methodologies, all is "soft," with intuition the only and best guide. The foregoing methodological statement was made as readable as the writer could manage within the terms of his mandate, but it was also drafted on the assumption that, read once over lightly in the manner of a literary essay in historiography, it could accomplish nothing. Its concepts, where unfamiliar, must be critically reviewed, mastered, and applied. Social science texts in which the fundamental propositions are formulated at sufficient length must be studied. Sophisticated social history requires adequate social theory even more than up-to-date statistical methods. What is "society"? If not just an aggregation of human bodies, then what? We use the term *social structure* to sustain a comforting illusion of physical reality, but when that has been recognized for the metaphor it is, we are left primarily with the dynamic processes: the ongoing actions and the systems of meaning from which they arise and to whose maintenance, or modification, they contribute. Phenomenology (the study of the nature of social realities) is, then, both the necessary starting point for well-founded social theory and the essential conceptual framework for systematic ethnography. In this dark, difficult field the author found Peter Berger and Thomas Luckmann's *The Social Construction of Reality: A Treatise in the Sociology of Knowledge* (Garden City, N.Y., 1967) most illuminating. It seeks to synthesize the insights into the nature of society arrived at by Marx, Weber, and Durkheim, with those of the phenomenologist Alfred Schutz. (For an introduction to the key writings of the latter, see Helmut R. Wagner, ed., *Alfred Schutz on Phenomenology and Social Relations* [Chicago, 1970].)

The encompassing concept of socially constructed reality—extending from marginal experiences (which tend to elude social controls), through everyday meanings, up to the overarching, legitimating, "symbolic universe"—provides a theoretical context in which both the elemental encounter ethnography of Erving Goffman and Clifford Geertz's exegesis of complex action-texts can be located. Goffman's approach can best be seen in *The Presentation of Self in Everyday Life* (New York, 1956) and *Interaction Ritual: Essays on Face-to-Face Behavior* (New York, 1967). Many of Geertz's most important contributions have been collected by him into a single volume: *The Interpretation of Cultures* (New York, 1973). The introductory essay, "Thick Description," offers a working concept of culture and, by implication, projects an action approach. This approach is finely developed in a number of essays that follow. See especially "Ritual and Social Change: A Javanese Example," and "Deep Play: Notes on the Balinese Cockfight."

The integrative operations of metaphors within cultural systems have been usefully outlined in Edmund Leach, *Culture and Communication: The Logic by which Symbols Are Connected* (Cambridge and New York, 1976). Victor

Turner is probably the field ethnographer who has been most persistent in his endeavors to systematize the study of metaphors enacted in ritual. His work, however, does not make easy reading and has to be understood as polemically addressed to the English school of structural-functionalist anthropologists descended from Radcliffe-Brown. See especially Victor Turner, *The Drums of Affliction* (Oxford, 1968); *The Ritual Process: Structure and Anti-Structure* (Chicago, 1969); and *Dramas, Fields, and Metaphors: Symbolic Action in Human Society* (Ithaca, N.Y., 1974). The writings of Kenneth Burke are rich in insights into the poetic-associational mode of thought to which metaphors belong and are also valuable for discussion of the relationship of this mode to rational-scientific systems. See *The Philosophy of Literary Form*, 3d ed. (Berkeley, Calif., 1974). Historians have scarcely begun such studies, but their potential is finely illustrated in Charles E. Rosenberg, "The Therapeutic Revolution: Medicine, Meaning, and Social Change in Nineteenth-Century America," *Perspectives in Biology and Medicine* 20 (1977): 485–506.

A sense of the dramatic is so much a part of our perception of the patterned interaction of human beings (and, by extension, other agents) that examples of its incorporation into social science abound. A brilliant essay at defining this mode of understanding and locating it in the context of other fundamental perspectives that enter into organized knowledge is found in Louis O. Mink, "History and Fiction as Modes of Comprehension," *New Literary History* 1 (1969–70): 542–58. A dramaturgical perspective on the communication and legitimation of power is explicitly developed in Clifford Geertz, "Centers, Kings, and Charisma: Reflections on the Symbolics of Power," in *Culture and Its Creators*, ed. J. Ben-David and T. Clark (Chicago, 1977), 150–71.

Interesting, albeit dated, anthropologists' comments on the relationship of their discipline to history may be found reprinted in E. Evans-Pritchard, *Anthropology and History* (Atlantic Highlands, N.J., 1961), and in A. L. Kroeber, *An Anthropologist Looks at History* (Berkeley, Calif., 1963). A more recent appraisal from the historians' end is Keith Thomas, "History and Anthropology," *Past and Present* 24 (1963): 3–24. Pungent commentaries on current uses and abuses are offered in E. P. Thompson's "Anthropology and the Discipline of Historical Context," *Midland History* 3 (1972): 41–55, and Eugene Genovese, "The Political Crisis of Social History: A Marxian Perspective," *Journal of Social History* 10 (1976): 205–20. An appropriate twist is given to interdisciplinary discussions in an essay that reviews the writing (and teaching) of history itself in an ethnographic perspective: G. M. Dening, "History as Social System," *Historical Studies, Australia and New Zealand* 15 (1971–73): 673–85. A valuable set of further references is to be found in the footnotes to that essay.

This frontispiece, an epigraph, consists of an observation by
William Faulkner, from *Requiem for a Nun*, placed on the
face of a lantern clock made by Daniel Hoskins ca. 1630.
(Drawing by Henry Glassie.)

Meaningful Things and Appropriate Myths: The Artifact's Place in American Studies

HENRY GLASSIE

Looking at the landscape, the monumental artwork of the world's people, Henry Glassie offers his aspirations for a history of American material life. As our mythology, history's central concern is the search for a meaningful human existence. But how are we to search for, or even to define, meaning? And how are we to push beyond meaning to the cultural values that structure society? As he extends the purpose of historical research from the reconstruction of past societies to the articulation of a philosophy of action, Glassie's essay demonstrates that any theory of history must be grounded in a theory of culture that allows us to conceive of individuals, their contexts, and their intentional actions as logical, systemically interrelated, and symbolic. To that extent, history will become a more anthropological pursuit.

Drawing upon the works of Jean-Paul Sartre, Claude Lévi-Strauss, Dell Hymes, James Joyce, Samuel Beckett, and Henry David Thoreau, Glassie maintains that people of the past are "theoretically comprehensible" if we attend to the lessons that material culture can teach. Attending to the written word alone is too easy and theoretically weak. For one thing, the men and women who wrote the kinds of documents we often find most informative—diaries, letters, sermons—were often themselves idiosyncratic people, either introverted, egotistical, or both. They were also invariably in the minority. But many other people in the past, the "written abouts" of American history, can be directly confronted in the houses and furniture they made, the songs they sang, or in the stories they told about local outlaws. These types of artifacts do survive, and challenge us to construct the democratically authentic story that the New History of the 1970s promised but never really delivered. In addition, even in a highly literate culture (like nineteenth-century America, for instance) different symbolic codes—words or things, songs or costumes, poems or houses—were used for different strategic purposes. Each kind of historical evidence, in other words, provided a context for all the others; hence, historians cannot read the words of a document without also accounting for the objects to which they were structurally linked in the creator's mind. Finally, as Glassie argues, the particular affective power or "mythic valence" of a given artifact can only be determined as it affected communication across different genres. In order to understand the contradictory logic of Thoreau's lament, for example, we need to read Walden *in relation to the fields, locomotives, town centers, and marketing depots he inhabited as he thought and wrote.*

As he links artifact study to literature, Glassie makes a simple yet powerful point: not all historical evidence is as direct, as efficient, for entering and penetrating the minds of dead people. The richest type of document pulses with myth, and artistic communication in any form—especially material objects—leads us directly into the creation of meaning. Yet historians are rarely trained to read artifacts. Inventory references to chairs are not the same as chairs, and photographs of houses do not open doors into worlds inhabited by alien minds. The study of material life, Glassie maintains, can make history a more ethical and theoretically more noble pursuit.

We quiet the inner voices that mock our free will, comforting ourselves that clocks in their turning kill time. But the past is not dead. It lives in mind, as mind. Our thoughts arise, our words appear, our deeds emerge out of the past. Subtly or obviously, now is made of then. The past tests our uniquely human birthright, lending us the strength to act freely and cajoling us to deny innate potentials and create the future in its image.

Unconsidered, the past swallows us into it. To guard against its power, to spring clear of its evil and control its virtues, we rise above it, bringing the past into awareness and arranging it into myth. In our society the functions of myth are filled mainly by history. History is myth, but not because it is false. All art, including history, obeys generic rules and uses small lies to approach large truths. All human products, including the facts out of which history is constructed, are available to intelligent discourse but not to final knowing: their truth lies always just beyond. History is myth because its elements are infinitely capable of new orderings, and these new orderings selectively explain the present in terms of the past and guide us in the creation of the moments out of which the future witlessly unfolds.

Historians are apt to term whiggish studies of the past designed to explain the evolution of current states of affairs. Still, the most disinterested, objective, and scientific exhumation and animation of the dead has its genesis in the psyches and social situations of individual scholars, and it will have repercussions throughout the scenes of their being. The relation of past to present surges unavoidably in the truth of time's flow. That relation would be better faced honestly, described, even used for human good, than deceitfully ignored in the name of rigorous study.

History should not become thrall to the issues of the day. The admirable effort to use history to cure social ills, the deplorable effort to use history to support the current regime—both destroy the serendipitous potential of historical study. Nor should history be released to reverberate in endless subjectivity. Without striving toward objectivity and submitting to the rigors of relativism (while not forgetting objectivity is impossible and relativism will be transvalued in judgment and action), we can only review what we know and learn nothing strange and beautifully new. Historians must plunge their thought in alien time, immersing their brains in past facts. But the facts will lead outward in ever-enlarging circles of context, tipping as they widen, spiraling backward and forward from vaporous beginnings to the present, blinding in its brightness, and spinning inexorably into the future that historians help to make and in which they must live. Ultimately, time's continuity

and the intimate relevance of past facts will demolish false distinctions between the synchronic and diachronic, the horizontal and vertical, and progressing and regressing will deny the estrangement of scholarship, compelling the historian's involvement. The scholar's imagination will approach dead others who are actually unknowable but theoretically comprehensible. It will enter them on some deep plane of human unity. The mind will obliterate chronology, electrically leaping periods and demanding the admission of a disciplined subjective. In a manner bravely inductive and responsibly theoretical, the historian will merge into history and research will not wither in self-indulgence. It will swell with meaning.

Meaning is the center of study. Yet one voice within asserts the meaninglessness of existence and praises the courage of enduring in such a world. Perhaps positivistic scientists defend their avoidance of meaning in those terms. Meaning is internal, invisible; it is the unverifiable issue of the marriage of unknowable intention with unknowable response. There is no way to measure it. Some modern thinkers hope that by describing all of the physical world, measuring all the houses, tabulating all the census data, recording all the texts, filming all the gestures, they will eventually outline the metaphysical. We have not time to wait. More importantly, such a materialistic positivism will never answer our central questions—matters of meanings and values. Studying only externalities yields classified lists of facts lacking purpose, lacking meaning; an enumeration of appearances; blackened pages, absurdity. The annihilation of self in methodology and the endless counting of sensate phenomena represent a failure of nerve, not its reverse, a shying from essentials. Willing to face the world as it is, godless, modern scholars can take the human mind—the intending, investigative mind realizing its potential for order—to be the prime mover of their universe. The acceptance of the inherent meaninglessness of existence is the beginning, not the end, of intellectual action. When evidence of the human wish for pattern and plan is discovered within the soul and abroad on the land, the modern scholar will find it courageous and right to suffuse the world with significance.[1]

Upon turning from our times to the void of the past, we cannot indulge in scientific despair or nihilistic antiquarianism. We fill the void with a few facts and interpret them as the result of intention, the embodiment of meaning. Thus is myth composed. Myth is history made meaningful. The emptiness of our symbols, the hollow meaninglessness of our present and past, tear us from hopefulness or sane affirmation, but meaning offers history to the person or nation wishing to act, wishing to strive toward fulfillment and humane liberation.

As a structure of scraps, history, our myth, does not liberate. But from it romantics take what they need to escape the limitations of the present and progressives take what they need to escape the enormity of the past; in it you and I develop our several selves. By enslaving itself to a political ideology or castrating itself in professionalistic particularity, bad history chains us to things as they are. By opening us to things as they were, good history explains our world and offers us options for overcoming it.

There is too much history, too many histories. It is current cant to argue that any study done well is worthwhile. Humbug. Graded on mechanical performances rather than venturesomeness of thought, developing scholars are coerced into intricate specializations within constricted disciplines. On achieving intellectual maturity, some scholars find their old fascinations satisfying, increasingly rich in themselves, expansive in their social significance.[2] Others sense the pressures of finite time and suffer, expertly bored. Essays, no matter how elegantly argued, hypothetico-deductive exercises, no matter how rigorously conceived, can be beside the point. Scholars cannot rely on editors who are bound into economic realities to censor them. They, we, must be serious and responsible as well as honest. We must be self-critical as well as careful. Histories should not just be written. The histories worth writing must be important and interesting and helpful.

Historians sometimes refuse to call biographies history. Yet, in these times of unrelieved individualism, the biography is a crucially important, helpful variety of historical writing. Even the biography that is only a chronological assemblage of facts about someone may hold implications for its reader by providing a consistent alternative for thought and action. But if the biography stresses personality and contingencies to record an individual struggling for authenticity within a particular tradition and set of circumstances, then it can stand as a model of the human condition, an inspiration and challenge for

people whose anxieties for unification are expressed constantly and aptly in today's argot: there is a deep-felt need to get it together, psychically and socially.

A concern for the lost lone actor pervades modern thinking. Modern novelists (think of André Gide and James Joyce) frequently position individuals in the middle of their works, fictionalizing biography and autobiography. Recoiling from superorganic simplicities, dissatisfied with immutable reifications of culture and society, modern anthropologists, sociologists, and psychologists are working to reestablish the individual as the constructor rather than the victim of mental patterns and social affinities. Individuals make history as surely as history makes them; the lone mind is the locus of all connection, and biography is the very type of historiography.

Biography is history's metaphoric frame. Nations and civilizations are born to flourish and die in narratives. Biography is history's real substance. The truism that history is about people, that history is a patchy composition of innumerable unique lives, carries important implications. Any study of human beings will build up to abstractions, but it must begin with something real. It will build up to institutions, cultures, and human universals, to periods and sweeping evolutionistic schemes—to the biography of Man. But these are phantasm and artifice. People are real. The biography is the epistemic entrance for the historian just as the encountered informant is for the social scientist. History, anthropology: all study of generalized, patterned humanity must begin with and proceed from an existential theory of the individual. Individuals exist in contexts, in space and time. In this they are like all things. Their human essence lies in what is called mind. Conditions are peripheries; mind is central, irreducible. At the base of a theory of the individual and, therefore, of all study of human being is a concept of mind.

Approaching the human subject, our daily acquaintances or dead heroes, we cannot claim to seriousness if we ignore the lessons taught by modern poets and novelists, philosophers, psychologists, and linguists. The mind is enormous in its complexity. Its power and wealth coil and resound vastly, surprisingly, remotely.

The great moderns, accepting their responsibilities as persons of the twentieth century, have come to mind and broken it apart to get some purchase on its complexities. Their analyses have been different, even contradictory, but their labors must force biographers and historians, like all students of humanity, to abandon commonsensically assembled notions of "human nature" in favor of the acceptance or construction of an adequately complicated theory of consciousness. Today's dominant theorists resort to metaphors of layering. Claude Lévi-Strauss's concept of mind was influenced by Sigmund Freud and by the geological idea of stratigraphy.

Mind's base stratum, its bedrock, is innate, genetic, universal, inalienably human. The shape of the innate, its content and the specificity of its processes, are matters on which agreement is slight; but extending from implications in the writings of Jean-Paul Sartre, Claude Lévi-Strauss, Kenneth Burke, and Noam Chomsky, I believe the mind must be seen to contain—biologically—the drive to freedom. The human animal both perceives and imagines. It actively accumulates percepts. And it arranges, blends, transforms, and negates them in an unstoppable process of building, destroying, and rebuilding concepts. We are genetically condemned to knowing what is, what is not, and therefore what ought to be.

The highest stratum, the mind's crust, is composed of something like a Jungian persona or a Yeatsian mask, taken from a reflection in the eye of the other, drawn through consciousness, and proposed in social dialectic as the public presentation of self. Mask covers the conscious, the stratum of self-awareness. Some hide this orderly interrelation of the personal and the cultural, the ego and the superego, behind their masks. Winslow Homer, feeling the most interesting part of his life was of no concern to the public, refused to cooperate with biographers and left us only the skins of his pictures. Others of a more confessional bent strive to fuse mask and awareness. François Mauriac considered André Gide virginal and pure because of his inability to lie—his pained attempt to expose his secret life in publication. Gide's self-analytic writings cry out, cooly and calmly, from anguished depths. Yet Mauriac's son finds Gide repressing and falsifying. Even his journals were a pose, and the autobiographical element in his novels, though disguised, distorted, and fictionalized, leads deeper into Gide's mind.[3]

Mind's deeper level, where, to use James Joyce's metaphor, day becomes night, might be called the subconscious. Sartre's cogent argument against the Freudians that one cannot suppress what one does not know makes the Sartrean formulation of the mind's deep well comparable not to the Freudian subconscious but to the Lévi-Straussian unconscious. The stratum of wild nighttime association lying beneath awareness, below the conscious, is not unknown, but known and unconsidered. In different people and at different times the twilit border between the two levels of consciousness shifts, sharpening, blurring. The linguist deduces into awareness the grammatical ability that operates for most people comfortably, capably in the unconscious. The poet or psychologist shocks into awareness desires that lurk for most people sleazily, radiantly in the subconscious. Neither unconscious nor subconscious is a good name, but both do point us toward the deepest level of consciousness where the brain's natural structuring, the genetic innate, joins animal nerve and melts through fundamental personal and cultural memories—the sticky and misty potent realm of mind that paradoxically resists articulation in any metalanguage, is never fully controlled in awareness and yet is volitionally, profoundly enacted in every truly human event.

The mind is not an earth, built up of stony strata. Nor is it an archaeological site, an onion, or a cake. It is more, as Walt Whitman said, unitary, a universe, "a soundless sea." Man is the cavern measureless to man. But scholars must try and in trying must avail themselves of false devices, such as models of mental stratigraphy.

Having gained some sense of mental complexity, biographers are obligated to get all the information they can. They need information about the subject— La Farge's impressions of Homer, Camus's of Gide— but it will always remain marginal, a delineation of the mask. The central, basic information will come directly from the subject, for only it can incorporate the fullness of conscious and unconscious mind. The information the subject presents, whether an open statement of intent—a pronouncement of the mask—or a subtle projection into art and tool, must be analyzed. It must be taken at face value, certainly, but the face of the fact has to be lifted away. Inner structures must be exposed and probed and opened to more and more delicate speculation. Exploring deeper, deeper, one analyst will discover writhing psychosis and grotesquely distorted sexuality where another finds the sublime balance of a universal logic, but they will agree upon the need for complex, forceful study. To do less is to deny what we know about people.

The dynamics of ambiguity, spontaneity, and metaphor allow artworks (Homer's paintings, Gide's novels) to deliver messages from deep in the psyche—messages that cannot be reduced to clear discourse or data or statistical summary. If I could say it, said Isadora Duncan, I would not have to dance it. Because they are aware of the arts as passages into the deeper recesses of the mind and soul, and because they are convinced of their subjects' intense individuality, art historians and literary critics are often capable biographers. Optimistically, they may underestimate the power of tradition and context in their portraits of the artist, but a complete structure of biography, of human existence, is present in the best of their works.

The structure of biography is erected on human absolutes. As displayed irrefutably in language play, in Whitman's "divine power to speak words," people are inherently disposed to order and to transcendent disorder, to syntactic structuring and poetic explosion, equilibrium and rebellion. This divine, satanic nature is configured uniquely in each person. In that difference is read the brilliance or dullness of individuals who are, nonetheless, wholly human. But as surely as people are genetically creative—free, responsible—they are situated—unfree, relieved of responsibility. They exist in nature among other objects. Within contexts composed of turnips and clay and wolves and policemen, air, earth, and sunshine, punishers and rewarders, old myth and new accident, people are coddled, prodded, and thwarted. In continual dialectic with context, the personality ascends to maturity and relaxes into senescence. The product and empirical record of that dialectic is action: postures, words, paintings, plowed fields, war.

Person, context, action: each is a pole of information. Proper biographers site themselves equidistantly between these poles and interpret each in terms of the other. The aspiration is not for answers, which are too easily come by, but for complex and useful, indispensible and ungraspable truth.

Once, understanding humankind was easy. There was this omniscient deity who kept the universe in order, winding the spring that drove people and planets in accord. Then a jealous folk, enlightened and inner lit, killed their clock-winding god, and order vanished into millions of separate skulls. Some mystics

sought desperate solace in the occult, and some scientists, in a last gasp of faith, attempted to find order in laws that governed human beings in the way the laws of physics govern blocks on inclined planes. The behavioral psychologists among them gave us valuable insights but failed when trying to extend their theories into philosophy. Content to comprehend people in terms of external forces, they could not deal with the central human fact of creativity. They had no workable, embracing vision of human nature. People remained unpredictable, unaccountable, and during our century—perhaps it is Freud's century—the mind has burgeoned hugely.

In such a situation, the biography is a safe study. Frightening troubles arise when the historian moves from explaining a person to explaining people. These theoretical troubles deeply engage thinkers today, uniting modern art and science in a single set of concerns. Given the complexity of each individual, how can people communicate, much less construct cultures enabling them to cohere in societies?

No contemporary thinker has faced these issues more squarely or wittily than the writer Samuel Beckett. As a young man he sat silently in James Joyce's rooms in Paris while Joyce was at work on *Finnegans Wake*. In *Ulysses*, Joyce had penetrated the partitions separating the interiors and exteriors of his characters, opening their thoughts to the reader as clearly as he described their motions. In the resplendent *Wake* he depicts mind from inside. Readers willing to follow the book's course as it pulsates and puns must surrender in disorientation, losing themselves to the "unconscious" mind's oppositional logic and powers of inclusion, connection, and reference. Samuel Beckett's problem was posed. How could he accept the message of *Finnegans Wake* and still write, and still live? Over the years he did solve the problem, and he has given us three pristine fictive meditations to mark the progress of his thought.

In *Watt*, Watt becomes one in a series of servants and observers of Mr. Knott. He informs us in great detail about the arrangements for feeding Mr. Knott and the hilarious protocol for dispensing of the leftovers. He describes the hundreds of ways Mr. Knott arranges the furniture in his bedchamber. We are given a vast amount of data about the man, but it is all external, therefore absurd, and, finally, Mr. Knott is a knot, untied, unrevealed: Mr. Knott is not. Knowing everything about Mr. Knott's context we know nothing about him at all. The book is the precise opposite of *Finnegans Wake*, a sleeper perceived from the outside. An anticipation of Andy Warhol's hangover Dada film, *Sleep*, it is a positivist's nightmare, a behaviorist's vision of hell. *Watt* alone should have put an abrupt stop to histories or ethnographies compounded of descriptive, exterior detail.

Watt reappears in *Mercier and Camier*, in which people bearing universes in their heads are allowed to interact. In the book, Beckett digresses astutely on the difficulties of knowing the unknowable in events of communication, but its solutions were premature. He delayed its publication for years and deposited the next landmark on the path of his philosophy at the end of his great trilogy.

In *Molloy*, the first of the novels, we watch in dim horror as people meet and bunglingly try to help each other. In the middle volume, Malone, the man alone, the ill one, the big sickness, lies abed writing and dying. We are carried inside him to learn his immediate anxieties. We know he owns some junk in the corner, that he has a room, the stub of a pencil, that they feed him. But how did he get there? And where is there? And why? We know him better, this purposeful, ethnographical Earwicker, than we did Mr. Knott. An inward view beats an outward one. But he passes, at last, unanswered and incomplete.

Malone dies, leaving us at the mercy of the Unnamable, around whom he orbits, about whom we know almost nothing for certain, not who he is or what or where, or what he is saying or doing, or even his name. We know only what he thinks, which is that he knows almost nothing for certain, not who he is or what or where, or what he is saying or doing, or even his name. He is not alone, it seems, but no communication breaks the membrane between him and them. His mind is consistent and logical; but unlinked to any exterior, it is closed in a circle of hopeless courage, spinning in relentless tautology. For no reason, save that he is, he must go on. The mentalist's inwardly tightening spiral leads closer to human essences than the positivist's outwardly loosening one, but *The Unnamable* names the fallacy of psychological formalism. Alone neither spiral describes the human reality. They must, like the double helix in W. B. Yeats's vision, interpenetrate.

The problem is how to present the inside and the outside simultaneously, looping them systematically together while letting them drift apart. In *Waiting for Godot*, the drama which *Mercier and Camier* prepared him to write, Beckett achieves a brilliant solution. His characters act what they say and say what they think. Normally we have to triangulate from trivial words and subtle gestures to the depths of covert thought. This process is inverted in *Godot*. If we care what the people say, we must turn the play inside out. When that is done, I find Vladimir and Estragon meeting on a rural lane in Ulster on two humdrum days, chattering about the weather and their health, then passing the time with a stuffy English tourist and his lackey. Being Irish countrymen, their strangeness and pain, their political outrage, their fears, boredom, sexuality, and creativity are hidden under simple conversation. But rather than losing their human depth Beckett revolves it to view, repressing their repression. These are real people, not puppets. They are capable of deep, weird thought, and they are capable of exploiting superficial conventions to develop shared interests and affection.

By seeming absurd *Waiting for Godot* is not, just as positivistic social science is absurd by pretending not to be. A surface of facts that looks complete, trim and prim, but has no reality beyond it, no meaning deep beneath it, will crack under our weight, dropping us into nothingness. A puzzling "nothing" that can happen twice disturbs us into searching below appearances. There we fumble and grope until, in astonishment, we touch its logic—the perfect reversal of normality—and almost get a grip on its great truths: that life is lived in time toward no goal except adapting to waiting, that cognition is wild but not entirely uncontrollable, that communication is difficult but somewhat possible. Genuine art, admitting confusion, startles us to make us live. False science, by turning its back on chaos, by ignoring real contradictions and the ultimate unknowability of things, braces and comforts us to let us die unachieved.

The complexities of cognition and communication, the issues stoutly faced by Samuel Beckett, preoccupy modern philosophers and social scientists. Sociologists, anthropologists, and folklorists are openly pondering them now, but the greatest advances have been made by linguists. Some behavioral theorists understood the crucially human and astoundingly complex ability to speak as developing in nurture by a process of reward and punishment. In radical opposition to them, Noam Chomsky located language in the generating, transforming—creative—

power of natural, innate mind. Here we have Beckett's problem again. The problem is not how to account for communication holistico-exteriodescriptively (as in a film of people talking and gesturing), nor deterministico-legalistically (as in a set of unwritten laws conversationalists must obey), nor positivistico-metaphoro-mechanistically (as in a circuit between black boxes, each transmitting and receiving, encoding and decoding). The problem is how to accept the rich and dynamic, powerful theory of linguistic competence Noam Chomsky has given us and still have both commonplace conversation and great poetry.

Our best answer is a gift from Dell Hymes (inspired by Kenneth Burke).[4] If we examine a person's performance, this casual greeting or that great epic, as the result of a mental connection between the performer's internal competence and an interiorization of external conditions—and if we realize that people are among each others' conditions—we can endow them with their own quirky integrity and with capacities for interaction. Hymes's solution is comparable to Beckett's. Though Dell Hymes formulated his theory in contention with Noam Chomsky, feeling Chomsky's to be formalistic and partial, Hymes's fine science may be read as incorporating Chomsky's philosophy of mind, much as Beckett's art incorporates Joyce's philosophy of mind.

Together people create situations that are at once instants of self-realization and occasions for the mutual transfer of thought and feeling. In these real and repetitious conjunctions of space and time, shared concepts are invented, modified, and destroyed. The communicating event results from and results in culture. And it exists integrally as the product of social and intellectual transaction. As memory and as artifact—book, barn, ruined limb, improved soil—the event lingers, forcing itself on time.

This theorizing that seems so important to artists, philosophers, and social scientists may seem obvious and unnecessary to historians. Although it has not been conceptualized in rigorous terms, historians have a theory of culture's construction: the school or movement. Using the idea of the movement, historians can modulate comfortably from biography to studies of people in groups.

At its worst the account of a movement is a gossipy pastiche that titillates the reader's voyeuristic predilictions. At its best the study of a movement describes how people, embedded in a particular environment, bring their psyches, talents, and learning into engagements where they shape new ideas that lead to new arts, new actions, new nations. Historians of the arts, knowing people's simple statements and complicated actions are often in conflict, and historians of politics, knowing noble pronouncements often cover intrigue, conspiracy, and evil, are especially well prepared to handle the multiplex reality of the movement.

John Adams asked, "Who shall write the history of the American Revolution?" "Nobody," Thomas Jefferson responded. Someone might present "merely its external facts," but its soul and life must remain forever unknown. Yet using biography and autobiography, public and private, fictional and factual expressions, using information about social, political, and economic conditions, using depictions of the personages, the artifacts they made and used, historians can turn into the light some of the shadowed inner form of a movement like that which produced the Declaration of Independence.

So long as the movement is conceived as consisting of people in direct contact, no theoretical riddles are posed. Historians can keep writing without heeding new thinking in the social sciences. When the movement is related to a larger human assemblage, unconnected by direct and immediate communication, then problems explode, and the need for social scientific guidance becomes unavoidable.

When Adams, Jefferson, and a few other prosperous, educated gentlemen met in Philadelphia to sign our declaration, how did their thought relate to that of the ladies they left at home, or that of the tradesmen laboring elsewhere in the city, the men trudging behind plow nags in rocky Vermont, the women baking hoecake in lonely Tennessee clearings, the manacled Africans newly arrived on a sandhill Carolina farm? The magnitude of an event like signing the declaration bleaches out of existence the multitude of doings that shared its day. As time increases, so does the great event's brilliance. The theoretical problem is lost in its glare. But the problem will reassert itself if we look at smaller movements, nearer to us in time. Black Mountain was important and worth years of a good scholar's life, but we cannot easily make it represent the thinking of many who were not its direct participants.[5] The hardscrabble farm people who shared its Appalachian setting would be obscured and offended if we did.

Now, look upon our days. Movements are gathering in lower Manhattan to create new thrills in the art galleries. Movements are gathering in Washington to create new upheavals in government. Future histories will be made of their results, but most of the bankers, housewives, and assembly line workers of America will find no expression in them and will die unruffled by them. Today's small artistic and political events do little more than fill a few minutes while the morning paper is drowsily perused between coffee and the beginning of work, and a few weary minutes more between televised terror and the sleep that work requires. Like Vladimir and Estragon, like Dilsey, we endure while notable movements break around us and the realities of our existence drain into nowhere, becoming invisible to history.

The historical problem is avoided if the movement is viewed as contained within the net of its own communications. While it must be related to its larger context, a movement like Black Mountain or Brook Farm or the Peninsular Campaign need not be presented as the only drama on the national stage. A populace can be imagined as comprising a vast quantity of simultaneous movements. Some will be successful, some not. Some will be ordered by programs and guided by manifestos, others will be loose and directionless. Some will engender new things, but most will serve only to pass the time, protecting their members against anomie. Most movements, that is, are groups like bowling leagues, bridge clubs, and the regulars who drink at Rod's. They attract sociologists but rarely historians. Historians tend to study groups that cry for attention by generating such surprises as coherent political ideologies or novel aesthetic philosophies, distinct concentrations of political power or extraordinary amounts of human misery. The historian who studies such movements for their intrinsic properties is vulnerable to the charge of elitism. It is a silly accusation. The careful study of a movement, whether composed of bourgeois poets or blue-collar radicals, holds implications for collective action and social life, just as the good biography implicitly teaches how to face the crises of heart, soul, and brain.

Studying the movement for itself, the historian is safe. But historians chafe in such confinement. Their fancies expand robustly, suggestively. Puritanism is not the theology of a small group of educated preachers and poets in seventeenth-century southern New England but the ethos of colonial Americans and their guilt-bedeviled descendents. The Hudson River School is not a group of landscape painters in the earlier nineteenth century but the national proclamation of an American Eden. William Faulkner's novels are not the visions of a singular genius but the howl of a region soaked in blood.

Such unbridled gallops over space and time are often theoretically irresponsible—and intellectually necessary. Recognizing multiplicity and diversity, we can draw a realistic depiction of humanity, unmystified by abstractions like culture, region, period, zeitgeist. And we can nestle comfortably into the trap of relativism, surrendering our responsibility to speak about excellence and significance.[6] Some movements, some people, some statements are more important than others.

Importance is contextually derived. Our own situations will dislodge some fragment of the past, making it loom large in our thought, whether it was important in its own era or not. Our angst over intellectual alienation draws us to movements like Brook Farm, the Pre-Raphaelite Brotherhood, and the Bloomsbury Group. Our hatred of the times brings us to a contradictory appreciation of individuals heroically at war with their contexts and draws us to revolutionaries like Giotto, John Brown, and Joyce. Or we might try to think in terms of historical ethnography. Then people, willingly grouped or sensual in their aloneness, become important not because we find them attractive but because their expressions embody a powerful and cogent distillation of ideas widely held in their own days. They might be socially peripheral, outsiders, deviants, elites; still, they might read the lines of their times accurately and compress them beautifully, memorably. Thomas Jefferson located himself above the farmers on the red clay hills around Monticello, but his early belief in the sanity of the agrarian way, his insistence on the rights to life, liberty, and property, were ideas his neighbors could share. Edgar Allan Poe was crazy and disdainful of the masses, yet his notion that the death of a beautiful woman was the most poetic of themes would have been instantaneously comprehensible to his contemporaries, whether the educated men of the English Pre-Raphaelite Brotherhood (Rossetti watched in sweet melancholy as Elizabeth Siddal faded; Millais painted her as Ophelia dead on the stream) or the illiterate mountaineers who made murdering a young woman (from Omie Wise in 1808 to Ellen Smith in 1893) the greatest southern ballad topic of the nineteenth century.

To make our own enthusiasms seem important, we scholars often argue that the people we study, in whom we have invested our own precious energies, do genuinely represent a larger mood. This rhetorical strategy is frequently adopted in American Studies. Cynics might say it is because the Americanists' subjects are inherently anemic. American poetry is not English poetry, American painting not French. The American people may have concentrated their hopes in directions less artistic and eternal, ones more quickly remunerative. Still, American scholars have not always looked in the right place for American artistic excellence. They have advocated our national literature with more excitement than our national architecture, though Sullivan, Richardson, and Wright have had more international impact than Hawthorne, Melville, and Twain. They have tried to add strength to our artistic treasures by covering them with a wash of enthusiasm and surrounding them with a nimbus of history, a glow of representativeness. Perhaps the American search for the representative was once explicable as an embarrassed twitching over identity. Today's motives are deeper. The ascendancy of the social sciences requires scholars in all fields to inspect their subjects' contexts: no genius, however eccentric, exists isolated from the conditions of his or her own milieu. The undeniable realities of injustice and of scholarship's role in perpetuating inequality implore scholars who began their careers as smug long-distance lovers of a particular poet or politician to figure out how to say something about the people en masse. Though pitifully underfed, a democratic spirit survives in American historiography.

And the geniuses themselves request to be read as representative. Walt Whitman not only saw and heard the American people; he became them, contained them. Their voice was his.

In his carefully crafted and brilliant book on the origins of American consciousness, Sacvan Bercovitch includes Whitman among the heirs to the Puritan unification of biography with national purpose.[7] The self does not rise and assert in lonely arrogance but as the embodiment of a democratic destiny. This simultaneous celebration and sacrifice of the person is an American tradition—and more. It is a post-Renaissance intellectual imperative, personified in men like W. B. Yeats and Albert Camus. Become an individual, free from religious limits and a fatalistic social organization, free to sing the ego, the modern man escapes vicious individualism by identifying with the locality, the nation, with all of humanity. Walt Whitman, prefiguring Joyce's Earwicker, was all of these: I, we, everybody.

Politicians and artists accept the claim scholars make in their behalf. I speak for the people, says every politico. The artist is the antenna of the race, says the poet. Free, fearlessly and cunningly, the young James Joyce sailed solo into exile to create "the uncreated conscience of my race." I think no artist since Dante came closer than Joyce in *Finnegans Wake* to compassing Western culture in a single mythic work. And I agree, too, with Padraic Colum that the people who inhabited the Dublin that Jim and Stephen and Bloom wandered would have regarded his project "as the quaintest of quaint conceits."[8] Strange that this odd, impoverished, bookish boy, that this self-proclaimed outlaw, this selfish writer of nearly unreadable prose should speak for us all. Preposterous. As surely as he is situated, like all people, the artist is alone.

In one sense the author of *Ulysses* or *Leaves of Grass*, of "Ulalume" or the Declaration of Independence, like every maker of ballads and carver of masks, speaks for himself only. The hope remains that some words or objects by virtue of immanent richness can lead us through their creators, out of the lone mind into confrontation with the conceptual and processual essences the creator shares with known and unknown contemporaries. In their search for these key cultural statements, historians are carried into anthropology.

The basic similarities of history and anthropology, and, therefore, the usefulness of one study for the other, are concealed under opaque layers of jargon. History is ethnology, vertically ordered, and the historian's interpretive difficulties parallel those of the ethnographer.

Anthropologists used to describe culture as if it were a consistent, invariant whole, as if it were an island awaiting discovery. Having done ethnography, I know its ways. You never find culture. Rather, you find individuals who are various and devious, open and closed, knowledgeable in this area, ignorant in that. Historians look for exceptional people and ethnographers for common ones, but the people ethnographers find most helpful are exceptional. They are outstandingly friendly and articulate. They have time to waste untangling a stranger's long skein of foolish questions. It is an odd person, not an average one, who produces the documents historians study, and it is an odd person who provides ethnographers with their most valuable statements. These statements—responses, comments, soliloquies, artworks—are not the culture. They are hypotheses, poised for testing against census data, constant observation, and repetitive interviewing. Then some statements come to represent more than a person or small group. They push the ethnographer toward a sense of consensus, an impression of pattern in consciousness, a theory of shared conceptualization—toward culture. Then some statements come to be myth, powerfully compacted, densely metaphoric, fecund presentations of a culture's soul.

Historians begin like ethnographers with particular statements, a landscape painting, a diarist's account of commercial adventuring. To make the statement represent not an individual or movement but a region or nation, it has to be evaluated, generalized, and exhaustively compared with information about, and information from, the less friendly, less verbose, less fortunate, more normal members of a society. It is they who give a minority the power to speak myth.

Myth is a word too much and too loosely used today. Myth pulses in forms, unhindered by media or social subdivisions. If a poem is myth, its idea will resonate through the folk song and sculpture and judicial decisions, through the daily rhythms of work and play of its moment, softly coaxing people while they construct their realities. Another poem, pretending to myth, might be no more than the reduction to doggerel of one man's whimsy. Another might fuse its poet with essential concerns; the loveliest and deepest of all, it cannot be held to myth as it snaps free of culture and soars away from time and place. Which poem is which, which tale or statue or history text is mythic? Here are subtle questions demanding disciplined study.

Things are even more complicated than that. Artworks do not come neatly packaged. They mix their possibilities. In some measure all poems (or dances or scientific experiments) are idiosyncratic and ephemeral, cultural and mythic, human and universal. It is not just a matter of locating statements that

are myths. The mythical valences of compound statements must be isolated. And that takes careful, attentive work.

It is work of the good old qualitative sort and of the good new quantitative sort—work that is annoying to scholars eager to leap from fact to myth, asserting the importance of a statement they have discovered or a generalization they have constructed. It is necessary to leap. Our work is never done. We are obliged to share our thoughts, even our premature and ill-formed thoughts, with those who share our interests. But there is a danger in the leap that is easily put. If we are not careful, we will offer and accept generalizations that fit more than a movement but less than a society. We will say Americans thought something when we really mean literate northern Protestants thought something. We will say Americans did something when we really mean middle-class American white men did something. We will say that American art underwent a revolution when we really mean that the artists retained by wealthy urbanites to enhance their prestige adopted a fashion from London or Paris. When our best intuitions prod us to leap, we cannot sail in bad faith, jumping because we are tired of hard work, because we believe the majority of people have no historical reality.

In taking the leap from the particular to the general, from statement to culture, fact to myth, scholars sometimes seem to be suggesting that most people have nothing to say. Or if they do have something to say, it is not important. Or if it is important, it only clumsily recapitulates what someone else can say better. Those are bad and untrue ideas.

If we assume without musing that the powerful, literate few speak plainly for the powerless, nonliterary many, we will be assuming that culture and society are static, consistent entities. If they were, any social fact or cultural expression would be a core sample, synecdochically representative of the whole. That notion will not stand up to a reading of social science or reality. Lacking dynamic, comprehensive—realistic—theories of culture and society, we will be lost for a reasonable theory of history.

Culture is an arrangement of ideas, a cognitive structure of generative principles, whirring and grinding in tension. Society is an arrangement of people who live within an order that dominates but cannot eliminate the animus for its own destruction. Culture and society arise out of wild, continual communicative confrontation. Both trope to closure without closing. They strain to unity while existing as the foci of forces in mad and utter opposition. Both are strong, even tyrannical; both are fragile, even vulnerable, expendable. Neither is homogeneously inert. We can speak of a culture like that of late nineteenth-century America as shifting toward secularization and still admit that the great popularity of gospel music, proved in the survival of thousands of uncollected, unexamined songbooks, reveals a counterurge toward the sacred. We can speak of the society of that era as adjusting to massively ordered industrial labor and still admit that the common contemporary ballads manifest a horror of the machine and glorify the lone, victimized worker. Georgie Allen, golden-haired engineer, Billy Budd's country cousin, is "murdered by the railway to be laid in a lonesome grave." "Too many men have lost their lives for the railroad company," but Steve Brady is ordered to make up lost time, his machine fails him, losing its air brakes on a downgrade, and his children are left fatherless. John Henry, the man who "ain't nothin but a man," outdrives the steam drill, breaking his poor heart, burying him "down in the sand."

If an aggregate of people is a society, it will not be ordered from without by a scholar's convenient schemes or a government's paid police. It will be ordered from within by culture. If culture is authentic it will expose itself mythically, not in little didactic exempla or insipid appeals to union, but in forms that are in themselves revelations of the paradoxes that throb at the culture's core.

Myths profoundly influence behavior. But they do not prescribe actions clearly. They establish a society's poles of argument, the terms of its major dialectics, by embracing warring forces. To Albert Camus the prime characteristic of tragedy is its counterposition of powers, which are equally strong and legitimate.[9] Myth is tragic. It reveals without conclusively solving the problems people must solve to live. Myth thrusts us into the heart of ambiguity, then commands us to act. This is an important point, deserving a pair of illustrations.

The forests had fallen to farmland and the meadows had been cut by the black tracks of trains. Factories bulked along the riverbanks. There was smoke in the sunset, quiet desperation in the breasts of laboring people. *Walden* was Henry David Thoreau's reaction. A sermon, it demands the renunciation of a

materialistic tradition and a return into nature.[10] But *Walden*'s rhetoric grinds against its narrative, nearly binding its ideological gears. The chapter named "Sounds" crescendos to the exultant cry that no path leads from Thoreau's door to the civilized world. Yet every day or two he strolled along the railroad causeway to loiter around the town. On other days, visitors came out to relieve his solitude.

Thoreau went into the woods and built a little house by a pond. But, as he is at great pains not to hide, he did not go far into the woods. In the book's first sentence he locates Walden within civilization—"in Concord." His house was no hut of natural substances. It was built of smooth hewn and planed lumber, of purchased, salvaged boards and bricks. He plastered it like a townhouse. If he sites his home excitedly in rhetorical wilderness, he locates his bean field less ecstatically as a mediator between nature and culture and pushes his metaphors across domains: the train is a hawk, a horse; the pond is glass, a mirror. That pond, font of his rebirth, was brushed—"touched"—by the railroad, whirling the pastoral into oblivion. Thoreau smirks at Thoreau.

Walden is read in youth as a hymn to innocence and in maturity as comic and ironic. Thoreau hates business, and he wryly totes his enterprise in a mock ledger. He will not have his senses sullied by the railroad, and he gazes in long rapture upon the smoking locomotive, "refreshed and expanded when the freight train rattles past" just as he is when observing nature. Against civilization, Thoreau says, "we need the tonic of wilderness." Against wilderness, Thoreau needed culture's petty medicine—the gossip of the village, "which, taken in homoeopathic doses, was really as refreshing in its way as the rustle of leaves and the peeping of frogs." He left the woods, as he tells us, for as good reason as he came in.

Walden argues honestly for natural purity while clearly describing its impossibility. Nature is beautiful—and savage and awful. The maniacal screech of the owl terrifies him, though less, it seems, than the nature alive in his own slimy viscera. Culture is enslaving—and necessary. He loves the open hearth's cheery glow, but on a cold morning, it may be admitted, there is "some virtue in a stove." The house was more appealing before it was plastered, but more comfortable after. Thoreau is not of nature; he must list himself, along with the woodcutters and railroad men, as a profaner of Walden. The book concludes triumphantly: things are as they are. Once lost, paradise cannot be regained . . . perhaps. John Cage was right to link Henry Thoreau with Marcel Duchamp as men who could say neither Yes nor No.[11]

Reading closely or openly, comparing narrowly or broadly, we can make *Walden* speak for its author, or for the Yankee intellectual movement in which he participated directly, or for the international movement, Romanticism, bound together by essays and poems in which people like Rousseau and Herder, Wordsworth and Coleridge, Ruskin and Morris—and Thoreau and Emerson—registered their protest against the materialistic, rationalist-capitalist, industrializing age that had them trapped. At an intermediate level of analysis, *Walden* breaks away from Europe and joins the canvases of the Hudson River School and the verse of the young women whose backs and minds ached in New England's mills to become an expression of the antebellum culture of the northeastern United States.

The attitudes shared by Henry Thoreau, Thomas Cole, and the Lowell Factory Girl were minority values. The majority report was sent in by the likes of Sam Colt and Eli Terry and was expressed less in poems than in cleared land and reaping machines, revolvers and muskets, locomotives, steamships, power looms, and clocks.

Yet the minority statement—if art—cannot be irrelevant to a society's dominant problematic.

When he was still a member, though a tough and independent member, of the loose circle around Emerson, Orestes Brownson declared the artist was no lone actor but the bound spokesman for society at large.[12] Art is a collective product. Brownson posed his argument against "Mr. Emerson and his friends," and Mr. Emerson's friend, Thoreau, would soon write that great art emanates from personal struggle. Art is an individual product. Those positions, that the artist is society's soldier, that the artist is an outlaw, have been separated, clarified, and crusted with emotion during debates lasting into our times. The positions, though, are not exactly antagonistic.

The artist's struggle is for authenticity. To prevent art from being false to the self, burned up in simple social assent and swept away as propaganda's ashes, the artist must exert against culture. But the confrontation of the artist with society and its conventions need not inevitably result in revolt, as it seems it must in a heart like Baudelaire's. Nor need it inevitably yield originality, as it must in a mind like Kandinsky's. For some artists—academic painters and ballad singers—can find a voice at once psychically satisfying, ethically supportive, and affirmatively conservative. Conversely, to prevent artworks from rising as cheap summaries of opinion or feeling, the artist must assert culture against the self, forcing the soul to mature in relation to external realities. In two ways, the artist's requisite quest for authenticity demands the test of contextual engagement: the personal and the collective mesh. If something is art and not mere reportage or doctrine, insincere confession or glib exercise, it will, even if rare and idiosyncratic, incorporate its place and time, mythically.

Although they were minority statements, *Walden* and Cole's *Oxbow* hummed with the tensions that generated much of the spirit of the times. There was no easy release from those tensions, the abrasive opposition of the old and the new, the cultural and the natural, for they were connected inextricably and unresolvably to conflicting visions of freedom. For Thoreau, conventions prevented freedom, and conventions could be eliminated only by submission to nature. For the industrialist, freedom rose out of nature's destruction. Only by making nature submit entirely to the progress of human planning and manipulation could the mind be set free. Individuals' actions differed, nearly diametrically, but they were affected and framed by the paradoxes smoldering in *Walden*.

Because it was a dominant concern of early English Romanticism, nature became an obvious focus of American Romanticism. Because they began their approach to America through the literature of nineteenth-century New England, many of the scholars who formulated American Studies emphasized the idea of nature, nature as sacred force, as symbol, in their own work. Surely, the relation of man and land is one of the great matters of American writing from Hariot to Jefferson to Turner to Faulkner, and it is worthy of the attention it receives from historians and geographers, art and literary historians. However, of at least equal importance in American consciousness is a theme that runs (though less obviously than nature) through Thoreau's writings, including *Walden*, and surfaces in "Civil Disobedience": the fury of a thinking individual within an imperfect society. This, our second example of mythic ambiguity, is the idea of the outlaw.

Henry Thoreau was a moral breaker of laws. If society, its customs and laws, are good, outlaws are bad. Since no social organization is closed and perfect, the responsible individual is forced to consider alternatives, to judge, perhaps to rebel. The Irish outlaw, the rapparee who rode the wild heaths, was sanctioned politically and religiously. A man like Black Francis Corrigan directed his robbery and outrage against the English colonizers of his native land, the Protestant oppressors of his religion. The moral position of the English outlaw is less clear. If some were defenders of customary law, others were brigands, footpads, and thieves. But the worst of the whole roguish lot were sentimentalized into heroes in ballad and legend. The popular mind revamped them as economic levelers. They did not have to be as good as Robin Hood, stealing from the rich to give to the poor; it was enough for a highwayman like Dick Turpin that his deeds were rakish and brave, that he robbed and humiliated the wealthy.

The American outlaw cuts his English progenitor's ambiguous figure. He breaks laws that must be upheld. He must be killed. But since the social order is imperfect, the adventures bringing him to that end are admirable and heroic. Counterfeiter and thief David Lewis, bank robber and murderer Jesse James, gather to them tales once told about Robin Hood, in which, for instance, a banker is robbed to pay the mortgage on a poor widow's farm. Not only is Jesse James lauded because he "took from the rich and gave to the poor"; his death is blurred, the chorus of his ballad underscoring the affection in which he is held by the living, and—at least in the version Carolina banjo-picker Thee Phillips sang to me—implying his uttermost reward will be Heaven: "I don't know where my poor old Jesse's gone, but I'll meet you in that land where we've never been before, and I don't know where my poor old Jesse's gone."

Fictively, the outlaw lives to deny and dies to maintain the social order. His artistic existence rides between life and death as an exposure of cultural confusion. The culture requires manliness of men. They must be competitive, aggressive, and brave. Ungrumblingly, they must labor hard hours in sweltering hayfields, damp mine pits, chilly construction sites, dreary factories, battlefields. And the culture requires restraint. Men must be docile, faithful husbands, poppas, servants. The outlaw is unrestrained. He is a bad man—a swaggering braggart, a pistol-packing bravo, a dandy womanizer. The culture preaches an egalitarian ethos. And the culture enforces subtle but harsh class distinctions and supports the radically unequal distribution of goods and well-being. The outlaw charges out of the demos to outwit, demean, and rob the bankers and lawyers who conspire to assure that the free enterprise system will be freer for some than for others.

Living and dying, the outlaw proves the disorder in order, manifesting the tensions in a culture both passive and aggressive, democratic and stratified. He personifies concretely the conflict Orestes Brownson, most politically aware of the Transcendentalists, stated abstractly in 1840: the head-on clash of capitalism and Christianity.

If capitalist ethics and Christian ethics are both good and if they are irreconcilably at odds, the citizen-worker is forced into a decision. One solution is deference to an afterlife. Christian laborers sing, "this world is not my home, I'm just a-travelin' through." Though miserable and surrounded by evildoers who reap the world's gain, they do not question for "farther along we'll understand why; cheer up my brother, live in the sunshine, we'll understand it all bye and bye." A world of pain, this vale of tears. Sweet Heaven when I die.

Henry Thoreau was a breaker of laws. He could understand the outlaw's morality, but Mirabeau was too much for him. The highwayman is manly but idle and desperate, less than sane. Thoreau would be no outlaw. When preparing for his exile, Thoreau's fellow artist, James Joyce, discoursed on the social need for rebellion and on the poetic excellence of one of his favorite ballads. He took its hero as a model, titling the early version of *A Portrait of the Artist as a Young Man, Stephen Hero*. "O rare Turpin hero" runs the refrain of the ballad recounting Dick Turpin's wild career, his assault on a lawyer and a judge, his hanging. Joyce, his antlers flashing, dashed into the woods to become a literary outlaw, gaily waylaying professors yet unborn.

The outlaw stands forth to be rejected or copied. The film *Bonnie and Clyde* cleverly portrays poor Clyde trying to live up to the image of the badman he received from tradition. Kinny Wagner, Mississippi lumberman, mule skinner, bronco buster, and circus roustabout, appropriated the pseudonym Harvey Logan from an outlaw ballad. He borrowed the badman's etiquette and guts from other songs and legends. Kinny Wagner became a killer, jailbreaker, and the subject of a ballad that had gained wide currency before his death in prison in 1958.

It takes superhuman courage or a heavy leaven of insanity to act the bandit, Clyde and Kinny style, but for an average individual the dilemma at the heart of the outlaw legend opens options for a personal synthesis of the thesis of Christianity and the antithesis of capitalism. The black man does not have to be the killer of the ballad, the lady killer of the toast "Staggerlee." But the badman jolts him. He does not have to be smilingly submissive either. If no murderer, he can still be muscular and scornful in the face of white society, taking on the Bad Nigger persona. It will get you in trouble, but the badass is a solid stance to strike before your colleagues on the corner, the cops in the alley. The white working-class man does not have to erupt like Jesse James or John Dillinger. Neither does he have to wait in meek obedience for admission to that cloudless, nightless land where there is no death, no pain or fear. He can accept society's law, bringing his heroes to the gallows, and he can detest the soft-handed, light-fingered politicians in Washington. He can drink as hard as he works, bloody his fists, cheat on his wife, and get saved for Christ once every couple of years.

People act. Myths are among the forces that make them. The old anthropological idea of myth as society's charter is not incorrect, but the charter is fraught with ambiguity. Actions can be at once cultural and unpredictably variable.

As students of the past, we must search for the real myths, folktales for children simultaneously encouraging aggression and restraint, governmental documents declaring the equality of men while denying freedom to black men, suffrage to women. As writers of the past, contributors to our own national mythos, we must not shy from confusion, contradiction, and complexity. Complexity is the inward and outward, cultural and social, reality. It is the essential precondition for change and, therefore, for history itself.

Simplicity is the enemy, the devil that counsels quick leaps. Simplicity lures historians to the delights of easy ideas, leaving them open to the drab, redundant charge of elitism.

Two types of simplicity tempt the historian. Thus far, we have been considering one of them, that which misrepresents history's horizontal dimension by accepting too much or too little as mythic or by offering a generalization—a selective construct or statistical contour—as an abstraction of the whole when it can truly account for only part of a culture or society, time or place. The vice of the usual horizontal perspective is consistency; its virtue is that it grows ultimately out of biography. It tends to be sophisticated in matters of mind—mind in context, minds in association—but to fail as the scholar's canvas is stretched to the edges of society. The other type of simplicity misrepresents history's vertical dimension. The tendency of the vertical view is to be sophisticated in its idea of society as a mechanical whole but naive in its understanding of mind and human experience.

The horizontal transforms into the vertical when we link the account of one age with the account of others in sequence to accomplish the necessary task of describing great changes. The difficulties of this task, of making the past into a cracking good story, cause us to drift into a concentration upon things that display change most vividly, thus smothering evidence of the human longing for stability under our need to split the past into reasonable periods.

Conceptually this problem appears in both spatial and temporal study. To gain geographic understanding, scholars divide space into regions. Features that distinguish one region from the next, aspects of geology or dialect or architecture, are isolated and compared so lines can be drawn on maps. The region might, then, be viewed as an assemblage of distinctive traits, but its true personality consists of features that connect as well as separate it from neighboring spatial subdivisions. In like manner, to gain historical understanding, scholars divide the past into periods on the basis of differentiating characteristics. Each period will share attributes with the eras from which it is broken away, the sharedness may even predominate, and the human course may have been more continuous than discontinuous, but we historians tend to overlook similarities in searching for details that can be built into narratives.

When historians lack a coherent model of culture, even the collection of temporally variable features may prove unwieldy, untidy, a task too large. Then we are circled into hermetic institutional chronicles. History breaks, brachiating. History is traded for histories, narratives of politics or economy or art or society, or more narrowly of government or industry or literature or the family, or still more narrowly of national government or industrial technology or lyric poetry or child raising. No matter how tightly those fascinations screw down, even into genealogy or some subject as arcane as the history of the hatband, they still squeeze our useful information. There is no denying the worth of these labors and no denying that they prepare us poorly for the necessary move from information to interpretation to explanation, from fact to correlation to causation.

Closed chronicles insidiously entreat us to interpret them internally, as if one legal code magically begat another, one pottery style the next, without the intervention of human agents in whose minds deep generative principles tie the creation of laws and pots into the creation of gardens, gods, and proper courting behaviors. Forgetfully we turn to explanation and find ourselves locked in prisons of our own devising. Walled in, we erect structures of causation among the facts we have assembled. Deterministic simplicity begins to look good, to satisfy. We cease sighing for freedom from academic conventions. Outside, history escapes.

It need not. The walls around us seem sturdy at first but turn out to be thin and easily breached. Good historians topple them handily, constructing correlations between arbitrarily separated chronicles. Facts from distinct areas of research intersect, interpenetrate. Grand patterns emerge.

But these are not history. They are history's husk, shell—shape, not essence.

The trouble comes clearly into view if we ask what the patterns mean. What significance did existence in one period or another have for the human beings who lived in it? One possible answer is deterministic. The economic, religious, and other factors typifying a period rage into a tide people cannot resist. It floods over them, swamping their psyches, sweeping them into obeying its mindless rule, carrying them unawares into the next period. Things seem like that, until they are examined closely. Then periods have predominant moods but always display tremendous, countervailing variety.

People have choices. As Eugene Genovese built a big book to show, black men and women in the pre-Civil War South could act intelligently and forcefully within the bitter limits of chattel slavery to create a society and maintain cherished parts of an ethos, African in origin.[13] The combined powers of the historical period are the circumstances of human being—the constraints not the determinants of culture.

The period is an environment. It is like the weather. Considering the impact of the weather on everyone's health and conversation, upon agrarian success and, therefore, everyone's food and life, it would be useful to have a history of the climate, tracing the succession of windy and still, hot and cold, wet and dry years. But that history would lack meaning, it would remain absurd until it was posed as culture's antagonist in a dialectical drama of adaptation—the war of will and weather as written in human products.

Natural and cultural circumstances are identified in *The Plague.* In that great novel, Albert Camus used struggle against pestilence to refer both to struggle against boredom from within and political oppressors from without. Human heroism, whatever the evil it stands against—that is what matters most. Still, for the writing of history there are differences between the conditions we make, those others make, and those madly loosed out of nature. A period's forces are not exactly like the weather. Most of them spring, however unpredictably, from human intentions.

Intentions arrive in the communicating event as one person's expressions and another's conditions. When history is based on the statements of a few people concerning the few areas of life that demonstrate great change, it becomes the story of the expressions of the few and the conditions of the many. And the historian's practice becomes ideographic mentalism for the few, who are honored as individual and volitional, and nomothetic behaviorism for the many, who are lost in the masses, racing witless ratwise.

History comes to lack human actors, being the product of a few gods, the climate for many beasts.

Now, that is unfair to many historians working to describe the life of past multitudes. And neither is it fair to many others who restrict their interests to the famous and make no pretence of accounting for all of society. But there is a tendency in historiography to deal sensitively with a minority (which, oddly enough, includes historians) and then to shrug off the majority as somehow muddling through. Millennia of people have muddled through millennia of weathers and political climates, but some have muddled with grace and some clumsily.

History's big events seem to crash above most people with all the logic and love of a thunderstorm.

Yet they are among the contexts within which people act, with which they interact to form valid personal statements. Take war. It is begun—caused—by a few men who take pleasure in ideological debates and byzantine machinations. It is directed by a few men who enjoy toying with tactics, chess players like Napoleon. But its reality is created by men who gamble their inner resources in a transaction with their fellow creatures and with conditions of control. In war they negotiate performances of self and present works as beautiful or absurd as those of the greatest dramatists. From one point of view, the people of war are politicians' puppets. From another, politicians are but the hands who clear the stage for the ultimate *commedia dell'arte.*

While history books list the external facts of battles and leaders, the folksongs of the American people disdain ideologies, disregard great names, ignore military specifics, and concentrate on individual realities, on the deaths of men, the woes of women. Historiographically, our ballads seem peripheral. Existentially, they are central.

Once I asked Eva Girvin, a fine singer of the Southern Appalachian tradition, about a favorite ballad of hers. When her mother sang it, it brought tears, and when she sang it, her clear voice rose over us, filling the kitchen of her home with strong sorrow. In the song, two men meet before battle. A pink boy talks of his mother, who has already lost a husband and son to war. A tall, dark man tells, in turn, of his sweetheart, whose picture he carries. They agree that should one of them die, the other will get the news to the woman who waits alone at home. They touch, the command is given, the armies meet with a terrible yell. Both are killed. The kitchen was quiet, a cool light spread on the table. I sat stunned in the atmosphere of her song; then, having been somewhere convinced such things are important, I asked Mrs. Girvin what army the men served in, for the song did not say. She said she didn't know. It didn't matter what army, what flag, what war. What mattered was the men, their friendship, their death.

We have returned to the midpoint of the historian's dilemma. It is necessary to paint time's vast seascape, depicting successive waves as they roll, break. Our view of the past, though, and our rendering of its patterns are closed down and conventionalized—limited in significance and utility—by the imp of simplicity. We are tempted to sacrifice culture's complex reality to ideas of homogeneity and false myth. We are beguiled into betraying the human being's complex reality in deterministic formulas.

The way out of the dilemma does not seem hard. In the group biography, the study of a movement, historians employ a three-point structure. Individual personalities are recognized, while a collective personality is developed. Outward facts are not merely listed, they are evaluated as to their salience. Expressions are used prismatically to separate the personal, the traditional, the contextual. Make history the biography of a people or of People and you will not be content with an absurd chronicle of conditions or with a list of exceptional persons and moments. The collective personality will unfold in all its schizophrenic splendor. The great event will sputter up not as the only event nor as one of a flat infinity of events. It will emerge accurately as having varying degrees of influence on real lives that flow on, now interrupted by, now oblivious to, the shenanigans of the famous. Expressions will open themselves as the record of the interchange between collective personality—culture—and conditions.

The biography of the American people would be difficult to write but easy to begin. In history and geography, we have much of the necessary contextual information. We need only attend to the expressions of the people themselves and see how culture and contexts constrained and directed the performances of which expressions are the available residue.

Our beginning cannot be made with one person's description of another. Whether trained ethnographer or casual journalist, one person always reads another in terms of tacit concepts of need and significance: the common folk are ennobled by romantics, slandered by progressives. No observer, neither psychiatrist nor poet, can draw out all the psyche of another. Our understanding of the mind, both philosophically and biologically, remains at an excruciatingly primitive level, but such hints as we do have require us to read people directly in their own statements, in which the fullness of consciousness might be caught, rather than indirectly through someone else's clinical report or judgmental commentary.

So, all we need is to look insistently, charitably, at the facts people create out of their compound selves: the ages at which they choose to wean children, the shelters they choose to erect, the poems they choose to sing, the ways they choose to die. It seems easy to do. Yet it is not done often. There are two main reasons why historians in great numbers have not brought under scrutiny the people's expressions in great numbers. One is easy to talk about, one not so easy. I will talk about the difficult one first.

"My experience with life," said Walt Whitman, "makes me afraid of historians: the historian, if not a liar himself, is largely at the mercy of liars." Like Jefferson, Whitman feared his war would evade history. The war he had seen in the cut-off arms and snuffed eyes of young men, "the real war," he said, "will never get in the books."[14]

It is cynical and even wrong to see historians as buzzing and fumbling in a cobweb of lies. But life's experiences breed distrust. No thinking person today is unaware of the biological equality of human brains. That sentence is not intended in its ridiculous literal sense but in its profound theoretical sense: no one who has access to the facts would argue that a Bushman because he is a Bushman, or a medieval serf woman because she is a medieval serf woman, is intellectually inferior to a professor of history because he is a modern Western man. The theories of the professor of history, in fact, are predicated on a unity of mind, or else his attempts to understand people removed from him in time and place would be all in vain. This relativism of mind is overtly proclaimed but seems gently to slip out of sight in historiographic practice.

Communities of farm people on the damp green drumlins of Ulster, in the stark piney woods of Mississippi, neighborhoods of poor black people locked in big city rifts, include as many smart and as many stupid people as any university faculty. I have lived in all these worlds and know that peasant villages and ivory towers both contain people who doze and nod by the fire, idiotically persisting without thought, and people who have at least once risen and left the hearth, walking into the night to stand under the circling stars and gaze plain on the void. They have passed the garden wall and gone alone to the edge, the very edge, and seen the stars and the void. And they have laughed lightly, understanding, and they have returned to the house, the hearth, knowing. We modern overreachers control many facts, it is true, but we own no exclusive license to epiphany or ex-

cellence or depth. Fortune, arrant whore, plays unequally with people, but people play equally with her.

Modern scholars announce a commitment to theoretical relativism, but their works rarely provide good evidence of that commitment. William Morris, the last century's fullest man, thought the Scots border ballads were the best of English language poetry.[15] An edition of the ballads was being planned at Kelmscott when he died, but where are the critical studies that treat the ballads—as art—with the dense intensity found in dozens of admirable works on Chaucer, Wordsworth, or Eliot? Even the scholar trained in literature will reduce the ballad from art to sociological fact, thereby demeaning it and its people. If you believe, as our science suggests you must, in theoretical human equality, then how can you not believe a ballad might be as fine as a sonnet, a quilt as fine as a painting, an epic sung by a Malian griot as excellent as a novel written by a deracinated cosmopolite? And what of social history? Edward Ives has written sensitive biographies of obscure northeastern poets. E. P. Thompson has written sensitive accounts of small movements that engendered no grand political revolutions.[16] Recent studies of colonial New Englanders and antebellum Afro-Americans herald good news for the future of the historian's community. But in most social history the "average" people of the past are not granted the respect biographers normally accord their subjects or political historians give to theirs.

That is because we scholars do not know the "average" people of the present, and even the most antiquarian of research must commence in the student's personal and existential concept of his or her own society. Jacques Barzun has criticized the new scientistic historians for burrowing into data, cuddling up to hardware, then talking about the public, political life they do not know experientially.[17] Of the old sort as well as the new, we historians are comfortable with shallow, nearly snide, characterizations of the masses because of the shallowness of our own contacts with the people who are supposed to make up the masses. *Masses* is a categorical term for the unknown members of one's own society.[18]

Scholars in disciplines grounded in fieldwork are fortunate that they are allowed to pass the time among people without puritanical goblins nagging them to burn their lives out amid musty paper or, worse yet, machines. Did not Yeats, like Camus anxious for a life both active and contemplative, say that the scholar's solitary light illumines truth and flickers from the tomb? Slow death in the study. Quick life in the streets.

This essay was conceived in a low dark bar by the tracks in a grim midwestern town. It is a tavern known for colorful fights—nothing beats a battle between women in the local aesthetic—but there were none that night. The band was driving hard, mixing mid-fifties rockabilly with cool current Nashville to produce the sound that typifies live roadhouse music today. A hard-working man in coveralls swung his heavy arms to its beat. A slim woman in black hotpants, coiffed like a lady of the court of Louis XIV, jitterbugged with a redhead in a softball uniform. It felt good, dancing free, spinning another bad week behind you. Long hours of standing on concrete floors assembling electronic contraptions evaporated in the beer and the rhythm and the darkness. It was an unexceptional night, so between chatting with the waitress, a bright young country woman trying to make it in town, and an old pal, a bright young man trying to make it in a mean university, I listened to the randy laughter, the shouts and slick guitar runs, and, struck again that this America was terra incognita to academe, thought about clotting more pages with words. Not that this essay is about bars, but my experiences in tough bars and hayfields, on civil rights marches and city streets at midnight, my waiting for Godot and view into the void, have caused me to distrust histories suspended cleanly above the pains, predicaments, and lovely flesh of people. My experiences form the ultimate ground for my scholarship, and so do yours.

Under this Emersonian plea for scholars to enroll in reality's school lies a simple logic. The things historians study are in themselves nothing. Here are curious little black spots on paper, there are bits of burned earth in the sand. Nothing. Scholars must act imaginatively to make them mean. First they are assumed to be the results of human intention. Mind is posited behind them. That mind, and therefore those marks and shards, can be understood only via compassion. The scholar presses his or her mind through tangible phenomena into the hollow vacated by a lost mind and fills it, becoming the writer of the document, the turner of the pot. The lost creator's mind becomes the scholar's mind. Quite simply, scholars must rely on themselves while performing this historical magic. If their contacts have been limited to people like themselves, other bourgeois intellectuals, then the act of inventing the absent other will be comparably limited.

The other will not be fully revealed, so scholarship must remain somewhat projective. But by experiencing diverse people, scholars might be able to locate a genuinely alien consciousness behind their sources. Ethnographic analogy, the transformation of space into time, is dangerous, but Albert Lord can gain insight into Homer's mode of composition by observing Yugoslavian epic-singers, and even so rigorous a theorist as Lewis Binford can use interviews with Eskimos to shine a sidelong light in Old World paleolithic data. I do not confuse modern Irish with premodern Americans, but my understanding of the people who inhabited old American houses was greatly enhanced by the months I spent visiting Irish men and women who lived without piped water or electricity, cooking on open hearths, entertaining themselves by dint of wit rather than machinery. I could have learned something by living alone, unencumbered by customary conveniences, but not much. Watching and talking with people who were experts at living that way checked and pricked my imagination, flashing me vague, fugitive, astonishing glimpses backward. The broader our human contacts, the less likely we will be to project our own psyches and prejudices full-scale into the past while accomplishing the necessary miracle of breathing life into dead minds.

There is nothing to be done or said about this point. If you cannot enter passionately into the life of your own times, you cannot enter compassionately into the life of the past. If the past is used to escape the present, the past will escape you. I am afraid we historians do not take the common people's expressions seriously because we do not think they are important, which is because we do not think the people are important, which is because we do not know them. The common people of present or past will seem remarkably uncommon once we get to know them. The second point to be made takes us out of personal matters and into general properties of historical disciplines.

If you agree history's forgotten people might be as complicated, ill, well, or wise as history's remembered ones, then all you have to do to write a truly democratic history is analyze their statements with care. That is easier said than done.

Although historians seem sometimes to prefer bad literature to good, their practice is literary. Much of their work is judged, and properly so, on the qualities of their transparent and vigorous prose. More importantly, they study not the past but the literary remains of the past. This methodological commitment to the written word has mired democratic historiography to the hubs. Most of the world's societies have been nonliterate. They left no literary remains. Within the confines of literacy most of the world's people have been illiterate. They left no literary remains. Among the literate, very few have elected to put their thoughts on paper. Such literary remains as we do have were left us by a miniscule minority of unusual people. And the richest of literature was produced by people who in Yeats's anguished formula traded life for art. It is not a contented, jovial, sociable individual who spends hours revising poems or talking into a journal. This means, simply, that a discipline based on writing is stuck with the job of writing about the culture of a small number of mostly white, mostly male, mostly urban, mostly prosperous, mostly strange people.

Happily, that is not entirely true. A few average people did leave us diaries and letters. But these are so overbalanced by the writings of exceptional people that they often amount to little more than curiosities, incapable of contradicting the large patterns historians contrive out of the documents forced upon them by the insistent, vociferous few. Old diaries convey human concerns clearly: soldiers' diaries concerned with hardtack, diarrhea, and long marches; mothers' diaries concerned with female friends and the health of children; farmers' diaries concerned with the weather and economic contracts. These are the realities. Still, it seems possible to root through those works, ignoring their loud messages, grubbing for trifles to reinforce the predetermined chronicle of big events.

Written facts do exist in numbers large enough to be drawn into patterns reflective of majority ways. Those are located in records of birth, marriage, and death, in inventories and wills. They must be handled with care, since they rarely come directly from the people they will be used to describe. There is every reason to suspect the information entered by census takers of our times and times long past. Im-

perfect, impeachable, indirect, such documents do include information about mass behavior, and they provide social historians with their readiest, most obvious source.

These documents have breadth, wide demographic coverage, but they are thin and brittle, mythically puny. They are not strong enough to resist the advances of an ardent theorist. They contain no ambiguity and therefore no meaning. No foreign consciousness is coiled within. Blank, bald data on infant mortality can be built into generalizations, but these remain meaningless, absurd, until explained. To explain statistical patterns is to discover mind behind them, motives and emotions in them. Since no guides to explanation wait in the patterns (they are invented by the historian, not by the people of the past), historians must import them from without. In putting explanations together, historians might rely on casual notions pulled out of the unexamined self. That is what happens when historians say they work without theory. More responsibly, they might carry in an established structure of explanation and erect it in the data, thus surrendering themselves to centerless eclecticism or trapping themselves in a cozy ideology. Marxists will have one explanation for the pitiful deaths of babies, capitalist apologists quite another. Usually today explanations are borrowed from psychology. During our century, anthropologists have proved that theories developed in the modern bourgeois West and supposed to be universal have had to be abandoned or much modified in non-Western locations. The use of Freudian concepts or modern clinical data to interpret, say, the rural seventeenth-century poor is—at the very best—deeply problematical.

No amount of quantification, no measure of Baconian optimism, will produce explanations. Carefully assembled and glued social historical models, despite their terrific potential, will be left to gather dust as dull monuments to the 1970s, or they will be dismembered and absorbed without a whisper into social psychology and elitist literary history, or they will be correlated with mythically fertile statements created by the same people who created the births and deaths out of which the models were built. I recommend the ballad.

Difficulties of dating and spottiness of field reporting make ballads, like other oral literature, an unreliable base for quantitative historical study. We have, though, hundreds of nicely indexed collections and indications enough of time depth and geographic distribution to make such texts the appropriate subjective correlatives of demographic models. The ballad, in particular, deals deeply with exactly the issues of family life intriguing to today's social historians. If the startling statistics on the deaths of children seem to suggest there was no love of parent for child among the seventeenth-century poor, the songs those people sang reveal that suggestion for the sham it is. Ballad children are murdered and abandoned. Ballad mothers are wrenched with guilt and grieving. They are paid sin's wages and damned to hell. Facing poetic statements in consort with mere and simple facts, modern scholars will be backed into subtler, more useful explanations.

Folk literature can be employed, like *belles lettres*, to pump blood through dry historical constructs. Historians will have to set aside some pleasant old prejudices and adopt some new complicated procedures, but social historians cannot be sincere in their search for truth and ignore the guidance available in story and song. At least they need not be forced out of the library or away from their reliance on words.

Adding folk literature to demographic models could yield social historical understanding, quantitative and qualitative, broad and deep. There are problems aplenty in this arithmetic. For one, the terms in the formula might not belong together. The quantitative incorporates no qualitative direction. The qualitative is not amenable to worthwhile quantification. Our information comes, and comes none too clearly, from people who are similar, perhaps, but not the same.

Quantification is necessary. Not because it gives historians the false assurance of a stylish scientific rhetoric—though that often seems to be study's sole end—but because the past, being malleable, can be built into too many patterns, and quantification throws into relief the patterns worth the effort of explanation. Explanation requires patterns to be compared with contemporaneous expressions rich enough to embody consciousness. Great literature and subliterature, such as letters and memoirs, are the obvious sources. E. P. Thompson has shown how newspaper accounts, protoethnographic descriptions, and court records can be analyzed, nimbly, gingerly, to make them speak for silent people. Folk literature is an underexploited resource of great value. The cor-

relation of the quantitative and qualitative will get us the results we need. History will be democratized or it will be a fatuous luxury. But we contort ourselves into attraction to the historical possibilities of quantifiable records and interesting literature, thus glossing over all manner of methodological problems, mainly to preserve the primacy of writing in our disciplines. It would be better to build upon a corpus of information—a data base they are calling it nowadays—which would be at once quantifiable and qualitative, socially broad and culturally deep. And to find such a source historians would, indeed, have to get out of the library and give over their dependence on words.

While historians go down into the archives to mine out scraps of paper and puzzle them delicately into frail, fragmentary constructions, the land spreads tremendous, a palimpsest, the people's own manuscript, their handmade history book.

Plowing, strip mining, laying brick upon brick in mortar, weeding, bulldozing: these are as much historical acts as scratching a pen over paper. The shapes of fields, the wrecked faces of hills, the houses and bridges, corrals, docks, temples, factories, prisons, switchyards, junkyards, graveyards, the highways on the plains, the paths in the woods—all are historical texts, overlaid, opposed, related into a single perfect structure, simultaneously spatial and temporal, qualitative, quantitative, as inclusive as the planet, as deep as time itself: a universal memory, a democratic historian's dream.

No, not a dream, but a reality, an abundant source for historians who take seriously their membership in a democratic society. The argument is simple. Few people write. Everyone makes things. An exceptional minority has created the written record. The landscape is the product of the divine average.

In the midst of a walk once in the Irish countryside, I found myself pondering the aesthetic energies the island's people have frozen materially. The beginnings, preserved in illuminated manuscripts and carved crosses, were auspicious. The recent artistic genius has been radiantly exhibited in literature, in oral narrative, and instrumental music; but in painting and sculpture, whether academic or folk, modern Ireland is curiously weak. My knowledge of history and my doctrinaire leftward politic had begun to nudge me toward a dreary and rather uninteresting theory, something about how oppressed people like the Irish and black Americans being denied material well-being choose to express themselves in nonmaterial arts, such as song, which they can possess fully and withhold from marauding police—I was thinking like that when the sun pierced a cloudbank and spotlit a whitewashed gable far up a gentle hillside. Gold glazed the gray and green. Suddenly I realized the entire island has been touched, molded by human beings. It is an artifact. From Fair Head in Antrim to Mizen Head in Cork, from dear dirty Dublin to rocky Connemara, Ireland is sculpture, a collective material artwork that dwarfs in beauty and conceptual magnificance the oeuvre of the proudest of nonanonymous sculptors. Let others chip stone or pat clay into representations, the Irish people have made the emerald isle. The land is art as Waldo Emerson exactly defined it: a blending of nature and will.

Our American land, too, is an artifact. It has been handled less tenderly than Ireland. Progress is a rough lover. But people, affectionate or rapacious, have made the land their expression, their testament and legacy. This, our inheritance, is ample, singular, consistent, comparable. You can measure—literally, with a tape measure—differences and similarities from period to period, region to region, class to class. You can set next to each other thickly rich phenomena, towns and houses and chairs, from the full range of the society and allow them to effervesce with meaning. The American artifact incarnates history enormously. It speaks, incessantly babbling myth.

We should learn the landscape's language.

Fascinated by words, historians must find listening to fields and empty houses insane, or more generously, metaphorically flamboyant. Yet from the publication of Owen Jones's influential *Grammar of Ornament* in 1856 to contemporary theoretical writings in archaeology, scholars of "material culture" have found the analogy of artifactual and verbal languages fruitful. Let me press it a bit harder before letting it drift back beneath my argument.

Normal people learn to speak and to make. In speaking, intangibly, in making, concretely, their own humanity is revealed to them. From birth the head is filled with constant sensations, a hum of sound, a shimmering of sights. The innate, brave will to order breaks these down and builds them up so the speaker possesses a set of discrete sounds and procedures for arranging and rearranging them, and the maker possesses a set of discrete shapes and proce-

dures for arranging and rearranging them. We have been taught by Noam Chomsky to think of this capacity in a formal, mathematical sort of way. The sounds and shapes are simple and limited in number. The ways to arrange them are also finite, but combinations and transformations can generate a theoretically infinite number of realities.

Analysts look into infinite reality. Agog with facts, they are not stymied. They develop a theory of basic entities, whether sounds or shapes, and a theory of the mental procedures governing the creation of infinite statements, sentences or artifacts. Here we have part of a grammar, its syntactic component.

Something in the environment or something in the soul calls. Muscles move. The speaker forms natural air into strings of words. The maker forms the natural earth into artifacts. The syntactic capacity has been bent to purpose. Here we have the remainder of a grammar. Sounds and shapes combine and appear phenomenally, offering themselves to meaning. Some of meaning is utility. Speech relays necessary information: the carpenter asks his apprentice for a hammer. The maker's object serves some use: the carpenter raises the hammer to nail shingles on the roof to keep snow out of the householder's soup. Another dimension of meaning, despite some thinkers' attempts, is not neatly reducible to usefulness. It is delight, play, art, mystification, an autoeroticism of word and thing. Speech becomes veiled, indirective, poetic. The hammer is used to smash up the tableware or chisel out nonobjective dream sculpture.

A grammar relates the formal ability, which is systematic, closed, and shared, to meaning, which is probably systematic, possibly closed, and is never completely shared. The formal abilities of speaker and maker, their syntactic competences, seem closely comparable. Possibly they employ an identical dynamic of mind. They can be described fully. Meaning is more complicated.

Even a speaker's informational statement is grounded on arbitrariness. We cannot understand it unless we know the language. Without knowing a people's artifactual language, we can still decipher degrees of utility in tools. By analogy with our own situations, we can understand some of the uses of a hammer or house made by alien people.

Our analytic potential seems reversed in domains of meaning unrestricted by utility. If we know the language, we assume a poem, no matter how obscure and personal, can be forced to open its semantic treasury. A splattered drippy canvas, apparently portraying nothing, might seem to lie beyond meaning. This is true and it is false. It is true because one painting is not in itself meaningful. But neither is one sentence. What is really being said is that the artifactual language is unknown and the communicational experience is not understood. If the viewer brings to this painting a memory of other paintings, it does not hang alone. It takes up residence in a structure of feeling and comprehension. The viewer's understanding does not depend on information from the artist. Jackson Pollock's comments are artworks themselves, bearing perhaps only tangentially on the idea in his paintings. Art historians will find his words helpful while constructing the reactions in which the circuit of meaning is completed most satisfactorily. But his words will prove no more helpful than other pictures by him, his contemporaries, or the earlier painters on whose canvases his are a comment. Art historians know the painter's language well. It is their business, their pleasure. But the language is not impenetrable to the uninitiated. Out of their experiences with nature and with artifacts, especially those of their own manufacture (mud pies, sandcastles, paper airplanes, do-it-yourself projects, gardens, hairdos, apple pies), people make a start toward meaning as soon as they confront an object. They ask themselves: What's that? And a comparative trip through memory brings them to a trial theory of the thing's meaning. The more it, and others of its tradition, are encountered, the deeper and narrower it becomes, the more clearly its meaning shows forth.

All the meaning of a painting or a hammer cannot be known. Neither can all the meaning of a poem or a straightforward political manifesto.

Up to now, I have developed the comparison of verbal and artifactual languages so they look substantially the same, like parallel aspects of a complete theory of semiotics. From the standpoint of a philosophy of mind, that is probably the most important insight. From the standpoint of history, more needs saying.

The world does not march two by two into the mind's ark. It exists in complacent unity. Though we are right to balk at the artificiality of dialectical analysis, modern thinkers like James Joyce and Claude Lévi-Strauss have taught us that dividing obvious unities into contrastive pairs helps us see reality more clearly, as sundered pairs achieve reunion surprisingly at deeper and higher planes. So I accepted the conventional grammatical dichotomy of the formal (syntactic) and meaningful (semantic) and I broke meaning into the useful (utilitarian) and playful (aesthetic), all the while knowing communication is organically single. Now, though knowing the mental procedures guiding speaking and making are consistent and connected from bottom to top, I will pretend we can talk about distinct deep and surface levels of form and meaning.

Formally the grammars of discourse and of artifacts are alike. At the surface we find complications that can be stripped away to expose simple essences. The rococo sentence and the austere one, which come so differently into the ear, are identical at the deepest level to the linguist. During the exhaustive development of a program of design for the domestic architecture of an area in rural Virginia, I discovered the pretentious, intricately appointed mansions shared fundamental formal principles with the humblest, plainest cabins. Basically the same, they were superficially different.

In folk art, the deep geometry of reason forces itself upward to the sensate surface, preventing characterological discursus, inhibiting the elaboration of incident, confining ornamentation, and manifesting itself in repetitive patterning. The bones of folk art show. Through time, the Western folk aesthetic, as displayed in the design and decoration of tales, songs, dramas, music, architecture, furniture, and textiles, holds a steady course between concealing and revealing its principles of construction. In the fine arts, fashions change. The styles of painting and furniture roll from the ornately baroque of the Georgian era through the clean and rational neoclassical and back into superficial complexity in Victoria's age. The later nineteenth century sent up architectural confections that obfuscated their basic formal properties and realistic dramas and novels that demurely hid their skeletons under draperies of diction and detail. In boredom and disgust, the makers of modern mind sought release from the materialistic complexity of their world in realms more spiritual and simple. William Morris went back to the Middle Ages, out to Iceland, forward to a socialized future—anywhere but here. In Mexico, Artaud; in Tahiti, Gauguin: "Civilization is falling from me. . . . I have escaped everything that is artificial, conventional, customary.

I am entering into the truth, into nature . . . a new man . . . purer and stronger." In Tahiti, Paul Gauguin could crush a timid, degenerate Europe and find it "simple to paint things as I saw them."[19]

The southern sun burns details away, scorching form into clarity. Purified forms compensate for cultural derangement. Supported by the folk arts, the classical and Oriental, many of the great early moderns could defy the shallow confusions shrieking about them, threatening their sanity. In the shadowless noons and bright seas of the hot latitudes, in the spiritual fires licking deep in the arts of peasant and savage, they searched for the vision of the child and true man, the seer and dreaming shaman; they simplified, cleaned, and freshened their works to see into the depths of natural, mystical mind. Think of W. B. Yeats, who went out to Sligo, stripping off his embroidered cloak to compose the soul's naked songs in a speaking tone, and D. H. Lawrence, who went out to Cornwall and Italy and Ceylon and Australia and Mexico, driving his prose to a primitive center. Think of Mondrian and Beckett working and reworking their projects, paring, peeling, polishing them down to the bare nubs of *Broadway Boogie-Woogie* and *The Lost Ones*. Or think of the architecture of Walter Gropius, the music of John Cage, the sculpture of the minimalists of the late 1960s. A sculpture that is a blue cube is not a blue cube only. It is a sweaty effort to present at once deep and surface structures, the exterior and formal essence of an artwork. It is the fusion into exposure of the wholeness of syntactic mind.

Formally, the mind's dynamic is the metamorphosis of simplicity. A Faulknerian sentence begins like one by Hemingway in the relation between a noun phrase and a verb phrase; the form of the Sistine ceiling like that of a hammer riffs off the rules of geometry. The formalist's task is writing an account of how the abstract and simple and single is permuted into the concrete, complex, and diverse. Formalistic writers of verbal and artifactual grammars will find their accounts similar. Both will posit at the mental floor an irreducible, principled unity. Both will sense at the surface an endless, shattering confusion.

There is no ready vocabulary for talking about the deep and shallow levels of meaning. I will, then, offer a pair of words, because here we must face an important difference between discourse and artifacts. At its surface, meaning is anecdotal. At base, meaning is mythic. In lyric poetry, anecdote is apt to consist of metaphor, which points to an infelicity in the terms I choose, but in a narrative the surface is made of sayings and doings—of anecdote.

Some discourse contains no mythic level and depends for deep meaning upon social context. A silly song's message arrives profoundly in the tongues and fingertips of lovers. A little memorat accumulates significance when used in a bar to thicken the relationship developing between drinking acquaintances. A cheap detective thriller or a set of bland demographic data become important when the scholar psychologizes them into meaningfulness. Within greater discourses, the anecdotal rides upon the mythic. A poem's metaphors flower out of humid depths. The actions and words of a tale's little gods at once cover and expose the world's fundament luminescently.

Anecdote attracts. It is easier for the literary critic to deal with the originality and snap of a poem's images, the realism and coherence of a novel's happenings, than with the vague philosophies roiling and expanding beneath the glittering surfaces of all good works. This is one reason for the critic's inability to find the excellence in folk literature. Anecdotally, folktales and songs are often trivial. Their metaphors are hackneyed, their plots redundant. Mythically, however, the best of them are terrifyingly powerful. That power is accessible only to critics willing to remove the gaudy, brittle skin of folk art and feel for its heart. Once grasped, its slippery beat will convince the critic to confuse no longer complexity with excellence.

Like the critic, the historian is drawn to the anecdote. It is clear, often warm and spicy. It is available for sprinkling through impersonal prose to add some sweetness and savor. Some historians seem hostile to subtle, searching analysis. The anecdote, the quote, the small story is the thing for them. It enlivens without challenging, fitting rather than testing preconceived schemes. This is one reason for the historian's lack of interest in the artifact as a source, a historical text. Artifacts generally lack a layer of anecdote.

When an artifact is a representation, an illustration, it carries anecdotes just as narratives do. Here we have a Crucifixion speaking openly at its surface of military indifference and viciousness, of a mother's grief, a dying man's pain. Then the surface blurs and vibrates, making us pry more deeply into the nature of reality, of life, of death: Does a human being, possessed of a soul, the wellspring of perfectibility, cease and rot like a tree, a toad? The painting will not say, nor will it let us not see. In myth, we confront the meaningfully unanswerable.

When an artifact is not obviously representational, when it is an abstract expressionist canvas or a hammer, its surface is built of forms, not anecdotes. Those forms refer us outward onto the utilitarian social terrain where the painting brings its author prestige and the hammer drives nails. We might follow that outward trajectory, concentrically, into an awareness of unpredictable consequences. Released out of control, the painting effects an unanticipated revolution in thought, and the hammer's hunger for nails increases lustily, ineluctably: it demands more and more nails, more iron, more mines and miners and ironmongers, more immigrants, flaming black furnaces, coal, mines, miners, open pits, soil erosion. . . . We can continue, endlessly mapping Mertonian latent functions and the Sartrean practico-inerte, or we can return to forms themselves and let them push us under, downward into a recognition of the assembled surface as an outgrowth of the seed tensions of personality and culture. The artifact is a symbolic essay in philosophy, whether or not it provides usable anecdotery.

It is a matter of vision. As our sensitivity and knowledge increase, black smears become Chinese characters, then a beautiful poem; a heap of rock and oak becomes a log cabin, then the myth of frontier life. Indolently we can let the world crumble around us, dying into meaninglessness, or we can actively, creatively see the world as Emerson did back in 1844:

> We are symbols and inhabit symbols; workmen, work, and tools, words and things, birth and death, all are emblems; but we sympathize with the symbols, and being infatuated with the economical uses of things, we do not know that they are thoughts. The poet, by an ulterior intellectual perception, gives them a power which makes their old use forgotten, and puts eyes and a tongue into every dumb and inanimate object.[20]

As historians we cannot forget economical uses, the functions of things. Nor can we refuse the role of poet. To allow a voice to the people of the past we must put tongues in inanimate objects. Following Sartre following Baudelaire, we can translate the material into the spiritual, sensing the tangible as the projection of the human psyche, knowing that manmade objects are both things and thoughts. Inspired by the brilliant work of the anthropologist Robert Plant Armstrong, we can see the artifact as an affecting presence, the perpetual, mythic enactment of a culture's essential structure.[21]

To prepare for the synthesis of historical study and modern social scientific theory I know to be necessary, I have compared artifacts with speech. That is because the mute artifact is an underused source, and historians must recognize it as grammatical, meaningful—useful. And it is because linguistics, the most highly developed of the human sciences, holds inspiration for all students of humanity. It was natural for me to employ a linguistic analogy. The great contributors to our theories of man, mind, and meaning have more often resorted to musical metaphors. What does music mean? At its surface of notes, nothing. Yet music moves us. Sounds on the air, in the ear, break out of time into new connections unifying different, sequential musical experiences into a structure of affect and association, investing the inherently meaningless with intense, nebulous significance.

We need only evoke the names Shakespeare and Michelangelo to be reminded that for centuries the goal in our greatest tradition was presenting excellence simultaneously at deep and superficial levels of meaning. During the eighteenth and nineteenth centuries artists seemed to obsess themselves increasingly with the anecdote, with matters of manners, with light as it flitted over visible forms. Myth atrophied. The angry great moderns reacted by piercing the surface to let the mythic, the musical, the emotive and profound, shine through.

"Epiphany" was their first attempt. The word was the choice of the youthful James Joyce, who ransacked reality for instants to isolate and record with such intense precision that they would funnel thought through the specific into the general, concentrating tiny, fleeting perceptions into large, timeless concepts. That is the Joyce of *Dubliners*. And it is the Baudelaire of the prose poems, the Gide of the black and white notebooks, the Manet whose exact depictions of Parisian moments provide a shockingly modern essay on alienation. Édouard Manet's people stare ahead, unmoving and alone in company, waiting for Samuel Beckett.

Epiphany melds the levels of meaning by seeming anecdotal and being mythic. It can be mistaken. The incidents in the works of Henry Thoreau and Winslow Homer—some are one thing, some the other. This drawing of a soldier is a soldier only; that soldier, with his accurately rendered kepi, shell jacket, and cape overcoat, his soft, rounded face and wistful gaze, that military boy is a conversation on the terrors of war. This fisherman, whose dory is awash on the wave, its tombstone transom and every sharp plank contrasting with the sea's seethe and sweep, this faceless fisherman is Everyman in Nature, but that one is just some fisherman. Joyce's epiphany, Gide's poetic moment of primary vision, is too near mere anecdote. The problem needed to be attacked more violently. The anecdote had to be scrambled, the surface blasted away to reveal mythic bedrock.

James Joyce called *Finnegans Wake* music and myth. Its simple story is nearly eradicated, its diction is confused beyond complete comprehension. Its point is its depth. The *Wake* will not let us loll in appearances. In fear and delight we must listen as it performs the primal, titanic symphony of consciousness. The painters of Joyce's period similarly proffered cruelly disorienting, untouchably weird surfaces. Maybe recent painters have wished to make thin surfaces, pretty patterns, with Rauschenberg erasing a de Kooning as the end of it all. But the early masters of the abstract and surreal valiantly killed the surface, destroying or distorting the objective, to let the mythic live. Invisible depths erupted into visibility. The nonobjective, nonanecdotal artwork seems to recapitulate chaos, mirroring the meaningless of modern life. Insofar as it is great and not vain, it does so to rouse us out of drowsy comforts, to make us admit the big and basic into awareness.

Art's intellectuals have been clear on the matter. The empirical, the objective and anecdotal, is not enough to make art great. It was John Ruskin, not first but most completely, who joined culture's aesthetic and ethical segments systematically together. Great art is beautiful and functional; it rises only out of great morality. In Ruskin's times, in the 1840s, Ralph Waldo Emerson argued that a poem is not phrases, rhymes, and meter but an important idea,

beautifully clothed. And Holman Hunt, a founder of the Pre-Raphaelite Brotherhood, said art should be strictly true to nature, but the purpose of realism is to convey the painting's essential morality to the viewer. Sensible beauty serves submerged human truth. About a century later, Jean-Paul Sartre would be writing that novels must be judged first on their metaphysical commitment, their appeal to freedom, and only secondarily on their writerly crafting. And Marcel Duchamp would be justifying his work, his ready-mades, glasses, erotic machinery, and non-paintings, as an attack on "retinal" superficiality. The charming Duchamp strove to bring profound concepts back into art. Sensible constructs serve inchoate philosophies.

The artistic effort has its parallel in social science. Some twentieth-century scientists, the academics of academe, have continued to follow antique directives, describing objects and compiling tallied lists of facts, while others have acted in courageous accord with the great artists of their era by cracking through objective surfaces to plunge into the depths where meanings flow. They have been more timid, less violent than artists. Modern scholars in the human sciences have not eliminated empirical facts but have structured them dialectically with theory. They have held to the worth of open communication, communal cohesion, and progress.

In their good fight to maintain community, scholars, like wise peasants, have strained to retain the best in their tradition. Tradition connects. At its worst this has resulted in codifying silly standards and whipping young thinkers through demeaning rites of passage. At its best it has involved a resistance to change for its own sake. Still, some old scientific desiderata have had to go. It would be nice if scientific work could be replicated, if propositions could be proved, if problems had answers. But unfortunately, achieving a method suitable to the study of people, rather than rocks and rats, has required a loss of neatness.

A loss of neatness does not necessitate a rise of egotism, a surrender into solipsism, and the death of science. Science is made better, not worse, by the disciplined incorporation of the scholar's subjective existence. Hidden it perverts, exposed it can be controlled for. Science is improved, not lost, when scholars recognize understanding not predictability to be the relevant end of human study. If the oxymoron be not too thick-witted, modern social science begins when things are discovered to be finally unknowable. Unreplicatable procedures and unprovable theories can still be judged on coherence, elegance, and usefulness. When scientists decide not to solve little puzzles but to front genuine problems, they can continue to approach and present their interests with rigor and clear minds.

Troubles remain. The scholar's cleverness can make things seem more recondite and grand than they are. Conversely, and more commonly, the old socially attractive desire for concise, accessible exposition, and the emotional need for denouement, can guide discourse too swiftly through reductions to answers that are less answers than keen hallucinations. The great modern artists had to learn self-censorship. Scientists will too. Unprovable, their works must be surrounded by introspection and founded on honesty. Their tradition cannot protect them: they must be sincere.

Only a few modern thinkers have tried to adhere to the virtues in a scientific tradition and, at the same time, to face great philosophical issues. The anthropologist Claude Lévi-Strauss is such a one. His attempt has been magnificent and, I think, sad, since it has been almost willfully misunderstood. His rare case would repay a closer look.

As a student, he heard the professors talk about everything except the central matter: meaning. This concerned him, powering him through field research in the Brazilian jungles. When his soul grew weary, he parodied science by counting the sticks of which huts were built and scribbling detailed entries in his notebooks. When his mind was lucid, his heart strong, he followed his quest for uncorrupted Rousseauian man, for the blood and bone true antithesis of the decadent, capitalistic, atomistic, meaninglessness he despised in Paris. At the end of his parallel journey up the Congo to the center of a savage continent, André Gide found an embrace, a dark breath. What Lévi-Strauss found at the end of his journey up the Amazon was no thrill before a noble man but humiliation before filthy children. His quest ended in disgust.[22] He discovered what Rousseau had told him, what Thoreau or Yeats could have told him: reality is, by definition, impure. Primitive man differs from Parisian man, not absolutely but by degree. A higher unity, the truth of universal mind, replaced the antinomy of the primitive and the civilized.

Claude Lévi-Strauss capped his field experience in an unfinished drama in which godliness is defined as the ability to live with things as they are: glorious, flyblown, and repulsive. Philosophy seeks the pure. Human science reveals impurity. The will is optimistic. The intellect is pessimistic. The man Lévi-Strauss learned to stand between, yearning for clarity, knowing ambivalence.

As a mature man he returned to the people of the Amazon interior. He did not cut through the jungles but journeyed in thought through their myths. In those tales he wanted to locate the operations of universal mind. He talked of syntactic structures and proposed mathematical formulas, but his philosophy prevented entrapment in formalism. Had he studied the shapes of myths, as others have studied the forms of sentences and folktales, he could have built a trim system, but the dynamic he wished to understand was that by which meaning is realized. His method was dialectic. It located oppositional pairs and the resolutions in which dichotomies dissolved. But since he was dealing in meaning, in open analogy, every resolution tied into a new opposition, every opposition into a new resolution. In volume after volume of his grand *Mythologiques*, final reductive resolutions eluded him and his work came to display the insight James Joyce took from Giordano Bruno to make *Finnegans Wake* work. To meaning there is no end; in reality, no purity; in myth, no resolution. Being profound, myths trick us into sensations of closure, while exposing constant ambiguity.

Some anthropologists have been slow to understand. Lévi-Strauss, they say, is a philosopher not a scientist. Yet he curbed his great writing talent and restrained his philosophies to work as scientifically as possible on a problem—human meaning—that science was not prepared to encounter. They ask him for clear statements, clean answers, when to offer clear statements would obscure his honest method, when to offer clean answers would falsify and destroy the subject he had the courage to write about. Myths mean, as music and abstract painting, as all poetic literature means: in endless, shifting, contracting and clearing, expanding and smoking, associations.

This is the statement we are ready for. If historians are going to write history they will have to take people seriously and stir into their schemes what we know about the nature of humanity, contextual complexity, and mental depth. To do that they will have to take the people's own expressions seriously. The land, manipulated nature, is the people's great work. The landscape offers little in the way of anecdotes, but it is redolent with mythic meanings. Historians, like old-time scientists, desire clarity. They demand answers. The danger is accommodating to that demand by reducing ambiguity to one of its elements, purifying complexity into a believable, reassuring lie. In truth all that can be done with the land's meanings is all that can be done with music or poetry, and that is to refine and clarify its paradoxes. That is much. Great, revealing discourse is possible. Understanding can be achieved. The land has no pat answers; patiently, serenely it awaits its analysts, holding immense quantities of historical information.

The painter glides the brush over canvas, guiding it to form a landscape, rectangular and one-dimensional. The gentlemen of the eighteenth century carried empty frames through which to view the scenery from their coaches. Modern travelers exhaust themselves, clicking film through machinery to capture views of Rome or the Rockies to throw through another machine to bore their friends. For most of humankind, the landscape has not remained out there, a distant vista, a remote object for reducing to representations. It has risen, an enemy. It has lain, a lover. Its experience has been direct and dirty. The land has had its creation, its exertion in the hands of men and women.

Frederic Edwin Church was one of the great American landscapists of the nineteenth century. His youthful paintings of North and South American scenes, meticulous and enormous, took the breath of his contemporaries, pleasing even John Ruskin with their verisimilitude. As an aging and ill man, he turned his energies into the third dimension, painting less, and less well, creating instead the real landscape of his estate above the Hudson. He built roads, moved trees, dug a lake, and wrote, "I can make more and better landscapes in this way than by tampering with canvas and paint in the Studio."[23] Church made the land itself. Like millions of tillers of the soil, he quietly anticipated the artists of our days who curl jetties into lakes and string curtains over valleys.

Patrick Kavanagh was one of the great poets of our times.[24] Better than anyone he got down on paper the bittersweet reality of country life. He had been a plowman on the rocky Irish dirt, and he spoke the happiness of thousands of makers of the land when he wrote:

> I turn the lea-green down
> Gaily now,
> And paint the meadow brown
> With my plough.

And he spoke their sadness when he wrote:

> O stony grey soil of Monaghan
> The laugh from my love you thieved;
> You took the gay child of my passion
> And gave me your clod-conceived. . . .
>
> You told me the plough was immortal!
> O green-life conquering plough!
> Your mandril strained, your coulter blunted
> In the smooth lea-field of my brow.

Here is the gentle and terrible, tangible, real landscape the people have painted, the human face of the earth in which is graved the unwritten, but legible, tale of the past.

Notes

1. I developed this modernist statement of the scholar's task with difficulty. It is an application to our realm of the Camusian formula fulfilled in *The Rebel* and announced in 1944 in Camus's "Letters to a German Friend," in *Resistance, Rebellion, and Death*, trans. Justin O'Brien (New York, 1974), 28.

2. Jean-Paul Sartre's essay, "A Plea for Intellectuals," in *Between Existentialism and Marxism*, trans. John Mathews (New York, 1976), 228–85, should be required reading for scholars and those planning toward that vocation.

3. Claude Mauriac, *Conversations with André Gide*, trans. Michael Lebeck (New York, 1965), esp. 75, 97, 152, 167, 230. In *Autumn Leaves*, trans. Elsie Pell (New York, 1950), 249, Gide comments that a journal loses its reason for being if it is touched up: yet, in the notebook (trans. Justin O'Brien) accompanying *The Counterfeiters* (New York, 1951), 383, Gide says psychological investigation can be pushed deeper in novels than in confessions: the singular first person pronoun—the mask—hinders complex exposure and revelation.

4. Dell Hymes's most complete statement is to be found in *Foundations in Sociolinguistics* (Philadelphia, 1974), but his early wonderfully influential papers must also be read, particularly: "Directions in (Ethno-) Linguistic Theory," in *Transcultural Studies in Cognition, American Anthropologist*, ed. A. Kimball Romney and Roy Goodwin D'Andrade,

66:3, 2 (Washington, D.C.: American Anthropological Association, 1964), 6–56: and "Introduction: Toward Ethnographies of Communication," in *The Ethnography of Communication, American Anthropologist,* ed. John J. Gumperz and Dell Hymes, 66:6, 2 (Washington, D.C.: American Anthropological Association, 1964), 1–34. Hymes's realistic linguistics can be related back to the deservedly famous pentad Kenneth Burke sets out in *A Grammar of Motives* (Berkeley, Calif., 1945; reprint ed., 1969), and to the theory of man Burke presents in the first section of *Language as Symbolic Action: Essays on Life, Literature, and Method* (Berkeley, Calif., 1968). Noam Chomsky's profoundly important concept of mind received an early application in *Syntactic Structures* (The Hague, 1957), and an early exposure in his crucial review of Skinner's *Verbal Behavior* in *Language* 35 (January–March 1959): 26–58; it is set forth accessibly in Noam Chomsky, *Problems of Knowledge and Freedom* (New York, 1971).

5. My reference is to Martin Duberman, *Black Mountain: An Exploration in Community* (Garden City, N.Y., 1973), a model study of a movement.

6. On relativism, I refer you to Clyde Kluckhohn's "Ethical Relativity: Sic et Non," in *Culture and Behavior: Collected Essays of Clyde Kluckhohn,* ed. Richard Kluckhohn (New York, 1962), chap. 16, and to Henry Glassie, *All Silver and No Brass: An Irish Christmas Mumming* (Bloomington, Ind., 1975), 76–77, 135–42, 148–49.

7. Sacvan Berocovitch, *The Puritan Origins of the American Self* (New Haven, Conn., 1975), chap. 5, esp. 181–86.

8. Mary Colum and Padraic Colum, *Our Friend James Joyce* (Garden City, N.Y., 1958), 58.

9. Albert Camus, "On the Future of Tragedy," in *Lyrical and Critical Essays,* ed. Philip Thody, trans. Ellen Conroy Kennedy (New York, 1970), 301.

10. I begin talking about *Walden* by parodying its treatment by R. W. B. Lewis in *The American Adam: Innocence, Tragedy, and Tradition in the Nineteenth Century* (Chicago, 1955); then I leave Lewis, because he does not apply his own good concept of myth to Thoreau. The mistake is reading *Walden* as if it were not a novel.

11. Moira Roth and William Roth, "John Cage on Marcel Duchamp: An Interview," in *Marcel Duchamp in Perspective,* ed. Joseph Masheck (Englewood Cliffs, N.J., 1975), 159.

12. Orestes A. Brownson, excerpted in Perry Miller, *The Transcendentalists: An Anthology* (Cambridge, Mass., 1960), 431–34.

13. Eugene D. Genovese, *Roll, Jordan, Roll: The World the Slaves Made* (New York, 1974).

14. Whitman's opinions are quoted from Daniel Aaron, *The Unwritten War: American Writers and the Civil War* (New York, 1975), 70; and Bliss Perry, *Walt Whitman: His Life and Work* (Boston, 1906), 155.

15. *A Note by William Morris on His Aims in Founding The Kelmscott Press, Together with a Short Description of the Press by S. C. Cockerell, and An Annotated List of the Books Printed Thereat* (London, 1898), 65.

16. Edward D. Ives, *Larry Gorman: The Man Who Made the Songs* (Bloomington, 1964); Ives, *Lawrence Doyle: The Farmer Poet of Prince Edward Island* (Orono, Me., 1971); Ives, "A Man and His Song: Joe Scott and 'The Plain Golden Band,'" in Henry Glassie, E. D. Ives, and John Szwed, *Folksongs and Their Makers* (Bowling Green, Ky., 1970), 69–146; E. P. Thompson, *The Making of the English Working Class* (New York, 1963); and Thompson, *Whigs and Hunters: The Origin of the Black Act* (New York, 1975).

17. Jacques Barzun, *Clio and the Doctors: Psycho-History, Quanto-History and History* (Chicago, 1974).

18. See Raymond Williams, *Keywords: A Vocabulary of Culture and Society* (New York, 1976), 158–63.

19. Antonin Artaud, *The Peyote Dance,* trans. Helen Weaver (New York, 1976), esp. 3–6, 46–49, 64–65; Paul Gauguin, *Noa Noa,* trans. O. F. Theis (New York, n.d.), 30–31, 41, 51. In his preface to *Paul Gauguin's Intimate Journals,* trans. Van Wyck Brooks (New York, 1921; reprint ed., 1970), Gauguin's son, Emil, says *Noa Noa* was so edited as to contain little of his father's spirit. Indeed, there is a great difference in style between the journals and *Noa Noa,* but whoever wrote the latter book produced a marvelously compressed statement of modern Romanticism.

20. Ralph Waldo Emerson, "The Poet," in *The Best of Ralph Waldo Emerson,* ed. Gordon S. Haight (Roslyn, N.Y., 1941), 236. Passages in "Nature" (84–85, 109–10) are also brilliantly perceptive on the meanings of things.

21. Jean-Paul Sartre, *Baudelaire,* trans. Martin Turnell (New York, 1950), 104, 172–79. I reviewed Armstrong's exciting books *Wellspring* and *The Affecting Presence* in "Source for a New Anthropology," *Book Forum* 2, no. 1 (1976): 70–77.

22. André Gide, *Travels in the Congo,* trans. Dorothy Bussy (New York, 1929), 187; Claude Lévi-Strauss, *Tristes Tropiques,* trans. John Russell (New York, 1970), esp. 39–46, 310, 340–41, 373–92.

23. David C. Huntington, *The Landscapes of Frederic Edwin Church: Vision of an American Era* (New York, 1966), 115–17.

24. The quotations are from Kavanagh's poems "Ploughman" and "Stony Grey Soil" in *The Complete Poems of Patrick Kavanagh,* ed. Peter Kavanagh (New York, 1972), 1, 73. Kavanagh left us with a rich assortment of autobiographical writings, most notably *The Green Fool* (London, 1938; reprint ed., 1971). Alan Warner has written a brief biography, *Clay Is the Word: Patrick Kavanagh, 1904–1967* (Dublin, 1973). His beginnings as a plowman are emphasized in W. G. McNeice's poem "In Memory of Patrick Kavanagh," in *Irish Poets: 1924–1974,* ed. David Marcus (London, 1975), 66.

Bibliography

This essay on the rationale of the artifact could only have been written during the year I spent as a fellow of the National Humanities Institute in New Haven, Connecticut. Our conversations were exciting, expansive, and endlessly informative. This essay consists of my reactions to them, my thefts from them. I am indebted to my colleagues in the Institute, both the fellows and our associates at Yale, for sharing their thoughts and taking mine seriously. I thank them all. In addition I wish to thank my friend Adam Horvath, who read a version of this essay and made amusing comments, and Kathleen Foster—much of what is of worth here emerged in conversations with her. My intellectual debts do not stop with my friends, so a bibliography follows. Its first section includes the works that guide me constantly. Listing them emphasizes the depth of my reliance and eliminates the need for repetitious footnoting. The bibliography's second section consists of a small number of works on material culture so that you can move beyond this essay, over it into the domain of artifactual research.

EPISTEMOLOGICAL

Armstrong, Robert Plant. *Wellspring: On the Myth and Source of Culture.* Berkeley, Calif., 1975.

Barthes, Roland. *The Pleasure of the Text.* Trans. Richard Miller. New York, 1975.

Bloch, Marc. *The Historian's Craft.* Trans. Peter Putnam. New York, 1953.

Burke, Kenneth. *A Grammar of Motives.* Berkeley, Calif., 1945; reprint ed., 1969.

Butterfield, Herbert. *The Whig Interpretation of History.* New York, 1965.

Camus, Albert. *The Rebel: An Essay on Man in Revolt.* Trans. Anthony Bower. New York, 1951; reprint ed., 1960.

Evans, E. Estyn. *The Personality of Ireland: Habitat, Heritage and History.* New York, 1973.

Hymes, Dell. *Foundations in Sociolinguistics: An Ethnographic Approach.* Philadelphia, 1974.

Lévi-Strauss, Claude. *The Raw and the Cooked: Introduction to a Science of Mythology,* Vol. 1. Trans. John and Doreen Weightman. New York, 1970.

Lévi-Strauss, Claude. *The Savage Mind.* Chicago, 1966.

Lévi-Strauss, Claude. *Structural Anthropology.* Trans. Claire Jacobson and Brooke Grundfest Schoepf. Garden City, N.Y., 1967.

Merton, Robert K. *On Theoretical Sociology: Five Essays Old and New.* New York, 1967.

Redfield, Robert. *The Little Community.* Chicago, 1960.

Sartre, Jean-Paul. *Being and Nothingness: An Essay on Phenomenological Ontology.* Trans. Hazel E. Barnes. London, 1943; reprint ed., 1972.

Sartre, Jean-Paul. From "Qu'est-ce que la littérature?" *Literature and Existentialism.* Trans. Bernard Frechtman. New York, 1947; reprint ed., 1972.

Sartre, Jean-Paul. *Search for a Method.* Trans. Hazel E. Barnes. New York, 1963.

Williams, Raymond. *The Country and the City.* New York, 1973.

Winch, Peter. *The Idea of a Social Science and Its Relation to Philosophy.* New York, 1958; reprint ed., 1973.

Yeats, W. B. *A Vision.* New York, 1925; reprint ed., 1966.

ARTIFACTUAL

Alexander, Christopher. *Notes on the Synthesis of Form.* Cambridge, Mass., 1971.

Armstrong, Robert Plant. *The Affecting Presence: An Essay in Humanistic Anthropology.* Urbana, Ill., 1971.

Bachelard, Gaston. *The Poetics of Space.* Trans. Maria Jolas. Boston, 1969.

Barley, M. W. *The English Farmhouse and Cottage.* London, 1961.

Binford, Sally, and Lewis Binford, eds. *New Perspectives in Archaeology.* Chicago, 1968.

D'Azevedo, Warren L., ed. *The Traditional Artist in African Societies.* Bloomington, 1974.

Deetz, James. *Invitation to Archaeology.* Garden City, N.Y., 1967.

Evans, E. Estyn. *Mourne Country: Landscape and Life in South Down.* Dundalk, 1951; reprint ed., 1967.

Fischer, J. L. "Art Styles as Cultural Cognitive Maps." *American Anthropologist* 63, no. 1 (1961):71–93.

Fitch, James Marston. *American Building: The Environmental Forces that Shape It.* Boston, 1948; rev. ed. 1972.

Fitch, James Marston. *American Building: The Historical Forces that Shaped It.* New York, 1948; rev. ed. 1973.

Fleming, E. McClung. "Artifact Study: A Proposed Model." *Winterthur Portfolio* 9 (1973):153–73.

Fontana, Bernard L., William J. Robinson, Charles W. Cormack, and Ernest E. Leavitt, Jr. *Papago Indian Pottery.* Seattle, 1962.

Glassie, Henry. "Archaeology and Folklore: Common Anxieties, Common Hopes." In *Historical Archaeology and the Importance of Material Things,* ed. Leland Ferguson. Special Publication, 2. Columbia, S.C., 1977.

Glassie, Henry. *Folk Housing in Middle Virginia: A Structural Analysis of Historic Artifacts.* Knoxville, 1975.

Glassie, Henry. *Pattern in the Material Folk Culture of the Eastern United States.* Philadelphia, 1969; reprint ed., 1976.

Glassie, Henry. "Structure and Function, Folklore and the Artifact." *Semiotica* 7, no. 4 (1973):313–51.

Glassie, Henry. "The Variation of Concepts within Tradition: Barn Building in Otsego County, New York." In *Man and Cultural Heritage: Papers in Honor of Fred B. Kniffen,* ed. H. J. Walker and W. G. Haag, 177–235. Baton Rouge, La., 1974.

Hart, John Fraser. *The Look of the Land.* Englewood Cliffs, N.J., 1975.

Hoskins, W. G. *The Making of the English Landscape.* Harmondsworth, Middlesex, 1970.

Jones, Michael Owen. *The Hand Made Object and Its Maker*. Berkeley, Calif., 1975.

Kandinsky, Wassily. *Concerning the Spiritual in Art*. Trans. Michael Sadleir. New York, 1912; reprint ed., 1964.

Klee, Paul. *On Modern Art*. Trans. Paul Findlay. London, 1969; first delivered 1924.

Kniffen, Fred. "Louisiana House Types." *Annals of the Association of American Geographers* 26 (1936):179–93.

Kouwenhoven, John. *The Arts in Modern American Civilization*. New York, 1948; reprint ed., 1967.

L'Orange, H. P. *Art Forms and Civic Life in the Late Roman Empire*. Princeton, N.J., 1972.

Ludwig, Allan I. *Graven Images: New England Stonecarving and Its Symbols*. Middletown, Conn., 1966.

Malraux, André. *Museum Without Walls*. Trans. Stuart Gilbert and Francis Price. Garden City, N.Y., 1967.

Mercer, Eric. *Furniture: 700–1700*. New York, 1969.

Montgomery, Charles. *American Furniture: The Federal Period*. New York, 1966.

Morris, William. *The Aims of Art*. London, 1887.

Norberg-Schulz, Christian. *Intentions in Architecture*. Cambridge, Mass., 1968.

Panofsky, Erwin. *Gothic Architecture and Scholasticism*. New York, 1957.

Panofsky, Erwin. *The Life and Art of Albrecht Dürer*. Princeton, N.J., 1943; reprint ed., 1971.

Reps, John. *Town Planning in Frontier America*. Princeton, N.J., 1969.

Ruskin, John. *The Stones of Venice*. 3 vols. London, 1851–53.

Thompson, Robert Farris. *African Art in Motion*. Berkeley, Calif., 1974.

Weiss, Richard. *Häuser und Landschaften der Schweiz*. Erlenbach, 1959.

Welsch, Roger. *Sod Walls: The Story of the Nebraska Sod House*. Broken Bow, Neb., 1968.

White, Lynn, Jr. *Medieval Technology and Social Change*. New York, 1964.

Part Two: New World Cultures

The Indians' New World: The Catawba Experience

JAMES H. MERRELL

Whether in New England, the mid-Atlantic colonies, or the South, the process of European colonization created many New Worlds, each defined at once by unpredicted social and cultural change and by a new material order. Most scholars emphasize the successful plantations established by white settlers expanding beyond the constricting cultural borders of England, Ireland, Germany, France, and the Netherlands. In this essay, James Merrell redirects our attention to the new worlds created by American Indian groups as they responded to the dramatic changes European settlers brought to their lives. Focusing on the Catawba Nation, an Indian confederation that arose in the early eighteenth century to consolidate the threatened peoples of the southern upland region, he stresses the conflict, accommodation, and survival of the group as they created new patterns of material life through trade, warfare, revitalization, and coexistence.

Three factors contributed to the Catawba experience and united them with other Indian groups along the eastern seaboard in the colonial period. First was the impact that European diseases had on native populations. Epidemics—"plagues" they were called by contemporaries—dramatically increased native mortality rates, and the major demographic upheaval that resulted immediately affected native economic life and the proper stewardship of natural resources. Disease also contributed directly to a series of migrations, each of which demanded the abandonment of a sacred landscape crucial to memory and cultural continuity. As their numbers dwindled, small groups joined forces and survived together as the Catawba Nation. The second major factor was European trade goods, curious and useful commodities that at first fit neatly into their established ritual structures. Soon, however, a failure to master the independent production of these objects made the Catawbas economically reliant on the colonists, especially since the easy availability of trade goods—guns, clothes, tools, and liquor—gradually undercut native skills and exchange relations. The coercive basis of the Indians' dependence on the white man's material culture became apparent during the Yamassee War of 1715; following this "material crisis" and others, Merrell maintains, the Catawbas sought to control their destiny with greater care. A final factor, white planters, emerged with the opening of the upland region to colonial agriculture during the 1730s. European farming patterns imposed a new structure of land use and a new discipline of legal restraint on the native landscape. Hostilities between white husbandmen and Catawbas were continual.

By the end of the colonial period, Merrell believes the material life of the Catawbas had been dramatically redefined. Embedded within a new, alien economy, they established a reservation in the early 1760s in order to secure a legal land base. As they gradually learned to play by the white man's rules, they also retained their own complex cultural traditions, making any theory of simple unilinear acculturation untenable. The whites had clearly taken over the territory, but the Catawba Nation endured.

In August 1608 John Smith and his band of explorers captured an Indian named Amoroleck during a skirmish along the Rappahannock River. Asked why his men—a hunting party from towns upstream—had attacked the English, Amoroleck replied that they had heard the strangers "were a people come from under the world, to take their world from them."[1] Smith's prisoner grasped a simple yet important truth that students of colonial America have overlooked: after 1492 native Americans lived in a world every bit as new as that confronting transplanted Africans or Europeans.

The failure to explore the Indians' new world helps explain why, despite many excellent studies of the native American past,[2] colonial history often remains "a history of those men and women—English, European, and African—who transformed America from a geographical expression into a new nation."[3] One reason Indians generally are left out may be the apparent inability to fit them into the new world theme, a theme that exerts a powerful hold on our historical imagination and runs throughout our efforts to interpret American development. From Frederick Jackson Turner to David Grayson Allen, from Melville J. Herskovits to Daniel C. Littlefield, scholars have analyzed encounters between peoples from the Old World and conditions in the New, studying the complex interplay between European or African cultural patterns and the American environment.[4] Indians crossed no ocean, peopled no faraway land. It might seem logical to exclude them.

The natives' segregation persists, in no small degree, because historians still tend to think only of the new world as the New World, a geographic entity bound by the Atlantic Ocean on the one side and the Pacific on the other. Recent research suggests that process was as important as place. Many settlers in New England recreated familiar forms with such success that they did not really face an alien environment until long after their arrival.[5] Africans, on the other hand, were struck by the shock of the new at the moment of their enslavement, well before they stepped on board ship or set foot on American soil.[6] If the Atlantic was not a barrier between one world and another, if what happened to people was more a matter of subtle cultural processes than mere physical displacements, perhaps we should set aside the maps and think instead of a "world" as the physical and cultural milieu within which people live and a "new world" as a dramatically different milieu demanding basic changes in ways of life.[7] Considered in these terms, the experience of natives was more closely akin to that of immigrants and slaves, and the idea of an encounter between worlds can—indeed, must—include the aboriginal inhabitants of America.

For American Indians a new order arrived in three distinct yet overlapping stages.[8] First, alien microbes killed vast numbers of natives, sometimes before the victims had seen a white or black face. Next came traders who exchanged European technology for Indian products and brought natives into the developing world market. In time traders gave way to settlers eager to develop the land according to their own

lights.[9] These three intrusions combined to transform native existence, disrupting established cultural habits and requiring creative responses to drastically altered conditions. Like their new neighbors, then, Indians were forced to blend old and new in ways that would permit them to survive in the present without forsaking their past. By the close of the colonial era, native Americans as well as whites and blacks had created new societies, each similar to, yet very different from, its parent culture.

The range of native societies produced by this mingling of ingredients probably exceeded the variety of social forms Europeans and Africans developed.[10] Rather than survey the broad spectrum of Indian adaptations, this essay considers in some depth the response of natives in one area, the southern piedmont (see fig. 1). Avoiding extinction and eschewing retreat, the Indians of the piedmont have been in continuous contact with the invaders from

Fig. 1. Indian peoples in the southern piedmont region. (Map by Linda K. Merrell.)

across the sea almost since the beginning of the colonial period, thus permitting a thorough analysis of cultural intercourse.[11] Moreover, a regional approach embracing groups from South Carolina to Virginia can transcend narrow (and still poorly understood) ethnic or "tribal" boundaries without sacrificing the richness of detail a focused study provides.

Indeed, piedmont peoples had so much in common that a regional perspective is almost imperative. No formal political ties bound them at the onset of European contact, but a similar environment shaped their lives, and their adjustment to this environment fostered cultural uniformity. Perhaps even more important, these groups shared a single history once Europeans and Africans arrived on the scene. Drawn together by their cultural affinities and their common plight, after 1700 they migrated to the Catawba Nation, a cluster of villages along the border between the Carolinas that became the focus of native life in the region. Tracing the experience of these upland communities both before and after they joined the Catawbas can illustrate the consequences of contact and illuminate the process by which natives learned to survive in their own new world.[12]

For centuries, ancestors of the Catawbas had lived astride important aboriginal trade routes and straddled the boundary between two cultural traditions, a position that involved them in a far-flung network of contacts and affected everything from potting techniques to burial practices.[13] Nonetheless, Africans and Europeans were utterly unlike any earlier foreign visitors to the piedmont. Their arrival meant more than merely another encounter with outsiders; it marked an important turning point in Indian history. Once these newcomers disembarked and began to feel their way across the continent, they forever altered the course and pace of native development.

Bacteria brought the most profound disturbances to upcountry villages. When Hernando de Soto led the first Europeans into the area in 1540, he found large towns already "grown up in grass" because "there had been a pest in the land" two years before, a malady probably brought inland by natives who had visited distant Spanish posts.[14] The sources are silent about other "pests" over the next century, but soon after the English began colonizing Carolina in 1670 the disease pattern became all too clear. Major epidemics struck the region at least once every generation—in 1698, 1718, 1738, and 1759—and a variety of less virulent illnesses almost never left native settlements.[15]

Indians were not the only inhabitants of colonial America living—and dying—in a new disease environment. The swamps and lowlands of the Chesapeake were a deathtrap for Europeans, and sickness obliged colonists to discard or rearrange many of the social forms brought from England.[16] Among native peoples long isolated from the rest of the world and therefore lacking immunity to pathogens introduced by the intruders, the devastation was even more severe. John Lawson, who visited the Carolina upcountry in 1701, when perhaps ten thousand Indians were still there, estimated that "there is not the sixth Savage living within two hundred miles of all our settlements, as there were fifty years ago." The recent smallpox epidemic "destroy'd whole Towns," he remarked, "without leaving one *Indian* alive in the Village."[17] Resistance to disease developed with painful slowness; colonists reported that the outbreak of smallpox in 1759 wiped out 60 percent of the natives, and, according to one source, "the woods were offensive with the dead bodies of the Indians; and dogs, wolves, and vultures were . . . busy for months in banqueting on them."[18]

Survivors of these horrors were thrust into a situation no less alien than what European immigrants and African slaves found. The collected wisdom of generations could vanish in a matter of days if sickness struck older members of a community who kept sacred traditions and taught special skills. When many of the elders succumbed at once, the deep pools of collective memory grew shallow, and some dried up altogether. In 1710, Indians near Charleston told a settler that "they have forgot most of their traditions since the Establishment of this Colony, they keep their Festivals and can tell but little of the reasons: their Old Men are dead."[19] Impoverishment of a rich cultural heritage followed the spread of disease. Nearly a century later, a South Carolinian exaggerated but captured the general trend when he noted that Catawbas "have forgotten their antient rites, ceremonies, and manufactures."[20]

The same diseases that robbed a piedmont town of some of its most precious resources also stripped it of the population necessary to maintain an independent existence. In order to survive, groups were compelled to construct new societies from the splintered remnants of the old. The result was a kaleidoscopic array of migrations from ancient territories and mergers with nearby peoples. While such behavior was not unheard of in aboriginal times, population levels fell so precipitously after contact that survivors endured disruptions unlike anything previously known.

The dislocations of the Saponi Indians illustrate the common course of events. In 1670 they lived on the Staunton River in Virginia and were closely affiliated with a group called Nahyssans. A decade later Saponis moved toward the coast and built a town near the Occaneechees. When John Lawson came upon them along the Yadkin River in 1701, they were on the verge of banding together in a single village with Tutelos and Keyauwees. Soon thereafter Saponis applied to Virginia officials for permission to move to the Meherrin River, where Occaneechees, Tutelos, and others joined them. In 1714, at the urging of Lt. Gov. Alexander Spotswood of Virginia, these groups settled at Fort Christanna farther up the Meherrin. Their friendship with Virginia soured during the 1720s, and most of the "Christanna Indians" moved to the Catawba Nation. For some reason this arrangement did not satisfy them, and many returned to Virginia in 1732, remaining there for a decade before choosing to migrate north and accept the protection of the Iroquois.[21]

Saponis were unusual only in their decision to leave the Catawbas. Enos, Occaneechees, Waterees, Keyauwees, Cheraws, and others have their own stories to tell, similar in outline if not in detail. With the exception of the towns near the confluence of Sugar Creek and the Catawba River that composed the heart of the Catawba Nation, piedmont communities decimated by disease lived through a common round of catastrophes, shifting from place to place and group to group in search of a safe haven. Most eventually ended up in the Nation, and during the opening decades of the eighteenth century the villages scattered across the southern upcountry were abandoned as people drifted into the Catawba orbit.

No mere catalog of migrations and mergers can begin to convey how profoundly unsettling this experience was for those swept up in it. While upcountry Indians did not sail away to some distant land, they, too, were among the uprooted, leaving their ancestral homes to try to make a new life elsewhere. The peripatetic existence of Saponis and others proved deeply disruptive. A village and its surrounding territory

were important elements of personal and collective identity, physical links in a chain binding a group to its past and making a locality sacred. Colonists, convinced that Indians were by nature "a shifting, wandring People," were oblivious to this, but Lawson offered a glimpse of the reasons for native attachment to a particular locale. "In our way," he wrote on leaving an Eno-Shakori town in 1701, "there stood a great Stone about the Size of a large Oven, and hollow; this the *Indians* took great Notice of, putting some Tobacco into the Concavity, and spitting after it. I ask'd them the Reason of their so doing, but they made me no Answer."[22] Natives throughout the interior honored similar places—graves of ancestors, monuments of stones commemorating important events—that could not be left behind without some cost.[23]

The toll could be physical as well as spiritual, for even the most uneventful of moves interrupted the established cycle of subsistence. Belongings had to be packed and unpacked, dwellings constructed, palisades raised. Once migrants had completed the business of settling in, the still more arduous task of exploiting new terrain awaited them. Living in one place year after year endowed a people with intimate knowledge of the area. The richest soils, the best hunting grounds, the choicest sites for gathering nuts or berries—none could be learned without years of experience, tested by time and passed down from one generation to the next. Small wonder that Carolina Indians worried about being "driven to some unknown Country, to live, hunt, and get our Bread in."[24]

Some displaced groups tried to leave "unknown Country" behind and make their way back home. In 1716 Enos asked Virginia's permission to settle at "Enoe Town" on the North Carolina frontier, their location in Lawson's day.[25] Seventeen years later William Byrd II came upon an abandoned Cheraw village on a tributary of the upper Roanoke River and remarked how "it must have been a great misfortune to them to be obliged to abandon so beautiful a dwelling." The Indians apparently agreed: in 1717 the Virginia Council received "Divers applications" from the Cheraws (now living along the Pee Dee River) "for Liberty to Seat themselves on the head of Roanoke River."[26] Few natives managed to return permanently to their homelands. But their efforts to retrace their steps hint at a profound sense of loss and testify to the powerful hold of ancient sites.

Compounding the trauma of leaving familiar territories was the necessity of abandoning customary relationships. Casting their lot with others traditionally considered foreign compelled Indians to rearrange basic ways of ordering their existence. Despite frequent contacts among peoples, native life had always centered in kin and town. The consequences of this deep-seated localism were evident even to a newcomer like John Lawson, who in 1701 found striking differences in language, dress, and physical appearance among Carolina Indians living only a few miles apart.[27] Rules governing behavior also drew sharp distinctions between outsiders and one's own "Country-Folks." Indians were "very kind, and charitable to one another," Lawson reported, "but more especially to those of their own Nation."[28] A visitor desiring a liaison with a local woman was required to approach her relatives and the village headman. On the other hand, "if it be an *Indian* of their own Town or Neighbourhood, that wants a Mistress, he comes to none but the Girl."[29] Lawson seemed unperturbed by this barrier until he discovered that a "Thief [is] held in Disgrace, that steals from any of his Country-Folks," "but to steal from the *English* [or any other foreigners] they reckon no Harm."[30]

Communities unable to continue on their own had to revise these rules and reweave the social fabric into new designs. What language would be spoken? How would fields be laid out, hunting territories divided, houses built? How would decisions be reached, offenders punished, ceremonies performed? When Lawson remarked that "now adays" the Indians must seek mates "amongst Strangers," he unwittingly characterized life in native Carolina.[31] Those who managed to withstand the ravages of disease had to redefine the meaning of the term *stranger* and transform outsiders into insiders.

The need to harmonize discordant peoples, an unpleasant fact of life for all native Americans, was no less common among black and white inhabitants of America during these years. Africans from a host of different groups were thrown into slavery together and forced to seek some common cultural ground, to blend or set aside clashing habits and beliefs. Europeans who came to America also met unexpected and unwelcome ethnic, religious, and linguistic diversity. The roots of the problem were quite different; the problem itself was much the same. In each case people from different backgrounds had to forge a common culture and a common future.

Indians in the southern uplands customarily combined with others like themselves in an attempt to solve the dilemma. Following the "principle of least effort," shattered communities cushioned the blows inflicted by disease and depopulation by joining a kindred society known through generations of trade and alliances.[32] Thus Saponis coalesced with Occaneechees and Tutelos—nearby groups "speaking much the same language"[33]—and Catawbas became a sanctuary for culturally related refugees from throughout the region. Even after moving in with friends and neighbors, however, natives tended to cling to ethnic boundaries in order to ease the transition. In 1715 Spotswood noticed that the Saponis and others gathered at Fort Christanna were "confederated together, tho' still preserving their different Rules."[34] Indians entering the Catawba Nation were equally conservative. As late as 1743 a visitor could hear more than twenty different dialects spoken by peoples living there, and some bands continued to reside in separate towns under their own leaders.[35]

Time inevitably sapped the strength of ethnic feeling, allowing a more unified Nation to emerge from the collection of Indian communities that occupied the valleys of the Catawba River and its tributaries. By the mid-eighteenth century, the authority of village headmen was waning and leaders from the host population had begun to take responsibility for the actions of constituent groups.[36] The babel of different tongues fell silent as "*Kàtahba*," the Nation's "standard, or court-dialect," slowly drowned out all others.[37] Eventually, entire peoples followed their languages and their leaders into oblivion, leaving only personal names like Santee Jemmy, Cheraw George, Congaree Jamie, Saponey Johnny, and Eno Jemmy as reminders of the Nation's diverse heritage.[38]

No European observer recorded the means by which nations became mere names and a congeries of groups forged itself into one people. No doubt the colonists' habit of ignoring ethnic distinctions and lumping confederated entities together under the Catawba rubric encouraged amalgamation. But Anglo-American efforts to create a society by proclamation were invariably unsuccessful;[39] consolidation had to come from within. In the absence of evidence, it seems reasonable to conclude that years of contacts paved the way for a closer relationship. Once a group moved to the Nation, intermarriages blurred ancient kinship networks, joint war parties or hunting expeditions brought young men together, and elders met in a council that gave everyone some say by including "all the Indian Chiefs or Head Men of that [Catawba] Nation and the several Tribes amongst them together."[40] The concentration of settlements within a day's walk of one another facilitated contact and communication. From their close proximity, common experience, and shared concerns, people developed ceremonies and myths that compensated for those lost to disease and gave the Nation a stronger collective consciousness.[41] Associations evolved that balanced traditional narrow ethnic allegiance with a new, broader, "national" identity, a balance that tilted steadily toward the latter. Ethnic differences died hard, but the peoples of the Catawba Nation learned to speak with a single voice.

*   *   *

Muskets and kettles came to the piedmont more slowly than smallpox and measles. Spanish explorers distributed a few gifts to local headmen, but inhabitants of the interior did not enjoy their first real taste of the fruits of European technology until Englishmen began venturing inland after 1650. Indians these traders met in upcountry towns were glad to barter for the more efficient tools, more lethal weapons, and more durable clothing that colonists offered. Spurred on by eager natives, men from Virginia and Carolina quickly flooded the region with the material trappings of European culture. In 1701 John Lawson considered the Wateree Chickanees "very poor in *English* Effects" because a few of them lacked muskets.[42]

Slower to arrive, trade goods were also less obvious agents of change. The Indians' ability to absorb foreign artifacts into established modes of existence hid the revolutionary consequences of trade for some time. Natives leaped the technological gulf with ease in part because they were discriminating shoppers. If hoes were too small, beads too large, or cloth the wrong color, Indian traders refused them.[43] Items they did select fit smoothly into existing ways. Waxhaws tied horse bells around their ankles at ceremonial dances, and some of the the traditional stone pipes passed among the spectators at these dances had been shaped by metal files.[44] Those who could not afford a European weapon fashioned arrows from broken glass. Those who could went to great lengths

to "set [a new musket] streight, sometimes shooting away above 100 Loads of Ammunition, before they bring the Gun to shoot according to their Mind."[45]

Not every piece of merchandise hauled into the upcountry on a trader's packhorse could be "set streight" so easily. Liquor, for example, proved both impossible to resist and extraordinarily destructive. Indians "have no Power to refrain this Enemy," Lawson observed, "though sensible how many of them (are by it) hurry'd into the other World before their Time."[46] And yet even here, natives aware of the risks sought to control alcohol by incorporating it into their ceremonial life as a device for achieving a different level of consciousness. Consumption was usually restricted to men, who "go as solemnly about it, as if it were part of their Religion," preferring to drink only at night and only in quantities sufficient to stupefy them.[47] When ritual could not confine liquor to safe channels, Indians went still further and excused the excesses of overindulgence by refusing to hold an intoxicated person responsible for his actions. "They never call any Man to account for what he did, when he was drunk," wrote Lawson, "but say, it was the Drink that caused his Misbehaviour, therefore he ought to be forgiven."[48]

Working to absorb even the most dangerous commodities acquired from their new neighbors, aboriginal inhabitants of the uplands, like African slaves in the lowlands, made themselves at home in a different technological environment. Indians became convinced that "Guns, and Ammunition, besides a great many other Necessaries, . . . are helpful to Man"[49] and eagerly searched for the key that would unlock the secret of their production. At first many were confident that the "*Quera*, or good Spirit," would teach them to make these commodities "when that good Spirit sees fit."[50] Later they decided to help their deity along by approaching the colonists. In 1757 Catawbas asked Gov. Arthur Dobbs of North Carolina "to send us Smiths and other Tradesmen to teach our Children."[51]

It was not the new products themselves but the Indians' failure to learn the mysteries of manufacture from either Dobbs or the *Quera* that marked the real revolution wrought by trade. During the seventeenth and eighteenth centuries, everyone in eastern North America—masters and slaves, farmers near the coast and Indians near the mountains—became producers of raw materials for foreign markets and found themselves caught up in an international economic network.[52] Piedmont natives were part of this larger process, but their adjustment was more difficult because the contrast with previous ways was so pronounced. Before European contact, the localism characteristic of life in the uplands had been sustained by a remarkable degree of self-sufficiency. Trade among peoples, while common, was conducted primarily in such commodities as copper, mica, and shells, items that, exchanged with the appropriate ceremony, initiated or confirmed friendships among groups. Few, if any, villages relied on outsiders for goods essential to daily life.[53]

Intercultural exchange eroded this traditional independence and entangled natives in a web of commercial relations few of them understood and none controlled. In 1670 the explorer John Lederer observed a striking disparity in the trading habits of Indians living near Virginia and those deep in the interior. The "remoter Indians," still operating within a precontact framework, were content with such ornamental items as mirrors, beads, "and all manner of gaudy toys and knacks for children." "Neighbour-Indians," on the other hand, habitually traded with colonists for cloth, metal tools, and weapons.[54] Before long, towns near and far were demanding the entire range of European wares and were growing accustomed— even addicted—to them. "They say we English are fools for . . . not always going with a gun," one Virginia colonist familiar with piedmont Indians wrote in the early 1690s, "for they think themselves undrest and not fit to walk abroad, unless they have their gun on their shoulder, and their shot-bag by their side."[55] Such an enthusiastic conversion to the new technology eroded ancient craft skills and hastened complete dependence on substitutes only colonists could supply.

By forcing Indians to look beyond their own territories for certain indispensable products, Anglo-American traders inserted new variables into the aboriginal equation of exchange. Colonists sought two commodities from Indians—human beings and deerskins—and both undermined established relationships among native groups. While the demand for slaves encouraged piedmont peoples to expand their traditional warfare, the demand for peltry may have fostered conflicts over hunting territories.[56] Those who did not fight each other for slaves or deerskins fought each other for the European products these could bring. As firearms, cloth, and other items became increasingly important to native existence, competition replaced comity at the foundation of trade encounters as villages scrambled for the cargoes of merchandise. Some were in a better position to profit than others. In the early 1670s Occaneechees living on an island in the Roanoke River enjoyed power out of all proportion to their numbers because they controlled an important ford on the trading path from Virginia to the interior, and they resorted to threats, and even to force, to retain their advantage.[57] In Lawson's day Tuscaroras did the same, "hating that any of these Westward *Indians* should have any Commerce with the *English*, which would prove a Hinderance to their Gains."[58]

Competition among native groups was only the beginning of the transformation brought about by new forms of exchange. Inhabitants of the piedmont might bypass the native middleman, but they could not break free from a perilous dependence on colonial sources of supply. The danger may not have been immediately apparent to Indians caught up in the excitement of acquiring new and wonderful things. For years they managed to dictate the terms of trade, compelling visitors from Carolina and Virginia to abide by aboriginal codes of conduct and playing one colony's traders against the other to ensure an abundance of goods at favorable rates.[59] But the natives' influence over the protocol of exchange combined with their skill at incorporating alien products to mask a loss of control over their own destiny. The mask came off when, in 1715, the traders—and the trade goods—suddenly disappeared during the Yamassee War.

The conflict's origins lay in a growing colonial awareness of the Indians' need for regular supplies of European merchandise. In 1701 Lawson pronounced the Santees "very tractable" because of their close connections with South Carolina. Eight years later he was convinced that the colonial officials in Charleston "are absolute Masters over the *Indians . . .* within the Circle of their Trade."[60] Carolina traders who shared this conviction quite naturally felt less and less constrained to obey native rules governing proper behavior. Abuses against Indians mounted until some men were literally getting away with murder. When repeated appeals to colonial officials failed, natives throughout Carolina began to consider war. Persuaded by Yamassee ambassadors that the conspiracy was widespread and convinced by years of ruthless commercial competition between Virginia and Carolina that an attack on one colony would not affect relations with the other, in the spring of 1715 Catawbas and their neighbors joined the invasion of South Carolina.[61]

The decision to fight was disastrous. Colonists everywhere shut off the flow of goods to the interior, and after some initial successes Carolina's native enemies soon plumbed the depths of their dependence. In a matter of months, refugees holed up in Charleston noticed that "the Indians want ammunition and are not able to mend their Arms."[62] The peace negotiations that ensued revealed a desperate thirst for fresh supplies of European wares. Ambassadors from piedmont towns invariably spoke in a single breath of restoring "a Peace and a free Trade," and one delegation even admitted that its people "cannot live without the assistance of the English."[63]

Natives unable to live without the English henceforth tried to live with them. No upcountry group mounted a direct challenge to Anglo-America after 1715. Trade quickly resumed, and the piedmont Indians, now concentrated almost exclusively in the Catawba valley, briefly enjoyed a regular supply of necessary products sold by men willing once again to deal according to the old rules. By midcentury, however, deer were scarce and fresh sources of slaves almost impossible to find. Anglo-American traders took their business elsewhere, leaving inhabitants of the Nation with another material crisis of different but equally dangerous dimensions.[64]

Indians casting about for an alternative means of procuring the commodities they craved looked to imperial officials. During the 1740s and 1750s native dependence shifted from colonial traders to colonial authorities as Catawba leaders repeatedly visited provincial capitals to request goods. These delegations came not to beg but to bargain. Catawbas were still of enormous value to the English as allies and frontier guards, especially at a time when Anglo-America felt threatened by the French and their Indian auxiliaries. The Nation's position within reach of Virginia and both Carolinas enhanced its value by enabling headmen to approach all three colonies and offer their people's services to the highest bidder.

The strategy yielded Indians an arsenal of ammunition and a variety of other merchandise that helped offset the declining trade.[65] Crown officials were especially generous when the Nation managed to play one colony off against another. In 1746 a rumor that the Catawbas were about to move to Virginia was enough to garner them a large shipment of powder and lead from officials in Charleston concerned about losing this "valuable people."[66] A decade later, while the two Carolinas fought for the honor of constructing a fort in the Nation, the Indians encouraged (and received) gifts symbolizing good will from both colonies without reaching an agreement with either. Surveying the tangled thicket of promises and presents, the Crown's superintendent of Indian affairs, Edmond Atkin, ruefully admitted that "the People of both Provinces . . . have I beleive [sic] tampered too much on both sides with those Indians, who seem to understand well how to make their Advantage of it."[67]

By the end of the colonial period, delicate negotiations across cultural boundaries were as familiar to Catawbas as the strouds they wore and the muskets they carried. But no matter how shrewdly the headmen loosened provincial purse strings to extract vital merchandise, they could not escape the simple fact that they no longer held the purse containing everything needed for their daily existence. In the space of a century the Indians had become thoroughly embedded in an alien economy, denizens of a new material world. The ancient self-sufficiency was only a dim memory in the minds of the Nation's elders.[68]

*   *   *

The Catawba peoples were veterans of countless campaigns against disease and masters of the arts of trade long before the third major element of their new world, white planters, became an integral part of their life. Settlement of the Carolina uplands did not begin until the 1730s, but once underway it spread with frightening speed. In November 1752, concerned Catawbas reminded South Carolina governor James Glen how they had "complained already . . . that the white People were settled too near us."[69] Two years later, five hundred families lived within thirty miles of the Nation and surveyors were running their lines into the middle of native towns.[70] "[T]hose Indians are now in a fair way to be surrounded by White People," one observer concluded.[71]

Settlers' attitudes were as alarming as their numbers. Unlike traders who profited from them or colonial officials who deployed them as allies, ordinary colonists had little use for Indians. Natives made poor servants and worse slaves; they obstructed settlement; they attracted enemy warriors to the area. Even men who respected Indians and earned a living by trading with them admitted that they made unpleasant neighbors. "We may observe of them as of the fire," wrote the South Carolina trader James Adair after considering the Catawbas' situation on the eve of the American Revolution, "'it is safe and useful, cherished at proper distance; but if too near us, it becomes dangerous, and will scorch if not consume us.'"[72]

A common fondness for alcohol increased the likelihood of intercultural hostilities. Catawba leaders acknowledged that the Indians "get very Drunk with [liquor] this is the Very Cause that they oftentimes Commit those Crimes that is offencive to You and us."[73] Colonists were equally prone to bouts of drunkenness. In the 1760s the itinerant Anglican minister, Charles Woodmason, was shocked to find the citizens of one South Carolina upcountry community "continually drunk." More appalling still, after attending church services "one half of them got drunk before they went home."[74] Indians sometimes suffered at the hands of intoxicated farmers. In 1760 a Catawba woman was murdered when she happened by a tavern shortly after four of its patrons "swore they would kill the first Indian they should meet with."[75]

Even when sober, natives and newcomers found many reasons to quarrel. Catawbas were outraged if colonists built farms on the Indians' doorstep or tramped across ancient burial grounds.[76] Planters, ignorant of (or indifferent to) native rules of hospitality, considered Indians who requested food nothing more than beggars and angrily drove them away.[77] Other disputes arose when the Nation's young men went looking for trouble. As hunting, warfare, and other traditional avenues for achieving status narrowed, Catawba youths transferred older patterns of behavior into a new arena by raiding nearby farms and hunting cattle or horses.[78]

Contrasting images of the piedmont landscape quite unintentionally generated still more friction. Colonists determined to tame what they considered a wilderness were in fact erasing a native signature on the land and scrawling their own. Bridges, buildings, fences, roads, crops, and other "improvements" made the area comfortable and familiar to colonists but un-

comfortable and unfamiliar to Indians. "The Country side wear[s] a New face," proclaimed Woodmason proudly;[79] to the original inhabitants, it was a grim face indeed. "His Land was spoiled," one Catawba headman told British officials in 1763. "They have spoiled him 100 Miles every way."[80] Under these circumstances, even a settler with no wish to fight Indians met opposition to his fences, his outbuildings, his very presence. Similarly, a Catawba on a routine foray into traditional hunting territories had his weapon destroyed, his goods confiscated, his life threatened by men with different notions of the proper use of the land.[81]

To make matters worse, the importance both cultures attached to personal independence hampered efforts by authorities on either side to resolve conflicts. Piedmont settlers along the border between the Carolinas were "people of a desperate fortune," a frightened North Carolina official reported after visiting the area. "[N]o officer of Justice from either Province dare meddle with them."[82] Woodmason, who spent even more time in the region, came to the same conclusion. "We are without any Law, or Order," he complained; the inhabitants' "Impudence is so very high, as to be past bearing."[83] Catawba leaders could have sympathized. Headmen informed colonists that the Nation's people "are oftentimes Cautioned from . . . ill Doings altho' to no purpose for we Cannot be present at all times to Look after them." "What they have done I could not prevent," one chief explained.[84]

Unruly, angry, intoxicated—Catawbas and Carolinians were constantly at odds during the middle decades of the eighteenth century. Planters who considered Indians "proud and deveilish" were themselves accused by natives of being "very bad and quarrelsome."[85] Warriors made a habit of "going into the Settlements, robbing and stealing where ever they get an Oppertunity."[86] Complaints generally brought no satisfaction—"they laugh and makes their Game of it, and says it is what they will"—leading some settlers to "whip [Indians] about the head, beat and abuse them."[87] "The white People . . . and the Cuttahbaws, are Continually at varience," a visitor to the Nation fretted in June 1759, "and Dayly New Animositys Doth a rise Between them which In my Humble opp[in]ion will be of Bad Consequence In a Short time, Both Partys Being obstinate."[88]

The litany of intercultural crimes committed by

each side disguised a fundamental shift in the balance of physical and cultural power. In the early years of colonization of the interior the least disturbance by Indians sent scattered planters into a panic. Soon, however, Catawbas were few, colonists many, and it was the natives who now lived in fear. "[T]he white men [who] Lives Near the Neation is Contenuely asembleing and goes In the [Indian] towns In Bodys . . . ," worried another observer during the tense summer of 1759. "[T]he[y] tretton the[y] will Kill all the Cattabues."[89]

The Indians would have to find some way to get along with these unpleasant neighbors if the Nation was to survive. As Catawba population fell below five hundred after the smallpox epidemic of 1759 and the number of colonists continued to climb, natives gradually came to recognize the futility of violent resistance. During the last decades of the eighteenth century, they drew on years of experience in dealing with Europeans at a distance and sought to overturn the common conviction that Indian neighbors were frightening and useless.

This process was not the result of some clever plan; Catawbas had no strategy for survival. A headman could warn them that "the White people were now seated all round them and by that means had them entirely in their power."[90] He could not command them to submit peacefully to the invasion of their homeland. The Nation's continued existence required countless individual decisions, made in a host of diverse circumstances, to complain rather than retaliate, to accept a subordinate place in a land that once was theirs. Few of the choices made survive in the record. But it is clear that, like the response to disease and to technology, the adaptation to white settlement was both painful and prolonged.

Catawbas took one of the first steps along the road to accommodation in the early 1760s, when they used their influence with colonial officials to acquire a reservation encompassing the heart of their ancient territories.[91] This grant gave the Indians a land base, grounded in Anglo-American law, that prevented farmers from shouldering them aside. Equally important, Catawbas now had a commodity to exchange with nearby settlers. These men wanted land, the natives had plenty, and shortly before the Revolution the Nation was renting tracts to planters for cash, livestock, and manufactured goods.[92]

Important as it was, land was not the only item Catawbas began trading to their neighbors. Some Indians put their skills as hunters and woodsmen to a different use, picking up stray horses and escaped slaves for a reward.[93] Others bartered their pottery, baskets, and table mats.[94] Still others traveled through the upcountry, demonstrating their prowess with the bow and arrow before appreciative audiences.[95] The exchange of these goods and services for European merchandise marked an important adjustment to the settlers' arrival. In the past, natives had acquired essential items by trading peltry and slaves or requesting gifts from representatives of the Crown. But piedmont planters frowned on hunting and warfare, while provincial authorities—finding Catawbas less useful as the Nation's population declined and the French threat disappeared—discouraged formal visits and handed out fewer presents. Hence, the Indians had to develop new avenues of exchange that would enable them to obtain goods in ways less objectionable to their neighbors. Pots, baskets, and acres proved harmless substitutes for earlier methods of earning an income.

Quite apart from its economic benefits, trade had a profound impact on the character of Catawba-settler relations. Through countless repetitions of the same simple procedure at homesteads scattered across the Carolinas, a new form of intercourse arose, based not on suspicion and an expectation of conflict but on trust and a measure of friendship. When a farmer looked out his window and saw Indians approaching, his reaction more commonly became to pick up money or a jug of whiskey rather than a musket or an ax. The natives now appeared, the settler knew, not to plunder or kill but to peddle their wares or collect their rents.[96]

The development of new trade forms could not bury all of the differences between Catawba and colonist overnight.[97] But in the latter half of the eighteenth century, the beleaguered Indians learned to rely on peaceful means of resolving intercultural conflicts that did arise. Drawing a sharp distinction between "the good men that have rented Lands from us" and "the bad People [who] has frequently imposed upon us," Catawbas called on the former to protect the Nation from the latter.[98] In 1771 they met with the prominent Camden storekeeper, Joseph Kershaw, to request that he "represent us when [we are] a grieved."[99] After the Revolution the position became more formal. Catawbas informed the South Carolina government that, being "destitute of a man to take care of, and assist us in our affairs," they had chosen one Robert Patten "to take charge of our affairs, and to act and do for us."[100]

Neither Patten nor any other intermediary could have protected the Nation had it not joined the patriot side during the Revolutionary War. Though one scholar has termed the Indians' contribution to the cause "rather negligible,"[101] they fought in battles throughout the southeast and supplied rebel forces with food from time to time.[102] These actions made the Catawbas heroes and laid a foundation for their popular renown as staunch patriots. In 1781 their old friend Kershaw told Catawba leaders how he welcomed the end of "this Long and Bloody War, in which You have taken so Noble a part and have fought and Bled with your white Brothers of America."[103] Grateful Carolinians would not soon forget the Nation's service. Shortly after the Civil War an elderly settler whose father had served with the Indians in the Revolution echoed Kershaw's sentiments, recalling that "his father never communicated much to him [about the Catawbas], except that all the tribe . . . served the entire war . . . and fought most heroically."[104]

Catawbas rose even higher in their neighbors' esteem when they began calling their chiefs "General" instead of "King" and stressed that these men were elected by the people.[105] The change reflected little if any real shift in the Nation's political forms,[106] but it delighted the victorious Revolutionaries. In 1794 the Charleston *City Gazette* reported that during the war "King" Frow had abdicated and the Indians chose "General" New River in his stead. "What a pity," the paper concluded, "certain people on a certain island have not as good optics as the Catawbas!" In the same year the citizens of Camden celebrated the anniversary of the fall of the Bastille by raising their glasses to toast "King Prow [sic]—may all kings who will not follow his example follow that of Louis XVI."[107] Like tales of Indian patriots, the story proved durable. Nearly a century after the Revolution one nearby planter wrote that "the Catawbas, emulating the examples of their white brethren, threw off regal government."[108]

The Indians' new image as republicans and patri-

ots, added to their trade with whites and their willingness to resolve conflicts peacefully, brought settlers to view Catawbas in a different light. By 1800 the natives were no longer violent and dangerous strangers but what one visitor termed an "inoffensive" people and one group of planters called "harmless and friendly" neighbors.[109] They had become traders of pottery but not deerskins, experts with a bow and arrow but not hunters, ferocious warriors against runaway slaves or tories but not against settlers. In these ways Catawbas could be distinctively Indian yet reassuringly harmless at the same time.

The Nation's separate identity rested on such obvious aboriginal traits. But its survival ultimately depended on a more general conformity with the surrounding society. During the nineteenth century both settlers and Indians owned or rented land. Both spoke proudly of their Revolutionary heritage and their republican forms of government. Both drank to excess.[110] Even the fact that Catawbas were not Christians failed to differentiate them sharply from nearby white settlements, where, one visitor noted in 1822, "little attention is paid to the sabbath, or religeon."[111]

In retrospect it is clear that these similarities were as superficial as they were essential. For all the changes generated by contacts with vital Euro-American and Afro-American cultures, the Nation was never torn loose from its cultural moorings. Well after the Revolution, Indians maintained a distinctive way of life rich in tradition and meaningful to those it embraced. Ceremonies conducted by headmen and folk tales told by relatives continued to transmit traditional values and skills from one generation to the next. Catawba children grew up speaking the native language, making bows and arrows or pottery, and otherwise following patterns of belief and behavior derived from the past. The Indians' physical appearance and the meandering paths that set Catawba settlements off from neighboring communities served to reinforce this cultural isolation.[112]

The natives' utter indifference to missionary efforts after 1800 testified to the enduring power of established ways. Several clergymen stopped at the reservation in the first years of the nineteenth century; some stayed a year or two; none enjoyed any success.[113] As one white South Carolinian noted in 1826, Catawbas were "Indians still."[114] Outward conformity made it easier for them to blend into the changed landscape. Beneath the surface lay a more complex story.

Those few outsiders who tried to piece together that story generally found it difficult to learn much from the Indians. A people shrewd enough to discard the title of "King" was shrewd enough to understand that some things were better left unsaid and unseen. Catawbas kept their Indian names, and sometimes their language, a secret from prying visitors.[115] They echoed the racist attitudes of their white neighbors and even owned a few slaves, all the time trading with blacks and hiring them to work in the Nation, where the laborers "enjoyed considerable freedom" among the natives.[116] Like Afro-Americans on the plantation who adopted a happy, childlike demeanor to placate suspicious whites, Indians on the reservation learned that a "harmless and friendly" posture revealing little of life in the Nation was best suited to conditions in post-Revolutionary South Carolina.

Success in clinging to their cultural identity and at least a fraction of their ancient lands cannot obscure the cost Catawba peoples paid. From the time the first European arrived, the deck was stacked against them. They played the hand dealt them well enough to survive, but they could never win. An incident that took place at the end of the eighteenth century helps shed light on the consequences of compromise. When the Catawba headman, General New River, accidentally injured the horse he had borrowed from a nearby planter named Thomas Spratt, Spratt responded by "banging old New River with a pole all over the yard." This episode provided the settler with a colorful tale for his grandchildren; its effect on New River and his descendants can only be imagined.[117] Catawbas did succeed in the sense that they adjusted to a hostile and different world, becoming trusted friends instead of feared enemies. Had they been any less successful they would not have survived the eighteenth century. But poverty and oppression have plagued the Nation from New River's day to our own.[118] For a people who had once been proprietors of the piedmont, the pain of learning new rules was great, the price of success high.

*　　*　　*

On that August day in 1608 when Amoroleck feared the loss of his world, John Smith assured him that the English "came to them in peace, and to seeke their loves."[119] Events soon proved Amoroleck right and his captor wrong. Over the course of the next three centuries, not only Amoroleck and other piedmont Indians but natives throughout North America had their world stolen and another put in its place. Though this occurred at different times and in different ways, no Indians escaped the explosive mixture of deadly bacteria, material riches, and alien peoples that was the invasion of America. Those in the southern piedmont who survived the onslaught were ensconced in their new world by the end of the eighteenth century. Population levels stabilized as the Catawba peoples developed immunities to once-lethal diseases. Rents, sales of pottery, and other economic activities proved adequate to support the Nation at a stable (if low) level of material life. Finally, the Indians' image as "inoffensive" neighbors gave them a place in South Carolina society and continues to sustain them today.

Vast differences separated Catawbas and other natives from their colonial contemporaries. Europeans were the colonizers, Africans the enslaved, Indians the dispossessed; from these distinct positions came distinct histories. Yet once we acknowledge the differences, instructive similarities remain that help to integrate natives more thoroughly into the story of early America. By carving a niche for themselves in response to drastically different conditions, the peoples who composed the Catawba Nation shared in the most fundamental of American experiences. Like Afro-Americans, these Indians were compelled to accept a subordinate position in American life yet did not altogether lose their cultural integrity. Like settlers of the Chesapeake, aboriginal inhabitants of the uplands adjusted to appalling mortality rates and wrestled with the difficult task of "living with death."[120] Like inhabitants of the Middle Colonies, piedmont groups learned to cope with unprecedented ethnic diversity by balancing the pull of traditional loyalties with the demands of a new social order. Like Puritans in New England, Catawbas found that a new world did not arrive all at once and that localism, self-sufficiency, and the power of old ways were only gradually eroded by conditions in colonial America. More hints of a comparable heritage could be added to this list, but by now it should be clear that Indians belong on the colonial stage as important actors in the unfolding American drama rather than as bit players, props, or spectators. For they, too, lived in a new world.

Notes

The author would like to thank the participants in the colloquium at the Institute of Early American History and Culture for their comments on a draft of this article. He is also grateful to Linda K. Merrell for preparing the map.

1. Edward Arber and A. G. Bradley, eds., *Travels and Works of Captain John Smith . . .*, vol. 2 (Edinburgh, 1910), 427.

2. Bernard W. Sheehan, "Indian-White Relations in Early America: A Review Essay," *William and Mary Quarterly*, 3d ser., 26 (1969): 267–86; James Axtell, "The Ethnohistory of Early America: A Review Essay," *William and Mary Quarterly*, 3d ser., 35 (1978): 110–44.

3. Benjamin W. Labaree, *America's Nation-Time: 1607–1789* (New York, 1976), cover, see also xi. Two exceptions are Gary B. Nash, *Red, White, and Black: The Peoples of Early America* (Englewood Cliffs, N.J., 1974), and Mary Beth Norton et al., *A People and a Nation: A History of the United States* (Boston, 1982), vol. 1. For analyses of the scholarly neglect of Indians in colonial America, see Thad W. Tate, "The Seventeenth-Century Chesapeake and Its Modern Historians," in Tate and David L. Ammerman, eds., *The Chesapeake in the Seventeenth Century: Essays on Anglo-American Society* (Chapel Hill, N.C., 1979), 30–32; Douglas Greenberg, "The Middle Colonies in Recent American Historiography," *William and Mary Quarterly*, 3d ser., 36 (1979): 415–16; and Neal Salisbury, *Manitou and Providence: Indians, Europeans, and the Making of New England, 1500–1643* (New York, 1982), 3–7.

4. Turner, "The Significance of the Frontier in American History," American Historical Association, *Annual Report for the Year 1893* (Washington, D.C., 1894), 199–227; Allen, *In English Ways: The Movement of Societies and the Transferal of English Local Law and Custom to Massachusetts Bay in the Seventeenth Century* (Chapel Hill, N.C., 1981); Herskovits, *The Myth of the Negro Past* (New York, 1941); Littlefield, *Rice and Slaves: Ethnicity and the Slave Trade in Colonial South Carolina* (Baton Rouge, La., 1981).

5. Allen, *In English Ways*; T. H. Breen, "Persistent Localism: English Social Change and the Shaping of New England Institutions," *William and Mary Quarterly*, 3d ser., 32 (1975): 3–28 and "Transfer of Culture: Chance and Design in Shaping Massachusetts Bay, 1630–1660," *New England Historical and Genealogical Register* 132 (1978): 3–17. More generally, others have argued that the European settlement of America marked an expansion of the Old World rather than a separation from it, "an extension of Europe rather than a wholly new world" (G. R. Elton, "Content-

ment and Discontent on the Eve of Colonization," in David B. Quinn, ed., *Early Maryland in a Wider World* [Detroit, Mich., 1982], 117–18; quotation from Quinn, "Why They Came," in Quinn, *Early Maryland*, 143).

6. Sidney W. Mintz and Richard Price, *An Anthropological Approach to the Afro-American Past: A Caribbean Perspective* (Philadelphia, 1976), 22; Nathan Irvin Huggins, *Black Odyssey: The Afro-American Ordeal in Slavery* (New York, 1977), 25–34.

7. While never thoroughly examined, the term has often been used this way by students of Indian history and others. For example, see Elizabeth A. H. John, *Storms Brewed in Other Men's Worlds: The Confrontation of Indians, Spanish, and French in the Southwest, 1540–1795* (College Station, Tex., 1975); Carolyn Gilman, *Where Two Worlds Meet: The Great Lakes Fur Trade* (St. Paul, Minn., 1982); Peter Laslett, *The World We Have Lost*, 2d ed. (New York, 1973); Edgar P. Richardson, Brooke Hindle, and Lillian B. Miller, *Charles Willson Peale and His World* (New York, 1982); and Irving Howe, *World of Our Fathers* (New York, 1976).

8. See T. J. C. Brasser, "Group Identification along a Moving Frontier," *Verhandlungen des XXXVIII Internationalen Amerikanistenkongresses*, vol. 2 (Munich, 1970): 261–62.

9. Salisbury divides the course of events into two phases, the first including diseases and trade goods, the second encompassing settlement (*Manitou and Providence*, 12).

10. For the societies created by Europeans and Africans, see James A. Henretta, *The Evolution of American Society, 1700–1815: An Interdisciplinary Analysis* (Lexington, Mass., 1973), esp. 112–16; Jack P. Greene, "Society and Economy in the British Caribbean during the Seventeenth and Eighteenth Centuries," *American Historical Review* 79 (1974): 1515–17; and Ira Berlin, "Time, Space, and the Evolution of Afro-American Society on British Mainland North America," *American Historical Review* 85 (1980): 44–78.

11. Among some Indian peoples a fourth stage, missionaries, could be added to the three outlined above. These agents did not, however, play an important part in the piedmont (or in most other areas of the southeast) during the colonial period. Lack of evidence precludes discussion of native religion among upland communities or the changes in belief and ceremony that occurred after contact. It is clear, however, that Indians there opposed any systematic efforts to convert them to Christianity. See Hugh Jones, *The Present State of Virginia: From Whence Is Inferred a Short View of Maryland and North Carolina*, ed. Richard L. Morton (Chapel Hill, N.C., 1956), 59.

12. Catawbas and their Indian neighbors have been objects of much study and considerable disagreement. Because these peoples lived away from areas of initial European settlement, detailed records are scarce, and archaeologists are only beginning to fill the gaps in the evidence. Important questions—the linguistic and political affiliations of some groups, their social structures, the degree of influence exerted by powerful societies to the east, west, and south, even their population—remain unanswered. But there are

many reasons to argue for a fundamental culture uniformity in this area beyond a common environment, hints of similar cultural traits, and the shared destiny of the region's inhabitants. Although these scattered villages fought with outsiders from the coast and the mountains, the north and the south, there is a distinct lack of recorded conflict among peoples in the piedmont itself. Peaceful relations may have been reinforced by a sense of common origin, for some (if not all) of these groups—including Saponis, Tutelos, Occaneechees, Catawbas, and Cheraws—spoke variant forms of the Siouan language and were descended from migrants who entered the area some seven centuries before Columbus arrived in America. Finally, other natives were cognizant of connections among these far-flung towns. The Iroquois, for example, called natives from the Catawbas to the Tutelos by the collective name "Toderichroone." For studies of these peoples, see James Mooney, *The Siouan Tribes of the East*, Smithsonian Institution, Bureau of American Ethnology, Bulletin 22 (Washington, D.C., 1894); Joffre Lanning Coe, "The Cultural Sequence of the Carolina Piedmont," in James B. Griffin, ed., *Archeology of Eastern United States* (Chicago, 1952), 301–11; Douglas Summers Brown, *The Catawba Indians: The People of the River* (Columbia, S.C., 1966); Charles M. Hudson, *The Catawba Nation* (Athens, Ga., 1970); and James H. Merrell, "Natives in a New World: The Catawba Indians of Carolina, 1650–1800" (Ph.D. diss., Johns Hopkins University, 1982).

13. Coe, "Cultural Sequence," in Griffin, ed., *Archeology of Eastern U.S.*, 301–11; Hudson, *Catawba Nation*, 11–17; William E. Myer, "Indian Trails of the Southeast," Bureau of American Ethnology, *Forty-Second Annual Report* (Washington, D.C., 1928), plate 15.

14. "True Relation of the Vicissitudes that Attended the Governor Don Hernando De Soto and Some Nobles of Portugal in the Discovery of the Province of Florida now Just Given by a Fidalgo of Elvas," in *Narratives of the Career of Hernando de Soto . . .*, ed. Edward Gaylord Bourne, vol. 1 (New York, 1904), 66. See also John Grier Varner and Jeannette Johnson Varner, trans. and eds., *The Florida of the Inca . . .* (Austin, Tex., 1951), 298, 315, and Henry F. Dobyns, *Their Number Become Thinned: Native American Population Dynamics in Eastern North America* (Knoxville, Tenn., 1983), 262–64.

15. South Carolina Council to Lords Proprietors, Apr. 23, 1698, in *Commissions and Instructions from the Lords Proprietors of Carolina to Public Officials of South Carolina, 1685–1715*, ed. Alexander S. Salley (Columbia, S.C., 1916), 105; Alexander Spotswood to the Board of Trade, Dec. 22, 1718, C.O. 5/1318, 590, Public Record Office (Library of Congress transcripts, 488); *South Carolina Gazette* (Charleston), May 4, 11, 25, June 29, Oct. 5, 1738. Catawba losses in this epidemic were never tabulated, but fully half of the Cherokees may have died (see John Duffy, *Epidemics in Colonial America* [Baton Rouge, La., 1953], 82–83; Catawbas to the governor of South Carolina, Oct. 1759, William Henry Lyttleton Papers, William L. Clements Library, Ann Arbor, Mich.; and *South Carolina Gazette*, Dec. 15, 1759). Dobyns constructs epidemic profiles for the conti-

nent and for Florida that offer a sense of the prevalence of the disease (*Their Number Become Thinned*, essays 1, 6).

16. See Edmund S. Morgan, *American Slavery, American Freedom: The Ordeal of Colonial Virginia* (New York, 1975), chaps. 8–9; Darrett B. Rutman and Anita H. Rutman, "Of Agues and Fevers: Malaria in the Early Chesapeake," *William and Mary Quarterly*, 3d ser., 33 (1976): 31–60; and several of the essays in Tate and Ammerman, eds., *Seventeenth-Century Chesapeake*.

17. Lawson, *A New Voyage to Carolina*, ed. Hugh Talmage Lefler (Chapel Hill, N.C., 1967), 232; see also 17, 34. The population figure given here is a very rough estimate. Lawson reckoned that Saponis, Tutelos, Keyauwees, Occaneechees, and Shakoris numbered 750 and that Catawbas (he called them "Esaws") were "a very large Nation containing many thousand People" (242, 46). Totals for other groups in the piedmont are almost nonexistent.

18. Philip E. Pearson, "Memoir of the Catawbas, furnished Gov. Hammond," MS (1842?), Wilberforce Eames Indian Collection, New York Public Library (typescript copy in the York County Public Library, Rock Hill, S.C.). For estimates of population losses, see *South Carolina Gazette*, Dec. 15, 1759; Arthur Dobbs to the secretary of the Society for the Propagation of the Gospel in Foreign Parts, Apr. 15, 1760, in *The Colonial Records of North Carolina*, ed. William L. Saunders, 10 vols. (Raleigh, N.C., 1886–90), 6:235, hereafter cited as *N.C. Col. Recs.*

19. Francis Le Jau to the secretary, June 13, 1710, in Frank J. Klingberg, ed., *The Carolina Chronicle of Dr. Francis Le Jau, 1706–1717* (Berkeley, Calif., 1956), 78.

20. John Drayton to Dr. Benjamin Smith Barton, Sept. 9, 1803, Correspondence and Papers of Benjamin S. Barton, Historical Society of Pennsylvania, Philadelphia. I am indebted to Maurice Bric for this reference.

21. Christian F. Feest, "Notes on Saponi Settlements in Virginia prior to 1714," Archaeological Society of Virginia, *Quarterly Bulletin* 28 (1974): 152–55; William Byrd, "The History of the Dividing Line betwixt Virginia and North Carolina Run in the Year of Our Lord 1728," in *The Prose Works of William Byrd of Westover: Narratives of a Colonial Virginian*, ed. Louis B. Wright (Cambridge, Mass., 1966), 315; H. R. McIlwaine et al., eds., *Executive Journals of the Council of Colonial Virginia*, 6 vols. (Richmond, Va., 1925–66), 4:269, hereafter cited as *Va. Council Jours.*; "A List of all the Indian names present at the Treaty held in Lancaster in June 1744," in Samuel Hazard, ed., *Pennsylvania Archives. Selected and Arranged from Original Documents . . .*, 1st ser., 1 (Philadelphia, 1852), 657.

22. Lawson, *New Voyage*, ed. Lefler, 173, 63.

23. Edward Bland, "The Discovery of New Brittaine, 1650," in *Narratives of Early Carolina, 1650–1708*, ed. Alexander S. Salley (New York, 1911), 13–14; William P. Cumming, ed., *The Discoveries of John Lederer . . .* (Charlottesville, Va., 1958), 12, 17, 19–20; John Banister, "Of the Natives," in *John Banister and His Natural History of Virginia, 1678–1692*, ed. Joseph Ewan and Nesta Ewan (Urbana, Ill., 1970), 377; William J. Hinke, trans. and ed., "Report of the Journey of Francis Louis Michel from Berne,

Switzerland, to Virginia, October 2, 1701–December 1, 1702," *Virginia Magazine of History and Biography* 24 (1916): 29; Lawson, *New Voyage*, ed. Lefler, 50; David I. Bushnell, Jr., "'The Indian Grave'—a Monacan Site in Albemarle County, Virginia," *William and Mary Quarterly*, 1st ser., 23 (1914): 106–12.

24. Lawson, *New Voyage*, ed. Lefler, 214.

25. Council Journals, Aug. 4, 1716, *N.C. Col. Recs.*, 2:242–43.

26. William Byrd, "Journey to the Land of Eden, Anno 1733," in Wright, ed., *Prose Works*, 398; *Va. Council Jours.*, 3:440.

27. Lawson, *New Voyage*, ed. Lefler, 35, 233.

28. Lawson, *New Voyage*, ed. Lefler, 184.

29. Lawson, *New Voyage*, ed. Lefler, 190.

30. Lawson, *New Voyage*, ed. Lefler, 184, 212, 24.

31. Lawson, *New Voyage*, ed. Lefler, 193.

32. Robert A. LeVine and Donald T. Campbell, *Ethnocentrism: Theories of Conflict, Ethnic Attitudes, and Group Behavior* (New York, 1972), 108.

33. Spotswood to the bishop of London, Jan. 27, 1715, in R. A. Brock, ed., *The Official Letters of Alexander Spotswood, Lieutenant-Governor of the Colony of Virginia, 1710–1722* (Virginia Historical Society, *Collections*, n.s., 2 [Richmond, Va., 1885]), 88, hereafter cited as Brock, ed., *Spotswood Letters.* See also Byrd, "History," in Wright, ed., *Prose Works*, 314.

34. Brock, ed., *Spotswood Letters*, 2:88.

35. Samuel Cole Williams, ed., *Adair's History of the American Indians* (Johnson City, Tenn., 1930), 236; The Public Accounts of John Hammerton, Esq., Secretary of the Province, in Inventories, LL, 1744–46, 29, 47, 51, South Carolina Department of Archives and History, Columbia, hereafter cited as Hammerton, Public Accounts; "Sketch Map of the Rivers Santee, Congaree, Wateree, Saludee, &c., with the Road to the Cuttauboes [1750?]," Colonial Office Library, Carolina 16, PRO (copy in Brown, *Catawba Indians*, plate 6, between 32–33); "Cuttahbaws Nation, men fit for warr 204 In the year 1756," Dalhousie Muniments, Gen. John Forbes Papers, Document #2/104 (copy in S.C. Dept. Archs. and Hist.).

36. J. H. Easterby, ed., *The Colonial Records of South Carolina: The Journal of the Commons House of Assembly, November 10, 1736–June 7, 1739* (Columbia, S.C., 1951), 481–82. Compare this to the Catawbas' failure to control Waccamaws living in the Nation a decade before (Journals of the Upper House of Assembly, Sept. 13, 1727, C.O. 5/429, 176–77 [microfilm, British Manuscripts Project, D 491]).

37. Williams, ed., *Adair's History*, 236.

38. Catawba Indians to Gov. Lyttelton, June 16, 1757, Lyttelton Papers (Santee Jemmy); Rev. William Richardson, "An Account of My Proceedings since I accepted the Indian mission in October 2d 1758 . . . ," Wilberforce Eames Indian Collection, entry of Nov. 8, 1758 (Cheraw George). South Carolina Council Journals (hereafter cited as S.C. Council Jours.), May 5, 1760, in William S. Jenkins, comp., *Records of the States of the United States*, microfilm ed. (Washington, D.C., 1950) (herafter cited as Records of States), SC

E.1p, reel 8, unit 3, 119 (Congaree Jamie); John Evans to Gov. James Glen, Apr. 18, 1748, in S.C. Council Jours., Apr. 27, 1748, Records of States, SC E.1p, 3/4 233 (Saponey Johnny); Hammerton, Public Accounts, 29, 51 (Eno Jemmy).

39. See, for example, Spotswood's efforts to persuade some tributary groups to join the piedmont Indians at Fort Christanna. *Va. Council Jours.*, 3:367; Spotswood to bishop of London, Jan. 27, 1715, in Brock, ed., *Spotswood Letters*, 2:88.

40. Easterby, ed., *Journal of the Commons House, 1736–1739*, 487.

41. See Brasser, "Group Identification," *Verhandlungen* 2 (1970): 261–65.

42. Lawson, *New Voyage*, ed. Lefler, 38.

43. William Byrd to [Arthur North?], Mar. 8, 1685/6, in Marion Tinling, ed., *The Correspondence of the Three William Byrds of Westover, Virginia, 1684–1776* (Charlottesville, Va., 1977), 1:57, Byrd to Perry and Lane, July 8, 1686, 64; Byrd to [Perry and Lane?], Mar. 20, 1685, 30; Byrd to North, Mar. 29, 1685, 31.

44. Lawson, *New Voyage*, ed. Lefler, 44–45; George Edwin Stuart, "The Post-Archaic Occupation of Central South Carolina" (Ph.D. diss., University of North Carolina, 1975), 133, fig. 72, B.

45. Lawson, *New Voyage*, ed. Lefler, 33, 63. Archaeologists have uncovered these arrowheads. See Tommy Charles, "Thoughts and Records from the Survey of Private Collections of Prehistoric Artifacts: A Second Report," Institute of Archeology and Anthropology, University of South Carolina, *Notebook* 15 (1983):31.

46. Lawson, *New Voyage*, ed. Lefler, 211, 18.

47. Lawson, *New Voyage*, ed. Lefler, 211; Robert Beverley, *The History and Present State of Virginia*, ed. Louis B. Wright (Chapel Hill, N.C., 1947), 182.

48. Lawson, *New Voyage*, ed. Lefler, 210. See also Craig MacAndrew and Robert B. Edgerton, *Drunken Comportment: A Social Explanation* (New York, 1969), chap. 5.

49. Lawson, *New Voyage*, ed. Lefler, 220.

50. One Santee priest claimed he had already been given this power by "the white Man above, (meaning God Almighty)," Lawson, *New Voyage*, ed. Lefler, 220, 26–27.

51. Catawba Nation to Gov. Dobbs, Oct. 5, 1757, encl. in Dobbs to Lyttelton, Oct. 24, 1757, Lyttelton Papers.

52. Immanuel Wallerstein, *The Modern World-System: Capitalist Agriculture and the Origins of the European World-Economy in the Sixteenth Century* (New York, 1974), esp. chap. 6.

53. Harold Hickerson, "Fur Trade Colonialism and the North American Indians," *Journal of Ethnic Studies* 1 (1973): 18–22; Charles Hudson, *The Southeastern Indians* (Knoxville, Tenn., 1976), 65–66, 316. Salt may have been an exception to this aboriginal self-sufficiency. Even here, however, Indians might have been able to get along without it or find acceptable substitutes. See Gloria J. Wentowski, "Salt as an Ecological Factor in the Prehistory of the Southeastern United States" (M.A. thesis, University of North Carolina, 1970). For substitutes, see Lawson, *New Voyage*, ed. Lefler, 89; Banister, "Of the Natives," in Ewan and Ewan,

eds., *Banister and His History*, 376; Beverley, *History*, ed. Wright, 180.

54. Cumming, ed., *Discoveries of Lederer*, 41–42.

55. Banister, "Of the Natives," in Ewan and Ewan eds., *Banister and His History*, 382.

56. "It is certain the Indians are very cruel to one another," Rev. Francis Le Jau wrote his superiors in England in April 1708, "but is it not to be feared some white men living or trading among them do foment and increase that Bloody Inclination in order to get Slaves?" (Le Jau to the secretary, Apr. 22, 1708, in Klingberg, ed., *Carolina Chronicle*, 39). Over the summer his worst fears were confirmed: "It is reported by some of our Inhabitants lately gone on Indian Trading that [Carolina traders] excite them to make War amongst themselves to get Slaves which they give for our European Goods" (Le Jau to the secretary, Sept. 15, 1708, in Klingberg, ed., *Carolina Chronicle*, 41). For an analysis of the Indian slave trade, see J. Leitch Wright, Jr., *The Only Land They Knew: The Tragic Story of the American Indians in the Old South* (New York, 1981), chap. 6. General studies of Indian warfare in the Southeast are John R. Swanton, *The Indians of the Southeastern United States*, Smithsonian Institution, Bureau of American Ethnology, Bulletin 137 (Washington, D.C., 1946), 686–701, and Hudson, *Southeastern Indians*, 239–57.

Evidence of an escalation in competition for hunting territories is sparse. But in 1702, only a year after Lawson noted that deer were scarce among the Tuscaroras, Indians in Virginia complained that Tuscarora hunting parties were crossing into the colony in search of game and ruining the hunting grounds of local groups. See Lawson, *New Voyage*, ed. Lefler, 65, and *Va. Council Jours.*, 2:275. It seems likely that this became more common as pressure on available supplies of game intensified.

57. "Letter of Abraham Wood to John Richards, August 22, 1674," in Clarence Walworth Alvord and Lee Bidgood [eds.], *First Explorations of the Trans-Allegheny Region by the Virginians, 1650–1674* (Cleveland, Ohio, 1912), 211, 215–17, 223–25; "Virginias Deploured Condition: Or an Impartiall Narrative of the Murders comitted by the Indians there, and of the Sufferings of his Maties. Loyall Subiects under the Rebellious outrages of Mr. Nathaniell Bacon Junr. to the tenth day of August A. o Dom 1676," Massachusetts Historical Society, *Collections*, 4th ser., 9 (Boston, 1871): 167.

58. Lawson, *New Voyage*, ed. Lefler, 64.

59. See Cumming, ed., *Discoveries of Lederer*, 41; Lawson, *New Voyage*, ed. Lefler, 210; and Merrell, "Natives in a New World," 74–77. For the competition between colonies, see Verner W. Crane, *The Southern Frontier, 1670–1732* (New York, 1981 [orig. publ. Durham, N.C., 1928]), 153–57, and Merrell, "Natives in a New World," 136–47.

60. Lawson, *New Voyage*, ed. Lefler, 23, 10.

61. The best studies of this conflict are Crane, *Southern Frontier*, chap. 7; John Phillip Reid, *A Better Kind of Hatchet: Law, Trade, and Diplomacy in the Cherokee Nation during the Early Years of European Contact* (University Park, Pa., 1976), chaps. 5–7; and Richard L. Haan, "The

'Trade Do's Not Flourish as Formerly': The Ecological Origins of the Yamassee War of 1715," *Ethnohistory* 28 (1981): 341–58. The Catawbas' role in the war is detailed in Merrell, "Natives in a New World," chap. 4.

62. Le Jau to [John Chamberlain?], Aug. 22, 1715, in Klingberg, ed., *Carolina Chronicle*, 162.

63. *Va. Council Jours.* 3:406, 412, 422.

64. Merrell, "Natives in a New World," 280–300, 358–59.

65. For an example of the gifts received by Catawbas, see the list of goods delivered to the Catawba Indians at the Congaree Fort, Feb. 14, 1752, in William L. McDowell, ed., *The Colonial Records of South Carolina: Documents Relating to Indian Affairs, May 21, 1750–August 7, 1754, ser. 2, The Indian Books* (Columbia, S.C., 1958), 217–18, hereafter cited as *Indian Affairs Docs.*

66. J. H. Easterby, ed., *The Colonial Records of South Carolina: Journals of the Commons House of Assembly, September 10, 1745–June 17, 1746* (Columbia, S.C., 1956), 132, 141, 173; George Haig to Gov. James Glen, Mar. 21, 1746, S.C. Council Jours., Mar. 27, 1746, Records of States, SC E.1p, 3/2, 74–75.

67. Atkin to Gov. William Henry Lyttelton, Nov. 23, 1757, Lyttelton Papers.

68. Treaty between North Carolina Commissioners and the Catawba Indians, Aug. 29, 1754, *N.C. Col. Recs.*, 5:144a.

69. Catawba King and Others to Gov. Glen, Nov. 21, 1752, *Indian Affairs Docs.*, 361.

70. Mathew Rowan to the Board of Trade, June 3, 1754, *N.C. Col. Recs.*, 5:124; Samuel Wyly to clerk of Council, Mar. 2, 1754, in S.C. Council Jours., Mar. 13, 1754, Records of States, SC E.1p, 6/1, 140.

71. Wilbur R. Jacobs, ed., *Indians of the Southern Colonial Frontier: The Edmond Atkin Report and Plan of 1755* (Columbia, S.C., 1954), 46.

72. Williams, ed., *Adair's History*, 235.

73. Treaty between North Carolina and the Catawbas, Aug. 29, 1754, *N.C. Col. Recs.*, 5:143. See also conference held with the Catawbas by Mr. Chief Justice Henley at Salisbury, May 1756, *N.C. Col. Recs.*, 5:581, 583; Matthew Toole to Glen, Oct. 28, 1752, *Indian Affairs Docs.*, 359; Catawbas to Lyttelton, June 16, 1757, Lyttelton Papers; and James Adamson to Lyttelton, June 12, 1759, *Indian Affairs Docs.*, 359.

74. Richard J. Hooker, ed., *The Carolina Backcountry on the Eve of the Revolution: The Journal and Other Writings of Charles Woodmason, Anglican Itinerant* (Chapel Hill, N.C., 1953), 7, 12; see also 30, 39, 53, 56, 97–99, 128–29.

75. S.C. Council Jours., May 5, 1760, Records of States, SC E.1p, 8/3, 119.

76. Robert Stiell to Gov. Glen, Mar. 11, 1753, *Indian Affairs Docs.*, 371; Gov. Thomas Boone to the Lords Commissioners of Trade and Plantations, Oct. 9, 1762, in W. Noel Sainsbury, comp., Records in the British Public Record Office Relating to South Carolina, 1663–1782, 36 vols., microfilm ed. (Columbia, S.C., 1955), 29:245–46, hereafter cited as *Brit. Public Recs., S.C.*

77. Treaty between North Carolina and the Catawbas,

Aug. 29, 1754, *N.C. Col. Recs.*, 5:142–43; Council Journal, Mar. 18, 1756, *N.C. Col. Recs.*, 5:655; Samuel Wyly to Lyttelton, Feb. 9, 1759, Lyttelton papers.

78. See, for example, Treaty between North Carolina and the Catawbas, Aug. 29, 1754, *N.C. Col. Recs.*, 5:142–43, and Catawbas to Lyttelton, June 16, 1757, Lyttelton Papers.

79. Hooker, ed., *Carolina Backcountry*, 63.

80. Augusta Congress, Nov. 1763, in Brit. Public Recs., S.C., 30:84.

81. Robert Stiell to Gov. Glen, Mar. 11, 1753, *Indian Affairs Docs.*, 371; Inhabitants of the Waxhaws to Samuel Wyly, Apr. 15, 1759, encl. in Wyly to Lyttelton, Apr. 26, 1759, Lyttelton Papers (colonists attacked). S.C. Council Jours., Feb. 6, 1769, Records of States, SC E.1p, 10/3, 9; King Frow to the governor, Mar. 15, 1770, in S.C. Council Jours., Mar. 27, 1770, Record of States, SC E.1p, 10/4, 56; "At a Meeting Held with the Catabaws," Mar. 26, 1771, Joseph Kershaw Papers, South Caroliniana Library, University of South Carolina, Columbia (Indians attacked).

82. Information of John Frohock and others, Oct. 10, 1762, *N.C. Col. Recs.*, 6:794–95.

83. Hooker, ed., *Carolina Backcountry*, 45, 52.

84. Treaty between North Carolina and the Catawbas, Aug. 29, 1754, *N.C. Col. Recs.*, 5:143; Catawbas to Glen, Nov. 21, 1752, *Indian Affairs Doc.*, 361.

85. Waxhaw inhabitants to Wyly, Apr. 15, 1759, encl. in Wyly to Lyttelton, Apr. 26, 1759, Lyttelton Papers: Meeting between the Catawbas and Henley, May 1756, *N.C. Col. Recs.*, 5:581.

86. Toole to Glen, Oct. 28, 1752, *Indian Affairs Docs.*, 358.

87. Toole to Glen, Oct. 28, 1752, *Indian Affairs Docs.*, 359; Meeting between the Catawbas and Henley, May 1756, *N.C. Col. Recs.*, 5:581.

88. John Evans to Lyttelton, June 20, 1759, Lyttelton Papers.

89. Adamson to Lyttelton, June 12, 1759, Lyttelton Papers.

90. Meeting between the Catawbas and Henley, May 1756, *N.C. Col. Recs.*, 5:582.

91. The Indians lobbied for this land beginning in 1757. Crown officials finally reserved it to them in Nov. 1763 and surveyed it in Feb. 1764. See Catawbas to Lyttelton, June 16, 1757, Lyttelton Papers; *S.C. Gaz.*, Aug. 9, 1760; S.C. Council Jours., May 15, 1762, Records of States, SC E.1p, 8/6, 497; Augusta Congress, Nov. 1763, Brit. Public Recs., S.C., 30:84, 104–6, 112–13; and "A Map of the Catawba Indians Surveyed agreeable to a Treaty Entered into with Them at Augusta in Georgia on the tenth Day of November 1763 . . . Executed, Certified and Signed by me the 22nd Day of February Anno Domini 1764, Sam[ue]l Wyly D[eputy] S[urveyo]r," Miscellaneous Records, H, 460, S.C. Dept. Archs. and Hist.

92. Brown, *Catawba Indians*, 283–84. For contemporary accounts, see Thomas Coke, *Extracts of the Journals of the Rev. Dr. Coke's Five Visits to America* (London, 1793), 148–49; "Travel Diary of Marshall and Benzien from Salem to South Carolina, 1790 . . . ," in Adelaide L. Fries et al., eds.

Records of the Moravians in North Carolina, 11 vols. (Raleigh, N.C., 1922–69), 5:1997; David Hutchison, "The Catawba Indians. By Request," *Palmetto-State Banner* (Columbia), Aug. 30, 1849 (copy in the Draper Manuscript Collection, ser. U, vol. 10, doc. #100 [Wisconsin State Historical Society, Madison]), hereafter cited as Hutchison, "Catawba Indians."

This land system broke down in 1840 when the Catawbas ceded their lands to South Carolina in exchange for promises of money and land to be purchased for them in North Carolina. By that time, the Nation's place in South Carolina society was secure enough to survive the economic and social shock of losing its land base. When plans to live in North Carolina fell through and the Indians drifted back to their ancient territory, no one forced them to leave. Instead, the state of South Carolina purchased a small reservation for them, a tract of land that has been the core of Catawba life ever since. See Brown, *Catawba Indians*, chaps. 13–14.

93. Affidavit of John Evans, S.C. Council Jours., Nov. 6, 1755, Records of States, SC E.1p, 7/2, 439; Affidavit of Liddy, Jan. 1, 1784, Kershaw Papers (horses). Report of the South Carolina Committee of Council, Apr. 19, 1769, Brit. Public Recs., S.C., 30:145–46; Hutchison, "Catawba Indians" (slaves).

94. John F. D. Smyth, *A Tour in the United States of America . . .*, vol. 1 (London, 1784), 193–94; Lucius Verus Bierce, "The Piedmont Frontier, 1822–23," in Thomas D. Clark, ed., *South Carolina: The Grand Tour, 1780–1865* (Columbia, S.C., 1973), 64; William Gilmore Simms, "Caloya; Or, The Loves of the Driver," in his *The Wigwam and the Cabin* (New York, 1856), 361–63.

95. Frank G. Speck, *Catawba Hunting, Trapping, and Fishing*, Joint Publications, Museum of The University of Pennsylvania and the Philadelphia Anthropological Society, no. 2 (Philadelphia, 1946), 10; Thomas J. Kirkland and Robert M. Kennedy, *Historic Camden, vol. 1: Colonial and Revolutionary* (Columbia, S.C., 1905), 58–59.

96. Compare, for example, the bitterness whites expressed to Adair before the Revolution (Williams, ed., *Adair's History*, 234) with the bemused tolerance in Simms's nineteenth-century fictional account of Catawbas and planters ("Caloya," in his *Wigwam and Cabin*, 361–429).

97. Besides the conflicts over hunting noted above, see Hooker, ed., *Carolina Backcountry*, 20; Lark E. Adams, ed., *The State Records of South Carolina: Journals of the House of Representatives, 1785–1786* (Columbia, S.C., 1979), 511–12; Journals of the House of Representatives, Dec. 5, 1792, Records of States, SC A.1b, 23/1, 83.

98. Catawba petition "To the Honourable the Legislature of the State of South Carolina now assembled at Charlestown," Feb. 13, 1784(?), Kershaw Papers. The Indians had made this distinction earlier; see S.C. Council Jours., Oct. 8, 1760, Records of States, SC E.1p, 8/5, 36.

99. "At a Meeting held with the Catawbas," Mar. 26, 1771, Kershaw Papers.

100. Catawba Petition to S.C. Legislature, Feb. 13, 1784(?), Kershaw Papers.

101. Hudson, *Catawba Nation*, 51.

102. The story of the Indians' service is summarized in Brown, *Catawba Indians*, 260–71.

103. "To the Brave Genl New River and the rest of the Headmen Warrieurs of the Catawba Nation," 1771 (misdated), Kershaw Papers.

104. A. Q. Bradley to Lyman C. Draper, May 31, 1873, Draper MSS, 14VV, 260. For other expressions of this attitude, see J. F. White to Draper, n.d., Draper MSS, 15 VV, 96; T. D. Spratt to Draper, May 7, 1873, Draper MSS, 107–8; Ezekiel Fewell to Draper, n.d., 318–19; and David Hutchison, "Catawba Indians."

105. Brown, *Catawba Indians*, 276.

106. The Nation's council "elected" headmen both before and after 1776, and kinship connections to former rulers continued to be important. For elections, see S.C. Council Jours., Feb. 20, 1764, Records of States, SC E.1p, 9/2, 40–41; Nov. 9, 1764, Record of States, 354; Feb. 12, 1765, Record of States, 9/3, 442–43; S.C. Commons House Jours., Jan. 27, 1767, Record of States, SC A.1b, 8/1, n.p. For later hereditary links to former chiefs, see John Drayton, *A View of South Carolina as Respects Her Natural and Civil Concerns* (Spartanburg, S.C., 1972 [orig. publ. 1802]), 98; Spratt to Draper, Jan. 12, 1871, Draper MSS, 15VV, 99–100.

107. *City Gazette* (Charleston), Aug. 14, 1794, quoted in Kirkland and Kennedy, *Historic Camden*, 320, 319.

108. Spratt to Draper, Jan. 12, 1871, Draper MSS, 15VV, 99. See also Hutchison, "Catawba Indians."

109. Smyth, *Tour*, 1:192; Report of the Commissioners Appointed to Treat with the Catawba Indians, Apr. 3, 1840, in A. F. Whyte, "Account of the Catawba Indians," Draper MSS, 1OU, 112.

110. W. J. Rorabaugh, *The Alcoholic Republic: An American Tradition* (New York, 1979), chap. 1. For reports of excessive drinking by whites along the Catawba River, see Records of the General Assembly, Petitions, N.D. (#1916), 1798 (#139), S.C. Dept. Archs. and Hist.; Journals of the Senate, Dec. 11, 1819, Records of States, SC A.1a, 25/3, 57; Journals of the House of Representatives, Nov. 23, 1819, Nov. 21, 1827, Records of States, SC A. 1b, 28/1, 8, 29/5, 15, 24.

111. Bierce, "Piedmont Frontier," in Clark, ed., *Grand Tour*, 66.

112. The story of the Catawbas' cultural persistence may be found in Merrell, "Natives in a New World," chap. 9, and "Reading 'an almost erased page': A Reassessment of Frank G. Speck's Catawba Studies," American Philosophical Society, *Proceedings*, 127 (1983): 248–62. For an interesting comparison of cultural independence in the slave quarter and the Indian reservation, see Thomas L. Webber, *Deep Like the Rivers: Education in the Slave Quarter Community, 1831–1865* (New York, 1978), chap. 18.

113. Hutchison, "Catawba Indians," Daniel G. Stinson to Draper, July 4, 1873, Draper MSS, 9VV, 274–77.

114. Robert Mills, *Statistics of South Carolina . . .* (Charleston, S.C., 1826), 773. See also the annual reports of the Catawba Agent to the Governor and State Legislature of South Carolina, 1841, 1842, 1848, 1849, 1860–64, in Legislative Papers, Indian Affairs, Governors' Correspondence, S.C. Dept. Archs. and Hist.

115. See Merrell, "Reading 'an almost erased page,'" 256 (names). Smyth, *Tour* 1:185; Coke, *Extracts*, 149; "Letter from the Country. Landsford, S.C., September 6, 1867," in *Courier* (Charleston), Sept. 12, 1867, 3 (language).

116. Catawba–black relations are analyzed in Merrell, "The Racial Education of the Catawba Indians," *Journal of Southern History* 50 (1984): 363–84.

117. Thomas Dryden Spratt, "Recollections of His Family, July 1875," (manuscript, South Caroliniana Lib.), 62.

118. See H. Lewis Scaife, *History and Condition of the Catawba Indians of South Carolina* (Philadelphia, 1896), 16–23, and Hudson, *Catawba Nation*, chaps. 4–6.

119. Arber and Bradley, eds., *Works of Smith*, 2:427.

120. Morgan, *American Slavery, American Freedom*, chap. 8.

Impermanent Architecture in the Southern American Colonies

CARY CARSON, NORMAN F. BARKA, WILLIAM M. KELSO, GARRY WHEELER STONE, AND DELL UPTON

Unlike students of material life in early New England, those who explore the first century of English settlement in the Chesapeake region have few surviving artifacts to study. The absence of early domestic buildings poses two methodological problems that the authors of this essay address. The first is simple; social historians who use material culture as primary evidence have had to team up with archaeologists in order to locate underground survivals. The second problem is more difficult. Archaeological discoveries must be embedded in contextual data sufficient to make them useful in interpretation. Both obstacles are overcome in this essay as it discovers in the impermanent buildings of early Maryland and Virginia a "starting place for a study of material life in the New World as it deviated little by little from the customs of the old."

The authors of this essay begin by focusing on a single, dominant type of housing in the early Chesapeake—those buildings erected by plantation "homesteaders" between the initial phase of temporary shelters and the arrival of permanent, often masonry, domestic forms on a widespread basis in the second quarter of the eighteenth century. Why were these impermanent houses built? The authors establish that lightly framed, earthfast structures had traditional antecedents in postmedieval England. In addition, recent research by demographic historians suggests that life in the malaria-ridden Chesapeake region was itself fragile. Society in seventeenth-century Maryland and Virginia seemed unstable and impermanent; perhaps individuals simply refused to invest their time and energy in structures that might outlast themselves. There was yet a third reason why small yeomen as well as large landowners preferred impermanent buildings; they were both participants in a tobacco economy that demanded intensive economic investment in land and labor. Logic argued that productive acreage warranted

more attention than housing. As it correlates the rise and fall of the tobacco economy with the persistence of small, lightly framed, clapboard-covered, earthfast houses, this essay takes a functionalist approach to the intersection of agriculture and architecture.

What, then, explains the emergence of permanent buildings in the eighteenth century? The authors argue that as the depressed tobacco economy stabilized and as planters gradually diversified into the production of cereal crops like corn and wheat, they profited from the sale of surplus crops on the open market. As they prospered in this new economic environment, they were able to "improve" their housing. Indeed, the authors conclude that "there is no denying that cash crops are a historian's best clue to predicting the time and the place of widespread rebuildings." As this essay suggests, cycles of environmental renewal in the New World were but patterned extensions of similar rebuildings that began in England in the mid-sixteenth century.

Impermanent building techniques were also maintenance-intensive, and these structures insured that the social relations of contractual obligation would also be frequently maintained. Cash crops changed the exchange relations that affect the choice of an appropriate building technology. Once cereals were available, the authors note, "marketing foodstuffs was less entangling." In turn, maintenance-free, "Georgian," permanent buildings were less socially entangling. Like the market, these new structures allowed for both personal freedom and personal alienation.

Once in a while someone slows down to read the historical marker that the state put up alongside the county road years before the site was actually found. Now the location is known for certain, but no one bothers to move the sign, because seventeenth-century Middle Plantation—down a side road and halfway across a soybean field in the rolling farm country west of Annapolis, Maryland—is nothing to look at anyway. Even when the excavation was in progress, there was little more to see than small dark stains in the mottled subsoil, the center of each pierced by a tobacco stick. The farmer who plowed the field had used the sticks to mark the stains that piqued his curiosity as they flashed by under the share. His own transformation into an excavator soon afterward followed almost literally the proverbial advice given to aspiring archaeologists: Get a bag of marbles and start collecting artifacts; every time you find one, replace it with a marble; when you have lost all your marbles, an archaeologist you will be. When the Maryland farmer had used up all his tobacco sticks, there were those who said he had to be a little daffy to see in their crazy pattern the houses, quarters, barns, and fencerows of a plantation that once belonged to one of Maryland's wealthiest and most successful merchant-planters.

To be told that the seventeenth-century civilization of England's largest and most populous American dominion, the Chesapeake colonies of Virginia and Maryland, has vanished almost without trace above ground, challenges credulity. Yet, that reality, stranger than fiction, is the inescapable testament of an impressive body of evidence recently accumulated in excavations on sites south from Middle Plantation to southern Maryland, to the northern neck of Virginia, and all along the York and James rivers. Its veracity is further borne out by the work of architectural historians, now in league with dendrochronologists. By careful examination of standing structures in the region they have reduced the probable number of surviving seventeenth-century buildings to fewer than six. So completely has time effaced the physical remains of early Chesapeake society that scholars have not bothered to look for catastrophes. Instead they believe that root causes can only be found in understanding the nature of material life in the New World, the pragmatic choices that faced all seventeenth-century settlers and homesteaders, and the special circumstances that prevailed in the southern colonies to perpetuate a meager and fragile material culture.

The last ten or twelve years have witnessed an extraordinary renascence of scholarly interest in seven-teenth-century Chesapeake history, an event that has received considerable notice in historical circles.[1] Less publicized, although not less remarkable, are the parallel efforts and comparable achievements of historians' opposite numbers in the fieldworking disciplines of archaeology and architectural history. Until ten years ago, the National Park Service had opened almost the only peephole on the material world of seventeenth-century Virginia by its excavation of Jamestown in the 1950s.[2] Since then, a few individuals and four major research institutions—St. Mary's City Commission (Maryland), Virginia Research Center for Archaeology (Williamsburg), Colonial Williamsburg, and Department of Anthropology, College of William and Mary (for a time affiliated with Southside Foundation)—have systematically explored over twenty-five sites in tidewater Maryland and Virginia (fig. 1). The structures brought to light have been almost without exception buildings whose framing members were in one manner or another *earthfast*, that is, standing or lying directly on the ground or erected in postholes.[3] While a few such impermanent structures were encountered in the excavations of Jamestown, no one suspected how prevalent they had been or how widely they were used for every sort of building from "manner houses" to hen coops. Earthfast building was overwhelmingly the predominant architectural tradition in the South; yet it has escaped the notice of everyone who has studied and written on the subject. The first purpose of this article, therefore, is to reintroduce the vernacular architecture of seventeenth-century Virginia and Maryland. For the first time, American historical archaeologists have in hand a body of evidence sufficiently large to support valid general observations comparable to those that numerous surviving buildings make possible in New England.

If American readers make their first acquaintance with earthfast buildings in these pages, English archaeologists will study them for another reason. Impermanent buildings are nothing unusual on Anglo-Saxon and medieval sites.[4] They have been found in regions where peasant houses were built of earth and

---

Fig. 1. Tidewater Maryland and Virginia showing locations of earthfast buildings. For key to numbers, see the detailed descriptions of specific sites and structures in "Appendix 2: Inventory of Earthfast Buildings in Maryland and Virginia," *Winterthur Portfolio* 16, nos. 2/3 (1981): 189–96.

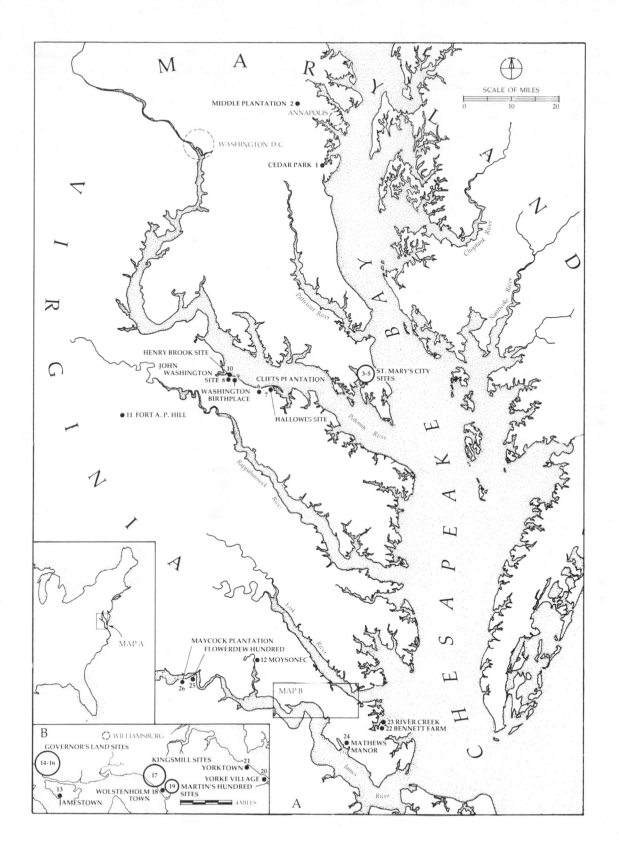

stone and, now that deserted medieval village sites are being explored in central England, in areas where timber building has an ancient ancestry.[5] Early results suggest a sequence of structural development that began with primitive, uncarpentered, earthfast buildings, evolved into ground-standing structures, and sometime in the thirteenth century culminated in prefabricated, fully framed buildings raised off the ground on stone pads or low foundation walls.[6] The archaeological evidence implies that the transformation was complete no later than the fourteenth century. This evolution in technology, English scholars believe, prepared the way for the professionally built, storied structures that survive in numbers from the latter half of that century onward.

But now from England's former American colonies comes complicating evidence to suggest that Englishmen kept alive certain very ancient and primitive building traditions well into the modern age. There is no question that the earthfast structures excavated along the eastern seaboard represent contemporary English practice transplanted to an American setting and are not New World inventions. The construction techniques described in this essay appear full-blown on sites occupied as early as 1618–19, scarcely ten years after the settlement of Jamestown. Thereafter they are encountered so consistently and widely throughout the Chesapeake area, and are known (mostly from literary sources) from as far away as New England, that independent invention must be ruled out as a plausible explanation. There has to have been a common source, and that source can only have been the colonists' homeland, England. English scholars, therefore, need to reassess their chronology and look again at fragmentary evidence from central Lincolnshire, south Somerset, Yorkshire, and elsewhere that hints at a coexistence of vigorous permanent and impermanent vernacular building traditions lasting possibly into the early nineteenth century.[7]

A variety of simultaneously current construction techniques, not a single evolutionary sequence, best explains the development of architectural traditions in the South. This key concept was first understood not by archaeologists so much as by the architectural historians who, since about 1968, have surveyed much of the Chesapeake Bay country county by county and house by house. Three nonacademic institutions led the way. The Maryland Historical Trust

and the Virginia Historic Landmarks Commission used federal survey grants to compile detailed inventories of historic structures in their respective states. That fieldwork led to the identification of the earliest buildings in the region. Those in Maryland the St. Mary's City Commission and the Maryland Historical Trust made the focus of a special recording project for the Historic American Buildings Survey.[8] Recently some of the oldest buildings have been revisited and sampled by the American Institute of Dendrochronology in a successful attempt to date construction and subsequent alterations.[9] All this research had two important consequences. By isolating the earliest extant structures, attention was focused on the building conventions that distinguished what contemporaries in the seventeenth century called the "Virginia house." Once those traits were recognized, connections could be traced back to specific regional traditions in English vernacular architecture.[10] Thus, the links were formed with archaic, timber building practices in England that finally led to the realization that colonists had known a whole range of building types—from the earthfast to the "fayre framed"—from which long experience had already accustomed them to choose whichever best suited the circumstances they encountered.

It is an easy step from such matters as these, which interest mainly archaeologists and architectural historians, to broader issues that command attention from social and economic historians. Choosing an appropriate building technology was a critical economic decision for anyone who set out to build a farm or a plantation. Thereafter it continued to be an important consideration if the enterprise prospered and earned profits that a farmer could reinvest in improvements and additions to his farmstead or could spend on better housing and a higher standard of living for his family. On the other hand, as the early history of the Chesapeake gives ample proof, financial reverses and other unforeseen setbacks postponed improvements and stalled farm economies in a perpetual state of incipient development. Such considerations figured so concretely in prospective settlers' perceptions of the opportunities that awaited them in the American colonies that, before setting out, many calculated the costs of different construction techniques down to the last halfpenny. "Tooling up" a plantation is a vital dimension to two questions that have come to dominate recent research in Chesapeake history — that is, to what degree the Tobacco Coast was a land of opportunity for small growers before 1660 and how did those who survived and acquired land and labor manage their resources. The subject leads from there to two other favorite topics, the gradual growth of a stable social order and the rise of a genuine consumer culture after 1700.

For once, written-record historians and their field-working brethren share a common plan of work. It is no coincidence. The institution most responsible for reviving interest in Chesapeake studies, St. Mary's City Commission, deliberately set out in 1969 to assemble a staff of archaeologists and social historians, and, that thing most rare, put them all to work on a single historical problem—to explore and to explain the transformation of Chesapeake society in the colonial period.[11] Their collaborative example has now spread to other institutions. As the circle of scholars expands and the slow work of archaeology advances, we look forward to a more regular flow of published site reports, architectural monographs, and, every now and then, our highest hope, an interpretive work of history. But for now this essay must serve all.

Discussion

To interpret correctly the buildings that archaeologists are now bringing to light one must start by making a distinction. These were not the makeshift shelters that sprang up in every new colony in the first days, weeks, and months following an expedition's landfall. Nor were they the improvised dwellings that later arrivals slapped together to huddle in while they cleared land for new farms or plantations. The early chronicles of almost every colony from Massachusetts Bay to the Carolinas clutter the landscape with shantytowns of huts, hovels, tents, cabins, caves, and dugouts.[12] Describing an aboriginal house form that a handful of iron nails transformed into an "English wigwam," one writer explained that such dwellings were the sort built for ten shillings "in the first 15. days whilst the ship at anchor is unlading and bound to diet and lodge the passenger."[13] Puncheon and hole-set buildings not only do not fit the descriptions of these earliest windbreaks, but archaeologists are now proving that such buildings lasted longer than the usual life span of wigwams and dugouts, which contemporaries reckoned at a few

months to three or four years at most.[14] Clearly, impermanence was a matter of degree.

The special fascination that primitive shelters held for an earlier generation of American architectural historians seems disproportionate today to their real importance.[15] For those who built them they were temporary, improvised expedients; for us such improvisations are as remote to a study of regional vernacular building traditions in American colonies as charcoal burners' huts and shepherds' *skali* are to the investigation of vernacular architecture in Great Britain and northern Europe. Much more important— then and now—were the buildings that came immediately afterward, for, although often "very meane and Little," they were, as one eyewitness observed, "Generally after the manner of . . . farme houses in England."[16] In other words, these were houses with antecedents. They were an architecture remembered from home. Hence, for us they are the starting place for a study of material life in the New World as it deviated little by little from the customs of the Old.

Whether they came to farm, to trade, or to follow some other occupation, most immigrants expected to make an investment in buildings. House construction and barn raising were inescapable first steps in a process of homesteading that was central to the American experience for over three hundred years. It required the planter-settler-pioneer-sodbuster to select from his or his carpenter's repertoire of building types and construction methods those best suited to immediate circumstances. A few could afford to gratify at once their ultimate aspiration for the best sort of building they had known at home. Many more could not or recognized the wisdom of choosing an easier, quicker, and cheaper form of building to meet their present needs. Such was the advice that experienced colonists gave to newcomers. Cornelius Van Tienhoven recommended that emigrants from the Low Countries time their departure so as to reach New Netherland in March or April.

Boors [farmers] and others who are obliged to work at first in Colonies ought to sail from this country in the fore or latter part of winter in order to arrive with God's help in New Netherland early in the Spring in March, or at latest in April, so as to be able to plant, during that summer, garden vegetables, maize, and beans, and *moreover employ the whole summer in clearing land and building cot-*

tages [that is, the dugouts that he describes later].

All then who arrive in New Netherland must immediately set about preparing the soil, so as to be able, if possible to plant some winter grain, and to proceed the next winter to cut and clear the timber . . .[including such trees] as are suitable for building, for palisades, posts and rails, which must be prepared during the winter, so as to be set up in the spring on the new made land which is intended to be sown, in order that the cattle may not in any wise injure the crops [in other words, fences first]. . . .

The farmer can get all sorts of cattle in the course of *the second summer*, when he will have more leisure to cut and bring home hay, also to *build houses and barnes for men and cattle.*

Van Tienhoven's report starts out seeming to imply that the dugouts or "cottages" were resorted to mainly by "those in New Netherland and especially in New England who have no means to build farmhouses." But later it explains that nearly everyone built huts the first summer and real "houses and barnes for men and cattle" the next.

[Even] the wealthy and principal men in New England, in the beginning of the Colonies, commenced their first dwelling-houses in this fashion for two reasons; first, in order not to waste time building and not to want food the next season; secondly, in order not to discourage poorer laboring people whom they brought over in numbers from Fatherland. In the course of three or four years, when the country became adapted to agriculture, they built themselves handsome houses, spending on them several thousands.[17]

The "poorer laboring people" presumably had to make do with their homestead houses and barns a good deal longer than the wealthy.

For many newcomers a hut was followed, as soon as could be, by a weatherproof but cheaply built house, which was not expected to last longer than it took its owner to accumulate enough capital to build yet another more substantial dwelling. Over and over again homesteaders on each new frontier moved in the same three steps from primitive shelters to temporary, impermanent buildings, to the "fayre houses" that many yeomen and even husbandmen were used

to from England. "If any one designs to make a Plantation in this Province," Thomas Nairne wrote from South Carolina in 1710, "the first thing to be done is, after having cutt down a few Trees, to split Palissades or Clapboards and therewith make small Houses or Huts to shelter the slaves."[18] In an area where neighbors had already moved on to the second or third stage of homesteading, only blacks needed to endure the worst hardships of getting started. The planter, his overseer, and his white indentured servants could expect to board "without any Charges" at nearby plantations. "And if the Person have any Wife or Children, they are commonly left in some Friend's House till a suitable dwelling Place and Conveniences are provided, fit for them to live decently." Decency and a modicum of convenience—these were all a newcomer should look forward to in the first few years. But Nairne reported that most settlers had hopes for a larger, better house in the future. A family's "small House," he said, "usually serves for a Kitchen afterwards when they are in better Circumstances."[19] One, two, three—hovel, house, home. In settlement after settlement that was the *beau idéal*, not for everyone, of course, and not invariably even for those so minded. Frontier communities often resembled the description of one in central North Carolina where the first inhabitants "built and lived in log Cabbins, and as they became more wealthy, some of them built framed clapboard houses with clay chimneys." Those were the years before 1800. "At present," said the writer in 1810, "there are many good houses, well constructed with brick chimneys, and glass lights. [Yet] there are no stone or brick walled houses, nor any that can be called edifices. . . . The greatest number of citizens yet build in the old stile." The standard was often easier to imagine than to meet.[20]

Can we be sure that for temporary houses homesteaders used inferior materials and methods of construction that were significantly cheaper, quicker, and consequently less durable than those employed in later permanent dwellings? Can we justifiably equate various perishable structures with an interim stage in the ideal homesteading process? In several specific cases the answer is unequivocally yes. Applied more generally the correlation still holds true, but with the important caveat that some earthfast building techniques passed into a mainstream tradition among southern housewrights by the close of the seventeenth century. The circumstances that prolonged their use to the point that they became an acceptable alternative to full frame construction are discussed in the concluding section of this paper. For the moment it is enough to show that many colonists just starting out regarded earthfast buildings as adequate for their immediate purposes but inferior to those they expected to construct later.

John Lewger, we know positively, built his house, St. John's, at St. Mary's City (fig. 2) four years after Maryland was founded and within half a mile of the original bivouac where the colonists took shelter in abandoned Indian wigwams. Similarly George Yeardley's party was accommodated at the main encampment on Jamestown Island before pushing on upriver to Flowerdew Hundred. Jamestown likewise served as the base camp for the founders of Wolstenholmtown, seven miles downstream. The archaeological evidence makes clear that few structures in any of these early settlements were primitive lean-tos, but neither were they "orderly, fair and well built" houses. The Flowerdew buildings lasted scarcely twenty-five years, although the town survived into the next century. The dwellings and storehouses destroyed at Wolstenholmtown in 1622 were followed by farmsteads comprised entirely of hole-set barns and farmhouses, which in their turn lasted only another twenty years or so. Nearby, on Littletown Quarter, Kingsmill, two dwellings—a tiny puncheon cabin and its hole-set frame successor—were built, used, and abandoned, all before 1650. St. John's was longer lived, partly because it was better built to begin with, but mainly because its underpinnings were renewed periodically and its accommodations enlarged and modernized. Like other buildings its dominant trait was its transience.

Written records multiply the small but growing archaeological sample of impermanent buildings associated with immigrants who were just getting settled. They also make explicit the inferences drawn from archaeological evidence. An anonymous pamphlet, published in 1684 to promote the new colony of Pennsylvania, gave "Such Persons as are Inclined to America" a virtual set of blueprints and a bill of particulars for "a mean way of Building," but one that "ordinary beginners" would find "sufficient and safest." It called for a medium-sized house, 30 feet long and 18 feet wide, with one partition near the middle and another to divide one end into two smaller rooms (fig. 3). "These houses," prospective settlers were assured, "usually endure ten years without Repair." It is easy to understand why not longer.

There must be eight Trees of about sixteen Inches square and cut off to *Posts* of about fifteen foot long, which the House must stand upon; and four pieces, two of thirty foot long and two of eighteen foot long, for *Plates*, which must lie upon the top of those *Posts* the whole length and bredth of the House for the *Gists* to rest upon. There must be ten *Gists* of twenty foot long to bear the Loft, and two false *Plates* of thirty foot long to lie upon the ends of the *Gists* for the *Rafters* to be fixed upon, twelve pare of *Rafters* of about twenty foot to bear the Roof of the House, with several other small pieces as *Wind-Beams, Braces, Studs*, etc. which are made of the Waste Timber. For Covering the House, Ends, and Sides, and for the Loft we use *Clabboard*, which is Rived feather-edged, of five foot and a half long, that well Drawn lyes close and smooth. The Lodging Room may be lined with the same and filld up between [with nogging], which is very Warm.[21]

The writer obviously spoke from firsthand experience ("we use *Clabboard*"), which he almost certainly learned from Chesapeake settlements immediately to the south. The construction techniques he described, in particular the so-called "false *Plates*" and the common-rafter roof, came straight out of a distinctive regional building tradition in Maryland and Virginia that had already developed away from English prototypes by the third quarter of the seventeenth century.[22] Here then, Pennsylvania notwithstanding, are the specifications for a southern planter's house, modest enough, the pamphlet tells us, for a newcomer to build within twelve months after his arrival, yet sufficiently substantial to last ten years. Afterward, if he prospered, the worn-out "first House" could be used, as the Carolina homestead was, for "a good out House till plenty will allow . . . a Better."

As with all promotional literature, the description repays careful reading between the lines. Its list of parts is informative not only for what it includes but also for what is left out, chiefly chimneys and ground sills. Although the writer explained that such houses were to "stand upon" the four pairs of 16-inch posts that composed the frame, it is only their length—15

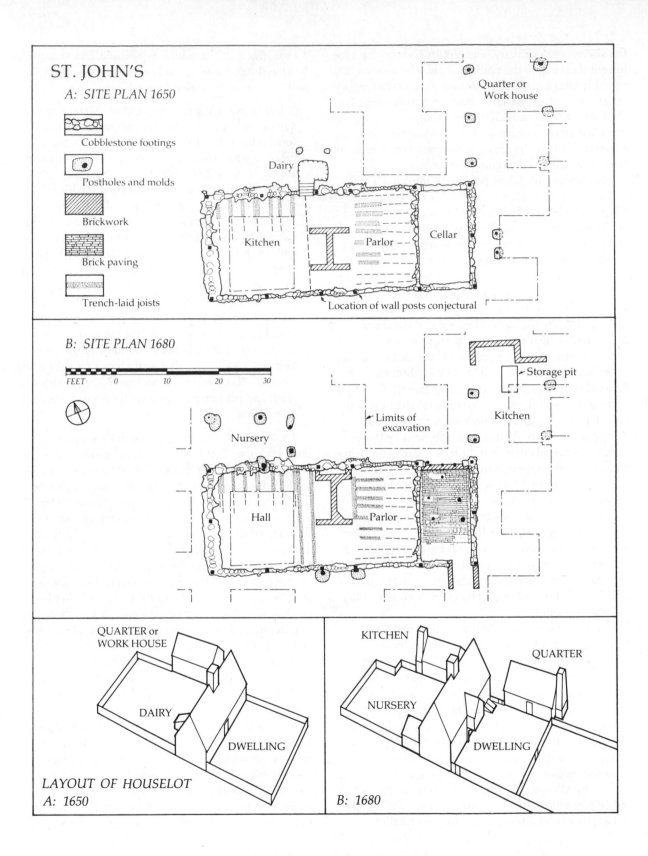

ST. JOHN'S

A: SITE PLAN 1650

Cobblestone footings

Postholes and molds

Brickwork

Brick paving

Trench-laid joists

Dairy

Kitchen

Parlor

Cellar

Quarter or Work house

Location of wall posts conjectural

B: SITE PLAN 1680

FEET   0   10   20   30

Nursery

Hall

Parlor

Limits of excavation

Storage pit

Kitchen

QUARTER or WORK HOUSE

DAIRY

DWELLING

LAYOUT OF HOUSELOT
A: 1650

KITCHEN

QUARTER

NURSERY

DWELLING

B: 1680

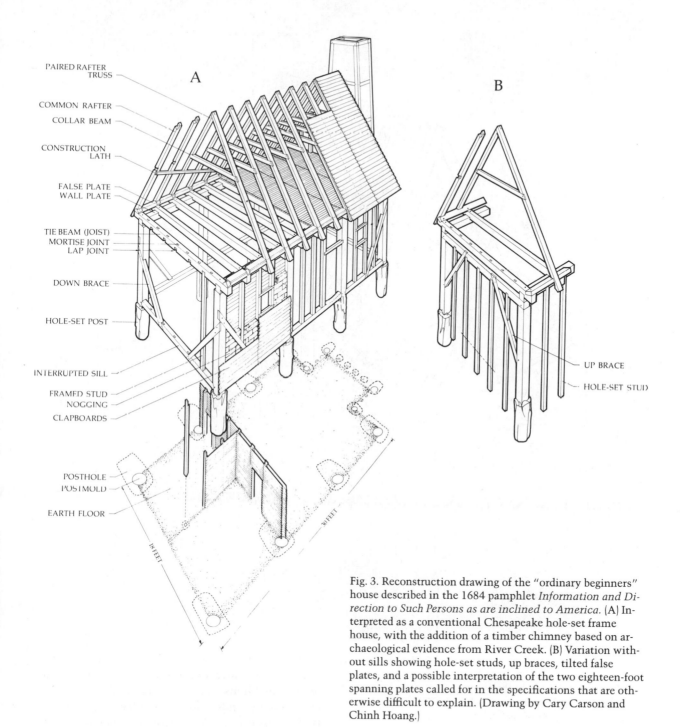

PAIRED RAFTER
TRUSS

COMMON RAFTER

COLLAR BEAM

CONSTRUCTION
LATH

FALSE PLATE
WALL PLATE

TIE BEAM (JOIST)
MORTISE JOINT
LAP JOINT

DOWN BRACE

HOLE-SET POST

INTERRUPTED SILL

FRAMED STUD
NOGGING
CLAPBOARDS

POSTHOLE
POSTMOLD

EARTH FLOOR

A

B

UP BRACE

HOLE-SET STUD

IN FEET

IN FEET

Fig. 3. Reconstruction drawing of the "ordinary beginners"
house described in the 1684 pamphlet *Information and Direction to Such Persons as are inclined to America*. (A) Interpreted as a conventional Chesapeake hole-set frame
house, with the addition of a timber chimney based on archaeological evidence from River Creek. (B) Variation without sills showing hole-set studs, up braces, tilted false
plates, and a possible interpretation of the two eighteen-foot
spanning plates called for in the specifications that are otherwise difficult to explain. (Drawing by Cary Carson and
Chinh Hoang.)

◀ Fig. 2. Development of St. John's, St. Mary's City, Maryland. The house was built in 1638, variously altered thereafter—extensively in 1678—and was finally leased as a tavern until about 1720. (Drawing by Shearon Vaughn and Cary
Carson.)

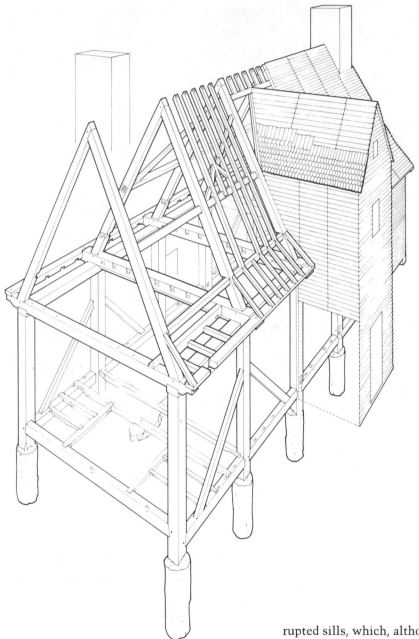

Fig. 4. Perspective view of the frame of Cedar Park, Anne Arundel County, Maryland, as built in 1702. (Drawing by Cary Carson and Chinh Hoang.)

feet—that tells us they were set up in postholes 4 or 5 feet deep, thus bringing the standing walls to the customary height of 10 or 11 feet. The studs, which *are* mentioned, may have been fastened to inter-rupted sills, which, although *not* referred to, may have been included among the "several other small pieces" that house builders were to salvage from left-over odds and ends. On the other hand, the inter-rupted sills used at Cedar Park (fig. 4) are heftier than that. It is perhaps more likely that the pamphleteer was remembering houses in which the studs, too, were buried in holes or trenches or were fastened to unframed lengths of sill beam laid in slots in the ground. Examples of both have been excavated at

Kingsmill tenements, Flowerdew Hundred, and Wolstenholmtown.

Both techniques draw attention to the further omission of ground-level floor joists from the list. Although the excavation of St. John's has shown that sleepers could be installed independently of any ground sills that a building may or may not have had, here there was no need. "The lower flour," the pamphleteer explained, "is the *Ground*; the upper *Clabbord*."[23] Probably many impermanent buildings had only earthen floors. Floors laid with expensive sawn planks were one feature, along with glazed windows and white limed walls, that John Hammond associated with the somewhat better built farmhouses he saw in Virginia in 1656.[24] Their absence elsewhere no doubt contributed to the "meanness" of poorer homesteaders' houses.

It was hard for anyone to avoid altogether the discomforts of settling in an overseas colony. All, no matter what their circumstances, were beginners. Take, for instance, a man like James Claypoole of Pennsylvania, whose letters describe step by step the process of planning, building, and improving a temporary house.[25] Claypoole was a merchant, a stockholder in William Penn's Free Society of Traders, and an owner of some five thousand acres of province lands. Wealthy as he was, he knew better than to lavish precious time and energy on a substantial first residence. He chose to avoid the rigors of hovel dwelling personally by sending indentured craftsmen ahead to Philadelphia to prepare a homestead for himself and his family according to specifications he drew up in London. The house they built early in 1683 following his instructions was "but a slight house like a barn with one floore of two Chambers" measuring overall "40 foot long and 20 broad" with a cellar underneath "to keep some wine and other liquors Cool in that I intend to take with me." Like the "ordinary beginners" houses, it had no chimney, not in August when the family finally arrived and not four months later in December when Claypoole cut short a letter to his brother "for cold, haveing no Chimney."[26] A flued cooking fire was more important, so, as the first improvement to his dwelling, Claypoole was building a twenty-foot kitchen provided with "a double Chimny." His neighbors, too, were busy bringing their properties up to standard; he wrote that "Wm Framton is on the other side of me building a great brewhouse." As adequate as Claypoole's house was to "hold us and our goods and keep us from the sunn and weather," it was a temporary expedient and nothing more. Even before leaving England he was making plans to build a brick house in the spring. He instructed his indentured bricklayer to find a good clay pit and "prepare as much clay as he can in the most convenient place to work upon come Springe." He himself would bring another carpenter, and he had asked his brother in Barbados to send "one or 2 good stout negroes" to help build the permanent house, which a man of his means could expect to occupy within less than a year after his arrival, although not without camping out in a barnlike stopgap in the meantime.[27]

Claypoole's letters offer only these few clues from which to guess what was slighted in making his "slight house." Fifty years earlier a New Englander of comparable social standing, Samuel Symonds, left much less to the discretion of the agent who supervised construction of his house in the frontier settlement of Ipswich, Massachusetts. "Concerneinge the frame of the howse," Symonds began his copious instructions,

I am indiferent whether it be 30 foote or 35 foote longe; 16 or 18 foote broade. I would have wood chimneys at each end, the frames of the chimnyes to be stronger than ordinary, to beare good heavy load of clay for security against fire. You may let the chimnyes be all the breadth of the howse, if you thinke good; the 2 lower dores to be in the middle of the howse, one opposite to the other. Be sure that all the dorewaies in every place be soe high that any man may goe upright under. The staiers I thinke had best be placed close by the dore. It makes noe great matter though there be noe particion upon the first flore; if there be, make one [room] biger than the other. Fore windowes, let them not be over large in any roome, & as few as conveniently may be; let all have current drawwindowes, haveing respect both to present & future use. I thinke to make it a girt howse will make it more chargeable then neede; however, the side bearers for the second story being to be loaden with corne, &c must not be pinned on, but rather eyther lett in to the studds or borne up with false studds, & soe tenented in at the ends; I leave it to you & the carpenters. In this story over the first, I would have a particion, whether in the middest or over the particion under, I leave it. In the garrett noe particion, but let there be one or two lucome windowes, if two, both on one side. I desire to have the sparrs reach downe pretty deep at the eves to preserve the walls the better from the wether, I would have it sellered all over, & soe the frame of the howse accordengly from the bottom. I would have the howse stronge in timber, though plaine & well brased. I would have it covered with very good oake-hart inch board, *for the present*, to be tacked on onely for the present, as you tould me. Let the frame begin from the bottom of the seller, & soe in the ordinary way upright, for I can hereafter (to save the timber within grounde) run up a thin brickwork without. I thinke it best to have the walls without to be all clapboarded besides the clay walls. It were not amisse to leave a dore-way or two within the seller, that soe hereafter one may make comings in from without, & let them be both upon that side which the lucome window or windowes be.[28]

Four features of the Symonds house are uncommon or unknown among surviving seventeenth-century buildings for precisely the reasons that recommended their use in circumstances where time and costs had to be held to a minimum. The pair of clay-daubed timber chimneys, one on each gable, must have resembled the "double clayed chimney" built in 1638 for the minister at the Agawam trading post (now Springfield, Massachusetts).[29] References to posted "Welsh chimneys" occur frequently enough in the seventeenth-century records of Maryland and Virginia to imply that wooden chimneys like Symonds's were used in insubstantial dwellings throughout the colonies.[30] Hole-set timber chimneys are regularly encountered on excavated sites (for example, Utopia Leasehold, James City County, Virginia), and one, River Creek in York County, Virginia, has produced unmistakable evidence of a chimney raised on corner posts with hole-set studs in between.

Symonds wanted the frame of his two-story house to be "strong in timber," yet, even so, it was to stand on posts set on or into the cellar floor. As his letter specifies, "Let the frame begin from the bottom of the seller, and soe in the ordinary way upright." It was ordinary for homestead structures perhaps but certainly not ordinary at all for the sorts of seventeenth-century houses that have lasted to the present day in New England. Symonds himself understood the difference, which he explained by saying, "I think to make it a girt house will make it more chargeable then neede." Instead of framing the ground-floor ceiling beams into girts and they in turn into the wall posts in the usual way, he called for "side bearers for the second story," or what we now term *clamps*. These were normally pegged to the inside surface of the posts and studs, in effect providing a shelf on which to rest the ends of the joists.[31] The technique required no mortises, which, being time-consuming, were costly. Clamps worked well where the floor above supported ordinary loads. But Symonds planned to store corn and other unusually heavy goods upstairs and, therefore, cautioned that the side bearers "must not be pinned on, but rather eyther lett in to the studds [in notches] or borne up with false studds, and soe tenented in at the ends." What he meant by false studs can only be guessed, perhaps secondary uprights fastened to the backs of the regular studs and snugged up under the clamps to bear their weight. As for tenoning the clamps "in at the ends," possibly he had in mind only a simple lap joint at their juncture with the posts. Otherwise, it is hard to understand how reinforced side bearers saved much over girts.

The final expedient was the roof, covered with oak boards "tacked on onely for the present." Apparently Symonds had plans to put on another kind of roof when time allowed or materials became available. Unlike Claypoole, the thrifty New Englander was building a house now that he could eventually improve to the point of making it more or less permanent without putting himself to the expense of building entirely anew. Not only was there the roof, the chimneys "stronger than ordinary," and the "draw-windowes" suited to "both the present and future use," but, knowing that inevitably the posts would rot, he anticipated that "I can hereafter (to save the timber within grounde) run up a thin brickwork without," in other words, brick foundation walls.[32] The same measure preserved another hole-set frame at Cedar Park.

Symonds's instructions for a make-do house in Ipswich, Claypoole's for his barnlike contrivance in Philadelphia, and the brochure for prospective builders of ordinary beginners' cottages in Penn's colony all state explicitly that the dwellings were interim structures. They demonstrate that a characteristic second stage in the process of making new settlements was often accompanied by the several sorts of earthfast structures that archaeologists have discovered in recent excavations. Such buildings plainly came after and were superior to newcomers' shanties. Just as plainly they preceded and were not as well built as the fully framed or brick houses that successful colonists set their sights on.

Between those two extremes the homesteader—the builder for here and now—might choose one of several construction techniques although, if British, he was likely to build a frame house covered with clapboards. "Such are almost all the English houses in the country," one traveler noted, failing only to observe that many (judging now from archaeological evidence) were raised on earthfast frames.[33]

Puncheon Buildings

The most primitive were buildings with driven posts and in fact were not really framed at all. Two dwellings excavated at the Maine, a 1620–30s plantation site opposite Jamestown, were hardly more than cabins, each nailed together around a rectangular pen of randomly placed uprights.[34] Their fragile remains recall a structure of similar size, plan, and date found underneath nearby Littletown Quarter. All were raised on poles and posts whose basal elevations varied so greatly as to rule out prefabricated walls or preassembled parts. Indeed, the absence of separately discernible postholes and molds suggests that the uprights were individually driven into the ground, making them what contemporaries knew as *punches*, or, when set close together, perhaps in prepared trenches, *pallisados*.[35] Puncheon buildings are mentioned in accounts of several early and widely separated settlements, often in terms that leave no doubt about their inferior and temporary character. It was reported from Virginia in 1623, for instance, that the settlers' houses "are onlie made of wood, few or none of them beeing framed houses but punches sett into the Ground And couered with Boards so as a firebrand is sufficient to consume them all."[36] Six years after Scituate, Massachusetts, was settled by Londoners and "men of Kent," a new arrival found nine dwellings in the village, "all wch," he noted, are "small plaine pallizadoe Houses."[37] Others are known to have been built in Connecticut,[38] in Plymouth,[39] and in Charlestown, which was merely a trad-

ing station before Massachusetts Bay was settled in 1630. In that year Capt. Roger Clap put into the Charlestown harbor and later described the village as having a few "wigwams and one House." The house was a "palisadoed and thatched" affair built in 1628, which, against all odds, was repaired, refurbished, and thereby kept standing for 150 years.[40] Its preservation may have been aided by ground-laid sills that provided a dry seat for the palisade walls. An early house in Yarmouth, Massachusetts, when razed about 1840, revealed wall construction of close-set (six-inch) palisades fitted into auger holes bored in parallel rows in the sills and plates and infilled with a packing of stones and clay.[41]

But silled palisade walls were exceptional. Most such buildings were puncheon buildings, which to housewrights then and to archaeologists since have usually meant ephemeral structures raised around a gaggle of earthfast uprights. Their builders may not even have planned them in the "bay" units so familiar to frame construction; occasional specifications for houses described as being so many "lengths of [riven clap-] boards" long, "alloweing 5 foote to each length," may betray a way of thinking in which the design of buildings was dimensioned in multiples of standard clapboard sizes rather than units of framing, an approach entirely consistent with the piecemeal manner of erecting puncheon structures.[42] It is hard to draw a line between houses like those at the Maine and the contraptions in which newcomers first took shelter. Indeed, a distinction (other than the relative longevity of the Maine houses) is probably not worth trying to make. Whether sturdy shacks or ramshackle homesteads, they are chiefly interesting now as the most primitive earthfast structures so far discovered, one end of a continuum that had at its other end elaborately framed, semipermanent, earthfast buildings like Cedar Park.

Hole-Set Framed Buildings

Most houses and barns that archaeologists are finding fall somewhere between the two extremes; usually they were laid out in regular bays formed by paired posts. By paying careful attention to the shape, orientation, and depth of the postholes and the location of the timber molds in those holes, excavators have made a start at telling apart hole-set buildings assembled in several different ways. The least sophis-

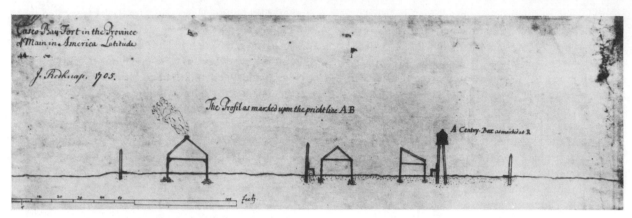

Fig. 5. Detail from a plat of "Casco Bay Fort in the Province of Main[e] in America" showing a cross-section through three hole-set buildings—a guard house and two store houses—inside the fortifications. The posts (upbraced in the largest structure) appear to be seated on rocks placed in the postholes. The drawing is signed and dated "J. Redknap. 1705." (Colonial Office Library, London; photograph courtesy of Yale University Library.)

ticated were those framed without any ground sills at all, not even interrupted sills. A technical drawing (1705) of buildings inside an English fort on Casco Bay, Maine, illustrates several methods of framing and bracing structures that derived most of their rigidity from their hole-set posts (fig. 5).[43] In buildings without sills the studs as well as the posts were embedded in the ground. Excavation of Kingsmill Tenement I (fig. 6) has produced the clearest archaeological evidence of this method, one that also left traces in written records. The Stafford County, Virginia, court for example, commissioned a small "prison house" in 1691, specifying "Locust posts Twelve Inches Square Studded with Locust Stoods [studs] three foot in the ground."[44] Houses and farm buildings, similarly constructed, are described as early as 1650.[45]

There may have been forms of construction that represented a cross between studded hole-set buildings and those with puncheon walls. An early structure at Flowerdew Hundred, thought to be a warehouse, could be one such case (fig. 7). It was erected on a bayed framework of hole-set posts, but the uncommonly wide bays (twenty feet), suggest that the smaller, earthfast uprights in between gave structural support to the wall plates in the manner of puncheons rather than of studs.

Embedded studs were sometimes improved upon when affixed to horizontal timbers laid into shallow trenches, a practice akin to the use of sills to waterproof the footings of palisade walls. Sites on Martin's Hundred along James River, including early Wolstenholmtown, have produced the remains of dwellings, farm buildings, and storehouses whose exterior walls stood on trench-laid sills interrupted at regular bayed intervals by hole-set framing posts. Firmly seated in the subsoil, such sill beams were probably not tenoned to the posts they abutted, thereby saving some costs. But even more important, it was a homesteader's willingness to make do with earthen floors that resulted in choosing this manner of construction in preference to interrupted sills raised entirely off the ground.

Higher was drier, and drier was definitely better. Many builders of hole-set structures must have agreed that a few more mortises and tenons were worth the expense of making interrupted sills an integral part of a framed house, for only the major uprights have left evidence in the ground on most sites. While traces of shallow earthfast studs and sills may since have been plowed to nothing, there are reasons to suppose that many house frames were entirely raised off the ground on hole-set posts. Several excavated sites preserve original grades, among them the kitchen yards at Gerret van Sweringen's tavern, at River Creek, and at Yorke Village. All yielded evidence of hole-set posts but not earthfast studs. Another indication is the growing preference among late seventeenth-century builders for silled buildings supported on wooden blocks (discussed on p. 129). Such construction appears to be a more logical outgrowth of silled frames standing on hole-set posts than frames with earthfast studs.

One of the clearest cases of a house with elevated sills is also one of the earliest structures excavated in Virginia. Built about 1620 in the clustered settlement on Flowerdew Hundred, its four-bay frame was erected on pairs of uprights set up in shallow construction trenches, not in separate holes (see fig. 7). Blocks of dressed siltstone (evidently reused ballast) were placed in the trenches between the uprights to

Fig. 6. Early structures at Kingsmill, James City County, Virginia. All were occupied ca. 1625–50. (Drawing by Shearon Vaughn and Cary Carson.)

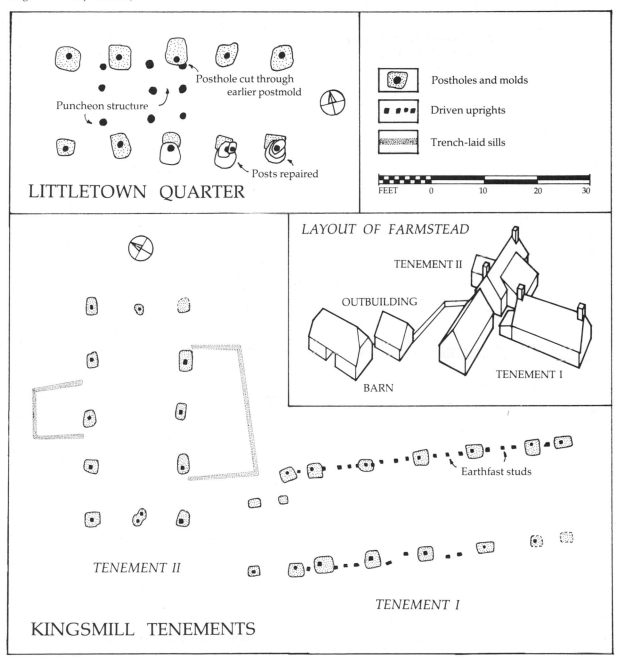

LITTLETOWN QUARTER

Puncheon structure

Posthole cut through earlier postmold

Posts repaired

Postholes and molds

Driven uprights

Trench-laid sills

FEET 0 10 20 30

LAYOUT OF FARMSTEAD

TENEMENT II

OUTBUILDING

BARN

TENEMENT I

TENEMENT II

Earthfast studs

TENEMENT I

KINGSMILL TENEMENTS

Impermanent Architecture

CARSON ET AL.

127

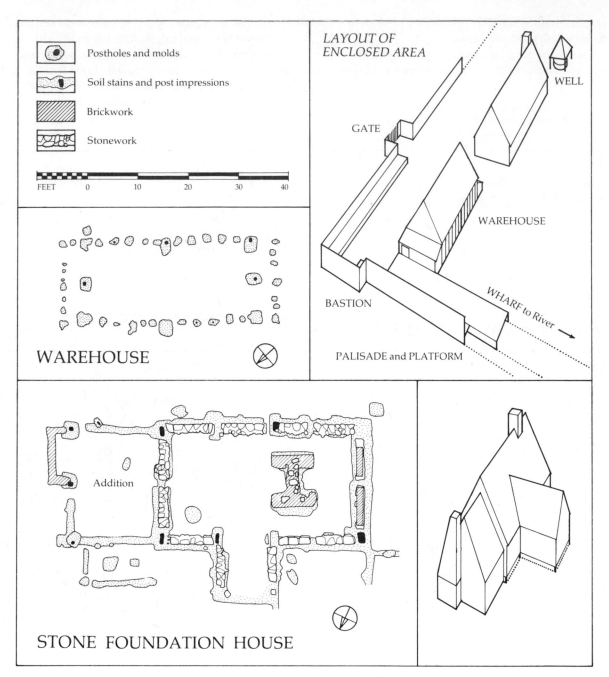

Fig. 7. Structures at Flowerdew Hundred, Prince George County, Virginia. Both date from the earliest settlement of Sir George Yeardley's particular plantation, ca. 1619–30. (Drawing by Shearon Vaughn and Cary Carson.)

make low foundation walls, the masons taking care to create a level surface. A topping of brickwork brought the plinth up evenly underneath what were surely interrupted sills; horizontal timbers mortised and tenoned to the uprights seated the studs and gave rigidity to the ground-standing frame.

Fully carpentered interrupted sills imply a fair degree of precision building. That confirms the impression that archaeologists have taken away from many excavations: post-in-the-ground buildings were often carefully planned, their parts prefabricated, and whole units preassembled. Raising preassembled frames, whether as walls or as tie-beam pairs, required postholes dug to a uniform depth to ensure that all horizontal members would come out level. At the John Hallowes site in Westmoreland County, Virginia, small stone shims were placed at the bottoms of some holes to raise the posts slightly, while other holes were first excavated to the approximate depth desired and then carefully scooped out to a measured bottom. Elsewhere it has been observed that loose dirt was sometimes thrown back into a freshly dug pit and tamped down to the correct level.

Irregular postholes or those with unusually small diameters hint that some hole-set buildings may have been set up one post at a time. Where frames were assembled in parts on the ground, as seems more often to have been the case, and once postholes were prepared, prefabricated units were tipped up in sections and lowered into place. These assembled modules were sometimes the plated side walls (resulting in what is known as "normal assembly") and sometimes post-and-tie-beam pairs ("reverse" or "bent assembly"). Each left its own telltale marks in the ground, which archaeologists are learning to distinguish. Normal assembly of side-wall frames was usually aided by positioning the rectangular postholes with the long axes at right angles to the length of the building. Their bottoms were sometimes sloped or stepped in the direction in which the wall was raised, each post coming to rest near the middle or far side of the pit at its deepest point. Similarly, it stands to reason that house frames raised on pairs of posts connected by tie beams were easiest to erect where the holes had their long axes parallel to the building's length. Kingsmill Tenement II (see fig. 6) and the first period dwelling at the Clifts (on Virginia's northern neck) suggest construction by reverse assembly. The two methods may have differed in another subtle respect. Careful measurement of the distances between post *molds* at St. John's Quarter has revealed that its bay intervals were calculated originally not post to post but from one outside corner to the *center* of the adjacent post, to the *center* of the one next to it, and so on to the opposite end. The carpenter dealt with the entire wall as a single design problem, the basic concept underlying all normal as-

sembly. Conceivably—and this supposition still awaits testing in the field—builders who practiced reverse assembly took a bay interval to be the space between pairs of posts, that is, the distance from the *side* of one tie-beam pair to the *nearest side* of the next one. That somewhat different way of dimensioning a building may sometimes be discernible on archaeological sites and hence another important indication of structures raised in bent frames.

Whatever future excavations reveal, the point is already well established that post-in-the ground buildings were sometimes so methodically planned and precisely dimensioned that their archaeological remains can validate conclusions that turn on fractions of an inch. To be sure, such exactitude was lacking in many earthfast structures where, presumably, costs outweighed advantages. But in the hands of master builders post-in-the-ground houses could be and sometimes were built as finely as the most professionally carpentered box-framed structures.

Framed Buildings on Hole-Set Blocks

Some structures were fully framed, yet "blocked up under the sills," a construction technique especially common toward the end of the seventeenth century and thereafter. Earthfast blocks left the kind of archaeological evidence observed in the excavation of an outbuilding on the Sweringen property in St. Mary's City (fig. 8).[46] Like hole-set frames, blocks reduced construction costs by compromising a building's durability, yet they offered a kind of limited liability. Always replaceable, they alone were subject to the decay that elsewhere put entire post-in-the-ground buildings at risk. A silled frame standing on structurally unrelated blocks was as impervious to damp as a framed building raised on brick foundations. What evidently began as a method of repairing older hole-set structures and rescuing frames built on ground-laid sills[47] gradually caught on in the eighteenth century as a technique equally suitable for new building.[48] Eventually it prevailed among clients too poor to afford brick, thus relegating hole-set posts to expendable "pole barns" and sheds. Its triumph signals the complete absorption of impermanent building practices into the dominant timber-frame tradition in the South, a matter that will receive fuller discussion later.

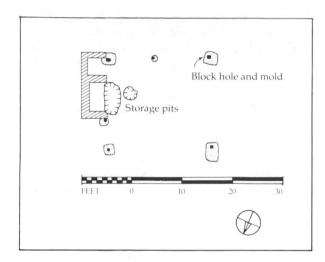

Fig. 8. An outbuilding, possibly a bakehouse and quarter, built by Gerret van Sweringen at St. Mary's City, Maryland. The silled frame was raised on hole-set blocks. (Drawing by Shearon Vaughn.)

Buildings Raised on "Cratchets"

Settlers in the Chesapeake colonies and the Leeward Islands knew how to build another kind of inexpensive, post-supported structure, one whose roof was raised on forked poles variously called "cratches," "cratchets," "crochets," "crotches," or "crutches." John Smith's account of Jamestown in 1608 includes a good description of such buildings and attests to their second place in the familiar, three-step homesteading sequence. The Jamestowners' first church, he explained, was "an old rotten tent, for we had few better . . . till we built a homely thing like a barne, set upon Cratchets," which the colonists roofed and walled with "rafts, sedge, and earth." He added that "the best part of our houses [was] of the like curiosity, but the most part farre much worse workmanship, that could neither well defend wind nor raine."[49] Smith's word *cratchets* has been taken by some to mean *crucks*, but he clearly meant slender, forked poles, for elsewhere in the same account he described some "poore [foot] bridges, only made of a few cratches thrust in the o[o]se, and three or foure poles laid on them."[50] His earlier choice of the phrase "like a barne" (the same analogy that Claypoole later used to describe his own temporary dwelling in Philadelphia) is suggestive, for poles with naturally forked tops were used in England throughout the seventeenth century to build seasonal farm buildings—pigsties, cart sheds, hop mangers, hayricks, and similar hovels "set upon crotches [defined as "forked Posts"] covered with poles and [a roof of sticks or] straw."[51] When fur traders from Virginia established a year-round camp on Kent Island in the upper Chesapeake Bay in 1631, they built "several thatch-roofed huts set on crotches and raftered with a covering of brush."[52] Occasionally the word *cratches* may have been used to describe hefty timbers—the "good and substantial cratches . . . erected [in 1668] for the making of a good, substantial, and firm cratched-house" on the island of Montserrat were apparently not mere poles.[53] But in most English and American contexts the term implies wall posts whose distinguishing characteristics, whenever described, are their slight size and forked tops.[54] Notwithstanding occasional claims to the contrary, no literary or archaeological evidence has yet come to light that proves or even strongly suggests that English settlers raised houses or barns on full-cruck trusses. Upper crucks, yes,[55] but not on timbers that reached from the footings to the ridge piece.

Raftered Houses

An ancient European building type brought to the Chesapeake was the house without walls, the primitive, ground-standing A-frame that Charles F. Innocent called a "roof hut."[56] A 1658 Virginia will mentions a 60-foot tobacco house "with rafters upon the ground."[57] Another tentlike tobacco house answering that description appears on a plat of Jamestown Island drawn in 1664.[58] The sketch shows an open gable with a central pole—conceivably a hole-set cratchet—supporting the ridge. The sloping sides are depicted as a grid of crisscrossed vertical and horizontal lines apparently representing rafters and thatching poles. Other roof huts may be inferred where records make a deliberate distinction between "wall plate tobacco houses" and "raftered" structures.[59] In the Chesapeake the technique seems to have been restricted to tobacco shelters.

Turf-, Earth-, and Log-Walled Houses

Commonplace as post-in-the-ground structures seem to have been in English settlements up and down the eastern seaboard, not all British colonists traded up from a wigwam or a dugout to a clapboard-covered frame house.[60] The author of a 1650 pamphlet promoting New Albion described "six sorts" of dwellings in America, the first being the newcomer's wigwam and the second "a clove board house nailed to posts," obviously the sort we have been looking at.[61] The third, fourth, and fifth were altogether different: "an Irish house of posts walled and divided with close watlle hedges, and thin turfed above, and thick turfs without below" (akin perhaps to the "sedge & earth" walled church and dwellings in Smith's description of Jamestown); "a log house of young trees 30. feet square notched in at corners"; and "a mud-wall house thatched or tiled." The sixth and last was the only unquestionably durable house type, "a brick house or square tower 3. stories high." Whether the author had seen all six in English settlements he does not say. Conceivably he had, for even log cabins had spread to Maryland and Virginia by 1655.[62]

Plank-Framed Houses

There was still another short-order construction technique in the British immigrant's repertoire. "The poor sort" who settled in East Jersey, according to an observer in 1684, "set up a house of two or three rooms themselves, after this manner: the walls are of cloven timber about eight or ten inches broad like planks, *set one end to the ground* and the other nailed to the raising [plate], which they plaster within."[63] Cloven-timber planks recall the tradition of plank-frame building common in southeastern Massachusetts. Although there the planks are fastened to sills in the earliest surviving structures of this type (houses built in the third quarter of the seventeenth century), the use of planks for walling goes back another forty or fifty years in the Plymouth region, perhaps to sill-less impermanent buildings where curtain walls stood directly in the ground.[64] If so, here is another case where the practice of embedding uprights directly into the ground was improved on by the addition of ground-laid sills. Recalling similar refinements in puncheon and stud-frame construction, silled plank-frame buildings demonstrate again that impermanence was a matter of degree, which is only another way of saying a matter of choice.

Newcomers to virtually all the American colonies

frequently exercised that choice in favor of building expediently for the present so as to husband their labor and capital for the future. He who said, "An ordinary House and a good Stock is the Planter's Wisdom," spoke for prudent homesteaders everywhere.[65] Such people had a selection of earthfast building types to choose from. Immigrants from the British Isles had probably known and built most of them back home, if not always as dwellings, then as farm buildings. Those origins are more than a little suggested by the oft-repeated analogy between Old World barns and New World first houses. It has been necessary to review the evidence for impermanent building throughout all the colonies in order to establish the overall validity of the homesteading process, for, as our attention turns now to the Chesapeake settlements in Maryland and Virginia, it will be their divergence from this general pattern that begs historical explanation.

*   *   *

Housewrights in the South used all but a few of the earthfast technologies known in seventeenth-century America. Their skills included puncheon, palisade, and cratchet building (most prevalent in the earliest Virginia settlements), log houses and frame buildings on blocks (increasingly common during the second half of the seventeenth century), and hole-set structures with and without interrupted sills (predominant throughout the seventeenth century and well into the next). Beyond that it is hard to generalize. While the most primitive structures tend to be among the earliest—Kingsmill Tenement I and cabins at the Maine for example—they have their equally early opposites in the ground-standing, silled house at Flowerdew Hundred and Col. Thomas Pettus's commodious and orderly farmstead at Littletown Plantation (fig. 9). Likewise it is tempting to interpret Cedar Park as representing the sophistication that some hole-set buildings had attained by the end of the seventeenth century. But that ignores the fact that many others still resemble the merchant's dwelling in Stafford County that was described as a "Shell of a house without Chimneys or particion and not one tittle of workmanship about it more than a Tobacco house work" (again, that allusion to barns).[66] Men's individual preferences and their personal wherewithal figured more in their choice of imper-

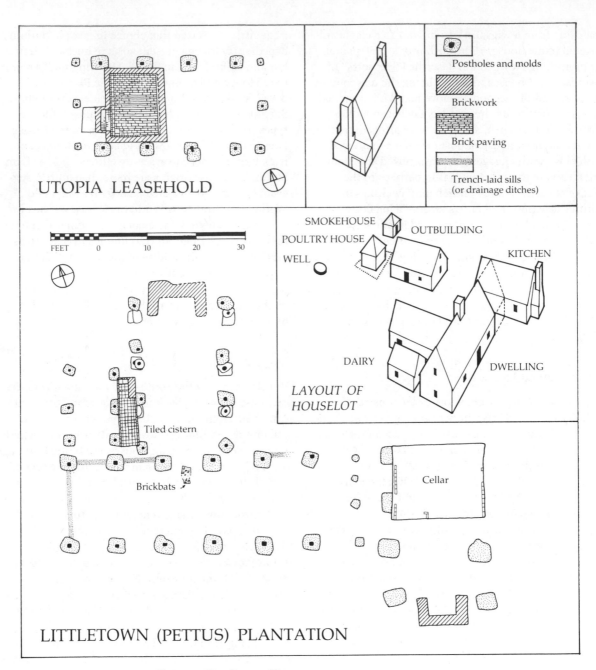

UTOPIA LEASEHOLD

Postholes and molds

Brickwork

Brick paving

Trench-laid sills
(or drainage ditches)

SMOKEHOUSE
POULTRY HOUSE
WELL
OUTBUILDING
KITCHEN
DAIRY
DWELLING

LAYOUT OF
HOUSELOT

FEET 0 10 20 30

Tiled cistern

Brickbats

Cellar

LITTLETOWN (PETTUS) PLANTATION

Fig. 9. Later structures at Kingsmill, James City County, Virginia. Colonel Thomas Pettus's plantation house complex was built and occupied ca. 1640–90; the outlying farmstead, Utopia, ca. 1660–1710. (Drawing by Shearon Vaughn and Cary Carson.)

manent building techniques, it appears, than in advances in the state of the art.

What all earthfast structures had in common were certain features that set them as "ordinary Virginia houses" apart from those "substantial good" dwellings that contemporaries referred to as "great houses," not necessarily brick, but, at a minimum, "English framed." Clearly they perceived and understood a difference, one that left prospective builders with a choice to make. Before exploring why planters in Maryland and Virginia made do for so long with second-best buildings in preference to those they regarded as affording more "comfortable [and] commodious accommodations," we first need to know in what respects the Virginia house was inferior.[67]

To speak merely of posts buried in holes in the ground can leave the wrong impressions. Earthfast building was perishable building, no doubt about it, but not all hole-set posts and blocks were equally vulnerable. It was not necessarily a contradiction in terms to talk of a "good Strong Substantial Virginia Built house."[68] Seventeenth-century carpenters gave careful attention to the preservation qualities of various woods, as had the Indians, whose lore in this matter Europeans heeded.[69] Both cultures chose those woods that experience showed were longest lasting. Sassafras, black locust, red cedar, and chestnut were known to be "very durable and lasting" and so were preferred, as one writer said of sassafras, "for Bowls, Timbers, Posts for Houses, and other Things that require standing in the Ground."[70] Black locust proved to be the favorite.[71] It was plentiful, and, if one can believe William Fitzhugh, who described a locust fence around an orchard on his Potomac River plantation, it was "as durable as most brick walls." Indeed by his reckoning, some heavier "locust Punchens," which "pallizado'd in" his yard, were actually "more lasting than any of our bricks."[72] Whether this was literally true, his and his contemporaries' savvy about the best woods for earthfast building has been borne out by modern experimentation. Cedar and black-locust fence posts tested by the Forestry Department at the University of Missouri were still going strong after 18 years (the conclusion of the test period). Sassafras was serviceable for 14. The oaks, normally as much a staple in America as in England, fared poorly, white oak failing after 12½ years and red and black oak lasting scarcely 3.[73] Charring the butts beforehand extended their serviceable life only marginally (four months on average), belying the benefits of a treatment prescribed in builders' handbooks and practiced by housewrights and barn builders in the Chesapeake colonies. The hardiest woods used for hole-set posts may sometimes have endured a great deal longer. The builder of Cedar Park felled the cedar trees nearby for his earthfast posts and interrupted sills and selected black locust for the sleepers; otherwise the frame is mostly oak. The sleepers are still in use after nearly three hun-

dred years; the posts and sills resisted decay for maybe fifty years, until the house was encased and underpinned with brickwork (inside of which some posts are perfectly sound today, including the butts).

Most hole-set structures were not so massively built, and force of habit may have disposed many builders to use oak regardless. Certainly archaeologists find over and over again that hole-set uprights had to be repaired and replaced periodically if they were to outlast their expected life span of a decade or so.[74] In the long run these buildings proved to be less durable—more impermanent if you will—than houses fully framed and set up on waterproof foundations. Many homesteaders expected no more; they had in mind to build better eventually anyway. But we must also entertain the possibility that others may have questioned that assumption, perhaps increasingly so as the seventeenth century wore on. The long run, after all, is something we are able to appreciate and even gain a sense of only in retrospect. The virtues we see in buildings able to last three centuries may have counted for nothing among many prospective builders in the seventeenth century for whom the short run was plenty long enough, either because they planned to replace their make-do houses regardless or because they planned not to, having learned to choose decay-resistant materials and make minimal repairs that could keep them standing in tolerable condition for thirty, forty, fifty years or more. To those of either persuasion, impermanence may have been a largely irrelevant consideration, and some may have come to regard posts in the ground as an acceptable, and less expensive, alternative to brick foundations no matter how everlasting.

Good enough, however, did not make such buildings "fair framed English houses." Nor were hole-set posts the only concession to economy. Those built with earthfast sills (or none at all) and earthen floors lowered costs by requiring less carpentry. Wooden chimneys[75] saved labor by eliminating any need to make brick. But the Virginia house was not merely a conventional building reduced to basics, not a standard box frame from which all frills had been stripped to provide affordable low-income housing for the poorer sort. Rather this primitive or archaic or impermanent vernacular architecture had traditions of its own, doubtless intermingled at many points in its development with the more familiar permanent building traditions in England and America, but in no oversimple sense a poor man's imitation of superior vernacular architecture. Throughout the colonial period and beyond impermanent buildings could be found alongside the more durable kind and, moreover, were probably built by poor and not so poor alike wherever special needs or circumstances dictated.[76]

The Virginia house is a case in point. Its origins can be traced to a little-known, archaic (but not earthfast), timber-frame tradition still practiced in southwestern England in the seventeenth century.[77] One among several primitive building types brought presumably from various parts of England to the Chesapeake region, it proved unusually adaptable to planters' requirements for a simplified, economical system of framing that minimized joinery and took full advantage of the structural quality of riven clapboards. The English prototype was essentially a reverse-assembled frame. Although standard wall plates occurred in modified versions, the salient feature was tie beams that extended beyond the wall lines and supported the principal rafters entirely independent of the posts. By thus effectively disjoining the wall frame from the frame of the roof, it avoided the complicated joinery necessary in buildings of normal assembly where plates, beams, and rafters all came together on each post. A carpenter had to know only two joints to build this more primitive structure, a straightforward mortise-and-tenon and variations on a lap joint. Chesapeake builders simplified it further (see fig. 3). By the third quarter of the seventeenth century, and maybe earlier, they had rediscovered the trussed-rafter roof, a roof composed entirely of collared common rafters. Their use of it appears to be a case of independent invention prompted by the discovery that short riven-oak or riven-chestnut clapboards nailed directly to the rafters lent an entire roof frame most of the longitudinal rigidity it needed. Wind-braces sometimes helped stiffen it; but with or without them, a light, tight covering of clapboards replaced the need for a heavily framed roof of principal rafters and purlins.[78] A lighter roof also simplified the problem of marrying it to the walls below. Unlike principal rafters, which concentrated the weight of a roof directly on the posts, common-rafter roofs distributed the burden evenly. Builders of Virginia houses capitalized on that inherent mechanical advantage by providing a tie beam for every pair of rafters (thereby also eliminating the many-jointed sum-

mer beams and common joists). Tie beams spaced uniformly every twenty to thirty inches along the whole length of a building were easily notched over (occasionally with a lap dovetail) and pinned down into the wall plates without regard to post positions. Each rafter couple was either mortised and tenoned to its tie beam or, simpler still, lapped over and nailed to a secondary plate. This member, called a "false plate" or "raising piece" by the Chesapeake builders who made it a virtual hallmark of their work, was borrowed from the same parent English prototype. In buildings of reverse assembly, it ran along the upper end of the tie beams and acted as the wall plate until the introduction of post-connected plates made it redundant. American builders retained it and eventually had the bright idea to tilt it forty-five degrees so that the common rafters could be hitched over its upper edge with barely a hatchet-made notch and a nail or two to hold them in place. Scantling for the rafters, collars, and false plates was sometimes split to size (like fence rails), other times hewn from small stock, but seldom sawn, since that was time-consuming and to be avoided where economy was the aim.[79]

The whole concoction was truly a made dish of things borrowed and things invented. We recognize some of its ingredients owing to the fortunate survival of a few archaic buildings in England. There must have been other influences that we can only guess at. Was, for instance, the technique of using clapboards as structural sheathing employed first in very primitive puncheon buildings (whose frames may have needed additional stiffening) and only afterward appropriated to "ordinary beginners" houses? Were multiple tie beams adopted from cratchet building? What does seem clear is that archaeologists and architectural historians must search among such recondite folkways as these for the real origins of vernacular architecture in the southern colonies. The Virginia house, however outlandish it appears to modern English eyes, had ancestors and even living relations back home to no less extent than those vernacular buildings whose genealogies are readily traced through generations of standing structures. Impermanent buildings merely descended from a different lineage, although ultimately, back beyond the "vernacular threshold," English archaeologists are beginning to find some common progenitors.

Americans must be content to affirm that seventeenth-century builders still practiced a variety of permanent and impermanent building techniques and chose whichever best suited their particular needs. Southerners built some structures in simple imitation of those left behind in England. Others they tinkered and dabbled with until, finally, they had custom made an impermanent structure that was the perfect accompaniment to a planter's special circumstances and way of life. They acknowledged its continuing utility by building and rebuilding it until it became almost second nature. But their acceptance of it was grudging. Needing it did not mean they had to like it. Its rotting posts and gray, unpainted clapboard walls and roofs were nagging reminders to many that their fondest aspirations remained unfulfilled.[80] We know because their own words betray their discontent. "The poverty of the countrey and want of necessaries here will not admitt a possibilitie to erect other then such houses as wee frequently inhabit," said their laws in 1647; or again in 1662, "our ability [is] not extending to build stronger" than "a house after the forme of a Virginia house."[81] A century later apologists were still complaining that, as run-of-the-mill farmhouses went, it was "impossible to devise things more ugly, uncomfortable, and happily more perishable."[82]

Historians ought to find it reassuring to hear southerners express the familiar hopes of homesteaders elsewhere for pretty, comfortable, and *im*perishable houses even though in practice they had good reasons to build otherwise. It helps narrow down the range of explanations for their choice by discounting the suggestion that some basic flaw in the southern character accounted for the region's long delay in achieving the degree of settledness that other colonists reached after only a generation or two. It directs attention instead to external circumstances that thwarted the ambition of ordinary Virginia and Maryland planters to build farmsteads that were a credit to themselves and an asset to their children. As we turn now to inquire into the nature of the considerations that weighed in a planter's decision to repair an old post-in-the-ground building or replace it with another no better, we have an opportunity rare for historians and archaeologists to peer inside the minds of people whose circumstances had brought them to that cultural divide we call the vernacular threshold. Those who crossed it and built an enduring architecture have understandably received more scholarly at-

tention than those who are the subject of this essay, the men and women who took stock of their needs and deemed them better served by an older, more rudimentary tradition of material culture.

Interpretation

Timing is critical to understanding the impetus to intensive rebuilding. Dates were the starting point for W. G. Hoskins when he formulated his "great rebuilding" thesis, and dates have been the matter most debated in reassessments of his work.[83] Timing also has a corollary in another consideration that deserves serious attention, the duration of the rebuilding process. The shorter or longer period of years it takes for a people to cross the vernacular threshold can have much to do with the manner of building that they eventually adopt. To put it another way, the longer that traditions of impermanent and permanent vernacular building coexist the more the former is likely to bequeath an inheritance directly to the latter.

New England's great rebuilding—its first one—was accomplished in the space of the five or six decades immediately following the settlement of Massachusetts in 1630. As early as midcentury settlers there could wonder that "the Lord hath been pleased to turn all the wigwams, huts, and hovels the English dwelt in at their first coming into orderly, fair, and well-built houses, well furnished many of them, together with Orchards filled with goodly fruit trees and gardens with variety of flowers."[84] Timber-framed houses were so much the rule by the turn of the century that a Boston woman traveling through the Narragansett country in 1704 could be surprised on coming upon a windowless, floorless cottage "suported with shores [meaning stakes, probably puncheons] enclosed with Clapboards laid on Lengthways." In all her experience, she confessed, that "little Hutt was one of the wretchedest I ever saw a habitation for human creatures."[85]

Modern scholarship confirms the implication of her remarks; primitively framed dwellings had been steadily replaced throughout the seventeenth century in New England to such an extent that those few that lasted past 1700 were oddities exciting curiosity. A recent study of vernacular buildings in Massachusetts has identified fully 10 extant houses built before 1660, another 61 before 1700, and over 100 in the period 1701–25, for a total of 257 known First Period houses in that one former colony alone (including 83 undocumented structures assigned to the period on stylistic grounds).[86] Others from northern New England, Rhode Island, and Connecticut add to their numbers. Most are timber framed, a few brick or stone, but all without exception would qualify as "orderly, fair, and well-built." As the promotional literature promised, homestead housing was punctually replaced in New England by people who not only were accustomed to higher standards in the English villages they came from but also whose circumstances in America were such that it made good sense to build soundly as soon as they were able. The process was a simple one of substitution.[87] The primitive, barnlike, but thoroughly English structures that immigrant builders resorted to for the purpose of launching their American plantations were replaced by thoroughly English houses of a very different kind—fully carpentered, timber-framed houses in keeping with New Englanders' view of their prospects for the future. Used for dwellings for so short a time, the technology of primitive building had almost no opportunity to modify the traditions of permanent vernacular architecture.[88] Consequently, surviving vernacular buildings in New England closely resemble their English counterparts.[89]

The experience of planters in Maryland and Virginia was very different. If the same two indicators—timing and duration—are applied, the late commencement of a general rebuilding throughout the region and its extreme prolongation stand in marked contrast to New England. In the South no buildings whatsoever survive from the first half of the seventeenth century despite the region's greater age, size, population, and prosperity. That is not to deny that no one built well. Excavations at Mathews Manor and Jamestown in Virginia and at St. John's in St. Mary's City, Maryland, have brought to light the foundations of some fairly substantial brick- and timber-framed dwellings, usually built (where the owners are known) by officials and other prominent citizens.[90] One of their kind, writing to Lord Baltimore in 1638, explained one reason for a colony's leaders to build well. He had under construction a house "of sawn Timber framed A story a half hygh, with a seller and Chimnies of brick," he said, "toe Encourage others toe follow my Example, for hithertoe wee Liue in Cottages."[91] Most ordinary planters were literally cottagers, but not everyone. Here and there a few lesser men managed to build "good and sufficient framed" houses too; none still stand, but they are occasionally described in building contracts. The terms almost always make specific mention of the major feature—groundsills "underpinned with bricks"—that set "framed worke" apart from the commonality of earthfast cottages.[92]

Were data available to draw a graph that showed the replacement rate for impermanent buildings in the southern colonies, the line would inch upward almost imperceptibly before 1700. A few buildings have survived from the period after 1660, but only a handful, a total of five or six from the entire region and most of those from the very end of the century or the first few years after 1700. They are far too few to tell us much of anything about the frequency of better-built houses, even among the small group of successful merchants and well-to-do planters to whom they belonged. Their significance is all the more obscured by offsetting archaeological evidence that indicates that other, equally wealthy, well-connected men were content to go on building and repairing earthfast farmsteads for decades. William Drummond, who lived on the Governor's Land near Jamestown, was one. Another was Col. Thomas Pettus (originally from Essex), a vestryman, councillor, land speculator, and builder of one of the largest post-in-the-ground domestic structures so far discovered (see fig. 9). Yet despite contradictions in the evidence, our imaginary replacement curve probably ought to show a blip or two near the close of the century, when a Frenchman traveling through Virginia in 1687 noted in his journal that "they have started making bricks in quantities, and I have seen several houses where the walls were entirely made of them."[93] This flurry of new construction continued, warranting by 1705 Robert Beverley's observation that "private buildings are of late very much improved," notably, he had to add in qualification, those of "several Gentlemen" who had recently "built themselves large Brick Houses."[94] Fifty years after rebuilding had transformed New England, the Chesapeake grandees were only getting started.

Less affluent neighbors had longer to wait. One effect of the recent archaeological excavations in the region has been to open historians' eyes to the fact that most plantation houses were small, poorly built, frequently repaired, and often rebuilt no better than before throughout the seventeenth century and much of the next. Typical was the complaint of planters living in the neighborhood of Charles City, Virginia, who reported that they were rebuilding "such houses as [they had] before and in them lived with continual repairs, and buildinge new where the old failed."[95] In rural localities housewrights could work for months and never set hand to a single "framed or English built" house as late as the 1690s, although, starting about then, impermanent buildings raised on blocks began to compete with hole-set framed houses.[96]

Small, fully framed dwellings, the kind that can last 250 years, only began to appear with some frequency in the 1710s, 1720s, and 1730s, the first period from which perhaps one hundred or more buildings survive. They include large houses in disproportionate number, as would be expected, but also a smattering of one-room dwellings. Consequently, our replacement curve should ascend more steeply after about 1720, but its rise should show only a steady, gradual improvement, no precipitous climb, for in fact primitive, impermanent, even earthfast, building continued in strength for years to come. Not until the 1740s, for example, were "post in the ground" and "bastard frame" buildings so uncommon on the upper eastern shore of Maryland that they were singled out for special mention in orphans court valuations, where they were sometimes further denigrated by the term *old-fashioned*.[97] Even twenty-five years later there were still houses in that neighborhood with open halls, some with chimneys, but others no doubt as rudimentary as the one that had "a little hole in ye roof to let out ye smoak."[98] Across the bay in Anne Arundel County the excavation of Middle Plantation (figs. 10, 11, 12) has dramatically demonstrated that whole farmsteads—houses, barns, kitchens, quarters, dairies, coolers, meat houses, root cellars, hen coops, everything—were continuously built and rebuilt through the middle of the century in a fashion that left behind archaeological evidence no more substantial than the site's fence-post holes and grave pits. Intensive rebuilding was delayed until after 1800 in the region's poorest districts—such backwaters as St. Mary's County, Maryland, parts of southside Virginia, and Albemarle Sound, North Carolina.[99] At the head of the bay in nearby Delaware "mud houses" lingered on to be recorded by tax assessors until the 1810s.[100] In short, throughout the Chesapeake region the replacement of homestead housing was slow to start and was then attenuated and prolonged for more than a century until it was finally subsumed in the first truly nationwide rebuilding of the early nineteenth century. Only at that point—1820–50—would trend lines for New England and the Old South finally converge.

Where hardy strains of impermanent architecture persevered for the better part of two centuries in the South, they had ample opportunity to exert a formative influence on the growth of the region's lasting vernacular building traditions. True, there were cases where homestead structures were replaced in good time by strictly English-framed buildings. Such cases of simple substitution would more likely have occurred, we expect, earlier rather than later in the seventeenth century—that is, before southern housewrights began improvising on impermanent building types from England to create the indigenous impermanent Virginia house previously described. Certainly every one of the few surviving houses from the late seventeenth and early eighteenth centuries, whether brick built or framed on sills, incorporates one or more features taken over from the Virginia house: its common-rafter roof frame, its system of tie beams and false plates, its clapboards used as structural elements, and so on. Indeed the magnitude of the southern builder's debt to the region's impermanent architectural tradition is only fully appreciated by looking ahead at the timber-framed house type that became absolutely standard and universal in the eighteenth century throughout Maryland, Virginia, the Carolinas, and eventually all those trans-Appalachian states settled by migrants from the tidewater South.[101] Virtually every member of its frame, save the continuous groundsills, can be traced back a hundred years or more to origins in the Virginia house.

The practice of repairing this and replacing that, when multiplied innumerable times over many years, in fact became the process by which southern architecture was transformed. The set of accounts that records the repeated renovations to a courthouse built in 1674 in Charles County, Maryland (fig. 13), reveals not only how specific buildings could be coaxed across the vernacular threshold but how thoroughly by the end of the seventeenth century an archaic building technology had become mainstream tradition. Eventually its vulnerable earthfast features—hole-set posts and studs and ground-laid

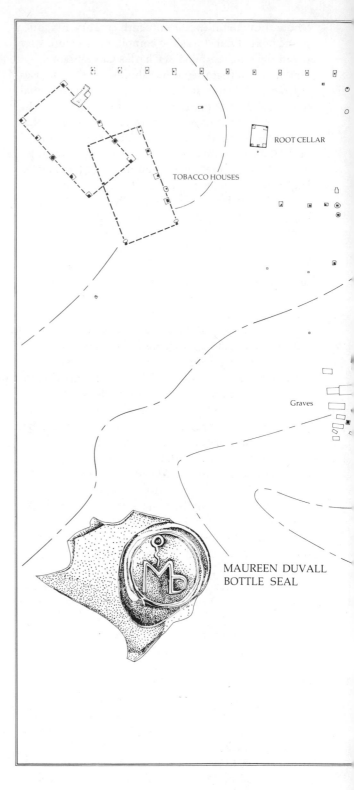

Fig. 10. Archaeological site plan of Middle Plantation, Anne Arundel County, Maryland, showing a merchant-planter's seventeenth-century farmstead overlain by an eighteenth-century tenement. (Drawing by William Deopkins, Garry Wheeler Stone, and Chinh Hoang.)

ROOT CELLAR

TOBACCO HOUSES

Graves

MAUREEN DUVALL
BOTTLE SEAL

sills—were winnowed out and eliminated in preference to wooden blocks, brick piers, and, finally, full foundations. But, for a considerable time, posts in the ground were acceptable to many builders of houses otherwise as strongly constructed as Cedar Park, because the two traditions had so thoroughly intermingled and because the process of rebuilding was so thoroughly an evolutionary one.

Archaeological evidence that forms such an unusual pattern of cultural development raises two important historical questions. Why were immigrants to the Chesapeake colonies so much slower than settlers elsewhere to establish an enduring material culture, and, when once a few began, what circumstances retarded its general acceptance? Were there chronic disabilities that plagued southern society, or, despite their protests to the contrary, were southerners really content to live from hand to mouth?

Indifference—a kind of cultural malaise—is an appealing explanation for some men's circumstances. Edmund Morgan has described Virginia in the 1620s as a boom country, a time and a place when the extraordinarily high price of tobacco produced a mining-camp mentality.[102] Planters were prospectors who came to strike it rich and looked on Virginia "not as a place of Habitacion but onely of a short sojourninge."[103] He finds the governing council of the Virginia Company complaining in 1626 that fortune seekers cared only for "a present Cropp, and their hastie retourne."[104] Easy come, easy go was the prevailing mood. Often as not planters gambled or drank away the profits from their yearly crop or squandered them on frippery like the "fresh flaming silkes" reportedly worn by the cow keeper at Jamestown or a collier's wife's "rough beaver hatt with a faire hatteband, and a silken suite therto correspondent."[105] Such people, the argument goes, had little use for well-built houses and sturdy farm buildings. Stopping places only, boom towns are shantytowns the world over. The archaeological record has to be stretched to fit this interpretation. Apart from some jewelry and fragments of gold and silver thread used to trim clothing, the artifacts recovered from sites of

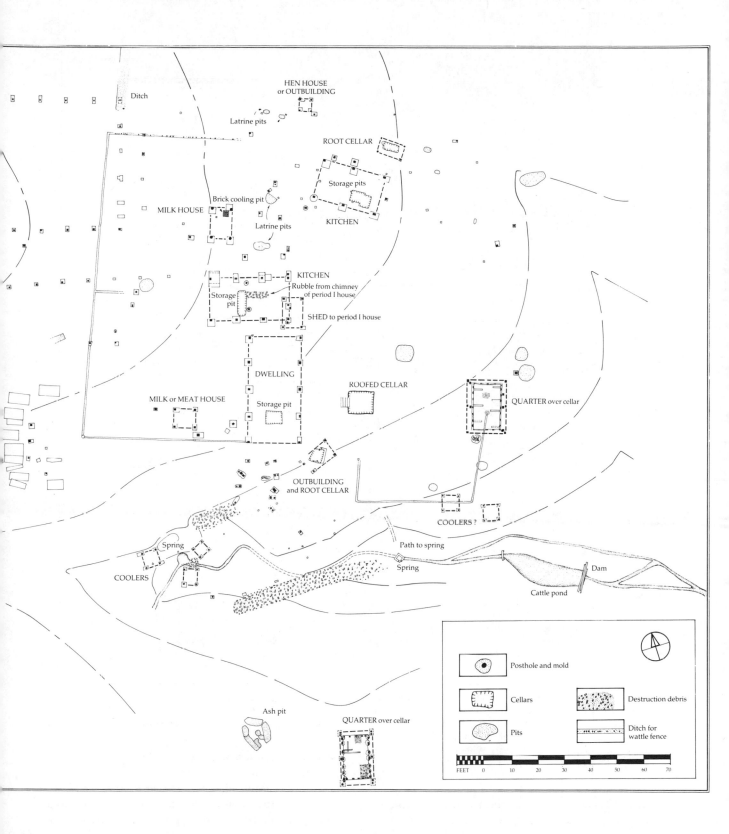

HEN HOUSE
or OUTBUILDING

Ditch

Latrine pits

ROOT CELLAR

Brick cooling pit

Storage pits

MILK HOUSE

Latrine pits

KITCHEN

KITCHEN

Rubble from chimney
of period I house

Storage
pit

SHED to period I house

DWELLING

ROOFED CELLAR

MILK or MEAT HOUSE

Storage pit

QUARTER over cellar

OUTBUILDING
and ROOT CELLAR

COOLERS ?

Path to spring

Spring

Spring

Dam

COOLERS

Cattle pond

Ash pit

QUARTER over cellar

Posthole and mold

Cellars

Destruction debris

Pits

Ditch for
wattle fence

FEET   0   10   20   30   40   50   60   70

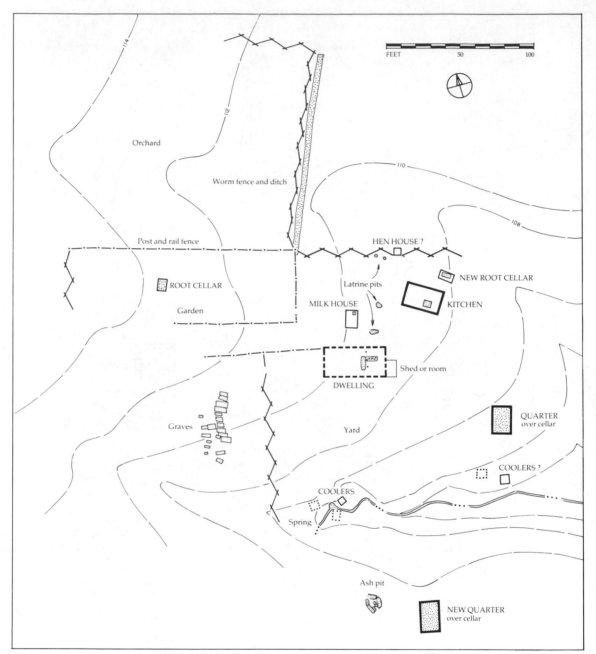

FEET 50 100

Orchard

Worm fence and ditch

Post and rail fence

HEN HOUSE?

NEW ROOT CELLAR

ROOT CELLAR

Latrine pits

MILK HOUSE

KITCHEN

Garden

DWELLING

Shed or room

Graves

Yard

QUARTER
over cellar

COOLERS?

COOLERS

Spring

Ash pit

NEW QUARTER
over cellar

Fig. 11. Conjectural reconstruction of Middle Plantation, Anne Arundel County, Maryland, ca. 1695–1700. The garden palings shown are from two different periods. Only those rail fences are shown whose locations are implied by other features. (Drawing by Garry Wheeler Stone and Chinh Hoang.)

the 1610s and 1620s do not bear witness to Virginia's sottish ways and tawdry vices. The most that can be said is that some sites present a notable contrast between the quantity and quality of discarded artifacts and the flimsiness of associated dwellings, barns, outbuildings, and enclosures.[106]

A more serious objection is that Morgan's boom-town hypothesis lays a false scent for the period as a whole. While tobacco mania may have had a contrib-

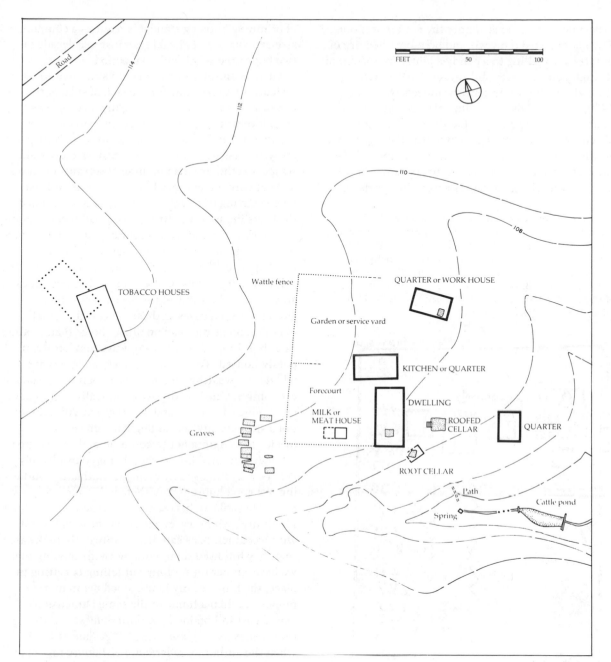

Fig. 12. Conjectural reconstruction of Middle Plantation, Anne Arundel County, Maryland, ca. 1730–35. (Drawing by Garry Wheeler Stone and Chinh Hoang.)

uting effect in encouraging construction of ramshackle housing during the second decade of the century, as an explanation it fails to fit the known facts. First, historians cannot substantiate the complaint about opportunists returning to England with tobacco fortunes salted away. No doubt individual cases can be found to show that some Virginia planters engaged in profit taking in the manner of cane planters on the sugar islands, but the bulk of evidence is in the other direction. Immigrants to the mainland colonies came to stay.

Beyond that, there is simply the matter of timing. The boom lasted ten years and no more, the price of best tobacco falling to a penny a pound by 1630 from its high point of three shillings in 1619.[107] Yet, throughout the whole century, indeed, well past 1750, the methods of building plainer sorts of farmhouses and barns changed hardly at all. As far as archaeologists can tell, the eighteenth-century builders at Middle Plantation, for instance, used most of the same techniques employed a century earlier in the boom towns along the James River. The persistence

Fig. 13. A surveyor's plat of 1697 showing the Charles County, Maryland, courthouse. The chimney is shown in its first location. Nearby are "P[hilip] L[ynes's] ordinary," two outhouses, and a "Parcell ould peach Trees" enclosed in a worm rail fence. (Reprinted from Margaret Brown Klapthor and Paul Dennis Brown, *A History of Charles County, Maryland, Written in Its Tercentenary Year of 1958* [La Plata, Md., 1958], facing p. 22.)

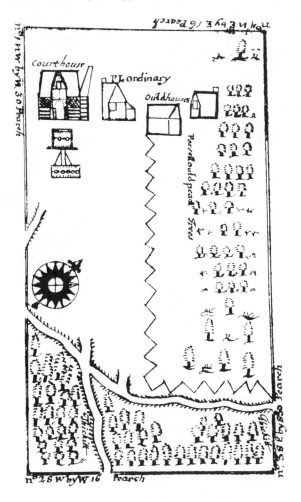

of primitive housing standards requires a comprehensive explanation applicable not just to a decade or two but to the whole colonial period.

There is another way to make a system of tobacco agriculture responsible for the lack of substantial housing. Tobacco was an unusually labor-intensive crop. It returned profits in direct proportion to the number of hands that a planter employed. New planters were wise to spend as much cash as they could scrape together on the purchase of servants or slaves and cut corners on capital improvements, at least when starting out. Unfortunately, no one itemized the costs incurred in setting up a small tobacco plantation until the eighteenth century, but there are probate inventories from the mid-seventeenth century that appraise "House and Plantacion" at less than the value of a single cow or at a figure only three times greater than the value of the decedent's suit of clothes.[108] Such cases as these suggest that small planters sometimes had no other choice than to allocate their limited resources in ways that left them poorly housed. They could scarcely do otherwise when even wealthy men found compelling reasons to economize. One was the astronomically high cost of employing carpenters and bricklayers. William Fitzhugh strongly advised an English correspondent headed for Virginia not to count on building "a great or English framed house, for labor is so intolerably dear & workmen so idle & negligent that the building of a good house to you there will seem insupportable." He spoke of his own recent experience. "When I built my own house & agreed as cheap as I could with workmen & as carefully & diligently took care that they followed their work, notwithstanding that we have timber for nothing but felling & getting in place, the frame of my house stood me in more money . . . than a frame of the same Dimensions would cost in London *by a third at least . . . & near three times as long preparing.*"[109] As late as 1775, when the author of *American Husbandry* tallied up the cost of settling a tobacco plantation in Virginia, the purchase price of twenty Negro field hands exceeded by five times the expense of building the "house, offices, and tobacco-house."[110]

Here again is the homesteader, living frugally and husbanding his resources in hopes of bountiful harvests and good markets. But if he were so unlucky as to be starting out in the third quarter of the seventeenth century, when tobacco prices began their thirty- to forty-year slide into the depths of depression, then the homesteader might have found himself stalled and trapped at a stage that other men in happier times had quickly passed through. Those who a few years earlier had looked forward to becoming small freeholders were increasingly likely to end up as tenants after 1680.[111] Tenancy encouraged the proliferation of impermanent buildings for reasons that made sense to both leaseholders and landlords. One of the latter, Fitzhugh, believed no sensible landowner would provide accommodations for tenants, there being many, he explained, who "for a seven year's Lease will build themselves a convenient dwelling & other necessary houses & be obliged at the expiration of their time to leave all in good repair." If anyone were foolish enough to build "an ordinary Virginia house" for lease to tenants, "it [would] be some Charge & no profit," he predicted, "& at the expiration of [the] tenant's time, the plantation [would] not be in better order than the way before proposed."[112] All things considered and given the state of the economy in Maryland and Virginia in the final decades of the seventeenth century, the absence of surviving buildings from that period should come as no surprise, nor should the evidence that many tenants and small freeholders spent those years patching, repairing, and shoring up dilapidated structures that had long since outlived their expected usefulness.

Tobacco madness in the 1620s and economic stagnation after 1680 were not the only obstacles to a settled way of life in the South. Disease and an abnormally high mortality rate among immigrants were fundamental sources of social instability. Figures alone tell the grim story. Male immigrants who lived to celebrate their twenty-second birthdays were already middle-aged. Seventeen percent of them would be dead before they were thirty, 41 percent before the age of forty, and 70 percent before fifty.[113] In contrast, a boy who reached his majority in New England in the same middle decades of the century could expect to live another fifty years; forty for those who grew up in rural England.[114] Contemporaries called the killer "seasoning," a process of adjusting to the Chesapeake climate in which malaria left its victims sickly and susceptible to other, fatal illnesses.[115]

The effect on family life was devastating. Few children grew up in the care of both their natural parents. Two of every three lost either a mother or a father before coming of age; one of three lost both. Orphans were legion; orphans and guardians and stepparents and half brothers and sisters sometimes all lived under one roof.[116] Fathers had no assurance that the wealth they accumulated would be passed on to their heirs in ways they could anticipate. Widows remarried, estates were broken up, and guardians not uncommonly despoiled their wards' inheritances. The law permitted the sale of orphans' property to preserve the value of their assets, but such action effectively dispossessed them of their fathers' farmsteads.[117] These were excellent reasons *not* to plan too far ahead or build things to last. Better to put profits back into production and spend disposable income on material comforts that could be enjoyed immediately. Planters 300 years ago may have made such choices deliberately. If so, their trash pits would yield just what archaeologists have found on most early sites in Maryland and Virginia, a wealth of utensils used for eating, drinking, and storing food, articles of apparel and personal adornment, farm tools, weapons, and even such architectural frills as delft fireplace tiles and fancy casement windows, all in association with buildings guaranteed to last a lifetime—a planter's lifetime—and not much more.

Still and all, it must have been human nature for healthy people to suppose that they would continue to be the lucky ones, that their lives would be spared. The survivors looked forward no doubt to improving their housing standards as soon as circumstances allowed. But, unfortunately, circumstances had a way of not allowing, not after 1680, because the market for tobacco went bad, and generally not throughout the period as a whole, because for many men and women both luck and life ran out. Fathers and mothers died, family assets were dispersed, old buildings fell hopelessly into disrepair, plantations were sold or neglected or exploited or simply minimally maintained by guardians, and years later the returning orphan sons or daughters had to begin all over again by building more temporary structures. Tenants came, built cheaply, and went away again. Freeholders stayed longer, but exceedingly high building costs encouraged repairs as long as possible and discouraged genuine improvements when finally irretrievably dilapidated structures had to be replaced. In short, the bay country was a perpetual frontier. Each generation was a homesteader generation; each frequently had to start from scratch.

The ill effects of an agriculture that required a continual supply of new recruits to replace the laborers who fell victim to seasoning held sway in the region as long as tobacco remained the exclusive market crop. The long depression after 1680, by breaking the labor-replacement cycle, set in train the events that eventually brought relief.[118] Low prices for the staple crop meant tight credit for planters, and that quickly stanched the flow of servants from England, Wales, and Ireland. The hardier, native-born population was thus given time to recover a more normal balance between the sexes, which in turn encouraged the formation of more numerous and longer-lasting families. Natural growth in the native population had already begun in the older settled areas, but sharply reduced numbers of British immigrants in the last decades of the century and their displacement by African slaves when the traffic in servants resumed hastened the ascendancy of a generation of colonists American born and bred.[119] As life assumed a more normal, settled character, planters learned to place greater confidence in the hope that the accumulated fruits of their labors could and would be handed down to their descendants.

All benefited from the general tendency toward demographic equilibrium and social stability, but not all at once. Wealthy men with large estates and many slaves, being best able to ride out hard times, were also best prepared to recover their fortunes first when tobacco prices improved.[120] These were the "Gentlemen" whose "large Brick Houses," newly built, received Robert Beverley's commendations in 1705. Homegrown patricians, they ruled their counties, married their cousins, and founded parochial dynasties that delighted in building architectural monuments to their self-esteem and their belief in a posterity. Others followed their lead as prosperity returned after 1715, with the result, already noted in regard to the region as a whole, that durable buildings of all sizes began to appear more frequently from the second quarter of the eighteenth century onward. Yet it must also be said that such buildings were far from commonplace before the 1780s; nor was their frequency everywhere uniform from one part of the Chesapeake to another. Unlike the northern colonies, where, once the process of replacing homestead housing began, impermanent buildings vanished almost completely from the older, longest-settled regions within a generation or two, rebuilding in Maryland and Virginia proceeded slowly and unevenly throughout the eighteenth century.

Historians searching for a working hypothesis to explain so protracted a course of development may find it useful to approach the problem as would a writer of detective fiction. Having established that demographic recovery provided a widespread *opportunity* to improve standards of living, the historical investigator must go on to prove that planters in the region had both a *means* and a *motive*. There is no question on either score so far as the great planters are concerned. But what of middling-sized, 350-acre planters, smaller freeholders, and even tenant farmers—the people whose numbers sustain vernacular traditions and in whom resides the collective genius of folk material culture?

The ability to replace inferior, worn-out buildings with better, longer-lasting ones varied from place to place and period to period. How and why requires a closer look at the behavior of subregional microeconomies in the period following the great end-of-the-century depression. The long years of unprofitable tobacco sales had forced many smaller operators to diversify their economic activities. Typically they resorted to by-employments, grew larger food crops, and made at home the manufactured goods—chiefly cloth and shoes—that they had previously purchased from abroad with income from the sale of the staple. The tobacco market's recovery in the 1710s brought a mixed response from smaller planters.[121] In a few localities they never went back to growing the crop, having developed in the meantime lucrative trades in specialized local products. The more common practice was to take up planting again but to supplement tobacco with other cash crops and exports. Meat, corn, wheat, fruits and vegetables, dairy products, firewood, naval stores, shingles, and staves found expanding markets in the islands, in the region's growing towns and cities, and in a hungry population that multiplied twelvefold in the hundred years ending in 1800. By that date, mixed farming and the craft activities needed to support it had replaced the region's heavy dependence on tobacco everywhere except in southern Maryland and southside Virginia.

While systematic surveys of vernacular architecture in the region are nowhere as advanced as studies of its local economies, county-by-county inventories of historic structures compiled by state preservation agencies in Maryland and in Virginia are now sufficiently numerous to be used to draw a map that shows the distribution of surviving buildings in several localities on both sides of the bay (fig. 14).[122] An intelligible pattern emerges at once, one that suggests how smaller planters acquired the means to take advantage of their brighter prospects after 1700. Incomplete as the architectural evidence still is, there is a pronounced correlation between areas and even neighborhoods that shifted to a diversified economy and the first appearance in those places of improved vernacular buildings.

Examples are too numerous to be explained as mere coincidence. Take Lower Norfolk County, Virginia, for instance (fig. 14, no. 1). Its planters gave up tobacco in the middle 1680s never to plant it again in marketable quantities. Between 1700 and the 1720s they turned overwhelmingly to the cultivation of cereal grains, mostly corn, but in the meantime they had avoided the worst rigors of depression by developing a brisk island trade in tar, pitch, and pork. It is surely significant that the earliest small brick houses in Virginia, buildings of the late seventeenth and very early eighteenth centuries, are concentrated in the Lynnhaven district of Lower Norfolk (later Princess Anne) County.[123] In the same general area a one-room frame house dated 1714 still stands along the banks of the Nansemond River.[124]

Across the mouth of the bay, the lower eastern shore of Virginia also grew less and less tobacco after 1700 and none to speak of by 1740 (no. 2). It, too, is a locality that boasts not only two of Virginia's earliest timber-framed buildings, both single-unit houses built sometime between 1680 and 1720 but also, in Northampton County, an unusual abundance of small, smart, mostly one-story, brick farmhouses from the middle decades of the eighteenth century, by which time tobacco patches there had mostly been plowed into cornfields.[125]

No region demonstrates the sensitive relationship between agriculture and vernacular building better than the bay-side counties on the lower eastern shore of Maryland (no. 3). Recent research suggests that tobacco production declined after 1680 in Somerset County. It recovered again in the 1730s, strongly in Monie, Manokin, and Annemessex hundreds but only marginally on the neck of land between the Wicomico and Nanticoke rivers (the area that became Wicomico County). There (no. 4) corn began to rival the traditional staple, and by the 1750s corn sur-

pluses were probably worth more than the tobacco crop. Be that as it may—and herein lies the instructive comparison—Somerset County (the three lower hundreds) produced corn, too, actually more per acre than Wicomico farms but never in quantities that matched the value of the tobacco crop. In short, both sections engaged in mixed farming, one favoring corn, the other tobacco.[126] Yet, rebuilding in the two areas followed different courses. A chronological distribution of surviving structures in Wicomico duplicates a pattern common to other early cereal-growing regions: permanent vernacular buildings began to appear in numbers when grain production overtook the export of tobacco, and their frequency increased steadily from then to the mid-nineteenth century. Rebuilding in Somerset by contrast gathered momentum little by little throughout the eighteenth century, then suddenly boomed after 1790 for a period of thirty or forty years. In so doing, it behaved like other regions where tobacco remained the dominant export. There seems no denying that cash crops are a historian's best clue to predicting the time and the place of widespread rebuilding.

There was no cash crop to bring wealth to the subsistence farms of Worcester County, hemmed in between the Pocomoke marshes and the Atlantic beaches (no. 5). Not surprisingly Worcester is poor in surviving eighteenth-century buildings. The same can be said of swampy Dorchester farther up the shore (no. 6), and the same explanation offered.[127]

The fertile plain above the Choptank River, the upper eastern shore, followed a different course (no. 7). It became the breadbasket of the Chesapeake in this period. The shift from tobacco to wheat was under way by the 1720s on farms at the head of the bay where wagons plied back and forth to Philadelphia. Wheat superseded tobacco as the major market crop in Kent County by 1750 and was becoming a significant source of income for planters as far south as Talbot County, although many, especially those seated near convenient navigation, continued to rely chiefly on tobacco until after 1775. By the fourth quarter of the century the rapidly expanding city of Baltimore added its demand to the market for locally grown foodstuffs (no. 8). Farmers responded accordingly, so much so that what was said of Baltimore County in 1794—"wheat has turned away Tobacco; and the erection of Grist Mills and the growing of Wheat go Hand in Hand, increasing yearly everywhere"—ap-

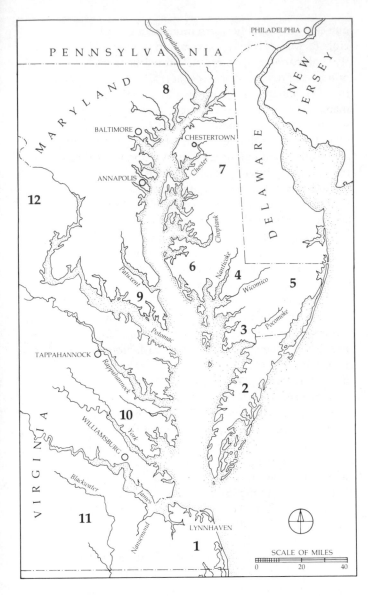

Fig. 14. Farming regions and farm building improvements in tidewater Maryland and Virginia, 1700–1800. Place names and numbered localities are identified in the text. (Drawing by Cary Carson.)

Anne's County, an area surveyed with great thoroughness, four of every five surviving eighteenth-century houses belong to the last quarter of the century and include the first extant frame houses in the county.[130] Less precise but similar numbers also hold for the upper western shore.[131]

Southern Maryland, that whole region lying between the bay and the navigable length of the Potomac, was premier tobacco country throughout the period, indeed to the Civil War (no. 9). Its planters grew just enough corn to eat and late in the century small quantities of grain to sell, but tobacco was almost as much the unchallenged cash crop in 1800 as it had been ever since the oldest part of Maryland was settled. Six early houses still stand in the area, but, even as exceptions that prove the rule, they are of limited significance considering that three of the frame structures[132] were only saved by the expedient of later encasing them inside brick walls and the single original brick dwelling[133] was the residence not of a true planter but of a wealthy merchant. The real history of rebuilding in southern Maryland is well represented by St. Mary's County. A comprehensive survey of all historic structures in the area shows even more clearly than Somerset the slight extent to which tobacco agriculture stimulated improved building standards.[134] Of more than 150 extent structures built before 1860 only four date from the early eighteenth century, not quite a score from the middle decades, and barely that number again from the last third of the century. There is no sign, in other words, of even the very gradually accelerated rate of rebuilding that the mixed economy of Somerset County sustained before the building boom that started there in the 1790s. The first burst of building activity in St. Mary's County came about ten years later. So did the first attempts at diversification, and then only successfully in the few coastal neighborhoods where broad alluvial plains provided enough tillable acreage for wheat fields. These were precisely the areas where many small, single-story, frame houses (described in the 1798 federal tax assessment) were replaced in the early 1800s by much larger, often two-story, brick dwellings. Once begun, the rebuilding continued unabated through the 1840s, its progress unaffected by the embargo on tobacco in 1808 and the crop's lackluster performance after 1820. Prices for wheat remained high throughout the period.

Farther south still, farmhouse-sized buildings on

plied generally to the northern counties on both shores.[128] Surviving vernacular buildings chart the progress of diversification from the head of the bay southward. A group of dated brick houses above Chestertown, Kent County, span the years from 1721 to the 1780s, but the greatest number record dates in the 1760s and the 1770s.[129] Below Kent in Queen the three great necks of land between the Potomac and the James (no. 10) have been neglected by scholars in proportion to their preoccupation with the celebrated mansions of the region. The absence of systematic fieldwork leaves a large hole in our distribution map, which is only poorly compensated for by the tentative observation that Virginia planters' devotion to tobacco in the area seems to have left the usual smattering of substantial brick farmhouses from the first half of the eighteenth century but virtually no small, frame houses (except perhaps around Tappahannock) until the 1770s, 1780s, and 1790s. By then investments in corn, wheat (especially in northern Virginia), and other diversified crops exceeded the commitment to tobacco with the predictable effect that rebuilding gathered force until at least the 1840s. Beyond that cautious statement nothing more can be said about improved housing standards in bay-side tidewater Virginia until reliable surveys are undertaken.

Vernacular buildings in the southern and southside counties of Virginia, except for a group of houses in the neighborhood of the Blackwater River dividing Surry from Sussex (no. 11), had received even less attention from architectural historians.[135] Like southern Maryland, Surry returned to growing tobacco after 1720 and kept up its production for as long as historians have followed the county's economic development. Surviving houses in the interior of that county are exceedingly rare even from the middle decades of the century. Finally in the 1780s and 1790s small, one- and two-room brick farmhouses made the kind of sudden appearance along the river that elsewhere heralded the advent of grain growing. If by now our hypothesis has acquired predictive powers, it can be supposed that diversification in Surry and Sussex will date from the closing years of the century.

All around the bay, then, wherever recent studies of local agricultural economies can be placed alongside surveys of vernacular architecture, a picture emerges of tobacco planters diversifying their cash crops and soon after replacing impermanent buildings with houses and barns substantial enough to have survived in considerable numbers to the present day. How mixed farming encouraged rebuilding is not yet clearly understood, but enough is known to attempt an explanation. New markets abroad and a growing population at home increased demand for wheat and flour, thereby creating opportunities for large and small producers alike, although each capitalized on them somewhat differently. The key was a farmer's access to labor and how he was able to employ it throughout the growing season. Tobacco and corn required regular attention from planting to harvest; wheat once sown was left unattended until reaping time, but then, in the space of a few critical weeks, all available hands were needed from sunup to sundown to bring in the vulnerable crop.[136] Slaveholders who owned enough land to grow wheat *and* tobacco could use their labor force to plant both and gamble that the grain would ripen by early summer after the young tobacco plants were transplanted. When the weather cooperated these larger planters got in two cash crops and two incomes with the same labor force.

Small producers could profit, too, even without owning slaves, because harvest was the only time when extra labor was needed; a man and his family could plant more acres in small grains than they themselves could harvest as long as hired hands or help from neighbors could be obtained when the ripened crop was ready to be gathered. Grain culture, therefore, opened up to small growers economic opportunities on a scale that in an exclusively tobacco economy required ownership of slaves or indentured servants.

Corn and wheat offered other advantages. They were much easier for farmers to process than tobacco, which, when cut, had to be hung, cured, taken down again, stripped, sorted, tied into hands, and packed into hogsheads. Throughout the Chesapeake wheat was efficiently threshed by horse treading, after which it, like shucked corn, was ready for milling or could be economically transported in the seed to local markets. Food crops destined for southern Europe or the West Indies were subject to many of the same hazards and expenses—and profits—of the tobacco trade. But foodstuffs sold locally or in regional trading networks spared farmers the high cost of overseas transportation, insurance, and faraway middlemen's services. Grain culture may also have lessened poorer planters' indebtedness to the storekeepers who extended them credit for essential manufactured goods as a lien against next year's crop.[137] Historians have not yet decided how tightly merchants held tobacco planters in debt, but one Marylander remembered that "as the culture of *wheat,* and the manufacturing it into *flour* travelled south-ward, the people became more happy, and independent of the British storekeepers who had kept them in debts and dependent."[138]

All in all, marketing foodstuffs was less entangling; sold locally it avoided the risks inherent in venturing a luxury crop in an unpredictable foreign market, it returned a steady, reliable annual income, and—basic to our explanation for the spate of rebuilding that finally removed most impermanent dwellings from the southern landscape—it minimized for small producers the disadvantage of not employing a large force of slave laborers. In short, corn and wheat built many modest fortunes. Profits from grain growing found their way into the pockets of even the poorest agriculturalists—tenant farmers. The dwellings of those who leased property on the proprietary manors of Maryland, when surveyed in 1767–68, were found to be smallest and meanest in southern Maryland, slightly more commodious in Kent and Baltimore counties (although still not much affected by the recent shift there to wheat production), and largest and best built on the lease lots of Monocacy Manor in Frederick County (no. 12), where wheat and rye had been major cash crops since the valley was settled in the 1740s. Not since the heyday of tobacco planting in the mid-seventeenth century had small farmers enjoyed such a favorable economic outlook. The difference this time was that, being more likely to live out their natural years and surer of an orderly inheritance, many solidified their gains and improved, not just replaced, old-fashioned homestead housing. Eighteenth-century property owners settled bequests on members of their immediate families much more often than had been the practice earlier and frequently with much greater attention to how the legacy was to descend to their children's children.[139] That more children lived to become heirs was only part of the reason; many testators now also had valuable improvements to endow them with.

Our explanation for the belated advent and long duration of the "great rebuilding" in the southern colonies has emphasized conditions largely beyond the control of individual planters. Demographic balance and social stability were, we have argued, prerequisites to the settled way of life that brought with it the opportunity to make a house a home. Even

then, normalcy and order were often insufficient in themselves to break tobacco's stranglehold on many smaller planters. Opportunity waited on means, and those means frequently were not forthcoming until still other external circumstances—new markets for new crops—enriched local agricultural economies. But why, it might be asked, did quite ordinary farmers choose to spend their profits from wheat and corn on better, not just newer, housing? Such choices imply preferences, and preferences raise questions about motives. When desire operates on a person's will causing it to act in certain ways, outside influences have been converted into intensely personal, internal impulses. Usually these are extremely difficult for historians to fathom, and this case is no exception. But the attempt is worth making, because mentalities are the real locus of cultural change. The "vernacular threshold" was a state of mind before it became an architectural reality.

Archaeologists have recently borrowed from social historians a hypothesis inspired by anthropological studies of peasant communities. It postulates that rural England and the American colonies underwent a fundamental social and psychological change, which was felt most intensely in the hundred years between 1650 and 1750. Less often explained than merely described as the transformation of "medieval folkways" into a "Georgian" or "modern world view," the interpretation lays heavy emphasis, so far as its effects on material culture are concerned, on an emergent self-awareness and a passion for self-expression.[140] They found outlet, so the argument goes, in a profusion of personal and household artifacts that displayed status and thereby increasingly conferred it. The idea is compelling not least of all because it receives reinforcement from scholars studying the same period from the different perspectives of economic and agrarian history and the history of the family. Yet, for all that, there is more that needs to be said. Like sociologists' "modernization theory," with which it has much in common, its usefulness lies chiefly in its descriptive power. In and of itself, it explains nothing. The temptation to attribute to a new and pervasive world view all the significant changes archaeologists have observed in early American material culture has to be resisted. Each case requires its own very careful demonstration and explanation.

As for impermanent architecture, this essay has

shown that it cannot simply be labeled "medieval" (although it employed some very ancient methods of construction), nor is it accurate to ascribe to its builders and users "peasant mentalities." On the contrary, as far back as southern planters can be heard expressing their sentiments about impermanent building—in the language of the statute of 1647, in Thomas Cornwaleys's observation that Maryland settlers lived in cottages, in John Smith's disparaging description of the barnlike "curiosities" at Jamestown—little more is revealed than a fine sense of expediency typical of people who found themselves in that special state of incipient economic growth that we have called homesteading. Homesteaders quickly learned that they must allocate time, energy, and resources to those activities that would contribute soonest to making a living. Once they had developed a fairly reliable livelihood and reestablished a self-sustaining family and community life, most of them expected as a matter of course to fence fields, plant orchards, breed livestock, raise barns, and build houses for the longer term. For some, we have suggested, those aspirations did not rule out such well-built, earthfast structures as Cedar Park, at least not in the seventeenth century. But if we are to take contemporaries at their word, there were always those who saw the practical advantage of buildings able to last many years without major repairs. A house or barn whose sills were raised off the ground on masonry foundations enhanced the value of a man's estate, thereby bringing a higher sale price or endowing his heirs with a richer patrimony. The desire to confer the wealth of one generation on selected beneficiaries of the next was a time-honored custom among country folk in England and much of western Europe.[141] If that impulse was intensified by the greater commitment parents were beginning to make to the upbringing and future prospects of their children, as some social historians believe, it is perhaps true after all that the decline of impermanent architecture owed something to the rise of what has been called "affective individualism."[142] But that seems to stretch a point. Compared to the fashionable appearance that a house might exhibit to those with educated tastes or the convenience that its plan might afford a family that had learned to value privacy, the mere fact that it stood on continuous sills or was made entirely of brick had little social signifi-

cance. Its real value was something an appraiser or a tax assessor could put a figure on, a monetary value. Its psychological value was the feeling of pride and accomplishment it must have engendered in men and women who had succeeded in overcoming the obstacles inherent in homesteading.

Few, if any, house-proud Chesapeake planters put into words that sense of achievement. One, Samuel Harrison of Anne Arundel County, left another kind of statement. His father had been one of the lucky survivors, living a long and prosperous life and leaving at his death in 1716 an estate of 5,500 acres. His home plantation he gave in life interest to his wife. Samuel received six large tracts of land, including a quarter called Holland's Hills (later corrupted to its present name, Holly Hill) on which a modest, one-story, two-bay, unpainted clapboard house was built in 1698, perhaps for an overseer or for Samuel himself, who was then nineteen. It was enlarged in 1713 by the addition of another room, a loft, a lean-to, and a brick chimney.[143] Whether or not its frame stood on earthfast posts, the house conformed in all other respects to the usual manner of building among tobacco planters in the region. But the Harrisons' circumstances were most unusual, and as soon as his inheritance was assured, Samuel set about rebuilding Holly Hill. The former cottage he enclosed with brick walls. He built a handsome new addition, also of brick, containing a fine large parlor, a generous stair hall, a dining room with a built-in "bowfat" for his china, and two upstairs chambers, the one over the parlor paneled and marbleized in hues of red, green, and cream. He retrimmed and repainted the old house throughout. When he was finished, he hired a limner to paint and frame a large wooden panel that still hangs above the parlor fireplace (fig. 15).[144] It depicts—platlike—the broad acres that he inherited from his father and that his descendants would continue farming for three generations. Down the right-hand margin are inscribed its precise metes and bounds. In the lower left-hand corner is a formal portrait of the house he had just improved (fig. 16). And across the top in block capitals (lest someone miss the point) is emblazoned the legend SAMUEL HARRISON'S LAND. The Harrisons had crossed the vernacular threshold. By a combination of prudence, longevity, and good timing the immigrant homesteader had waxed rich, weathered the depression,

Fig. 15. Samuel Harrison's plantation, Holly Hill, Anne Arundel County, Maryland, before 1733. Oil on wood, 42¾" × 54⅝". The painting is signed "AS." (Mr. and Mrs. Brice Clagett; photograph courtesy of The Colonial Williamsburg Foundation.)

and stubbornly refused to die until the very year that tobacco prices began improving. His American-born son inherited an opportunity that the father had worked a lifetime for and provided the means to achieve. The son accomplished the rest. It was the way founding a family in the American colonies was supposed to happen but in the South so seldom did.

Notes

Five authors incur debts to friends and colleagues five times over. Some were the field supervisors and laboratory conservators who helped excavate and analyze the sites described. Others excavated other sites or conducted architectural surveys and have generously shared unpublished infor-

mation about them. A number have helped interpret sites and buildings, have brought useful documents to our attention, or have reviewed the manuscript. Those we must thank by name are N. W. Alcock, Nathan Altshuler, Michael Barber, Guy Beresford, Peter Bergstrom, Michael Bourne, Ronald Brunskill, Paul Buchanan, Lois Carr, Barbara Carson, Edward Chappell, John Cotter, William Deopkins, Walter Diggs, Jr., Andrew Edwards, Mark Edwards, Junius Fishbourne, Jr., H. Chandlee Forman, Patricia Gibbs, Harold B. Gill, Leverette Gregory, J. C. Harrington, David A. Harrison III, David Hazzard, Edward F. Heite, John Hemphill II, Charles Hodges, Carter Hudgins, Ivor Noël Hume, Barbara Hutton, Robert Keeler, Kevin Kelly, Polly Longsworth, Nicholas Luccketti, Edwards McManus, Robert Machin, Bayly Marks, Russell Menard, George Miller, Henry Miller, James Moody, Jr., Alexander Morrison II, Alain and Merry Outlaw, Susan Peters, J. Richard Rivoire, Orlando Ridout V, James Shey, J. T. Smith, James Smith, Merry Stinson, Vinson Sutlive, Jr., Jane Townes, Ransom True, Shearon Vaughn, Lorena Walsh, and E. H. D. Williams. Finally, especial thanks go to Fraser D. Neiman, whose help and insights make him virtually a sixth collaborator, and whose published works first raised important questions about impermanent architecture in the Chesapeake.

Fig. 16. Detail of figure 15. The frame house of 1698 and the addition made to it in 1713 were encased in brick when the right-hand wing was built, probably in the 1720s. Note the unusual piazza surmounted by a small pedimented roof.

1. Thad W. Tate, "The Seventeenth-Century Chesapeake and Its Modern Historians," in *The Chesapeake in the Seventeenth Century: Essays on Anglo-American Society*, ed. Thad W. Tate and David L. Ammerman (Chapel Hill, 1979), 3–50; reviewed and the scholarship further commented on by John M. Murrin in *William and Mary Quarterly*, 3d ser., 38, no. 1 (1981): 115–21.

2. John L. Cotter, *Archeological Excavations at Jamestown, Virginia* (Washington, D.C., 1958); John L. Cotter and J. Paul Hudson, *New Discoveries at Jamestown* (Washington, D.C., 1957). Reports on excavations of three other early sites were published in this period: Louis R. Caywood, *Excavations at Green Spring Plantation* [Virginia] (Yorktown, Va., 1955); Ivor Noël Hume, *Excavations at Tutter's Neck in James City County, Virginia, 1960–1961*, Museum of History and Technology Paper no. 53 (Washington, D.C., 1966); Hume, "Mathews Manor," *Antiques* 40, no. 6 (1966): 832–

36. The masonry foundations of several presumed seventeenth-century structures encountered in the restoration of Colonial Williamsburg have never been reported on. Sites described in Henry Chandlee Forman, *Jamestown and St. Mary's, Buried Cities of Romance* (Baltimore, 1938), have mostly been reexcavated and reinterpreted by National Park Service and St. Mary's City Commission.

3. The general term *earthfast* refers throughout this essay to timbers embedded in the ground any way at all; *hole-set* and the contemporary phrase "posts in the ground" specifically denote uprights erected in postholes; *ground-standing, ground-laid,* and *trench-laid* are modern terms for members set directly on the ground surface or embedded in trenches too shallow to give the structure rigidity. Other building terms used in this essay are described in fig. 3.

4. Maurice Beresford and John G. Hurst, eds., *Deserted Medieval Villages* (London, 1971), 78–100; David M. Wilson, ed., *The Archaeology of Anglo-Saxon England* (London, 1976), 49–97. The vernacular threshold between permanent and impermanent architecture is discussed in Eric Mercer, *English Vernacular Houses* (London, 1975), 1–9, 23–39, and in J. T. Smith, "The Evolution of the English Peasant House to the Late Seventeenth Century: The Evi-

dence of Buildings," *Journal of the British Archaeological Association*, 3d ser., 33 (1970): 122–46.

5. Guy Beresford, *The Medieval Clay-Land Village: Excavations at Goltho and Barton Blount* (London, 1975); "Excavation of a Moated House at Wintringham in Huntingdonshire," *Archaeological Journal* 134 (1977): 194–286; "Excavations at the Deserted Medieval Village of Caldecote, Hertfordshire: An Interim Report," *Hertfordshire's Past* 4 (1978): 3–13. See also interim notes on Faxton, Northamptonshire, in *Medieval Archaeology* 10 (1966): 214; 11 (1967): 307; 12 (1968): 203; 13 (1969): 279; D. G. Hurst and John G. Hurst, "Excavations at the Medieval Village of Wythemail, Northamptonshire," *Medieval Archaeology* 13 (1969): 167–203; P. V. Addyman, *The Work of the York Archaeological Trust, 1976* (York, 1976) and *The Work of the York Archaeological Trust, 1977* (York, 1977), which Barbara Hutton brought to our attention.

6. G. Beresford, "Wintringham," 225–29.

7. David L. Roberts, "The Persistence of Archaic Framing Techniques in Lincolnshire," *Vernacular Architecture* 5 (1974): 18–20; 6 (1975): 33–38; fieldwork in Somerset by Cary Carson and E. H. D. Williams to be reported on at a future date. As this essay went to press we learned from J. T. Smith that an extant seventeenth-century hole-set structure has been discovered in Lincolnshire.

8. Filed at the Library of Congress, Washington, D.C.

9. Dates established by tree-ring analysis hereafter indicated as, for example [1703].

10. See p. 134.

11. The collaborative character of the commission's research was the principal feature of two National Endowment for the Humanities grants entitled "Plantation Society in Colonial Maryland: A Research Partnership between History and Historical Archaeology," nos. RO–6228–72–468 (1972–74) and RO–10585–74–267 (1974–76).

12. These are conveniently collected in S. Fiske Kimball, *Domestic Architecture of the American Colonies and of the Early Republic* (New York, 1922), 3–9, and recently for Massachusetts in Abbott Lowell Cummings, *The Framed Houses of Massachusetts Bay, 1625–1725* (Cambridge, Mass., and London, 1979), 18–21.

13. Edmund Plowden [Beauchamp Plantagenet], *A Description of the Province of New Albion* (1650). The authors are grateful to Clifford Lewis III for giving them a photostatic copy of the exceptionally rare 1650 edition, the first to include a description of the "six sorts" of American houses. Excerpted in "American Notes," *Journal of the Society of Architectural Historians* 15, no. 3 (1956): 2, and discussed in G. Carroll Lindsay, "Plantagenet's Wigwam," *Journal of the Society of Architectural Historians* 17, no. 4 (1958): 31–34.

14. Cornelius Van Tienhoven reported that colonists to New Netherland had kept "dry and warm in these [dugout] houses with their entire families for two, three, or four years" ("Information Respecting Land in New Netherland," in *Pennsylvania Archives*, 19 vols., 2d ser. [Harrisburg, 1874–1900], 5:183).

15. Harold R. Shurtleff, *The Log Cabin Myth: A Study of the Early Dwellings of the English Colonists in North America* (Cambridge, Mass., 1939), 20–35.

16. *Archives of Maryland*, 65 vols. (Baltimore, 1883–1919), 5:266.

17. Van Tienhoven, "New Netherland," 181–83 (emphasis added).

18. Thomas Nairne, *A Letter from South Carolina* (London, 1710), 49–50. He too agreed that "the properest Time to begin a settlement is in September or, at fartherest, before the first of December."

19. This was true of a small log cabin that Charles Yates instructed an agent to build on his lot in newly laid out Bath Town, Berkeley Co., Va., in 1778: the cabin "may in future be turned into a Kitchen [consequently] it should be so placed on the Lott as to be convenient to a Better House which will stand on the best front in the Lott" (Charles Yates Letter Book, 1773–83, folio 200–201, Alderman Library, University of Virginia, Charlottesville).

20. William Dickson to Thomas Henderson, Nov. 24, 1810, Thomas Henderson Letter Book, 1810–11, Division of Archives and History, North Carolina Department of Cultural Resources, Raleigh.

21. *Information and Direction to Such Persons as are Inclined to America, More Especially Those Related to the Province of Pennsylvania* (n.p., n.d.), 2. (Copy of the Pennsylvania Historical Society is reproduced by photostat in the Massachusetts Historical Society Americana Series [Boston, 1919], no. 122). The tract is dated 1684 and attributed to William Penn in John Whiting, *A Catalogue of Friends' Books . . .* (London, 1708). The date is accurate or nearly so, for the Huntington Library owns a second edition printed in London in 1686, but Penn's authorship, we are kindly informed by Edwin Bronner of Haverford College, is more doubtful.

22. Cary Carson, "The 'Virginia House' in Maryland," *Maryland Historical Magazine* 69, no. 2 (1974): 185–96. The earliest documented reference to a "false plaite" is 1678, at which time it was old enough to need repair; Charles County Court and Land Records H, no. 1, folio 139, Maryland Hall of Records, Annapolis.

23. The practice of flooring (and ceiling) attic rooms with riven clapboards continued to the end of the eighteenth century. Examples in Maryland include Cloverfields (QA–2), Enfield (SM–115), and the Raley House (SM–236) (map identifications refer to the inventory by Maryland Historical Trust, Annapolis).

24. John Hammond, "Leah and Rachel; or, The Two Fruitful Sisters Virginia and Maryland: The Present Condition . . . ," in *Tracts and Other Papers . . .*, ed. Peter Force, 4 vols. (Washington, D.C., 1836–46), 3: 18, tract 14.

25. James Claypoole Letter Book, 1681–84, Historical Society of Pennsylvania. A brief biographical sketch of Claypoole appears in Albert Cook Myers, ed., *Narratives of Early Pennsylvania, West Jersey, and Delaware* (New York, 1912), 292, n. 33.

26. Houses without chimneys figure in accounts of other fledgling colonies. In Massachusetts, for example, a small house "made all of clapboards," one of the first in the

settlement of Watertown, burned down in 1632 "by making a fire in it when it had no chimney" (James Savage, ed., *The History of New England from 1630 to 1649, by John Winthrop, Esq. . . .*, 2 vols. [Boston, 1853], 1:104).

27. Two-story frame houses built in 1691 on Front Street in Philadelphia "were founded under ground on a layer of sap clapboards," which were still "hard and sound" when the houses were razed about 1810 (John Fanning Watson, *Annals of Philadelphia* [Philadelphia and New York, 1830], 290).

28. Samuel Symonds to John Winthrop, Jr., n.d. [after February 1638], *Boston Collections*, Massachusetts Historical Society Collections, 4th ser., vol. 7 (Cambridge, Mass., 1865), 118–20. The editors note that Symonds, a gentleman, emigrated from Yeldham, Essex. From internal evidence it is clear that the letter in the collections of the Essex Institute, Salem, Massachusetts, was written after Symonds's arrival in Massachusetts.

29. Samuel Eliot Morison, *Builders of the Bay Colony* (Boston and New York, 1958; reprint ed., Boston, 1981), 346.

30. For example, *Archives of Maryland*, 41:281–82, contains a deposition concerning housing built by one Hugh Bevin (obviously Welsh himself), whose duties included putting up "the Posts of the Welch Chimney." Timber chimneys were sometimes backed with brick. John Mercer, building a frame house in Marlborough, Virginia, in 1730, paid his carpenters for "covering my house and building a Chimney" and "plaistering my House and making 2 brick backs" (Mercer Ledger B [1725–32], Bucks County Historical Society, Doylestown, Pennsylvania). Mercer, an English merchant, took shelter in a small, abandoned house on first moving to Marlborough in 1726, for him the equivalent of a hut or a wigwam. Four years later he built a frame house with wooden chimneys and sixteen years after that a permanent dwelling, a fine brick mansion. See C. Malcolm Watkins, *The Cultural History of Marlborough, Virginia: An Archaeological and Historical Investigation of the Port Town for Stafford County and the Plantation of John Mercer* (Washington, D.C., 1968), 17–20, 34–39, 85–99.

31. Clamps, adopted in the second half of the sixteenth century as a method of inserting first floors into older open halls, "came to be regarded as a cheap alternative, structurally, by both carpenter and customer during the seventeenth century. The use of these obviated the use of girths, the inclusion of which was expensive" (Cecil A. Hewett, "Some East Anglican Prototypes for Early Timber Houses in America," *Post-Medieval Archaeology* 3 [1969]:109). Hewett illustrates two early seventeenth-century Essex (England) houses with original clamps in *Post-Medieval Archaeology* 3 (1969): 102–4; 5 (1971): 79–80.

32. In specifying that the windows were to be smallish and as few as possible Symonds was again saving time and money. An itemized list of repairs carried out on a house at Snow Hill Manor, Maryland, in 1639 shows that "making framed windows" could be extremely time-consuming, at Snow Hill taking more than twice as long as covering the roof (*Archives of Maryland*, 4:110).

33. Bartlett B. James and J. Franklin Jameson, eds., *Journal of Jasper Dankaerts, 1679–1680* (New York, 1913), 97.

34. To be discussed at length in a forthcoming report by Alain Outlaw, Virginia Research Center for Archaeology.

35. The different terms applied to fence construction, too, as the case of Gerret van Sweringen of St. Mary's City demonstrates. In 1684 his cattle broke into a garden by pushing "between the palisadoes" (*Archives of Maryland*, 17:300–301). When excavated, the fence was found to have been constructed of closely spaced, heavy riven posts.

36. Susan Myra Kingsbury, ed., *The Records of the Virginia Company of London*, 4 vols. (Washington, D.C., 1906–35), 4:259.

37. Recorded in the diary of Rev. John Lothrop under the heading "The Houses in ye planta[tion] Scituate Att my Comeing hither, onely these wch was aboute end of Sept. 1634," *New England Historical and Genealogical Register* 10 (1856): 42.

38. Norman Morrison Isham and Albert F. Brown, *Early Connecticut Houses* (Providence, R.I., 1900), 12–13. Isham collected other references to palisade buildings in an unpublished and untitled history of Massachusetts architecture, now deposited in Society for the Preservation of New England Antiquities, Boston.

39. Harold Shurtleff believes that the phrase "palisadoed house," when found in New England records, meant a house surrounded by a stockade (*Log Cabin Myth*, 88n). Sometimes it did (see Samuel Maverick, "A Briefe Description of New England . . .[ca. 1660]," *Proceedings of the Massachusetts Historical Society*, 2d ser., 1 [1885]: 234–36), but not always. For example, a thief broke into a dwelling house in Plymouth in 1646 "by putting aside some loose pallizadoes" (Nathaniel B. Shurtleff and David Pulsifer, eds., *Records of the Colony of New Plymouth*, 12 vols. [Boston, 1855–59], 2:111).

40. Alexander Young, ed., *Chronicles of the First Planters of the Colony of Massachusetts Bay* (Boston, 1846), 348–49, 374–75.

41. Amos Otis, *Genealogical Notes of Barnstable Families*, ed. Charles Swift (Barnstable, Mass., 1880–82), 202–3. French settlers in Canada and along the Mississippi Valley built walls much the same way (see Fred Kniffen and Henry Glassie, "Building in Wood in the Eastern U.S.: A Time-Place Perspective," *Geographical Review* 56, no. 1 [1966]: 50–54, and Kenneth E. Kidd, *The Excavation of Ste Marie I* [Toronto, 1949], 37–42, 53–59, 61–64). Whether New World builders were merely following a very old practice still current in seventeenth-century England and France is part of the larger question we hope this essay reopens—that is, how extensively ancient methods of impermanent building may have survived into fairly recent times.

42. Surry County, Deeds and Wills, book 1, folios 55 (1651), 96 (1657), Virginia State Library, Richmond; these and other State Library references are courtesy of the Association for Preservation of Virginia Antiquities' Virginia Settlers Research Project.

43. Archer Butler Hulbert, ed., *The Crown Collection of Photographs of American Maps*, ser. 3 (London, n.d.): plate 167, cat. no. 11.

44. "Notes from the Records of Stafford County, Virginia, Order Books," *Virginia Magazine of History and Biography* 46, no. 1 (1938): 20.

45. They were recommended for building silkworm houses by E. W. Gent[leman], "Virginia: More especially the South part thereof, Richly and truly valued" (1650) in Force, *Tracts*, 3: 36–37, tract 11; a dwelling built this way in 1658 may be the correct interpretation of the description of a house in *Archives of Maryland*, 41:281–82.

46. A typical reference: When the vestrymen of Truro parish, Virginia, undertook to build a new vestry house in 1750, they specified a building sixteen feet square, including an inside wooden chimney, all of "framed work" (that is, box framed), clapboard covered, floored with plank, and lofted with more clapboards, the entire structure to be "raised on Blocks" (*Minutes of the Vestry, Truro Parish, Virginia, 1732–1785* [Lorton, Va., 1974], 58). Blocked barns and granaries in Maryland are described in Queen Anne's County Deed Book RT, no. F, folios 145, 173, Hall of Records, Annapolis.

47. The ground-laid sills under the Third Haven Meeting House (1682), Talbot County, Maryland (T–46), were raised on cedar blocks in 1698 and the building new floored; Minute Book, 1676–1746, Third Haven Friends Meeting, folios 158, 170, Maryland Hall of Records, Annapolis.

48. The suggestion has been made that English builders may have set sill beams on temporary blocks while raising a frame, later replacing them with low plinth walls; Richard Harris, *Discovering Timber-Framed Buildings* (Princes Risborough, Aylesbury, Bucks, U.K., 1978), 16–17. So far no evidence of that practice has been observed on early American sites or in American buildings. Here blocks were hole-set to prevent easy dislocation. Earthfast blocks cannot have been wholly unfamiliar to English housewrights, for Richard Neve's *Builder's Dictionary* (London, 1736) recommends that "the Stem or Stump of a Tree," if charred "to a Coal" before it was set in the ground, would "continue a long Time without rotting." The virtue of charring or tarring earthfast posts was still appreciated at the end of the eighteenth century (see *Encyclopedia; or, A Dictionary of Arts, Sciences, and Miscellaneous Literature . . .* [Philadelphia, 1798], s.v. "posts").

49. Edward Arber and Arthur G. Bradley, eds., *Travels and Works of Captain John Smith*, 2 vols. (Edinburgh, 1910), 2:957.

50. Arber and Bradley, *John Smith*, 2:405.

51. Thomas Tusser, *Five Hundred Points of Good Husbandry* (1580), ed. Dorothy Hartley (London, 1931], 111, 127. It includes *Tusser Redivivus* (1710), which not only attests to the longevity of the farming practices Tusser describes but enlarges on them.

52. Nathaniel C. Hale, *Virginia Venturer: A Historical Biography of William Claiborne, 1600–1677* (Richmond, Va., 1951], 152. Roofs of heaped-up brush were excellently suited to structures framed no higher than the ceiling joists; see J. E. C. Peters, "The Solid Thatch Roof," *Vernacular Architecture* 8 (1977):825.

53. Richard S. Dunn, *Sugar and Slaves: The Rise of the Planter Class in the English West Indies 1624–1713* (New York and London, 1972), 289.

54. Significantly, the dialect word *crotch* occurs in English sources outside the region where cruck building was still current in the sixteenth century; see R. de Z. Hall and N. W. Alcock, "A Note on the Word Cruck," *Vernacular Architecture* 7 (1976): 11–14. The 1783 tax assessment for Charles County, Md., records several dwellings and tobacco barns "supported by [or "with"] crutches" (Alphabetical List of Lands, District 6, 1783 tax assessment, Maryland Historical Society). Various meanings can be guessed at— upper crucks possibly, or maybe shores or braces, considering that the structures in question are almost always further described as "old," "very old," or "like old age." Other evidence strongly favors an interpretation that makes the term an archaic dialect word for hole-set posts (with or without forked tops). Farmers in southern Maryland were still calling the hole-set posts they used to build pole barns "crutches" as late as the 1870s (see Edwin W. Beitzell, ed., "Diary of Dr. Joseph L. McWilliams, 1868–1875," *Chronicles of St. Mary's* 25, no. 10 [1977]: 8). Meriwether Lewis and William Clark, both of Virginia, were still sufficiently acquainted with cratchet buildings to employ hole-set forked poles in framing the temporary shelters they built on their western expedition in 1806 if we can believe a description and illustration in Patrick Gass, *A Journal of the Voyages and Travels . . . of Capt. Lewis and Capt. Clarke* (Philadelphia, 1810), 60–61.

55. Upper crucks support the roof of Ocean Hall [1703], Bushwood, Maryland (SM–111); see measured drawings, Historic American Buildings Survey, Library of Congress.

56. Charles Frederick Innocent, *The Development of English Building Construction* (Cambridge, 1916), 7–25. The house type endured into modern times; see Gwyn I. Meirion-Jones, "Some Early and Primitive Building Forms in Brittany," *Folk Life* 14 (1976): 46–64.

57. York County Deeds, Orders, and Wills, book 3, folio 35, State Library, Richmond.

58. Forman, *Jamestown and St. Mary's*, front endpaper and 129.

59. Surry County Deeds and Wills, book 1, folios 368–69, State Library, Richmond; *Archives of Maryland*, 54:54. *Raftered houses* continued to be mentioned in early eighteenth-century records in contexts that suggest roof huts unless the term had other meanings, too.

60. The prevalence of hole-set framed buildings is demonstrated best in the southern colonies where many more sites have been excavated than elsewhere. There are, however, shreds of evidence to suggest that Samuel Symonds was not alone among New Englanders in his preference for buildings erected on "posts . . . standing in the ground," a phrase William Bradford used to describe a clapboarded trading post built before 1627 at Aptuxcet (Samuel Eliot Morison, ed., *Of Plimoth Plantation, 1620–1647* [New York, 1952], 280). The 1630 Isaac Allerton house of Kingston, Mass., the first hole-set structure excavated in New En-

gland, is described in James Deetz, "Plymouth Colony Ar chitecture: Archaeological Evidence from the Seventeenth Century," in *Architecture in Colonial Massachusetts*, ed. Cummings (Boston, 1979), 49–53.

61. Plowden, *Description of New Albion.*

62. York County Deeds, Orders and Wills, book 1, folio 101, State Library, Richmond, Va.; *Archives of Maryland,* 53:357. John Nevill's "loged house" had already served some time as his homestead dwelling; he was building a new and better house in 1662 (*Archives of Maryland,* 53:232).

63. Samuel Smith, *The History of the Colony of Nova-Caesaria, or New-Jersey* (Philadelphia, 1765), 180 (punctuation and emphasis added). The account was written by another Welshman, Gawen Lawrie. "Raised piece" meant false plate in Virginia (according to Paul Buchanan, Colonial Williamsburg Foundation); Joseph Moxon's *Mechanick Exercises* (London, 1678) uses "raising piece" as a synonym for wall plate.

64. Richard M. Candee, "A Documentary History of Plymouth Colony Architecture, 1620–1700," *Old Time New England* 59, no. 3 (1969): 59–71, and 60, no. 2 (1969): 37–53. Ernest A. Connally, "The Cape Cod House: An Introductory Study," *Journal of the Society of Architectural Historians* 19, no. 2 (1960): 47–56. The oldest standing structure in the Plymouth Colony region seems to be the Harlow House (ca. 1667) in the town of Plymouth.

65. *Information and Direction,* 2.

66. William Fitzhugh to Nicholas Hayward, Jan. 30, 1686/ 87, in Richard Beale Davis, ed., *William Fitzhugh and His Chesapeake World, 1676–1701: The Fitzhugh Letters and Other Documents* (Chapel Hill, N.C., 1963), 203.

67. William Fitzhugh to Nicholas Hayward, Jan. 30, 1686/ 87, in Davis, ed., *Fitzhugh,* 202.

68. Middlesex County Deeds [1], 1687–1750, folio 10, State Library, Richmond. The description occurs in articles of agreement for the building of a courthouse in 1692, the county having failed in an attempt several years earlier to erect a "good Strong Brick House" the equal of the "Brick Courte house lately Built in Gloucester County" (Middlesex County Order Book no. 2, 1680–94, folio 201, State Library, Richmond).

69. Colonel Norwood, shipwrecked on the eastern shore of Virginia in 1649, was taken to a local Indian chief's lodge, which he observed was raised on "locust posts sunk in the ground at corners and partitions" ("A Voyage to Virginia," n.d., in Force, *Tracts,* 3:35, tract 10).

70. John Lawson, *A New Voyage to Carolina* (London, 1709), 94–100.

71. Specified in many orphans court valuations, for example, Queen Anne's County Deed Book RT, no. E, folio 62 (Hall of Records, Annapolis).

72. William Fitzhugh to Dr. Ralph Smith, Apr. 22, 1686, in Davis, ed., *Fitzhugh,* 175.

73. J. C. Wooley, *The Durability of Fence Posts,* Missouri Agricultural Experiment Station Bulletin no. 312 (Columbia, Mo., 1932), 2–3.

74. The estimate of the anonymous writer of the *Information and Direction* that hole-set houses for "ordinary beginners" "usually endure ten years without Repair" is corroborated by a growing body of archaeological evidence.

75. Such chimneys were still commonplace in rural Maryland when the federal tax assessment was made in 1798 (Maryland Historical Society, Baltimore).

76. Impermanent structures persisted in England, too. Their use as seasonal farm buildings has already been noted. Some laborers' cottages also employed primitive timber framing. Robert Machin believes that as late as the late eighteenth century estate owners still provided such housing (Machin to Cary Carson, July 12, 1979); see also entry for Thomas Gale in a 1604 survey of Thurleigh published by N. W. Alcock in *Bedfordshire Archaeological Journal* 4 (1969): 62. Large earthfast buildings with carpentered roofs still made acceptable barns for some gentry farmers in the seventeenth century (one built in 1607 is described and illustrated in C. B. Robinson, ed., *Rural Economy in Yorkshire in 1641, Being the Farming and Account Books of Henry Best of Elmswell in the East Riding,* vol. 33, Publications of the Surtees Society [Durham, 1857], 47, 170–71).

77. Specifically, south-central Somerset, although the area in which surviving structures have been recorded is likely to be smaller than their original extent.

78. Carson, "The 'Virginia House' in Maryland," 188–90; Dell Upton "Board Roofing in Tidewater Virginia," *APT Bulletin* 8, no. 4 (1976):22–43.

79. Garry Wheeler Stone, "Sarum, Charles County, Maryland: Notes on the Woods and Carpentry of the Period I Structure," memorandum, July 5, 1979, St. Mary's City Commission.

80. Builders often esteem well-built structures not because they guarantee a longer future but because they reflect favorably on their owners in the present: "We tend to take it for granted that buildings are solidly constructed so that they may last for a long time. But permanence is not likely to be the most elementary consideration. Any concern with the future or the past is less immediate than a concern with the present. Firmness and solidity are, first of all, a property of the present state of things and serve as the perceptual equivalent of what has value. If I make something of durable material, I express my conviction that the thing is good, often without the rationalization, and therefore I want it to last" (Rudolph Arnheim, "Thoughts on Durability: Architecture as an Affirmation of Confidence," *AIA Journal* 66, no. 7 [1977]: 48–50).

81. William Waller Hening, ed., *Statutes at Large; Being a Collection of All the Laws of Virginia . . . ,* 13 vols. (Richmond, Va., 1809–23), 1:340; 2:76.

82. Thomas Jefferson, *Notes on the State of Virginia* [1787], ed. William Peden (Chapel Hill, N.C., 1955), 152.

83. William G. Hoskins, "The Rebuilding of Rural England, 1570–1640," *Past and Present* 4 (November 1953): 44–59; Robert Machin, "The Great Rebuilding: A Reassessment," *Past and Present* 77 (November 1977): 33–56.

84. John Franklin Jameson, ed., [*Edward*] *Johnson's Won-*

der-Working Providence, 1628–1651 (New York, 1910), 211; Timothy H. Breen, "Transfer of Culture: Chance and Design in Shaping Massachusetts Bay, 1630–1660," *New England Historical and Genealogical Register* 132, no. 1 (1978): 3–17.

85. Malcolm Freiberg, ed., *The Journal of Madam Knight* (Brookline, Mass., 1972), 13.

86. Abbott Lowell Cummings, "Massachusetts and Its First Period Houses: A Statistical Survey," in *Architecture in Colonial Massachusetts*, 113–21.

87. Notwithstanding cases like Samuel Symonds's where an impermanent house was later substantially improved, the more likely practice is spelled out in a building contract of 1679 between John Williams of Boston and a housewright who was engaged to raze an older house before building Williams a new one (Cummings, "Massachusetts and Its First Period Houses," 204).

88. Possible exceptions are plank-framed houses.

89. Hewett, "East Anglican Prototypes," 110–21; Cummings, *Framed Houses*, esp. chaps. 1 and 6.

90. Hume, "Mathews Manor," 834; Cotter, *Excavations at Jamestown*, 11–159.

91. *Calvert Papers, Number One*, Maryland Historical Society Fund Publication no. 28 (Baltimore, 1889), 174.

92. Surry County, Deeds and Wills, book 1, folios 176–77 (1643), 10–11 (1652), State Library, Richmond; *Archives of Maryland*, 41:367 (1659); "Westmoreland County Records," *William and Mary Quarterly*, 1st ser., 15, no. 3 (1907): 181–82 (1661).

93. Durand de Dauphiné, *A Huguenot Exile in Virginia*, ed. Gilbert Chinard (New York, 1934), 119–20.

94. Robert Beverley, *The History and Present State of Virginia*, ed. Louis B. Wright (Chapel Hill, N.C., 1947), 289.

95. H. R. McIlwaine, ed., *Journals of the House of Burgesses of Virginia, 1619–1658/9*, 13 vols. (Richmond, 1915), 1:33.

96. The workload of two carpenters between August and November 1691 is described in Charles County Court and Land Records R, no. 1, folio 513, Hall of Records, Annapolis.

97. This is based on analysis of Queen Anne's County Deed Book RT, nos. D, E, and F, as interpreted in a letter from Garry Wheeler Stone to Cary Carson, Dec. 7, 1977.

98. Orlando Ridout V, who kindly brought this reference to our attention, will publish the full text in a forthcoming study of vernacular buildings in Queen Anne's County. It will include references to other open halls.

99. Cary Carson and Merry Stinson, unpublished survey of all historic structures in St. Mary's County built before ca. 1860; Dell Upton, "Early Vernacular Architecture in Southeastern Virginia," (Ph.D. diss., Brown University, 1979); and Carl Lounsbury, "The Development of Domestic Architecture in the Albemarle Region," in *Carolina Dwelling: Towards Preservation of Place*, ed. Doug Swaim (Raleigh, N.C., 1978), 46–61. In *Poverty in a Land of Plenty: Tenancy in Eighteenth-Century Maryland* ([Baltimore and London, 1977], 56–84), Gregory A. Stiverson includes an excellent discussion of tenant housing in the late 1760s,

buildings that a traveler in St. Mary's County described thus: "Some have their foundations in the Ground, others are built on Puncheons or Logs, a Foot or two from the Earth [what we have been calling blocks], which is more airy, and a Defence against the Vermin" (Edward Kimber, "Observations in Several Voyages and Travels in America," *William and Mary Quarterly*, 1st ser., 15, no. 3 [1907]: 153).

100. Bernard L. Herman to Cary Carson, Oct. 24, 1978.

101. Paul E. Buchanan, "The Eighteenth-Century Frame Houses of Tidewater Virginia," in *Building Early America: Contributions toward the History of a Great Industry*, ed. Charles E. Peterson (Radnor, Pa., 1976), 54–73.

102. E. S. Morgan, *American Slavery, American Freedom: The Ordeal of Colonial Virginia* (New York, 1975), 108–30.

103. Kingsbury, ed., *Records*, 1:566.

104. Kingsbury, ed., *Records*, 4:572.

105. Kingsbury, ed., *Records*, 3:221.

106. Ivor Noël Hume, "First Look at a Lost Virginia Settlement," *National Geographic* 155, no. 6 (1979):735–67.

107. Russell R. Menard, "A Note on Chesapeake Tobacco Prices, 1618–1660," *Virginia Magazine of History and Biography* 84, no. 4 (1976): 401–10, and "Farm Prices of Maryland Tobacco, 1659–1710," *Maryland Historical Magazine* 68, no. 1 (1973): 80–85.

108. *Archives of Maryland*, 4:387, 499. The author of the 1684 pamphlet promoting settlement in Pennsylvania reckoned that an "ordinary beginners" house and a barn "of the same Building and Dimensions" ought to cost 16.1% of his expenses the first year, which were estimated to be £30.2.6 for an immigrant family's passage and passage and clothes for two servants, £1.0.0 for two month's lodging "till a house be built," £15.10.0 for the house and barn (including £3.10.0 for nails and hardware), £16.17.6 for one year's provisions, and £24.10.0 for livestock (*Information and Direction*, 2).

109. William Fitzhugh to Nicholas Hayward, Jan. 30, 1686/87, in Davis, ed., *Fitzhugh*, 202–3 (emphasis added).

110. Harry James Carman, ed., *American Husbandry* (1775; reprint ed., New York, 1939), 168–70. "Posted" slave quarters on such plantations were valued at £5 apiece, one-third the cost of building a frame house for an overseer; Loyalist Claims, AO 13/27, Public Record Office, London.

111. Russell R. Menard, "From Servant to Freeholder: Status Mobility and Property Accumulation in Seventeenth-Century Maryland," *William and Mary Quarterly*, 3d ser., 30, no. 1 (1973): 37–64; Lorena S. Walsh, "Servitude and Opportunity in Charles County, Maryland, 1658–1705," in Aubrey C. Land, Lois Green Carr, and Edward C. Papenfuse, eds., *Law, Society, and Politics in Early Maryland* (Baltimore and London, 1977), 111–33; Lois Green Carr and Russell R. Menard, "Immigration and Opportunity: Servants and Freedmen in Early Colonial Maryland," in Tate and Ammerman, eds., *Chesapeake in Seventeenth Century*, 206–42; Willard F. Bliss, "The Rise of Tenancy in Virginia," *Virginia Magazine of History and Biography* 58, no. 4 (1950): 427–41: Stiverson, *Poverty in a Land of Plenty*, 1–55, 85–103.

112. William Fitzhugh to Nicholas Hayward, Jan. 30, 1786/87, in Davis, ed., *Fitzhugh*, 202.

113. Lorena S. Walsh and Russell R. Menard, "Death in the Chesapeake: Two Life Tables for Men in Early Colonial Maryland," *Maryland Historical Magazine* 69, no. 2 (1974): 211–27; Menard, "Immigrants and Their Increase: The Process of Population Growth in Early Colonial Maryland," in Land, Carr, and Papenfuse, eds., *Law, Society and Politics*, 88–110.

114. Maris A. Vinovskis, "Mortality Rates and Trends in Massachusetts before 1860," *Journal of Economic History* 32, no. 1 (1972): 184–213; Lawrence Stone, *The Family, Sex and Marriage in England, 1500–1800* (New York, 1977), 72.

115. Darrett B. Rutman and Anita H. Rutman, "Of Agues and Fevers: Malaria in the Early Chesapeake," *William and Mary Quarterly*, 3d ser., 33, no. 1 (1976): 31–60.

116. Darrett B. Rutman and Anita H. Rutman, " 'Now-Wives and Sons-in-Law': Parental Death in a Seventeenth-Century Virginia County," in Tate and Ammerman, eds., *Chesapeake in Seventeenth Century*, 153–82; Lorena S. Walsh, " 'Till Death Us Do Part': Marriage and Family in Seventeenth-Century Maryland," in Tate and Ammerman, eds., *Chesapeake in Seventeenth Century*, 126–52; Daniel Blake Smith, "Mortality and Family in the Colonial Chesapeake," *Journal of Interdisciplinary History* 8, no. 3 (1978): 403–27.

117. Lois Green Carr, "The Development of the Maryland Orphans' Court, 1654–1715," in Land, Carr, and Papenfuse, eds., *Law, Society, and Politics*, 41–62; E. McN. Thomas, "Orphans' Courts in Colonial Virginia" (M.A. thesis, College of William and Mary, 1964), esp. 23–24, 43–44, for abuses by guardians.

118. Russell R. Menard, "The Tobacco Industry in the Chesapeake Colonies, 1617–1730: An Interpretation," *Research in Economic History* 5 (1980): 109–77; Menard, "From Servants to Slaves: The Transformation of the Chesapeake Labor System, 1680–1710," *Southern Studies* 16 (1977): 355–90.

119. Carole Shammas, "English-born and Creole Elites in Turn-of-the-Century Virginia," in Tate and Ammerman, eds., *Chesapeake in Seventeenth Century*, 274–96; David W. Jordan, "Political Stability and the Emergence of a Native Elite in Maryland," in Tate and Ammerman, eds., *Chesapeake in Seventeenth Century*, 243–73.

120. Gloria L. Main, "Maryland and the Chesapeake Economy, 1670–1720," in Land, Carr, and Papenfuse, eds., *Law, Society, and Politics*, 134–52.

121. For the region as a whole, see Arthur P. Middleton, *Tobacco Coast: A Maritime History of Chesapeake Bay in the Colonial Era* (Newport News, Va., 1953), pt. 2; Aubrey C. Land, "Economic Behavior in a Planting Society: The Eighteenth-Century Chesapeake," *Journal of Southern History* 33, no. 4 (1967): 469–85; Allan Kulikoff, "The Colonial Chesapeake: Seedbed of Antebellum Southern Culture?" *Journal of Southern History* 45, no. 4 (1979): 513–40; Peter V. Bergstrom, "Markets and Merchants: Economic Diversification in Colonial Virginia, 1700–1775" (Ph.D. diss., University of New Hampshire, 1980); and Lois Green Carr,

P. M. G. Harris, and Russell R. Menard, "The Development of Society in the Colonial Chesapeake," National Endowment for the Humanities Grant no. RS–23687–76–431 (1976–79), St. Mary's City Commission, St. Mary's City.

122. County surveys of vernacular buildings on file with Virginia Historic Landmarks Commission, Richmond, and Maryland Historical Trust, Annapolis. Studies of local agricultural economies used in the following analysis include, besides Bergstrom, "Markets and Merchants," and Carr, Harris, and Menard, "Development of Society in Colonial Chesapeake," Paul G. E. Clemens, *The Atlantic Economy and Colonial Maryland's Eastern Shore: From Tobacco to Grain* (Ithaca, N.Y., 1980); Carville V. Earle, *The Evolution of a Tidewater Settlement System: All Hallow's Parish, Maryland, 1650–1783*, University of Chicago, Department of Geography Research Paper 170 (Chicago, 1975); James B. Gouger III, "Agricultural Change in the Northern Neck of Virginia, 1700–1860" (Ph.D. diss., University of Florida, 1976); Harold B. Gill, Jr., "Wheat Culture in Colonial Virginia," *Agricultural History* 52, no. 3 (1978): 380–93; Ronald Hoffman, *A Spirit of Dissension: Economics, Politics, and the Revolution in Maryland* (Baltimore and London, 1973), 6–15; Kevin P. Kelly, "Economic and Social Development of Seventeenth-Century Surry County, Virginia" (Ph.D. diss., University of Washington, 1972); Allan Kulikoff, "Tobacco and Slaves: Population, Economy, and Society in Eighteenth-Century Prince George's County, Maryland" (Ph.D. diss., Brandeis University, 1976); Bayley Marks, "Economics and Society in a Staple Plantation System: St. Mary's County, Maryland, 1790–1840" (Ph.D. diss., University of Maryland, 1979); Michael Lee Nicholls, "Origins of the Virginia Southside, 1703–1753: A Social and Economic Study" (Ph.D. diss., College of William and Mary, 1972); Stiverson, *Poverty in a Land of Plenty*; Lorena S. Walsh, "Charles County, Maryland, 1658–1705: A Study of Chesapeake Social and Political Structure" (Ph.D. diss., Michigan State University, 1977); Robert A. Wheeler, "Lancaster County, Virginia, 1650–1750: The Evolution of the Southern Tidewater Community" (Ph.D. diss., Brown University, 1972).

123. Lynnhaven House (134–37), Thoroughgood House (134–33), Weblin House (134–31). Numbers refer to historic building survey inventory done by Virginia Historical Landmarks Commission.

124. Old Woodward House (133–41).

125. Pear Valley, Northampton County (65–52), Red Hill (destroyed), Accomac County (01–133). See Bernard L. Herman and David G. Orr, "Pear Valley et al.: An Excursion into the Analysis of Southern Vernacular Architecture," *Southern Folklore Quarterly* 39, no. 4 (1975): 307–27.

126. The authors are grateful to Lois Green Carr for permission to cite these yet unpublished findings. For vernacular buildings in Somerset, Wicomico, and Worcester counties, see Maryland Historical Trust, *Historic Sites Inventory II* (Annapolis, Md., 1973).

127. Dorchester County survey, Maryland Historical Trust; information from Michael Bourne, Chestertown, Md.

128. William Strickland, *Journal of a Tour in the United*

States of America, 1794–1795, ed. J. E. Strickland (New York, 1971), 223.

129. Kent County survey, Maryland Historical Trust; information from Marsha Fritz, Annapolis, Md.

130. Queen Anne's County survey, Maryland Historical Trust; information from Orlando Ridout V, Annapolis, Md. A comprehensive survey of Caroline County turned up no pre-Revolutionary houses whatsoever; see Michael Bourne, *Inventory of Historic Sites in Caroline County*, ed. Christopher Weeks (Annapolis, Md., 1980).

131. Information for Harford (formerly Baltimore) County compiled by Bel Air American History Club and kindly provided by David Hill, Bel Air, Md.

132. Sarum [after *1714*], Charles County (CH–15); Cedar Park [*1702*], Anne Arundel County (AA–141); and Holly Hill [*1698* and *1713*], Anne Arundel County (AA–817). Morgan Hill farm [*1725*], Calvert County (CT–61) and Sotterley (ca. 1710), St. Mary's County (SM–7), have always remained frame dwellings.

133. Ocean Hall [*1703*], St. Mary's County (SM–111). Both Sotterley and Cedar Park were built by merchants, too.

134. Carson and Stinson, survey, St. Mary's County; for Charles and Calvert counties, see Maryland Historical Trust, *Historic Sites Inventory I* (1973; rev. ed., Annapolis, Md., 1980).

135. Upton, "Early Vernacular Architecture."

136. Stiverson, *Poverty in a Land of Plenty*, 85–103.

137. Stiverson, *Poverty in a Land of Plenty*, 99–100, n. 38.

138. John Beale Bordley, *Essay and Notes on Husbandry and Rural Affairs*, 2d ed. (Philadelphia, 1801), 301. The adverse effect of tobacco culture on the independence and self-sufficiency of small farmers can be seen from a modern example to work in reverse—that is, where diversified crops are given up to grow tobacco, sharecroppers and small producers experience the declining standards of living described by Harry Crews in his recollections of Bacon County, Ga., in the 1920s: "Before tobacco came into Bacon County, the farmers were self-sufficient in a way they were never to be again. In the days before tobacco they grew everything they needed and lived pretty well. Since they were too far south to grow wheat, they had to buy flour. But almost everything else they really wanted, they could grow. . . . But tobacco took so much of their time and energy and worry that they stopped growing many of the crops they had grown before. Consequently, they had to depend upon the money from the tobacco to buy what they did not grow. A failed tobacco crop then was a genuine disaster that affected not just the individual farmer but the economy of the entire county" (Harry Crews, *A Childhood: The Biography of a Place* [New York, 1978], 27).

139. James W. Deen, Jr., "Patterns of Testation: Four Tidewater Counties in Colonial Virginia," *American Journal of Legal History* 16, no. 2 (1972): 154–63. The trend appears to continue after 1720 according to preliminary observations from the York County Project, National Endowment for the Humanities Grant no. RS—00033–80–1604 (1979–81), Research Department, Colonial Williamsburg Foundation, Williamsburg, Va.

140. James Deetz, *In Small Things Forgotten: The Archaeology of Early American Life* (Garden City, N.Y., 1977), 28–43; Cary Carson, "Doing History with Material Culture," in *Material Culture and the Study of American Life*, ed. Ian M. G. Quimby (New York, 1978), 58–64.

141. John Goody, Joan Thirsk, and E. P. Thompson, eds., *Family and Inheritance: Rural Society in Western Europe, 1200–1800* (New York, 1976); Alan Macfarlane, *The Origins of English Individualism: The Family, Property, and Social Transition* (Oxford, 1978).

142. Stone, *Family, Sex and Marriage*, 211–69.

143. Measured drawings in the Historic American Buildings Survey, Library of Congress, correct a somewhat inaccurate description in Carson, "The 'Virginia House' in Maryland," 186–91. Recent dendrochronological analysis dates the first and second construction periods precisely.

144. The authors are grateful to Mr. and Mrs. Brice Clagett for permission to photograph and illustrate the painting.

Village and Community in Early Colonial New England

JOSEPH S. WOOD

At a basic level, settlement plans structured material life and social relations in colonial New England. Scholars have long associated one form of settlement, the nucleated plan, with the desire of Puritan leaders to maintain control of local societies and to insure that their covenanted communities would remain cohesive and "loving." Complementing this line of thought, the appearance of dispersed settlements was typically explained as the symbolic expression of spiritual declension as material temptations pried the Puritan heart from its concern for the common good. Indeed, William Bradford of Plymouth first sketched the "declension theory" when he lamented the exodus of acquisitive farmers to nearby Duxbury and Marshfield in the late 1620s and early 1630s.

Joseph S. Wood challenges this orthodoxy in two ways. First, he demonstrates that the nucleated settlement was only one of many settlement types in early seventeenth-century England. Typically, it was most often found in the English midlands. Alongside it, New England immigrants from England's southeastern counties and from parts of the west country transplanted their equally "traditional" dispersed plans. As Wood argues, "no singular folk tradition or set of rules and material forms existed" in early modern England; New England, by extension, was complicated from the beginning. Wood's conclusion is clear: dispersion, in fact, was an option available beginning in the 1620s and emphatically not a consequence of community breakdown. A second reason Wood offers concerns the frequent appearance of "villages" established from parent towns—places like Salem Village (formed from Salem in 1640) and Medfield (formed from Dedham in 1649). Once we overcome a belief that these villages were imperfect offspring of "real" (that is, nucleated) parent towns and were in fact very common, we realize that the dispersed settlement form of villages was the dominant scheme that prevailed in New England throughout the colonial period. Here, Wood con-

cludes that "community," as a social web grounded in reciprocal relations and bonds of kinship and realized through face-to-face interaction, could function as well in a dispersed settlement as it could in a nucleated settlement.

Over the course of the eighteenth century, as the pressures of agrarian reform and an expanding post-Revolutionary market economy shot a jolt of mercantile prosperity into tired hinterland settlements, new buildings—shops, libraries, banks, small milling operations—sprang up around old churches initially built in remote locations. This new federal-period town center was a nucleated response to a new centralization of rural capitalism and must not be confused with the dynamic processes of historical change that led to its ultimate appearance.

Early New England colonists, it is widely believed, established nucleated settlements, and these nucleated settlements enhanced community life.[1] This correlation between community function and settlement form was so important, it is further believed, that community was diminished in the eighteenth century as settlement form was loosened and many community members dispersed from nucleated villages to individual farms. But was community forbearance so dependent upon nucleated settlement? Or has the rhetoric about Puritan community been so linked with the particular settlement form of the New England town as "to effect an implicit definition of community as the ideal Puritan town" and so confuse the settlement form with community?[2] The argument that follows suggests that a simple correlation between community function and nucleated settlement form in early colonial New England is mistaken. Highly structured communities were established; but, as in England, whence the colonists came, new communities—often called villages—de veloped and survived quite well without the necessity of nucleated settlement.

Community is a "social web" or, more explicitly, "a network of social relations marked by mutuality and emotional bonds."[3] Community is dependent upon common purpose, shared understanding and values, a sense of obligation and reciprocity, and collective action. As traditional community interaction was interpersonal and frequent, common space is also implied in most definitions. Space and place denote common experience, and, in the traditional view, community as experience and community as place were one.[4] The organization of the common space—the settlement form—reflects in large measure the configuration or spatial structure of the social web.[5]

The prevalent settlement form attributed to the place associated with traditional, preindustrial community is the village, or "collection of dwelling houses and other buildings, forming a centre of habitation in a country district."[6] Village and community, like place and community, are often considered one and the same and the terms used interchangeably; but, in the primary definition of village, nucleation is strongly implied:[7] a kind of cosmological prediction to have a nucleated settlement located at the center of a community's area prevails and, in the geographical literature, is reinforced by a spatial view based on Von Thünen land-use rings, agglomeration economies, and central places. Quite simply, nucleated forms provided the functional requirements for successful community and economy.[8]

No settlement form would have better ensured community forbearance as seventeenth-century colonists ventured into the wilderness of New England. The conventional view that New England's colonial communities formed compact villages gathered around a central meetinghouse correlates nicely with an idealized social order attributed to hard-bitten, theocratic Puritans, with recorded plans for villages, with literary and circumstantial historical reference to villages, with nineteenth-century maps and sketches of villages, and with present-day landscape. Yet, for all that has been said about community and settlement form in New England, it is instructive to examine once more the New England village. First, a number of scholars have shown that villages need not be nucleated settlement forms at all. Villages in Europe, including England, have ranged in form from quite compact, to linear, to widely dispersed neighborhoods.[9] Dispersed villages were common in southeast England, the major source area of New England colonists in the seventeenth century.[10] Second, recent studies of New England communities have dealt largely with the question of the essence of preindustrial village life in New England, the extent to which this way of life reflected its particular English origins, and the particularly American experience of those communities.[11] As a result of these studies, it has become evident to some historians that nucleation was not the constant rule for settlement form in early colonial New England.[12]

Close inspection of seventeenth-century New England villages—places specifically called "villages" in records of towns and governing colonial assemblies—suggests that "village" was an official designation of a community, like "town," and that villages were subordinate to towns. Also like towns, villages were not necessarily nucleated in form. Indeed, detailed accounts of settlement form indicate that the modal form of settlement was dispersed from the 1630s onward, and even many nucleated settlements were short-lived.[13] Nevertheless, New England communities existed and functioned quite well. Even when social structure or settlement form was altered, the social web that constituted community persisted. Village status encouraged such community forbearance by providing a community with land resources and by placing the community and its assigned land under the auspices, guidance, and taxing power of a parent town. This status enabled the community to establish its own ecclesiastical society, or parish, or, if unsettled, to undertake settlement beyond the pale of what in time might become a town in its own right.

"In the Village Manner"

New England colonists' yearning for land was great, and available land was a critical factor in the establishment of New England villages. Civil and religious liberty was important for settlers who came to New England, of course, but owning land and all that it implied were the most impelling reasons for initial colonization and inland settlement alike.[14] The goal of Puritan settlement in New England was noble; there was to be a covenanted community of men established in a new England, a congregation of individuals bound by special compact. But abundant land had an unsettling effect. Settlement expansion took place by replication, by increasing the number of communities, not by enlarging any one. Not satisfied with crowding along the shoreline, in Salem or about Boston Bay, settlers spread inland when and wherever they could. Much of New England is hardscrabble; once salt marshes, old Indian fields, and riverine meadows called intervales were taken, settlers were forced to settle land more marginal than what the first settlers had found. As New Englanders spread across the land, they established a settled landscape of places, many called villages and all designed to foster community well-being.

The New England town system was designed to bring order to these communities. The town was a community of settlers incorporated as an administrative unit to encourage settlement and establish political and religious institutions within clearly defined geographic boundaries and, thus, perpetuate community. But a town was not a settlement. Only through land proprietors, in whom was vested local authority and who were responsible for distributing land, did towns become instruments of settlement. Colonial magistrates made extensive grants of land to town proprietors and to individuals in their favor, so, according to Governor Winthrop, "that (when the towns should be increased by their children and servants growing up, etc.) they might have place to erect villages, where they might be planted, and so the land improved to the more common benefit."[15]

These "villages or plantations" were to be developed into new, freestanding communities, and certain conditions were required to assure their success.[16] The town of Lynn, Massachusetts, one of the original towns around Massachusetts Bay, was especially in need of the grant for Lynn Village. The fifty families that came to Lynn in 1630 had laid out farms from ten to two hundred acres in size and had settled these farms in all parts of the original town grant.[17] But by 1639 more land was required, and the General Court was generous:

The petition of the inhabitants of Linn for an inland plantation at the head of their bounds is granted them 4 miles square, as the place will affoard, upon condition that the petitioners shall within 2 years make some good proceeding in planting, so as it may bee a village fit to conteine a

convenient number of inhabitants, which may in dewe time have a churche there, & so as such as shall remove to inhabit there shall not with all keepe their accomodations in Linn above 2 years after their removall to the said village, upon paine to forfeit their interest in one of them, at their owne election, except this Court shall see just cause to dispense further with them; & this village is to bee 4 mile square at least by just content.[18]

New England towns were thus settled, according to Timothy Dwight, widely traveled president of Yale College, in *the village manner: the inhabitants having originally planted themselves in small towns."*[19] Dwight continued:

A town in the language of New England, denotes a collection of houses in the first parish, if the township contains more than one, constituting the principal, and ordinarily the original, settlement in the Parish. . . . A Street is the way, on which such a collection of houses is built; but does not at all include the fact, that the way is paved. . . . *Nor is it intended that the houses are contiguous, or even very near to each other.*[20]

While Dwight's statement is characteristic of the eighteenth-century landscape with which he was familiar, his description is appropriate for the seventeenth century as well. A century and a half before Dwight wrote, Capt. Edward Johnson described Watertown, like Lynn one of the original towns around Massachusetts Bay, as:

a fruitful plat, and of large extent, watered with many pleasant Springs, and small Rivulets, running like veines throughout her Body, which hath caused her *inhabitants to scatter in such manner*, that their Sabbath-Assemblies prove very thin if the season favour not.[21]

Similar descriptions, individual town records and maps, and even idiosyncratic town histories confirm that seventeenth-century settlements, like Lynn or Watertown, were more often than not settled in a dispersed fashion.

Dispersal was especially characteristic of places explicitly called villages in colonial records (fig. 1). Some of these places, like Billerica, first mentioned as a village in the colonial records of Massachusetts Bay in 1642, received new grants of land:

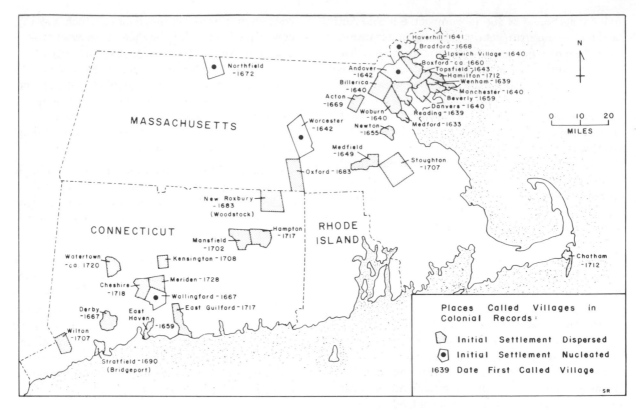

Fig. 1. Places called villages in colonial records and their corresponding settlement forms. (Map by Joseph S. Wood.)

All the land lying upon Saweshine Ryver & between that & Concord Ryver, & between that & Merrimack Ryver, not formerly granted by this Court, are granted to Cambridge, so as they may erect a village there within 5 yeares, & so as it shall not extend to prejudice Charlstowne village [Woburn], or the village of Cochitawit [Andover], nor the farmes formerly granted to the now Governor of 1260 acres.[22]

By 1660 over forty families had established farms in Billerica, forming a settlement that partially paralleled the Concord River but was otherwise dispersed (fig. 2).[23] Such other villages as Manchester, Beverly, and Salem Village, now the town of Danvers, were outlying neighborhoods of the original town of Salem. The dispersed inhabitants of Salem Village, called the "farmers of Salem," broke off from "Salem Town," where Salem's merchants resided. Salem Town was not becoming too crowded for farmers, but

farmers had long before moved out into an interstitial area beyond the reach of comfortable weekly commuting to the meetinghouse.[24] As in many other towns in Massachusetts and Connecticut, Salem's settlers were simply too widely dispersed from homesteading on great lots, distant divisions of land, not to split into more manageable social, religious, and eventually political units—villages.

The Meaning of Village

A number of issues follow from the manner in which the term *village* was used in early colonial New England. First, not all settlements were called villages, and not all villages were dispersed settlements. Villages seem generally to have been secondary settlements, for a time part of or subordinate to another town. None of the first settled towns in either Massachusetts Bay or Connecticut, and few primary or first-order towns, granted independently of any other town, were called villages.[25] There were three exceptions. Andover and Haverhill were first-order towns reserved by the Massachusetts Court as villages and granted to companies of men from a number of the original towns around Massachusetts Bay. The nucleated settlements of both towns were short-lived. As at Sudbury and Dedham, nucleated forms proved useful for establishing initial settlements in the deep woods but not for general farming, and farmers dispersed within a generation, leaving no nucleated settlement in Andover and only a small commercial settlement in Haverhill.[26] The vicinity of Worcester in Massachusetts Bay was first mentioned for a village in 1642 because of the presence of lead mines, but the venture did not succeed. In 1667 a committee was established to view the vicinity of Quinsigamond Pond for a village. Worcester was settled and abandoned twice, however, before permanent settlement occurred in 1713. The relatively compact but linear form of settlement that came to prevail in Worcester was important for defense, and later for central-place activities, but not for open-field farming.[27] The second-order settlements of Northfield, Massachusetts, and Wallingford, Connecticut, were also more clustered than dispersed. Riverine topography favored linear settlement in both places, and both were threatened by Indians. Wallingford had to be abandoned in 1675; Northfield was not permanently settled until after 1713.[28] In all other settlements expressly called villages in colonial records, dispersed settlement prevailed.

Though such villages were established throughout the first century of settlement in Massachusetts Bay and Connecticut, the meaning of the term *village* seems to have changed over time. In Massachusetts Bay, where the term was generally used only in the seventeenth century and thus earlier than in Connecticut, a village charter was an instrument of land distribution and town formation. Population was greater in Massachusetts Bay than in Connecticut, and inland settlement proceeded more quickly. Hence, Massachusetts Bay towns were subdivided or required new land grants earlier, often within a decade or generation of initial settlement. The area allocated for a town in Massachusetts Bay could hold only so many people before the community either split into new communities or overflowed. In Connecticut, on the other hand, dispersed settlements divided from older towns as well, but only long after the same process had generally occurred in Massachusetts Bay. In contrast to Massachusetts Bay, En-

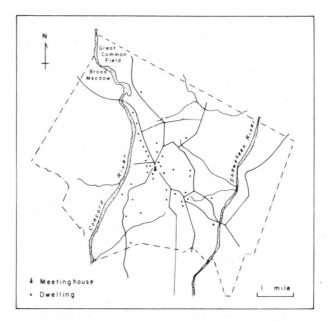

Fig. 2. Billerica, Massachusetts, ca. 1660. Settlers in early Billerica did not establish a nucleated settlement. (Map by Joseph S. Wood.)

glish agricultural practice, including common-field agriculture, persisted longer in Connecticut, larger reserves of land were held for future generations, and stricter control was placed on land division. Moreover, with a smaller initial population, population pressure took longer to build up. Hence, there were fewer requests for new communities, and until the end of the seventeenth century the Connecticut Court and Assembly were reluctant to grant new villages liberally.[29]

By then, *village* had come to mean something different in Connecticut than in Massachusetts. As early as 1659, some dispersed inhabitants of New Haven, Connecticut, were asking to become a separate village of East Haven. They agreed to meet conditions of their "Village grant" by laying out a five-acre meetinghouse lot, constructing a meetinghouse, and settling a minister.[30] Village status was finally granted in 1707, and records of the subsequent dialogue between inhabitants of East Haven and the Connecticut Assembly reveal the changing meaning of village:

This Assembly considering the petition of the East Village of New Haven, do see cause to order that they shall be a village distinct from the township of Newhaven, and invested and privileged with all immunities and privileges that are proper and necessary for a village for the upholding of the publick worship of God, as also their own civil concerns; and in order thereunto, do grant them libertie of all such offices as are proper and necessary for a town, and to be chosen by themselves in order and form as allowed by law for each and any town. . . . As also the said village have libertie to have a school amongst themselves with the privilege of the fortie schillings upon the thousand pound estate as every town hath by law; and also shall free their own village charge, and maintain their own poor, as all towns are obliged by law to do; and be fully freed from paying any taxes to the town of Newhaven.[31]

East Haven residents read more into their charter than the Assembly had meant to concede them, and in 1710 the order had to be qualified to read that "there is nothing in the said act that concerns property of lands, or that excludes the village from being within the township of New Haven."[32] Even this failed to settle the matter. In 1716, East Haven was "to have no other powers than those that are common to other parishes."[33] In short, land distribution was no longer the purpose or prerogative of the village, but a village still formed a community for social and religious functions. Consequently, when the inhabitants of Wilton petitioned for separation from Norwalk in 1726, the assembly was quite specific about what village had come to mean in Connecticut: "Upon the petition . . . praying to be a village by themselves enjoying parish privileges, and that they may be called by the name of Wilton Parish: This Assembly do hereby grant the said inhabitants be one village."[34]

Occasional references not specifying any particular place suggest that village was used by some to mean any settlement, especially any recent or prospective settlement.[35] But in most cases, a village was self-consciously and legally ordained as a community. In the seventeenth century, a village had sufficient independent status and authority to establish and foster spiritual as well as economic, social, and political well-being for its inhabitants while still constituting a part of a parent town. By the eighteenth century, a village was at least an ecclesiastical parish.

The Cultural Context

The traditional view that colonial New England villages were necessarily nucleated settlements housing rural communities practicing open-field agriculture is based on the premise that New Englanders were so predisposed. That is what the English were supposed to do. Moreover, nucleated settlements met the requirements of both mutual protection in the wilderness and Puritan tenets about how communities should be organized spatially to maximize political and religious order.[36] But though English colonists shared a common heritage, England was hardly homogeneous in social structure. The English came from a variety of social backgrounds and regional subcultures. Most had some familiarity with agriculture, but rural England in the seventeenth century was not composed exclusively, even largely, of corn-and-stock peasants farming open fields and living in nucleated settlements. Areas devoted more to livestock and less to grain tended towards dispersed settlement.[37] Thus, no singular folk tradition or set of rules and material forms existed. No single model of how an agricultural community was to operate or how a settlement was to be formed prevailed.[38] The English village that many colonists left behind was not necessarily a nucleated cluster of dwellings and outbuildings adjacent to a church and manor and encircled by common fields. How an English village functioned to provide a sense of community was more important than the form it took. The village was an interdependent, rural society carrying on family-oriented agriculture. The village functioned to provide economic security for its inhabitants, and its inhabitants shared a common social purpose.[39]

Not only did England embody a heterogeneous landscape of settlement forms, but the society colonists were leaving behind in England was in the throes of significant institutional change, including changes in land division and tenure. England was experiencing a crumbling of old customs of farming in the face of subtly increasing commercialization of agriculture and voluntary enclosure. The bulk of New England colonists, though not necessarily the dispossessed, came from portions of the east and south of England that were especially undergoing change. They brought with them to New England a strong notion that land ownership would provide both prestige and economic security.[40] Their desire for land was compounded by a spirit of individualism in politics, society, and ideas that had grown and developed in sixteenth- and seventeenth-century England. Hence, New England settlement must be viewed in the context of a tension between a longing for individual private control of land in a garden—and individual economic security—and a communal forbearance in a wilderness—social security. In all of their endeavors, large numbers of English colonists were driven to seek individual expression and convenanted communities alike.[41]

Driven as they were, and with no vested interests in a complex and finely woven cultural landscape as in England, the intricate weave of social structure that was itself undergoing change in England would not be rewoven in the same fashion. The English in New England could mold a new cultural landscape. Thus, while colonists drew on familiar forms and ways of doing things, they probably brought with them little excess cultural baggage, few vestiges of medieval institutions in community, church, governance, or agricultural practice. As a result, English local institutions were reshaped within each New England community to meet the particular needs and the particular English backgrounds of the inhabitants.[42] Because people of common cultural heritage but different social backgrounds and regional subcultures, each with their own customs and material forms, were intermingling, further reduction of vestigial ways and forms and a process of adaptation and innovation eventually took place. Such intermingling led towards more common ways of doing things and more common material culture.[43] By the end of the seventeenth century, much individual town distinctiveness inherited from England was gone.[44]

Both the common English notion of community and dispersed settlement survived the cultural transfer of English ways to the wilderness of New England. Such community could not only accommodate the centripetal requirements of venturing into the wilderness but, in its English variety of settlement forms, could also accommodate the variety of individual needs and experiences of New England's colonists. Requirements of defense and economic and spiritual well-being easily gave way to direct transfer from England of well-established cultural predispositions for certain kinds of economic endeavor, land-division practices, and preferences for particular environmental conditions that could not all be accommodated in a nucleated settlement form. Because livestock raising was especially significant in early colonial New England, settlers were prompted to secure as much intervale or salt marsh as they could while still remaining loyal to the evolving concept of the New England town.[45] One could choose either nucleated or dispersed settlement; but the modal form of community settlement that characteristically emerged in an early colonial New England, torn between individual expression and community covenant, was the dispersed village and English custom encouraged it.

Village and Community

What is important from the foregoing discussion of settlement form is not only that villages were often not nucleated settlements in early colonial New England but that villages functioned as communities regardless of settlement form. No one doubts that community was achieved in early colonial New England villages. The process of community building was not necessarily easy; but, aided by the common English heritage of the colonists, by the fact that many communities were purposefully gathered from parent communities in England or were formed in New England of old neighbors or acquaintances, and by the provision for land distribution, community building was accomplished. As in England, village meant community. As in England, villages were well-knit rural societies carrying on family-oriented agriculture, constituting distinct social and religious groups, and providing collective security for inhabitants. Indeed, community cohesion may have grown stronger in New England, and New Englanders continued to nourish such localism as a value to be cherished.[46] Congregational control of the church and local political control, including collective regulation of land distribution, encouragement of local enterprise, and coordination of communal activities, provided for a distinctive sense of community identity. Shared ideology insured societal uniformity and cohesion. Even economic exchange was fundamentally local. Trading relationships were familiar and intimate. Moreover, available land had released colonists from an age-old cultural tradition of communal frugality in land use. Finally, available land meant that political responsibility based on freeholding could be more widely held within the community.[47]

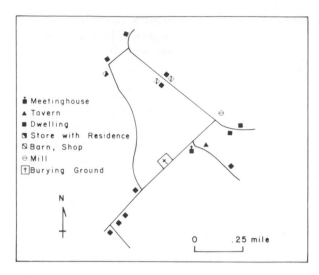

Fig. 3. The central portion of Meriden, Connecticut, ca. 1780. Meetinghouses were the symbolic and geographic centers of New England communities, but meetinghouses were not necessarily the centers of nucleated settlements. (Map by Joseph S. Wood.)

Dispersed settlement did not necessarily imply remoteness and isolation, a denial of community, even in a society driven to individual expression. Interaction caused by daily, weekly, seasonal, and annual congregational and political responsibilities took place within an established social structure, and the interaction itself was more important than the degree to which settlement was nucleated. The real colonial New England village was a network of social and economic linkages—a social web, not a cluster of dwellings. Within the social web, a basic conflict between human striving for individual expression and a similar strong need for collective experience and a place to belong was played out. People were villagers within an umbrella of social control and economic security, while living dispersed upon their own farms.

The New England community's network of interaction had a physical manifestation. Common cultural features of colonial maps of New England villages and towns are a node, paths, and edges—or the meetinghouse, roads, and town boundaries. Other buildings or dwellings and property boundaries are less often shown, especially on the earliest extant maps. The meetinghouse, the focus of community activity, was often exaggerated beyond proportion to indicate its location. Indeed, the meetinghouse, well situated often at an elevation, standing alone or accompanied by a parsonage, in time a tavern, perhaps a blacksmith, and by chance a farmhouse or two, was the dominant feature of the village landscape throughout the colonial period. No particular sacredness was attached to the meetinghouse itself, but the meetinghouse was the embodiment of the community, a tangible manifestation of the intangible political and religious life of the community—even if it stood alone as Capt. Edward Johnson described the meetinghouse in Roxbury, Massachusetts, in the 1630s. "Their streets are large, and some fayre Houses, yet they have built the House of Church-assembly, destitute and unbeautified with other buildings."[48] One hundred and fifty years later, community centers looked little different, as Meriden, Connecticut, first called a village in 1728, illustrated (fig. 3).[49] The town road network, extended to interconnect dispersed farmsteads, enhanced the situation of the meetinghouse, providing access for all in the community. The physical circumscription of bounds added to the sense of place, and the annual perambulation and intertown contentiousness over bounds recorded by provincial assemblies attest to the significance of town boundaries.[50]

Bounds, of course, could not be too extensive, or intratown contentiousness also recorded by town meetings and provincial assemblies might arise and a new community might need to be established. Equitable organization of space within reasonable bounds for dispersed settlements was the overriding consideration in the formation of new communities. As seventeenth-century settlement reached into extensions of land granted for villages and plantations and more distant settlers were required to travel considerable distances to meeting and so often petitioned to establish a separate community, a village with its own meetinghouse could be sanctioned and social order maintained. As residents withdrew still further from the affairs of the original community—the town—they might petition for their own separate town incorporation. Because parent towns were often reluctant to release such communities within their bounds and thus reduce their tax base, as residents of East Haven, Connecticut, had learned, such division was slow. Nevertheless, division of dispersed communities into new villages and towns was an important process in the evolution of the New England settlement landscape.[51] As long as social and economic linkages remained unbroken, community prevailed. When linkages were stretched too far, the effect was hardly a rejection of the idea of community. As in 1630, when too many settlers had gathered on the shores of Massachusetts Bay to form a single community, division created new communities.[52] By the end of the colonial period, early settled towns had been subdivided and more recently settled towns granted in such a fashion that the landscape of New England came to resemble a great mosaic of equal-sized communities.

Also by the end of the colonial period, the notion of community as it had been known in early colonial New England was being challenged. Economic and social linkages that maintained community were strained. Yet the informal and intimate relationship of self-conscious, colonial communities bridged differences, including the new abstract theological differences of the Great Awakening that had given rise to dissenting congregations within communities and that had assumed great rhetorical importance in provincial politics. A multiplicity of operating cultures—a pragmatic, family-based community culture concerned with local economic and social affairs, superficially overlain by a more abstract culture concerned with religious and political issues, all interpenetrated by emerging external associations—helps explain the apparent persistence of "peaceable kingdoms" well into the eighteenth century. Community was not necessarily diminished; it simply accommodated change; and settlement form, long dispersed, had little to do with it.[53] Methods of land distribution within towns, on the other hand, increasingly individualistic and competitive rather than community-based as the colonial period passed, may have had much to do with transforming what was recognized as community in the seventeenth century to a form of community more appropriate to the eighteenth century.[54] That, however, is another study.

Conclusion

David Lowenthal reminds us that the preservation of relict artifacts may overemphasize the role an artifact played in a past landscape.[55] The village encountered in New England today, white-painted, black-shuttered, classical-revival dwellings, churches, and stores abutting a tree-shaded green, reflects not continuity with New England's colonial past but a most dramatic change. The change took place in the federal period—the last generation of the eighteenth century and the first generation of the nineteenth century. Economic affairs became increasingly regional, and New Englanders broke out of traditional cultural molds to create a landscape of commercial places where meetinghouses had long stood alone.[56]

Only then, as the form of settlement changed to become nucleated, did the term *village* take on its present-day connotation. To early colonial New Englanders, who were not necessarily predisposed towards nucleated settlement, village only meant community. The New England town was the source of land for most individuals and thus the initial instrument for providing economic security and encouraging settlement. A well-bounded corporate space, inhabited by people who sensed they composed a community distinct from any other, was sufficient to provide the order and cohesion long attributed to nucleated settlement. Indeed, closely interdependent, collaborative communities of colonial New England themselves allowed nucleated settlement, where it had been implanted, to wither. Social order did not require nucleation. In the colonial meaning, the village was a social web in which Puritan tenets worked well enough.[57]

Notes

1. On settlement form, see Edna Scofield, "The Origin of Settlement Patterns in Rural New England," *Geographical Review* 28 (1938): 652–63; Glenn T. Trewartha, "Types of Rural Settlement in Colonial America," *Geographical Review* 36 (1946): 568–96; F. Grave Morris, "Some Aspects of the Rural Settlement of New England in Colonial Times," in *London Essays in Geography*, ed. L. D. Stamp and S. W. Wooldridge (New York, 1951), 219–27; and D. R. McManis, *Colonial New England: A Historical Geography* (New York, 1975). On New England communities, see Sumner Chilton Powell, *Puritan Village: The Formation of a New England Town* (Middletown, Conn., 1963); Richard L. Bushman, *From Puritan to Yankee: Character and Social Order in Connecticut, 1690–1765* (Cambridge, Mass., 1967); Kenneth A. Lockridge, *A New England Town: The First Hundred Years* (New York, 1970); Philip J. Greven, Jr., *Four Generations: Population, Land, and Family Life in Andover, Massachusetts* (Ithaca, N.Y., 1970); and Bruce C. Daniels, *The Connecticut Town: Growth and Development, 1635–1790* (Middletown, Conn., 1979).

2. Darrett B. Rutman, "The Social Web: A Prospectus for the Study of the Early American Community," in *Insights*

and Parallels: Problems and Issues of American Social History, ed. William L. O'Neill (Minneapolis, Minn., 1973), 58.

3. Rutman, "Social Web," 62–63; Thomas Bender, Community and Social Change in America (New Brunswick, N.J., 1978), 7 (including n. 4).

4. Yi-Fu Tuan, Space and Place: The Perspective of Experience (Minneapolis, Minn., 1977), 3; see also Bender, Community and Social Change, 61; Rutman, "Social Web," 62–63; and Harold R. Kaufmann, "Toward an Interactional Conception of Community," Social Forces 38 (1959): 9–17.

5. Milton B. Newman, "Settlement Patterns as Artifacts of Social Structure," in The Human Mirror: Material and Spatial Images of Man, ed. M. Richardson (Baton Rouge, La., 1974), 339–61.

6. Oxford English Dictionary, 1st ed., s.v. "village."

7. Webster's New International Dictionary, 3d ed., s.v. "village."

8. Albert Demangeon, "La géographie de l'habitat rural," Annales de géographie 36 (1927): 1–23, 97–114; W. Christaller, Central Places of Southern Germany (Englewood Cliffs, N.J., 1966). As an objective measure, Martyn J. Bowden of Clark University (personal communication to author) has suggested that a nucleated settlement be one in which more than four neighbors dwell purposefully within hailing distance of one another, perhaps 100 meters. Four houses located by chance at a crossroads need not be considered a nucleated settlement.

9. Robert E. Dickinson, "Rural Settlements in the German Lands," Annals of the Association of American Geographers 39 (1949): 239–63; Gottfried Pfeifer, "The Quality of Peasant Living in Central Europe," in Man's Role in Changing the Face of the Earth, ed. W. L. Thomas (Chicago, 1956), 240–77.

10. Joan Thirsk, "The Farming Regions of England," in The Agrarian History of England and Wales, 1500–1640, vol. 4, ed. Joan Thirsk (Cambridge, 1967), 1–112; see also George C. Homans, "The Explanation of English Regional Differences," Past and Present, no. 42 (1969): 18–34.

11. See, for example, Powell, Puritan Village; Lockridge, New England Town; and Greven, Four Generations.

12. Rutman, "Social Web," 67, n. 29; T. H. Breen, "Persistent Localism: English Social Change and the Shaping of New England Institutions," William and Mary Quarterly, 3d ser., 32 (1975): 20; Breen, "Transfer of Culture: Chance and Design in Shaping Massachusetts Bay, 1630–1660," New England Historical and Genealogical Register 132 (1978): 9.

13. Joseph S. Wood, "The Origin of the New England Village" (Ph.D. diss., Pennsylvania State University, 1978), 58–202.

14. David Grayson Allen, In English Ways: The Movement of Societies and the Transferal of English Local Custom to Massachusetts Bay in the Seventeenth Century (Chapel Hill, N.C., 1981); T. H. Breen and Stephen Foster, "Moving to the New World," William and Mary Quarterly, 3d ser., 30 (1973): 189–222; James T. Lemon, "Early Americans and Their Social Environment," Journal of Historical Geography 6 (1980): 119–21.

15. John Winthrop, The History of New England from 1630–1649, 2 vols. (New York, 1825), 2:263. See also Records of the Governor and Company of Massachusetts Bay, ed. Nathaniel B. Shurtleff, 5 vols. (Boston, 1853–55), 2:135 (hereafter MBR).

16. W. Haller, Jr., The Puritan Frontier: Town Planning in New England Colonial Development, 1630–1660 (New York, 1951); H. R. McCutcheon, "Town Formation in Eastern Massachusetts, 1630–1802: A Case Study in Political Area Organization" (Ph.D. diss., Clark University, 1970).

17. Alonzo Lewis and John R. Newhall, History of Lynn, Essex County, Massachusetts (Boston, 1865), 131; Richard Brigham Johnson, "Swampscott, Massachusetts, in the Seventeenth Century," Essex Institute Historical Collections 109 (1973): 251.

18. MBR, 1:272; 3:7.

19. Timothy Dwight, Travels in New England and New York, 4 vols. (New Haven, Conn., 1821–22), 1:216.

20. Dwight, Travels in New England, 1:216 (emphasis added).

21. Edward Johnson, Wonder-Working Providence of Sion's Saviour in New England (1654; reprint ed., Andover, Mass., 1867), 46 (emphasis added).

22. MBR, 2:17.

23. H. A. Hazen, History of Billerica, Massachusetts (Boston, 1883), 24–26.

24. MBR, 5:247–48; Charles W. Upham, Salem Witchcraft (Boston, 1867); Sidney Perley, "Part of Salem Village in 1700," Essex Institute Historical Collections 52 (1916): 177–91; Paul Boyer and Stephen Nissenbaum, Salem Possessed: The Social Origins of Witchcraft (Cambridge, Mass., 1974); Richard P. Gildrie, Salem, Massachusetts, 1628–1683: A Covenanted Community (Charlottesville, Va., 1975). The use of the term town in this context suggests that, like village, it could be ambiguous in colonial New England. In New England as in England, town could refer to a major market center, like Salem or Boston, as well as an incorporated town. For additional comments, see Carville E. Earle, "The First English Towns in North America," Geographical Review 67 (1977): 34–50.

25. On the classification of towns by order, see McCutcheon, "Town Formation."

26. MBR, 1:306, 319; 2:10–11, 17; A. Abbot, History of Andover from its Settlement to 1829 (Andover, Mass., 1829), 12, 47, 74–76; Philip J. Greven, Jr., "Old Patterns in the New World: The Distribution of Land in Seventeenth-Century Andover," Essex Institute Historical Collections 101 (1965): 133–48; G. W. Chase, The History of Haverhill, Massachusetts, from its First Settlement, in 1640, to 1860 (Haverhill, Mass., 1861), 42, 61. See also Powell, Puritan Village, and Lockridge, New England Town.

27. MBR, 2:11; 4, pt. 2:408–9; W. Lincoln, History of Worcester, Massachusetts (Worcester, Mass., 1837), 6–7, 30–31, 43.

28. MBR, 4, pt. 2:528–29; J. H. Temple and George Sheldon, History of the Town of Northfield, Massachusetts (Albany, N.Y., 1875), 165; Public Records of the Colony of Connecticut, 1636–1776 (Hartford, Conn., 1850–90), 2:255;

3:1 (hereafter *PRC*); C. H. S. Davis, *History of Wallingford, Connecticut, from its Settlement in 1670 to the Present Time* (Meriden, Conn., 1870), 78–79.

29. Wood, "Origin of New England Village," 102–7, 117–36; Daniels, *Connecticut Town*, 97; and Bender, *Community and Social Change*, 72, n. 70.

30. S. E. Hughes, *History of East Haven* (New Haven, Conn., 1908), 67–75; D. Deming, *The Settlement of Connecticut Towns* (New Haven, Conn., 1933), 68.

31. *PRC*, 4:15–16.

32. *PRC*, 4:123–24.

33. *PRC*, 5:63.

34. *PRC*, 5:521.

35. *PRC*, 3:190; *MBR*, 5:213–14, 311–12.

36. Scofield, "Origin of Settlement Patterns"; Trewartha, "Types of Rural Settlement."

37. Thirsk, "Farming Regions of England;" Homans, "Explanation of English Regional Differences." See also Allen, *In English Ways*, for more detailed discussion of several distinct source communities.

38. A significant statement on this point is Allen, *In English Ways*.

39. Peter Laslett, *The World We Have Lost* (New York, 1965), 53–80, may overstate the case. See also R. Cole Harris, "The Simplification of Europe Overseas," *Annals of the Association of American Geographers* 67 (1977): 471, esp. n. 6; Joan Thirsk, "Enclosing and Engrossing," in *Agrarian History of England and Wales*, ed. Thirsk, 225.

40. Christopher Hill, *Change and Continuity in Seventeenth-Century England* (London, 1974); Thirsk, "Farming Regions of England," 6–7; Howard S. Russell, *A Long Deep Furrow: Three Centuries of Farming in New England* (Hanover, N.H., 1976), 26–27; John R. Stilgoe, "Pattern on the Land: The Making of a Colonial Landscape, 1633–1800" (Ph.D. diss., Harvard University, 1976).

41. Michael Zuckerman, "The Fabrication of Identity in Early America," *William and Mary Quarterly*, 3d ser., 34 (1977): 183–214; see also P. N. Carroll, *Puritanism and the Wilderness: The Intellectual Significance of the New England Frontier, 1629–1700* (New York, 1969), 133, 140–47, 182–87.

42. Allen, *In English Ways*; Breen, "Transfer of Culture," 5, n. 5; G. B. Warden, "Law Reform in England and New England," *William and Mary Quarterly*, 3d ser., 35 (1978): 687–88.

43. Harris, "Simplification of Europe Overseas," elaborates on this process; see also Robert D. Mitchell, "Comment on the Simplification of Europe Overseas," Adrian Pollock, "Commentary—Europe Simplified," and Harris "Comment in Reply," all in *Annals of the Association of American Geographers* 69 (1979): 474–80; Allen, *In English Ways*, 222, argues that the trend away from open fields was faster in New England than was possible in England. On material culture, see Abbott Lowell Cummings, *The Framed Houses of Massachusetts Bay, 1625–1725* (Cambridge, Mass., 1979).

44. Allen, *In English Ways*, 231–32.

45. McManis, *Colonial New England*, 92–102.

46. John Murrin, "Review Essay," *Historical Theory* 11 (1972): 231.

47. Bender, *Community and Social Change*, 63–68, provides a full summary of community in New England. See also Rutman, "Social Web"; James A. Henretta, "Families and Farms: *Mentalité* in Preindustrial America," *William and Mary Quarterly*, 3d ser., 35 (1978): 3–32; T. H. Breen and Stephen Foster, "The Puritans' Greatest Achievement: A Study of Social Cohesion in Seventeenth-Century Massachusetts," *Journal of American History* 60 (1973): 5–22; Breen, "Transfer of Culture."

48. *PRC*, 6:121; Davis, *History of Wallingford*, 125; C. B. Gillespie, comp., *A Century of Meriden* (Meriden, Conn., 1906).

49. Johnson, *Wonder-Working Providence*, 44.

50. Tuan, *Space and Place*, 166. James T. Lemon, "The Weakness of Place and Community in Early Pennsylvania," in *European Settlement and Development in North America: Essays in Honour and Memory of A. H. Clark*, ed. J. R. Gibson (Toronto, 1978), 198–99, argues that a critical difference between community in Pennsylvania and community in New England was the fixing of parish or town bounds to provide a strong sense of place for community groups.

51. McCutcheon, "Town Formation," and Daniels, *Connecticut Town*, are good sources on the division of towns. The process of towns dividing into smaller units or sending out new villages, parishes, or towns has long been called "hiving off." The analogy is inappropriate because it suggests a nucleated settlement splitting to form another nucleated settlement, or hive.

52. Bender, *Community and Social Change*, 72–73; Rutman, "Social Web," 68.

53. Zuckerman, *Peaceable Kingdoms: New England Towns in the Eighteenth Century* (New York, 1970). Bender argues that a historically grounded concept of community is one that allows the alteration of its social structure, and by implication its spatial structure, to meet new conditions without necessarily breaking down (*Community and Social Change*, 3–13, 75–78).

54. See Daniels, *Connecticut Town*, 173, and Lemon, "Early Americans," 129–30.

55. David Lowenthal, "Age and Artifact: Dilemmas of Appreciation," in *The Interpretation of Ordinary Landscapes*, ed. D. W. Meinig (New York, 1979), 103–27.

56. Wood, "Origin of New England Village," 203–85.

57. The University Research Committee, the University of Nebraska at Omaha, has funded portions of the research reported in this paper.

"Shining in Borrowed Plumage": Affirmation of Community in the Black Coronation Festivals of New England, ca. 1750–1850

MELVIN WADE

Processions and festivals articulated one ritual dimension of American material life as they merged social and artifactual realms in dynamic displays of music, toasts, and dance carried on by masked figures sporting wild costumes of rags, grass, and military emblems. In addition to marking celebrations, festivals and parades served a variety of symbolic functions. In this exploration of black coronation festivals in eighteenth- and nineteenth-century New England, Melvin Wade describes the coronations as a complex genre of artistic exchange between blacks and whites that was securely anchored in African tradition. He also demonstrates that Afro-American cultural connections were crucial to black identity in New England, even though most existing scholarship concentrates on the persistence of black consciousness among slaves in the American South.

Wade shows that the black coronation festivals were one way that New England blacks celebrated their own social structure within the dominant Anglo-American order; the festivals also manifested in visible and kinetic form their continuing attachment to their African cultural homeland and the importance of ancestors, and also served as a complex metaphor of patriarchal kinship structure. The form of the festivals, while varying widely from one place and time to another, derived from the Odwira festival of the Ashanti people, a ritual of social purification in which negative social forces were purged while ancestors were honored.

As he outlines the structure and functions of the coronations, we see how black New Englanders, like their counterparts in the South, succeeded in asserting and preserving their cultural autonomy through expressive forms. And while the ritual inversions effected by the coronation festivals were circumscribed by the legal restraints of Yankee culture, the
forms and texture of the accompanying parades— their music, strutting, and enthusiastic rounds of toasts—made a lasting impact on the form and content of parades in America's official culture during the first half of the nineteenth century.

In colonial and antebellum New England, the stringent measures restricting interaction between black Americans failed to prevent them from orienting and ordering their relations with each other. By the middle of the eighteenth century, black Americans in New England had established the modal pattern of the customary event known as Negro Election. The earliest recorded instance of this "Negro's hallowday" dates back to May 27, 1741, when Benjamin Lynde, Sr., noted the attendance of Scipio and William, captives from his household, at the occasion.[1] By 1755 the coronation had definitely emerged as the central feature of Negro Election in Newport, Rhode Island, whose black population numbered 1,300 residents. Subsequent observances of the occasion during the 1760s were reported in Hartford and Norwich, Connecticut. By 1790 the practice had reached a peak, spreading to no fewer than eighteen other towns in New England, among them Boston, Massachusetts; Providence, Rhode Island; Portsmouth, New Hampshire; and New Haven, Connecticut. Entering a period of decline by the turn of the century, the rites survived in Connecticut until the 1850s.[2]

Succeeding General Election Day, the principal holiday in the calendar year of white New Englanders, the gala event took place annually during the late spring and early summer seasons, in May or June. In Connecticut, the occasion began the Saturday after the white elections in May. In Massachusetts, the rites occurred over four days, beginning the last Wednesday in May or encompassing the entire week. In Rhode Island, the celebrations were held around the third Sunday in June.[3]

As microcosms of the black communities that created their basic format, the black coronation festivals embodied a number of processes characteristic of the emergence of social systems: (1) *communication*— "the process by which information, decisions and directives are transmitted among actors and the ways in which knowledge, opinions and attitudes are formed or modified by interaction"; (2) *boundary maintenance*—"the process whereby the identity of the social system is preserved and the characteristic interaction pattern maintained"; (3) *systemic linkage*—"the process whereby one or more of the elements of at least two social systems is articulated in such a manner that the two systems in some ways and on some occasions may be viewed as a single unit"; (4) *socialization*—"the process through which the social and cultural heritage is transmitted"; (5) *social control*—"the process by which deviancy is either eliminated or somehow made compatible with the functioning of the social groups"; and (6) *institutionalization*—"the process through which organizations are given structure and social action and interaction made predictable."[4] The intent of this paper is to investigate the black coronation festivals of New England as cultural events in which black communities celebrated their existence as social systems. While the prevailing academic opinion dismissed the festivals as mere mimicry of white election practices, a counternotion of African survivals began to emerge as a minority viewpoint in the scholarship beginning with Hubert H. S. Aimes. Extending this line of analysis, William G. Piersen accomplished the most significant breakthrough, examining the festivals as an African-derived, European-influenced cultural phenomenon common throughout the New World, distinct in style and custom. More recently, Joseph Reidy has suggested that the festivals have their cultural origins primarily in the rites of the Ashanti of Ghana. The current analysis, building upon Aimes, Piersen, and Reidy, treats the festivals as cultural events intended to preserve community among blacks in New England, emphasizing Africa as homeland, African ancestors as authority figures, and patriarchy as social organization.

Communication in the Black Coronation Festivals

In colonial and antebellum New England, black communication systems were apparently most stable and complex in the black communities of the larger towns along the seacoast and river valleys. Surpassing similar social units within the region in population density and ethnic and social class diversity, these communities evolved such networks of organizations as lodges, churches, schools, mutual aid societies, and fraternal and sororal societies. Membership in these organizations derived principally from the black captives and freedpersons residing in the town. Though these organizations may not have formally supported the black coronation festivals, their formal meetings and auxiliary events, such as church-raisings and house-raisings, provided excellent opportunities for the dissemination of information about Negro Election. During the early nineteenth century, the black community of Providence evolved a town-centered communication network, which was served by the Hiram Lodge Number Three, initiated in 1799; the African Union School, founded in 1819; and the African Union Meeting House, a church organized in 1820.[5]

Complementing the town-centered networks were communication networks among blacks in rural areas of New England. Based on work alliances formed around the kitchens, gardens, the stables, and the fields, these informal networks were effective information systems. During the late eighteenth century, blacks in the Narragansett country of Rhode Island coordinated their social relations through a rural-centered network. Their autumnal corn-huskings brought together entire contingents of black captives from neighboring forms for work and play.[6] It is probable that house servants, artisans, chauffeurs, grooms, and free blacks were the primary conduits of information.

The most influential communication networks in several black communities of New England, however, were the organizational hierarchies of the black coronation festivals. In most instances, the structure of these hierarchies emerged during the elective and military holidays within the white social calendar— particularly General Election, when the white governor was inaugurated, and Training Day, or Muster Day, when a company or an entire regiment engaged in ceremonial drill on the local parade grounds. When the whites assembled in state capitals or other prominent towns to elect their public officials, to review the results of elections, or to celebrate their military traditions, black captives often accompanied them in some menial capacity. Left to their leisure, the captives from rural areas interacted with their fellow captives and freedpersons living in town. Together they planned and conducted rump festivals, electing, appointing, or commemorating their own kings, governors, lieutenant-governors, sheriffs, deputies, justices of the peace, or other officials with title and responsibility, sometimes for annual terms, other times for more lengthy periods. These festivities linked communities of blacks through networks that stressed interpersonal communication, disseminating information by word of mouth. Churches, lodges, meetinghouses for blacks as well as public taverns and workplaces provided forums for discussion. The efficiency of the communication networks was attested to by the audiences and participants often drawn from a number of towns or counties. In such towns as Hartford and Newport, ritual officials sometimes claimed jurisdiction over an entire state.[7]

Boundary Maintenance in the Black Coronation Festivals

The three-tiered model of social stratification envisioned by the white male population in colonial and antebellum New England generally featured white men occupying the highest stratum, white women the middle rank, and red and black men and women the lowest rungs of the social ladder. According to the assumptions of the model, blacks epitomized the marginal personality, their perceptual and behavioral norms often exerting pressure on the margins of society rather than at its center. The maintenance of rigid social, economic, political, and cultural boundaries was intended to prevent these normative differences from disturbing the social order. Lamenting the apathy and irreverence associated with late nineteenth-century observances of General Election Day, James Newhall of Lynn, Massachusetts, rationalized black normative differences on grounds of social deviance:

So long as slavery existed in Massachusetts, our colored brethren—who were allowed by their mas-

ters an annual vacation of four days, beginning with the day on which the General Court made their elections—were accustomed then, in imitation of their masters, to assemble on Boston Common or in some other convenient place, and proceed to elect rulers from their own ranks; or rather imitation rulers, rulers without authority and without subjects. They engaged in their sportive political ceremonies with a keen relish, the more so perhaps from having no real interest to be anxious about, and wound up with scenes of unlimited jollity. And the whole of their vacation was marked by excesses such as might be expected from a class so ignorant and so excitable when freed from restraint.[8]

To Newhall and his contemporaries, the relaxation of boundaries threatened to create an epidemic of social deviance in New England, allying the blacks with the white lower classes in their rejection of the civil authorities. Inasmuch as the white election ceremonies paid homage to those who held military and political office, these occasions were believed to intensify the boundaries between the authorities and other citizens, and between citizens and marginals. Given a certain gravity by their setting, the election ceremonies were conducted for the most part in the public squares, the public meetinghouses, and the statehouses usually situated in the heart of town. The overt sense of formal boundaries was further enhanced by the presence of the clergy and the virtual exclusion of blacks and women from prominent roles.[9]

Emerging from the vacuum of exclusivity practiced by the white male electors, the black coronation festivals enabled their partisans to realign social, temporal, spatial, and symbolic boundaries—even though the transformations were momentary. The festivals, in their infancy, collapsed social boundaries more so than did any other social event in colonial New England, deriving their participants and spectators across lines of race, sex, class, and generation.[10] As focal events for the gathering of marginals, the festivals were commonly held in an open field on the outskirts of town, with the parade route winding its way through the streets of town. In Salem, Massachusetts, the festival was held on the plain near the Collins farm; in Hartford, it was held on the Neck near the north burial grounds; in Derby, Connecticut, at Hawkins Point; in South Kingston, Rhode Island, on Pine Hill and in Potter's Woods; and in Newport, by the tree at the head of Thames Street.[11] In Puritan New England, where secular celebrations of Christmas, Easter, and Whitsuntide were prohibited, the festivals offered popular outlets for marginal behavior, the length of time allotted to them increasing from a single day to a period of four to six days.[12]

The open character of the festivals and the dissolution of conventional social, spatial, and temporal boundaries created a climate sufficient for the emergence of *communitas*,[13] a transitory state of social and physical integration in which individuals interact with each other, displaced from conventional constraints of role and status, acutely conscious of their commonality. The principal catalyst for this communitas was the symbolic inversion of roles within the festivals. In Lynn, "the masters did not interfere till the utmost verge of decency had been reached, good-naturedly submitting to the hard hits levelled against themselves, and possibly profiting a little by some shrewd allusion."[14] As conventional role and status boundaries were manipulated, the social hierarchy of white-over-black was temporarily leveled, calling into play a revised model of social stratification. In the emergent model, performance skills in music, dance, and speaking—as well as observance of traditional rules of demeanor and decorum—became primary normative criteria for ascribing social rank. Implicit within this model was criticism of the prevailing white models of social stratification in which race overpowered all other criteria.

Systemic Linkage in the Black Coronation Festivals

In their systemic relations with other social groups the black communities of colonial and antebellum New England embodied a model of social adaptation based on cultural "creolization." Hybrid in their cultural composition, the ways of life of these dominated communities reflected the tangible artifacts of the dominating social system in combination with the subtle value structure of the parent culture, the former often apprehended consciously and the latter usually perceived unconsciously. As events that intensely focused cultural and social energies, the black coronation festivals publicly displayed the link of black communities with both their African ancestors and their European-American captors.

The majority of the testimonies, reminiscences, and secondhand reports contemporary to the events posited that the black festivals were imitations of the white election ceremonies, however imperfect the copy.[15] A more accurate assessment would have been that there was much free and open exchange of cultural traits within the festivals by both blacks and whites. The titles of the elective offices, the occasional formal balloting, the apparent prohibition of women from elective status, the procession on horseback, the firing of military salutes, the mode of military garb and formal dress, the indoor staging of the election ball, and the majority of the musical instrumentation provide likely examples of ethnic borrowing by blacks from whites. Conversely, the tradition of the inaugural parades, the diversity of musical instrumentation within the parade ensemble, the polytonal texture and upbeat rhythms of the music, its percussive emphasis, and the strutting and baton-twirling of the marchers were equally apparent instances of borrowing by whites from blacks. Moreover, other customs—the pre-election "parmateering" (parliamenteering), the order of march during the procession, the prominence accorded military traditions, the precision drilling of troops, and the inaugural oration represented probable convergences of traits evident in both the African and European-American cultural pasts.

While considerable borrowing and convergence of cultural traits occurred between blacks and whites, the deepest links in the black coronation festivals related the descendants of Africa to their parent culture. Most accounts of the British colonies in the Americas identify the Fanti and Ashanti peoples of Ghana as the groups that established the predominant mold of black culture toward which other black captives adjusted. Colonial and antebellum New England fits well the modal pattern of the British colonies in the Americas, the confirmation of Fanti and Ashanti presence found in the common usage of day-names such as Quashee (Sunday) and Quamino (Saturday) and the widespread mention of "Gold Coast" blacks in newspaper advertisements seeking the return of fugitive captives.[16]

Those descended from African royalty had a formidable advantage in competing for positions of title. King Pompey of Lynn, Massachusetts, King Prince

Robinson of South Kingston, Rhode Island, Governor Tobiah of Derby, Connecticut, and his son Gov. Eben Tobias were reliably reported to be scions of African royal lineages. Even those who could recall specific knowledge of their African lineage were excellent prospects for elective office. King Nero Brewster of Portsmouth, New Hampshire, and Governors Boston of Hartford, Quash Freeman of Derby, and London of Wethersfield, all in Connecticut, knew of their African past. Govs. Cuff and Quaw of Hartford, Roswell Quash Freeman of Derby, Quash Piere of New Haven, Boston Trowtrow of Norwich, and Jubal Weston and his sons, Nelson and Wilson, of Seymour, all in Connecticut, were likely to have had knowledge of their African background. Since at least sixteen of the thirty-one black kings and governors reported by William Pierson apparently possessed an acquaintance with their African heritage, it can be concluded that black celebrants of the festivals attached considerable significance to their ritual patriarchs as representatives of a living cultural heritage.[17]

The emphasis on knowledge of the African past suggests that blacks in New England closely resembled their Ashanti forefathers in their conceptions of the patriarchal office. The Ashanti anthropologist Kofi A. Busia has described the role of the *Omanhene*, the paramount chief of state of the Ashanti, as symbol of lineage and ethnic group and as intermediary to the ancestors:

> An Ashanti chief . . . is important not only as a civil ruler who is the axis of the political relations of his people and the one in whom the various lineages that compose the tribe find their unity; he is also the symbol of their identity and continuity as a tribe and the embodiment of their spiritual values . . . he is the link, the intermediary, between the living and the dead; for, according to the conception which the Ashanti share with other Akan tribes, the dead, the living, and those still to be born are all members of one family.[18]

The method of electing the ritual patriarch among the blacks of New England bore resemblance to the elective process among the Ashanti. In Hartford, Eben E. Bassett, the son of Gov. Eben Tobias, recalled that the electorate chose the new patriarch "more by *viva voce* and caucus than by ballot."[19] Consensus within the community was at the heart of the Ashanti elective process, too.

During the lifetime of a chief there is generally a member of the royal house who has been marked out to succeed the reigning chief on the death of the latter. He is the heir apparent and is called in Ashanti the *badiakyiri*. His selection is, to all outward appearances, in the hands of the chief and the queen-mother. In one sense, therefore, it would appear that they select the successor. This, however, is not the case. There is in the vernacular one of those sayings or proverbs which have all the force of legal maxims. It states . . . one of the royal blood does not place a chief on a stool. . . . Nominally, it will be seen that it is the queen-mother who does so . . . although in every enstoolment it is she who publicly nominates the successor to the late chief, she does so only after discussion, consultation, and agreement in private with the *mpanyimfo* (elders), who in turn take good care to find out the wishes of the majority of the populace.[20]

Moreover, the black coronation festivals evoke comparison with their Ashanti background in the overall patterning of the cultural events. The most definite parallel to the festivals can be found in the *Odwira* festival, "the rite of purification,"[21] among the Ashanti. The intent of Odwira was to purge negative spiritual forces from the community, to sanctify the chief and the community, and to propitiate the ancestors, thereby preparing the community for the transition from the old to the new year.[22]

Demarcating the New Year in the Ashanti calendar, Odwira was oriented around the vernal equinox, the first of two times during the year when the sun crosses the equator.[23] Occurring around March 21, causing day and night to be equal in length, the vernal equinox heralds the coming of spring. Because spring signified freshness, newness, rebirth, the Ashanti associated it with the renewal of the earth, the growth of life. As a rite of spring, Odwira celebrated the revitalization of the communal *kra*, the "life force," through the symbolic rejuvenation of the chief's powers. Similarly, the black coronation festivals were oriented to Easter, whose observance was scheduled in relation to the first full moon after the vernal equinox. Symbolic of the death and resurrection of Christ, Easter was appropriate for the themes of personal and communal renewal. The coronation of the ritual patriarch culminated this period of renewal, perhaps initiating for some the New Year.[24]

In a fashion resembling Odwira, the black coronation festivals were preceded by a traditional period of moderation, fasting, and introspection. Following the format of Odwira, the program of activities within the festivals featured the presentation of the patriarch to the public gathering, the procession of the patriarch and his entourage, the firing of military salutes in tribute to the patriarch, the precision drilling of the militia, the public address by the patriarch, the reception of allegiance, and communal feasting, singing, and dancing. In some Ashanti communities, Odwira was affiliated with the *Apo* festival, literally, the "whole entity," the "making whole" of the community, characterized by a period of free and open exchange of ritual insults without fear of penalty.

> "The great day of abuse" . . . is said to have been founded in the belief that the grievances and evil wishes harboured secretly by one person against another endanger . . . the process of growth. To avert this, everybody is permitted to say openly what he thinks of his neighbours, and can insult them without punishment; he may even insult the *Omanhene* and queenmother.[25]

As a model for the black coronation festivals, Odwira hardly represents a perfect fit. Several common features of Odwira—the "clearing of the path" to the ancestral shrines, the ritual bathing of the *Omanhene*, the pouring of libations, the sacralization of the stools of the royal lineage, the parading of the first fruits of harvest, and the ritual sacrifice of a black hen—were apparently absent from the coronation festivals. However, modes of behavior always experienced modification in their transfer from one locale to another—whether the carriers of tradition were European or African in lineage. Culture change within the festivals occurred as a consequence of changes in the total environment of blacks and whites transplanted to New England; it cannot ultimately be reduced to a simple equation based on the status of the black captives relative to the status of those who held them in captivity.

Socialization in the Black Coronation Festivals

The principal means of socialization in the black coronation festivals of New England were their rituals. By focusing energies, rituals serve to heighten consciousness, to transfer authority, to enhance charisma, to condense messages—all processes supportive of socialization.

> A ritual is a stereotyped sequence of activities involving gestures, words, and objects . . . designed to influence preternatural entities or forces on behalf of the actors' goals and interests. Rituals may be seasonal, hallowing a culturally defined moment of change in the climatic cycle or the inauguration of an activity such as planting . . . or they may be contingent, held in response to an individual or collective crisis.[26]

The rituals of the festivals commenced with the arrival of the celebrants, families of them approaching the site of the events along the major thoroughfares. Exchanging greetings and engaging in gossip and repartee, the black captives—the most visible participants in the early stages of the festivals—promenaded in their borrowed finery. "The horses of the wealthy landowners were on this day all surrendered to the use of the slaves, and with cues, real or false, heads pomatumed and powdered, cocked hat, mounted on the best Narragansett pacers, sometimes with their master's sword, with their ladies on pillions, they pranced to election."[27] The attention devoted to "fancy speech" and "fancy dress" promoted a class consciousness among both captives and free persons, who waged competition with each other over proper observance of norms of decorum and demeanor. The preliminary round of activities was often highlighted by a parade escorting the retiring patriarch to the gathering site. Once the retiring patriarch had been sufficiently feted, the transfer of power from the old to the new was concluded with an electoral campaign—speeches, singing, and drumming for candidates—culminating in an election, appointment, or, in some instances, commemoration of the ritual patriarch by consensus.

Though details of the accession of the new patriarch are sketchy, it is probable that the installation ceremony was witnessed only by a select few—in keeping with the parent Ashanti tradition. The accession was completed once the symbols of royalty were conferred, ranging from the flowers of King Pompey of Lynn and the feathers, flowers, and ribbons of Gov. Eben Tobias of Derby to the crown and sword of King Caesar of Durham and the engraved gold-headed cane of Governor Quash Piere of New Haven.[28]

The main event of the festivals was the coronation

parade, which usually followed a meandering course, drawing black, white, and red people, men, women, and children of all social classes as participants and spectators. Usually clad in military uniform—the formal dress of the period—the patriarch was the center of attention. Music, from the solemn military march to festive strutting and prancing rhythms, keyed the opening and closing of the parade. In Hartford, the parade featured "drums beating, 'colors flying' and fifes, fiddles, clarionets, and every 'sonorous metal' that could be found, 'uttering martial sound.'" In Newport, the voices of the black celebrants were in their "highest key . . . all the various languages of Africa, mixed with broken and ludicrous English, filled the air accompanied with the music of the fiddle, tambourine, the banjo, drum, etc." Drums, fifes, and brass horns provided the most conventional instrumentation for the parades in New England.[29]

While the musicians preceded the patriarch in the order of march, the entourage accompanied the patriarch, separating him from the spectators. In Norwich, the escort marched on either side of the black governor. In Hartford, the escort numbered as many as one hundred marching double-file or mounted. The larger the entourage, the more intense the ritual focusing of energies on the patriarch and, consequently, the greater the investment of prestige and authority by the community in its champion. During the parade, the entourage commonly addressed military salutes to the patriarch and other ritual dignitaries. In Salem, Massachusetts, the beating of drums accompanied the ceremonial volleys of gunfire. In Derby, it was common for the salute to be fired after the procession arrived at the home of the black justice of the peace. This round was usually concluded with an oration by the patriarch and the precision drilling of troops, usually members of the entourage. Through parade, the black celebrants symbolized change in the seasonal cycle, transition from the old social order to the new, and the renewal of positive spiritual energies. According to the conventional wisdom of the era, parades organized by whites in New England to inaugurate their governors were modeled on black coronation parades.[30] It is probable that the percussive diversity of the music, the flashy baton-twirling, the festive strutting and prancing were the enduring legacy of blacks to European-American conceptions of parade.

Following the parade was the communal feast, often referred to as the "election treat." Prominent on the menu were "election cake, a sort of rusk rich with fruit and wine," and "election beer," brewed from barks and roots customarily gathered and sold by old squaws during early May.[31] In the Narragansett country, the first responsibility of the defeated candidate attending the election treat was to drink the initial toast to the winner, his second duty to be seated to the left of the victor.[32] In Newport, the reconciliation of the contestants amid feasting was a decided departure from the usual aftermath of white elections of the period, the latter often ending with "broken head and bloody nose."[33] Such allegiance to the patriarch placed communal interests above individual ones, upholding the office of the king or governor as symbolic of the welfare of the community. Once the feasting was completed, it was customary for the patriarch to receive his subjects and enjoy the homage paid him. In Hartford, the governor retired to special quarters to receive the good wishes of the gathering, favoring them with greetings, advice, and appointments. Singing and dancing usually marked the final phase of the festival proper, the violin or fiddle serving as the featured musical instrument. In the towns with larger black populations, the dancing was sometimes formalized into an election ball.[34]

By paying homage to their ritual patriarch, blacks similarly paid homage to their African forefathers. Through their rituals, captives and free persons countered the forces of social and cultural fragmentation to which they were subjected. In some instances, festivals preserved African speech or songs or symbology; in other instances, festivals promoted a consciousness of Africa; and in still other cases, the festivals merely struck a note of unity, facilitating the survival of Africa in the unconscious, its most effective medium of transmission under duress.

Social Control in the Black Coronation Festivals

Once committed to the practice of black bondage, whites sought persistently to exercise social control over blacks. In larger New England towns, the festivals generated a stable, quasi-governmental hierarchy that was empowered by whites to adjudicate charges of misdemeanors and other minor grievances against blacks that arose during its term of office. The king, sheriff, deputy, and other officers in Portsmouth tried cases involving petty charges, those usually brought by captor against captive, and executed punishment. The magistrate in Newport, an appointee of the governor, tried cases initially, with the governor sitting as judge in cases of appeal, and his court levying the punishment.[35] Clearly, whites intended the black governments as buffers between themselves and the captives, deflecting criticism away from themselves. In describing the harsh punishment apparently administered by a black court in Rhode Island, Orville Platt explained the rationale behind white tolerance of the courts.

> Masters complained to the Governor and magistrates of the delinquencies of their slaves, who were tried, condemned and punished at the discretion of the court. The punishment was sometimes quite severe, and what made it the more effectual, was that it was the judgment of their peers, people of their own rank and color had condemned them, and not their masters, by an arbitrary mandate.[36]

While whites of the period often regarded the black courts as extensions of white social hegemony over blacks, blacks frequently perceived the festivals as extensions of black social control over themselves. During the colonial era, the black governors in Hartford and Newport believed their influence so great that they claimed jurisdiction over the entire black populations of their respective states. Even in smaller towns, the sanctity of his office caused the patriarch to be revered as counselor and opinion leader among his people. His authority over matters of social conduct was thought to be a measure of self-governance.[37]

> He was consulted as to the settlement of many petty disputes among his black brothers, and his decision was law. His office thus had a certain power, and commanded some respect among white people, who through him could obtain small settlements and adjustments, and arrange many matters in their relations with the negroes, without the trouble of personal effort.[38]

Occasionally, the influence of a black king or governor extended significantly beyond the bounds of his constituents. Governor Quash Freeman of Derby, a captive to Agar Tomlinson, was said in the Tomlinson family history to have effectively reversed the conventional relationship between captor and captive.[39]

> He was a man of herculean strength, a giant six-footer, and it is said of him that he could take a bull by the horns and the nose and at once prostrate him to the ground. No one ever dared to molest or tried to make him afraid, and when he was approaching from a distance he awakened the sense of a coming thunder cloud.[40]

After his election, "his dignity and self-importance were so sensibly affected that it was commonly said that 'Uncle Agar lived with the Governor.'" The prevailing opinion was that Governor Quash managed affairs in his district.[41]

Though the courts attendant to the festivals were accorded a degree of patronizing tolerance by whites, the festivals themselves came under a barrage of invective from the white establishment. Anxieties focused on the underlife peripheral to the festivals that constituted for white public officials a persistent threat to law and order. Some black and white festival-goers attended the rites principally to try their hand at "shaking pawpaw,"[42] pitching pennies, and tossing quoits. An atmosphere of license was further engendered by the generous supplies of beer, eggnog, flip, and muddy ale, which were sold at the festival grounds, along the main thoroughfares, and in taverns and dance halls. As the festivals grew in popularity, white clergymen, politicians, and other public figures joined in a chorus of criticism, attributing race and class antagonisms to the rites. While the primary thrust of the attacks was predictably directed against the blacks, James Newhall further speculated that "these excesses of the negroes gave rise to the vile manner in which the season was observed by the lower class of some of our own complexion; and perhaps, also, 'election time' extended to four days, in accordance with the limit of the vacation allowed the slaves."[43] By the last decade of the eighteenth century, the criticism had become a major factor in bringing about the gradual decline of the festivals. Responding to the shift in white public opinion, Connecticut changed the date of its white elections to October, and Massachusetts switched its balloting to January.[44] The change of dates disrupted the traditional significance of the affiliated black festivals since these rites no longer marked the coming of spring or initiated the ritual New Year.

Most prior interpretations of Negro Election, usually focusing on the role of the black courts, have posited that whites held absolute dominance over blacks. Under such hermetic conditions, New England blacks were supposedly unable to achieve enough autonomy to proceed beyond mere mimicry of white culture. When the courts are considered in the context of the festivals, this viewpoint becomes parochial. Black captive and white captor existed in a relationship of give-and-take that permitted enough autonomy for blacks to assert themselves in a culturally continuous and complex fashion. Having their labor and their sex to barter, blacks creatively used the social niche in which they found themselves.

Institutionalization in the Black Coronation Festivals

In the natural history of societies, new institutions and modes of behavior and thought appear in the developmental process at more complex systemic levels; this evolution of forms is the consequence of the interaction and adaptation of organisms to modified circumstances. The quality embedded in these forms—emergence—characterized the subtle patterns of sociation within the black coronation festivals. One form of emergent relations derived from the symbiotic connection between white patron and black contestant. As the amount of money, goods, services, and labor invested in the festivals increased, the amount of prestige mushroomed, attracting the wealthiest and most socially conscious white landowners as patrons and spectators.

By the middle of the eighteenth century, the festivals were widely perceived by whites as opportunities for "deep play";[45] relative to what could be afforded, the ratio of capital investment was so high that the agon of competition was transformed from material rivalry into status rivalry. At the periphery of the festivals, individuals were pitted against each other for profit, fun, and personal pride. However, the festivals themselves matched black captives representing households, towns, or counties competing for the sake of social class pride, household honor, and town loyalty. On another level, the competition between blacks masked the rivalry between whites for the sake of masculine pride. The maintenance of the proper decorum by whites in the face of what was deliberate provocation by blacks was a means of promoting a positive image in the eyes of neighbors. Rank among white celebrants was allocated on the basis of the success of the black competitors as well as the maintenance of a decorum befitting social superiors.[46]

Just as white landowners often perceived the festivals as a contest between black captives representing white interests, blacks often viewed the festivals as a competition of white landowners representing black interests. During the colonial era, blacks learned to exploit the paternalistic attitudes of their captors, directing their appeals to vanity. Aware of the intense consciousness of public image among whites, blacks argued that the captors had a social stake in publicly presenting the captives in lavish style. The festivals provided the ideal occasion, it was said, for the white patron to offer undeniable proof of his prosperity, his beneficence, and his competitive acumen. According to the conventional wisdom, it was "degrading to the reputation of the owner if the slave appeared in inferior apparel, or with less money than the slave of another master of equal wealth."[47] The irony of whites depending on blacks for the fulfillment of their status expectations provided blacks a rich range of comic and satiric options. Rank among black celebrants was ascribed on the basis of creativity in exploiting white vanities as well as on the mastery of such traditional performance skills as speaking, singing, and dancing.

Another form of emergent relations was generated by the symbiotic connection between black celebrants and the transcendent world of their ancestors. The psychic reality of this ancestral domain was confirmed by the widespread belief of New England blacks in the transmigration of souls after death.[48] According to Zephaniah Swift, "to them the messenger of death is an angel of peace and they fondly believe that they shall have a day of retribution in another existence in their native land."[49] Abducted from Africa at the age of twelve, Jin Cole, a black woman sold to the family of Parson Jonathan Ashley of Deerfield, Massachusetts, in 1739, was typical of those who believed that they would return to their motherland at death.

She fully expected at death, or before, to be transported back to Guinea; and all her long life she was gathering, as treasures to take back to her motherland, all kinds of odds and ends, colored rags, bits of finery, peculiar shaped stones, shell buttons, beads, anything she could string. Nothing came amiss to her store.[50]

Though her son Cato spent all his life in New England, he too collected memorabilia for the journey to Africa until his death in 1825.

It was commonly believed that the living could only apprehend the domain of the forefathers by entering into a state of heightened consciousness. Seeking to promote this heightened consciousness, the black coronation festivals sought to recreate Africa as a means of propitiating their ancestors, the ritual patriarch functioning as the mediator of the process. The most graphic clue that the festivals were being performed for a sacred audience was the demeanor of the patriarch. In Norwich, Frances Caulkins was perplexed at the contrast between the noble deportment of the governor and the genuflected status of a captive:

> This sham dignitary after his election . . . puffing and swelling with pomposity . . . moving with a slow, majestic pace, as if the universe was looking on. When he mounted or dismounted, his aides flew to his assistance . . . bowing to the ground before him. The Great Mogul . . . never assumed an air of more perfect self-importance than the Negro Governor at such a time.[51]

In the conceptions of self and role reflected in the elegant demeanor of the patriarch and the stylized deference of the entourage, there were close parallels to the code of normative prescriptions circumscribing the ritual behavior of the chief in Ashanti society.

> The chief is believed to have been brought into a peculiarly close relationship with his ancestors. Thereupon his person becomes sacred. This is emphasized by taboos. He may not strike or be struck by anyone; he should not walk bare-footed; and as the drummer regularly reminds him on the talking drums, he should always tread "gently, gently; a chief walks gently, majestically," lest he stumble; his buttocks must never touch the ground. The occurrence of any of these incidents would, it is believed, cause some misfortune to befall the community, unless the expected calamity be averted by a sacrifice.[52]

By invoking the ancestors, the black celebrants so-cially constructed a world whose past glory contrasted with their own present status. This emergent world had its point of orientation in Africa, its superordinate roles enacted by the ancestors, and its warrant bound up with deeply embedded notions of ethnicity. In the black celebrants' own social world, rank was influenced by social and cultural proximity to the ancestors.

Conclusion

Encoded within the black coronation festivals of colonial and antebellum New England was a model of the black community organized according to the principles of patriarchy. At the apex of the hierarchy of the living members of the community was the ritual patriarch. An intermediary between the ancestors and the living, the king or governor occupied an office exclusively reserved for men. Through the king or governor, the ethnic line of descent was symbolically linked to Africa. Even the supporting cast of elected officials was a male domain. The status of women was almost wholly defined in relation to men, and the roles women enacted were usually low-profile ones removed from a formalized political process.

In this milieu, patriarchy emerged as a vehicle for focusing and channeling positive energies that could be tapped by the community. Whether captive or free, the patriarch was expected to be personally prosperous or affiliated with a prosperous patron. It was widely believed that the prosperity of the patriarch was transmitted to his constituency; the lavish postelection dinner, the fancy dress, the elegant bearing, the influential favors and appointments were regarded as omens of good fortune. Similarly, the patriarch was expected to embody cultural proximity to Africa. A knowledge of African traditions, whether it was the recollection of the family surname or the knowledge of African words or etiquette was interpreted as demonstrating respect for age and experience. These attributes were essential in maintaining harmonic relations with the ancestors. The common belief was that the ancestors would ultimately reward their descendants with autonomy. It is when one pursues the model of black society in colonial and antebellum New England as an African-derived, European-influenced cultural system of captives, patriarchally stratified, bound by its folk traditions, that the portrait of a community "shining in borrowed plumage"[53] emerges.

Notes

An earlier version of this paper was presented at the November 1978 meeting of the Conference of African and African-American Folklorists held in College Park, Maryland. I owe a special debt of gratitude to William D. Piersen, Fisk (Tennessee) University, whose conversation and research stimulated my interest in the topic. I am also indebted to Archie Green, University of Texas (Austin), for numerous hours of critical discussion during the revision process.

1. *The Diaries of Benjamin Lynde and of Benjamin Lynde, Jr.* (Cambridge, Mass., 1880), 109.

2. William D. Piersen, "Afro-American Culture in Eighteenth Century New England" (Ph.D. diss., Indiana University, 1975), 217–20.

3. Piersen, "Afro-American Culture," 220.

4. Charles P. Loomis, *Social Systems: Essays On Their Persistence and Change* (Princeton, N.J., 1960), 30–36.

5. Julian Rammelkamp, "The Providence Negro Community, 1820–1842," *Rhode Island History* 7 (January 1948): 26–27.

6. Alice Morse Earle, *Customs and Fashions in Old New England* (New York, 1909), 231–32.

7. Jane Shelton, "The New England Negro: A Remnant," *Harper's New Monthly Magazine* 88 (March 1894): 533–38; Telfer H. Mook, "Training Day in New England," *New England Quarterly* 11 (December 1938): 675–97; and Wilkins Updike, *History of the Episcopal Church in Narragansett, Rhode Island* (New York, 1847), 178.

8. James Newhall, *History of Lynn, Massachusetts, 1864–1890* (Lynn, Mass., 1890), 236.

9. Edward A. Kendall, *Travels Through the Northern Parts of the United States*, 2 vols. (New York, 1809), 1:1–7.

10. Samuel E. Morison, "A Poem on Election Day in Massachusetts about 1760," *Proceedings of the Colonial Society of Massachusetts* 18 (February 1915): 54–61, and Nathaniel B. Shurtleff, "Negro Election Day," *Massachusetts Historical Society Papers* 13 (1873): 45–46.

11. James D. Phillips, *Salem in the Eighteenth Century* (Boston, 1937), 272; Samuel Orcutt, *History of the Old Town of Derby, Connecticut, 1642–1880* (Springfield, Mass., 1880), 550; Isaac Stuart, *Hartford in the Olden Time* (Hartford, Conn., 1853), 34; Thomas R. Hazard, *Recollections of Olden Times* (Newport, R.I., 1879), 121; and Henry Bull, "Memoir of Rhode Island," *Rhode Island Republican*, August 19, 1837, 1/1.

12. See Lorenzo J. Greene, *The Negro in Colonial New England* (Port Washington, N.Y., 1966), 245–48, and Mook, "Training Day in New England," 675–97.

13. Victor W. Turner, *The Ritual Process: Structure and Anti-Structure* (Chicago, 1969), 96, 177.

14. Newhall, *History of Lynn*, 236.

15. See Shelton, "The New England Negro: A Remnant,"

535; Updike, *History of Episcopal Church*, 177; and Newhall, *History of Lynn*, 236.

16. See Hubert H. S. Aimes, "African Institutions in America," *Journal of American Folklore* 18 (1905): 15–32, for an early formulation of the African origins of the festivals. Among the more recent arguments linking the black men and women of New England to Ashanti origins, see especially Piersen, "Afro-American Culture," 20–23; Joseph P. Reidy, "Negro Election Day and Black Community Life in New England, 1750–1860," *Marxist Perspectives* 1 (Fall, 1978): 108–9; and Melville Herskovits, *The Myth of the Negro Past* (Boston, 1941), 50.

17. Piersen, "Afro-American Culture," 247, 318.

18. Kofi A. Busia, "The Ashanti," in *African Worlds*, ed. C. Daryll Forde (New York, 1954), 202.

19. Orville Platt, "Negro Governors," *New Haven Colony Historical Society Papers* 6 (1900): 332.

20. Robert S. Rattray, *Ashanti Law and Constitution* (Kumansi, Ghana, 1956), 85.

21. See Reidy, "New Election Day," for a similar comparison of the black coronation festivals with the *Adae* and *Apo* ceremonies of the Ashanti, Odwira is the ceremony denoting the ninth and concluding *Adae*—a cycle of forty days culminating in propitiation of the ancestors.

22. Ranging from a week to a fortnight, Odwira, also known as the Yam Festival, was characterized by considerable individual variation within the general model, much like the black coronation festivals of New England. See Busia, "The Ashanti," 203–4, and A. A. Opoku, *Festivals of Ghana* (Accra, 1970), 7–27.

23. Eva L. Meyerowitz, *The Sacred State of the Akan* (London, 1951), 149–56, 171–77.

24. Morison, "A Poem on Election Day," 60–61.

25. Meyerowitz, *Sacred State of the Akan*, 153–54.

26. Victor W. Turner, "Symbols in African Ritual," in *Readings in Anthropology* (1977–78): 100–101.

27. Updike, *History of Episcopal Church*, 178.

28. Piersen, "Afro-American Culture," 227, 241, 264.

29. Stuart, *Hartford in Olden Time*, 39; Bull, "Memoir of Rhode Island," 1/1.

30. Frances M. Caulkins, *History of Norwich, Connecticut* (Hartford, Conn., 1866), 330; Stuart, *Hartford in Olden Time*, 39; Joseph B. Felt, *Annals of Salem from Its First Settlement*, 2 vols. (Salem, Mass., 1827), 2:419; and Shelton, "New England Negro," 537.

31. Earle, *Customs and Fashions in Old New England*, 225–26.

32. Updike, *History of Episcopal Church*, 178.

33. Bull, "Memoir of New England," 1/1.

34. Stuart, *Hartford in Olden Time*, 39; Shelton, "New England Negro," 535–37; Earle, *Customs and Fashions in Old New England*, 226; Bull, "Memoir of New England," 1/1; *The Diary of William Bentley, D.D.*, 4 vols. (Salem, Mass., 1914), 4:457; and Frances McDougall, *Memoirs of Elleanor Eldridge* (Providence, R.I., 1840), 35–36.

35. Thomas B. Aldrich, *An Old Town by the Sea* (Boston, 1893), 78, and Platt, "Negro Governors," 321–24.

36. Platt, "Negro Governors," 324.

37. Platt, "Negro Governors," 325.

38. Alice Morse Earle, *In Old Narragansett* (New York, 1898), 81.

39. Samuel Orcutt, *Henry Tomlinson and His Descendants in America* (New Haven, Conn., 1891), 53, and Shelton, "New England Negro," 536.

40. Orcutt, *Henry Tomlinson*, 549.

41. Shelton, "New England Negro," 536.

42. Pawpaw was a gambling game named after Dahomean captives from the port of Popo. Played by shaking and throwing cowry shells, it closely resembled dice. See Earle, *Customs and Fashions in Old New England*, 226.

43. Newhall, *History of Lynn*, 236.

44. Shurtleff, "Negro Election Day," 45.

45. For an explanation of this concept, see Clifford Geertz, "Deep Play: Notes on the Balinese Cockfight," in *The Interpretation of Cultures*, ed. Geertz (New York, 1973), 412–53.

46. Aldrich, *Old Town by the Sea*, 78; Platt, "Negro Governors," 318; and Updike, *History of Episcopal Church*, 177–78.

47. Updike, *History of Episcopal Church*, 177.

48. Piersen, "Afro-American Culture," 182–84.

49. Zephaniah Swift, *Oration on Domestic Slavery* (Hartford, Conn., 1791), 15.

50. George Sheldon, *A History of Deerfield, Massachusetts, II* (Deerfield, Mass., 1896), 897–98.

51. Caulkins, *History of Norwich*, 330–31.

52. Busia, "The Ashanti," 202.

53. Mook, "Training Day in New England," 686.

Part Three: The Production and Control of Property

A Small Planter's Profits: The Cole Estate and the Growth of the Early Chesapeake Economy

RUSSELL R. MENARD, LOIS GREEN CARR, AND LORENA S. WALSH

Two forces consistently blur a clear vision of material life in seventeenth- and eighteenth-century America. One is the "great man" approach to research and writing that highlights the achievements of a few politically influential and wealthy men while it ignores the daily routines and struggles of everyone else. The second, closely related force is the role many museums play in supporting this image of the past in their presentations of objects owned and domestic environments lived in by the privileged few. Both approaches offer a distorted view of prosperity and comfort that only systematic fieldwork, archival research, and disciplined curating can correct. In the following essay Russell R. Menard, Lois G. Carr, and Lorena S. Walsh ask a simple question aimed at remedying these biases: What was daily life like for an "average" small plantation owner in the economy of the early Chesapeake?

The authors explore this question by examining one small planter—Robert Cole of St. Clement's Manor in St. Mary's County, Maryland—in great detail. Although Cole died at the young age of thirty-five in 1662, his estate was carefully managed and its financial affairs recorded between his death and 1673. From surviving accounts for that eleven-year period, the authors offer new interpretations of material life in seventeenth-century Maryland; their efforts demonstrate the potentials of quantitative methods coupled with an imaginative approach. First, we discover that Cole was not the slovenly, tobacco-crazed planter we might expect. He was, after all, an Englishman with an Englishman's belief that beauty derived from the experience of order. In the midst of tobacco cultivation, we find Cole making orderly decisions about land use and crop yield. He located his plantation with variations in local soil quality firmly in mind. He also maintained his farmstead; he worried over his outbuildings, tended his livestock, and took time to raise fruit trees. Because he was such a "careful husbandman," Cole fared well in the unpredictable Chesapeake economy. Although he did not die a wealthy man, he rested securely at the midpoint of local wealth structures and had respectable investments in land, labor, and household goods. His moderate success was due to his skill in balancing market involvement with self-sufficiency. He realized any reliance on foreign imports like shoes, cloth, and tools demanded that a farm family produce at least enough food for its own year-round use.

In recounting Cole's activities and decisions, the authors alter our image of early Maryland material life. While previous historians have described the decades from 1650 to 1680 as years of prolonged depression, Menard, Carr, and Walsh discover that Cole in fact experienced small but steady economic growth throughout the period. Such incremental growth suggests that the mid-seventeenth century was for some a time of increasing security rather than risk. This new security derived from the process of "farm-building" or "homesteading," an interval when a high percentage of agricultural income was reinvested in productive capital resources like land, slaves, new buildings, or tools. The economic growth that resulted from plowing earnings back into the ground permitted Cole and others to accumulate property, to enjoy some leisure time, and to achieve a new mastery of the cultural landscape.

Most historians now agree that small plantations predominated on the tobacco coast during the seventeenth century, but few have studied them closely. Basic questions are still unanswered. Did small planters grow most of the food their families consumed? What surpluses did they produce besides to-bacco? How did they spend their income? What pro-portion went to wages, rent, clothing, tools, or taxes? Were nearly all their earnings exported or was a sub-stantial proportion spent locally, in the domestic economy? How profitable were their operations? Was income merely adequate to keep a planter afloat, or did small plantations afford opportunities for tenants to become landowners and yeoman farmers to join the local gentry? How did small planters cope with the recurring depressions in the Chesapeake econ-omy, with the secular decline of tobacco prices, and with the gradual increase in the costs of land and labor?

One result of the ongoing renaissance of Chesa-peake studies has been the accumulation of a consid-erable body of knowledge concerning the lives of small planters. Much work remains to be done, but we know a good deal about their opportunities, their demographic characteristics, their familial structure, and their changing position in politics and society.[1] However, we know little about the domestic econ-omy of the small planter, and it will be a long time before the needed evidence is uncovered. In fact, ex-tensive grubbing among reluctant materials is neces-sary merely to determine whether sufficient data ex-ist to support a detailed inquiry into the business of farming along the tobacco coast during the seven-teenth century. Nevertheless, enough information is now at hand for a beginning. A set of accounts for Robert Cole's plantation in St. Mary's County sur-vives at the Hall of Records in Annapolis. These rec-ords detail income and expenditures from 1662 to 1673. They are far from perfect, but when combined with bits and pieces from other sources and inter-preted with the help of some educated guesswork, they yield new insight into the economy of the fam-ily farm.[2]

Robert Cole (ca. 1627–1662) was about twenty-five years old when he arrived in Maryland in 1652 or 1653 with his wife, Rebecca, four children (at least two were hers by a previous marriage), and two ser-vants. The Coles were Roman Catholics, which may explain the attraction Maryland had for them. Robert Cole had a "kinsman," Benjamin Gill, who had lived and prospered in Maryland for a decade. Perhaps re-ports of Gill's success had reached Robert in En-gland.[3] Cole came with some capital, probably enough to purchase land and begin a plantation im-mediately. He apparently moved to St. Clement's Manor and bought a 300-acre tract there soon after arriving in Maryland. He also surveyed 350 acres of unimproved land on the Nangemoy River in Charles County in 1654. He sold the tract within four years, however, and seems to have done nothing to de-velop it.

Dr. Thomas Gerard had patented St. Clement's in 1639. The manor occupied a broad neck of land on the Potomac between the Wicomico River and St. Clement's Bay. It originally contained only 1,030 acres, but Gerard enlarged and repatented it as a 6,000-acre tract in 1641. In 1678, when Gerard's heirs had the manor resurveyed, it was found to contain 11,400 acres, eloquent testimony to the amateurism of Maryland's first surveyors. By the time of Cole's arrival, Gerard was emerging as one of Maryland's most successful estate developers, perhaps the only man to give more than a fleeting substance to Lord Baltimore's manorial vision. Beginning with a little capital of his own and about £175 sterling borrowed from a brother-in-law, Gerard used intelligent man-agement, a judicious credit policy, the marriages of his several daughters, and the force of his personality to build an impressive landed empire.[4]

It is not clear why Cole chose to live on St. Clem-ent's Manor, nor is it certain what impact the choice had on his life in Maryland. Perhaps the existence of functioning manorial courts created a more inte-grated neighborhood with a stronger sense of com-munity than had yet developed elsewhere in the province, although the high rate of population turn-over suggests that this was not the case.[5] The manor possessed other attractive features, but they could be found elsewhere in Maryland. There were several men living on St. Clement's who could provide the capital needed to begin a plantation. Robert Slye, Gerard's son-in-law and perhaps the wealthiest mer-chant in Maryland, offered adequate marketing and supply facilities. Although the soil was not the best in the country for tobacco, it was more than adequate for the staple, and its characteristics would attract farmers who planned a diversified agriculture. Since the manor occupied a peninsula drained by several creeks, even interior locations offered the easy access to water transport often sought by tobacco planters. Cole's residence on St. Clement's burdened him with a few minor duties—attendance at annual courts, for example—but apparently did not sharply distinguish him from the majority of small planters who avoided manorial obligations.

Cole's plantation was on the east side of the manor on Tomakokin Creek. Descriptions of the soils on the farm are available only from twentieth-century surveys, and surface soil characteristics may have changed since Cole's time. However, if these surveys at all reflect seventeenth-century conditions, some interesting speculations are possible. The site may have seemed a choice location to a seventeenth-century English farmer. The soil is a mixture of Mattapex and Othello sandy and silt loams, which together are well suited to diversified agriculture. The Mattapex is fairly well drained and performs adequately with corn and English grain and garden crops. The Othello is less fertile, but its poor drainage system offers a hedge against unusually dry years. Livestock could flourish on the natural meadows and in the low, marshy areas of the plantation. That Cole actually entertained such considerations in choosing a farm site is of course purely conjectural. Still, he was apparently descended from an English yeoman family, and it is possible that his decisions were as much informed by traditional English agricultural wisdom as by the lore of tobacco culture.[6]

Other aspects of Cole's farm operation also suggest that he worked within an English agricultural tradition modified by the demands of tobacco production under New World conditions. He was not the stereotypical tobacco planter, a slovenly husbandman who devoted all his energies to the staple, neglected his livestock, and ravaged his land in pursuit of quick profits. Cole built a dairy; he purchased nails for a hog pen just before he died; and his administrator later built a henhouse on the plantation, suggesting some concern for the condition of farm animals. Tobacco was the most important source of income, but its rhythms did not wholly dominate plantation work routines. Substantial grain, orchard, and garden crops were made, and livestock products accounted for a high proportion of farm income. The care with which Robert Cole inventoried his possessions and instructed his overseers on the eve of a voyage to England suggests a careful, intelligent farmer. Cole was not what would later be known as an "improving farmer": he did not own a plow or a harrow, nor is there evidence that he rotated crops or manured his fields. Nevertheless, it would seem inaccurate to characterize him as wasteful or destructive; given the abundance of land and short supplies of labor in the colonial economy, his farming practices seem altogether sensible. "Where land is cheap and labour dear," George Washington explained more than a century after Cole's death, "men are fonder of cultivating much than cultivating well."[7] Cole does not easily fit into the traditional picture of the seventeenth-century Chesapeake planter. He was perhaps more careful and certainly better educated than the average yeoman, but he probably more closely represents reality than does the old caricature.

Cole's life as a Maryland tobacco planter proved short. He planned a trip to England in 1662, only a decade after he first set foot in the New World. Knowing the hazards of an Atlantic crossing, he made elaborate preparations for the care of his children and the management of his estate in case he died. He prepared a detailed inventory of his possessions in March and, in April, wrote a will. Within that brief interval his wife of over a decade, Rebecca, must have died: she is mentioned in the inventory but not in the will. Her death did not change Robert's plans. He charged two of his Maryland neighbors, Luke Gardiner and William Evans, and a London cousin, Henry Hanks, with the care of his children and property and left for England, probably in the spring of 1662. By September 1663 he had died (exactly when and where is uncertain), leaving seven orphan children for his executors to raise and a small farm for them to operate.

Ten years later, in 1673, Robert's son, Robert Jr., and his son-in-law, Ignatius Warren, brought Luke Gardiner, the only surviving executor, to court over his management of the estate. Judge Philip Calvert chastised Gardiner for general sloppiness in record keeping and his failure to adhere to the letter of the law. In particular, Gardiner had not taken the executor's oath, had not appraised the estate, had on occasion failed to record the "Express time of the Delivery or to whome or for what account," and had not kept "such an account . . . as he dares absolutely Sweare to as an Executor ought to doe." Gardiner's errors were minor ones, however, and Calvert exonerated him of all charges of dishonesty or serious mismanagement. In fact, Gardiner's improvements of the estate's value, particularly the livestock, overrode his technical shortcomings and he escaped severe penalty. The court ordered him to submit his accounts of the estate, which the judge examined, "Rectified in many particulars," and entered into the record.[8] The documents describe Gardiner's administration of the Cole plantation for nearly twelve years, from Robert's departure for England in early 1662 until the initiation of the suit in mid-1673. Gardiner's bookkeeping may not have satisfied the court, but the accounts provide more information about the economy of a small plantation than any other single source yet discovered.

Fixing Robert Cole's place within Maryland society is not without difficulty. At his departure in 1662, he hovered at the vague line that separated the majority of planters from the county gentry. Maryland society at mid-century was still highly fluid, lacking the firm definition it would later acquire.[9] Cole, along with many of his contemporaries, was improving his estate and his social position when death stopped his progress. He had started in Maryland as a small farmer with two servants, a modest capital, and, one imagines, hopes of prosperity for himself and his family. In 1662, with an operating farm, four servants, an estate doubtless much larger than that he began with, and four sons who would soon be old enough to join the plantation work force, he was well on the way to realizing those hopes. Despite this success, he called himself "yeoman" in his will, suggesting that he still worked in the fields and considered himself an ordinary small planter. Yet he could have styled himself "gentleman" had he so chosen. He was not rich, even by the standards of the Chesapeake frontier, but his estate was larger than that of most planters. Although his role in local government was limited to frequent jury service and an ensign's post in the militia, his wealth equaled and even surpassed that of many men who served on the county bench and sat in the provincial assembly. He had also gained some recognition of his achievement. Beginning in 1660, he was occasionally but not always called "mister" or "gentleman" in the public records, a clerical inconsistency reflecting the transitional stage he had reached in his career. Perhaps if Cole had lived much beyond the age of thirty-five he would have stopped thinking of himself as a yeoman, assumed the designation "gentleman," and joined his close friends William Evans and Luke Gardiner on the county bench.

A comparison of Cole's assets with those of his neighbors helps to place him in his society. In the inventory Cole made of his possessions in 1662, he priced only a few items but estimated the total value of his personal property. By using data from other inventories taken in the early 1660s, one can fill in the missing values.[10] Cole's movable estate was worth about £154 currency, more than twice the mean estate probated in St. Mary's County from 1658 through 1665 and just over four-and-one-half times the median (see table 1).[11] Robert Cole, it would seem, was substantially better off than most residents of the tobacco coast. However, a different perspective is gained by looking at his place on the scale of movable wealth left by probated decedents. He ranked fifth of thirty-nine in the county, but the four above him (the richest 10 percent) held 48 percent of the movable wealth.

These figures, furthermore, omit land, a crucial component of wealth in an agricultural society. When land is included in Cole's wealth, his distance from most planters who died in the same period narrows.[12] His total wealth then comes to £212, or 1.7 times the mean probated estate in St. Mary's County between 1658 and 1665, and less than three times the median (table 1). As the reference group is defined more tightly, the gap continues to shrink. If the ten men who did not head households are eliminated, Cole's estate is only 1.3 times larger than the mean, although still 2.4 times the median. When the four tenant farmers are also left out and Cole is compared to landowning household heads, his estate is only 1.1 times the mean and less than twice the median. He ranked sixth in the whole group of thirty-nine, in the top 15 percent, but the top five owned 53.7 percent of the wealth. If the group is restricted to landowning households, the five men wealthier than he owned 57 percent of the wealth. Cole's overall wealth thus put him in the bottom half of the scale of total wealth, although near the top of that half.

A look at the composition of Cole's estate in comparison to that of others also helps fix his position. Land and the labor to work it were the prime assets of a planter. A man needed 20 acres per full working hand for continuous tobacco production. He also needed at least 2 acres per hand for corn, the basic food crop, and additional land for pasture and wood.[13] Lists of St. Mary's County holdings compiled for 1659 and 1705 suggest that 50 acres was the minimum size for a viable farm. However, the man who hoped to use the labor of his sons and then provide them with land would require more, and the great majority of farms were larger. In 1659 the median holding in St. Mary's County was 250 acres.[14] Robert Cole died possessed of 300 acres and rights to 650 more. Clearly, he had intended to put future profits into acquiring additional land that would have made him a major landowner. As it was, among probated householding landowners, his holdings were well below the mean of 733.6 acres but above the median of 200 acres.[15]

Cole had less of his estate invested in land (27 percent) than the great majority of landowning decedents and much less than any of those wealthier than he. Nevertheless, he had all he needed for the profitable employment of many more hands than he was using. If he worked alongside his three male servants, he would have needed eighty acres for continuous tobacco production and another eight or ten acres for corn. There was ample acreage for additional men to work whenever Cole could afford to expand his labor force or when his sons reached the age to contribute. He was being a careful husbandman.

Cole invested in movable assets in some surprising ways. His investment in labor and livestock was not unusual for estates of that size, although somewhat less might have been in livestock and somewhat more in labor. But he had more in tools and farm equipment than did any other estate, as well as a much higher investment in consumer goods than his place in the scale of wealth would lead us to expect.

The degree to which Cole's investment in farm equipment and tools was unusual is probably exaggerated. The inventories of eleven of the twenty-nine householders list none, yet these decedents must have owned at least an axe and a hoe. These items, worth little, may have been overlooked or included in a category such as "old iron" or "old lumber." Their omission understates actual investment in such goods. Cole took his inventory himself and was meticulous in listing everything. Still, his investment was exceptional. He was the only decedent to own a cart, which alone was more valuable than the tools on all but two of the other estates. His plantation was one of only two equipped for making shoes. Other inventories list only axes and hoes and sometimes a few carpenter's tools. Before 1680, only a few of the richest estates showed more variety of equipment. The value and variety of tools are further indications of Cole's concern to be a careful husbandman.

Table 1. Comparison of the Estate of Robert Cole with the Estates of All St. Mary's County Decedents, 1658–1665, in £ Currency, Constant Value

	Labor	Livestock	Tools	Other Capital	Total Capital	Consumer Goods	Total Movables	Land	Total Estate Value
Cole	27.14	56.79	2.55	3.95	90.43	63.48	153.91	58.01	211.92
All Estates (N = 39)									
Mean	14.21	22.25	.39	17.56	54.31	14.51	68.82	57.37	126.14
Ratio, Cole to Mean	1.91	2.55	6.54	.22	1.67	4.37	2.24	1.01	1.68
Median	0.00	11.22	.11	4.46	25.11	7.62	33.96	36.01	72.86
Ratio, Cole to Median		5.06	23.18	.89	3.60	8.33	4.53	1.61	2.91
Householders (N = 29)									
Mean	19.11	29.41	.50	20.82	69.84	18.52	88.36	74.99	163.29
Ratio, Cole to Mean	1.42	1.93	5.10	.19	1.29	3.43	1.74	.77	1.30
Median	5.21	16.54	.26	4.02	37.25	8.33	39.79	41.42	88.34
Ratio, Cole to Median	5.21	5.06	9.81	.98	2.43	7.62	3.87	1.40	2.40
Householders with Land (N = 25)									
Mean	21.96	32.65	.56	22.74	77.91	20.34	98.25	86.99	185.16
Ratio, Cole to Mean	1.24	1.74	4.55	.17	1.16	3.12	1.57	.67	1.14
Median	6.13	16.85	.38	4.46	40.25	8.85	53.98	54.14	108.74
Ratio, Cole to Median	4.43	3.37	6.71	.89	2.25	7.17	2.85	1.07	1.95

Sources: Cole Plantation Accounts, Testamentary Proceedings, 6:118–47; St. Mary's City Commission, "Social Stratification in Maryland, 1658–1705" (project funded by the National Science Foundation, 1972).

The biggest surprise in the inventory is the value of Cole's consumer goods. His household furnishings, provisions, cloth for clothing his family, and so on were valued at £63, well above the average for men of his wealth level. Nevertheless, his household arrangements were not unusually elaborate or comfortable; he owned no silver plate, fine furniture, or delicate tableware. In part, the high value in consumer goods reflects the size of his family, large for this period in Chesapeake history. But it also reflects the appearance in Cole's inventory of items only rarely found in the probate records. Provisions seldom appear in inventories, since the administrator was allowed to feed the family from the produce of the farm, while only the decedent's clothing was appraised, and often even his was missing. Cole, however, left more than £13 in provisions and over £21 in cloth and clothing, reflecting his intention to equip his family for eight months—the length of time he expected to be absent—and his care to list all supplies on hand. Were such items removed from Cole's estate, the difference between him and others of his rank would largely disappear.[16]

*   *   *

Robert Cole can stand as a broadly representative figure in southern Maryland around mid-century. He was not a great planter and he did not live like one. He was comfortable but not rich, better off than most

but not so much better off that his life-style was sharply different from that of the majority of planters. Further, and for reasons this essay hopes to illuminate, the position he had achieved was within reach of even the poorest freeman in his neighborhood. Cole was an entirely typical planter. Little about his life distinguished him from others of his class or justifies our concern to assemble his biography and fix his place in early Chesapeake society. What does distinguish Cole occurred after he died. For eleven years following Robert's departure for England, from 1662 through 1672, Luke Gardiner administered the Cole plantation and kept a detailed record of income and expenditures. It is to that record that we now turn.

Table 2 reports the revenue earned on the market by the Cole plantation by year and in various categories from 1662 to 1672. Over the entire period the estate earned an average annual gross income of just under 8,700 pounds of tobacco. This works out to roughly £38 in local currency, an apparently handsome return for a farm with a market value of just over £200 in 1662. Revenues were fairly steady, falling between £30 and £40 in most years, but there were some sharp variations. Earnings were especially low in 1666—in the midst of a severe depression when war disrupted trade and extreme weather destroyed crops throughout the region—and especially high in 1668, at the beginning of a short but strong

Table 2. Income, Cole Plantation, in £ Currency, Constant Value

	1662	1663	1664	1665	1666	1667	1668	1669	1670	1671	1672	Total	Annual Average
Tobacco Crop	30.62 77.4%	27.77 50.2%	32.43 76.9%	31.24 84.2%	13.97 88.0%	20.14 78.7%	37.58 45.4%	17.37 54.0%	19.28 70.1%	23.77 73.1%	22.48 73.1%	276.65	25.15 65.6%
Livestock		17.29 31.2%	6.99 16.6%	4.94 13.3%	.51 3.2%	4.67 18.2%	32.53 39.2%		8.23 29.9%	6.51 20.0%	6.15 20.0%	87.82	7.98 20.8%
Dairy		3.47 6.3%			.32 2.0%							3.79	.34 0.9%
Grains										1.09 3.3%	1.03 3.3%	2.12	.19 0.5%
Orchard					1.09 6.8%		3.22 3.9%					4.31	.39 1.0%
Misc./ Unknown	8.93 22.6%	6.84 12.3%	2.76 6.5%	.94 2.5%		.78 3.0%	9.54 11.5%	14.82 46.0%		1.15 3.5%	1.09 3.5%	46.85	4.26 11.1%
Total	39.55	55.37	42.18	37.12	15.89	25.59	82.87	32.19	27.51	32.52	30.75	421.54	38.32

Source: Cole Plantation Accounts, Testamentary Proceedings, 6:118–47.

postwar recovery. The pattern suggests the importance of foreign trade to a small plantation.[17]

The table provides further evidence of the dominant role of the export sector. The tobacco crop was clearly the major source of market income on the plantation. Tobacco production averaged about 5,800 pounds per year, worth roughly £25 currency. There were short crops in 1666, 1669, and 1670, and an unusually large one in 1668—reflecting both fluctuations in the work force and inconsistencies in climate—but output was fairly steady, in most years ranging between 5,000 and 7,000 pounds. Tobacco accounted for two-thirds of total revenue earned on the market over the eleven years for which the accounts were kept, never less than 45 percent and in two years more than 80 percent. In addition, such a direct measure underestimates the importance of the staple. There was a clear inverse relationship between total income earned in a year and the share of all income produced by the tobacco crop. Tobacco's contribution to income grew (and income fell) with the approach of the severe depression in the export sector of 1665 to 1667, fell (while total income rose) with the sharp recovery of 1668, and then rose again as the economy slid into a minor slump in the early 1670s. Income from tobacco and income from other sources, it would seem, were directly related on the Cole plantation—and, we would argue, in the economy as a whole—apparently because prosperity in the industry encouraged expansion and created markets for livestock and foodstuffs, while depressed markets for the staple led to a general contraction in economic activity. Diversified agriculture as yet provided only the slightest hedge against the uncertainties of producing a staple crop for the international market.[18]

But if the hedge was slight, the supplement was substantial. Livestock and livestock products—meat, tallow, hides, butter, and cheese—produced on average more than 20 percent of the farm's income, and a few shillings could be earned by occasional sales of corn or cider. These figures, furthermore, slight the contribution of livestock, grain, and the orchard because most items in the residual category are small bills paid by local residents for unspecified goods and services, doubtless often for agricultural products other than tobacco. All or nearly all plantation products except tobacco were sold locally, and the domestic market in the region grew rapidly during the third quarter of the seventeenth century as demand for tobacco led to the creation of many new farms, which in turn provided opportunities for established planters. The local market was an important source of income to the Cole's plantation and in many years proved the difference between profit and loss.[19]

Not all the goods and services produced by the

Table 3. Sources of Revenue on the Cole Plantation, 1662–1672, in £ Currency, Constant Value

Year	A. Estimated Value of Subsistence Production	B. Export Earnings	C. Local Exchanges	D. Total Revenue
1662	30.47	30.62	8.93	70.02
1663	35.90	27.77	27.60	91.27
1664	41.33	32.43	9.75	83.51
1665	38.07	31.24	5.88	75.19
1666	30.46	13.97	1.92	46.35
1667	26.10	20.14	5.45	51.69
1668	27.19	37.58	45.29	110.06
1669	29.36	17.37	14.82	61.55
1670	27.19	29.28	8.23	64.70
1671	28.28	23.77	8.75	60.80
1672	25.01	22.48	8.27	55.76
Mean	30.85 (44.0%)	26.06 (37.2%)	13.17 (18.8%)	70.08 (100.0%)
Standard Deviation	5.29	7.13	12.57	18.84
Coefficient of Variability	.171	.274	.954	.269

Source: Cole Plantation Accounts, Testamentary Proceedings, 6:118–47.

Cole plantation entered the market: a substantial proportion was consumed on the spot. The farm was nearly self-sufficient in foods; all members of the household were provided shelter, fuel, and other incidental services; and the small children were supervised and nurtured. It is impossible to know the precise value of such goods and services, but we can offer an estimate. There are occasional references in other records to the purchase of room and board by adult males in Maryland during the seventeenth century: these describe an average price of about £4.35 currency per year. If we assume that women and adolescents could purchase room and board for three-quarters the price charged a man, and children under twelve could do so for one-half the man's cost, we can, given the composition of the Cole household, estimate the annual value of subsistence production on the plantation. The results appear in column A of table 3. The estimates suggest two points worth noting. Most important is the share of total income generated by self-sufficient activities. They accounted for nearly 45 percent of the total, more than twice the share earned through local exchange and nearly 25 percent more than that gained by the sale of tobacco to foreign markets. Second, the income earned through self-sufficient production was much less variable than that earned on the market. While the degree of stability in subsistence income evident in table 3 reflects our method of estimation, we suspect that it approximates reality as well: the substantial degree of self-sufficiency achieved on tobacco plantations had the important effect of stabilizing the standard of living against sharp fluctuations in the foreign sector and in opportunities for local exchange.[20]

Table 4. Expenditures on the Cole Plantation, 1662–1672, in £ Currency, Constant Value

	1662	1663	1664	1665	1666	1667	1668	1669	1670	1671	1672	Mean	Total
Clothing	13.41	13.82	12.58	16.75	7.02	9.99	14.22	10.97	16.14	12.38	11.71	12.64	138.99
Tailor's Wages	1.89	1.44	1.69	.52	1.58	3.12	1.17	.74	1.54	1.21	1.14	1.46	16.04
Indentured Servants	9.67	10.21				5.54	7.27	18.70				4.67	51.39
Maid's Wages		3.33	4.67	4.29	2.72							1.36	15.01
Provisions	1.79	.47	.90	1.72	.95	2.42	1.41	3.16	4.66	3.36	3.18	2.19	24.02[a]
Tools	1.03	1.31	1.71	.13								.38	4.18
Cask		2.28	2.10	2.68	.91	1.38	2.72	1.81	.46	.78	.74	1.44	15.86
Rent		2.42						2.04	2.06	.64	.60	.71	7.76
Taxes	.90	1.59	1.87	2.00	1.39	1.41	3.86	1.42	.83	1.21	1.14	1.60	17.62[b]
Building Repairs		1.88		4.94			1.82		.55			.84	9.19
Medical, Education	.05	1.40	.93	5.19	3.81	6.18	4.54		1.83	.86	.82	2.33	25.61[c]
Misc. Local Goods and Services	2.75	6.00	12.17	.77	.16	4.57	5.33	2.87	7.50	1.15	1.09	4.03	44.36[d]
Misc. Imported Goods and Services	3.34	.39	.27	.24	.50	.99	.85	2.79	2.12	1.80	1.70	1.36	14.99
Unidentified	11.20	4.30			.11					1.82	1.72	1.74	19.15
Total	46.03	50.84	38.89	39.23	19.04	35.71	43.19	44.50	37.69	25.21	23.84	36.74	404.17

Source: Cole Plantation Accounts, Testamentary Proceedings, 6:118–47.
[a]£8.01 in local provisions and £16.01 in imported provisions.
[b]£12.76 in taxes paid the government and £4.86 in donations to the church.
[c]£3.09 in medical expenses; £22.52 for education.
[d]Includes £16.84 in administrative expenses.

Table 4 describes the annual expenditures of the Cole plantation in several categories; these are summarized and compared to market earnings in table 5. Expenditures were closely tied to income, and the data carry a clear suggestion of belt-tightening when earnings were low and of more lavish spending during good years. But the relationship was not perfect and expenditures show much less variation than income. Gardiner was able, either by drawing on earnings or by purchasing on credit, to run in the red for a year or two when necessary, to smooth out the effects of fluctuations in income, and to ride out bad years without greatly sacrificing standards of consumption. For planters who were less well off, less able to draw on the good years of the past or to borrow on the expectation of better years to come, the impact of depressed tobacco markets or a poor crop must have been more immediate and painful.[21]

Perhaps the point about the pattern of expenditures on the Cole plantation that deserves the most emphasis is the large share, more than 55 percent, that went to imported goods and services. Cloth, clothing, shoes, and the like, virtually all of English manufacture, were by far the most important items, accounting for more than a third of the total and leading the list in all years but one. Indentured servants also commanded substantial outlays, on average nearly 13 percent of the total. Cole had left instructions that his servants "be imployed for the most benefitt and

good of my Children, and when or as they be free such or so many other may be put in their roomes to serve my Children Jointly."[22] Gardiner did not follow the injunction strictly, but he apparently tried to maintain a work force of four to five men, including Robert Cole's adult sons, a strategy that required the purchase of single servants in 1662, 1663, 1667, and 1668, and of two servants in 1669. Although the plantation was nearly self-sufficient in provisions, some items not made locally—chiefly spices, liquor, and soap—were purchased on a regular basis. The work force required few tools, although the table understates the amounts spent because tools were sometimes lumped with other manufactured goods in the accounts. Axes, hoes, and knives were sufficient for the simple agricultural operations along the bay. Gardiner purchased little in the way of household goods, cooking utensils, tableware, furniture, and the like, perhaps reflecting the peculiar situation of the Cole plantation. The absence of such purchases, doubtless an important item in the budgets of most households of similar wealth, makes the high share of income spent on imports even more striking. The spending pattern of the Cole plantation is clear evidence of the "colonial" structure of the Chesapeake economy and underscores the developmental problems faced by export-led plantation regions that watched much of their earnings flow to the metropolis to purchase essential goods and services.[23]

Table 5. Summary of Income and Expenditures on the Cole Plantation, 1662–1672, in £ Currency, Constant Value

Year	Income	Expenditures	Balance
1662	39.55	46.03	− 6.48
1663	55.37	50.84	4.53
1664	42.18	38.89	3.29
1665	37.12	39.23	− 2.11
1666	15.89	19.04	− 3.15
1667	25.59	35.71	− 10.12
1668	82.87	43.19	39.68
1669	32.19	44.50	− 12.31
1670	27.51	37.69	− 10.18
1671	32.52	25.21	7.31
1672	30.75	23.84	6.91
Mean	38.32	36.74	1.58
Standard Deviation	17.90	10.06	
Coefficient of Variability	.467	.274	

Source: Cole Plantation Accounts, Testamentary Proceedings, 6:118–47.

While the spending patterns of the Cole plantation support the traditional picture of the Chesapeake economy as one that laid out most of its income on imports, they also suggest that the domestic sector was more important than is usually allowed. Roughly 40 percent of the expenditures went to purchase locally produced goods and services. Wages—to the tailor for making and mending clothes, to the cooper for tobacco casks, to the maid who kept house and cared for the younger children, to the carpenter for construction and repairs—were the principal expense, accounting for about 14 percent of the total and 35 percent of the portion spent locally. Gardiner paid a few medical bills and bought an occasional barrel of corn when the plantation's supply fell short of its needs. He also paid for the education and apprenticeship of the several children. This was an unusual expense for that time and place, but one consistent with Robert Cole's request that his sons be taught "to write and read and cast account," and his daughters "to read and sew with their Needle."[24] Rent and taxes consumed little income: the Cole estate reminds one of Adam Smith's colonial farmer who had "no rent, and scarce any taxes to pay," and therefore had "every motive to render as great as possible a produce which is thus to be almost entirely his own."[25]

The data in the accounts are sufficiently detailed to permit an estimate of the share of expenditures devoted to maintaining the work force and the plantation.[26] These can be subtracted from gross earnings to yield a net figure for market income (table 6). The Cole plantation showed an average annual net income from market transactions of £12.59 over the eleven years that the accounts were kept. While this seems a rather meager return on an investment worth roughly £200, it must be remembered that the figure does not include food, shelter, and fuel consumed by the children: if these are added, the total rises to £21.49. Further, the ratio of savings to income on the Cole plantation was very high, and, as a consequence, the estate increased markedly in value over the period.

Just how substantially its value increased is revealed by an inventory of the plantation that Gardiner took in 1673 (table 7). Movables on the Cole estate were then worth £245, a gain of more than £90 since 1662. All the growth was accounted for by livestock, which had increased fourfold. Indeed, every other category—labor, tools, miscellaneous capital, and consumer goods—fell in value during the period. The value of the land and its improvements had also increased, from £58 to £75, and Gardiner had acquired 525 additional acres for Cole's three sons—200 acres for Robert, 210 for William, and 115 for Edward—all unimproved and together worth about £40. Summing up, the Cole estate was worth nearly £360 in 1673, up sharply from just over £210 in 1662. The annual rate of increase was nearly 5 percent, an impressive performance by any standards.[27]

The Cole plantation obviously did well. We have

Table 6. Net Income, Cole Plantation, 1662–1672, in £ Currency, Constant Value

Year	Market Income	Expenses of Maintaining Work Force and Plantation	Net Market Income	Net Subsistence Income	Total Net Income
1662	39.55	25.31	14.24	14.16	28.40
1663	55.37	37.42	17.95	11.98	29.93
1664	42.18	32.59	9.59	13.06	22.65
1665	37.12	25.98	11.14	9.80	20.94
1666	15.89	10.41	5.48	9.80	15.28
1667	25.59	18.36	7.23	8.70	15.93
1668	82.87	33.61	49.26	5.44	54.70
1669	32.19	38.76	−6.57	11.96	5.39
1670	27.51	22.70	4.81	9.79	14.60
1671	32.52	18.26	14.26	6.52	24.04
1672	30.75	19.67	11.08	3.26	14.34
Mean	38.32	25.73	12.59	9.50	22.38

Source: Cole Plantation Accounts, Testamentary Proceedings, 6:118–47.

Table 7. Value of Cole Plantation in 1662 and 1673, in £ Currency, Constant Value

Category	1662	1673
Labor	27.14	15.70
Livestock	56.79	217.07
Other Capital	6.50	.28
Consumer Goods	63.48	11.71
Total Movables	153.91	244.76
Home Plantation	58.01	74.91
Other Land		39.57
Total Land	58.01	114.48
Total Estate Value	211.92	359.24

SOURCE: Cole Plantation Accounts, Testamentary Proceedings, 6:118–47.

now assembled the data needed to calculate how well—to estimate, that is, the internal rate of return for the estate across the eleven years of the accounts: the value of the assets in 1662, the net income earned between 1662 and 1673, and the value of the plantation in 1673. The calculation itself is straightforward, but there are alternative methods of estimating the several values, particularly the worth of the estate in 1673. It is sufficient to report here that a return of 20 percent per annum represents a lower-bound measure. Despite our conservative assumptions, it is clear that the plantation performed handsomely.[28]

How representative was this earnings performance? Perhaps the earnings were somewhat below average. For one thing, the plantation was without the labor of its owner, which meant not only that management had to be purchased (Gardiner collected annual fees for his administrative duties) but that the individual with the most powerful incentives for hard work, savings, and investment was absent. For another, administrators had different incentives from owners. An administrator who substantially increased the value of an estate would reap only slight benefits; one who let that value diminish could pay dearly. Hence an administrator was more likely to avoid risk than an owner; he would sacrifice income and growth for security and stability. There is a suggestion of such behavior in Gardiner's choices: he invested in livestock rather than labor. The strategy paid off, but one wonders if the Cole estate would have done even better had Gardiner sold off some cattle or horses to purchase servants. On the other

hand, the plantation may have been fortunate, its returns higher than average. There were no deaths among the indentured workers, livestock herds grew rapidly (although well below the maximum biologically possible), and the dependency ratio, high at first, declined sharply over the life of the accounts.[29] Obviously, we would like to argue that these considerations balanced each other and that earnings on the Cole plantation were typical. But in the absence of comparative data for other estates such an argument would rest on a flimsy base.

There are, however, some data to suggest this was the case, that the performance of the Cole estate was not unusual. Despite assertions that this was an era of prolonged depression in the Chesapeake region,[30] a variety of measures indicate that rapid growth in wealth levels was a central characteristic of the southern Maryland economy in the third quarter of the seventeenth century. Real, nonhuman, physical wealth per capita, for example, grew at roughly 2.7 percent per year from the 1650s to the 1680s on Maryland's lower Western Shore. Mean movable estate values among probated decendent householders grew faster still. Further, there is evidence that this was not merely a local phenomenon, peculiar to southern Maryland. Rapid increases in wealth per capita in regions of recent settlement, with rates of growth that seem high even by modern standards and that are truly spectacular for preindustrial societies, were perhaps a regular feature of the colonial economy and of frontier societies generally.[31]

The Cole account yields some insight into this rapid growth in wealth characteristic of newly settled regions and sheds light on its impact on welfare. There is little in the account to suggest that exports were the dynamic force in the growth of the Cole plantation. Income from tobacco did not increase over the period 1662–73; rather, it declined slightly. In this, the plantation mirrors the economy as a whole. Despite an enormous increase in aggregate output and major gains in productivity early in the century, the growth of the Chesapeake tobacco industry was an extensive rather than an intensive process, achieved more through the addition of new farms and new workers than by the more efficient use of existing factors; measured on a per household, per capita, or per worker basis, income from tobacco did not increase during the seventeenth century. This is not to slight the importance of tobacco to the

Chesapeake economy. The weed attracted immigrants and capital, made possible the rapid growth of population and settled area during the seventeenth century, and shaped the structure of Chesapeake society, the distribution of wealth and power, and the concerns of public life, while its rhythms influenced intimate events of human relationships. Tobacco placed a floor, albeit an unstable one, under incomes in the Chesapeake and, we would argue, kept those incomes higher than in colonies where exports were less central. But it was a floor quickly reached and one that offered few opportunities for further growth.[32]

The Cole account suggests a similar conclusion for income from the local market, although in this regard we are less confident in generalizing to the economy as a whole. Earnings from local exchange, like income from the export sector, did not increase. Given the growth of the Cole livestock herds and what we know about productivity in grains, this reflects a failure of the market rather than a constraint on supply. The market for agricultural produce in the Chesapeake was small and quickly saturated. Planters needed to purchase basic foods only early in the process of farm making. Once they had cleared sufficient land and built up adequate herds, they supplied those needs internally, turning to their neighbors only when faced with an occasional shortage. It was not until the eighteenth century, when Chesapeake planters began to penetrate markets in the West Indies, the Wine Islands, and southern Europe, that food production significantly increased incomes and offered chances for growth.[33]

By our estimation, subsistence income per capita—the value of goods and services produced and consumed on the plantation—did not increase on the Cole estate. That, of course, is an artifact of our method, and the conclusion may require some qualification. Perhaps, for example, meat consumption increased with the growth of livestock herds. More generally, we would argue that subsistence production was a major source of growth early in the history of the region and early in the life of particular plantations. That is, there were real gains to the economy as a whole as the colonies became self-sufficient in food, and real gains to families as they became able to supply their needs internally. But there were limits to this as a source of growth, and those limits were quickly reached. Over the first decade or so of a farm's existence, a family might see its real income grow as land was cleared and fenced, herds of cattle, horses, and swine were raised, and an orchard was cultivated. But once those things were accomplished and the needs of the family met, the absence of a lively market for food meant that there would be little opportunity or incentive for further growth. We suspect that the Cole plantation had nearly reached this stage by the time the accounts begin.

Why, then, did wealth increase, both on the Cole estate and in newly settled regions generally? And what impact did those gains have on income? The Cole account suggests that most of the gains could be captured under the heading of "farm building" or "pioneering," which was, as Percy Wells Bidwell noted, "a process of capital making."[34] New settlements in British North America were initially characterized by low levels of wealth, but the process of constructing working farms provided substantial opportunities for saving, investment, and accumulation. As a consequence, wealth grew rapidly in the decades following settlement as planters cleared land, erected buildings and fences, built up livestock herds, planted orchards, began vegetable gardens, improved their homes, and the like. The Cole account suggests that this period was marked by a high ratio of savings and investment to income. There are several ways of calculating such a ratio, but they all point to the same conclusion. A comparison of the total increase in estate value (£147.32) with net income from subsistence and the market plus that increase (£393.53) yields an investment-to-income ratio of 37 percent. Clearly, a substantial part of the income generated by the estate was reinvested—plowed back into the plantation. The rapid increase of wealth in the region indicates that other planters must have saved at similar rates.[35]

It is important to note that such high rates of saving were not achieved primarily by limiting current consumption, although that was part of the process. One might, for example, keep meat consumption low until herds were large enough that harvesting could satisfy needs, or one might forgo the purchase of furniture to acquire an additional servant. But one could clear an additional acre, plant an orchard, fence a field, or tend more animals without major cash outlays. And the opportunity costs of such activities were low. Tobacco was a demanding, labor-intensive crop, but it left time for other activities without diminishing output and sacrificing export earnings. Farm building was not costless, but most of what was given up was leisure time. Further, since this was a society of unfree labor, it was often someone else's leisure that the householder spent.[36]

The Cole account also indicates that this early growth process was characterized by a rising ratio of wealth to income. Again, alternative calculations are possible but all point to the same conclusion: the income generated by the plantation did not keep pace with the growth in the value of the estate. The wealth/income ratio rose by roughly 80 percent over the period covered by the accounts: in the early 1660s the estate generated £1 in income for each £2.4 in wealth; by the early 1670s it took £4.3 of wealth to produce £1 in annual income. The rising ratio of wealth to income suggests that there were limits to the growth process in the early stages of settlement, limits that the Cole plantation was fast approaching. In the absence of dependable markets for any crop but tobacco, diminishing returns quickly lowered the incentives to further farm-building activities. Once enough land had been cleared and fenced to meet the household's need for food, once livestock herds had become large enough to satisfy meat and dairy requirements, once the plantation had a fruitbearing orchard and a comfortable house, there was little else most farmers could do to improve family welfare. We do not know the experience of the Cole plantation after 1672, but in southern Maryland as a whole the early growth spurt ended in the 1680s. From then until the late 1740s, when world food shortages created new opportunities and the terms of trade shifted in favor of primary producers, wealth levels, however measured, showed no tendency to rise.[37]

Still, the accumulation of wealth early in the settlement process led to some important welfare gains. For one thing, there were additions to income: our point is not that income failed to grow but only that it failed to grow as fast as wealth. For another, leisure increased as the process neared completion. Once the hard work of making a farm was accomplished, a planter faced the demanding but less arduous task of maintaining it and forcing it to yield a living. Further, the process created major opportunities for poor people, most of them former servants, to accumulate property and become full members of a community. Elsewhere we have described those opportunities in detail and have shown that ex-servants

in early Maryland, if they lived long enough, had a good chance to establish families, acquire land, build estates, participate in local government, and achieve respectability.[38] Farm building helped to provide those opportunities, for it yielded ample rewards to persistent hard work. Finally, there were major gains in security and flexibility. With developed, working farms in full operation, families were assured of food and shelter despite the uncertainties of the international tobacco market. They could take risks without facing destitution, and they could pursue strategies of import substitution not possible earlier. It was easier to ride out a depression if one were assured of enough to eat and could counter its impact by clothing oneself in crude homespun, by making one's own shoes, utensils, and furnishings, and by experimenting with export commodities other than tobacco—with grains, meat, and wood products, for example. Life in the Chesapeake colonies was harsh and uncertain throughout the seventeenth century, but the process of accumulation revealed by the Cole accounts helped to make it less so.

Notes

Support for this project was provided by the St. Mary's City Commission with funds from the National Endowment for the Humanities (RS–23687–76–431) and the National Science Foundation (GS–32272), and by the University of Minnesota Computer Center. The essay has benefited from the comments of Paul Clemens, Stanley Engerman, David Galenson, and George Green, and from presentations to the Social History Seminar at the University of Minnesota and the Economic History Workshop, University of Chicago.

1. For a survey of the recent literature, see Thad W. Tate, "The Seventeenth-Century Chesapeake and Its Modern Historians," in Tate and David L. Ammerman, eds., *The Chesapeake in the Seventeenth Century: Essays on Anglo-American Society* (Chapel Hill, N.C., 1979), 3–30; Allan Kulikoff, "The Colonial Chesapeake: Seedbed of Antebellum Southern Culture?" *Journal of Southern History* 45 (1979): 513–40; and John J. McCusker and Russell R. Menard, *The Economy of British America, 1607–1790: Needs and Opportunities for Study* (Chapel Hill, N.C., 1985), chap. 7. Tate and Ammerman, eds., *Chesapeake Essays*, and Aubrey C. Land et al., eds., *Law, Society, and Politics in Early Maryland* (Baltimore, 1977), are representative selections of recent studies.

2. The documents are in Cole Plantation Accounts, Testamentary Proceedings, 6:118–47, Maryland Hall of Records, Annapolis. A detailed analysis of these records, stress-

ing the changing relationships of individual plantations to the local community, appears in Lorena Seebach Walsh, "Charles County, Maryland, 1658–1705: A Study of Chesapeake Social and Political Structure" (Ph.D. diss., Michigan State University, 1977), 262–305. We hope to publish the accounts and related documents, along with a more detailed commentary, in a book now in preparation, tentatively titled *Robert Cole's World: Agriculture and Society in Early Maryland.*

3. Unless otherwise noted, biographical information is drawn from the biographical files of the St. Mary's City Commission, housed at the Maryland Hall of Records.

4. On Gerard, see Edward C. Papenfuse et al., *A Biographical Dictionary of the Maryland Legislature, 1635–1789,* vol. 1 (Baltimore, 1979), 348–49.

5. Only 8 of the 39 adult males who lived on the manor between 1659 and 1661 were still there in 1670. William Hand Browne et al., eds., *Archives of Maryland . . . ,* vol. 53 (Baltimore, 1936), 627–37.

6. On soil characteristics, see S. O. Perkins, *Soil Survey of St. Mary's County, Maryland* (Washington, D.C., 1928), and Joseph W. Gibson, *Soil Survey of St. Mary's County, Maryland* (Washington, D.C., 1978).

7. Washington to Arthur Young as quoted in H. J. Habakkuk, *American and British Technology in the Nineteenth Century: The Search for Labour-Saving Inventions* (Cambridge, 1962), 100–101.

8. Cole Plantation Accounts, Testamentary Proceedings, 6:119.

9. This characterization of Maryland society is elaborated in Russell Robert Menard, "Economy and Society in Early Colonial Maryland" (Ph.D. diss., University of Iowa, 1975), esp. chap. 5.

10. The first estimate came within 8% of Cole's total. Values attached to individual items were then adjusted to yield Cole's sum. We are confident that the results of this process are reliable, so that the prices assigned particular commodities are reasonably close to their market values. The documents used in this essay report nearly all values in pounds of tobacco, the money of account in Maryland before the early 1680s. We have translated those values into local currency and then reduced figures in local currency to a constant-value series by a commodity price index (CPI, 1700 = 100) at the following rates:

	Price of Tobacco in pence	
Year	per pound	CPI
1658	1.55	135
1659	1.55	135
1660	1.55	135
1661	1.53	121
1662	1.60	138
1663	1.55	120
1664	1.35	120
1665	1.10	106.5
1666	0.90	103
1667	1.10	116

	Price of Tobacco in pence	
Year	per pound	CPI
1668	1.25	114.5
1669	1.15	113
1670	1.15	104.5
1671	1.05	114
1672	1.00	115.5
1673	1.00	103.5

For details of the construction of both series, see Menard, "Farm Prices of Maryland Tobacco, 1659–1710," *Maryland Historical Magazine* 68 (1973): 80–85, and "A Note on Chesapeake Tobacco Prices, 1618–1660," *Virginia Magazine of History and Biography* 84 (1976): 401–10; and Lois Green Carr and Lorena S. Walsh, "Inventories and the Analysis of Wealth and Consumption Patterns in St. Mary's County, Maryland, 1658–1777," *Historical Methods* 13 (1980): 96–101.

11. Comparison of Cole's estate with a larger pool of decedents drawn from three southern Maryland counties—St. Mary's, Charles, and Calvert—yields results nearly identical to those reported in table 1. We have here confined our attention to St. Mary's County decedents because of the superior quality of the information on their wealth in real estate. The data are drawn from a project of the St. Mary's City Commission, "Social Stratification in Maryland, 1658–1705" (funded by the National Science Foundation, GS–32272).

12. Estimating the value of landholdings in early Maryland is problematic. Too few deeds have survived to support an annual series, and these report sharp price variations according to the degree of improvement. The following table summarizes the available evidence:

	Improved Tracts		Unimproved Tracts		All Tracts*	
Years	N	pence/ acre	N	pence/ acre	N	pence/ acre
1652–57	4	65.68	2	19.88	6	50.41
1658–64	8	79.60	3	24.80	14	57.16
1665–68	12	66.25	3	14.70	21	46.14
1669–74	10	83.67	4	18.71	16	62.05

*Includes some tracts unknown as to improvements.

Source: The data are drawn from a variety of sources. Details are available in the files of the St. Mary's City Commission.

Since the mean size of tracts that could be identified as improved was about 200 acres, in valuing land we assumed that each householder's first 200 acres should be considered improved and that any additional acreage should be valued at the price for unimproved land.

13. For minimum tobacco acreages, see Carville V. Earle, *The Evolution of a Tidewater Settlement System: All Hallow's Parish, Maryland, 1650–1783* (Chicago, 1975), 29, and Gregory A. Stiverson, *Poverty in a Land of Plenty: Tenancy in Eighteenth-Century Maryland* (Baltimore, 1977), 95–96.

Through the 1660s, Maryland law required each hand working in tobacco to raise two acres of corn.

14. Menard, "Economy and Society in Early Colonial Maryland," 242.

15. Acreage for 5 of the 26 decedent landowners could not be determined but seems clearly to be less than 350. To estimate their holdings we took the mean size of all known holdings less than this amount, 150 acres, and assigned that to the 5.

16. For a more detailed analysis of consumption patterns based on probate inventories, see Lois Green Carr and Lorena S. Walsh, "Changing Life Styles in Colonial St. Mary's County," *Working Papers of the Regional Economic History Research Center*, vol. 1 (1978): 73–118. With 7 children in 1662, Cole's family was among Maryland's largest. Wills probated in the province between 1660 and 1665 report an average of 1.83 children (Menard, "Economy and Society in Early Colonial Maryland," 198). See also Lois Green Carr and Lorena S. Walsh, "The Planter's Wife: The Experience of White Women in Seventeenth-Century Maryland," *William and Mary Quarterly*, 3d ser., 34 (1977): 552–53.

17. For the timing of cycles in the tobacco trade see Russell R. Menard, "The Tobacco Industry in the Chesapeake Colonies, 1617–1730: An Interpretation," *Research in Economic History* 5 (1980): 128–42. In the Cole plantation accounts, income and expenditures for the years 1671 and 1672 are lumped together. We assumed that equal amounts of tobacco were earned and spent in the two years. Differences reported in the several tables therefore reflect only changes in the price of tobacco and the exchange rate as reported in n. 10, above.

18. The relationships between shifting fortunes in the tobacco industry and other sectors of the economy are described in Menard, "Tobacco Industry in the Chesapeake Colonies," 123–28. On the Cole plantation, the relationship between the value of the tobacco crop and the share of total income produced by that crop over the years 1662 through 1672 yields a Spearman's Coefficient of Rank-Order Correlation of $-.53$. A more direct test of the relationship of income from tobacco and income from other sources yields a correlation coefficient $(r) = .63$ in a regression of the form

$\log y = 1.72 \log x - 1.39$, where $y =$ all market income other than tobacco and $x =$ income from tobacco.

19. A rapid growth in the size of the local market is suggested by the sharp increase in the number of taxables, total population, and households in southern Maryland during the 1660s and early 1670s. See the data assembled in Russell R. Menard et al., "Opportunity and Inequality: The Distribution of Wealth on the Lower Western Shore of Maryland, 1638–1705," *Maryland Historical Magazine* 69 (1974): 175–77, and in Menard, "Economy and Society in Early Colonial Maryland," 457–59. We know little as yet about the operation of the local market in the early Chesapeake, but see the discussion in Walsh, "Charles County, Maryland," 262–305.

20. For examples of contracts for room and board, see Charles County Court and Land Records, R#1, fols. 125, 156, 181, Maryland Hall of Records. We know little about subsistence activities in the Chesapeake, but useful discussions of the growth of plantation self-sufficiency appear in Earle, *Evolution of a Tidewater Settlement System*, 101–42, and Gerald W. Mullin, *Flight and Rebellion: Slave Resistance in Eighteenth-Century Virginia* (New York, 1972), 3–34. The composition of the Cole household, necessary for the calculation of column A in table 3, has been reconstructed from evidence in the accounts (see table below).

21. The correlation coefficient $(r) - .589$ in a regression of the form $x = 24.05 + .33y$, where $x =$ expenditures in year t and $y =$ income in year t. The hypothesis that Gardiner behaved in such a fashion—that he attempted to smooth out the impact of short-term fluctuations in income on plantation living standards by adjusting expenditures to the average, rather than the annual, income earned on the plantation—finds support in further analysis of the data. Regression with a slightly smoothed income term produces a much better fit: $r = .703$, $x = 14.2 + .56y$, where $x =$ expenditures in year t and $y =$ the average of income in years t and t-1.

22. Wills I, 184, Maryland Hall of Records.

23. The literature on export-led growth in early America is surveyed by David W. Galenson and Russell R. Menard, "Approaches to the Analysis of Economic Growth in Colo-

Year	Male Servants Age 16+	Sons Age 16+	Adult Women	Children 12–15	Children Under 12	Total
1662	3	0	1	1	5	10
1663	4	0	2	1	4	11
1664	5	0	2	2	3	12
1665	4	1	2	1	3	11
1666	3	1	1	1	3	9
1667	3	1	0	2	1	7
1668	3	2	0	1	1	7
1669	2	2	0	3	1	8
1670	2	2	0	3	0	7
1671	2	3	0	2	0	7
1672	2	3	0	1	0	6
1673	3	1	0	0	0	4

nial British America," *Historical Methods* 13 (1980): 3–16.

24. Wills I, 184. The children, Cole added, were to "be kept from Idleness but not to be keept as Common servants." They were to receive this education before reaching age eighteen, "and after such learning so bestowed" Cole requested "that such care be taken of my Children that they may not forgett their Learning before they do come to the age as aforesaid."

25. Smith, *An Inquiry into the Nature and Causes of the Wealth of Nations,* ed. Edwin Cannan (New York, 1937 [orig. pub. London, 1776]), 532.

26. In most cases the account itself makes clear which expenditures were made to maintain the work force and the plantation, but some entries simply record purchases for food, cloth, or unspecified goods and services. We allocated such expenditures to the work force according to the ratio of servants to total residents of the household as detailed in n. 20. For example, in 1662, when the household contained four servants among its ten residents, we multiplied such unclassified expenditures by .4 and allocated the result to the costs of maintaining the work force and plantation.

27. Some of the cattle and swine were distributed to the older children before this inventory was taken. If we include that livestock in the estate and make a reasonable allowance for its increase, the value of the livestock would rise to roughly £265, the estate to over £400, and the 1662–73 growth rate to more than 6% per year. The documents convey the impression that Gardiner was less careful in constructing the inventory of the plantation in 1673 than Cole had been in 1662. Were that the case, it would account for some of the decline in the several categories of assets revealed in table 7 and would lead to an underestimate of the rate of growth in total worth over the period.

28. The internal rate of return is calculated using the formula:

$$C1662 = \sum_{t=1}^{11} \frac{R}{(1 + i)^t} + \frac{C1672}{(1 + i)^{11}}$$

Where: C = the value of capital on the plantation (land, labor, livestock, tools, etc.; see table 7)

R = the annual net income from all sources earned on the plantation (see table 6)

t = a subscript or exponent designating a year

i = the internal rate of return

For the calculation and some useful comparative material, see Robert William Fogel and Stanley L. Engerman, "The Economics of Slavery," in Fogel and Engerman, eds., *The Reinterpretation of American Economic History* (New York, 1971), 321–28, 338–39, and Paul G. E. Clemens, *The Atlantic Economy and Colonial Maryland's Eastern Shore: From Tobacco to Grain* (Ithaca, N.Y., 1980), 150–61.

29. For the dependency ratio on the plantation, see n. 20, above. Our comments about the rate of increase among livestock are based on detailed records preserved among York County, Virginia, probate materials analyzed by Carr. She intends to publish the results shortly. For evidence of the importance of livestock in the Chesapeake economy, espe-

cially in bequests and in the estates of orphans, see Edmund S. Morgan, *American Slavery, American Freedom: The Ordeal of Colonial Virginia* (New York, 1975), 136–40, 168–70. Although rates of seasoning mortality (the likelihood that an immigrant would die shortly after arrival) had declined sharply since the early seventeenth century, they remained high enough during the years covered by the accounts to produce occasional complaints of a shortage of servants due to exceptional death rates. See, for example, William Wakeman to Joseph Williamson, Apr. 22, 1670, S.P. 29/274, no. 213, Public Record Office. See also the general discussion in Henry A. Gemery, "Emigration from the British Isles to the New World, 1630–1700: Inferences from Colonial Populations," *Research in Economic History* 5 (1980): 185–90, and in Russell R. Menard, "The Growth of Population in the Chesapeake Colonies: A Comment," *Explorations in Economic History* 18 (1981): 401–3.

30. See, for example, Morgan, *American Slavery, American Freedom*, 180–95. For a contrary view, note Wesley Frank Craven's suggestion that historians "have drawn a darker picture of economic conditions in Virginia through the third quarter of the century than is warranted" (*White, Red, and Black: The Seventeenth-Century Virginian* [Charlottesville, Va., 1971], 21).

31. Russell R. Menard, "Comment on Paper by Ball and Walton," *Journal of Economic History* 36 (1976): 124–25; Menard et al., "Opportunity and Inequality," *Maryland Historical Magazine* 69 (1974): 169–83; P. M. G. Harris, "Integrating Interpretations of Local and Regionwide Change in the Study of Economic Development and Demographic Growth in the Colonial Chesapeake, 1630–1775," *Working Papers of the Regional Economic History Research Center*, vol. 1 (1978): 35–72; Terry L. Anderson, "Wealth Estimates for the New England Colonies, 1650–1709," *Explorations in Economic History* 12 (1975): 151–76; McCusker and Menard, *Economic History of British America*, chaps. 7, 15.

32. For income from tobacco on the Cole plantation, see table 3, above. The description of the Chesapeake tobacco industry offered in this paragraph is elaborated in Menard, "Tobacco Industry in the Chesapeake Colonies," 109–77.

33. The literature on the diversification of Chesapeake exports during the eighteenth century is large. See especially David C. Klingaman, "The Significance of Grain in the Development of Tobacco Colonies," *Journal of Economic History* 29 (1967): 268–78; Peter Victor Bergstrom, "Markets and Merchants: Economic Diversification in Colonial Virginia, 1700–1775" (Ph.D. diss., University of New Hampshire, 1980); and Clemens, *Atlantic Economy and Colonial Maryland's Eastern Shore*.

34. Percy Wells Bidwell and John I. Falconer, *History of Agriculture in the Northern United States, 1620–1860* (Washington, D.C., 1925), 82. Aubrey C. Land has emphasized the importance of this process in capital formation along the Chesapeake ("Economic Behavior in a Planting Society: The Eighteenth-Century Chesapeake," *Journal of Social History* 33 [1967]: 469–85).

35. Alternatively, one could measure the savings rate as the ratio of income devoted to maintaining the work force

and plantation to total income, or as the ratio of income devoted to maintaining the operation plus the increase in estate value to total income plus that increase. Such measures also suggest a high rate of savings.

36. Ester Boserup puts the issue as follows: "The first important thing to note about agricultural investment is that a large share of it can be carried out by the cultivators themselves. Furthermore, it is normal for cultivators to have shorter or longer periods of leisure each year when current agricultural work is at a minimum so that working capacity for additional investment is normally available. In other words, the question is not whether the cultivators are able and willing to restrain consumption in order to invest. The question is whether an increasing family provides sufficient incentive to additional work and whether the system of land tenure is such that the cultivators have access to additional cultivable land or sufficient security of tenure to make land improvements a worthwhile investment" (*The Conditions of Agricultural Growth: The Economics of Agrarian Change under Population Pressure* [London, 1965], 88). See also Julian L. Simon, *The Economics of Population Growth* (Princeton, N.J., 1977).

37. The following table presents a calculation of the wealth/income ratio on the Cole plantation. It assumes that the value of the estate increased at a constant annual rate and defines income as the sum of the total earned on the market, the estimated value of subsistence production, and the annual increase in the value of the estate:

Year	Estimated Value of Estate	Estimated Gross Income	Wealth/Income
1662	£212	£80	2.6
1663	222	102	2.2
1664	233	95	2.5
1665	245	87	2.8
1666	257	59	4.4
1667	269	65	4.1
1668	282	124	2.3
1669	296	76	3.9
1670	311	74	4.2
1671	326	81	4.0
1672	342	73	4.7
1673	359		

Alternative calculations—all of which describe a similar pattern—could assume that the estate value increased in equal annual increments, could confine the definition of wealth to capital goods, or could define income as net of expenditures to maintain the work force and plantation or as only that income earned on the market. Alice Hanson Jones offers an informed discussion of colonial wealth/income ratios in *Wealth of a Nation to Be: The American Colonies on the Eve of the Revolution* (New York, 1980), 61–64, 369–74.

For the pattern of growth in Chesapeake wealth levels after 1680, see n. 31, above; Allan Kulikoff, "The Economic Growth of the Eighteenth-Century Chesapeake Colonies,"

Journal of Economic History 39 (1979): 275–88; and Clemens, *Atlantic Economy and Colonial Maryland's Eastern Shore*, 228–32.

38. Russell R. Menard, "From Servant to Freeholder: Status Mobility and Property Accumulation in Seventeenth-Century Maryland," *William and Mary Quarterly*, 3d ser., 30 (1973): 37–64; Lorena S. Walsh, "Servitude and Opportunity in Charles County, Maryland, 1658–1705," in *Law, Society, and Politics in Early Maryland*, ed. Land et al., 111–33; Lois Green Carr and Russell R. Menard, "Immigration and Opportunity: The Freedman in Early Colonial Maryland," in *Chesapeake Essays*, ed. Tate and Ammerman, 206–42.

Work and Culture: The Task System and the World of Lowcountry Blacks, 1700–1880

PHILIP D. MORGAN

Perhaps no aspect of material life in the seventeenth, eighteenth, and nineteenth centuries has left deeper wounds in American identity than slavery, a process of labor exploitation and a legally sanctioned institution through which African and American Indian men, women, and children were themselves converted into alienable property, objects to be manipulated for the good of their owner. In recent years, different scholars have demonstrated that despite the work-discipline imposed on them by their masters, black slaves were still able to construct a culture of their own and, within limits, to create their own distinct history; in the South, for example, African traditions survived and new Creole languages and art forms flourished. In the following essay, Philip D. Morgan extends the investigation of everyday life in the quarters as he explores a much-overlooked variant of slave labor organization: the "task system" that characterized black life on the rice plantations of lowcountry South Carolina and Georgia, an agricultural region whose low-maintenance crops demanded an alternative to the "gang-labor" method of working slaves that obtained in other areas of the antebellum South.

As he surveys three stages in the development of the task system from the early eighteenth century through the Civil War, Morgan concentrates on the domestic economy and attitude of slaves who, once they had completed their assigned daily "task," could use their "time" as they saw fit. What makes the task system stand out is the stimulus it provided for industrious and hardworking slaves to acquire their own material possessions, accumulate real estate, and, ironically, in some instances to buy their freedom with cash they had earned and saved while enslaved. Two advantages, Morgan argues, made the task system flourish. Because it allowed slaves to determine the actual length of their working day, the system allowed slaves free time, hours that quickly

became sacrosanct. On their own time they could grow their own subsistence crops, including traditional African foods like groundnuts, sesamen, peppers, calabashes, and African varieties of corn, on their own plots. Spare hours also allowed them to work for profit; with their earnings, many highly skilled black artisans bought or bartered for their own horses, pigs, boats, and wagons. Indeed Morgan reveals that on the eve of the Civil War some slaves were described by whites as being "pretty well off," "more than usually prosperous," and "just like a white man except [for] his color." Such accumulation led to competition between slaves—evidenced in the ostentatious display of prized horses—as well as engendering notions of upward social mobility in the midst of chattel bondage.

But while the task system extended white hegemony by rewarding with property slaves who were hardworking and frugal, it also led to what Morgan aptly describes as an "internal economy" controlled by slaves who could purchase, exchange, and even inherit property. This hidden economy reveals the views that slaves and, after emancipation, black freedmen had toward work and the dominant white culture. In their hesitancy to engage market capitalism, their rejection of northern wage-labor reformers, and their reluctance to move away from subsistence-oriented local exchange values, Morgan suggests that they nurtured a "peasant mentalité" similar to that of Caribbean societies studied by anthropologists.

Who built Thebes of the seven Gates?
In the books stand the names of Kings.
Did they then drag up the rock-slabs?
And Babylon so often destroyed,
Who kept rebuilding it?
In which houses did the builders live
In gold-glittering Lima?
Where did the brick-layers go
The evening the Great Wall of China was finished?

. . .

Even in legendary Atlantis
Didn't the drowning shout for their slaves
As the ocean engulfed it?

. . .

So many reports
So many questions.

—Bertolt Brecht (1939)

Within the realm of slavery studies there has been a pronounced preoccupation with the external or institutional aspects of the slave system. Despite repeated clarion calls for investigations of life in the slave quarters, little scholarly attention has been directed to the domestic economy of the slaves, their work routines, their attitudes toward resource allocation, their attempts to accumulate, and their patterns of consumption.[1] This academic shortsightedness is more easily identified than remedied. Attitudes toward work and patterns of work constitute an area of inquiry that sprawls awkwardly across academic demarcations: the subject is all too easily neglected.[2] In addition, the genre to which this type of history is most akin, namely, labor history, often suffers from its own myopia: studies that begin by aiming to uncover the experience of workers can all too readily focus instead on management priorities.[3] Moreover, what has been said with respect to the English farm laborer applies even more forcefully to the Afro-American slave: "No one has written his signature more plainly across the countryside; but no one has left more scanty [written] records of his achievements."[4]

Mindful of these difficulties and pitfalls, this essay accepts the challenge posed by Brecht's questions: it attempts to bring history closer to the central concerns of ordinary people's lives—in this case, the lives of Afro-American slaves in the lowcountry region of South Carolina and Georgia. In this light, perhaps the most distinctive and central feature of low-country slave life was the task system. In Lewis Gray's words, "Under the task system the slave was assigned a certain amount of work for the day, and after completing the task he could use his time as he pleased," whereas under the gang system, prevalent in most Anglo-American plantation societies, "slaves were worked in groups under the control of a driver or leader . . . and the laborer was compelled to work the entire day."[5] While previous commentators have drawn attention to the task system, few have explored how this peculiarity arose and how it structured the world of those who labored under it. In order to shed light on the first matter, I shall open three windows onto different phases in the development of this labor arrangement: its origins in the first half of the eighteenth century, its routinization during the Revolutionary era, and its full flowering by the time of the Civil War. I shall also explore the ramifications of the task system for the slaves by analyzing its most distinctive feature so far as they were concerned: the opportunities it provided for working on their own behalf once the stipulated task had been completed.[6] I shall argue, then, that a particular mode of labor organization and a particular domestic economy evolved simultaneously in the colonial and antebellum lowcountry.[7]

This argument can best be secured by broadening our horizons to take in not only colonial and early national developments but also those of the antebellum and even postbellum years. On the one hand, such a strategy will show how colonial developments bore directly on nineteenth- and even twentieth-century realities. To take a minor example, the basic task unit still current in the minds of freedmen in the 1930s will be shown to have had a precise colonial origin. On the other hand, the opportunities that the task system presented slaves can be understood only in the light of mid-nineteenth-century experiences. To take a more significant example, the resemblance between the experiences of some low-country slaves and of the protopeasants found among the slaves of certain Caribbean plantation societies emerges most clearly from a glance at the behavior of slaves and freedmen in the years surrounding the Civil War.[8] In other words, to understand the evolution of the task system and its concomitant domestic

Production and Control of Property

economy, we shall need a telescope rather than a microscope.

* * *

If the Negroes are skilful and industrious, they plant something for themselves after the day's work
—Johann Bolzius (1751)

The earliest, fragmentary descriptions of work practices in the lowcountry rice economy indicate that a prominent characteristic of the task system—a sharp division between the master's "time" and the slave's "time"—was already in place. In the first decade of the eighteenth century the clergy of South Carolina complained that slaves were planting "for themselves as much as will cloath and subsist them and their famil[ies]." During the investigation of a suspected slave conspiracy in mid-century, a lowcountry planter readily acknowledged that one of his slaves had planted rice "in his own time" and could do with it as he wished.[9] The most acute observer of early work practices, Johann Bolzius, described how slaves, after "their required day's work," were "given as much land as they can handle" on which they planted corn, potatoes, tobacco, peanuts, sugar and water melons, and pumpkins and bottle pumpkins.[10] The opportunity to grow such a wide range of provisions on readily available land owed much to the early establishment and institutionalization of the daily work requirement. By mid-century the basic "task" unit had been set at a quarter of an acre. Moreover, other activities, outside of the rice field, were also tasked: in pounding the rice grain, slaves were "tasked at seven Mortars for one day," and in providing fences lowcountry slaves were expected to split one hundred poles of about twelve feet in length (a daily "task" that remained unchanged throughout the slave era, as table 1 indicates).[11] These tasks were not, of course, easily accomplished, and occasionally planters exacted even higher daily requirements; but, as Bolzius noted, the advantage to the slaves of having a daily goal was that they could, once it was met, "plant something for themselves."[12]

A tried and tested model of labor organization—the gang system practiced on both tobacco and sugar plantations—was available when lowcountry planters discovered their own plantation staple. In fact,

many of the first immigrants were from Barbados, where they must have had direct experience of operating gangs of slaves.[13] Why did they and others decide to adopt a new system? U. B. Phillips claimed that temporary absenteeism was responsible: "The necessity of the master's moving away from his estate in the warm months, to escape the malaria, involved the adoption of some system of routine which would work with more or less automatic regularity without his own inspiring or impelling presence." However, while absenteeism may have contributed to the attractiveness of this system, it seems an insufficiently powerful agent to account for its inception. The example of Caribbean sugar production is pertinent here; if the withdrawal of an inspiring master encouraged the development of tasking, why did not sugar planters in the West Indies, where absenteeism began relatively early, adopt the system?[14]

The absence of masters may be an unconvincing explanation for the development of a task system, but perhaps the presence of particular slaves can serve in its place. Peter H. Wood and Daniel C. Littlefield have pointed out that some black immigrants to early South Carolina were already familiar with the techniques of rice cultivation.[15] These slaves' expertise, it might be argued, accounts for the evolution of a system that would operate more or less automatically. It has even been suggested, in this regard, that a work pattern of alternating bouts of intense labor and idleness tends to occur wherever men are to some degree in control of their own working lives (need one look any further than authors?).[16] By displaying their own understanding of the basic requirements of rice cultivation, lowcountry slaves might have gained a measure of control over their lives, at least to the extent of determining the length of their working days. While this is an attractive argument, it is not without problems. The coastal regions that seem to have supplied a majority of slaves to early South Carolina were not rice-producing areas; lowcountry whites have left no record of valuing the knowledge of rice planting that some slaves might have displayed; and familiarity with rice planting is hardly the same as familiarity with irrigated rice culture, practiced in South Carolina from early days.[17] Slaves undoubtedly contributed a great deal to the development of South Carolina's rice economy; but, on present evidence, it would be rash to attribute the development of a task system to their prowess, especially when that prow-

Table 1. Tasking Requirements, ca. 1750–ca. 1860

Representative Tasks	1750s[1]	1770s[2]	1820s[3]	1830s[4]	1840s[5]	1850s–1860s[6]
Rice						
Turning up land	¼a		¼a	¼a	¼–½a	¼a
Trenching/Covering	½a		¾a	¾a	¾a	½a
First Hoeing	¼a		¼–½a	½a	½a	¼–½a
Second Hoeing				½a	½a	
Third Hoeing	½a			¾a	20c	
Reaping					¾a	¾a
Threshing			600s	600s	600s	600s
Pounding	7m					
Ditching			600sf	700sf	500sf	600sf
Cotton						
Listing			¼a	¼a	½a	¼–½a
Bedding			¼a	¼a	⅜a	¼–½a
Hoeing			½a	½a	½a	½a
Picking			90–100lbs	70–100lbs		
Assorting			30–50lbs	60lbs		
Ginning			20–30lbs	30lbs		20–30lbs
Moting			30–50lbs	30lbs		
General						
Splitting rails	100	100	100	100		100–125
Squaring timber		100'	100'	100'		100'

a = acre   c = compasses   s = sheaves   sf = square feet   m = mortars

[1]"Bolzius Answers a Questionnaire," trans. and ed. Loewald et al., 258; Garden to the Royal Society, Apr. 20, 1755, Guard Book 1, 36.

[2]John Gerar William De Brahm, *Report of the General Survey in the Southern District of North America*, ed. Louis De Vorsey, Jr. (Columbia, S.C., 1971), 94.

[3]"Estimate of the Daily Labour of Negroes," *American Farmer* 5 (1823–24): 319–20; [Edwin C. Holland], *A Refutation of the Calumnies Circulated against . . . Slavery . . .* (New York, 1969 [orig. publ. Charleston, S.C., 1822]), 53; Basil Hall, *Travels in North America in the Years 1827 and 1828*, vol. 3 (London, 1829), 219–23.

[4]"A Memorandum of Tasks," *Southern Agriculturalist* 7 (1834): 297–99; W. H. Capers, "On the Culture of Sea-Island Cotton," *Southern Agriculturalist* 8 (1835): 402–11.

[5]Edmund Ruffin, *Report of the Commencement and Progress of the Agricultural Survey of South-Carolina for 1843* (Columbia, S.C., 1843), 118; J. A. Turner, *The Cotton Planter's Manual* (New York, 1865), 285.

[6]Frederick Law Olmsted, *A Journey in the Seaboard Slave States . . .* (New York, 1968 [orig. publ. 1856]), 434–35; Francis S. Holmes, *Southern Farmer and Market Gardener* (Charleston, S.C. 1852), 234–36; Weehaw Plantation Book, 1855–61, South Carolina Historical Society, Charleston; "Tasks for Negroes," *Southern Cultivator* 18 (1860): 247; Col. A. J. Willard to W. H. Smith, Nov. 13, 1865 (A7011); testimony of Harry McMillan, 1863 (K78) (see below, n. 81, for explanation of these notations); Turner, *Cotton Planter's Manual*, 133–35. See also George P. Rawick, ed., *The American Slave: A Composite Autobiography* (Westport, Conn., 1972), 2: pt. 2, 302; 3: pt. 3, 92; 3: pt. 4, 117.

ess went largely unrecognized and may not have been significant.

A consideration of staple-crop requirements provides the most satisfactory, if not complete, answer to the question of the system's origins. The amount of direct supervision demanded by various crops offers at least one clue to the puzzle. Unlike tobacco, which involved scrupulous care in all phases of the production cycle and was therefore best cultivated by small gangs of closely attended laborers, rice was a hardy plant, requiring a few relatively straightforward operations for its successful cultivation.[18] The great expansion of rice culture in seventeenth-century Lombardy, for instance, was predicated not on a stable, sophisticated, and well-supervised labor force but on a pool of transient labor drawn from far afield.[19] Nor did rice production require the strict regimentation and "semi-industrialised" production techniques that attended the cultivation of sugar and necessitated gang labor.[20] However, the Caribbean plantation experience does offer parallels to the lowcountry rice economy: in the British West Indies,

Production and Control of Property

crops that required little supervision or regimentation—notably coffee and pimiento—were, like rice, grown by a slave labor force organized by tasks rather than into gangs.[21]

In addition to the degree of direct supervision required by a crop, the facility with which the laborers' output could be measured also shaped different forms of labor organization. For example, the productivity of a single coffee and pimiento worker could be measured accurately and cheaply, particularly in the harvesting cycle. It was easy to weigh an individual's baskets of coffee or pimiento berries, and tasking may have first developed in this stage of the respective crop cycles before being extended to other operations. Conversely, the much larger volumes involved in the cane harvest would have proved far less easy and much more expensive to measure on an individual "task" basis; not surprisingly, gang labor was employed at this and other stages of the sugar cycle.[22] In the case of rice, it was less the harvesting and more the cultivation of the crop that lent itself to inexpensive and efficient measurement. As Phillips pointed out, drainage ditches, which were necessary in lowcountry rice cultivation, provided convenient units by which the performance of tasks could be measured (fig. 1).[23] The ubiquity and long-standing history of the quarter-acre task suggest that the planting and weeding stages of the rice cycle provided the initial rationale for the task system; once tasking became firmly established, it was extended to a whole host of plantation operations.

Thus various staple-crop requirements seem to have served as the most important catalysts for the development of particular modes of labor organization. Undoubtedly other imperatives contributed to the attractiveness of one or the other labor arrangement: absenteeism and the ease with which slaves took to rice cultivation may well have encouraged a more widespread and rapid diffusion of the task system in the lowcountry than might otherwise have been the case. Moreover, once a task system had been tried, tested, and not found wanting, it could be extended to crops that were produced elsewhere by means of gang labor. In other words, once tasking became a way of life, means were found to circumvent the otherwise powerful dictates of the various staple crops.[24]

Whatever the origins of the task system, its consequences soon became apparent. Indeed, the way in

Fig. 1. Rice fields at Mulberry Plantation, ca. 1935. Mulberry Plantation was established on the west branch of the Cooper River in 1714 by Thomas Broughton. (Photograph by Frances Benjamin Johnson, reprinted from Samuel Gaillard Stoney, *Plantations of the Carolina Low Country*, ed. Albert Simons and Samuel Lapham, Jr. [Charleston, S.C., 1938], 107.)

which slaves chose to spend their own "time" created unease among ruling South Carolinians. One of the earliest laws relating to slaves, enacted in 1686, prohibited the exchange of goods between slaves or between slaves and freemen without their masters' consent. A decade later, slaves were expressly forbidden from felling and carrying away timber on lands other than their masters'. In 1714 the legislature enacted its stiffest prohibition; slaves were no longer to "plant for themselves any corn, peas or rice."[25] While this stark ban appears definitive, later legislation suggests its ineffectiveness. In 1734, for example, an act for the better regulation of patrols allowed patrollers to confiscate "all fowls and other provisions" found in the possession of "stragling negroes." That slaves produced provisions independently is further implied in a 1738 act for the licensing of hawkers and pedlars, which aimed to stamp out the illicit traffic in rice and provisions between slaves and itinerant traders. By 1751 the legislators bowed to the inevitable. By outlawing the sale of slaves' rice and corn to anybody other than their masters, they were implicitly recognizing the right of slaves to cultivate such crops.[26] The law of 1714 had thus died a natural death.

From the evidence of plantation account books and estate records, the act of 1751 simply brought the law closer into line with social practice. In 1728 Abraham, a Ball family slave, was paid £1 10s. for providing his master with eighteen fowls, while a female slave received £8 for supplying hogs. In 1736 twenty-two Ball family slaves were paid more than £50 for supplying varying amounts of rice to their master.[27] The extent of this trade in provisions was occasionally impressive; over the course of two years, the slaves belonging to James Hartley's estate were paid £124 for supplying 290 bushels of their corn.[28] Henry Ravenel not only purchased his slaves' provision goods, consisting of corn, fowls, hogs, and catfish, but also their canoes, baskets, and myrtle wax.[29]

Masters undoubtedly benefited from these exchanges while displaying their benevolence, but we should not assume that there was no bargaining, however unequal, between the parties. Henry Laurens, for example, advised one of his newly appointed overseers to "purchase of your own Negroes all [the provisions] that you know Lawfully belongs to themselves at the lowest price that they will sell it for."[30] If a master refused to give slaves a fair price for their produce, they could take it elsewhere. One of the most persistent complaints of lowcountry planters and legislators concerned illicit trading across plantation boundaries.[31] A slave who produced rice "in his own time" also traveled more than fifteen miles up the Cooper River to sell a barrel of his crop to his brother, who resided on another plantation.[32] A white boatman, implicated in a slave conspiracy, openly acknowledged that he had exchanged his hog for a slave's deer skin.[33] The records of one lowcountry estate even register payments to a neighboring planter's slaves for their seed rice.[34] In other words, once slaves were allowed to produce provisions, they would al-

ways find ways to market them, be it to passing traders, neighboring whites, or fellow slaves.

Lowcountry slaves took the opportunity to raise a wide array of agricultural products, many of which reflected their African background. In the third decade of the eighteenth century Mark Catesby observed two African varieties of corn in the lowcountry but only among the "Plantations of *Negroes*." When William Bartram visited the lowcountry in the 1770s he noticed that the tania or tannier (a tuberous root found in the West Indies and tropical Africa) was "much cultivated and esteemed for food, particularly by the Negroes."[35] Bernard Romans claimed that slaves had introduced the groundnut into South Carolina; by the early nineteenth century, according to David Ramsay's informants on Edisto Island, groundnuts were "planted in small patches chiefly by the negroes, for market."[36] Romans also attributed the introduction of the "sesamen or oily grain" to lowcountry slaves; they used it, he maintained, "as a food either raw, toasted or boiled in their soups and are very fond of it, they call it *Benni*." Over one-and-a-half centuries later, a black sea islander was to be found planting what he called "bene." He used it in the same ways that his ancestors had done. Most significant, when asked where he acquired the seed, he said "his parents always had it and he was told 'Dey brung it fum Africa.'"[37] Apparently peppers were also the preserve of slaves. Knowing that his slave old Tom "plants a good deal of pepper," Elias Ball desired him to send "sum Read pepper pounded and corked up in a pint Bottle." In 1742, when Eliza Lucas sent her friend some of the same product, she referred to it, in revealing fashion, as "negroe pepper."[38] The only tobacco grown in early eighteenth-century South Carolina belonged to the slaves.[39] Janet Schaw was so impressed by the way in which Carolina slaves used their "little piece[s] of land" to grow vegetables, "rear hogs and poultry, sow calabashes, etc." that she thought they cultivated them "much better than their Master[s]." Furthermore, she believed that "the Negroes are the only people that seem to pay any attention to the various uses that the wild vegetables may be put to."[40]

The cultivation and subsequent exchange of provisions allowed some slaves to claim more substantial items of property. In 1714 the South Carolina legislature denied the slaves' claim to "any stock of hogs, cattle or horses." This directive apparently fell on

PART THREE   Production and Control of Property

deaf ears, for in 1722 it became lawful to seize any hogs, boats, or canoes belonging to slaves. Moreover, this later act referred to the "great inconveniences [that] do arise from negroes and other slaves keeping and breeding of horses"; not only were these horses (and cattle) to be seized, but the proceeds of their sale were to be put to the support of the parish poor. The irony of slave property sustaining white paupers was presumably lost on South Carolina legislators but perhaps not on the slaves. Once again, legislative intentions seem to have been thwarted, for in 1740 more complaints were to be heard about those "several owners of slaves [who] have permitted them to keep canoes, and to breed and raise horses, neat cattle and hogs, and to traffic and barter in several parts of this Province, for the particular and peculiar benefit of such slaves."[41] The most dramatic example of property ownership by a lowcountry slave in the first half of the eighteenth century involved not horses or canoes but men. According to a deed of manumission, a slave named Sampson "by his Industry and the Assistance of Friends" had purchased and "procured in his owne Right and property and for his owne Use" another slave named Tom. Sampson then exchanged his slave Tom for "fifty years of his [that is, Sampson's] Life time and Servitude (to come)."[42] If the task system had created the opportunities for Sampson's "Industry" to manifest itself in this way, it truly was a potent force.

*   *   *

Once a slave has completed his task, his master feels no right to call on him.

—Daniel Turner (1806)

By the late eighteenth century the task system had taken deep root in the lowcountry. Tasks were set for almost all operations—from clearing new ground (one-eighth of an acre) to the weekly task of a pair of sawyers (600 feet of pine or 780 feet of cypress).[43] However, the basic unit, a quarter-acre, was still the yardstick for virtually all rice-planting operations (fig. 2).[44] In recognition of this reality, one Georgia absentee in 1786 sent a chain "for running out the Tasks" to his plantation manager. "It is 105 feet long," he noted, "and will save a great deal of time in Laying out the field, and do it with more exactness." Henry Ferguson, an East Floridian who had spent seventeen years in South Carolina and Georgia, was able to specify precisely how much land his slaves had cleared "from the Tasks which he set to his Negroes having measured the Ground frequently for that purpose." He added that "a Task was a quarter of an Acre to weed p. day."[45] Even opponents of the task system testified to its pervasiveness. William Butler, a keen observer of rice culture, argued in 1786 that slaves "should always be Kept in Gangs or parcels and not scattered over a field in Tasks as is too generally done, for while in gangs they are more immediately under the Superintendants Eyes, [and] of course may be much better and more immediately inspected" (fig. 3).[46]

The extension of the task system to the cultivation of sea island cotton confirms the failure of Butler's advice. Since both the long- and short-staple varieties of cotton required close attention, especially in the tedious hoeing and thinning phases of their cultivation, they were ideal candidates for gang labor. Most upcountry South Carolina planters adopted this arrangement from the first, and sea island planters were encouraged to do the same: one lowcountry planter from Georgia advised his South Carolina colleagues that "there is no possibility of tasking Negroes" in cotton culture. However, his peers proved him wrong. By the early nineteenth century the tasking requirements of all sea island cotton operations were well established. They remained substantially unchanged throughout the nineteenth century (see table 1).[47]

Perhaps the profits being generated under the existing task system discouraged lowcountry planters from adopting gang labor, for they were not likely to restructure an arrangement that was so patently successful. In 1751 James Glen reported that South Carolina planters expected a slave to pay for himself within four to five years. Dr. Alexander Garden calculated that in 1756 planters made between £15 to £30 sterling for every slave they employed in the field, which he noted was "indeed a great deal." At that rate, a slave would pay for himself in two to three years. In 1772 a visitor to South Carolina noted that indigo planters made from £35 to £45 sterling for every able slave; in this case, a newly purchased slave paid for himself in less than two years.[48] The rate of return of a two-hundred-acre rice plantation, employing forty slaves in the late colonial period, was estimated to be 25 percent, more than double the opportunity cost of capital.[49] And although the Revo-

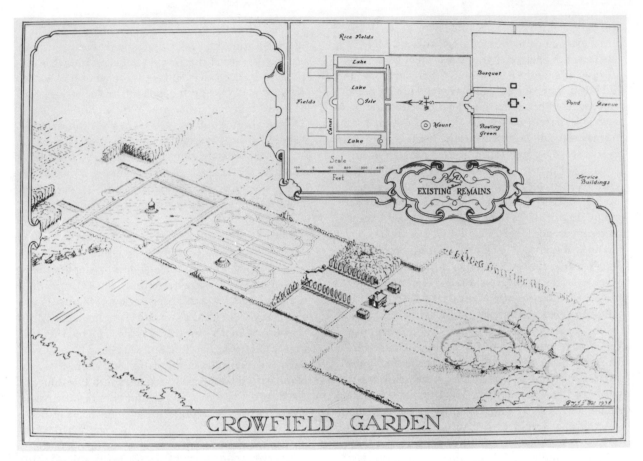

Fig. 2. Reconstructed plan of Crowfield Plantation, ca. 1730. Crowfield Plantation was the seat of William Middleton, given to him by his father, Edward, in 1729. Named after a family property in England, its layout—using canals, a lake, a mount, a bosque, and bowling green to separate the rice fields from the main house—was fully in keeping with English landscape ideals of the time. (Reprinted from Samuel Gaillard Stoney, *Plantations of the Carolina Low Country*, ed. Albert Simons and Samuel Lapham, Jr. [Charleston, S.C., 1938], 123).

lutionary war was enormously disruptive of the low-country economy, the 1790s were boom years for planters, since they replaced one highly profitable secondary staple (indigo) with another (sea island cotton). So profitable was this second staple that planters on Edisto Island in 1808 averaged a return of between $170 and $260 for every field hand.[50]

Crucial to the continuing profitability of rice plantations was the wholesale transfer of production from inland to tidal swamps, a process that was well underway by the late eighteenth century. John Drayton, writing at the turn of the century, identified some of the advantages of this shift in location: "River swamp plantations, from the command of water, which at high tides can be introduced over the fields, have an undoubted preference to inland plantations; as the crop is more certain, and the work of the negroes less toilsome." Surely it was a tidewater rice plantation that a Virginian witnessed in 1780 when he observed that "after the ground is once well cleared little cultivation does the ground [need] being soft by continual moisture."[51] In short, the development of tidewater rice culture reduced the heavy hoeing formerly required of slaves in the summer months. As might be expected, the daily task unit expanded, and squares of 150 feet (approximately a half-acre) appeared in tidewater rice fields.[52] The other side of this coin was the increase in heavy labor required of slaves in the winter months, for tidewater cultivation demanded an elaborate system of banks, dams, canals, and ditches. By the turn of the century, no doubt, lowcountry laborers were as familiar with the daily ditching requirement (about 600 to 700 square feet, or ten compasses) as they had ever been with the quarter-acre task.[53]

Although the precise definition of daily tasks had advantages from the slaves' point of view, the potential conflict that stereotyped tasks and their careless assignment could engender should not be underestimated. Indeed, the evidence of conflict should alert us to a battle that undoubtedly was being waged but that rarely surfaces in the historical record; namely, the constant warring between taskmaster (fig. 4) and laborers (figs. 5, 6) over what constituted a fair day's work. After one such altercation between a black driver and a group of slaves, the latter took their case to their master in Charleston. When he asked them "why they could not do their Tasks as well as the rest," they answered that "their Tasks were harder." The master was sympathetic, knowing that "there is sometimes a great difference in Tasks, and Paul told me he remembered that Jimmy had a bad Task that Day. I was sorry to see poor Caesar amongst them for I knew him to be an honest, inoffensive fellow and tho't if any will do without severity, he will. I inquired his fault, & Paul told me . . . he had been 2 days in a Task."[54] Hoeing was at issue in this dispute; on another plantation, threshing became a source of conflict. Three slaves belonging to George Austin—Liverpool, Moosa, and Dutay—"ran off early in December, for being a little chastis'd on Account of not finishing the task of Thrashing in due time."[55] By the early nineteenth century, a modus vivendi had apparently been reached on most lowcountry plantations. One South Carolina planter reckoned that the "daily task does not vary according to the arbitrary will and caprice of their owners, and although [it] is not fixed by law, it is so well settled by long usage, that upon every plantation it is the *same*. Should any owner increase the work beyond what is customary, he subjects himself to the reproach of his neighbors, and to such discontent amongst his slaves as to make them of but little use to him."[56] The task system's requirements were hammered out just as much in conflicts with the work force as in the supposedly inevitable march of technological progress.

However onerous tasking could become for some slaves, the system at least had the virtue of allowing the slave a certain latitude to apportion his own day, to work intensively in his task and then have the balance of his time. With the institutionalization of the task system, the slave's "time" became sacrosanct. The right not to be called on once the task had been completed was duly acknowledged by lowcountry masters.[57] One of the advantages of such a right is neatly illustrated in an incident that befell a Methodist circuit rider, Joseph Pilmore. On March 18, 1773—a Thursday—he arrived at the banks of the Santee River in the Georgetown district of South Carolina. After waiting in vain for the appearance of the regular ferry, he was met by a few blacks. Presumably they told him that they "had finished their task," for that is how he explained their availability in his journal. He then hired their "time" so that he could be ferried across the river. The actual time was about three o'clock in the afternoon.[58] Slaves could not only complete their work by midafternoon; they might then earn money on their own account.

In the same year that Pilmore visited the Georgetown district, another observer of lowcountry society, "Scotus Americanus," testified more fully to the advantages that a fully institutionalized task system presented to slaves:

Their work is performed by a daily task, allotted by their master or overseer, which they have generally done by one or two o'clock in the afternoon, and have the rest of the day for themselves, which they spend in working in their own private fields,

Fig. 3. A. R. Waud, *Rice Culture on the Ogeechee, Near Savannah, Georgia*, 1867; detail of slaves working a lowland Georgia rice field. (Reprinted from A. R. Waud, "Sketches on a Rice Plantation," *Harper's Weekly*, Jan. 5, 1867, 8.)

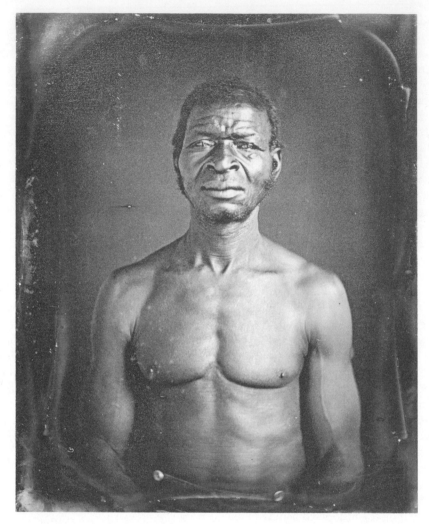

Fig. 4a. A black African slave driver in South Carolina. The caption on the rear of this daguerrotype, taken at the request of Professor Louis Agassiz, reads: "Jack (driver) Guinea. [Edgehill] Plantation of B. F. Taylor, Esq., Columbia, S.C., daquerrotype by J. T. Zealy, March 1850." (Photograph courtesy of the Peabody Museum, Harvard University; print made by Hillel Burger, no. 35-5-10/53043 [neg. N27430].)

consisting of 5 or 6 acres of ground, allowed them by their masters, for planting of rice, corn, potatoes, tobacco, &c. for their own use and profit, of which the industrious among them make a great deal. In some plantations, they have also the liberty to raise hogs and poultry, which, with the former articles, they are to dispose of to none but their masters (this is done to prevent bad consequences) for which, in exchange, when they do not chuse money, their masters give Osnaburgs, negro cloths, caps, hats, handkerchiefs, pipes, and knives. They do not plant in their fields for subsistence, but for amusement, pleasure, and profit, their masters giving them clothes, and sufficient provisions from their granaries.[59]

As we shall see, planting for "amusement, pleasure, and profit" continued to be a prerogative of lowcountry slaves.

Pilmore and Scotus Americanus alert us to the ways in which lowcountry slaves continued to acquire money. It should hardly surprise us, then, that lowcountry bondmen still aspired to the ownership of more substantial items of property. In spite of the acts of 1714, 1722, and 1740, slaves remained singu-

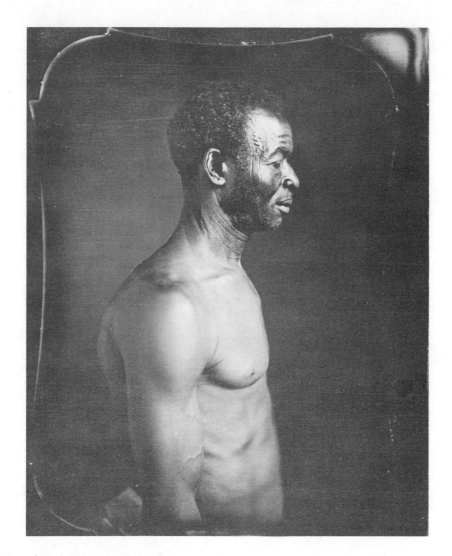

Fig. 4*b*. A side view of "Jack"; note ritual scarification on his cheek. (Photograph courtesy of the Peabody Museum, Harvard University; print made by Hillel Burger, no. 35-5-10/53044 [neg. N27433].)

larly reluctant to relinquish their claims to horses. In 1772 the Charleston District Grand Jury was still objecting to "Negroes being allowed to keep horses . . . contrary to Law."[60] In a transaction that bore a remarkable similarity to the one effected by Sampson a half-century earlier, a slave named Will showed even less regard for the law by exchanging his horses for his freedom. A witness to the exchange heard Will's master, Lewis Dutarque, say to

old fellow Will that he had been a faithful servant to him and if he had a mind to purchase his freedom he should obtain the same by paying him three hundred pounds old currency and says he Will you have two horses which will nearly pay me. I will allow you hundred pounds old currency for a Roan Gelding and forty five currency for your Gray for which the fellow Will readily consented to the proposals and Mr. Dutarque took possession of the Horses and the fellow Will was to pay the Balance as soon as he could make it up. Mr. Dutarque also borrowed of the fellow Will a small Black mare which he lost and he said she was worth six Guineas and would allow him that price for her.[61]

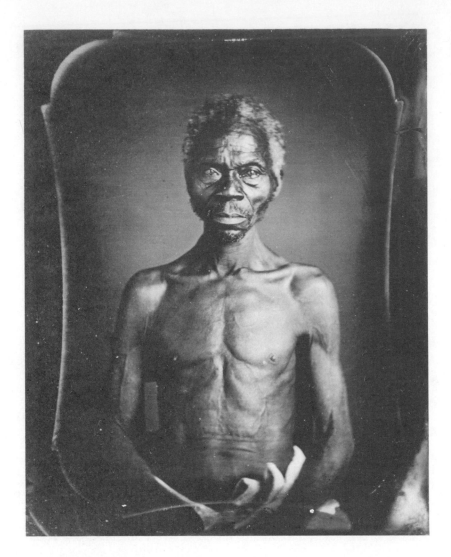

Fig. 5. J. T. Zealy, "Renty," an elderly field hand who worked on the Edgehill Plantation of B. F. Taylor in Columbia, S.C. Daguerrotype taken in March 1850. He is identified as a Congo slave. (Photograph courtesy of the Peabody Museum, Harvard University; print made by Hillel Burger, no. 35-5-10/53037 [neg. N27432].)

One begins to wonder how many horses Will possessed. Horse trading may even have been possible within the slave community, if a notice placed in a South Carolina newspaper in 1793 is any indication: "On Sunday last was apprehended by the patrol in St. George's parish, a certain negro man who calls himself *Titus* and his son about 10 year who is called *Tom*; he was trading with the negroes in that neighbourhood, and he had in his possession 2 horses . . .

one poultry cart, and several articles of merchandise, consisting of stripes, linens, and handkerchiefs."[62] Given these examples, one lowcountry master was perhaps right to be sanguine about an unsuccessful hunt that he had launched for a group of seven absentees. He was "convinced these runaways would not go far, being connected at home, and having too much property to leave."[63]

*   *   *

Q. You think that they have a love for property?
A. Yes, Sir; Very strong; they delight in accumulating.
—Testimony of Rufus Saxton (1863)

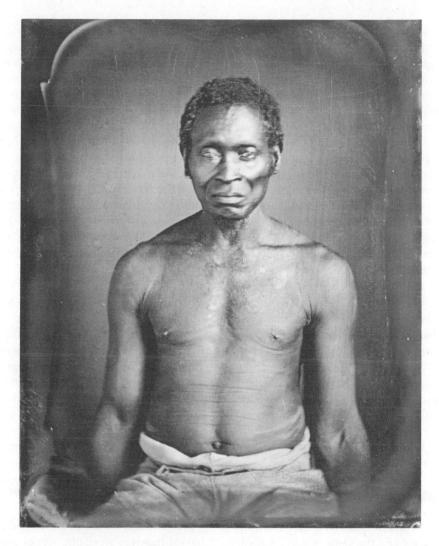

Fig. 6. J. T. Zealy, "Fassena," a Mandingo slave who worked as a carpenter on the plantation of Col. Wade Hampton near Columbia, S.C.; note probable evidence of ritual scarification on his stomach. Daguerrotype taken in March 1850. (Photograph courtesy of the Peabody Museum, Harvard University; print made by Hillel Burger, no. 35-5-10/53048 [neg. N27533].)

By the middle of the nineteenth century the task system dominated agricultural life in the lowcountry. Indeed, the term so pervaded the region's agricultural terminology that its varied meanings have to be disentangled. For example, a lowcountry planter might say that he had planted "seven tasks (within one task of two acres, as a planter well knows)." At this time, a slave was expected to be able to sow two acres of rice a day; this is presumably what this planter had in mind when referring to the single task of two acres. And yet, the early eighteenth-century definition of a task as measuring one-quarter of an acre was still very much current. It was possible, therefore, to speak of seven units, measuring one-quarter of an acre each, within a larger unit measuring two acres.[64] Similarly, a planter might say that he had penned "thirty head of cattle on a task for one week" (the "task" here refers to one-quarter of an acre); or he might mention setting a "task" of three rice barrels a day for his cooper.[65] In other words, in common usage the term *task* not only referred to a unit of labor (a fixed or specified quantity of labor exacted from a person is the dictionary definition) but also to a unit of land measurement (almost invariably one-quarter of an acre, or an area 105 feet square).

Slaves were completely conversant with this terminology, as the recollections of ex-slaves attest. Testifying before Southern Claims Commissioners in 1873, Peter Way knew precisely what constituted a "task" as a unit of land measurement. "Five poles make a task," he noted authoritatively, "and there is twenty-one feet in a pole."[66] Using the term in this sense, former slaves might say that "Mr. Mallard's house was about four or five tasks from Mr. Busby's house" (about 420 or 525 feet distant), or that Sherman's troops were "about three tasks off in the woods. I could see [them] from [my] house" (about 315 feet away).[67] When Mason Crum interviewed an old black woman (a former slave) in the 1930s, she told him that she owned her land "and that she had in the tract t'ree acres and a tass'," by which she meant three-and-a-quarter acres.[68] When freedmen referred to the crops that they had produced for themselves in "slavery times," they used the units acres and "tasks" interchangeably (tasks here again refer to quarter-acre plots).[69] At the same time, ex-slaves used the term "task" to connote a unit of labor. A freedman, referring to the terms of the contract that he had signed with his employer, spoke of giving "five tasks, that is, I work five tasks for him and plant everything he has a mind to have it planted in for all the land myself and wife can cultivate."[70] The dual meaning of the term is nowhere better illustrated than in the words of one former slave, interviewed in the 1930s, who in one and the same breath recalled "de slave [having] but two tasks ob land to cultivate for se'f" (by which he meant half an acre) and "in daytime [having] to do his task" (by which he meant a quantity of labor depending on the operation at hand).[71]

Tasking was so much a way of life in the antebellum lowcountry that virtually all crops and a whole host of plantation operations were subject to its dictates. The cultivation of corn was discussed in terms of the number of hills in a "task-row" and the number of "beds" in a task.[72] Sea island cotton had its own task-acre as distinct from the task-acre used in tidewater rice culture.[73] Even when lowcountry planters experimented with sugar cultivation in the 1820s and 1830s, they attempted to retain the notion of a task: a hundred plants, according to one author-

ity, were to be put in a task-row, and two hands could then both plant and cut a task a day.[74] On Hopeton plantation, where sugar was grown on a large scale, task work was "resorted to whenever the nature of the work admits of it; and working in gangs as is practiced in the West Indies and the upper country, is avoided. The advantages of this system are encouragement to the labourers, by equalizing the work of each agreeably to strength, and the avoidance of watchful superintendance and incessant driving."[75] Whether this attempt to adapt sugar cultivation to the task system contributed to the failure of lowcountry sugar production is difficult to say; but it is possible that sugar, unlike cotton, just could not be successfully grown without gang labor.

Tasking was ubiquitous in another sense: those slaves not able to benefit from the system's opportunities had to be compensated in other ways. The proposition that drivers, as a group, suffered discrimination is barely credible, but in the lowcountry, at least, such was the case. As one ex-slave recalled, "I suppose the Foreman had advantages in some respects and in others not, for he had no task-work and had no time of his own, while the other slaves had the Evenings to themselves." The son of a Georgia planter remembered that his father's driver was "obliged to oversee all day," whereas the field hands "were allowed to work in any way they chose for themselves after the tasks were done."[76] By way of compensation, lowcountry drivers were entitled to receive a certain amount of help in tending their own crops. Thomas Mallard's driver "had the privilege of having hands to work one acre of corn and one acre of rice" on his behalf; the driver on Raymond Cay's plantation had Cay's field hands plant one acre of corn and three to five "tasks" in rice on his account.[77] One ex-slave recalled that "drivers had the privilege of planting two or three acres of rice and some corn and having it worked by the slaves"; and, in order to dispel any misimpressions, he emphasized that "these hands worked for [the drivers] in the White people's time."[78] Other occupational groups received different forms of compensation. A former slave plowman recalled that he "didn't work by the task but at the end of the year [his master] gave [him] 6 bushels of corn" by way of redress. A former slave carpenter recollected that "when [he] worked carpentering [his] master allowed [him] every other saturday and when [he] worked farming [his master] gave him tasks."[79] In this man's mind, apparently, these "privileges" were about equal.

The central role of the task system in lowcountry life can best be gauged by investigating its fate immediately after emancipation. Throughout the postwar cotton South freedmen firmly rejected most of the elements of their old system of labor; from the first, gang labor was anathema.[80] At the same time, however, freedmen in the lowcountry were tenaciously striving to retain—and even extend—the fundamentals of their former system. A Freedman's Bureau official, resident in lowcountry Georgia in 1867, identified a basic response of the former slaves to their new work environment when he observed that they "usually stipulate to work by the task."[81] Lowcountry freedmen even demonstrated their attachment to the task system when they rejected one element of their former slave past by refusing to do the ditching and draining so necessary in rice and sea island cotton cultivation.[82] This work was arduous and disagreeable, of course, and since ditching was more amenable to gang labor than any other operation in lowcountry agriculture, blacks appropriately sought to avoid it at all costs. But in an 1865 petition a group of planters from Georgetown district touched on an even more compelling reason for the freedmen's refusal to perform this familiar task. They pointed out that "it is a work which, as it does not pertain to the present crop, the negroes are unwilling to perform." The recipient of this petition, Colonel Willard, was a sympathetic and sensitive observer, and his elaboration of this rationale penetrates to the heart of the issue. The freedmen's real fear, he explained, was that having prepared the ditches for the forthcoming crop, the planters would "insist on having them by the month." This arrangement would be absolutely unacceptable, because the freedmen had "been accustomed to working by the task, which has always given them leisure to cultivate land for themselves, tend their stock, and amuse themselves." If they gave way on this issue, he continued, "their privileges will go and their condition will be less to their taste than it was when they were slaves."[83]

Precisely to avoid such a condition was the overriding imperative governing the actions of lowcountry freedmen. Once this is understood, the multifarious and fluid labor arrangements that characterized the postwar lowcountry become comprehensible. In 1865 and 1866 two basic forms of labor contract (with many individual variations) were employed in the lowlands of South Carolina and Georgia. Either the freedmen worked for a share of the crop (anywhere from one-half to three-quarters, a higher share than found elsewhere in the South), with the freedmen's share being divided among them on the basis of tasks performed, or they hired themselves for the year, with payment being made on the basis of the numbers of tasks completed (usually fifty cents a task, although payment was by no means always made in cash).[84] Whatever the mode of reimbursement, the task was central to most early contracts.

In 1866 a third labor arrangement arose that soon became general throughout the lowcountry. Known as the "two-day" or, less frequently, "three-day" system, it simply extended the concept of task labor, for it drew an even more rigid demarcation between the planters' "time" and the laborers' "time." The Freedmen's Bureau agent for eastern Liberty County, Georgia, observed as early as February 1867 that there were in his district no freedmen working by the month and only a few for wages. Some were working for a share of the crop, but most were employed by the "two-day" system, working a third of the time on the employers' crop and receiving land to work on their own account for the remainder of the time.[85] The agricultural census of 1880 reported that the "two-day" system was ubiquitous on the South Carolina sea islands. For ten months of the year, slaves worked two days in each week for their employers and received in return a house, fuel, and six acres of land for their own use, free of rent. Proprietors were said to dislike the system because their employees only cultivated about two acres in the owners' "time." However, the report continued, "the laborers themselves prefer this system, having four days out of the week for themselves." As a result, "they are more independent and can make any day they choose a holiday."[86]

The reasons for the slaves' (and the freedmen's) attachment to the task system should be readily apparent, but the subject is worth a moment's extra consideration because we are in the privileged and rare position of being able to listen to the participants themselves. The most obvious advantage of the task system was the flexibility it permitted slaves in determining the length of the working day. Working from sunup to sundown was the pervasive reality for most antebellum slaves; but ex-slaves from the low-

Fig. 7. Early nineteenth-century slave quarters on Hermitage Plantation near Savannah, Chatham County, Georgia, as they appeared ca. 1880–1910. (Photograph courtesy of the Georgia Department of Archives and History.)

country recall a different reality. Richard Cummings, a former field hand, recalled that "a good active industrious man would finish his task sometimes at 12, sometimes at 1 and 2 oclock and the rest of the time was his own to use as he pleased." Scipio King, another former field hand, reckoned, as he put it, that "I could save for myself sometimes a whole day if I could do 2 tasks in a day then I had the next day to myself. Some kind of work I could do 3 tasks in a day."[87] Exhausting as task labor undoubtedly was, its prime virtue was that it was not unremitting.

A second advantage concerned the relationship between the slaves' provisions and the planters' rations.

Whatever slaves produced beyond the task was regarded as surplus to, not a substitute for, basic planter allocations of shelter (fig. 7), food, and clothing. One former slave recalled that his master continued to dispense rations "no matter how much they [the slaves] made of their own . . .[which] they could sell . . . if they chose." July Roberts, another ex-slave, emphasized that "every week we drew our rations no matter what we raised." When one former slave claimed the loss of corn, rice, and clothing taken by Federal troops, an attempt was made to deny him his title because these represented rations and "so belonged to the master." The response of this freedman's attorneys no doubt reflected the prevailing attitude of former slaves: "It is obvious to remark that if these things had not been taken from the claimant by the army, he would have had them after 'freedom came' and were to all intents his property."[88] Not only did slaves plant in their own time for "amusement, pleasure, and profit," they claimed the master's rations as their own to do with as they wished.

In view of these advantages, we might expect the scale and range of property owning by slaves to have assumed significant dimensions by the middle of the nineteenth century. An analysis of the settled claims submitted by former slaves to the Southern Claims Commission for loss of property to federal troops provides the best test of this hypothesis.[89] Taking the Liberty County, Georgia, claimants as a sample, former field hands outnumber all other occupational groups. While most were mature adults when their property was taken, 30 percent were under the age of thirty-five. In terms of occupation and age these claimants constitute a relatively broad cross-section of the slave population. Moreover, whether field hands or artisans, young or old, virtually all had apparently been deprived of a number of hogs, and a substantial majority listed corn, rice, and fowls among their losses. In addition, a surprising number apparently possessed horses and cows, while buggies or wagons, beehives, peanuts, fodder, syrup, butter, sugar, and tea were, if these claims are to be believed, in the hands of at least some slaves. The average cash value (in 1864 dollars) claimed by Liberty County former slaves was $357.43, with the highest claim totaling $2,290 and the lowest $49.[90]

Some claims were spectacular. Paris James, a former slave driver, was described by a neighboring white planter as a "substantial man before the war [and] was more like a free man than any slave."[91] James claimed, among other things, a horse, eight cows, sixteen sheep, twenty-six hogs, and a wagon. Another slave driver, according to one of his black witnesses, lived "just like a white man except his color. His credit was just as good as a white man's because he had the property to back it." Although the claims commissioners were skeptical about his alleged loss of twenty cows—as they explained, "twenty cows would make a good large dairy for a Northern farmer"—his two white and three black witnesses supported him in his claim.[92] Other blacks were considered to be "more than usually prosperous," "pretty well off," and "hardworking and money-saving"—unremarkable characterizations, perhaps, but surprising when the individuals were also slaves.[93] Alexander Steele, a carpenter by trade and a

former house servant of Chatham County, Georgia, submitted a claim for $2,205 based on the loss of his four horses, mule, silver watch, two cows, wagon, and large quantities of fodder, hay, and corn. He had been able to acquire these possessions by "trading" for himself for some thirty years; he had had "much time of [his] own" because his master "always went north" in the summer months. He took "a fancy [to] fine horses," a whim he was able to indulge when he purchased "a blooded mare," from which he raised three colts. He was resourceful enough to hide his livestock on Onslow Island when Sherman's army drew near, but some of the federal troops secured boats and took off his prize possessions. Three white planters supported Steele in his claim; indeed, one of them recollected making an unsuccessful offer of $300 for one of Steele's colts before the war. Lewis Dutarque's Will, a horse owner of note in the late eighteenth century, had found a worthy successor in Alexander Steele.[94]

The ownership of horses was not, however, confined to a privileged minority of slaves. Among the Liberty County claimants, almost as many ex-field hands as former drivers and skilled slaves claimed horses. This evidence supplies a context for the exchange recorded by Frederick Law Olmsted when he was being shown around the plantation of Richard J. Arnold in Bryan County, Georgia. Olmsted noticed a horse drawing a wagon of "common fieldhand negroes" and asked his host

"[do you] usually let them have horses to go to Church?"
"Oh no; that horse belongs to the old man."
"Belongs to him! Why, do they own horses?"
"Oh yes; William (the House Servant) owns two, and Robert, I believe, has three now; that was one of them he was riding."
"How do they get them?"
"Oh they buy them."[95]

Although a few freedmen recalled that former masters had either prohibited horse ownership or confined the practice to drivers, most placed the proportion of horse owners on any single plantation at between 15 and 20 percent.[96] A former slave of George Washington Walthour estimated that "in all my master's plantations there were over 30 horses owned by slaves. . . . I think come to count up there were as many as 45 that owned horses—he would let them own any thing they could if they only did his work."[97] Nedger Frazer, a former slave of the Reverend C. C. Jones, recalled that on one of his master's plantations (obviously Arcadia, from Frazer's description) there were forty working hands, of whom five owned horses; and on another (obviously Montevideo) another ten hands out of fifty owned horses.[98] This, in turn, supplies a context for an interesting incident that occurred within the Jones's "family" in 1857. After much soul-searching, Jones sold one of his slave families, headed by Cassius, a field hand. A man of integrity, Jones then forwarded Cassius the balance of his account, which amounted to $85, a sum that included the proceeds from the sale of Cassius's horse.[99] Perhaps one freedman was not exaggerating when he observed in 1873 that "there was more stock property owned by slaves before the war than are owned now by both white and black people together in this county."[100]

The spectacular claims and the widespread ownership of horses naturally catch the eye, but even the most humdrum claim has a story to tell. Each claim contains, for instance, a description of how property was accumulated. The narrative of John Bacon can stand as proxy for many such accounts: "I had a little crop to sell and bought some chickens and then I bought a fine large sow and gave $10.00 for her. This was about ten years before the war and then I raised hogs and sold them till I bought a horse. This was about eight years before freedom. This was a breeding mare and from this mare I raised this horse which the Yankees took from me."[101] This was not so much primitive as painstaking accumulation; no wonder one freedman referred to his former property as his "laborment."[102] And yet, occasionally, the mode of procurement assumed a slightly more sophisticated cast: some slaves recall purchasing horses by installment;[103] some hired additional labor to cultivate their crops;[104] two slaves (a mill engineer and a stockminder) went into partnership to raise livestock;[105] and a driver lent out money at interest.[106] Whatever the mode of accumulation, the ultimate source, as identified by virtually all the ex-slaves, was the task system. As Joseph James, a freedman, explained, "They all worked by tasks, and had a plenty of time to work for themselves and in that way all slaves who were industrious could get around them considerable property in a short time."[107]

By the middle of the nineteenth century, in sum, it is possible to speak of a significant internal economy operating within a more conventional lowcountry economy. According to the depositions of the freedmen, this internal economy rested on two major planks. The first concerns the degree to which some slaves engaged in stock raising. One white planter, testifying on behalf of a freedman, recalled that "a good many" slaves owned a number of animals; he then checked himself, perhaps realizing the impression that he was creating, and guardedly stated that "what I mean was they were not allowed to go generally into stock raising."[108] And yet some slaves seem to have been doing just that. One ex-slave spoke of raising "horses to sell"; another claimed to have raised fourteen horses over a twenty-five-to-thirty-year period, most of which he had sold; and one freedwoman named some of the purchasers, all of whom were slaves, of the nine horses that she had raised.[109] The other major foundation of this internal economy was the amount of crop production by slaves. Jeremiah Everts observed that the slaves in Chatham County, Georgia, had "as much land as they can till for their own use."[110] The freedmen's recollections from all over the lowcountry support this statement: a number of ex-slaves reckoned that they had more than ten acres under cultivation, while four or five acres was the norm.[111] The proprietorial attitude encouraged by this independent production is suggested in one freedman's passing comment that he worked in his "own field."[112] Through the raising of stock and the production of provisions (together with the sale of produce from woodworking, basketmaking, hunting, and fishing), slaves were able to attract money into their internal economy. Robert W. Gibbes knew of an individual slave who received $120 for his year's crop of corn and fodder; Richard Arnold owed his slaves $500 in 1853 when Olmsted visited him.[113] Thus, while produce and livestock were constantly being bartered by slaves— "swapping" was rife, according to the freedmen—one observer of the mid-nineteenth-century lowcountry was undoubtedly correct when he noted that "in a small way a good deal of money circulated among the negroes, both in the country and in the towns."[114]

The autonomy of this internal economy is further indicated by the development of a highly significant practice. By the middle of the nineteenth century, if not before, slave property was not only being produced and exchanged but also inherited. The father of Joseph Bacon bequeathed him a mare and all his other children fifty dollars each.[115] Samuel Elliot claimed a more substantial legacy, for his father "had 20 head of cattle, about 70 head of hogs—Turkeys Geese Ducks and Chickens a Plenty—he was foreman for his master and had been raising such things for years. When he died the property was divided among his children and we continued to raise things just as he had been raising."[116] The role of less immediate kin was also not negligible. Two freedmen recalled receiving property from their grandfathers; another inherited a sow from his cousin; and William Drayton of Beaufort County, South Carolina, noted that when his father died he "left with his oldest brother, my uncle, the means or property he left for his children," and Drayton bought a mule "by the advice of my uncle who had the means belonging to me."[117] There were rules governing lines of descent. One female claimant emphasized that she had not inherited any of her first husband's property because she had borne him no children; rather, his son by a former marriage received the property.[118] The ability to bequeath wealth and to link patrimony to genealogy serves to indicate the extent to which slaves created a measure of autonomy.

The property rights of slaves were recognized across proprietorial boundaries as well as across generations. Slaves even employed guardians to facilitate the transfer of property from one plantation to another. Thus when Nancy Bacon, belonging to John Baker, inherited cattle from her deceased husband who belonged to Mr. Walthour, she employed her second cousin, Andrew Stacy, a slave on the Walthour plantation, to take charge of the cattle and drive them over to her plantation. According to Stacy, Mr. Walthour "didn't object to my taking them [and] never claimed them."[119] The way in which slave couples took advantage of their divided ownership is suggested by Diana Cummings of Chatham County, Georgia. Her husband's master, she explained, "allowed him to sell but mine didn't," so Diana marketed her crops and stock through her husband and received a part of the proceeds. On her husband's death, she received all his property for, as she put it, her "entitle" (surname) was then the same as her husband's. She had since changed it, through remarriage to Sydney Cummings, but she noted that Cummings had "no interest in [the] property [being claimed]."[120]

By the middle of the nineteenth century the ownership of property by lowcountry slaves had become extensive and had assumed relatively sophisticated dimensions. This, in turn, gives rise to an obvious question. What significance was attached to the practice by the slaves? What was the *mentalité*, the moral economy, of this property-owning group? Certainly some freedmen spoke of "getting ahead" and of "accumulating" under slavery.[121] Jacob Monroe, a freedman, admitted that as a slave under the task system he "could go and come when [he] pleased, work and play after [his] task was done," but he pointedly emphasized that "he chose to work."[122] Competitiveness was also not alien to the slave quarters. One freedman recalled how the young adults on one plantation "were jealous of one another and tried to see which would get their days work done first."[123] William Gilmore referred to the disparities in property ownership that characterized Raymond Cay's slaves; he likened them to the "five wise and five foolish" and disparaged those who "slept and slumbered the time away."[124] Similar impressions are derived from those Northerners who came into contact with sea island blacks in the early 1860s. B. K. Lee observed that "they are very acquisitive indeed"; Henry Judd described their "passion for ownership of horses or some animal"; and Rufus Saxton was impressed to find that "they regard the rights of property among themselves. If a man has a claim upon a horse or sow he maintains his right and his neighbours recognize it."[125]

Acquisitiveness and respect for property had other overtones, as Rufus Saxton's resonant phrase—"they delight in accumulating"—suggests.[126] Display and ostentation, while not on any grand scale, of course, seem an accurate characterization of some slaves' behavior. The ownership of horses undoubtedly had practical purposes—one freedman explained that "some of the slaves had families a good ways off and they used their horses to visit them. The masters said it was for their interest to have us own horses so that we could get back home to work."[127] But the exhibition of status appears also to have been involved. William Golding's ownership of a horse and saddle was proved because "he was given to riding about on Sundays." Frederick Law Olmsted not only witnessed a head house-servant mount his horse after church service but, in true paternalistic fashion, slip a coin to the boy who had been holding its reins.[128] Ex-slaves commonly justified their ownership of a horse and wagon by their need to go to church on Sunday. This was not just a practical matter: Leah Wilson could not disguise the sense of status she derived from being able to drive "right along together with our master going to church."[129] A horse, as Edward Philbrick observed in 1862, was more than a means of transport; it was "a badge of power and caste." Sea island blacks had no respect for people who could not present themselves on a horse. "They will hardly lift their hats to a white man on foot," he noted, and viewed a "walking nigger" with contempt.[130]

Although we find elements of display, of accumulation for its own sake, and of "getting ahead," the *mentalité* of the slaves cannot be reduced to any one of these traits and was indeed much more. We can uncover better the meaning and limits of such behavior by exploring, once again, the slaves' immediate response to freedom. In terms of their attitude toward labor, the freedmen firmly resisted the overtures of Northern reformers and proclaimed a resounding attachment to what may be resonantly characterized as a task-orientation. Employers and Freedmen's Bureau officials alike constantly bemoaned the impossibility of persuading the freedmen to "perform more than their allotted tasks."[131] In 1867 Frances Butler Leigh observed freedmen who begged "to be allowed to go back to the old task system" when the agent of the Freedmen's Bureau attempted to have them work by the day. "One man," she reported, "indignantly asked Major D——what the use of being free was, if he had to work harder than when he was a slave."[132] Few freedmen would work a full day, a full week, "and very seldom a full month steady," complained one employer.[133] One Northerner advocated the confiscation of the freedmen's boats so that instead of continuing in their ways of "precarious living," they might develop "habits of steady industry."[134] The freedmen were said to work "when they please and do just as much as they please"; they then relied on hunting and fishing "to make up for what they lose in the field."[135]

This clash between the proponents of Northeastern business methods and a laboring population wedded to an alternative work ethic reverberated throughout the postwar lowcountry. The conflict is neatly illustrated in an exchange that occurred in 1865 between Colonel Willard, a man generally sympathetic to the freedmen's plight, and two ex-slaves who were saw-

mill workers. Willard was approached by the harassed owner of the mill, who was unable to impress upon his workers the virtues of "steady" work: they claimed, for example, at least two hours of rest during their work day. From the standpoint of a Northern businessman, Willard's argument to the two representatives of the work force was impeccable: "Laborers at the North," he pointed out, "got less wages, and worked from sunrise to sunset, this season of the year, only having an hour at noon." The freedmen's reply was equally forceful: "We want," they emphasized, "to work just as we have always worked." Willard was left to expostulate that these former slaves "have no just sense of the importance of persistent labor."[136]

The freedmen's attitude toward the accumulation of property, much like their attitude toward work, was decisively shaped by their former experience under the task system. The argument that "the more they cultivate, the more they gain" had, as one Northern army officer discovered, no appeal. In 1868 Frances Butler Leigh made a similar discovery when she found that some freedmen refused wages and rations, preferring to "raise a little corn and sweet potatoes, and with their facilities for catching fish and oysters, and shooting wild game, they have as much to eat as they want, and now are quite satisfied with that."[137] In short, lowcountry freedmen apparently wished to avoid an unlimited involvement in the market, favoring production for sale only within the familiar context of an assured production for subsistence. This explains, in large measure, why the freedmen would not forego their hunting and fishing activities for a greater concentration on cash crops, why they aspired to the ownership or rental of land, and why they refused to work for wages.[138] The degree to which subsistence (in this case, hunting) formed the priorities of one freedman is captured in a brief anecdote. A special agent, who toured the lowcountry in 1878 investigating disputed claims, visited the home of Samuel Maxwell, a former slave. He was not impressed with this particular claimant's adaptation to freedom and advised him to participate more fully in the wider society. For a start, he suggested, why not raise hogs rather than dogs? To which Maxwell replied: "A pig won't help us catch coons and rabbits."[139]

The preferences and ambitions of the freedmen reflected, above all, a desire for autonomy not only

PART THREE   Production and Control of Property

from the impersonal marketplace but also from individual whites. As one would-be employer found out in 1866, the freedmen who rejected wages and wanted to supply their own seed were expressing a fundamental desire to "be free from personal constraint."[140] They sought, in other words, to build upon a foundation that the task system had laid, consisting of that part of a day, that plot of land, or those few animals that they, as slaves, had been able to call their own. Thus for many, if not most, lowcountry freedmen, the central priorities of subsistence and autonomy shaped whatever propensity for material accumulation and for "getting ahead" they may have had. And what these goals of subsistence and autonomy signally call to mind, of course, are nothing more than the central priorities of peasants throughout the world.[141]

The freedman's quest for a measure of autonomy from individual whites should not be construed, however, as a desire for total disengagement from whites, particularly in the immediate postemancipation years. The moral universe of lowcountry slaves apparently contained notions of social equity and of reciprocal obligations between blacks and whites that were not jettisoned when freedom came.[142] Henry Ravenel's slaves, for example, voluntarily presented themselves before their master in March 1865 and "said they would be willing to take a certain piece of land which they would cultivate for old Master—that they would not want a driver or overseer, but would work that faithfully for him—and that they would take another piece of land to work for their own use." Another set of plantation blacks dumbfounded their former owner in July 1865 when they told him that they now considered the land as their own; perhaps more striking, however, was their readiness to grant "Master" a portion of the crop as "a free gift from themselves."[143] When the promise of land dimmed, the freedmen could be expected to assume a more hostile posture. While evidence of such hostility exists, some sensitive observers were still aware of a basic and continuing paradox. Thus Joseph Le Conte, writing of Liberty County, Georgia, freedmen in the 1890s, noted their refusal to be tied to whites and their rejection of wage labor based, in his view, on their ability to "live almost without work on fish, crawfish, and oysters." At the same time, however, he referred to "the kindliest feelings" existing "among the blacks . . . toward their former masters." While

Le Conte may have been guilty of some self-deception, similar observations from his fellow whites suggest the reality of this paradox.[144] Once again, this aspect of the freedmen's world view is strikingly reminiscent of a central feature of peasant life that, according to one authority, is permeated by the moral principle of reciprocity.[145]

*　　*　　*

The significance of the particular conjunction that this essay set out to explore—the conjunction between a certain mode of labor organization and a particular domestic economy—can now be assessed. From the short-run perspective of masters, this conjunction had a number of benefits. They could escape their plantations in the summer months, they were supplied with additional provisions, and their slaves were *relatively* content, or so they believed. Oliver Bostick, a Beaufort County planter, explained that he "allowed [his] slaves to own and have their property and have little crops of their own for it Encouraged them to do well and be satisfied at home." Rufus King, another lowcountry master, was satisfied that "no Negro with a well-stocked poultry house, a small crop advancing, a canoe partly finished or a few tubs unsold, all of which he calculates soon to enjoy, will ever run away."[146] From the short-run perspective of the slaves, this conjunction increased their autonomy, allowed them to accumulate (and bequeath) wealth, fed individual initiative, sponsored collective discipline and esteem, and otherwise benefited them economically and socially.[147] In other words, on a much reduced scale, there were lowcountry slaves who resembled the protopeasants found among Caribbean slaves. This similarity was derived from very different origins: in the lowcountry, from a particular mode of labor organization; in the Caribbean, from the need for slaves to grow most of their own food and provision the free population. There was, in short, a much wider "peasant breach in the slave mode of production" in the Caribbean than in the lowcountry.[148]

Still, the parallel is suggestive, for in the same way that protopeasant adaptations had a comparable short-term significance for masters and slaves in both Caribbean and lowcountry, there were comparable long-term results. Wherever there were significant protopeasant activities among the slaves, there emerged after emancipation a class of people who had acquired the requisite skills that helped them escape, at least in part or temporarily, their dependence on the plantation.[149] In the lowcountry, the course of the war, the capital requirements of its major staple crop, and the development of phosphates production go some way toward explaining the particular shape of its postwar labor history.[150] But surely certain elements of this configuration had deeper roots, roots that without exaggeration can be traced all the way back to the early eighteenth century. The imperatives so dear to generations of lowcountry slaves achieved a measure of realization in the more distinctive features of the region's postwar labor arrangements. By

Fig. 8. Free black women hulling rice with traditional mortar and pestle, Sapelo Island, Georgia, ca. 1890–1915. (Photograph courtesy of the Georgia Department of Archives and History.)

1880 the percentage of farms sharecropped in the coastal districts of South Carolina and Georgia ranked among the lowest in the South; the proportion of rural black landowners was one of the highest in the South; it is possible to speak of a "black yeomanry" in the late nineteenth-century lowcountry; and by 1880 one observer in coastal Georgia could describe how most of the Negroes in his county had "bought a small tract of land, ten acres or more [on which they made] enough rice . . . to be perfectly independent of the white man" (figs. 8, 9).[151] To paraphrase Sidney Mintz, nothing else during the history of lowcountry slavery was as important as the task system and its concomitant domestic economy in making possible the freed person's adaptation to freedom without the blessings of the former masters.[152]

Fig. 9. Leigh Richmond Miner, "Woman with Hoe." Print from glass-plate negative of ca. 1900–1910 showing Adelaide Washington of St. Helena Island, South Carolina, setting off for gardening work. Note the traditional Sea Island use of two belts and the distinctive Afro-American sweetgrass basket and work hat she carries. According to Miss Rossa Cooley, a Vassar graduate who was principal of the Penn Community School in the early twentieth century, the second belt or cord tied around her hips was common among women and believed to provide extra strength. (Photograph courtesy of the Penn Center, St. Helena Island.)

Notes

The author wishes to thank members of an Institute of Early American History and Culture colloquium, panel members at a Southern Historical Association meeting, and Stanley Engerman and Edward Steiner for their comments on an earlier version of this essay. He is also grateful to Ira Berlin, Joseph Reidy, and particularly Leslie Rowland for their help in guiding him through the very valuable files of the Freedmen and Southern Society Project at the University of Maryland.

1. Comparative studies of slavery have been especially prone to the institutional or external perspective. Even one of the best studies of slave life—Eugene D. Genovese's *Roll, Jordan, Roll: The World the Slaves Made* (New York, 1974)—devotes only a few pages to the domestic economy of the slaves (535–40), although slave work routines (285–324) and aspects of consumption patterns (550–61) are explored sensitively and at length.

2. Anthropologists, for example, have been criticized for neglecting the subject. See the introduction to Sandra Wallman, ed., *Social Anthropology of Work*, Association of Social Anthropologists, Monograph 19 (London, 1979).

3. The labor history that is practiced in *History Workshop* and in the volumes published in the *History Workshop* series is the kind to which this article aspires. Also noteworthy is a recent trend in American labor history that treats the reality of work as the focus, or starting point, of investigation. See David Brody, "Labor History in the 1970s: Toward a History of the American Worker," in *The Past before Us: Contemporary Historical Writing in the United States*, ed. Michael Kammen (Ithaca, N.Y., 1980), 268.

4. Alan Everitt, "Farm Labourers," in *The Agrarian History of England and Wales, Vol. 4*, ed. Joan Thirsk (Cambridge, 1967), 396.

5. Lewis Cecil Gray, *History of Agriculture in the Southern United States to 1860*, 2 vols., (Gloucester, Mass. 1958 [orig. publ. Washington, D.C., 1933]), 1: 550–51.

6. Equally, we could investigate more fully than will be possible here the special role of the black driver, the marketing opportunities, or the occupational structure that a rice tasking system produced.

7. The word *particular* is important here because I do not intend to suggest that the independent production of goods and the accumulation of property by slaves was necessarily predicated on a task system. From situations as diverse as a sugar plantation in Jamaica to an iron foundry in the United States, slaves were often able to control the accumulation and disposal of sizable earnings and possessions. Rather, in the lowcountry, a particular conjunction arose that probably led—but this would need much greater space for comparative presentation—to a distinctive internal economy among the slaves.

8. In exploring these resemblances, I have found the work of Sidney W. Mintz to be particularly helpful. See "The Origins of Reconstituted Peasantries," in *Caribbean Transformations* (Chicago, 1974), 146–56, and "Slavery and the Rise of Peasantries," in *Roots and Branches: Current Directions in Slave Studies*, ed. Michael Craton (Toronto, 1979), 213–42.

9. "The Instructions of the Clergy of South Carolina given to Mr. Johnston, 1712," A8/429, Society of the Propagation of the Gospel, London; testimony of Thomas Akin and Ammon, Feb. 7, 1749, Council Journal, no. 17, pt. 1, 160, South Carolina Department of Archives and History, Columbia.

10. "Johann Martin Bolzius Answers a Questionnaire on Carolina and Georgia," trans. and ed. Klaus G. Loewald et al., *William and Mary Quarterly*, 3d ser., 14 (1957): 259.

11. Dr. Alexander Garden to the Royal Society, Apr. 20, 1755, Guard Book 1, 36, Royal Society of Arts, London; "Bolzius Answers a Questionnaire," trans. and ed. Loewald et al., 258.

12. "Bolzius Answers a Questionnaire," trans. and ed. Loewald et al., 256.

13. Richard S. Dunn, "The English Sugar Islands and the Founding of South Carolina," *South Carolina Historical Magazine* 72 (1971): 81–93; Richard Waterhouse, "England, the Caribbean, and the Settlement of Carolina," *Journal of American Studies* 9 (1975): 259–81.

14. Ulrich Bonnell Phillips, "The Slave Labor Problem in the Charleston District," in *Plantation, Town, and County: Essays on the Local History of American Slave Society*, eds. Elinor Miller and Eugene D. Genovese (Urbana, Ill., 1974), 9. For Caribbean absenteeism, see Richard S. Dunn, *Sugar and Slaves: The Rise of the Planter Class in the English West Indies, 1624–1713* (Chapel Hill, N.C., 1972), 101–3, 161–63.

15. Peter H. Wood, *Black Majority: Negroes in Colonial South Carolina from 1670 through the Stono Rebellion* (New York, 1974), 56–62; Daniel C. Littlefield, *Rice and Slaves: Ethnicity and the Slave Trade in Colonial South Carolina* (Baton Rouge, La., 1981), 74–114.

16. E. P. Thompson, "Time, Work-Discipline, and Industrial Capitalism," *Past and Present* 38 (1967): 73.

17. Of those slaves imported into South Carolina before 1740 and for whom an African coastal region of origin is known, I calculate that 15% were from rice-producing areas. Unfortunately, we know little or nothing about the regional origins of the earliest slave vessels to South Carolina. The first association between an African region and the cultivation of rice that I have found comes late in the day and may have been no more than a mercantile gambit. In 1758 the merchant firm Austin and Laurens described the origins of the slave ship *Betsey* as the "Windward and Rice Coast" (*South-Carolina Gazette* [Charleston], Aug. 11, 1758). Whites in other areas of North America are on record as valuing the familiarity with rice planting that some Africans displayed (see Henry P. Dart, "The First Cargo of African Slaves for Louisiana, 1718," *Louisiana Historical Quarterly* 14 [1931]: 176–77, as referred to in Joe Gray Taylor, *Negro Slavery in Louisiana* [Baton Rouge, La., 1963], 14). For the West Africans' widespread unfamiliarity with irrigation, see Littlefield, *Rice and Slaves*, 86, and the issue of *Africa* 51:2 (1981) devoted to "Rice and Yams in West Africa." A fuller discussion of all these matters will be presented in my *Slave Counterpoint: Black Culture in the Eighteenth-*

Century Chesapeake and Lowcountry (Chapel Hill, N.C., forthcoming).

18. In 1830 one Cuban planter, with little historical sense, could even argue that the culture of the tobacco plant "properly belongs to a white population, for there are few plants requiring more attention and tender treatment than this does" (Joseph M. Hernandez, "On the Cultivation of the Cuba Tobacco Plant," *Southern Agriculturalist* 3 [1830]: 463).

19. Domenico Sella, *Crisis and Continuity: The Economy of Spanish Lombardy in the Seventeenth Century* (Cambridge, Mass., 1979), 121–22.

20. Dunn, *Sugar and Slaves*, 189–200. The connection between sugar cultivation and gang labor was not absolutely axiomatic, at least in the postemancipation era. See Douglas Hall, *Free Jamaica, 1838–1865: An Economic History* (New Haven, Conn., 1959), 44–45; Jerome Handler, "Some Aspects of Work Organization on Sugar Plantations in Barbados," *Ethnology* 4 (1965): 16–38; and James McNeill and Chimman Lal, *Report to the Government of India on the Conditions of Indian Immigrants in Four British Colonies and Surinam* in *British Parliamentary Papers*, 1915, Cd. 7744, 7745 (I am indebted to Stanley Engerman for the last reference).

21. B. W. Higman, *Slave Population and Economy in Jamaica, 1807–1834* (Cambridge, 1976), 23–24, 220; a Jamaican bookkeeper reported that the only work on a coffee plantation *not* carried out by tasks was the drying of the berries, because "this required constant attention" (p. 23).

22. Barry Higman suggested this to me in a personal communication.

23. Ulrich Bonnell Phillips, *American Negro Slavery: A Survey of the Supply, Employment and Control of Negro Labor as Determined by the Plantation Regime* (Baton Rouge, La., 1966 [orig. publ. New York, 1918]), 247.

24. See the relevant discussion, above, pp. 209, 216, of how the task system was extended to the cultivation of cotton and even sugar in the late eighteenth- and early nineteenth-century lowcountry.

25. Thomas Cooper and David J. McCord, eds., *The Statutes at Large of South Carolina* (Columbia, S.C., 1836–41), 2: 22–23; 7: pt. 2, 368.

26. Cooper and McCord, eds., *Statutes of South Carolina*, 3: 398, 489; 7: 423.

27. Ball Family Account Book, 174, 32, and unpaginated memorandum, Jan. 21, 1736, South Carolina Historical Society, Charleston.

28. Administration of James Hartley's estate, Aug. 1758–July 1760, Inventory Book 5: 160–75, South Carolina Department of Archives and History, Columbia.

29. Henry Ravenel's Day Book, particularly for the years 1763–67, South Carolina Historical Society, Charleston.

30. George C. Rogers et al., eds., *The Papers of Henry Laurens*, vol. 5 (Columbia, S.C., 1976), 41.

31. Apart from the acts already mentioned, see Cooper and McCord, eds., *Statutes of South Carolina*, 7: 407–9, 434–35. See also Charlestown Grand Jury Presentments, *South Carolina Gazette*, Nov. 5, 1737.

32. Testimony of Thomas Akin and Ammon, Feb. 7,

1749, Council Journal, no. 17, pt. 1, 160.

33. Testimony of Lawrence Kelly, Jan. 30, 1749, Council Journal, 17, pt. 1, 85.

34. Administration of David Caw's estate, Oct. 20, 1761, Inventory Book 5, 12–19.

35. Mark Catesby, *The Natural History of Carolina, Florida and the Bahama Islands . . .*, vol. 2 (London, 1743), xviii; Francis Harper, ed., *The Travels of William Bartram* (New Haven, Conn., 1958), 297.

36. Bernard Romans, *A Concise Natural History of East and West Florida . . .*, vol. 1 (New York, 1775), 131; David Ramsay, *The History of South Carolina*, vol. 2 (Charleston, S.C., 1808), 289. The groundnut is a South American cultivated plant that was disseminated so widely and rapidly within Africa that some have postulated an African origin. This is not the case, but Africans apparently introduced the plant into North America (A. Krapovickas, "The Origin, Variability and Spread of the Groundnut," in *The Domestication and Exploitation of Plants and Animals*, ed. Peter J. Ucko and G. W. Dimbleby [London, 1969], 427–41).

37. Romans, *History of East and West Florida*, 1:130; Orrin Sage Wightman and Margaret Davis Cate, *Early Days of Coastal Georgia* (St. Simons Island, Ga., 1955), 163.

38. Elias Ball to Elias Ball, Feb. 26, 1786, Ball Family Papers, University of South Carolina, Columbia; Elise Pinckney, ed., *The Letterbook of Eliza Lucas Pinckney, 1739–1762* (Chapel Hill, N.C., 1972), 28.

39. "Bolzius Answers a Questionnaire," trans. and ed. Loewald et al., 236; John Glen to the Board of Trade, Mar. 1753, C.O. 5/374, 147, Public Record Office; Bernhard A. Uhlendorf, trans. and ed., *The Siege of Charleston: With an Account of the Province of South Carolina . . .* (Ann Arbor, Mich., 1938), 353. The cultivation of tobacco spread rapidly through West Africa during the seventeenth century, so that eighteenth-century black immigrants to South Carolina might well have been familiar with the crop. See, for example, Jack R. Harlan et al., eds., *Origins of African Plant Domestication* (The Hague, 1976), 296, 302, and Philip D. Curtin, *Economic Change in Precolonial Africa: Senegambia in the Era of the Slave Trade* (Madison, Wis., 1975), 230.

40. Evangeline Walker Andrews and Charles McLean Andrews, eds., *Journal of a Lady of Quality . . .* (New Haven, Conn., 1923), 176–77.

41. Cooper and McCord, eds., *Statutes of South Carolina*, 7: 368, 382, 409.

42. "Mr. Isaac Bodett's Release to a Negro for Fifty Years, Nov. 13, 1728," Records of the Secretary of the Province, Book H, 42–43, South Carolina Department of Archives and History, Columbia.

43. John Gerar William De Brahm, *Report of the General Survey in the Southern District of North America*, ed. Louis De Vorsey, Jr. (Columbia, S.C., 1971), 94.

44. William Butler, "Observations on the Culture of Rice," 1786, South Carolina Historical Society, Charleston. One plantation journal recorded completed daily tasks and acres planted: the quarter-acre task was uniformly applied throughout the planting season. See Plantation Journal, 1773, Wragg Papers, South Carolina Historical Society.

45. J. Channing to Edward Telfair, Aug. 10, 1786, Telfair

Papers, Duke University, Durham, N.C.; Wilbur H. Siebert, ed., *Loyalists in East Florida, 1774 to 1785*, vol. 2 (DeLand, Fla., 1929), 67.

46. Butler, "Observations," 1786. There was a parallel debate in England at this time between the advocates of regularly employed wage-labor and the advocates of "taken-work." One of those who censured the recourse to taken-work made a point similar to that of Butler: people only agreed to tasking, this critic alleged, in order "to save themselves the trouble of watching their workmen" (Thompson, "Time, Work-Discipline, and Industrial Capitalism," 78–79).

47. Letter to printers, *City Gazette* (Charleston), Mar. 14, 1796. The readiness with which sea island planters extended the task system to sea island cotton planting suggests prior familiarity, which in turn suggests that indigo planting had been subject to tasking. No direct evidence of this connection is available, so far as I am aware. Few upland cotton plantations employed a thoroughgoing task system. One that did—the Silver Bluff plantation belonging to Christopher Fitzsimmons, subsequently owned by James Henry Hammond—was run as an absentee property and was more than likely populated by slaves already inured to tasking when resident on Fitzsimmons's tidewater plantation (Drew Gilpin Faust to author, personal communication).

48. James Glen to the Board of Trade, July 15, 1751, C. O. 5/373, 155–57, P. R. O.; Garden to the Royal Society, May 1, 1757, Guard Book 3: 86; G. Moulton to [?], Dec. 20, 1772, Add. MSS 22677, 70, British Library.

49. John Gerar William De Brahm, *History of the Province of Georgia . . .* (Wormsloe, Ga., 1849), 51; Ralph Gray and Betty Wood, "The Transition from Indentured to Involuntary Servitude in Colonial Georgia," *Explorations in Economic History* 13 (1976): 361–64.

50. Ramsay, *History of South Carolina*, 2: 278–80. High rates of profit continued to characterize the large rice plantation (see Dale Evans Swan, *The Structure and Profitability of the Antebellum Rice Industry, 1859* [New York, 1975]).

51. John Drayton, *A View of South-Carolina as Respects Her Natural and Civil Concerns* (Spartanburg, S.C., 1972 [orig. publ. Charleston, S.C., 1802]), 116; James Parker's Journal of the Charlestown Expedition, Feb. 5, 1780, Parker Family Papers, 920 PAR I 13/2, Liverpool City Libraries, Liverpool, England.

52. Timothy Ford speaks of half-acre tasks (Joseph W. Barnwell, ed., "Diary of Timothy Ford, 1785–1786," *South Carolina Historical Magazine* 13 [1912]: 182). However, the first specific reference that I have so far found to the 150-feet-square task is in Edmund Ruffin, *Report of the Commencement and Progress of the Agricultural Survey of South-Carolina for 1843* (Columbia, S.C., 1843), 104.

53. See table 1. Time and space do not permit an investigation of the effect of developments in machinery on slave work routines. However, to give but one example, the pounding task of the early eighteenth century was, by the end of the century, redundant. Agricultural manuals in the nineteenth century do not set daily tasks for pounding.

54. Richard Hutson to Mr. Croll, Aug. 22, 1767, Charles Woodward Hutson Papers, University of North Carolina, Chapel Hill.

55. Josiah Smith to George Austin, Jan. 31, 1774, Josiah Smith Letterbook, University of North Carolina, Chapel Hill.

56. [Edwin C. Holland], *A Refutation of the Calumnies Circulated against . . . Slavery . . .* (New York, 1969 [orig. publ. Charleston, S.C., 1822]), 53. In the antebellum era, the role of the laborers continued to be significant in the evolution of the task system. For a particularly good example of the difficulty in modifying a long-established task (in this case, threshing), see James M. Clifton, ed., *Life and Labor on Argyle Island: Letters and Documents of a Savannah River Rice Plantation, 1833–1867* (Savannah, Ga., 1978), 8–9. Frederick Law Olmsted also noted that "in all ordinary work custom has settled the extent of the task, and it is difficult to increase it." If these customs were systematically ignored, Olmsted continued, the planter simply increased the likelihood of "a general stampede to the 'swamp'" (*A Journey in the Seaboard Slave States* [New York, 1968 [orig. publ. 1856]], 435–36). James Henry Hammond waged what appears to have been an unsuccessful battle with his laborers when he tried to impose gang labor in place of the task system much preferred by his slaves (Drew Gilpin Faust, "Culture, Conflict, and Community: The Meaning of Power on an Ante-bellum Plantation," *Journal of Social History* 14 [1980]: 86).

57. Daniel Turner to his parents, Aug. 13, 1806, Daniel Turner Papers, Library of Congress (microfilm). Equally sacrosanct, at least to some slaves, was the product of their "time." Thus, in 1781 a set of plantation slaves attempted to kill their overseer because he tried to appropriate the corn that they were apparently planning to market (*South-Carolina and American General Gazette* [Charleston], Jan. 20, 1781).

58. Frederick E. Maser and Howard T. Maag, eds., *The Journal of Joseph Pilmore, Methodist Itinerant: For the Years August 1, 1769 to January 2, 1774* (Philadelphia, 1969), 188.

59. ["Scotus Americanus"], *Information Concerning the Province of North Carolina, Addressed to Emigrants from the Highlands and Western Isles of Scotland* (Glasgow, 1773), reprinted in William K. Boyd, "Some North Carolina Tracts of the Eighteenth Century," *North Carolina Historical Review* 3 (1926): 616. This account almost certainly refers to the Cape Fear region of North Carolina. For slightly less-detailed accounts, see François Alexandre Frédéric, duc de La Rochefoucauld-Liancourt, *Travels through the United States of North America . . . ,* vol. 1 (London, 1799), 599; Drayton, *View of South Carolina*, 145; and Edmund Botsford, *Sambo & Tony, a Dialogue in Three Parts* (Georgetown, S.C., 1808), 8, 13, 34.

60. Charlestown District Grand Jury Presentments, *South Carolina Gazette*, Jan. 25, 1772.

61. Declaration of John Blake, Apr. 25, 1788, Miscellaneous Record Book VV, 473, South Carolina Department of

Archives and History, Columbia.

62. *State Gazette of South-Carolina* (Charleston), Oct. 26, 1793.

63. William Read to Jacob Read, Mar. 22, 1800, Read Family Papers, South Carolina Historical Society, Charleston. For another description of property owning by low-country slaves in the early nineteenth century, see Sidney Walter Martin, ed., "A New Englander's Impressions of Georgia in 1817–1818: Extracts from the Diary of Ebenezer Kellogg," *Journal of Southern History* 12 (1946): 259–60.

64. A Georgian, "Account of the Culture and Produce of the Bearded Rice," *Southern Agriculturalist* 3 (1830): 292. For the evidence that about two acres was the sowing "task," see "A Memorandum of Tasks," *Southern Agriculturalist* 7 (1834): 297, and Ruffin, *Report of the Commencement and Progress of . . . South Carolina,* 118.

65. A Plain Farmer, "On the Culture of Sweet Potatoes," *Southern Agriculturalist* 5 (1832): 120; for the cooper's task, see the sources cited in the footnotes to table 1.

66. Testimony of Peter Way, claim of William Roberts, July 4, 1873, Liberty County, Georgia, Case Files, Southern Claims Commission, Records of the 3d Auditor, Record Group 217, Records of the U.S. General Accounting Office, National Archives. Hereafter, only the name and date—county and state will be added whenever a claim originates from an area other than Liberty Co., Ga.—will be given, followed by the abbreviation SCC.

67. Testimony of Philip Campbell, claim of Windsor Stevens, July 12, 1873, SCC; claimant's deposition, claim of Diana Cummings, June 17, 1873, Chatham County, Ga.; see also testimony of Henry LeCount, claim of Marlborough Jones, July 30, 1873.

68. Mason Crum, *Gullah: Negro Life in the Carolina Sea Islands* (Durham, N.C., 1940), 51; for a similar use of the term, but by a son of former slave parents, see Wightman and Cate, *Early Days of Coastal Georgia,* 81.

69. For example, see the claim depositions of James Anderson, William Cassell, Prince Cumings, Hamlet Delegal, and Thomas Irving of Liberty Co., Ga., SCC.

70. Claimant's deposition, claim of Marlborough Jones, July 30, 1873, SCC; see also claimant's deposition, claim of Somerset Stewart, July 30, 1873.

71. George P. Rawick, ed., *The American Slave: A Composite Autobiography,* vol. 3 (Westport, Conn., 1972), pt. 3: 200–201. A black Edisto Islander, born in 1897, interviewed in 1970, was also conversant with the dual meaning of the term *task* (Nick Lindsay, trans., *An Oral History of Edisto Island: The Life and Times of Bubberson Brown* [Goshen, Ind., 1977], 27, 46–47, 50, 53).

72. "Memoranda of a Crop of Corn Grown in St. Andrew's Parish," *Southern Agriculturalist* 3 (1830): 77; "Account of the Mode of Culture Pursued in Cultivating Corn and Peas," *Southern Agriculturalist* 4 (1831): 236. An intensive application of tasking to operations that ranged from the construction of post-and-rail fences to the digging of groundnuts can be found in the "Plantation Journal of Thomas W. Peyre, 1834–51," esp. 259, 332, 365, South Carolina Historical Society, Charleston. (I am grateful to Gene

Waddell, Director of the Society, for bringing this to my attention).

73. Even Lewis Gray and U. B. Phillips, the two standard authorities on the task system, are confused on this issue. The task-acre in tidewater rice cultivation ideally took the form of a field 300' × 150', divided into two half-acre "tasks" of 150' square. The task-acre on inland rice and sea island cotton plantations was ideally a square of 210', divided into four quarter-acre squares, each side 105' in length. See R. F. W. Allston, "Sea-Coast Crops of the South," *De Bow's Review* 16 (1854): 596, 609; cf. Phillips, *American Negro Slavery,* 247, 259, and Gray, *History of Agriculture,* 1: 553.

74. Jacob Wood, "Account of the Process of Cultivating, Harvesting and Manufacturing the Sugar Cane," *Southern Agriculturalist* 3 (1830): 226.

75. The Editor, "Account of an Agricultural Excursion Made into the South of Georgia in the Winter of 1832," *Southern Agriculturalist* 6 (1833): 576.

76. Testimony of William Winn, claim of David Stevens, July 17, 1873, SCC; testimony of James Frazer, claim of John Bacon, July 7, 1873.

77. Claimant's deposition, claim of Joseph Bacon, Aug. 12, 1873, SCC; testimony of Peter Way, claim of Silvia Baker, Aug. 9, 1873.

78. Testimony of Tony Law, claim of Linda Roberts, July 19, 1873, SCC. See also D. E. Huger Smith, *A Charlestonian's Recollections, 1846–1913* (Charleston, S.C., 1950), 29.

79. Claimant's deposition, claim of John Crawford, Mar. 3, 1874, SCC; claimant's deposition, claim of Frank James, Mar. 14, 1874.

80. See, for example, Leon F. Litwack, *Been in the Storm So Long: The Aftermath of Slavery* (New York, 1980), 410.

81. Lt. Douglas G. Risley to Col. C. C. Sibley, June 2, 1867 (A123), Freedman and Southern Society, files of documents in the National Archives, University of Maryland, College Park. (Hereafter reference to documents read at the Society will be given in parentheses.) But cf. Litwack, *Been in the Storm,* 410.

82. Bvt. Maj. Gen. Charles Devens to Bvt. Lt. Col. W. L. M. Burger, AAG, Oct. 29, 1865, and Nov. 13, 1865 (C1361, pt. 1, C4160, pt. 1); Brig. Gen. W. T. Bennett to Bvt. Lt. Col. W. L. M. Burger, AAG, Oct. 11, 1865 (C1361, pt. 1).

83. Ben Allston et al. to Col. Willard, Oct. 30, 1865 (C1602, pt. 2); Lt. Col. A. J. Willard to Capt. G. W. Hooker, AAG, Nov. 7, 1865 (C1614, pt. 2).

84. This information was derived from Lt. Col. A. J. Willard to Capt. G. W. Hooker, AAG, Nov. 7, 1865, and Dec. 6, 1865 (C1614, pt. 2, C1503, pt. 1); case #104, James Geddes v. William B. Seabrook, Feb. 11, 1867 (C1534, pt. 1); contract between William H. Gibbons and 120 Freedmen, Chatham Co., Ga., Mar. 1, 1866 (A5798); Maj. Gen. James B. Steedman and Bvt. Brig. Gen. J. S. Fullerton to E. M. Stanton, June 4, 1866 (A5829); Capt. Henry C. Brandt to Lt. Col. A. W. Smith, Jan. 12, 1867 (A5395). See also John David Smith, "More than Slaves, Less than Freedmen: The 'Share Wages' Labor System during Reconstruction," *Civil War History* 26 (1980): 256–66, for the example of a contract,

not the analysis that accompanies it. A detailed analysis of the labor contracts in operation in these years would undoubtedly enrich, and perhaps modify, this section.

85. A. M. McIver to Lt. J. M. Hogg (SAC), Feb. 28, 1867 (A5769); see also Lt. W. M. Wallace to Capt. E. W. H. Read, Jan. 8, 1867 (C1619); D. M. Burns to [?], Mar. 17, 1867 (A7188); and Joel Williamson, *After Slavery: The Negro in South Carolina during Reconstruction, 1861–1877* (Chapel Hill, N.C., 1965), 135–36.

86. Harry Hammond, "Report on the Cotton Production of the State of South Carolina," in U.S. Census Office, *Tenth Census, 1880* (Washington, D.C., 1884), 6: pt. 2, 60–61.

87. Testimony of Richard Cummings, claim of Lafayette Delegal, July 11, 1873, SCC; claimant's deposition, claim of Scipio King, July 9, 1873. A number of lowcountry freedmen made similar statements. For the general recollections of ex-slaves see George P. Rawick, *From Sundown to Sunup: The Making of the Black Community* (Westport, Conn., 1972), and Paul D. Escott, *Slavery Remembered: A Record of Twentieth-Century Slave Narratives* (Chapel Hill, N.C., 1979), 38.

88. Testimony of Peter Stevens, claim of Toney Elliott, Aug. 8, 1873, SCC; testimony of July Roberts, claim of Nedger Frazer, Feb. 27, 1874; report of R. B. Avery and testimony of Gilmore and Co., attorneys for claimant, claim of Jacob Dryer, Nov. 1, 1873.

89. The settled or allowed claims from ex-slaves for Liberty and Chatham counties, Ga., and Beaufort, Charleston, and Georgetown counties, S.C., were investigated. For a fuller presentation of my findings, see "The Ownership of Property by Slaves in the Mid-Nineteenth-Century Lowcountry," *Journal of Southern History* 49 (1983): 399–420.

90. The Liberty Co., Ga., claims are the most numerous and most detailed. They contain few urban claimants and form the ideal sample for the purposes of this study. Eighty-nine former slaves from this county submitted claims that were settled: 50 of the 89 were field hands and 25 of 86 were under the age of 35 when their property was taken. For a fuller discussion of the reliability of these claims and an analysis of the claimed property, see my article cited in n. 89.

91. Testimony of Raymond Cay, Jr., claim of Paris James, June 2, 1874, SCC. Cay also said that he "looked upon [James] as one of the most thrifty slaves in Liberty County." His claim totaled $1,218.

92. Testimony of W. A. Golding, claim of Linda (and Caesar) Roberts, July 19, 1873, SCC. His claim noted $1,519.

93. Report of R. B. Avery, claim of Jacob Quarterman, July 5, 1873, SCC; report of R. B. Avery, claim of Prince Stewart, July 29, 1873; report of the Commissioners of Claims, claim of James Stacy, Aug. 15, 1873.

94. Claimant's deposition and testimony of John Fish, claim of Alexander Steele, Aug. 17, 1872, Chatham Co., Ga., SCC.

95. Charles E. Beveridge et al., eds., *The Papers of Frederick Law Olmsted*, vol. 2 (Baltimore, 1981), 182. Twenty-four field hands, out of a total of 53 slaves, claimed horses.

96. Two Liberty Co. freedmen testified to a ban on horse ownership on their plantations; 3 recalled that only drivers had horses; and 14 supplied the proportions mentioned here.

97. Claimant's deposition, claim of Paris James, June 2, 1874, SCC.

98. Claimant's deposition, claim of Nedger Frazer, Feb. 27, 1874, SCC. This is the same Niger, as he was known as a slave, who objected to being hired out in 1864 because he was unable, as he put it, to "make anything for himself," and who pretended to have yellow fever so that Sherman's troops would not deprive him of his property (see Robert Manson Myers, ed., *The Children of Pride: A True Story of Georgia and the Civil War* [New Haven, Conn., 1972], 1162, 1237).

99. Myers, ed., *Children of Pride*, 244, 306.

100. Testimony of W. A. Golding, claim of Linda (and Caesar) Roberts, July 19, 1873, SCC.

101. Claimant's deposition, claim of John Bacon, July 7, 1873, SCC.

102. Report of R. B. Avery, claim of Robert Bryant, Oct. 6, 1877, Beaufort Co., S.C., SCC.

103. Claimant's deposition, claim of William Drayton, Feb. 20, 1874, Beaufort Co., S.C., SCC; testimony of Sterling Jones, claim of Sandy Austin, July 21, 1873.

104. James Miller, for example, recalled that "many times I would get some one to help me, and get along that way, I would pay them whatever they asked according to the time they worked" (report of R. B. Avery, claim of James Miller, July 29, 1873, SCC). See also claimant's deposition, claim of Pompey Bacon, Aug. 7, 1873.

105. Claimant's deposition, claim of Edward Moddick and Jacob Hicks, Mar. 17, 1873, Chatham Co., Ga., SCC.

106. Report of J. P. M. Epping, claim of Pompey Smith, n.d., Beaufort, Co., S.C., SCC.

107. Testimony of Joseph James, claim of Linda and Caesar Jones, Aug. 1, 1873, SCC.

108. Testimony of T. Fleming before R. B. Avery, claim of Prince Wilson, Jr., July 28, 1873, Chatham Co., Ga., SCC. The widespread ownership of animals is also indicated in the records of one lowcountry plantation. In 1859 almost 40 slaves, over half the adult males on the plantation, owned at least one cow, cow and calf, steer, or heifer. Only about 10 of the 40 held skilled or privileged positions (Weehaw Plantation Book, 1855–61, 87, South Carolina Historical Society, Charleston).

109. Testimony of Fortune James, claim of Charles Warner, Aug. 6, 1873, SCC; claimant's deposition, claim of Prince Wilson, Jr., July 28, 1873, Chatham Co., Ga.; claimant's deposition, claim of Jane Holmes, July 21, 1873.

110. Jeremiah Everts Diary, Apr. 5, 1822, Georgia Historical Society, Savannah, as quoted in Thomas F. Armstrong, "From Task Labor to Free Labor: The Transition along Georgia's Rice Coast, 1820–1880," *Georgia Historical Quarterly* 64 (1980): 436.

111. The Liberty Co. claimants who mention such acreages include Daniel Bryant, William Cassell, Prince Cumings, George Gould, Ned Quarterman, Paris James, and

Richard LeCounte. The Chatham Co. claimants include Dennis Smith and Alfred Barnard. The Beaufort Co. claimants include John Morree, Andrew Riley, Pompey Smith, Moses Washington, and Benjamin Platts. When James Miller's brother, Lawrence, a student at Howard University, was asked whether the 100 bushels of rice claimed by his brother was not excessive, he replied, "I should not think so—not in his condition." James's "condition" was only that of a field hand, but he was the "director" of the family, and the family planted five acres (testimony of Lawrence Miller, claim of James Miller, July 29, 1873, SCC).

112. Claimant's deposition, claim of Adam LeCount, Feb. 26, 1874, SCC.

113. Robert W. Gibbes, "Southern Slave Life," *De Bow's Review* 24 (1858): 324; Olmsted, *Journey in the Seaboard Slave States*, 443. Fanny Kemble noted that two carpenters on the Butler estate sold a canoe to a neighboring planter for $60 and that slaves could earn large sums by collecting Spanish moss (Frances Anne Kemble, *Journal of a Residence on a Georgian Plantation in 1838–1839*, ed. John A. Scott [New York, 1961], 62, 364). Unfortunately, there are no estimates of the proportion of money circulating among the slaves. The handling of money certainly gave rise to some discernment: one freedman remembered paying $60 in "good money" for a horse. He continued, "I call silver good money, I call confederate money wasps' nests" (claimant's deposition, claim of Simon Middleton, June 2, 1873, Chatham Co., Ga., SCC).

114. Alice R. Huger Smith, *A Carolina Rice Plantation of the Fifties* (New York, 1936), 72.

115. Claimant's deposition, claim of Joseph Bacon, Aug. 12, 1873, SCC.

116. Claimant's deposition, claim of Samuel Elliott, July 17, 1873, SCC.

117. Claimant's deposition, claim of York Stevens, Mar. 2, 1874, SCC; claimant's deposition, claim of Edward Brown, Feb. 20, 1874; Beaufort Co., S.C.; claimant's deposition, claim of William Roberts, July 4, 1873; claimant's deposition, claim of William Drayton, Feb. 20, 1874, Beaufort Co., S.C.

118. Claimant's deposition, claim of Jane Holmes, July 21, 1873, SCC. Twenty-three Liberty Co. freedmen referred to inheriting property within the same plantation.

119. Claimant's deposition and testimony of Andrew Stacy, claim of Nancy Bacon, Mar. 14, 1874, SCC; Stacy performed the same service for Clarinda Porter (claimant's deposition, claim of Clarinda Porter, Feb. 18, 1874). Nine Liberty Co. freedmen referred to inheriting property across plantation boundaries.

120. Claimant's deposition, claim of Diana Cummings, June 17, 1873, Chatham Co., Ga., SCC.

121. See, for example, claimant's deposition, claim of Silvia Baker, Aug. 9, 1873, SCC; claimant's deposition, claim of Hamlet Delegal, Mar. 7, 1874; and claimant's deposition, claim of William Golding, May 16, 1874.

122. Claimant's deposition, claim of Jacob Monroe, July 18, 1873, SCC.

123. Testimony of Joshua Cassell, claim of George Gould,

Aug. 11, 1873, SCC.

124. Testimony of William Gilmore, claim of York Stevens, Mar. 2, 1874, SCC.

125. Testimony of B. K. Lee, 1863 (K72); testimony of Henry G. Judd, 1863 (K74); testimony of Brig. Gen. Rufus Saxton, 1863 (K70).

126. Testimony of Saxton, 1863 (K70).

127. Testimony of Lafayette Delegal, claim of Richard Cummings, Feb. 28, 1874, SCC.

128. Report of R. B. Avery, claim of William Golding, May 16, 1874, SCC; Olmsted, *Journey in the Seaboard Slave States*, 428.

129. Testimony of Leah Wilson, claim of Prince Wilson, Jr., July 28, 1873, Chatham Co., Ga., SCC. See also the claim depositions of William Gilmore and Hamlet Delegal, and the testimony of Simon Cassell, Henry Stephens, and Fortune James in the claims of Jacob Monroe, Clarinda Porter, and Charles Warner, respectively.

130. Edward S. Philbrick to Pierce, Mar. 27, 1862 (Q12).

131. Bvt. Lt. Col. R. F. Smith report in Bvt. Maj. Gen. R. K. Scott to O. O. Howard, July 9, 1866 (C1428, pt. 1). See also Bvt. Lt. Col. B. F. Smith to O. A. Hart, Apr. 25, 1866 (C1617).

132. Frances Butler Leigh, *Ten Years on a Georgia Plantation* (London, 1883), 55.

133. E. T. Wright to Lt. Col. H. B. Clitz, Oct. 6, 1865 (C1361, pt. 1).

134. J. G. Foster to [?], Sept. 20, 1864 (C1334, pt. 1).

135. Joseph D. Pope to Maj. Gen. Q. A. Gilmore, June 29, 1865 (C1472).

136. Lt. Col. A. J. Willard to W. H. Smith, Nov. 13, 1865 (A7011).

137. Smith report in Scott to Howard, July 9, 1866 (C1428, pt. 1); Leigh, *Ten Years on a Georgia Plantation*, 124.

138. I have been influenced by Eric Foner, *Politics and Ideology in the Age of the Civil War* (New York, 1980), 97–127; Willie Lee Rose, *Rehearsal for Reconstruction: The Port Royal Experiment* (New York, 1976 [orig. publ. Indianapolis, Ind., 1964]), 226, 303, 406; and the works by Mintz cited in n. 8, above.

139. Report of R. B. Avery, claim of Samuel Maxwell, June 8, 1878, SCC.

140. J. R. Cheeves to A. P. Ketchum, Jan. 21, 1866 (A7058).

141. Apart from the standard works on peasants by Wolf, Shanin, and Mintz, I found the general implications of James C. Scott, *The Moral Economy of the Peasant: Rebellion and Subsistence in Southeast Asia* (New Haven, Conn., 1976) particularly helpful.

142. For antebellum slaves, and on a general level, this is the argument of Genovese, *Roll, Jordan, Roll*, esp. 133–49.

143. Arney Robinson Childs, ed., *The Private Journal of Henry William Ravenel, 1859–1887* (Columbia, S.C., 1947), 216; Capt. H. A. Storey to C. B. Fillebrown, July 9, 1865 (C1468). Ravenel still considered his plantation hands to be slaves in Mar. 1865.

144. William Dallam Armes, ed., *The Autobiography of*

Joseph Le Conte (New York, 1903), 234. Long after emancipation, when he had ceased to be a landowner, Daniel E. Huger Smith still shared in "the same interchange of small gifts of eggs or a chicken or two on the one side and perhaps an article of clothing on the other" that had characterized master-slave relations many years before (*A Charlestonian's Recollections*, 127).

145. Scott, *Moral Economy of the Peasant*, 157–92.

146. Testimony of Oliver P. Bostick, claim of Andrew Jackson, Mar. 10, 1874, Beaufort Co., S.C., SCC; Rufus King, Jr., to William Washington, Sept. 13, 1828, in *American Farmer* 10 (1828): 346.

147. See Mintz, "Slavery and the Rise of Peasantries," 241.

148. The phrase was coined by Tadeusz Lepkowski, referred to by Sidney W. Mintz, "Was the Plantation Slave a Proletarian?" *Review* 2 (1978): 94. I would also suggest that there was a significantly wider peasant breach in the slave mode of production in the lowcountry than elsewhere in North America where "incentives," in the forms of garden plots, opportunities to earn money, and so forth, were accorded slaves. More comparative work is obviously needed, but evidence from one area of the antebellum South supports my supposition (Roderick A. McDonald, "The Internal Economics of Slaves on Sugar Plantations in Jamaica and Louisiana" [paper, presented at Southern Historical Association Meeting, 1981]). In any case, I am reluctant to describe the task system as an incentive system; it was more a way of life.

149. Mintz, "Slavery and the Rise of Peasantries," esp. 226–33. In the same way that I consider there to have been a wider peasant breach in the slave mode of production in the lowcountry than elsewhere in North America (though it was certainly not absent elsewhere), I also believe—and this is almost a corollary—that the ability to escape the plantation, while not unique to the lowcountry, was more effectively secured here than elsewhere in North America.

150. As we might expect, lowcountry freedmen, particularly sea islanders, proved an unreliable source of labor for the phosphate mines. Their plots of land took precedence, and their earnings from mining formed only a welcome supplement to the income derived from farming (Tom W. Schick and Don H. Doyle, "Labor, Capital, and Politics in South Carolina: The Low Country Phosphate Industry, 1867–1920" [typescript], 11).

151. Roger L. Ransom and Richard Sutch, *One Kind of Freedom: The Economic Consequences of Emancipation* (Cambridge, 1977), 91–93; Williamson, *After Slavery*, 155; W. E. B. DuBois, "The Negro Landholder of Georgia," *Bulletin of the United States Department of Labor* 6, no. 35 (1901): 647–77; T. J. Woofter, *Black Yeomanry* (New York, 1930); *Morning News* (Savannah), Jan. 30, 1880, quoted in Armstrong, "From Task Labor to Free Labor," *Georgia Historical Quarterly* 64 (1980): 443. This last-mentioned article makes a similar argument to the one here.

152. Mintz, "Was the Plantation Slave a Proletarian?" 95.

The Material Lives of Laboring Philadelphians, 1750–1800

BILLY G. SMITH

Although many objects survive both above and below ground from America's seventeenth and eighteenth centuries, few students of material culture face up to a simple, undeniable truth: a culture as lived cannot be reduced to its artifacts. Other social processes that came into constant play—daily work routines, individual attitudes toward upward mobility and physical comfort, and those concrete economic realities of scarcity or abundance we define as a "standard of living"—no longer exist in either country or city. Without attending to the systematic reconstruction of these often mundane details, we can easily paint too rosy a picture of everyday life in the past. In this pathbreaking account of the household budgets, work schedules, and real wages of laborers and mariners, shoemakers and tailors in Philadelphia from 1750 to 1800, Billy G. Smith attacks three illusions we commonly have about the material lives of working people in the eighteenth century: that they received high wages in a labor-scarce society, that they lived in a state of physical comfort, and that they enjoyed the prospect of upward mobility in a fluid economy.

Using 1762 as his index year, Smith demonstrates that working people needed at least £63 in annual income in order to maintain subsistence levels of food, housing, fuel, and clothing. Yet this figure changed as each decade brought new fluctuations due to war, depression, stagnation, and currency inflation. Food, for example, cost about £10 per annum in 1762, but over the rest of the eighteenth century its average cost more than doubled. Housing grew more expensive as property in central Philadelphia rose in price and was seized by acquisitive merchants; working people were pushed to the city's territorial margins, where they lived in crowded, ramshackle, wood-framed structures. Fuel costs rose as Philadelphia's wooded hinterlands were deforested, and clothing proved affordable only if it was homemade. Women and children in most laboring families had to work to make ends meet. These conditions worsened when seasonal layoffs, injury, and sickness interrupted household earnings, and in years of economic stagnation, local almshouses were filled.

The material lives of working people were always precarious and often subject to unpredictable change. Some artisans—master shoemakers and tailors, for example—prospered if they were careful to protect their authority in the trades through rules for prices. But unpropertied journeymen were chronically underpaid and their skills exploited; ultimately, they helped to stimulate radical labor activity in the opening years of the nineteenth century. Making it in eighteenth-century Philadelphia, Smith argues, was difficult at best. Most working people remained unaffected by the rising mercantile wealth of the port, as productive capital most often stayed in the coffers of merchants and real estate speculators. For the urban laboring classes, staying afloat and keeping bread on the table was challenge enough.

John Shenton, a Philadelphia mariner, sailed four times to Antigua on the snow *Mary* between October 1750 and November 1752. He earned between £13 and £15 per voyage, plus 3s. 6d. for each day he may have worked unloading or stowing cargo, for an annual income of approximately £32 during those years. Shenton's personal expenses must have been minimal, for room and board were provided on ship, and the only financial difficulties he may have encountered would have resulted from supporting a wife and children, if he had such. The material conditions that he and his hypothetical family experienced, however, are not clear to us.

Fifteen years later, Joseph Graisbury earned about £180 annually by outfitting some of Philadelphia's wealthiest citizens in the latest fashions from Holland-cloth breeches to silk vests. He bought a house worth £120 in Lower Delaware ward, in which he resided with his wife, at least seven children, all under eight years of age, and a slave. But the standard of living provided by his tailoring, and the ways it varied during the decade before the Revolution, is unknown.

Late in the 1780s, John and Elizabeth Baldwin performed occasional jobs for the Pennsylvania Hospital for the Sick Poor. John whitewashed fences and walls for 5s. 5d. per day and spread dung on the hospital's garden for 1s. 6d. per day. Elizabeth washed clothes, cleaned rooms, made candles, cooked, and nursed, usually for 2s. 6d. per day. The couple and their two children lived in a "brick tenement" rented from the hospital for £12 annually and may at times have paid 9d. for a meal at the hospital. Again, the material circumstances of their lives and the nature of their struggle to make ends meet cannot be clearly understood from these fragmentary data.[1]

These vignettes provide glimpses into the material world of urban laboring people in America during the second half of the eighteenth century. They are a summons to research the day-to-day lives of ordinary Americans rather than a basis for easy generalizations about their physical existence. Despite limited evidence, historians usually describe the living standards of the urban lower classes as comfortable, perpetuating the hoary myth that labor scarcity in early America inevitably meant high wages for anyone who cared to work. Thus Sam Bass Warner finds Revolutionary Philadelphia a city of "abundance for the common man." "An unskilled laborer without connections," Warner claims, "could find work with board and wages to begin accumulating a little money for tools," and the "earnings of the ordinary artisan . . . could support a wife and children without having to take outside employment."[2] Carl Bridenbaugh states that the "lower sort" received "very high wages" and that "a hard-working man could support his wife and family and even lay by a little money for the future."[3] Philadelphians in particular, Bridenbaugh believes, "enjoyed continuing prosperity and a steady rise in the standard of living."[4] In the Quaker City as in the colonies generally, according to John J. McCusker, "not only were the rich getting richer but the poor were also."[5] Jackson Turner Main concurs: "The general standard of living was high."

Indeed, conditions in the Pennsylvania capital were so favorable that even the "poor laborer," Main avers, "could normally expect to become a small property owner."[6]

Similarly, paucity of evidence has not restrained historians from using the supposedly favorable economic circumstances of laboring people to interpret their political motivations and behavior. Charles S. Olton argues that "the mechanic class" in Revolutionary Philadelphia was "preponderantly composed of independent entrepreneurs" whose "common interests" help explain their political activity.[7] Other historians, generalizing on the meaning of the Revolution, assert that it did not result from "belly factors" or "rising misery" but "took place in a basically prosperous . . . economy." Americans in general, it is said, did not confront, and were not roused to rebellion by, the "predicament of poverty."[8]

Little has been done to test the comfort of the urban "lesser sort" by measuring their living standards. Reviewing the literature, Philip S. Foner concludes that "we can but guess at the actual wages of eighteenth-century workers"—a fundamental issue—because "we have no reliable statistics on pay scales."[9] Main's work on the social structure of Revolutionary America took a tentative step in this direction, but we have not advanced far since then.[10] Recent studies of the Philadelphia poor by Gary B. Nash and John K. Alexander contradict the prevailing rosy view of the lives of laboring people.[11] Nash discovers growing problems of poverty and unemployment during the late colonial period, which he regards as symptoms of structural weaknesses in the urban economy, and he undertakes to show how changes in the "material conditions of life . . . for city dwellers" generated a "revolutionary commitment within the middle and lower ranks of colonial society."[12]

We still lack a systematic investigation sensitive to changes in the material welfare of the urban laboring classes during the late eighteenth century. Historians have not studied the relation between wages and living costs, the regularity of employment opportunity, or the cyclical factors that affected income, prices, and work availability. Basic questions consequently remain unanswered. How did the supposed high wages translate into purchasing power? How did the seasonality of work affect income? How close to the margin did working people live, and how seriously did fluctuations in the economy affect them? How often did they experience periods of hardship or prosperity? Were the material conditions of their lives generally improving or deteriorating? The evidence available to answer such questions is more limited than that for the study of the wealthy or even of the institutionalized poor for whom government records exist. But it is possible, nonetheless, to find out a good deal about the material lives of laborers and artisans—and this inquiry is essential to a full understanding of the social, political, and economic history of the period.

My purpose in this article is to measure as precisely as the sources permit the household budgets, wages, and material conditions of Philadelphia's lower sort—those people who lived just above the poverty line and generally did not receive public assistance—during the second half of the eighteenth century. A large range of property, wealth, and economic interests existed among urban laborers, and the failure of historians clearly to specify the people being examined has generated some of the current confusion in studies of eighteenth-century labor.[13] To avoid compounding this confusion, this article focuses on two categories of less-skilled artisans—cordwainers (shoemakers) and tailors—and two unskilled groups—laborers and mariners. Several factors determine the selection of these four groups. Of all major occupations, they were the most heavily concentrated near the bottom of the economic order; tax collectors assessed two-thirds of their members the minimum rate in 1772. The four groups composed not only a substantial portion of the lower sort, accounting for almost half of those in the bottom third of the tax structure in 1772, but also a sizable segment of the city's population—at least one-third and probably one-half of the free male workers.[14] The variety of economic functions performed by members of these groups should make their experiences representative of Philadelphia's laboring people. Mariners and many laborers served in the maritime sector; other laborers depended on the construction and shipbuilding industries as well as on a host of miscellaneous jobs; cordwainers and tailors worked as artisans supplying consumer goods and services.

The following pages give an account of the costs of four basic necessities—food, rent, fuel, and clothing—in order to construct a typical household budget. A consideration of actual and real wages (the latter adjusted by the cost of living), of income, and of the material conditions of the four occupational groups will follow.[15]

* * *

Food was the most important item in every household budget. The series of eighteenth-century Philadelphia wholesale prices developed by Anne Bezanson and her associates cannot be used to make accurate estimates of expenditures for food because neither the retail mark-up nor the effect of the international market on wholesale prices can be deduced from these data.[16] Fortunately, accounts of daily purchases, specifying the quantity and price of each commodity, by the Pennsylvania Hospital from the mid-1750s until well into the nineteenth century provide a wealth of information about the retail prices of food and the consumption standards of Philadelphia's lower sort.[17]

The hospital's purchases reveal that Philadelphians could select from an impressive variety of food. Flour, bran, oats, barley, and rice products constituted a large part of their diet; they also dined on fresh and salted pork, mutton, veal, beef (including calf's head), chicken, goose, turkey, pigeon, and rabbit, as well as such seafoods as shad, herring, oysters, and clams. Vegetables included white and sweet potatoes, turnips, parsnips, corn, beans, peas, asparagus, and cucumbers, and Philadelphians ate apples, oranges, peaches, lemons, raisins, currants, and cranberries in season. Butter, cheese, and eggs seem to have been plentiful, while salt, pepper, mustard, horseradish, sugar, molasses, syrup, and vinegar were used to flavor food. The Quaker City residents washed all this down with milk, coffee, several types of tea, chocolate, and unfermented cider, and they lifted their spirits with hard cider, rum (both the local and the more expensive West Indian variety), wine, and "small" and "strong" beer.

The cost of items purchased by the hospital provides an annual average retail price of each foodstuff during the second half of the century.[18] To construct an accurate food-budget index that measures the cost of food for an individual or family, a weighting system based on the quantity of each of the foodstuffs consumed is necessary. For the purposes of the present investigation, reliable food consumption patterns of Philadelphia's lower sort can be derived from the records of the Pennsylvania Hospital. Because the hospital was a publicly funded institution established for the poor, and because it experienced continuous financial problems, we may reasonably assume that the types and proportions of foods eaten by laboring Philadelphians resembled the diet of the patients.[19]

To establish a reliable laborer's diet, I have computed the proportion of each of the nineteen most common foodstuffs purchased by the hospital in 1772.[20] The caloric requirements of laboring Philadelphians have been used to determine the amount of each food they consumed. Nutritionists consider that a twentieth-century man of average physical activity needs between 3,000 and 3,200 calories each day; men engaged in heavy labor require approximately 4,550.[21] Men of the colonial period perhaps needed somewhat fewer calories because of their slightly smaller stature, though this may well have been offset by the additional energy required in the absence of modern labor-saving machinery.[22] It seems unlikely that an eighteenth-century laborer could long have been adequately sustained on fewer than 3,000 to 3,200 calories daily. Accordingly, I have constructed a diet of 3,000–3,200 calories in which the nineteen foodstuffs were consumed in the same proportion as they were purchased by the Pennsylvania Hospital (table 1).[23]

Although the method of establishing this diet is not completely satisfactory, comparisons with other real and estimated patterns of food consumption indicate that the Philadelphia laborer's diet was minimal in both quality and cost. Grains constituted the mainstay of the American table generally. Daily rations of the Continental army in 1775 included one pound of bread and a small amount of cornmeal.[24] Prisoners in early nineteenth-century Philadelphia ate 1.25 pounds of bread, supplemented by cornmeal.[25] James T. Lemon finds that the wills of Pennsylvania farmers specified that their widows should receive five hundred pounds annually, or 1.37 pounds daily, of grain products.[26] The proposed diet of laboring Philadelphians, which allows 1.31 pounds of grains daily, closely resembles that of soldiers, prisoners, and widows. Meat furnished a significant proportion of the caloric intake of Americans. The Continental army allotted one pound of beef a day to soldiers; Philadelphia prisoners ate one-half pound; .41 pounds has been estimated as the daily fare of both Pennsylvania widows and American adults generally.[27] The laborer's diet, as constructed, includes

Table 1. Estimated Philadelphia Laborer's Diet

Foodstuff	Annual Quantity Consumed	Daily Caloric Intake	1762 Cost per Week in Pence
Wheat flour[a]	365.0 lb.	1600	12.73
Cornmeal	45.0 lb.	199	.71
Rice	15.7 lb.	68	.68
Bran	52.6 lb.	110	.69
Meat		528	11.65
beef	100.2 lb.		
mutton	18.2 lb.		
pork	9.1 lb.		
veal	47.0 lb.		
Potatoes	6.6 lb.	7	.19
Turnips	27.6 lb.	12	.50
Butter	12.8 lb.	117	5.09
Milk	38.1 gal.	281	7.81
Salt	21.9 lb.	[b]	.37
Pepper	.1 lb.	[b]	.06
Sugar	16.8 lb.	83	2.16
Molasses	4.9 gal.	174	3.16
Beverages			.92
coffee	.7 lb.	[b]	
tea	.2 lb.	[b]	
chocolate	.2 lb.	[b]	
Total		3179	46.72

[a]Includes both middling and common flour.
[b]Not included in caloric calculations.

.48 pounds of meat daily, similar to that of prisoners and widows, and to the overall American consumption, but not quite half the rations of soldiers. Contemporary comments indicating that "most labourers and mechanics eat a portion of [meat] at breakfast and supper" suggest that, if anything, the diet estimate cuts the meat allotment to the bone.[28] Milk, sugar, and molasses served as less important energy sources. Most Americans apparently drank milk even though it soured quickly in warm weather. Both Bostonians of the "middling figure" in the early eighteenth century and Continental soldiers during the Revolution consumed a quart daily; Philadelphia laborers are estimated to have drunk .4 quart per day.[29] Sugar and molasses were important food flavorings, and the latter was also used in making the "small beer" popular among Pennsylvanians.

If the laborer's diet included more grains and less meat than other real and estimated patterns of consumption, it was also cheaper to purchase. Retail prices gathered from the hospital records indicate that in 1762 (the base year for all the indices constructed in this essay) Philadelphians would have paid 3.88s. per week, or £10.12 per year, for the diet served up in table 1.[30] Estimates by Main and David Klingaman exceed this amount. Main puts the cost of food for a single man at £10–13 annually during this period, and Klingaman calculates the per capita food budget in Philadelphia at £11.88 per year between 1768 and 1772. The Continental army rations, because they included more meat than the diet specified in table 1, cost even more: £14.38 per year at Philadelphia 1762 prices.[31] Other miscellaneous records of expenditures for food corroborate the conservative nature of this budget.[32]

Although the diet in table 1 is imprecise, for the purposes of this study it need be only a reliable estimate, and it does appear a reasonable, if minimal, diet for Philadelphia's lower sort both in pattern of consumption and in price. In any case, minor alterations in the diet will not significantly affect the overall conclusions of this investigation.

Using this diet and the food-price series above, I have constructed a food-budget index that measures the cost of the diet in each year relative to its cost in 1762 (table 2, column 1).[33] For example, in 1762 the diet cost £10.12; in 1770 its cost was 90 percent of that, or £9.11. Food prices climbed more than 20 percent from the war years of the 1750s to 1763 (see fig. 1),[34] fell to their prewar level by the late 1760s, and then rose gradually until the outbreak of the Revolutionary War. The diet's cost was 50 percent higher during the early 1780s but decreased steadily until 1788, when it again began to rise steeply, increasing more than 100 percent by the mid-1790s.

The food-budget index functions as a barometer of a family's food expenditures. Nutritionists consider that, on average, an adult female and a child require 83 and 60 percent, respectively, of the calories needed by an adult male.[35] The median size of families in the four occupational groups in Philadelphia during the mid-1770s was four—two adults and two children—and that composition forms the basis of all computations of house-hold budgets in this article.[36] Consumption at these rates, when applied to the £10.12 cost of the diet in table 1 in 1762, produces an esti-mated family food budget of £30.66 for the base year of the food-budget index.

Even though Philadelphia was located in a grain- and animal-producing region, its people could not buy food as cheaply as might be expected. Because foodstuffs composed the primary exports of the area, overseas demand drove up local prices and caused rapid and wide fluctuations in food costs. The assize of bread, for example, was legally bound to the price of wheat or flour, and as the export prices of those commodities increased, so did the price of loaves in the city's bakeries.[37]

During difficult times, laboring families adopted several strategies to trim food costs. They could produce their own food, although the crowded alleys where most lived made gardening impractical and the possession of a cow even less feasible.[38] Many undoubtedly kept hogs, notching their ears for identification and allowing them to roam freely through the streets to feed on garbage. Poorer Philadelphians most often reduced their food costs by eating larger quantities of flour, cornmeal, and rice, foods with the highest caloric yield for the money. Carried to its extreme—the consumption of grains only—a family food budget could be trimmed by as much as 45 percent, though this resulted in a bland, unnutritious diet. Such a strategy would have been debilitating, increasing susceptibility to the diseases that plagued the city.[39] "Most who are used to hard labour without doors begin to fail soon after [age] thirty," one contemporary wrote, "especially if they have been obliged to live on a poor diet that afforded but little nourishment or was unwholesome."[40]

The cost of shelter constituted the second major component of the household budget. Constables' returns and tax assessors' reports for various years provide sufficient data to construct an index of rents (table 2, column 2).[41] Laboring families lived predominantly as tenants and boarders; fewer than one in ten owned their homes.[42] In 1767, laborers, mariners, cordwainers, and tailors paid average annual rents of £10.08, £11.86, £21.98, and £22.81, respectively. During the decade before Independence housing costs remained stable, as cheap dwellings multiplied on the outskirts of the city. Rents of poorer Philadelphians doubled during the Revolutionary War, reflecting the general inflation, declined during the Confederation era, and then climbed slightly during the following decade.

Table 2. Household Budget Indices (Base Year = 1762)

Year	(1) Food-Budget Index: 19 Items Weighted by Laborer's Diet	(2) Rent Index	(3) Firewood Price Index[b]	(4) Clothing Price Index	(5) Household Budget Index[e]
1754	94		59[c]	92	89[f]
1755	89		60	83	84[f]
1756	99		52		92[g]
1757	98[a]		78[c]		95[g]
1758	80[a]		56[c]		76[g]
1759	89		95[c]		90[g]
1760	95		91		94[g]
1761	86		88		86[g]
1762	100	100	100	100	100
1763	115		91	100	107
1764	101		116[c]	94	102
1765	91		96[c]	82	94
1766	90		58[c]	73	90
1767	94	112	81[c]	88	96
1768	86		71	81	90
1769	81		71	83	88
1770	90		73	88	94
1771	96		71	79	95
1772	99		91	85	99
1773	90		76[d]	76	92
1774	100		61	79	96
1775	89	111	76	80	92
1776	97		82	251	121
1783	154	252	118	188	180
1784	147		160	99	164
1785	123		116	92	143
1786	124		111	110	142
1787	119		105	99	134
1788	99		74	139	123
1789	107	165	76	82	115
1790	134		79	92	131
1791	130		97	92	131
1792	131		106	110	136
1793	143		111	119	144
1794	161		130	137	158
1795	207		197	114	186
1796	227		215	132	201
1797	192		212	150	185
1798	183	184	182	129	176
1799	188		174	105	174
1800	201		177	125	185

[a] Interpolated from the wholesale cost of nine food items in Anne Bezanson, Robert D. Gray, and Miriam Hussey, *Prices in Colonial Pennsylvania* (Philadelphia, 1935), 422–23.

[b] Includes oak and pine wood only. Mean prices for April, May, and June of each year are used to construct the index unless otherwise indicated.

[c] Index based on mean price for entire year.

[d] Interpolated from price in 1772 and 1774.

[e] Budget based on expenditure for food, fuel, clothing, and rent unless otherwise indicated.

[f] Based on food, fuel, and clothing costs.

[g] Based on food, fuel, and rent costs.

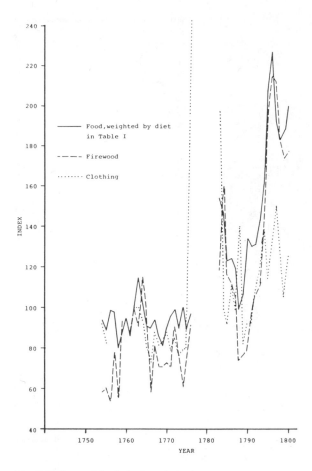

Fig. 1. Indices of food, fuel, and clothing costs, Philadelphia, 1750–1800.

Laboring Philadelphians commonly crowded into small, narrow, wooden houses (fig. 2). Typically, Philip Mager, a tailor with a wife and four children, leased a two-story wooden tenement twelve feet wide and eighteen feet deep. Mariner Richard Crips and his family rented an eleven-by-fourteen foot, single-story dwelling in the northern suburbs. In his two-story wooden box, eighteen feet square, in Harmony Alley, tailor William Smith may have found himself in even more cramped quarters. Like many other poor men, he did not have a separate kitchen, so his wife prepared meals in the fireplace not only for their three children but also for two boarders.[43] Many families saved expenses by taking in lodgers or by doubling up with other families. Laborer Martin Summers and his family, for example, lived with cordwainer Henry Birkey, his wife, and three chil-

dren, and divided the £18 annual rent. With his wife and four young children, Christian Fight, a Knight of St. Crispin, shared his abode and £12 lease with fellow shoemaker Christian Nail and his family.[44] By contrast, wealthier citizens frequently occupied three-story brick houses of comparable width but two or three times as deep, with such outbuildings as kitchens, wash houses, and stables (fig. 3). Many owned two-story brick kitchens of a size equal to or greater than most of the dwellings of the lower sort.[45]

Before the Revolutionary War, laboring Philadelphians inhabited back alleys and rooming houses scattered throughout the city, though they tended to congregate on its perimeters. As the rapidly expanding population pressed on available housing, central-city estate values rose and tenements were hurriedly constructed in the suburbs. During the final quarter of the century poorer Philadelphians radiated increasingly to the fringe areas of the city—to Mulberry Ward and the Northern Liberties in the north (fig. 4), and Dock Ward and Southwark in the south. A 1795 ordinance prohibiting the erection of wooden structures in the city both reflected and stimulated residential change. Judged from the ratio of taxpayers to houses, conditions in poorer areas must have deteriorated during the second half of the century. In Mulberry Ward the number of houses rose at an annual rate of 2.5 percent, while taxpayers increased by 3.1 percent each year; simultaneously, both houses and taxpayers grew by only .4 percent annually in Walnut Ward in the middle of the city.[46] By the close of the century, expensive two- and three-story brick houses filled the center of the city, while laborers and less-skilled artisans crowded into frame tenements in the fringe wards and suburbs (fig. 5). Though still blurred, a distinctly modern pattern of residential segregation by economic strata began to emerge by 1800.[47]

Philadelphians cooked their meals and heated their homes with firewood, an essential ingredient in their household budgets. Private business documents and records of the Pennsylvania Hospital permit the construction of an index of firewood prices (table 2, column 3).[48] Only the costs of oak and pine are tabulated, for these were the cheapest available fuels and the ones most likely used by the lower sort. The cost of wood spiraled upward from the war years of the 1750s to a peak in 1764 (see fig. 1), plummeted for the next two years, then fluctuated until Independence. Like food prices and house rents, firewood

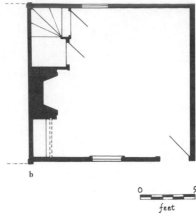

Fig. 2. *a*, Wood-framed houses of laboring people, 726–728 South Front Street, Philadelphia, ca. 1750 (now destroyed). (Photograph courtesy of the Philadelphia Historical Commission.) *b*, plan of one-room house built by Robert Moffatt, waterman, at 33½ Catherine Street, Southwark, Philadelphia, ca. 1790. (Drawing by Robert Blair St. George after original in Historic American Building Survey.)

Fig. 3. *a*, Town residence of merchant Samuel Powell, originally built for merchant Charles Stedman, now at 244 South Third Street, Philadelphia, ca. 1765–66. The grandest Georgian town house of its day, this house boasted ornate plaster-work ceilings, marble fireplace surrounds, and some of the finest furniture in colonial Philadelphia. (Photograph by Robert Blair St. George.) *b*, plan of first floor. (Drawing by Robert Blair St. George.)

Fig. 4. Brick rental houses for laboring people, 530–534 Quarry Street, Northern Liberties, Philadelphia, ca. 1760–80. (Photograph courtesy of the Philadelphia Historical Commission; taken Mar. 23, 1931.)

prices climbed during the Revolutionary War, declined during the 1780s, and rose again in the subsequent decade.

In 1762 Philadelphians spent an average of 22s. 11d. for the cheapest cord during the spring months. Poorer citizens, frequently buying quantities smaller than a full cord and most often during the winter, when prices were at their peak, may well have paid two or three times that amount.[49] The quantity of wood burned by a typical household is difficult to determine because of the paucity of evidence and seasonal variations in the use of fuel. Four journeyman silversmiths employed by John Fitch each burned an average of 4.88 cords annually from 1772 to 1775.[50]

This appears at least a fair indication of use by laboring Philadelphians; much less would hardly have sufficed for their cooking and heating requirements, particularly in their drafty wooden homes. Thus a poor family spent a substantial sum, an estimated £5.60 in 1762, for fuel.[51]

The great demand for wood by both private and commercial users undoubtedly drove up its cost. Households alone burned more than 20,000 cords in 1772. Bakers, brickmakers, blacksmiths, and iron manufacturers likewise needed fuel, while coopers, house carpenters, shipwrights, and lumber exporters must have added to the city's wood requirements. So vital was firewood that local regulations proscribed its purchase for resale in the city between September and March.[52] As the forests surrounding the city were depleted, small boats brought wood from New Jersey

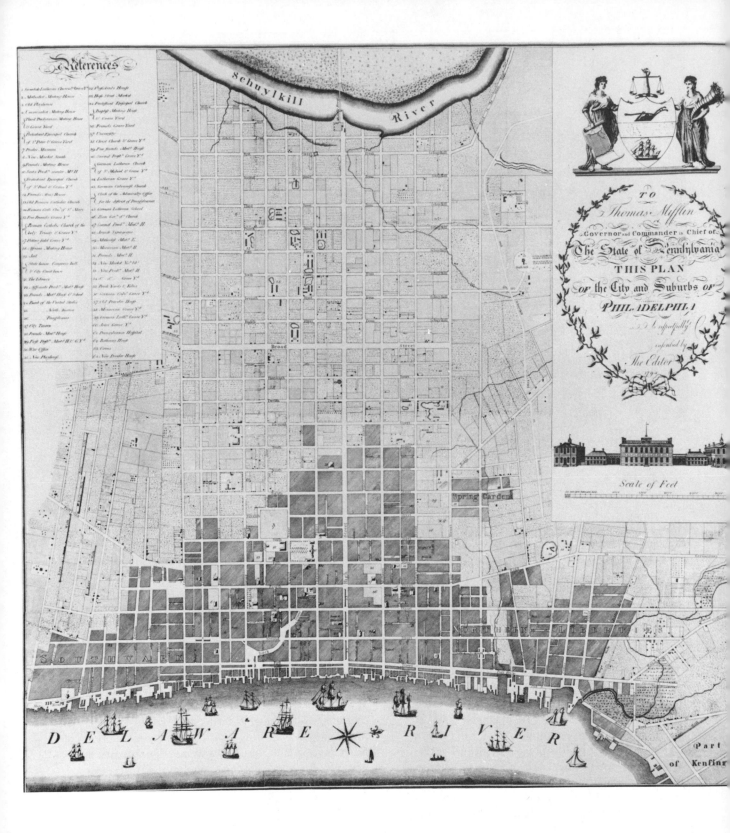

and the Delaware Valley; as the carrying distance increased, so did the price of fuel. The problem evoked numerous charity drives to supply wood to the city's poor, as well as recurrent demands to regulate the amount charged by carters and boatmen for carrying firewood.[53]

Reasonable estimates of clothing costs can be made. The city's workhouse spent at least £3 annually to outfit John Peter Operting, a "labouring lunatic," during the 1760s. Main has calculated £4.17 as an average annual clothing allowance for adult males during this period.[54] In 1770, the most essential and least expensive attire could be purchased in Philadelphia for about £3.74. For that sum a man could buy a pair of coarse laborer's shoes (9s.), a pair of stockings (2s. 6d.), a pair of cloth breeches (15s. 7d.), a cloth coat (29s. 5d.), two shirts (6s. 2d. each), and a felt hat (6s.).[55] This wardrobe would have been minimal, not quite equaling the standard of dress annually issued to the inmates of the city's almshouse during the early nineteenth century and far inferior to the silk garments fashionable among wealthier citizens.[56] If materials were purchased, and the coat, breeches, and shirts made at home, clothing costs could be cut to £2.5.[57] This figure, 40 percent below Main's estimate, can be used to compute the clothing costs for a laboring family. The price of women's dress probably matched that of men's, while cordwainers' and tailors' records indicate that children's shoes, breeches, and coats cost about 70 percent of those of men.[58] Thus in 1770 a laboring family of four would have spent roughly £8.5 for clothing. Prices for basic articles of clothing other than shoes are unavailable for the entire period, but an index constructed from the cost of materials—thread, flax, tow, flannel, and linen—for certain articles of apparel (stockings, breeches, shirts, and coats) can serve as a proxy for the changes in the cost of clothing.[59] This index, combined with the price index of shoes and each index weighed according to its proportion of the 1770 clothing budget estimate given above, provides a clothing-price index (table 2, column 4) graphed in figure 1.

The family budget for laborers, mariners, cordwainers, and tailors constructed from calculations of the price of food, rent, fuel, and clothing averaged £60.82 in 1762.[60] The costs of the items in this budget are below other observed costs and estimates made by other historians. Not only is the budget thus minimized, but many necessities for a "decent competency" are excluded. Rum, apparently a vital element of the lives of eighteenth-century Americans,[61] may have cost laboring Philadelphians £3 annually but has not been included in the household budget. Taxes likewise are excluded; they amounted to £2–3 per year for poorer Philadelphians at the end of the colonial period.[62] Although the Pennsylvania Hospital provided low-cost services, medical treatment was expensive. Smallpox variolation cost £3, not including wages lost during the required quarantine period of one or two weeks, and the inoculation had to be renewed every four or five years.[63] Death imposed a financial burden; in the early 1760s interment in private cemeteries could cost as much £11.[64] Childbearing also was dear: midwives charged about 15s. before the Revolutionary War.[65] All of these necessities, along with soap, starch, candles, chamber pots, brooms, cutlery, and furniture, have been excluded from the estimated budget.

The index of the average household budget of the four occupational groups, which measures the relative cost of purchasing the 1762 budget in nearly every year from 1754 to 1800, appears in table 2, column 5, and is graphed in figure 6.[66] The cost of this budget increased sharply toward the end of the French and Indian War, fell precipitously in 1765 to its prewar level, and rose gradually during the following decade. The significant jump in 1776 marked the beginning of the exorbitant inflation during the Revolutionary War. The index plummeted from 1783 to 1789, then climbed rapidly to a peak more than twice as high as in the 1770s.

*　　*　　*

Laborers, mariners, cordwainers, tailors, and their families frequently found it hard to earn enough money to meet their basic expenses. Relatively low wages (compared to the cost of living) and irregular employment made life unpredictable for laboring people and undercut their attempts to achieve more

Fig. 5. *Plan of the City and Suburbs of Philadelphia,* engraving by R. Scot and S. Allardice, 1794. The shaded area in the map's center represents the densely settled portion of the city. Adjacent to the river at the left is the city's Southwark section, to the right the Northern Liberties. (Photograph courtesy of The Historical Society of Pennsylvania.)

Table 3. Indices of Laborers' Wages (Base Year = 1762)

Year	Laborers' Actual Wages	Laborers' Real Wages	Number of Observations	Sources
1751	92		6	a
1752	90		11	a
1753	89		15	a
1754	86	97	18	a,i
1755	85	101	28	a,b,c
1756	92	100	11	a
1757	92	97	1	c
1758	90	118	13	b,c
1759	92	102	7	b,d
1760	118	126	34	b,e,m,p,t
1761	116	135	3	r,v
1762	100	100	17	b,c,k,p,w
1763	90	84	18	b,h,p,y
1764	86	84	12	b,c,f,m,x
1765	92	98	3	b,c,k
1766	105	117	6	b,f,k
1767	105	109	10	b,f,k
1768	101	112	11	f,k,m,s
1769	84	95	14	b,c,j,m
1770	89	95	35	b,m,n,q
1771	87	92	12	b,n
1772	82	83	5	b,z
1773	68	74	12	b,n,o,z
1774	79	82	13	b,m
1775	74	80	13	b
1776	93	77	8	b,m
1783	125	69	9	b,x
1784	110	67	22	b,u,x,z[1]
1785	126	88	57	b,l,n,u,x,z[1]
1786	120	84	16	b,u,x
1787	104	78	29	b,u,x,z[1]
1788	117	95	15	b,u
1789	88	77	17	b,m,x,z[1]
1790	86	66	14	b,l,z[1]
1791	97	74	25	b,g,z[1]
1792	119	88	15	b,z[1]
1793	117	81	11	b,n,z[1]
1794	143	90	28	b,z[1]
1795	174	94	12	b,l,z[1]
1796	170	85	12	b,z[1]
1797	178	96	2	b,z[1]
1798	197	112	9	b,z[1]
1799	197	113	11	b,z[1]
1800	162	88	10	b,l,z[1]

The location for all sources below is The Historical Society of Pennsylvania, Philadelphia, unless otherwise noted.

a. Bills and receipts, Coates and Reynell Papers, Boxes 1751–54 and 1755–67.
b. Matron and Steward's Cash Books, Pennsylvania Hospital Records, American Philosophical Society, Philadelphia.
c. Minutes of the County Commissioners.
d. Ledger of Isaac Zane, 1748–59.

than a minimal degree of physical well-being or economic security. The following section compares the wages and incomes of the four groups with the cost of their household budget and considers the factors responsible for their struggle to maintain their subsistence.

Contradicting Carl Bridenbaugh's contention that "few day laborers . . . were to be found in any [colonial] city," Philadelphia's tax lists reveal that laborers formed the second largest occupational group in the city, their number exceeded only by mariners.[67] Laborers composed between 5 and 14 percent of taxpayers during the second half of the century. Their proportion of the working population undoubtedly was greater than this percentage, however, because many

poorer citizens were excused from paying taxes and many taxpayers with undesignated occupations probably were unskilled. Laborers were concentrated at the very bottom of the tax hierarchy: in 1772, assessors appraised nine of every ten laborers at the minimum rate. Many worked in construction or shipbuilding or hauled goods to and from ships, warehouses, and stores; others found jobs in breweries and distilleries or as street pavers, hay mowers, potato diggers, dung spreaders, whitewashers, swamp drainers, sawyers, chimney sweeps, and the like.

Using data on laborers' earnings contained in the ledgers of the Pennsylvania Hospital, government records, and a host of private business accounts, I have constructed an index of laborers' actual wages, and I have used the household budget index as an inflationary scale to produce an index of laborers' real wages (table 3).[68] Real wages peaked during the French and Indian War (fig. 7), plunged during the last two years of that conflict, rose during the mid-1760s, and then declined steadily during the last dec-

Notes to table 3, cont.

e. Clifford Papers, Correspondence, vol. 2, 1760–62.
f. Account Book, Folder: Brigantine *Elizabeth* Accounts, Richard Waln Collection.
g. Dutilh and Wachsmuth Papers, Miscellaneous Box 1704–1800, folder 32.
h. Isaac Norris Cash Book.
i. The accounts of building the addition to the statehouse in the early 1750s are in the Norris Fairhill Papers.
j. Minutes of the Friendship Carpenter's Company, 1768–76.
k. Minutes of the Commissioners for Paving Streets.
l. U.S. Department of Labor, "Wages and Hours of Labor," *Bulletin of the United States Bureau of Labor Statistics*, vol. 128 (Washington, D.C., 1913), 21.
m. Bill, receipts, and accounts, Shippen Family Papers, vols. 28–30.
n. Cadwalader Collection, Incoming Correspondence, bills and receipts, Boxes 1–6, 12–14.
o. Ledgers of Joshua Humphreys, 1766–77, 1772–73, 1784–1805, Joshua Humphreys Papers.
p. Ledger of Mifflin and Massey, 1760–63.
q. Journal of John and Peter Chevalier.
r. Ledger of Joseph Wharton, Wharton Papers.
s. Business Papers of Levy Hollingsworth, Hollingsworth Collection, Sec. 7: bills, 1751–89; Sec. 3: invoices, 1764–89.
t. Samuel Morris Day Book, 1755–67, and Ledgers, 1755–72, 1761–63.
u. Thomas A. Biddle Shipbook.
v. Forde and Reed Papers.
w. Account of Richard Meadow, Ball Papers.
x. Business Records of Stephen Girard, American Philosophical Society, Philadelphia.
y. Philip Benezet's Account with Sloop *Sally*, Dreer Collection.
z. *Minutes of the Supreme Executive Council of Pennsylvania: Colonial Records of Pennsylvania* (Harrisburg, Pa., 1852).
z[1]. Donald R. Adams, Jr., "Wage Rates in Philadelphia, 1790–1830" (Ph.D. diss., University of Pennsylvania, 1967).

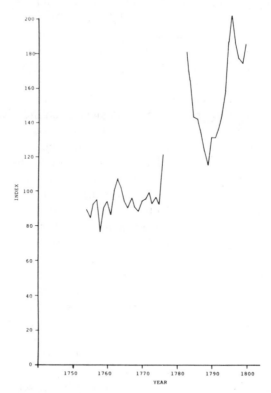

Fig 6. Index of household budgets for laboring Philadelphians, 1750–1800.

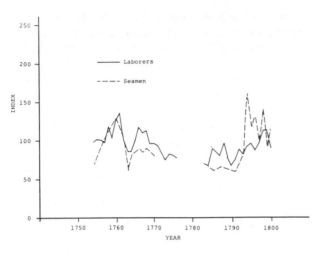

Fig. 7. Index of real wages for unskilled laborers and seamen, Philadelphia, 1750–1800.

ade before the Revolutionary War. Although they fluctuated, real wages in the 1780s approximated those of the 1770s and began to rise during the final decade of the century.

If employed for six days each week throughout the year, a laborer would have earned £59.3 in 1762, the base year of the wage indices. Because this hypothetical annual income assumes full employment, however, it must be considered a high figure, rarely if ever attained. The supply of jobs depended on a variety of factors, among them the cycles of nature that affected activity in the city nearly as much as on the farm. Severe winter weather halted maritime commerce, shipbuilding, and housing construction. Ice in the Delaware River, as well as the seasonal shipment of agricultural produce, caused ship arrivals during January and February to average less than a third their usual number for the rest of the year.[69] Jobs for outdoor workers declined correspondingly. Newspaper and broadside commentators characterized winter as a season when the city had "little occasion . . . for the labour of the Poor," and when "for want of Employment, many . . . are reduced to great Straits and rendered burthensome to their neighbors."[70] Thus when laborer James Thompson for "want of work" entered the almshouse in January 1789, he joined many laboring Philadelphians in similar circumstances who annually swelled the ranks of the institutional poor during the winter months.[71] Cyclical variations in the cost of living corresponded to the seasonality of employment. During the winter,

firewood prices often doubled or tripled, and the variety of foodstuffs available in the markets narrowed, restricting the options of the lower sort in limiting their food budgets. "Winter is fast approaching," wrote John Edgworth, a laborer, "whose dire effects the very Rich and oppulent will feel, much more [the] poor."[72] Another Philadelphian noted that "collections (time immemorial) have been made every winter, either by means of charity sermons among the different sects, or private subscriptions, for the poor."[73]

Epidemics, illness, and injury also limited the regularity of work. Recurrent smallpox and yellow fever epidemics caused mass evacuations of the city, so that laboring people who, in the words of one observer, "have neither place to remove to, or funds for their support," were left without work for long periods until panic subsided.[74] It is sadly ironic that during the 1790s, just as laborers' wages increased, their earning capacity was badly disrupted by the serious epidemics of that decade. Philadelphians who worked outdoors were peculiarly susceptible to such ailments as rheumatism and frostbite, and to on-the-job injuries. And, as a contributor to the *Pennsylvania Journal* observed, "a labouring man, who has a wife and children, if he falls into sickness . . . falls into distress."[75] Thus laborer Eneos Lyon, injured while sinking a pump and rendered "incapable of labouring for a livelyhood," had little choice but to enter the almshouse. When mariner Thomas Loudon was admitted, the almshouse clerk noted that he suffered from the "casualties, and accidents in his Way of life, and the vicissitudes of fortune to which such men are liable seems now to manifest itself."[76]

Cyclical variations in the city's economy also influenced the amount of work available to unskilled workers. Two examples will suffice. Economic dislocations following the French and Indian War curtailed employment opportunities for many poor citizens. In 1764 city leaders complained about the "want of Employment, which was reducing a large number of residents to great Straits."[77] Two years later, Philadelphia's grand jury admitted that many "labouring People & others in low Circumstances . . . who are Willing to work cannot obtain sufficient Employment."[78] During the 1790s, on the other hand, Philadelphia's rapidly expanding maritime commerce brought a high demand for the services of laborers and mariners.[79]

A comparison of incomes and household budgets discloses the nature of the struggle to make ends meet. In 1762, a laborer would have spent about £55 for food, rent, fuel, and clothing for himself and his family. If fully employed, his total annual wages of nearly £60 met these basic expenses. If he were partially employed (a more reasonable assumption) for five out of every six work days, or ten of every twelve months, his income fell £6 shy of these necessities. Other members of his family therefore had to work to secure its subsistence. For example, Rachel, the wife of weaver James Brown, made rifle cartridges and soldiers' clothing during the Revolutionary War to earn needed money.[80] After the war, laborer Samuel Cryndal found that in addition to "what little he Earned . . . his wife's Industry" was essential for his family to make "out a living although a very Poor one."[81] Women toiled for the Pennsylvania Hospital as nurses, clothes washers, chimney sweeps, potato diggers, cooks, maids, whitewashers, soap makers, and bakers, and in wealthier homes as servants. The range of money-making activities for children was more limited. They gathered twigs to sell for firewood, tended cattle, and carried dairy produce from the countryside. Children in poorer households undoubtedly were often apprenticed at a young age because of the financial burden they posed.

Limited evidence suggests that women received roughly one-half the wages of men, and children somewhat less than that.[82] A working woman in 1762 thus might have contributed an additional £25 to the household. This would have covered the deficit for the four necessities and the extra expenses of taxes, medical bills, candles, soap, and other miscellaneous items, while perhaps even providing a few luxuries such as rum, tobacco, or "sweet meats." This degree of comfort was most likely to have been achieved when the index of real wages was one hundred or greater, as during the French and Indian War, the mid-1760s, and the late 1790s.

Much more prevalent was a situation in which the income of a family barely matched the cost of basic necessities. This condition characterized the postwar depression of 1762–65 and most of the 1770s, 1780s, and early 1790s, when real wages fluctuated 20–25 percent below their 1762 level and posed severe economic problems for laborers and their families. At the partial level of employment assumed above, a laborer's earnings would have averaged £14 below the cost of essentials. The combined income of husband and wife would barely have covered food, fuel, rent, and clothing, and the few remaining pounds could not have met additional expenses, much less permit savings or minor luxuries.[83]

Unskilled workers and their families in Philadelphia generally lived on the edge of, or occasionally slightly above, the subsistence level; simply to maintain that level both spouses had to work. Life was hard at the best of times and disastrous at the worst. Consequently, institutional aid to the poor rose to unprecedented levels during the second half of the century.[84] When Hugh Porter's rheumatism became inflamed, Lenoard [sic] Croneman broke his thigh, and John Drew suffered frostbitten feet, they joined hundreds of laborers who depended on public or private assistance for fuel, clothing, and food.[85] Others, like laborer Samuel Cryndal, were forced to take more drastic measures; his financial problems during the post-Revolutionary depression "obliged him to bind his Eldest child out, tho very young," because Cryndal could not support the boy.[86]

A detailed examination of the causes of variations in real wages and material conditions is beyond the scope of this study, but some tentative explanations can be offered. The supply of unskilled laborers and the demand for their services determined their economic condition. Migration patterns influenced the size of the labor pool, while fluctuations in the city's economy, particularly in maritime commerce, housing construction, and shipbuilding—the areas in which most unskilled workers were employed—defined the demand side of the economic equation. During the quarter century preceding the Revolutionary War, Philadelphia's population, augmented by heavy European immigration, grew faster than these three sectors of its economy. Between 1756 and 1774, laborers increased from 5 to 14 percent of the taxable work force. Simultaneously, when the volume of the three economic sectors is measured on a per capita basis—the best available indicator of the relative numbers of jobs in these areas—one finds that Philadelphia's maritime commerce remained stagnant, housing construction grew only slightly, and shipbuilding declined. This accounts for much of the gradual decrease in laborers' real wages before the Revolutionary War.[87]

After booming briefly at the close of the war, the city's shipbuilding and maritime commerce slumped during the 1780s, and the housing industry remained dormant throughout the decade. The real wages of laborers, who composed a constant 7 percent of the taxable workforce, were correspondingly depressed until the early 1790s. Better times returned with the outbreak of hostilities between France and England in 1793. Philadelphia's neutral carrying and re-export trades flourished, and this commercial expansion underlay much of the vigorous shipbuilding and housing construction during the decade. As laborers declined from 7 percent of the work force in 1789 to 5 percent in 1798, their real wages and material conditions improved.

Mariners composed the largest occupational group in the city during the late eighteenth century, accounting for as much as 20 percent of the free male work force on the eve of the Revolutionary War. They numbered only about 5 percent of taxpayers, since their mobility and poverty excluded the vast majority of them from the tax rolls.[88] Only 164 seamen appear on the 1772 tax list, for example, but other sources indicate a much greater number of sailors in the city. During the 1770s, about two hundred ship captains belonged to Philadelphia's Society for the Relief of Poor and Distressed Masters of Ships, Their Widows and Children.[89] Since vessels averaged approximately six crew members, the city probably contained roughly 1,200 merchant seamen in the early years of the decade. Between July 1, 1770, and July 1, 1771, custom officials collected a tax of 71,164 pence from Philadelphia sailors at the rate of sixpence for each month they drew wages.[90] This suggests a total of 1,186 seamen in the city, assuming each mariner worked ten months during the year, and a larger number if they worked less than that. Corroborating this estimate is a remark by the customs house officer in 1770 that "there are not less than a thousand Seamen here at this time."[91]

Most sailors were concentrated at the bottom of the economic ladder of freemen; tax collectors assessed 70 percent of them the minimum tax in 1772. A sizable majority of Philadelphia mariners spent a considerable portion of their lives as common seamen, forming a kind of deep-sea proletariat. Some of the rest came from farms near the city and served only briefly before the mast, while others occasionally signed on for short voyages and worked in less-skilled jobs when ashore. Most mariners were men with few skills, lured to the sea neither by a sense of adventure nor by hopes for advancement but by the opportunity for employment.[92]

From mariners' wage rates recorded by merchants engaged in the overseas trade, I have constructed indices of the actual wages of seamen, mates, and captains, and, deflating by the household budget, an index of seamen's real wages (table 4).[93] In 1762, common seamen earned an average of £4.1 per month, and mates £5.4.[94] The maximum annual income of seamen, £49, fell short of the cost of the four basic necessities and also of the maximum earnings of day laborers. Longer periods of continual employment and the food and lodging supplied sailors on board ship somewhat offset this difference. As with laborers, however, periodic unemployment prevented seamen from earning the maximum income. Job opportunities varied seasonally; mariners paid only 12 percent of their taxes during the winter months. More important was the turnaround time of ships in port, on the order of thirty-six days in Philadelphia at midcentury.[95] In foreign ports sailors filled part of that slack period unloading and stowing cargo. In Philadelphia, however, in the words of an Admiralty Court judge, "merchants find it more for their interest . . . to hire other than the mariners to lade and unlade vessels" because it was cheaper to employ stevedores by the day than to pay the crew monthly wages and supply them with provisions.[96]

Living on the edge of subsistence, merchant seamen with families faced many of the same economic problems as did laborers. When John Machman was unable to get a berth on a ship during winter, when John Quail suffered from rheumatism and venereal disease, when James Union came down with a fever, they landed in the almshouse, and their families suffered. Mary Lewis and Mary Winger, wives of sailors on the frigate *City of Philadelphia* in 1800, ended up in the almshouse when unable to support themselves, the former because she was pregnant and the latter because she was ill. Even mariners' wives who had jobs struggled to provide for themselves and their children. When a constable picked up eight-year-old William Thomas for begging in the street, the boy explained that while his father "has been gone to sea" his mother "goes out washing of Cloaths for a livelihood . . .[and] leaves him at home to take care of his Brother." When his brother cried from hunger, William went soliciting bread.[97]

The pay of mariners responded to fluctuations in

Table 4. Indices of Mariners' Wages (Base Year = 1762)

Year	Seamen's Actual Wages	Seamen's Real Wages	Mates' Actual Wages	Captains' Actual Wages
1750	73		79	80
1751	72		79	80
1752	69		78	80
1753	65		79	80
1754	61	69	74	80
1755	67	80	74	80
1756	85	92	84	80
1757	98	103		107
1759	109	121		107
1760	121	129	130	
1762	100	100	100	100
1763	67	63	93	107
1764	83	81	91	93
1765	79	84	93	93
1766	79	88	93	93
1767	82	85	93	93
1768	81	90	93	93
1770	76	81	86	93
1772				93
1784	109	66	139	160
1785	82	57	130	133
1786	82	58	112	107
1787	80	60	93	107
1789				100
1790	77	59	93	120
1791	77	59	93	120
1792	95	70	95	113
1793	121	84	125	120
1794	255	161		
1795	218	117	216	
1796	264	131	209	180
1797	182	98	233	250
1798	246	140	223	250
1799	155	89	265	250
1800	209	113	233	250

Sources: Coates and Reynell Papers, Boxes 1751–54; Clifford Papers, Correspondence, vol. 2, 1760–62; Account Book, Folder: Brigantine *Elizabeth* Accounts, Richard Waln Collection; Ships and Shipping Folder, Etting Papers; Customs House Papers; Dutilh and Wachsmuth Papers, Miscellaneous Boxes 1726–1856 and 1704–1800; Thomas Mason's Journal, 1775, Miscellaneous Letters of Thomas and John Mason, Henry Pleasant's Papers; Journal of John and Peter Chevalier; Philip Benezet's Account with Sloop *Sally*, Dreer Collection; Biddle Shipbook, 1784–92—all at HSP; Business Records of Girard, American Philosophical Society; Adams, "Wage Rates in Philadelphia," 213.

the city's economy in much the same fashion as did that of laborers. The demand for sailors, and the significant role that war played in shaping that demand, were key factors determining their material comfort. Their wages were abnormally high during the French and Indian War, partly because privateering attracted many men who hoped to strike it rich and left few able seamen in the city.[98] As shipping activity slackened during the early 1760s and again in the 1780s, so did mariners' wages. The boom in the export and re-export trades during the 1790s raised seamen's wages after 1793.

Cordwainers and tailors formed the two largest groups of artisans, each accounting for about 5.6 percent of the taxable workforce during the second half of the century. Although cordwainers were scattered throughout the tax structure except at the very top, most found a place near the bottom of the economic scale. Forty percent were assessed the minimum tax in 1772.

More than 250 bills for shoes contained in the Pennsylvania Hospital records and merchants' papers permit construction of individual price series for a variety of shoes. Price relatives of each of these have been weighted equally to produce a retail price index for shoes (table 5, column 1).[99] This index does not accurately indicate cordwainers' wages, since the costs of raw materials and labor are included in the price of shoes. However, this retail price index and a price index of raw materials can be employed to create an index of cordwainers' wages. According to a broadside issued during the Revolutionary War, the cost of raw materials in 1774 averaged 57 percent and labor 43 percent of the retail price of shoes.[100] The Philadelphia wholesale price index of leather, hides, and shoe leather developed by Anne Bezanson represents the cost of raw materials for shoes (table 5, column 2).[101] Using the actual price of raw materials in 1774, Bezanson's wholesale price index, and the retail price index of shoes computed above, I have calculated an index of cordwainers' wages for their labor (table 5, column 3) and, adjusting for the cost of the household budget, an index of their real wages (table 5, column 4).[102]

Except for a large increase reflecting the rapid inflation of late 1776, cordwainers' actual and real wages remained stable during the years immediately preceding Independence (see fig. 8). Real wages were markedly lower in 1783 than before the war and con-

tinued at about the same level until the early 1790s. They more than doubled in 1793 and remained relatively high for much of the rest of the period.

Though evidence is sparse, a few available sources permit rough approximations of the earnings of cordwainers. Their incomes can be estimated from information contained in their 1779 broadside and in the labor conspiracy trial of Philadelphia journeyman shoemakers in 1806. The broadside indicates that in 1774 a master cordwainer received 4s. 9d. for the craftmanship involved in each pair of shoes.[103] Journeymen testified at the trial that they produced about six pairs of common shoes per week.[104] A master thus might have earned 28.5s. weekly, or £74.1 in 1774, if fully employed. Masters collected an additional shilling on every pair made by their journeymen, so each journeyman might have contributed as much as £15.6 to his master's income in 1774.[105]

Master cordwainers enjoyed a relatively comfortable material position during most of the period. Food, rent, fuel, and clothing would have cost £62.9 in 1774. In that year a master, working without assistants, might have earned £74.1 if fully employed. Thus he would need to have been employed 85 percent of his possible working time to meet the cost of those four necessities. If he enjoyed the services of a journeyman or a few apprentices, the profits accrued from their labor would have covered his family's additional miscellaneous expenses. If he worked alone, however, earnings by his wife or children probably would have been required. Assuming that his wife could earn approximately one-half the income of a male laborer, her contribution of £19.4 would have helped to provide the four necessities and some minor luxuries, with perhaps a bit left over for savings. The relatively favorable circumstances of master cordwainers deteriorated after the Revolution. The combined incomes of husband and wife, even if both employed full-time, could not quite meet the cost of the four necessities.[106] Master cordwainers who hired journeymen, and the few who owned servants and slaves, were in the best position to survive the economic dislocations of the 1780s, but nearly all were forced to cut their living standards drastically until the early 1790s.

Journeyman cordwainers earned appreciably less than their masters. In 1774 they received 3s. 9d. for a pair of shoes, yielding £58.5 for a year of full employment. But, as they testified at their trial, work was

Production and Control of Property

Table 5. Indices of Shoe Costs and Cordwainers' Wages for Workmanship (Base Year = 1762)

Year	(1) Retail Prices of Shoes	(2) Wholesale Prices of Raw Materials	(3) Cordwainers' Actual Wages for Workmanship	(4) Cordwainers' Real Wages for Workmanship
1762	100	100	100	100
1763	115			
1764	112			
1767	92			
1768	88			
1769	88			
1770	91	90	92	98
1771	96	90	104	109
1772	97	90	106	107
1774	96	96	96	100
1775	94	97	90	98
1776	181	133	243	201
1783	103	113	88	49
1784	100	110	86	52
1785	94	103	82	57
1786	91	113	62	44
1787	87	102	64	48
1788	89	99	77	63
1789	88	101	72	63
1790	89	113	58	44
1791	90	110	63	48
1792	91	107	75	55
1793	150	107	206	143
1794	115	110	122	77
1795	151	121	190	102
1796	117	93	149	74
1797	146	86	225	122
1798	136	103	178	101
1799	113	107	131	75
1800	124	108	144	78

Sources: Bills, receipts, and accounts, Shippen Family Papers, vols. 28–30, 1754–1822; bills and receipts, Coates and Reynell Papers, HSP; Matron and Steward's Cash Books, Pennsylvania Hospital Records.

seasonal, and winter was usually a slack period.[107] Although slightly better off than common laborers, journeymen shoemakers were hard pressed to meet the £64.3 cost of basic necessities during the early 1770s. The depression of the 1780s severely affected their material condition, not only by driving wages down but by limiting the available work. Hugh Dugan, sent into the almshouse as a pauper in 1789, was one of many cordwainers forced to rely on public assistance.[108] Even during good times, journeymen made little money to spare. At their trial they declared that they earned 45s. per week, or £117 annually during the late 1790s.[109] But their estimated family budget during that period averaged £120 per year, so that their income barely matched the cost of the four necessities. As a result, a number of shoemakers, like John and Esther Dougherty and their three children, spent time in a relief institution.[110]

Shoemaking was organized on a small scale during the colonial period, and on the eve of the Revolution as many as half of Philadelphia's taxable cordwainers functioned as masters.[111] Few owned a shop; nearly all toiled at home, mainly on "bespoke work," that is, shoes made to order for local customers. Masters invested in few unfree laborers; 7 percent owned servants and only one possessed a slave in 1772, although some directed as many as three or four apprentices.[112] Through their organization of the Cordwainers Fire Company, which served as a guild, and their political activity, master cordwainers were able to control shoe prices and the wages of their journeymen and to maintain their profits at a fairly constant level before the Revolutionary War.[113] When England dumped shoes on the American market after the war, Philadelphia's cordwainers were hard hit: the profits of masters and wages of journeymen were alike depressed. Both groups consequently pushed for protective legislation for their products.

The rising demand for Philadelphia-made footwear, in conjunction with several national tariffs on shoes beginning in 1789, stimulated higher prices for shoes during the final decade of the century. Locally, the growth in the city's inhabitants, and thus their demand for shoes, outstripped the increase in the number of shoemakers. Between 1789 and 1798, the proportion of cordwainers in the taxable work force declined from 7.5 to 5.2 percent. Simultaneously, protective tariffs enlarged the national market, and European wars created a greater international need for American shoes.[114] During the 1790s, the United States shifted from a net importer of eighty thousand pairs of shoes annually to a net exporter of fifty thousand pairs.[115] Masters and journeymen struggled with one another for the greater profits on their product, as each group formed its own organization to further its interests. Their conflict culminated in America's first labor conspiracy trial in 1806.[116]

Tailors and breeches-makers were the wealthiest of the four occupational groups considered in this article, but they still clustered near the bottom of the tax hierarchy. Assessors taxed 41 percent of them the minimum rate in 1772. But one-fourth of them, those who catered to the city's wealthy citizens, appeared in the top third of the tax structure. Tailors' bills scattered through merchants' papers and the Pennsyl-

vania Hospital's records can be used to determine their earnings.[117] These bills distinguish the charge for labor from the cost of materials and are sufficiently detailed to permit construction of individual series of wages for making a number of articles of clothing.[118] Wage relatives for labor costs for sewing these articles have been weighted equally to create an index of tailors' wages (table 6, column 1). When this index is adjusted by the household budget, an index of real wages results (table 6, column 2).

Because the amount of available work fluctuated, the real wages of tailors do not translate exactly into their real incomes. But, as in the case of cordwainers, it is unlikely that wages varied inversely with demand for clothes. Real wages and real income should have been isomorphic, and changes in the former should be indicative of changes in the latter. Real wages varied little before the Revolutionary War (fig. 8), perhaps reflecting the success of the Taylors Company of Philadelphia, formed in 1771 by masters in an attempt to standardize their pay.[119] This wealthiest of the four occupational groups was hard hit after the war as real wages fell 25–40 percent and remained at a low level during the 1790s.

Tailors' incomes and living standards can be roughly approximated from the few available sources. Naturally, a crucial determinant of a tailor's income was his status as either journeyman or master. Journeymen probably made up 40 or 50 percent of the tailors in the city during the second half of the century.[120] The master tailors of the Taylors Company limited journeymen to a maximum of 4s. per day, which, assuming full employment, would have yielded £62.4 annually during the years immediately preceding the Revolutionary War.[121] Journeyman tailors thus had to work full-time at maximum wages to earn the £63 cost of essentials, but their work, like that of cordwainers, varied seasonally.[122] During the two decades following the war, their economic condition deteriorated seriously.

An appraisal of the income of master tailors is more difficult. The ledger of Joseph Graisbury records his average income from 1765 to 1769 at £182 per year, but he was one of the wealthiest tailors in the city.[123] His tax rate in 1767 exceeded the median tailor's assessment nearly fourfold, and he was even more exceptional in owning both his home and a slave. The majority of master tailors must have earned considerably less than Graisbury though still

Table 6. Indices of Tailors' Wages for Workmanship (Base Year = 1762)

Year	(1) Tailors' Actual Wages	(2) Tailors' Real Wages
1762	100	100
1763	100	93
1764	99	97
1765	98	104
1766	98	109
1767	99	103
1768	99	110
1769	97	110
1770	97	103
1771	98	103
1772	98	99
1773	99	108
1774	96	100
1775	100	109
1776	104	86
1783	132	73
1784	124	76
1785	84	59
1786	82	58
1787	78	58
1788	84	68
1789	79	69
1790	100	76
1791	82	63
1792	109	80
1793	82	57
1794	123	78
1795	90	48
1796	112	56
1797	100	54
1798	110	62
1799	102	59
1800	134	72

Sources: Bills, receipts, and accounts, Shippen Family Papers, vols. 28–30, 1754–1822; bills and receipts of John Cadwalader, Cadwalader Collection; bills and receipts, Coates and Reynell Papers; Business Papers of Hollingsworth, Hollingsworth Collection, Sec. 7: bills, 1751–89; Sec. 3: invoices, 1764–89; Samuel Morris Day Book, 1755–67; ledger of Graisbury—all at HSP; Matron and Steward's Cash Books, Pennsylvania Hospital Records.

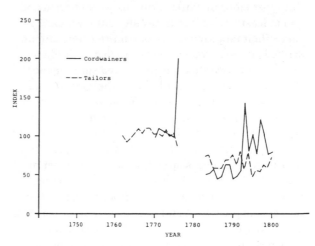

Fig. 8. Index of real wages for workmanship by cordwainers and tailors, Philadelphia, 1750–1800.

similar living standards before Independence, but tailors' real wages plummeted during the 1780s and continued at a much lower plateau during the century's final decade.

*   *   *

The findings of this study challenge the customary maxims concerning the elevated wages, comfortable material conditions, and abundant opportunities for economic advancement enjoyed by laboring people in early American urban society. Its analysis of the incomes and living costs of the lower sort in one city paints a markedly darker portrait of their economic circumstances than that generally limned by historians. A knowledge of the material position of laboring people during the latter half of the eighteenth century in British America is essential if we are to assess such vital issues as the effect of class structure on the turbulent political events of the period or the eventual impact of industrialization on the lives of Americans.

Unskilled workers and journeyman artisans in the "lesser" crafts in Philadelphia often encountered very serious difficulties in meeting their families' basic needs. Many, if not most, lived in poverty or on its edge. The severity of their struggle simply to maintain, or rise slightly above, the subsistence level depended to a great extent on the size and composition of their households. Unmarried, healthy males generally found it easy enough to earn a living wage.

more than journeymen, perhaps on the order of £100 annually during the prewar years. This estimate is congruent with the appraisal of the income of master cordwainers. Masters in both crafts probably enjoyed

But most laboring Philadelphians were married and had at least two children, usually quite young.[124] Because their employment opportunities were circumscribed and their wages low, women and children rarely could earn their keep, but as a supplement to the wages of the household head, their income was essential to the maintenance of the family. Only in the best of times, as during the French and Indian War or the late 1790s, could male heads of household in the four occupational groups earn enough money to pay for basic necessities. Those a step higher in the economic hierarchy, like master cordwainers and tailors, who were able to profit from the labor of journeymen, apprentices, and in a few instances servants and slaves, enjoyed a more comfortable existence. However, in periods of depression, such as the early 1760s and the 1780s, they, too, faced serious hardships, and other members of their households had to contribute to the family income.

The number of urban laboring people in colonial America was greater, and their economic plight more precarious, than has been commonly assumed. It has been estimated that about one-third of the residents of eighteenth-century European cities were laboring poor who frequently became destitute at times of crisis.[125] A similar proportion of Philadelphians—perhaps between one-fourth and one-third of the free population—experienced analogous conditions. Their material position was extremely vulnerable, and they were easily driven below the subsistence level by such ordinary occurrences as business cycles, seasonal unemployment, illness, injury, pregnancy or child-care requirements, or epidemics that disrupted the city's economy. As a result, private and public aid to the poor rose to unprecedented levels during the late colonial period and the 1780s, and increasingly not only the aged, infirm, widowed, and orphaned but able-bodied working men and women as well found themselves on the charity rolls.[126]

The late colonial period was not one during which Philadelphia's laboring people enjoyed steadily increasing prosperity. Indeed, they lived so near subsistence before the Revolutionary War that there appears to have been no lower level from which they could have risen. The increasing wealth usually thought to have characterized the colonies in general and Philadelphia in particular during this period did not trickle down to the lower sort. If anything, the opposite occurred. Philadelphia's poorer residents experienced relative prosperity during the late 1750s and early 1760s but generally suffered declining living standards from the end of the French and Indian War until Independence. For the city's laboring people, the Confederation era was a period of adversity that ended for many, although not all, only by the mid-1790s.

The material standards of Philadelphia's laboring people were spartan. The budgets constructed in this article are extremely lean ones, generally based on estimates of minimal expenditures for four necessities and omitting many essentials of a decent competency. If the lower sort met the cost of the budget, they still lived very sparely, even by contemporary standards, for they dined like prisoners, dressed in the same fashion as almshouse inmates, and crowded into cramped quarters. Any reduction in income or increase in expenses meant significant sacrifices. Hard-pressed families ate more grains, doubled or tripled up in houses, went without essential clothing, shivered through winters with insufficient fuel, forewent smallpox inoculation but were unable to flee the city in times of epidemic. Some undoubtedly were pushed into an underground economy, stealing their necessary provisions. Others turned to public and private charities, and many landed in relief institutions that often were little more than prisons for the poor. The specter of poverty and deprivation haunted their lives. In these circumstances, dreams of wealth or home ownership, if such dreams existed, would have been shattered by a reality where even a decent competency was difficult to maintain. If this were the best poor man's country for urban laboring people at the time (and that remains a disputed question), it still was a world requiring constant vigilance and struggle to survive.

Notes

The author wishes to thank David E. Dauer, Gary B. Nash, John K. Alexander, Michaele Cohen, P. M. G. Harris, and Carole Strole for their critical comments. An earlier form of this article appears in Billy G. Smith, "'The Best Poor Man's Country': Living Standards of the 'Lower Sort' in Late Eighteenth-Century Philadelphia," *Working Papers of the Regional Economic History Research Center* 2, no. 4 (1979): 1–70; see also Smith, "Struggles of the 'Lower Sort' in Late Eighteenth-Century Philadelphia," *Working Papers of the Regional Economic History Research Center* 3, no. 2 (1979): 1–30.

1. These vignettes are drawn from information in the U.S. Bureau of the Census, *Heads of Families of the First Census of the United States taken in the Year 1790: Pennsylvania* (Washington, D.C., 1908), 245, and in the following manuscript records: Business Papers of Samuel Coates and John Reynell, 1755–67, Coates and Reynell Papers, Historical Society of Pennsylvania, Philadelphia (hereafter HSP); ledger of Joseph Graisbury, 1759–73, Forde and Reed Papers, HSP, hereafter cited as ledger of Graisbury; transcripts of the 1767 Tax Assessors' Reports, Van Pelt Library, University of Pennsylvania, Philadelphia; Philadelphia City Constables' Returns for 1775, Philadelphia City Archives, City Hall Annex; and Matron and Steward's Cash Books, Pennsylvania Hospital Records, American Philosophical Society, Philadelphia.

2. Sam Bass Warner, Jr., *The Private City: Philadelphia in Three Periods of Its Growth* (Philadelphia, 1968), 7. See also David Hawke, *In the Midst of a Revolution* (Philadelphia, 1961), 38, and Stephen E. Lucas, *Portents of Rebellion: Rhetoric and Revolution in Philadelphia, 1765–76* (Philadelphia, 1976), 20.

3. *Cities in Revolt: Urban Life in America, 1775–1776* (New York, 1955), 148, 284.

4. Carl Bridenbaugh and Jessica Bridenbaugh, *Rebels and Gentlemen: Philadelphia in the Age of Franklin* (New York, 1942), 10–11, 13.

5. "Sources of Investment Capital in the Colonial Philadelphia Shipping Industry," *Journal of Economic History* 32 (1972): 146–57. In this same volume, see also James F. Shepherd and Gary M. Walton, "Trade, Distribution, and Economic Growth in Colonial America"; see also Alice Hanson Jones, "Wealth Estimates for the American Middle Colonies, 1774," *Economic Development and Cultural Change* 18 (1970): 127–40.

6. Jackson Turner Main, *The Social Structure of Revolutionary America* (Princeton, N.J., 1965), 279, 194.

7. Charles S. Olton, *Artisans for Independence: Philadelphia Mechanics and the American Revolution* (Syracuse, N.Y., 1975), 8–9.

8. Hannah Arendt, *On Revolution* (New York, 1963), esp. chap. 1. See also Bernard Bailyn, "The Central Themes of the American Revolution: An Interpretation," in *Essays on the American Revolution*, ed. Stephen G. Kurtz and James H. Hutson (Chapel Hill, N.C., 1973), 12.

9. Philip S. Foner, *Labor and the American Revolution* (Westport, Conn., 1976), 12.

10. While Main's collection in *Social Structure of Revolutionary America* of massive amounts of data is admirable, his methodology at times is imprecise and faulty. Examining the economic mobility of taxpayers in two Philadelphia wards, for example, he draws optimistic conclusions about the material circumstances of urban laborers (192–94, 195, n. 49). However, no laborers lived in either of the two wards in the year he chose. For a darker view of the economic mobility of poor Philadelphians, see Gary B. Nash, "Up from the Bottom in Franklin's Philadelphia," *Past and Present* 77 (November 1977): 57–83. For other criticism of Main, see Jesse Lemisch, "The American Revolution Seen from the Bottom Up," in *Towards a New Past: Dissenting Essays in American History*, ed. Barton J. Bernstein (New York, 1968), 8, 33.

11. Nash, "Poverty and Poor Relief in Pre-Revolutionary Philadelphia," *William and Mary Quarterly*, 3d ser., 33 (1976): 3–30, and "Urban Wealth and Poverty in Pre-Revolutionary America," *Journal of Interdisciplinary History* 6 (1976): 545–84. A recent excellent study that focuses more on the responses of wealthier Philadelphians to poverty is John K. Alexander, *Render Them Submissive: Responses to Poverty in Philadelphia, 1760–1800* (Amherst, Mass., 1980).

12. Gary B. Nash, "Social Change and the Growth of Prerevolutionary Urban Radicalism," in *The American Revolution: Explorations in the History of American Radicalism*, ed. Alfred F. Young (DeKalb, Ill., 1976), 7; Nash, *The Urban Crucible: Social Change, Political Consciousness, and the Origins of the American Revolution* (Cambridge, Mass., 1979).

13. Historians have defined the lower sort imprecisely, partly because eighteenth-century terms were imprecise. Staughton Lynd, for example, used the term "mechanics" as it was employed in the eighteenth century, as "all groups below merchants and lawyers," including "anyone who worked with his hands" ("Mechanics in New York Politics, 1774–1788," *Labor History* 5 [1964]: 225–46). Herbert Morais equated "craftsmen" and "lower class" ("Artisan Democracy and the American Revolution," *Science and Society* 6 [1942]: 227–41). Eric Foner has described several divisions within Philadelphia's middle and lower orders (*Tom Paine and Revolutionary America* [New York, 1976]). James H. Hutson mistakenly identified a highly skilled group of ship carpenters as part of the "lower sort" in "An Investigation of the Inarticulate: Philadelphia's White Oaks," *William and Mary Quarterly*, 3d ser., 28 (1971): 3–25. See also Jesse Lemisch and John K. Alexander, "The White Oaks, Jack Tar, and the Concept of the 'Inarticulate,'" *William and Mary Quarterly*, 3d ser., 29 (1972): 109–34; in this same volume, see also Simeon J. Crowther, "A Note on the Economic Position of Philadelphia's White Oaks," 134–36, and Hutson, "Rebuttal," 136–42.

14. These four groups composed about one-third of the city's taxables on seven tax lists between 1756 and 1798. This must represent a minimum figure for their proportion of the entire working population, since many of the poor, because of their mobility or poverty, were missed or excused by the assessors and thus did not appear on the rolls. The underrepresentation of mariners on the tax lists is discussed in detail below. The 1756 tax list was published in Hanna Benner Roach, comp., "Taxables in the City of Philadelphia, 1756," *Pennsylvania Genealogical Magazine* 22 (1961): 3–41. Transcripts of the Tax Assessors' Reports for 1767 are in the Van Pelt Library. The 1772, 1780, 1789, and 1798 provincial tax lists are in the City Archives. Figures for the 1774 tax list are based on an analysis in Jacob M. Price, "Economic Function and the Growth of American Port Towns in the Eighteenth Century," *Perspectives in American History* 8 (1974): 123–86.

15. A word of caution concerning the data in this article should be offered. No historical statistics are completely accurate, and statistics from the colonial period are generally less accurate than those from later eras of American history. The best one can hope for are reliable estimates. In this study the relative values—the indices of change of prices, budgets, and wages—are generally more reliable than the estimates of absolute budgets and wages.

16. Anne Bezanson, Robert D. Gray, and Miriam Hussey, *Prices in Colonial Pennsylvania* (Philadelphia, 1935), and *Wholesale Prices in Philadelphia, 1784–1861*, 2 vols. (Philadelphia, 1936–37); Bezanson et al., *Prices and Inflation during the American Revolution: Pennsylvania, 1770–1790* (Philadelphia, 1951).

17. Matron and Steward's Cash Books, Pennsylvania Hospital Records. Since the hospital purchased in bulk, it probably bought food at a discount. Estimations of the food budget of laboring people based on these retail prices thus probably err on the conservative side.

18. To account for seasonal variation in the cost of food, prices from February, May, August, and November of each year have been collected, and the mean prices during each of the four months have been weighted equally to compute the average annual price of each commodity. The price relative of each commodity and the evenly weighted index of all items are available in Smith, "'The Best Poor Man's Country,'" 50, 64–68.

19. William H. Williams, "The 'Industrious Poor' and the Founding of the Pennsylvania Hospital," *Pennsylvania Magazine of History and Biography* 97 (1973): 431–43; Nash, "Poverty and Poor Relief," 7–8. Eighteenth-century medical practice discouraged wealthier citizens from entering hospitals, and the diet standards provided there undoubtedly reflected that fact.

20. The amount the Pennsylvania Hospital spent on various foods between May 3, 1772, and May 3, 1773, is in its report to the assembly. See Charles F. Hoban, ed., *Votes of the Assembly* (Samuel Hazard et al., eds., *Pennsylvania Archives*, 8th ser. [Philadelphia and Harrisburg, Pa., 1852–1949]), 7: 7069, hereafter cited as *Votes of Assembly*.

21. Mary Davis Rose, *Laboratory Handbook for Dietetics*, ed. Clara Mae Taylor and Grace Macleod, 5th rev. ed. (New York, 1949), 15–36, hereafter cited as Rose, *Laboratory Handbook*.

22. Eighteenth-century Americans apparently were not as short as is sometimes believed. Sixty-seven inches was the mean height of 130 mariners who applied for certificates of citizenship in Philadelphia between 1795 and the end of the century. Seamen's Protective Certificate Applications to the Collector of Customs for the Port of Philadelphia, Records of the Bureau of Customs, Record Group 36, National Archives.

23. Caloric estimates are from Rose, *Laboratory Handbook*. Neither fish nor peas are included in the diet because the method of purchasing them does not permit calculating their unit price.

24. U.S. Bureau of the Census, *Historical Statistics of the United States: Colonial Times to 1970*, vol. 2 (Washington, D.C., 1975), 1175.

25. James Mease, *The Picture of Philadelphia . . .* (Philadelphia, 1811), 167.

26. James T. Lemon, "Household Consumption in Eighteenth-Century America and Its Relationship to Production and Trade: The Situation among Farmers in Southeastern Pennsylvania," *Agricultural History* 41 (1967): 63–64, 68.

27. These figures are computed from *Historical Statistics*, 2: 1175; Mease, *Picture of Philadelphia*, 167; Lemon, "Household Consumption," 63; and David Klingaman, "Food Surpluses and Deficits in the American Colonies, 1768–1772," *Journal of Economic History* 31 (1971): 559–60.

28. Mease, *Picture of Philadelphia*, 121. The proportional relationship of the foodstuffs composing the diet in table 1 closely resembles the proportions of foodstuffs issued occupants of Philadelphia's almshouses during the late eighteenth century. In 1792 and 1793 the almshouse supplied its inhabitants with .32 pounds of meat for every pound of cereals, while the diet in table 1 allots .36 pounds of meat for every pound of cereals. Daily Occurrences Docket, Feb. 5, 1793, Guardians of the Poor, Philadelphia City Archives, hereafter cited as Daily Occurrences Docket.

29. *Historical Statistics*, 2: 1175; Bridenbaugh, "The High Cost of Living in Boston, 1728," *New England Quarterly* 5 (1932): 800–811.

30. All values in this article are in Pennsylvania currency unless otherwise indicated. Conversion rates to sterling before the Revolution are available in *Historical Statistics*, 2: 1198. For the 1790s, values are converted from dollars to Pennsylvania pounds at the rate of 7.5s. per dollar. The superior data on prices and wages available for the year 1762 determined its selection as the base year for all indices in this article. For accuracy and convenience, money values are given in decimal notation: £10.12 is £10. 2s. 5d.

31. The currency of Main's estimate is unclear. If it is pounds sterling, the equivalent in Pennsylvania currency is between £16.67 and £21.67 (*Social Structure*, 115). Klingaman's estimate in pounds sterling is converted into Pennsylvania currency at the rate of .6 pounds sterling per each Pennsylvania pound and then adjusted to the 1762 food prices found in this article ("Food Surpluses," 567). Data on the Continental army rations are in *Historical Statistics*, 2: 1175.

32. During the third quarter of the eighteenth century, 1s. per day "diet money" was customarily allowed both sea captains and their "boys" (Journal of John and Peter Chevalier, Nov. 29, 1770, July 19, 1773; Clifford Papers, vol. 3, 1760–62; bills and receipts, Coates and Reynell Papers, boxes 1751–54 and 1755–67, all at HSP). In the 1770s, John Fitch's journeyman silversmiths paid 8s. 2d. weekly for board (ledger of John Fitch, Case 3, HSP). Simultaneously, master tailors thought that it cost 1.5s. per day to feed a journeyman (calculated from information in the minutes of the Taylors Company, HSP). Ten shillings per week was the cost for board in the Pennsylvania Hospital and the workhouse before the Revolution. After the Revolution, the hospital both paid and charged workmen 9d. per meal, while the lowest price for patients' board fluctuated between 7s. 6d. and 12s. 6d. per week (Matron and Steward's Cash

Books, Pennsylvania Hospital Records).

33. The formula used to construct this index is

$$I = \frac{\sum\left[P_0 Q\left(\frac{P_i}{P_0}\right)\right]}{\sum P_0 Q}$$

where I = food-budget index; P_0 = prices of each foodstuff in base year 1762; P_i = prices of each commodity in a given year; and Q = quantities of each food consumed by families in 1772. This is the most widely used measurement in cost-of-living studies. A slight upward bias is built into this measurement, as it is assumed that the pattern of consumption remains constant. Consumption patterns change, however, as consumers tend to purchase more of those items the prices of which rise least or fall most over time. Arithmetic rather than geometric indices are used in this essay because the former make more economic sense even though the latter possess superior mathematical qualities. For an explanation of the construction of an index and a discussion of the benefits and liabilities of arithmetic and geometric indices, see R. G. D. Allen, *Index Numbers in Theory and Practice* (Chicago, 1975), 1–48, and Irving Fisher, *The Making of Index Numbers: A Study of Their Varieties, Tests, and Reliability*, 3d rev. ed. (New York, 1927).

34. Rising food prices during the early 1760s may have been even more dramatic than the food-budget indicates. In 1761 the assembly passed a law regulating the assize of bread; in changing the measurement of loaves from troy to avoirdupois weight, the law reduced the size of the cheapest loaf by approximately 25%. James T. Mitchell and Henry Flanders, eds., *The Statutes at Large of Pennsylvania from 1682 to 1801* (Philadelphia and Harrisburg, Pa., 1896–1911), 2: 61–63, 6: 69–71, hereafter cited as *Pa. Statutes*.

35. Rose, *Laboratory Handbook*, 15–36.

36. Household size is calculated by matching people in the four occupational groups on the 1772 tax list with the Constables' Returns of 1775, City Archives, which give the name of the household head and composition of the household.

37. *Pa. Statutes*, 2: 61–63; 6: 69–72; 8: 130–38, 308–9, 429–35; 14: 510–11. Philadelphians continually complained that forestalling and engrossing drove up the cost of food. Because of these "different manoeevers," one drayman grumbled, "a number of worthy families were sorely distressed, and the common day laborers almost starved" ("A Drayman," *Independent Gazetteer* [Philadelphia], Apr. 9, 1791).

38. Only 3% of the members of the four occupational groups were taxed for a cow in 1772.

39. On the threat of disease and high mortality in Philadelphia, see Billy G. Smith, "Death and Life in a Colonial Immigrant City: A Demographic Analysis of Philadelphia," *Journal of Economic History* 37 (1977): 863–89.

40. "Phileleutheros," *Pennsylvania Gazette and Weekly Advertiser* (Phila.), Feb. 2, 1780. Other comments on the inferior quality of food consumed by poorer citizens are "Citizens," *Gazette of the United States* (Phila.), Mar. 23, 1796, and "A Speculator," *Pennsylvania Gazette*, Mar. 16, 1785.

41. Rents are calculated from information contained in the Constables' Returns of 1762 and 1775 and the tax lists of 1783, 1789, and 1798, all at City Archives, and from the 1767 Tax Assessors' Reports, Van Pelt Library. These computations represent the minimal expense for shelter since they do not include the ground rent and taxes that many tenants complained they had to pay. "A Poor Tradesman," *Pennsylvania Packet, and Daily Advertiser* (Phila.), Oct. 20, 1784; "A Tenant," *Pennsylvania Evening Herald, and American Monitor* (Phila.), July 16, 1785. For a complete explanation of the method of determining rents, see Billy G. Smith, "The 'Lower Sort' in Revolutionary Philadelphia" (Ph.D. diss., University of California at Los Angeles, 1981), chap. 3.

42. Only 4% of laborers and mariners, and 14% of cordwainers and tailors, owned their homes, based on the 1767 Tax Assessors' Report, Van Pelt Library, the tax lists of 1772, 1783, 1789, 1798, and the Constables' Returns of 1775, City Archives. This contradicts Main's assertion that the "great majority of artisans . . . were homeowners" (*Social Structure*, 80). In the same work (p. 132), Main argues that over half of cordwainers owned their homes and that "three-fourths of all artisans were homeowners."

43. These conditions are reconstructed from descriptions of dwellings contained in United States Direct Tax of 1798: South Ward, 26, Form A, reel 2, frame 169; East Northern Liberties, 43, Form A, reel 3, frames 51, 122, City Archives. Occupational information is from Cornelius William Stafford, *The Philadelphia Directory, for 1797* . . . (Philadelphia, 1797), 51, 122, 169. Information on family composition is in U.S. Census Office, *Return of the Whole Number of Persons within the Several Districts of the United States: Second Census* (Washington, D.C., 1800), reel 8, frames 74, 134, and reel 9, frame 90.

44. Constables' Returns for 1775, North Ward, City Archives.

45. See, for example, the descriptions of houses in High Street Ward in U.S. Direct Tax of 1798, 1, Form A, reel 1, City Archives. For a good survey of laboring people's housing in Southwark, see Margaret B. Tinkcom, "Southwark, A River Community: Its Shape and Substance," *Proceedings of the American Philosophical Society* 114, no. 4 (1970): 327–42. The houses of the wealthy are described and illustrated in Thomas M. Doerflinger, *A Vigorous Spirit of Enterprise: Merchants and Economic Development in Revolutionary Philadelphia* (Chapel Hill, N.C., 1986), 20–36.

46. Mulberry Ward contained 488 and 1,343 houses in 1749 and 1790, respectively, and 309 and 1,372 taxpayers in 1741 and 1789. During the same years, houses in Walnut Ward increased from 104 to 125, and taxpayers grew from 98 to 122. The numbers of houses in 1749 and taxables in 1741 are given in John F. Watson, *Annals of Philadelphia, and Pennsylvania, in the Olden Times* . . . (Philadelphia, 1884), 2: 404–7; 3: 236. Taxables in 1789 are from my analysis of the 1789 Provincial Tax List, City Archives. The number of houses in 1790 is from Benjamin Davies, *Some Account of the City of Philadelphia* . . . (Philadelphia, 1794), 17.

47. This analysis of residential patterns is based on information in Smith, "'Lower Sort' in Revolutionary Philadelphia," chap. 6.

48. Matron and Steward's Cash Books, Pennsylvania Hos-

pital Records. The following are at HSP: Samuel Morris's Day Book, 1755–67; bills, receipts, and accounts of the Shippen family, vols. 28–30, 1754–1822; Journal of John and Peter Chevalier; bills and receipts of John Cadwalader, Cadwalader Collection; business papers of Levy Hollingsworth, Hollingsworth Collection, Sec. 7: bills, 1751–89, and Sec. 3: invoices, 1764–89; and Thomas A. Biddle Shipbook.

49. The price of firewood varied seasonally, often costing twice as much in winter as in spring. Moreover, in his construction of a working-class Philadelphia family budget in the early nineteenth century, Matthew Carey estimated that a cord was nearly twice as high when bought in small parcels (*An Appeal to the Wealthy of the Land* . . . [Philadelphia, 1833], 10).

50. Ledger of John Fitch, Case 33, HSP. One contemporary estimated that a "genteel" Philadelphia family burned 25 cords annually during the 1790s; estimate of Joseph Nourse in Ellis Paxson Oberholtzer, *Philadelphia: A History of the City and Its People*, vol. 1 (Philadelphia, n.d.), 400.

51. The £5.60 figure is the product of the 1762 average price per cord, 22.92s., and the estimated 4.88 cords burned per year. An artisan in Charleston, S.C., thought firewood cost him £3 sterling each year, or £5 Pennsylvania currency, and winters are much milder in Charleston than in Philadelphia. Main, *Social Structure*, 118.

52. Mease, *Picture of Philadelphia*, 125–26; Bridenbaugh, *Cities in Revolt*, 27, 235.

53. Bridenbaugh, *Cities in Revolt*, 27, 235, and *Rebels and Gentlemen*, 235.

54. Gertrude MacKinney, ed., *Votes and Proceedings of the House of Representatives of the Province of Pennsylvania* (Samuel Hazard et al., eds., *Pennsylvania Archives*, 8th ser.), 6: 5451, 6345; *Pennsylvania Gazette*, July 14, 1763; Main, *Social Structure*, 116.

55. Ledger of Graisbury; Matron and Steward's Cash Books, Pennsylvania Hospital Records.

56. Clothing Issues Ledger, 1805–31, Guardians of the Poor, City Archives.

57. Spinning the yarn and weaving the cloth domestically might save a bit more money, but this would have been difficult for many poorer households because of the considerable time and skill required as well as the substantial investment. A spinning wheel cost £1, or about four days' wages for a laborer, in 1788 (Matron and Steward's Cash Books, Pennsylvania Hospital Records).

58. Ledger of Graisbury. Main estimates that the cost to clothe a child ran about 80% of the expense of outfitting an adult, or about £3.33 (Pa. currency) annually during this period (*Social Structure*, 116).

59. Prices of these articles are from the Matron and Steward's Cash Books, Pennsylvania Hospital Records. Unfortunately, these records are incomplete and do not contain any data on clothing costs from 1756 through 1761.

60. In 1762, food, fuel, and clothing cost £30.66, £5.60, and £9.66, respectively. Laborers, mariners, cordwainers, and tailors paid rents of £9, £10.58, £19.63, and £20.37, respectively, or an average of £14.90 for the four groups.

61. W. J. Rorabaugh, *The Alcoholic Republic: An American Tradition* (New York, 1979), 7–11.

62. Nash, "Up from the Bottom," 76.

63. George W. Norris, *The Early History of Medicine in Philadelphia* (Philadelphia, 1886), 112.

64. Norris Stanley Barratt, *Outline of the History of Old St. Paul's Church, Philadelphia, Pennsylvania* (Philadelphia, 1917), 43.

65. Matron and Steward's Cash Books, Pennsylvania Hospital Records.

66. Except for the years 1754 through 1761, the annual costs of food, rent, fuel, and clothing are summed for each year and divided by the estimated 1762 budget to compute the index of household budgets. Because of limitations in the data, the household-budget index for 1754 and 1755 is calculated by dividing the total expenditure for food, fuel, and clothing in those years by the total cost of these items in 1762. Similarly, the index for 1756 through 1761 is constructed by dividing the outlay for food, fuel, and rent in those years by the total price of these items in 1762. Rent and clothing accounted respectively for 25% and 14% of the total 1762 household budget. Unless the costs of those two items fluctuated very significantly during the few years for which the data are not extant—and there is no reason to believe that they did—the household-budget index for 1754–61 should accurately reflect variations in the cost of the budget.

67. Bridenbaugh, *Cities in Revolt*, 148. The proportion of the taxpayers who were laborers is from my analysis of the tax lists cited in n. 14.

68. Only laborers performing unskilled tasks and receiving wages "not found" (not supplied board) are considered. Hardly any short-term laborers were supplied board. The indices of all real wages in this article are calculated by solving the following equation for each year:

$$I_R = I_W/I_H$$

where I_R = index of real wages, I_W = index of actual wages, and I_H = index of household budget.

69. This is based on ship arrivals in 1756, 1759, and 1762, reported weekly in the *Pennsylvania Gazette* during these years.

70. *Pennsylvania Packet*, Dec. 12, 1787; *Whereas the Number of Poor In and around this City* . . . [Philadelphia, 1764], broadside, Evans no. 9870, as quoted in Alexander, *Render Them Submissive*, 14–15.

71. Daily Occurrences Docket, Jan. 20, 1789.

72. Records of Pennsylvania's Revolutionary Governments, Clemency File, 1775–90, RG 27, roll 38, frame 642, Pennsylvania State Archives, Harrisburg, hereafter cited as Recs. of Pa.'s Revolutionary Governments.

73. *Independent Gazetteer*, Dec. 12, 1785, as quoted in Alexander, *Render Them Submissive*, 16.

74. "A Useful Hint," *Mercury Daily Advertiser* (Phila.), Aug. 19, 1797, as quoted in Alexander, *Render Them Submissive*, 130. During the last half of Oct. 1793, at the peak of a yellow fever epidemic, one quarter of the families in the city received money, provisions, and firewood distrib-

uted at city hall. Many Philadelphians were reduced to begging their daily bread from bakers. "Money, Provisions, and Firewood," *Federal Gazette and Philadelphia Daily Advertiser*, Nov. 2, 1793, and "Loaf Bread Baker," *Federal Gazette and Philadelphia Daily Advertiser*, Nov. 6, 1793.

75. *Pennsylvania Journal and Weekly Advertiser* (Phila.), Sept. 27, 1786, as quoted in Alexander, *Render Them Submissive*, 12.

76. Daily Occurrences Docket, Apr. 29, Nov. 17, 1800.

77. *Whereas the Number of Poor*, Evans no. 9870.

78. *Votes of Assembly*, 7:5830.

79. For a detailed analysis of Philadelphia's economic cycles, see Smith, "'Lower Sort' in Revolutionary Philadelphia," chap. 5.

80. Petitions for Revolutionary War Pensions, W 15879, National Archives.

81. Recs. of Pa.'s Revolutionary Governments, roll 37, frames 1242–43.

82. Women employed by the Pennsylvania Hospital earned about half the wages paid men even when performing the same jobs. This also appears to have been a common wage proportion between the sexes in the nineteenth century. See Edith Abbot, *Women in Industry: A Study in American Economic History* (New York, 1910), 262–316.

83. In 1774, the cost of the four basic necessities was £52.72, while a laborer, employed at 83% of full capacity, and his wife might earn £58.30. The resulting per capita estimated income of £8.74 sterling for a laborer's family of four agrees with the calculations of other historians. David Klingaman computes the per capita income in Philadelphia in about 1770 at between £6.5 and £9 sterling ("Food Surpluses and Deficits," 569). Alice Hanson Jones figures a range of £8.4 to £14 sterling per capita income in the American colonies in 1774 ("Wealth Estimates," *Economic Development and Cultural Change* 18, pt. 2 [1970]: 128, table 51).

84. Nash, "Poverty and Poor Relief," 3–30; George W. Geib, "A History of Philadelphia, 1776–1789" (Ph.D. diss., University of Wisconsin, 1969), 203–5.

85. Daily Occurrences Docket, Mar. 1, June 2, 1800, June 22, 1801.

86. Recs. of Pa.'s Revolutionary Governments, roll 37, frames 1242–43.

87. This and the following paragraph are based on an analysis of the city's economy in Smith, "'Lower Sort' in Revolutionary Philadelphia," chap. 5.

88. The county commissioners recorded the names of citizens too poor to pay taxes. Three volumes of their minutes, from 1718 to 1766, are in the City Archives. Another volume, from 1771 to 1774, is at HSP, and a final volume, from 1774 to 1776, is in the Tax and Exoneration Records, Pennsylvania State Archives.

89. Quarterly Payments, 1768–76, HSP.

90. By an act of Parliament in 1696, this tax, which supported the Greenwich Hospital for disabled seamen, was assessed on every sailor who served on a ship owned by a citizen of the British Empire. The collections from Philadel-

phia mariners during 1770–71 are recorded in the Customs House Papers, vol. 11, 1409, HSP.

91. Customs House Papers, vol. 10, n.p.

92. This paragraph is based on an analysis of several hundred seamen in the Ship's Crew Lists and the Seamen's Protective Certificate Applications, Records of the Bureau of Customs, RG 36, National Archives, and the Maritime Records of the Port of Philadelphia, 1789–1860, Library of Congress. Samuel Eliot Morison mistakenly characterizes most seamen as young, adventure-seeking boys attracted by the romance of the sea and kept there by hopes of promotion or rum (*The Maritime History of Massachusetts, 1783–1860* [Boston, 1921], 106).

93. Business Papers, Boxes 1751–54, 1765–67, Coates and Reynell Papers; Clifford Papers, Correspondence, vol. 2, 1760–62; Account Book, Folder: Brigantine *Elizabeth* Accounts, Richard Waln Collection; Ships and Shipping Folder, Etting Papers; Customs House Papers; Dutilh and Wachsmuth Papers, Miscellaneous Boxes 1726–1856 and 1704–1800; Thomas Mason's Journal, 1775, Miscellaneous Letters of Thomas and John Mason, Henry Pleasant's Papers; Journal of John and Peter Chevalier; Philip Benezet's Account with Sloop *Sally*, Dreer Collection; Claude W. Unger Collection; Boats and Cargoes, Society Miscellaneous Collection; Biddle Shipbook, 1784–92—all at HSP; Business Records of Stephen Girard, American Philosophical Society. Donald R. Adams, Jr., "Wage Rates in Philadelphia, 1790–1830" (Ph.D. diss., University of Pennsylvania, 1967), 213.

94. These figures do not include the privilege of carrying their own freight aboard ship to sell in their home port, but this was more often reserved for captains than for the entire crew.

95. James F. Shepherd and Gary M. Walton, *Shipping, Maritime Trade, and the Economic Development of Colonial North America* (Cambridge, 1972), 198.

96. *Admiralty Decisions in the District Court of the United States, for the Pennsylvania District, by the Hon. Richard Peters . . .* (Philadelphia, 1807), 1:255, 2:413. The practice of hiring men other than mariners to stow and unload the cargo seems to have been common in pre-Revolutionary Philadelphia as well. See Business Papers, Box 1755–67, Coates and Reynell Papers, HSP.

97. Daily Occurrences Docket, Feb. 6, 1790, Jan. 18, 1793, Mar. 17, Apr. 7, May 22, 1800, Aug. 29, 1801.

98. Included in the wills recorded in Philadelphia between 1755 and 1760 are those of many lower-class men who were going to sea on privateers (Will Book K [1752–57], Will Book L [1757–60], Register of Wills, City Hall Annex, Philadelphia). See also Virginia D. Harrington, *New York Merchants on the Eve of the Revolution* (New York, 1935), 303–7.

99. Price series for slippers, "channel pumps," "dress shoes," and "ordinary" shoes for adult males, as well as for "Negroes shoes," boys' shoes, and cobbling charges for "soaling" and "heel-taping," are constructed from bills, receipts, and accounts, Shippen Family Papers, vols. 28–30, 1754–1822, and bills and receipts, Coates and Reynell Pa-

pers, HSP; Matron and Steward's Cash Books, Pennsylvania Hospital Records.

100. *To the Inhabitants of Pennsylvania* . . . (Philadelphia, 1779), broadside, HSP.

101. Bezanson et al., *Prices and Inflation*, 332–42; Bezanson, Gray, and Hussey, *Wholesale Prices in Philadelphia*, 1: 385.

102. The index of cordwainers' wages was calculated by solving the following equation for each year:

$$I_W = \frac{I_P - (.57)I_M}{.43}$$

where I_W = index of cordwainers' wages, I_P = retail price index of shoes, and I_M = price index of raw materials.

103. *To the Inhabitants*, broadside, HSP.

104. Job Harrison testified that in 1799 he earned about 48.75s. ($6.50) per week making shoes for 9s. each. At this rate, he must have produced 5.4 shoes in a week of work. Those shoes had linings and required slightly more time to make than common shoes, so the latter could probably be made at the rate of six shoes per week. Philadelphia's cordwainers frequently observed the holiday of "Saint Monday" in the alehouse and thus probably averaged slightly more than one pair of common shoes per day. John R. Commons et al., eds., *A Documentary History of American Industrial Society, Vol. 3: Labor Conspiracy Cases, 1806–1842*, pt. 1 (Cleveland, 1910), 63, 73–74, 83–84, 121–24, hereafter cited as *Documentary History*; Foner, *Tom Paine*, 36.

105. In 1774 masters typically sold shoes for 11s., of which they paid 6s. 3d. in material costs and 3s. 9d. in journeymen's wages, leaving a profit of 1s; *To the Inhabitants*, broadside, HSP.

106. The hard times of the 1780s are reflected in the "value" of cordwainers' occupations assessed by tax collectors in 1783 and 1789. In 1783, the occupations of 17.5% of cordwainers were assessed at £25 or less. By 1789, 40% of cordwainers were assessed that amount. Tax lists for 1783 and 1789, City Archives.

107. *Documentary History*, 3: pt. 1, 114, 123–24. Work also fluctuated annually. The shoe market in 1769, for instance, was said to be "much overdone," and few jobs were then available (Thomas Clifford to Edward and William Gravena, May 23, 1773, Thomas Clifford Letter Book, Clifford Papers, 1767–73, HSP).

108. Daily Occurrences Docket, Feb. 18, 1789.

109. Because many journeymen were forced to do "market work," which paid only half as much as "bespoke work," this probably was near a maximum. *Documentary History*, 3: pt. 1, 73–74, 86.

110. Daily Occurrences Docket, Aug. 23, 1800.

111. While no records indicate the total number of masters and journeymen during this period, several sources give clues to the proportion of each. By identifying as many masters and journeymen as possible and then determining their common and distinguishing characteristics, an approximation of their numbers can be obtained. For a complete explanation of the methodology, see Smith, "'Best Poor Man's Country,'" 23, n. 103, and Thomas Smith, "Re-

constructing Occupational Structures: The Case of Ambiguous Artisans," *Historical Methods Newsletter* 8 (1975): 136–46.

112. These figures are calculated from the tax list of 1772 and the Account of Servants and Apprentices Bound before John Gibson, Dec. 5, 1772, to May 21, 1773, HSP.

113. Olton, *Artisans for Independence*, 21–22; minutes of the Cordwainers Fire Company, HSP.

114. Olton, *Artisans for Independence*, 102–3; Blanche Evans Hazard, *The Organization of the Boot and Shoe Industry in Massachusetts before 1875* (Cambridge, Mass., 1921), 39–40.

115. Adam Seybert, *Statistical Annals* . . . (New York, 1969 [orig. publ. 1818]), 94–95, 100–101, 108, 160–61, 162–63.

116. For changes in shoemaking during this period, see Hazard, *Organization of the Boot and Shoe Industry*, 24–45, and *Documentary History*, 3: pt. 1, 19–58.

117. Bills, receipts, and accounts, Shippen Family Papers, vols. 28–30, 1754–1822; bills and receipts of John Cadwalader, Cadwalader Collection; bills and receipts, Coates and Reynell Papers; Business Papers of Hollingsworth, Hollingsworth Collection, Sec. 7; bills, 1751–89; Sec. 3: invoices, 1764–89; Samuel Morris Day Book, 1755–67; ledger of Graisbury—all at HSP; Matron and Steward's Cash Books, Pennsylvania Hospital Records.

118. Individual series of wages for making each of the following articles of clothing have been constructed: cloth and "superfine" suits, cloth and silk breeches, cloth coats, damask and silk vests, Holland "draws," "ordinary" shirts and trousers, and "Negroes" cloth coats and breeches.

119. Members of the society agreed to abide by only two articles: neither to charge a lower price for workmanship than that agreed upon by the society, nor to pay more to journeymen than the society specified. Disciplinary action was taken several times against members who violated these rules (minutes of the Taylors Company, HSP).

120. These estimates have been arrived at by the method described in n. 111.

121. Minutes of the Taylors Company, HSP.

122. Winter was invariably a slack season for Joseph Graisbury (ledger of Graisbury, passim).

123. Ledger of Graisbury, passim.

124. It is important to note the significance of life cycle in assessing the situation of the "lower sort." Studying the career patterns of the members of the four occupational groups considered in this article, I found an extremely weak correlation between their life cycle and either their tax assessment or occupational status. Most of the unskilled and the "lesser" artisans remained in the same economic circumstances for the duration of their residence in the city. See Smith, "'Lower Sort' in Revolutionary Philadelphia," chap. 4.

125. Jeffry Kaplow, "The Culture of Poverty in Paris on the Eve of the Revolution," *International Review of Social History* 12 (1967): 278–91.

126. Nash, "Poverty and Poor Relief," 3–30; Geib, "History of Philadelphia," 203–5.

Furniture and the Domestic Environment in Wethersfield, Connecticut, 1639–1800

KEVIN M. SWEENEY

Students of social history and material culture converge in a single question: what kinds of possessions did people in the past actually own? In addressing this central but difficult problem, scholars from different disciplines have made particular use of estate inventories, or lists of the real (land and buildings) and personal (household movables) property individuals owned at the time of their death. These documents are not without their inherent biases. They typically tell us more about the possessions of the old than the young, of men than women, of the rich than the poor. But once these biases are recognized and taken into full account, inventories can provide extremely detailed glimpses into how much land people owned, whether they ate with forks and knives, what they named their favorite cattle, and how they furnished their household space. As he uses inventories to explore the furniture forms owned by residents of Wethersfield, Connecticut, between 1639 and 1800, Kevin M. Sweeney discovers changing patterns of accumulation and room use and a gradual, if uneven, rise in the community's standard of living.

Sweeney breaks the seventeenth and eighteenth centuries into four periods. During the first, from 1639 to 1670, people had a few basic possessions— beds, tables, stools, chests—and wealthy individuals simply had more of these same forms than did their social inferiors. Between 1671 and 1720, as the town's population and mercantile economy grew, local merchants began to import objects from Boston and London, while Wethersfield joiners began to make their own distinctive furniture for nearby patrons. A few rich householders now had exotic looking glasses and sets of urbane upholstered chairs in their parlors. By 1720, the town's elites were already acquiring sets of china dishes as well as such new furniture forms as "dressing tables" and writing desks. With these trappings of gentility, Wethers-field's gentry engaged in polite anglophilic rituals like tea drinking and semipublic grooming. These people, not producers themselves, were in the vanguard of a frenzied consumerism that linked all corners of England's mercantile (and aesthetic) empire.

This rising tide of consumer consciousness, forged on the circulation of anonymous commodities, was more apparent in Wethersfield between 1720 and 1760. In response to local demand, the town's cabinetmakers, some of whom were urban émigrés in search of expanding hinterland markets, produced a greater diversity of objects; new descriptive terms defined the intended function of chairs, tables, and chests with surprising specificity. By 1760 the sheer amount and variety of one's household possessions were trusted indices of social status and aspiration in Wethersfield. Between 1760 and 1800, fashionable objects formerly seen only in gentry houses diffused down the social scale. As the town's post-Revolutionary population continued to climb, local woodworkers made objects in greater quantity; prices came down and comfort grew more enviable and affordable.

Yet as late eighteenth-century fashion diffused from court circles in London through Boston and New York to Wethersfield's Main Street, its force was always compromised by the selective power of local traditions with seventeenth-century roots. The persistence of this dialectical tension between the rapid acceptance of novelty and the deep retention of familiar ways suggests that the rise of market capitalism in the broader Atlantic economy was uneven at best and did not translate into any mechanistic acceptance of material "progress."

O n October 27, 1639, Andrew Ward and Richard Gyldersly of Wethersfield went to the home of their neighbor, Widow Brundish, to inventory the worldly possessions of the late John Brundish. To satisfy the demands of creditors who were owed £61 and to protect the inheritance of John Brundish's five young children, an accurate accounting of the decedent's personal estate (household furnishings, livestock, harvested crops, tools, and debts receivable) and real estate (land and buildings) was required. Beginning with Brundish's wearing apparel, Ward and Gyldersly proceeded to record and appraise the contents of the house. The furniture consisted of two beds worth £6; one chest, a box, a small cupboard, and a table valued together at £3; and cushions, stools, and chairs appraised at a mere 10s. The brass and pewter, presumably stored in the small cupboard, came to £5, while the cooking utensils around the fireplace were valued at £1 5s. The largest portion of the estate's value lay in real estate, £130; livestock, £103; crops and hay, £30 6s; debts receivable, £15; and husbandry tools, £4 5s. The inventory compiled by Ward and Gyldersly was submitted to the court in Hartford and duly recorded by the clerk of the court.[1]

The inventory of the estate of John Brundish was the first probate inventory recorded for a resident of Wethersfield. During the seventeenth and eighteenth centuries, the procedure followed by Ward and Gyldersly would be repeated hundreds of times in the town. Almost eight hundred probate inventories taken in Wethersfield before 1800 survive, and, when analyzed as a group, they provide insight into the structure of social and economic hierarchies, changing standards of living, and shifts in fashion.[2]

The use of probate inventories to study the economic and social history of Wethersfield or any colonial New England town is not without its problems, and these pitfalls must be noted at the outset.[3] The surviving probate inventories do not provide a complete record of all the possessions of all the residents of Wethersfield who died before 1800. Most probated decedents were adult males; women were probated infrequently and only if they were widows or spinsters who owned some personal or real property. Inventories do not survive for all adult males who died in town. During the seventeenth century, the estates of most males—80 to 90 percent—appear to have been inventoried and a copy filed with the probate court, but in the eighteenth century the surviving inventories represent perhaps only 60 to 70 percent of

the male population.[4] Poorer men with little property were less likely to be probated than their wealthier counterparts, though it is hard to generalize. The estate of Joseph Webb, Sr., the wealthy merchant who built Wethersfield's stylish Webb House, for example, was not inventoried.

In addition to gender and wealth biases in the overall sample of surviving inventories, particular biases inherent to individual inventories must also be taken into account. The age at which a person died affected the quantity of possessions in the estate. Middle-aged men owned more than either younger men just starting out in life or older men, who had often begun to pass along land and personal belongings to their sons and daughters. A spouse's possessions formed part of a given household but were usually excluded from her husband's estate. This meant that the widow's wearing apparel and any other household goods or furnishings—often some textiles and a chest or a trunk—that were recognized as her personal property, and not her deceased husband's, might be omitted from the inventory of the household. Certain items seem to have been systematically excluded from inventories because they were regarded as having no readily transferable or marketable value. Whether because of their numbers or their short life span, chickens rarely appear in inventories. Such personal pets as dogs were never inventoried, and family portraits also sometimes escaped inventory since in most cases the value of such possessions was more personal than monetary.

Specific problems exist that bedevil any study of furniture forms and their period usage. Probate inventories indicate only that a person owned a given item at the time of his or her death; they do not indicate when the item had been purchased, nor, in the case of furniture, do they tell precisely when a given form or stylistic vocabulary was first introduced. Terminology used in probate inventories was not consistent and differs greatly from that used today by most private collectors, antiques dealers, and museum curators. Recovering correct period nomenclature and understanding its use can provide insight into both contemporaries' attitudes towards and their use of particular furniture forms, but the process of deciphering period terminology is not easy. Word usage varied over time and space, and even within a given town variation existed. A chair called a bowback in the 1760s or 1780s was probably a rush-seat,

PART THREE   Production and Control of Property

crooked-back, or frame chair (misleadingly called today a transitional or country Queen Anne chair); a
bowback chair in the 1790s was more likely to be a
type of Windsor chair.[5] A description of a chair as a
black chair can obscure as much as it reveals. Was it
a black slat-back (today's "ladder-back") chair, or was
it a black crown (often today's "heart and crown")
chair, or was it a black crooked-back or frame chair?
Sometimes the value assigned to the chair or table or
chest in question can help recover some of its meaning, but appraised value is not an infallible guide because it was affected by age and condition, and the
inflation of the mid-1700s and the currency changes
of the mid-1750s and mid-1790s sometimes make
comparisons difficult. Finally, the reappearance of
the same unusual piece of furniture in the subsequent inventory of an heir can give a false impression
of the frequency with which a particular item was
found in the town. It is clear that during the late seventeenth century and early eighteenth century the
same set of leather chairs appears in two, possibly
three, inventories of members of the Chester family,
while in the late eighteenth century the same desk-
and-bookcase appears in two or possibly even three
inventories.

Even with these drawbacks and difficulties, probate
inventories remain an invaluable and revealing
source. By categorizing, quantifying, and studying
comparatively the furniture forms mentioned in
Wethersfield inventories, it is possible to measure
changes in standards of living and in how wealth was
accumulated and displayed. Analyzing patterns of
furniture usage and placement also provides insight
into changes in domestic architecture during this period. Indeed, a full understanding of domestic architecture requires an integrated study of houses and
furniture.[6]

1639–1670

Unlike neighboring towns to the north, Wethersfield was not settled by a united church of pious Puritans shepherded out of Massachusetts by a charismatic pastor. The original ten adventurers who came
to Wethersfield from Watertown, Massachusetts,
were led by a merchant, John Oldham, and a minor
English gentleman, John Chester. These settlers
came to the banks of the Connecticut River primarily to find a better life in this world, though their

deeply held, often incompatible beliefs about the
next world led to a series of bitter and divisive religious disputes. Before 1660 the newly established
town suffered three sizable emigrations by disaffected
brethren.[7] For those who stayed, however, the promise of agricultural prosperity was fulfilled. Standards
of material life compared favorably with those found
elsewhere in the American colonies.[8]

Regrettably, the surviving probate inventories
taken between 1639 and 1670 say relatively little
about the actual appearance of Wethersfield furniture
during this early period. Few references to furniture
forms are preceded by descriptive adjectives indicating the type or color of the chairs, chests, or tables
recorded. In many instances the actual quantities of
furniture are not recorded. Entries simply refer to
"chairs," "stools," "tables," or "chests." Few entries
state the particular value of specific furniture forms,
because in most cases all the references to furniture
in a given inventory or in a specific room within an
inventory are enumerated on a single line for which
only a total sum is given.

Despite these frustrating shortcomings, the thirty-
eight inventories that date from between 1639 and
1670 do reveal useful information about the types of
furniture available and their use in households of the
period. The basic furniture forms—bedsteads, tables,
chairs, stools, and chests—resembled those found in
contemporary provincial England. The quantities of
furniture recorded indicate that most households
were sparsely furnished. The average inventory contained two beds, one or two chests, possibly a few
stools, and a "form" (that is, a backless bench) or
some chairs (see tables 1 and 2). In some households
people possibly sat on boxes or chests, and children
may have stood while eating. Only about one-quarter
of the inventories mention cupboards. Built-in
shelves or cupboards undoubtedly provided storage
space in some houses.

Surviving inventories that list their contents by location suggest how particular furniture forms were
used and placed within the house. Approximately
one-third (thirteen) of the thirty-eight inventories
taken between 1639 and 1670 list their contents with
some room designations indicated. Examples come
from all economic levels of society except the lowest
third, which consisted primarily of youthful heads of
families, the elderly poor, and such transients as mariners.

Table 1. Percentages by Decade of Wethersfield Probate Inventories Containing Selected Furniture Forms, 1639–1800

Decade	Number of Inventories	Beds (%)	Tables (%)	Stools (%)	Chairs (%)	Chests (%)	Cases of (or with) drawers (%)	Cupboards (%)	Boxes (%)	Looking Glasses (%)
1640s	14	86	50	36	21	71	—	7	29	—
1650s	12	100	50	33	58	83	—	25	17	—
1660s	12	100	58	33	83	67	—	25	33	16
1670s	23	87	65	22	57	78	—	43	43	17
1680s	43	93	63	16	81	91	—	23	56	12
1690s	31	90	74	16	81	68	—	39	35	26
1700s	30	77	63	13	73	87	—	37	40	37
1710s	68	85	71	19	79	84	—	31	50	38
1720s	29	79	72	14	69	90	—	21	66	45
1730s	59	88	83	12	86	80	12	27	44	61
1740s	50	88	82	14	84	88	26	12	54	66
1750s	81	91	88	9	90	91	40	31	36	73
1760s	63	92	87	10	84	95	56	21	38	70
1770s	98	96	90	3	91	99	52	16	17	76
1780s	91	92	88	—	88	95	58	20	11	69
1790s	82	91	91	—	89	91	55	9	—	77

The dash [—] indicates percentages of 2% or less.

Note: Decades on this table and for all other tables are defined in the following manner: 1640s = 1639–50; 1650s = 1651–60; 1660s = 1661–70, and so forth. This method was chosen to make the analysis comparable to a companion project being carried out in Concord, Massachusetts.

The pattern of room use and furniture placement revealed by the inventories with room designations is fairly consistent across all levels of society. While it is true that rooms were often multifunctional, it is misleading to view these domestic interiors as simply undifferentiated or unordered stages for improvisation. Conventions determined by usage and a sense of what was appropriate ordered the interiors of seventeenth-century houses.[9]

Usually the parlor served as the sleeping quarters of the head of the household; the decedent's wearing apparel often appears to have been in the parlor. In at least one instance, a seventeenth-century Wethersfield inventory refers to the "parlor or little bedroom."[10] The parlor often contained the most expensive bed, which was sometimes called the "best bed" or "great bed," and occasionally a second bed (see table 3). The great bed or best bed, which when fully furnished with pillows, bolster, sheets, coverlets, and curtains could be worth six to eight pounds, often exceeded the value of the remainder of the furniture (exclusive of other beds) in the house. The presence of the best bed richly furnished with textiles established the parlor as a place in which the family's most prized possessions could be displayed. Cupboards may have been placed in parlors to display ceramics, pewter, or silver if the family possessed any. Chests in the parlors contained such other important possessions as fine linens and clothing.[11]

On occasion the parlor was used for dining and entertaining. About one-half of the parlors mentioned in the thirteen room-by-room inventories had a table and chairs or stools and forms. Stools and forms or a pair of forms would have been the most appropriate seating for a long table in the parlor, and such seating would not necessarily have been cheaper than chairs. The six joined stools in merchant John Harrison's 1666 inventory were valued at fifteen shillings, while most contemporary chairs were worth about one to two shillings. Tradition and a sense of what was appropriate determined the use of stools and forms. Stools and forms maintained the social distance be-

Table 2. Mean Quantities of Furniture in Wethersfield, Connecticut, Probate Inventories, 1639–1800

Decade	Number of Inventories	Beds	Tables	Stools	Chairs	Chests	Cupboards	Boxes	Looking Glasses
1640s	14	2.2	.9	.7	.4	1.3	—	.4	—
1650s	12	1.9	1.1	.8	1.8	1.7	.3	—	—
1660s	12	3.2	1.2	1.3	2.8	1.6	.3	.5	—
1670s	23	2.5	1.0	.7	2.4	2.4	.5	.7	—
1680s	43	1.9	.9	.7	2.6	2.0	.3	.9	—
1690s	31	3.0	2.0	.8	5.9	1.7	.5	.7	.3
1700s	30	1.8	1.1	.4	4.5	2.1	.5	1.0	.4
1710s	68	2.5	1.3	.4	6.0	2.2	.4	.9	.4
1720s	29	2.3	1.4	—	6.1	2.6	—	1.0	.6
1730s	59	2.8	2.1	—	10.5	2.4	.3	.8	.9
1740s	50	2.7	2.1	—	9.4	2.6	—	.9	.9
1750s	81	2.6	2.5	—	10.4	3.0	.3	.6	1.0
1760s	63	3.1	3.2	—	12.5	3.4	—	.8	1.5
1770s	98	3.1	3.2	—	12.3	3.9	—	—	1.4
1780s	91	2.8	3.3	—	12.6	3.5	—	—	1.2
1790s	82	3.2	3.5	—	15.8	3.4	—	—	1.7

The dash [—] indicates mean quantities of .2 or less.
Note on method: For the purposes of computing the means for each form for each decade, all plural references such as "chests," "chairs," "tables," etc., were treated as indicating two items. This probably underestimated the items in some cases, particularly in references to chairs, but this method was chosen as the most conservative and least likely to skew the results.

tween the head of the family, who would have been seated in a chair, and other family members.

The hall, or "dwelling room" or "outward room," as it was sometimes called, functioned as the center of family life.[12] It had to be a more public and more flexible space than the more intimate and restricted parlor, or "inner room." Furnishings had to be readily movable to adjust to the hall's more varied functions. Chests heavy with stored textiles and large, fully hung beds had no place in the hall. Fragile valuables and textiles were also safer in the parlor; the smoke and soot generated by the hall's constantly burning fire would have hastened the deterioration of linen sheets and woolen bed hangings.

People usually ate in the hall, and in many houses without a separate kitchen, food was prepared in the hall. The hall was even more likely than the parlor to have a table and chairs or stools and forms. Tablewares of wood, pewter, and, in rare instances, ceramic were often stored in the hall either in a freestanding cupboard or in or on a built-in cupboard or shelves. A cupboard would have been the largest piece of furniture in the hall. Separate kitchens, when listed in inventories, served almost exclusively as places of food preparation. Kitchens usually did not contain beds, tables, seating furniture, or storage furniture in this early period. They appear to have been used solely as workspaces.

Upstairs rooms, called chambers, were sparsely furnished. Fragmentary evidence indicates that most beds in a given household were on the ground floor—in the parlor or in other first-floor rooms located in a lean-to or in other additions to the main house. In no case do the inventories taken before 1671 indicate a second-floor location for the best bed. Beds located on the second floor often shared the chamber with no other furniture than another bed. In some chambers chests held stored textiles. Other chambers contained nothing but grain stored in bags or meal chests. The relative absence of tables and chairs suggests that people spent little time in these upper rooms. Governor Thomas Wells's possible use of his porch chamber—which had two chairs and a table—as a study was exceptional.

Table 3. Placement of Furniture Forms in Probate Inventories with Room Designations, from Wethersfield, Connecticut, 1639–1670

	Parlor	Hall	Kitchen	Bedroom	Chamber	Garret	Cellar	Other Rooms	Unknown	Total
Total Number of References:	11	8	4	—	14	3	3	5	—	—
Furniture Form:										
Best Bed	7							1	5	13
Other Beds	5				4[a]			2	13	24[a]
Tables	4[a]	4[c]	1		3				1	13[d]
Stools	[b]	[c]			3[a]				6[a]	18[c]
Forms	2[a]	[b]	[a]						3	6[c]
Chairs	[a]	[c]	3[a]		5				5[b]	13[g]
Chests	7[b]				3[a]			2[a]	6[a]	18[c]
Cupboards	2	2	1							5
Looking Glasses									1	1

Note: This table draws upon information from thirteen inventories with room designations. In some instances the inventories did not specify the exact number of tables, stools, or chests, but did indicate that more than one table, stool, or chest was present by the use of the plural, *tables, stools,* or *chests.* The occurrence of such references is indicated by the use of superscript letters: [a] indicates that one inventory had a reference to *tables, stools, chests, etc;* [b] indicates that there were two references to just *tables, stools, chests, etc;* [c] indicates that there were three such references, and so forth.

Other rooms includes references to rooms designated only by points of the compass, references to lower room, inner room, middle room, as well as references to backhouse, backroom, and lean-to. Most, if not all, of the rooms so designated were downstairs.

Unknown includes all references to furniture for which the location was not designated in the room by room inventories consulted.

Best Bed refers to the most expensive bed in the inventory.

Furnishings and domestic architecture did make the homes of the wealthy recognizable. The houses of Gov. Thomas Wells, merchant John Harrison, and other wealthy residents had on the average more rooms than the houses of poorer residents of Wethersfield. Inside the home of one of Wethersfield's wealthier residents, the quantities and types of furniture forms set its occupants apart. Prosperous individuals such as Wells, who died in 1660, typically owned more than an average quantity of chairs and tables; the number of chests they owned, however, does not appear to have been closely related to their wealth or status. Governor Wells also owned a livery cupboard worth one pound, five shillings, a "drawing table," or draw table worth one pound, ten shillings, and a round table worth fifteen shillings. Most tables cost four to six shillings at the time, and later seventeenth-century inventories reveal that most cupboards were valued at less than a pound. John Lattamore, who died in 1662 possessed of the most valuable estate probated before 1671, owned a looking glass. The 1662 inventory of Thomas Lord, the town's schoolmaster and the offspring of a wealthy Hartford mercantile family, listed the only other looking glass during this period. Clearly, a looking glass, with its suggestion of worldly vanity and self-reflexivity, was an item of conspicuous consumption. Before 1671 few Wethersfield residents purchased these relatively inexpensive looking glasses.

1671–1720

The relationship between the possession of certain furniture forms and status became more marked during the late seventeenth and early eighteenth centuries. The town's population grew from 349 in 1670 to approximately 1,000 in the early 1700s.[13] Commercial activity in Wethersfield increased during the period as six warehouses were built at the north end of Main Street.[14] The increase in the mean quantities of selected furniture forms in all inventories suggests that overall standards of living rose gradually during the half-century between 1671 and 1720 (see table 2). The quantities and variety of furniture forms found in the wealthiest 10 percent of probate estates indicated that local merchants and members of the gentry benefited most from the town's growth and the increase in commercial activity. Before 1671 the wealthiest 10 percent of the decedents' inventories included that of John Lattamore, a substantial yeoman farmer; John Harrison, a shoemaker who became a prosperous merchant; James Boosey, the town's first joiner; and Gov. Thomas Wells. Between 1671 and 1720, the wealthiest 10 percent of estates inventoried included those of four merchants surnamed Chester, four other merchants (including John Buttolph and Capt. John Blackleach), four gentlemen magistrates, four yeomen farmers, two woodworkers, and one individual who may have been a ship owner and trader.[15] It is evident from their inventories that these individuals, especially the merchants, invested some of their profits in substantial case pieces, upholstered chairs, and handsomely furnished beds.

The average quantities of all furniture forms found in the inventories gradually increased during the late seventeenth and early eighteenth centuries. The average number of chests per inventory increased to two, and chests of drawers appeared in a few inventories for the first time (see tables 2 and 4). Tables were found with greater frequency in inventories, though most estates still possessed only one table (see tables 1 and 2). The ownership of chairs became more com-

Table 4. Totals of Chests by Type in Wethersfield, Connecticut, Probate Inventories, 1639–1800

	1640s	1650s	1660s	1670s	1680s	1690s	1700s	1710s	1720s	1730s	1740s	1750s	1760s	1770s	1780s	1790s
Number of Inventories	14	12	12	23	43	31	30	68	29	59	50	81	63	98	91	82
Total Chests:	4[g]	16[b]	15[b]	50[c]	74[f]	51[a]	62[a]	144[c]	80	144	132	244	216	361	320	279
Chests by type:																
Unspecified	3[g]	15[b]	15[a]	48[c]	59[f]	47[a]	50[a]	107[c]	44	75	37	80	78	150	113	84
Great			[a]		8	2	3	6			6	2	2	2	2	
Wainscot					1		1	1	2	1	1	2	1	1		1
Carved								1	1		3	1	3	3	4	
Red					1				1	1	5	4	7	13	17	13
Plain					3		3	5	17	18	23	35	28	13	9	10
Board								12	1		1†	1†	1†			
Flowered											1					
Colored											2	2			1	1
Spanish							1									
Black											1				1	2
Blue											1		1	2	1	1
Green															1	
Pine															2	
Sea Chest	1	1			1		1			2	1	7	7	8	12	12
High Chest							1				1					2
Chest of Drawers				2	1	2	2	10	6	15	17	24	4	7	4	8
Chest with Drawers								2	8	14	26	50	40	100	89	64
Case of (or with) Drawers										9	15	36	44	62	63	68
Bureau															1	13

Note: The superscript letters serve the same purpose as in table 3.
† Creased Chest—a board chest with shadow molding made with a creasing plane.

mon (see table 5), while stools and forms went out of fashion. After 1720 these latter two types of seating furniture rarely appeared in inventories (see table 6). Ownership of boxes and looking glasses increased. The relationship between wealth and the possession of looking glasses became more obvious. Even though most looking glasses still cost only four to six shillings, over two-thirds of the looking glasses were found in estates ranking among the wealthiest one-fourth of the estates probated during this period.

Trundle beds, which could slide under other beds, constituted a growing percentage of the beds listed in inventories (see table 7). Presumably used for small children, they provided a way of expanding the available sleeping places while conserving floor space. Trundle beds frequently appear in association with the best bed or a great bed. More often than not, they were located in the parlor. They were twice as likely to appear in a downstairs room as in an upstairs chamber.

Certain other furniture forms appear for the first time in Wethersfield in the inventories taken between 1671 and 1720. Desks are explicitly referred to for the first time in the 1670s (see table 8). It is possible that before this decade (and even in later decades of the seventeenth century) some of the boxes listed in the inventories served as writing surfaces and containers for papers and writing implements. As a rule, items called desks are valued at six to ten shillings while boxes range in value from one to four shillings. The desk worth ten shillings in the 1697 inventory of merchant John Chester and the desk with drawers valued at eight shillings in the 1703 inventory of merchant John Blackleach may have been freestanding writing surfaces supported by their own legs. For the few individuals owning desks—seven of them belonged to John Blackleach—the possession of a desk appears to be related directly to professional or business concerns. Ownership of these modestly valued desks indicated occupational status, not merely wealth or conspicuous consumption.

Large case pieces for storing textiles or displaying valued possessions do appear to have functioned more obviously as objects of conspicuous display. Analysis of the inventories reveals a striking relationship between cupboards worth over a pound—most were valued at two to three pounds—and wealth. These large cupboards, which would probably be

called "court cupboards" today, differed in kind from the more common, more strictly utilitarian cupboards worth anywhere from three to eighteen shillings. Designed to store table linens and tablewares, these more expensive cupboards functioned socially as massive wooden ornaments that were in turn showcases for more fragile ornaments. The association of the following successive entries in John Chester's 1697 inventory is suggestive: "Earthenware on the Cupboard 6 s[hillings]; To silver tankard, spoons, pottiner [porringer] and wine cup at £10; To Cupboard & Cloth £2–10." Individuals having estates valued among the top 10 percent of those probated between 1671 and 1720 owned 60 percent of the more expensive cupboards listed in inventories during the period. At least fifteen of the nineteen inventories that made up the wealthiest 10 percent of the estates probated had such a cupboard. Some of the court cupboards not owned by wealthy individuals were owned by the heirs or relatives of the wealthy, by ministers, or, interestingly, by woodworkers capable of making such a display piece. Obadiah Dickinson, a joiner of middling status, owned the most expensive of these court cupboards, which was valued at three pounds, fifteen shillings when he died in 1698.

Like expensive cupboards, presses were largely the property of the wealthy. Presses served as freestanding closets to hang clothes in and were invariably found in association with beds. As a rule, presses that held and attested to the possession of valuable textiles represented a somewhat more conservative, though no less expensive, statement than a cupboard displaying silver, pewter, and ceramics. Parlors or downstairs bedrooms were the usual locations for what was a relatively uncommon furniture form in Wethersfield (see table 8). Presses usually ranged in value from one to two pounds, though Samuel Deming's 1709 inventory listed an exceptional press worth four pounds.

Chests of drawers, which appeared in Wethersfield inventories for the first time during the 1670s, represented a somewhat newer furniture form than the cupboard or press. Designed for an urban, bourgeois market, the chest of drawers was a more specialized, more precisely ordered storage container than a board or joined chest with a lift top. Ownership of these chests of four or five drawers remained relatively restricted to wealthier households before 1700. The chests, which were usually valued at one pound to

Table 5. Totals of Chairs by Type in Wethersfield, Connecticut, Probate Inventories, 1639–1800

	1640s	1650s	1660s	1670s	1680s	1690s	1700s	1710s	1720s	1730s	1740s	1750s	1760s	1770s	1780s	1790s
Number of Inventories	14	12	12	23	43	31	30	68	29	59	50	81	63	98	91	82
Total Chairs	c	14[d]	22[f]	48[d]	83[o]	166[i]	128[d]	388[i]	173[a]	615[c]	466[a]	843[a]	781[b]	1202	1142[c]	1286[d]
Chairs by type:																
Unspecified	c	6[d]	22[f]	48[d]	83[o]	142[i]	109[d]	362[i]	110[a]	279[c]	172[a]	226[a]	337[a]	622	478[b]	320
Great							9	14	21	60	40	66	54	92	78	76
Black								6	38	115	102	218	146	124	101	90
Turned		6														21
Joined		2												1		
Leather						12	10	6		8		8	8			
High						12				10	19	2[†]	1			
Cane										6	7				6	
White									4	17	29	75	11[a]	30	7	2
Yellow										7			6			
Red										9	6[@]	11	10	50	34	47
Slat Back*										71	39	71	71	78	127	141
Crown										27	30	49	8	75	99[a]	99
Bannister											10	6	16	6		
Crooked Back										6	6		6		9	
Frame											6	37	33	12	62	72
Brown												24	9			6
Flat Back												18	35	2		6
Split Back												9			4	
Kitchen												10				26
Maple												6				6
Bowback													6	16	25	71[a]
Round Back													1	14		
Square Back													6			6
Brigden														27	31	27
Cloth-Bottom													3			
Plush-Bottom														14	4	
Easy Chair													1	2	1	2
Straight Back														6	12	6
Worked-Bottom														8	8	a
Cushion Chair															10	
Scalloped Top															5	
Cherry															12	26
Leather-Bottom															6	9
Green															10	40
Windsor															7	109[a]
Rocking															1	3
Fiddle Back																12
Mahogany																24
Miscellaneous												7	22	14	5	39[a]

Note: The superscript letters serve the same purpose as in table 3. Chairs are categorized on the basis of form and then on the basis of color or wood. A black crown chair is a crown chair. A green Windsor chair is a Windsor chair.

[@] Six colored chairs.

[†] Two little high chairs. These two are probably children's high chairs.

* Slat Back chairs includes plain chairs, common chairs, two-back chairs, three-back chairs, four-back chairs, etc.

Table 6. Seating Furniture Other than Chairs—Stools, Forms, Benches, Couches, and Settles in Wethersfield, Connecticut, Probate Inventories, 1639–1800

	1640s	1650s	1660s	1670s	1680s	1690s	1700s	1710s	1720s	1730s	1740s	1750s	1760s	1770s	1780s	1790s
Number of Inventories	14	12	12	23	43	31	30	68	29	59	50	81	63	98	91	82
Stools	e	4c	7d	15	25c	25a	10b	22b	5	12	13	9	7	3	1	
Staining Stools					a				1							
Forms	b	10	2	5	8a	8	4	5	1					4		2
Benches	a														1	
Couches						1							2		1	
Settles												2	1			1

Note: The superscript letters serve the same purpose as in table 3.

Table 7. Beds by Type in Wethersfield, Connecticut, Probate Inventories, 1639–1800

	1640s	1650s	1660s	1670s	1680s	1690s	1700s	1710s	1720s	1730s	1740s	1750s	1760s	1770s	1780s	1790s
Number of Inventories	14	12	12	23	43	31	30	68	29	59	50	81	63	98	91	82
Total Beds	25	21a	30d	53b	78a	91a	55	157e	67	166	134	208	195	305	254	261
Beds by Type:																
Unspecified	25	20a	28d	52b	68a	83a	43	129e	55	134	110	178	174	279	230	236
Trundle Beds			2	1	10	8	11	28	12	28	22	27	14	19	19	18
Sea Beds		1					1				2	1	2		3	2
Negro Beds										4		2	5	5	1	2
Bunks																2
Camp Beds														1		
Press Beds														1	1	1
Cradles		2	2	1	9	9	1	15	6	9	10	13	9	10	12	11

Note on method: In the seventeenth and eighteenth centuries the term *bed* referred to the stuffed sack or mattress that sat upon a bedstead. The term is being used here in a more modern manner to refer to sleeping units. A bed can be a bed, bedstead, and furniture. It can be a reference to a bedstead without a bed or mattress. It can also refer to a bed or mattress or two beds without a bedstead that presumably rest directly on the floor. In some instances the inventories did not specify the exact number of beds or bedsteads but did indicate that more than one bed or bedstead was present by the use of the plural, *beds and bedsteads.* The occurrence of such references is indicated by the use of superscript letters: ᵃ indicates that one inventory had a reference to *beds, bedsteads,* or *bedding;* ᵇ indicates that there were two references to *beds, bedsteads,* or *bedding;* ᶜ indicates three such references, and so forth.

one pound, ten shillings, never challenged the position of the cupboard as a stage for display, nor did they replace lidded chests and presses as preferred storage furniture for quantities of textiles and other possessions. By the early years of the eighteenth century, chests of drawers could be found in the homes of wealthy merchants and in the homes of artisans and yeomen farmers of middling status.

Merchant John Blackleach owned still more ostentatious and avant-garde case furniture. In addition to a cupboard worth three pounds, he owned a high chest valued at two pounds, ten shillings, a Spanish

Table 8. Storage Furniture Other than Chests—Cupboards, Presses, Cabinets, Trunks, Boxes, Desks, and Bookcases—in Wethersfield, Connecticut, Probate Inventories, 1639–1800

	1640s	1650s	1660s	1670s	1680s	1690s	1700s	1710s	1720s	1730s	1740s	1750s	1760s	1770s	1780s	1790s
Number of Inventories	14	12	12	23	43	31	30	68	29	59	50	81	63	98	91	82
Cupboards	1	3	3	10[a]	11	15	14	24	7	18	8	26	15	18	22	7
Presses				2	2	1	2	4	1	3	1	4	1	1		
Cabinets								4								
Trunks	3[b]	2	2	6	6	21	13	28	10	60	42	34	59	49	42	61
Total boxes:	3[a]	2	2[b]	12[b]	33[b]	21	27[a]	59[b]	31	43[a][†]	46	46	48[*]	24[††]	14	2
Boxes by type:																
Unspecified	3[a]	2	2[b]	12[b]	32[b]	18	26[a]	55[b]	28	37[a]	41	37	41	19	12	2
Carved					1	1	1	2	1	1						
Flowered										1	2	3	2	2		1
Painted						1			1	1			4	1	4	
Boxes with Drawers						1		2			2	3	2		1	
Desks				1			3	8	3	8	4	11	22	30	29	40
Desks and Bookcases													4	3	3	4
Bookcases										1	1		3			1
Writing Table														1		

Note: The superscript letters serve the same purpose as in table 3.
† Includes two veneered boxes.
* Includes two footed boxes.
†† Includes one japanned box.

chest valued at three pounds, and cabinets. Assembled with the use of dovetails, the high chest and cabinets may have been the work of a cabinetmaker instead of a local joiner. The Spanish chest may have come from Iberia or the Caribbean.[16] These oversized chests, which were five to six feet wide, were usually made of cedar and exotic woods and decorated on the front (fig. 1). Blackleach's Spanish chest, high chest, and cabinets document the more unusual possibilities available to, but usually shunned by, Wethersfield's mercantile elite of the late seventeenth and early eighteenth centuries.

The greater frequency with which prices were recorded for individual items and the occasional presence of descriptive adjectives make it easier to sort out some of the other varieties of chests used in Wethersfield between 1671 and 1720 than was the case in earlier inventories. Surviving examples of Wethersfield furniture from the late seventeenth and early eighteenth centuries document the existence of carved oak chests with one, two, or no drawers; six-board chests of pine with or without decoration; and chests with painted decoration (see table 4). While few of the chests in the inventories are referred to as "carved," "wainscot [oak]," board or "plain," it is possible to make some determinations based on value. The 1712 inventory of Jonathan Riley lists a "joiner's chest" worth sixteen shillings and two "board chests" worth ten shillings. Other references to "wainscot chests," to "plain" or board chests, and to "great chests" also suggest that chests worth three to seven shillings (and occasionally as much as nine shillings) were undoubtedly board (plain) chests, while those valued at twelve or more shillings were probably joined chests. The evidence suggests that board chests, made from six pine boards nailed together, outnumbered joined chests, usually made of oak, by almost three to one (fig. 2).[17] Both joined and

Fig. 1. A cedar "Spanish chest" of the type that may have been owned by John Blackleach of Wethersfield. The chest dates from ca. 1700–1725 and is located in St. Brannock's Church, Braunton, Devon, England. (Photograph courtesy of the "British Influence on American Furniture" research project sponsored by the Kaufman Americana Foundation, Museum of Early Southern Decorative Arts.)

Fig. 2. Pine, board, or plain chest with shadow moldings applied with a "crease plane"; probably Hartford County, Connecticut, or Hampshire County, Massachusetts, ca. 1675–1725; yellow pine. Some of the board or plain chests mentioned in Wethersfield inventories had similar decoration. (Photograph courtesy of the Yale University Art Gallery, Mabel Brady Garvan Collection.)

Fig. 3. Chest with two drawers, probably Wethersfield, Connecticut, ca. 1680–1700; oak. This chest descended through female lines of the Belding, Churchill, and Hanmer families of Wethersfield. (Photograph courtesy of The Connecticut Historical Society.)

board chests could be undecorated or adorned with carved, painted, or punch-work decoration.

Even though joined chests appear to have been relatively less common and more expensive than board chests, it should not be assumed that only the wealthy could afford joined chests of oak (fig. 3). Both types of chests were found in households at almost all economic levels of society. Carved chests and carved boxes valued at ten to fifteen shillings and three to four shillings, respectively, furnished the parlors of yeomen and artisans of middling status as

well as the rooms of wealthy merchants. Board chests could also be found in the parlors of the well-to-do.

The inventories of the late seventeenth and early eighteenth centuries provide less insight into the types of chairs and tables available in Wethersfield at the time (see tables 5 and 9). Inventory takers valued most chairs at only one to two shillings and made no effort to describe them further. Most of these chairs were probably turned chairs with rush, or "flag bottom," seats. Sets of these chairs appear to have been the exception rather than the rule. Chairs with arms were typically called "great chairs" and usually valued at two to four shillings each. More valuable but much less common were the sets of "leather chairs" owned by members of the Blackleach and Chester

Table 9. Totals of Tables by Type in Wethersfield, Connecticut, Probate Inventories, 1639–1800

	1640s	1650s	1660s	1670s	1680s	1690s	1700s	1710s	1720s	1730s	1740s	1750s	1760s	1770s	1780s	1790s
Number of Inventories	14	12	12	23	43	31	30	68	29	59	50	81	63	98	91	82
Total Tables:	4[d]	13	10[b]	24	33[c]	61[a]	33	83[a]	42	124	105	205	201	313	299	286
Tables by type:																
Unspecified	4[d]	10	9[b]	18	27[c]	41[a]	17	52[a]	25	48	41	34	39	34	35	27
Great				2	2	4	6	10	5	2	4	3		4		1
Long						1	4	1		3	5	7	10	11	3	5
Little		1	1	3	3	10	6	15	4	14	11	21	15	16	21	9
Drawing		1														
Round		1					1	1	4	21	11	34	37	60	56	40
Oval										9	10	16	26	29	27	10
Square						2		1	3	11	12	64	39	85	80	57
Kitchen										2			1	2	3	9
Dressing										3[a]	1	9	8	21	22	17
Table Frames					1			1			1	2	2		2	
Slate								1		5	1		3	1		1
Tea										3	2	7	8	13[†]	7	14
With Drawers								1		1	1	1	2	2	1	
Flowered										1						
Walnut										1						
Japanned											1					
Black											1					
Red											1	1		1	1	
Colored											1	1				
With Leaves											2	2	3	1	1	5
Table Chest									1			1			1[*]	
Cherry												1	2	9	15	46
8-Square											1	2				
Stand Table													2	11	14	20
Buttonwood													1	1	1	
Pine														4	1	2
Rule Joint													2		1	2
Square Leaf														2		5
Tavern																2
Mahogany																5
Card																1
Breakfast																3
Dining																1
Miscellaneous													1	4	5	4

Note: The superscript letters serve the same purpose as in table 3. Tables are categorized on the basis of form and then on the basis of color or wood. A mahogany card table is a card table.

ᵃ Includes a chamber table.

† Includes two coffee tables.

* Cupboard table. The cupboard table and the two table chests could be what are usually referred to as chair-tables.

families. These chairs, valued at five to twelve shillings each, may actually have been leather-covered back-stools (today often called "Cromwellian chairs"); these inventory references are too early for leather-bottomed, crooked-back Boston chairs. Two major varieties of table are distinguishable: long or great tables worth between fifteen shillings and one pound, and smaller, less expensive tables worth four to six shillings. The continued use into the early eighteenth century of the long table as the usual dining table, even in the parlors and halls of the wealthy, documents the persistence of traditional forms and dining practices. More avant-garde was the slate table, valued at three pounds, seven shillings, listed in the 1712 inventory of merchant John Chester. It may have been used as a mixing or serving table.

Despite the first appearance of a slate table, leather chairs, desks, and a high chest (presumably a case of drawers), furniture forms and their use did not change markedly in the half-century between 1671 and 1720 or, for that matter, in the century between 1630 and 1730. The board or joined chest with lift top (the so-called blanket chest) remained the most common form of storage furniture well into the early years of the eighteenth century. More fashionable round or oval tables rarely appeared in households where the older forms of long and square tables still held sway. Only the shift in seating furniture from stools and forms to chairs and great chairs documented a definite change in fashion and usage during this period.

The placement of furniture within houses changed little from the mid-1600s until the mid-1700s (see table 10). The forty-two probate inventories with some room designations that date from between 1671 and 1715 show little change in room use despite the fact that these inventories disproportionately represent the homes of wealthy decedents. Half of these forty-two inventories are valued in the upper 20 percent of estates probated during the period, and few of the inventories with room designations include examples from the lower 50 percent of the estates probated. Still, these forty-two inventories reveal the continuation of established patterns of room use.

Table 10. Placement of Furniture Forms in Probate Inventories with Room Designations from Wethersfield, Connecticut, 1671–1715

	Parlor	Hall	Kitchen	Bedroom	Chamber	Garret	Cellar	Other Rooms	Unknown	Total
Number of References	24	11	15	3	69	6	11	26	—	—
Furniture Form:										
Best Bed	19		1	1	10			9	2	42
Other Beds	20	2	1	2	71[a]	[a]		16	17[a]	129[c]
Tables	14	13[a]	10		8			14	40[a]	99[b]
Stools	10	8[a]	5[a]		12			17	14[a]	66[c]
Forms	1	4	1		1			3	9	19
Chairs	65[a]	83	24[b]		13[a]			60[b]	114[g]	359[m]
Chests	22	4		2	40[a]		1	2[a]	43[b]	114[d]
Chests of Drawers	3							2	2	7
Cupboards	6	5			3			4	11	29
Presses	2		1		2				3	8
Looking Glasses	8	1			1			4	8	22

This table draws upon information from forty-two inventories with room designations.
Note: The use of superscript letters is the same as in table 3.

Most parlors still contained beds; only two of the twenty-four parlors cited did not. In almost half of the inventories the best bed stood in the parlor. Parlors also contained tables and chairs and cupboards with pewter or silver, indicating that many parlors remained places of entertainment and display.

The status of halls improved somewhat as kitchens increasingly became the place in which food was prepared and the hall the place in which it was consumed. Valuable cupboards and an occasional looking glass or carved box appeared in halls in addition to tables and chairs. Gradually, the multipurpose hall or dwelling room was evolving into the more specialized family sitting room of the mid- to late eighteenth century. But in the late seventeenth and early eighteenth centuries the evolution was still in its early stages. Another just discernable change was the increased use of chambers. A clear majority of beds and one-quarter of the best beds in the inventories now stood in upstairs chambers. In some inventories of the wealthy, tables and chairs and an occasional cupboard were located in chambers. As a rule, tables and chairs were infrequently found in chambers, and the older pattern of using chambers to store grain persisted in some households.

1721–1760

During the mid-eighteenth century, the quantity of furniture found in Wethersfield inventories increased significantly. The growing number of tables, chairs, and looking glasses found in most inventories reflected and proclaimed the town's continued prosperity based on trade and commercial agriculture. The town's population stood at 2,483 in Connecticut's 1756 census.[18] Shipping tonnage owned by Wethersfield taxpayers doubled between 1730 and 1750.[19] The raising of livestock and the cultivation of such cash crops as onions and tobacco provided a ready surplus for export. Landowning descendants of the town's seventeenth-century gentry families—the Robbinses, Treats, Welleses, and Wolcotts—and merchants, some sea captains, and others with commercial interests did especially well during the mid-eighteenth century and distanced themselves from even well-to-do yeomen and artisans.[20] These families provided a healthy market for the native-born and migrating joiners, cabinetmakers, and chairmakers who worked in Wethersfield during the 1740s and 1750s.

By then, the average Wethersfield inventory contained two to possibly three times the amount of furniture listed in inventories one hundred years earlier (see tables 1 and 2). The statistically average inventory of the mid-eighteenth century had two or three beds—one of which in one-third of the inventories was likely to be a trundle bed—two to three chests—one of which was a chest of drawers, case of drawers, or chest with drawers—two to three tables, ten to twelve chairs, a box, and probably a looking glass. Cupboards, groups of stools, and forms appeared less frequently than in the previous century (see tables 6 and 8). Even when possible differences within the composition of the surviving sample of inventories are taken into account, it is evident that the average mid-eighteenth-century household would have had more furniture in it than its seventeenth-century counterpart of the same social and economic status.

The outward appearance of furniture as well as the increased quantities of it would have distinguished many households of the mid-eighteenth century from households of the previous century. More was involved than just a shift in stylistic vocabulary. The construction, materials, and shape of furniture changed. Some furniture forms fell into disfavor while new forms gained in popularity. Lighter cases of drawers of pine, poplar, maple, and cherry, made by cabinetmakers who dovetailed and nailed their cases together, gradually supplanted the heavier joined chests with drawers, chests of drawers, and oak cupboards. The variety of chairs increased dramatically, and such specialized tables as tea and dressing tables made their first appearance in Wethersfield during the 1730s.

These changes can be documented with precision throughout this period because of the growing specificity with which all items, including furniture, are described in the inventories. By the 1730s a majority of chests, chairs, and tables were preceded by a descriptive adjective of some sort (see tables 4, 5, and 9). In part, these more detailed descriptions were a direct result of the increased quantities of household goods; to record accurately the contents of an estate before it was divided among the heirs, it was no longer adequate just to say chairs if the number of chairs was now twenty-four instead of just four. At the same time, the appearance in Wethersfield of such new varieties of chairs as "crown chairs," "frame chairs," and "bannister chairs" either encouraged or forced consumers and inventory takers to look with greater discrimination at the goods around them. Some of the furniture forms described in detail for the first time during the 1720s and 1730s—flowered boxes, chests with drawers, carved chests of drawers, carved cupboards, and slat-back chairs—had been introduced earlier but were now being recorded as such to distinguish them from cases of drawers and the new varieties of chairs. There also appears to have been present a previously unarticulated awareness of style and fashion that found its most obvious expression in the description of "old fashioned" being applied to some tables, cupboards, and presses during the 1730s.

Beginning in the early eighteenth century, a few round tables and oval tables (today called "gateleg" tables) began to appear in Wethersfield inventories (see table 9). Initially introduced into eastern Massachusetts in the mid- to late 1660s, these tables with leaves, or "falls," and turned legs had gradually replaced the traditional long table as the form preferred by wealthier individuals for dining.[21] The shift in fashion only became evident in Wethersfield in the 1730s and 1740s, as round and oval tables valued usually at one pound, ten shillings supplanted the massive long tables and smaller square tables that had been commonly used in the seventeenth century.

By the late 1740s and 1750s, Wethersfield cabinet-makers and joiners made tables of cherry. Some of these oval fall-leaf tables or square-leaf or round tables undoubtedly had cabriole legs, or "deer's feet," as they were sometimes called in Wethersfield and elsewhere in the lower Connecticut River Valley (fig. 4).[22] John Calder, an English or Scottish merchant who died in Wethersfield in 1749, owned a square table with "bears Claw Legs" worth thirty shillings, a fall-leaf table with "Four Legs Bear Claws" worth five pounds, and a square tea table with "Bears Claws" legs valued at forty shillings. These rustic descriptions may possibly refer to cabriole legs with heavy, hairy, ball and claw feet executed in a style that some English furniture historians associate with the reign of George II. The pace with which such new stylistic vocabulary was introduced into Wethersfield clearly quickened, though John Calder's tables with "Bears Claws" legs did not have any immediate impact on locally produced furniture.

Fig. 4. Oval or round fall-leaf table with "deer's feet," Wethersfield, Connecticut, ca. 1750–1780; cherry. This table was owned in the Stevens family of Wethersfield. (Photograph courtesy of the Wethersfield Historical Society.)

In addition to suggesting the introduction of new stylistic impulses during the mid-eighteenth century, tables of the period clearly document a concern with display, comfort, and gentility among the town's wealthier residents. Tables served as the focal point at meals and at such new genteel social rituals as the serving of tea (see the essay by Rodris Roth elsewhere in this volume). The tables on which these events transpired made important public statements. The heightened concern with the stylishness of tables and the purchase of specialized tea tables or tea stands—John Calder owned a japanned tea stand—indicate that some of Wethersfield's residents—usually its merchants and wealthier landowners—took these events, which both defined and maintained social boundaries, very seriously.

The expenditure of money on candlestands and dressing tables attested to a growing interest in "improving" and refining the domestic environment as a moral enclave. While the ownership of lighting devices generally increased during the period, not all residents chose to spend money on furniture forms designed primarily to hold a single candlestick (see table 11). Despite the relatively modest price of candlestands—two to five shillings—such an expenditure bespoke conspicuous consumption and possibly a more than average interest in transcending localism through reading. The designation or special purchase of a table for use as a dressing table suggested an active interest in personal grooming and the possession of greater than average wealth.

Those individuals who purchased dressing tables occasionally did so in combination with the purchase of a case of drawers.[23] A few inventories of the 1730s and 1740s list together a case of drawers (or a high chest of drawers) and a dressing table. The case of drawers (today usually called a "high chest" or occasionally a "highboy") first appeared in Wethersfield in measurable quantities during the 1730s (see tables 2 and 4). Usually valued at five to eight pounds in the rapidly inflating currency of the period, the case of drawers was an expensive possession initially found primarily, but not exclusively, in the homes of the wealthy. Over 60 percent of the cases of drawers and chests of drawers valued at seven to eight pounds were found in the top 20 percent of the estates probated in the 1730s. In the late 1740s and 1750s, the close relationship between wealth and the ownership of cases of drawers begins to break down, although some of the cases of drawers in these inventories were low cases of drawers (a low chest of four to five drawers) and not the high cases of drawers. The ownership of the more expensive high cases of drawers never became common even in the late eighteenth century, when only one out of five inventories contained such an item.

The appearance of quantities of cases of drawers in Wethersfield coincides exactly with the arrival in Wethersfield in 1730 of cabinetmaker William Manley (ca. 1703–87), who came from Charlestown, Massachusetts. The timing of Manley's arrival and the production of the first cases of drawers in Wethersfield explains the apparent absence of cases of drawers with turned legs in the so-called William and Mary style. The first cabinetmakers to arrive in the Connecticut River Valley region came relatively late, and they arrived already fluent in a new style today called "Queen Anne." The first cases of drawers had cabriole or "deer's feet" legs and flat tops (fig. 5). The preferred woods were initially pine, poplar, or maple, often painted red. By the late 1740s or early 1750s, cabinetmakers also used cherry. In the mid-1750s Wethersfield cabinetmaker Elihu Phelps made cases of drawers with "Crown tops," which today might be called "scrolled" tops or "bonnet" tops. Once again the evidence suggests more rapid changes in stylistic vocabulary and in fashion during the mid-eighteenth century than would be discerned in the probate inventories of the 1600s.[24]

With its introduction and relatively rapid acceptance during these years, the case of drawers assumed the position of preeminence previously held by cupboards and presses. In the 1720s and 1730s, the wealthiest 10 percent of the inventories probated still contained valuable cupboards, even as their owners began acquiring the new case of drawers. By the 1740s cupboards had ceased to be highly valued possessions. The values recorded for cupboards drop to a few shillings as they came to be used primarily in kitchens or cellars. The press fell out of favor even earlier, and most of the examples recorded in the 1720s and 1730s were described as "old fashioned," their role overtaken in part by the appearance of clos-

Table 11. Totals of Stands, Candlestands, and Screens in Wethersfield, Connecticut, Probate Inventories, 1639–1800

	1640s	1650s	1660s	1670s	1680s	1690s	1700s	1710s	1720s	1730s	1740s	1750s	1760s	1770s	1780s	1790s
Number of Inventories	14	12	12	23	43	31	30	68	29	59	50	81	63	98	91	82
Stands											3	7	12	16	32	20
Candlestands										1	1	4		7	8	32
Screens					1					1				4	2	1

Fig. 5. Case of drawers, probably Wethersfield, Connecticut, ca. 1740–55; poplar and pine with traces of original red coloring. This case of drawers descended in the Robbins family of Wethersfield. (Photograph courtesy of The Webb-Deane-Stevens Museum.)

conjunction of aesthetic concern and wealth. The case of drawers, on the other hand, was often part of a more complete and more integrated aesthetic statement of gentility, comfort, and accomplished taste. Cases of drawers in the 1730s and 1740s sometimes came *en suite* with a dressing table and were usually found in association with sets of chairs such as crown or frame chairs. The same individuals who bought cases of drawers and dressing tables were also likely to buy tea tables and stands; the probability that a tea table would appear only in an inventory containing a dressing table was better than fifty-fifty throughout the mid- to late 1700s. This more obviously unified approach to furnishing discrete rooms or an entire household was apparent by the 1660s in eastern Massachusetts and was probably present in the parlors of the Blackleaches and Chesters by the late 1690s but did not become more common in Wethersfield until the middle of the eighteenth century.[25]

The purchase of chairs in sets of six or twelve and occasionally eight becomes noticeable in inventories beginning in the 1740s. During the period from 1721 to 1760 the average number of chairs in an inventory increased from six to almost eleven (see table 2). Such quantities of chairs exceeded the usual needs of the average family and evince greater concern with sociability and interaction with neighbors.

Possession of increased varieties of chairs went along with the increased numbers owned. The number of chairs as well as tables in the wealthiest 10 percent of the inventories probated was more than average—eighteen chairs—but the increased quantities did not represent the mere acquisition of more of the same. Those who owned more chairs usually owned a set of bannister-back crown chairs valued at three shillings each (after adjusting for inflation) or in the 1750s a set of maple (or possibly cherry) crooked-back frame chairs valued at four to five shillings each (when adjustments are made for inflation) as well as a set or two of slat-back, common, or plain chairs worth one to two shillings each (after adjusting for inflation) (figs. 6 and 7). The different sets would have been disposed strategically throughout the house to indicate the relative importance of various rooms.

The same relationship between increasing quantities of furniture and the purchase of different varieties of any single item can also be seen in the types of looking glasses found in Wethersfield inventories re-

ets built into newer houses. By the 1760s and 1770s, inventory takers rarely valued presses at more than five to nine shillings.

The replacement of the cupboard by the case of drawers marked more than just the replacement of one furniture form by another. The cupboard had been a focal point of conspicuous display in the parlor, in some instances the hall, or more infrequently in the bed chamber. The cupboard and the valuable items both in and on it had usually been a singular

Fig. 6. Crooked-back or frame chair with rush seat, probably Wethersfield, Connecticut, ca. 1740–60; maple. This chair resembles examples known to have been owned in Wethersfield. (Photograph courtesy of The Webb-Deane-Stevens Museum.)

Fig. 7. Chair, possibly Wethersfield, Connecticut, ca. 1735–90; poplar and birch. This type of chair is frequently found with a history of ownership in Wethersfield. (Photograph by John Giamatteo, courtesy of the Wethersfield Historical Society.)

corded during the mid-eighteenth century. Between 60 and 70 percent of the inventories during the period listed a looking glass (see table 1). A relationship between the possession of a looking glass and wealth still existed. Inventories valued among the wealthier half of those probated were twice as likely as those in the lower half to contain looking glasses. Wealthy households were also more likely to contain more valuable looking glasses. While appraisers valued most looking glasses at two to six shillings (after ad-

justing for inflation), larger, presumably framed, looking glasses could cost two to five pounds. Increased availability and affordability made such modest luxuries as imported looking glasses more common, but opportunities for the demarcation of status did not diminish. Now that more people had a relatively inexpensive looking glass, there was a greater awareness of the statement made by an oversized, framed (and in some cases gilded frame) looking glass (fig. 8). After all, people can only appreciate hyperbole when they speak the same language.

Surprisingly, the increasing numbers of looking glasses, chairs, and tables did not dramatically alter established patterns of using domestic space, nor did they drive out all traditional furniture forms. Even in the households of the wealthiest, older furniture forms and patterns of domestic order could be found coexisting with more genteel manners. At social levels below that occupied by merchants, prosperous sea captains, and large landowners, the persistence of older patterns in both furniture forms and usage was more obvious. Chests with lift tops with no, one, or two drawers could be found in almost all inventories (fig. 9). The majority of chairs in all inventories were

Fig. 8. Looking glass, probably English but possibly American, ca. 1740–70; frame of walnut and pine. This example was probably owned by Col. Thomas Belden (1732–82) of Wethersfield. (Photograph courtesy of The Webb-Deane-Stevens Museum.)

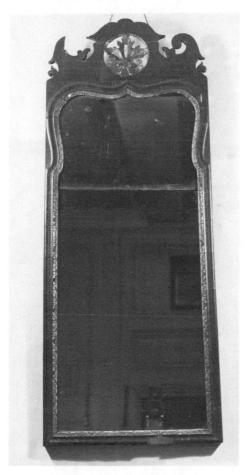

Fig. 9. Chest with two drawers, Wethersfield, Connecticut, ca. 1750–80; pine. This type was more commonly owned than either cases of drawers or chests of drawers in eighteenth-century Wethersfield. The scalloping of the front skirt board closely resembles that found on the skirts of cases of drawers owned in Wethersfield during the period. (Photograph by John Giamatteo, courtesy of the Wethersfield Historical Society.)

still turned chairs with rush, or "flag bottom," seats valued at one to two shillings. The entry for "10 varnished bannister" chairs worth an impressive twelve pounds in the widow Sarah Goodrich's inventory of 1747 may be the only inventory reference before the 1760s to chairs with slip, or "cushion," seats. Comfort had not yet descended to the chair bottoms of even the wealthiest in Wethersfield.

The distribution of beds in the twenty-nine inventories taken between 1721 and 1760 that list the location of sleeping furniture indicates that the parlor remained the location of the most expensive bed and furnishings (see table 12).[26] In almost half of the twenty-nine estates inventoried, the best bed stood in the parlor, and in another 30 percent it stood in another first-floor room. All told, however, at least 40 percent of the beds stood in chambers or garrets, and

Table 12. Placement of Beds in Probate Inventories with Room Designations from Wethersfield, Connecticut, 1639–1800

Decade	Number of Inventories	Parlor	Hall	Kitchen	Lower Room	Bedroom	N. Room	S. Room	W. Room	E. Room	Chambers	Garret	Other Rooms	Unknown	Total
1640s	3	3									1		1	5	10
1650s	6	5									2[a]			6	13[a]
1660s	4	4		1							1		1	7	14
1670s	8	10		1				3			13		2	4	33
1680s	8	6		1	2	2					9		1	5	26
1690s	10	5					1	1			25	[a]	7	4	43[a]
1700s	4	4									9		1	1	15
1710s	14	15	2	1	1	1					30		5	5	60
1720s	5	4	1								10			10	25
1730s	7	3				2	1	1	1	3	15	2		5	33
1740s	7	5		1	1	3	1				12			8	31
1750s	10	8		1			2	2	2	1	14		3	12	45
1760s	17	2	2	1		14		5	2	6	29		1	22	84
1770s	19	6	3			13	7	6		1	25		2	21	84
1780s	18	1	1		2	12	6	1	3	2	29		2	21	80
1790s	19	1		1		26	4	1			37	2	2	17	91

Note: The superscript letters serve the same purpose as in table 3.

Note on method: Bed is defined for the purposes of this table in the same manner in which it is defined in the note for table 7. *Hall* includes references to dwelling room and outward room.

Other Rooms includes references to new room, great room, minor room, and middle room, as well as lean-to, backroom, and back house.

only 34 percent definitely stood on the first floor.

Admittedly inconclusive evidence supplied by a few inventories that do list most or all of their contents by room indicates that in the homes of the wealthy the best chamber assumed increasing importance during the mid-eighteenth century. The best bed chamber could be the location of the best bed and of such new furniture forms as a case of drawers and a dressing table. Sets of chairs and tables were also sometimes placed in the best chamber, suggesting that formal entertaining or visiting could occur upstairs. Captain Gideon Wells, who died in 1740, had a large "old fashioned" table worth £1, a tea table worth £1, a desk, a looking glass worth £5, and a set of black chairs worth £1 3s. in his east room (a hall or sitting room); two beds, two tables, a looking glass worth 10 shillings, eight chairs worth £1, and a cupboard worth £2 in his west room (a traditional parlor); and his most expensive bed, five chairs worth £2 10s., a looking glass worth £1, a case of drawers worth £7, and a table, possibly a dressing table, worth £3 in the east chamber. Evidence for the enhanced status of the best chamber increases later in the eighteenth century.

1761–1800

Wethersfield continued to grow during the prosperous years of the late 1760s and early 1770s. The town's population stood at 3,489 in 1774.[27] Commercial opportunities still attracted such men as English-born William Beadle and Peter Verstile and Groton native Silas Deane who moved to Wethersfield hoping to make a fortune in trade. The Revolution cruelly shattered the hopes of Beadle, Deane, Verstile, and others, but it helped make the fortune of Capt. Ashael Riley and others with commercial and shipping interests. The town weathered the economic and social disruptions of the Revolution and the postwar depression with its economic vitality undiminished.

Evidence for the town's continued economic well-being is found in the probate inventories, which reveal no decline in the standard of living in Wethersfield. The quantities of given types of furniture in the inventories continue to increase. By the late eighteenth century, an average inventory usually contained three beds, two sets of chairs (twelve chairs), three to four chests (including a chest of drawers and possibly a case of drawers or bureau), three or four tables, one or two looking glasses, and possibly a stand.

The actual furniture forms in the inventories remained largely unchanged throughout the second half of the eighteenth century. Turned chairs still made up the largest percentage of seating furniture in any given household (see table 5). Most of these turned chairs were slat-back, plain, common, or white chairs (all ladder backs) worth a shilling or two (fig. 10). Appearing first in the 1780s, Windsor chairs, valued at four to five shillings, found their way into an increasing number of Wethersfield households by the 1790s (fig. 11). These versatile chairs were used in sitting rooms, best chambers, and possibly even parlors. The crown chairs declined somewhat in price—usually only two to three shillings in the 1780s and 1790s—and in status, but this chair type still found favor with Wethersfield residents. For those who

Fig. 10. Slat-back or four-back great chair, Wethersfield, Connecticut, ca. 1740–70; maple and ash. This chair, owned by members of the Buck family, is one of the few slat-back chairs to survive with a firm history of ownership in Wethersfield. (Photograph by John Giamatteo, private collection.)

Fig. 11. Fanback-type Windsor chair, possibly Wethersfield or Hartford, Connecticut, 1780–1800; poplar, hickory, and maple. This chair was owned in Wethersfield by a member of the Woodhouse or Robbins family. Chairs like this became increasingly common in the 1790s and early 1800s. (Photograph courtesy of The Webb-Deane-Stevens Museum.)

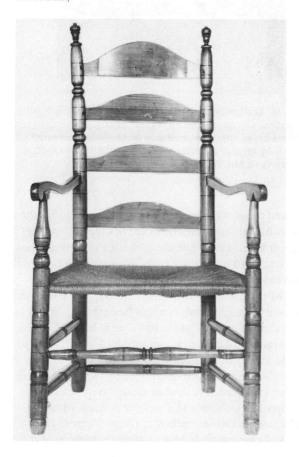

could afford them, a set of crooked-back frame chairs with rounded or bowed crests and rush seats served as the best chairs in the house. A particularly distinctive framed chair made by chairmakers Thomas and Michael Brigden was highly prized in the 1770s and 1780s, but it declined somewhat in popularity and value in the 1790s. At most only 6 to 8 percent of the chairs inventoried between 1761 and 1800 were frame chairs.

Chairs with slip seats made up only a minuscule percentage—maybe 3 percent—of the chairs recorded in inventories from 1761 to 1800. Easy chairs, which were presumably upholstered arm chairs, were even scarcer (see table 5). Chairs with slip seats appeared in the inventories as "plush-bottom," "green-bottom" (probably referring to a seat covering of green wool), "worked-bottom" (crewel embroidered), "leather-bottom," "cushion chair," "mahogany chairs" worth twenty-two shillings each, and "cherry chairs" worth twelve to eighteen shillings each. As a general rule, chairs with slip seats were worth more than six shillings each; most were worth eight to twelve shillings. By the 1790s a few of these relatively rare chairs with slip seats may have been in the so-called Chippendale style, but the presence or absence of such frequently used stylistic categories says little about the design of the vast majority of the chairs in Wethersfield in the late eighteenth century (fig. 12).

Stylistic change also had relatively little impact on most case furniture during the period. Board chests and chests with drawers remained a fixture in all households (see table 4). Cases of drawers, in most instances low cases with four to five drawers worth about one pound, became more common. By the 1790s some inventory takers recorded bureaus; some of these bureaus were undoubtedly low cases of drawers, while others may have been chests of drawers with bracket feet in a late Chippendale style. It is unlikely that these references to bureaus referred to case furniture in a neoclassical style.

Ownership of high cases of drawers valued at two pounds, ten shillings to five pounds was still limited primarily, though not exclusively, to estates in the wealthiest 20 percent of the inventories probated; the concentration of ownership among the merchants, professionals, and large landowners who possessed the wealthiest 20 percent of the estates probated was very high.[28] Most of these high cases of drawers con-

Fig. 12. Leather-bottom chair, probably East Windsor or Hartford, Connecticut, 1785–1800; cherry. According to local tradition, this side chair was purchased in the early 1790s by Frederick Butler of Wethersfield. (Photograph courtesy of The Webb-Deane-Stevens Museum.)

tinued to be made in the Queen Anne style. For those desiring a more distinctive case of drawers, mahogany or walnut could be used, though the inventories list only two mahogany cases of drawers and one walnut case of drawers.

The popularity of desks increased in the latter decades of the eighteenth century (see table 8). While less than one estate in six had a desk before 1751, over one-third of the estates probated after 1760 had a desk, and most of these were valued at one to two pounds. Desks valued in the one-to-two pound price range were probably dual-purpose case pieces with drawers for storage and a writing surface for work. While most estates ranked in the wealthiest 10 percent of those probated had a desk, ownership of this furniture form became well distributed throughout all but the lowest stratum of society as time went on. Still, the desk was regarded as both a work surface and a statement of status, suggesting both literacy and economic pursuits that involve written records and accounts. The frequent placement of desks in parlors or best chambers underscores their dual role as places for solitary work and as status objects intended to be seen by others on certain occasions.

The combination desk-and-bookcase provided an even more powerful statement of economic status, learning, and possible commercial pursuits (fig. 13). Desk-and-bookcases first appeared in Wethersfield inventories in the 1760s. Generally, a desk-and-bookcase was valued at twice the value of a desk and slightly more than a case of drawers; most were appraised at four pounds, ten shillings to five pounds, though some were appraised at only two pounds, ten shillings to three pounds. While almost one-half of the owners of desk-and-bookcases were merchants or professionals with estates valued among the top 10 percent of those probated, desk-and-bookcases could also be found in the inventories of less wealthy individuals. Occupation and the possession of an unusually large number of books undoubtedly influenced the decision to buy a desk-and-bookcase as much as mere wealth.

Tables continued to be the most sensitive barometer of changing fashions, status, and living standards. Tea tables of various descriptions and varying values continued to be scarce, while dressing tables with three or four drawers and valued at twelve to fourteen shillings came to be found with more regularity (see table 9). Still, over half of the dressing tables (fig. 14) were found in the estates of merchants, professionals, and prosperous yeomen and artisans who made up the top 20 percent of the estates probated after 1761. An even closer association existed between the possession of a "stand table" and wealth. Some of the references to stand tables in the inventories appear to be to candlestands, but other references are to a type of tripod-based, pedestal table with a large round top that tipped or swiveled as John Calder's 1749 inventory described it: "1 [table] stand fashion swivel leaf." Approximately 60 percent of all stand tables recorded were owned by individuals with estates among the wealthiest 20 percent probated. The relationship between the ownership of expensive stand tables worth fifteen shillings to one pound and

Fig. 13. Desk-and-bookcase, eastern Massachusetts, 1760–90; mahogany. This desk-and-bookcase was owned in Wethersfield by Rev. John Marsh (1742–1821) and shows that not all Wethersfield-owned furniture was locally made. (Photograph courtesy of Historic Deerfield, Inc.)

wealthy merchants, like Calder, was even closer.

Despite this one innovation of the mid-eighteenth century that became somewhat more popular by the 1780s and 1790s, table forms changed little. Round,

Fig. 14. Dressing table, Wethersfield, Connecticut, ca. 1740–60; mahogany. This example, valued at one pound, four shillings in the inventory of its original owner, Col. Thomas Belden, is the only known example of a dressing table made in Wethersfield of mahogany. (Photograph courtesy of The Brooklyn Museum.)

oval, and square tables that could be used for dining or tea drinking were the forms most frequently used for entertaining. Even more commonly owned were simpler square and rectangular tables without leaves valued at four to eight shillings. Except for a few late examples, references to dining tables, card tables, and breakfast tables are not found in the inventories.

While the basic furniture forms and styles introduced in the mid-eighteenth century remained dominant, some subtle but significant developments occurred between 1761 and 1800. These developments suggest increased concern with refining domestic interiors at all levels of society. Most inventories had one looking glass, and many had two (see tables 1 and 2). Stands and candlestands, which had been listed in less than one inventory out of six in the 1750s, could be found in over half of the inventories probated in the 1790s (see table 11). The ownership of clocks was less widespread, but, beginning in the

1770s, it increased to surprisingly high levels (see table 13). By the 1790s the use of cherry stained dark to resemble mahogany was widespread on cases of drawers, tables, and stands and could be found in a majority of inventories (see table 9).

Those who sought to go one better than the owners of cherry furniture bought chairs, desks, bedsteads, and case furniture of genuine imported mahogany. The numbers of those who did so remained small. Members of older established mercantile families such as Col. John Chester, Col. Thomas Belden, and Edward Bulkley purchased an occasional piece of mahogany furniture. New arrivals and recently enriched merchants such as James Adams (died 1791) from Killingly, Connecticut, and Silas Deane (probated 1792) from Groton, Connecticut, bought entire rooms of mahogany furniture.

A more commonly shared and more revealing development involved beds and sleeping arrangements. While the average quantity of beds per inventory gradually and marginally increased in the later 1700s, the character of beds changed more dramatically (see tables 2 and 7). Before 1720 few beds appear to have been fully or partially curtained.[29] Evidence suggests that in the seventeenth and early eighteenth centuries only one out of ten or eleven beds had hangings, and less than one out of six inventories had at least one curtained bed. During the period from 1720 to 1760, the portion of all inventories listing bed curtains and valances approached 40 percent, and perhaps as many as one bed in five was a partially or fully curtained high-post bed. After 1760, over 60 percent of the inventories listed beds with hangings, and one bed in four was probably curtained.

Such beds not only displayed wealth in the form of textiles but also provided for increased comfort and privacy within the household. With its curtains drawn, a fully hung bed became a room within a room. Several scholars have recently written about the growing concern with privacy in the eighteenth century and have pointed to architectural changes.[30] It is also evident that changes to enhance privacy could occur within traditional housing plans. Increased use of curtained beds and the decreased use of trundle beds provided more privacy when sleeping (see table 7). The placement of the best bed—the parents' bed—in an upstairs chamber or in a first-floor bedroom used solely as a sleeping apartment could provide more privacy even in a traditional, though

Table 13. Looking Glasses and Clocks in Wethersfield, Connecticut, Probate Inventories, 1639–1800

	1640s	1650s	1660s	1670s	1680s	1690s	1700s	1710s	1720s	1730s	1740s	1750s	1760s	1770s	1780s	1790s
Number of Inventories	14	12	12	23	43	31	30	68	29	59	50	81	63	98	91	82
Total Looking Glasses			2	4	5	10	11	27	19	53	46	87	96	140	111	139
Looking Glasses by type:																
Unspecified			2	4	5	10	11	27	19	53	46	80	76	114	89	107
Small												6	15	16	13	27
Stacia												1	5	10	9	5
Clocks				1				1		3		1	2	8	9	15

often enlarged, version of the central-chimney house (see table 12).[31] By the 1790s, inventories with room designations placed 87 percent of the best beds and at least 70 percent of all beds in first-floor bedrooms or chambers that appear to have been used almost exclusively for sleeping.

Elsewhere in the houses of Wethersfield residents, even wealthy residents, much remained the same. Parlors or rooms still functioning as traditional parlors contained beds—perhaps no longer the best bed, but a valuable bed. The parlor in William Hurlburt's 1791 inventory had a fully curtained bed, a case of drawers, a desk, and twelve chairs, while his "outward room" (or sitting room) had a clock, an old desk, a great table, and eighteen less-expensive chairs. In other inventories of the 1790s, the pattern remained the same, while the names of the rooms changed: a northern or western room contained a bed, a table, a case piece, and a set of chairs, while a southern or eastern room contained a table and often a tea table and one or two sets of chairs. Only in the homes of merchant Col. Thomas Belden (died 1782), Samuel Foster (died 1797), a New York state native, and perhaps a few other residents did both front rooms downstairs lack a bed and serve exclusively as entertaining and sitting rooms.

The tenacity with which traditions in room use and furnishings persisted into the late eighteenth century in the Connecticut River Valley occasionally evoked amused or disgusted comments from those acquainted with more urbane practices. During a 1771 visit to Middletown, John Adams dined with Dr. Eliot Rawson, whose house was "handsome without, but neither clean nor elegant within, in furniture or anything else." "His [Rawson's] dining Room is crouded with a Bed and a Cradle, &c. &c."[32] Rawson's "dining Room" was undoubtedly a traditional parlor, and his furniture probably very similar to the majority of that found in neighboring Wethersfield, since one of Middletown's leading cabinetmakers, Timothy Boardman (1727–92), and one of the town's chairmakers, Thomas Brigden, Jr., were both raised and trained in Wethersfield. If given the opportunity to visit most homes in Wethersfield, Adams would have been similarly unimpressed with the seemingly conservative furnishings. Like their Middletown neighbors, Wethersfield residents in the later eighteenth century were still far from the more advanced styles and pretentions found in urban Boston and New York, but they had come a great distance from the material world of their forefathers.

*   *   *

A thorough analysis of the results of this study of furniture found in Wethersfield probate inventories must be comparative. As similar studies of other communities in colonial North America are undertaken and published, a more meaningful interpretation of the Wethersfield data will be possible.

It is possible to suggest, tentatively, some larger conclusions on the basis of the Wethersfield findings and of studies done elsewhere. The evidence from the seventeenth- and early eighteenth-century Wethersfield inventories underscores Abbott L. Cummings's observation on seventeenth-century furnishings that "this period was at one and the same time more richly elaborate and more starkly primitive than we realize."[33] In Wethersfield, conservative versions of rich and elaborate furnishings could be found in the homes of the wealthy, but most residents lived a simpler, if not necessarily primitive, material existence. Compared to the households of individuals living in more isolated farming communities of inland New England and those of the average residents of the Chesapeake Bay region, the homes of Wethersfield's middling yeomen and artisans were relatively well furnished.[34] It is also clear that the examples of Wethersfield furniture that survive from the seventeenth century are late examples of relatively substantial furniture.

The increase in the quantities and changes in the types of furniture found in Wethersfield inventories of the mid-eighteenth century were not isolated phenomena. Like other communities throughout Britain and its colonies, the town of Wethersfield clearly added to the growing demand for goods in the early and mid-1700s that produced a consumer revolution and helped launch the industrial revolution in England.[35] In each locality, the growing demand for certain types of household goods, such as furniture, must have resulted in increased production by local artisans as well. The same pattern of increasing possessions found in the Wethersfield inventories of the mid-1700s can be found up the Connecticut River in Deerfield, Massachusetts; to the east in Concord, Massachusetts; and far to the south in the Chesapeake Bay region.[36] Differing levels of economic activity and prosperity and the particular preferences of local consumers shaped the character of local demand, but the same basic trend existed in disparate communities participating in the Atlantic economy.

The change in Wethersfield, as elsewhere, was qualitative as well as quantitative. Some scholars have spoken of the emergence during the mid-eighteenth century of a new cultural outlook, a "Georgian world view."[37] New emphases on individualism, privacy, and order are seen as characterizing this new cultural outlook. The appearance of sets of chairs, of more fully curtained beds, and of rooms furnished *en suite* suggests that furnishings were acquired to promote a more obviously ordered environment, one that intensified the desire for greater privacy and enhanced the rituals of genteel civility.

It would be wrong, however, to conclude that the mahoganized surfaces of cherry tables and sets of chairs indicate the complete triumph or undigested reception of a new world view or cultural outlook. The continued presence of parlors with beds, chests with lift tops, and turned chairs with slat backs forcefully suggests that in Wethersfield, as in other communities, older patterns, habits, and cultural outlooks also persisted with tenacity at least until 1800 at all levels of society and in the minds of most residents.

Notes

The transcription and preliminary analysis of the 786 probate inventories used in this article were undertaken by present and former members of the staff at the Webb-Deane-Stevens Museum: Helen Lewis, Christina Perugini, Charlotte Stiverson, and the author. The inventory research project was part of the museum's contribution to the 1982 *Two Towns: Concord and Wethersfield* exhibition and catalog, which was supported by the National Endowment for the Humanities. The author would also like to acknowledge the comments and suggestions of Donald R. Friary and Robert F. Trent.

1. *The Public Records of the Colony of Connecticut*, ed. J. Hammond Trumbull (Hartford, 1850), 1:444.

2. Most of the Wethersfield probate inventory transcripts used in this study were based on the file copies of the estate papers at the Connecticut State Library in Hartford. In the 1600s and 1700s, Wethersfield was part of the Hartford Probate District.

3. Some of the problems inherent in the use of probate inventories are discussed in Jackson T. Main, "The Distribution of Property in Colonial Connecticut," in *The Human Dimensions of Nation Making*, ed. James Kirby Martin (Madison, 1976), 54–57, and Lois Green Carr and Lorena S. Walsh, "Inventories and the Analysis of Wealth and Consumption Patterns in St. Mary's County, Maryland, 1658–1777," *Historical Methods* 13, no. 2 (1980): 81–82; Gloria L. Main, "Probate Records as a Source for Early American History," *William and Mary Quarterly*, 3d ser., 32, no. 1 (1975): 89–99.

4. Main, "Distribution of Property in Connecticut," 56.

5. The 1768 probate inventory of Jacob Griswold has an entry for "4 Bowbacks or framed chairs, 18 shillings." Estate of Jacob Griswold, 1768, Hartford Probate District, File no. 2436, Connecticut State Library (hereafter CSL).

6. The latter point is made forcefully in Robert Blair St. George, "A Retreat from the Wilderness: Pattern in the Domestic Environments of Southeastern New England, 1630–1730" (Ph.D. diss., University of Pennsylvania, 1982), esp. xxii.

7. Sherman W. Adams and Henry R. Stiles, *The History of Ancient Wethersfield*, 2 vols. (New York, 1904), 1:135–69, and John P. Demos, *Entertaining Satan: Witchcraft and the Culture of Early New England* (New York, 1982), 340–67.

8. Carter L. Hudgins, "Exactly as the Gentry Do in England: Culture, Aspirations, and Material Things in the Eighteenth Century Chesapeake" (paper given at a conference on "The Colonial Experience: The Eighteenth Century Chesapeake," Sept. 13–15, 1984), 18, table 7; Kathleen E. Eagan, "We Got Plenty of Nothin': Furniture Styles, Forms, and Amounts Found in Deerfield Inventories" (Historic Deerfield Summer Fellowship paper, 1975); Mary Tigue, "Colonial Standards of Living: Economic Progress in Deerfield, Massachusetts" (Historic Deerfield Summer Fellowship paper, 1980); and unpublished data on Concord, Mass., probate inventories supplied to the author by Peter Benes; see also Cary Carson and Lorena Walsh, "The Material Life of the Early American Housewife" (paper presented at a conference on "Women in Early America," November 5–7, 1981, Williamsburg, Va.), esp. tables 1A, 1B, 4, and 5; Jack Michel, " 'In a Manner and Fashion Suitable to Their Degree': A Preliminary Investigation of the Material Culture of Early Rural Pennsylvania," *Working Papers of the Regional Economic History Research Center* 5, no. 1 (1981): 12, table 3.

9. Both John Demos, *A Little Commonwealth: Family Life in Plymouth Colony* (New York, 1970), 33, 39, 44, and Karen Andressen, "A Layered Society: Material Life in Portsmouth, New Hampshire, 1680–1740" (Ph.D. diss., University of New Hampshire, 1982), 116, stress the fluid and undifferentiated character of interior spaces. For a contrasting view, see Robert Blair St. George, " 'Set Thine House in Order': The Domestication of the Yeomanry in Seventeenth-Century New England," in *New England Begins: The Seventeenth Century*, ed. Jonathan L. Fairbanks and Robert F. Trent, 3 vols. (Boston, 1982), 2:168–73.

10. Estate of John Buttolph, 1693, Hartford Probate District, File no. 1042, CSL.

11. The 1690 probate inventory of Ens. Samuel Wright contains the following: "The Contents of the chest marked DW mentioned on the other side are as follows:" 1 pair of worsted stockings, 6s.; 1 hat, 12s.; 1 serge coat, £2; 1 belt and 1 black ribbon, 4s.; 1 black scarf, 10s.; 1 red scarf or sash, 8s.; 2 yards of broad cloath, £2 10s.; 12 yards of drugct £1 8s.; 8 yards of Kentin, £1 12s.; pins and a marking iron, 2s.; and a bag of money totaling £16 8s.

12. St. George, " 'Set Thine House in Order,' " 168–73, and Abbott L. Cummings, *Rural Household Inventories* (Boston, 1969), xvii–xviii.

13. *The Wyllis Papers*, ed. Albert C. Bates, *Collections of the Connecticut Historical Society* 21 (Hartford, 1924), 191, and Evarts B. Greene and Virginia D. Harrington, *American Population before the Federal Census of 1790* (New York, 1932), 58.

14. Adams and Stiles, *Ancient Wethersfield*, 1:542–43.

15. The composition of this group was determined by ranking inventories on the basis of gross personal wealth.

16. I am indebted to Robert F. Trent, Curator of the Connecticut Historical Society, for clarifying this reference.

17. A study by William N. Hosley, Jr., finds a ratio closer to two to one; William N. Hosley, Jr., and Philip Zea, "Decorated Board Chests of the Connecticut River Valley," *Antiques* 119, no. 5 (1981):1146.

18. Greene and Harrington, *American Population*, 58.

19. The comparison is based on shipping tonnage taxed in Wethersfield in 1730 and 1751, Wethersfield Tax Abstracts, box 11, CSL.

20. References to this economic elite and other references to the economic patterns of furniture ownership for this section are based primarily on material from the period 1721–50. Inflation and the currency change in the 1750s made use of information on wealth from the 1750s impossible.

21. See catalog entry no. 286 ("Draw Table") in *New England Begins*, ed. Fairbanks and Trent, 2:289–90.

22. Estate of Simeon Griswold, 1785, Hartford Probate District, File no. 2466, and estate of Timothy Boardman, 1792, Middletown Probate District, File no. 447, CSL.

23. Period terminology for describing what are today often called "highboys" was not consistent, especially in the 1730s and 1740s. The case of drawers worth £3 4s. in the 1753 probate inventory of Martin Kellogg was undoubtedly the chest of drawers worth £3 11s. in the 1754 probate inventory of his widow, Dorothy Kellogg. A mahogany case of drawers and matching dressing table now at the Brooklyn Museum were recorded in Col. Thomas Belden's 1782 probate inventory as "1 Mahogany chest with drawers £3–10" and "1 Mahogany dressing table £1–4."

24. See Kevin M. Sweeney, "Furniture and Furniture Making in Mid-Eighteenth Century Wethersfield, Connecticut," *Antiques* 125, no. 5 (1984): 1156–63.

25. Cummings, *Rural Household Inventories*, xxvi–xxvii, and Robert F. Trent, *Historic Furnishings Report: Saugus Iron Works National Historic Site, Saugus, Massachusetts* (Harpers Ferry, W. Va., 1982), 56–57.

26. After 1715, inventory takers tended to group furniture and other items in a household categorically instead of by room location. Some inventory takers did indicate the location of beds, and these scattered references have been used to compile table 12.

27. Greene and Harrington, *American Population*, 58.

28. References to this economic elite and to the economic patterns of ownership in this section are based primarily on an analysis of inventories probated between 1761 and 1770 and between 1781 and 1790. Inflation in the late 1770s and a currency change in the mid-1790s made using those decades difficult.

29. A more detailed study of bed hangings and other textiles found in Wethersfield probate inventories is being prepared by Christina Perugini and Charlotte Stiverson.

30. David Flaherty, *Privacy in Colonial New England* (Charlottesville, Va., 1972), 25–44, and James Deetz, *In Small Things Forgotten: The Archaeology of Early American Life* (New York, 1977), 115–17.

31. Analysis of surviving structures and valuation lists for Wethersfield reveals that between 1750 and 1800 newly constructed central-chimney houses outnumbered central-

hall houses by a ratio of two or three to one. See Dione Longley, "Neat Mansions of Comfort and Independence: Wethersfield's Role in Architecture, 1750–1800" (Carleton Internship paper, Webb-Deane-Stevens Museum, 1981), esp. 3, 10.

32. *Diary and Autobiography of John Adams*, ed. L. H. Butterfield, 4 vols. (Cambridge, Mass., 1961), 2:31.

33. Cummings, *Rural Household Inventories*, xx.

34. See studies cited in nn. 3, 8.

35. John Brewer, J. H. Plumb, and Neil McKendrick, *The Birth of a Consumer Society: Commercialization in Eighteenth-Century England* (Bloomington, Ind., 1982).

36. See studies cited in nn. 3, 8.

37. Deetz, *In Small Things Forgotten*, 39–43, 111–17.

Women and Property in South Carolina: The Evidence from Marriage Settlements, 1730–1830

MARYLYNN SALMON

Whether in Pennsylvania, in New England, or in the South, in city or in country, the control and production of household property and its proper management were often linked to marriage, a legally and ecclesiastically sanctioned union of material estates as well as an emotional bond. Through marriage men often found a means of holding women in submission to patriarchal rule. As Marylynn Salmon demonstrates in the following essay, the dominance of men through marriage certainly found support in the common law of property, which severely restricted the property rights of women. Yet in marriage settlements—essentially agreements in which a husband allowed his wife or wife-to-be to retain control of the goods she brought to their marriage—permitted under the equally valid system of equity law, she discovers an effective mechanism through which South Carolina women could and did seize control of both real and personal property and, in so doing, exercise some of the same privileges men enjoyed.

The primary sources Salmon draws on are particularly rich. Between 1730 and 1830, a sample of some 638 marriage settlements from South Carolina allow her to explore the people who entered into such agreements and the different ways in which these nuptial contracts functioned. In some instances settlements guaranteed aristocratic women or their trustees that their inherited estates would not be endangered if their husbands proved insolvent. Yet the settlement was used widely by people of middling status as well; carpenters and shoemakers entered into such agreements with their spouses. In many such cases, women retained the right to their own estates, often comprising one or two slaves, a cow, or some bedding and household furniture. Their concern for the relative autonomy of their few possessions, Salmon argues, can only suggest that these South Carolina women were worried less about the welfare of their unborn grandchildren than about planning for their own security in a world not espe-cially kind to propertyless women.

As she discusses various strategies used by women entering into settlements, Salmon highlights their importance to widows whose prior experience in marriage sharpened an appreciation for the legal independence that such agreements could provide. Widows, for example, often had property from their deceased first husband's estate that needed protection. With children from a prior marriage perhaps already mature and adequately provided for, widows entering into new settlements seemed less worried about property passing directly to their children. Unlike many single women, widows frequently stipulated that they be permitted to write their own wills. Salmon concludes that widows above all wanted "absolute control" as managers of their own property. Between the eighteenth and early nineteenth centuries, the percentage of settlements allowing women to write wills fell dramatically; the drop suggests that as women came to share with husbands more power over household business, their need to protect property both in life and after death became less intense. When marriage settlements were made in the early national period, they paradoxically often recognized the increased real authority of women within marriage by actually demanding joint control of all family property.

During the eighteenth and early nineteenth centuries two distinct sets of legal principles—those of the common law and equity law—governed the status of women in the British-American colonies and the American states. Complications arose when the rules contradicted each other, as they did, for example, with regard to property ownership. Under the common law, a married woman (feme covert) could not own property, either real or personal. All personalty a woman brought to marriage became her husband's. He could spend her money, sell her stocks or slaves, and appropriate her clothing and jewelry. He gained managerial rights to her lands, houses, and tenements and decided if land was to be farmed by the family or leased.[1] He also controlled the rents and profits from all real estate. With regard to conveyances, however, women held a single note of power. No husband could sell real property without the consent of his wife. The common law sanctioned conveyances only when wives freely agreed to them, although "free" consent was sometimes quite difficult to determine in court.[2]

Since women could not own property under the common law, they could not exercise legal controls over it. A feme covert could not make a legally binding contract. She could not sell or mortgage property that she brought to the marriage or that she and her husband acquired. She possessed no power to execute a deed of gift or write a will unless her husband consented, and even then her power was restricted to personal property. During widowhood, the law allowed a woman dower rights in one-third of her husband's real property. Hers was a life interest only, and she gained no right to sell or mortgage the land. With regard to personal property, widows could claim absolute ownership of one-third, but only if the estate were free of debts. If a husband died heavily indebted or insolvent, his wife lost all her personal property (and in some jurisdictions her real property as well), even though she had exercised no control over the accumulation of her husband's debts. Regarding property, then, women were virtually powerless under the common law.[3]

Equity law as administered by the British and American courts of chancery was not similarly harsh. Through formal contracts called marriage settlements, femes covert owned and controlled property.[4] In their various forms, marriage settlements allowed women full or partial managerial rights over property. Separate clauses gave women the right to sell or mortgage property, give it away, or write wills. Some marriage settlements stated explicitly the traditional rights that men relinquished by signing them. Many settlements barred husbands from "intermeddling" with their wives' estates in any way and, perhaps most important, stated that settlement property could not be taken by creditors to pay a husband's debts. Separate estates for women

also frequently included clauses guaranteeing the inheritances of children. Once women or their relations protected property from the possible business misfortunes of their husbands, it could safely be passed through the maternal line.

Marriage settlements were designed, then, to serve several functions. They gave women a measure of financial security during marriage and widowhood. They protected a portion of family property from creditors. They provided grandparents with the assurance that family fortunes would not be spent before grandchildren came of age. Historians of aristocratic society in seventeenth- and eighteenth-century England have tended to emphasize this last function of marriage settlements. They have found that beginning in the late sixteenth century, fathers created trust estates for their daughters in an effort to prevent sons-in-law from controlling, and perhaps squandering, family fortunes. For a man who wanted to guarantee the inheritances of his grandchildren, a trust presented an alternative to turning property over to an outsider—his daughter's husband. According to this interpretation, the primary purpose of English marriage settlements was to create and preserve large family estates.[5]

Historians of early America have tended to discount the importance of the British perspective on trust estates. Instead, scholars such as Richard B. Morris and Mary R. Beard stressed the utilitarian function of settlements for the feme covert. Pointing to the existence of equity law and trust estates, Beard and Morris claimed that in America (and Beard also applied the argument to England), women functioned virtually on a legal par with men. If a woman could own property, make contracts, and write wills under equity law, then common law restrictions on her activities lost meaning.[6] Thus the most generally accepted interpretation of equity law in America has emphasized its ability to elevate the legal status of women from subservience to relative independence.

Historians of women in early America have relied on this interpretation of equity law to help define the status of the feme covert. The hypothesis of equality has contributed to the assumption that colonial women enjoyed a legal and social status superior to that of both their English contemporaries and their nineteenth-century descendants.[7] For if, as Morris claimed, marriage settlements were "widely employed" in America, and if, as Beard believed, they were interpreted liberally, then women of all classes in the colonies enjoyed the rights of wealthy Englishwomen. In the view of these historians, the common use of settlements in the eighteenth century reflected a beneficial legal climate for American women. Similarly, the decline of equity law in the nineteenth century demonstrated the advantages enjoyed by eighteenth-century matrons.[8]

Neither Morris nor Beard studied marriage settlements in detail. They knew that equity law contained rules allowing women to own property and that some marriage settlements existed, but they did not know how frequently settlements were employed or what specific powers women exercised through them. Historical understanding of equity law and the use of marriage settlements has been based on scant research and impressionistic evidence. The current lively debate over the nature of women's legal and social status in the colonial and early national periods makes it important, however, to understand equity law more precisely.[9] We must learn who used marriage settlements, how often they were used, and for what purposes. Such information should reveal the degree to which settlements provided women with financial security and whether they were written to benefit women, or children and grandchildren, or all three groups.

Before the role of equity law in America can be understood, many separate studies of settlements must be conducted, because each colony and state handled principles of equity law differently.[10] Large numbers of settlement deeds must also be scrutinized, even though the informality of American recording practices frequently makes such analysis difficult. This essay reports findings for South Carolina, for which a wealth of information is available. The extent of the documentation makes South Carolina a good place to begin an investigation into the nature of equity law. The legal record reveals remarkably liberal attitudes toward women's property rights—quite possibly the most liberal of all the colonies and states, although that supposition must be tested by comparative study.[11]

In 1720 the colony established a court of chancery that handled cases concerning marriage settlements in a sophisticated manner, imitating the English Chancery Court in style and decisions.[12] The court kept good records and remained active throughout the colonial and early national periods. The legisla-

ture did not require registration of marriage settlements until 1785, but before that date prudent persons frequently recorded their settlements with the secretary of state in Charleston. After 1785, all settlements had to be recorded within three months of their creation to be considered valid.[13] Altogether some 2,000 settlements have survived from the colonial and early national periods.[14] For this study, an attempt was made to discover and analyze all recorded marriage settlements for the colonial and Revolutionary periods. For the period 1785–1830, when the law required settlements to be recorded and the number increased accordingly, a sample consisting of all deeds registered in Charleston in every fifth year has been analyzed, for a total of 638 (see table 1). Each settlement gives the names of the parties, the dates of creation and recording, the type of property settled, and the terms of the settlement. Also frequently noted are the occupations of the parties, their residence, their marital status, the name of the owner(s) of the property, and the location and amount of the property.

Table 1. Marriage Settlement Sample Size

Years	N	% of Total
1730–1740	23	4
1741–1750	35	5
1751–1760	55	9
1761–1770	107	17
1771–1780	107	17
1781–1790	88	14
1791–1800	51	8
1801–1810	54	8
1811–1820	49	8
1821–1830	69	11
1730–1780	327	51
1781–1830	311	49
1730–1830	638	100

*   *   *

Proper marriage settlements were complicated documents, usually made in the form of trusts. Before the English case of *Rippon* v. *Dawding* (1769), all valid settlements were required to include trustees who nominally owned the property in the name of the feme covert (the *cestui qui trust*).[15] After 1769, in England and in some American jurisdictions, simple marriage settlements—contracts made directly between a man and a woman without the intervention of trustees—also sufficed to create separate estates.[16] In their handling of simple marriage settlements, equity courts initially referred to the husband as trustee for his wife. This language soon disappeared from most cases, however, perhaps as courts realized the irony of naming husbands trustees for their wives' separate estates. In South Carolina, judges disliked simple agreements, and trusts remained the most common form for separate estates. Trust estates composed 91 percent (582) of the deeds studied. Only 9 percent (56) were simple marriage settlements, indicating the reluctance of South Carolinians to abandon the formality of trusts.[17]

To create a trust estate in the normal fashion, the man, woman, and trustee(s) all joined in the execution of an "indenture tripartite," a contract stipulating the terms of the settlement. This form guaranteed the knowledge and consent of the parties, as required by law. In cases involving separate estates, equity standards demanded that men be fully apprised of the terms of their wives' settlements. Judges refused to support a woman who deceived her fiancé or husband into expecting property at marriage, only to secure it to herself through a trustee.[18] They viewed such action as a fraud against the husband's marital rights and held that "he [or she] that hath committed Iniquity, shall not have Equity."[19]

Settlements granting women separate estates could be written either before or after marriage, but most couples executed them prior to marriage. For the period under study, 87 percent (552) of the settlements were prenuptial. There was no significant change in this pattern over time, indicating the constancy of women's desire to secure separate property at the point when they exercised the greatest bargaining power over men.[20] Postnuptial settlements usually resulted when a wife inherited property unexpectedly or when her husband encountered financial difficulties that made it necessary to secure some family property against creditors.

For understandable reasons, creditors disliked trust estates, particularly those made after marriage. They resented the ability of a feme covert to deny them access to her separate estate and argued that husbands as well as wives could find protection under the terms of marriage settlements. A man who lost his own estate through business misfortunes or extravagant living, they claimed, could fall back on the income from his wife's trust property. Indebted or insolvent husbands might even attempt to preserve a portion of their own fortunes by fraudulently settling property on their wives.[21]

Evidence from South Carolina undermines the argument that settlements commonly benefited husbands rather than wives. Women who wrote marriage settlements usually wanted to control the property they brought to their marriages, not their husbands' property. Eighty-two percent (523) of the settlements studied included only the wife's estate; 11 percent (68), only the estate of the husband; and 5 percent (35), property from both the husband and wife. (In twelve cases, 2 percent, it is unknown who owned the property.) No man put his entire estate into a trust for his wife. These figures demonstrate no general attempt by men to protect their property through marriage settlements. They benefited, of course, when women held property that could not be confiscated for family debts, but they did not usually safeguard their own estates. The need for credit in money-scarce economies gave men reasons to avoid trusts. In addition, by the end of the eighteenth century strict recording requirements made deceit difficult, for creditors could easily discover the status of a family's estate and refuse to extend credit on settled property.

Cases of fraudulent trusts demonstrate judicial solicitude for the rights of creditors. The recording statute of 1785 served primarily as a means of informing creditors about separate estates. In addition, chancellors refused to enforce trusts made to deny creditors their just claims.[22] But the South Carolina Court of Chancery also demonstrated sensitivity to the needs of debtors who wanted to create trust estates. A debtor could execute a valid settlement for the benefit of another person if he possessed assets to repay his debts above the value of the trust property.[23]

In the case of *Tunno* v. *Trezevant* (1804), to take a well-documented example, we find that a man consented to the marriage of his niece only after her fiancé agreed to create a settlement including all her property and some of his own.[24] The young man was a merchant whose credit appeared to be good at the time of his marriage (the uncle made inquiries), but within a year he became an insolvent debtor hounded by creditors who demanded payment out of both his business and his private property. From testimony the court found that he had not created his marriage settlement with any fraudulent purpose in mind. Both he and his bride-to-be had honestly believed that their financial position was secure when they executed the deed. In situations such as theirs, when a settlement was created for the "valuable consideration" of marriage, the court of chancery enforced it against the claims of creditors. In this instance the judges regarded the settlement as "a *bona fide* discharge of a moral duty" and refused to "weigh it too nicely." They did not attach the settlement property to discharge the husband's debts, acting on the fundamental principle that "marriage is not only a *bona fide* and valuable consideration, but the very highest consideration in law; this Court will therefore always support marriage settlements, if there is no particular evidence of fraud made out, showing an intention to deceive or defraud creditors."[25]

Tunno v. *Trezevant* clearly demonstrates the advantages of separate estates for women and their children. Through marriage settlements, families possessed a source of income that was free from obligations of the male head, either business or, if the estate were so designed, personal. Since separate estates could prove so beneficial, it is important to know how many women actually employed them. In this regard the documentation for colonial South Carolina is sadly limited. Before 1785, the absence of a recording statute makes it impossible to discover the total number of settlements. For the period 1785–1810, however, when virtually all marriage settlements were recorded in Charleston and when accurate census records are available for the state, it is possible to arrive at a rough estimate of the number of couples with settlements. During those years, approximately 3 percent of marrying couples created separate estates.[26] Settlements apparently were far from the common occurrence that some historians have believed, at least in South Carolina. Few women had either means or reason to use them.

Who, then, did create marriage settlements? Perhaps the small number of deeds indicates use of settlements only among the wealthy, landed families of South Carolina in the manner of the English aristocracy. Fortunately, the detailed information available in the deeds allows us to discover something about the status of couples who employed trust es-

tates and marriage settlements. This can be done by analyzing the value of settled property and by noting the occupations of husbands. (We cannot consider the occupations of wives, because few identified themselves by occupation.) The following discussion investigates property values first, and then turns to male occupations.

Analysis of property values presents some difficulty. Many settlements do not specify the amount or type of property but refer to it as "everything" or "all her property both real and personal." When these deeds are excluded, 456 (71 percent) remain for analysis, but even these, while listing such specific types of property as slaves, cattle, or land, rarely give property values. Consequently, only broad, comparative categories will be considered here, and not specific property valuations.[27]

The upper ranks of South Carolina society relied on settlements more often than people of middling status. It appears that 69 percent (316/456) of the estates that specified types of property included property worth more than £500 sterling, or more than five slaves, or more than one town lot with appurtenances, or a plantation of more than three hundred acres.[28] Settlements of more than ten slaves and hundreds of pounds sterling were common. One settlement included one hundred slaves, another £50,000 sterling, and still another forty-four slaves and over four thousand acres of land. A number of settlements included more than ten slaves, land, and at least one town lot with appurtenances—the traditional estate of a wealthy South Carolina planter family.

Although the elite employed marriage settlements most often, persons with small amounts of property also used them. Settlements sometimes included only one or two slaves, a few articles of household furniture, or the woman's clothing and household goods. Approximately 9 percent (41/456) of the settlements included property estimated to be worth less than £150 sterling, or included only one slave, or a part of a house. Another 22 percent (99) included property estimated at £151–500 sterling, or contained two to five slaves, or one house, or 100 to 299 acres of land. The settlement of John Darrell and Elizabeth Legeaux is typical of contracts made by persons from the middling ranks of society:

This is to certify to all whom it may concern that I John Smith Darrell of the city of Charleston and

State aforesaid Mariner being now about to be joined in the holy Bond of Wedlock to Miss Elizabeth Browne Legeaux conceiving it just and right that she should continue after marriage to hold what property she might have at that time I do therefore by this Instrument Secure to her and the heirs of her body for ever all right and title to Two Negroes left to her by her Father (Vizt.) the Woman Named Constant and her son Caesar together with any other Issue that the said Constant may have. I do also secure to her her Bed Bedding and the household furniture that she now possesses reserving to myself the Services of the said Negroes during my Natural life.[29]

While Elizabeth Legeaux's estate of two slaves might have been enviable by eighteenth-century standards, it was hardly that of an heiress. The motivation for creating a trust estate of small value undoubtedly stemmed from more than a desire to protect the inheritances of future generations. A woman who went to the trouble and expense of creating a separate estate for her household furniture was concerned about herself and her own position in life at least as much as with the well-being of her children. Although the desire to protect family property for future generations may have motivated some of the wealthy couples with settlements, the preservation of family status was not the dominant consideration for all. Given the wide range of individuals with separate estates—from a woman with one slave, to an heiress with one hundred—we cannot rely on the traditional English interpretation of settlements.

Most women who made settlements owned personal rather than real property. Very few of the settlements included real estate to the exclusion of personalty (10/456), and only one-third (147) included some real estate. The other two-thirds (301) involved only personal property. In South Carolina, women's marriage settlements most often included slaves, money, cattle, and household goods, but not land. Such a pattern may indicate that fathers gave their land to sons, while daughters received slaves or money. In the absence of comparative probate materials, it is impossible to be sure. What is clear, however, is that settlements consisting entirely of personal property appeared twice as often in the sample as settlements including any real property. Given the fact that under the common law men acquired absolute ownership of their wives' personal estates at marriage, while they exercised only managerial rights over real property, this is not surprising. Settlements were more useful to women who owned personal property.

This consideration may explain why a substantial number of settlements involved slaves. Eighty-two percent (372) of the deeds that specify the nature of the property included at least some slaves, and 28 percent (129) included only slaves. No other type of property appears so frequently in the settlements. Moreover, settlements including only a few slaves appeared in the sample as often as those with many slaves. When settlements including only slaves are singled out, we learn that fully 32 percent (41/129) contained five slaves or fewer, and that an additional 19 percent contained six to ten slaves. Women with slaves appreciated the importance of protecting their property.

More may be learned about the function of settlements by studying the occupational status of the men who made them. Of the whole number of deeds analyzed, 68 percent (434) noted the husband's occupation (see table 2). Over half of these (228) involved planters (30 percent, N = 131) or gentlemen (22 percent, N = 97). From the settlements, we can learn no more about the status of these men than the words they used to describe themselves. We do not know, for example, how many of the planters were large landowners and therefore considered members of the social elite. The word *planter* stood for all farmers and landowners in South Carolina, large and small. The fact that 22 percent of the sample referred to themselves as "gentlemen," however, reveals the high social standing of a significant proportion of settlement holders.

Merchants composed the next largest group of men with settlements, 13 percent (58/434). Perhaps the volatile fortunes of merchant families gave them special incentives to protect their property from creditors. Indentures tripartite involving merchants frequently alluded to the financial risks of trade. The settlement of William Edwards and Elizabeth Moore in 1774, for example, gave the couple joint control over her property—seven slaves and a £6,000 current money bond—"unless it shall happen that the said William Edwards shall become Bankrupt or meet with losses or misfortunes in Trade or Business so as

Table 2. Male Occupations

Title	N	%
Planter	131	30
Gentlemen and professionals		
Gentleman, esquire	97	22
Merchant	58	13
Physician	30	7
Lawyer, judge	13	3
Minister	6	1
Schoolmaster	2	—
Shipmaster	1	—
Officials		
Military officer	6	1
Government official	3	1
Shopkeepers and innholders		
Shopkeeper	5	1
Factor	5	1
Clerk	5	1
Innholder, tavernkeeper	3	1
Trader	1	—
Indian trader	1	—
Grocer	1	—
Artisans		
Carpenter	10	2
Cordwainer	9	2
Tailor	8	2
Blacksmith	4	1
Cabinetmaker	4	1
Baker	3	1
Bricklayer	3	1
Butcher	1	—
Cooper	1	—
Breechesmaker	1	—
Watchmaker	1	—
Frame mole knitter	1	—
Carver	1	—
Spinner	1	—
Saddler	1	—
Coachmaker	1	—
Wheelwright	1	—
Periwigmaker	1	—
Shipwright	1	—
Painter	1	—
Distiller	1	—
Mariner	10	2
Free black	1	—
Total	434	100

to be unable to support himself and family."[30] In that case, Elizabeth Edwards would have full managerial rights, free from "interference" by her husband. In 1787 James Stephenson and Elizabeth Scott were equally careful. Their settlement stated that if James became insolvent "by losses in trade or otherwise by accumulation of debts by accident or misfortune," the trustees would give Elizabeth £350 current money for her separate use, "to the intent that the said Elizabeth may have a resource left."[31] The overseas expeditions of merchants could place wives and children in precarious financial situations. Before Josiah Smith left on a "sea voyage," he took out the 1789 equivalent of flight insurance. He settled six slaves on his wife for her sole and separate use, free from his debts, if he never returned.[32] The case of *Tunno* v. *Trezevant*, discussed above, suggests that it was wise for a woman to be wary when entering marriage with a South Carolina merchant.

Almost as many artisans, innkeepers, and mariners made marriage settlements as gentlemen—20 percent (86/434). Although we cannot learn the economic standing of these men from the settlements (and some of them may have owned considerable amounts of property), the fact that they identified themselves by trade rather than by status indicates that they were not a part of the South Carolina elite. Even persons at the lowest social level could make use of equity law, as demonstrated by the appearance of a free black man in the sample. On the basis of male occupations, then, it is possible to state that marriage settlements were not made exclusively by the South Carolina aristocracy. Couples from the middling and even the lower ranks of society also sometimes took the precaution of establishing separate estates for wives.

It is easy to understand why the wife of a merchant or a mariner might want a separate estate, yet not all merchants' wives utilized equity provisions, and not all mariners followed in the footsteps of John Darrell, whose settlement appears above. Moreover, it is not as obvious why a planter's wife, or a physician's or a cordwainer's, might desire this special protection. Why did a particular gentleman and his fiancée step into the office of the secretary of state to register a settlement, given the fact that most genteel families did not? The motivations of individuals cannot be conclusively established; but by investigating the provisions for control and descent of settlement property and by analyzing the court cases concerning specific disputes over settlement terms, we may learn more about the use of separate estates.

Each marriage settlement contained various clauses for delineating control over settlement property. Couples could place property under the management of trustees, or they could give trustees no managerial powers at all, reducing them to figureheads. Some husbands retained control over their wives' estates, and in many cases, as will be shown below, femes covert managed their own property. The powers retained by women became significant for determining their level of independence. Some trusts gave women extensive authority over their own property, while others gave them none at all but instead directed trustees to pay them the rents and profits of their estates. Some settlements gave women one privilege of control while denying others. For example, if a deed granted a feme covert the right to devise, she could not also sell or mortgage her estate; those powers had to be granted in a separate clause. In the same vein, a woman whose settlement gave her rights to the rents and profits of her property could not regulate the principal, which remained in the hands of trustees who made all investment decisions.[33]

Although most South Carolina settlements were trust estates, trustees rarely managed property. Only 3 percent (16) of the deeds gave trustees sole powers of control. In 93 percent (591) trustees were vested with minimal powers, such as the right to approve a property sale initiated by the feme covert, or were not employed at all. In 5 percent of the settlements (31), control was shared by the trustee and the couple or the arrangement is unknown. Settlement terms demonstrate that many creators of separate estates, whether parents, relatives, or the women themselves, wanted women rather than trustees—or husbands—to manage their own property. Over the entire period studied, 40 percent (254) of the women administered their estates alone. In 28 percent (180) of the deeds, husbands and wives managed settlement property together, and in 25 percent (157), men possessed exclusive managerial rights (see table 3).

Some change in this division of authority occurred over time (see fig. 1). There was a small but steady decline in the number of women who managed their own estates, offset by an increase in the number of husbands and wives who shared control. With the exception of a slight rise between 1780 and 1800, the number of men who managed settlement property alone remained fairly constant, at about 22 percent. What we see, then, is a shifting pattern, away from exclusive privileges for women and toward joint privileges for couples.

A plausible explanation for this pattern may be found in Mary Beth Norton's study of marital relationships in the eighteenth and early nineteenth centuries. Norton discovered that before the Revolution wives rarely played an active role in family business beyond their sphere of domestic concerns. They de-

Table 3. Control of Settlement Property

Years	Woman		Man		Couple		Trustee		Mixed/ Unknown		No. Deeds
	N	%	N	%	N	%	N	%	N	%	
1730–1740	12	52	7	30	4	17	0	0	0	0	23
1741–1750	20	57	6	17	6	17	0	0	3	9	35
1751–1760	29	53	12	22	9	16	3	5	2	4	55
1761–1770	44	41	25	23	32	30	2	2	4	4	107
1771–1780	44	41	25	23	31	29	4	4	3	3	107
1781–1790	34	39	28	32	22	25	1	1	3	3	88
1791–1800	14	27	18	35	16	31	2	4	1	2	51
1801–1810	19	35	13	24	18	33	2	4	2	4	54
1811–1820	17	35	8	16	16	33	1	2	7	14	49
1821–1830	21	30	15	22	26	38	1	1	6	9	69
Total	254	40	157	25	180	28	16	3	31	5	638

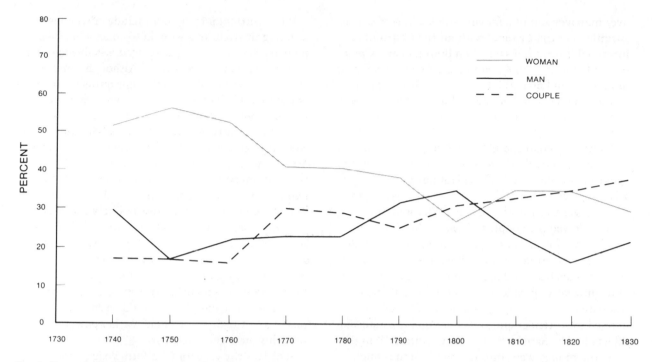

Fig. 1. Control of settlement property, South Carolina, 1730–1830.

ferred to their husbands on most questions and relied on men to manage family finances. By the end of the century, however, this deferential relationship was changing. Marriages became more egalitarian, as wives abandoned passivity to participate in broader decisions concerning family affairs. The need for female autonomy in regulating separate estates would decrease as relationships between spouses became more equal over time. Femes covert might no longer desire total independence in managing their own estates precisely because they exercised more authority over the general fund of family property.

For the 180 settlements involving coadministration, we cannot know who actually managed the property. Perhaps men dominated in all cases, and the figure should be combined with that for sole male control. Total freedom for all husbands in this category is unlikely, however, for many of the joint control settlements restricted husbands in various ways. Some required that the wife consent to all conveyances made by her husband (16 percent, N = 29). In others, either the trustee or both the trustee and the wife had to consent to all transactions (5 percent,

N = 9). More important, the fact that a feme covert wielded authority with her spouse says a great deal about the way she wanted the property handled, that is, under her management as well as her husband's. Since many women did possess managerial rights, we can assume they wanted to take part in decisions concerning their property. At the very least they exercised a veto power over sales and investments stronger than that provided by the common law, which offered only weak protection in the form of private examinations.

Most important for limiting the degree of power exercised by men in joint-control settlements were clauses restricting creditors' interests. Although the principal sums of settlements could never be taken to pay husbands' debts, rents and profits could be so applied if the settlement terms gave men access to them. To avoid this danger, yet still allow husbands the use of separate estates, many couples relied on clauses that explicitly denied creditors' rights. Martha Baker and Allen Bolton wrote such a settlement in 1765. They agreed that Allen, a planter, could "have Receive and take the use enjoyment profits and interest" of Martha's £5,000 estate as long as he continued "in good Circumstances." If his affairs suffered, however, Martha would be permitted to take over management of her own estate. The settlement specified her right to act "without the Controul or Intermeddling of the said Allen Bolton or any Creditors of his in the same manner as if she were sole and unmarried and no part [of her estate] thereof or the interest thereof shall be thereafter liable to any Debts Contracts or engagements of the said Allen Bolton."[34]

Another woman and her fiancé took similar precautions. Although Thomas Bee considered himself a "gentleman," he and Susanna Holmes thought it wise to place £1,000 of her money in a trust as protection against future insolvency. The settlement terms allowed the couple full use of the money, unless "by misfortunes or losses (which God avert) the present occupation calling or business of him the said Thomas Bee as a Planter or otherwise, shall fail or decline very considerably, and there shall be manifest danger, or probability, that he will be reduced and obliged to surrender quit or deliver up his Estate and Effects for the Satisfaction of his Creditors."[35] In that case, the money went into the hands of the couple's trustees, who were directed to pay them the annual interest, safe from creditors' demands. Similar stipulations commonly appeared in settlements throughout the period. Over half (51 percent, N = 326) of the women demanded this explicit protection. Without clauses denying creditors' claims on settlement property, husbands' debts, poor business decisions, fraud, or, simply, financial misfortunes could destroy the utility of a separate estate.

Carefully constructed settlements specified each restriction or power of control separately and included sections allowing or disallowing certain basic changes in the settled property. For example, when creating trusts for the benefit of daughters or other female relatives, some individuals perceived a need to forbid future changes in the settlements. They feared the power of their beneficiaries to annul the protective function of their trusts by conveying them to their husbands or making use of the principal.[36] To protect women from male coercion or prevent them from making damaging business decisions, creators of settlements sometimes employed clauses forbidding changes or certain kinds of potentially harmful dispositions. A deed of settlement might state that it could not be altered in any way, or it might include provisions allowing a feme covert control over the rents and profits but not the principal of her estate.

When settlements did not include provisions restricting the right of a woman to control her own property, she could change or even dissolve her marriage settlement at any time.[37] Although some women wanted to alter settlement terms for the benefit of their husbands, more often wives acted to transfer controls from husbands to themselves. At the time of marriage it might seem appropriate for a woman to give her husband powers of active control over her property, without any reference to contingency arrangements in the event he encountered difficulties. Many women, unlike Martha Baker and Susanna Holmes, did not express publicly their fears for the future. But if a husband later suffered financial setbacks threatening his wife's estate, she might want to rescind his powers. By inserting a clause in her settlement allowing unspecified changes in her trust, a woman who initially wanted to leave property in her husband's hands could do so, confident that at a future date she could use her power to restrict his managerial capacity.

Such was the case for Charlotte Poaug, whose prenuptial settlement gave her husband control over the rents and profits of her real property.[38] John Poaug was a merchant who became indebted several years after his marriage. In 1771, to prevent John's creditors from seizing their estate, the Poaugs changed the terms of their settlement. In the new document, Charlotte retained all powers of control for herself. Clearly, a safety valve of this nature was invaluable for families with uncertain fortunes.

Unfortunately, some individuals did not understand the importance of precision. They wrote loose documents, failing to delineate specific powers of control. Occasionally, friends or relatives failed to clarify the fact that they were creating a separate estate for a feme covert through a deed of gift or a devise. They gave a woman property, meant for her separate use, but failed to say so explicitly. In South Carolina, when settlements were vague and disputes brought couples into court, judges in equity did everything in their power to protect women. The intent of settlements, gifts, or wills, however haphazardly designed, governed judicial decisions.

Court records indicate that by the early nineteenth century, South Carolina jurists interpreted unclear words in a deed of gift or marriage settlement consistently for the benefit of women. For example, following the English Chancery case of *Tyrrel* v. *Hope*

(1743), the South Carolina court ceased requiring the specific words "to her sole and separate use" for the creation of a separate estate.[39] Instead, chancellors began to assume that any conveyance to a married woman was meant for her own use, whether the donor said so explicitly or not. If it appeared from other evidence, either parol evidence concerning the donor's intent or the wording of the document in question, that the property was intended for the sole use of a woman, the standard phrase could be omitted.

The South Carolina case of *Johnson* v. *Thompson* (1814) exemplifies judicial practice in this regard.[40] Here a father made a bequest of personal property to his married daughter. Her husband claimed the property and disposed of it. After the woman's death, her children contested his disposition. They stated that their grandfather intended the property to descend to his daughter as a separate estate, free from the control of her husband. In deciding favorably for the children, the court of appeals noted that since the devise was made to a feme covert, its wording had to be examined closely to determine intent. Here the words "fairly inferred" that the estate was designed to be a separate one, and therefore the woman's husband possessed no right to dispose of it. The implementation of this liberal policy in South Carolina indicates strong support for marriage settlements as a legal form.

South Carolina chancellors also interpreted unclear words in settlements for the benefit of married women. When coercion was not an issue, judges assumed that the absence of restrictive clauses meant freedom to exercise control.[41] In *Lowndes' Trustee* v. *Champneys' Executors* (1821), the chancellor declared that it was "immaterial in what form or phrase a trust of this nature creating a seperate [sic] estate for the Wife is described—technical language is not necessary—All that is requisite is that the intention of the gift should appear manifestly to be for the wife's seperate enjoyment."[42] An inference, or the circumstances of a gift or devise, could induce the court to rule in favor of separate estates.

The favorable perspective on marriage settlements in South Carolina equity courts is also demonstrated by acceptance of the doctrine called "equity to a settlement." Settlements became so respectable, and chancellors supported them so wholeheartedly, that by the mid-eighteenth century in England and by 1762 in South Carolina, equity courts regarded them

as a positive right for all married women.[43] Under certain circumstances, chancellors ordered men to give their wives separate estates. Most often chancellors made such orders when the executor of an estate refused to give a woman her proper inheritance under a will, thereby forcing her and her husband to sue in Chancery for possession. Before awarding them the property, the chancellor would order the husband to settle all or part of it on his wife. The amount of the settlement depended on the man's financial situation. In this way, chancellors knew that they were not giving property to men who could take it for themselves, providing their wives—the rightful owners—no benefits from it.

South Carolina equity courts closely followed English law on the wife's equity to a settlement. Chancellors maintained that any man who sued in an equity court for the property of his wife assumed a moral obligation to settle at least a part of it on her as a separate estate. Thus in *Mathewes and others* v. *The Executors of Mathewes et al.* (1762), the court ordered the creation of a trust for Mary Lloyd.[44] Her husband, Thomas, had refused to appear in court for hearings concerning the execution of his father-in-law's estate. What other transgressions Thomas may have committed are unclear, but the court refused to give him Mary's inheritance. The chancellor ordered division of the deceased's estate and distribution among the heirs, "except the Share and proportion claimed by the Defendant Thomas Lloyd in right of his said Wife Mary." His share was ordered invested, and the proceeds paid to Mary "for her own and separate use, and after her Death the said Money to go to and become the property of the said Thomas Lloyd the Son, if he be then living, if not, then the Interest of said Money shall be paid to the said Thomas Lloyd the Defendant during his Natural life."[45]

Chancellors ordered the creation of a separate estate when the financial situation of a husband caused them concern for his wife's well-being. Men of good standing in the community were not usually handled as harshly as Thomas Lloyd. When William Henry Drayton, a prosperous planter, member of the Governor's Council, and subsequently chief justice of South Carolina, won a chancery suit against his father-in-law's executors, he did not have to place the property into a trust.[46] Undoubtedly the court believed that his respectable position, added to the fact that his wife already possessed a settlement, made the order unnecessary.

In another similar case, the court ordered no settlement for Mrs. Postell, a plaintiff with her husband in the suit of *Postell and wife, and Smith and wife* v. *The Executors of James Skirving* (1789).[47] The chancellor explained his omission carefully for the record. "The court having in private examined Mrs. Postell, who has attained twenty-one years of age, and the said Mrs. Postell being very desirous that no settlement should be made on her; and it appearing to the court that Mr. and Mrs. Postell have constantly lived together in the greatest harmony; and he being a gentleman of fortune in his own right, it is not requisite that he should make any settlement on his said wife."[48] With regard to the other plaintiff, Mrs. Smith, the court was not so trusting of the husband. She received a settlement, and the words of the chancellor demonstrate his opinion about the importance of female separate estates. "With regard to Mr. O. B. Smith," he wrote, "his wife is not of age to make such request as Mrs. Postell has done, (although the court entertains a similar opinion of him as of Mr. Postell), they find themselves bound to order that the said O. B. Smith do make the usual settlement on his wife, of the fortune she is entitled to from her father."[49] The "usual" settlement gave the Smiths joint control over her property, with descent to the survivor and then to their children. Presumably in a case of this nature, Mrs. Smith could void her own trust upon reaching her majority. As previously noted,

such action could be taken under the law and occasionally was.

On one point South Carolina chancellors were not willing to make liberal interpretations. Unless a settlement explicitly gave a feme covert power to write a will, she could not do so.[50] Women and their benefactors were careful, therefore, to include this right as a clause in settlements. It appeared frequently, particularly during the first two decades under study, when 62 percent (36/58) of the women specified the power to make a will. The figure rises to 71 percent if we include those women who possessed the right to bequeath in the event they outlived their husbands. Over the course of the eighteenth century, this figure fell, but until 1800 more than half of the women with settlements possessed testamentary powers. After the turn of the century the figure declined until fewer than one-third of all femes covert could write wills under the stated terms of their settlements. From 1801 to 1830, 26 percent (45/172) of the settlements sampled gave women this privilege, while 29 percent (50/170) gave it to either the feme covert or the survivor of the marriage (see table 4). As the number of settlements allowing women to write wills declined, those arranging for automatic descent to children increased (fig. 2).

The reasons for this decline are not clear. One explanation may lie in the increasing standardization of settlements. As the chancellor noted when ordering creation of a trust for Mrs. Smith, there was a

Table 4. Descent of Settlement Property

Years	Woman Controls		Survivor Controls		Combined*		Automatic to Children		Mixed/ Unknown		No. Deeds
	N	%	N	%	N	%	N	%	N	%	
1730–1740	12	52	4	17	16	70	3	13	4	17	23
1741–1750	24	69	1	3	25	71	10	29	0	0	35
1751–1760	26	47	3	5	29	53	24	44	2	4	55
1761–1770	37	35	9	8	46	43	52	49	9	8	107
1771–1780	50	47	6	6	56	52	45	42	6	6	107
1781–1790	39	44	6	7	45	51	43	49	0	0	88
1791–1800	20	39	1	2	21	41	29	57	1	2	51
1801–1810	15	28	2	4	17	31	30	56	7	13	54
1811–1820	14	29	1	2	15	31	27	55	7	14	49
1821–1830	16	23	2	3	18	26	47	68	4	6	69
Total	253	40	35	5	288	45	310	49	40	6	638

*Woman Controls and Survivor Controls

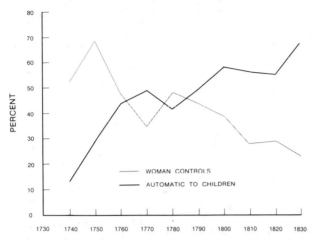

Fig. 2. Descent of settlement property, South Carolina, 1730–1830.

"usual" settlement. It consisted of joint control for husband and wife, with descent to their children. Over the period studied, we have seen an increase in settlements allowing for joint control, as well as descent to children. Chancellors ordered this kind of settlement in most cases coming under their jurisdiction, and the increasing use of automatic descent provisions may demonstrate female acceptance of a standard form on this point. Moreover, as marriages became less patriarchal over the period, women may have regarded the right to make wills as less vital to their financial autonomy. The desire to exert control after death dwindled as more women possessed authority during life. Most mothers undoubtedly divided their estates equally among children, even when they did write wills. The change to automatic descent probably represents little difference in the way estates were administered but does demonstrate a weakening of women's desires for explicit protection and control.

Some mothers were fully aware of the potential power of testamentary rights. Mary Ladson, marrying for the first time in 1760, included a clause in her settlement allowing her to write a will. She wanted her estate to be divided among her children "in such shares and proportions and at such times as the said Mary by her last Will and Testament shall give Limit." The widow Jane Wilkie was equally explicit about her desire to decide what property should go to her children. In 1774 she wrote in her settlement, "All such Child or Children shall possess & enjoy all

such part & proportion in the manner & form as she the said Jane Wilkie shall point out & direct." Even after the turn of the century, when fewer women possessed the legal ability to write wills, some women still realized the power they held. Elizabeth Legare wrote in 1825 that she intended to use her estate during her lifetime for the provision of her children "at her own discretion," and not otherwise.[51]

*   *   *

Women who had already experienced married life, such as Jane Wilkie and Elizabeth Legare, took special care to protect their property rights in marriage settlements. Most single women were not so careful. Comparison of settlements made by widows and single women proves valuable for understanding some individuals' needs for separate estates. A woman's marital status frequently acted as a motivating force for the creation of a settlement and for the inclusion of female managerial and testamentary powers.[52]

Of the 638 settlements sampled, 532 recorded a marital status for the woman. During the period 1730 to 1780, widows appeared in over half of the settlements giving status, 56 percent (159/286), while single women constituted 44 percent (127) of the sample. Even if we take into account the high mortality rate in colonial South Carolina and the use of the state as a Revolutionary battlefield, the high percentage of widows is surprising. After 1780, the number of widows declined, but they still made settlements in 40 percent (98/246) of the sample.

When we compare the powers of control exercised by widows with those held by single women, it becomes clear that experienced matrons were more emphatic about managing their own property than were women marrying for the first time (see table 5). Widows held complete managerial powers and specified the right to make wills at more than double the rate of first brides. Rather than directing settlement property by themselves, most single women divided between giving their husbands authority and arranging for coadministration. They also provided for automatic descent of settlement property in fully two thirds of their deeds, whereas widows did so less than one-third of the time. The settlements of first brides thus demonstrate a less protective attitude than those of experienced matrons. Moreover, after 1740 there was remarkably little change in this pattern either for control or descent (see figs. 3, 4).

Clearly, the experience of marriage affected the attitudes of women toward property control and management. Before entering a second union, many women demanded the right to administer their own property. Widows' desire for active control may have reflected the fact that their estates were no longer simply gifts from parents and friends but property they had worked for themselves, either alone or with their former husbands. Parents who initiated the settlements of new brides concerned themselves primarily with protecting property from husbands' creditors. They did not seek to provide daughters with the power to control and devise property as much as they created a fund for family income. Widows, however, frequently demanded the right to manage the property that they had obtained themselves. Elizabeth Meshaw's settlement in 1736 observed, "The said Elizabeth Meshaw since the Death of her said Husband hath by her great pains care Labour and Industry acquired a considerable addition to the Estate and Interest so left her. . . . [P]articularly [she] hath purchased a Tract of Land containing two Hundred and Fifty Acres." Elizabeth retained the right to devise her estate as she saw fit, without the interference of her new husband. When Christiana Hoff purchased a slave through her own labor, she wrote a settlement in 1772 explicitly denying her husband

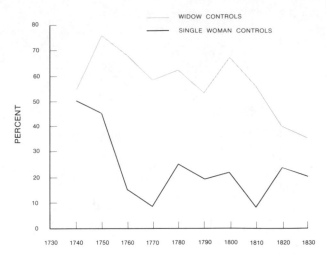

Fig. 3. Descent of settlement property, South Carolina, 1730–1830.

any rights to it. The case of Elizabeth Baxter may be most revealing. Before Elizabeth, a "merchant," consented to marry Thomas Robinson, a "mariner," in 1771, she executed a settlement of all her personal estate and business property. She reserved absolute control over the property for herself "in order the better to enable her to support & maintain her & her children & which the said Thomas Robinson is at present rendered incapable of doing."[53] Elizabeth was taking no chances. If Thomas could not support her,

Fig. 4. Settlements with provisions for children, South Carolina, 1730–1830.

Table 5. Widows and Single Women Compared

	Widows		Single women	
	N	%	N	%
Control				
Woman	133	52	59	21
Man	50	19	90	33
Couple	55	21	107'	39
Trustee	3	1	10	4
Mixed/unknown	16	6	9	3
Total	257	99	275	100
Descent				
Woman controls	150	58	53	19
Survivor controls	10	4	19	7
(Combined)	160	62	72	26
Automatic to children	79	31	185	67
Mixed/unknown	18	7	18	7
Total	257	100	275	100

Production and Control of Property

she would arrange to do so herself. Women such as Elizabeth, who knew the dangers of marriage and widowhood, took special care for their own and their childrens' futures.

Although the number of widows who provided for children in their settlements increased throughout the period, widows remained less likely than young brides to arrange for automatic descent. Widows such as Elizabeth Baxter had the responsibility of caring for the children of their previous marriages and undoubtedly felt pressure to include protective clauses for children in their settlements, yet did so at half the rate of single women. Thus Mrs. Baxter retained the right to devise her estate. Although she clearly was concerned with providing for her children, she did not think it necessary to arrange for their inheritances when she wrote her settlement. Such dispositions could be made later, when she was closer to death. For the moment she worried primarily about living in a male-dominated world with a new husband who could not support her. The failure to arrange for automatic descent implies that many widows did not view settlements primarily as a means of guaranteeing the inheritances of their children. More than anything else, they wanted absolute control over management decisions and the right to bequeath to whomever they pleased. When they chose to remarry, they did so with strings attached.

Although the comparative powers of widows and single women remained largely the same throughout the eighteenth and early nineteenth centuries, one development in the settlements of single women may indicate an increasing desire on their part to exercise authority. There was a gradual but steady increase in the number of settlements allowing couples joint powers of administration. Single women did not feel the need to exercise sole control to the same degree as widows, but they did become less willing to give husbands absolute managerial rights. From 1730 to 1780, only 32 percent (41/127) of their settlements gave couples joint powers of administration, whereas 45 percent (66/148) did so from 1781 to 1830. The number of men with sole powers fell from 39 percent (49/127) to 28 percent (41/148). With regard to the management of property, therefore, the settlements of widows and single women became slightly more uniform over time, with both groups favoring partnerships in managing separate estates.

*　　*　　*

Widows, heiresses, merchants' wives, the wives of debtors, and women whose parents warned them about the dangers of married life—these were the South Carolina matrons with trust estates. They were frequently women of wealth with a great deal to lose if their husbands proved wasteful or unfortunate in business. Sometimes they were women of small fortunes intent on protecting what little they had. They were intelligent, or experienced, or protected by concerned parents. Above all, given the legal status of women under the common law, they were fortunate.

Courts of chancery in South Carolina offered liberal support for marriage settlements. Judges regarded separate estates as the right of every feme covert, necessary for women's security in many cases and helpful to society in providing some families with economic support. Judges consistently ruled in favor of the creation of separate estates and enforced liberal precedents for administering them. Realizing the delicate position of married women under the common law, chancellors acted to mitigate legal hardships by wholeheartedly supporting women's rights to separate estates. Judicial acceptance of settlements increased in the period studied, demonstrating expansion of women's property rights under equity law. As seen in the cases of *Postell and Smith* v. *Skirving's Executors, Johnson* v. *Thompson*, and *Lowndes' Trustee* v. *Champneys' Executors*, equity law promoted the legal rights of South Carolina women. Historians of colonial American law may have been overly optimistic in positing wide use of settlements among femes covert, but they were correct in stressing the legal importance of equity law. Women with separate estates in eighteenth- and early nineteenth-century South Carolina enjoyed many of the legal rights of men. It remains to be seen if other jurisdictions duplicated this pattern.

Although chancellors supported the use of separate estates, settlements were rare, used either by wealthy women with valuable family interests to protect or by women with an uncommon perspective on their legal status. Equity provided invaluable to such women as the widow Elizabeth Holson, who wanted to enjoy her own estate without "the Least or Smallest Controul or intermeddling" of her husband, but Elizabeth was one of only a small number of women with marriage settlements.[54] We still do not know why so few women relied on separate estates. Either they were satisfied with their common law status, or they did not regard equity law as a viable alternative. In South Carolina, it may be important that settlements were not necessary to confer feme sole trader status. Independent businesswomen functioned under the common law as long as their husbands demonstrated tacit consent to their activities. But more important, the majority of women apparently regarded equity law protections as superfluous to their needs. For women without much property or for women who perceived their legal status as secure, separate estates served no purpose.

We must learn more about the application of common law principles before we will fully understand the meaning of equity law. Perhaps the harshness of common law rules were mitigated in practice, making separate estates largely unnecessary. If most women did not feel a need to use equity law, then we must reevaluate the effect of common law restrictions on women's lives. We must also consider an alternative possibility: that social custom so oppressed women, they did not consider the possibility of employing separate estates. Community scorn or family opposition may have prevented women from acting on their desire for separate estates. There is some evidence to show that the fear and distrust women exhibited by creating settlements antagonized men. The wording of settlements, for example, occasionally reveals attempts to appease men's feelings. Some women wrote that their desire for separate estates arose from a fear of the system, not the individual. Such public statements relieved men of responsibility for the anxiety experienced by women and thus saved them face in the community. Otherwise, the mere existence of a settlement attested to the insecurity of a particular woman.

At this point it is impossible to be sure whether male antipathy to settlements prevented most women from making them. Final conclusions await further research on the social customs of families in the South and on the use of common law rules pertaining to the rights of women. Perhaps the words of Sarah Ann Baxter demonstrate, as well as anything we now have, the attitude of women who wrote settlements. Sarah's settlement stated that its object was to protect her separate interests so that she would not be "defeated or defrauded" out of her property "by the collusive act or device" of her husband.

The job of Sarah's trustees was to sue her husband in case he "bargained, sold, or inveigled away" her lands and to demand damages from the court "for any waste which he may commit upon the said lands or injury he may commit upon the said personal or any of the said personal property."[55] There can be no doubt that Sarah Ann did not trust her husband-to-be. It is unlikely that most couples began married life with such distrust. Undoubtedly women as well as men preferred to demonstrate hope, rather than fear, on the day of their marriage. But if experience proved women naive, then we can understand why so many widows insisted on the creation of settlements, and we can also comprehend why they carefully reserved managerial rights for themselves.

Notes

The author wishes to thank Mary Maples Dunn, Mary Beth Norton, and the members of the 1979–1980 seminar of the Philadelphia Center for Early American Studies for their critical comments on this and an earlier version of the essay. The invaluable technical assistance of Joseph O'Rourke is also gratefully acknowledged.

1. William Blackstone, *Commentaries on the Laws of England . . .*, 4 vols. (Oxford, 1765–69), 2:132, 136, 255, 293, 355; Thomas Smith, *De Republica Anglorum: A Discourse on the Commonwealth of England*, ed. Leonard Alston (Cambridge, 1906), 127; William Holdsworth, *A History of English Law*, 16 vols. (London, 1903–66), vol. 3 (5th ed.), 193, 195–96, 249; *An Essay on the Nature and Operation of Fines and Recoveries* (London, 1728), 68–69; *The Laws Respecting Women . . .* (Dobbs Ferry, N.Y., 1974 [orig. publ. London, 1777]), 181; James Kent, *Commentaries on American Law*, 4 vols. (New York, 1826–30), 2:151–54; Samuel Church, "Lectures on Law by Tapping Reeve, Esq." (1806) (notebook, Cornell University Law Library, Ithaca, N.Y.).

2. Tapping Reeve, *The Law of Baron and Femme, of Parent and Child, of Guardian and Ward, of Master and Servant, and of the Powers of Courts of Chancery . . .* (New Haven, Conn., 1816), 1–8, 22–30, 60–63, 192–93; *Laws Respecting Women*, 148–63; Blackstone, *Commentaries on the Laws of England*, 1:430–32; 2:433–36.

3. No comprehensive study of the legal status of early American women has yet been written. The best general discussion is still Reeve, *Baron and Femme*. *Laws Respecting Women* is a good survey of English law and is available in a reprint edition. Holdsworth's impressive overview of the history of English law is also helpful. The most commonly cited discussion of the legal rights of early American women is Richard B. Morris, *Studies in the History of American Law, with Special Reference to the Seventeenth and Eighteenth Centuries* (New York, 1930), chap. 3. This

should be used with care, however, since it is only a cursory study and unreliable.

4. Holdsworth cited Avenant v. Kitchen (1581) as the first case in which an equity court supported the right of a woman to hold property separately from her husband by the force of a prenuptial contract. Within a short period of time, the Chancery Court permitted women to exert active control over settlements. Decisions recognized the right of women to enter into binding contracts (1582), write wills (1594), make presents to their husbands (1614), and convey to strangers (1619). Holdsworth, *History of English Law*, vol. 1 (7th rev. ed.), 494; 5:303, 310–15; Richard Francis, *Maxims of Equity . . .* (London, 1728), 5; Reeve, *Baron and Femme*, 222–23, 238; *Laws Respecting Women*, 179; Zephaniah Swift, *A System of the Laws of the State of Connecticut: In Six Books*, 2 vols. (New Haven, Conn., 1795–96), 1:200–201.

5. Christopher Clay, "Marriage, Inheritance, and the Rise of Large Estates in England, 1660–1815," *Economic History Review*, 2d ser., 21 (1968): 503–18; H. J. Habakkuk, "Marriage Settlements in the Eighteenth Century," Royal Historical Society, *Transactions*, 4th ser., 32 (1950): 15–31; Lawrence Stone, *The Crisis of the Aristocracy, 1558–1641* (Oxford, 1965).

6. Morris, *Studies in the History of American Law*, 126–55; Mary R. Beard, *Woman as Force in History: A Study in Traditions and Realities* (New York, 1962 [orig. publ. 1946]).

7. In fact, historians usually depict the colonial period as a golden age for women. In addition to Morris's legal study, books by Elisabeth Anthony Dexter (*Colonial Women of Affairs: Women in Business and the Professions in America before 1776* [Boston, 1924] and *Career Women of America, 1776–1840* [Francestown, N.H., 1950]) and Mary Sumner Benson (*Women in Eighteenth-Century America: A Study of Opinion and Social Usage* [New York, 1935]) helped to build the theory of a liberal legal and social climate for colonial women. More recently the theory has been supported by the work of John Demos in *A Little Commonwealth: Family Life in Plymouth Colony* (New York, 1970); Roger Thompson in *Women in Stuart England and America: A Comparative Study* (London, 1974); Mary P. Ryan in *Womanhood in America: From Colonial Times to the Present* (New York, 1975); Ann D. Gordon and Mari Jo Buhle in "Sex and Class in Colonial and Nineteenth-Century America," in *Liberating Women's History: Theoretical and Critical Essays*, ed. Berenice A. Carroll (Urbana, Ill., 1976), 278–300; and Joan R. Gundersen and Gwen Victor Gampel, "Married Women's Legal Status in Eighteenth-Century New York and Virginia," *William and Mary Quarterly*, 3d ser., 39 (1982): 114–34. In her pathbreaking study of American women between 1750 and 1800, Mary Beth Norton revises significantly the old interpretations, concluding that women possessed both a low status and a low self-image during the colonial period. The status of women changed as a result of the American Revolution, improving on some points such as self-esteem but remaining ambiguous in the areas of politics and law (*Liberty's Daughters: The Revolutionary Experience of American Women, 1750–1800* [Bos-

ton, 1980]). Linda K. Kerber has also demonstrated that women's lives changed after the American Revolution, but she emphasizes points on which women lost rights, especially in the law (*Women of the Republic: Intellect and Ideology in Revolutionary America* [Chapel Hill, N.C., 1980]). Kerber's contention that the legal status of women deteriorated in the nineteenth century is not proved. For a revisionist study of the legal rights of women, see Marylynn Salmon, *Women and the Law of Property in Early America* (Chapel Hill, N.C., 1986), esp. 185–93.

8. Morris, *Studies in the History of American Law*, 138; Beard, *Woman as Force in History*, 151.

9. There appears to be a growing split among women's historians concerning the changing status of women after 1800. Scholars such as Norton, and Kerber to a lesser degree, see a widening of the female sphere during the early national period away from the subservience and dependence of colonial women. Other historians still maintain that colonial women occupied a privileged position compared to nineteenth-century women, who lost status and economic power with the rise of industrialism. Most recently, Gerda Lerner has made the latter argument in a review of the Norton and Kerber books, "What the Revolution Meant for Women," *Washington Post Book World* 15 (January 4, 1981): 9.

10. Some colonies, such as Massachusetts, Connecticut, and Pennsylvania, did not have separate courts of equity in the English fashion. On the problem of equity law in early America, see Stanley N. Katz, "The Politics of Law in Colonial America: Controversies over Chancery Courts and Equity Law in the Eighteenth Century," *Perspectives in American History* 5 (1971): 257, and Swift, *A System of the Laws . . . of Connecticut*, 2:419–60. For a full discussion of regional comparisons on the administration of marriage settlements, see Salmon, *Women and the Law of Property*, 81–140.

11. Salmon, *Women and the Law of Property*, 37–40, 45–49, 79–80, 156–60, 169–72.

12. Anne King Gregorie, ed., *Records of the Court of Chancery of South Carolina, 1671–1779* (Washington, D.C., 1950), 5–7.

13. "An Act to oblige persons interested in Marriage Deeds and Contracts, to record the same in the Secretary's office of this state," in Thomas Cooper and David J. McCord, eds., *The Statutes at Large of South Carolina* (Columbia, S.C., 1836–41), 4:656–57.

14. Marriage Settlements, vols. 1–10 (1785–1830); Records of the Register of the Secretary of the Province, vols. A–I (1721–33); Miscellaneous Records of the Secretary of State, Charleston Series, vols. AB, BB–XX (1735–89). All manuscripts cited are located in the South Carolina State Archives, Columbia, unless noted otherwise.

15. Rippon v. Dawling, Ambler, 565 (1769).

16. Reeve reported in 1816 that settlements without trustees had become "no uncommon thing" (*Baron and Femme*, 163). One of the earliest American cases to deal with a simple marriage settlement appeared on the docket of the Pennsylvania Supreme Court in 1793. See Barnes Les-

see v. Hart, 1 Yeates 221 (1793). The case is analyzed in Marylynn Salmon, "Equality or Submersion? *Feme Covert* Status in Early Pennsylvania," in *Women of America: A History*, ed. Carol Ruth Berkin and Mary Beth Norton (Boston, 1979), 91–113.

17. South Carolina courts preferred women to use formal trusts rather than direct agreements with their husbands. In Barret v. Barret, 4 S.C. Eq. (4 Des.) 491 (1814), and Dupree v. McDonald, 4 S.C. Eq. (4 Des.) 209 (1812), the judges noted their disapproval of settlements made without trustees. See also the arguments of counsel in Executors of Smelie v. Executors of Smelie, 2 S.C. Eq. (2 Des.) 72 (1802).

18. Holdsworth, *History of English Law*, 5:313; George W. Keeton and L. A. Sheridan, *Equity* (London, 1969), 442–43; Reeve, *Baron and Femme*, 236. In the South Carolina case of Cape v. Adams, 1 S.C. Eq. (1 Des.) 567 (1797), a man tried to create a settlement of his wife's property for his own benefit without her knowledge or consent. The court disallowed his deed.

19. Francis, *Maxims of Equity*, 5.

20. Reeve noted the significant role of parents and guardians in bargaining with the suitors of young women (see *Baron and Femme*, 174).

21. Some men did attempt to settle property on their families after contracting debts. Examples of cases involving fraudulent trusts include Drayton v. Pritchard (1816), Charleston District Equity Decrees, 3:161; Peigne v. Snowden, 1 S.C. Eq. (1 Des.) 591 (1800); Peace v. Spierin, 2 S.C. Eq. (2 Des.) 500 (1807); and Croft v. Townsend's Administrators, 3 S.C. Eq. (3 Des.) 223 (1811).

22. The preamble to the recording statute of South Carolina noted the problem. It read, "The practice prevailing in this State of keeping marriage contracts and deeds in the hands of those interested therein, hath been oftentimes injurious to creditors and others, who have been induced to credit and trust persons under a presumption of their being possessed of an estate subject and liable to the payment of their just debts" (Cooper and McCord, eds., *Statutes of South Carolina*, 4:656).

23. Reeve, *Baron and Femme*, 176. In Croft v. Townsend's Administrators, Chancellor Desaussure ruled against a settlement that included too much of an indebted man's property. See especially his comments on p. 2. In Taylor v. Heriot, 4 S.C. Eq. (4 Des.) 227 (1812), a legal opinion noted that indebted men were fully justified in creating settlements of their future wives' estates before marriage.

24. Tunno v. Trezevant, 2 S.C. Eq. (2 Des.) 264 (1804).

25. Tunno v. Trezevant, 2 S.C. Eq. (2 Des.) 269–71 (1804).

26. There are no accurate marriage rates for South Carolina in the period under study. Population figures are available, however, and by applying the earliest available marriage rate, that of 1860 (1/115), we can arrive at a rough percentage of marrying couples with settlements. Thus in 1790, when the free population was 141,801, the estimated number of marriages was 617. Twenty-two settlements were written in that year and therefore the percentage of marrying couples with settlements was 3.5. The next federal census (1800) revealed a population figure of 199,185, making

the estimated number of marriages 866. Since 28 settlements were written in 1800, the percentage of marrying couples with settlements was 3.2. *The Statistical History of the United States: From Colonial Times to the Present* (New York, 1976), 1168; *Population of the United States in 1860* (Washington, D.C., 1869), xxxvi.

27. For determining the approximate values of property included in marriage settlements, the work of Alice Hanson Jones was indispensable. See *American Colonial Wealth: Documents and Methods*, 2d ed., 3 vols. (New York, 1977). Equally useful for determining exchange rates for South Carolina in the eighteenth century was John J. McCusker, *Money and Exchange in Europe and America, 1600–1775: A Handbook* (Chapel Hill, N.C., 1978), 223–24. Throughout the eighteenth century, approximately £7 South Carolina currency equaled £1 sterling.

28. For the purpose of making comparative statements concerning settlement property, I assigned estimated values to certain types of property, based on information provided in Jones, *American Colonial Wealth*, vol. 3. A slave was valued at £85, one acre of improved land at £1, one head of cattle at £10, one riding horse at £75, one town lot with appurtenances at less than £500, and more than one town lot with appurtenances at more than £500. Settlements with a single slave were all classified as containing property of a value less than £150, as were settlements containing only part of a house. Settlements including only slaves, numbering two to five, were all classified in the £150–500 range. All pounds are pounds sterling. Although estimated valuations such as these are extremely unreliable for determining absolute wealth, they enable us to distinguish between individuals of great and middling wealth.

29. Marriage Settlement between Elizabeth Legeaux and John Smith Darrell (1809), Marriage Settlements, 5:522–23.

30. Marriage Settlement between Elizabeth Moore and William Edwards (1744), Miscellaneous Records, RR, 212–13.

31. Marriage Settlement between Elizabeth Scott and James Stephenson (1787), Marriage Settlements, 1:338.

32. Marriage Settlement between Mary Smith and Josiah Smith (1789), Marriage Settlements, 1:446–47.

33. Reeve, *Baron and Femme*, 162–63, 170–73; Price v. Michel (1821), Charleston District Equity Decrees, 3:377; Kent, *Commentaries on American Law*, 2:164–65.

34. Marriage Settlement between Martha Baker and Allen Bolton (1765), Marriage Settlements, 1:110.

35. Marriage Settlement between Susanna Holmes and Thomas Bee (1761), Marriage Settlements, 1:170.

36. In any case in which it appeared conclusively that a man forced his wife to transact a certain agreement against her will, she was not held liable for the agreement. Reeve, *Baron and Femme*, 165; Bethune v. Beresford, 1 S.C. Eq. (1 Des.) 174 (1790). The evidence had to be positive, however, for once a woman possessed separate property jurists defined her as a feme sole rather than a feme covert and did not regard her as susceptible to coercion. In the mid-nineteenth century a debate arose in Maryland and South Carolina over the need for women with trust estates to

undergo private examinations when conveying their property. Maryland decided that women did not need private examinations because they were legally femes sole. South Carolina decided just the opposite. See Tiernan v. Poor, 1 G. & J. 216 (1829); Brundige v. Poor, 2 G. & J. 1 (1829); Ewing v. Smith, 3 S.C. Eq. (3 Des.) 467 (1811). The South Carolina stance indicates concern with protecting women from male coercion. See Marylynn Salmon, " 'Life, Liberty, and Dower'. The Legal Status of Women after the American Revolution," in *Women, War, and Revolution*, ed. Carol R. Berkin and Clara M. Lovett (New York, 1980), 85–106.

37. Reeve, *Baron and Femme*, 162–63; Curtis v. Duncan (1821), Charleston District Equity Decrees, 3:468; Price v. Michel (1821), Charleston District Equity Decrees, 3:377; Garner v. Garner's Executors, 1 S.C. Eq. (1 Des.) 477 (1795); Dupree v. McDonald, 4 S.C. Eq. (4 Des.) 209 (1812). In *Garner*, the court corrected nonsensical words in a deed of settlement that had the effect of denying a woman all rights to her property until after her own death. The court opinion noted that it was the duty of a chancellor to correct such errors. In *Dupree*, the court interpreted a poorly worded settlement to benefit the feme covert and her son against the claims of the woman's second husband, who attempted to seize all of her property after her death.

38. Marriage Settlement between Charlotte Poaug and John Poaug (1771), Marriage Settlements, 1:78.

39. Tyrrel v. Hope, 2 Atkyns 561 (1743); Reeve, *Baron and Femme*, 164; Lowndes' Trustee v. Champneys' Executors (1821), Charleston District Equity Decrees, 3:354.

40. Johnson v. Thompson, 4 S.C. Eq. (4 Des.) 498 (1814).

41. During the period under study, only one case indicated a judicial reluctance to support female powers of control, and there the controversial subject of divorce clouded the issue. See Barret v. Barret, 4 S.C. Eq. (4 Des.) 491 (1814).

42. Lowndes' Trustee v. Champneys' Executors (1821), Charleston District Equity Decrees, 3:354.

43. Reeve, *Baron and Femme*, 9, 178–79. Favorable decisions include McPike v. Hughes and Rumph (1816), Charleston District Equity Court Decrees, 3:175; Tatnell v. Fenwick's Executors, 1 S.C. Eq. (1 Des.) 147 (1786); Greenland v. Brown, 1 S.C. Eq. (1 Des.) 196 (1791); and Postell and Smith v. Skirving's Executors, 1 S.C. Eq. (1 Des.) 158 (1789).

44. Gregorie, ed., *Chancery Records*, 507–11.

45. Gregorie, ed., *Chancery Records*, 510.

46. Gregorie, ed., *Chancery Records*, 551–52; Marriage Settlement between Dorothy Golightly and William Henry Drayton (1764), Marriage Settlements, 2:185–92.

47. Postell and Smith v. Skirving's Executors, 1 S.C. Eq. (1 Des.) 158.

48. Postell and Smith v. Skirving's Executors, 1 S.C. Eq. (1 Des.) 158.

49. Postell and Smith v. Skirving's Executors, 1 S.C. Eq. (1 Des.) 158–59.

50. Women without the right to make wills through marriage settlements could bequeath personal property if their husbands consented. See Grimke v. Grimke, 1 S.C. Eq. (1 Des.) 366–82 (1794), and Smelie v. Smelie, 2 S.C. Eq. (2 Des.) 66–79 (1802). The law on this point is discussed in Blackstone, *Commentaries*, 2:498, and *Laws Respecting Women*, 178–79. Without valid marriage settlements, however, women could never devise real property. Smith, *De Republica Anglorum*, ed. Alston, 127; *Laws Respecting Women*, 149; Holdsworth, *History of English Law*, 3:185; Kent, *Commentaries on American Law*, 2:130–31.

51. Marriage Settlements between Mary Ladson and Thomas Poole (1760), Miscellaneous Records, MM, 41–44; Jane Wilkie and Charles Cogdell (1774), Miscellaneous Records, RR, 314–16; Elizabeth Legare and William B. Legare (1825), Marriage Settlements, 9:185–87.

52. For a discussion of one enterprising widow's experience, see Mary Beth Norton, "A Cherished Spirit of Independence: The Life of an Eighteenth-Century Boston Businesswoman," in *Women of America*, ed. Berkin and Norton, 48–67. Although the woman Norton describes was a Bostonian, the same influences governed her actions in creating a marriage settlement as governed the actions of many South Carolina women.

53. Marriage Settlements between Elizabeth Meshaw and Thomas Snipes (1736), HH, 27–28; Christiana Hoff and John Hoff (1772), PP, 254; Elizabeth Baxter and Thomas Robinson (1771), PP, 6–8, Miscellaneous Records.

54. Marriage Settlement between Elizabeth Holson and John Harth (1779), Marriage Settlements, 1:152.

55. Marriage Settlement between Sarah Ann Baxter and Joseph Binnikes (1825), Marriage Settlements, 9:159.

Hog Meat and Cornpone: Foodways in the Antebellum South

SAM B. HILLIARD

In the following essay, Sam B. Hilliard explores the distinctive foodways of Southern whites and blacks before the Civil War. He demonstrates that food— the only type of created artifact that men and women literally "consume"—served at once to define the South as a cultural region and to demarcate recognized social boundaries. Probably no cultural region in America stirs up such forceful images of local cuisine; the tourist or nostalgic native dreams of pork ribs, pork chops, hog maws, chitlins, grits, fatback, collard greens, and turnips. In part these modern stereotypes are grounded in historical reality. But in the late eighteenth and nineteenth centuries Southern foodways were much more complex, with wide variation in recipes and access to imported products making urban centers distinct from inland villages. "Traditional" foodways, like ballads and fiddle tunes, were invented and continued to evolve in a specific historical context.

The cultural construction of a regional diet, Hilliard points out, is firmly lodged in economic life. When white planters were first breaking fields and setting fenceposts, a lack of improved arable acreage forced them to rely strongly on wild game. But as forests yielded first to the ax and then to the plow, both grain and livestock prospered. By the late eighteenth century, Southern farmers depended most heavily on the two products they could raise with the least amount of intensive husbandry: corn and pigs. Throughout the antebellum years, these two mainstays dominated the diet, with support from a few vegetables: turnip greens, yellow peas, sweet potatoes, and squash. Southern culture developed in relation to the sowing and harvesting of corn and the slaughtering and smoking of pork. Other grains and meats—wheat, oats, poultry, beef, and mutton, to name just a few—provided an occasional release from monotony but never threatened to displace the two staples. As the Atlantic market economy extended through the South during the mid-nineteenth century, whites in urban centers and large country

towns benefited from an impressive range of imported foodstuffs, including everything from brandy to fruitcake to ice cream. But most poorer white planters ate a more restricted variety of foods; their diet was similar to that of slaves: pork (much of it fat), greens, sweet potatoes and turnips, and an occasional chicken. Slaves modified the narrow range of their rations with additional vegetables and chickens they raised. Still, the diet of poor whites and slaves alike was protein- and vitamin-deficient; the "traditional" Southern food system paradoxically became most entrenched among those who suffered most its nutritional shortcomings.

As food habits drew cultural lines around biological needs, they also linked diet to medicine and the world of popular beliefs that in part defined a nineteenth-century understanding of the human body. The consumption of pork, Hilliard explains, was believed to be ideal for slaves involved in heavy field labor but unfit for "delicate" Southern women. Herbs and teas served both in seasoning and in folk healing. Beliefs similarly conditioned the consumption of beverages; the "evils" of alcohol, for example, were portrayed by temperance workers as both physically and morally debilitating. What Southerners ate derived from where they lived, their state of economic ease or hardship, their relative freedom, and from the way they imagined the metaphysics of food.

There is a pleasant land, not far from the sea-shore of a celebrated Southern State, watered by the Waccamaw, Great Pedee, and Winyah, noble rivers. . . . A land it is of jonnycakes and waffles, hoe-cakes and hominy, very agreeable to look back upon.[1]

An essential element in any discussion of Southern culture is the distinctive character of its foodways. Nowhere in the nation has a cultural pattern become so outstanding nor certain foods become so identified with a single area as in the South. While it is true that recent trends indicate a mass homogenization of American food habits, the notable food preferences of eighteenth- and nineteenth-century Southerners and the persistence of these choices into the twentieth century have consistently distinguished the region from other parts of the country. Perhaps owing to low production costs or ready availability of certain foods, the area developed and maintained strong food preferences. Most Southern foods were not unique; many were frontier staples in other parts of the country. Yet the South came to depend so strongly on such items as pork, corn, turnips, sweet potatoes, okra, and peas that they often are regarded as distinctly "Southern" foods. This essay deals with the development of Southern food habits and describes the foodways of whites and blacks as they existed during the antebellum period. It also comments on the nutritional aspects of Southern diet and the persistence of food preferences through time.

The scientific study of diet is essentially a post-Civil War phenomenon. Detailed information is not available for the antebellum period, leaving us the problem of extracting bits of material from scattered sources that do not deal specifically with foodways. Some information can be gleaned from the writings of travelers in the South, who commented frequently on food they encountered while touring the area. More comes from the extant diaries and daybooks of planters and farmers who kept records of foodstuffs produced or purchased. Finally, a number of studies published toward the end of the nineteenth century and in the twentieth century indicate fairly precisely the food habits in a few specific areas.[2] From these rather scattered sources it is possible to glean bits of information about Southern food habits, and with what we know about contemporary food habits we can sketch a generalized picture of conditions as they existed during the pre-Civil War period. Southern food habits during the antebellum period stemmed in part from those existing in the Atlantic seaboard South during the late eighteenth and early nineteenth centuries and were tempered by "frontier" conditions and the availability of food items suited to conditions—slavery among them—in the South.

Foodways of White Planters

During the early years of settlement, food choices were dictated by frontier conditions and the state of agricultural progress. Since settlement was not instantaneous, economic conditions varied from place to place and from time to time. In Virginia, along the South Carolina coast, and in lower Louisiana, settlement was accomplished quite early and the inhabitants enjoyed a variety of foods. In the interior lower South no such conditions existed. Even as late as 1840 parts of Georgia, Alabama, and Mississippi were scarcely inhabited and few amenities were available. Our best, though most critical, descriptions of the interior come from travelers. Much of the area was considered wilderness and was avoided by all but the most adventurous tourists. Those curious enough to venture into the interior found that conditions changed markedly as they moved from the more settled areas into the back country. Before 1835 or 1840, many travelers reported an almost total lack of luxury items in the interior and often complained about the coarse food. On an overland trip from New Orleans to Charleston in the 1830s Thomas Hamilton described the food in the interior of Alabama: "We were now beyond the region of bread, and our fare consisted of eggs, broiled venison, and cakes of Indian corn fried in some kind of oleaginous matter." He reported this menu again and again, though at times there were no eggs.[3] In the backcountry there was a strong dependence on game, and travelers found it wherever they went.[4]

This was also true of the more settled areas. Fanny Kemble, while a resident on the Butler plantation in Georgia in 1838 and 1839, stated that their "living consists very mainly of wild ducks, wild geese, wild turkeys and venison."[5] This fare was not exclusively a rural one since there was a sizable market for venison in the port cities. Tyrone Power described the Mobile market as "abundantly supplied with provisions, fish, and game of every variety."[6] New Orleans markets were similarly stocked with "Game of all kinds, venison, woodcock, pheasant, snipe, plover, etc."[7] Even in the more settled areas game was not entirely absent from the urban market. In 1840 the *Southern Cabinet* described the Charleston market as being "abundantly supplied with game . . . as in former years."[8] Nearly two decades later Frederick Law Olmsted found deer still plentiful in South Carolina. In the up-country he referred to a farmer who had "lately shot three deer," while near Charleston the sons of his host returned from a night hunt "with a boatload of venison, wild fowl and fish." He added that "the woods and waters around us abound . . . with game."[9]

The transition from wild to domestic food was gradual; most people depended less on forest and stream as their farms began to produce and as the supply of game diminished. During the first year on a farm or plantation practically everything was in short supply; even corn, the universal staple, had to be brought in from the settled areas or purchased from neighbors whose farms were already producing.[10] Most settlers, whether large or small landholders, planted corn as soon as possible to provide food for the coming year. Usually, they owned a few cattle and hogs, which were expected to increase and provide dairy products and meat.

Pork was the most common domestic meat during the early years, and a broodstock of hogs was considered essential on all new holdings. It increased rapidly and, even in remote areas, salt pork competed very strongly with venison as the staple meat. In the 1830s Harriet Martineau complained that travelers found "little else than pork, under all manner of disguises."[11] One complained about the toughness of Virginia chickens but remarked that they would have been relished "in Alabama, where bacon and sweet potatoes constitute the only delicacies."[12] He described a meal offered him near Columbus, Georgia, which, with the possible exception of the milk, probably represented the usual fare.

> In the middle of the table was placed a bottle of whiskey, of which both host and hostess partook in no measured quantity, before they tasted any of the dishes. Pigs' feet pickled in vinegar formed the first course; then followed bacon with molasses; and the repast concluded with a super-abundance of milk and bread, which the land-lord, to use his own expression, washed down with a half a tumbler of whiskey. The landlady, a real Amazon, was not a little surprized to see a person refusing such a delicacy as bacon swimming in molasses.[13]

In 1837 a traveler near Berrien, Georgia, reported the addition of rice to the usual "fryed middlen [sic], cornbread and coffee."[14] Early settlers in Mississippi could seldom offer much variety, as James Creecy complained: "I had never fallen in with any cooking so villainous. Rusty salt pork, boiled or fried . . . and musty corn-meal dodgers, rarely a vegetable of any description, no milk, butter, eggs, or the semblance of a condiment—was my fare often for weeks at a time." Again: "But few, indeed, of the early settlers gave a thought to gardens or vegetables, and their food was coarse corn-meal bread, rusty pork, with wild game . . . and sometimes what was, most slanderously, called coffee."[15]

Corn and pork were dietary mainstays and were the domestic food items most avidly sought; while other foods were added as settlers devoted more time and space to gardens, orchards, and poultry, the primary foods remained corn and hog meat. A good crop for new settlers was turnips. Providing greens in only a few weeks, the plants were ideal for new clearings and were quite common on newly opened landholdings. The overseer of a new plantation in Mississippi proudly reported to the owner that he had "sode four acre of turnips" that would serve as food.[16] Even if the prospective farmer or planter arrived at the site in late summer or fall there was always time for sowing turnips.

As more land was cleared for farming, a greater variety of foods became available. A garden was planted, orchards were set out, the cattle and hogs increased, and poultry became more common. Moreover, the sale of such cash crops as cotton made possible the purchase of a few luxury items. Thus, the typical fare of new settlers underwent gradual improvement in variety. During the first year there was almost complete reliance on nondomestic foods and pork, corn, sweet potatoes, turnips, and a few chickens, but most farmers had to wait a few years until sufficient stock of animals was accumulated, thus providing an abundance of meat. Perhaps by the third or fourth year the fields and pastures began to yield adequately and by the fifth or sixth the orchard trees were bearing, but a decade might pass before the farm or plantation could offer a good variety of food. Even then, only the most foresighted could maintain an assorted fare throughout the year.

While the more settled parts of the South underwent some change in food habits as the variety of foods increased, most farmers and planters retained a number of their frontier eating habits, keeping game, fish, and gathered food from the large areas of unimproved land on the table up until the Civil War.

Moreover, corn and pork remained the dietary staples throughout the antebellum period and into the twentieth century.

The primary meat in the South was pork. In fact, this could be said for the remainder of the country as well. Not only was it the most important meat on American tables, but the total consumption of meat was very high in comparison with other countries. This heavy consumption of meat together with the preponderance of pork tended to give European travelers the impression that Americans consumed little else. In commenting on diet in America, Mrs. Trollope remarked, "They consume an extraordinary quantity of bacon. Ham and beefsteaks appear morning, noon, and night."[17] One estimate placed the per capita pork consumption during the period at three times that of Europe.[18] In the South and West, the tendency was to rely even more strongly on pork, with most white people having it every day. One story has it that an immigrant Irishman wrote home that he commonly "took meat" twice a day. When asked why he so distorted the truth, he replied that if he said "three times a day" he would have been called a liar.[19]

In the Deep South pork was the undisputed "king of the table." Olmsted stated that bacon "invariably appeared at every meal."[20] As a long-time student of the South, Emily Burke believed that "the people of the South would not think they could subsist without their [swine] flesh; bacon, instead of bread, seems to be THEIR staff of life. Consequently, you see bacon upon a Southern table three times a day either boiled or fried."[21]

Many people thought pork to be high in "energy" and considered it the best meat for working people. And, although some physicians were beginning to plead for less pork and more vegetables in the diet, most thought it best for heavy laborers and slaves.[22] Dr. John S. Wilson of Columbus, Georgia, one of the most outspoken doctors in the South, frequently attacked the overuse of pork. In one of his numerous articles on diet and health he delivered a scathing attack on pork-eating and cooking with lard.

The United States of America might properly be called the great Hog-eating Confederacy, or the Republic of Porkdom. At any rate, should the South and West . . . be named dietetically, the above appellation would be peculiarly appropriate; for in many parts of this region, so far as meat is concerned, it is fat bacon and pork, fat bacon and pork only, and that continually morning, noon, and night, for all classes, sexes, ages, and conditions; and, except the boiled bacon and collards at dinner, the meat is generally fried, and thus supersaturated with grease in the form of hogs' lard. But the frying is not confined to the meat alone: for we have fried vegetables of all kinds, fried fritters and pancakes . . . fried bread not infrequently, and indeed fried everything that is fryable, or that will stick together long enough to undergo the delightful process . . . hogs' lard is the very oil that moves the machinery of life, and they would as soon think of dispensing with tea, coffee, [or] tobacco . . . as with the essence of hog.[23]

The dominance of pork led to a great deal of experimentation with production, slaughter, and preservation methods. The system of pork-packing that had developed in the Ohio River Valley was well organized by 1840 and, due to the dominance of large packing houses, exhibited considerable uniformity. With no organized packing industry in the Deep South, pork production was largely confined to farms and plantations; consequently, variety was the order of the day, with each person having his or her own "pet" methods of slaughtering and curing. The most common curing method was dry-salting followed by smoking. The carcass was cut up into six or more pieces, placed in a meat box, and covered with salt. After a few weeks (sometimes as long as six), the meat was removed, washed, and hung in the smokehouse over a slow fire. Although not a universal practice, some producers preferred to sprinkle the meat lightly with salt and let it lie overnight to "draw out the blood" before placing it in the meat box.

An alternative to this method was pickling in casks filled with brine solution. Pickling offered advantages in that it permitted slaughtering in warmer weather without fear of spoilage and eliminated the laborious process of salting, hanging, and smoking. Moreover, awkward pieces, such as the head, could be preserved more easily than by smoking. While pickled meat was less likely to become spoiled than smoked meat, it required soaking in water to remove enough salt to make it palatable.[24] Moreover, most Southerners much preferred the salt-smoke process since it produced, to their taste at least, better flavored meat. Consequently, it must have been the most commonly used method. Emily Burke reported from Georgia: "Pork at the South is never to my knowledge, salted and barreled as it is with us, but flitches as well as hams are hung up without being divided, in the house built for that purpose, and preserved in a smoke that is kept up night and day."[25]

These general descriptions of pork processing hardly do justice to the myriad individual variations that existed. The above methods were employed commonly in making large quantities of pork, such as that needed for slave meat on large plantations, but meat destined for the use of planter or farmer received special treatment. The carcass was carefully cut up, the joints trimmed to shape, and the spine, ribs, and tenderloins separated from the abdominal sides, which were cured into bacon. Excess fat was rendered into lard, while lean pieces went into sausage, "souse," and "head cheese." The backbone and ribs, liver, tongue, and brains often were consumed fresh. The kidneys, heart, and lungs were occasionally eaten, but few Southerners cared for them. Chitterlings (the large intestine), reputedly treasured only by blacks, were relished by whites as well, and the traditional "chitlin supper" came to be an annual epicurean event. Curing techniques were matters of personal pride—each farmer or planter added his own flourishes to the basic method. Pepper, alum, ashes, charcoal, cornmeal, honey, sugar, molasses, saltpeter, mustard, and a host of other seasonings were added, and each producer fancied his own meat to be "not inferior to the best Wesphalian hams."[26] The preferred cuts were the hams, shoulders, sausage, and perhaps the tenderloin, but each part of the animal had its devotees, and all were consumed, in one manner or another, through the winter and well into the summer. On occasion the entire animal was roasted. Apparently, the famous Southern barbecue was in practice before the Civil War, as a young bride in North Carolina wrote her parents in New York:

Not until you come here can you imagine how entirely different is their mode of living here from the North. They live more heartily. . . . Red pepper is much used to flavor . . . the famous barbarque [sic] of the South . . . which I believe they esteem above all.[27]

The use of meat other than pork by the white people of the Deep South is easy to underestimate.

Beef was not relied on very heavily because it was hard to preserve in a manner to suit Southern tastes. Most beef was eaten fresh, but it was occasionally pickled, and there is some evidence that it was also dried.[28] Except in winter, fresh beef has to be consumed rather quickly in order to prevent spoilage. On a farm or plantation with a large labor force beefs were slaughtered one at a time and the meat divided among the families, to be consumed in a few days. Occasionally planters and farmers formed cooperatives in which each family periodically killed and divided the meat among the participants.[29] Apparently, this became a common practice among the French in Louisiana.[30] In other cases, neighbors simply borrowed fresh meat and repaid later as their own animals were slaughtered.[31]

Because of the tendency to run short of pork in summer, there was probably a rise in beef consumption in that season. Cattle were fatter in summer and, after months of salt pork, beef was a welcome relief.[32] One Southern writer, pleading for agricultural reform and higher pork production, cited planters who were forced to kill beefs so often that "the cows are afraid to come home at night."[33]

Such frequency was not the rule and, except the piney woods grazers who kept large cattle herds, it is unlikely that beef was eaten regularly by the poorer whites. Among the diversified farmers and better planters beef was more common. Most operators slaughtered one or two animals each year, while the larger planters may have killed more.[34] Susan Dabney Smedes refers to beef as if it were common, and it is likely that beef-eating was the rule among the herders in the southern portion of the Deep South.[35] Beef consumption by most Southerners, however, must have been sporadic and the total amount small relative to pork. This was not true where cooperative slaughtering was practiced, but one questions just how widespread the cooperative system might have been.

Apparently, there were no regionally characteristic ways in which Southerners prepared their beef. Travelers referred to "beefsteaks" but seldom with any hint as to their preparation.[36] In restaurants or hotels it was prepared in a variety of ways. Olmsted noted that the menu of the Commercial Hotel in Memphis included a number of beef dishes: corned beef, Kentucky Beef (roasted), beef heart, and kidney.[37] Frying was a common cooking method and was well suited to places where few utensils were available.[38]

Traditionally, Southerners have not been considered consumers of mutton. In fact, in his monumental work on the history of Southern agriculture, Lewis C. Gray concludes that "there was a strong prejudice in the South against mutton, a prejudice that must have been widespread, judging from frequent references to it."[39] Undoubtedly, mutton was a minor food on Southern tables, but its use was not uncommon, and in many areas it was actively sought.[40] As one visitor along the rice coast remarked, "so far from mutton being dispised, as we have been told, it was much desired."[41] In Louisiana mutton was well liked; even in the interior of the Deep South there appears to have been a sizable demand.[42] In fact, some evidence argues that sheep were kept *primarily* for their flesh rather than for wool. Solon Robinson met a planter in Louisiana who kept two hundred to five hundred sheep to feed his slaves, and he hinted that the practice was common along the Mississippi.[43] Writing to the Patent Office in 1849, a Mississippi agriculturist revealed a surprising concern for mutton sheep: "Few planters keep more sheep than enough to supply their own tables with that most excellent dish, a saddle of Mississippi mutton."[44] Another wrote, "I do not think it an object with our planters to increase their flocks to a greater extent to supply their family wants. The sheep is valued with us more for his flesh than for his fleece. The mutton, we think, is quite equal to any in the world."[45]

Mutton was without doubt more common among the affluent than among poorer whites and slaves. The larger farmers and planters were more likely to keep sheep, and most planned to slaughter several each year, a practice that resulted in mutton becoming a periodic supplement to the regular meat supply.[46] Some planters, however, kept sheep enough to have lamb or mutton quite often. Fanny Kemble, while visiting along the rice coast, remarked that, "we have now not infrequently had mutton at the table, the flavor of which is quite excellent."[47] A Mississippi planter butchered as often as twice a week during spring and summer.[48] And on *Rosedew*, a Georgia coastal plantation, lambs were slaughtered weekly and sent to market, indicating some demand in urban areas.[49]

While mutton and beef offered periodic respites from pork, poultry served as a regular meat dish throughout the year. Chickens, turkeys, ducks, geese, and guinea fowl were common on most Southern landholdings and were important elements in the white diet, possibly more than either beef or mutton. Even if the total quantity of poultry did not equal the amount of beef and mutton consumed, it was available more regularly and was therefore more important in breaking the monotony of the usual meat routine.

Poultry was regarded as a semiluxury item, and the implication of the term "chicken on Sunday" was accurate. The more astute farmers and planters were able to have poultry frequently, and the visitor was plied with both chicken and turkey.[50] Most planters had their own flocks and some supplemented this supply with purchases from their slaves who kept poultry. The smaller landholder had fewer fowls but still depended on poultry for special occasions. Southern pots were often filled in expectation of the preacher or other guest. For example, Olmsted's request for breakfast in northern Mississippi was promptly fulfilled after a group of black children chased and caught a hen in the backyard.[51] The occasional visitor, the family get-togethers on Sundays, or the periodic visits by the preacher were times for slaughtering a fryer or nonlaying old hen. A favorite story in the rural South portrays barnyard fowls becoming so "educated" to the Sunday slaughter that when a "genteel-looking" person approached the house they fled to the woods.

The preparation of poultry meat was simple, with few Southern flourishes added. The most notable dish was fried chicken, but frying required a young bird, often unavailable. Those too old and tough for frying were roasted or boiled until tender, and leftover chicken or turkey carcasses were converted into pies with large dumplings made of wheat flour. While poultry flesh helped relieve the monotony of a pork-dominated diet, eggs added even more variety. Commonly used as ingredients in breads, cakes, and pies, they also were used as food items themselves and were surprisingly common as food for travelers.[52] Although the quantity of eggs consumed is unknown, they must have been eaten regularly during summer by most white families. The seasonal character of egg-laying, however, meant a dearth in the winter.

Southerners took game of all kinds throughout the year, but fall and winter were the preferred hunting seasons. This provided game during the period when poultry and eggs were least abundant. Wild turkey, rabbit, and squirrel tended to replace domestic poultry and eggs in the diet during winter. The cooking of game was similar to that of domestic meats. Frying was a favorite method of preparing young rabbit, but older animals were boiled.[53] Squirrel meat was tougher than rabbit and required more cooking, but the results were considered superior to rabbit dishes. Squirrel broth or pie with dumplings were considered delicacies.[54] Opposum was certainly not confined to the black diet; most whites also ate the animal and many sought them eagerly. One can imagine the satisfaction of the Southern hunter who proudly entered in his diary the results of a night's hunt: "Caught three fine Possums last night."[55] Young ones could be fried, but the preferred cooking method was roasting and serving with sweet potatoes. An ex-slave commented on their gastronomical worth, saying, "verily there is nothing in all butcherdom so delicious as a roasted 'possom.'"[56]

Perhaps the game most sought were the various kinds of fowls. Along the Atlantic coast and Mississippi flyways waterfowl were numerous and provided excellent food. However, wild turkey was the favorite since it abounded throughout the area. A South Carolina hunter revealed his enthusiasm for the hunt. "Today I saw a lot of wild turkeys," wrote David Harris in his farm journal for 1858, "and among the others was one fine old goblar [sic]; I have marked him as mine—and if he does not leave the neighborhood I will be sure to eat him."[57]

Like game, fish and seafood were important minor foods in much of the area, but near the coasts and in the larger rivers they were relied on quite heavily. The oyster was the easiest of the marine foods to harvest, but other kinds were taken by nets and seines in large quantities. Shrimp and mullet were taken with "cast nets," and, with luck, a large catch could be had in a few hours' casting.[58] One source describes a bachelor Carolina planter who owned five or six slaves and lived off fish, shrimp, potatoes, and game. Apparently, he spent "half of his time hunting and fishing and the rest in making shrimp nets and fishing tackle."[59]

Farther inland the catfish became the prize catch. They were found in all rivers including those of the Tennessee, Mississippi, and Alabama-Tombigbee systems, as well as the many smaller streams that flow directly into the Atlantic. River "cats" were easy to catch, and many were large enough to feed an entire family. And, while some whites expressed disgust on seeing their first live catfish, their reservations disappeared when confronted with steaming platters of fillets or steaks. Both whites and blacks came to relish catfish, and, indeed, it has come to be the fish commonly identified with the area. The fish were taken in large quantities, and considerable evidence indicates that many people depended strongly on them for food.[60] Catches could be quite large; on the Davis plantation in Alabama, several dozen were caught daily. Occasionally, large cats weighing 30 to 40 pounds were caught.[61] In the Mississippi River's channels and tributaries, extremely large fish sometimes were taken. On one plantation two were caught that weighed 104 and 108 pounds.[62]

During season shad were taken from the Atlantic-flowing streams of the South. From the James to the Altamaha these fish moved upstream annually to be taken by seine and net. Charles Stevenson states that they moved as far as four hundred miles upstream and were taken in large quantities to be consumed fresh or salted for later use.[63] This estimate on distance would have placed shad above the fall zone cities and well within the reach of many inland inhabitants, and there is evidence that they were caught far inland. Shad are extremely easy to catch, and, given any constriction in the channel, dip nets can yield dozens of fish in a night.[64] In coastal North Carolina, where shad fishing was quite well developed, many planters gained considerable income from fishing; some even issued regular fish rations to their slaves.[65]

Frying was the most common method of preparing fresh fish, and, no matter what the species, the fish was rolled in cornmeal and then fried. Saltwater fish were treated in the same manner. Near the coast, shellfish, too, were so prepared, though often they were roasted unshucked over an open fire or made into a stew.

As mentioned previously, Indian corn (maize) was the companion food to pork, and together they were dietary mainstays of the South. Corn was used in myriad ways. While still green during early summer, it often was boiled on the cob, cut off the cob and creamed (called "fried corn"), or simply roasted in the shuck.[66] After the ears had ripened and dried there were other ways it could be prepared. The most common was to grind it into meal, from which an almost endless variety of breads were concocted. The most common was cornbread, which, in its simplest form, was a baked cake, or "pone," made from meal, salt, and water. Variations on this included the addition of milk, buttermilk, shortening, or eggs. After hog-killing, bits of crisp "cracklings" left over from the lard-rendering process were added to make "crackling bread." The variations were legion; even today, one encounters dozens of recipes for Southern cornbread.

The dominance of cornbread as *the* bread for the South is unquestionable. Whether in the mountains or near the coast, Olmsted constantly commented about being fed cornbread; apparently, it was the bread he most often encountered.[67] U. B. Phillips refers to corn as the food of the "plain people," but there is little to indicate that cornbread was exclusively a poor man's food. It is true that the more affluent could afford wheaten bread, but most did not abandon cornbread as they "moved up" to the use of other cereals. Charles Lyell found that even in "some rich houses maize, or Indian corn, and rice were entirely substituted for wheaten bread."[68] Harriet Martineau, in describing a fantastically sumptuous plantation menu, lists "hot wheat bread . . . corn bread, biscuits" as if corn and wheat breads were commonly served together.[69] Phillip Gosse, while visiting in Alabama, concluded that cornbread was "even preferred to the finest wheaten bread."[70]

The popularity of cornbread is not easy to explain. Its use for slave food presumably was due to the cheapness of cornmeal compared with wheat flour, but one wonders why it was so well liked by all. It was easy to make but, unlike most European breads, did not remain fresh very long. Perhaps this is one of the reasons why Southern women came to think of hot bread as an essential element of every meal. In the absence of other reasons for its popularity one can only conclude that Southerners learned to like the taste of cornbread when it was all they had and have continued to demand it though they might well have afforded wheaten bread. However, such persistence was not so notable in such other areas as the Old Northwest, where corn was the principal "frontier" cereal.

Cornmeal was used to make a number of other items besides cornbread. Some, such as corn dodgers, hoecake, corn muffins, and egg bread, were simply variations of cornbread, while other dishes were quite different.[71] Often cornmeal was made into mush (porridge), griddle cakes, or waffles.[72] Sometimes it was mixed with wheat flour and occasionally with rice to make bread. On some occasions, cornmeal was mixed with milk or water, put in a warm place to sour, and made into "sourings," which served as bread.[73]

In addition to the use of corn as meal, Southerners converted it into hominy and grits. This involved a lye-soaking process that removed the husk (not the shuck) from the grain. Hominy consisted of whole grain corn boiled and eaten as a vegetable. When hominy grains were dried, ground into a coarse meal, and boiled, the dish was called grits. The preparation of grits varied depending upon personal preference, but they usually were cooked into a thick porridge. Contrary to popular opinion, neither grits nor hominy ever came close to being universally used in the area before the Civil War. Both were common, but, compared to the other uses to which ground corn was put, they were certainly subordinate. Since the Civil War grits have become a common complementary dish to ham, sausage, or bacon and eggs for breakfast, but there is little evidence that grits were used nearly as much as cornbread during the antebellum period.

Other cereals have had much less notable places in the Southern diet. Buckwheat, rye, and oats have never been particularly liked and seldom were used. Wheat and rice were the most common minor cereals. Wheat bread was commonly used by Virginia and Carolina colonists, and its use was retained throughout the antebellum period. But the relatively low production of the grain within much of the area and the high cost of imported flour tended to cut down wheat consumption. Travelers often complained about the lack of wheat bread, and when available some considered it "doughy" because of the addition of too much shortening (hog lard, of course).[74] Wheaten bread undoubtedly was more commonly used in the older states of the South than in the areas settled later. More wheat flour was consumed per capita in Virginia and North Carolina than in Georgia, and more in Georgia than in either Mississippi or Alabama. Wheat bread and other wheaten items were by no means rare, but among less affluent people they were "something special," available perhaps on Sundays or two or three times each week. The day-to-day bread was cornbread. Moreover, much of the wheat flour was used for pastries, cakes, waffles, and pancakes rather than for bread.

Rice consumption was quite high along the Carolina and Georgia coasts, yet outside the "rice area" rice was a minor item. Extremely high production along the coastal counties of Georgia and South Carolina, and correspondingly low costs—especially for the less marketable kinds—made it a staple in the diet of both blacks and whites. Charles Lyell noted that rice, together with cornbread, took the place of wheaten bread in the rice area of South Carolina.[75] Olmsted commented quite favorably on a breakfast roll made with rice flour.[76] Another visitor noted that it was one of the principal dishes: "I always eat from this dish of rice at breakfast, because I know it to be very wholesome. People generally eat it with fresh butter, and many mix with it also a soft-boiled egg."[77] The high consumption of rice in limited areas of the South is an excellent example of a food preference being determined by the ready availability of an item. Although rice is no longer grown in coastal Georgia and South Carolina, the local preference has persisted.

The favorite Southern vegetables were sweet potatoes, turnips, and peas. More than any others, these were the items to which Southerners commonly turned for vegetable food. The sweet potato (commonly and confusingly referred to simply as "potato") was useful in that it was highly nutritious, kept well during winter, and could be cooked in a number of ways. Baking or roasting in ashes was a common method of cooking; this left the skin on the tuber, making it easy to carry and suitable for hunting trips or for snacks. Olmsted noted both black and white boys roasting potatoes in the ashes of a campfire at a religious service; later the children crawled around on the church floor carrying "handfuls of cornbread and roasted potatoes about with them."[78]

Turnips were grown for their roots and greens, and both were eaten in large quantities. Both were invariably boiled (seemingly for hours), and Southerners preferred the greens boiled with a large "chunk" of bacon in the pot. Cabbage, collards, other greens, beans, and peas (field peas or cowpeas) were all cooked in this manner. A by-product of this process of boiling with a piece of bacon was the "pot-likker." This was a concentrated broth combining juices from both the vegetables and meat and was eaten with cornbread. Although this practice might not appeal to today's discerning tastes, it was extremely impor-tant that the more nutritious juices were consumed rather than discarded. In addition to boiling, many vegetables were fried, including white potatoes, eggplant, okra, squash (Southerners preferred the yellow summer squash), and even sweet potatoes, sliced and rolled in meal.

Fruits and melons were popular in season and were easily preserved for winter use.[79] For desserts, fruits were made into pies or served fresh. Surplus fruits were either dried or preserved by some sugaring process. Dried peaches, apples, and other fruits were served in winter, while apples, peaches, various grapes including scuppernongs and muscadines, blackberries, strawberries, and even watermelons were converted to sweets for off-season use. Additional sweetening came in the form of molasses, syrup, and honey (both wild and domestic).[80] The molasses and syrup used in the South were of two basic kinds. In areas near the South Atlantic and Gulf coasts, especially in Louisiana, the most common syrup was molasses made from sugar cane. It was an important trade item and was the sweetening most frequently issued to slaves. The major sources were Louisiana or the West Indies. On landholdings not producing sugar, syrup was made from sorghum cane and was referred to as sorghum, ribbon cane, or cane syrup, but occasionally as "molasses," too.

The Southern attitude toward beverages has changed markedly since antebellum times. While there was a small temperance movement before the Civil War, the great, almost universal, condemnation of alcoholic drinks came in the late nineteenth and early twentieth centuries. During the antebellum period, whiskey and wine were consumed in huge quantities by all whites who could afford them, with whiskey being preferred by the less well-to-do.[81] Wine was common among the affluent. A number of visitors noted its use; apparently claret was the favorite.[82] This preference for claret is further confirmed by the statistics for wines imported into the country, which show the major part of the claret moving into New Orleans.[83]

Nonalcoholic drinks included coffee, tea, and milk. Coffee was a favorite, but tea was also fairly common. Milk was consumed fresh or sour (curds) or made into buttermilk. Both sour milk and buttermilk were quite popular, and even today a favorite dish is cornbread crumbled into buttermilk to make a soupy mixture.[84] It was common to serve plain water at meals, and between meals a gourd of cool spring water was a summer treat invariably offered to visitors.

A number of towns and cities, notably New Orleans, Mobile, Savannah, and Charleston, offered a variety of luxury foods not available in the more remote rural stores. The inland towns functioned much as did the coastal cities but on a smaller scale. Raleigh, Columbia, Augusta, Macon, Milledgeville, Columbus, Montgomery, Selma, Florence, Decatur, Jackson, Vicksburg, and Natchez were all centers where luxury foodstuffs were available. Stores, restaurants, and hotels as well as factors handled imported wines, liquors, spices, cheese, and other items for the affluent. Lewis Atherton's study of country stores in the South revealed a surprising variety of goods available in many rural areas as well. All stores carried sugar, coffee, tea, salt, and whiskey, but a number went far beyond this simple list. Some rural towns had specialty stores where luxury items were sold. A house in Huntsville advertised "loaf and lump sugar, pineapple cheese, allspice, ginger, pepper, raisins, almonds, nutmegs, mustard, . . . tea, and wine."[85] In Talladega, Alabama, a store advertised "liquors, brandies, wines, whiskies, ale, porter [and] schnapps."[86] A wholesaler in Athens listed an almost unbelievable array of gourmet items. Furthermore, many towns had confectioners where "candies, cordials, fruit cakes" were offered.[87] J. S. Buckingham noted (even in the 1840s) that Columbus, Georgia, had "more than the usual number of . . . 'Confectionaries,' where sweetmeats and fruits are sold." He apparently found a similar situation in Alabama but noted that the cordials were alcoholic and that some confectioner's shops were only gentlemen's bars.[88]

Perhaps the most notable innovation affecting popular diet was the availability of ice. It became available in port cities early in the century and by the 1850s had penetrated the interior as well. Ice was sold in Selma in 1840 and by 1855 had reached most urban places located near rivers or on railroads.[89] The availability of ice increased the variety offered by the confectionery, and the true soda fountain came into being. Just before the war an Alabama store advertised:

The subscribers have put up a soda fountain in their establishment, and have arrangements to be supplied with ice. . . . The syrups will be of the richest and most choice variety, consisting of rose, lemon, pineapple and strawberry, vanilla, sarasparilla, sassafras, ginger, almond, and peach.[90]

As ice became available the year round, ice-cream making became possible. It was made in the area before the 1840s, but few machines were in use. A freezer, roughly the same as the freezer now used, began to be marketed during the 1850s, and presumably some moved into the South.[91]

With such items available, the urban inhabitant as well as white planters and farmers living nearby had opportunities to vary their food intake with unusual or exotic goods. It is unlikely that people indulged in such luxuries very often, but there must have been occasions when even small farmers purchased a few special items. The infrequent trip to town, the birthday, or the trip to take a son away to the academy were occasions calling for treats that offered a welcome variety in the day-to-day fare.

The availability of these items, together with a disparity of wealth among Southerners, led to variations in foodways among economic classes. Unfortunately, most detailed menu descriptions come from the pens of affluent planters or writers who visited the larger and better managed plantations, most of which were in the older or more developed settlements such as the Georgia–Carolina coast or lower Louisiana. Such descriptions reveal an almost incredible opulence. At one meal on the Alston plantation along the rice coast a sumptuous table was laden with

turtle soup at each end [and] two parallel dishes, one containing a leg of boiled mutton and the other turtle steaks and fins. Next was a pie of Maccaroni in the center of the table and on each side of it was a small dish of oysters. Next . . . were two parallel dishes, corresponding with the two above mentioned, one of them turtle steak and fins, and the other a boiled ham. When the soups were removed, their place was supplied at one end by a haunch of venison and at the other by a roast turkey. . . . [A second course included] bread pudding . . . jelly . . . a high glass dish of ice cream . . . [and] a pie. . . . [After the second course came] . . . two high baskets . . . one of bananas and the other of oranges. One larger . . . of apples.

During the meal Madeira, sherry, and champagne were served and, after dessert, Hermitage, Madeira, and cordials.[92] John Grimball described another meal for eight with four courses that included two soups, ham, turkey with oyster sauce, a leg of mutton, a haunch of venison, three wild ducks, turtle steaks and fins, four vegetables, apple pudding, custards, cheese, and bread. All this was followed by dessert.[93] Apparently overindulgence was not unknown, as he complained of another meal:

> Dined yesterday with Mr. Vanderhorst. . . . [T]he table absolutely groaned under the load of meats. . . . [T]he wines were good. . . . I mixed the wines and drank more than my stomach would bear, and when I came home was made quite ill.[94]

The tables of less wealthy whites were not so abundantly supplied, yet it was common to have more than one meat at a single meal. A traveler in Mississippi in the 1850s described a table: "Here we have excellent ham, boiled whole, a surloin of Venison, and a dainty steak from 'Old Bruin.'"[95] Small planters and farmers served abundant and wholesome but not sumptuous meals. In Virginia a traveler was fed soup, cabbage and bacon (boiled together), fowl, both wheaten and corn bread, potatoes, green corn, and apple dumplings for dinner. Breakfast was made up of "coffee, small hot wheaten rolls [probably biscuits], batter bread, and hoe-cake . . . milk, eggs, and rashers of bacon."[96] But these modest meals were not available to all whites. Many Southern tables saw only pork, cornbread, and a vegetable or two day after day, week after week. This was particularly true in winter when vegetables were fewer and there was a strong dependence on cured meat and semiperishable cereals and vegetables. Even more restricted throughout the colonial and antebellum periods were the foods available to the ever-increasing population of black slaves.

Foodways of Black Slaves

The diets of blacks and whites had many similarities, but the basic differences in the two groups' social, legal, and economic positions led to marked differences in the kind, quality, and (possibly) the quantity of foods consumed. To be sure, many slaves received the same foods as whites—even dining at the same tables—and many whites lived little better than slaves; yet one must recognize the fundamental fact that whites had greater opportunity to vary their diets as food availability and economic means might have permitted. Living in close proximity and often subsisting on the same kinds of foods, both blacks and whites developed the same likes and dislikes, yet there seems little doubt that most whites had a much better and more varied diet than the great bulk of the slave population.

The simplicity of the slave diet coupled with the numerous contemporary references to slave food make it relatively easy to describe slave foodways. In fact, a great deal more is known with confidence about slave food consumption than about that of the white population. There are still blanks in our knowledge, but, on the whole, the picture of slave diet is much clearer than that of Southern whites during the same period.[97]

Slaves had three primary sources for the food they consumed. The bulk came as daily or weekly rations issued by the master and consisted principally of a regular allowance of corn and pork supplemented by periodic doles of sweet potatoes, other vegetables, and fruits. Occasionally, molasses, salt, coffee, and a few other items were added, but the basic ration was composed of corn, pork, and vegetables. The second source was the food raised by slaves themselves, either by keeping animals or growing vegetables in their own provision plots. The third major source was gathering, hunting, and fishing. Not all slaves could exploit the last two sources, and the extent to which each was used depended upon the location of the plantation, the attitude of the master, and the resourcefulness of the slave.

The slave ration (usually doled out weekly) almost invariably contained corn, which in some cases was unground, but most planters preferred to issue cornmeal since it saved the time required to grind the corn. The usual ration was a peck to every hand each week. Cornmeal was a major segment of the slave's diet; in most cases the recommended allowance was followed carefully, but some planters allowed unlimited access to the meal bin. It was consumed primarily in the form of cornbread, but from time to time mush was made. Occasionally, grits and hominy were issued, but by far the most common issue was cornmeal.

Although the slave's cornmeal supply usually was ample, the pork allowance was another matter. Masters varied in their notions of what constituted a proper meat ration, and there was always a possibility that it would be discontinued if supplies ran short. The usual ration was from two to five pounds each week. This was not universal, however, and many operators varied considerably both above and below these figures depending on the slave's age, condition, work load, and season of the year. As mentioned earlier, blacks were thought by many to require large amounts of pork while laboring heavily and were more generously supplied with meat during the working season.

The kind of hog meat commonly issued to slaves is not an easy matter to determine. Most references describe it as either "pork" or "bacon," but precisely what is meant by these terms is not absolutely clear. The common assumption today is that bacon was cured middlings (the relatively fat abdominal walls, commonly called "fatback" or "sowbelly") and that such meat made up the bulk of the slaves' meat rations. When purchased meat was used or when both whites and blacks were fed from the same source, the slave undoubtedly received the middlings and poorer cuts. For example, on small holdings, a slaughtered animal might be divided between slaves and whites, in which case the better meat cuts (or at least a large portion of them) went to the whites. In some cases, planters living off the premises left orders for a certain amount of choice meat to be sent to them.[98] Apparently a surfeit of such choice items was not unknown, as an overseer of the Telfair plantation in Jefferson County, Georgia, wrote his master concerning leftover hams: "After sending the usual Quantity of hams to Savannah I gave the ballance out to the Negroes in the Early Part of the season while they were good as I did not expect you would wish any of them sent down in the fall season."[99]

Although *fat* pork and bacon were used commonly as slave food, it is extremely difficult to imagine the majority of slaves living off "fatback" the year round. For one thing, there was simply not enough side meat produced from the hogs slaughtered on each landholding to feed the slave population. Apparently, many operators maintained a supply of "meat hogs" for the use of the slaves and kept a few special hogs for family use, in which case the two meat supplies were separate. Furthermore, on plantations that were overseer operated (often he was the only white on the plantation), the great majority of the hogs were killed and made into pork for the slaves. With an annual slaughter of fifty to one hundred hogs, it is almost certain that the entire part of nearly all the hogs was consumed by the slave force.

Where written records of slave rations are examined, the usual reference is to "bacon" or "pork" and it appears that the terms did not refer exclusively to the sides but to all or most of the hog. Frequently, the meat was described as "good clean bacon" or "clean meat" or "clear meat" or "bacon-clean of bone," with an implication that the term did not always mean simply side meat.[100] In fact, some planters varied the weekly ration depending on the kind available, especially since some thought fat pork was better for working persons, blacks in particular, than the leaner meat.[101] Records from a number of sources support this observation. A Sumter County, Alabama, planter fed his hands one pound per day while feeding the "boney parts" (presumably the backbone and ribs, feet, head, and neck), four pounds a week while feeding joints (hams and shoulders), and three and one-half pounds when feeding middlings.[102] A perennial contributor to antebellum Southern agricultural periodicals, *Agricola*, states that he allowed three and one-half pounds of bacon if middlings were issued and four pounds if the allowance was of shoulder.[103] Apparently, these people shared the notion that fat meat was more nutritious than lean and increased the allowance accordingly.

Therefore, the terms most commonly used, "bacon" and "pork," referred to more than simply pork sides and must have included at least the shoulders and, on occasion, all the joints. Meat that was labeled "pork" could have been either salted or pickled meat, but that referred to as "bacon" underwent an additional smoking process that took several weeks.[104] Apparently, these terms applied in the packing plants in the West as well. Charles Cist described the Cincinnati packing industry's output: "The different classes of cured pork packed in barrels, are made up of the different sizes and conditions of hogs—the finest and fattest making clear and mess pork while the residue is put up into prime pork or bacon."[105] Part of the output of the packing houses was sent to smokehouses to be cured into bacon. Usually, bacon was made up of most parts of the hog, but the individual parts must have been put up separately since it was possible to buy "bacon sides" or "bacon hams." According to Cist, prime pork was the class most often

PART THREE   Production and Control of Property

shipped south for plantation use, and this consisted of: "Two shoulders, two jowls, and sides enough to fill the barrel."[106]

In answer to the question originally raised, it appears that pork issued slaves varied depending on the situation. Where the pork was made on the plantation, the slaves were most likely fed the entire animal. On smaller holdings where the proportion of white inhabitants to slaves was relatively high, the better cuts went to the whites. And, when meat was purchased, it probably contained some joints, although much of it was bacon sides.

While pork made up the great bulk of the slaves' meat supply, on occasion they received beef and mutton. Considering the large numbers of cattle in the area, it is surprising that beef was on the menu so infrequently. Apparently, it was because beef was considered harder to cure and, when fed, was believed to be nutritionally poorer than pork. For this reason, when beef was fed to slaves the allowance was generally higher than that for pork. On rice plantations, where beef was more commonly issued, the usual ration was "one pound of pork or two of beef."[107] A Mississippi planter issued three pounds of fresh beef a day (this would amount to twenty-one pounds per week).[108] Another factor in the low consumption of beef may well have been that the slaves simply preferred pork to beef. Solon Robinson, in discussing Southern pork production, cites black prejudice as the reason for the little use of beef.[109] Some individuals, of course, advocated feeding beef, mutton, or even goat in order to get away from the heavy dependence on pork, but few Southerners were convinced that pork was anything but the best possible slave meat.[110]

Beef and mutton were seldom relied on as steady meat sources for slaves but were usually reserved for such special occasions as holidays and weddings. Apparently, a common practice was to celebrate notable occasions with a barbecue. Some planters had annual affairs toward the end of the season where pigs, beefs, lambs, and goats were roasted over coals.[111] Such occasions were the delight of the participants, of course, and were important interruptions in the slave's routine, yet they were relatively infrequent and short-lived. More important to the overall slave diet was the practice of slaughtering one or more beefs periodically to be divided and issued as fresh

meat. For example, on the Telfair plantation in Georgia there was a standing order to kill in July, August, and September.[112] On other plantations, beef or mutton was slaughtered weekly, and where practiced, such a system could easily yield several pounds of meat per family at each occasion.[113] Mutton and beef may have been issued more commonly on holdings near the Atlantic coast than on cotton plantations. Apparently, the daily ration of cured pork was not the rule on most rice plantations, where the meat supply came primarily from periodic slaughterings of either hogs, cattle, or sheep.[114]

Estimating the importance of poultry consumed by slaves presents a problem. It is known that slave-owned poultry was fairly common, but the practice of selling or trading their own poultry and eggs must have reduced severely the amount actually consumed. For the same reason one must question the general use of slave-owned swine as food for the slaves. It was very common for slave-owned pigs to be sold rather than eaten; in fact, many slaves never thought of eating their own animals but kept them solely for ultimate sale either to merchants or to a planter to augment his supply of pork.[115] It is conceivable, of course, that the slave's own swine might have been slaughtered and issued back to him as a part of the weekly ration.[116]

While the staple ration for the slave was corn and meat, most slave owners attempted to provide vegetables as well. This was probably due more to the desire to cut down on costly meat consumption than any recognition of their nutritive qualities. The variety of vegetables was limited. Apparently, the plants were chosen for their yield and ease of cultivation. The most common were turnips, sweet potatoes, peas, cabbage, collards, and pumpkins. Such others as onions, okra, and squash were known, but most operators concentrated on the items most common in the area. Where slaves had their own gardens they often planted the same items as they were regularly issued (peas, turnips, and sweet potatoes) but augmented these crops with vegetables remembered from Africa: tania root, groundnuts, calabashes, and sesamen (see the essay by Philip D. Morgan in this volume). Most slaves could usually count on some kind of garden vegetable as a regular ration, but they did not always receive a variety at one time, nor were vegetables available at every meal. Slaveowners attempted to provide vegetables daily but may not have been able to do so consistently.[117] Most slaves probably ate at least one vegetable each day, but the limited variety with perhaps only one or two vegetables available at a given season led to a monotonous routine. During late summer and fall, sweet potatoes were heavily relied on; in winter, turnips and greens served as staples; but by spring and summer a few more items were available. Peas, either fresh or dried, could be had the year round.

The consumption of fruit by slaves was fairly common. Recognizing their nutritive value, most planters provided some fruits, mostly peaches, for their hands.[118] Hugh Davis planned and planted a large orchard at Beaver Bend plantation in Alabama, and M. W. Philips of Mississippi was noted for his fruit culture. Philips constantly wrote articles about fruit growing and boasted that he had "more fruit to the number of persons, than any man in Mississippi."[119] Although generally critical of the slave's fare, a temporary resident on an Alabama plantation observed that the orchard "affords them [the slaves] considerable help." In commenting further he remarked: "Peaches are now ripe. . . . So highly is the fruit esteemed, that every farm has large tracts planted with it, as orchards, to one of which the slaves have liberty of access when they please."[120] Fruits were cooked on occasion, but the great bulk—both wild and domestic—was probably consumed raw.

Slaveholders issued molasses and syrup periodically. Exact amounts are difficult to determine, and the practice was by no means universal. On some plantations a molasses ration, such as a quart each week, was regularly issued, but on other holdings it was considered a special treat.[121] Other planters purchased molasses by the barrel, in which case it was used as the slaves pleased.[122] Other minor items were occasional dabs of coffee, tea, and whiskey. Salt was the only seasoning the slave tasted regularly; other condiments were unknown.

Although the foodways of whites and blacks were similar in many respects, one of the greatest differences was in the relative amounts of dairy products consumed. Some masters attempted to provide milk for their slaves, but the amount must have been minuscule. Dairy products, when consumed by slaves, were most often in the form of buttermilk. Whole milk was occasionally given, but butter seldom and cheese almost never.[123] The primary reason,

of course, was the extremely low milk production in the area. Almost all farmers and planters kept lactating cows during summer, but the production was never enough to provide substantial quantities for the hands. Any small milk surplus that was produced usually went to the slave children.[124]

In many respects, the preparation of slave food was quite like that of whites', the primary difference being in the variety of food available, the utensils used, the time taken to prepare food, and the knowledge of cooking methods. Having the same basic foods with which to work and living under the close supervision of white masters, it was almost inevitable that slaves would develop similar cooking methods. Where cooking was done individually, a lack of utensils and cooking knowledge hampered the cook; where communal cooking was the rule, the necessity for cooking large amounts inhibited any great variation. The dearth of utensils (a complaint common to most frontier areas) often necessitated cooking several items together and may have been the factor that led to the Southerner's (both white and black) liking for meat and vegetables cooked together. While the Southern white has been noted for odd food combinations, the black had an even greater reputation for seemingly incongruous mixtures, and this tendency probably was due to both the persistence of African traditions and having to cook and eat with a minimum of equipment.

Vegetables were usually cooked in a large pot with pieces of meat, while corn pone was baked on the hearth or occasionally in a pan. If cooking was communal, there was probably an oven for baking bread.[125] Toward the end of the antebellum period, the communal kitchen apparently came to be the preferred, though not universal, place of cooking. This probably grew out of an attempt to cut down food waste and increase the efficiency of the field hand's labor. There seemed to be a growing realization that the employment of a few plantation cooks allowed field hands more working time in the field and more rest at night. Furthermore, some masters felt that slaves seldom had time to prepare their food properly. There was a strong feeling that some foods, especially vegetables, should be cooked a long time, and a well-supervised plantation kitchen was a means of ensuring against poorly cooked food.[126] One Georgia planter showed a surprising concern for the slaves' food as he gave orders in a letter to his overseer to "look into the cook pot to see if the victuals are well cooked and [the] utensils clean."[127] This insistence on "well-cooked" food has remained with many Southerners and may be partially responsible for overcooked vegetables and the coolness toward some raw vegetable salads in the rural South today.[128]

Foodways and nutrition

Though perhaps peripheral to the main theme of this essay, it seems useful to raise a few questions about the nutritional adequacy of Southern foods and speculate on the overall quality of Southern diets. It is certain that a strong obstacle to good nutrition in the South (or any other part of the country at the time) was the lack of detailed knowledge about human physiology. The study of nutrition was poorly developed before the Civil War, and not until the late nineteenth century were any detailed dietary studies done in the South. Apparently, there was a marked improvement in the quality of diet in the nation after about 1840, but this was due primarily to greater food availability and a higher standard of living rather than any significant development in the science of nutrition.[129] Most planters (and perhaps many doctors) felt that the foods Southerners commonly used were quite nutritious and adequate for human health. For example, pork was believed to have been difficult to digest, yet it was favored for persons doing heavy labor. It was ideal for the slave who was considered a "low heat producer" but was looked upon as the worst possible food for the "delicate" Southern white female.[130]

Even if not very soundly based in theory, it must be said in defense of the antebellum physician that his food recommendations were not wholly inconsistent with today's practices. His explanations for prescribing certain foods may not have been sound, but had planters and farmers listened to his advice and adhered more closely to his recommendations, they and their chattels would have fared much better. Most doctors recommended meat, bread, vegetables, fruit, milk, sugar, and molasses, which, if abundantly supplied, would have provided a fairly decent diet.[131] It appears, then, that the lack of knowledge about nutrition was only one of the factors that led to poor diet. In addition, there was often an inability (or lack of concern) on the part of the planter to provide an adequate supply of the foods commonly recommended. Furthermore, it is probable that the variety of foods, particularly fruits and vegetables, was so limited that many nutritionally desirable items such as yellow vegetables (supplying vitamin A) and citrus fruits (vitamin C) were missing.[132]

There seems little doubt that the predominance of pork contributed to a high energy diet with less protein than had other meats been used. Where fat side-meat was predominant the protein intake was probably one-third that of a beef diet. Where more lean pork was included, the protein increased but did not reach the level that beef would have provided.[133] This protein deficiency may not have been critical among whites, but some slaves, whose supply of meat was low or irregular, almost certainly suffered critical protein shortages during a part of the year. The large quantities of corn consumed probably did little to help, since some animal proteins are essential to good health and cannot be replaced by cereal proteins. Whites had advantages over blacks in securing these animal proteins in that they had more milk, eggs, and beef and often had access to larger game. The use of pork did, however, provide a high-energy diet. This was especially true where fat pork was used, since fat yields considerably more calories per pound than does either protein or carbohydrate.[134]

Corn provided considerable bulk in the diet as well as the major part of the carbohydrates. Where meat consumption was low it also provided much of the energy. Corn supplied few vitamins, however, and little protein. To make matters worse, Southerners preferred white corn, which, unlike yellow corn, has virtually no vitamin A.[135]

Garden vegetables, when consumed in sufficient quantities, provide many of the essential minerals and vitamins needed for adequate nutrition. Shortages of these essentials probably occurred among the slave population fairly frequently, especially in winter, and on occasion among whites. It is probable that the deficiencies were severe enough in winter to cause pellagra and other related deficiency diseases. After studying plantation records and diaries of planters, William Postell concluded that notations suggested such diseases were most common during the time of the year when vegetable consumption was relatively low.[136]

An additional unfortunate characteristic of the Southern diet was the frequent omission of green and yellow vegetables. Turnip greens and cabbage were common, but when supplies ran short, there were few other green vegetables to replace them. Furthermore, those people not engaged directly in farming, such as urban dwellers and laborers, probably consumed a disproportionate amount of cowpeas and potatoes (items more often offered in markets than green and yellow vegetables). Such food choices easily could have led to deficiency diseases, since they lacked the antipellagra factor (niacin) as well as other such essential vitamins as vitamin A.[137] Table 1 lists some of the more common Southern foods with comments on their nutritive qualities.

Dietary studies made in various parts of the South in the late nineteenth and early twentieth centuries provide some clues about Southern nutrition, and, while there certainly had been some dietary change in the half-century or more since antebellum times, the studies have general applicability. In an Alabama

Table 1. General Characteristics of Some Major Southern Foods

Food	Nutritional Characteristics	Remarks
Beef and mutton	High in protein.	Too little consumed, especially among slaves.
Pork	A good protein source if not too fat. High in energy.	Made up a disproportionate part of most diets.
Fish	Excellent source of many nutrients.	Too little available. However, it may well be that fish and seafood were the major sources of protein along the coasts and rivers.
Game	Good source of many nutrients.	Much more important for whites than slaves. In many areas probably replaced beef.
Poultry and eggs	Excellent source of many proteins. Easy to kill and eat. No preservation problems.	May have been very important for whites. Blacks, unfortunately, sold much of their poultry and eggs.
Turnips (roots and tops)	Rich in vitamins and iron.	A very good source of vitamins. Might well have saved many from serious deficiency diseases.
Sweet potatoes	Very high in many nutrients. Good vitamin source.	An excellent food choice combining ease of production and preservation with good nutrition.
Molasses	Rich in energy, calcium, and iron.	Together with sweet potatoes and turnips was the "savior" of many Southern diets.
Peas	High in energy, fairly high in protein and some vitamins.	Many were eaten green but large quantities were dried for later use.
Dairy products	High in calcium, protein, and fat.	Too little consumed, especially by slaves. White consumption was low but probably not critically so.
Fruits	Rich in vitamins. Dried fruit high in energy.	Especially rich when dried.
Corn	Provided adequate bulk, carbohydrates, and energy. Low in protein and some vitamins.	Whites had a fair amount; slaves probably had less than they needed.

study done in the 1890s the most common diet was found to have been very high in energy but deficient in protein.[138] Studies in Mississippi in the 1920s revealed similar diets. They found few black diets to be substandard in calories but many that were deficient in iron, calcium, phosphorus, and protein (in that order).[139] In Georgia, the same general pattern was found, though the deviation from the accepted "norm" was much less. In general, the intake of meats, eggs, dairy products, fruits, and vegetables was low while that of fats, sweets, and cereals was high.[140]

The use of these late nineteenth- and early twentieth-century dietary studies to explain conditions a half-century or more earlier has its limitations, but it is tempting to speculate on the similarities between the two periods. There is little doubt that many of the food preferences existing during the antebellum period were carried over to the twentieth century and survive as relics in the rural South today. On the other hand, gradual dietary changes accompanying the rise of sharecropping after the Civil War may have made the typical Southern diet around 1890–1920 significantly different from, though not necessarily superior to, that of the 1850s. The rise in sharecropping, in particular, may have had a detrimental effect on diet in the years following the war. The effects on the black population undoubtedly were greater than on the whites who remained landowners. Nevertheless, some deterioration in diet occurred as a consequence of the decrease in standard of living accompanying the process by which landowning whites became croppers. The restriction to certain small plots of land, the encouragement to grow as much cotton as possible in order to raise cash, the rise of the "furnish" system with its accompanying "crop liens" that led to increased credit-buying at the local or plantation store, all led to a system that decreased the amount of home-raised foods, resulting in a diet poor in variety and nutritive quality. Blacks suffered the same as the white croppers but, having lived under the "protective" aegis of slavery, were handicapped further by less knowledge about food production, preservation, and cooking, as well as nutrition.

The total meat consumption in America remained fairly high after the Civil War, but it is likely that there was a gradual decline in the amount of meat consumed during the period 1860–1920.[141] However, while the remainder of the nation shifted away from a heavy consumption of pork, much of the South may have actually increased the proportion of pork in the diet. It is true that the beef industry in the South has increased markedly during the twentieth century, but this increase is primarily a post–World War II phenomenon, and little of it was reflected in the diets of sharecroppers or tenants (white or black) before 1940. Moreover, there is good reason to suspect a higher intake of lean meat prior to the Civil War than in the 1890–1930 period. Considering the relatively small and lean Southern hog of the 1840s and 1850s in comparison to the larger (and fatter) animal of the early twentieth century, it is difficult not to conclude that fat meat consumption increased during the 1860–1930 period. Furthermore, there was probably an increase in the proportion of purchased meat (as opposed to home cured) by tenants, which by 1890 or 1900 almost invariably meant sidemeat, or "sowbelly."[142]

Other items in the diet may have been altered materially from the antebellum period up to the time of the Atwater, Woods, and Dickens dietary studies. Plantation orchards, while scarcely adequate before the war, must have deteriorated rapidly as plantations became fragmented by the granting of share-plots or, in many cases, became restricted to the owner and his family. Gardens, too, probably suffered more for care after the war than before; in fact, a common fault of the cropping system was that it encouraged the cropper to produce as much cotton as possible, often leaving little time or space for gardens. Before the days of acreage restrictions an outstanding characteristic of the cotton belt landscape was the absence of gardens around cropper's cabins. Felice Swados concluded that fresh vegetables were probably a more common part of the black diet before 1860 than in the early 1940s, and there seems little reason to quarrel with his observation.[143]

Conclusion

Conclusions regarding Southern diet and food preferences during the antebellum period can never be precise. The inevitable loss of information involved in the passing of a century casts doubt on the knowledge of both quality and quantity of Southern foods. Considered in the light of nineteenth-century customs, habits, and technology, it is very unlikely that many whites in the South were underfed. The lack of methods of food preservation and an apparent unwillingness to accept and encourage the production of a wider variety of foods, however, led to relatively monotonous foodways with less variety than was the rule in the remainder of the nation. The slave diet was characterized by the same monotony but, in addition, was frequently nutritionally inadequate. Part of the blame for these diets, which ranged from "tolerable" to "inadequate," must go to the lack of information about human nutrition. Additional blame can be placed on a cotton monoculture in which food crops were often neglected. Finally, the institution of slavery itself must be held largely responsible for the poor diet of blacks and may be further indicted as being partially responsible for the continuation of the low dietary standards that were characteristic of Southern blacks during the postbellum period.

Perhaps the most significant aspect of southern foodways is the persistence of food preferences once they were established. The most obvious characteristic of Southern food habits was the strong dependence on corn and pork, which endured throughout the nineteenth century and, indeed, survives to the present day. During the colonial period both were staples all along the Atlantic coast including New England. Both were staples in the South and West during the first few decades of the nineteenth century. But by the 1830s and 1840s food habits in the East and West were undergoing significant changes. There was a general rise in standard of living after about 1840 with a consequent change in food habits. Better methods of food preservation and transportation increased the variety available to the consumer. At the same time, waves of immigrants from all parts of Europe introduced new food habits into the increasingly complex cultures of the East and West. The South, on the other hand, shared little in these changes. Instead of being strongly affected by these factors, it became increasingly isolated during the years before the Civil War. Perhaps even more important was the continuation of these processes after the war. Emancipation did little to alter the economic position of Southern blacks, nor did it greatly alter the agricultural commodity emphases. If anything, there was an intensification of the cotton economy. Moreover, the effects of sharecropping reduced many former white landowners to tenancy and a lower level of living. Without the cultural "shock" of immigrants moving into the South and handicapped by

a lower standard of living than other regions, many elements of the Southern diet persisted through the nineteenth and well into the twentieth century. Thus, traditional Southern foodways have survived the settlement years, a civil war, and more than a century of time to become a frontier "relic" in the midst of twentieth-century American life.

Notes

1. An anonymous English traveler quoted in Katharine M. Jones, *The Plantation South* (Indianapolis, Ind.; 1957), 204.

2. Edgar W. Martin, *The Standard of Living in 1860* (Chicago, 1942), 57–64; Wilbur O. Atwater and Charles D. Woods, *Dietary Studies with Reference to the Food of the Negro in Alabama in 1895 and 1896*, U.S. Dept. of Agriculture, Office of Experiment Stations Bulletin 38 (Washington, D.C., 1897); Richard O. Cummings, *The American and His Food: A History of Food Habits in the United States* (rev. ed.; Chicago, 1941); Margaret Cussler and Mary L. De Give, *'Twixt the Cup and the Lip: Psychological and Socio-Cultural Factors Affecting Food Habits* (New York, 1952); Dorothy Dickens, *A Study of Food Habits of People in Two Contrasting Areas of Mississippi*, Mississippi Agricultural Experiment Station Bulletin 245 (1927); and Rupert B. Vance, *Human Factors in Cotton Culture* (Chapel Hill, N.C., 1929).

3. [Thomas Hamilton], *Men and Manners in America*, 2 vols., 2d ed. (London, 1834), 2:255, 258, 262.

4. [Hamilton], *Men and Manners in America*, 2:255, 258, 262, and Harriet Martineau, *Retrospect of Western Travel*, 2 vols. (London, 1838), 1:212.

5. Frances A. Kemble, *Journal of a Residence on a Georgia Plantation in 1838–1839*, ed. John A. Scott (New York, 1961), 58.

6. Tyrone Power, *Impressions of America*, 2 vols. (London, 1836), 2:224.

7. Henry B. Whipple, *Bishop Whipple's Southern Diary 1843–1844*, ed. Lester B. Shippee (Minneapolis, Minn., 1937), 103.

8. *Southern Cabinet of Agriculture, Horticulture, Rural and Domestic Economy* 1 (1840): 125.

9. Frederick L. Olmsted, *Journey in the Seaboard Slave States* (New York, 1859), 411.

10. J. D. Anthony, "Cherokee County, Alabama: Reminiscences of Its Early Settlements," *Alabama Historical Quarterly* 8 (1946): 331; John S. Bassett, *The Southern Plantation Overseer as Revealed in His Letters* (Northampton, Mass., 1925), 44–45; Martin B. Coyner, "John Harwell Cocke of Bromo: Agriculture and Slavery in the Ante-Bellum South" (Ph.D. diss., University of Virginia, 1961), 408–9; George Powell, "A Description and History of Blount County," *Transactions of the Alabama Historical*

Society (1855): 40–42; and Bayrd Still, "The Westward Migration of a Planter Pioneer in 1796," *William and Mary Quarterly*, 2d ser., 21 (1941): 320.

11. Harriet Martineau, *Society in America*, 3d ed. (London, 1837), 203.

12. C. D. Arfwedson, *The United States and Canada, in 1832, 1833, and 1834*, 2 vols. (London, 1834), 2:415.

13. Arfwedson, *United States and Canada*, 2:11.

14. William H. Wills, "A Southern Sulky Ride in 1837, From North Carolina to Alabama," *Southern History Society Publications* 7 (1903): 12.

15. James R. Creecy, *Scenes in the South* (Washington, D.C., 1860), 84, 106.

16. Bassett, *Southern Plantation Overseer*, 74.

17. Frances M. Trollope, *Domestic Manners of the Americans* (London, 1832), 238.

18. *Southern Cultivator* 13 (1855): 23.

19. *Southern Cultivator* 13 (1855): 23.

20. Frederick L. Olmsted, *A Journey in the Back Country* (New York, 1863), 161.

21. Emily Burke, *Reminiscences in Georgia* (Oberlin, Ohio, 1850), 233.

22. John C. Gunn, *Gunn's Domestic Medicine; or, Poor Man's Friend . . .* (Philadelphia, 1840), 182.

23. John S. Wilson, "Health Department," *Godey's Lady's Book* 60 (1860): 178.

24. See *Cotton Planter and Soil* 3 (1859): 306; *Southern Cultivator* 1 (1843): 172, 175, 195, 208; 7 (1849): 114; Burke, *Reminiscences in Georgia*, 223; and Weymouth T. Jordan, *Herbs, Hoecakes and Husbandry: The Daybook of a Planter of Old South* (Tallahassee, Fla., 1960), 45, 47–48, 52–54, for descriptions of the curing processes used.

25. Burke, *Reminiscences in Georgia*, 222.

26. *Southern Cultivator* 1 (1843): 174; 17 (1859): 339.

27. Letter from Sarah Williams to Samuel Hicks of New Hartford, N.Y., Dec. 10, 1853, in Sarah Hicks Williams Papers, File no. 3210, Southern Historical Manuscript Collection, University of North Carolina, Chapel Hill (hereafter SHMC).

28. George G. Smith, Jr., *The History of Methodism in Georgia and Florida from 1785 to 1865* (Macon, Ga., 1877), 306.

29. George E. Brewer, "History of Coosa County," *Alabama Historical Quarterly* 4 (Spring 1942): 127, and Ulrich B. Phillips, *Life and Labor in the Old South* (Boston, 1929), 92.

30. T. Lynn Smith and Lauren C. Post, "The Country Butchery: A Co-operative Institution," *Rural Sociology* 2 (1937): 335–37.

31. Ervin E. William, "Journal for 1846," entry for Nov. 17, 1846, SHMC.

32. *Patent Office Report* (1850): 287, and William P. Dale, "A Connecticut Yankee in Ante-Bellum Alabama," *Alabama Review* 6 (1953): 63.

33. *Soil of the South* 2 (1852): 294.

34. Louise Gladney, "History of Pleasant Hill Plantation, 1811–1867" (M.A. thesis, Louisiana State University, 1932), 45–46; William J. Dickey, "Diaries, 1858–1859" (Manu-

script Collection, University of Georgia, Athens); and Edward M. Steel, "A Pioneer Farmer in the Choctaw Purchase," *Journal of Mississippi History* 16 (1954): 235.

35. Susan Dabney Smedes, *A Southern Planter: Social Life in the Old South* (New York, 1900), 81, and *DeBow's Review* 30 (1861): 645.

36. Adam Hodgson, *Letters from North America*, 2 vols. (London, 1824), 1:21, 31, and Martineau, *Society in America*, 306.

37. Olmsted, *Journey in the Back Country*, 127.

38. Sub Rosa [Paul Ravesies], *Scenes and Settlers of Alabama* [Mobile, Ala., 1885], 9.

39. Lewis C. Gray, *History of Agriculture in the Southern United States to 1860*, 2 vols. (New York, 1941), 2:832.

40. J. S. Buckingham, *The Slave States of America*, 2 vols. (London, 1842), 1:404; Herbert A. Kellar, *Solon Robinson: Pioneer and Agriculturalist* (Indianapolis, Ind., 1936), 161; Benjamin M. Norman, *New Orleans and Environs* (New Orleans, 1845), 56; Power, *Impressions of America*, 2:250; and Kemble, *Journal of a Residence*, 184.

41. Martineau, *Society in America*, 44.

42. *Patent Office Report* (1848): 516; Buckingham, *Slave States of America*, 1:404; Kellar, *Solon Robinson*, 161; Norman, *New Orleans and Environs*, 56; Power, *Impressions of America*, 2:250; Smedes, *Southern Planter*, 82; and Francis Pulszky and Theresa Pulszky, *White, Red, Black: Sketches of American Society* (New York, 1853), 97.

43. Kellar, *Solon Robinson*, 161.

44. *Patent Office Report* (1849): 161.

45. *Patent Office Report* (1850): 365.

46. Gladney, "History of Pleasant Hill," 46, and Wendell H. Stephenson, "A Quarter-Century of a Mississippi Plantation," *Mississippi Valley Historical Review* 23 (1936): 367.

47. Kemble, *Journal of a Residence*, 184.

48. Smedes, *Southern Planter*, 82; and Elizabeth W. A. Pringle, *Chronicles of Chicora Wood* (Boston, 1940), 89.

49. Kolloch Plantation Books, vol. 5, File no. 407, SHMC.

50. Martineau, *Society in America*, 306; [Charles A. Clinton], *A Winter from Home* (New York, 1852), 38; and Margaret H. Hall, *The Aristocratic Journey* (New York, 1831), 209, 221.

51. Olmsted, *Journey in the Back Country*, 140.

52. [Hamilton], *Men and Manners in America*, 2:255–58; Martineau, *Retrospect of Western Travel*, 1:212; Fredrika Bremer, *The Homes of the New World: Impressions of America*, trans. Mary Howitt (New York, 1853), 280, 288; William F. Gray, *From Virginia to Texas, 1835* (Houston, Tex., 1909), 40, 51; Frederick L. Olmsted, *The Cotton Kingdom* (New York, 1861), 86; Olmsted, *Journey in the Seaboard Slave States*, 565; and Wills, "Southern Sulky Ride," 473, 481.

53. Sub Rosa, *Scenes and Settlers of Alabama*, 10; Martineau, *Retrospect of Western Travel*, 1:212; and [Hamilton] *Men and Manners in America*, 2:255, 258, 262.

54. Philip H. Gosse, *Letters from Alabama* (London, 1859), 128.

55. Everard G. Baker, Diaries, vol. 1, entry of Oct. 30, 1849; File no. 41, SHMC.

56. Solomon Northup, *Twelve Years a Slave* (New York, 1855), 201.

57. David G. Harris, Farm Journals, Jan. 7, 1858, File no. M-982, SHMC.

58. [Clinton], *Winter from Home*, 14, and Rosser H. Taylor, *Ante-Bellum South Carolina: A Social and Cultural History* (Chapel Hill, N.C., 1942), 15.

59. Diary of W. Thacker, quoted in Taylor, *Ante-Bellum South Carolina*, 15.

60. Sub Rosa, *Scenes and Settlers of Alabama*, 9; Weymouth T. Jordan, *Hugh Davis and His Alabama Plantation* (University, Ala., 1948), 126; and Joe G. Taylor, *Negro Slavery in Louisiana* (Baton Rouge, La., 1963), 108.

61. Jordan, *Hugh Davis and His Alabama Plantation*, 126.

62. John Q. Anderson, "Dr. James Green Carson, Ante-Bellum Planter of Mississippi and Louisiana," *Journal of Mississippi History* 18 (1956): 261.

63. Charles H. Stevenson, "Fisheries in the Ante-Bellum South," in *Economic History, 1607–1865*, ed. James C. Ballagh, in *The South in the Building of the Nation*, vol. 5 (Richmond, Va., 1909), 267.

64. Buckingham, *Slave States of America*, 1:157, and John C. Butler, *Historical Record of Macon and Central Georgia* (1897; reprint ed., Macon, Ga., 1958), 162. Martineau, *Retrospect of Western Travel*, 1:217.

65. Grimes Family Papers, Box 2, File no. 3357, SHMC, and Edward Wood, Greenfield Fishery Records, File no. 1598, SHMC.

66. *DeBow's Review* 15 (1853): 70.

67. Olmsted, *Journey in the Back Country*, 198, 200, 240; *Cotton Kingdom*, 86; *Journey in the Seaboard Slave States*, 564.

68. Charles Lyell, *A Second Visit to the United States of North America* (New York, 1849), 144.

69. Martineau, *Society in America*, 306.

70. Gosse, *Letters from Alabama*, 46–47.

71. *DeBow's Review* 15 (1853): 70; David W. Mitchell, *Ten Years in the United States* (London, 1862), 23; and A. De Puy Van Buren, *Jottings of a Year's Sojourn in the South* (Battle Creek, Mich., 1859), 46.

72. Gosse, *Letters from Alabama*, 46; Olmsted, *Journey in the Back Country*, 242; Lyell, *Second Visit to United States*, 34; and William E. Dodd, *The Cotton Kingdom* (New Haven, Conn., 1921), 91.

73. Olmsted, *Journey in the Seaboard Slave States*, 478, and Charles Lanman, *Adventures in the Wilds of the United States and British American Provinces* (Philadelphia, 1856), 137.

74. Hall, *The Aristocratic Journey*, 245; [Hamilton], *Men and Manners in America*, 2:241; and Olmsted, *Journey in the Back Country*, 161–62.

75. Lyell, *Second Visit to United States*, 144.

76. Olmsted, *Journey in the Seaboard Slave States*, 478.

77. Bremer, *Homes of the New World*, 280.

78. Olmsted, *Journey in the Seaboard Slave States*, 454–55.

79. The process of canning in tins was in its infancy during the antebellum period, but other methods of keeping fruits preserved by sugar were well developed. Thus, while the true canning of vegetables and meats was essentially a postwar phenomenon, there was an abundance of preserves, jellies, and jams. See Martin, *Standard of Living in 1860*, 27–33; Cummings, *The American and His Food*, 85; and Myrtie L. Candler, "Reminiscences of Life in Georgia during the 1850's and 1860's," *Georgia Historical Quarterly* 30 (1949): 118.

80. Olmsted, *Journey in the Back Country*, 162; *Cotton Kingdom*, 86; Herbert Weaver, *Mississippi Farmers, 1850–1860* (Nashville, Tenn., 1945), 50; John F. H. Clairborne, "Trip through the Piney Woods," *Publications of the Mississippi Historical Society* 9 (1906):522; and Bennie C. Mellown, *Memoirs of a Pre-Civil War Community* (Birmingham, Ala., 1950), 18.

81. Arfwedson, *United States and Canada*, 2:11, and Taylor, *Ante-Bellum South Carolina*, 169.

82. Lyell, *Second Visit to United States*, 158; Martineau, *Retrospect of Western Travel* 1:221; *Society in America*, 1:307; Olmsted, *Journey in the Seaboard Slave States*, 625; Timothy Flint, *Recollections of the Last Ten Years* (Boston, 1826), 365; and James Stuart, *Three Years in North America* (New York, 1833), 123.

83. U.S. Treasury Dept., *A Report of the Commerce and Navigation of the United States for 1856*, House Ex. Doc. vol. 13, 34th Cong., 3d sess., 459–63.

84. Gosse, *Letters from Alabama*, 47; Van Buren, *Jottings of a Year's Sojourn*, 46; Lyell, *Second Visit to United States*, 158; Mitchell, *Ten Years in the United States*, 23; and Martineau, *Retrospect of Western Travels*, 1:212.

85. Lewis E. Atherton, *The Southern Country Store, 1800–1860* (Baton Rouge, La., 1949), 78–79.

86. Wellington Vandiver, "Pioneer Talladega, Its Minutes and Memories," *Alabama Historical Quarterly* 16 (1954): 131.

87. Earnest C. Hynds, Jr., "Ante-Bellum Athens and Clarke County, Georgia" (Ph.D. diss., University of Georgia, 1961), 258, and Atherton, *Southern Country Store*, 79–80.

88. Buckingham, *Slave States of America*, 1:246, 251, 287.

89. Hynds, "Ante-Bellum Athens and Clarke County, Georgia," 259, and John Hardy, *Selma: Her Institutions and Her Men* (1879; reprint ed., Selma, Ala., 1957), 117. For detail on the ice trade during the prerefrigeration period, see Richard O. Cummings, *The American Ice Harvest: A Historical Study in Technology, 1800–1918* (Berkeley and Los Angeles, 1949).

90. Vandiver, "Pioneer Talladega," 130–31.

91. "Modern Ice Cream, and the Philosophy of Its Manufacture," *Godey's Lady's Book* 60 (1860): 460–61; Martineau, *Society in America*, 1:307; Martineau, *Retrospect of Western Travel*, 1:221; and Lyell, *Second Visit to United States*, 158.

92. John B. Grimball, Diaries, entry of Oct. 18, 1832, SHMC.

93. Grimball, Diaries, entry of Oct. 16, 1832.

94. Grimball, Diaries, entry of July 7, 1832.

95. Van Buren, *Jottings of a Year's Sojourn*, 46.

96. Mitchell, *Ten Years in the United States*, 23, 37.

97. For discussions of slave food, see Charles S. Davis, *Cotton Kingdom in Alabama* (Montgomery, Ala., 1939); James B. Sellers, *Slavery in Alabama* (University, Ala., 1950); Ralph B. Flanders, *Plantation Slavery in Georgia* (Chapel Hill, N.C., 1933); Joe G. Taylor, *Negro Slavery in Louisiana*; Rosser H. Taylor, *Slaveholding in North Carolina*; "Feeding Slaves," *Journal of Negro History* 9 (1924): 139–43; Charles S. Sydnor, *Slavery in Mississippi* (New York, 1933); Ulrich B. Phillips, *American Negro Slavery* (New York, 1918); and Kenneth M. Stampp, *The Peculiar Institution: Slavery in the Ante-Bellum South* (New York, 1956). For contemporary views on the subject, see *Southern Cultivator* 8 (1850): 162–64; *Southern Agriculturist*, n.s., 6 (1846): 224–27; and *DeBow's Review* 3 (1847): 419–20; 7 (1849): 380–83; 14 (1853): 177–78; 25 (1858): 571–72.

98. Charles S. Sydnor, *A Gentleman of the Old Natchez Region: Benjamin L. C. Wailes* (Durham, N.C., 1938), 98.

99. Ulrich B. Phillips, ed., *Plantation and Frontier Documents: 1649–1863*, vols. 1 and 2 of the *Documentary History of American Industrial Society* (Cleveland, 1909), 1:332.

100. See *DeBow's Review* 7 (1849): 380–82; *Cotton Planter and Soil* 2 (1858): 113; *Southern Cultivator* 12 (1854): 205; James D. B. DeBow, *The Industrial Resources, Statistics, Etc., of the United States*, 3 vols. in 1 (New York, 1854), 2:331.

101. One doctor actually recommended fat meat for slaves because he thought it to be an excellent "heat generating" substance. This is despite the fact that he considered fat meat and grease detrimental to Southern whites; *Cotton Planter and Soil* 4 (1860): 126, and *DeBow's Review* 19 (1855): 359.

102. Davis, *Cotton Kingdom in Alabama*, 82.

103. *DeBow's Review* 19 (1855): 358–59.

104. *Soil of the South* 3 (1853): 753; *Southern Cultivator* 1 (1843): 172, 175; 7 (1849): 114; *Cotton Planter and Soil* 3 (1859): 306.

105. *DeBow's Review* 12 (1852): 69–70.

106. *DeBow's Review* 12 (1852): 69–70.

107. *DeBow's Review* 24 (1858): 325.

108. Gladney, "History of Pleasant Hill," 25.

109. Kellar, *Solon Robinson*, 149.

110. *Southern Cultivator* 8 (1850): 4, and *Southern Agriculturist*, n.s., 5 (1845): 314.

111. Weymouth T. Jordan, *Hugh Davis and His Alabama Plantation* (University, Ala., 1948), 84; Ralph B. Flanders, "Two Plantations and a County of Ante-Bellum Georgia," *Georgia Historical Quarterly* 12 (1928): 11; Francis Butler Leigh, *Ten Years on a Georgia Plantation since the War* (London, 1883), 233; Taylor, *Ante-Bellum South Carolina*, 54; William H. Holcombe, "Sketches of Plantation Life," *Knickerbocker Magazine* 57 (1861): 621.

112. Phillips, *Plantation and Frontier Documents*, 1:129.

113. Kellar, *Solon Robinson*, 367; Smedes, *A Southern Planter*, 82–84; Pringle, *Chronicles of Chicora Wood*, 89; Davis, *Cotton Kingdom in Alabama*, 56.

114. DeBow, *Industrial Resources*, 2:425; David Doar, *Rice and Rice Planting in the South Carolina Low Country*, The Charleston Museum Contributions, no. 8 (Charleston, S.C., 1936), 32.

115. Olmsted, *Journey in the Seaboard Slave States*, 439; Kellar, *Solon Robinson*, 367; *DeBow's Review* 24 (1859): 325; Fredrika Bremer, *America of the Fifties; Letters of Fredrika Bremer*, ed. Adolph B. Benson (New York, 1924), 111; V. Alton Moody, "Slavery on Louisiana Sugar Plantations," *Louisiana Historical Quarterly* 7 (1924): 255; and M. B. Hammond, *The Cotton Industry* (New York, 1897), 91.

116. Evidence bearing this out appears in journal entries. For example, Ben Sparkman records paying for hogs at four and five cents per pound from people named "Sam," "Toby," "Prince," and "Lindy," suggesting he was buying pork from his own slaves. Ben Sparkman, Plantation Record, 1853–59, Dec. 22, 1853, Jan. 24, 1854, and Sparkman Family Papers, vol. 7, 1858, SHMC.

117. Jordan, *Hugh Davis and His Alabama Plantation*, 128–29; Sydnor, *A Gentleman of the Old Natchez Region*, 101; DeBow, *Industrial Resources*, 2:331; *DeBow's Review* 14 (1853): 177; *Southern Cultivator* 7 (1850): 162; and *Southern Agriculturist*, n.s., 6 (1846): 225.

118. *Southern Cultivator* 2 (1844): 204; James Ewell, *The Planter's and Mariner's Medical Companion* (Washington, D.C., 1807), 197.

119. *Southern Agriculturist* 6 (1846): 225, and Jordan, *Hugh Davis and His Alabama Plantation*, 123, 129.

120. Gosse, *Letters from Alabama*, 194, 253.

121. *DeBow's Review* 13 (1852): 193; Sydnor, *Slavery in Mississippi*, 35; Anderson, "Dr. James Green Carson, Antebellum Planter of Mississippi and Louisiana," 246; John Berkley Grimball, Diary, Dec. 25, 1832; William E. Sparkman, Plantation Record, Mar. 1844–Jan. 1846; Letter from Sarah Williams of North Carolina to her parents in New Hartford, N.Y., Dec. 10, 1853, in Sarah Hicks Williams Papers. In a letter to his overseer, R. J. Arnold instructed him to "give a little molasses occasionally to the children once a day." R. J. Arnold to A. M. Sanford, May 19, 1840, Arnold-Scriven Papers. The last four items are in SHMC.

122. Olmsted, *Cotton Kingdom*, 180, and Kellar, *Solon Robinson*, 381.

123. *DeBow's Review* 14 (1853): 177; Sellers, *Slavery in Alabama*, 89; Phillips, *American Negro Slavery*, 266; John B. Cade, "Out of the Mouths of Ex-Slaves," *Journal of Negro History* 20 (1935): 299–301; John F. H. Clairborne, *Life and Correspondence of John A. Quitman*, 2 vols. (New York, 1860), 1:80.

124. Cade, "Out of the Mouths of Ex-Slaves," 300.

125. Cade, "Out of the Mouths of Ex-Slaves," 299–301; Flanders, "Two Plantations and a County," 7; Pulszky and Pulszky, *White, Red and Black*, 105; DeBow, *Industrial Resources*, 2:331; *DeBow's Review* 24 (1860): 359; and Guion G. Johnson, *A Social History of the Sea Islands* (Chapel Hill, N.C., 1930), 136.

126. *Southern Agriculturist*, n.s., 6 (1846): 225; *Southern Cultivator* 8 (1850): 162; Cade, "Out of the Mouths of Ex-

Slaves," 299–301; Sellers, *Slavery in America*, 95–97; *De-Bow's Review* 7 (1849): 382; 14 (1885): 177; 25 (1858): 571; 22 (1857): 39, 376; *Cotton Planter and Soil* 2 (1858): 293.

127. Letter from R. J. Arnold to A. M. Sanford, May 19, 1840, Arnold-Scriven Papers, SHMC.

128. Dickens, *Food Habits in Mississippi*, 33; Dickens, *A Nutrition Investigation of Negro Tenants in the Yazoo Mississippi Delta*, Mississippi Agricultural Experiment Station Bulletin 254 (1928), 37.

129. Cummings, *The American and His Food*, 74.

130. *Cotton Planter and Soil* 4 (1860): 126–27; Wilson, "Health Department," 178; Gunn, *Gunn's Domestic Medicine*, 182.

131. *Cotton Planter and Soil* 2 (1858): 293; 4 (1860): 126–27; Ewell, *Medical Companion*, 65, 197; William D. Postell, *The Health of Slaves on Southern Plantations* (Baton Rouge;, La., 1951), 32–34.

132. For details on the general health of slaves and medical care in the South, see Postell, *Health of Slaves*; Felice Swados, "Negro Health on the Ante-Bellum Plantation," *Bulletin of the History of Medicine* 10 (1941): 460–72; Richard H. Shryock, "Medical Practice in the Old South," *South Atlantic Quarterly* 29 (1930): 160–78; Weymouth T. Jordan, "Plantation Medicine in the Old South," *Alabama Review* 3 (1950): 83–107; Victor H. Bassett, "Plantation Medicine," *Journal of the Medical Association of Georgia* 29 (1940): 112–22.

133. For a discussion of the relative nutritional values of Southern foods, see Atwater and Woods, *Dietary Studies*, 12–15. These data on food values are somewhat out of date, but they may be more representative of the values of some nineteenth-century Southern foods than present-day tests.

134. Lloyd B. Jensen, *Man's Foods: Nutrition and Environments in Food Gathering Times and Food Producing Times* (Champaign, Ill., 1953), 189.

135. Mark Graubard, *Man's Food, Its Rhyme or Reason* (New York, 1943), 120. The appearance of vitamin A seems related to the amount of yellow pigment present in vegetables. Carrots are rich in vitamin A but were not widely consumed in the area. Some varieties of sweet potatoes (generally the yellow tubers) were helpful since they contained sizable amounts of the vitamin. See Barnett Sure, *The Vitamins in Health and Disease* (Baltimore, 1933), 28ff., and Henry C. Sherman, *Chemistry of Food and Nutrition* (New York, 1952), 482–84, for discussion of this relationship.

136. Postell, *Health of Slaves*, 85.

137. Postell, *Health of Slaves*, 85; Graubard, *Man's Food, Its Rhyme or Reason*, 120; Sherman, *Chemistry of Food and Nutrition*, 416; Sure, *Vitamins in Health and Disease*, 128ff.; Josué de Castro, *The Geopolitics of Hunger* (Boston, 1952), 127ff. See also E. J. Underwood, *Trace Elements in Human and Animal Nutrition* (New York, 1956).

138. Atwater and Woods, *Dietary Studies*, 64–69.

139. Dickens, *Nutrition Investigation of Negro Tenants* 15–17, 26.

140. Susan B. Mathews, *Food Habits of Georgia Rural People*, Georgia Experiment Station Bulletin 159 (n.d.), 27. For additional evidence, see H. D. Frissell and Isabel Bevier, *Dietary Studies of Negroes in Eastern Virginia*, U.S. Department of Agriculture, Office of Experiment Stations Bulletin 71 (1897–98).

141. Cummings, *The American and His Food*, 258.

142. As sharecropping and tenancy become entrenched throughout the cotton belt, the plantation store came to be a landmark. In the store were stored goods sold or "furnished" to the tenants, of which "side meat" was one of the more important items. Many people today can recall seeing the "meat box" in the corner of these stores filled with large pieces (perhaps fifteen by thirty inches in size and four inches thick) of white salt meat. Many, too, can remember seeing warehouses in Memphis, Nashville, Atlanta, Montgomery, or Jackson filled with stacks of such white slabs. It is this writer's opinion that extreme dependence on these white slabs of sidemeat by tenants in the South during the early twentieth century has influenced students of Southern history to assume that Southern pork during the antebellum period was similar. Of course, there was a great deal of fat meat consumed before the war, but it appears unlikely that it reached the proportions prevalent by the turn of the century.

143. Swados, "Negro Health on the Ante-Bellum Plantation," 471, and Emily S. Maclachlan, "The Diet Pattern of the South: A Study in Regional Sociology" (M.A. thesis, University of North Carolina, 1932), 22.

Part Four: Landscapes of Social Distance

Artifacts of Regional Consciousness in the Connecticut River Valley, 1700–1780

ROBERT BLAIR ST. GEORGE

Students of American material culture frequently atomize the cultural landscape into discrete "regional cultures," or areas marked by similar styles or variants of form and linguistic dialect. Although these regions are empirically defined and of great diagnostic use in identifying the geographic origins of diverse artifacts, few scholars have explored the historical processes that underlay the formation of regional culture. In this essay on the emergence of regional consciousness in the Connecticut River Valley during the eighteenth century, Robert Blair St. George discovers that the stylistic uniformity of many surviving objects from that area cloaks an underlying tension between small yeomen freeholders and local elites.

Elites in the Connecticut River Valley styled themselves River Gods. Several wealthy families— the Williamses, the Pynchons, the Stoddards, the Dwights, and others—controlled most of the property and, by exercising their economic and political muscle, profited as middlemen in trade networks that linked the region to such colonial ports as Boston, Newport, New London, and New York. These same individuals assumed the role of cultural brokers and shaped the distribution of news and channels of communication to their advantage. In the century of economic and cultural growth before 1730, their secure hold on the region was carefully mediated through the strategic perpetuation of socially "open" forms: open fields, "traditional" central-chimney houses, chests without drawers. These objects created a symbolic identity between them and their social inferiors; in other words, elites coercively manipulated the landscape to hold the existing social hierarchy firmly in place.

But by the 1730s, local farmers began to resent the autonomy of these hereditary aristocrats. They

openly criticized the ostentation of newly built mansions and complained that rents were higher than greedy landlords need exact. No longer able to manipulate everyone in their towns, and striving to assume the airs of the English landed gentry, the River Gods withdrew into a new environment of controlled anonymity. Large houses with elaborate doorways provided impenetrable façades of order; inside, rooms remained oddly unfinished, symbolic statements of disarray beneath a calm surface. The efforts of the River Gods to use the landscape as a means of mystifying their power during the decades from 1750 to 1780 suggest that class solidification, rather than an easy consensus, underlay the "regional style" that marks many surviving (and economically biased) artifacts. If we fail to recognize beneath the guise of surface unity a series of deep fissures encoding themselves in coercive artifice, we, like the River Gods themselves, may confuse nostalgia with critical history.

Anyone who has seen the Connecticut River at dusk knows its seductive force. As it glides past Hadley and twists its current into the Ox-Bow at Northampton, the river seems knowable, even reassuring. Its surface is calming. But as the river winds its way into our historical imagination, its gently sloping banks are sometimes awash with violent currents. For even today this "great river" curses the benevolence of New England's most fertile fields with occasional flooding that leaves crops and farmers in ruin. In the nineteenth century this river lifted Thomas Cole to transcendental visions and at the same time powered mills that produced cloth and a new genera-

Artifacts of Regional Consciousness

ST. GEORGE

335

tion of entrepreneurial capitalists straining to control the growing strength of industrial workers. And in the eighteenth century, it supported a regional culture shaped by the actions of individuals whose lives were similarly defined by tension and conflicting values.

Samuel Porter was one such individual. Like many of his neighbors in early eighteenth-century Hadley, Porter owned a farm and raised grain and livestock. At night he retired to his house, a six-room, central-chimney structure that resembled most of the others in town. By these indices he seems to have been a farmer among farmers in this prosperous agrarian community. But if we follow Porter's life farther, the dry details of his 1722 estate inventory reveal he kept a "Treading Shop." From this small structure adjacent to his house, Porter sold expensive textiles ("East-Endia Silk," "Mohare," "Canteloon," and "Caleminko"), pewter, glassware, spectacles, spices, sugar, buttons, and imported sewing implements; these commodities marked the arrival of a consumer revolution that had begun in London in the mid-seventeenth century and within fifty years had affected the everyday lives of settlers in England's most distant colonies. In 1722 Porter was worth more than £7,790, roughly fifty times what the average yeoman in the Connecticut River Valley was likely to have amassed during a life of constant toil and little earthly reward. When he died, in addition to household furnishings worth £388 and livestock valued at £131, he had 114 gallons of rum at Hartford ready for shipment upriver, furs worth £148 waiting to leave Boston for London, and trade goods in London valued at £196 loaded for shipment home.[1]

Samuel Porter is just one of many people whose lives raise questions concerning the internal complexities and apparent contradictions that characterized routine social relations in the Connecticut River Valley during the eighteenth century. If the distance between Porter and his neighbors was already evident in 1722, it gained visibility for his son in the 1740s and was glaring when his grandson inherited the farm in the 1760s. Yet in the decades between 1750 and 1780, the regional culture that emerged in the Connecticut River Valley derived an ironic coherence as the Porters and other elite families struggled to perpetuate specific economic and social inequalities on which their grasp of local affairs depended. This brief moment of coherence raises more questions than it

answers about eighteenth-century New England society. How useful is the "regional culture" approach in discovering meaningful linkages between social history and artifact study? In what ways were social and economic relations distinctive in the Connecticut River Valley?

Despite its long and complex history, the concept of regional culture remains an inexact analytical tool for two reasons. First, its meaning is weakened by definitions that extend imprecisely in all directions. Howard W. Odum and Harry Estill Moore, the great advocates of American regionalism and theorists of regional culture, claimed in 1938 that five distinct "types of regions" exist for study: the "natural region" (like a river valley); the "metropolitan region," in which a city is the center and focus of adjacent areas; a "loosely defined region," or provincial locality bound together by common loyalties and "folkways"; the "region for convenience," or area that is articulated for political or bureaucratic purposes"; and the "group of states" region, such as the Northeast. Odum and Moore classified other regions on the basis of disciplinary approaches to the study of culture and society. Here they included the "functional regions" of geographers, the "mercantile regions" of economists, the "administrative regions" of political scientists, and the "aesthetic and literary regions" of art historians and literary critics.[2] The problem with all of this is apparent; a quick glance shows that *all* these definitions partially describe the Connecticut River Valley during the eighteenth century and suggests they are ahistorical categories external to the culture as it was actually lived.

Fortunately, there is a practical common denominator to the confusion. Whether plotting demographic activity, exchange relations, or the distribution of isolable "culture traits" like material artifacts, the identification of regional culture is at one level a spatial activity fundamentally geographic in nature. Ideally, when maps detailing singular patterns are superimposed, the area of overlap indicates genuine regional boundaries based on all available evidence. In an attempt to chart cultural regions with greater precision, geographers and folklorists have relied on extensive fieldwork. Fred Kniffen, dean of American cultural geographers, was among the first to superimpose maps when, in the course of testing "the diagnostic power of folk housing" as an indicator of regional boundaries, he noted the overlapping distributional patterns of domestic architecture and speech dialect in the eastern United States. Based on additional field study, Henry Glassie in 1968 extended and revised Kniffen's work and, in so doing, grounded the reality of regional culture in the rigorous analysis of artifacts that vary predictably from place to place.[3]

Materials have already been studied in the Connecticut River Valley that, in deviating from related forms found elsewhere in New England, assert its integrity as a regional culture during the middle decades of the eighteenth century. Here the evidence—and the boundaries—are above dispute. Hans Kurath found that historical patterns of local speech dialect united the valley in Connecticut and Massachusetts but broke sharply once north of the Vermont border, a boundary that Amelia Miller's detailed and systematic study of eighteenth-century doorways confirms. Miller's findings in the lower valley provide an architectural complement to John T. Kirk's studies of household furniture and to Dr. Ernest Caulfield's exhaustive research on Connecticut gravestones.[4]

The efforts of cultural geographers, folklorists, and students of the decorative arts demonstrate one point clearly: it is one thing to chart the boundaries of a distinct cultural region, but quite another to explain the constitutive logic of its assumed underlying cultural unity. Here we confront the second reason why the regional culture concept is analytically impoverished; its advocates have always stopped short of fully explaining why apparent similarities emerge. Indeed, they have systematically neglected its utility in exploring conflicting social values and emergent forms of class consciousness.

Perhaps the oversight results from their diverse methods and theoretical goals. Students of folklore, geography, social history, and the decorative arts usually ask different questions of their data, and, in the end, they tell different stories. The lack of conceptual precision that characterizes studies of American regional artifacts results directly from the fact that most students have asked questions *about* the artifact and not *of* it. Studying shadowy references to objects in probate records, tax lists, and account books more often than real objects, they fail to confront the values that artifacts actively assert.[5] The principal question that community and regional studies must ask of the artifact is not "How much did it cost?" or "Does this demonstrate the spread of the consumer

revolution?" or even, *pace res semiotica*, "Is it a sign, a moment of 'nonverbal communication'?" The challenge instead lies in addressing anew an issue raised without conclusion by John Demos fifteen years ago: "How did people *feel* about this or that object?"[6]

This single question urges us to place the surviving fragments of eighteenth-century culture in the Connecticut River Valley within a specific structure, a structure whose context frames the period aesthetic standards and the values—or conflicts—that characterized that society as a whole. In defining this structure, Raymond Williams reminds us that "we are talking about characteristic elements of impulse, restraint, and tone; specifically affective elements of consciousness and relationships: not feelings against thought, but thought as felt and feeling as thought: practical consciousness of a present kind, in a living and interrelating continuity. We are then defining these elements as a 'structure': as a set, with specific internal relations, at once interlocking and in tension."[7] To fuse thought with feeling, to collapse our need to isolate intellect from emotion, to see the history of ideas and the history of their material enactments as a unity basic to human experience in past and present: these are prerequisites of establishing a social history that transforms the descriptive study of regional culture into the analytical exploration of regional consciousness.

Regional consciousness in the valley defined a series of felt tensions between social homogeneity and social fragmentation, wealth and poverty, and mobility and stasis. It affected and in part was derived from the valley's agrarian economy, from the gentry's purposeful use of houses, doorways, and gravestones to create both a distance from and a paradoxical reliance on local craftsmen, and from the resulting dependence and occasional resentment of laboring people for their elite neighbors. Because the valley's regional culture defined a tension between community and class, between communication and the maintenance of social distance, it allows us to link artifacts as enactments of cultural values to other power structures in local society.

Although previous writers have stated that social homogeneity and a consensus in values characterized the Connecticut River Valley during the eighteenth century,[8] regional consciousness in the valley derived first from a form of agrarian capitalism that made a consensus of values logically impossible. Like its counterpart in eighteenth-century rural England, Connecticut River Valley society was built on a single great contradiction: while its economy gestured to a market run by individuals acting as free agents of profits, its political and social structures were based on a system of aristocratic preference linked by an intricate web of kin relations.[9] We can begin an analysis of how regional consciousness emerged by examining each side of this contradiction separately.

English settlement in the Connecticut River Valley was market oriented from its beginnings and quick to turn a profit from the land, river, and forests. In Connecticut, sons of prominent English families—men like George Wyllys of Hartford and John Chester of Wethersfield—recreated with remarkable speed the well-capitalized farms and system of tenant labor they remembered from their gentle upbringings. These first-generation landlords shared a vision of society essentially the same as that expressed by John Winthrop when he explained that the "rich and mighty" were morally charged to nurture qualities of "love, mercy, gentleness, and temperance" and urged "not to eat up the poor." In return for their love and protection, the "poor and inferior sort" were to practice "faith, patience, and obedience" so as not to "rise up against their superiors and shake off their yoke." In Massachusetts, William Pynchon concurred as he profited from the lucrative fur trade. By 1650 he had created a fiefdom that his descendants would inherit and rely on as a power base for the next century.[10]

The goal of large landowners in the valley was not mere self-sufficiency but rather to "improve" a surplus of goods to sell to Boston merchants at a high profit. Describing New England in 1645, Robert Child of Boston attested to the level of production already occurring in parts of the lower valley. "The next jurisdiction is Connecticut river," he wrote, "where Mr. Hooker lives contayning 5 or 6 good plantations, exceedingly abounding in corne. the last yeare they spared 20000 bushell, and have already this yeare sent to the bay 4000 bushell at least of corne. these are the fruitfullest places in all new England."[11] Within one or two decades of settlement, the Connecticut River Valley was inextricably bound up in the destiny of the colonial marketplace. By the close of the seventeenth century, mercantile dependence on the Connecticut River as a trade route was widely recognized. After a poor harvest in 1695, the Massachusetts assembly ordered that "no grain of any sort, bisket or flower shall be exported or carried out of this province by land or water (except what is brought from the western towns to Hartford, in order to be transported from thence to Boston)."[12]

Agricultural specialization emerged by the mid-1730s. Wethersfield farmers raised onions. Yeomen in Hadley, Hatfield, and Deerfield fattened livestock for Boston slaughterers and meat packers. Householders in Enfield, Longmeadow, and Northampton grew the wheat that made their area the "breadbasket of New England," and farmers in Glastonbury, Windsor, and East Hartford cultivated tobacco. On the one hand, this economic system fostered an interdependence between towns that lent the region coherence and integration. On the other hand, it gave the merchants in Springfield, Hartford, Middletown, Colchester, and East Haddam an unrivaled opportunity for profit as middlemen.[13]

Like many market-oriented rural landscapes, the Connecticut Valley was a meeting place for individuals with different visions of how society should work, to whose advantage it should work, and whose interests should dominate local affairs. In this contest for social and political influence, a local gentry made up of recognized River Gods and a series of lesser aristocrats arose as the clear victor. In brief, their power was grounded in mercantile activity supported by the control of large areas of land during a period of rapid population growth. They maintained their hegemony by performing real and ceremonial functions of leadership that skillfully balanced assertions of social difference against benevolent rituals of moral identification.[14]

The trappings of proclaimed social difference were immediately apparent. Some local elites were officers in the county militia who led local troops both in drills and in field duty. Others enhanced their authority as lawyers and magistrates. Colonel Fisher Gay of Farmington, for example, owned such basic texts as the "Connecticut Law Book," "Jacobs Law dictionary," "Woods Institutes," "Everyman his own Lawyer," and "Burns Justice 4 vol." when he died in 1779.[15] Still other elites served as physicians and through the mystification of medical knowledge took control of people's bodies. In the "Surgeons Shop" worth £60 on his Wethersfield estate in 1775, Ezekiel Porter kept the tools of his trade ready for use, including "3 Cases of Surgeons Instruments," "2 Sets Do. for Drawing teeth," and "1 Set of amputating [Do.]."[16] Finally, the authority of ministers extended over the spiritual welfare of those beneath them. The power of the clergy was in part due to their role in perpetuating an orthodox covenant theology with roots in seventeenth-century social structure. The library of the Reverend William Russell of Windsor, Connecticut, who died in 1775 with an impressive estate of £1,416, illustrates how conservative accepted doctrine was; his favorite authors included such well-known seventeenth-century Puritan ministers as William Perkins, John Preston, Thomas Hooker, and Richard Baxter.[17] In its emphasis on the sanctity of a hierarchic society ruled by wise patriarchs, such conservative doctrine legitimized the unchallenged authority of the Connecticut River Valley gentry into the third quarter of the eighteenth century. Without doubt, local elites in the 1770s would have appreciated the Reverend Solomon Stoddard's sense of hierarchy when he urged, "authority must be kept up . . . and . . . we must take heed that we don't Suffer people to trample upon us."[18]

The social differences manifest in holding civil and religious power over the body and souls of other men and women were intensified as the gentry exploited positions of prestige for personal gain. Local merchants like Samuel Porter played a vital role in sustaining their communities, while at the same time controlling prices and availability so that laws of supply and demand worked to their own advantage. As Kevin M. Sweeney has pointed out, merchants who served as subcommissaries in the militia stood to gain if they could make clever use of government bills of credit extended to them during wartime. The shrewd handling of £6,000 in drafts on the Royal Paymaster General in London made Joseph Dwight a fast personal fortune in 1748, at the same time that it ensured his Hampshire County troops their pay before going to war. In addition, merchant subcommissaries decided which local farmers could sell their produce to the militia, thus enabling them to bless certain plebeians with their favor while denying it to others.[19]

The gentry also made the most of their frequent stints as justices of the peace, the one job that all of the known River Gods in Massachusetts at one point held, as did many of their fathers. John Adams summarized the social distance that justices experienced as a result of their power, especially in rural districts.

"The Office of a Justice of the Peace," he wrote in 1774, "is a great Acquisition in the Country, and such a Distinction to a Man among his Neighbours as is enough to purchase and corrupt almost any man."[20] Once in power, justices could easily define the public good in terms of personal agendas. As a result, the political goals of the Connecticut River Valley gentry were typically parochial and concerned principally with jurisdictional issues and military allocations that would guarantee their return to office and insure the protection of their own landholdings in case the French or Indians were to attack.[21]

Joseph Hawley of Northampton, for example, in 1754 considered using his power as a representative to the Massachusetts assembly in order to block the nomination of a rival for a military post he wanted. Threatening to stop military allocations that his local constituents coveted, he wrote to Israel Williams that if his own goals could not be realized, "it seems to me *all our separate designs and projections* will be likely to prove abortive. I don't think that in my private capacity I am of much importance as to such matters," he continued, "but as a member of the House it is possible I may be, for I have always spoke my mind in the House and sometimes have been heard."[22] Despite how subtly or how overtly they fought their own private battles, members of the valley gentry—merchants, ministers, magistrates, and militia officers—would have agreed that the fulfillment of personal interests was a necessary privilege of being atop the "natural order" of their society.

When a single individual filled more than one of these roles, that person could become extremely powerful. Samuel Porter, our original protagonist, was a merchant who also dispensed legal advice from the pages of the "Province Law-Book" he kept in the "hall," or public room, of his house. Most powerful was Israel Williams of Hatfield, whose position of unchallenged authority caused his political opponents in Boston to call him the "monarch of Hampshire." Local plebeians acknowledged his River God status literally by calling him "our father."[23] The hegemony that Williams and others enjoyed derived directly from a structure of wealth based on radical inequalities in land ownership that also informed the political economy and its ecclesiastical outposts. While most yeomen worked farms that may have grown as large as 100 acres, the gentry had vast holdings that often included the most productive acreage. Samuel

Porter owned 2,801 acres of land in Hadley worth £1,194. Seth Wetmore of Middletown died in 1778 with an estate valued at £14,535. Of this, his 1,282 acres of land accounted for £9,129 (63 percent). The 164 animals he owned accounted for another £394 (3 percent), while an additional £1,083 (7.5 percent) was invested in the "Old Mansion house & out houses with 17 Acres Meadow east of house & 3 Acres West [of] where the house stands." Members of the gentry who relied on tenant farmers to work their estates were called "Landlord" in return.[24]

The unequal distribution of property extended beyond land to engage a system of explicit status markers that the gentry depended on as a means of glorifying their own social position. From these artifacts they built a theater of class dominance and control that functioned in two ways. First, it created symbolic barriers between themselves and their neighbors. Second, it used these barriers to link their own authority to the authority of God. Most evident in this new disjunctive landscape were the large, elaborately carpentered houses they built, the doorways with which they dramatized the front (and occasionally the side) doors of these structures, and the impressive gravestones they placed over their dead relatives.

A brief examination of roof structures clarifies one aspect of architectural difference. The yeoman's house in the Connecticut River Valley was normally roofed in one of two ways. One system employed a series of principal rafters joined together by principal purlins, or horizontal timbers that were framed between each pair of rafter couplings and steadied the trusses. Typically, the outside surface of these purlins supported a second set of smaller, secondary rafters. The other type relied on a series of common rafters steadied by the horizontal roof boards. Like similar examples built at Massachusetts Bay and in Rhode Island, the surviving Connecticut River Valley examples, such as those at the Buttolph-Williams house in Wethersfield and the Joseph Hollister house in Glastonbury (fig. 1), have clear antecedents in postmedieval timber framed buildings in England.[25] Under their peaked timbers, these roofs afforded a small garret suitable for the storage of processed grains, spare tools, or old furniture in the space around a massive central chimney stack.

The difference between these roofs and the large gambrel roof that merchant Joseph Webb put on his

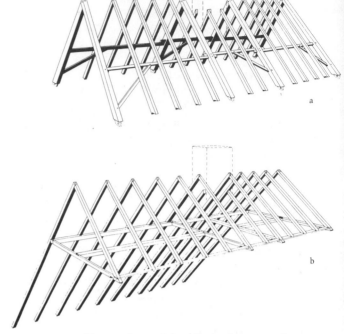

Fig. 1. *a*, Roof frame of Buttolph-Williams house, Wethersfield, Connecticut, ca. 1695–1700. (Drawing by Robert St. George, based on fieldwork conducted by Robert St. George and R. Trent, October 1984.) *b*, Second roof frame of Joseph Hollister's house, South Glastonbury, Connecticut, ca. 1740.(Drawing and fieldwork by Robert St. George, November 1984.)

new Wethersfield house in 1752 is immediately apparent (fig. 2). At one level, the design of Webb's gambrel frame gestured to bookish prototypes available in the standard eighteenth-century English building manuals of Batty Langley and Francis Price.[26] The form of his roof was foreign to the domestic experience of most of his fellow townsmen and may have been calculated to put them in awe of his knowledge of the world beyond their farm fences. It was also a roof type that, when built locally, was commonly reserved for public buildings and for the houses of justices of the peace. In short, it carried associations of political authority.[27]

In its structural complexity, Webb's roof signaled his ability to pay for materials and for the labor of Judah Wright, the carpenter who masterminded the project. Webb's overt consumption of skill was remarkable, as his account for Wright's work indicates.

For carpentry work alone, Webb credited Wright with a total of almost £169.[28] In addition, Webb bought 5,100 pine shingles in July 1752 from William Eastman of Hadley[29] and probably purchased dressed red sandstone foundation blocks in Middletown, making the completed structure a tour de force of his ability to exploit trade connections and obligations throughout the Connecticut River Valley. Other members of the gentry also consumed labor on a regional basis. When Roger Wolcott of Windsor, governor of the Connecticut colony, died in 1767, his executors insisted that his body rest beneath a table stone ordered from Thomas Johnson's Middletown quarry. And, as we might expect, the cost of the monument increased due to the labor required to get it to Windsor:

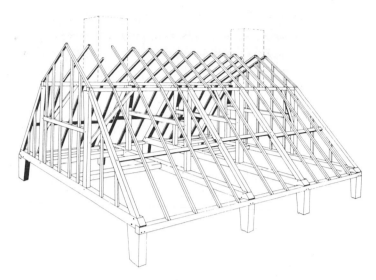

Fig. 2. Roof frame of Joseph Webb's house, made by Judah Wright, 1752. (Drawing by Robert St. George, based on fieldwork by Robert St. George, R. Trent, and Kevin Sweeney, November 1984.)

	[£.	s.	d.]
To Cash to Thomas Johnson for a Table Stone	6	15	0
To boating the Stone from Middletown	0	10	0
To Carting the Stone from the River	0	3	0
To Cash to Matthew Grant for Setting up the Stone	0	3	5
[Total:	£7	11	5][30]

The domestic environments of the Connecticut River Valley gentry became more impressive as they exploited available labor. As testimonials to such consumption, houses and gravestones were appropriate icons of an underlying moral code that also sanctioned the ownership of black slaves. Indeed, the architectural facades adopted by valley elites bear comparison with those of Southern planters; the more frail and dangerously unequal the social structure, the more architecture moves toward symmetry and control.[31]

The theater of dominance in the Connecticut River Valley also relied on the elaborate doorways that Amelia Miller has studied in detail.[32] Like the framing system of Joseph Webb's roof, these doorways (fig. 3) gestured to a world of architectural uniformity at the same time that they admitted individual variations by local woodworkers. These doorways glorified the status of the gentry perhaps more than any other artifact. Probate inventories of known doorway owners indicate a mean estate of nearly £4,500 and $8,500, both sizable sums. Josiah Dwight, a Springfield merchant whose doorway is now at the Winterthur Museum and whose house is now reconstructed in Deerfield, was worth nearly £9,500 in 1768. Like

Fig. 3. Doorway on Elijah Williams's house, Deerfield, Massachusetts, built ca. 1760. (Photograph by Robert St. George, August 1975.)

the gambrel roofs they sometimes accompanied, these doorways invoked authority because their size and workmanship were associated with large public buildings; in New Haven, the "State House" (1763), the first Episcopal church (1753), and the third meetinghouse (1757) all had impressive portals. So did Christ Church (Episcopal) at Stratford (ca. 1744–48) and the second meetinghouses of Bethlehem (1767), Longmeadow (1767), and Northfield (1762).[33]

In their large size and indulgent exterior decorations, the houses of the Connecticut River Valley participated, albeit at a distance, in the "ideology of the country house" that had already made a similar impression on the English landscape. In this context, houses like those of Samuel Porter, Josiah Dwight, and Joseph Webb were intended "to break the scale, by an act of will corresponding to their real and systematic exploitation of others." In so doing, they provided "a visible stamping of power, of displayed wealth and command: a social disproportion which was meant to impress and overawe." And, always, this power and command had its roots in the extent to which the gentry could fuse its mercantile interests with its control of increasing agricultural specialization.[34]

The public display of class prerogative was occasionally complemented by the furnishings inside a local gentry household; objects that comprised one side of a dialectic that existed between the private, inner world of selected acquaintances and the public, outer world of less specific impressions. Without doubt, the gentry relied on local craftsmen to produce their most public artifacts—houses, doors, gravestones—and in so doing fulfilled their moral responsibility to lend visible support to their neighbors, some of whom might even be less successful relatives. They even relied on neighborhood craftsmen for some of their most polite furniture, like the "Cherry Desk & Book Case" worth £3.10.0 owned by Ezekiel Porter of Wethersfield in 1775.[35] While they owned locally made objects, the gentry also used their interiors to reveal their interest in the world beyond the familiar faces of their towns. Because at least two-thirds of the River Gods had risen to power as merchants,[36] they were in a position to acquire imported objects and participate in levels of the foreign marketplace that their less prosperous neighbors would never know. Throughout the eighteenth century, objects arrived in valley homes from Boston,

Newport, New York, Philadelphia, and London and provided a jarring counterpoint to the wares of local artisans. In the early eighteenth century, Hezekiah Wyllys of Hartford exploited his mercantile ties in New York City to obtain a tankard made by silversmith Bartholomew Schaats (fig. 4). Ebenezer Plummer, Glastonbury's leading mid-eighteenth-century merchant, displayed a printed view of Quebec executed by the prominent Boston engraver Thomas Johnston in 1759 (fig. 5). And the Reverend Eliphalet Williams had a Staffordshire tea service delivered to his East Hartford mansion in the decade before the Revolution (fig. 6). The gentry's simultaneous patronage of local workers and need to identify with their perceived social equals in urban centers of "taste" supports Lewis Mumford's belief that "a genuine regional tradition lives by two principles. One is, cultivate whatever you have, no matter how poor it is; it is at least your own. The other is, seek elsewhere for what you do not possess; absorb whatever is good

Fig. 4. Bartholomew Schaats, tankard, New York City, 1700–1720. Silver; h. 6¾"; w. at base 5". (Photograph by John Giammateo, courtesy of Historic Deerfield, Inc.)

QUEBEC, *The Capital of* NEW-FRANCE, *a Bishoprick, and Seat of the Soverain* COURT.

1. *The Citadel.* 2. *the Castle.* 3. *Magazine.* 4. *ÿ Recolets.* 5. *Ursulines.* 6. *Jesuits.* 7. *Cathedral of Our Lady.* 8. *The Palace* 9. *ÿ Seminary.* 10. *The Hôtel Dieu.* 11. *St Charles River.* 12. *The Common Hospital.* 13. *The Hermitage of the Recolets.* 14. *The Bishop's House.* 15. *The Parish Church of the Lower Town.* 16. *The Upper Town* 17. *ÿ Lower Town.* 18. *The Platform & Battery of Cannon.* 19. *The Isle of Orleans.* 20. *Point Lievi.*

Engrav'd & Printed By Thos Johnston for Step Whiting.

Fig. 5. Thomas Johnston, *Quebec, The Capital of New-France, A Bishoprick, and Seat of the Soverain Court*, Boston, Massachusetts, 1759. Line engraving; 8″ × 9⁵⁄₁₆″. (Photograph by Robert Bitondi, courtesy of The Connecticut Historical Society.)

wherever you may find it; make it your own."[37]

Like their drive to consume labor as a sign of power, the need to assert an extensive identity based on possessing foreign artifacts separated the gentry from their neighbors. Doorways were fragile membranes separating the outer world of the locally made from the inner world of elite fashion. They were portals through which only the chosen few, the socially elect, could pass. Once securely inside, the fortunate few could enjoy a world supplied with sensual de-

lights, the exotic fruits of merchant capital. In essence, a River God's doorway was a disjunctive icon that enforced divisions of social class through the symbolic invocation of legitimizing religious dogma. The distance separating the River Gods and their local supplicants in this world metaphysically suggested, in a moment of continuity with seventeenth-century thinkers like Edward Taylor of Westfield, the ordained separation of those souls elected for salvation and the reward of heavenly delights (approached through a portal or gate) from those who would never know the bliss of God's kingdom. "Death is the portal to eternity, and carries men over to an unchangeable state," wrote Samuel Willard in 1726.[38] Indeed, inheriting the crown of glory in resurrection must have been the typological basis for the popularity of "crown-topped" doors, "crown-topped" high chests, "crown" looking glasses, and "crown" chairs among the local gentry.

The eighteenth-century gravestones of the Connecticut River Valley gentry refer frequently to the "portal of death." The souls of the dead rise through scroll-topped pediments (fig. 7), pass through scroll-topped doorways into Eternity (fig. 8), or cross the thresholds of literal doorways on the way to the next world (figs. 9, 10).[39] Entering one's home through an elaborate ceremonial doorway, like entering the gates of Heaven, was probably seen by the gentry as a divinely sanctioned act of self-glorification designed to inspire the earthly congregation. And to make the metaphor complete, both kinds of doorways enabled elites to pass to an unseen world—one hidden from neighbors of a lesser status, the other invisible to all mortals. Once admitted to this hopefully "unchangeable state," they would dwell in the house of a River God, or in the house of the Lord. Doorways further intensified the power of disjunction and changing states as they endowed wood with the appearance of other materials. In the Elihu White doorway from Hatfield, for example, yellow pine attains both the rigidity of stone and the delicacy of a grapevine.[40]

As they transcended substance, doorways—like the houses they adorned—also vibrated with symmetry. Like their first-generation ancestors, eighteenth-century people in the Connecticut River Valley be-

Fig. 7. Detail of Capt. Simon Colton stone, 1796, Longmeadow, Massachusetts. (Photograph by Robert St. George, December 1984.)

Fig. 8. Detail of Martha Welch stone, 1773, Storrs, Connecticut. (Photograph by Robert St. George, December 1984.)

Fig. 6. Teapot, Staffordshire, England, 1760–75. Creamware with copper green glaze; h. 4⅝". (Courtesy of Wadsworth Atheneum; bequest of Mrs. Gurdon Trumbull.)

lieved that symmetry invoked God's perfect formation of the human body, and they were aware of the perfect symmetry of their own frames as the "type" of artifactual frames. As Thomas Anburey observed in 1778, Connecticut elites "appear here with much stiffness and reserve: they are formed by symmetry."[41] The bilateral logic of houses, doorways, and gravestones was grounded in an ambivalent admixture of physical and metaphysical meanings and in a tension between the person-ness and thing-ness of everyday objects.[42]

The affective power of doorways and gravestones, as portals marking the entrances to two different houses of deference and belief, derived from tensions on different levels. On one level, their size and cost set them apart from the physical worlds of lesser yeomen and artisans. In short, they were ostentatious performances of social dominance. On another level, they referred to foreign sources but admitted domes-

tic tradition and modification by familiar craftsmen. And they were ambivalent for several reasons. First, they were icons that blurred the clear boundaries of public and private domains. Doors suggested public buildings as they led into private dwellings, while gravestones were private markers in public yards. Second, at the same time that they provided a substantive portal they played with its materiality, making wood resemble stone or flowers, or making stone look like trees and vines. Finally, as their symmetry drew metaphysical connections between the houses and bodies of the gentry and of God, they blurred basic distinctions between objects and subjects. Owning these powers, doorways, houses, and gravestones affectively linked the gentry's aesthetic authority to their economic and political power in local society.[43]

Fig. 10. Elisha Dickinson stone, 1813(?), Hadley, Massachusetts. (Photograph by Robert St. George, 1984.)

Fig. 9. Samuel Dwight stone, 1763, Enfield, Connecticut. (Photograph by Robert St. George, December 1984.)

Only part of the Connecticut River Valley gentry's longevity in power was due to their assertions of social difference. The rest was due to their success in assuring their poorer neighbors that they had their best interests at heart. Here the elites were being more practical than altruistic, for if we look back, we see a line of popular protest and rebellion against the hegemony of the River Gods as continuous as that inscribed by the sure progress of agrarian capitalism. Such resentment was apparent on a local level as early as 1716, when the Reverend Stephen Williams of Longmeadow worried over his neighbors' criticism of his new mansion. Williams realized that an ostentatious house could easily alienate more of his parishioners than it might inspire: "This morning I heard that my neighbor Brooks is uneasy because of my house being so stately. I have heard of others that speak meanly and reproachfully of me. God forgive them and help me heartily to do it. O Lord, help me to walk inoffensively, so that none may have occasion to speak ill of me; help me, O Lord, to do my duty, and by no means to neglect that, to curry favor with man. Man had better be angry with me than God."[44] For Williams, as for his many relatives in positions of power, maintaining the landscape of social distance and forgiving the moral infractions of resentful plebeians were part of one's "duty" to God.

Opposition to gentry authority found a voice on the provincial level as well. Early in 1766, known River Gods from Hampshire County were among those indicted by radicals for having supported the Stamp Act. "They are justly to be accounted *enemies of the country*," claimed the insurgents. "Whosoever contributes to enslave posterity, and bring a lasting ruin on his country, his name shall descend, with all the marks of infamy, to the latest times." In 1770 Israel Williams of Hatfield, having refused to join other Massachusetts merchants in a boycott of English goods, was derided as one of "those Persons . . . that preferred their little private Advantage to the common Interest of all the Colonies . . . who with a design to enrich themselves, basely took Advantage of the generous self denial of their Fellow Citizens for the common Good." And after the Consolidation Act of 1781 imposed an excise tax on Massachusetts residents to rebuild the post-Revolutionary economy— an event that led to the prosecution of hapless debtors, massive migrations of insolvent farmers to New York state and the Western Reserve, and to Shays' Re-

bellion—one Hampshire County village protested the government. Their diction appropriately recalled Winthrop's advice that rulers should not "eat up the poor": "Honoured sirs are not these imprisonments and fleeings away of our good inhabitants very injurious to the credit or honour of the Commonwealth: will not people in the neighboring states say of this state: altho the [people of] Massachusetts bost of their fine constitution their government is such that it *devours their inhabitants*."[45]

Indeed, the surviving artifacts suggest that, along with a theater of dominance, the River Gods built a self-interested "ideology of community" in three ways. First, as we have already seen, they actively patronized local artisans and relied on their skills rather than importing urban craftsmen whose understanding of neoclassical style and architectural theory may have been more "correct." In addition, they chose to actively participate in the perpetuation of a range of "socially open" forms that typically correspond to a closed, hierarchically ordered social structure. Such socially open forms include common field agriculture, central-chimney, hall-and-parlor houses, and room usage that retained the hall as the center of domestic functions in the public front of the house (fig. 11). In short, socially open forms give the impression of social integration and "community" values. This is one reason why the seventeenth-century style persisted in the Connecticut River Valley into the second half of the eighteenth century.

Nucleated villages surrounded by common fields, for example, survived in some places until the mid-eighteenth century (Deerfield and Northfield), even though they had given way to dispersed settlement and enclosed fields in eastern Massachusetts and coastal Connecticut by the early 1660s. These eighteenth-century towns, whether inland or on the banks of the river, were still conceived of as a series of concentric social rings. The meetinghouse stood at the symbolic center, surrounded by the houses of the gentry and more prosperous yeomen on the large house lots along the town's main street. On smaller lots tucked in side streets stood the small, one-and-one-half story cottages of lesser farmers, beyond which the fields extended in neat progression. When one of John Adams's hosts in the Connecticut River Valley in 1771 boasted "there was not such another Street in America as this at Weathersfield excepting

Fig. 11. House on Route 116, Amherst, Massachusetts, ca. 1770. (Photograph by Robert St. George, August 1979.)

one at Hadley," he was describing the promenade of mansions that defined the secular center of such towns. These houses, according to one New England settler in 1634, were "orderly placed to enjoye comfortable comunion" and to assert the authority of the "rich and mighty" upon whose shoulders the weight of leadership pressed. Cotton Mather saw in such order the "Sacred Geography of God's Kingdom."[46]

Domestic houses in the Connecticut River Valley retained index features of seventeenth-century form and style until the third quarter of the eighteenth century. Many members of the gentry continued to live in houses of the same form as those of their yeomen neighbors; a hall and a parlor were separated by a large central chimney, while a shed enclosing the working kitchen and service rooms ran across the rear of the house. Bracketed jetties and angular lean-tos articulated internal divisions of space, making the social use of the house legible from the street. Inside, people furnished their houses in similar ways as

well. Despite a marked rise during the 1730s and 1740s in the amount and range of interior furniture used, gentry and yeomen alike followed established seventeenth-century practices, such as displaying plate on cupboards, through the late 1730s. While the houses of the wealthy were larger and more ornate than those of farmers, they still gestured toward consensus in terms of how space was organized and used. Visitors to Connecticut River Valley towns must have had a reaction similar to that of Thomas Anburey, who, after passing through Enfield and Suffield in 1778, recalled that "I could not help remarking that the houses are all after the same plan."[47]

Yet their use of similar forms does not only suggest that the gentry shared the values of those beneath them. Equally, it suggests that they realized that these forms were necessary linkages of identification that might help to ensure deference. In other words, the gentry seem to have manipulated "traditional" images to their own advantage. Here, too, the River Gods could have cited the precedent of John Winthrop and other gentlemen, who at first built on a humble scale, "in order not to discourage poorer laboring people whom they brought over in numbers from [the] fatherland."[48]

Beginning in the late 1740s some merchants and magistrates began building houses with a radically different plan. With four rooms arranged symmetrically around a central hall or passageway, these "Georgian" houses effectively cast aside the importance of identification, or the assertion of feigned commonality, as a basis of deference. In opting out of consensual forms, these houses may seem to show a new confidence on the part of the gentry, but they also betray their owners' fear that their social position was weakening. Displays of social distance followed by acts of calculated generosity no longer alone ensured that the gentry's will would be done. As they witnessed the rise of "modern" attitudes toward privacy and individualism, these houses also announced the loosening of the River Gods' hold on local society.[49]

The final way that the Connecticut River Valley gentry preserved the image of corporate communalism to their own advantage was through gifts, chief among which were silver objects donated to the local congregation, itself the single most powerful symbol of consensus. In performing these calculated acts of largesse, members of the gentry were perpetuating a tradition with seventeenth-century roots. "These great acts of generosity," wrote Marcel Mauss in his classic study *The Gift*, "are not free from self interest. . . . Between vassals and chiefs, between vassals and their henchmen, the hierarchy is established by means of these gifts. To give is to show one's superiority, to show that one is something more and higher. . . . To accept without reimbursing or repaying more is to face subordination, to become a client and subservient."[50] Thus, when Gov. Roger Wolcott donated in 1756 a pair of silver beakers to the First Church of East Windsor, he did so knowing that the inscription bearing his initials would be quickly recognized and that the congregation, unable to repay him, would not only be subservient but grateful for his benevolent gesture. Individuals like Jonathan Allen, a deacon of the First Church of Middletown for forty years who willed £10 for the purchase of "a Suitable Cup or Vessel for the Communion Table," were, among other things, anxious to have people remember them as benevolent and continue paying homage to their heirs.[51]

The fact that local elites were concerned to secure for their descendants the deferential prerogative they had enjoyed suggests that while some leaders may not have sufficiently felt that peculiar mixture of confidence and fear needed to build Georgian houses, they nonetheless must have worried that their days in power were numbered. By the early 1770s some of the River Gods had suffered dramatic economic losses, due in part to their failure to amass sufficient capital to free them from a reliance on Boston merchants. In addition, many of the wealthiest elites had much of their estates either in land or else outstanding in "notes of hand" on which they charged interest, and thus lacked the freedom that liquid assets afford. Of Fisher Gay's total estate of £5,222, some £2,286 (44 percent) were due in such notes; £4,288 (58.7 percent) of Alexander Allyn's Windsor estate, worth a total of £7,307, were similarly tied up.[52]

Caught between visions of grandeur and grim financial realities, some local aristocrats built houses complete on the outside but left partially unfinished inside. Looking at the large houses near Enfield late in 1778, Anburey noticed that "most of them were only one half finished, the other half having only the rough timbers that support the building . . . but as the houses are entirely compleat on the outside, and the windows all glazed, they have the appearance of being finished, but on entering a house, you cannot help lamenting that the owner was unable to complete it." When their houses were furnished, not all were as impressive as a passerby might have guessed. Visiting Dr. Eliot Rawson in Middletown in 1771, Adams remarked that his house was "handsome without, but neither clean nor elegant within."[53]

As they sensed themselves losing power, individual elites reacted by spending additional cash on the outward trappings of wealth, hollow though they often were. If the appearance of elaborate doorways between 1750 and 1780 can be read as a sign of perceived social insecurity, their distribution suggests that such anxieties were most pronounced in the northern valley towns of Deerfield, Hatfield, and Northampton (table 1), where the need of the Porters, Williamses, Hawleys, and Partridges to assert a fading aristocratic legacy was the greatest and where the socal structure was the frailest.[54] Because control of land and mercantile activity easily assured his authority, Samuel Porter had no need of an elaborate doorway by 1722. If anything, such ostentation might have needlessly polarized public opinion and under-

Table 1. Connecticut River Valley Towns Having at Least Four Doorways, 1755–1780

Town*	Doorway Type				Total
	Scroll-top	Triangular-top	Segmental-top	Flat-top	
Massachusetts					
Deerfield	3	2	6	—	11
Hatfield	6	2	2	1	11
Hadley	2	1	3	—	6
Northampton	1	8	3	—	12
Springfield	1	4	2	—	7
Westfield	2	1	3	—	6
Longmeadow	1	3	1	—	5
Connecticut					
Enfield	—	—	5	1	6
Suffield	4	—	—	—	4
Windsor	—	2	4	—	6
S. Windsor	3	5	—	—	8
Hartford	2	2	1	—	5
E. Hartford	1	1	2	—	4
Farmington	1	—	5	—	6
Wethersfield	4	1	2	—	7
Glastonbury	1	2	1	—	4
Middletown	2	1	1	—	4
New Haven	3	1	3	—	7
Saybrook	—	—	4	—	4
Total	37	36	48	2	123

Source: Amelia F. Miller, *Connecticut River Valley Doorways: An Eighteenth-Century Flowering* (Boston, 1983), 20, 66, 86, 90. Incorporation dates as they existed for Massachusetts towns in 1780 have been followed, as given in Frederic W. Cook, *Historical Data Relating to Counties, Cities, and Towns in Massachusetts* (Boston, 1948). The total of 123 doors here represents 55.9% of the 220 doors listed by Miller.
*Towns are listed from north to south, geographically.

cut the communal image he needed to exploit. Porter perhaps knew of plebeian disdain for the Reverend Stephen Williams's mansion in Longmeadow and wanted to avoid any similar grumblings. Porter's son Eleazer, who died in 1757, did not need a doorway either. Yet by the early 1760s, his grandson Eleazer, Jr., must have felt sufficiently unsure of his aristocratic lineage to erect an impressive scroll-topped doorway on the house.[55]

Living in their strangely low-key interiors behind increasingly false images of authority, elites of the 1760s and 1770s had good reason to be paranoid that others were gradually usurping their control. After all, as they sought to separate themselves from the plebeians beneath them, they effectively put more liquid capital into the hands of those on whose skills they relied for markers of social difference. As a re-sult, artisans had more work and prospered like never before. By 1768 a tailor, a shoemaker, and a joiner had placed elaborate doorways on their own houses, blurring distinctions of status and threatening outright the "natural order" of the River Gods' society.[56]

The third quarter of the eighteenth century marked a point at which, in being prisoners of one another, elites and artisans were oddly equal in controlling different kinds of power on which the other relied. Since the seventeenth century, the gentry had depended on artisans for the houses, doorways, and furniture they needed to perpetuate their commanding presence on the land. And artisans had always depended on the gentry for the cash resources they needed to expand their markets and diversify into new industries. But in the Connecticut River Valley this relationship had not approached equality before the mid-eighteenth century. The balance of different powers and interdependent resources that occurred in the valley between 1750 and 1780 lay at the heart of regional consciousness. For here was a distinctive social phenomenon without precedent in local memory; the aesthetic economy controlled by skilled workers and the money economy controlled by the gentry had reached a point of precarious, interlocking equilibrium.

In this brief "interregnum" between the fall of a secure aristocracy and the rise of defined social classes neither group could exist without the other. Local arts flourished during this "interlude of release" as artisans fulfilled the demands of patrons eager to have variation for the social advantages it implied.[57] Between 1750 and 1780 workmen in the Connecticut River Valley produced a series of extremely energetic artifacts for a weakened aristocracy whose habitual control of local affairs blinded them from fully realizing that their brand of power could no longer logically endure. These same artisans made equally energetic objects for ambitious individuals eager to rise despite the dominant presence of the established River God clans.

Deriving from such tension, the artifacts of regional consciousness themselves assert a conflict of values. On one hand, the gentry used houses, doorways, furniture, and gravestones as a means to create a theater of dominance and the stage for a coercive image of community that functioned to their own advantage. Yet on the other hand, these objects freely indulged the idiosyncratic skills of specific artisans. Details like molding profiles, carved rosettes, and tobacco-leaf capitals were the signatures of known workers—men like John Steele, Oliver Easton, and Parmenas King—whose reputations soon obtained for them contracts throughout the valley.[58] During the interregnum decades from 1750 to 1780, valley artisans for the first time realized that their skills were a base for power, which, if safeguarded, they could use for social purposes. By August 1792, for example, the "Cabinet-Makers" of Hartford formally convened "for the purposes of regulating the prices of our work." After agreeing "in the principle of dealing in CASH," the members resolved that they would "strictly conform to the prices which are or shall be affixed to our work; a deviation therefrom, shall be deemed a forfeiture of *word* and *honour*."[59] The house-joiners of Hatfield organized four years later.

Ultimately, the artifacts of regional consciousness in the Connecticut River Valley owe their power to a series of social relations that emerged in the local transition from agrarian to industrial capitalism. Selected artifacts embody a sense of genuine community among artisans that led, when challenged, to a greater sense of occupational solidarity in the closing years of the eighteenth century. Of course, this was built on a solid base of kinship ties that had linked craftsmen together since the settlement of the region. Nowhere are the linkages between distinct artisans more directly revealed, nowhere is communication through migration and diffusion more emphatically declared, than in the so-called "sunflower" and "Hadley" chests (figs. 12, 13). In these joinery traditions, the earliest phases of which date as far back as the 1670s, similar construction details and decorative motifs appear in towns as far distant from one another as Middletown, Enfield, Northampton, and Deerfield. As these objects suggest, the ties created by apprenticeship and patronage throughout the valley resulted both in a shared vision of appropriate design and, ironically, in the uneven distribution of affective power in local society. The emphasis on the values of one's "*word* and *honour*" in the

Fig. 12. "Sunflower-type" chest with drawers, attributed to Peter Blin, Wethersfield, Connecticut, ca. 1675–1700. Red oak, yellow pine, and white pine; h. 39½"; w. 43¾"; d. 19¾". (Photograph by Robert Bitondi, courtesy of The Connecticut Historical Society.)

Fig. 13. "Hadley-type" chest with drawers, vicinity of Springfield, Massachusetts, ca. 1690–1710. White oak, yellow pine, and beech; h. 34"; w. 49½"; d. 19". (Courtesy of the Henry Francis duPont Winterthur Museum.)

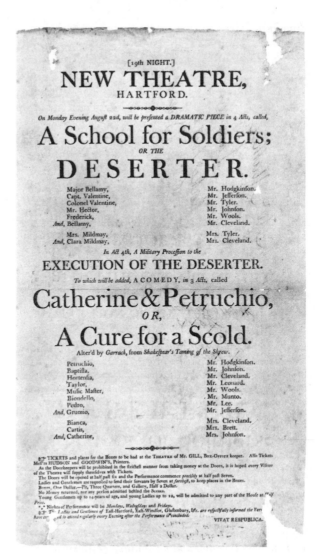

Fig. 14. Theater broadside, attributed to Hudson & Goodwin, printers, Hartford, Connecticut, 1796. Ink on paper; 17¾" × 9⁷⁄₁₆". (Photograph by Robert Bitondi, courtesy of The Connecticut Historical Society.)

Hartford agreement shows that the commonality among artisans was firmly rooted in the "traditional" moral code plebeians had cherished in the face of the River Gods.

At the same time, the artifacts owe their energy to local elites retreating in the face of ideological pluralism. Rather than demonstrating a rise to power, Georgian houses, doorways, and gravestones suggest that the steady *withdrawal* of the gentry began as early as the 1740s. As the eighteenth century became the nineteenth, the wealthy took control of newly formed philanthropic, educational, and charitable organizations while cherishing memories of lost authority. In this role, for example, they established a theater in Hartford (fig. 14), which they conceived of as "a school of morality" that they hoped "will be a great source of instruction . . . to those who visit it."[60] Along with town libraries, literary clubs, museums, and dancing academies, the new theater was a form of education—an "engine of cultural acceleration (or estrangement)"[61]—on which their continued assertion of social exclusivity depended.

By 1800 the Connecticut River Valley already afforded a painful vista of urban wealth and rural poverty, factory owners and millworkers, and dirt poor farmers trying to buck the arrival of fast-talking businessmen in slick suits selling a new brand of agrarian reform. A Hartford newspaper editor had even ad-

mitted the previous year that society was "composed of men of all *classes.*"[62] Into such complexity rode Timothy Dwight in 1815. Himself a River God's descendant, the fact that he could still warm to the belief that the "inhabitants of this valley may be said . . . to possess a common character" demonstrates his inherited inability to give up the nostalgic belief that these people were all one, big, happy family living under imagined parental guidance.[63] In taking it on himself to assess the "character" of these "inhabitants" as a whole, Dwight confirmed the gentry's retreat to moral judgment as a means of asserting superiority.

By 1800 the frail regional culture held together by the multiple tensions of a fading aristocratic social order had all but vanished. In its wake were poor farmers, aggressive businessmen, new ranks of industrial workers and management, and a few old River Gods trying to preserve their divinity. Because his perception of social affinities in the Connecticut River Valley was born of trenchant nostalgia, Timothy Dwight described a consensus that not only never existed but by 1815 was blatant in its absence.

Notes

This essay is for David Dangremond, whose enthusiasm as a teacher first sparked my interest in eighteenth-century Connecticut River Valley culture. Helpful suggestions have come in conversations with Robert F. Trent, Henry Glassie, John Brooke, Alice Gray Read, and David D. Hall, and from the works of E. P. Thompson, Raymond Williams, Peter Burke, and, in particular, from Kevin M. Sweeney's work on eighteenth-century society and material culture in the Connecticut River Valley.

1. Inventory of Samuel Porter of Hadley, Hampshire County Probate Records, box 177, no. 25 (1722), Probate Court of Hampshire County (hereafter HCPR), Northampton, Mass. Porter's position in the economic hierarchy of the region is based on evidence for Hartford County in Jackson Turner Main, "The Distribution of Property in Colonial Connecticut," in *The Human Dimensions of Nation Making: Essays on Colonial and Revolutionary America*, ed. James Kirby Martin (Madison, Wis., 1976), 68, table 4. On the origins and spread of consumer revolutions, see Joan Thirsk, *Economic Policy and Projects: The Development of a Consumer Society in Early Modern England* (Oxford, 1978), and Chandra Mukerji, *From Graven Images: Patterns of Modern Materialism* (New York, 1983), 30–130.

2. Howard W. Odum and Harry Estill Moore, "The Implications and Meanings of Regionalism," in *American Regionalism: A Cultural-Historical Approach to National Integration*, ed. Odum and Moore (New York, 1938), 29–34. For further discussion of the meaning of "region" in American scholarship, see Vernon Carstensen, "The Development and Application of Regional-Sectional Concepts, 1900–1950," in *Regionalism in America*, ed. Merrill Jensen (Madison, Wis., 1951), 99–118.

3. Fred Kniffen, "Folk Housing: Key to Diffusion," *Annals of the Association of American Geographers* 55, no. 4 (1965): 568–69, 577; Henry H. Glassie, *Pattern in the Material Folk Culture of the Eastern United States* (Philadelphia, 1968), 34–39. Glassie adds that although his own work was modeled after Kniffen's, he feels their conclusions differ; Glassie states (p. 34n) that Kniffen may have underestimated the influence of the Tidewater area on inland Southern culture. Glassie's maps (pp. 37–39) should be compared with those in Kniffen, "Folk Housing: Key to Diffusion," 560, 570, 572, 573, and with those in Hans Kurath, *A Word Geography of the Eastern United States* (Ann Arbor, Mich., 1949), figs. 2, 3; see also the comments in Glassie, "Eighteenth-Century Cultural Process in Delaware Valley Folk Building," *Winterthur Portfolio* 7 (1972): 31–32. Regions are analytically useful because of their historical integrity, a point made by Louis Wirth: "The regional idea owes its scientific vitality to the fact that it offers a naturalistic and empirically verifiable theory for the interpretation of history. It affords a check on other competing theories in that it keeps the investigator's feet planted on the solid ground of the physical conditions of existence" ("The Limits of Regionalism," in *Regionalism in America*, ed. Jensen, 381).

4. Kurath, *Handbook of the Linguistic Geography of New England* (Providence, R.I., 1939), 8–10, 18–22; Amelia F. Miller, *Connecticut River Valley Doorways: An Eighteenth-Century Flowering* (Boston 1983); John T. Kirk, *Connecticut Furniture, Seventeenth and Eighteenth Centuries* (Hartford, Conn., 1967). Furniture patterns are also clarified in Michael K. Brown, "Scalloped-Top Furniture of the Connecticut River Valley," *Antiques* 117 (1980): 1092–99; Kevin M. Sweeney, "Furniture and Furniture Making in Mid-Eighteenth-Century Wethersfield, Connecticut," *Antiques* 125 (1984): 1156–63; and Leigh Keno, "The Windsor-Chair Makers of Northampton, Massachusetts, 1790–1820," *Antiques* 117 (1980): 1100–1108. An important linkage between the diffusionist dialectal work of Kurath and furniture study is suggested in Kirk, *American Chairs: Queen Anne and Chippendale* (New York, 1972), 105–8. Scholarship on gravestones is dominated by Caulfield; see, among others, his "Connecticut Gravestones III [:Ebenezer Drake]," *Bulletin of the Connecticut Historical Society* 18, no. 4 (1953): 25–32; "Connecticut Gravestones V [:Thomas Johnson / Thomas Johnson II / Thomas Johnson III]," *Bulletin of the Connecticut Historical Society* 21, no. 1 (1956): 1–21; and "Connecticut Gravestones XIV, Part I: William Buckland (1727–1795)," *Bulletin of the Connecticut Historical Society* 41, no. 2 (1976): 33–56.

5. While semiotic approaches to artifact study suggest that objects are empty vessels whose "meanings" are provisionally assigned and shift situationally, some artifacts in all cultures are less context-dependent than others. My own interest here is to discover the values that some artifacts actively assert irrespective of situation. This approach, at once phenomenological and structural, is discussed in Robert Plant Armstrong, *The Affecting Presence: An Essay in Humanistic Anthropology* (Urbana, Ill., 1971), 3–54, and made relevant to American materials in Henry Glassie, "Meaningful Things and Appropriate Myths: The Artifact's Place in American Studies," in this volume.

6. John Demos, *A Little Commonwealth: Family Life in Plymouth Colony* (New York, 1970), 21. The work of E. P. Thompson has helped me worry productively about the methodological difficulties of reconstructing the values and moral configurations of past societies. As artifacts enact cultural values, they address what Thompson sees as a major gap in Marxist theory; see "Interview with E. P. Thompson (1976)," in *Visions of History*, ed. Harry Abelove et al. (New York, 1984), 20. See also the critical comments in Raphael Samuel, "Art, Politics, and Ideology: Editorial Introduction," *History Workshop* 6 (Autumn 1978): 101–6, and Geoff Eley and Keith Neild, "Why Does Social History Ignore Politics?" *Social History* 5, no. 2 (1980): 268–69.

7. Raymond Williams, *Marxism and Literature* (New York, 1977), 132.

8. On social homogeneity, see Marshall E. Dimock's comment that "regionalism results from the growth of a sense of community, in turn dependent upon common traditions, interests and aspirations," quoted in Odum and Moore, "Implications and Meanings of Regionalism," in *American Regionalism*, ed. Odum and Moore, 23; Rupert B. Vance's suggestion that "each region must differ from neighboring regions, but must approximate a mode of homogeneous characteristics if it is to possess identity," in Vance, "The Regional Concept as a Tool for Social Research," in *Regionalism in America*, ed. Jensen, 123; and Michael K. Brown's assertion that the distinctive scalloped-top case furniture of the Connecticut River Valley proves "the homogeneity of the population of the valley" in Brown, "Scalloped-Top Furniture," 1096–97. On consensus as the goal of regional studies, see the comments of Odum and Moore in these two papers: Odum, "The Role of Industry in Regional Development," in *Folk, Region, and Society: Selected Papers of Howard W. Odum*, ed. Katherine Jocher et al. (Chapel Hill, N.C., 1964), 143: "The theme of American regionalism is, after all, essentially that of a great American Nation, the land and the people, in whose continuity and unity of development . . . must be found not only the testing grounds of American democracy but, according to many observers, the hope of American civilization"; and Odum and Moore, "Implications and Meanings of Regionalism," in *American Regionalism*, ed. Odum and Moore, 4: "Regionalism is a symbol of America's geographic as opposed to occupational representation; of *popular as opposed to class control*" (emphasis added).

9. "Regional consciousness" is E. P. Thompson's term; see his "The Moral Economy of the English Crowd in the Eighteenth Century," *Past and Present* 50 (February 1971): 100; Raymond Williams, *The Country and the City* (New York, 1973), 182. The family ties among the valley gentry are treated selectively in Kevin M. Sweeney, "River Gods in the Making: The Williamses of Western Massachusetts," in *The Bay and the River, 1600–1900*, ed. Peter Benes (Boston, 1982), 101–16, and in Robert Zemsky, *Merchants, Farmers, and River Gods: An Essay in Eighteenth-Century American Politics* (Boston, 1971), 28–76; see also Edward M. Cook, *Fathers of the Towns* (Baltimore, 1976), 177.

10. John Winthrop, "A Model of Christian Charity," in *The Puritans*, ed. Perry Miller and Thomas H. Johnson, 2 vols. (New York, 1963), 1:195. See Stephen Innes, *Labor in a New Land: Economy and Society in Seventeenth-Century Springfield* (Princeton, N.J., 1983).

11. Letter from Robert Child to Samuel Hartlib, Dec. 24, 1645, reprinted in G. H. Turnbull, "Robert Child," in *Publications of the Colonial Society of Massachusetts* 38 (1959): 51.

12. *The Acts and Resolves . . . of the Province of Massachusetts Bay*, 21 vols. (Boston, 1869–1922), 1:226 (emphasis added). The extent to which an individual could contribute to the market was an overt basis of taxation and an index of social status; see the March 1669/70 "List of Families in Windsor with Quantity of Grain in Possession of Each," and similar lists for Hartford and Wethersfield in *Wyllys Papers*, in *Collections of the Connecticut Historical Society* 21 (1924): 190–97. Good discussions of regional economic history include W. Isard, "Regional Science, The Concept of Region, and Regional Structure," and M. E. Garnsey, "The Dimensions of Regional Science," both in *Papers and Proceedings of the Regional Science Association* 2 (1956): 13–26, 27–39; see also Preston E. James, "Toward a Further Understanding of the Regional Concept," *Annals of the Association of American Geographers* 42, no. 3 (1952): 195–222.

13. On the role of merchants in controlling the growth and structure of agrarian capitalism, see E. P. Thompson, "Eighteenth-Century English Society: Class Struggle without Class?" *Social History* 3, no. 2 (1978): 139: "We are habituated to think of capitalism as something that occurs at ground level, at the point of production. In the early eighteenth century wealth was created at this lowly level, but it rose rapidly to higher regions, accumulated in great gobbets, and the real killings were to be made in the distribution, cornering and sale of goods or raw materials (wool, grain, meat, sugar, cloth, tea, tobacco, slaves), in the manipulation of credit, and in the seizure of the offices of State." See also Williams, *The Country and the City*, 60, 104. While clinging to a myth of a "subsistence economy" mediated by progressive merchants, Margaret E. Martin, "Merchants and Trade of the Connecticut River Valley, 1750–1820," *Smith College Studies in History* 24, nos. 1–4 (October 1938–July 1939), ably describes the wealth and range of activities that specific individuals pursued. See also Richard Bushman, *From Puritan to Yankee: Character and the Social Order in Connecticut, 1690–1765* (New York, 1970), 61–64, 114, and Richard B. Sheridan, "The Domestic Economy," in *Colonial British America: Essays in the New History of the Early Modern Era*, ed. Jack P. Greene and J. R. Pole (Baltimore, 1984), 71.

14. In particular, see Sweeney, "River Gods in the Making"; Sweeney, "Mansion People: Kinship, Class, and Architecture in Western Massachusetts in the Mid-Eighteenth Century," *Winterthur Portfolio* 19, no. 4 (1984): 231–55; and Robert H. Taylor, *Western Massachusetts in the Revolution* (Providence, R.I., 1954); Howard Newby, "The Deferential Dialectic," *Comparative Studies in Society and History* 17, no. 2 (1975): 149–50; see also J. G. A. Pocock, "The

Classical Theory of Deference," *American Historical Review* 81, no. 3 (1976): 516–23.

15. Inventory, Col. Fisher Gay, Farmington, 1779, Farmington District, file 1051, Connecticut State Library (hereafter CSL), Hartford.

16. Inventory, Ezekiel Porter, Wethersfield, 1775, Hartford District, file 4344, CSL.

17. Inventory, Rev. William Russell, Windsor, 1775, Hartford District, file 4686, CSL.

18. Quoted from Stoddard in the Diary of Rev. Stephen Williams of Longmeadow, Mass., Aug. 10, 1721; see Sweeney, "River Gods in the Making," 104.

19. Sweeney, "River Gods in the Making," 113–14; Joseph Dwight's business dealings are summarized in Zemsky, *Merchants, Farmers, and River Gods*, 54–56.

20. Quoted in Robert Gross, *The Minutemen and Their World* (New York, 1976), 37.

21. Zemsky, *Merchants, Farmers, and River Gods*, 32–33.

22. Quoted in Zemsky, *Merchants, Farmers, and River Gods*, 58. For a summary of how other Massachusetts merchants used political offices and "charitable trusts" and social welfare institutions of their own creation for personal ends, see Peter Dobkin Hall, "Family Structure and Economic Organization: Massachusetts Merchants, 1700–1850," in *Family and Kin in Urban Communities, 1700–1930*, ed. Tamara K. Haraven (New York, 1977), 47–49, 58.

23. Inventory, Samuel Porter, Hadley, 1722, box 117, no. 25, HCPR, quoted in Sweeney, "River Gods in the Making," 114, 115.

24. Inventories, Samuel Porter, Hadley, and Seth Wetmore [Whitmore], Middletown, Middletown District, file 3853, CSL. For period references to individuals being called "landlord," see John Montague Smith, *History of the Town of Sunderland, Massachusetts, 1673–1899* (Greenfield, Mass., 1899), 194, and John H. Lockwood, *Westfield and Its Historic Influences, 1669–1919: The Life of an Early Town* (Springfield, Mass., 1922), 567.

25. See Abbott Lowell Cummings, *The Framed Houses of Massachusetts Bay, 1625–1725* (Cambridge, Mass., 1979), 98, 101–3, 116; Robert Blair St. George, "'Set Thine House in Order': The Domestication of the Yeomanry in Seventeenth-Century New England," in *New England Begins*, ed. Jonathan L. Fairbanks and Robert F. Trent, 2 vols. (Boston, 1982), 2:166–67, 200–201. "Theater of dominance" is Thompson's phrase; see "Eighteenth-Century English Society," 150.

26. See Batty Langley, *The Builder's Jewel; Or, The Youth's Instructor and Workman's Remembrancer . . .* (London, 1746), plates 89, 90, 92, and Francis Price, *The British Carpenter; Or, A Treatise on Carpentry* (London, 1733), plate I–K (B). I am indebted to Robert F. Trent and Kevin M. Sweeney for helping me measure the Webb house roof.

27. Sweeney, "Mansion People," 242.

28. Account book, Joseph Webb, Sr., Wethersfield, 1751–59, 121, Connecticut Historical Society. I am indebted to Kevin M. Sweeney for sharing this reference with me.

29. Account book, Joseph Webb, Sr., 121.

30. Inventory, Roger Wolcott, Windsor, 1767, Hartford District, file 6200, CSL. Sweeney, "Mansion People," 239–40, discusses the similar "region-wide" building campaign of Elisha Williams in 1751–54; these examples suggest that the extensive use of labor was an important social component in the definition of an elite architectural "style."

31. Among the many slaveholders in the Connecticut River Valley, Rev. William Russell of Windsor owned "a Negro Man Named Dan" worth £50, Thomas Seymour of Hartford owned "a Negro Man named Tam" and "One Negro Named Neptune" together valued at £80, and Seth Wetmore of Middletown owned "6 Negroes" valued at £300 (inventories of William Russell, Hartford District, file 4686; Thomas Seymour, Hartford District, file 4808; and Seth Wetmore, Middletown District, file 3853, CSL). See also Gwendolyn Wright, *Building the Dream: A Social History of Housing in America* (Cambridge, Mass., 1981), 46–47.

32. Miller, *Connecticut Valley Doorways*.

33. The average estate values are based on inventories in HCPR and CSL for those individuals who were responsible for erecting doorways as listed in Miller, *Connecticut Valley Doorways*; inventory of Josiah Dwight of Springfield, 1768, box 51, no. 25, HCPR; Miller, *Connecticut Valley Doorways*, 21, 26–27, 36–39, 79; Sweeney, "Mansion People," 248–49.

34. Williams, *The Country and the City*, 106; Williams adds that during the period of eighteenth-century agrarian improvement, "much of the profit of a more modern agriculture went not into productive investment but into that explicit social declaration: a mutually competitive but still uniform exposition, at every turn, of an established and commanding class power." The axis of domestic authority in gentry households defined a one-point physical and social perspective; see Thompson, "Eighteenth-Century English Society," 136: "the great house is at the apex, and all lines of communication run to its dining-room, estate office or kennels." On the transferal of strategies of gentry dominance in general, see Bushman, "American High Style and Vernacular Cultures," in Greene and Pole, *Colonial British America*, 360–67. I argue here that Bushman's proposed "top-down" model of social diffusion was conditioned by the selective adoption of only those features needed to perpetuate a "traditional" aristocratic social order in a specific locale. For introductory comments on reading the landscape with concepts of power in mind, see Edward W. Soja, *The Political Organization of Space*, Commission on College Geography Resource Paper no. 8 (Washington, D.C., 1971).

35. Inventory, Ezekiel Porter, Wethersfield, 1775, Hartford District, file 4344, CSL.

36. See the list of occupations for 35 known River Gods in Sweeney, "Mansion People," 255 (appendix); an abstracted list for Hampshire County is in Sweeney, "River Gods in the Making," 109, table 2.

37. Lewis Mumford, "Orozco in New England," *New Republic* 80 (1934): 235.

38. Samuel Willard, *A Compleat Body of Divinity* (Boston, 1726), 233. The doorway as a disjunctive icon engages directly Erving Goffman's definition of a region as "any

place that is bounded by some degree by barriers to perception" (*Presentation of Self in Everyday Life* [Garden City, N.Y., 1959], 106).

39. Allan I. Ludwig, *Graven Images: New England Stonecarving and Its Symbols, 1650–1815* (Middletown, Conn., 1966), 73 (plate 3a–d), 132 (plate 48a), 169 (plate 77b), 400 (plate 237b, c), 402 (plate 238a). Ludwig discusses the Samuel Dwight stone on pp. 142–43 (plate 56a), 233, related to the Dwight stone is the Gamaliel Ripley stone, 1799, Scotland, Conn., p. 144 (plate 57b). The Martha Welch stone is discussed on pp. 135–36 (plates 50–51), but to a different end than I am using it here. The Dwight and Welch stones memorialize wealthy individuals; Dwight was worth £2,918 at his death in 1763, while Welch, the wife of Rev. Daniel Welch of Storrs, was, as her epitaph notes, "the only daughter of Mr. Moses Cook & Mrs. Deborah Cook of Hartford." Moses Cook's estate totalled £420 in 1778; inventories of Samuel Dwight, Enfield, 1764, Hartford District, file 1792, and of Moses Cook, Hartford, 1778, Hartford District, file 1384, CSL.

40. Miller, *Connecticut Valley Doorways,* 56–57. Miller adds that buff-colored paint was used to enhance the appearance of rusticated stone on the doorway to Ichabod Camp's Middletown mansion (p. 26).

41. Thomas Anburey, *Travels through the Interior Parts of America,* ed. William Harding Carter, 2 vols. (Boston, 1923), 2:41.

42. Armstrong, *The Powers of Presence: Consciousness, Myth, and Affecting Presence* (Philadelphia, 1981), 5–8, locates one aspect of the aesthetic power of an object in the tension between person-ness and thing-ness.

43. On the crucial relationship of powers "owned" by artifacts to the assertion of values in society, see Armstrong, *The Affecting Presence: Wellspring: On the Myth and Source of Culture* (Berkeley, Calif., 1975); and *The Powers of Presence;* see also Yi-Fu Tuan, "The Significance of the Artifact," *Geographical Journal* 70, no. 4 (1980): 464–65; and Suzanne Preston Blier, "Houses Are Human: Architectural Self-Images of Africa's Tamberma," *Journal of the Society of Architectural Historians* 42, no. 4 (1983): 371–82.

44. Quoted from the diary of Rev. Stephen Williams in *Proceedings at the Centennial Celebration of the Incorporation of Longmeadow, October 17th, 1883, with Numerous Historical Appendices and a Town Genealogy* (Longmeadow, Mass., 1884), 34.

45. Quoted in Gross, *The Minutemen and Their World,* 38; *Boston Town Records, 1770–1777,* in *A Report of the Record Commissioners of the City of Boston* (Boston, 1887), 18:16; quoted in John L. Brooke, "Society, Revolution, and the Symbolic Uses of the Dead: An Historical Ethnography of the Massachusetts Near Frontier, 1730–1820" (Ph.D. diss., University of Pennsylvania, 1982), 288 (emphasis added).

46. On the persistence of common fields in the upper valley, see J. H. Temple and George Sheldon, *History of the Town of Northfield, Massachusetts, for 150 Years* (Albany, 1875), 22, 219–20. *Diary and Autobiography of John Adams,* ed. Lyman H. Butterfield, Leonard Faber, and Wendell D. Garrett, 4 vols. (Cambridge, Mass., 1962), 2:28; "Essay on the Laying Out of Towns, &c," *Collections of the Massachusetts Historical Society,* 5th ser., 1 (1871): 479; Cotton Mather, "Triparadisus," ca. 1720 MSS, octavo vol. 49, f. 1, Mather Family Papers, 1613–1819, American Antiquarian Society, Worcester, Mass. I am indebted to David Watters for telling me about this manuscript. On the circular form of common-field villages, see John Barrell, *The Idea of Landscape and the Sense of Place, 1730–1840: An Approach to the Poetry of John Clare* (Cambridge, 1972), 103–6.

47. See the quantitative data from inventories discussed earlier in Kevin M. Sweeney, "Furniture and the Domestic Environment in Wethersfield, Connecticut, 1639–1800," table 1 and table 2; Anburey, *Travels through America,* ed. Carter, 2:152–53.

48. Cornelius v. Tienhoven, "Information Relative to Taking Up Land in New Netherland, in the Form of Colonies or Private Boweries (1650)," in *Remarkable Providences: 1600–1760,* ed. John Demos (New York, 1972), 48.

49. Here I mean to complicate current theory on the cultural meaning of "Georgianization." Most see in it the emergence of a new set of values supporting individualism, privacy, and control that undercut the collective mentality of the "peasant community"; Henry Glassie, in "Eighteenth-Century Cultural Process in Delaware Valley Folk Building," states that Georgian houses define a landscape in which "there is also the beginning and fulfillment of the dominant style of America, loose, worried, acquisitive individualism," while in pre-Georgian "traditional" houses "there is a lingering sense of the tightness of the English or German peasant with his clustered, corporate modes" (p. 57). Building on this key insight, I suggest the following: agrarian capitalism and radical social inequality based on separate value systems were in fact part of the New England settlement process itself. I maintain here that elites already nurtured these values while strategically identifying their houses with those of their social inferiors. Whether in England, Virginia, Pennsylvania, or New England, "Georgian" houses invariably appeared as the clarity and force of social hierarchy came under direct attack during periods of rapid population growth, shifting exchange relations, and occupational mobility; the fact that merchants rarely "fit" neatly into established categories of social rank accounts for their building such "modern" houses before most others in England (1630–50), Boston (1670–1710), and in the Connecticut River Valley (1740–60). From this point of view, such houses paradoxically represent not only the "beginning . . . of a dominant style" but also the anxious gasps of fading aristocrats whose retreat to self-mystification and "worried" anonymity was their last base of authority.

50. Marcel Mauss, *The Gift: Forms and Functions of Exchange in Archaic Societies,* trans. Ian Cunnison (New York, 1967), 72; see also Newby, "Deferential Dialectic," 161–63.

51. Peter Bohan and Phillip Hammerslough, *Early Connecticut Silver, 1700–1840* (Middletown, Conn., 1970), 40 (plate 17), 114 (plate 90). A few valley elites even had sets of

communion vessels carved on their gravestones, symboliz-ing at the same time their gifts to the earthly congregation and their hope for communion with God in death; see Lud-wig, *Graven Images*, 177 (plate 83), 178 (plate 84a–c), 179 (plate 85a).

52. Sweeney, "River Gods in the Making," 116; invento-ries of Col. Fisher Gay of Farmington, 1779, Farmington District, file 1051, and of Alexander Allyn, Windsor, 1790, Hartford District, file 77, CSL.

53. Anburey, *Travels through America*, 2:152–53; quoted in Sweeney, "Furniture and the Domestic Environment in Wethersfield," in this volume, p. 287; see the additional in-stances cited in Sweeney, "Mansion People," 249–50.

54. See Miller, *Connecticut Valley Doorways*, 20, 66, 86, 90.

55. Miller, *Connecticut Valley Doorways*, 50.

56. The tailor: Capt. Nathaniel Talcott of Glastonbury; the shoemaker: Jacob Griswold of Wethersfield; the joiner: Judah Woodruff of Farmington. Woodruff built his house in 1762; see Miller, *Connecticut Valley Doorways*, 24 (no. 7), 129–30.

57. The concepts of "interregnum" and "interlude of re-lease" are explained in a related Latin American context in George A. Kubler, "The Arts: Fine and Plain," in *Perspec-tives on American Folk Art*, ed. Ian M. G. Quimby and Scott T. Swank (New York, 1980), 237–38. It is precisely this moment of interregnum that is characterized by class con-sciousness but not an articulated, abstract concept of "class"; see Thompson, "Eighteenth-Century English Soci-ety," 151.

58. Miller, *Connecticut Valley Doorways*, 120–30 sum-marizes the working careers of known doorway makers.

59. The 1792 Hartford agreement is reprinted in Irving W. Lyon, *The Colonial Furniture of New England* (1891; re-print ed., New York, 1977), 267–70.

60. *The Connecticut Courant*, Aug. 10, 1795, quoted in John Warner Barber, *Connecticut Historical Collections* (New Haven, Conn., 1836), 56.

61. Thompson, "Eighteenth-Century English Society," 152.

62. *Hartford Courant*, Dec. 30, 1799, quoted in Barber, *Connecticut Historical Collections*, 58. On the impact of industrialization on one valley town, see Agnes Hannay, *A Chronicle of Industry on the Mill River* (1936; reprint ed., New York, 1977).

63. Dwight, *Travels*, 2:229. Dwight's idealism in hind-sight reinforces Thompson's belief that "paternalism as myth or as ideology is nearly always backward looking" ("Eighteenth-Century English Society," 136).

White and Black Landscapes in Eighteenth-Century Virginia

DELL UPTON

In the following essay, Dell Upton explores a basic, though often ignored, historical question: can we describe the living, experiential encounters between people and the landscapes they create? If so, how? With the exception of objects in museum installations, we seldom if ever confront artifacts in isolation. Instead, fields, fences, buildings, and household furniture form a structured totality, which we perceive differently as we move through it. Our perception of a building is conditioned by who we are, where we have already been, what we have already seen, and where we believe we are headed. In leading us into the carefully contrived landscapes of white and black Virginians in the eighteenth century, Upton argues that if architecture structured daily experience on plantations, then it also served as a subtle and effective means of manipulating time and consciousness. The landscape, then, was an extension of ideological process.

We can break the landscape of eighteenth-century Virginia into two contingent segments. The world of the great white planters consisted of contrived collections of buildings and spaces ordered by sequences of social barriers: rows of trees, terraces, dependencies, the kitchen. Finally, the house itself confronted the white visitor with more barriers: portico, doorway, grand stair hall, chambers for waiting, chambers for formal talking, chambers for formal dining. The whole was a carefully orchestrated exercise in the definition of status; every barrier successfully passed was a mark of preference. Each great house was a vortex of local power sustained through its centrality in commerce, education, rituals of hospitality, and politics. And this highly structured but fluid white domestic landscape was metaphorically reenacted in ecclesiastical life (in churches), judicial affairs (in courthouses), and popular entertainments (in horse-racing and cockfighting).

In contrast to the dominant white landscape, spaces structured by blacks (and poor whites) were sparsely furnished, one- or two-room houses segregated in Quarters distant from the big house. The domain of blacks extended from these flimsy cottages into adjacent work areas—fields, shops, and gardens. Despite the barriers the main house offered to white visitors, blacks could pass into its back entries directly, invisibly. As Upton points out, this informal access allowed slaves a meaningful, if limited, opportunity to undercut the contrived quality of white planter society. Living in a world that offered them little real authority, blacks and poor whites viewed the landscape from a different perspective. Rather than living in a dynamic environment whose aesthetic power was rooted in movement—perhaps the white planters' interest in defending rigid social hierarchy forwarded "movement" as a disguise for maintaining the status quo—slaves conceived of the landscape as a series of fixed points between which movement often seemed indeterminate at best. As much as the great planters and their impressive houses seemed to dominate the landscape, their hegemony was never total. The white and black landscapes of eighteenth-century Virginia merge into a single polyvocal text whose divergent messages compete for our close attention.

For me, one of the most engaging problems in architectural history is to understand the social experience of architecture.[1] To the extent that such an effort is possible, it requires us to account for the entire range of spatial divisions from the scale of furnishings to that of settlement patterns. An individual's perception of a landscape changes with the experience of moving through it. It is less obvious but equally true that an apparently unified landscape may actually be composed of several fragmentary ones, some sharing common elements of the larger assemblage. Indeed, this may be the only way to make sense of certain historical landscapes, such as

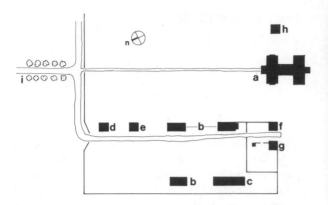

Fig. 1. Tuckahoe plantation, Goochland County, Virginia; site plan showing the main house (*a*), slave houses (*b*), a slave house converted to a stable (*c*), storehouse (*d*), smokehouse (*e*), office or dairy (*f*), kitchen (*g*), schoolhouse (*h*), and cedar lane (*i*). Buildings *a, b* (except the northwest slave house), *e, f,* and *h* date from the eighteenth century; the rest of the structures were built in the nineteenth century. (Drawing by Dell Upton.)

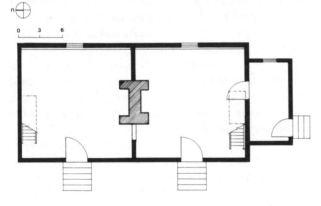

Fig. 2. Plan of slave house at Tuckahoe, Goochland County, Virginia, built in eighteenth century. (Drawing by Carol Silverman.)

Fig. 3. Slave house at Tuckahoe. (Photograph by Dell Upton.)

architectural history worked to create a landscape meant to be experienced dynamically, one that depended on memory and the rapid dissolution and reformulation of individual experiences to establish its meanings.[3] Though similar methods and similar visual forms were used in Europe, what is distinctive about Virginia is the way that they were adapted to a particular, extant, social setting.

Against the plantation houses and their surroundings, we can set the houses of slaves. While a relatively large number of planters' mansions have survived to be studied, and while contemporary descriptions of them are available, slave houses are less well documented. Native whites rarely mentioned them, although comments on slave life were an obligatory element in travelers' accounts in the last quarter of the eighteenth century. These and the few surviving slave houses suggest a variety of conditions of slave life, centering around readily described norms. Slaves lived in houses of many sizes and equally varied quality. The extant structures misrepresent the norm in both their size and quality but can serve to illustrate those norms.

A group of four slave houses at Tuckahoe, Goochland County, includes three that were probably built in the second half of the eighteenth century. All are

that of pre-Revolutionary Virginia, with its racially and socially stratified population.

The twentieth-century obsession with time as experienced by individuals, time as evanescent states of consciousness linked by memory, has roots in the eighteenth century. The modern concept of history is a product of that century, and the attempt to represent and manipulate time and consciousness in architecture also originated then.[2] Virginians shared in that effort. The elite builders of the great eighteenth-century mansions that are familiar from traditional

Fig. 4. Slave house at Howard's Neck plantation, Goochland County, Virginia, built in the mid-nineteenth century. (Photograph by Dell Upton.)

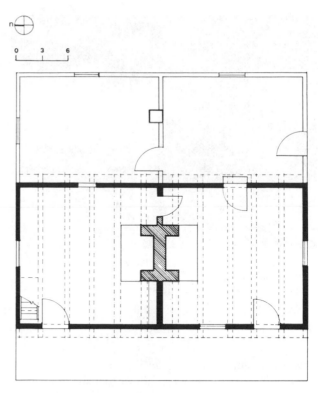

Fig. 5. Plan of slave house at Howard's Neck. (Drawing by Carol Silverman.)

one-story frame buildings with two rooms, each with an exterior door, and separated by a central chimney (figs. 1, 2). In the best-preserved structure, the interior opening between the rooms is a nineteenth-century alteration. Thus, while the building appears relatively large, it really consists of two separate one-room units, one with access to a loft, the other without. A single room and possibly a loft above, shared by six to twenty-four people, was the standard slave dwelling in eighteenth-century Virginia, though a favored slave like Landon Carter's Johnny or Joseph Ball's Jo might have a one- or even a two-room dwelling to himself.[4] The rooms in the Tuckahoe quarter illustrated here are relatively large by eighteenth-century standards. According to such documentary evidence as newspaper advertisements, building contracts, and court records, slave houses might be as little as twelve by eight feet in size. Dwellings larger than sixteen by twenty feet were divided, as the Tuckahoe houses were, into two units.

Quality varied as much as size. Again, the surviving structures are misleading. The houses at Tuckahoe were upgraded in the nineteenth century and are now well-finished framed buildings with glazed windows, plastered interiors, and painted exteriors (fig. 3). Other eighteenth-century slave houses were built of brick. Most, though, were less well constructed. From the third quarter of the eighteenth century, log was the dominant material for the houses of a

large proportion of Virginia's slaves. Two of three nineteenth-century quarters at Howard's Neck, Goochland County, are well-preserved examples of better-quality log slave houses of a sort that were common in the eighteenth century (fig. 4). None survives from that period. They are V-notched hewn-log structures that stand on brick piers about a foot from the ground at the east and three feet at the west. The central building is the best preserved, though all were originally identical in form and the two log buildings in detail as well. As usual, each room in plan has a front door, and an original interior door connects the two rooms of the house. A brick chimney and a log partition that stops a foot from the ceiling separate the two rooms (fig. 5). A ladder stair, its foot almost against the wall, gives access to an unfinished loft from the southwest corner of the western room. The ceiling joists are round logs about seven inches in diameter, which pass through the walls and form eaves about a foot deep on the front and the rear (fig. 6). All original windows except one on the rear wall of the west room are gone. The opening on the rear wall is a

Fig. 6. Interior of slave house at Howard's Neck, showing whitewashed finish, round-log joists in ceiling, fireplace, and original window opening with shutter track. (Photograph by Dell Upton.)

Fig. 7. Back wall of slave house at Howard's Neck, showing log construction and original exterior treatment. (Photograph by Dell Upton.)

two-foot-square hole set two feet from the floor and closed by a single wooden shutter that slid from side to side in a track. A scar shows that the door leading from the east room to the rear lean-to replaces a similar rear window there. If there were any windows on the end walls of the house, they were similar to the surviving opening. There were no windows in the front wall until the twentieth century.

The addition of sheds to the rear of the quarter protects the original exterior treatment there, which consisted of whitewash applied directly to the logs (fig. 7). The inside was decorated in the same way with whitewash on log. Other interior treatment includes holes drilled in the front wall between the window and the partition in the west room. These one-inch-diameter piercings were intended to hold sticks that supported shelves or served as hooks. Alterations made after slavery to adapt all the houses are telling: the buildings were covered with weatherboards, kitchen-bedroom sheds were added, finished floors and glazed windows were installed, and porches were built along the front.

The Howard's Neck quarters illustrate the lack of built-in furniture and storage space that characterized eighteenth- and nineteenth-century quarters. The slave occupants of the houses probably installed many fittings and furnishings privately. These might

include shelves, either fixed in a niche next to the fireplace or of a movable variety supported on round sticks set into holes drilled into the wall, like those at Howard's Neck. Similarly, spikes might be driven into the rafters for drying herbs and other plants, a common practice in Virginia houses of all sizes. Less evident but probably equally common were cubby holes and root cellars, which are small holes, about three feet in every direction, similar to one described in Booker T. Washington's nineteenth-century boyhood home in Franklin County, Virginia: "In the center of the earthen floor [was] a large, deep opening covered with boards, which was used as a place in which to store sweet potatoes during the winter."[5]

The amenity mentioned most often was a bed, which might be the only comfort provided. A French visitor to the Shenandoah Valley found a house with "a box-like frame made of boards hardly roughed down, upheld by stakes [and] some wheat straw and cornstalks, on which was spread a very short-napped woolen blanket that was burned in several places."[6] Aside from these items, few owners provided much beyond an iron pot for cooking. To augment them slaves occasionally appropriated to themselves small things from the plantation stock and purchased or made other personal possessions. The most conspicuous of these in travelers' accounts were the musical instruments, particularly fiddles and banjos, that many slaves could play.[7]

One can think of the quarters as standing for the houses of all black and white people who were not great planters, for in many respects the physical characteristics of the quarters—small, flimsy, and sparsely furnished—merely reflected the slaves' status as poor people in Virginia. Their houses were indistinguishable in size, elaboration, and quality from those of white "common planters." But where poor whites' spartan conditions reflected their lack of economic success, the poverty of slaves on large plantations was the result of the appropriation of their labor to the enrichment of the planter and his decision not to return much of it to the slaves in the form of either material goods or time to produce them. But what of the landscape?

The quarter extended beyond its walls. The space around the building was as important as the building itself. At Howard's Neck, for example, the three surviving quarters are set in a line at precisely one-hundred-foot intervals, allowing for ample development of the surroundings (fig. 8). Here slaves socialized. Their chickens and dogs lived here. More important, here were the gardens where slaves grew produce to supplement their diets and to give them something to barter with or to give away in return for services. All eighteenth-century observers agreed on the importance of these "little Spots allow'd them [to] cultivate, at Vacant times."[8]

Slave quarters were parts of two intersecting landscapes. They fit into a white landscape centered on the main house in one way and into a black landscape centered on the quarters in another. From the master's point of view, slave quarters were part of a working landscape that dictated to some degree their siting and location. Quarters for house slaves were often close to the main house on large plantations, and they were carefully ordered in rows or "streets."

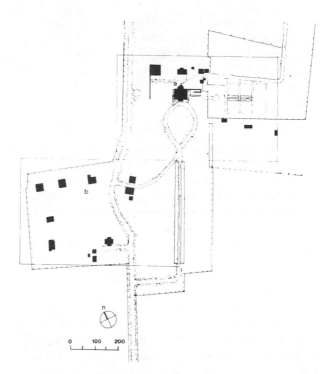

Fig. 8. Howard's Neck plantation, Goochland County, Virginia; site plan showing main house area (a) and slave quarter area (b), based on fieldwork by Dell Upton and by the Agricultural Buildings Project, Colonial Williamsburg Foundation. (Drawing by Carol Silverman.)

If they were visible from the house, they were arranged on the site and treated on their exteriors with an eye to the visual effect from the main house. Other planters hid them from the eye, and in those cases they were usually plainer but were nevertheless carefully sited and arranged. The Howard's Neck quarters are part of this sort of arrangement. Howard's Neck is an extensive complex on the north side of the James River. The domestic buildings, which were occupied in 1825, include a large brick house, a brick kitchen, and an orangerie, along with several other frame structures. This group sits on a knoll at the top of a rise that falls away irregularly to the south and west toward the river. Southwest of the house at the edge of the lawn are some frame worksheds and stables, and behind these stretches the quarter complex.[9]

William Hugh Grove saw similar plantation groups as he sailed up the York River in 1732. Like many other travelers in the seventeenth and eighteenth centuries, he likened them to villages. The river, he wrote, "has pleasant Seats on the Bank which Shew Like little villages, for having Kitchins, Dayry houses, Barns, Stables, Store houses, and some of them 2 or 3 Negro Quarters all Seperate from Each other but near the mansions houses which make a shew to the river of 7 or 8 distinct Tenements, tho all belong to one family."[10]

The outsider's image of the village is important in understanding the white and black landscapes of the slave society, for it provides a means with which to grasp the different views that the two groups held of it and the different roles each performed in it. From the first years of settlement, white Virginians expressed concern over the failure to create a city- and village-based society with a hierarchical institutional structure. While some historians have pointed out that the public institutions that towns provided were present in Virginia in dispersed locations before the mid-eighteenth century, it is more useful for our purposes to concentrate on the village metaphor. The private plantation usurped in many respects the functions of the town, and the planter appropriated to himself the prerogatives and the good of the community. In effect, the plantation *was* a village, with the planter's house as its town hall. But the economic activities of this village were intended to enrich a single individual, so far as it was in his power to control them, and the economic health of the community was judged by the planter's profits.[11]

The plantation complex was a commercial center, where the goods of the common planter were gathered and shipped with those of the great planter to Europe. Here the common planter could purchase imported goods. The plantation was an educational center. The planter often kept a school at which his own and other children were tutored. More important, the plantation was a social center, at which formal entertainments—balls and house parties—were held, friends invited to dine and to stay, and strangers given the benefit of the planter's hospitality. Most of all, the plantation complex was a kind of governmental center of the plantation's residents. In this respect the plantation's resemblance to a village went beyond mere appearance. On large holdings like those of the Northern Neck planters Landon and Robert Carter, John Tayloe, or George Washington, where there were many outlying Quarters, the plantation was a kind of county seat, an administrative center

that affected the lives even of those slaves farming the Quarters, who might come to the home house only rarely.[12]

The great planter intended that his landscape would be hierarchical, leading to himself at the center. His house was raised above the other buildings and was often set off from the surrounding countryside by a series of barriers or boundaries—fences and terraces. It was tied to the public landscape by carefully conceived roads and drives. Thomas Anburey, a traveler, noted that planters felt free to alter the public road courses for their convenience. Where the planter was particularly dominant, as Robert "King" Carter of Corotoman in Lancaster County was, his house might be connected to an important public institution like the church by a similar drive. Corotoman and Christ Church stood as equal termini of a two-way drive, with Carter as the leading figure at each end. Similar formal paths at other plantations might link the outbuildings with the main house. The schoolhouse where the tutor John Harrower lived and taught was "a neat little house at the upper end of an Avenue of planting at 500 yds. from the Main house." Philip Fithian, a more famous tutor, left an account of Nomini Hall that presents a vivid picture of this formal, hierarchical kind of landscape (fig. 9). The main house was

large, & stands on a high piece of Land [and] it may be seen a considerable distance; I have seen it at the Distance of six Miles—At equal Distances

Fig. 9. Nomini Hall plantation, Westmoreland County, Virginia, ca. 1750–75; site plan reconstructed from Philip Fithian's description, showing main house (a), schoolhouse (b), stable (c), dairy, bakehouse, and other domestic outbuildings (d), kitchen (e), coach house (f), work or wash house (g), and poplar lane to main road (h). (Drawing by Dell Upton.)

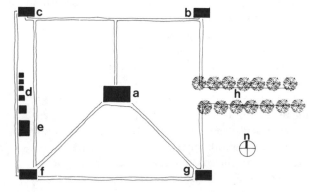

from each corner of this Building stand four other considerable Houses. . . . Due East of the Great House are two Rows of tall, flourishing, beautiful, Poplars, beginning on a Line drawn from the School to the Wash-House; these Rows are something wider than the House, & are about 300 yards Long, at the Easter[n]most end of which is the great Road leading through Westmorland to Richmond [County Court House]. These Rows of Poplars form an extremely pleasant avenue, & at the Road, through them, the House appears most romantic, at the same time that it does truly elegant—The Area of the Triangle made by the Wash-House, Stable, & School-House is perfectly levil, & designed for a bowling-Green, laid out in rectangular Walks which are paved with Brick, & covered over with burnt Oyster-Shells—In the other Triangle, made by the Wash-House, Stable, & Coach House is the Kitchen, a well-built House, as large as the School-house, Bake-House; Dairy; Store-House & several other small Houses; all which stand due West, & at a small distance from the great House, & form a handsome Street. These Building[s] stand about a quarter of a Mile from a Fork of the River Nomini, one Branch of which runs on the East of us, on which are two Mills.[13]

The white landscape, or more precisely the great planter's landscape, was both articulated and processional. It was articulated in the sense that it consisted of a network of spaces—rooms in the house, the house itself, the outbuildings, the church with its interior pews and surrounding walled churchyard, the courthouse and its walled yard—that were linked by roads and that functioned as the settings for public interactions that had their own particular character but that worked together to embody the community as a whole.[14]

The formalized layout of a great plantation complex facilitated the operation of this landscape in one form. One set of meanings, that is, was derived from moving through this microlandscape that had the individual planter at its center. At Mount Airy, the Tayloe house in Richmond County, for example, the visitor's route to the house involves passing a series of physical barriers that are also social barriers (fig. 10). One approaches along a drive that skirts a sunken park (fig. 11). The informal park contrasts with the formal layout of the house on its terraces and serves

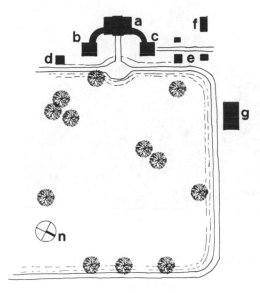

Fig. 10. Mount Airy plantation, Richmond County, Virginia, ca. 1760; site plan showing main house (*a*), family wing (*b*), kitchen and working wing (*c*), schoolhouse (*d*), eighteenth- and nineteenth-century domestic outbuildings (*e*) arranged along a street, orangerie (*f*), and early nineteenth-century stable (*g*). (Drawing by Dell Upton.)

Fig. 11. Mount Airy from the park. (Photograph by Dell Upton.)

to make the terraces appear even higher than they are. The curved drive shows the visitor the house from a variety of tantalizing prospects and ends as he or she arrives on the lower of the two terraces. The upper terrace forms a forecourt that is defined by the two advance buildings. These were originally free-standing and were connected to the house sometime

Fig. 12. Mount Airy, north facade. (Photograph by Dell Upton.)

Fig. 13. Christ Church, Lancaster County, Virginia, ca. 1730–35. The largest pews, in the chancel, were reserved for the Carters, the dominant gentry family in Lancaster County. In general, the size of the pews and the elaboration of their paneling corresponds to the social standing of the parishioners assigned to them. (Photograph by Dell Upton.)

later in the eighteenth century. The connection served to heighten the constriction of space that accompanied the passing of social barriers and the ascent of terraces and steps. Having climbed a few steps onto a terrace and then crossed it, a much higher flight of steps led one not to the main entry but to a recessed loggia (fig. 12). Then one entered a large living hall through the front door. More exclusive, but still public, rooms opened off this hall. If one came to visit the Tayloes, one would pass through a series of seven barriers before reaching one's goal, which might be the dining room table, the ritual center of Virginia hospitality. Each barrier served to reinforce the impression of John Tayloe's centrality, and each in addition affirmed the visitor's status as he or she passed through it.

The largest meanings of the articulated processional landscape, however, were perceived in the continual dissolutions and reformulations of social groups that occurred as many planters moved from one place to another within the public landscape of which the great plantation was a part. A planter moved from being the planter-among-his-family-and-slaves, for instance, to being the planter-among-his-peers doing business in the churchyard before Sunday service. The group dissolved again, and filed into the church, each to find his own pew, and thus regrouped as the planter-in-his-ranked-community (fig. 13). Or planters traveled to the courthouse village, gathered in the yard or the recessed loggia, and then went into

court, where some were arrayed on the bench as the planter-among-his-fellow-magistrates (fig. 14; see the essay by A. G. Roeber elsewhere in this volume). Each social grouping had a specific character and a particular physical manifestation that was integrated within the articulated processional landscape. In the movement from one grouping to another, from one collective pose to another, the white landscape achieved its fullest meaning.[15]

While the planter's landscape offered the image of an orderly society that focused on himself and linked him to his peers, the slave's landscape took a different form. No accounts by eighteenth-century slaves, and few by other people, give us a direct statement of their perceptions of their surroundings. Nevertheless it is possible to form a few impressions from the material evidence and to augment these with hints collected from the documents.

The black landscape, or landscapes, had several aspects. Some were reflexive; that is, they consisted of the slaves' responses to the planter's landscape. In some respects slaves shared the position of the white common planter, but their status as slaves worked in other ways to alter and even to undercut the intended effects of the processional landscape. Within the confines of the plantation, for instance, the common planter would be subject to the full effect of the for-

Fig. 14. King William County Courthouse, King William County, Virginia, ca. 1730. (Photograph by Dell Upton.)

mal route through it, but it is unlikely that he could progress as far along the route as a Carter or a Tayloe could. The common white planter, that is, was part of the intended audience of the processional landscape, and it served to affirm his *lack* of standing in it. The slaves were not intentionally a part of the audience. Few white planters imagined that slaves were susceptible to the legitimating functions of white society; they recognized that the slave's lack of standing made force the only sure legitimizer. At Mount Airy the slave's route began in the street of outbuildings that lay outside the kitchen door, west of the

house. It moved through the kitchen and, originally, from there through a small pedimented doorway on the west end of the house directly into the dining room (fig. 15). After the addition of the connecting quadrants, the route passed through them, into the stair hall, and then into the dining room. These routes mirrored the private routes that led family intimates from the rooms in the east wing into the secondary passage at the east end of the main block. The family entry was marked by a rusticated three-part opening (fig. 16) that was larger and more elaborate than the corresponding slave doorway at the opposite end of the house. Since the meaning of spaces depends as much on how we got there as it does on our being in them—on the shifting states of awareness as we pass one barrier after another—it is evident that in circumventing the formal barriers of the processional entrance, both the private and the slaves' route undercut the social statement made by the formal approach.

In this kind of landscape, blacks could pass almost at will, while whites from outside had to observe the formalities. The traveler Alexander Macaulay was annoyed to find this so when he visited Christiana Campbell's house in Williamsburg in 1783. The house had a "cold, poverty struck appearance; a large cold room on the left hand," the parlor, was occupied by several blacks. After inquiring for Mrs. Campbell, Macaulay was not shown into this private room, but left to stand in the entry; "But as I did not approve of waiting for her in the passage, I led Betsey into the cold parlour."[16] This is not to say that there were no

Fig. 15. Mount Airy, schematic plan showing formal, family, and slave entry and work routes. Key: H = hall; L = loggias; D = dining room. (Drawing by Dell Upton.)

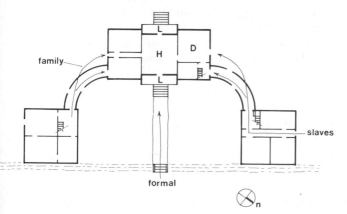

Fig. 16. Family entrance, Mount Airy, east facade. (Photograph by Dell Upton.)

barriers to slaves at all. They generally stood in the passage when waiting on their masters and mistresses in the parlors and dining rooms. But it was a less mystified landscape than that planters created for their peers.[17]

The slave also faced an absence of clear barriers in public, once he or she had passed the major one—permission to be off the master's property. At church, for instance, there was no definite seating arrangement for those few slaves who chose to attend or who were permitted to do so. The "slave gallery" of the nineteenth century was a rarity in the eighteenth. The colonial church gallery was usually reserved for private seating or, less often, for "the public"—those whites who did not have their own pews. Slaves might sit in or adjacent to their masters' pews, or they might share a section at the rear set aside for them.

If the master's landscape was a network that implied connection and movement, the landscape of the slave was a static one of discrete places. A comparison of landscape descriptions by elite and black Virginians is instructive. The elements of movement and commanding position built into such complexes as Mount Airy were objects of explicit admiration among the upper classes. Philip Fithian was able to capture their qualities to convey the feelings that they aroused. He caught sight of ladies riding, their red cloaks streaming, their hair protected by white kerchiefs. His description of his young pupils' dancing was based on the same perceptions of time and evanescent consciousness that the built landscape of the gentry embodied. He found it "beautiful to admiration, to see such a number of young persons, set off by dress to the best Advantage, moving easily, to the sound of well performed Music, and with perfect regularity, tho' apparently in the utmost Disorder." On another occasion, he noted his fondness for walking on the high hills near Nomini Hall, "where I can have a long View of many Miles & see on the Summits of the Hills Clusters of Savin Trees, through these often a little Farm-House, or Quarter for Negroes."[18] To be above it all, to see and not to be seen, were values increasingly cherished by the gentry. In church, they moved from their pews in the chancel, the most conspicuous part of the church, to galleries, private galleries, and hanging pews, above the heads of their fellow parishioners. Whereas Mount Airy could see and be seen, by 1770 Monticello

was set to command a view of the landscape for miles around—most visitors noted this—but could not be seen until one was quite close to the house.[19] Both qualities—of movement through the landscape, and of dominating large tracts—were alien to the conception of the landscape embodied in the slaves' directions.

Benjamin Henry Latrobe twice got directions from slaves who used as landmarks discrete, static barriers to be passed in moving from one point to another. The sense of a larger articulated network was missing. Indeed there was no acknowledgment that the barriers existed in any relation to other features not currently of interest. Thus Latrobe found it necessary "to make minute enquiry after all the byeroads and turnings which I am to avoid. By this mode of enquiry I in general astonish my directors by discoveries of difficulties they never thought of before. This was the case with my old negroe." In this kind of landscape, all points are related to one's own customary location rather than to the current position of the observer. The slaves' landscape was described from the point of view of someone surrounded by other people's power, and its landmarks were plantation houses and fields differentiated by ownership. It was not a way of thinking of the landscape that was necessarily confined to slaves but perhaps characterized all those who had nowhere to go themselves. Similar directions to those that Latrobe got from slaves in the 1790s were given by white farmers to Thomas Anburey in 1779. The local, Anburey wrote, "tells you to keep the right hand path, then you'll come to an old field, you are to cross that, and then you'll come to the fence of such a one's plantation, then keep that fence, and you'll come to a road that has three forks . . . then you'll come to a creek, after you cross that creek, you must turn to the left, and then you'll come to a tobacco house . . . and then you'll come to Mr. such a one's ordinary." If similar descriptions have been produced in other times and places, it remains true that the gentry perception of the landscape stands in striking and illuminating contrast to those of the slave and the common planter and that the failure to conceive of the landscape dynamically and systematically was a trait that elite observers found exasperating and characteristic of their social inferiors.[20]

In addition to the master's world of work and possession in which slaves operated they had another, private, landscape of personal life and prerogative. The slave house itself was the center of this life, and though many slaves had few possessions, some nevertheless had locks on their doors that they could use to lock out their fellow slaves and even their masters. Landon Carter was prevented from punishing his slave William when "he rushed in, bolted his door, and as the people were breaking in to him he broke out of the window and run off."[21] William's action showed a strong sense of territorial and personal rights that many visitors noticed in eighteenth-century Virginia quarters. Isaac Weld, for example, noted that while slaves on large plantations had to work certain hours, they had "ample time to attend to their own concerns," and that this time was devoted to their own gardens and poultry and to furnishing their houses and making them comfortable in minor ways, even if the masters' allocation of labor and materials rarely allowed for significant improvements to the buildings.[22]

Slave landscapes went beyond the immediate vicinity of the quarters. They included the woods and fields, where some measure of seclusion and secrecy was available. Landon Carter's slaves went to the woods when they wished to quit their master for awhile. By moving back and forth from the woods to the quarter, some of Carter's slaves were able to elude him for weeks or even months without actually leaving Sabine Hall's grounds. Nineteenth-century accounts mention religious meetings held in the woods, and Frederick Law Olmsted encountered casual groups of blacks who were gathered in woodland clearings during their leisure time.[23]

Slaves and masters shared traditional Anglo-American attitudes about workers' rights in their jobs and workplaces. From this point of view, all work areas other than the main house were the slaves' domain, a division of space made clear by the frequent juxtaposition of work buildings and slave houses, as at Tuckahoe, an eighteenth-century complex in Goochland County (fig. 17). Philip Fithian attended slaves' cockfights at the stables. He clearly thought of the shops and stables as black areas and recorded with disapproval his pupil Harry Carter's fondness for spending time "either in the Kitchen, or at the Blacksmiths, or Carpenters Shop." The slaves enforced this division of space and work rights. Thus Fithian was obliged to pay a forfeit of seven and one-half pence to the baker for an unspecified trespass on

Fig. 17. Slavehouses and smokehouse at Tuckahoe. (Photograph by Dell Upton.)

the prerogatives of his trade and another to Natt the plowman for touching the plowlines.[24]

Finally, the slaves' private landscape extended to other Quarters and plantations by means of unofficial ties with friends, relatives, spouses, and lovers. The increase in the size of many Quarters after the mid-eighteenth century helped to stabilize slave life and to promote a distinctive group existence as larger groups of slaves increasingly lived away from direct white control. Their separation from much white control allowed slaves to form communities that were held together by their mastery of the slave landscape of woods, fields, and waterways. Slaves formed neighborhoods, black landscapes that combined elements of the white landscape and of the quarters in a way that was peculiar to them and that existed outside the official articulated processional landscape of the great planter and his lesser neighbors.[25]

Much of the architectural historiography of early Virginia revolves around the gentry style. Its elements have been cataloged, its sources probed, its dominance assumed. Yet these approaches miss the dynamic quality of gentry self-presentation that was the style's greatest strength and greatest weakness. Elements of movement through the landscape were built into its forms, and architectural details were disposed along it in a carefully planned sequence. Experienced as intended, it could be a powerful and intense ideological statement. But the duties and personal experience of slaves circumvented this experience. Blacks were not drawn into the social posturing of gentry society, and whites did not expect them to be. Raw power replaced ideological persuasion. With this realization we are spurred on to see the physical landscape in a new light. It must be read as a whole; it was neither uniform nor entirely dominated by the gentry. The meaning of the landscape can be read in more than one way.

Notes

1. This paper draws on continuing work on pre-Revolutionary Virginia architecture for its data and, in particular, on Dell Upton, "Slave Housing in Eighteenth-Century Virginia: A Report to the Department of Social Cultural History, National Museum of American History, Smithsonian Institution" (MS, Smithsonian Institution, 1982 [contract no. SF2040940000]), and Upton, *Holy Things and Profane: Anglican Parish Churches in Colonial Virginia* (New York and Cambridge, Mass., 1986). In addition, I am grateful to Karen Kevorkian, John Vlach, and Edward Chappell for assistance with the fieldwork and to Edward Chappell and the Colonial Williamsburg Foundation for additional site drawings of Mount Airy and Howard's Neck.

2. The origins of historical consciousness and its implications for architecture are discussed in Peter Collins, *Changing Ideals in Modern Architecture* (Montreal, 1967).

3. The standard account of Virginia's upper-class houses is Thomas T. Waterman, *The Mansions of Virginia, 1706–1776* (Chapel Hill, N.C., 1944).

4. Landon Carter, *The Diary of Colonel Landon Carter of Sabine Hall, 1757–1778*, ed. Jack P. Greene (Charlottesville, Va., 1965), 291; entry of Feb. 8, 1743, Joseph Ball Letter Book, MS, Library of Congress (I am indebted to John Vlach for the references to the Ball Letter Book); for the occupancy of slave houses, see Upton, "Slave Housing," 26–28.

5. Booker T. Washington, *Up from Slavery* (New York, 1955), 2–3.

6. Ferdinand-Marie Bayard, *Travels of a Frenchman in Maryland and Virginia*, trans. and ed. Ben C. McCary (Williamsburg, Va., 1950), 13.

7. Philip Fithian, *Journal and Letters of Philip Vickers Fithian, 1773–1774: A Plantation Tutor of the Old Dominion*, ed. Hunter Dickinson Farish (Charlottesville, Va., 1957), 96; John Harrower, *The Journal of John Harrower, An Indentured Servant in the Colony of Virginia, 1773–1776*, ed. Edward Miles Riley (Williamsburg, Va., 1963), 89.

8. Edward Kimber, "Observations in Several Voyages and Travels in America in 1746," *William and Mary Quarterly*, 1st ser., 15 (1907): 148; Isaac Weld, Jr., *Travels through the United States of North America* (London, 1799), 85; Fithian, *Journal*, 96, 140.

9. Quarter groupings on outlying subsidiary farms appear to have been less formally arranged. Little evidence for their layout remains, but the quarters illustrated in the eighteenth-century map of York County reproduced by Rhys Isaac, for instance, are not so rigidly arranged as those of Howard's Neck (Rhys Isaac, *The Transformation of Virginia, 1740–1790* [Chapel Hill, N.C., 1982], 54–55, but see p. 41). In this paper I have used *quarter* to designate the individual slave house, and *Quarter* to refer to the outlying farm. I am indebted to Robert L. Alexander, Edward Chappell, and Richard Cote for information about the history and site of Howard's Neck that supplements my own field examination.

10. William Hugh Grove, "Virginia in 1732: The Travel Journal of William Hugh Grove," ed. Gregory A. Stiverson and Patrick H. Butler III, *William and Mary Quarterly*, 3d ser., 85 (1977): 26.

11. Dell Upton, "Early Vernacular Architecture in Southeastern Virginia" (Ph.D. diss., Brown University, 1980), chap. 1; Upton, "The Origins of Chesapeake Architecture," in *Three Centuries of Maryland Architecture* (Annapolis, Md., 1982), 44–57; Upton, "Vernacular Domestic Architecture in Eighteenth-Century Virginia," *Winterthur Portfolio* 17 (1982): 102; Joseph A. Ernst and H. Roy Merrens, "'Camden's Turrets Pierce the Skies!': The Urban Process in the Southern Colonies during the Eighteenth Century," *William and Mary Quarterly*, 3d ser., 30 (1973): 554, 568–73; John C. Rainbolt, "The Absence of Towns in Seventeenth-Century Virginia," *Journal of Social History* 35 (1969): 343–60; Carville Earle and Ronald Hoffman, "Staple Crops and Urban Development in the Eighteenth-Century South," *Perspectives in American History* 10 (1976): 7–78.

12. Aubrey C. Land, "Economic Base and Social Structure: The Northern Chesapeake in the Eighteenth Century," in *Shaping Southern Society*, ed. T. H. Breen (New York, 1976), 238–40; Edmund S. Morgan, *Virginians at Home: Family Life in the Eighteenth Century* (Williamsburg, Va., 1952), chaps. 1, 4; Harrower, *Journal*, 83; Isaac, *Transformation of Virginia*, 70–79. Decisions about working and transferring slaves on the outlying Quarters were made at the plantation center. In addition, the Quarter frequently served as a kind of colony or service center for the main plantation. Charles Carter's Edge-Wood plantation in Hanover County, for instance, supplied meat to his other properties, including his seat at Shirley, Charles City County (Richard S. Dunn, "A Tale of Two Plantations: Slave Life at Mesopotamia in Jamaica and Mount Airy in Virginia, 1799 to 1828," *William and Mary Quarterly*, 3d ser., 34 [1977]: 44–45; Carter Berkeley, Edge-Wood, Hanover County, to Charles Carter, Shirley, Charles City County, Oct. 19, 1802 [MS, Virginia Historical Society, Richmond]).

13. Thomas Anburey, *Travels through the Interior Parts of America*, 2 vols. (1789; reprint ed., Boston, 1923), 2:196; Harrower, *Journal*, 41; Fithian, *Journal*, 80–82. For a conjectural reconstruction drawing of Nomini Hall, which burned in the mid-nineteenth century, see Waterman, *Mansions*, 137.

14. For more on the concept of the articulated proces-

sional landscape, see Upton, *Holy Things and Profane*, 214, 227, and chap. 9, *passim*.

15. Isaac, *Transformation of Virginia*, 58–63; Rhys Isaac, "Religion and Authority: Problems of the Anglican Establishment in Virginia in the Era of the Great Awakening and the Parsons' Cause," *William and Mary Quarterly*, 3d ser., 30 (1973): 3–36; Upton, *Holy Things and Profane*, 179–80, 187–94, 204–6, 214, 220; A. G. Roeber, "Authority, Law, and Custom: The Rituals of Court Day in Tidewater Virginia, 1720–1750," later in this volume.

16. "Journal of Alexander Macaulay," *William and Mary Quarterly*, 1st ser., 11 (1903): 187.

17. Daniel Blake Smith, *Inside the Great House: Planter Family Life in Eighteenth-Century Chesapeake Society* (Ithaca, N.Y., 1980), 43.

18. Fithian, *Journal*, 29, 33, 178.

19. See the descriptions of the views from Monticello and Mount Vernon in Luigi Castiglioni, *Luigi Castiglioni's Viaggio: Travels in the United States of North America, 1785–87*, trans. and ed. Antonio Pace (Syracuse, N.Y., 1983), 112, 185–86.

20. Benjamin Henry Latrobe, *The Virginia Journals of Benjamin Henry Latrobe, 1795–1798*, ed. Edward C. Carter II and Angeline Polites (New Haven, Conn., 1977), 137–41; Anburey, *Travels*, 2:196–97; Fithian, *Journal*, 178. For a perceptive discussion of social landscapes, see Isaac, *Transformation of Virginia*, 52–57.

21. Joseph Ball Letter Book, Feb. 18, 1743, Nov. 4, 1746, April 1754; Carter, *Diary*, 845.

22. Weld, *Travels*, 85.

23. Isaac, *Transformation of Virginia*, 328–36; Charles L. Perdue, Thomas E. Barden, and Robert K. Phillips, eds., *Weevils in the Wheat: Interviews with Virginia Ex-Slaves* (Charlottesville, Va., 1976), 124; Frederick Law Olmsted, *A Journey in the Seaboard Slave States* (New York, 1856), 89.

24. Fithian, *Journal*, 37, 88, 201.

25. Dunn, "Tale of Two Plantations," 38–39, 42, 44–45; Allan Kulikoff, "The Origins of Afro-American Society in Tidewater Maryland and Virginia, 1700 to 1790," *William and Mary Quarterly*, 3d ser., 35 (1978): 248; Sarah Shaver Hughes, "Slaves for Hire: The Allocation of Black Labor in Elizabeth City County, Virginia, 1782 to 1810," *William and Mary Quarterly*, 3d ser., 35 (1978): 263–73; Kimber, "Observations," 217.

Rewalking the "Walking City": Housing and Property Relations in New York City, 1780–1840

BETSY BLACKMAR

Although we may commonly think of urban space as a static record of well-integrated social and economic structures, its complexity increases when we realize that spatial patterns—streets and parks, slums and "respectable" neighborhoods—are charged with social meanings that derive from concrete historical changes. Spatial patterns do not just happen; they are caused. As Betsy Blackmar explains in this essay, New York City between 1785 and 1840 witnessed a series of dramatic transformations in the distribution and management of mercantile wealth. These changes altered the definition and use of social space and, in so doing, allowed for new forms of exploitation of laboring people by those in control of the real estate and housing markets.

In New York City's colonial period, artisans often had land and housing adequate to their economic livelihoods. Shops and domestic quarters were in the same building, and apprentices and journeymen lived under the master's roof. Artisans owned land next-door to merchants. Yet by the 1750s, merchants and landed gentry families had taken several steps to use urban space—its land and housing—as an investment to generate profits. Drawing on linkages of intermarriage and political interest, these elites solidified their holdings by buying up multiple lots in the old port city; they also bought extensive tracts of land north of the town center, where between 1740 and 1770 they established their country houses, pastoral retreats to which they could invite favored guests and from which they could view the city at a comfortable distance. Soon artisans and laborers looked to this unsettled acreage with plans to rent land and build small houses. By 1775 the country gentlemen, many of them Loyalists, had become landlords.

After the Revolution New York's rapid economic growth led to three important shifts. As population increased and as more and more land fell into fewer and fewer hands, property values rose more than sevenfold between 1785 and 1815. Master artisans expanded production and moved away from their old integrated houses and shops, forcing journeymen and apprentices to find their own lodgings. As the "household system of labor" broke down, trade and domestic shelter became physically separate. New ranks of dispossessed working people moved to the city's periphery, yet even there rents were rising. As merchant rentiers and speculative developers tightened their grip on land ownership, Blackmar argues, they effected a second major shift: an urban "enclosure movement" in which cash was the crop produced. Those in control of the "land system" mystified their identity and distanced themselves socially from a landless underclass by establishing mediating layers of agents, brokers, leaseholders, and sub-landlords.

The third transformation came as "class neighborhoods" emerged in the early years of the nineteenth century, a trend fueled in part by changes in the building trades. As laboring people sought alternatives to high rents, they developed strategies of overcrowding and transience; subdivided houses in old artisan neighborhoods emerged as the domain of the city's poor. Worried that these areas were both unhealthy and morally dangerous, middle-class citizens moved into blocks of restrained, single-family Federal-style row housing. As it explores the consequences of these three rifts in New York's social fabric, this essay suggests that urban space was an active political arena in which upper class prerogative could be more precisely defined and its power extended.

We can look at the organization of space in cities of the past in three ways. We can view the urban landscape in a two-dimensional frame and, from pictures and maps, gain an impression of the design and shape of buildings, streets, and neighborhoods. Or, with our imaginations, we can move through a city and note the location of different structures and people in relation to one another. Or again, as historians, we can walk the urban landscape through a fourth dimension and observe not only the forms but how those forms have changed, both internally and externally, over time. But however we approach the city, we always confront the same question: what are the social meanings of the spatial patterns and forms we see?

In describing late eighteenth- and early nineteenth-century American seaports, some historians have looked for an answer to this question in Sam Bass Warner's concept of the "walking city," where houses, shops, and storehouses were clustered within a two-mile "walking" radius of the wharves.[1] Warner and his followers have suggested, on the strength of this image, that the spatial compactness of the walking city contributed to social harmony and deference among classes of merchants, artisans, and laborers who lived and worked in close proximity to one another. Other historians, such as David Gordon, have refined the concept of the walking city by noting that because of the differentiation of land values, classes settled in different areas of the city, thus revealing spatially the economic stratification of mercantile society.[2] Allowing for these distinctions, however, historians have continued to argue that spatial concentration and integration encouraged and supported social cohesion, cooperation, and deference.

At first glance, viewed through maps, prints, and contemporary descriptions, the eighteenth-century landscape of Manhattan matches the visual representations of the "walking city."[3] Two- and three-story wood and brick townhouses, containing both trade and domestic workspace, fronted streets that encircled the Battery. Some geographic separation of different social classes in Manhattan is also evident. Economic elites, primarily merchants, established themselves near their wharves and stores in the vicinity of Wall Street; laborers and the poor settled on less expensive property at the western and northern edges of the port. Between these two extremes, artisans clustered, often by trade, on side streets, while shopkeepers, grocers, and tavern keepers situated themselves on corners and along such well-traveled thoroughfares as Broadway and the Bowery. Yet,

though these patterns appear to conform visually to the paradigm of the walking city, they do not confirm prevalent social interpretations of that landscape.

Interpretations of geography and built form that view spatial organization as being merely emblematic of social organization project a static conception of space, class, and the relation between the two. By approaching space from the outside and by reading surface patterns schematically for social content, we fail to understand how social relations actively shape and transform the organization of space. In this essay I propose that we try to penetrate the facades and maps of Manhattan in order to understand the forces that formed and changed the city landscape between 1785 and 1840. By examining the distribution and management of land, the changes in household labor relations, the formation of the urban real estate and housing markets, and the reorganization of the building industry, we can consider how and why Manhattan residents changed their spatial arrangements for living and working and how these changes revealed changing social relations among households. In this way, rewalking the walking city through time, I hope to suggest, albeit schematically, how we can begin to explore the emergence of new, class-based social relations.

I

In seventeenth- and early eighteenth-century New York City, land distribution accommodated both the social need and the social hierarchy of a colonial port engaged in mercantile shipping and simple commodity production. The majority of householders controlled the space that was a resource for their own productive activity. Through land grants, estate inheritances, and purchases on the private market, merchants and independent artisans acquired town lots and built houses for their workshops, stores, kitchens, and sleeping quarters. A geographic surplus of land before 1740 allowed successful craftsmen to establish their shops near the wharves. In 1730, over two-thirds of the port's taxpayers (out of a total population of eight thousand) owned property in Manhattan, concentrated within a one-mile area.[4]

For artisans and merchants in the colonial city, the internal integration of house and shop, of trade and domestic space, was social as well as spatial. In exchange for labor, master artisans, merchants, or widowed heads-of-house provided living accommodations for their household labor force—family and additional dependent members such as servants, apprentices, journeymen, and slaves. Master artisans found accommodations for their apprentices and journeymen either within the master house or through board in the neighborhood. Heads of households provided shelter for journeymen and family members with the expectation that these dependents would eventually accumulate the means—out of wages, patrimony, or advantageous marriage—to acquire a town lot and establish their own house and shop, or, for merchants, house and stores.

Colonial elites—merchants, church and government officials, and Hudson River patroon families—sought Manhattan land not simply as a resource for their own livelihoods but as a secure investment for the profits of trade and as an emblem of social status. Prosperous merchants used their capital, family connections, and political influence to accumulate multiple town lots, water lots along both shores of the island, and large farm tracts to the north of the port.[5] In the 1740s and again in the 1760s, Manhattan witnessed its first episodes of gentrification as wealthy New Yorkers purchased country estates that also provided summer retreats (figs. 1, 2). By the 1770s, land beyond the core city of 23,000 people (north of Chambers Street) had been divided into approxi-

mately 136 estates owned by fewer than one hundred families (fig. 3).[6] Six farms dominated the land most accessible to the interior built city. As the port expanded, this social monopoly at the periphery drew new class lines in the distribution and development of land.

The social geography of Manhattan began to change in the mid-eighteenth century. Though successful artisans continued to reside in the center city, as commercial expansion increased demand for space near the wharves in the 1760s and 1770s, some mechanics began to migrate west and north in search of cheaper land. Large proprietors held the territory at the periphery as a long-term investment; and because aggregate demand was still low and because potential residents were seldom wealthy, they did not subdivide and sell their country estates in lots to individual artisans. Instead, eighteenth-century Manhattan landowners became rentiers by adopting the English long-term agricultural lease and renting out lots for terms running from twenty-one to ninety-nine years.[7]

Ground rents of from two to eight pounds, fixed by twenty-one-year leases, enabled artisans and laborers to establish proprietorship without the burden of purchasing property outright. In the 1760s and 1770s, Trinity Church, for example, granted nearly two hundred leases for lots on its farm west of Broadway (see

Fig. 1. "Richmond Hill," country house built by Maj. Abraham Mortier in 1766–67 as his rural retreat overlooking the Hudson River (see fig. 3"E" for location); engraved by Cornelius Tiebout, 1798. Ink on paper, 3⅝″ × 6⅝″. (Photograph reprinted from I. N. P. Stokes, *The Iconography of Manhattan Island* [New York, 1914], vol. 1: plate 55.)

Fig. 2. Henry Rutgers's mansion house, built before 1768 on the Rutgers Farm above the East River (see fig. 3"D" for location); lithograph on paper. (Photograph reprinted from Daniel T. Valentine, *Manual of the Corporation of the City of New York, For the Year 1858* [New York, 1858], facing p. 606.)

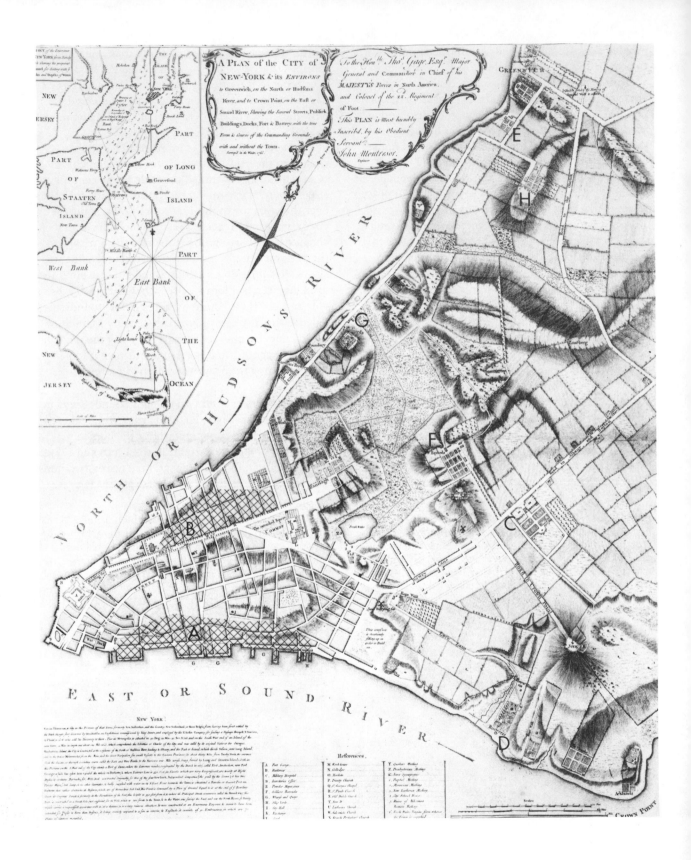

PART FOUR   Landscapes of Social Distance

fig. 3,"B"), many to cartmen, carpenters, and mechanics who could no longer compete with merchants for land near the wharves and whose trade allowed them to relocate.[8] These artisan leaseholders
built or commissioned their own modest wood and
brick front houses. Before 1785, few landowners systematically developed their property or collected
rents from their own buildings.[9] Loyalist James Delancey, who owned a 220-acre farm immediately
north of the city (see fig. 3,"C"), for example, leased
out over 80 acres but owned only four houses himself. In his 1784 petition for reparations for his confiscated estate, Delancey explained the prevalent
leasehold practice to English officials: "Every tenant
has permission by the terms of his lease to remove
his house at the expiration of his lease, leaving the
lands under fence. They were wooded houses in the
suburbs of the city."[10] Thus, in the first phase of geographic differentiation by class within Manhattan's
walking city, low ground rents and long lease terms
gave mechanics at the periphery a measure of control
over the use of leased land and the opportunity to establish their own houses and shops for production.
At the same time, rentiers skimmed off a portion of
the value produced by the labor of those households.

Though the payment of ground rents drew the artisans and merchant rentiers into landed market relations, class relations were less apparent in the distribution of housing in the colonial city. Colonial
builders produced houses primarily for simple commodity exchange—that is, for their purchase by
known customers who put up the capital and consumed the "use value" of a shelter for their household's livelihood.[11] That craftsmen selling their
houses occasionally advertised not only a building
but the "stock in trade" of the premises or its suita-
bility for a particular craft suggests their own close

Fig. 3. John Montresor, surveyor, *A Plan of the City of New
York & its Environs . . .*, London, 1766; engraved by P. Andrews. Ink on paper, 20⅝″ × 23⅜″. Key to locations indicated: (A) Wharf District; (B) Trinity Church Farm area; (C)
James Delancey Farm; (D) Henry Rutgers Farm; (E) Abraham Mortier estate, "Richmond Hill"; (F) William Bayard
Farm; (G) Leonard Lispenard Farm; (H) Lady [Peter] Warren
Farm. Note that the upper boundary of the Common, now
the site of City Hall, corresponds approximately to present-
day Chambers Street. (Photograph courtesy of the Prints
and Photographs Division, Library of Congress.)

association of housing with their trade. We must not
romanticize the access of all colonial artisans to their
own houses as a means of production. Because building by commission required a substantial personal
outlay of capital, independent mechanics before the
Revolution also secured domestic quarters and workspace through the rearrangement and sharing of existing houses and especially through boarding.

Boarding also provided living accommodations for
the city's transient population of mariners and laborers, for widows, for unmarried journeymen, and for
new arrivals to the city. Within houses, extra space
for boarders depended on family and household life
cycles, but both wealthy and middling households
characteristically occupied their houses intensively
rather than consuming extra space in greater personal
privacy. Unlike ground rents, which flowed from artisans to the landowning merchant elite, rent for
shared housing circulated within artisan ranks. Yet
internal adaptations of houses to create specialized
living space for boarders not connected to household
production prefigured the external separation of trade
and domestic workspace and the production of housing as a commodity for a general market.

II

Economic and demographic growth following the
Revolution transformed the underlying property relations of the walking city. The number of people in
New York County (Manhattan) increased from
23,000 in 1785 to 31,131 in 1790 and doubled to
60,529 in 1800. As peace restored both European
markets and lines of credit, New York shipping expanded and local craft production embraced a new
American market. The accompanying transformation
of property relations and housing, however, involved
more than an inevitable market response to increased
demand for land from immigration and/or to new
capital from expanding production. New York landowners systematically altered their methods of managing and distributing real estate to capture investment capital. Furthermore, changes in the social
structure fundamentally changed the nature of demand for housing.[12]

By the end of the eighteenth century, "transience"
and "detachment" were becoming permanent conditions for the formerly attached population of journeymen and for increasing numbers of unskilled laborers

in Manhattan. Master craftsmen, reorganizing and expanding production for the market, ceased to provide living accommodations for their workers and moved away from their shops. We find evidence for the demise of the household system of labor in Manhattan in the decline of apprenticeship, in the formation of separate and antagonistic journeymen and employers' trade organizations, and in the uneven increase in shop size. Even those workers who continued to work in their domestic quarters—women in the cloth-making industry or shoemakers, for example—returned to master shops to pick up their materials and wages. The steady growth of the city's wage-earning class, from laborers to clerks, and the expansion of its bourgeoisie of merchants and entrepreneurs, prompted what geographer James Vance has called the "formation of a generalized housing market," that is, the widespread social need for domestic shelter separate from centers of production and commerce.[13]

In the late 1780s and in the 1790s, as investors with capital from the prospering mercantile economy anticipated the new demand for housing, their speculations in city land sent prices soaring. Historian Edmund Willis estimates that between 1785 and 1815, land values on Manhattan rose by nearly 750 percent.[14] With the rapid inflation of land prices and the rising number of Manhattan residents, land ownership became increasingly concentrated in the first thirty years following the Revolution, despite the opening of streets and subdivision of land north of Chambers Street.[15] The merchant rentier monopoly on real estate at the periphery of the port meant that the immediate benefits of economic and geographic growth—the appreciation of land values—flowed into the hands of this elite proprietary class. The real estate market as an investment market dominated the process and timing of land subdivision and sales. Those who owned large tracts of land also exercised the power to hold it back from the market when prices dropped and to promote its sale in subdivided blocks to those with capital to invest. Though in the 1780s artisans were able to purchase single lots in the sale of such confiscated loyalist estates as the Delancey farm, investors acquired larger and multiple tracts.[16] In some instances, these speculative landowners held property for thirty years or more before subdividing and selling in a favorable market.

Landowners who held real estate as a long-term investment continued to rely on ground leases to extract an annual return. But as rentiers perceived the emerging gap between income from ground rents and income from building rents, as well as the differentiation of land values according to land use, they adopted strategies to promote development and to enhance the value of their holdings.[17] Some owners began to intervene in tenants' use of leased lots by adding restrictive covenants to their leases. After 1790, for example, Henry Rutgers—the third-generation proprietor of an estate on the Lower East Side (see fig. 3, "D")—and Trinity Church required their leaseholders to build a "substantial well-built two or three story brick house." Covenants for the landlord to purchase back improvements at the expiration of the lease further encouraged the construction of substantial buildings as an investment by leaseholders. Other covenants restricted tenants from engaging in such nuisance industries as bone-boiling or tanning that might depress land values.

These policies added a new financial burden to renting land and attracted a class of leaseholders who, viewing long-term groundleases as marketable interests in land, were willing to assume the cost of construction as part of their own investment. In place of independent artisans looking for space to build their own integrated houses and shops, investors—merchants, entrepreneurs, brokers, shopkeepers, and speculative builders—acquired twenty-one-year leases and advanced the capital for improvements. Then they either sold the lease with new buildings for the remainder of the lease term to a leaseholder/landlord who made back the cost, plus a profit, by collecting housing rents or they became landlords themselves. In many instances, the owners of houses on leased land in turn sublet those buildings to other individuals who collected multiple rents from tenants. Thus, in place of a low ground rent and the cost of building his own house, the Manhattan tenant began to pay a house rent that returned an annual profit to the rentier who owned the land, to the leaseholder who owned the building, and to the sublandlord who leased the building.

Landowners' lease policies and the competition of investors squeezed out the former leasing class of mechanics who could not afford to construct or purchase required lease improvements for their own use. By 1812, cartmen and laborers, for example, had begun to move from the lots on Trinity Church's farm north to undeveloped property that remained less expensive due to both geographic inconvenience and the absence of restrictive covenants (fig. 4).[18] As land values, ground rents, and the cost of construction continued to rise in the first half of the nineteenth century, the option of land ownership at the periphery faded. Rents consumed earnings. In a process analogous to agricultural enclosures, urban rentiers who managed their property with an eye to the market, together with speculative leaseholders who became landlords, appropriated both land and houses from independent producers who could no longer control space as a resource for their own livelihoods. In the urban instance, "enclosed" land produced building rents rather than cash crops.

The reorganization and management of land and houses for the market both reflected and affected changing social relations of production—the formation of New York's wage-earning class. But the elaborate tiered system of property distribution mystified the social relations of property in the walking city by obscuring the flow of profits out of rents. For rentiers and large proprietors who stood at the head of the land system, income from ground rents and the profits from sales—like the dividends from stocks and interest from bonds—was a medium of capital accumulation, capital that could be reinvested to create more capital. Yet large landowners' use of agents and brokers to manage their holdings created an aura of "absenteeism," though they often resided in the vicinity of their rental property.[19] The social distancing of landowners reinforced the impersonal structure of a housing market that undermined whatever the proximity of the walking city may have achieved in deferential or harmonious social relations.

Real estate also gave those independent producers who became entrepreneurs an investment opportunity that helped establish the most successful among them in the ranks of the capitalist class previously dominated by merchants. When such master artisans as shipwright Noah Brown or tanner Jacob Lorillard became landlords as well as employers, they collected back as rent the cash they paid out in wages.[20] As real estate added to the wealth of the city's economic elite, the gap between propertied and unpropertied widened.

On another level, grocers, shopkeepers, tavern keepers, and building tradesmen, who were most often able to raise the capital necessary for purchas-

Fig. 4. View from West Eleventh Street, looking toward Manhattan, 1825. Watercolor on paper. Note enclosed work yard adjacent to house and fencelines separating property divisions. (Photograph courtesy of the Museum of the City of New York.)

ing leases and buildings as a small investment, became a dominant leaseholding group in the city and thus direct landlords to multiple wage-earning tenant households (fig. 5).[21] Many small proprietary landlords—and their sublandlords—with from one to three houses, looked to rental income for part of their own livelihood—that is, income to be consumed rather than reinvested. Among this middling class of landlords, participation in the leasehold housing market was often as transitory as tenants' tenure in houses. Carpenters and masons, for example, sublet buildings and became landlords during recessions when there was high unemployment in their trade. Unlike rentiers hidden behind their agents, landlords and sublandlords, who often resided in or near the houses they rented out and who collected rents in person, remained highly visible to their tenants and became the public villains of New York's mid-nineteenth-century housing crisis. Paying ground and house rents to rentiers or leaseholders, as well as the costs of maintenance, these landlords and sublandlords tried to counteract the high turnover rates and low rent-paying power of their working-class tenants by crowding more and more of those tenants into less and less space.

In the 1790s and early 1800s, Manhattan journeymen protested their deteriorating social status and argued that their wages were insufficient against the

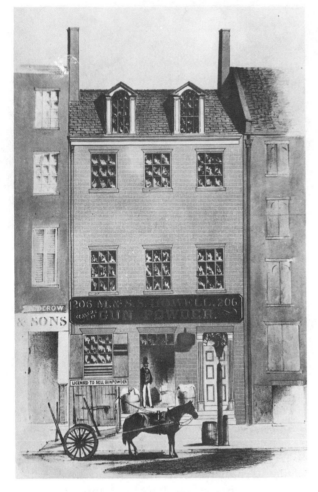

Fig. 5. House at 206 Front Street built as shop and domestic space by grocer Matthew Howell in 1798. Watercolor on paper. Door at right of structure leads to passage to rear domestic workspaces and living quarters, and to stairs leading to private chambers above. (Photograph courtesy of the Museum of the City of New York.)

Though the new social need for domestic quarters had become apparent by the first decade of the nineteenth century, different solutions to that need reveal the contradictions inherent in the formation of a class-divided market society. Despite the development of investment instruments and strategies for a rental housing market, the realization of profits from house rents or sales depended on the social income of a predominantly wage-earning population. Unable to afford single-house rents, Manhattan journeymen and laborers, and their families, developed their own strategies of rent sharing—the more intensive occupation of houses—and of mobility—moving around to find lower rents or absconding.

Boarding, the provision of lodging and meals, offered the first systematic multi-tenant housing solution from within the mechanic classes. Proprietors of boarding houses—and households that took boarders—produced living accommodations for the market. Longworth's *New York Directory*, the most public though still incomplete record, listed 50 commercial boarding houses in 1790 and over 150 ten years later as the city's population doubled. Women, often widows, operated from one-half to three-fifths of these advertised establishments, renting out rooms in houses they generally leased from the owner. The management of boarding houses transformed domestic labor into a service commodity. Throughout the nineteenth century, for families who continued to take boarders as a strategy to increase household income, the value of this labor remained disguised by its location in what was called the "private sphere."

Though notices for boarding houses and the prevalent but less publicized practice of taking boarders were the most common evidence of New York wage earners' move to shared and specialized living space, boarding did not solve the long-term social problem of housing wage-earning families. Other forms of shared domestic space also emerged in the early years of the nineteenth century. Notices for rooms "with the use of the kitchen" or "with separate kitchen" heralded the arrival of the apartment dwelling in New York long before the appearance of formally designed apartment houses.[23] With commercial tenants in front, landlords offered the upper stories and back-

steadily increasing cost of living and especially of housing.[22] But as Engels pointed out in his analysis of European proposals for housing reform, the "housing question" was but one arena of class struggle and could not be understood or solved without confronting the social relations of production in a capitalist society. Still, in Manhattan, where the transformation of production occurred gradually in the first half of the nineteenth century, new class relations perhaps became most dramatically visible in the reshaping of domestic space and the immiserization of working class housing.

rooms of once unified old buildings for separate residences. Speculative leaseholders and landlords who commissioned or built substantial new houses preferred the stability of a single resident tenant with a one- or five-year lease. But when they could not find tenants able to pay the rent for an entire house, they also leased or sublet single-family dwellings to landlords who in turn broke them up for multiple occupancy.

Manhattan tenants who paid cash rents out of wages and who shared domestic quarters experienced a similar class condition in housing though their paid working conditions still varied widely. The interchangeability of rental housing as a commodity, like the interchangeability of labor power to capitalist production, forced working-class tenants to move around in order to find accommodations within the price limit set by wages that had become their only means of livelihood. In the early decades of the nineteenth century, tenant districts that became the city's first slums—Five Points (fig. 6), Church and Chapel streets on the Trinity Church Farm (fig. 7), and streets on the Lower East Side (fig. 8)—rose from within wood and brick-front houses erected by artisans who had once leased land and built houses for their own use. Thus, as individual tenants moved or crowded together, multifamily housing fixed their

Fig. 7. Baroness Hyde de Neuville, painting of artisans' wood-framed houses and shops, corner of Warren and Greenwich streets on the Trinity Church Farm, New York, January 1809. Watercolor on paper; 8" × 13½". (Photograph courtesy of the Museum of the City of New York, bequest of Mrs. J. Insley Blair.)

class identity as a permanent feature of the walking city.

Against the background of the urban working class sharing domestic space, the ideal of the single-family dwelling emerged as part of the definition of middle-class status. As master artisans became petty manufacturers, they removed themselves both from the activity and the place of production. The city's middle class of professionals and even clerks joined the merchants and entrepreneurs in demanding living space

Fig. 6. "The Five Points in 1859," intersection of Baxter, Park, and Worth streets, New York. Lithograph on paper. (Photograph reprinted from Daniel T. Valentine, *Manual of the Corporation of the City of New York, For the Year 1860* [New York, 1860], facing p. 396.)

Fig. 8. "Old Houses, Corner of Pearl & Elm Streets," New York. Lithograph on paper. (Photograph reprinted from Daniel T. Valentine, *Manual of the Corporation of the City of New York, For the Year 1860* [New York, 1860], facing p. 492.)

Rewalking the "Walking City"

PART FOUR   Landscapes of Social Distance

that departed from the traditional integrated housing forms. The "genteel" urban dwelling (fig. 9), with its emphasis on convenience to a separate workplace, healthfulness, and family comfort, replaced the merchant house, which had often included an office or counting room and which had been situated on streets near the wharves—the area of the city believed most vulnerable to summer epidemics.

In the first decades of the nineteenth century, "class neighborhoods" in Manhattan emerged in the form of "class streets" or even parts of streets divided into "respectable" and "nonrespectable" blocks. Stores, offices, and workshops persisted on primarily residential streets, but they ceased to house a resident labor force. As the city grew, the pressure of rising commercial rents in the wharf district combined with the threat of exposure and contact with the "dangerous classes" and disease to push the middle class out of the central city toward the safer terrain of Greenwich Village or land north of Fourteenth Street.[24] This gradual geographical separation of residential houses into class neighborhoods between 1800 and 1840 depended both on the strength of middle-class purchasing power and on the reorganization of the building industry to produce houses for that generalized market.

To a large extent, Manhattan builders and developers created new social neighborhoods through the quality and the uniformity of the houses they constructed. House-building shifted from an eighteenth-century craft directly tied to the capital and instructions of the customer to a stratified industry of investors, developers, builders, subcontractors, and laborers developing a product for a socially constructed but anonymous market.[25] In the building industry's "infant years," the heavy personal investment of individual speculators, and their dependence on credit, underscored the high risk involved in the extensive production of housing as a ready-made good. Furthermore, fluctuations in the money market and repeated recessions in the years 1790 to 1840

confirmed the risk. The extreme vulnerability of the construction industry meant that during building booms—in the mid-1820s and again in the mid-1830s—builders concentrated on supplying the most secure and immediately lucrative market—commercial buildings and middle-class dwellings. This interest in secure profits from new construction also enhanced the return of landlords who invested in and subdivided existing housing stock for "unreliable" working-class tenants.

While New York's elites established themselves within the uniformly developed residential enclaves of Hudson Square, Washington Square, Union Square, and Gramercy Park, the social geography of the rest of the city continued to evolve out of ad hoc adaptations to the unstable income of the city's wage earners.[26] Between 1825 and 1835, Manhattan builders constructed an average of one thousand houses a year, but the anticipated middle-class market for these dwellings was not growing as fast as working-class needs.[27] "Over produced" single-family houses had to be rapidly subdivided for four or five families, the sum of whose rent could meet the rental price for a single house. Unlike the residential parks and uniform block-fronts raised by speculative developers for the elite, new construction in working-class districts was uneven, with small-scale builders and investors erecting one, two, or three dwellings at a time. These marginal and eclectic two- and three-story houses could not adequately absorb the numbers of tenants that increased while the buildings themselves deteriorated. To create additional living space at little expense, landlords rented out cellars and attics and added wooden rear houses to back lots.[28] The waves of immigrants who arrived in New York between 1825 and 1850 had no choice but to settle in space filtered from within working-class neighborhoods.

Thus where Manhattan's capitalist class had the means to command new residential building in their own behalf,[29] the city's working class continued to depend on the continuous adaptation of existing housing stock to new and more intensive use. Despite forty years of multi-tenant practice, however, no new housing form emerged to accommodate Manhattan's wage-earning households until the 1840s. Since New York's laboring population before 1850 did not constitute an industrial labor force comparable to the operatives of a Manchester or Birmingham, employers did not produce workers' housing

Fig. 9. A row of houses on the west side of State Street, facing Battery Park, New York, ca. 1864. This 1790s uniform Federal-style block front was the prototype of the genteel houses erected by builder-entrepreneurs for Manhattan's middle class. (Photograph courtesy of the New-York Historical Society.)

along the lines of the English back-to-back cottages.[30] Indeed, through the sweating system, New York manufacturers saved rents by forcing workers to pay the "shop" overhead through house rents.

In spite of all the new construction and expansion of the Erie Canal era, by the 1830s the walking city experienced a crisis in housing and public health. In the mid-1830s, the first evidence of designed multi-tenant houses also suggests that Manhattan builders and investors were beginning to understand that six-or-more working-class rents equalled one genteel rent. But the Panic of 1837 brought new construction to a halt. The institutionalization of the class-based social geography of Manhattan, the systematic construction of tenement housing for the working class, and the city's full transformation into an "industrial city" of specialized land-use and geographically segregated classes—all of this did not begin until the late 1840s. It had already become clear, however, that though New York's social classes still lived within walking distance of one another, the social distance between them had grown immeasurably.

Notes

The author would like to thank Thomas Bender, Edwin Burrows, Christine Rosen, and Rachel Bernstein for comments on an earlier draft of this essay and Jean-Christophe Agnew, Gary Kornblith, Roy Rosenzweig, and Michael Wallace for rewalking the present version with her. The description and analysis of Manhattan property relations in this essay is further expanded in Elizabeth Blackmar, *The Quality of Rents: Property and Housing Relations in New York City 1785–1850* (Ithaca, N.Y., forthcoming 1988), in which more complete documentation can also be found.

1. Sam Bass Warner coined the phrase "walking city" for contemporary use in *Streetcar Suburbs: The Process of Growth in Boston, 1870–1900* (New York, 1973); he developed the image of the mercantile city in *The Private City: Philadelphia in Three Periods of Its Growth* (Philadelphia, 1968), 10–11, 16, 21, and 50. John K. Alexander reexamines the Philadelphia case in "Poverty, Fear, and Continuity: An Analysis of the Poor in Late Eighteenth-Century Philadelphia," in *Peoples of Philadelphia, 1790–1940: A History of Ethnic Groups and Lower Class Life*, ed. Allen F. Davis and Mark H. Haller (Philadelphia, 1973), 13–37, esp. 32.

2. See, for example, David Gordon, "Capitalism and the Roots of Urban Crisis," in *The Fiscal Crisis of American Cities*, ed. Roger E. Alcaly and David Mermelstein (New York, 1977), 82–112, esp. 99–100.

3. The Ino and Stokes collections of Manhattan prints and maps in the Prints Division of the New York Public Library provide a visual record of the city's growth. For eighteenth-century social geography, see Carl Abbott, "The Neighborhoods of New York City, 1760–1775," *New York History* 55 (April 1976): 35–53, and Bruce Wilkenfield, "Social and Economic Structure of the City of New York, 1695–1795" (Ph.D. diss., Columbia University, 1973), 173–74, 196. Selections from contemporary descriptions can be found throughout I. N. P. Stokes, *Iconography of Manhattan Island, 1498–1909*, 6 vols. (New York, 1914–28), 4:248–940, and in Stokes's manuscript compilation of contemporary observations on the city under "Slums" file, Manuscripts Division of the New York Public Library.

4. Wilkenfield, "Social and Economic Structure," 85.

5. I. N. P. Stokes, "Original Grants and Farms," in Stokes, *Iconography of Manhattan*, 4:66–177. See also "Map of the City of New York Showing . . . the Location of the Different Farms and Estates" in *Manual for the City of New York*, ed. D. T. Valentine (New York, 1853).

6. Evert Bancker, Jr., "List of Farms on New York Island, 1780," *New-York Historical Society Quarterly* 1 (April 1917): 8–11. The six farms belonged to Trinity Church, James Delancey, Henry Rutgers, Nicholas Bayard, the heirs of Peter Warren, and the Stuyvesant family.

7. Representative long-term leases for this period can be found in the microfilmed Libers of Deeds and Conveyances for New York County in the Office of the City Registrar; in the New York City Papers, miscellaneous MSS, New-York Historical Society; in the Beekman, Byvanck, Delancey, DePeyster, Duane, Leake, and Trinity Church papers in the New-York Historical Society; and in the Bayard-Pearsall-Campbell Papers of the New York Public Library Manuscripts Division.

8. Trinity Church Papers, Miscellaneous MSS (box 29), New-York Historical Society.

9. An inventory of patriot real property holdings at the time of the Revolution, for example, showed that while nearly half of the patriot proprietors owned more than one house, only 11% owned more than three houses in one ward and that only 11 out of 170 patriots owned four or more houses. "Estimates of Value of the Real Estate Belonging to Persons Now in Actual Rebellion," in *Fascimile of Manuscripts in European Collections Relating to America, 1773–1783* (London, 1889–93), 12:1234–35.

10. Delancey's testimony is found in the transcripts of the *Manuscript Book and Papers of the Commission of Enquiry into the Losses and Services of American Loyalists*, 41:292–314, in the New York Public Library Manuscripts Division.

11. My analysis of colonial building and patterns of occupancy is based on a close reading of newspaper advertisements. Notices are reprinted in three volumes compiled by Rita Susswein Gottesman, *The Arts and Crafts in New York: Advertisements and News Items from New York City Newspapers*, in *New-York Historical Society Collections* 64 (1938) for 1726–76; 81 (1954) for 1776–99; 82 (1965) for 1800–1804; in "Old New York and Trinity Church," *New-York Historical Society Collections* 3 (1870), and in David

T. Valentine, comp., *Manual for the City of New York* (1854), 672–739; (1855), 726–839; (1866), 617–724. Observations on housing density are based on population and housing figures in Evarts Greene and Virginia Harrington, *American Population before the Federal Census of 1790* (New York, 1932).

12. For discussion of the economic development of New York City in this period, see Sidney I. Pomerantz, *New York: An American City, 1783–1803* (New York, 1938); Allan R. Pred, *Spatial Dynamics of Urban Industrial Growth, 1800–1914* (Cambridge, Mass., 1966), 163–85; and for later years, R. G. Albion, *The Rise of New York Port, 1815–1860* (New York, 1939). For changes in the city's social structure, see Raymond Mohl, *Poverty in New York, 1783–1825* (New York, 1971); Howard B. Rock, *Artisans of the New Republic: The Tradesmen of New York City in the Age of Jefferson* (New York, 1979); Christine Stansell, *City of Women: Sex and Class in New York 1789–1860* (New York, 1986); Sean Wilentz, *Chants Democratic: New York City and the Rise of the American Working Class, 1788–1850* (New York, 1984); and Edmund Willis, "Social Origins and Political Leadership in New York City from the Revolution to 1815," (Ph.D. diss., University of California, Berkeley, 1967), esp. chap. 3.

13. James Vance, "Housing the Worker: The Employment Linkage as a Force in Urban Structure," *Economic Geography* 42 (1966): 309–25.

14. Edmund Willis, "Social Origins and Political Leadership," 113.

15. While 70.5% of the city's taxpayers owned land in 1730, by 1796 only 54% were proprietors. Among voters, property ownership declined from 29.6% in 1795 to 19.5% in 1815. As a proportion of the entire city population, these figures from tax and voting records do not take into full account women, blacks, and that portion of the population that did not own enough personal property to appear in the tax rolls. See Bruce Wilkenfield, "Social and Economic Structure," 208; Edmund Willis, "Social Origins and Political Leadership," 113–19; and the 1807 Electoral Census in *Minutes of the Common Council* (New York, 1917), 4:649–52.

16. Harry Yshope, *The Disposition of Loyalist Estates in the Southern District of the State of New York* (New York, 1939), 28–31, 154–56.

17. My analysis of landlords' policies and the effects of the leasehold system on social geography are based on the private papers and rent rolls in, among others, the Astor, Johnson, Leake, McComb, Morris, Probyn, Rhinelander, and Trinity Church papers in the New-York Historical Society. For the management of the Rutgers, Stuyvesant, Bleecker, and Pell lands, I studied transactions recorded in the Libers of Deeds and Conveyances and indexed by location in the *Block Index of Reindexed Conveyances*. Long-term and building leases were regularly recorded in the city clerk's office.

18. Observations on the changing social geography are based on the street surveys of Evert Bancker, Jr., 1779–1800, in the Bancker Papers, New-York Historical Society; on

Longworth's New York Directory for the years 1799–1820; and, for 1812, on *Trow's New York Directory*, organized by streets.

19. See, for example, Henry Livingston's letter to his agent requesting the latter to remove a family of black rag pickers who rented the stable behind the Livingstons' house on Leonard Street. Henry Livingston to Charles Osborn, Aug. 25, 1843, in the Osborn Papers, New York Public Library.

20. G. W. Sheldon, "The Old Ship Builders of New York," *Harper's Magazine* 65 (1882): 221–41; Frank Norcross, *A History of New York Swamp* (New York, 1901); and the holdings of Brown and Lorillard in Libers of Deeds and Conveyances.

21. My observation on the tiers of landlords in the housing market are based on the account books of agents Charles Osborn (1814–28) and his sons Charles and George L. Osborn (1842–51) in the Manuscript Division, New York Public Library; for further discussion see Blackmar, *Quality of Rents*, chap. 7.

22. For labor discontent, see Alfred Young, "The Mechanics and the Jeffersonians: New York, 1789–1801," *Labor History* 5 (1964): 260–64, and Howard B. Rock, "The American Revolution and the Mechanics of New York City: One Generation Later," *New York History* 57 (July 1976): 367–94.

23. Advertisements for housing in the *Commercial Advertiser*, 1800–1820, are extremely valuable in revealing the process of breaking up houses for new patterns of occupancy.

24. In her diary (1799–1806), in the New York Public Library, Elizabeth Bleeker reported numerous "incidents" that illustrate the perils "respectable" Manhattanites encountered by living in the port district. For example, on Nov. 28, 1804, Bleeker found "a mob at the door occasioned by a black woman who was intoxicated and had a little milatoe [*sic*] girl with her whom she had given liquor."

25. See *History of Architecture and Building Trades of Greater New York* (New York, 1899); Real Estate Record, *A History of Real Estate, Building, and Architecture in New York City* (New York, 1898); and Samuel B. Ruggles Papers, New York Public Library. The numerous court cases involving building contracts and liens provide dramatic illustrations of the controversies and risks that dominated New York's building industry in this period.

26. For the creation of middle-class streets and neighborhoods through the building of set-back townhouses, see Charles Lockwood, *Bricks and Brownstones: The New York Row House, 1783–1929* (New York, 1972). For the formation of the city's slums, see the excellent descriptive essay in James Ford, *Slums and Housing* (New York, 1937), 72–204.

27. *A Summary Historical, Geographical, and Statistical View of the City of New York* (New York, 1836), 17; James Hardie, *A Census of the New Buildings Erected in this City in the Year 1824* (New York, 1825).

28. In the early 1840s, New York City inspectors began to call attention to the extreme shortage of adequate housing

and especially to the use of cellars and rear houses in their *Annual Reports.* The Annual Reports of the New York Association for Improving the Condition of the Poor, beginning in 1845, also provided statistical documentation of the city's housing crisis. In his *Sanitary Conditions of the Laboring Population of New York* (New York, 1845), John Griscom argued that it was economically unhealthy for the city to lose the labor power of its working class to disease and epidemics exacerbated by poor housing.

29. From 1834 to 1849, the Annual Report of New York City Inspectors contained a census of new building each year, giving the height, materials, and streets of new houses.

30. Anthony Sutcliffe, *Multi-Story Living: The British Working Class Experience* (London, 1974).

Pawtucket Village and the Strike of 1824: The Origins of Class Conflict in Rhode Island

GARY KULIK

At the close of the eighteenth century, the look and feel of the American landscape began to change radically. In Pawtucket, Rhode Island, in the 1790s, a series of ambitious textile mills and proprietors' houses sprang up in the midst of what had since the seventeenth century been a community used to the seasonal rhythms of farming, shipbuilding, and ironworking. By 1824 these new industrial buildings dwarfed the smaller houses, barns, and shops of yeomen, artisans, and newly recruited mill workers; their dissimilarities of scale, materials, and inhabitants represented the social structure of inchoate industrial capitalism. In 1824 a major strike in protest of increased work hours, and low wages for some female weavers, articulated the new class consciousness that had mobilized local workers in opposition to Samuel Slater and his Quaker merchant backers from nearby Providence. As he explains the causes and contexts of the 1824 strike, Gary Kulik reveals the growing inequalities that shaped American material life in the early nineteenth century.

The Pawtucket strikers were not an unruly mob acting without reason. Their acts of protest were carefully planned to achieve specific ends. As farm people, most townsmen were ill prepared for the work discipline imposed on their lives by the mills. Before the 1790s, they had made free use of local rivers and streams to fish and to power local saw- and gristmills. The mill owners "enclosed" the rivers. Before industrialization, time passed in irregular intervals defined by work as a social activity. After Slater's arrival, bells signaled the beginning and end of work, and clocks ticked out regular wages. Before 1790, all the houses in town were wooden. After the mill owners came, three-story brick mansions broke the horizon of local morality with a new sense of self-proclaimed authority. Now even churches had to compete with belfried mill buildings as landmarks for travelers. When wages dropped in the 1820s, the ability of mill workers and local artisans to acquire and maintain property was threatened.

The strikers drew on recognized forms of English popular culture in their protest of having their labor appropriated as a commodity. Eighteenth-century traditions of workers' "combinations," for example, were revived as models for protective trade union groups. When these and other measures proved insufficient to gain redress, their activity escalated. Sometimes they resorted to violence. Street mobs threatened the houses of mill owners, windows in mills were broken, and anonymous arsonists tried to burn the mills down. In response, mill owners had boys pull floats boasting textile machinery through the Pawtucket streets, making the contest for property a form of folk theater. While the landscape of social distance in Pawtucket was reshaped by mill owners eager to gain control of public space and local resources, it was also a stage on which workers fought to retain some control over their own lives.

Ⅰn the late spring of 1824, approximately five hundred textile workers closed the spinning and weaving mills of Pawtucket in a week-long strike. The strike, the earliest in the North American textile industry and the first of any kind to involve women, laid bare deep social cleavages in this Blackstone River village (fig. 1). During this week, mill owners faced determined and well-organized workers, the hostility of angry village crowds, and the threat of arson. Community outrage was sufficient to compel a compromise settlement. Such a settlement, in a period when workers generally lost strikes, is noteworthy and indicates both a measure of worker power and the community's ability to impose effective sanctions on the behavior of mill owners.[1]

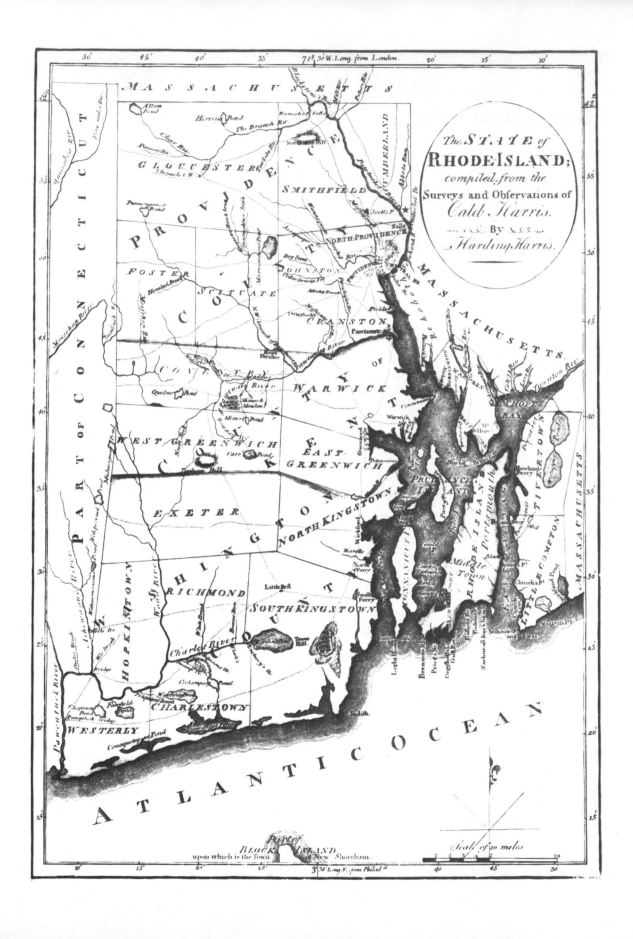

The STATE of RHODE-ISLAND; compiled, from the Surveys and Observations of Caleb Harris. By Harding Harris.

Though the strike dramatically underlined the attitude of villagers to the textile mills, it was neither the first act of community resistance nor the last. Resistance to the village's textile industry had been visible since 1790, when the famous English immigrant Samuel Slater established the first Arkwright spinning mill in America in a former clothier's shop at Pawtucket Falls. Through the 1830s, resistance was intermittently punctuated by conflict over water rights, taxes, work routines, and the recording of factory time. This conflict was engendered by the rapid expansion of the textile industry in the years before 1830 and the substantial social changes it brought in its wake. The most important of these changes were the increased use of unskilled labor and the new definitions of time, work, and leisure that accompanied the rise of industrial capitalism; the far more extensive use of waterpower and the challenge this posed for customary notions of water rights; and the increasing efforts of mill owners to achieve cultural and political authority commensurate with their economic power.

The events of 1824 in Pawtucket—and by implication similar events elsewhere—can only be understood in the context of a long tradition of local resistance to textile mills and mill owners. The existence of such traditions has usually been ignored or denied by American historians, who prefer the notion that capitalism sank its roots into American society quickly and without opposition. But the more closely one examines the values and beliefs textile workers brought into the mills, and the more carefully one traces the origins of those beliefs in rural culture and democratic thought, the more apparent it becomes that the "triumph" of capitalism was at best difficult and incomplete.

In this essay I develop themes similar to those suggested by Herbert Gutman and, more recently, by Alan Dawley. Gutman, in a series of influential articles, has argued two positions that bear directly on early nineteenth-century Pawtucket. First, in a study of industrial communities in the Ohio River Valley in the 1870s, Gutman argued that values "alien to industrialism" were stronger and more vibrant in relatively small hinterland towns recently subjected to the new pressures of industrial capitalism and that those values were manifested in widespread community support for workers during strikes. Second, drawing on the work of E. P. Thompson, Gutman has argued that first-generation migrants to industrial capitalism brought with them preindustrial values, which persisted and formed the core of private and, at times, collective resistance to the values of industrial capitalism. Alan Dawley, in his book *Class and Community: The Industrial Revolution in Lynn*, has pressed these points further and has succeeded in attaching a name to those values that nurtured resistance to the growing power of industrial capital. For Dawley, the belief in "equal rights," rooted in the producer ethic common to both rural and artisan culture, was the ideological source of labor's nineteenth-century oppositional tradition. Whether or not one chooses to call the tradition "equal rights," it is clear that some such oppositional tradition fed the artisan and working-class movement of the 1830s and that its origin antedated that movement. In Pawtucket, an oppositional tradition grew out of the patterns and expectations of rural and artisan culture, the democratic thought of the Revolutionary period, and the experience of adjusting to the vast changes wrought by the introduction of the textile mills.[2]

Pawtucket came to nourish that oppositional tradition because of the particular pattern of its industrial development. A settled artisan community before the introduction of textile mills, Pawtucket was relatively free of those institutions of mill owner control—company-owned houses, stores, and churches—that prominently marked other New England textile villages. Moreover, the presence of artisans provided mill workers with additional sources of support during times of crisis. It is my further purpose to suggest the quality of the relationship between mill workers and artisans and to assess the strengths and limits of that relationship.

From 1790 to approximately 1820, the village of Pawtucket, located on the banks of the Blackstone River and straddling the Rhode Island–Massachusetts border, was the most important industrial village in the United States. The water-powered cotton textile industry began here in 1790 with Samuel Slater's introduction of the Arkwright system of carding and spinning. By the early 1820s, this village of close to three thousand inhabitants supported eight textile

Fig. 1. *The State of Rhode Island by Caleb Harris*, Philadelphia, 1814. Star shows location of Pawtucket. (Photograph courtesy of the Rhode Island Historical Society.)

mills, six of them likely involved in both spinning and weaving. The largest and most important of the mills were: the two-story, wood-frame Slater Mill (fig. 2), built in 1793 and owned by the English immigrant Slater and the Providence merchants William Almy and Smith Brown, the latter two kinsmen of the wealthy Quaker merchant Moses Brown; the White Mill, built in wood about 1800 (fig. 3), expanded in stone in 1813, and owned by the skilled and upwardly mobile artisan Oziel Wilkinson and three of his sons-in-law; the four-story Yellow Mill, built in 1805, expanded in 1813, and owned by a group of prominent local merchants, including Maj. Ebenezer Tyler, Nathaniel Croade, Oliver Starkweather, and Eliphalet Slack; and the four-story, stone Wilkinson Mill (fig. 4), built in 1810–11 by Oziel Wilkinson and operated by his son, David. By the early 1830s, the village's textile industry ran approximately fourteen thousand spindles, over 350 looms, and employed slightly fewer than five hundred workers.[3]

Textile mills did not wholly dominate the local economy. Pawtucket had been an ironworking center since the mid-seventeenth century. By the early nineteenth century, the village produced anchors, nails, screws for linseed and fish oil presses (some cast, the others turned on David Wilkinson's screw-cutting machine—the American forerunner of the slide-rest, industrial lathe), cannons, hollow ware, and assorted castings. The work was done in numerous small

Fig. 3. *Pawtucket Falls, 1812*, from *Polyanthus* 1 (1812). (Photograph courtesy of the Rhode Island Historical Society.)

forges located along the river and in a rolling and slitting mill operated by the Wilkinsons. In addition to the ironworking shops, Pawtucket's artisans ran a gristmill, a tannery and bark mill, three snuff mills, one linseed oil mill, three fulling mills, and a clothier's works. The village also had a sizable shipbuilding industry. Between 1794 and 1805, one builder, George Robinson, employed nineteen to twenty ship carpenters and built seventeen vessels ranging in size from 80 to 280 tons. This local industry provided a market for the village's ironworkers, but when shipbuilding collapsed during the embargo years, most of the ship-related iron business collapsed with it. The growth of the textile industry, however, provided a

Fig. 2. Slater Mill, Pawtucket, Rhode Island, 1793 and later. (Photograph by Robert Blair St. George.)

Fig. 4. Wilkinson Mill, Pawtucket, Rhode Island, 1810–11. (Photograph by Robert Blair St. George.)

new market for the village's ironworks. A few artisans, such as the Wilkinsons, had previous experience in building textile machinery, but significant expansion did not occur until 1812–13. By 1819, on the Rhode Island side alone, there were "six shops engaged in the manufacture of machinery." One year later, the census taker remarked that the machine shops employed "a great number of hands" and built "all kinds of mill machinery." This was a sophisticated and nationally important industry, nurturing such prominent inventors and machine builders as David Wilkinson, Asa Arnold, John Thorp, Larned Pitcher, and James Brown.[4]

Pawtucket, like many English towns, was an industrial village before the introduction of textile mills. Unlike the large urban complexes on the Merrimack River or the smaller villages on the Blackstone and Pawtuxet rivers, Pawtucket experienced capitalist industrialization in a context of both rural experience and artisan tradition. This was not a village like Slatersville, Rhode Island, for example, where the entire physical plant—mills, canals, and class-structured housing—was implanted in an isolated rural community, crystallizing at once a set of hierarchical relationships that would seem to later generations to be both permanent and inevitable. Pawtucket in 1800 was a community of artisans and farmers with distinct industrial and preindustrial traditions, a community in which wealth, status, and power had not coalesced in a consistent pattern.[5]

Class, and class consciousness, emerged in Pawtucket as the textile industry developed. A new and distinct class consisting of textile mill owners and wealthy merchants with textile investments formed itself before 1820. The common needs of textile capitalists to recruit and discipline labor, to secure uncontested rights to waterpower, and to exercise political and social control in the village, drew Pawtucket's mill owners together in fundamental ways. Despite early conflict between Moses Brown and Samuel Slater over the building of the White Mill, Brown wrote in 1802 that "in order to save the business from immediate ruin we thought best to so far unite so as not to interfere with each other in workmen nor wages."[6] This early agreement set the tone for future cooperation. By the 1820s, Pawtucket's mill owners were accustomed to meeting together to regulate hours and wages and to discuss matters of common interest.[7]

Economic interest was reinforced by kinship and religion. Oziel Wilkinson had three of his sons, Abraham, Isaac, and David, and four sons-in-law, Samuel Slater, Timothy Greene, Hezikiah Howe, and William Wilkinson, involved with him in textile mill ownership. A few of the owners, like the Wilkinsons and the Browns, were Quakers, and a distinct network of Quaker businessmen developed along the East coast for the sale and distribution of yarn. Other owners were Baptist or Episcopalian, but sectarian ties were never strong enough to limit cooperation. Mill owners of different religions dominated the founding of Pawtucket's Sunday school and, along with their wives, played a critical role in the formation and administration of the Baptist and Episcopal churches, the Pawtucket Moral Society, and the Female Beneficent Society. Such activity expressed more than a simple, shared piety. In forming these institutions, mill owners attempted to convey their own standards of industry, propriety, and religion to a community of laborers and artisans with frequently distinct standards.[8]

The mill owners were most conspicuously different from their poorer neighbors in their patterns of consumption and display. Though they were the village's sole owners of carriages, their stately houses were the most visible manifestation of their wealth. Ebenezer Tyler's house, built about 1800 on the corner of Main Street and East Avenue, was "then the only three story dwelling in the place."[9] Samuel Slater and his second wife finished a brick structure (fig. 5), begun by Hezikiah Howe, on three East Avenue

Fig. 5. The Slater mansion, ca. 1820. (Photograph courtesy of the Slater Mill Historic Site.)

lots. Bought from Howe in 1819 for $6,500, the "Slater mansion" was richly decorated. Wallpaper depicting Oriental scenes embellished one parlor, while the walls of another featured scenes from Sir Walter Scott's *Lady of the Lake.* On the east side of the river, Oliver Starkweather built his "mansion house" about 1800. The Starkweather house's elaborate detail, quoined corners, ornate entrance, and gabled dormers rivaled the finest Federal houses of the period. In 1815, Col. Eliphalet Slack, involved with Starkweather and Tyler in mill ownership, built an imposing brick house for himself: "For a long period these two were the finest dwellings in Pawtucket on either side of the river. The Walcotts and the Pitchers, who were interested in the cotton manufacture and other industries, erected mansion houses about this time."[10] Here was starkly visible evidence of the changes brought by the advance of the textile industry. The stately houses of Pawtucket's newly rich were not isolated in rural retreats or even in separate neighborhoods, as they would be later, but were built in more than one neighborhood and in the midst of ruder housing. For some they were affronts to the traditional order (fig. 6), and for the striking textile workers of 1824, they served to focus community animosity.[11]

Fig. 6. Plan of artisan-laborer's cottage, Pawtucket, Rhode Island, ca. 1758. (Drawing by Robert Blair St. George.)

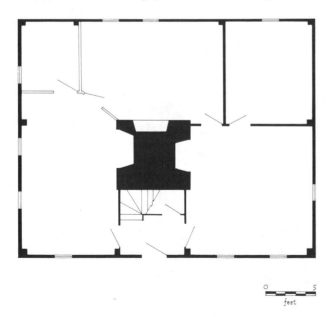

0   5
feet

As late as 1820, Pawtucket was a community primarily composed of artisans. A few, like the metalworking Jenkses, had deep roots both in the village and in their trade, but the majority were recent migrants from the countryside who entered Pawtucket in the period of industrial expansion that followed the Revolution. The term *artisan*, or *mechanic* (as they were then known), encompassed a variety of trades and masked subtle differences in status, work routine, wealth, and power. Some master artisans, like the highly skilled Wilkinsons, were critical of the development of the textile industry, and their values and allegiances developed accordingly. For every master, however, there were many more apprentices and journeymen, as well as others for whom the customary forms of apprenticeship were largely meaningless. The village's ship carpenters, for example, worked as wage laborers under a single master ship builder in gangs as large as twenty and with little opportunity for advancement.[12] And with the rapid growth of textile machine shops in the years of embargo and war, many machinists and metalworkers became increasingly subject to distinctively capitalist forms of business organization. These artisans thus experienced a loss of autonomy similar to, though not as extreme as, that which confronted the village's textile workers.[13]

Pawtucket's artisans were men poised in the middle, with the lure of independent proprietorship on the one side and the disgrace of downward mobility into the ranks of factory labor on the other. Historians know more about the successful—those such as Oziel Wilkinson who rose to industrial prominence and took a leading part in town politics. But for every Wilkinson there were many more like the Smithfield shoemaker Stafford Benchley, forced to give up his trade and to enter a local textile mill with his family in order to meet mounting debts.[14]

The chance for upward mobility affected whether artisans identified with those above them or with those below them in the new industrial hierarchy. Craftsmen and laborers like the ship carpenters, nail makers, and others whose time was hired by master artisans, were likely to identify with the village's textile workers. The ship carpenters, in particular, whose work was seasonal and who returned to local farms in the winter, adhered to a loose and traditional pattern of work close to the rhythms of agricultural life. Stigmatized by the local Baptist minister as "wanting in stability," the ship carpenters were the natural allies of the textile workers, whose behavior invoked identical, if harsher, comment. Other artisans, particularly those master machinists who saw their fate directly linked to the textile industry, accepted the values and ideology of mill owners. In their attitudes and behavior, in their standards of work, time discipline, and moral propriety, they were among the village's "respectables."

Independent proprietorship and "respectable" behavior, however, did not necessarily imply deference to mill owners. Direct conflict between artisans and mill owners occurred remarkably early. When the Slater Mill was built in 1793 it was necessary to build a second dam on the Blackstone a short distance upstream of Pawtucket Falls. The building of the Slater Mill dam restricted the flow of water available to the ironworkers John, Stephan, and Eleazer Jenks, whose ancestors were the first to use the Pawtucket Falls water privilege. The Jenkses responded, in the words of the court case that followed, by "illegally and violently" pulling down the upper dam. This act of sabotage was only the first instance in a prolonged and acrimonious local conflict over the fair apportioning of the Blackstone's power.[15]

Even other "respectable" artisans, who seemed to subscribe to the values of mill owners, were often ambivalent. In the early 1820s, local artisans formed the Pawtucket Mechanics Society apart from the prior organization of the mill owners and their agents. None of the society's numerous officers were mill owners. At a dinner meeting of the society held in the Smithfield Hotel on March 20, 1828, the artisans offered toasts to the "American System," to Henry Clay (the "Champion of Freedom"), and to General Jackson: "In the hands of a mad opposition he would cut the throat of his country." Each of the toasts reflects a political culture shared by mill owners and artisans. However, the meeting was held in celebration of the traditional ending of the use of artificial light for late-afternoon labor in the textile mills. This was an authentic element of working-class culture in New England mill towns. In Lowell, "blowing out" balls customarily marked the twentieth of March, and the practice continued in Rhode Island at least into the 1850s.[16]

It is not surprising that Pawtucket artisans identified with those below them in the new industrial hierarchy. Many had directly experienced the changes brought by capitalist organization. Others observed for themselves the increased use of unskilled labor, the new discipline of the factory, and the emergence of a wealthy elite. In the bonds of experience, common culture, and kinship, the lives of lesser artisans and mill workers were linked. These links strengthened and made more visible Pawtucket's resistance to the claims of capital. There is an important and growing literature on the centrality of artisan leadership both to the American and to the European trade union movement. But the evidence from Pawtucket indicates relatively little direct leadership by artisans, at least before the 1830s. During this decade, local artisans played a critical role in the formation of the area's first labor paper, the *New England Artisan*, and in the establishment of the first regional labor organization, the New England Association of Farmers, Mechanics, and Other Workingmen. The strike of 1824 was led not by artisans but by the young women weavers. The artisan presence was important, however, because it provided mill workers with additional resources of experience and support. This alliance between mill workers and artisans was most noticeable during times of crisis. Yet at other times, and increasingly through the 1830s, for reasons to be explored in the conclusion, that alliance appeared fragile and incomplete, its promise never fully realized.[17]

Pawtucket's textile workers were generally recruited in family units from nearby farms. Large families were prized by the early spinning mills because of the industry's need for child labor. In 1820, children constituted more than two-thirds of Pawtucket's textile workforce. A sizable number of adults and some children were, however, employed outside the factories, for the industry was only partially mechanized. In its first twenty to thirty years, the spinning mills of Pawtucket depended on handloom weavers and hand pickers. The latter were workers who, in their own homes, opened the raw cotton by hand, separated the fibers, and removed the excess dirt and seeds. The weavers, often farmers or members of farm families, produced finished cloth from yarn furnished by the mills at a rate fixed by the mill owners. Because of the nature of production, numerous local families came into direct contact with the new textile industry.[18]

The mechanization of picking and weaving in cotton textiles took place between 1814 and 1825 and was essentially complete in Pawtucket by 1824. Machine pickers and power looms increased production and altered the composition of the workforce. More young women entered the factories to tend the new power looms. Labor was sufficiently scarce throughout this period to require mill owners to lure their new labor with cash wages. One Pawtucket company advertised in 1821 for "Twenty-four good Water Loom Weavers, to whom good wages will be given, part cash, or all, if particularly required." The increased rate of work made it difficult for small children to keep pace, and by the mid-1820s they were rarely used as production workers. Children remained in the mills in a variety of auxiliary jobs, most of which involved moving stock from one point in the production process to the next. The percentage of children in Pawtucket's cotton mills declined from almost 70 percent of the total workforce in 1820 to approximately 40 percent in 1831. Over the same period, the percentage of women increased from about 16 percent to over 30 percent, while the percentage of adult men increased from about 15 percent to about 25 percent. By 1824, Pawtucket's textile mills exhibited a fully mature factory system, a system that necessarily incorporated a much larger number of adult workers.[19]

Pawtucket's mill workers did not adjust easily to the demands of industrial capitalism. Freshly drawn from the tasks of farm labor, they were not yet accustomed to the methodical, attention-demanding, and repetitive nature of factory work, nor to the new strictures of a day's work solely defined by the factory bell. They expressed their independence from the mill owners in a number of critical ways. During various times in the industry's first decade, parents disrupted production by removing their children from the Slater Mill at random moments in the day; handpickers refused to work with dirty cotton; children refused to clean ice from the water wheel; five to six male workers left Slater's employ in a dispute over wages to begin a mill of their own; and during berry-picking season in July 1796, most of Slater's outworkers chose to pick whortleberries rather than clean cotton.[20]

The village's textile workers expressed their independence outside the factory as well, to the discomfort of such moralists as the Baptist minister David Benedict:

> The cotton mill business had brought in a large influx of people who came in the *second-class* cars.

Such was the prejudice against the business that few others could be had, and the highways and hedges had to be searched even for them. . . . There was a set of old and staid inhabitants of a very respectable class, who made up their minds to live here the best way they could. But when strangers came here who had been accustomed to a good state of society, they made loud complaints, and their censures were frequent and free. *Bang-all*, *Hard-scrabble*, *Bung-town*, *Pilfershire*, etc., were with them appropriate epithets for the place.[21]

Elsewhere, Benedict referred to Pawtucket as a "nest of corruption and disorder,"[22] and one of the village's nineteenth-century historians argued that the first generation of local mill workers had a reputation for "rough, rude, and boisterous behavior, for drunkenness and debauchery."[23]

These are of course class-biased comments, but they indicate the extent to which Pawtucket's workers lived beyond the comfortable propriety of churchgoing mill owners. By all accounts, local mill workers drank heavily. The village's dozen taverns were not closely licensed, and local production of liquor was extensive. In 1820, there were sixteen cider mills in North Providence producing nine hundred barrels a year. In the same year, a single local resident, Oliver Holmes, brewed eight hundred barrels of beer, and a local cooper, Edmund Shelton, worked full-time in the production of rum barrels. The minister and deacons of Pawtucket's First Baptist Church continually expressed concern over the drinking habits of church members. The church elders were equally preoccupied with sexual misdeeds. Even among church members (a decided minority of the population) the incidence of pre- and extramarital sex was marked, though only women seem to have been singled out for the ritualized investigations. Such investigations were most often followed by confession, excommunication, and, on occasion, by readmission to church "fellowship." In their drinking habits and their sexual behavior, the village's workers conformed to the more openly secular standards of the late eighteenth century, a period noted for its alcoholic consumption and for its high rate of premarital pregnancy, the highest of any period in American history before the 1960s.[24]

The mill workers also distinguished themselves from the mill owners and their supporters by their recreation. The primary summer sport for both children and adults consisted of swimming in the Black-stone. The nude swimming of adolescent boys elic-ited middle-class outrage, but not as much as the practice of high diving. It became customary for boys, swimming both at the noon hour and after work, to challenge each other to jump from large rocks at the river's edge and from the Main Street bridge into the eddy below the falls. The "boldest" of the jumpers was mule spinner Sam Patch, who began his short but brilliant career as a nationally promi-nent daredevil by jumping off the four-story Yellow Mill into the river. Patch, the best-known Pawtucket resident of his time, attracted large local crowds and, according to one account, left the village after "people began to object" to his performances. He be-came a traveling "professional," immortalized in nineteenth-century folklore.[25]

The mill owners made concerted efforts to control the behavior of the village's workers by establishing churches, moral reform societies, and temperance or-ganizations, all designed to buttress the values and ideology of industrial capitalism. Their efforts, re-flecting a desire to achieve cultural hegemony in the village, were similar to those of American industrial-ists elsewhere in this period. Paul Faler, in his study of Lynn, Massachusetts, in the early nineteenth cen-tury, has described the attempt of local manufactur-ers to create an "industrial morality," emphasizing order, inner discipline, propriety, and the work ethic.[26] Pawtucket's mill owners adhered to the same morality and attempted to extend its reach to the en-tire village. In 1815, two years after a significant ex-pansion in textile mill capacity, the owners formed the Pawtucket Moral Society to "combat the irreli-gion and licentiousness" said to be connected with rapid population increase. Mill owner Timothy Greene was its first president, Oliver Starkweather and Samuel Slater, its first vice presidents. Its objects were to "suppress intemperance," "profane swear-ing," and "breaches of the Sabbath."[27] The last prob-lem was particularly vexing. It became customary for the Baptist church to appoint a committee each year "to preserve order in and about the meeting house in time of service."[28] Like the children of Slatersville, Rhode Island, who in this period played ball "before the doors" of the meeting house "all the time of ser-vice," most of Pawtucket's workers viewed Sunday not as a day of religious observance but as a time for rest and recreation.[29] Recognizing the difficulty of changing the behavior of workers through voluntary

organizations, local mill owners also attempted to in-crease police power. In June 1814, mill owners and their supporters petitioned the Rhode Island General Assembly for authorization to form a local police force "for the punishing of such persons who may be disturbers of the peace." The twenty-five signers ad-mitted that "it has often been found difficult to pre-serve order and due subordination."[30]

Throughout this period few mill workers joined churches. Over all, no more than 15 percent of the area's population belonged to Pawtucket's churches. First Baptist, formed in 1805 and dominated by mill owners Starkweather, Tyler, Croade, and Slack, had fewer than 200 members in 1820. Some mill workers joined the church, particularly in periods of eco-nomic depression, but they did not do so in great numbers. St. Paul's, an Episcopal church formed in 1815 with the active support of Slater, David Wilkin-son, Barney Merry, and the Greenes, had 309 mem-bers in 1824, many of whom were children. For a time, it faced the village's "bitter hostility," perhaps because of its associations with British aristocracy and high-church ritual. It is likely that the only workers who joined were recent British immigrants like Edward Jones, who in 1820 lived in a mill worker tenement. The one church free of mill-owner influ-ence at its inception was the Free-Will Baptist, formed by Ray Potter in 1820 with only 60 to 70 members. In 1821, mill owner and church member Daniel Greene, hostile to Potter's encouragement of revivalism and religious "enthusiasm," set a portion of the congregation against Potter and gained control of the church. Potter's published defense was cast in the form of a sermon on the biblical text "Do not rich men oppress you? Io to ye rich men, weep and howl for the miseries that shall come upon you." Greene's successful bid to control Free-Will Baptist established the authority of mill owners over the vil-lage's only evangelical sect, whose beliefs were im-plicitly democratic and whose practice was, on occa-sion, disruptive of public order.[31]

The independence of Pawtucket's mill workers was nurtured on the rocky and unyielding soil of New En-gland's hard-scrabble farms and derived in part from standards of work, leisure, and customary right char-acteristic of noncommodity production, a form that Michael Merrill has termed the household mode of production. This was a cultural inheritance re-inforced by the responses of farmers themselves to the coming of the spinning mills. Many mill workers who migrated from local farms in the first thirty years of textile mill development carried with them the knowledge that their neighbors and kinsmen had previously defied the encroachment of textile mill owners and other industrialists. The farmers of Waterford, Rhode Island, for example, opposed the building of a woolen mill and "placed all the obstacles which they could in its way." Other farmers contested mill owners over matters of tax policy, road building, and town division. But the most pervasive form of conflict saw farmers invoking stout definitions of customary right in a long series of disputes over waterpower. In so doing, their actions evoke the outlines of what E. P. Thompson has identified as a "moral economy of the poor" in eighteenth-century England: "a traditional view of social norms and obligations, of the proper economic functions of several parties within the community."[32]

Dams built to provide waterpower for textile mills or iron furnaces had two serious consequences for those farmers who lived above the dams. First, the building of a new dam sufficient to power those industries that required a substantial, continuous flow significantly raised water levels upstream and frequently flooded arable farmland. This occurred in Valley Falls, Scituate, and Manville, Rhode Island. In two of the cases, the aggrieved farmers won court cases against the mill owners, but the fines imposed were not high, and the upstream lands remained underwater. The flooding of good farmland caused bitterness. One resident of Valley Falls, a Blackstone River mill town just above Pawtucket, pointedly complained that "one of two of the best farms in the region [was] forever submerged under the waters of the created [mill] pond."[33] Second, the building of dams the width of the river forced curtailment of the seasonal fish runs. This had serious consequences for farmers and fishermen accustomed to the traditional spawning of shad, alewives, and salmon at Woonsocket Falls. Before the extensive damming of the Blackstone, according to one report, "salmon were very plentiful, so much so that they formed the chief article in the farmer's bill of fare."[34] Conflict over fishing rights had divided the village previously. In 1714, local residents cut a fishway, known as Sargeant's Trench, around the Pawtucket Falls on the west bank. When the fishway failed in its purpose, anti-industrial interests were strong enough to have the Rhode Island General Assembly declare the

Blackstone a "public" river and to make it lawful to break down or blow up the rocks at Pawtucket Falls to "let fish pass up."[35] The controversy festered until the damming of the river in 1792–93, and the refusal of both the Court of Common Pleas in Taunton, Massachusetts, and the Rhode Island General Assembly to act against the mill owners effectively ended any hope of redress for the farmers and fishermen.[36]

The oppositional elements of eighteenth-century rural culture were given political direction by the popular democratic thought of the Revolutionary period. The villagers were active partisans of the Revolution and maintained strong democratic values. Some of Rehoboth's farmers, for instance, participated in Shays' Rebellion and gained the support of a majority of the town's freemen, and the voters of North Providence played an important and continuing part in efforts to expand the restrictive Rhode Island suffrage. As a consequence of such traditions, many of the villagers opposed the textile mills as a British importation. It was, of course, not uncommon in this period for many Americans to view British manufacturing as a threat to democratic liberties and as an assault on equality. According to Benedict, there was prejudice against Slater because he was an Englishman, prejudice that "lasted some time, and attached to everything pertaining to cotton manufacturing." Pawtucket's textile workers thus inherited a democratic and egalitarian culture, suspicious of textile mill owners and resistant to "industrial" values, a culture with its roots in eighteenth-century agricultural life and the traditions of the Revolutionary period.[37]

This oppositional culture formed a common heritage for many textile workers throughout New England, but it was especially vibrant in Pawtucket because mill owners had to build their institutions and impress their values within a preexisting community with strong internal ties. In their first thirty years in Pawtucket, textile mill owners altered the physical landscape with their large mills and stately houses, greatly increased the numbers of unskilled laborers by employing women and children, introduced new definitions of time, work, and leisure, and attempted to secure political and cultural control of the village. Their hegemony, however, was never secure. Despite their wealth and despite the increasingly restrictive Rhode Island suffrage, they rarely controlled town politics. This meant that they not only had to face recalcitrant work habits but could not mobilize a majority of freemen in their efforts to win uncontested rights to waterpower, freedom from local taxes, and a free hand in disciplining their child laborers. Moreover, this was a village that had no rows of company housing, and no church until 1805. There was one company-run store, but it had no monopoly of local business since it sold its wares alongside numerous other stores. The buttressing institutions of early capitalism were weaker here than elsewhere in New England. Pawtucket was also a community in which the experiential ties among lesser artisans, farmers, and mill workers were especially strong and likely reinforced by kinship and marriage. This became increasingly evident after the introduction of the power loom, when large numbers of young, unmarried women, the daughters of local artisans, farmers, and mill workers, entered the mills to tend the new looms (fig. 7). Unlike the young mill women of Lowell, who developed strong and cohesive ties to each other but had none to the local community (and who consequently lost their strikes of the early 1830s), the weavers of Pawtucket drew strength not only from each other but from the community as well. This was a lesson brought home to the village's mill owners in the spring of 1824.[38]

The strike of 1824 was precipitated by the decisions of local mill owners on May 24 to run their mills one hour longer and to reduce, by approximately 25 percent, the wages of "those who weave by the yard." The owners, acting in concert, intended the changes to take effect June 1. Increasing the workday was to be accomplished by reducing the "time allowed at the several meals." This would bear equally on all workers. Reducing weaving piece-rates, however, would affect only the young women weavers.[39]

The owners' rationale was explicit. They referred to conditions of "general depression" in a report justifying their actions, which was published after the strike. They believed themselves to be paying 10 to 20 percent more for the same work than "any manufacturing district in the union." Their factories were running fewer hours than others to their knowledge. One newspaper report mentioned the recent tariff as a cause of the mill owners' action, but the owners themselves did not discuss it. The owners displayed a remarkable willingness to reveal their competitive

Fig. 7. *Women Winding Shuttle Bobbins,* after a drawing by Winslow Homer in C. Bryant's *Song of the Sower,* 1871. (Photograph courtesy of the Museum of American Textile History.)

disadvantages. If economic arguments were insufficient to convince a hostile community that their actions were responsible, the owners summoned one further argument. They claimed that the women weavers made two dollars a week "above their board" and that this was "generally considered to be extravagant wages for young women." It was, the owners continued, much more than the women could earn elsewhere and was a sum "out of proportion to the wages of other help." This latter statement can be interpreted to mean that some weavers, at least, were making more money than unskilled men.[40]

There is no evidence of "general depression" in 1824. It is clear, however, that by the early 1820s the cotton textile industry was first feeling the effects of the capitalist trade cycle. Earlier periods of economic crisis could be traced partly to political causes. The stronger producers had weathered the overexpansion of the embargo years and the subsequent dumping of British goods at the close of the War of 1812. Beginning in 1819–20, though, the entire industry began to experience periodic bursts of overproduction and declining cloth prices in the context of a volatile and largely uncontrolled market—conditions that haunted the industry throughout the nineteenth century. In the early nineteenth century markets could not be created fast enough or be sufficiently stabilized to keep pace with the thrusts of technological innovation.[41]

Productivity, measured by annual cloth output, rose from 1820 to 1824 by a factor of four, from 13,844,000 yards to 55,777,000 yards. This was primarily the result of the introduction of the power loom. Over the same period, and following the same logic, the average annual price of brown sheeting on the New York market dropped precipitously, from 24.4 cents per yard to 14.6 cents per yard, the sharpest drop coming between 1823 and 1824 (20.7 cents per yard to 14.6 cents per yard). Combined with a steep rise in the average annual price of middling cotton (11.4 cents per pound in 1823, 14.8 cents per pound in 1824), these figures suggest that New England textile mill owners found themselves during the spring of 1824 in deteriorating economic circumstances.[42]

These trends were generally reflected in Pawtucket. The Pawtucket Cotton Manufacturing Company (the name of the Yellow Mill company by 1832) experienced a decline in the price of brown shirting from 30 cents per yard in 1816 to 12.5 cents per yard in 1824. Profits for 1824 were 8 percent, compared to 15 percent the year earlier and to 10 percent in each of the two subsequent years. The early 1820s were also years of serious drought in Pawtucket. Lack of water forced mills to lie idle in the late summer, further contributing to the economic difficulties of local mill owners.[43]

It is not surprising, therefore, that Pawtucket mill owners sought to cut labor costs, for these were the only major costs over which they had control. Their decision to reduce the rates of women weavers may be seen as shrewd calculation. The weavers were the newest entrants to the factory system. Since no real labor market existed for women before textile mill development, it can be assumed that young female weavers had no highly developed sense of a custom-

ary wage. The mill owners evidently believed that the weavers would not respond to a wage cut as forcefully as male laborers. And since piece rates for power weaving were a new and still experimental form of payment, it is likely that female weavers of sufficient skill and dexterity were able to make more money than unskilled males, as the owners seemed to charge. The owners were willing to exploit the issue, perhaps assuming that it would divide the workforce. They miscalculated badly.[44]

Though the increase in hours and reduction in rates were not to go into effect for a week, the workers responded immediately. The local manufacturers' press provided a detailed account of the beginning of the "turnout": "When the laboring part of the community learned the result of the meeting [this was the meeting of owners on May 24], they very generally determined to work only the usual hours; and when the bell rang to call them to their employment, they assembled in great numbers, accompanied by many who were not interested in the affair, round the doors of the mill, apparently for the purpose of hindering or preventing the entrance of those [willing to work], no force, however, was used."[45] The turnout closed all the textile mills in the village and was supported by "many" who did not work in the mills. Moreover, it elicited the spontaneous and militant action of the young women weavers. The *Manufacturers' and Farmers' Journal* continued its account with patriarchal disdain: "The female weavers assembled in parliament to the number, it is stated, of one hundred and two—one of the most active, and most talkative, was placed in the chair, and the meeting, it is understood, was conducted, however strange it may appear, without noise, or scarcely a single speech. The result of the meeting was a resolution to abandon their looms, unless allowed the old prices."[46]

Though the young women weavers very quickly took a leading role in the turnout, they did not act alone. They were supported by a substantial part of the village, and this was made clear on the evening of May 26. According to the *Journal:*

On Wednesday evening a tumultuous crowd filled the streets, led by the most unprincipled and disorderly part of the village, and made an excessive noise—they visited successively the houses of the manufacturers, shouting, exclaiming and using every imaginable term of abuse and insult. The window in the yellow mill was broken in—but the riot, considering the character of those who led, and the apparent want of all reflection in those that followed, was not so injurious to property and personal security, as might have been reasonably apprehended. The next day the manufacturers shut their gates and the mills have not run since.[47]

Like the eighteenth-century mobs analyzed by recent historians, the crowd in Pawtucket acted with restraint and deliberation to defend accepted community standards and a broadly defined notion of the public good. The owners' intention to cut wages and increase hours, while justified by the new standards of capitalist entrepreneurship, threatened to degrade the village's mill laborers and to intensify their exploitation. The community's immediate and unambiguous response served notice of a different set of standards, one rooted in an artisan culture with a profound sense of the dignity of labor. It is significant that the community chose the mill owners' houses as objects of its anger, for they were the village's chief symbols of aristocratic pretense, the physical embodiments of the antidemocratic thrust of textile industrialism.[48]

The strike continued through the remainder of the week and into the next. The *Journal*'s account, published on May 31, indicates continued unrest: "The citizens of Pawtucket have, for a few days past, been in a state of excitement and disorder, which reminds us of the accounts we frequently read of the tumults of manufacturing places in England, though unattended with the destruction and damage usually accompanying those riots."[49] There is no record of further organized and public activity by the strikers. However, early on the morning of June 1, a fire broke out in a section of the Yellow Mill. The *Journal* remarked that it was "evidently the work of an incendiary."[50] Fire enveloped seven bales of cotton near a window but was discovered quickly enough to prevent major damage.

The deliberate burning of textile mills was not uncommon in early nineteenth-century New England. One historian of industrial Rhode Island asserts that "many of the early mill fires were reported to be of incendiary origin."[51] In Pawtucket alone more than five attempts were made to burn cotton mills or related structures in the period 1811–20. On October 5,

1811, at 1:30 A.M., the iron-slitting mill of Oziel Wilkinson was burned, and the fire spread to a workshop owned by Almy, Brown, and Slater, causing considerable damage.[52] Three nights later, fire was discovered in the Slater Mill but was put out before serious damage was done. Samuel Slater, in a letter to Almy and Brown, stated that "[m]any are of opinion it was set on fire wilfully," though Slater himself did not wish to believe it.[53] On February 1, 1814, the *Rhode Island American* reported that "[s]everal attempts have been made to set fire to the cotton mills in Pawtucket." The newspaper interpreted the attempts as political attacks against the Federalist mill owners.[54] Then, in early May 1820, three fires were set in a five-day period, two of which involved cotton mills.[55] These acts were a form of anonymous resistance to the textile industry and the factory system and part of a larger underground tradition employing arson for the redress of grievances both public and private. And if we wish to glimpse something of the attitude of mill workers to the burning of their mills, there is the remarkable statement of a nineteenth-century Rhode Island historian who, in commenting on the changing relations of workers and owners since the depression of 1837, asserted that "[n]o body of men would now stand by and cheer at the destruction of their employers' mill, as they did when that of William Harris, at Valley Falls, was being devoured by the flames."[56]

The burning of textile mills seems to have declined by the 1830s as the working-class movement became increasingly committed to public organization and agitation; yet at its high point, this form of resistance was vigorous enough to prompt changes in mill construction. By the 1820s, the majority of new textile mills were constructed of stone rather than wood, and in the same decade, Rhode Island mill owner Zachariah Allen developed a form of "slow-burning" interior construction designed to resist the effects of fire. Wood beams of large cross-section and floors three to four inches thick replaced the traditional smaller beams, joists, and single-ply floors. Adopted as a response both to the "normal" fire hazards of buildings full of loose cotton and fast-running machinery, as well as to the high incidence of arson, masonry mills with "slow-burning" interiors became commonplace by the 1830s.[57]

Mill owners in this period were well aware of the possibility of arson. The attempt to burn Walcott's

Mill may have encouraged Pawtucket's owners to settle quickly, for the strike came to an end almost immediately after this incident. Only two pieces of evidence relate to the strike's conclusion. On June 3, the *Journal* reported that the "ferment" in Pawtucket had "subsided," and the mills were "generally in operation." On June 5, the *Providence Patriot* stated that "the Pawtucket mills are again in operation, under a compromise between the employers and the employed." This is not unqualified victory, but the compromise settlement underscores both the inability of Pawtucket's mill owners to dominate the village and the strength of the community's opposition.[58]

On June 2, the day after the fire at Walcott's Mill, the mill owners met at Blake's Hotel. A committee of five was appointed to draft a statement for the local newspapers. Among other things, the statement was designed to refute "a report . . . industriously circulated" that the recent changes were "for the purpose of tyrannizing over, and oppressing the people employed in [the owners'] factories." Two days later, after the strike had been finally settled, the owners met "at the usual place" to issue their report. This is the same report that freely and candidly revealed the wage scale, the hours of operation, and the comparative disadvantages of Pawtucket's mill owners. The tone is defensive, and the act of writing deliberate. This was no hasty or poorly conceived response but the act of a committee proceeding with due consideration, attentive to public opinion. The strike was clearly perceived as a matter of consequence. The owners took seriously the threat to their reputation and went to unusual lengths to "remove all impressions . . . prejudicial to the manufacturers" of their village. On one level, this reflected the owners' fear that if such impressions gained currency, they would have a harder time recruiting workers. On another, more fundamental level, the owners' response was an indication of the incomplete and still fragile hegemony of industrial capitalism. Despite the workers' recourse to the strike, a weapon both new and of doubtful legality, it was the owners who felt called upon to defend themselves.[59]

The text of the owners' report is significant, not simply for what it says but for what it does not say. With the exception of the owners' aggressive stance on the wages of women weavers, they made no direct attack on the workers. They did not mention the or-

ganized crowd, the insults and epithets, the damage to property, or the attempted arson. Within the developing ideology of industrial capitalism, the owners could have used any or all of these incidents to mount a damning attack on Pawtucket's workers. Yet they did not do so. Given the history of Pawtucket, the mill owners' defensiveness is understandable. They knew that a direct attack on the workers would not have been supported by the community. This is not the sort of defensiveness one expects to find among nineteenth-century capitalists, but in 1824 the future success of industrial capitalism was far from assured. If the mill owners of Pawtucket did not act like men confident of their own values, the reasons for it were deeply rooted in the village's past.

In the immediate aftermath of the strike, a special meeting of the North Providence Town Council was called. With authorization provided by the annual town meeting two days earlier, Abraham Wilkinson, Timothy Greene, and Caleb Drown petitioned the council to appoint a night watch in the fire district of Pawtucket. The town granted the petition, and the three were authorized to select a watch and to "provide a suitable building as a Watch house and Bridewell to confine any person or persons . . . disturbing the peace and quiet."[60] The watch, established because of the owners' fear of continued arson, was organized to guard the town and the owners' property from 9:00 P.M. to sunrise. The cost, however, was to be borne, not by the town, but by the petitioners. While seemingly sympathetic to the owners' fears, the good citizens of the town had no intention of paying for the mill owners' protection.

While the mill owners and freemen of North Providence considered the role of local government in protecting private property, local mule spinners were busy organizing. For approximately three weeks, both the *Journal* and the *Patriot* carried notices announcing a meeting of "Mule-Spinners in the State of Rhode Island and vicinity" to be held July 5 at Joseph Randall's Inn, Smithfield, just one mile from Pawtucket. The purpose of the meeting was to organize a society of mule spinners and "to establish rules and regulations for the government thereof." In many ways it was a remarkable notice, indicative of the spinners' newly felt power. The spinners could have met on the previous day. They chose instead to meet in the middle of a workday, curtailing production for the time they were out. Unfortunately, we know nothing more. The press carried no account of the meeting, and organizational records have not survived.[61]

In the face of the workers' efforts to organize, the mill owners continued their attempts to establish cultural control. In the fall of 1826, two hundred residents met in the Pawtucket Hotel in support of the newly organized temperance movement. A petition signed by the village's leading figures was addressed to the Rhode Island General Assembly asking for authorization to pass more stringent licensing laws. It was granted immediately but, because of local opposition, could not be effectively implemented in the village.[62] On July 4, 1827, the owners sponsored their most impressive act of public theater. Three hundred to four hundred young boys from the village's Sunday schools, wearing "the look of health, cheerfulness and prosperity," paraded alongside a gala float drawn by six white horses. The float contained a loom and spinning frame operated by a crank leading from one of the axles: "On a flag floating over the machinery, were the names, H. Clay, H. Niles, and M. Carey [three of the manufacturers' most effective propagandists], and attached to the flag-staff was a placard '*Encourage National Industry, under this we prosper.*'"[63] The loom wove, in the course of the parade, eight or fifteen yards of cloth, depending on accounts.[64]

The effectiveness of these institutions was limited. Most of Pawtucket's workers remained unruly and resistant to the values of the mill owners. In March 1828, the mill owners on the Massachusetts side offered one answer. After a petition to the Massachusetts legislature, the town of Pawtucket, Massachusetts, was constituted as a distinct entity. Its first town clerk was J. C. Starkweather, and mill owners comprised its three selectmen and five of its seven tax assessors. For the first time, mill owners controlled at least part of the village. Rhode Island mill owners made similar efforts. At the August town meeting, they proposed to split Pawtucket from North Providence. The proposal was first postponed and later dropped. Pawtucket was not separated from North Providence until 1874.[65]

The mill owners' efforts at political control aroused new opposition. In the fall of 1828, the editorial column of the *Pawtucket Chronicle* gave notice of a significant, and perhaps unique, effort at community alliance against the mill owners. The villagers had "promptly and liberally" raised five hundred dollars, at public subscription, for a town clock to be placed in the new Congregational church then being built on the Massachusetts side. The *Chronicle* expressed the need for such a clock with clarity: "A time-piece which can be depended upon as a regulator, located in so central and public a situation as the new Congregational Church, will be of *great utility* in this village—All are aware of the vexatious confusion occasioned by the ringing of the factory bells at this time, and which can only be remedied by erecting a clock that will always give '*the time of day.*'"[66] The clock was erected to counter the mill owners' monopoly of public time. In the absence of such a public clock, the village and its workers were at the mercy of the factory bells and the owners' definition of time. Thomas LeFavour, before becoming a mill owner himself, worked from dawn to 7:30 P.M., "or what they called half-past seven, for the clock used to be figured to suit the owners."[67] Even advertisements for workers carried references to a workday defined not by the number of hours but by the factory bell. J. Underwood and Company advertised in the fall of 1821 for twenty to thirty weavers "willing to work six whole days in each week, and attend their Looms all bell hours."[68] The clock, as the *Chronicle* indicated, would reduce confusion, but, more importantly, it would directly challenge the mill owners' power to define public time. The erection of the clock represented a genuine victory for Pawtucket's workers, but the victory had been won on terms set by the mill owners. Workers would now have a public standard to gauge and resist the owners' capriciousness, but the new clock sanctioned the concept of industrial time and limited the scope of future conflict.

Two conflicting trends are visible in the 1830s. The early years of the decade saw the first flowering of national labor unrest as trade societies, labor newspapers, regional labor associations, and workingmen's parties were formed. But the militance of such labor radicals as the Providence carpenter Seth Luther was at times tinged with despair. Luther saw the power and influence of labor slipping away. He believed that the press was not open to the laboring class and feared both that the control of mill owners over their workers was becoming more overt and that the possibility for education was increasingly beyond the grasp of working people. In this period, mill owners consolidated their power, tightened discipline in the factory, and increased the pace of production. Potential labor alliances were weakened because of the small number of mill workers who participated in sustained organization.[69] The New Haven delegates to the third convention of the New England Association of Farmers, Mechanics, and Other Workingmen complained in October 1833: "The absence of delegates from the factory villages gives reason to fear that the operatives in the factories are already subdued to the bidding of their employers—that they have felt the chains riveted upon themselves and their children and despair of redemption. The Farmers and Mechanics, then, are the last hope of the American people."[70]

The organization of mill workers in this period was fraught with difficulty. Textile factory hands were divided by age, sex, and skill and were peculiarly subject to the imposition of a competitive work culture structured by piece rates and divisive of group solidarity. Further, they were a mobile and transitory population, described by one contemporary source as a "succession of learners," and not yet imbued with a sense of permanence as a factory proletariat. And finally, they were largely isolated in small rural villages, frequently without access to taverns or halls not owned by the mills. This isolation restricted their contact, not only with other mill workers but with the artisan radicals who played such a major role in the labor movement of the 1830s.[71]

Beyond this, however, the alliance between mill workers and artisans, as important as it was in Pawtucket during times of crisis, was in other respects fragile and incomplete. No firm explanation for this is yet possible, but two reasons may be suggested. Paul Faler has argued that the artisan radicals of Lynn adhered to a form of "industrial morality," which embraced temperance, frugality, moral discipline, and propriety. Through their emphasis on education, self-help, and organization, these workers turned this morality against the claims of capital. For many textile workers who adhered to a more traditional sense of time, work, and leisure, this was a stern and unattractive morality. Cultural differences could be overcome, but they were a hindrance to sustained and organized collective action. Second, although there was a strong identity of interest and experience between mill workers and lesser artisans, the scope and depth of that identity was limited by the attenuated development of the American textile industry.

Unlike Britain, the United States had no large network of traditional textile craftsmen, weavers, framework knitters, and wool croppers whose trades were threatened by foreign competition, price-cutting, and the introduction of machine technology. The displaced British artisans, through their own experience, grasped the central contradictions of the new economic order: increased productivity attended by unemployment and the promise of a new machine age accompanied by the tyranny of the factory and the degradation of the craft. Through such understanding they provided the radical leaven for the British working-class movement and thereby narrowed the ideological gap between the producer ethic, with its powerful and continuing artisan vision of individual proprietorship, and the class consciousness of industrial workers. The absence of these crafts in the United States eliminated one level of resistance and a major link between mill workers and artisans. The labor movement of the 1830s was unable to make up the deficiency through its own resources.[72]

Despite the absence of mill workers in the counsels of the New England Association, Pawtucket's tradition of opposition to textile industrialism did not die entirely. Its outlines were visible throughout the early 1830s in the continued conflict over the mill owners' definition of time, in the organization of a cooperative store, and in the formation of the *New England Artisan*. With the depression of 1837, the base for continued opposition was weakened. The depression took its toll, closing mills and scattering workers. Pawtucket did not recover until the coming of the railroad and the Irish in the late 1840s. Even in the 1840s, however, one sees evidence of a continuation of Pawtucket's antiauthoritarianism. Like other mill villages, Pawtucket provided critical support for the prosuffrage party of Thomas Dorr. The effort to revise the colonial charter and to expand the suffrage beyond its restrictive property qualifications was first led by laborers and artisans. Though the movement was later dominated by middle-class elements and its goals watered down, its primary popular support was found in the mill villages of the Blackstone and Pawtuxet river valleys. But the prosuffrage forces lost the Dorr War, and the Irish quickly replaced the Yankees in Rhode Island's mills in the late 1840s and early 1850s. The possibilities for sustained class consciousness had been weakened by depression, loss of the free suffrage fight, and the encroaching power of the mill owners. With wholesale demographic change, the owners would be faced with the new problems of disciplining a second group of preindustrial migrants to the work habits of industrial capitalism. But they would not have to face a culturally unified working class with a forty-year tradition of opposition to textile industrialism.[73]

Notes

1. On the strike, see John Commons et al., *History of Labour in the United States,* vol. 1 (New York, 1918), 156. Commons refers to it as the "first instance of women participating in the activities of labour organization." He does not argue that it is the first textile strike in North America, but I have found no reference to one earlier.

2. Gutman, "The Workers' Search for Power: Labor in the Gilded Age," in *The Gilded Age: A Reappraisal,* ed. H. Wayne Morgan (Syracuse, N.Y., 1963), and "Work, Culture, and Society in Industrializing America, 1815–1919," *American Historical Review* 78 (June 1973): 531–88; Thompson, *The Making of the English Working Class* (London, 1963), and "Time, Work Discipline, and Industrial Capitalism," *Past and Present* 38 (December 1967): 56–97; Dawley, *Class and Community: The Industrial Revolution in Lynn* (Cambridge, Mass., 1976).

3. Massena Goodrich, *Historical Sketch of the Town of Pawtucket* (Pawtucket, R.I., 1876), 5, 15; *1820 U.S. Census* (Washington, D.C., 1821); William Bagnall, *The Textile Industries of the United States, 1639–1810,* vol. 1 (Cambridge, Mass., 1893), 253–56, 379–82; Robert Grieve, *An Illustrated History of Pawtucket, Central Falls, and Vicinity* (Pawtucket, R.I., 1897), 136ff.; Louis McLane, *Report of the Secretary of the Treasury, 1832: Documents Relative to the Manufactures in the United States,* 2 vols. (Washington, D.C., 1833).

4. David Wilkinson, "Reminiscences," in *Transactions of the Rhode Island Society for the Encouragement of Domestic Industry in the Year 1861* (Providence, R.I., 1862), 76–99; see also 101–18; Timothy Dwight, *Travels in New England and New York,* 4 vols. (New Haven, Conn., 1821), 2:27; *1820 Census of Manufactures,* Schedule for Massachusetts and Rhode Island; *Pawtucket Past and Present* (Pawtucket, R.I., 1917), 27.

5. On mill village development, see Caroline Ware, *The Early New England Cotton Manufacture* (Providence, R.I., 1939). On the problems of wealth, status, and power, I have benefited from a research project of Lisa Krop's (data on file at the Slater Mill Historical Site) and from Jonathan Prude, *The Coming of Industrial Order: Town and Factory Life in Rural Massachusetts, 1810–1860* (New York, 1983).

6. Moses Brown to Elisha Waterman, February 23, 1802;

Almy, Brown, and Slater Papers, Rhode Island Historical Society, Providence, hereafter cited as *ABSP.*

7. See the charter of the Pawtucket Association of Mechanics and Manufacturers, Rhode Island Charters, July 1810, Rhode Island State Archives, and the "Petition of Cotton Manufacturers of Providence and Vicinity to the Senate and House of Representatives," October 1815, Timothy Pickering Papers, Massachusetts Historical Society, Boston.

8. Grieve, *Illustrated History,* 80, 84–87; Records of the Catholic Baptist Society, December 1792–March 1838, bound, and Records of the First Baptist Church, August 1805–November 1837, bound, First Baptist Church, Pawtucket; Rhode Island Petitions, 1811–12, p. 60, Rhode Island State Archives; Rev. Edward H. Randall, *A Discourse Commemorative of the 50th Anniversary of the Consecration of St. Paul's Church, Pawtucket, R.I.* (Pawtucket, R.I., 1868); Goodrich, *Historical Sketch of Pawtucket,* 152–53.

9. Grieve, *Illustrated History,* 136–37.

10. Grieve, *Illustrated History,* 136–37.

11. Grieve, *Illustrated History,* 54–56, 100, 140.

12. *1820 Census of Manufactures;* McLane, *Report; Transactions . . . ,* 101–18. Rich sources for artisan life in this period are the depositions in the Sargeant's Trench Case, Ebenezer Tyler et al. v. Abraham Wilkinson et al., 1826, Federal Case no. 14,312,4, Mason 397, Federal Records Center, Waltham, Mass.; *Pawtucket Past and Present,* 27.

13. Rhode Island Petitions, 1815, p. 11, Rhode Island State Archives, Providence.

14. *Report of the Centennial Celebration of the 24th of June, 1865, at Pawtucket, of the Incorporation of the Town of North Providence* (1865), 87; Grieve, *Illustrated History,* 98–99.

15. Moses Brown, "Deposition," Aug. 31, 1792, cited in *The Flyer* (January 1972), publication of the Slater Mill Historic Site; Grieve, *Illustrated History,* 104ff.; David Green, "Battle for Water Power: The Sargeant's Trench Case, Pawtucket, 1826" (MS, Slater Mill Historic Site, 1976).

16. *Manufacturers' and Farmers' Journal,* Aug. 23, 1824; *Pawtucket Chronicle,* Aug. 29, 1829, and Mar. 22, 1828. See also membership list of the artisans' militia unit, the Fayette Rifle Corps (Grieve, *Illustrated History,* 218). It included no mill owners. On the "blowing-out" balls, see the *Pawtucket Gazette and Chronicle,* Mar. 18, 1852, and Hannah Josephson, *The Golden Threads: New England's Mill Girls and Magnates* (New York, 1949).

17. *Pawtucket Chronicle,* Apr. 25, 1829; Grieve, *Illustrated History,* 98–99; *New England Artisan.* The *Artisan* was published in Pawtucket from January 1832, when it was founded, until October 1832, when it moved to Boston. The best history of the New England Association is still that written by Helen Sumner for John Commons et al., *History of Labour in the United States,* vol. 1 (New York, 1918). On artisans, see Thompson, *The Making of the English Working Class;* Dawley, *Class and Community;* and Bernard Moss, *The Origins of the French Labor Movement: The Socialism of Skilled Workers, 1830–1914* (Los Angeles, Calif., 1976).

18. Ware, *Early Cotton Manufacture*, 198–235; *1820 U.S. Census*.

19. *Manufacturers' and Farmers' Journal*, June 18, 1821; *1820 U.S. Census*; McLane, *Report*.

20. Slater to Almy and Brown, Sept. 25, 1795, and July 19, 1796, *ABSP*; George S. White, *Memoir of Samuel Slater* (Philadelphia, 1836), 98–106.

21. David Benedict, "Reminiscences No. 23," *Providence Gazette and Chronicle*, Oct. 28, 1853.

22. *Report of the Centennial Celebration*, 88.

23. Grieve, *Illustrated History*, 94.

24. *1820 Census of Manufactures*; Records of the First Baptist Church (see n. 8), meetings of Dec. 5, 1818, Jan. 7, July 28, 1819, Feb. 5, Mar. 1, Aug. 7, Sept. 28, 1820, and June 28, 1821. See also Bruce Laurie, "'Nothing on Compulsion': Life Styles of Philadelphia Artisans, 1820–1850," *Labor History* 15 (Summer 1974): 337–66, and Daniel Scott Smith and Michael Hindus, "Pre-marital Pregnancy in America, 1640–1971," *Journal of Interdisciplinary History* 5 (Spring, 1975): 537–70.

25. Grieve, *Illustrated History*, 100–101; Richard M. Dorson, "The Wonderful Leaps of Sam Patch," *American Heritage* 18 (December 1966).

26. Faler, "Cultural Aspects of the Industrial Revolution: Lynn, Massachusetts, Shoemakers and Industrial Morality, 1826–1860," *Labor History* 15 (Summer 1974): 367–94.

27. *Rhode Island American*, Sept. 8, 1815.

28. Records of the First Baptist Church.

29. Rev. E. A. Buck, *An Historical Discourse Delivered at the . . . Anniversary of the Slatersville Congregational Church, September 9, 1866* (Woonsocket, R.I., 1867), 14.

30. Rhode Island Petitions, 1815, p. 43, Rhode Island State Archives. See also North Providence Town Meeting Records, 1808–55, meeting of Nov. 18, 1812, Pawtucket City Hall.

31. Membership computed from *Manual of the First Baptist Church, Pawtucket, Rhode Island* (Providence, R.I., 1884) and the records of the First Baptist Church; from the vital records, St. Paul's Church, Pawtucket; Randall, *Discourse*, 6; *1820 U.S. Census*; Ray Potter, *A Poor Man's Defense* (Providence, R.I., 1823), 10; Grieve, *Illustrated History*, 179–80. For the democratic thrust of evangelical religion, see William G. McLoughlin, *New England Dissent, 1630–1833: The Baptists and the Separation of Church and State*, 2 vols. (Cambridge, Mass., 1971).

32. William Bagnall, "Contributions to American Economic History," vol. 2, ed. V. S. Clark (typescript, 1908, Baker Library, Harvard University), 999; E. P. Thompson, "The Moral Economy of the English Crowd in the Eighteenth Century," *Past and Present* 50 (February 1971): 76–136; Michael Merrill, "Cash Is Good to Eat: Self-Sufficiency and Exchange in the Rural Economy of the U.S.," *Radical History Review* 3 (1977): 42–71. For a more detailed analysis of water rights in northern Rhode Island during the period see Gary Kulik, "Dams, Fish, and Farmers: Defense of Public Rights in Eighteenth-Century Rhode Island," in *The Countryside in the Age of Capitalist Transformation*, ed.

Steven Hahn and Jonathan Prude (Chapel Hill, N.C., 1985), 25–50.

33. Lillie B. C. Wyman, *Elizabeth Buffam Chace, 1806–1899*, vol. 1 (Boston, 1914), 73.

34. R. Bayles, *History of Providence County*, vol. 2 (New York, 1891), 235.

35. Grieve, *Illustrated History*, 105.

36. James L. Conrad, Jr., "The Evolution of Industrial Capitalism in Rhode Island, 1790–1830" (Ph.D. diss., University of Connecticut, 1973), 91.

37. Leonard Bliss, Jr., *The History of Rehoboth, Bristol County, Massachusetts* (Boston, 1836), 158; North Providence Town Meeting Records, meeting of Jan. 20, 1797; *Report of the Centennial Celebration*, 87–88; Brenden F. Gilbane, "A Social History of Samuel Slater's Pawtucket," (Ph.D. diss., Boston University, 1969), 364–67.

38. North Providence Town Meeting Records; Conrad, "Evolution of Industrial Capitalism," 122–23; Gilbane, "Slater's Pawtucket," 282–83; Grieve, *Illustrated History*, 93; Bliss, *Rehoboth*, 235; Thomas Dublin, *Women at Work: The Transformation of Work and Community in Lowell, Massachusetts, 1826–1860* (New York, 1981).

39. *Manufacturers' and Farmers' Journal*, June 7, May 31, 1824; *Providence Patriot*, May 29, 1824.

40. *Manufacturers' and Farmers' Journal*, May 31, June 7, 1824; *Providence Patriot*, May 29, 1824.

41. Ware, *Early Cotton Manufacture*, 39–59.

42. Robert Brooke Zevin, *The Growth of Manufacturing in Early Nineteenth-Century New England* (New York, 1975), tables 1, 3; John M. Cudd, *The Chicopee Manufacturing Company, 1823–1915* (New York, 1974), appendix 16.

43. McLane, *Report* (Mass. Doc. 3, No. 51).

44. Bagnall, "Contributions," 3:1918.

45. *Journal*, May 31, 1824.

46. *Journal*, May 31, 1824.

47. *Journal*, May 31, 1824.

48. Pauline Maier, "Popular Uprisings and Civil Authority in Eighteenth-Century America," *William and Mary Quarterly*, 3d ser., 27 (1970): 3–35; Dirk Hoerder, "Boston Leaders and Boston Crowds: 1765–1776," in *The American Revolution*, ed. Alfred F. Young (DeKalb, Ill., 1976).

49. *Journal*, May 31, 1824.

50. *Journal*, June 3, 1824; *Patriot*, June 5, 1824.

51. Joseph Brennen, *Social Conditions in Industrial Rhode Island, 1820–1860* (Washington, D.C., 1940), 33.

52. Slater to Almy and Brown, Oct. 9, 1811, *ABSP*.

53. Slater to Almy and Brown, Oct. 9, 1811, *ABSP*.

54. *American*, Feb. 1, 1814.

55. *Pawtucket Gazette and Chronicle*, Aug. 2, 9, 16, 1861.

56. Erastus Richardson, *History of Woonsocket* (Woonsocket, R.I., 1876), 173.

57. On changes in mill construction, see Kulik, "Introduction," in *Rhode Island, An Inventory of Historic Industrial and Engineering Sites* (Washington, D.C., 1978), 1–25.

58. *Journal*, June 3, 1824; *Patriot*, June 5, 1834.

59. *Journal*, June 7, 1824.

60. North Providence Town Meeting Records, meetings of June 7, 9, 1824.

61. *Patriot*, June 16, 19, 1824; *Journal*, June 14, July 1, 1824.

62. Rhode Island Petitions, 1826–27, p. 47, Rhode Island State Archives; North Providence Town Meeting Records, Apr. 15, 1829, Sept. 17, 1831.

63. *Journal*, July 5, 1827; *Pawtucket Chronicle*, July 7, 1827.

64. *Journal*, July 5, 1827; *Pawtucket Chronicle*, July 7, 1827.

65. Town Meeting Records, Pawtucket, Mass., Mar. 4, 1828; North Providence Town Meeting Records, Aug. 26, 1828, Apr. 15, 1829; Grieve, *Illustrated History*, 126.

66. *Chronicle*, Oct. 18, 1828.

67. David Benedict, "Reminiscences," *Pawtucket Gazette and Chronicle*, June 10, 1853.

68. *Journal*, Sept. 27, 1821.

69. Seth Luther, *An Address to the Working-Men of New England* (Boston, 1832).

70. Quoted in Commons, *History of Labour*, 1:306.

71. On the effect of piece rates, see Samuel Ogden, *Thoughts: What Probable Effect the Peace with Great Britain Will Have on the Cotton Manufactures of This Country* (Providence, R.I., 1815).

72. Faler, "Cultural Aspects"; on the importance of textile workers to the emergence of class consciousness in Britain, see John Foster, *Class Struggle and the Industrial Revolution: Early Industrial Capitalism in Three English Towns* (New York, 1974), and the review by Gareth Stedman Jones in *New Left Review* 90 (March–April 1975).

73. Grieve, *Illustrated History*, 102; Dan King, *The Life and Times of Thomas Wilson Dorr* (1859; reprint ed., Freeport, N.Y., 1969), 147–48; Marvin Gettleman, *The Dorr Rebellion* (New York, 1973), 18ff., 130–34.

Part Five: Ritual Space

Seating the Meetinghouse in Early Massachusetts

ROBERT J. DINKIN

The history of early New England at times seems dominated by Puritanism, that complex admixture of academic theology and popular belief whose distinctive force helped to cast the collective mentalité of the region into a single "mind." A concern for the power of Puritanism has almost made such terms as "Half-Way Covenant," "closed corporate Christian utopian communities," and the "politics of declension" household words for historians, and their book titles—Errand into the Wilderness, Meetinghouse Hill, The Faithful Shepherd, A Little Commonwealth—bear equal witness to its influence. Yet for all their attention to the hold that the mythic structures of reformed Protestantism had over the ordinary lives of New England yeomen, few scholars have focused on the meetinghouse itself as a ritual space. In the following essay, Robert J. Dinkin draws on church records and town histories as he explores an aspect of meetinghouse design that was crucial to the reflexive representation of local social structure: "seating" the congregation.

"Seating" was the process by which a hierarchy of spaces in the meetinghouse was assigned to town residents. As such, it made the act of attending worship an event that drew attention to and legitimized a specific set of power relations in local society. Dinkin situates the seating ritual in two broad frames. The first is the established debate among historians concerning the relative democratic or deferential quality of Massachusetts towns. To this question he gives a clear answer: New England society was always deferential, in that individuals of high status received prize seats near the pulpit or in the front rows of galleries. As one moved to the rear and sides of the meetinghouse, one found middling and then poorer farmers and artisans. Under the galleries and on the stairs sat (and often stood) children, Indians, and blacks. Week after week, the meetinghouse presented those in attendance with an exposed schematic view of community structure and their place in it. Yet the basis of one's assigned place

in that structure changed over time. Initially seating was assigned on the basis of a few qualities of white men: their age, their place in local affairs, their utility to the town, and their wealth. Some communities took great care to insure that everyone—whether young or old, disabled or healthy—was treated fairly. Yet by the time of the Revolution, as towns grew more crowded and people saw one another less frequently, wealth arose as the single uniform factor that determined one's seating position.

Dinkin's second point is to locate seating as a culminating ritual within the more extended symbolic process of literally building a congregation. Several steps were necessary: deciding that a new meetinghouse was necessary, finding an appropriate location, locating a builder (or "undertaker"), settling on the "just price" of work. The actual construction of the meetinghouse climaxed in a raising, an occasion marked by a feast for the congregation and the symbolic driving of a pin by the minister. Authority was then transferred to a seating committee, on whose shoulders fell the onerous task of "dignifying the seats." Because their plan defined the order of local hierarchy for several years to come, their work was symbolically charged. By viewing seating as one step in a larger ritual process, Dinkin helps us avoid seeing churchgoing as an episodic digression from secular affairs. Indeed, Massachusetts farmers seem always to have been involved in one phase of congregation-making or another.

In the goodly house of worship,
　　where in order due and fit,
As by public vote directed,
　　classed and ranked the people sit,
Mistress first and good wife after,
　　clerkly squire before the clown,
From the brave coat, lace-embroidered,
　　to the gray frock shading down.*

Fig. 1. Second meetinghouse ("Old Ship"), Hingham, Massachusetts, built 1681–84 by Joseph Stockbridge of Scituate, Massachusetts. (Photograph by Robert Blair St. George.)

There has been much debate in the past three decades about whether early Massachusetts was a democratic or deferential society. Professor Robert E. Brown insisted that it was democratic, while J. R. Pole and others argued that it was not.[1] A study of one of the major practices in the society, the seating of the meetinghouse, would seem to support the latter view.

It is clear that in colonial and provincial Massachusetts when people attended the meetinghouse (figs. 1, 2) they were assigned specific places according to their standing in the community. In a truly democratic society, one would certainly not expect to find an ordered delineation of status among its members, yet numerous local histories and church records reveal that the custom of seating the inhabitants by social rank prevailed in nearly all Massachusetts towns.

Fig. 2. Second meetinghouse, Cohasset, Massachusetts, built 1747. (Photograph by Robert Blair St. George.)

From the beginning of the first permanent English settlement the colony always had some form of segregated church seating. As Darrett Rutman has stated, the earliest church officers usually sat "apart from the congregation on raised benches."[2] In 1638, at Anne Hutchinson's trial before the First Church in Boston, members and nonmembers of the church were separated for the first time. At the inception of the trial, John Leverett, one of the elders, said that it had been decided "to request those that are Members of the Congregation, that they would draw as neare togeather as they can, & into such places as thay may be distinguished from the rest of the Congregation, that whan thear Consent or Dissent is required to the Things which shall be read: we know how thay do

*Quoted in *Magazine of American History* 24 (September 1890): 216. The practice of seating is mentioned in more than one hundred town histories. Though the subject is not touched on in a number of other volumes, nowhere is it specifically stated that the institution did not exist.

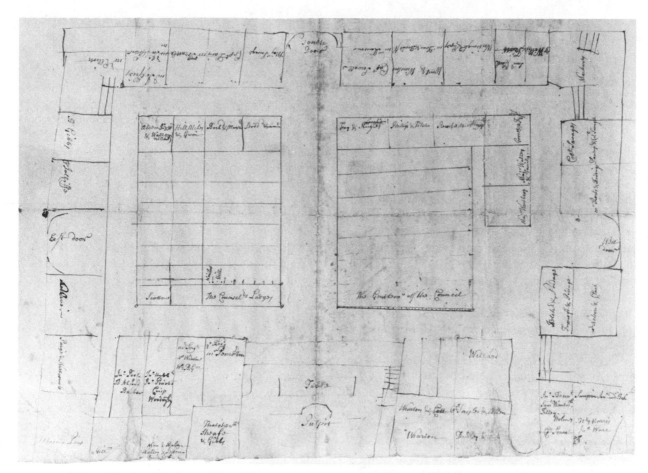

Fig. 3. Seating plan, first meetinghouse of Boston's Third ("Old South") Church, ca. 1675. (Photograph by Robert Blair St. George, courtesy of Old South Meetinghouse, Inc.)

express themselves ayther in the allowinge or condemninge of them."[3]

The earliest known record mentioning a systematic seating of the meetinghouse is one for the town of Sudbury in 1645. In the first Sudbury meetinghouse, people had a right to purchase seats and to dispose of them if they departed from the settlement, "provided that they leave the seating of the persons to whom they sell, to the church officers, to seat them if they themselves go out of town."[4] By the 1660s, the practice of assigning seats in the meetinghouse seems to have become quite customary. It had already been adopted in many towns, including Andover, Billerica, Charlestown, Dorchester, Haverhill, Newbury, Reading, and even in the distant frontier communities of Hatfield and Northampton.[5] The ear-

liest surviving seating plan shows the arrangement in Boston's Third Church ("Old South") in the mid-1670s (fig. 3).

A person occupying a seat other than the one allocated to him or her was subject to heavy fine. In Reading, it was ordered in 1662 that "no women, maid nor boy nor gall shall sit in the south alley and east alley of the meeting house, under penalty of 12d. for every day they shall sit in the alley after this present day."[6] The town of Haverhill in 1665 exacted a fine of 2s. 6d. from those refusing to comply with the seating arrangements, though it lowered it to 12d. in corn in 1684.[7] On April 28, 1669, John Wolcott and Peter Toppan appeared before the court at Ipswich "for disorderly going and setting in a seat belonging to others" in the meetinghouse. They were admonished for their offense and forced to pay the costs of the hearing.[8]

As time went on, with new towns being incorporated and new meetinghouses being erected, seating became a colonywide phenomenon. A few of the older localities might not have inaugurated seating plans in the old barnlike structures with long benches that served as houses of worship during the mid-seventeenth century. However, the situation was changed in the new spacious edifices that began to dot the countryside in the following period.

The new buildings constructed in the late seventeenth and early eighteenth centuries often took a few years from the planning stage to their completion. There was always some haggling over the location, each section of the town wanting the site in its own domain. Then came a struggle over the finances, with some people desiring that a subscription be taken, others wishing that the money be advanced from the town treasury. Severe weather frequently caused delays in building, but eventually the structure was completed. At the time of the raising of the frame it was usually ordered "to provide victuals and drink for as many men as the selectmen should think convenient."[9] Finally, a committee was appointed to "seat the meeting house," or to "dignify the seats."

The seating committee was generally composed of the selectmen plus the elders and deacons of the church or a special committee chosen for the purpose. Seating was considered very serious business and often the most prominent persons in the town took part. In Northampton, the Reverend Solomon Stoddard and Joseph Hawley, Sr., were among the seaters.[10] Sometimes the task of the committee proved extremely difficult since it was hard to please everybody. Thus, to avoid animosities, a second group was appointed to "seat the seating committee."[11]

The rules and instructions in regard to seating differed from place to place and over the years even changed within specific towns. In most cases, monetary worth and age were the two most important considerations, though such other factors as high political office could also be influential. In Sutton, the committee was instructed to emphasize "age and rate and office."[12] Deerfield ordered that people be judged according to "age, estate, place, and qualifications."[13] For Hatfield, seats were allocated on the basis of "age, estate, and places of trust."[14] Watertown voted that the committee stress "Age, Honor, Usefulness; also to go according to real and personal estate."[15] When figuring the relative value of age and estate, usually one year of age was taken as the equivalent of one or two pounds in the assessment of real and personal estate.[16] Thus, a man sixty years old possessing an estate valued at £100 was accepted on a par with someone thirty-five years of age who owned property rated at £125 or £150. Framingham had an even more detailed method. In that town, 1d. was added to the assessed rate for persons between fifty and sixty, 5d. was tacked on for persons sixty to seventy, while those over seventy were honored at the discretion of the seating committee.[17]

Probably the most elaborate system was that in effect at the First Parish Church in Beverly. Although far from typical, this scheme illustrates the relative importance of such various factors as military standing and parentage. The plan differed from all others in the use of "degrees" for the possession of certain attributes. On one occasion the committee voted

that every male be allowed one degree for every complete year of age he exceeds twenty-one; that he be allowed for a captain's commission twelve degrees; for a lieutenant's eight, and for an ensign's four degrees; that he be allowed three degrees for every shilling for real estate in the last parish tax, and one degree for every shilling for personal estate and faculty; every six degrees for estate and faculty of a parent alive, to make one degree among his sons, or, where there are none, among the daughters that are seated; every generation heretofore living in this town to make one degree for every male descendant that is seated; parentage to be regarded no farther otherwise than to turn the scale between competition for the same seat; that taxes for polls of sons and servants shall give no advancement for masters or fathers, because such sons or servants have seats; that no degree be allowed on account of any one's predecessors having paid toward building the meeting house, because it had fallen down before now, but for repairs since made; that some suitable abatement be made, where it is well known the person is greatly in debt; that the tenant of a freehold for term of years shall be allowed as many degrees as half the real estate entitles him to, and the landlord the other half; that the proprietor of lands in any other parish shall be (if under his own improvement) allowed as much as he would be if they lay in this parish, but, if rented out, only half as much.[18]

Toward the middle of the eighteenth century, wealth became more and more the dominating factor in influencing the manner of seating. In 1707, Northampton had instructed its committee "1st to have regard to person's age 2. to Estate 3. to have some regard to men's usefulness."[19] But in November, 1737, when the new meetinghouse was completed, it was "1. Voted that . . . the committee have respect principally to men's estate. 2. To have regard to men's age. 3. Voted that there be some regard and respect to men's usefullness but in a less degree."[20]

The assignment of pews and pew space in the eighteenth century also showed the greater importance of wealth in connection with placement in the house of worship. The small seventeenth-century meetinghouses seldom contained room for many pews, the construction of more than a few being prohibited. Even in places where there was available space, many towns denied requests for the building of more

pews.[21] However, as the years passed, a number of these towns relented. At the same time, the structures built in the eighteenth century began to be projected with the idea of pew space in mind so that pews could later be added. Pews and pew spots were designated by a committee in the same manner as were seats, except that real and personal estate or subscription to the cost of the new meetinghouse appeared to be the only factors considered.[22] Yet one exception to this last rule was Cotton Mather's Old North Church, where the pews other than those awarded to the proprietors were distributed among such buyers "as it had been thought for the interest of the society to allow to become their purchasers."[23]

Although Boston was the only town in the province that supported its houses of worship by subscription rather than from local or ministerial taxes, it did not differ from the others on the question of seating. Among the regulations passed by the committee for the New Brick Meeting House, built by the congregation of the First Church in 1712 (fig. 4), were "That no seat or pew appropriated to any person

Fig. 4. *View of the Old Brick Meeting House in Boston, 1808.* Aquatint, 4¼" × 6⅛". This structure, known as the "New Brick" when erected in 1712, was the third meetinghouse of Boston's First Church. (Photograph courtesy of the Massachusetts Historical Society.)

shall be transferred or disposed of by such persons to another without the approbation and allowance of the committee," and "That all persons keep the seat and places assigned them by the committee, and remove not to any other seat or place without the committee's appointment. That so ordered and decency may be observed."[24]

When a member of the elite in Massachusetts purchased a large amount of property in a certain area and desired to have a pew built in the local meetinghouse, his wishes were quickly granted. Thomas Hutchinson, who bought a sizable estate on Milton Hill, wanted to have a place set aside for a pew in the Milton meetinghouse. Soon afterward, the town voted that for Mr. Hutchinson, "six inches be taken off the women's stairs if need be to make room for a pew."[25]

The emergence of pews in the meetinghouse brought about a major social change in the seating. Previously, women had been placed on the opposite side of the aisle from the men, wives in the same position in order as their husbands and widows given a spot in relation to the status of their late spouses. But with the creation of pews, men who possessed them were permitted to have their wives as well as other female relatives sit with them.[26] Yet in the remainder of the house the separation of the sexes was still maintained.

Pew holders were also allowed certain other privileges. In Brookline, it was voted "that Captain Corey be granted liberty . . . to cut a window in his pew at his own expense provided he cuts no braces,—and that Mr. Moses White's window be moved as far as may be, without being carried out of his pew."[27] However, pew owners also had responsibilities. At the First Church in Boston, the proprietors of pews were expected to adhere to the recommendation that "upon lecture days and other occasional solemnities, they receive and accommodate so many strangers, or of their particular friends invited to take a seat with them, that the pews may be conveniently filled."[28]

Other members of the community—minors, Indians, and blacks—also had specific places. In a few instances children were seated in accordance with their family's standing,[29] but most frequently they were assigned gallery seats, the rear seats, or the stairs. In Middleborough, it was ordered "that the hind seat below in the meeting house and the hind seat in each of the men's galleries shall be for the boys to sit in and

that . . . two of the tithingmen . . . shall be empowered to have inspection over the boys to prevent their playing at the meeting."[30]

In some localities, Indians were entitled to many of the privileges of the other inhabitants in regard to public worship. The selectmen in Grafton consulted the Indians as to where they wished to sit, though they were eventually given a less than desirable spot—on either side of the front door against the walls of the house, the men on one side, the women on the other.[31]

Although blacks were also usually granted full religious privileges, they too were given seats that were far from being the best. In Milton, they were ordered "to sit in the two hindermost seats of the uppermost gallery."[32] The Brattle Street Church in Cambridge recommended "that the Negroes be directed to leave the back seats of the lower and go into those of the upper gallery."[33] Where meetinghouses possessed many pews, blacks were sometimes directed to fill the highest, most distant ones.[34]

Although between one-fourth and one-fifth of the population in Massachusetts "had little property of any sort,"[35] according to Jackson T. Main, there are few references to the seating of "poor folks"[36] and servants.[37] This is in contrast to the numerous statements concerning the placing of blacks.[38] It is possible, of course, that when seating committees considered people's estates or wealth, those with little or no property were included under these categories. Furthermore, a few localities disclosed certain limitations within which persons were to be seated. A committee for the West Cambridge precinct of Arlington in 1781 voted "to seat such part of the inhabitants as should be thought proper,"[39] while the town of Dover in 1767 seated only those who paid a tax on real and personal estate.[40]

Seating arrangements had to be revised every few years to take into account the changes in wealth and the expansion of population, especially in the newer towns. The meetinghouse in Amherst first seated in August 1749 was reseated in January 1750, March 1755, March 1760, February 1762, January 1767, and January 1771.[41] Generally, alterations in the seating plan took place once in three, five or ten years.[42]

The seating of the meetinghouse on the basis of wealth and social distinctions did not go without opposition. Nevertheless, most persons accepted the practice as within the "natural" order of things. Actually, the bulk of criticism, at least in the first half of the eighteenth century, was directed less at the system as a whole than at the specific arrangements made by the various seating committees. Most people did not seem to dislike the idea of seating as long as they were able to obtain a coveted spot for themselves. In order to remove some of the grounds for possible grievances, a number of towns made certain locations in the house that seemed less desirable equal in dignity to the better seats nearest the pulpit. This process was known as "dignifying the seats." For instance, the committee in Marlborough voted that "the front seats in the gallery should be next in dignity to the second seats below, and that the fore seats in the end gallery should be next in dignity to the third seats below."[43] Some towns had much more detailed plans for dignifying the seats. In Sunderland, it was decided

the great pew to be the first; the corner pew to be next and the foreseat in the body to be next; and the second seat in the body to be next, and the next to that is the front gallery and next is the third pew, and next to that is the third seat in the body, next to that the pew under the stairs; and next [to] that is the pew in the front gallery; and next to that is the foreseat in the upper tier in the gallery and next is the fourth seat in the body and next [to] that is the foreseat in the town tier in the gallery and next to it is the second seat in the front gallery and next is the last seat in the body.[44]

Since the dignifying of seats in this manner did not alleviate all the dissatisfaction, certain towns adopted regular channels for appeal. Persons unhappy with their placement could register their protest with the local seating committee.[45] Richard Hazzen of Haverhill made a request to build a small pew, maintaining that he had "no place to sit but upon the courtesy of Mr. Eastman or crowding into some fore seat, too honorable for me."[46] In 1723, four inhabitants of the same town desired a new place, complaining that they were "obliged to sit squeezed on the stairs where we cannot hear the minister and so get little good by his preaching, though we endeavor to ever so much."[47] Sometimes the number of dissatisfied individuals was large enough to force the committee to undertake a complete reseating.[48]

By the second quarter of the eighteenth century, there are indications of disenchantment with the seating system. During a town meeting in Deerfield on November 23, 1730, numerous questions related to seating were discussed. From the motions made it can be seen that many divergent views were put forth, including one designed to do away with the whole concept of seating requirements.

Voted to seat men and their wives in the pews.
Voted to leave it with the seaters to dignify the pews and seats.
Voted to seat without having regard to qualifications [emphasis added].
Voted to seat by rules of age and estate.
Voted that a pound rateable estate as in the list shall be accepted equal with a year's age.
Voted to seat by rules of age, estate and qualifications.

Toward the end of the meeting, however, it seems that those opposed to major changes dominated, for it was voted "that the above written votes made on this adjournment shall be void and of non-effect." Finally, it was decided to seat the meetinghouse on the basis of age, estate, and qualifications, although one month later, the seating committee was again called on to make further alterations.[49]

In Worcester in 1750 the seating problem was so acute that a town meeting was called to try "to come into some method that people may sit in the seats assigned to prevent disorders and that they don't put themselves too forward." The selectmen were ordered to "give tickets to such people as have not taken their seats properly, according to the last seating, directing them to sit where they ought."[50]

The practice of seating according to qualifications met with even greater opposition in the next two decades. In 1757, there was a general disapproval of the seating arrangements in the town of Acton, and someone even suggested that the leading sinners ought to be granted the closest seats to the pulpit since they most needed to hear the minister. Later, that person admitted that his proposal would in no way reduce the problems of the seating committee.[51] Three years afterward, in Hadley, many people refused to take the seats assigned to them and moved into the higher seats, disrupting the whole congregation.[52]

The town of Conway furnished another example of dissatisfaction. Nathaniel Dickinson, a wealthy property holder from Deerfield, who later engaged with Israel Williams in what was considered a treasonable correspondence with General Gage, owned land in Conway and sometimes attended services in the meetinghouse there. It was said that he "thought himself a little above the common level" and always occupied an armchair that he had provided for himself and that was placed near the deacon's seat. Arriving late on one occasion, Dickinson "found his chair among the missing," and, much to his own disgust but to the satisfaction of the rest of the congregation, he was forced to take a seat "side by side with the common people." Some time afterward, his chair was found "on the top of Dr. Hamilton's hill hanging in a hemlock."[53]

Yet few towns abandoned the practice abruptly as a result of this agitation. The termination of seating in a few places at that time seems more directly related to renovation or changes in meetinghouse construction. The interiors of many buildings were being largely turned over to pews, while many new houses of worship were being erected with similar floor plans. There is no reference to seating in Watertown after the new multi-pewed edifice was constructed in 1755,[54] nor is there any for the town of Wenham following the installation of pews in its meetinghouse in 1765.[55] With the making of pews on a large scale and with all the prominent citizens of a community being granted one, many town leaders probably felt that to continue to assign the remaining seats would not be worth the trouble. This attitude was reinforced by the mounting criticism of their work.

Nevertheless, it was not until the Revolution and its aftermath that the majority of towns agreed to abandon the institution. At this time, the decision to end seating was made regardless of whether the floor of the meetinghouse was wholly given over to pews (figs. 5, 6). Many people were no longer willing to accept the status-conscious dictates of seating committees. Needham and Amherst abolished the system after 1771.[56] Topsfield, Manchester, Princeton, and Townsend disbanded it around 1780.[57] The town of Stow made its last vote for seating in 1790, Weston in 1791, and Framingham in 1794, while Newton decided to "disannul the ancient mode of seating parishioners" in 1800.[58]

In order to raise money for their meetinghouses, a number of towns began selling pews by auction rather than appointing them as before.[59] Though

wealthy persons usually bought most of the best locations, some people of lesser status were now able to purchase desirable pews if they were willing to pay the price.

However, at the same moment that many communities were getting rid of the old system, new towns incorporated at the time of the Revolution were adopting it. Middlefield, in Berkshire County, incorporated in 1783, seated its new meetinghouse in 1791 under the stipulation that "five years of age shall be to one pound of the valuation."[60] Boxborough, established in the same year, was seating individuals in 1796,[61] and Ludlow, founded in 1774, voted a committee to appoint seats in its meetinghouse in 1797.[62] At least one newly settled town seems to have been torn between the accepted use of seats and the newer

Fig. 5. *The Worcester, Massachusetts, Meeting House (Old South), 1763, as it appeared in 1776.* (Reprinted from Albert A. Lovell, *Worcester in the War of the Revolution* [Worcester, Mass., 1876], frontispiece.)

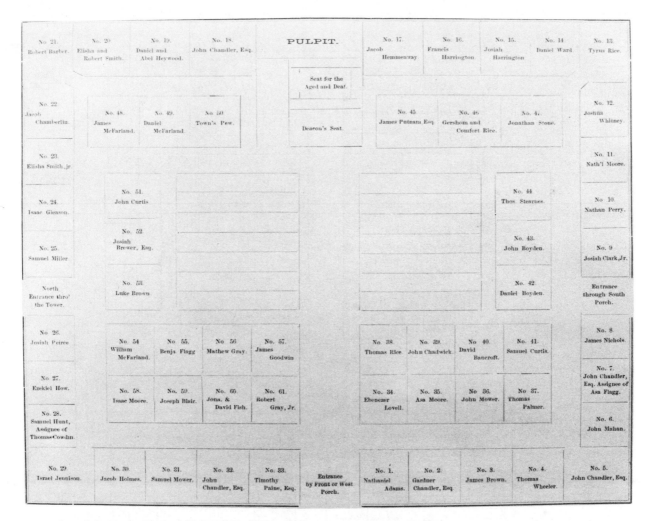

Fig. 6. *Plan of the Lower Floor of the Meeting-House, 1763,* Worcester, Massachusetts. (Reprinted from Albert A. Lovell, *Worcester in the War of the Revolution* [Worcester, Mass., 1876], facing p. 6.)

popularity of pews; when Berlin raised its first meetinghouse in 1779, it fitted its interior with some of each (fig. 7). In so doing, the new town was likely copying the ca. 1763 seating plan at nearby Worcester (see fig. 6).

Other towns settled much earlier continued the practice of seating well into the nineteenth century. Acton followed the custom during the entire existence of its old meetinghouse—down to 1808.[63] The seating in Leicester was still in place in 1815 (fig. 8). Deerfield, which had displayed a great deal of opposi-

tion toward the system many decades earlier, still retained it in the second decade of the new century.[64] Northfield seated its meetinghouse anew every five to eight years until 1830,[65] while the town of Dover hoped to prevent the continuous problem of assigning places in its new house of worship by voting in 1812 "to seat the meeting house for forty years."[66]

Thus, within the "democratic" framework of Massachusetts society, where a majority of the people owned at least some property and a majority of adult males had the right to vote, there existed a highly ordered social system that ranked persons according to their standing in the community. As Charles Adams has written, "a degree of deference now almost unknown was on the Sabbath day systematically paid

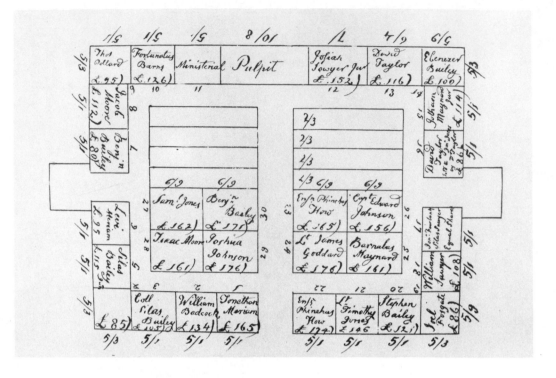

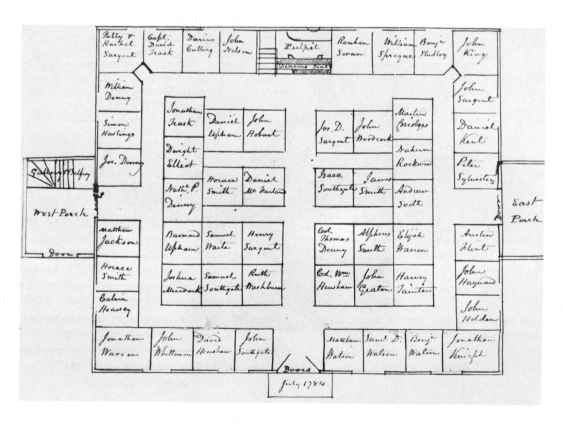

Fig. 7 (top, left). Seating plan, first meetinghouse, Berlin, Massachusetts, 1779–91. (Reprinted from William A. Houghton, *History of the Town of Berlin . . . From 1784–1895* [Worcester, Mass., 1895], facing p. 112.)

Fig. 8 (bottom, left). Seating plan, first meetinghouse, Leicester, Massachusetts, ca. 1815. (Photograph courtesy of the American Antiquarian Society.)

---

within the walls of the meeting house, not only to age and official standing, but to social and family distinctions."[67] The system pervaded the entire province and continued throughout the colonial and provincial periods. The practice declined only in the last quarter of the eighteenth century, while remnants of it persisted even during the Jacksonian era.

Notes

1. Robert E. Brown, *Middle-Class Democracy and the Revolution in Massachusetts, 1691–1780* (Ithaca, N.Y., 1955); J. R. Pole, *Political Representation in England and the Origins of the American Republic* (London, 1966), pt. 2, sec. 1.

2. Darrett Rutman, *Winthrop's Boston: Portrait of a Puritan Town, 1630–1649* (Chapel Hill, N.C., 1965), 126.

3. "A Report of the Trial of Mrs. Anne Hutchinson before the Church in Boston, March, 1638," *Proceedings of the Massachusetts Historical Society*, 2d ser., 4 (1887–89): 162.

4. Alfred S. Hudson, *The History of Sudbury, Massachusetts, 1638–1889* (Boston, 1889), 102.

5. Sarah L. Bailey, *Historical Sketches of Andover* (Boston, 1880), 412; Henry A. Hazen, *History of Billerica, Massachusetts* (Boston, 1883), 169; Richard Frothingham, Jr., *History of Charlestown, Massachusetts* (Charlestown, Mass., 1845–49), 160; *Records of the First Church at Dorchester, 1636–1734*, ed. S. J. Barrows et al. (Boston, 1891), 46; George W. Chase, *The Sketch of the History of Newbury . . .* (Boston, 1845), 64; Lilley Eaton, *Genealogical History of the Town of Reading, Massachusetts* (Boston, 1874), 17; Daniel W. Wells and Reuben F. Wells, *History of Hatfield* (Springfield, Mass., 1910), 60; James R. Trumbull, *History of Northampton*, 2 vols. (Northampton, Mass., 1898–1902), 1:121–23.

6. Eaton, *Genealogical History of Reading*, 17.

7. Chase, *The History of Haverhill, Massachusetts, from Its First Settlement in 1640 to the Year 1860* (Haverhill, Mass., 1861), 106, 140–41.

8. John J. Currier, *History of Newbury, Massachusetts, 1635–1902* (Boston, 1902), 318.

9. John J. Babson, *History of the Town of Gloucester* (Gloucester, Mass., 1860), 216.

10. Trumbull, *History of Northampton*, 1:517.

11. Samuel Sewall, *The History of Woburn* (Boston, 1868), 84; Chase, *History of Haverhill*, 141.

12. William A. Benedict and Hiram A. Tracy, *History of the Town of Sutton, Massachusetts, 1704–1876* (Worcester, Mass., 1878), 42–43.

13. George Sheldon, *A History of Deerfield*, 2 vols. (Greenfield, Mass., 1895–96), 1:205.

14. Wells and Wells, *History of Hatfield*, 138.

15. J. G. Bartlett and Elizabeth Bartlett, eds., *Watertown Records*, 6 vols. (Watertown, Mass., 1894–1919), 4:211.

16. William S. Tilden, ed., *History of the Town of Medfield, Massachusetts* (Boston, 1887), 130. John M. Smith, *History of the Town of Sunderland, Massachusetts* (Greenfield, Mass., 1899), 54.

17. Josiah H. Temple, *History of Framingham, Massachusetts, 1640–1880* (Framingham, Mass., 1887), 198.

18. *The First Parish Church, Beverly, Massachusetts* (Beverly, Mass., 1942), 34–35; Christopher T. Thayer, *An Address Delivered in the First Parish, Beverly* (Boston, 1868), 35–36.

19. Trumbull, *History of Northampton*, 1:517.

20. Trumbull, *History of Northampton*, 2:74.

21. Mortimer Blake, *A History of the Town of Franklin, Massachusetts* (Providence, R.I., 1879), 29; Sylvester Judd, *History of Hadley* (Springfield, Mass., 1905), 312; Lucius Paige, *History of Hardwick, Massachusetts* (Boston, 1883), 182; J. G. Metcalf, ed., *Annals of the Town of Mendon* (Providence, R.I., 1880), 161.

22. *Records of the Church in Brattle Square, 1699–1872* (Cambridge, Mass., 1902), 6; Elias Nason, *A History of the Town of Dunstable* (Boston, 1877), 96–97; Caleb Butler, *History of the Town of Groton* (Boston, 1848), 309; Josiah Kent, *Northborough History* (Newton, Mass., 1921), 17; Eaton, *Genealogical History of Reading*, 162.

23. Chandler Robbins, *A History of the Second Church, or Old North* (Boston, 1852), 177.

24. Arthur B. Ellis, *History of the First Church of Boston, 1630–1880* (Boston, 1881), 175–76.

25. A. K. Teele, *The History of Milton, Massachusetts, 1640–1887* (Milton, Mass., 1888), 283.

26. Harold R. Phalen, *History of the Town of Acton* (Cambridge, Mass., 1954), 45; Charles M. Hyde, *Historic Celebration of the Town of Brimfield* (Springfield, Mass., 1879), 120; Teele, *History of Milton*, 282; Trumbull, *History of Northampton*, 2:74; Smith, *History of Sunderland*, 53.

27. *Muddy River and Brookline Town Records, 1634–1838* (Boston, 1875), 338; see also Phalen, *History of Acton*, 46.

28. Ellis, *History of the First Church of Boston*, 176.

29. Edward C. Smith and Philip M. Smith, *A History of the Town of Middlefield, Massachusetts* (Menasha, Wis., 1924), 84; Henry M. Burt, *The First Century of the History of Springfield*, 2 vols. (Springfield, Mass., 1898), 1:126.

30. Thomas Weston, *History of the Town of Middleboro, Massachusetts* (Boston, 1906), 570. See also Hyde, *Historic Celebration of . . . Brimfield*, 120; Trumbull, *History of Northampton*, 2:314.

31. Frederick C. Pierce, *History of Grafton* (Worcester, Mass., 1879), 171.

32. Teele, *History of Milton*, 282.

33. *Records of the Church in Brattle Square*, 21.

34. Judd, *History of Hadley*, 313.

35. Jackson Turner Main, *The Social Structure of Revolutionary America* (Princeton, N.J., 1965), 41.

36. Hyde, *Historic Celebration of . . . Brimfield*, 120; Frank Smith, *A History of Dover, Massachusetts* (Boston, 1897), 38.

37. Thayer, *Address Delivered in . . . Beverly*, 35; Silas R. Coburn, *History of Dracut, Massachusetts* (Lowell, Mass., 1922), 191.

38. Phalen, *History of Acton*, 46; Benjamin Cutter and William R. Cutter, *History of the Town of Arlington, Massachusetts* (Boston, 1880), 35; Andrew E. Ford, *History of the Origin of the Town of Clinton, Massachusetts* (Clinton, 1896), 88; Sheldon, *Deerfield*, 2:905; Judd, *History of Hadley*, 313; Charles Hudson, *History of the Town of Lexington*, 2 vols. (Boston, 1868), 1:482; Teele, *History of Milton*, 282; Currier, *History of Newbury*, 360; Bradford Kingman, *History of North Bridgewater, Massachusetts* (Boston, 1866), 95; William S. Heywood, *History of Westminster, Massachusetts, 1728–1893* (Lowell, Mass., 1893), 277.

39. Cutter and Cutter, *History of Arlington*, 94.

40. Smith, *History of Dover*, 37.

41. Edward W. Carpenter and Charles F. Morehouse, *History of the Town of Amherst* (Amherst, Mass., 1896), 38–39.

42. Josiah H. Temple, *History of North Brookfield, Massachusetts* (Boston, 1887), 254; Temple, *History of Framingham*, 146; Temple and George Sheldon, *A History of the Town of Northfield, Massachusetts* (Albany, N.Y., 1875), 316; Charles Hudson, *History of the Town of Marlborough* (Boston, 1862), 112.

43. Hudson, *History of Marlborough*, 112.

44. Smith, *History of Sunderland*, 53; see also *First Parish Church, Beverly*, 36; Sheldon, *History of Deerfield*, 1:205; John H. Lockwood, *Westfield and Its Historic Influences, 1669–1919*, 2 vols. (Springfield, Mass., 1922), 1:144.

45. Josiah H. Temple, *History of the Town of Palmer, Massachusetts* (Springfield, Mass., 1889), 159; Francis E. Blake, *History of the Town of Princeton, Massachusetts*, 2 vols. (Boston, 1915), 1:131.

46. Chase, *History of Haverhill*, 252–53.

47. Chase, *History of Haverhill*, 265.

48. Phalen, *History of Acton*, 53; Judd, *History of Hadley*, 312; Trumbull, *History of Northampton*, 1:123.

49. Sheldon, *History of Deerfield*, 1:482.

50. Franklin P. Rice, ed., *Worcester Town Records . . . [1722–1848]*, 7 vols. in 6 (Worcester, Mass. 1879–95), 2:114–15.

51. Phalen, *History of Acton*, 53–54.

52. Judd, *History of Hadley*, 312.

53. Charles B. Rice, *Celebration of the Hundredth Anniversary of the Incorporation of Conway, Massachusetts* (Northampton, Mass., 1867), 32n.

54. Barrett and Barrett, eds., *Watertown Records*, 5:50, 157–61.

55. *Wenham Town Records, 1730–1775* (Salem, Mass., 1940), 173, 194–95.

56. George K. Clarke, *History of Needham, Massachusetts, 1711–1911* (Cambridge, 1912), 200; Carpenter and Morehouse, *History of Amherst*, 38–39.

57. *Town Records of Topsfield, Massachusetts*, 2 vols. (Topsfield, Mass., 1919–20:), 2:325; *Town Records of Manchester*, 2 vols. (Salem, Mass., 1889), 1:163; Blake, *History of Princeton*, 1:132; Ithamar B. Sawtelle, *History of the Town of Townshend* (Fitchburg, Mass., 1878), 135.

58. Duane Hamilton Hurd, ed., *History of Middlesex County, Massachusetts*, 3 vols., (Philadelphia, 1890), 1:644; *Town of Weston, Records of the First Precinct, 1746–1754 and of the Town, 1754–1803* (Boston, 1893), 418; Temple, *History of Framingham*, 198; Francis Jackson, *History of the Early Settlement of Newton, 1639–1800* (Boston, 1854), 142.

59. Phalen, *History of Acton*, 118; William D. Herrick, *History of the Town of Gardner, Massachusetts* (Gardner, Mass., 1878), 485; J. M. Stowe, *History of Hubbardstown* (Gardner, Mass., 1881), 124; C. M. Hyde and Alexander Hyde, *Centennial History of the Town of Lee* (Springfield, Mass., 1878), 230; Jackson, *History of Newton*, 142; Temple, *History of Palmer*, 213; Heywood, *History of Westminster*, 273.

60. Smith and Smith, *History of Middlefield*, 84.

61. Lucie C. Hager, *Boxborough: A New England Town and Its People* (Philadelphia, 1891), 38.

62. Alfred Noon, *The History of Ludlow* (Springfield, Mass., 1912), 130.

63. Hurd, ed., *History of Middlesex County*, 1:243.

64. Sheldon, *History of Deerfield*, 1:202.

65. Temple and Sheldon, *History of Northfield*, 316.

66. Smith, *History of Dover*, 39.

67. Charles F. Adams, *Three Episodes of Massachusetts History*, 2 vols. (Cambridge, Mass., 1893), 2:733.

Authority, Law, and Custom: The Rituals of Court Day in Tidewater Virginia, 1720–1750

In eighteenth-century Virginia, as in other British colonies, the court was the institution charged with safeguarding property rights. On one level, local legal affairs were mundane. Magistrates heard cases, reached decisions, and pronounced judgments; fees were levied, punishments meted out, and injured parties perhaps vindicated. But on another level, the law was a complex symbolic system that both established and defended key cultural values. In this essay A. G. Roeber examines court-day ritual in the Old Dominion as a display of legal authority. By correctly managing the tension in tidewater society between the formal and the familiar, court day allowed the gentry to define the gradations in rank, power, and obligation that structured society.

Roeber unfolds the significance of court day as a drama in four acts. The first act involves contempt-of-court cases in which justices asserted their authority over detractors. Justices came from established gentry families. Born into wealth, they were well educated and knew the benefits of propertied existence. They were, in the words of one less fortunate Virginian, "beings of a superior sort" whose success in office derived from their skill in combining a knowledge of local customary relations with the abstract authority of legal power. In defending their prerogative, they sought to legitimize social hierarchy as a natural order. When people tested the boundaries of this order by speaking out against the court, the law put them back in their proper place in the social firmament. The second act concerns debt cases, which were frequent in Virginia's cash-poor tobacco economy. Poor and middling planters were in debt to their rich neighbors, who in turn owed money to factors in London and Bristol. As Roeber suggests, the court forced a recognition of deferential rule as it demanded the face-to-face reconciliation of debt in public. A third act—the impaneling of grand jurymen—turns our attention to another group of propertied Virginians who, while of lesser

status than the justices, were crucial to the law's effective mediation of formal authority and local custom. A final act admitted the presence of servants and slaves on court days, suggesting that propertied people recognized their obligations to those on whose obedience they depended.

These four acts of the court-day ritual encapsulate the structural relationships in Virginia society that law defined and supported. As part of the ritual process, the courthouse setting itself insisted on hierarchy. Without property, slaves and servants were commonly prevented from entering the building that stood for property's defense. Instead, they sat near open windows or peeked in open doors to witness the costumed actors on the judicial stage inside. On entering the courthouse itself, spectators passed the rooms for the jury on their way to benches in the main seating area. Bars separated this public space from the seats for the justices, which were raised off the floor in the "upper" end of the building. Like the law itself, the courthouse as a ritual space defined social relationships and carefully guarded boundaries of status. As Roeber's essay demonstrates, people, texts, and material surroundings were interdependent parts of a performance in which local custom and sanctioned hierarchy were "commingled" in moments of symbolic exchange.

The *Laws* of a country are necessarily connected with every thing belonging to the people of it; so that a thorough knowledge of *them*, and of their progress, would inform us of everything that was most useful to be known about them.[1]

In July 1746 the *London Magazine* published the travel notes of a young Englishman recently returned from a tour of the American colonies. Of Virginia, he reported that "the principle [sic] Meetings of the

Rituals of Court Day

Country are at their Court-Houses, as they call them; which are their Courts of Justice." Describing York-town, he noted that "the Court-House is the only considerable publick Building, and is no unhandsome Structure." Of the sessions in Williamsburg, he commented that they were conducted "with a Dignity and Decorum, that would become them even in Europe."[2] These observations were correct but under-stated. In fact, the English traveler's sense of the importance of court day in colonial Virginia would have been strengthened considerably had he remained longer and noted more closely the events of that occasion. No institution was more central to tidewater Virginia culture than the county court in both physical eminence and practical consequence. Yet historians have generally neglected to pay attention to the "Dignity and Decorum" of court rituals—the dramaturgical exercises—in which propertied authority and communal custom defined the shared values of the culture by means of the law.[3]

Virginians of the mid-eighteenth century lived in a world both formal and familiar. The tension produced by exchanges between formal and familiar styles enabled the gentlemen justices of the peace and the county residents over whose legal affairs they presided once a month, every month, to define social rank, mutual obligation, and shared values. To do this, the law itself and its procedures had to embody the formal and familiar qualities of Virginia life. Clearly, power and authority belonged to the propertied, and the body of rules that was Virginia law constituted the dimensions and boundaries of conduct, obligation, and order. The authoritative and customary institutions that the Old Dominion had inherited from England were celebrated in such public statements as the one Sir William Gooch made to the General Court grand jurors in 1730. Informing them that they should see to the safety of their community, Gooch reminded the jurors that ancient procedures and laws were only as good as the "execution of them, is *punctual* and *exact.*" Virginians concurred. A writer to the *Virginia Gazette* argued for the regular enforcement of law, since "Law is a dead Letter, and lives only in the due Administration thereof." For Virginians, "the Laws of *England* are our best Inheritance, the Ties of harmonious Society, and Defence of Life, Liberty, and Property. . . . *English* Law (from Antiquity not to be traced) hath preserved it's Purity, and Certainty," and "this Purity, and Cer-

tainty of Law, hath been transmitted to us."[4] Virginians participated in discovering the meaning of law—ancient, formal, but customary. The degree of participation varied, depending on social distance from the authorities who dominated the center of power that was the courthouse. In a semiliterate society, it was not in printed opinions of authors but in ritual actions, in face-to-face familiar meetings in the courthouse, that the reality of law unfolded in a formal setting modulated by routine and repetition.[5]

The key that unlocks the meaning of court day is *action*—action that proceeded as a kind of dramatic play, whose setting we can reconstruct from contemporary records. Certain "acts" in this cultural pageant are especially worthy of our attention, for they informed Virginians where they stood in society, what obligations they owed to social superiors and inferiors, and what constituted the accepted norms of social conduct. Those norms were defined not merely by authority and power but by communal sanction. The oath of the justice told the county that he must "do equal right, to the Poor, and to the Rich," and do so with "cunning, wit" (that is, intelligence and skill), and "power." As the Virginia correspondent to the *Gazette* observed, law lives only in its administration; and it is particularly in four select but similar patterns of action that we glimpse the interplay of authority and custom within the theater of court day. The "acts" to watch are (1) contempt of court, (2) settlement of debt cases, (3) the meeting of the grand jury, and (4) the use of the court by the propertyless. In these are mirrored the justices' attempts to "do equal right to all manner of people, great and small, high and low, rich and poor . . . without favour, affection, or partiality," according to their rank and station.[6]

The principles of the drama in which the entire county played a part were His Majesty's gentlemen justices, the planters who had risen from humble and fractious seventeenth-century antecedents and who, by the 1720s, were secure in their rank and claim to deference. Familial pedigrees had for the most part been established a generation or two earlier. The justices included both elite magnates and lesser squireens, allied by marriage, who as a rule handed down their seats from father to son, from uncle to nephew.[7]

The passing on of a seat to a junior member of the family also meant that the public rank of the assembled bench was visibly proclaimed not only according to the degree of propertied wealth possessed but also according to age. The rank of the justices was immediately obvious since the commission of the peace named the senior justices "of the Quorum" first. Quorum justices were regarded as more learned in the law than their associates because of their experience; the counties came to rely on them as customary leaders. These stalwarts were essential to the functioning of the court: at least one of them had to be present for a lawful court to sit. Deference to the gray locks of the colony's patriarchy encouraged the courts to press the governor into appointing even aged men like Francis Thornton, who had refused one commission already, "alledging that he was Sickly and uncapable," and Leonard Hill, who declined "because he is now antient & thinks himself uncapable." Lancaster County mourned the loss of Edwin Conway in 1752 when he refused to sit after serving forty years. The seventy-one-year old retired "for that his Sense of hearing is much impaired and he is far advanced in Years." As late as 1787, Essex County pointed out to the governor the necessity of nominating two mature men even though the loyalty of one of them to the Revolution had been questionable. Since John Upshur and James Edmondston could no longer sit, the next two most experienced justices were essential because "they . . . as senior magistrates would keep more Order and decorum in Court."[8]

Property, family, and experience were important, and literacy in a largely aural culture also set the bench apart from the people of the country. Yet the unlearned folk and learned gentry had a common cultural experience. From the fragmentary literary remains of the gentry one can glean the sense that literacy was coupled in their minds with familiar wisdom. Since barristers, attorneys-at-law, and even attorneys of fact who were not also gentlemen were scarce in Virginia before 1750, the gentlemen justices took a peculiar pride in their literate, if homely, legal ability. As one planter observed, "It is a shame for a gentleman to be ignorant of the laws of his country and to be dependent on every dirty pettifogger," but highly "commendable . . . for a gentleman of independent means, not only [not] to stand in need of mercenary advisers, but to be able to advise his friends, relations, and neighbors of all sorts." Justice Landon Carter aptly defined the proper use of literate knowledge when a lawyer accused him of not knowing how to bring a suit to trial. The feisty colonel retorted that "it pleased me to find a Gentleman Pique himself on a little Mechanical knowledge . . . Attorneys were always lookt upon as so many Copyers and their knowledge only lay in knowing from whom to Copy Properly." Such an attitude helps to explain the lack of a licensing law for attorneys in Virginia from 1690 to 1732; the rarity of these professionals even after that latter date until 1750 enabled the justices both to sustain their singular authority and to deal in direct, familiar terms with the people and cases before them.[9]

Those cases, and the administrative details of local life, were the stuff of which the court's extensive powers were made. Monthly courts in the Virginia counties had originally exercised jurisdiction over civil cases and petty criminal causes. By the 1660s these courts were called county courts; the justices by then had acquired a broad range of duties that included caring for roads, bridges, and ferries, probating wills, trying cases at law and in equity, and examining white suspects in order to determine whether they should be sent to trial for felony before the General Court in Williamsburg or whether an immediate punishment on a lesser charge should be imposed in the county. Sitting under a commission of oyer and terminer, the justices tried slaves for both petty crimes and capital offenses. As the eighteenth century dawned, the county court enforced a host of statutes purposefully drawn broadly to give the justices wide-ranging discretionary powers over nearly every aspect of local life.[10]

*   *   *

An overture established the tone of the drama by which the justices put law in motion. Standing in the door of the courthouse, the deputy clerk or under-sheriff issued an archaic bidding that coupled the formal authoritative bench—the locus from which power emanated—with the familiar gatherings on the piazza, on the green, in the nearby ordinary: "Oyez, Oyez, Oyez, silence is commanded in the court while his Majesties Justices are sitting, upon paine of imprisonment. All manner of persons that have any thing to doe at this court draw neer and give your attendance and if any one have any plaint to enter or suite to prosecute lett them come forth and they shall be heard. God Save the King." By this means were all bidden to "draw neer" to those gentlemen justices who sat with tricorns on their wigs before the uncovered ranks of society.[11]

The dramaturgy of this opening spectacle was not less effective for being humbler than in England or, for that matter, in the General Court of the colony. There was no preliminary sermon, no formal procession from parish church to shire hall, no parade of judicial gowns or gold-laced coats, no tip-staffs leading the way. Yet justices in Virginia could expect the deference due them as "beings of a superior order," in the words of Devereux Jarratt, who recalled from boyhood that "when I saw a man riding the road, near our house, with a wig on . . . I would run off." In those times, he believed, "Such ideas of the difference between *gentle* and *simple* were . . . universal among all of my rank and age." The vivid visual symbols of propertied "quality" were awesome, even frightening, outside the context of court day. Within the setting of the courtroom, county folk heard the well-defined rules according to which justice was to be done in return for their deference. The oath sworn by each justice in order of seniority defined and limited authority's obligations in public, oral fashion. No magistrate was permitted to serve as counsel in a cause before him, unless a litigant needed representation and could not afford an attorney; all proceedings, whether taken before one justice or before the whole bench, would be public and recorded—print culture would operate for the simple as well as for the gentle; and no justice was allowed any "fee, gift, or gratuity, for any thing to be done by virtue of [his] office." The rule-making quality of law here limited the otherwise illimitable power of the gentlemen justices but demanded deference from the ruled while assuring them of familiar and regular administration of the law, applied with "cunning, wit, and power."[12]

As we examine the ritual actions of court day, we must place ourselves on the set or stage where the drama took place. The courthouse was located at a crossroads near the center of the county, on a green with a tavern or ordinary close at hand (fig. 1; see also fig. 13, p. 142). By the 1720s, the old wooden frame courthouses were giving way to new buildings that were the boasts of the shires. Most of the new tidewater courthouses were patterned after models first developed at the capital in Williamsburg. The Virginian who came riding up to the courthouse beheld a public meeting place that was markedly superior to his own dwelling. Most Virginia houses in the early

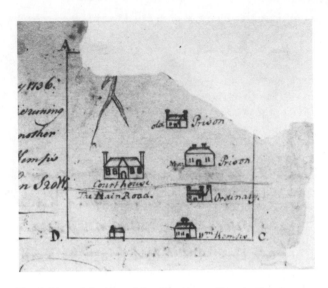

Fig. 1. Plan of the site of the Gloucester County Courthouse, Gloucester, Virginia, 1754. (Photograph courtesy of The Colonial Williamsburg Foundation.)

eighteenth century were still of the English "puncheon," or earth-fast, type, susceptible to termites and rotting (see the essay by Carson et al., p. 113 in this volume). A contemporary described for a London correspondent the house of a neighbor as a "Shell, of a house without Chimneys or partition, & not one tittle of workmanship about it more than a Tobacco house work."[13] The courthouse, in contrast, was an impressive place. Outside, the county standard flew in the morning air, and, as coaches and horsemen arrived and gentlemen took early draughts in the ordinary, the red brick of the courthouse on its green stood in sharp contrast to the surrounding woods. When viewed from their entry sides, eighteenth-century Virginia courthouses presented facades of two types, both of which were impressive. Perhaps a majority had a plain front elevation. More intimidating, however, were courthouses like those in Hanover County (fig. 2) and King William County (see fig. 14, p. 365), structures that presented an arcaded loggia of five rounded arches and a flagged pavement. This porch was usually occupied by servants, slaves, and smallholders who milled about, hawked wares, quarreled, or listened to the proceedings inside. The arcaded piazza had recently become an integral part of public symbolism and display in Virginia and was used to connect the large main houses of the greater

Fig. 2. Hanover County Courthouse, Hanover, Virginia, mid-eighteenth century. (Photograph courtesy of The Cook Collection, Valentine Museum.)

planters to lesser buildings, or "dependencies." The "dependent" nature of the lesser orders of society who occupied these piazzas was ratified in the architecture of the courthouse, just as the interior of that building signified that it was particularly the place of authority, formality, and power.[14]

On entering the courthouse proper, the spectator immediately understood the structure of local law. Passing through the front door of a simple rectangular plan courthouse like the one in Amelia County (fig. 3), he or she would have seen the two rooms reserved for the jury to the right. On the left, his or her gaze would have met the seats of the justices. On entering the arcaded courthouse in Hanover County (fig. 4), the sense of processual drama was heightened as the spectator saw to his or her immediate right and left the two jury rooms. Attention would then have been drawn quickly to the point from which the action of court day sprang. The social ranking of the county was confirmed as he or she walked the length of the building gazing at portraits of the royal family or colonial officials in ascending order of significance along the side walls. The wall above the bench was dominated by the king's arms, and immediately below the royal emblem were arrayed the seats of the gentlemen justices (figs. 5, 6) ranging behind the bench that was raised above the floor at least one foot and sometimes three. A jury box was affixed directly below the bench; clerk, deputy king's attorney, and sheriff each had a place within the bar, and the walls of this space were wainscoted, in contrast to the plastered and whitewashed interior of the public area. The county's perception that the bar was a place somewhat apart from the larger room was modified by the architectural device of a "neat Mondillion Cornice all round the whole" room.[15]

Not a little imposing, this scene was nonetheless a familiar one. County residents marked the rhythm of their communal lives by the events that unfolded here. As winter ended in March, courts convened after inclement weather that often forced cancellations of sessions in December and January. Suits were brought; freeholders were notified to be on hand in May to sit as participants in the "Grand Inquest" of the county. Public claims and grievances were often settled in the spring; the grand jury met in May; summer sessions wilted in the merciless heat and humidity of the low country. In September cooler weather and the ripening of crops occasioned constables' complaints of farmers tending "seconds," or inferior stalks of tobacco; every fourth year that month the vestries "beat the bounds" of the parishes

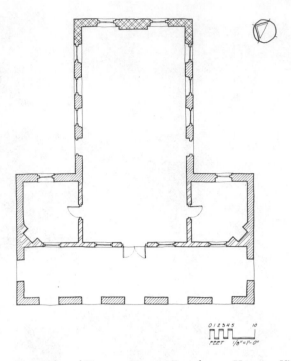

Fig. 4. Plan of Hanover County Courthouse, Hanover, Virginia, mid-eighteenth century: *diagonal shading*, original fabric; *crossed lines*, restorations done in late nineteenth century; *double lines*, fabric rebuilt in 1954. (Drawing by Doug Taylor, courtesy of The Colonial Williamsburg Foundation.)

Fig. 3. Plan of Amelia County Courthouse, Amelia, Virginia, 1767. (Drawing by Doug Taylor after original in Amelia County Records, courtesy of The Colonial Williamsburg Foundation.)

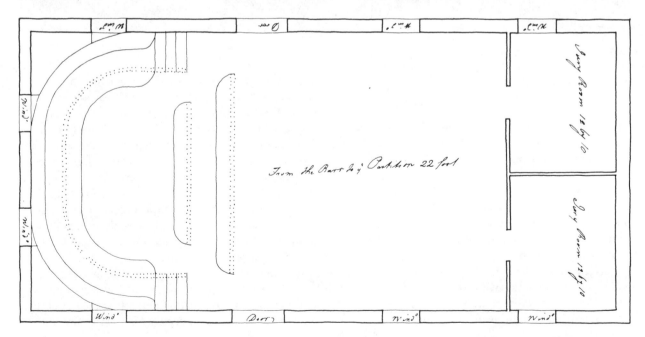

and made a return of their processioning to the court. Orphans' estates were inquired into in late autumn, and the county gathered again in November for another biannual examination of petty sins and misde-meanors. In December the county levy was laid. Punctuating this yearly cycle were the "called courts" and oyer and terminer sessions, whose meetings were infrequent and, though important, mere reflections of the monthly gatherings of the county court. On those regular, repeated occasions we can pierce the curtain of time as it rose to reveal the law in action.[16]

Fig. 5. View of wainscoted magistrate's seating area, Chowan County Courthouse, Edenton, North Carolina. (Photograph by Willie Graham, courtesy of The Colonial Williamsburg Foundation.)

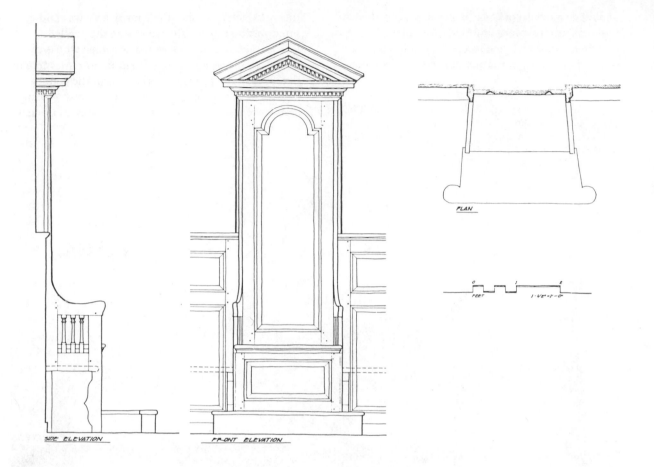

SIDE ELEVATION

FRONT ELEVATION

PLAN

Fig. 6. Chief Magistrate's chair, Chowan County Courthouse, Edenton, North Carolina, mid-eighteenth century. (Drawing by Doug Taylor, courtesy of The Colonial Williamsburg Foundation.)

Act 1. Authority and Deference: Contempt of Court

Court sessions opened to a medley of affairs. Sometimes the justices estimated the age of slaves brought in for public record of tithable status, appointed road surveyors, or heard immediately a case docketed from an earlier session. The county got down to participating at once, the formal anthems of the king's law intoned over a *continuo* line of scuffling and murmuring. Flies buzzed in and out of open doors and windows; sounds intruded from the courthouse porch and nearby ordinary where business transactions and the peddlars' hawking competed for atten-

tion with racehorses pounding across the green. Inside, the court directed action on the formal stage to the keeping of the king's peace.

That peace was interrupted from time to time by Virginians clearly not intimidated by gentry authority to such a degree that they remained silent. Like the hierarchical culture itself, their obstreperous behavior was graduated in seriousness, as was the response of the court. The collective identity of the justices was routinely invoked whenever someone challenged their dignity. Always referring to themselves as "this Court," the justices carefully guarded their authority. When Allen Hawthon came into the room with his hat on, the justices noted that such an act "appeared to this Court an Insolent behaviour." Hailed before the bench, Hawthon, "readily acknowledging his fault & humbly Begging pardon for the same," was able to satisfy the justices that he had not meant to affront them. The predictable response: they were "well satisfied" and "it is therefore ordered he be released out of Custody paying fees." Hawthon was reminded of his inferior rank; the justices confirmed their authority. He was called on to explain and apologize; the court thereupon administered a minimal correction. On such ritual occasions, face-to-face encounters with authority took place within carefully circumscribed limits according to commonly accepted linguistic exchanges.[17]

The intensity of such encounters naturally varied with the grossness of the offense and the rank of the offender. Culprits were treated firmly but in the light of the justices' recognition of the temptations of the nearby tavern. Magistrates were accustomed to hearing an offender confess that his behavior stemmed from "being much in drink." The court was thus only temporarily startled by Richard Patterson "by his Looking in at the Court and Speaking out a Loud 'Come here You Dogs and Fight.'" Fined twenty-nine shillings and put in the stocks until the court rose, he was remanded to the sheriff's custody and ordered "before the court Tomorrow Morning (when perhaps he may be sober)." Another planter through his vivid, albeit vulgar, language threatened the natural order of society from his "appearing Drunk and Insolent by his bidding Benjamin Weeks undersheriff Kiss his Arse in the face of the Court." Though fined for his behavior, three weeks later "the said Davis came now into Court in a very submissive manner and asked pardon for the high offence he had been guilty of & promises for the future to take care never to be guilty of an offense of the Like nature." The court's formulaic response graciously proclaimed to all that "this Court being willing to Show & grant Compassion etc. do therefore retract their said order" that Davis be fined.[18]

Planters and lawyers who questioned the integrity of the court's decisions could expect a higher penalty for their outrages. Richard Lowe had to pay five pounds current money, which was not remanded, for saying that the sheriff, justices, and clerk were rogues for charging him more than his taxable status allowed, "which Impudent, base, false, and scandalous Speeches were fully proved against him . . . by Sundry Witnesses." William Kennan, one of the few attorneys appearing in the county courts during this era, paid the same sum for asserting the court had made "a Roguish order in favor of one Moses Self in a Suit." Similarly, when John Bolling, a former justice, burgess, and wealthy Henrico planter, came into court and behaved "himself after a very rude manner to the Justices by calling them Puppies and calling on God to damn them together with other misdemeanours," he was taken into custody and fined.[19]

Yet the court knew where custom and social convention set limits to its use of the law. Its treatment of two important but distinct groups of men guilty of the same sort of "contempt" signaled this recognition to the county. When a new commission of the peace appeared under the governor's hand, the sitting justices of Westmoreland County sent the sheriff to the tavern to request that the new nominees appear in court. Several did, but the court sent the sheriff out again; he returned to report that five of the gentlemen were still in the ordinary, and, when asked why they would not come in and swear, he stated that "the Reason they gave him was they would come into court when they See fit."[20]

This exchange set in motion a definition of rank and authority that had to be moved forward with great delicacy. The sitting justices rose to the occasion. One of their number, George Lee, demanded that the recalcitrants be forced to give up their law books, copies of which were sent to each county for use by the court. The men who had issued such a peremptory challenge to their equals on the bench were summoned and threatened with a fine. Perhaps to prove their magisterial rank, they kept the court waiting for eighteen months, then surrendered the books, whereupon the fines were discontinued. Apparently some of the lesser planters misread this symbolic exchange and some time later also failed to appear in court when summoned for jury duty. The justices irately noted that even after the court "was So Indulgent to Send the Sheriff out to Call them who it Seems were in the ordinary," they ignored this officer's summons and "Informed the Court that they . . . would Come when they had done dinner." Standing upon its collective dignity, the magisterial gentry noted that "for [this] Contempt this Court do hereby Inflict the fine of Twenty Shillings upon Each of them." Moreover, the fines were not remanded.[21]

These acts involving authority and the deference due it moved in predictable patterns and in varying degrees of importance as demanded by the nature of the exchanges. The various presentations and definitions of self and rank were publicly acted out, with no intermediaries between bench and community. Once authority's rightful place had been defined, another action—another dramatic exchange of a different sort—could proceed on the stage of court day.

Act II. Law and Mutual Obligations: Debt Cases

Law is a form of social control, and its application by officials shows how the rules of society work. Eighteenth-century definitions of law described it as the "rule of justice," or "giving to every man what is his due."[22] In order to insure that every person received his or her due, the law defined obligations and set the boundaries by which people could tell what to expect from one another in public intercourse. For Virginians living in a plantation economy dominated by the staple crop, tobacco, this meant that the law had to deal with indebtedness. So chronic was debt that one observer noted the "great number of Litigious suits" and concluded that "to be arrested for debt is no scandal here."[23] The reason was that the law recognized social and economic reality: in a society with little circulating specie, where debts were paid in tobacco, the condition of everyone from planter magnate to yeoman was at least modestly leveled by dependence on the market. Hence, the law ensured social order and guaranteed that every man would receive his due—the money owed him—when it provided the forum for face-to-face meetings where the propertied majority settled obligations before the justices.

The personal quality of such encounters was aided by the fact that lawyers were forbidden to involve themselves in small debt cases. The prescribed way to settle such issues was to move for judgment by petition. The plaintiff stood and presented his claim; most debtors readily "confessed judgment" to the sum owed; payment was agreed on according to schedule. If the schedule was not met, a creditor requested that the court declare for him the rightness of his demand for the sum, and this was routinely done. At this point, a rather more elaborate game of face-saving sometimes began, with the debtor intervening before a creditor could get the court's judgment against the recalcitrant. Declaring that he protested the plaintiff's bill and "saved to himself" all exceptions to it, the debtor pleaded for time "to imparl," a request that was always granted. By imparl-

ing, the debtor hoped to come to an agreement with the plaintiff out of court. From the frequency with which planters resorted to this device and from the numerous notations, "dismissed, the parties being agreed," one may conclude that mutual obligations were upheld, and public honor maintained, by those debtors who did not immediately "confess judgment."[24]

Even justices of the peace had to submit to these procedures. In Henrico County, Peter Randolph, a planter, sued justice John Ellis, who admitted that the action "against him is Just for Ten pounds Current money." Ellis was ordered by his fellows on the bench to honor the debt and to pay costs. If a planter grew impatient for payment of a sum after judgment had been made in his favor, the law specified that he wait a year and a day before seeking a writ of *scire facias* to recover the debt. Reluctance to become harsh about payment reveals itself in one planter's regretful decision to proceed "against John Ward on a Judgment obtained by the said Bolling of a longer Date than ten Years."[25]

This ongoing ritual action of suing and being sued kept planters and farmers coming to court every month to see who was recovering against whom and what their own role in the drama might be at any given moment. Exactly this state of affairs kept Ralph Wormeley of Middlesex County constantly attuned to what was happening at court day. For months Wormeley dunned his neighbors, especially John Turberville of Hickory Hill, for their debts, so that they should "not oblige me, contrary to my wish, to adopt another mode of applying, which necessity only shall urge me upon." Wormeley's preference for an amicable settlement was heightened by his need to hold *his* creditor Thomas Reid at bay. Finally obtaining an execution against Turberville, which was served at court, Wormeley quickly scribbled to the sheriff of Westmoreland County: "Sir: Please to pay to the order of M. Tho. Reid of Northumberland the sum of £100 (the first paid into yr. hands) out of the money made by virtue of the Exec. levied on the estate of J. T. Esq. of Hiccory Hill—& for so doing this shall be your warrant."[26]

In those rare instances where a case of debt was genuinely contested, a defendant still invoked the community's awareness of mutual obligation by "praying oyer" of his cause and "putting himself upon the county," asking that a jury hear his case.

The assembled county then heard the clerk demand of the plaintiff, "A.B. come forth and prosecute the action against C.D. or else thou will be nonsuit," and then of the defendant, after the plaintiff (who rarely failed to appear) had entered his declaration, "C.D. come forth and save thee and thy bales or else thou wilt forfeit thy recognizance." Though the jury's participation helped to ensure that communal custom and experience were part of the decision, the law and the final declaration rested with authority—the justices before whom the case was argued. Except when the jurors delivered a verdict in these disputes, debts—at all times the single most numerous civil cause before the county courts—were settled between the two parties alone, in face-to-face definitions of mutual obligation in a public forum.[27]

Act III. The Legal Authority of Communal Sanction: The Grand Jury

A third kind of action cast the spotlight of public attention farther from the bench, into circles broader than that of the propertied planters and farmers. The biannual convening of the grand jury was a familiar ritual in which twenty-four "grave and substantial freeholders" gathered after being notified two months in advance by the sheriff to attend the May or November court. From the twenty-four, fifteen at least were impaneled, and as the court came to order the clerk stood and called out: "You good men that be returned to enquire for our Sovereign Lord the King, and the body of this county . . . answer to your names, every man at the first call, and save your fines." Though the justices were clearly the head of the "body of the county," the grand jurors also functioned with authority, swearing three at a time to uphold the oath their foreman took with his hand on the Gospels. Jurymen were bound to "present no man for hatred, envy, or malice, neither [to] leave any man unpresented for love, fear, favour, or affection, or hope of reward; but [to] present things truly, as they come to . . . knowledge, according to the best of your understanding. So help you God."[28]

Though the freeholders of the county, as grand jurymen, shared in the authority of the court, they did not thereby earn the opportunity of rising from jury box to magistrates' bench. Grand jurymen did not become justices. Faithful servants of the court, they often continued to appear for jury duty time after

time, in addition to holding other county offices. The Rust family of Westmoreland County may be fairly representative of their counterparts in neighboring tidewater communities. Peter Rust served as grand juryman and foreman during the 1740s and 1750s. A man of modest means but excellent parts, he was forced to ask the court to bind out to various masters three orphans left to his care because their estate could not sufficiently compensate him. He served as road surveyor, a duty shared with George and Vincent Rust. Vincent, also a grand juryman, was given the lucrative post of tobacco inspector, let his rank go to his head, and was fined for insolence, but four months later was back in good grace and received a license to keep a tavern. Jeremiah Rust served the court with his relatives, though in humbler fashion: he was paid 540 pounds of tobacco for cleaning the courthouse. Despite long years of service in various capacities, the Rusts never did become justices.[29]

Farmers and planters like the Rusts, once sworn to their duty, rose to the clerk's bidding to "stand together and hear your charge," as the county at large was admonished to keep silent "under paine of imprisonment" while the charge was given. A formulaic summary of general moral principles as well as of types of offenses to be investigated, the charge was delivered by the senior justice or the deputy king's attorney. Modeled on such English examples as those contained in Richard Chamberlain's *The Complete Justice,* it reminded listeners that religion and morality were "the only Foundations whereon Society and civil government subsist." Man's laws should reflect God's and were sadly necessary since conscience alone would never suffice to restrain "Fashionable Vices" in the "depraved state" of human existence. It was the purpose of law to deter men from evil, promote the general good, and ensure that the "particular Rights of every individual may be preserved & maintained."[30]

It was for this dual reason—to sustain the common weal and protect individuals—that the jurymen were to present offenders who violated God's laws or were guilty of civil nuisances. The grand jury was exhorted to name all whom they found to have violated the Sabbath, missed church, scoffed at the sacraments or scripture, blasphemed, or got drunk. In second order of importance were offenders who sold drink without a license, failed to keep up roads, let their mill dams fall into disrepair, or "conceale[d] Tithable persons to the great Griefe and Damage of the Inhabitants of this County." The court further delegated its power to use "wit and cunning" to the jurors by reminding them that they were to present "all those who you know are guilty of any hanious Crime Either against almighty God, the King & Queens Maj[es]ties, or Wronge done to your Neighbour—although the said Cryme be not Expresly nominated or Sett downe." Having withdrawn to consider this weighty charge, the jury drew up the list of persons to be presented according to their own knowledge or on information given by the churchwardens or by two witnesses, carefully noting the names of the informants under each presentment. When the jury reentered the courtroom, the foreman read out the presentments, which were then entered on the record. The court thanked the jury and it was dismissed, the clerk crying out to the undersheriffs, "Make way for the gentlemen of the grand inquest."[31]

Having played their mediatory role between authority and community, the grand jurymen resumed their seats in the courtroom, and the action shifted back to the principals—the justices of the peace—who ordered the accused to appear at the next court. There the court artfully combined "cunning, wit, and power" in a manner guaranteed to uphold authority and communal custom by putting offenders to shame on the public stage of court day. That Virginians recognized the impact of shame on their public personalities is revealed in the vast number of nonappearances to answer presentments. Such "non-action" was a presumptive admission of guilt and was so considered by the court, which levied an appropriate fine on all persons "being thrice solemnly called but appearing not." Nonappearance enabled the court to exact monies for the relief of the county's poor, a practice that had the additional advantage of relieving the tax burden on propertied gentry and yeomen. The occasional outright confession of guilt confirmed the utility of the courts' practices, as when John Stuard was presented for profanity, failed to appear, and had the sheriff tell the court that he "confessed himself to be guilty and was ashamed to appear before the Court, but would Willingly Submitt to the Courts Judgement."[32]

Formal authority itself was not immune to this sort of corrective pressure; indeed, holding public office and exemplifying propertied personality made justices even more subject to psychological and so-

cial sanctions. A great wagging of tongues therefore assailed the sensitive justice Landon Carter when he had to step down from the bench and admit the rightness of a presentment for swearing, pay the fine, and resume his place. The mortification of Robert Wormeley Carter was eloquent, though privately confessed. To his diary Carter confided about his presentment, "I take shame to myself it being for swearing; I recollect the matter; an insolent fellow accused me of usury; which provoked me & put me off guard. May God pardon me." This awareness that formal authority could be subjected to customary sanctions through the law may have tempered the severity of judgments. When John Forrister was presented for operating "a tip'ling house" without a license, the court discovered he could not pay his fine but accepted his earnest promise never again to sell liquor illegally. The justices declared that they knew him "to be very poor and that he hath a Wife and Several Children." In view of their familiarity with this case, the justices "in Compassion beg leave to Recommend him to the Governor as an object of Charity."[33]

In all such instances arising from the grand jury's sitting, formal authority mingled with familiar custom. Authority was shared with the grand jurors, and the communal nature of acts involving ritual confession and expiation of sin was heightened. Since shaming affected the great as well as the simple, such acts touched all free members of the county. (For the most part, slaves and servants were dealt with by their masters on the plantations.) Freeholders guilty of missing church, failing to keep up their roads, having illegitimate children, swearing, or getting drunk were publicly identified and reproved.[34] Beneath them in the social order, and usually at court day restricted to the porch, were the unpropertied of Virginia. Yet even to them, whose lives only occasionally were touched by the justices on the bench, the public stage of court day was accessible, and they, too, played a part in the drama that displayed qualities both formal and familiar.

Act IV. Authority and Its Obligations before the Law: Slaves and Servants

So far we have observed exchanges between the formal and familiar spheres of Virginia life that involved those propertied actors whose public personalities and identities received definition and confirmation at court day. Beyond the circles of the great and middling ranks of the society, however—at the periphery of these exchanges—stood men and women in varying degrees of unpropertied servitude. If law was something more than a coercive tool employed solely to the advantage of the propertied gentry, court day must reveal that additional quality. The recognition of the significance of slaves and servants by the court was signaled by its actions, both in its treatment of such persons and in the props and appurtenances deemed appropriate for their rank.[35]

The presence of the lowest members of Virginia society on the courthouse porch was recognized in August 1750 when the Richmond County Court ordered its sheriff to "employ some person to rail in a Yard with good saw'd Whiteoak Rails and Locust posts Twenty foot in Wedth from each Corner of the Courthouse five foot high, The rails to be within three inches of one another, And to sett up four Benches in each of the Piazzas and one under each of the Windows in the body of the Courthouse of a Convenient hight and Breadth for people to set on."[36] Such an order, though not intended exclusively for the benefit of servants, and not at all for that of slaves, nonetheless testifies to the court's awareness of the lower orders of society whose standing and due were confirmed by the court's actions in regard to them and on their behalf.

The formal authority of the justices was invoked by servants as a reminder of obligations owed these denizens of the piazza who were themselves a species of property and possessors of very little. Occasionally a servant's plea was brought by an intermediary but more often by the servant him or herself. The "wit and cunning" of the court, as well as social standards of rank based on race, were in full play as servant Thomas Cox complained against his master, William Woodson. The justices listened, agreed "that the said Cox hath not been kept as a white servant ought to be," and ordered that in future his master should provide him with "Sufficient diet, lodging, and cloathing, and . . . not immoderately Correct him."[37]

White servants had rights above those of black servants or slaves, as the above instance demonstrates. Yet obligations incumbent on authority to give black Virginians their due were occasionally, if infrequently, invoked with success by Afro-Americans. Beaten and imprisoned by Elias Newman, a black woman named Sarah argued that she was over twenty-one and free, contrary to Newman's claim that she was his wife's slave. In this instance, an attorney-at-law, John Martin, acted as Sarah's representative, though whether appointed by the court for her in forma pauperis, as was sometimes the case, we do not know. Newman's protests to Sarah's bill were ruled insufficent, and he was forced to carry his case on appeal to Williamsburg, where we lose sight of it.[38]

Servants, black and white alike, usually came into court of their own volition and were not represented by an attorney but, like the rest of society, stood in face-to-face meeting with authority. And it was precisely the justices' jealous sense of that authority that worked for the lesser ranks of the social order. Certainly this is the reason why the court ordered a planter publicly whipped for beating the slave of another without the sanction of the law. Cruel or arbitrary punishment was not opposed for its own sake but rather because of the threat to constituted authority—its own—which the court protected. Yet here again, the interplay of authority and custom, formal and familiar, is obvious, and both types of actors in the drama got something out of the situation. This same quality of the law—that it protected both the public, propertied personality of authority while intervening for dependents as well—moved the farmer Job Shadrick to complain to his patron, Augustine Washington, a gentleman justice. Abused by John Bayes, the captain of a troop of soldiers, Shadrick insisted that Bayes "suffered them to beat him in a Barbarous manner." Washington had written to Bayes for an explanation, "but instead of Complying he flung the Letter in the fire and said Col. Washington might kiss his backside." For his insult, Bayes was arrested, brought into the public forum, and forced to give security for his good behavior.[39]

In some degree, qualities we have seen in other acts—shame, intercession by the "gentle" members of society for inferiors, jealous protection of authority—all seem to have coalesced in the act that revealed the rank and rights of the lower orders. Thus one indentured servant's canny use of the court provides a fitting climax to the dramatic play we have been observing. Captured and brought into court after attempting to run away, Alexander Stewart loudly demanded protection since he was "inhumanely rased as well In his Diett and Great Severity" by his master, John Livingston, Jr. Sensing the spectacular potential of his position, Alexander maneuvered the court into ordering that he be "stript in Court and it appearing to the said Court that the said Alexander has bin severely whipped by ye many Stripes on his Naked Skin Contrary to any authority by Law for so doeing," the justices issued a public reprimand. Though Alexander was to return to Livingston's service, the court admonished the master to treat his servant "in a more Christian and Human Manner than he before has and that he doe Not suffer him to be used any otherwise," lest upon "further Complaint and Just Occation & Cause" he be dealt with severely by the court.[40]

Though the justices of the counties did not regularly interfere with the private law administered on the plantations to servants—and never, as far as we can tell, with regard to slaves—it is nevertheless true that law held meaning and consequence for the lesser ranks of society. The trials of slaves for felony in oyer and terminer sessions were a kind of spectacle that deserves separate treatment; yet even there one finds that the formal letter of the law was regularly moderated by familiar custom. The king's law functioned in those instances, too, where Afro-Americans stood on trial for their lives before the justices. Yet it is perhaps significant that those sessions were separate from the regular meetings of court day, and we should not try to force a total unity of action on a culture whose prevailing views were ambiguous and tortured at best, in that slaves were regarded simultaneously as human beings and as chattel property.[41]

*   *   *

Planters and farmers, free blacks and mulattoes, servants and tenants—all left the stage of court day in tidewater Virginia secure in the sense that communal affairs had been shaped and ratified by themselves, that the rhythm of public life continued, and that customary institutions were firmly guided by the authority of the gentry. That authority, expressed through the application of law, upheld the defense of property and, through that, the public identities, the well-being, and the security of most of society. The law could give every person his or her due only if it was replete with suasive images, commonly accepted values. Where it failed, it did so because the Virginia society failed to grapple with the contradictions inherent in chattel slavery based on race. Besides being a mode of social control whereby authority was sanc-

tioned and norms of behavior were enforced, the law regularly, predictably, appeared as a sentinel guarding the boundaries and defining relationships between the worlds of formal authority and customary, familiar county life.

Contemporary English opinion, so highly valued in eighteenth-century Virginia, wisely held (though it failed to put into practice) the conviction that law should rarely be enforced through the mere fear of punishment. Rather, it should promote acquiescence among a people persuaded of its value. "We find by experience," wrote Richard Chamberlain in 1681, "that it is not frequent punishment that prevents offences . . . It is better preventing, than redressing offences."[42] As long as the routine, the rituals, the repetition of the "acts" we have observed continued—as long as shared perceptions were publicly expressed and communication between various ranks of society was guaranteed—court day flourished. In their deft handling of the occasional displays of violence, hauteur, and vulgarity, and the ills attendant on chattel slavery, Virginia's justices promoted the interplay between formality and familiarity in county life. Whether the existence of court day with its attendant controls of public opinion and censure had a beneficial effect on private law in the plantations, we can only speculate. Certainly one senses that in its formal architecture, its dramaturgy, its visual and aural symbolism, the courthouse was a sort of "everyman's plantation." To a degree, everyone in the county "belonged" there and rightly expected to receive what was due them as they defined themselves, their rank, their relationships to others. Authority, in the persons of the justices, managed to give various ranks of Virginians what was theirs, as the law was supposed to do, by a judicious mixture of "cunning, wit, and power." At its best, court day was the arena in which authority, law, and custom mingled in ritual exchanges. Deference to authority was expected all down the line. Mutual obligations had to be acted out as well, as both business and self-images were advanced in the settlement of debt. Communal sanction served to ratify authority's presence by mediating that presence by means of the grand jury, and in exchange for deference, obligations were set on superiors as well. Over all, the public law, the public authority of the king's court, loomed large in everyone's mind.

Sir Edward Coke, the great expositor of the ancient,

customary nature of English law, would have been pleased at the commingling of formality and familiarity wrought by the gentlemen justices of the peace in Virginia. Of the commission of the peace, he had once said that it was "such a forme of subordinate government for the tranquillity and quiet of the Realm, as no part of the Christian world hath the like, if the same be duly executed."[43] The due execution of the office by Virginia's justices kept court day alive as the stage upon which the dynamic between authority and custom, formality and familiarity, guided the vigorous evolution of a culture intensely proud of English law "from antiquity not to be traced." While the dialectic lasted, court day continued to be the occasion for "the principal meetings of the Country."

Notes

A version of this essay was delivered February 18, 1979, as a public lecture at the American Antiquarian Society, where the author was an NEH Fellow. The author wishes to thank Clifford Geertz, Rhys Isaac, Harry Stout, Warren Billings, John Murrin, and Charles Wetherell for comments on this article and the supporting literature.

1. Joseph Priestley, *Lectures on History*, 2 vols. (London, 1793), 1:149, and quoted on the title pages of William Waller Hening, ed., *The Statutes at Large; Being a Collection of all the Laws of Virginia . . .* (Richmond, Va., 1819–23), hereafter cited as *Statutes at Large*.

2. "Observations in Several Voyages and Travels in America in the Year 1736. (From *The London Magazine*, July 1746)," *William and Mary Quarterly*, 1st ser., 15 (1907): 147, 222–23. The Englishman also observed a great number of lawyers at Williamsburg and York; this grouping of attorneys around the capital began in the late seventeenth century. See Philip Alexander Bruce, *Institutional History of Virginia in the Seventeenth Century: An Inquiry into the Religious, Moral, Educational, Legal, Military, and Political Conditions of the People*, vol. 1 (New York, 1910), 570–87. On the training of Virginia lawyers, see Alan McKinley Smith, "Virginia Lawyers, 1680–1776: The Birth of an America Profession" (Ph.D. diss., Johns Hopkins University, 1967). For a different interpretation explaining the low number of lawyers in outlying counties in contrast to professional growth around Williamsburg, see A. G. Roeber, *Faithful Magistrates and Republican Lawyers: Creators of Virginia Legal Culture, 1660–1810* (Chapel Hill, N.C., 1981), and "'The Scrutiny of the Ill-Natured Ignorant Vulgar': Lawyers and Print Culture in Virginia, 1716–1775," *Virginia Magazine of History and Biography* 91 (1983): 387–417.

3. In addition to Bruce's institutional studies of the courts, see Albert Ogden Porter, *County Government in Virginia: A Legislative History, 1607–1904* (New York, 1947), and George Lewis Chumbley, *Colonial Justice in Virginia: The Development of a Judicial System . . .* (Richmond, Va., 1938). More useful on specifics of procedure and application of law are Arthur P. Scott, *Criminal Law in Colonial Virginia* (Chicago, 1930), and, on the General Court, Hugh F. Rankin, *Criminal Trial Proceedings in the General Court of Colonial Virginia* (Charlottesville, Va., 1965). The exceptional, if impressionistic, study of Charles S. Sydnor, *Gentleman Freeholders: Political Practices in Washington's Virginia* (Chapel Hill, N.C., 1952), first suggested the value of looking at court-day rituals, an insight developed in the 1970s by Rhys Isaac, especially in "Evangelical Revolt: The Nature of the Baptists' Challenge to the Traditional Order in Virginia, 1765–1775," *William and Mary Quarterly*, 3d ser., 31 (1974): 345–68. For an overview of the literature on ideas and social action, see Richard R. Beeman, "The New Social History and the Search for 'Community' in Colonial America," *American Quarterly* 29 (1977): 422–43. Beeman's survey reveals the paucity of studies on the law and legal institutions; such studies should be fitted into the emerging and cultural historiography.

4. "A Charge to the Grand Jury" (Williamsburg, Va., 1730), in *William Parks, Printer and Journalist of England and Colonial America*, ed. Lawrence C. Wroth (Richmond, Va., 1926), 33. *Virginia Gazette* (Parks), Oct. 3–10, 1745. On the "customary" and "immemorial" qualities of common law thinking, see J. G. A. Pocock, *The Ancient Constitution and the Feudal Law: A Study of English Historical Thought in the Seventeenth Century* (Cambridge, 1957), 30–70. Virginians like William Beale appealed to antiquity and custom in the county courts, even in defiance of English common law prohibitions: see Richmond County Orders, June 4, 1739, where Beale defended his right to stop up a public way, "setting forth that he and his ancestors here for a Long time Enjoyed the conveniency of keeping gates upon the severall roads Leading through his land without which he could not have the benefitt of a pasture." All county orders and inventories are at the Virginia State Library Archives, Richmond.

5. The main point of departure among historians of colonial America for methods of historical anthropology has been the work of Clifford Geertz, on which the present essay depends heavily. See especially Geertz, "Thick Description: Toward an Interpretive Theory of Culture," in *The Interpretation of Cultures . . .* (New York, 1973), 3–32; Geertz, "Centers, Kings, and Charisma: Reflections on the Symbolics of Power," in *Culture and Its Creators: Essays in Honor of Edward Shils*, ed. Joseph Ben-David and Terry Nichols Clark (Chicago, 1977), 150–71. On the importance of ritual action in a world of oral communication, see Walter J. Ong, *The Presence of the Word: Some Prolegomena for Cultural and Religious History* (New Haven, Conn., 1967), and *Interfaces of the Word: Studies in the Evolution of Consciousness and Culture* (Ithaca, N.Y., 1977). On the literacy rate in Virginia, see Kenneth A. Lockridge, *Literacy*

in Colonial New England: An Enquiry into the Social Context of Literacy in the Early Modern West (New York, 1974), 77–78, 90, 93. Lockridge concludes that the literacy rate may have begun to stagnate after 1750; at best, two-thirds of able-bodied white males may have been literate in Virginia. On the importance of personal meetings in such a culture, see the ideas advanced by Erving Goffman in *The Presentation of Self in Everyday Life* (New York, 1959), *Behavior in Public Places: Notes on the Social Organization of Gatherings* (New York, 1963), and *Interaction Ritual: Essays on Face-to-Face Behavior* (Chicago, 1967).

6. The oath of justice is in *Statutes at Large*, 3:508–9 (quotations are italized in original). The method used here combines quantification of the most numerous types of action in twelve tidewater county courts over most of the eighteenth century with the analysis of such action as symbolic, ritualized summation of such key cultural concepts as deference, hierarchy, dependence, and property. On action-as-text, see Paul Ricoeur, "The Model of the Text: Meaningful Action Considered as a Text," *Social Research* 38 (1971): 529–62; Robert K. Merton, "The Unanticipated Consequences of Purposive Social Action," *American Sociological Review* 1 (1936): 894–904; Alfred Schutz, "Concept and Theory Formation in the Social Sciences," in *Philosophy of Social Sciences: A Reader*, ed. Maurice Natanson (New York, 1963), 231–49, esp. 247–49; and Schutz, "Common-Sense and Scientific Interpretation of Human Action," in *Philosophy of Social Sciences*, ed. Natanson 302–46, esp. 342–46. The selected patterns of action spring from a broad sampling and were significant in ritual and symbolic fulness for the participants. The twelve counties studied are York, Henrico, Warwick, Charles City, Middlesex, Essex, Caroline, Lancaster, Richmond, Westmoreland, King George, and Northumberland. For quotations, see *Statutes at Large*, 3:509.

7. Inventories of justices at death, sampled for the various counties, reveal a wide range of wealth, but with every member's personal wealth counted in hundreds of pounds current money. Courts were kept running by a faithful group of magistrates, for example, three Randolph brothers in Henrico, and Taylors, Taliaferros, and Buckners in Caroline. Great magnates sat irregularly; the eminent Corbin, Beverley, and Baylor families in Caroline were allied by marriage with the above-named faithful magistrates but sat infrequently; the same was true of the Carters and Byrds in their counties, with the exception of the highly conscientious Landon Carter in Richmond. On Caroline, see T. E. Campbell, *Colonial Caroline: A History of Caroline County, Virginia* (Richmond, Va., 1954), 349. Campbell found that no justice ever owned fewer than one thousand acres. Family connection and tradition, however, were just as important. In York, Thomas Barber, whose family had served on the bench since the 1650s, refused to sit, and the court ordered the sheriff to wait on him to plead with him. When he died, his total inventory was only £105 10s. (York Orders, Mar. 19, 1710/11, May 18, 1713). Barber's fellow justice Robert Reade owned 22 slaves and 2 indentured mulattoes, with other chattels (York Orders, May 18, 1713). King

George justice William Strother's personal estate was valued at £858 19s. 3½d. (King George Inventories, 1721–44). At the other end of the spectrum were men like Augustine Washington, whose personal inventory in the King George Inventories read: July 1, 1743, £824 8s. 3d., including 27 slaves and surveyor's instruments in that county; in Westmoreland, June 28, 1743, £409 10s. 8d.; and in Stafford, £287 8s. Washington's rank would have been comparable to that of James Burwell of York, whose inventory totaled 42 slaves and other servants, as well as a personal estate worth £2,386 18s. 10d. (York Orders, Mar. 16, 1718).

8. On the value of older men, see David Hackett Fischer, *Growing Old in America: The Bland-Lee Lectures . . .* (New York, 1977), and his disagreements with Lawrence Stone in "Growing Old: An Exchange," *New York Review of Books*, Sept. 15, 1977. For Stone's views, see *The Family, Sex and Marriage in England, 1500–1800* (New York, 1977), 58–60, 125–218, 403–4. For the examples cited for Virginia, see York Orders, July 21, Aug. 19, 1719; on Edwin Conway, Lancaster Orders, June 19, 1752, and Horace Edwin Hayden, *Virginia Genealogies: A Genealogy of the Glassell Family of Scotland and Virginia* (Wilkes-Barre, Pa., 1891), 238–44; on Essex, justices to Gov. Randolph, Mar. 27, 1788, in William P. Palmer, ed., *Calendar of Virginia State Papers and Other Manuscripts*, vol. 4 (Richmond, Va., 1884), 417–19.

9. Charles Carroll of Doughregan Manor to Charles Carroll of Carrollton, Oct. 16, 1759, in *Unpublished Letters of Charles Carroll of Carrollton*, ed. Thomas M. Field (New York, 1902), 33–34, and quoted in Richard Beale Davis, *Intellectual Life in the Colonial South, 1585–1763*, vol. 3 (Knoxville, Tenn., 1978), 1588. Jack P. Greene, ed., *A Diary of Colonel Landon Carter of Sabine Hall, 1752–1778* (Charlottesville, Va., 1965), 92–93. Virginia licensed attorneys as early as 1643 but repeatedly reversed policy; by 1690 all attempts had been given up (*Statutes at Large*, 4:357–62). Between 1732 and 1750 the profession began to grow at a prodigious rate, judging from the number of licenses presented in the county courts by men swearing the oath of an attorney. Eventually, of course, the rise of the profession altered the personal quality of going-to-law on court day. For details of the growth of the profession and its impact, see Roeber, *Faithful Magistrates and Republican Lawyers*, and "Scrutiny of the Ill-Natured," passim. As few as three attorneys were in active practice between 1732 and 1750 in some of the tidewater counties, as many as ten in more heavily populated areas and sites of merchant activity such as, for example, Essex County.

10. For summaries of the court's duties, see Porter, *County Government*, and the sample of seventeenth-century laws and orders and the introductory essay on local government in Warren M. Billings, ed., *The Old Dominion in the Seventeenth Century: A Documentary History of Virginia, 1606–1689* (Chapel Hill, N.C., 1975), 69–103. No white person could be tried for felony in the counties. My survey of "Called Courts" reveals that, for example, in Caroline 21 separate examinations resulted in only 9 people being sent to Williamsburg, on charges of horse-stealing, breaking and entering, and theft. The remainder were found

not guilty or were summarily punished (at times at their own request) or bound over to the grand jury session to await a bill of indictment. Likewise, in King George County during 1730–50, 30 examinations sent 18 culprits to Williamsburg, primarily for burglary but also for murder, forgery, and accidental shooting. Twenty-five were whipped, fined, found not guilty, or remanded to the grand jury on a lesser charge. In York, 24 sessions examined 29 people, sent 15 to Williamsburg for theft and murder, 1 for forgery, 1 unspecified, and dealt with another dozen in the county. Slaves were tried by the justices for felony and executed as well under the county court's power derived from the commission of oyer and terminer; on slave trials, see below.

11. The "stile" for calling the court is in *Statutes at Large*, 2:59–60, 72. Forms used for swearing jurors and officers and those cited hereafter in conducting the order of business are drawn from one of the most common manuals of the day, *The Office of the Clerk of Assize: . . . Together with the Office of the Clerk of the Peace* . . . (London, 1676). Americans adapted such treatises to local conditions; see James Parker's *Conductor Generalis; or, The Office, Duty, and Authority of the Justice of the Peace* . . . (New Jersey, 1764), modeled on Richard Burn's *The Justice of the Peace and Parish Officer* (London, 1755), 505–16. On the manuals and law treatises in Virginia, see William Hamilton Bryson, *Census of Law Books in Colonial Virginia* (Charlottesville, 1978), 31–82.

12. *The Life of the Reverend Devereux Jarratt* . . . (Baltimore, 1806), 14. On General Court ritual and appointments, see Rankin, *Criminal Trial Proceedings*, 63–87. The oath of a justice is in *Statutes at Large*, 3:508–9.

13. Fitzhugh to Nicholas Hayward, Jan. 30, 1686, quoted in Richard Beale Davis, ed., *William Fitzhugh and His Chesapeake World, 1676–1701* (Chapel Hill, N.C., 1963), 203, 208, n. 4.

14. On courthouse architecture and the evolution of a public style of display in plantations and government buildings, see Marcus Whiffen, *The Public Buildings of Williamsburg: Colonial Capital of Virginia, an Architectural History* (Williamsburg, Va., 1958), 50, 152–61; Whiffen, "The Early County Courthouses of Virginia," *Journal of the Society of Architectural Historians* 18 (1959): 2–10; Frederick Doveton Nichols, "Palladio's Influence on American Architecture," in *Palladio in America* (Milan, 1976), 101–25, esp. 105–7 on the arcaded loggia; and C. Malcolm Watkins, *The Cultural History of Marlborough, Virginia* . . . (Washington, D.C., 1968), 115–22. On contemporary houses and their evolution see Henry Chandlee Forman, *Virginia Architecture in the Seventeenth Century* (Williamsburg, 1957).

15. See Lancaster Orders, Aug. 8, 1740. On Elizabeth City's old 1693 courthouse, see William Montgomery Sweeny, "Gleanings from the Records of (Old) Rappahannock County and Essex County, Virginia," *William and Mary Quarterly*, 2d ser., 18 (1938): 297–313, esp. 307; Campbell, *Colonial Caroline*, 125–27; and Evelyn Taylor Adams, *The Courthouse in Virginia Counties, 1634–1776* (Hamilton, Va., 1966). The concept of "otherness" or "nou-

menal" space set aside from the "phenomenal" familiar world is developed by Rudolf Otto, *The Idea of the Holy: An Inquiry into the Non-Rational Factor in the Idea of the Divine and Its Relation to the Rational*, trans. John W. Harvey, 2d ed. (New York, 1950), 65–68; Mircea Eliade, *Images and Symbols: Studies in Religious Symbolism*, trans. Philip Mairet (New York, 1961); and Wendell C. Beane and William G. Doty, eds., *Myths, Rites, Symbols: A Mircea Eliade Reader*, 2 vols. (New York, 1976). See also Peter L. Berger, *The Sacred Canopy: Elements of a Sociological Theory of Religion* (New York, 1967), and Berger and Thomas Luckmann, *The Social Construction of Reality: A Treatise in the Sociology of Knowledge* (New York, 1966). That ritual actions in a legal context should be viewed as a species of quasireligious definition of life in semiliterate cultures can be seen in Victor W. Turner, *The Ritual Process: Structure and Anti-Structure* (Chicago, 1969), and *Dramas, Fields, and Metaphors: Symbolic Action in Human Society* (Ithaca, N.Y., 1974); Max Gluckman, *The Judicial Process among the Barotse of Northern Rhodesia* (Manchester, 1955), and *The Ideas in Barotse Jurisprudence* (New Haven, Conn., 1965); Lloyd A. Fallers, *Law without Precedent: Legal Ideas in Action in the Courts of Colonial Busoga* (Chicago, 1969); and Paul Bohannan, *Justice and Judgment among the Tiv* (Oxford, 1957).

16. The cycle was dictated by statutes drawn by Burgesses who had been justices and would be again when they finished their terms of office or were turned out. See Jack P. Greene, "Foundations of Political Power in the Virginia House of Burgesses, 1720–1776," *William and Mary Quarterly*, 3d ser., 16 (1959): 488–506; four-fifths of the members during this era were former justices. Of the 39 lawyers Greene identifies, 28 sat after 1745—another index of the growing importance of lawyers after 1750.

17. Westmoreland Orders, July 31, 1728.

18. The use of alcohol and tobacco in the courtroom was forbidden. Drunkenness, even on the part of sitting justices, had marred many seventeenth-century proceedings. A statute of 1676/7 warned that drunken magistrates would be fined and, on a third offense, removed from office (*Statutes at Large*, 2:384). No instances of drunken behavior, grand jury presentments, or reprimands by the council against justices for the period 1700–1750 have been found. Examples of contempt and apology cited are found in Essex Orders, Nov. 21, 22, 1727, and Westmoreland Orders, May 29, 1739, Jan. 29, 1744/5, and Mar. 26, 1746.

19. Westmoreland Orders, June 28, 1738; Henrico Orders, June 6, 1720. Attorneys were obviously expected to behave as officers of the court. The few instances (8) of contempt by an attorney before 1750 in the counties studied resulted from a lawyer's questioning the justices' legal expertise. See Roeber, *Faithful Magistrates and Republican Lawyers*, chap. 3.

20. Westmoreland Orders, Feb. 22, 1736/7.

21. Westmoreland Orders, Apr. 1, 1741, Mar. 1, Aug. 31, Oct. 31, 1738.

22. Samuel Johnson, *A Dictionary of the English Language* . . . (London, 1755), s.v. "Law" and "Justice." A useful

definition of law as a "rule-making" process, where "primary rules" are elaborated in action, or at a "secondary" level by officials, is in H. L. A. Hart, *The Concept of Law* (Oxford, 1961), 77–96, at 92. This functional definition is protested by Lon Fuller, who insists that moral questions are not so easily separated from functional, positive aspects of law. See the exchange between the two men in Frederick A. Olafson, ed., *Society, Law, and Morality: Readings in Social Philosophy* (Englewood Cliffs, N.J., 1961), 439–505, and Lon L. Fuller, *The Morality of Law* (New Haven, Conn., 1964). On the relationship between law and property, see below.

23. Journal of Nicholas Cresswell, Dec. 12, 1774, Leesburg, Loudon County, Va., MSS, Colonial Williamsburg Foundation.

24. The law forbade a lawyer to take a fee in any cause brought by petition for a small debt, and for detinue and trover by petition for any sum under £5 (*Statutes at Large*, 4:426–28); an exception was made in 1736 for collecting debts on behalf of a client in another county when the plaintiff could not be present (*Statutes at Large*, 4:486–87). Imparling was in use from the 1730s onward; see any county order book.

25. For the *scire facias* action, brought by John Bolling, Jr., see Henrico Orders, June 3, 1753, and Henrico Orders, Randolph v. Ellis, Mar. 1, 1762.

26. Entries for Dec. 20, 1783, May 17, July 2, 1784, Aug. 23, 1788, Mar. 1792, Jan. 23, 1795, in Letterbook of Ralph Wormeley, 1783–1802, MSS, Alderman Library, University of Virginia, Charlottesville. The time involved here was extraordinarily long; nonetheless, it was quite common for debt causes to grind on for several years, especially if an actual trial of the issue took place.

27. The clerk's words were prescribed by statute (*Statutes at Large*, 2:59–60). For examples of cases see any county order book. Jury trial of debt cases before 1750 was rare—usually not more than three to seven per year, but increasing steadily thereafter as economic growth, indebtedness, and the legal profession all expanded. Judgment by petition was the most common action in debt cases.

28. The grand juries met in April and December in the late seventeenth century (*Statutes at Large*, 2:74), and courts were admonished to hold a session at least once a year (*Statutes at Large*, 2:407–8). Juries were to meet in May and November after 1705; courts were warned that failure to call the grand inquest would result in a fine of 400 pounds of tobacco against each justice (*Statutes at Large*, 3:368). Surveying the county records between 1720 and 1750, one finds that no grand jury ever presented its justices for failure on this head, nor were fines levied against the justices by the General Court, as far as the records show. Nevertheless, though most counties always called at least one jury in a calendar year, in small counties where population was scattered (for example, Northumberland) the courts did not always see fit to call two juries a year. The best record was York's, which missed only one grand jury—in November 1726. Middlesex and King George, on the other hand, were quite remiss, neglecting at least a dozen

times to call the juries; in Middlesex entire years were skipped—in 1734, 1737, 1745. Gaps in county records make an average estimate nearly impossible, but for counties with fairly complete runs of order books the generalization that courts regularly held the grand inquest seems valid.

29. On the Rusts, see Westmoreland Orders, Jan. 29, 1754, Nov. 28, 1753, May 27, 1755, Mar. 29, July 25, Nov. 28, 1758. In Caroline, Campbell found that out of 343 jurors only 28 ever attained magisterial rank (*Colonial Caroline*, 351–56). David Alan Williams found the same absence of former jurors on the benches of Middlesex and Surry ("Political Alignments in Colonial Virginia Politics, 1678–1750" [Ph.D. diss., Northwestern University, 1959], 91–101). See also Williams, "The Small Farmer in Eighteenth-Century Virginia Politics," *Agricultural History* 42 (1969): 91–101. The differentiation between magisterial and grand jury planters seems to have been emerging in the late seventeenth century. See Kevin P. Kelly, "Economic and Social Development of Seventeenth-Century Surry County, Virginia" (Ph.D. diss., University of Washington, 1972). Most grand jurymen owned about five hundred acres during their time of service in the first half of the eighteenth century.

30. Chamberlain, *The Complete Justice* (London, 1681), 470–85. See "Charge to a Grand Jury" (n.d.), Latané Family Papers, 1667–1800, Alderman Library. Chamberlain's work contains the model in "A Compendious Charge to be given at the Quarter Sessions," which follows a discussion of the law divided into its two parts: "first the Laws Ecclesiastic for the peace of the Church, and Laws Civil, or Temporal, for the peace of the Land" (*Complete Justice*, 470).

31. The county charge quoted here is also divided, with moral offenses first and civil nuisances second. See "Some helps for the Grand Jury of Middlesex, 1693/4," Middlesex County, Virginia Deeds, etc., 1679–94, no. 2 [1a], Virginia State Library, Richmond. I wish to thank Anita Rutman for this reference.

32. Henrico Orders, July 6, 1741.

33. Richmond Orders, July 4, 1745; entry of Aug. 9, 1791, Robert Wormeley Carter Diary, Earl Gregg Swem Library Special Collections, College of William and Mary, Williamsburg; Henrico Orders, Aug. 4, 1746.

34. Tabulation of presentments reveals that missing church was the most common offense in Middlesex, Essex, Lancaster, and Northumberland, and second most common in York, Caroline, King George, Richmond, and Westmoreland. Women presented for bastardy represent the second most numerous offense; prosecution on this head was high, as it was for missing church. The presentments are not an index of bastardy in Virginia. To these figures one would have to add informations and complaints of churchwardens and masters against servant women. No county attempted to prosecute putative fathers with any rigor before 1750. A new law of 1769 encouraged free white women (not servants or slaves) to come into court and accuse the reputed father, provided he was not a servant (*Statutes at Large*, 8:374–77). The new law abolished the practice of whipping women who were unable to pay the 20s. fine. A man could be jailed if he failed to pay a recognizance bond of £10; if

found guilty, he was liable for child support at a rate determined by the court. Tabulation of presentments for 1750–70 reveals a marked drop of bastardy presentments. Since bastard children had to be bound out at the parish's expense and constituted a public charge on property, one can only wonder why sanctions against property in the form of fines were not more regularly imposed and why fathers were not more vigorously pursued for child support. Whether the reluctance to shame a planter or farmer by bringing him into court on this charge outweighed the monetary burdens imposed by supporting illegitimate children at the public's expense is a tantalizing but unresolvable question.

35. Property, far from constituting merely "possessions," embraced everything that was "held" by or "pertained" to the person, no matter how humble. Thus one's religion, social obligations and rights, vesture, and diet all fall under this heading. Clearly, persons of great wealth held the most properties, of various sorts, including that property around which so much of English common law revolved—land. The upholding of the gentry's rights to property, however, was important not only to them but also to the lower orders, who had a right to expect *their* property to be guaranteed them at law. See the following discussions of the symbolic and public nature of private property and its ties to "fundamental rights": G. P. Gooch, *Political Thought in England: Bacon to Halifax* (London, 1914); David Little, *Religion, Order, and Law: A Study in Pre-Revolutionary England* (New York, 1969), 176–89; Howard Nenner, *By Colour of Law: Legal Culture and Constitutional Politics in England, 1660–1689* (Chicago, 1977), 36–39. The potential abuses of the law of property and the often unintended consequences wrought by authority's actions have been insightfully treated by Douglas Hay in "Property, Authority, and the Criminal Law," in *Albion's Fatal Tree: Crime and Society in Eighteenth-Century England*, ed. Hay et al. (New York, 1975), 17–64, and by E. P. Thompson in *Whigs and Hunters: The Origin of the Black Act* (London, 1975), 258–69.

36. Richmond Orders, Aug. 6, 1750.

37. Henrico Orders, Mar. 5, 1722/3.

38. Essex Orders, Nov. 20, 1745. For examples of courts providing an attorney *in forma pauperis* (usually the deputy king's attorney), see King George Orders, Apr. 1, 1737; Middlesex Orders, June 2, 1747, for freedom dues for Mulatto Frank (Frank won the case July 7); and Richmond Orders, Apr. 2, 1739. The King George justices provided the king's attorney to a poor widow who wished to sue the sheriff for maladministration of her deceased husband's estate.

39. York Orders, June 17, 1728; Westmoreland Orders, Apr. 21, 1757. The Westmoreland Court drove home its patronage powers by locking up the unfortunate Bayes until "two good Securitys" could be found to guarantee his behavior. The justices then offered two of their most eminent fellows in Virginia, Thomas Ludwell Lee and Richard Henry Lee, as securities.

40. Essex Orders, May 19, 1752.

41. Philip J. Schwarz of Virginia Commonwealth University has kindly shared with me his preliminary conclusions on slave trials ("Slave Crimes in Eighteenth-Century Virginia," work in progress). He contends that by the 1770s, 60% to 80% of the slaves tried were pardoned, their sentences were commuted, or the goods they stole were devalued. Like the whites accused of felony, the overwhelming majority of slaves tried were not executed for felony, and, as with whites, their most numerous offenses were breaking and entering and theft of goods. In every county on which the conclusions of the present essay rest, white offenders far exceeded blacks in numbers, and there were many more Called Courts than oyer and terminer sessions. See Gerald W. Mullin's excellent evocation of Virginia's patriarchal culture, and the figures for Richmond County, in *Flight and Rebellion: Slave Resistance in Eighteenth-Century Virginia* (New York, 1972). Mullin's conclusions, like my own, differ from those of Edmund S. Morgan, who contends that slavery in eighteenth-century Virginia was based on a "competitive" rather than a "paternalist" set of values. See Morgan, *American Slavery—American Freedom: The Ordeal of Colonial Virginia* (New York, 1975), 325–26, n. 33.

42. Chamberlain, *Complete Justice*, 485.

43. Edward Coke, *Fourth Part of the Institutes of the Laws of England* (London, 1644), 170. Rhys Isaac has suggested that during the 1760s the Baptist conventicles provided a novel sense of communal order and social sobriety in a formerly chaotic society. Isaac sees those qualities as very potent in the tidewater, "where no cultural tradition existed as preconditioning for the communal confession, remorse, and expiation that characterized the spread of the Baptist movement" (Isaac, "Evangelical Revolt," 359). On the contrary, I suggest that precisely because religion, order, and law were vital elements of gentry culture as expressed in the ritual of court day, Isaac's Baptists were (correctly) perceived as direct threats to an already-existing liturgical and dramatic occasion. Hence there is a small but significant difference in our interpretations. The decline of court day in the 1760s requires separate treatment.

Tea-Drinking in Eighteenth-Century America: Its Etiquette and Equipage

RODRIS ROTH

In this essay Rodris Roth explores the ritual significance of tea-drinking in eighteenth-century American domestic life through an impressive array of evidence: portraits, prints, estate inventories, travelers' accounts, newspaper advertisements, and surviving artifacts. Introduced into Europe from China by the early seventeenth century, tea was but one of many exotic eastern imports that fueled a Western fascination for things Oriental. Tea-drinking was initially favored for its medicinal value—relieving headaches, curing "agues" and fevers—and restricted to consumers wealthy enough to afford its high cost. But as merchants secured a ready supply and advertised its virtues, tea's popularity rose dramatically. Drinking tea, Roth argues, moved through society like many other genteel habits. It began as an upperclass English custom requiring expensive objects and an emphatic consciousness of leisure time but was soon imitated by individuals of the "lesser sort." By the mid-eighteenth century, the rage for tea-drinking across all levels of American society suggests that the power of rising "consumerism" derived in part from the East India Company's successful attempt to create demand by shaping aesthetic "taste" in emulation of aristocratic traditions.

Tea-drinking transformed select rooms of the eighteenth-century house into ritual space. Like a good field ethnographer, Roth offers a detailed description of the tea ceremony. We encounter through a rare sketch the actual seating (and standing) arrangement used at teatime in an elite Philadelphia household. And we learn the ways in which material objects disciplined human action. Only specific kinds of tables, trays, and tablecloths and distinct types of silverware, glassware, and sets of cups and saucers were deemed appropriate. Tea-drinkers also had to know rules for proper etiquette: how to hold a cup, whom to sit with, and how to signal silently that no more tea was desired. Even the brewing and serving of tea could be minor artistic performances.

What, then, did tea-drinking actually accomplish? As she describes what people actually did during teatime—gossiping, discussing business affairs, courting, celebrating marriage—Roth presents two functions that transformed the dwelling house, however briefly, into a center of ritual activity. On the one hand, tea-drinking provided a form through which select individuals realized group membership. It enhanced this sense of commonality through hospitality, since entertaining others entailed a network of reciprocity that ensured a continual reenactment of social ties. On the other hand, tea-drinking was also a disjunctive ritual that separated those familiar with genteel tradition from the uninitiated. Keeping up with the latest minute changes in teapot decoration or the newest fad in sugar-tong design, knowing how to cheat at whist, and mastering the fine art of teacup holding—these were special kinds of knowledge that made distinction the necessary basis of social life. The tea ceremony allowed a new order of household magistrates—well-dressed ladies and their gentle admirers—to pronounce aesthetic judgments.

The Americans "use much tea," noted the Abbé Robin during his visit to the United States in 1781. "The greatest mark of civility and welcome they can show you, is to invite you to drink it with them."[1]

Tea was the preferred social beverage of the eighteenth century; serving it was a sign of politeness and hospitality, and drinking it was a custom with distinctive manners and specific equipment. Most discussions of the commodity have dealt only with its political, historical, or economic importance; however, in order to understand the place tea holds in

America's past, it is also important to consider the beverage in terms of the social life and traditions of the Americans. As the Abbé Robin pointed out, not only was tea an important commodity on this side of the Atlantic, but the imbibing of it was an established social ritual.

An examination of teatime behavior and a consideration of what utensils were used or thought appropriate for tea-drinking help to reconstruct and interpret American history as well as to furnish and recreate interiors of the period, thus bringing into clearer focus the picture of daily life in eighteenth-century America.

Tea had long been known and used in the Orient before it was introduced into Europe in the early seventeenth century. At about the same time two other new beverages appeared, chocolate from the Americas and coffee from the Near East. The presence of these commodities in European markets is indicative of the vigorous exploration and active trade of that century, which also witnessed the successful settlement of colonies in North America. By the mid-seventeenth century the new beverages were being drunk in England, and by the 1690s they were being sold in New England. At first chocolate was preferred, but coffee, being somewhat cheaper, soon replaced it and in England gave rise to a number of public places of refreshment known as coffeehouses. Coffee was, of course, the primary drink of these establishments, but that tea also was available is indicated by an advertisement that appeared in an English newspaper in 1658. One of the earliest advertisements for tea, it announced: "That Excellent, and by all Physitians approved, *China* Drink, called by the *Chineans*, *Tcha*, by other nations *Tay alias Tee*, is sold at the *Sultaness-head*, a *Cophee-house* in *Sweetings* Rents by The Royal Exchange, London."[2]

For a time tea was esteemed mainly for its curative powers, which explains why it was "by all Physitians approved." According to an English broadside published in 1660, the numerous contemporary ailments that tea "helpeth" included "the headaches, giddiness, and heaviness." It was also considered "good for colds, dropsies and scurvies and [it] expelleth infection. It prevents and cures agues, surfeits and fevers."[3] By the end of the seventeenth century, however, tea's medicinal qualities had become secondary to its fashionableness as a unique drink. Tea, along

with such other exotic and novel imports from the Orient as fragile porcelains, lustrous silks, and painted wallpapers, had captured the European imagination. Though the beverage was served in public pleasure gardens as well as coffeehouses during the early 1700s in England, social tea-drinking in the home was gradually coming into favor. The coffeehouses continued as centers of political, social, and literary influence as well as of commercial life into the first half of the nineteenth century, for apparently Englishmen preferred to drink their coffee in public rather than in private houses and among male rather than mixed company. This was in contrast to tea, which was drunk in the home with breakfast or as a morning beverage and socially at afternoon gatherings of both sexes. As tea-drinking in the home became fashionable, both host and hostess took pride in a well-appointed tea table, for a teapot of silver or fragile blue-and-white Oriental porcelain with matching cups and saucers and other equipage added prestige as well as elegance to the teatime ritual.

At first the scarcity and expense of the tea, the costly paraphernalia used to serve it, and the leisure considered necessary to consume it limited the use of this commodity to the upper classes. For these reasons, social tea-drinking was, understandably, a prestige custom. One becomes increasingly aware of this when looking at English paintings and prints of the early eighteenth century, such as *Family Group* (fig. 1), painted by Gawen Hamilton about 1730. Family members are portrayed in the familiar setting of their own parlor with its paneled walls and comfortable furnishings. Their pet, a small dog, surveys the scene from a resting place on a corner of the carpet. Teatime appears to have just begun, for cups are still being passed around and others on the table await filling from the nearby porcelain teapot. It seems reasonable to assume, since the painting is portraiture, that the family is engaged in an activity that, although familiar, is considered suitable to the group's social position and worthy of being recorded in oil. That tea-drinking was a status symbol is also indicated by the artist's using the tea ceremony as the theme of the picture and the tea table as the focal point.

Eighteenth-century pictures and writings are basic source materials for information about Anglo-American tea-drinking. (For those paintings used in researching this essay and those mentioned in the text, see the appendix on p. 459.) A number of the pictures are small-scale group or conversation piece paintings of English origin in which family and friends are assembled at tea, similar to *Family Group*, and they provide pictorial information on teatime modes and manners. The surroundings in which the partakers of tea are depicted also reveal information about the period and about the standard of living enjoyed in the better homes. Paneled walls and comfortable chairs, handsome chests and decorative curtains, objects of ceramic and silver and glass—all were set down on canvas or paper with painstaking care and sometimes with a certain amount of artistic license. A careful study of these paintings provides an excellent guide to the material surroundings of eighteenth-century social customs—even to such small details as objects on mantels, tables, and chests—and thus complements data from newspapers, journals, publications, and writings of the same period.

In America, as in England, tea had a rather limited use as a social beverage during the early 1700s. Judge Samuel Sewall, recorder-extraordinary of Boston life at the turn of the eighteenth century, seems to have mentioned tea only once in his copious diary. In the entry for April 15, 1709, Sewall wrote that he had attended a meeting at the residence of Madam Winthrop where the guests "drunk Ale, Tea, Wine."[4] At this time ale and wine, in contrast to tea, were fairly common drinks. Since tea and the equipment used to serve it were costly, social tea-drinking was restricted to the prosperous and governing classes who could afford the luxury. The portrayal of the rotund silver teapot and other tea-drinking equipment in such an American painting as the 1730 portrait of *Susanna Truax* (fig. 2), by an unknown painter, indicates not only that in America as in England was the tea ceremony of social importance but also that a certain amount of prestige was associated with the equipage. Indeed, the very fact that an artist was commissioned for a portrait of this young girl suggests the more than ordinary social status of the sitter and activity depicted.

English customs were generally imitated in America, particularly in urban centers. Of Boston, which he visited in 1740, Joseph Bennett observed that "the ladies here visit, drink tea and indulge every little piece of gentility to the height of the mode and neglect the affairs of their families with as good grace as

Fig. 1. Gawen Hamilton, *Family Group*, England, ca. 1730. The tea set, undoubtedly of porcelain, includes cups and saucers, a cream or milk container, and a sugar container with tongs. (Photograph courtesy of The Colonial Williamsburg Foundation.)

Fig. 2. *Susanna Truax*, Hudson River Valley of New York, 1730. On the beige, marblelike table top beside Susanna—who wears a dress of red, black, and white stripes—are a fashionable silver teapot and white ceramic cup, saucer, and sugar dish. (Photograph courtesy of the National Gallery of Art.)

the finest ladies in London."[5] English modes and manners remained a part of their social behavior after the colonies became an independent nation. Visitors to the newly formed United States were apt to remark about such habits as tea-drinking, as did Brissot de Warville in 1788, that "in this, as in their whole manner of living, the Americans in general resemble the English."[6] Therefore, it is not surprising to find that during the eighteenth century the serving of tea privately in the morning and socially in the afternoon or early evening was an established custom in many households.

The naturalist Peter Kalm, during his visit to North America in the mid-eighteenth century, noted that tea was a breakfast beverage in both Pennsylvania and New York. From the predominantly Dutch town of Albany in 1749 he wrote that "their breakfast is tea, commonly without milk." At another time, Kalm stated: "With the tea was eaten bread and butter or buttered bread toasted over the coals so that the butter penetrated the whole slice of bread. In the afternoon about three o'clock tea was drunk again in the same fashion, except that bread and butter were not served with it."[7] This tea-drinking schedule was followed throughout the colonies. In Boston the people "take a great deal of tea in the morning," have dinner at two o'clock, and "about five o'clock they take more tea, some wine, madeira [and] punch," reported Baron Cromot du Bourg during his visit in 1781.[8] The Marquis de Chastellux confirmed his countryman's statement about teatime, mentioning that the Americans take "tea and punch in the afternoon."[9]

During the first half of the eighteenth century the limited amount of tea, available at prohibitively high prices, restricted its use to a proportionately small segment of the population. About mid-century, however, tea was beginning to be drunk by more and more people, as supplies increased and costs decreased, due in part to the propaganda and merchandising efforts of the East India Company. According to Peter Kalm, tea, chocolate, and coffee had been "wholly unknown" to the Swedish population of Pennsylvania and the surrounding area before the English arrived, but in 1748 these beverages "at present constitute even the country people's daily breakfast."[10] A similar observation was made a few years later by Israel Acrelius. "Tea, coffee, and chocolate are so general," he claimed, "as to be found in the

most remote cabins, if not for daily use, yet for visitors, mixed with Muscovado, or raw sugar."[11]

America was becoming a country of tea drinkers. Then, in 1767, the Townshend Acts imposed a duty on tea, among other imported commodities. Merchants and citizens in opposition to the acts urged a boycott of the taxed articles. A Virginia woman, in a letter to friends in England, wrote in 1769 that "I have given up the Article of Tea, but some are not quite so tractable; however if wee can convince the good folks on your side the Water of their Error, wee may hope to see happier times."[12] In spite of the tax many colonists continued to indulge in tea-drinking. By 1773 the general public, according to one Philadelphia merchant, "can afford to come at this piece of luxury," while one-third of the population "at a moderate computation, drink tea twice a day."[13] It was at this time, however, that efforts were made to enforce the English tea tax, and the result was that most famous of tea parties, the Boston Tea Party.

Thereafter, an increasing number of colonists abstained from tea-drinking as a patriotic gesture. Philip Fithian, a tutor at Nomini Hall, the Virginia plantation of Col. Robert Carter, wrote in his journal on Sunday, May 29, 1774: "After dinner we had a Grand & agreeable Walk in & through the Gardens—There is great plenty of Strawberries, some Cherries, Goose berries &c.—Drank Coffee at four, they are now too patriotic to use tea." And indeed they were patriotic, for by September the taste of tea had almost been forgotten at Nomini Hall, as Fithian vividly recounted in his journal:

> Something in our palace this Evening, very merry happened—Mrs. *Carter* made a dish of Tea. At Coffee, she sent me a dish—& the Colonel both ignorant—He smelt, sipt—look'd—At last with great gravity he asks what's this?—Do you ask Sir—Poh!—And out he throws it splash a sacrifice to Vulcan.[14]

Other colonists, in their own way, also showed their distaste for tea (fig. 3). Shortly before the outbreak of the American Revolution there appeared in several

---

Fig. 3. *A Society of Patriotic Ladies*, engraving published by R. Sayer and J. Bennet, London, 1775. These ladies at Edenton, North Carolina, are pledging to drink no more tea. (Photograph courtesy of Prints and Photographs Division, Library of Congress.)

We the Ladye
of Edenton do
hereby Solemnly
Engage not to Conform
to t Pernicious Custom
of Drinking Tea, or that we the
aforesaid Ladys will not Promote y wear
of any Manufacture from England
untill such time that all Acts
which tend to Enslave this our
Native Country shall be Repealed

newspapers an expression of renouncement in rhyme, "A Lady's Adieu to Her Tea-Table," which provides a picture of contemporary teatime etiquette and equipage:

> FAREWELL *the Tea-board with your gaudy attire,*
> *Ye cups and ye saucers that I did admire;*
> *To my cream pot and tongs I now bid adieu;*
> *That pleasure's all fled that I once found in you.*
> *Farewell pretty chest that so lately did shine,*
> *With hyson and congo and best double fine;*
> *Many a sweet moment by you I have sat,*
> *Hearing girls and old maids to tattle and chat;*
> *And the spruce coxcomb laugh at nothing at all,*
> *Only some silly work that might happen to fall.*
> *No more shall my teapot so generous be*
> *In filling the cups with this pernicious tea,*
> *For I'll fill it with water and drink out the same,*
> *Before I'll lose* LIBERTY *that dearest name,*
> *Because I am taught (and believe it is fact)*
> *That our ruin is aimed at in the late act,*
> *Of imposing a duty on all foreign Teas,*
> *Which detestable stuff we can quit when we*
>   *please.*
> LIBERTY's *The Goddess that I do adore,*
> *And I'll maintain her right until my last hour,*
> *Before she shall part I will die in the cause,*
> *For I'll never be govern'd by tyranny's laws.*[15]

Many people gave up tea for the duration of the war and offered various substitute beverages, such as coffee and dried raspberry leaves, "a detestable drink" which the Americans "had the heroism to find good," remarked a postwar visitor, Léon Chotteau.[16] Although the colonists had banished tea "with enthusiasm," the tea habit was not forgotten. Chotteau further noted that "they all drink tea in America as they drink wine in the South of France." Tea-drinking continued to be an important social custom in the new nation well into the nineteenth century.

The tea ceremony, sometimes simple, sometimes elaborate, was the very core of family life. Moreau de St. Méry observed in 1795, during his residence in Philadelphia, that "the whole family is united at tea, to which friends, acquaintances and even strangers are invited."[17] That teatime hospitality was offered to the newest of acquaintances or "even strangers" is verified by Claude Blanchard. He wrote of his visit to Newport, Rhode Island, on July 12, 1780, that "in the evening there was an illumination. I entered the

house of an inhabitant, who received me very well; I took tea there, which was served by a young lady." And while staying in Boston, Blanchard mentioned that a new acquaintance "invited us to come in the evening to take tea at his house. We went there; the tea was served by his daughter."[18]

In the daily routine of activities when the hour for tea arrived, Moreau de St. Méry remarked that "the mistress of the house serves it and passes it around."[19] In the words of another late eighteenth-century diarist, the Marquis de Barbé-Marbois, those present might "seat themselves at a spotless mahogany table, and the eldest daughter of the household or one of the youngest married women makes the tea and gives a cup to each person in the company." *Family Group* (see fig. 1) provides an illustration of this practice in the early part of the century. During the tea hour social and economic affairs were discussed, gossip exchanged, and, according to Barbé-Marbois, "when there is no news at all, they repeat old stories."[20] Many entries in Nancy Shippen's journal between 1783 and 1786 indicate that this Philadelphian passed many such hours in a similar manner. On March 11, 1785, she wrote: "About 4 in the Afternoon Dr Cutting came in, & we spent the afternoon in the most agreable chit-chat manner, drank a very good dish of Tea together & then separated." Part of an undated entry in December 1783 reads: "This Afternoon we were honor'd with the Company of Genl Washington to Tea, Mrs & Major Moore, Mrs Stewart Mr Powel Mr B Washington, & two or 3 more." If acquaintances of Nancy's own age were present or the company large, the tea hour often extended well into the evening with singing, conversing, dancing, and playing of whist, chess, or cards. Of one such occasion she wrote:

> Mrs Allen & the Miss Chews drank Tea with me & spent the even'g. There was half a dozen agreable & sensible men that was of the party. The conversation was carried on in the most sprightly, agreable manner, the Ladies bearing by far the greatest part—till nine when cards was proposed, & about ten, refreshments were introduced which concluded the Evening.[21]

Obviously, young men and women enjoyed the sociability of teatime, for it provided an ideal occasion to get acquainted. When the Marquis de Chastellux was in Philadelphia during the 1780s he went one afternoon to "take tea with Madam Shippen" and found musical entertainment to meet with his approval and a relationship between the sexes that had parental sanction. One young miss played on the clavichord, and "Miss Shippen sang with timidity but a very pretty voice," accompanied for a time by Monsieur Otto on the harp. Dancing followed, noted the marquis, "while mothers and other grave personages conversed in another room."[22] In New York as in Philadelphia teatime was an important part of the younger set's social schedule. Eliza Bowne, writing to her sister in January 1810, reported that "as to news—New York is not so gay as last Winter, few balls but a great many tea-parties."[23] The feminine interest and participation in such gatherings of personable young men and attractive young women was expressed by Nancy Shippen when she wrote in her journal after such a party: "Saturday night at 11 o'clock. I had a very large company at Tea this Evening. The company is but just broke up, I dont know when I spent a more merry Even[g]. We had music, Cards, &c &c."[24] A masculine view of American tea parties was openly voiced by one foreign visitor, Prince de Broglie, who, on arrival in America in 1782, "only knew a few words of English, but knew better how to drink excellent tea with even better cream, how to tell a lady she was pretty, and a gentleman he was sensible, by reason whereof I possessed all the elements of social success."[25] Similar feelings were expressed by the Comte de Ségur during his sojourn in America in the late eighteenth century when, in a letter to his wife in France, he wrote: "My health continues excellent, despite the quantity of tea one must drink with the ladies out of gallantry, and of madeira all day long with the men out of politeness."[26]

Festive tea parties such as the ones described above are the subject of some of the group portraits or conversation pieces painted about 1730 by the English artist William Hogarth. *The Assembly at Wanstead House* illustrates quite an elegant affair taking place in a large, richly decorated English interior. The artist has filled the canvas with people standing and conversing while a seated group plays cards at a table in the center of the room. To one side near the fireplace a man and two women drinking tea are seated at an ornately carved, square tea table with a matching stand for the hot water kettle. On a dish or circular stand in the center of the table is a squat teapot with

matching cups and saucers arranged in parallel rows on either side.

Tea-drinking guests seem to have been free to sit or stand according to their own pleasure or the number of chairs available, and Barbé-Marbois noted that at American tea parties "people change seats, some go, others come." The written and visual materials offer little in the way of evidence to suggest that in general men stood and women sat during teatime. In fact, places at the tea table were taken by both sexes, even at such formal tea parties as the one depicted in *The Assembly at Wanstead House.*

A less formal but more usual tea scene is the subject of another Hogarth painting, *The Wollaston Family.* The afternoon gathering has divided into two groups, one playing cards, the other drinking tea. An atmosphere of ease and comfort surrounds the party. The men and women seated at the card table are discussing the hand just played, while the women seated about the square tea table in front of the fireplace are engaged in conversation. A man listens as he stands and stirs his tea. Each drinker holds a saucer with a cup filled from the teapot on a square tile or stand in the center of the table. One woman is returning her cup, turned upside down on the saucer, to the table. More about this particular habit later.

The same pleasant social atmosphere seen in English paintings seems to have surrounded teatime in America, as the previously cited entries in Nancy Shippen's journal suggest. Her entry for January 18, 1784, supplies a description that almost matches *The Wollaston Family:* "A stormy day, alone till the afternoon; & then was honor'd with the Company of M[r] Jones (a gentleman lately from Europe) M[r] Du Ponceau, & M[r] Hollingsworth at Tea—We convers'd on a variety of subjects & play[d] at whist, upon the whole spent an agreable Even[g]."[27]

Tea was not only a beverage of courtship; it also was associated with marriage. Both Peter Kalm in 1750 and Moreau de St. Méry in the 1790s report the Philadelphia custom of expressing good wishes to a newly married couple by paying them a personal visit soon after the marriage. It was the duty of the bride to serve wine and punch to the callers before noon and tea and wine in the afternoon.[28]

Tea seems to have been the excuse for many a social gathering, large or small, formal or informal. And sometimes an invitation to drink tea meant a rather elegant party. "That is to say," wrote one cosmopoli-

tan observer of the American scene in the 1780s, the
Marquis de Chastellux, "to attend a sort of assembly
pretty much like the *conversazioni* [social gather-
ings] of Italy: for tea here, is the substitute for the
rinfresco [refreshment]."[29] A view of such an event
has been depicted in the English print *Conversazioni*
(fig. 4), published in 1782. We can only hope that the
stiffly seated and solemn-faced guests became more
talkative when the tea arrived. However, this tea
party may have been like the ones Ferdinand Bayard
attended in Bath, Virginia, of which he wrote, "The
only thing you hear, while they are taking tea, is the
whistling sound made by the lips on edges of the
cups. This music is varied by the request made to
you to have another cup."[30] Sometimes wine and
punch were served at teatime, and "in summer," observed Barbé-Marbois, "they add fruit and other
things to drink."[31] Coffee too might be served. As the
Frenchman Claude Blanchard explained, "They [the
Americans] do not take coffee immediately after dinner, but it is served three or four hours afterwards
with tea; this coffee is weak and four or five cups are
not equal to one of ours; so that they take many of
them. The tea, on the contrary, is very strong. This
use of tea and coffee is universal in America."[32] Dealing with both food and drink at the same time was
something of an art. It was also an inconvenience for
the uninitiated, and on one occasion Ferdinand Bayard, a late eighteenth-century observer of American
tea ritual, witnessed another guest who, "after having taken a cup [of tea] in one hand and tartlets in the
other, opened his mouth and told the servant to fill it
for him with smoked venison!"[33]

While foreign visitors recognized that the "greatest
mark of courtesy" a host and hostess could offer a
guest was a cup of tea, hospitality could be "hot
water torture" for foreigners unless they understood
the social niceties not only of holding a cup and tart-
let but of declining without offending by turning the
cup upside down and placing a spoon upon it. The
ceremony of the teaspoon is fully explained by the
Prince de Broglie who, during his visit to Philadelphia in 1782, reported the following teatime incident
at the home of Robert Morris:

> I partook of most excellent tea and I should be
> even now still drinking it, I believe, if the [French]
> Ambassador had not charitably notified me at the
> twelfth cup, that I must put my spoon across it

Fig. 4. W. H. Bunbury, *Conversazioni*, England, 1782. (Photograph courtesy of Prints and Photographs Division, Library of Congress.)

when I wished to finish with this sort of warm
water. He said to me: it is almost as ill-bred to refuse a cup of tea when it is offered to you, as it
would [be] indiscreet for the mistress of the house
to propose a fresh one, when the ceremony of the
spoon has notified her that we no longer wish to
partake of it.[34]

Bayard reports that one quick-witted foreigner, unin-
formed as to the teaspoon signal, had had his cup
filled again and again until he finally "decided after
emptying it to put it into his pocket until the replen-
ishments had been concluded."[35]

The gracious art of brewing and serving tea was as
much an instrument of sociability as was a bit of music or conversation. This custom received the attention of a number of artists, and it is amazing what
careful and detailed treatment they gave to the acces-
sories of tea. We are familiar with the journals, newspaper advertisements, and other writings that provide
contemporary reports on this custom, but it is to the
artist we turn for a more clearly defined view. The
painter saw, arranged, and gave us a visual image—
sometimes richly informative, as in *Man and Child
Drinking Tea* (fig. 5)—of the different teatime items
and how they were used. The unknown artist of this
painting, done about 1725, has carefully illustrated
each piece of equipment considered appropriate for
the tea ceremony and used for brewing the tea in the
cups held with such grace by the gentleman and
child.

Throughout the eighteenth century the well-equipped tea table would have displayed most of the items seen in this painting: a teapot, slop bowl, container for milk or cream, tea canister, sugar container, tongs, teaspoons, and cups and saucers. These pieces were basic to the tea ceremony and, with the addition of a tea urn, which came into use during the latter part of the eighteenth century, have remained the established tea equipage up to the present day. Even a brief investigation of about twenty estate inventories—itemized lists of the goods and property of deceased persons that were required by law—reveal that in New York between 1742 and 1768 teapots, cups and saucers, teaspoons, and tea canisters were owned by both low and high income groups in both urban and rural areas.

The design and ornament of the tea vessels and utensils, of course, differed according to the fashion of the time, and the various items associated with the beverage provide a good index of stylistic change

Fig. 5. *Man and Child Drinking Tea,* England, ca. 1725. The silver equipage includes (left to right) a sugar container and cover, hexagonal tea canister, hot water jug or milk jug, slop bowl, teapot, and (in front) sugar tongs, spoon boat or tray, and spoons. The cups and saucers are Chinese export porcelain. (Photograph courtesy of The Colonial Williamsburg Foundation.)

in the eighteenth century. The simple designs and unadorned surfaces of the plump pear-shaped teapot in *Man and Child Drinking Tea* (fig. 5) and the spherical one seen in the portrait *Susanna Truax* (fig. 2) mark these pieces as examples of the late baroque style popular in the early part of the eighteenth century. About mid-century, teapots of inverted pear shape, associated with the rococo style, began to appear. The restrained decoration and linear outlines of the teapot illustrated in the print titled *The Old Maid* (see fig. 11) and the straight sides and oval shape of the teapot belonging to a late eighteenth-century child's set (see fig. 9) of Chinese export porcelain are characteristics of the neoclassical style that was fashionable at the end of the century. Tea drinkers were extremely conscious of fashion changes and, whenever possible, set their tea table with stylish equipment in the prevailing fashion. Newspaper advertisements, journals, letters, and other written materials indicate that utensils in the "best and newest taste" were available, desired, purchased, and used in America.

Tea furnishings, when in use, were to be seen on rectangular tables with four legs, square-top and circle-top tripods, and Pembroke tables. Such tables were, or course, used for other purposes, but a sampling of eighteenth-century Boston inventories reveals that in some households all or part of the tea paraphernalia was prominently displayed on the tea table rather than stored in cupboards or closets. A "Japan'd tea Table & China" and "a Mahog[any] Do. & China," both in the "Great Room," are listed in Mrs. Hannah Pemberton's inventory recorded in Boston in 1758. The inventory of Joseph Blake of Boston recorded in 1746 lists a "tea Table with a Sett of China furniture" in the back room of the house, while in the "closett" in the front room were "6 Tea Cups & Saucers" along with other ceramic wares.[36]

The most popular type of tea table apparently was the circular tripod: that is, a circular top supported on a pillar with three feet. This kind of table is seen again and again in the prints and paintings (see figs. 1, 2, 7, 11) and is listed in the inventories of the period. These tables, usually of walnut or mahogany, had stationary or tilt tops with plain, scalloped, or carved edges. Square or round, tripod or four-legged, the tables were usually placed against the wall of the room until teatime, when, in the words of Ferdinand Bayard, "a mahogany table is brought forward and

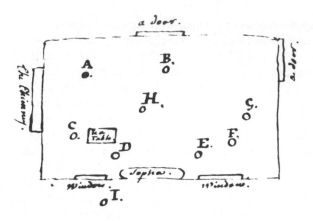

Fig. 6. A sketch by Louis Guillaume Otto enclosed in a letter to Nancy Shippen of Philadelphia, ca. 1780. The sketch indicates the placement of the furniture in the Shippen parlor and the location of the tea-party participants. The "Explication" accompanying the drawing reads: "*A.* Old Dr. Shippen sitting before the Chimney . . . *B.* Mr. Lee walking up and down, speaking and laughing by intervalls . . . *C.* Miss Nancy [Shippen] before the tea table . . . *D.* Mrs. Shippen lost in sweet meditations. *E. F. G.* Some strangers which the Spy [Mr. Otto] could not distinguish. *H.* Cyrus [the butler] standing in the middle of the room—half asleep. *I.* Mr. Otto standing before the window." (Photograph courtesy of Manuscripts Division, Library of Congress.)

placed in front of the lady who pours the tea."[37] This practice is depicted in a number of eighteenth-century pictures, with the tea table well out in the room, often in front of a fireplace, and with seated and standing figures at or near the table (see fig. 1). Evidence of such furniture placement in American parlors is recorded in a sketch and note Nancy Shippen received from one of her beaus, who wrote in part, "this evening I passed before Your house and seeing Company in the parlour I peep'd through the Window and saw a considerable Tea Company, of which by their situation I could only distinguish four persons. You will see the plan of this Company upon the next page."[38]

In the sketch (fig. 6), a floor plan of the Shippen parlor, we can see the sofa against the wall between the windows, while chairs and the tea table have been moved out in the room. The table is near the fireplace, where Miss Shippen served the tea. In the eighteenth century such an arrangement was first and foremost one of comfort, and perhaps one of taste. The diary of Jacob Hiltzheimer indicates that

in 1786 the first signs of fall were felt on August 1, for the Philadelphian wrote: "This evening it was so cool that we drank tea by the fire."[39] In the South as in the North, tea—or, at the time of the American Revolution its patriotic substitute, coffee—was served by the fire as soon as the first winter winds were felt. Philip Fithian, while at Nomini Hall in Virginia, wrote in his journal on September 19, 1774, "the Air is clear, cold & healthful. We drank our Coffee at the great House very sociably, round a fine Fire, the House and Air feels like winter again."[40]

Table cloths—usually square white ones (as in fig. 7) that showed folds from having been stored in a linen press—were used when tea was served, but it is difficult to say with any certainty if their use depended on the whim of the hostess, the type of table, or the time of day. A cloth probably was used more often on a table with a plain top than on one with scalloped or carved edges. However, as can be seen in *Family Group* (see fig. 1), it was perfectly acceptable to serve tea on a plain-top table without a cloth. Apparently such tables were also used at breakfast or morning tea, because Benjamin Franklin, in a letter from London dated February 19, 1758, gave the following directions for the use of "six coarse diaper Breakfast Cloths," which he sent to his wife: "they are to spread on the Tea Table, for nobody breakfasts here on the naked Table, but on the Cloth set a large Tea Board with the Cups."[41] Some of the eighteenth-century paintings depicting tea tables with cloths do deal with the morning hours, as indicated by their titles or internal evidence, as in *The Honeymoon* (fig. 7) painted by John Collet about 1760. In this scene of domestic confusion and bliss, a tray or teaboard has been placed on the cloth, illustrating Franklin's comment about English breakfast habits. Cloths may also be seen in pictures in which the time of day cannot be determined. Therefore, the use of a cloth at teatime may in truth have depended upon the hostess's whim, if not her pocketbook.

In addition, trays or teaboards of various sizes and shapes were sometimes used. They were usually circular or rectangular in form, occasionally of shaped or scalloped outline. Some trays were supported on low feet; others had pierced or fretwork galleries or edges to prevent the utensils from slipping off. Wood or metal was the usual material, although ceramic trays were also used. At large gatherings a tray was often employed for passing refreshments (see fig. 4).

Fig. 7. John Collet, *The Honeymoon*, England, ca. 1760. In the midst of a domestic morning scene replete with homey details, the artist has depicted with care the tea table and its furnishings, including a fashionable tea urn symbolically topped with a pair of affectionate birds. (Photograph courtesy of The Colonial Williamsburg Foundation.)

"A servant brings in on a silver tray the cups, the sugar bowl, the cream jugs, pats of butter, and smoked meat, which are offered to each individual," explained Ferdinand Bayard.[42] The principal use of the tray was, of course, to bring the tea equipage to the table. Whether placed on a bare or cloth-covered table, it arrived with the cups and saucers, spoons, containers for sugar and cream or milk, tongs, bowls, and dishes arranged about the teapot.

Such tea furnishings of ceramic were sold in sets;

that is, all pieces were of the same pattern. Newspaper advertisements in the 1730s specifically mention "Tea Setts," and later in the century ceramic imports continue to include "beautiful compleat Tea-Setts." In the early eighteenth-century, tea sets of silver were uncommon if not unique, though pieces were occasionally made to match existing items, and, in this way, a so-called set similar to the pieces seen in *Man and Child Drinking Tea* (see fig. 5) could be formed. However, by the latter part of the century, the wealthier hostesses were able to purchase from among a "most elegant assortment of Silver Plate . . . compleat Tea and Coffee services, plain and rich engraved."[43] When of metal, tea sets (fig. 8) usually consisted of a teapot, containers for sugar and cream or milk, and possibly a slop bowl, while ceramic sets,

Fig. 8. John McMullin, silver tea set consisting of teapot, sugar bowl, container for cream or milk, and waste bowl, Philadelphia, ca. 1800. The matching coffee and hot-water pot at the left were made at about the same time by Samuel Williamson, also of Philadelphia. The letter "G," in fashionable script, is engraved on each piece of the set. (Photograph courtesy of the National Museum of American History, Smithsonian Institution.)

such as the one seen in *Family Group* (see fig. 1), included cups and saucers as well.

While the tea set illustrated in *Family Group* appears to have all the basic pieces, it can hardly be considered a "complete" tea set when compared with the following porcelain sets listed in the 1747 estate inventory of James Pemberton of Boston:

One sett Burnt [china] Cont[aining] 12 Cups & Saucers   Slop Bowl   Tea Pot   Milk Pot boat [for spoons]   tea Cannister   Sugar Dish 5 Handle Cups   plate for the Tea Pot & a wh[i]t[e] Tea Pot   Value   } [£]20

One set Blue & white do. contg. 12 Cups & saucers   Slop Bowl   2 plates   Sugr. Dish Tea Pot   6 Handle Cups & white tea Pot Value   } [£]10

In addition, the Pemberton inventory lists a silver tea

pot and "1 pr. Tea Tongs & Strainer," items that were undoubtedly used with the ceramic sets.[44]

Tea sets were even available for the youngest hostess, and the "several compleat Tea-table Sets of Children's cream-colored [ceramic] Toys" mentioned in a Boston advertisement of 1771 no doubt added a note of luxury to make-believe tea parties during playtime.[45] The pieces in children's tea sets, such as the ones pictured from a child's set of Chinese export porcelain (fig. 9), were usually like those of regular sets and differed only in size. Little Peggy Livingston of Philadelphia must have been happy indeed, when her uncle wrote that he had sent "a compleat tea-apparatus for her Baby [doll]. Her Doll may now invite her Cousins Doll to tea. & parade her teatable in form. This must be no small gratification to her. It would be fortunate if happiness were always attainable with equal ease."[46]

The pieces of tea equipage could be purchased individually. For instance, teacups and saucers, which are differentiated in advertisements from both coffee and chocolate cups, regularly appear in lists of ceramic wares offered for sale, such as "very handsome Setts of blue and white China Tea-Cups and Saucers," or "enamell'd, pencill'd and gilt, red and white, blue

Fig. 9. Part of a child's tea set of Chinese export porcelain, or "painted China," China, ca. 1790. The painted decoration is of pink roses and rose buds with green leaves; the border is orange, with blue flowers. At one time this set probably included containers for cream or milk and sugar, as did the adult "tea table setts complete" advertised in period newspapers. (Photograph courtesy of the National Museum of American History, Smithsonian Institution.)

Fig. 10. Hand-painted creamware teacup, Staffordshire, ca. 1780–1800. This teacup was excavated at the site of a probable eighteenth- and early nineteenth-century china shop in Newburyport, Massachusetts. Decoration consists of a brown band above a vine border with green leaves and blue berries over orange bellflowers. The spiral fluting on the body and the slight scalloping on the edge of this cup are almost identical with that on the cup held by Mrs. Calmes in figure 12. (Photograph courtesy of the National Museum of American History, Smithsonian Institution.)

and white, enamell'd and scallop'd [fig. 10], tea-cups and saucers."[47] These adjectives used by eighteenth-century salesmen usually referred to the types and the colors of the decorations that were painted on the pieces. "Enameled" most likely meant that the decorations were painted over the glaze, and "penciled" may have implied motifs painted with a fine black line of pencil-like appearance, while "gilt," "red and white," and "blue and white" were the colors and types of the decoration. Blue and white china was, perhaps, the most popular type of teaware; it regularly appears in newspaper advertisements and inventories and among sherds from colonial sites.

Concerning tea, Abbé Robin went so far as to say in 1781 that "there is not a single person to be found, who does not drink it out of china cups and saucers."[48] However exaggerated the statement may be, it does reflect the popularity and availability of Chi-

nese export porcelain in the post-Revolutionary period when Americans were at last free to engage in direct trade with East Asia. Porcelain for the American market was made in a wide variety of forms, as well as in complete dinner and tea sets, and was often decorated to special order. Handpainted monograms, insignia of various kinds, and patriotic motifs were especially popular. A tea set decorated in this way was sent to Dr. David Townsend of Boston, a member of the Society of the Cincinnati, by a fellow member of the society, Maj. Samuel Shaw, the American consul at Canton. In a a letter to Townsend from Canton, China, dated December 20, 1790, Shaw wrote:

Accept, my dear friend, as a mark of my esteem and affection, a tea set of porcelain, ornamented with the Cincinnati and your cypher. I hope shortly after its arrival to be with you, and in company with your amiable partner, see whether a little good tea improves or loses any part of its flavor in passing from one hemisphere to the other.

Appended to the letter was the following inventory, which provides us with a list of the pieces deemed essential for a fashionably set tea table:

2 tea pots & stands
Sugar bowl & d[itt]o
Milk ewer
Bowl & dish
6 breakfast cups & saucers
12 afternoon d[itt]o[49]

Porcelain, however, had long been a part of China-trade cargos to Europe and from there to America. The early shipments of tea had included such appropriate vessels for the storage, brewing, and drinking of the herb as tea jars, teapots, and teacups. The latter were small porcelain bowls without handles, a form that the Europeans and Americans adopted and continued to use throughout the eighteenth century for tea, in contrast to the deeper and somewhat narrower cups, usually with handles, in which chocolate and coffee were served. Even after Europeans learned to manufacture porcelain early in the eighteenth century, the ware continued to be imported from China in large quantities and was called by English-speaking people "china," from its country of origin. Porcelain also was referred to as "India china ware," after the English and continental East India companies, the original traders and importers of the ware.

Whatever the ware, the teacups and saucers, whether on a tray, the cloth, or a bare table, were usually arranged in an orderly manner about the teapot, generally in rows on a rectangular table or tray and in a circle on a round table or tray. In the English conversation piece painting titled *Mr. and Mrs. Hill in Their Drawing Room*, by Arthur Devis about 1750, the circular tripod tea table between the couple and in front of the fireplace is set in such a way. The handleless teacups on saucers are neatly arranged in a large semicircle around the rotund teapot in the center that is flanked on one side by a bowl and on the other by a jug for milk or cream and a sugar container. Generally, cups and saucers were not piled one on the other but spread out on the table or tray, where they were filled with tea and then passed to each guest.

Pictures show male and female guests holding both cup and saucer or just the cup. An English satirical print, *The Old Maid* (fig. 11), published in 1777, unusually depicts an individual using a dish for tea, or, to be exact, a saucer. In the eighteenth century a dish of tea was in reality a cup of tea, for the word "dish" meant a cup or vessel used for drinking as well as a utensil to hold food at meals. A play on this word is evident in the following exchange reported by Philip Fithian between himself and Mrs. Carter, the mistress of Nomini Hall, one October forenoon in 1773: "Shall I help you, Mr. Fithian, to a Dish of Coffee?—I choose a deep Plate, if you please Ma'am, & Milk."[50] The above suggests that the practice of saucer sipping, while it may have been common among the general public, was frowned on by polite society. The fact that Americans preferred and were "accustomed to eat everything hot" further explains why tea generally was drunk from the cup instead of the saucer. According to Peter Kalm, "when the English women [that is, of English descent] drank tea, they never poured it out of the cup into the saucer to cool it, but drank it as hot as it came from the teapot."[51] From this it would appear that "dish of tea" was an expression rather than a way of drinking tea in the eighteenth century. On the table a saucer seems always to have been placed under the cup whether the cup was right side up or upside down.

Teaspoons, when in use, might be placed on the saucer or left in the cups. The portrait titled *Mrs. Calmes* (fig. 12), painted by G. Frymeier in 1806, in-

Fig. 11. *The Old Maid*, English cartoon, 1777. Although the Englishwoman apparently is defying established tea etiquette by drinking from a saucer and allowing the cat on the table (it, too, drinks from a saucer), her tea furnishings appear to be in proper order. The teapot is on a dish, and the teakettle is on its own special stand, a smaller version of the tripod tea table. (Photograph courtesy of Prints and Photographs Division, Library of Congress.)

Fig. 12. G. Frymeier, *Mrs. Calmes*, America, 1806. The cup and saucer (or bowl), possibly hand-decorated Staffordshire ware or Chinese export porcelain, are decorated with dark blue bands and dots, wavy brown bands, and a pink rose with green foliage. (Photograph courtesy of the Chicago Historical Society, Calmes-Wight-Johnson Collection.)

dicates that handling a cup with the spoon in it could be accomplished with a certain amount of grace. Teaspoons also were placed in a pile on the table or in a silver "Boat for Tea Spoons," or more often in such ceramic containers as "Delph Ware . . . Spoon Trays," or blue-and-white or penciled china "spoon boats."[52]

Tongs were especially suited for lifting the lumps of sugar from their container to the teacup. During the eighteenth century both arched and scissor-type tongs were used. Instead of points, the latter had dainty flat grips for holding a lump of sugar (fig. 13). The early arched tongs were round in section, as are the pair illustrated in *Man and Child Drinking Tea* (see fig. 5), while tongs made by arching or bending double a flat strip of silver (fig. 14) date from the second half of the eighteenth century. These articles of

tea equipage, variously known as "tongs," "tea tongs," "spring tea tongs," and "sugar tongs," were usually made of silver, though "ivory and wooden tea-tongs" were advertised in 1763.[53] According to the prints and paintings of the period, tongs were placed in or near the sugar container. Teaspoons were also used for sugar, as illustrated in the painting *Susanna Truax* (see fig. 2). Perhaps young Miss Truax is about to indulge in a custom favored by the Dutch population of Albany as reported by Peter Kalm in 1749: "They never put sugar into the cup, but take a small bit of it into their mouths while they drink."[54]

Shallow dishes, such as the one seen in the portrait *Susanna Truax*, and hemispherical bowls were used as containers for sugar. Often called "sugar dishes" or just "sugars," they were available in delftware, glass (fig. 15), and silver, as well as in blue-and-white, burnt, enameled, and penciled china. Some contain-

Fig. 13. Jacob Hurd, silver sugar tongs in the rococo style, Boston, ca. 1750. (Photograph courtesy of the National Museum of American History, Smithsonian Institution.)

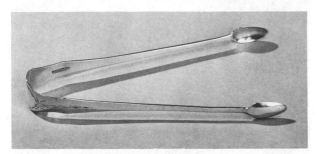

Fig. 14. William G. Forbes, silver sugar tongs in the neoclassical style, New York, ca. 1790. The engraved, or "brightcut," decoration of intersecting lines is typical of the neoclassical style. A variant of this popular motif appears as the painted border on the creamware teacup from the same period illustrated in figure 10. (Photograph courtesy of the National Museum of American History, Smithsonian Institution.)

Fig. 15. "Stiegel-type," cobalt blue glass sugar dish with cover, America, ca. 1770. (Photograph courtesy of the National Museum of American History, Smithsonian Institution.)

ers were sold with covers, and it has been suggested that the sugar-shaped cover of the hemispherical sugar dish or bowl, fashionable in the first half of the eighteenth century, also served as a spoon tray. However, in the painting *Man and Child Drinking Tea* (see fig. 5) the cover is leaning against the bowl and the spoons are in an oval spoon tray or boat.

Silver sugar boxes, basins, and plated sugar baskets were other forms used to hold sugar,[55] which, in whatever container, was an important commodity. As Moreau de St. Méry noted, Americans "use great quantities in their tea."[56]

Containers for cream or milk may be seen in many of the eighteenth-century teatime pictures and are found in the advertisements of the period under a variety of names. There were cream pots of glass and pewter and silver (figs. 16, 17), jugs of penciled and

burnt china, and in the 1770s one could obtain "enameled and plain three footed cream jugs" from Henry William Stiegel's glass factory at Manheim, Pennsylvania. There were cream pails, urns, and ewers of silver plate and plated cream basins "gilt inside."[57] Milk pots, used on some tea tables instead of cream containers, were available in silver, pewter, ceramic, and "sprig'd, cut and moulded" glass.[58] Although contemporary diarists and observers of American customs seem not to have noticed whether cream was served cold and milk hot or if tea drinkers were given a choice between cream and milk, the Prince de Broglie's comment already cited concerning his ability to drink "excellent tea with even better cream" and the predominance of cream over milk containers in eighteenth-century advertisements would seem to indicate that in this country cream rather than milk was served with tea in the afternoon. While Americans, as did Europeans, added cream or milk and sugar to their tea, their use of lemon with the beverage is doubtful. Nowhere is

Fig. 16. Myer Myers, silver creamer, New York, ca. 1750. The fanciful curves of the handle and feet are related to the rococo design of the sugar tongs illustrated in figure 13. (Photograph courtesy of the National Museum of American History, Smithsonian Institution.)

Fig. 17. Simeon Bayley, silver creamer, New York, ca. 1790. Aside from the beaded border at top and bottom, the only ornamentation is the engraving of the initials "RM" below the pouring lip. (Photograph courtesy of the National Museum of American History, Smithsonian Institution).

there any indication that the citrus fruit was served or used with tea in eighteenth-century America.

Often a medium-sized bowl, usually hemispherical in shape, is to be seen on the tea table, and it is most likely a slop bowl or basin. According to advertisements these bowls and basins were available in silver, pewter, and ceramic.[59] Before a teacup was replenished, the remaining tea and dregs were emptied into the slop bowl. Then the cup might be rinsed with hot water and the rinsing water discarded in the bowl. The slop basin may also have been the receptacle for the mote or foreign particles—then inherent in tea but now extracted by mechanical means—that had to be skimmed off the beverage in the cup. In England this was probably done with a small utensil

known to modern scholars as a mote spoon or mote skimmer. Although the exact purpose of these spoons remains unanswered, it seems likely that they were used with tea. It has been suggested that the perforated bowl of the spoon was used for skimming foreign particles off the tea in the cup and the tapering spike-end stem to clear the clogged-up strainer of the teapot spout. The almost complete absence of American-made mote spoons suggests that these particular utensils were seldom used here. Possibly the "skimmer" advertised in 1727 with other silver tea pieces was such a spoon.[60] No doubt, tea strainers (fig. 18) were also used to insure clear tea. The tea dregs might then be discarded in the slop bowl or left in the strainer and the strainer rested on the bowl. However, only a few contemporary American advertisements and inventories have been found that mention tea strainers.[61] Punch strainers, though generally larger in size, seem to have doubled as tea strainers in some households. The 1757 inventory of Charles Brockwell of Boston includes a punch strainer, which is listed not with the wine glasses and other pieces associated with punch but with the tea items: "1 Small . . . [china] Milk Pot   1 Tea Pot   6 Cups & 3 Saucers & 1 Punch Strainer."[62] Presumably, the strainer had last been used for tea.

The teapot was, of course, the center of the social custom of drinking tea; so, it usually was found in the center of the tray or table. At first, only teapots of East Asian origin imported with the cargos of tea were available, for the teapot had been unknown to Europeans before the introduction of the beverage. However, as tea gained acceptance as a social drink

Fig. 18. James Butler, silver (tea?) strainer, Boston, ca. 1750. The handle's pierced pattern of delicate, curled vines distinguishes this otherwise plain strainer. (Photograph courtesy of the National Museum of American History, Smithsonian Institution.)

and the demand for equipage increased, local craftsmen were stimulated to produce wares that could compete with the Chinese imports. Teapots based on Chinese models and often decorated with Chinese motifs were fashioned in ceramic and silver. No doubt many an eighteenth-century hostess desired a silver teapot to grace her table and add an elegant air to the tea ceremony. A lottery offering one must have raised many a hope, especially if, as an advertisement of 1727 announced, the "highest Prize consists of an Eight Square Tea-Pot," as well as "six Tea-Spoons, Skimmer and Tongs." By the end of the century "an elegant silver tea-pot with an ornamental lid, resembling a Pine-apple" would have been the wish of a fashion-conscious hostess. Less expensive than silver, but just as stylish according to the merchants' advertisements were "newest fashion teapots" of pewter or, in the late eighteenth century, Britannia metal teapots. The latest mode in ceramic ware could also be found on the tea table. In the mid-eighteenth century it was "English brown China Tea-Pots of Sorts, with a rais'd Flower" (probably the ceramic with a deep, rich brown glaze known today as Jackfield-type ware), "black," "green and Tortois" (a pottery glazed with variegated colors in imitation of tortoise shell), and "Enameled Stone" teapots. At the time of the American Revolution, teaware imports included "Egyptian, Etruscan, embossed red China, agate, green, black, colliflower, white, and blue and white stone enamelled, striped, fluted, pierced and plain Queen's ware tea pots."[63]

Sometimes the teapot, whether ceramic, pewter, or silver, was placed on a dish or small, tile-like stand with feet. These teapot stands served as insulation by protecting the surface of the table or tray from the damaging heat of the teapot. Stands were often included in tea sets but were also sold individually, such as the "Pencil'd China . . . tea pot stands," advertised in 1775, and the "teapot stands" of "best London plated ware" imported in 1797.[64] The stands must have been especially useful when silver equipage was set on a bare table top; many of the silver teapots of elliptical shape with a flat base, so popular in the latter part of the eighteenth century, had matching stands raised on short legs to protect the table from the expanse of hot metal. On occasion the teapot was placed on a spirit lamp or burner to keep the beverage warm.

In most instances it was the hot water kettle rather

than a teapot that sat on a spirit lamp or burner. Kettles were usually related to the form of contemporary teapots but differed in having a swing handle on top and a large, rather flat base that could be placed over the flame. Advertisements mention teakettles of copper, pewter, brass, and silver, some "with lamps and stands."[65] The actual making of tea was part of the ceremony and was usually done by the hostess at the tea table. This necessitated a ready supply of boiling water close at hand to properly infuse the tea and, as Ferdinand Bayard reported, it also "weakens the tea or serves to clean up the cups."[66] Thus, the kettle and burner on their own individual table or stand were placed within easy reach of the tea table.

Both pictures and advertisements reveal that by the 1770s the tea urn was a new form appearing at teatime in place of the hot water kettle. Contrary to its name, the tea urn seldom held tea. These large silver or silver-plated vessels, some of which looked like vases with domed covers, usually had two handles on the shoulders and a spout with a tap in the front near the bottom. "Ponty pool, japanned, crimson, and gold-striped Roman tea urns" imported from Europe were among the fashionable tewares advertised at the end of the eighteenth century.[67] The urn might be placed on a stand of its own near the table or on the tray or table in the midst of the other equipage, as it is in the painting titled *The Honeymoon* (see fig. 7). Wherever placed, it signified the newest mode in teatime furnishings. One Baltimorean, O. H. Williams, in a letter dated April 12, 1786, to a close friend, enthusiastically explained that "Tea & Coffee Urns plated (mine are but partially plated and are extremely neat) are the genteelest things of the sort used now at any House & tables inferior to the first fortunes."[68]

The tea canister (fig. 19), a storage container for the dry tea leaves, was yet another piece of equipment to be found on the table or tray. Ceramic canisters of blue and white, and red and gold, could be purchased to match other tea furnishings of the same ware, and silver tea canisters were often fashioned to harmonize with the silver teapots of the period. Individual canisters, as well as canisters in sets of two or three, were produced. A set of canisters was usually kept in the box in which it came, a case known as a tea chest or tea caddy, such as the "elegant assortment of Tea-caddies, with one, two and three canisters" advertised in 1796.[69] Canister tops if dome-shaped were

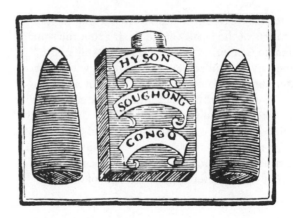

Fig. 19. The sign of "The Tea Canister and Two Sugar Loaves," used by a New York grocer and confectioner in the 1770s. Other "tea" motifs for shop signs in the eighteenth century included "The Teapot," used by a Philadelphia goldsmith in 1757, and "The Tea Kettle and Stand," which marked the shop of a Charleston jeweler in 1766. (Photograph courtesy of the National Museum of American History, Smithsonian Institution.)

used to measure out the tea and transfer it to the teapot. Otherwise, small, short-handled spoons with broad, shallow bowls, known as caddy spoons and caddy ladles, were used. However handled, the tea could have been any one of the numerous kinds available in the eighteenth century. Although Hyson, Soughong, and Congo, the names inscribed on the canister in figure 19, may have been favored, there were many other types of tea, as the following advertisement from the *Boston News-Letter* of September 16, 1736, indicates: "To be Sold . . . at the Three Sugar Loaves, and Cannister . . . very choice Teas, viz: Bohea Tea from 22 s. to 28 s. per Pound, Congou Tea, 34 s. Pekoe Tea, 50 s. per Pound, Green Tea from 20 s. to 30 s. per Pound, fine Imperial Tea from 40 s. to 60 s. per Pound."[70]

In the eighteenth century tea-drinking was an established social custom with a recognized etiquette and distinctive equipage, as we know from the pictures and writings of the period. At teatime men and women gathered to pursue leisurely conversations and enjoy the sociability of the home. A study of *An English Family at Tea* (fig. 20) will summarize the etiquette and equipage of the ritual.

On the floor near the table is a caddy with the top open, showing one canister of a pair. The mistress of the house, seated at the tea table, is measuring out dry tea leaves from the other canister into its lid. Members of the family stand or sit about the square tea table while they observe this first step in the ceremony. A maidservant stands ready with the hot water kettle to pour the boiling water over the leaves once they are in the teapot. In the background is the tripod kettle stand with a lamp, where the kettle will be placed until needed to rinse the cups of diluted tea. From the right enters a male servant carrying a tall silver pot, which may contain chocolate or coffee. These two other social beverages of the eigh-

teenth century were served in cups of a deep cylindrical shape, like the three seen on the end of the table. The shallow, bowl-shaped, handleless teacups and the saucers are arranged in a neat row along one side of the table. The teapot rests on a square tile-like stand or dish that protects the table from the heat. Nearby is a bowl to receive tea dregs, a pot for cream or milk, and a sugar bowl.

The teatime ritual has begun.

Fig. 20. *An English Family at Tea*, attributed to Joseph Van Aken, England, ca. 1720. (Photograph courtesy of the Tate Gallery, London.)

PART FIVE   Ritual Space

Appendix: Chronological List of Pictures Consulted

1700 ca.   *Portrait Group of Gentlemen and a Child.* Believed to be English or Dutch. Reproduced in Ralph Edwards, *Early Conversation Pictures from the Middle Ages to about 1730* (London, 1954), 117, no. 73.

1710 ca.   *The Tea-Table.* English. Reproduced in Ralph Edwards and L. G. G. Ramsey, eds., *The Connoisseur Period Guides: The Stuart Period, 1603–1714* (New York, 1957), 30.

1720 ca.   *A Family Taking Tea.* English. Reproduced in Edwards, *Early Conversation Pictures*, 132, no. 95.

        Two Ladies and a Gentleman at Tea. Attributed to Nicolaas Verkolje, Dutch. Reproduced in Edwards, *Early Converstation Pictures*, 96, no. 42.

        An English Family at Tea (fig. 20). By Joseph Van Aken(?). Reproduced in Percy Macquoid and Ralph Edwards, *The Dictionary of English Furniture*, rev. and enlarged ed., 3 vols. (London, 1954), 1:10, fig. 16.

1725 ca.   *Man and Child Drinking Tea* (fig. 5). English. Reproduced in Helen Comstock, "Williamsburg Revisited," *Antiques* 68 (November 1955): vi, following p. 460.

1730 ca.   *The Assembly at Wanstead House.* By William Hogarth, English. Reproduced in Edwards, *Early Conversation Pictures*, 125, no. 87.

        Family. By William Hogarth, English. Reproduced in R. H. Wilenski, *English Painting* (London, 1933), plate 11a.

        Family Group (fig. 1). By Gawen Hamilton, English. Reproduced in "Paintings and Prints" [at Colonial Williamsburg], *Antiques* 60 (1953): 270.

        A Family Party. By William Hogarth, English. Reproduced in G. C. Williamson, ed., *English Conversation Pictures of the Eighteenth and Early Nineteenth Century* (London, 1931), plate 10.

1730   *Susanna Truax* (fig. 2). American. Reproduced in Frank O. Spinney, "Portrait Gallery of Provincial America," *Art in America* 42 (May 1954): 101.

        The Wollaston Family. By William Hogarth, English. Reproduced in Edwards, *Early Conversation Pictures*, 126, no. 88.

1731   Painting on lobed, square delft tea tray. Dutch. Reproduced in C. H. De Jonge, *Oud-Nederlandsche majolica en delftsch aardewerk* (Amsterdam, 1947), 241, fig. 209.

1732   *A Tea Party at the Countess of Portland's.* By Charles Philips, English. Reproduced in Edwards, *Early Conversation Pictures*, 132, no. 94.

        Thomas Wentworth, Earl of Stafford, with His Family. By Gawen Hamilton, English. Reproduced in Edwards, *Early Conversation Pictures*, 130, no. 92.

1735 ca.   *The Western Family.* By William Hogarth, English. Reproduced in Sacheverell Sitwell, *Conversation Pieces* (New York, 1937), no. 14.

1736 ca.   *The Strode Family.* By William Hogarth, English. Reproduced in Oliver Brackett, *English Furniture Illustrated* (New York, 1950), 168, plate 140.

1740 ca.   *The Carter Family.* By Joseph Highmore, English. Reproduced in *Connoisseur* 94 (1934): xlv (advertisement).

1743   Painting on lobed, circular Bristol delft tea tray. English. Reproduced in F. H. Garner, *English Delftware* (New York, 1948), plate 54.

1744 ca.   *Burkat Shudi and His Family.* English. Reproduced in Philip James, *Early Keyboard Instruments from Their Beginnings to the Year 1820* (New York, 1939), plate 48.

1744   *Shortly after Marriage,* from *Marriage à la Mode* series. By William Hogarth, English. Reproduced in *Masterpieces of English Painting* (Chicago, 1946), plate 3.

1745 ca.   *The Gascoigne Family.* By Francis Hayman, English. Reproduced in *Apollo* 66 (October 1957): vii (advertisement).

1750 ca.   *Mr. and Mrs. Hill in Their Drawing Room.* By Arthur Devis, English. Reproduced in *The Antique Collector* 28 (June 1957): 100.

1760 ca.   *The Honeymoon* (fig. 7). By John Collet, English. The Colonial Williamsburg Foundation.

1765 ca.   *Paul Revere.* By John Singleton Copley, American. Reproduced in John Marshall Phillips, *American Silver* (New York, 1949), frontispiece.

1770 ca.   *Lord Willoughby and Family.* By John Zoffany, English. Reproduced in Lady Victoria Manners and Dr. G. C. Williamson, *John Zoffany, R. A.* (London, 1920), plate preceding p. 153.

        Mr. and Mrs. Garrick at Tea. By John Zoffany, English. Reproduced in Manners and Williamson, *John Zoffany, R. A.*, plate facing p. 142.

        Sir John Hopkins and Family. By John Zoffany, English. Reproduced in Manners and William son, *John Zoffany, R. A.*, 2d plate following p. 18.

The Squire's Tea. By Benjamin Wilson, English. Reproduced in Marion Day Iverson, "Slipcovers of Past Centuries," *Antiques* 60 (October 1951): 310.

1775   *A Society of Patriotic Ladies* (fig. 3). Engraving published by R. Sayer and J. Bennet, London. Prints and Photographs Division, Library of Congress.

1777   *The Old Maid* (fig. 11). English. Prints and Photographs Division, Library of Congress.

1780 ca.   *The Tea Party.* By William Hamilton, English. Reproduced in *Art in America* 42 (May 1954): 91 (advertisement).

1782   *Conversazioni* (fig. 4). By W. H. Bunbury, English. Prints and Photographs Division, Library of Congress.

1785 ca.   *The Auriol Family* [*in India*]. By John Zoffany, English. Reproduced in Manners and Williamson, *John Zoffany, R. A.*, plate facing p. 110.

1786   *Dr. Johnson Takes Tea at Boswell's House.* By Thomas Rowlandson, English. Reproduced in Charles Cooper, *The English Tea Table in History and Literature* (London, 1929), plate facing p. 150.

1790 ca.   *Black Monday, or the Departure for School.* Engraved by J. Jones after Bigg, English. Reproduced in *Antiques* 64 (September 1953): 163 (advertisement).

1792   *Tea at the Pantheon.* By Edward Edwards, English. Reproduced in William Harrison Ukers, *The Romance of Tea* (New York, 1936), plate facing p. 214.

1806   *Mrs. Calmes* (fig. 12). By G. Frymeier, American. Reproduced in "Primitives on View in Chicago," *Antiques* 58 (November 1950): 392.

Notes

1. Claude C. Robin, *New Travels Through North America: In a Series of Letters . . . in the Year 1781* (Boston, 1784), 23.

2. *Mercurius Politicus*, Sept. 23–30, 1658.

3. Edward Wenham, "Tea and Tea Things in England," *Antiques* 54 (October 1948): 264.

4. Samuel Sewall, *Diary of Samuel Sewall, 1674–1729*, in *Collections of the Massachusetts Historical Society*, 5th ser., 6 (1879): 253.

5. Quoted in John Marshall Phillips, *American Silver* (New York, 1949), 76.

6. Jacques-Pierre Brissot de Warville, *New Travels in the United States of America Performed in 1788* (London, 1794), 80.

7. Peter Kalm, *The America of 1750; Peter Kalm's Travels in North America*, ed. and trans. Adolph B. Benson, 2 vols. (New York, 1937), 1:346; 2:605.

8. Baron Cromot du Bourg, "Journal de mon séjour en Amérique," *Magazine of American History* (1880–81), quoted in Charles H. Sherrill, *French Memories of Eighteenth-Century America* (New York, 1915), 155.

9. Marquis de Chastellux, *Voyages de M. le Marquis de Chastellux dans l'Amérique septentrionale* (Paris, 1788), quoted in Sherrill, *French Memories of Eighteenth-Century America*, 190.

10. Kalm, *The America of 1750*, 1:195.

11. Israel Acrelius, *A History of New Sweden: or, The Settlements on the River Delaware*, trans. and ed. William M. Reynolds (Philadelphia, 1894), 158.

12. Letter from M. Jacquelin, York, Va., to John Norton, London, Aug. 14, 1769, in *John Norton and Sons, Merchants of London and Virginia, Being the Papers from Their Counting House for the Years 1750 to 1795*, ed. Frances Norton Mason (Richmond, Va., 1937), 103.

13. Letter from Gilbert Barkly to the directors of the East India Company, May 26, 1773, in *Tea Leaves: Being a Collection of Letters and Documents . . .* , ed. Francis S. Drake (Boston, 1884), 200.

14. Philip Vickers Fithian, *Journal and Letters of Philip Vickers Fithian, 1773–1774: A Plantation Tutor of the Old Dominion*, ed. Hunter Dickinson Farish (Charlottesville, Va., 1957), 110, 195–96.

15. Quoted in R. T. H. Halsey and Charles O. Cornelius, *A Handbook of the American Wing* (New York, 1924), 111–12.

16. Léon Chotteau, *Les français en Amérique* (Paris, 1876), quoted in Sherrill, *French Memories of Eighteenth-Century America*, 96.

17. Médéric-Louis-Elie Moreau de Saint-Méry, *Moreau de St. Méry's American Journey*, ed. and trans. Kenneth Roberts and Anna M. Roberts (Garden City, N.Y., 1947), 266.

18. Claude Blanchard, *The Journal of Claude Blanchard, Commissary of the French Auxiliary Army Sent to the United States during the American Revolution, 1780–1783*, ed. Thomas Balch and trans. William Duane (Albany, N.Y., 1876), 41, 49.

19. Moreau de Saint-Méry, *Moreau de St. Méry's American Journey*, 266.

20. François, Marquis de Barbé-Marbois, *Our Revolutionary Forefathers: The Letters of François, Marquis de Barbé-Marbois during His Residence in the United States as Secretary of the French Legation, 1779–1785*, ed. and trans. Eugene Parker Chase (New York, 1929), 123.

21. Nancy Shippen, *Nancy Shippen, Her Journal Book*, ed. Ethel Armes (Philadelphia, 1935), 167, 229, 243.

22. Chastellux, *Voyages de M. le Marquis de Chastellux*, quoted in Sherrill, *French Memories of Eighteenth-Century America*, 40.

23. Eliza Southgate Bowne, *A Girl's Life Eighty Years*

Ago: Selections from the Letters of Eliza Southgate Bowne, ed. Clarence Cook (New York, 1887), 207.

24. Shippen, *Nancy Shippen, Her Journal Book,* 167.

25. Prince de Broglie, "Journal du Voyage," in *Mélanges de la Société des Bibliophiles Français* (Paris, 1903), quoted in Sherrill, *French Memories of Eighteenth-Century America,* 13.

26. Comte de Ségur, *Mémoires, ou souvenires et anecdotes* (Paris, 1826), quoted in Sherrill, *French Memories of Eighteenth-Century America,* 78.

27. Shippen, *Nancy Shippen, Her Journal Book,* 175.

28. Kalm, *The America of 1750,* 2:677; Moreau de Saint-Méry, *Moreau de St. Méry's American Journey,* 286.

29. Marquis de Chastellux, *Travels in North America in the Years 1780–81–82* (New York, 1827), 114.

30. Ferdinand-Marie Bayard, *Travels of a Frenchman in Maryland and Virginia, with a Description of Philadelphia and Baltimore in 1791,* ed. and trans. Ben C. McCary (Ann Arbor, Mich., 1950), 48.

31. Barbé-Marbois, *Our Revolutionary Forefathers,* 123.

32. Blanchard, *Journal of Claude Blanchard,* 78.

33. Ferdinand-Marie Bayard, *Voyage dans l'intérieur des Etats-Unis* (Paris, 1797), quoted in Sherrill, *French Memories of Eighteenth-Century America,* 93.

34. Claude-Victor-Marie, Prince de Broglie, "Narrative of the Prince de Broglie," trans. E. W. Balch, *Magazine of American History* 1 (1877): 233.

35. Bayard, *Voyage dans l'intérieur des Etats-Unis,* quoted in Sherrill, *French Memories of Eighteenth Century America,* 93.

36. Suffolk County Probate Records, Suffolk County Courthouse, Boston, Mass. (hereafter SCPR), 53:444 (inventory of Mrs. Hannah Pemberton, Boston, June 22, 1758); 39:185 (inventory of Joseph Blake, Boston, Sept. 18, 1746). Among other Suffolk County inventories listing tea tables with tea equipment thereon were those of Sendal Williams, Boston, Mar. 13, 1747 (43:407); Rev. Benjamin Colman, Boston, Sept. 1, 1747 (40:266); Nathaniel Cunningham, Boston, Feb. 6, 1748 (42:156); Joseph Snelling, Boston, Dec. 8, 1748 (42:60); Elizabeth Chauncy, Boston, May 28, 1757 (52:382); Gillam Tailer [Taylor], Boston, Oct. 18, 1757 (52:817); and Jonathan Skinner, Boston, Oct. 30, 1778 (77:565).

37. Bayard, *Travels of a Frenchman in Maryland and Virginia,* 47.

38. "Letter from [Louis Guillaume] Otto [to Nancy Shippen]," undated, Shippen Papers, box 6, Manuscripts Division, Library of Congress; the letter is dated about 1780 by Ethel Armes in Shippen, *Nancy Shippen, Her Journal Book,* 8.

39. Jacob Hiltzheimer, *Extracts from the Diary of Jacob Hiltzheimer of Philadelphia, 1765–1798,* ed. Jacob Cox Parsons (Philadelphia, 1893), 94.

40. Fithian, *Journal and Letters,* 193.

41. Benjamin Franklin, letter to Mrs. Deborah Franklin, Feb. 19, 1758, London, in *The Writings of Benjamin Franklin,* ed. Albert Henry Smyth, 10 vols. (New York, 1907), 3:432.

42. Bayard, *Voyage dans l'intérieur des Etats-Unis,* quoted in Sherrill, *French Memories of Eighteenth-Century America,* 93.

43. *Boston Gazette,* Apr. 25, 1737; *Boston News-Letter,* June 24, 1762; *New-York Gazette,* Jan. 8, 1799. These and all other newspaper references have been taken variously from the following sources: George Francis Dow, *The Arts and Crafts in New England, 1704–1775* (Topsfield, Mass., 1927); Rita Susswein Gottesman, *The Arts and Crafts in New York, 1726–1776* (New York, 1938); Gottesman, *The Arts and Crafts in New York, 1777–1799* (New York, 1954); and Alfred Coxe Prime, *The Arts and Crafts in Philadelphia, Maryland, and South Carolina, 1721–1785* (Topsfield, Mass., 1929).

44. SCPR, 39:499, inventory of James Pemberton, Boston, Apr. 8, 1747.

45. *Boston News-Letter,* Nov. 28, 1771.

46. Shippen, *Nancy Shippen, Her Journal Book,* 215. No doubt make-believe teatime and pretend tea-drinking were a part of some aristocratic children's playtime activities. Perhaps many young girls played at serving tea and dreamed of hosting a tea party of their own; but few were probably as fortunate as Peggy Livingston, who, at about the age of five, was allowed to invite "by card . . . 20 young misses" to her own "Tea Party & Ball." She "treated them with all good things, & a violin," wrote her grandfather. There were "5 coaches at ye door at 10 when they departed. I was much amused [for] 2 hours" (Shippen, *Nancy Shippen, Her Journal Book,* 248).

47. *Boston News-Letter,* Oct. 4, 1750; *Maryland Journal,* Nov. 20, 1781.

48. Robin, *New Travels Through North America,* 23.

49. W. Stephen Thomas, "Major Samuel Shaw and the Cincinnati Porcelain," *Antiques* 27 (May 1935): 178. The letter and the tea set are now in the collections of Historic Deerfield, Inc., Deerfield, Mass.

50. Fithian, *Journal and Letters,* 133.

51. Kalm, *The America of 1750,* 1:191. Later in the century another naturalist, C. F. Volney, also noted that "very hot tea" was "beloved by Americans of English descent" (Volney, *Tableau du climat et du sol des Etats-Unis* [Paris, 1803], quoted in Sherrill, *French Memories of Eighteenth-Century America,* 95).

52. *Boston News-Letter,* Mar. 24, 1774, Nov. 18, 1742, Apr. 4, 1771; *New-York Journal,* Aug. 3, 1775.

53. *New-York Gazette,* Apr. 3, 1727; *Boston Gazette,* June 4, 1759; *Boston News-Letter,* Jan. 9, 1772; *Maryland Gazette,* May 13, 1773; *Pennsylvania Journal,* Dec. 15, 1763.

54. Kalm, *The America of 1750,* 1:347.

55. *Boston News-Letter,* Apr. 4, 1771, Nov. 18, 1742, Jan. 9, 1772; *New-York Gazette,* Feb. 14, 1757; *Pennsylvania Gazette,* Jan. 25, 1759; *Rivington's New York Gazetteer,* Jan. 13, 1774; *New-York Journal,* Aug. 3, 1773; *Boston Gazette,* Sept. 11, 1758; and *New-York Daily Advertiser,* Jan. 21, 1797.

56. Moreau de Saint-Méry, *Moreau de St. Méry's American Journal,* 38.

57. *New-York Gazette,* Feb. 14, 1757; *Boston Gazette,*

May 14, 1764; *Maryland Gazette*, Jan. 4, 1759; *New-York Journal*, Aug. 3, 1775; *Pennsylvania Gazette*, July 6, 1772, Oct. 31, 1781; *Boston News-Letter*, Apr. 4, 1771, Jan. 9, 1772; and *New-York Daily Advertiser*, Jan. 21, 1797.

58. *New-York Mercury*, Oct. 30, 1758; *Pennsylvania Journal*, Apr. 25, 1765; *Boston News-Letter*, Jan. 17, 1745; and *New-York Gazette*, Dec. 6, 1771.

59. *Pennsylvania Gazette*, Jan. 25, 1759; *Pennsylvania Journal*, Apr. 25, 1765; and *Independent News Journal* [New York], July 23, 1785.

60. *New-York Gazette*, Apr. 3, 1727.

61. *Maryland Gazette*, Jan. 4, 1759; *Pennsylvania Chronicle*, Jan. 29, 1770; SCPR, 52:324, inventory of John Procter, May 13, 1757.

62. SCPR, 52:327, inventory of Rev. Charles Brockwell, May 13, 1757.

63. Quotations variously taken from *New-York Gazette*, Apr. 3, 1727, Aug. 2, 1762; *Commercial Advertiser* [New York], Oct. 10, 1979; *Boston Gazette*, July 26, 1756; *New-York Daily Advertiser*, May 7, 1793; *Boston News-Letter*, Oct. 18, 1750; and *Pennsylvania Evening Post*, July 11, 1776.

64. *New-York Journal*, Aug. 3, 1775; *New-York Daily Advertiser*, Jan. 21, 1797.

65. *Pennsylvania Packet*, May 29, 1775; *American Weekly Mercury* [Philadelphia], Jan. 1736; *Boston Gazette*, May 3, 1751, Sept. 11, 1758; and *Pennsylvania Journal*, Aug. 1, 1771.

66. Bayard, *Voyage dans l'intérieur des Etats-Unis*, quoted in Sherrill, *French Memories of Eighteenth-Century America*, 92.

67. *New-York Daily Advertiser*, May 7, 1793.

68. Letter from O[tho] Holland Williams to Dr. Philip Thomas, Apr. 12, 1786, Williams Papers, vol. 4, letter no. 320; manuscript collection, Maryland Historical Society, Baltimore.

69. *Boston News-Letter*, Apr. 4, 1771; *Pennsylvania Gazette*, Oct. 31, 1781; *Minerva, & Mercantile Evening Advertiser* [New York], Aug. 4, 1796.

70. *Boston News-Letter*, Sept. 16, 1736.

"For Honour and Civil Worship to Any Worthy Person": Burial, Baptism, and Community on the Massachusetts Near Frontier, 1730–1790

JOHN L. BROOKE

The interpretation of gravestones and the social history of death and dying are fertile fields for the study of ritual space in pre–Civil War America. Many of us have stopped in the low, raking light of a sunny winter afternoon to admire the intricate local variations in New England gravestone iconography. Considering the sheer number of dated stones that survive in their original locations, relatively few scholars have tried to "read" them in the context of the culture that made and used them. John L. Brooke shows in this essay the subtlety required to decode gravestones in relation to ongoing changes in local religion and social structure. Yet, unlike most students of the subject, he goes beyond the analysis of individual markers to situate the stones in a broader view of how the location of churches and burial grounds in central Massachusetts enacted opposing concepts of spiritual renewal.

Brooke's essay is significant in two ways. In relying not only on gravestones and local maps but also on vital statistics, church records, diaries, and sermons, he ably demonstrates the range of evidence demanded by the interdisciplinary study of ritual space. The point of his methodology is clear: when exploring the symbolic world of the living through their texts on dying, one must be able to trade in metaphors. What seem on the surface to be "face-decorated" gravestones become community elders looking down from their "city on a hill" to the earthly congregation, icons of cultural memory intended to keep the faithful bound to covenant theology. In making many such connections, this essay represents the first time that the elusive relationship between the ritual and symbolism of death and religious change has been examined on a local level.

Brooke argues convincingly that existing generalizations concerning change in gravestone decoration and the "decline" of orthodox Puritanism are based on superficial correlations ungrounded in the day-to-day reality of any specific community. Beyond this, he is able to connect beliefs about death to the ways in which divergent religious groups urged a vision of moral economy on themselves.

The affective power of the church and burial ground as ritual spaces in New England culture ultimately lay in the way they shaped the different histories of the standing Congregational order and Baptist dissenters. Ritual space, in other words, had a distinctly temporal meaning. Whether high on a hill or low in a boggy river valley, whether dominated by images of earth or of water, the communities on Massachusetts's Near Frontier that Brooke explores structured a landscape that was both emotionally intense and intellectually demanding. Ritual space brought into focus and presented for conscious contemplation a variety of factors at once: rites of passage, concepts of sin and grace, the meanings of baptism and burial, and how the congregation made its own history through the construction of tangible forms that fused physical substance with spiritual energy.

The diary of Benjamin Gilbert, the son of minor gentry parents in the North Parish of Brookfield, Massachusetts, shows him to have been a rowdy young man of the Revolutionary era. Returning home on leave from the garrison at Albany in January 1778, he recorded his disappointment with the hospitality shown him at a house in Great Barrington. "[T]heir was four Girls, two Sick and two well. The well ones wanted Company Very Much, But the Oold man was so full of Grace that it would not do." Setting out on a tardy return to Albany one month later, Gilbert and his companions stopped at his cousin's tavern in Brookfield's West Parish and "Drinkt Sling till we all got well Sprung." In the camps on the Hudson River Gilbert never attended religious meetings but did meet in Capt. Daniel Shays's tent to observe the secular rites of Freemasonry. After resigning from the army, Gilbert recorded in detail his comings and goings in North Brookfield for eight months in 1780 and 1782. His diary reveals a repetitive pattern. Work early in the week was followed by a round of all-night visiting with neighbors, friends, and relatives, playing cards, drinking, and dancing. This social round took him to widely separated sections of the parish and intersected with the collective gatherings and rituals of quiltings, house-raisings, weddings, "arbitrations," and town and parish meetings. But, significantly, and in sharp contrast to his camp routine, Gilbert attended morning and afternoon meetings every Sunday with his father's family and, in February 1780, attended the funeral of Mrs. Samuel Hinckley, walking with the procession "to the Grave in the South parrish."[1] Thus, even for a seemingly dissolute soldier of the Revolution, the formal ritual observances of the New England town maintained their proscriptive hold. The traditional obligations of the covenanted community had not been completely eroded under the impact of war and social upheaval.

In this essay I explore a central dimension of these traditional obligations: the collective ritual practice of a complex culture of death. The symbolic rituals of death, burial, and remembrance observed in orthodox communities throughout eighteenth-century New England were important means by which townsmen publicly reaffirmed their commonality in the face of ever-present threats of disharmony and disunion. In a sense, the culture of death was continuous with the ongoing round of visitation and collective conviviality in which Benjamin Gilbert participated so heartily. Both brought people together from various neighborhoods; both were lubricated with the ever-present sling or rum-flip.[2] But death and burial were structurally and symbolically powerful events, bringing crises to the individual, the household, and the community and requiring the mobilization of formal religious categories, the manipulation of material symbols, and the binding of the community to the province's mythic past.

These considerations make the public culture of death a rich focus of study. The emphasis here on the "public" aspects of death is deliberate; this essay does not deal directly with the problem of the individual's experience of death or that of a household's breach and restructuring at the passing of a family member. These questions have been explored with great insight by social historians of early modern Europe and America.[3] Rather, the focus here is the relationships between the symbolism and attendent rituals of death and the broader problems of community definition, formal religion, and civil order. We need first to examine the emergence of an elaborated culture of death against the transformation of Massachusetts Bay "from colony to province."[4] Only after this process is clarified can we explore the structure and meaning of death ritual in the "contrasting communities" on the Massachusetts Near Frontier.[5] In that region, orthodox Congregationalists and dissenting Separate Baptists followed drastically different interpretations of the nature of death and earthly burial, interpretations that were interwoven with patterns of human geography, social organization, individual life cycle, and collective *mentalité*.

*   *   *

Eighteenth-century Congregationalists treated death and the dead far differently than did early seventeenth-century Puritans. Hinging on the transformation of the New England Way from exclusive sect to inclusive church, this difference had roots in a specific historical context; eighteenth-century Congregationalists inherited a highly ritualized culture of death that had itself been invented in the final quarter of the previous century to take the place of that destroyed by the reforming impulse of early Puritanism.[6]

The anonymous "Essay on the Laying out of Towns" (ca. 1634) and the physical form of many early towns attest to the power of the nucleated village ideal for the Puritans of the Great Migration. But the town descriptions in Edward Johnson's *Wonderworking Providence* and an extensive secondary literature also document the progressive erosion of that ideal. Tightly clustered villagers rapidly gave way to

Table 1. Meetinghouse and Burial Ground Locations: Middlesex and Worcester Counties, 1630–1775[a]

Relationship of Meetinghouse and Burial-ground	1630–1669	1673–1701	1712–1740	1741–1775	Total, 1673–1775
Middlesex County					
Adjacent	2 (17%)	4	7	6	17 (57%)
Separate[b]	10 (83%)	2	10	1	13 (43%)
Known	12 (100%)	6	17	7	30 (100%)
Unknown	1		1		1
TOTAL	13	6	18	7	31
Worcester County					
Adjacent		1	12	17	30 (65%)
Separate[b]	3 (100%)		6	10	16 (35%)
Known	3	1	18	27	46 (100%)
Unknown			1	3	4
TOTAL	3	1	19	30	50
Both counties					
Adjacent	2 (13%)	5	19	23	47 (62%)
Separate[b]	13 (87%)	2	16	11	29 (38%)
Known	15 (100%)	7	35	34	76 (100%)
Unknown	1		2	3	5
TOTAL	16	7	37	37	81

Sources: Samuel A. Drake, *History of Middlesex County, Massachusetts*, 2 vols. (Boston, 1880); *History of Worcester County, Massachusetts*, 2 vols. (Boston, 1879); *County Atlas of Middlesex, Massachusetts* (New York, 1875); *Atlas of Worcester County, Massachusetts* (New York, 1870; reprinted Rutland, Vt., 1971); and individual town histories.

[a]Table reflects the geographic relationship of meetinghouses and burial grounds as initially arranged at the towns' settlement, but not later changes in this relationship.

[b]Between 400 feet and ½-mile in distance.

scattered "outlivers," as the lure of open lands overwhelmed Puritan and English inhibitions.[7] The shape of the earliest Puritan villages had certainly involved their inhabitants in daily face-to-face interaction, close contact that certainly required the "principles and practice of peace" for the avoidance of conflict.[8] Yet, given the scattered shape of later New England settlements, the principles and practices of union were of equal importance to those of peace. Indifferences growing out of isolation, rather than contention rooted in close quarters, threatened the public life of the eighteenth-century town.

If New England townsmen had by the eighteenth century abandoned the town center as a living place, that center had not lost its social meaning. An important symbolic inversion had occurred, an inversion that indicated a dramatic change in the physical and ritual relationship between the living and the dead. In at least some early seventeenth-century Puritan settlements, the living had clustered in nuclear villages. Indeed, most towns buried their dead with little ceremony at a distance from the community center. But in the eighteenth-century New England town, the living scattered themselves onto their dispersed lands and buried their dead with great ceremony at the center of the community. The emergence and continual elaboration of a complex culture of death were important means by which eighteenth-century townsmen stated and restated the moral and civil union of communities composed of widely scattered and isolated households.

The flow of population and institutional forms from the Massachusetts Bay settlements, particularly southern Middlesex County, into the Near Frontier of Worcester County over the course of the eighteenth century allows a broad analysis of the arrangement of the dead on the public landscape in these two counties (table 1).[9] During the four decades following the Great Migration of 1629–30, burial grounds were laid out at a distance from central meetinghouses in the Puritan settlements, signaling a marked segregation of the dead from the center of civil and religious life. Among fifteen towns established in Middlesex County before the 1670s, thirteen (87 percent) had established such a separation of public spaces, ranging from four hundred feet in Woburn to a half-mile in Charlestown. On the Near Frontier, this early seventeenth-century pattern was manifest in the 1665 settlement at Quaboag (later Brookfield), where the meetinghouse sat at the center of a nucleated village and the burial ground lay a half-mile to the north, beyond the townspeoples' houselots.[10]

This separation was a radical departure from the traditional English pattern of the consecrated churchyard surrounding the parish church and was bound up in Puritanism's departure from the sacramentalism of the Anglican establishment. Puritan iconoclasm and deritualization had roots in Henry VIII's destruction of the Catholic church in England, in a particular doctrinal focus on conversion and the millennium, and in the Protestant effort to radically compress mediation between man and God. English Puritans and sectarians gutted churches, smashed funerary sculpture, and stripped their own funeral rites of all religious content. In their differentiation between the place of religious worship and the place of civil burial, the early New England Puritans were following a general Reformed rejection of the significance of death as a passage between worldly and glorified states.[11]

But, if the dead were pushed to the periphery of early seventeenth-century communities, the end of the century saw the reversal of this pattern. Starting in the 1670s, new towns in Middlesex County (and in the region that in 1730 would become Worcester County) established their meetinghouses and burial places in immediate proximity (see table 1). Overall, among seventy-six towns, districts, and parishes incorporated during the century preceding the Revolution, forty-seven (62 percent) built meetinghouses next to burial grounds to form an integrated corporate center. In similar fashion, some older towns, among them Cambridge, Reading, Groton, and Marlborough, rearranged existing seventeenth-century alignments to bring their own centers into conformity with the new ideal. In Groton this rearrangement

immediately followed the town's destruction in King Philip's War. Marlborough had built its meetinghouse a half-mile from the town burying ground in 1663 but, unlike Groton, reestablished this spatial arrangement in the post war resettlement. The town rearranged its public spaces in 1706, voting "that the land exchanged with John Parry Taylor adjoining the meetinghouse . . . shall lay for a Trayning place and Burying place forever." This new location was not plow land but neither was it waste; Taylor made sure that he received "other lands of the proprietors in the cow common."[12] In eastern Middlesex, new parishes and districts carved out of older towns in the early eighteenth century could not always achieve this ideal. The middle and western districts of Watertown, for example, were granted the right to establish graveyards in 1703, only to have a new distribution of population determine a different meetinghouse site when they were incorporated as the districts of Waltham and Weston in 1721.[13]

By contrast, on the tabula rasa of the new towns and districts of the Near Frontier, the new arrangement of public space could be achieved from the start, without friction from a preexisting human geography. Proprietors' meetings established this new relationship by repeatedly setting aside or buying land for the corporate center of a new town. In Southborough land was acquired before incorporation for "a training field, buryal place, and a meetinghouse," while in Athol in 1741 eight acres were "to lie in common for a Burying Place and Meetinghouse." In Spencer two acres were given in 1740 "for the accomodation of a meetinghouse and for a training field and for such other public uses as the town shall direct forever." Here, as in all other towns, these "public uses" included the graveyard; the first burial in this plot dates to 1742.[14]

Such public places were not randomly located but were situated at a carefully agreed upon central location. In Oakham they were to be at the "santer or next convenient place"; in New Braintree it was the "center of land already laid off."[15] In every town the interests of the various outlying neighborhoods had to be delicately balanced to establish what was in effect the physical manifestation of an inclusive moral economy. The meetinghouse and training field were literally the common ground for a scattered townspeople, providing gathering places both in- and out-of-doors for the acting out of collective, corporate

Fig. 1. Gravestone of John Person, Wakefield, Massachusetts, 1679. (Photograph by Daniel Farber and Jessie Lee Farber.)

blems of death that continued to be popular for devotional purposes in Protestant New England. The appearance of these images on the gravestones was not unique. They were also used to decorate a wide variety of mourning paraphernalia, including horse furniture, printed sermons, broadside elegies, and the enameled gold rings given to prominent participants in funeral processions.[18]

Occasional literary references to these emblems suggest that they were seen as general reminders of mortality rather than as images of departed souls. It was in this sense that an elegaic poem written in 1645 told an aging Thomas Dudley that "a deaths head on your hand you need not weare"; being advanced in years, he needed no mourning ring to remind him of his approaching death. Writing at the end of the seventeenth century, Cotton Mather reiterated this theme of the image as an emblematic reminder of mortality. "Let us look upon everything as a sort of Death's-Head set before us, with a *Memento mortis* written upon it." Like those jeremiad funeral sermons of the 1670s and 1680s that presented the "death of usefull men" as an example of God's displeasure, the death's head image was presented as an exemplum that would turn people's minds toward questions of preparation, death, and salvation.[19]

However, at various points during the first half of the eighteenth century, New England's gravestone carvers began to abandon the death's head in favor of a diverse assemblage of more lifelike images, reverting in effect from an early modern emblem of death toward a late medieval effigy of the dead. In some cases this shift was a gradual, in others a rapid transformation. Portraits carved by eastern "urban" workshops were clearly images of the dead in life, and rural carvers' occasional practice of putting the deceased's initials on either side of the winged face provides strong evidence that these images were intended to depict the souls of the dead (fig. 2).[20] Thus, while the death's head functioned as an emblem of mortality, the soul effigies that populated New England's graveyards in the eighteenth century paradoxically kept the faces of the dead alive before the community. They transcended the liminal boundary of death; fulfilling the biblical type of Abel, the face-decorated gravestones provided a medium through which the deceased town elders could, "though dead, yet speak."[21]

Despite this apparent religious function, the grave-

civil and religious duties and privileges. Whenever they gathered at the town center, the people would also be confronted with their own past, with the place where previous members of the corporate community lay waiting for the Resurrection in the common ground of the graveyard.[16]

The mere presence of the dead was not the only element that shaped the new context of the corporate center. Beginning in the mid-1670s an elaborate symbolism began to appear on stone monuments in the graveyards of Massachusetts Bay, replacing impermanent wooden post-and-rail markers and inscribed, but otherwise unornamented, stones.[17] Initially, the dominant sign in this new visual language was that of a winged death's head (fig. 1). This image, with its supporting cast of coffins, shrouds, crossbones, imps of death, hourglasses, picks, and shovels, was drawn from a late medieval repertoire of conventional em-

Fig. 2. Detail of tympanum on gravestone of Ann Porter, Hadley, Massachusetts, 1756. (Photograph by Daniel Farber and Jessie Lee Farber.)

stones were formally recognized as coming under civil jurisdiction. In *A Testimony from the Scripture against Idolatry and Superstition*, first published in 1672, Samuel Mather made a rare direct commentary on funerary symbolism, excluding it from the Second Commandment's injunction against the use of "graven images."

> [I]t is not meant of Images for Civil use, but for worship; thou shalt not bow down to them, nor serve them. For the Civil use of Images is lawful for the representation and remembrance of a person absent, for honour and Civil worship to any worthy person, as also for ornament, but the scope of the Command is against Images in State and use religious.[22]

Although Mather inveighed against religious "uses," gravestones in eighteenth-century New England drew their symbolic power from the same conflation of spheres that characterized the corporate town. Just as the meetinghouse combined civil and religious roles and the orthodox minister was supported by town rates under penalty of civil law, a seemingly religious symbolism, explicitly denoted as "civil worship," was planted in the civil context of the town graveyard.

A gradual evolution in the ritual of funeral and burial was intimately bound up with the changing location and marking of the dead. The funeral procession and burial in New England never took on the efficacious value of Anglican or Catholic rites for the dead. But late in the seventeenth century they underwent a transformation that brought into particular focus the corporate town center of meetinghouse and burying ground and the linkage between the religious and civil roles of the Congregational minister.

Funerals in seventeenth-century New England were civil ceremonies at which the minister might be present but in which he would not participate in his clerical capacity.[23] The turn of the eighteenth century brought an interdependent set of changes as both the procession's route and the minister's role were altered. The route of the seventeenth-century funeral procession, which sometimes wound through the streets of larger towns for maximum dramatic display, usually moved directly from household to graveyard. With increasing frequency in the eighteenth century, however, processions stopped at the meetinghouse for prayers and, particularly for prominent persons, a funeral sermon by the minister. Following the custom begun in the late seventeenth century, funeral sermons drew on the jeremiad tradition, placing death firmly in the context of the community's responsibility to the covenant.[24] Prayers and a sermon in the meetinghouse were followed by graveside prayers in the adjacent burying ground. This new role for the minister in the civil ritual of burial was paralleled by a new role in another sphere: the first occasion of prayers at a funeral in 1685 was followed in 1686 by the first marriage performed by a minister. But if the funeral ceremony was intended to show "every token of respect . . . and friendship" for both the living and the dead and gave the minister an opportunity to deliver an exhortation to the community, it was not intended to influence the fate of the deceased's soul.[25] Rather than an individual religious function, the attendance of minister and community at funerals served collective social purposes, thickening the ritual connections that bound an increasingly scattered and contentious people.

Most importantly, the emergence and elaboration of the visual and spatial elements of the death ritual must be seen as interwoven with a critical transformation of religious piety and polity in late seventeenth-century Massachusetts Bay. Whereas conversion had been all-important to early seventeenth-century Puritan elders as a means of defining the exclusive church of the elect, their children increasingly failed to experience conversion. Beginning in the 1650s and 1660s, the younger ministers of Massachusetts Bay responded to the threat of memberless churches by urging a more inclusive polity on their congregations. Their argument was rooted in Federal theology. As the spiritual descendants of the Old Testament nation of Israel, the people of New England were entitled to that special dispensation first enjoyed by Abraham and his "seed": a birthright contract of divine protection and human obedience between God and His chosen people. Despite initial lay resistance, the resulting Half-Way Covenant was widely implemented in the final quarter of the seventeenth century. It allowed the unconverted children of full church members both to "own the covenant" and to come under church discipline; in turn it extended the privilege of baptism to their children, thus binding successive generations to the obligation and promise of a national covenant. In actual practice, many churches began to allow the children of unconverted members to "own the covenant" and extended baptism to include almost the entire population of the town.[26] While they remained within the wider Reformed tradition, eighteenth-century Congregationalists were no longer Puritans.

Alongside this shift from exclusive, conversionary sect toward inclusive, territorially defined church came an intensified focus on the place of the dead in a symbolic order. The willingness of particular congregations to adopt extended baptism was mirrored and, in some way, anticipated by their arrangement of meetinghouse and burial ground as public spaces. The churches of the two early Middlesex County towns that first built their meetinghouses adjacent to their graveyards, Sudbury and Chelmsford, adopted the Half-Way Covenant by 1657 and 1665, respectively, well before the majority of the churches in Massachusetts Bay. Overall, among eleven churches in Essex, Middlesex, and Suffolk counties practicing extended baptism before 1670, six were in towns with adjacent meetinghouse and graveyard. In at least one case, the extension of baptism was clearly linked with the relocation of a meetinghouse. In Reading, where the Half-Way Covenant had been adopted in 1669, the death of the town's minister in 1688 was preceded by an "awakening" of unchurched "adult children" and the baptism of their offspring and was followed in 1689 by the building of a new, larger meetinghouse close to the old graveyard.[27]

By contrast, all six churches known to have opposed or delayed implementation of the Half-Way Covenant were in towns where the meetinghouse and graveyard were separated by a tenth to four-fifths of a mile.[28] Similarly, churches in Plymouth Colony resisted adoption of the Half-Way Covenant until the early eighteenth century, and their towns had multiple, scattered graveyards. At another level, the adoption of the Half-Way Covenant and of the death's head carvings were linked. The graveyards in Reading, Cambridge, and Concord, whose churches were among the first to adopt the Half-Way Covenant, contain early death's head carvings by the anonymous "Charlestown carver" dating from the 1670s (see fig. 1); Dedham and Woburn resisted the measure, and the first death's head carvings in their graveyards date from 1689 and 1690, respectively.[29]

By the turn of the century both extended baptism and an elaborated culture of death were widespread. In short, the symbolism of the graveyard had become the material equivalent of the Half-Way Covenant—genealogical references united the people of particular communities in crises of birth and death just as they were increasingly scattered in their daily lives.

A change in civil topography completes the picture of the inversion of the symbolic order of the town landscape. Before the New England Indians' desperate assault on English settlements in 1675, villages were generally "planted" on the banks of rivers, replicating the settlement pattern of both the English countryside and of the Algonkians themselves. However, in the wake of forty years of intermittent warfare, the towns established on the Near Frontier after the Peace of Utrecht of 1713 took a very different form. Rather than centering on river valleys with higher peripheral elevations, towns were laid out so that their centers could be located on more easily defended hilltops.[30] With the decline of Indian attacks in the 1720s, this new topographical logic lost its potential strategic coherence, although it continued to affect the symbolic and institutional life of eighteenth-century towns. Thus, a particular ideal of the proper arrangement of public space guided the voters of the district of Hubbardston in the early 1770s. Having abandoned their original common as inconvenient for some, they exchanged land for another location and met in 1773 "to see if the district will vote what way or manner they will come into for clearing up the common for burial-place and meeting-house." The previous year they had decided "to build a meeting-house . . . betwixt Mr. Parker's and the burying ground on the height of land."[31]

Though they were slow in implementing their decision, the people of this new district had a clear image of how their public spaces should be arranged: convenient to all inhabitants, adjacent to each other, and located on high ground. Quite literally, the dead had replaced the living as inhabitants of the "city upon a hill." In the early seventeenth century, the perceived ideal of close and watchful living stood as social evidence of a special covenant with God and a mission in the world. But the rapid collapse of this settlement ideal and of the uniform religious purity that it came to represent set the stage for a refiguration of church, society, and symbolic forms. Throughout the eighteenth century, the material symbolism at the empty and silent town centers, especially the winged faces of the dead, stood as mute evidence of the continued allegiance of New England townsmen to that covenant tradition.

*   *   *

By the mid-eighteenth century, the orthodox way of the standing order no longer defined the limits of religious belief or expression in New England. The Great Awakening spawned a new people. In "an extraordinary outpowering of the spirit," religious dissenters "venture[d] on upon a naked promis." Feeling that those of the orthodox way "were all going Blindfold to destruction," they separated themselves into exclusive and pure meetings of regenerate saints.[32]

One important result of the Great Awakening on Worcester County's Near Frontier was that after the mid-eighteenth century the cultural landscape of the region's towns came to be defined by two opposed ritual paradigms (fig. 3). The inclusive umbrella of the Federal Covenant was the "unclean thing" that drove the dissenters out of the Congregational meetinghouses; "unclean" because it legitimated the baptism of unconverted children and drew the unregenerate into halfway membership. And those who remained within the standing order's Federal Covenant continued to follow a unifying ritual practice that focused on the burial of the dead at upland public centers. By contrast, when dissenters rejected in-

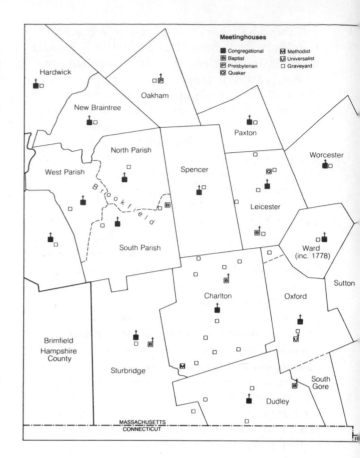

Fig. 3. Towns, meetinghouses, and graveyards in southwest Worcester County, Massachusetts, 1730–90. (Map by John L. Brooke and Lori Wall.)

fant baptism, they also abandoned the established culture of death. For many people living in lowlands on the edges of towns, the implied ideals of height, earth, and centrality apparently clashed with the concrete reality of their own low, wet, and peripheral situation. Rather than continuing to go to the orthodox meetinghouse "upon a hill," many people in outlying valley neighborhoods found legitimacy in the waters flowing through their midst.

The division between orthodoxy and dissent on the Near Frontier did not fade as the passions of the Great Awakening subsided but rather crystallized into opposing institutional and theological positions. The preaching of George Whitefield in Brookfield in 1740 set off a revival among some of the Congregational churches in the region, and a number of established ministers adopted an evangelical, New Light orientation.[33] Yet, as the revivals' impact waned, even these New Light Congregational churches returned to an inclusive polity. Congregational churches in the region typically maintained the Half-Way Covenant until well after the Revolution, giving it up in two waves in the 1790s and 1810s during the Second Great Awakening.[34] In the decades separating the two Great Awakenings, the classical Puritan balance proved impossible to maintain on the Near Frontier as Congregationalists put territorial community before theological purity.

The dissenters followed a path that institutionalized their polity and theology in a distinctly opposite form. Following their charismatic withdrawal from communion in the standing order, they embarked on a course of religious experimentation that by the 1770s brought them to the common ground of closed-communion, Separate Baptist polity and doctrine. Baptism by immersion as an exclusive sign of admission to a closed communion emerged as the central religious ritual among these dissenting churches.[35] In adopting Baptist ritual practice they turned their backs on the particular Protestant tradition that Massachusetts society had inherited and transmuted from seventeenth-century Puritan experience.

The withdrawal of the dissenters threatened the standing order on the most basic level. In refusing to pay ministerial taxes they undermined the moral economy of towns dependent on a united commitment to intertwined civil and religious duties and privileges. However, while producing a fluid enthusiasm that threatened the structures of orthodoxy, the Awakening also helped to build an alternative set of institutions that counterbalanced the influence of the standing order and provided an institutional focus for particular social groups.

Dissenting opinion was restricted to particular neighborhoods in southwest Worcester County and to groups of people already linked by ties of kinship and common "mechanical" occupations. In four Baptist churches gathered in the region between 1731 and 1797, almost three-quarters of the initiating membership (95 of 129) was already linked by kinship before church formation.[36] Similarly, the sources of their marriage partners ran counter to the intratown pattern of the Congregationalists; men who joined Baptist churches were far more likely to marry women from adjacent towns. Among male Baptists

in Charlton, Sturbridge, Leicester, and East Brookfield for whom there is complete information, fully one-half (36 of 71) had married across town lines before joining the church. Among similar Congregationalists in Spencer, Sturbridge, and the North Parish of Brookfield less than one in five (12 of 71) had done so.[37] In addition, the occupational orientation of the two groups contrasted distinctly. Within the rudimentary division of labor on the Near Frontier, dissenters made up a disproportionate amount of the "mechanical" population. Evidence for eighteenth-century occupations available for Leicester and the North Parish of Brookfield suggests that as many as one-half of all male dissenters were mechanics and tradesmen or were the sons of such men, as compared to roughly one-fifth of the Congregationalists (table 2). Baptists were particularly inclined toward all kinds of milling and ironworking as well as the trades of potting, tanning, masonry, sieve making, and spinning-wheel manufacturing. While they by no means had a monopoly on rural industry on the Near Frontier, the dissenters certainly had a consistent relationship with it.[38]

These characteristics of marriage and occupation interwove with another dimension: Baptist households clustered in clearly defined and consistently located neighborhoods. A series of lot maps and lists of covenant signers, church members, and pewholders allow the reconstruction of the geography of religious communities in Leicester, Spencer, and the north and east parts of Brookfield (fig. 4). In each case, the households of Congregational church members were located predominantly on upland lots surrounding the central meetinghouse, while the majority of the Baptists' were located in the lowlands on town peripheries, with their meetinghouses adjacent to important millstreams. Baptist meetinghouses were built in similar locations in Sturbridge, Charlton, Sutton, Dudley, South Brimfield, Wilbraham, and Granby. Importantly, in two communities for which reliable evidence exists, the settlement of future Baptists in the lowlands predated the formation of the Baptist church—by at least a decade in Leicester and by a half-century in Brookfield.[39]

A distinctive, self-selecting constellation of households united in new dissenting meetinghouses. One form of separatist, evangelical religion, a "walk . . . to and in the good old way," provided an institutional and symbolic focus for peripheral, lowlying, particu-

Table 2. Mechanical Trades in Eighteenth-Century Leicester and North Brookfield: Congregationalists, Baptists, and Quakers

| | Total on List | Linked with: | | | | Total Mechanical Trades |
		Milling[a]	Ironworking[b]	Woodworking[c]	Other Trades[d]	
North Brookfield Congregational church members on 1783 Valuation	69	7[e]	2[e]	5	0	14 (20.3%)
Leicester Congregational pewholders, 1783	40	0	4[e]	1	2[e]	7 (17.5%)
East Brookfield Baptists, 1778–97[f]	29	6	4	1	5	16 (55.2%)
Leicester Baptist subscribers, 1776–85	37	9	0	1	6	16 (43.2%)
All Leicester Baptists, 1732–1800	85	14	5	2	7	28 (32.9%)
Leicester Quakers, 1758	10	1	1	3	0	5 (50.0%)

Sources: Josiah H. Temple, *History of North Brookfield, Massachusetts* (North Brookfield, Mass., 1887), 11–15, 266–68, 282; *The Confession of Faith and Covenant of the First Congregational Church in North Brookfield, Mass., with a Catalogue of Members (1752–1878)* (West Brookfield, Mass., 1878), 24–37; 1783 Valuation, North Brookfield (State Library, Boston); Leicester General Records, 1745–85, 338–40; Greenville (Leicester, Mass.) Baptist Church Records, vol. 1 (Trask Library, Andover-Newton Theological Seminary); Hiram C. Estes, "Historical Discourse," in *The Greenville Baptist Church* (Worcester, Mass., 1887), 18–25; Emory Washburn, *Historical Sketches of the Town of Leicester, Massachusetts* (Boston, 1860), passim; Charles H. Lincoln, "The Antecedents of the Worcester Society of Friends," *Worcester Historical Society Publications*, n.s., 1 (1928): 31; Holmes Ammidown, *Historical Collections* (New York, 1877), 2: 176–79.

[a]saw, grist, fulling, and cider mills.
[b]blacksmith, gunsmith, ironworks.
[c]cabinetmaker, joiner, carpenter, cooper, wheelwright, housewright.
[d]potter, mason, tanner, sieve maker, saddler, spinning-wheel manufacturer.
[e]One N. Brookfield miller, two N. Brookfield iron-masters, three Leicester blacksmiths, and one Leicester tanner also linked to Baptists.
[f]Six Brookfield residents who joined Baptist churches in Leicester, Charlton, and Woodstock, 1778–83, and 23 signers of the 1797 E. Brookfield Baptist petition.

larly mechanical neighborhoods.[40] The key ritual practice that bound these people was that of believer's baptism: the full immersion of a capable, converted individual in the waters of a river or millpond by an elder with the assembled members and "attenders" gathered on the bank. The establishment of Baptist polity and practice in the lowland neighborhoods effected a crucial shift in the ritual use of the landscape, a shift that had centrally important repercussions for the eighteenth-century culture of death. At the same time that they found a new legitimacy in the waters defining the topography of their local world, the Baptists turned their backs on the material symbols of orthodoxy and territorial union at the town centers. The places in which they buried their dead and the manner in which they marked their graves provide an entry into a critical dimension of their rejection of the orthodox way.

The Baptist rejection of the traditional material culture of death, when seen on the level of both context and artifact—graveyard and gravestone—stands in sharp contrast to the Congregational commitment to these symbols. In towns, districts, and parishes where the Congregational (or in one case, Presbyterian) church remained the sole religious institution throughout the eighteenth century, the central graveyard remained the only burying place until well into the nineteenth (see fig. 3). An analysis of the face-decorated gravestones placed in these central graveyards confirms their close association with the Con-

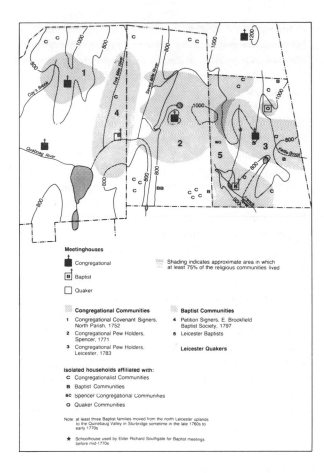

Fig. 4. Religious communities and topography in Brookfield, Spencer, and Leicester, Massachusetts, 1730–90. (Map by John L. Brooke and Lori Wall.)

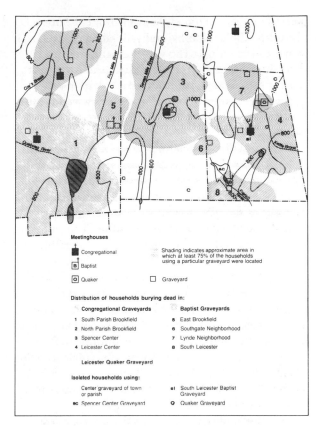

Fig. 5. Graveyards and topography in Brookfield, Spencer, and Leicester, Massachusetts, 1730–90. (Map by John L. Brooke and Lori Wall.)

gregational church. In Spencer 84 percent (37 of 44) of these stones can be linked within nuclear families to Congregational church members or pewholders; in the three parishes of Brookfield the figure is 86 percent (85 of 99), in Sturbridge 78 percent (40 of 51), in Leicester 64 percent (9 of 14) and in Charleston 60 percent (3 of 5).[41] And it must be stressed that these face-decorated stones were not reserved for full church members. In the three parishes where complete membership information is available, only 40 percent of these stones were erected for full Congregational church members; the remainder commemorated people of the broader orthodox orbit. If the dead spoke to the living through these face-images, it was not in their capacity as visible saints but as former

inhabitants of particular corporate localities.[42]

But in towns where religious unity was fractured from an early date, separate graveyards were established in widely scattered neighborhoods (fig. 5). The withdrawal of the dissenters from central meetinghouses paralleled their withdrawal from central graveyards. Four peripheral graveyards were established in eighteenth-century Leicester, three of them by Baptist households and one by Quakers; individual burials were scattered in at least four other places in the town. In Charlton the strength of the dissenters and the corresponding weakness of the standing order resulted in an equally dispersed pattern of burial: nine graveyards and isolated burial places were used in the eighteenth century. The same pattern of separate graveyards for dissenting communities, or isolated plots for dissenting families, appeared in nearby Dudley, South Brimfield, Sutton, East Brookfield, Granby, and Wilbraham, as well as in other towns lying to the west in Hampshire and Berkshire counties.[43] Overall, there was a clear pattern of scattered distribution of the dead in those places where the structural unity of town and church had been eroded by religious pluralism and contention.

Centrally placed upland graveyards were one critical feature of the Congregational culture of death; gravestones ornamented with images of the faces of the dead were another. Just as they avoided the central graveyards, the dissenters failed to invest these face-decorated gravestones with value. This failure was emphatically not a function of wealth (tables 3, 4). Among taxpaying church members listed in the 1783 valuations of Sturbridge, Leicester, and Charlton, 11.1 percent (3 of 27) of the Baptists in the wealthiest quintile can be linked to face-decorated gravestones, as compared to 40.7 percent (35 of 86) of the Congregationalists in the top quintile in Sturbridge, Spencer, and the three parishes of Brookfield. Overall, just 6 percent of the Baptists and 23 percent of the Congregationalists on these valuations can be linked with face-decorated gravestones.[44]

Avoiding professionally carved gravestones ornamented with winged heads, the Baptists marked the graves of their dead with roughly shaped fieldstones sometimes crudely inscribed with the initials of the deceased and with dates of birth and death. Such rough fieldstones were used throughout the Near Frontier before the mid-eighteenth century and can be found in orthodox graveyards at Sturbridge, Sutton, and the south parish of Brookfield. A few of those at Sturbridge can clearly be dated to the 1740s and were put in by Congregational families. However, while the Congregationalists moved away from these crude markers as soon as professionally carved stones with personal imagery became available, the Baptists continued to use them throughout the century.

The Congregationalists, of course, were participating in an elaborate culture of death that had emerged as the standing order in the late seventeenth century moved away from an exclusive, voluntary sect toward an inclusive, territorial church polity. The dissenters rejected this new symbolic tradition as firmly as they had rejected the prior theological transformation. In avoiding corporate burying places at town centers, in burying their dead in sectarian and private grave-

yards, and in refusing to acknowledge the iconic power of face-decorated gravestones, dissenters rejected a symbolism of "civil worship" that reinforced the legal association of civil and religious in the orthodox way.

Thus the acceptance or rejection of an elaborate eighteenth-century material culture of death on the Near Frontier was bound up in a matrix of competing religious institutions and divergent definitions of the role of civil power, the boundaries of distinct neighborhoods and communities, and the appropriate ritual uses of the landscape. The rituals of burial and baptism intersected with the landscape at the burying ground and the riverbank. They also intersected with another critical dimension: the life cycles of the individual members of the opposing communities. As such, they constituted crucial rites of passage as people moved through highly charged points in time and space, acting out pivotal religious roles in imitation of sacred biblical "types," roles that were a sign—if not an efficacious means—of the promise of salvation. An examination of the relationships between religious belief, ritual practice, and personal life cycle opens a useful window onto the places of death and the dead in these opposed worlds of orthodoxy and dissent.

*　　*　　*

The admission of "graceless" persons had driven the Separate Baptists out of the established order in the Great Awakening. By stressing the continuity of Abraham's contract between the Lord and his "chosen nation," the orthodox ministers had undermined the central dynamic of Calvinism; the Separates withdrew to their "pure" gospel churches to restore the primacy of election by grace alone. The Separate Baptists in fact expanded this critique by effectively denying the validity of the Old Testament covenant of Abraham and basing all hopes for salvation on Christ's death and resurrection—the central event of the new dispensation.[45] Both Congregationalists and Baptists scoured the Bible for "types," believing that the flow of grace depended on the shaping of lives and institutions in strict imitation of scriptural form. The conflicting interpretations of the biblical "revealed word" informed drastically different configurations of religious ritual, the rites of passage that punctuated individual life cycles.[46]

The Congregationalist minister's contribution to

Table 3. Congregationalists, Face-Decorated Gravestones, and the 1783 Valuation

Quintile, 1783 Valuation	Brookfield Individuals[a]	Stones	Sturbridge Individuals	Stones	Spencer Individuals	Stones	Total Individuals	Stones
1st: FDGS[b]	21 (39.6%)	40	9 (52.9%)	13	5 (31.2%)	9	35 (40.7%)	62
No FDGS	32	—	8	—	11	—	51	—
2d: FDGS	5	5	4	4	4	5	13	14
No FDGS	40	—	7	—	7	—	54	—
3d: FDGS	5	9	0	—	2	3	7	12
No FDGS	31	—	7	—	5	—	43	—
4th: FDGS	0	—	1	1	0	—	1	1
No FDGS	18	—	2	—	3	—	23	—
5th: FDGS	0	—	0	—	0	—	0	—
No FDGS	9	—	5	—	1	—	15	—
Total: FDGS	31	54	14 (32.5%)	18	11 (28.9%)	17	56 (23.1%)	89
No FDGS	130	—	29	—	27	—	186	—
TOTAL	161	—	43	—	38	—	242	—

Sources: Survey of cemeteries in West, North, and South Brookfield, Spencer, and Sturbridge; Valuation, 1793 (Massachusetts State House, Boston); *Catalogue of the Members of the Congregational Church in West Brookfield* (West Brookfield, Mass., 1861); *The Confession . . . of the First Congregational Church in North Brookfield* (West Brookfield, Mass., 1878); *Rules of Order . . . of the Evangelical Congregational Church in Brookfield* (West Brookfield, Mass., 1878); *Manual . . . of the Congregational Church, in Sturbridge* (West Brookfield, Mass., 1843); Membership Book, First Congregational Church of Spencer, Mass. (MS., church collection).
[a] Individual church members identified on 1783 Valuation.
[b] FDGS: Face-decorated gravestone linked to individual[a] within nuclear family (see n. 44).

Table 4. Baptists, Face-Decorated Gravestones, and the 1783 Valuation

Quintile, 1783 Valuation	Leicester Individuals[a]	Stones	Sturbridge Individuals	Stones	Charlton Individuals	Stones	Total Individuals	Stones
1st: FDGS[b]	1	2	2	4	0	—	3 (11.1%)	6
No FDGS	8	—	6	—	10	—	24	—
2d: FDGS	0	—	1	2	0	—	1	2
No FDGS	5	—	7	—	10	—	22	—
3d: FDGS	0	—	1	1	0	—	1	1
No FDGS	5	—	4	—	3	—	12	—
4th: FDGS	0	—	0	—	0	—	0	—
No FDGS	2	—	2	—	3	—	7	—
5th: FDGS	0	—	0	—	0	—	0	—
No FDGS	1	—	2	—	6	—	9	—
Total: FDGS	1	2	4	7	0	—	5 (6.3%)	9
No FDGS	21	—	21	—	32	—	74	—
TOTAL	22	—	25	—	32	—	79	—

Sources: Survey of cemeteries in Leicester, Sturbridge, and Charlton; Valuation, 1783 (Massachusetts State House, Boston); Records of the Greenville Baptist Church, Leicester, Mass., vol. 1 (MS., Trask Library, ANTS); Hiram C. Estes, "Historical Discourse," in *The Greenville Baptist Church* (Worcester, Mass., 1887), 26ff.; Henry Fisk, "The Testimony of a People . . ." (Backus Papers, ANTS); The Records of the Baptist Church of Christ in Sturbridge (Old Sturbridge Village, Mass.); Holmes Ammidown, *Historical Collections* (New York, 1877), 2:176–79.
[a] Individual male church members, elders, deacons, certificators, and messengers to the Warren Association.
[b] FDGS: Face-decorated gravestone linked to individual[a] within nuclear family (see n. 44).

Table 5. Baptisms in Eight Congregational Parishes, Southwest Worcester County, 1729–1792

	Years of recorded baptisms	Baptisms	Families in 1764[a]	Polls in 1764[a]	Estimated procreating families[b]	Baptisms per year	Baptisms per decade per estimated procreating family
Oxford	1761–1782	453	165[c] (1771)	238 (1771)	117	21.3	1.82
Holden	1742–1773	520	75	109	53	16.7	3.15
Sutton	1729–1779	1210	370	510	268	24.2	.90
Dudley	1744–1790	857	119	173[c]	84	18.6	2.21
Brookfield							
West Parish	1757–1775	290	71	110	49	16.8	3.43
North Parish	1750–1775	426	107	167	74	17.0	2.29
South Parish	1758–1775	366	105	162	73	22.2	3.04
Hubbardston	1770–1792	740	100[c] (1781)	132 (1781)	74	33.6	4.54

Sources: George F. Daniels, *History of the Town of Oxford, Mass.* (Oxford, Mass., 1892), 56, 266; Samuel C. Damon, *History of Holden, Mass., 1667–1841* (Worcester, Mass., 1841), 138–39; David Hall, *A Sermon Preached at Sutton* (Worcester, Mass., 1781), 26–27; James H. Francis, "Discourse Delivered on Fast-Day, April 9, 1835," (n.p., 1892); Nathan Fiske, "An Historical Account of the Settlement of Brookfield," *Massachusetts Historical Society Collections*, ser. 1, 1 (1792): 267; John M. Stowe, *History of Hubbardston* (Hubbardston, Mass., 1881), 90; Evarts N. Greene and Virginia D. Harrington, eds., *American Population before the Federal Census of 1790* (New York, 1932), 25–26; Nancy Osterud and John Fulton, "Family Limitation and the Age at Marriage: Fertility Decline in Sturbridge, Massachusetts, 1730–1850," *Population Studies* 30 (1976): 481–94.

[a]Or year indicated.

[b]Families minus 20% of polls (see n. 48).

[c]Estimated from a poll/family ratio of 1.5.

Distribution of families and polls in three Brookfield parishes extrapolated from 1776 record in "Brookfield, Mass., Local Records, 1673–1860," AAS.

the stability of his town lay in great part in his maintaining a parallel series of civil and religious states from birth to death in the lives of his people. Administering the covenant through an ordered sequence of rituals, he used his legitimating authority to bind the individual to the community while overseeing a gradual growth in saving grace as individuals moved from birth through marriage to death. By contrast, the Baptist believer followed a fundamentally different path through social time and space. Rather than an ordered sequence of rites of passage, the life of the Baptist centered on a single ritual—adult baptism by immersion—linked to a spasmodic emotional crisis. Importantly, the concepts of baptism and burial played equally important but distinctly different roles in the belief and ritual practice of both groups.

The Abrahamic command that the offspring of "God's covenanted people" receive the "seal of the righteousness of the faith," as transfigured into infant baptism under the new dispensation, stood at the heart of these opposed patterns of life crisis and rit-

ual. Infant baptism was central to the covenanted Congregational polity; among the Baptists, "infant sprinkling . . . went away like the chaff on the summer threshing flore."[47] Records of baptisms for eight Congregational churches on the Near Frontier indicate the impact of these beliefs (table 5). Measured against an index figure of "estimated procreating families,"[48] these records suggest that the ratio of Congregational baptisms per total births varied significantly with the state of religious orthodoxy in different towns and parishes. Sutton, Dudley, and the North Parish of Brookfield had relatively low rates of baptism, given the presence of Baptists in varying numbers. However, in places without such a presence, like Holden, Hubbardston, or the west or south parishes of Brookfield, the rates of baptism probably ran as high as 80 percent of births. Among Congregationalists the rite of baptism provided the newborn an admission to the "promise" of the covenant, whereas the children of Baptist parents had to wait until they could "repent and believe."

Table 6. Timing of Marriage and Church Admission: Congregational Males

Years between marriage and church admission:	Brookfield 1758–1800		Sturbridge 1751–1767		Spencer 1745–1800		Combined total	
	total	with wives	total	with wives	total	with wives	total	with wives
+ 11 to 40	12	8	5	3	25	14	42	25
+ 6 to 10	12	7	4	1	9	8	25	16
+ 3 to 5	33	28	2	2	14	9	49 (22%)	39 (17%)
+ 1 to 2	66	60	4	4	10	10	80 (35%)	74 (33%)
0	8	4	2	2	3	1	13 (6%)	7 (3%)
− 1 to 6	12	1	1	0	3	0	16	1
Total known	143	108	18	12	64	42	225 (100%)	162
Total unknown	35	17	18	8	19	8	72	33
TOTAL	178	125	36	20	83	50	297	195

Sources: *Vital Records,* and sources cited for table 3; see also n. 49.
With wives: Husband and wife joined church in the same year (same day in north and west parishes of Brookfield and in Spencer).
Unknown: Date of marriage unknown.

Table 7. Timing of Marriage and Church Admission: Baptist Males

Years between marriage and church admission:	Charlton 1762–1800		Sturbridge 1776–1800		Charlton and Sturbridge combined		Leicester 1776–1800	Charleton, Leicester, and Sturbridge combined
	total	with wives	total	with wives	total	with wives	total	total
+ 11 to 40	18	5	8	4	26	9	10	36
+ 6 to 10	9	4	4	3	14	7	3	16
+ 3 to 5	6	4	4	4	10 (12%)	8 (10%)	4	14 (13%)
+ 1 to 2	3	0	0	0	3 (4%)	0	2	5 (5%)
0	6	1	4	0	10 (12%)	1 (1%)	0	10 (9%)
− 1 to 6	15	3	6	1	21	4	5	26
Total known	57	17	26	12	83 (100%)	29	24	107 (100%)
Total unknown	22	3	7	2	29	5	25	54
TOTAL	79	20	33	14	112	34	49	161

Sources: *Vital Records,* and sources cited for table 4; see also n. 49.
With wives: Husband and wife joined church in same two-year period.
Unknown: Date of marriage unknown.

The Abrahamic injunction to baptize the "seed" of the covenanted people had a similar impact on a second set of civil and religious states. Congregationalists had a close association between family formation and church membership; Baptists had no such association (tables 6, 7). Among male Congregational church members in Spencer, Sturbridge, and the three parishes of Brookfield, 41 percent (93 of 225) joined the church in the first two years following their marriage, and 63 percent (142 of 225) within five years of their marriage. By contrast, comparable figures for the male church members of the Baptist churches in Charlton and Sturbridge were only 16 percent (13 of 83) and 28 percent (23 of 83), respectively. Even more dramatically, 53 percent (120 of 225) of the male Congregational church members joined the church within five years of marriage and in the same year as their wives (usually on the same day), while only 11 percent (9 of 83) of Baptist men joined both within five years and within *the same two-year span* as their wives. Among Congregationalists, church membership was a covenant "duty" to the new generation and, when paired with family formation, comprised the second in a series of rituals tied to specific life crises.[49] Spurning this covenantal and generational imperative, Baptist believers could join the church at any time in an adult lifespan.

Finally, Congregationalists and Baptists had drastically different interpretations of the nature and significance of earthly burial, differences of critical importance in their concern for the central event of the New Testament. While death and burial had important links in Congregational theology to the covenant of the Old Testament, the laying out of the dead in the graveyard was explicitly and literally patterned on the death, burial, and Resurrection of Christ. Of all the religious events in a Congregational believer's experience, his burial most faithfully imitated the scriptural type. The beliefs that underlay this typological fulfillment were spelled out most explicitly in a Congregational funeral sermon delivered in Brookfield in 1788.

> JESUS . . . visited the tomb, and explored the silent mansions of the dead; but this Prisoner proved too mighty for the King of Terrors; on the third day he revived, he burst asunder the marble bars of death, came forth, and shewed himself the very CHRIST. . . . He has bought the grave, it is no longer a prison, but a house, yea, his inner chamber, here the saints of the Most High God may rest in hope, till the last grand revolution.[50]

The metaphor of sleep pervaded the imagery of death in all its manifestations. The dead had "fallen asleep in Jesus," and would rise at the Resurrection.

> Their bodies that were purchased by Christ, and the temples of the Holy Ghost, shall come forth at the dawn of the everlasting day, beautiful and immortal, fashioned like unto Christ's glorious body: Yes, their faithful monuments will render back their dust, and with their bodies, their characters shall rise, and their righteousness go forth.[51]

Thus the religious life of the Congregationalist stretched from birth to Resurrection; death and burial acted as an initial and pivotal transformation of status within that continuum.

Arguments made by two Baptist ministers in tracts and sermons reveal the place of death and burial in the Baptist world, and permit the equation of the core ritual practices followed by Congregationalists and Baptists. Following an argument for the discontinuity of the Old Testament covenant and the inability of infants, Baptist minister Benjamin Foster of Leicester focused his attention on the scriptural precedents of the opposed modes of baptism used by Congregationalists and Baptists: a sprinkling of water versus the full immersion, or "plunging," of the body into a baptismal pool. In this context, he proceeded to establish a parallel between the "plunging" form of baptism and Christ's burial and Resurrection.

> "How is plunging a living body into the water a lively representation or resemblance of laying Christ's *dead and embalmed* body in the tomb hewn out of rock?" . . . As a burial has relation to a *grave*, so has baptism to *water*.— When Christ was buried, he was *laid down in the grave*; so are we *laid down in the water*, when we are baptized. After Christ's burial, he *arose out of* the grave; so, after our burial in baptism, we *arise out of* the water. To these circumstances the apostle evidently refers when he says, "buried with him in baptism, wherein also we are risen with him, through the faith of the operation of God, who hath raised him from the dead."[52]

In an earlier tract, Foster had quoted from an "ancient authority" on the "primitive" mode of baptism an argument that "plunging . . . signified the immersion of the old and the raising of the new man" and again made the parallel with Christ's death and Resurrection.[53] The rite of immersion, in other words, was implicitly linked with the evangelical conception of the converted being "dead to sin." Another Baptist minister who had grown up in south Leicester put the argument in somewhat more combative terms in a 1790 sermon.

> [Can] it be with propriety admitted, that a corpse is buried, if only laid in a grave with a little dust sprinkled on the coffin? I conclude not. Baptism is a representation of Christ's burial and resurrection: and when we submit to this ordinance, the very manner of our conduct in being baptized, publicly manifests our faith in the death, burial, and resur-

rection of the Son of God; and our own hope of a glorious resurrection from the dead.[54]

Summarized by Isaac Backus as "burying in baptism,"[55] these beliefs provide a pivotal explanation for the Baptist neglect of the traditional material culture of death and permit a summary of their attitudes toward rites of passage. The Baptists avoided the ritual symbolism of death because it worked to reinforce the blending of church and state central to the orthodox way. They also avoided a focus on death and burial because the religious function of these events as imitations of sacred types had already been accomplished in the plunging of converted souls into the baptismal pool. Rather than the ordered sequence of rites of passage that ascriptively tied Congregationalists to their territorial community, Baptists telescoped the rites of baptism, church admission, and burial into one cathartic and voluntaristic event. The explicit association of believer's baptism with Christ's death and Resurrection allows an important equation: baptism functioned for the Baptists in the same way that burial served the Congregationalists. Both were explicitly drawn from the same religious "type," and both marked the same liminal passage between the old and the new, the same transformation from the worldly to the glorified.

The patterned oppositions in human geography, social organization, personal life cycle, and religious belief and practice dividing orthodoxy and Baptist dissent encouraged and found reinforcement in metaphorical analogies to "earth" and to "water." Elaborating on a favorite text from Isaiah, one Congregational minister told the people of Spencer that "man at first sprung from the ground, as well as the grass, and the flower of the field—he is of the earth, earthy, and must soon fade and return to his original dust."[56] In the midst of the massive Baptist revival of 1779, the Baptist church at Wilbraham wrote to the Warren Association that "i[t] is wonderful to behold the change that has been in the space of one year with us. . . . God is to us a place of broad rivers." South Brimfield wrote that "[t]he Lord, of his mercy, is come down among us . . . like the showers of rain upon the mown grass."[57]

Those who remained within the established Congregational way were expected to "do duty and receive privilege" in both the material and spiritual components of a territorial community. For their mutual benefit, they were to accept and to participate in the collective regulation of town and church. Their final reward would come when they were laid to rest in the plot of earth reserved for the dead, where the corporate community literally arranged itself for the Resurrection. In sharp contrast, rather than being defined by an ascriptive territoriality, the Baptist community was made up of those who had experienced an intense, emotional moment of conversion, joining in a pure church and sharing in the covenant of grace. As did the local rivers, these dissenters ranged freely across town lines, disregarding the religious "duties" and "privileges" of any particular incorporated locality. A watery immersion freed the Baptist from the customary expenses of ministerial support and of the material culture of death; dead to sin and no longer of this world, he or she could pursue a personal calling without consideration for the reciprocal obligations of a corporate moral economy.[58] Where the earth was used to reinforce the Congregationalist's commingling of the civil and religious, the secular and sacred, the Baptists used water as the medium by which they kept these spheres rigidly differentiated.

Ultimately, their ritual uses of earth and water point to their contrasting relationship with a mythical and historical past. As they immersed themselves at conversion, the Baptists manifested their rejection of the Abrahamic covenant. In their refusal to mark their graves with traditional face-decorated gravestones, they refused to contribute to a received and continuous history. The Abrahamic covenant and the elaborate memorialization of the dead were central to the Congregational way. The covenant, they believed, had been transmitted to them by the "founders" through the "Great Migration." Those of the standing order owed a debt to the past for this "blessing." Through their commitment to the traditional culture of death they paid their respects to "usefull men," in effect symbolically and physically creating a new history continuous with the old. The "honorable dead" thus became a new "city upon a hill," speaking from beyond the grave through face carvings and epitaph inscriptions. Their "faithful monuments" stood as evidence of the townspeoples' continuing commitment to that organic established way; gravestones, in other words, worked to exhort the earthly Congregation to persist in that commitment.

*　　　*　　　*

The landscape of belief and ritual in early New England reveals two dimensions of the public culture of death. Without question, the dramatic elaboration of the symbolic and ritual ordering of death and the dead in the eighteenth century had roots in a general transformation of religion and society in the late seventeenth century. As exclusive congregations of the Puritan elect evolved into inclusive orthodox parishes, extended baptism, the Half-Way Covenant, and the "civil worship" of the dead provided means of expressing the moral unity of the corporate, covenanted community. Yet the evangelical dissenters of the Great Awakening and the New Lights, particularly the Separate Baptists, rejected the symbolism of death for precisely this reason. Just as they rejected the interweaving of civil and religious states of the orthodox way, so too they repudiated a constellation of beliefs, practices, and "graven images" that to them literally objectified that "unclean thing." Working in a contrasting configuration of ecology, society, and belief, they adopted a parallel ritual practice of adult baptism that anchored a profoundly different relationship of individual, family, and community.

Moving from the specific context of seventeenth- and eighteenth-century New England to the broader frame of Western Europe as a whole, we encounter difficulties in reconciling the complexity of local traditions in the New World with interpretive narratives built by historians with a Continental perspective. Indeed, in this case as in many others, evidence from the densely symbolic life of "provincial" culture complicates our understanding of what transpired at the supposed centers of France, England, Germany, or Italy. Philipe Ariès, for example, has argued that the development of "western attitudes toward death" can be viewed in a progressive sequence from a medieval conception of "death tamed" that focused on collective ritual and the certainty of salvation, through an early modern focus on the individual's struggle with death and judgement, to a romantic nineteenth-century focus on the mourning survivors.[59] Yet even in seemingly uniform New England this interpretation does not fit the evidence. Clearly, there were dramatically different attitudes toward death among the orthodox and the dissenters. In short, the material discussed here cannot be reduced to Ariès's sequence. Perhaps the dissenters were moving toward a romantic and sentimental conception of family and the

dead; certainly the Puritan settlers had rejected the collective medieval ritualism of death in favor of a focus on the individual and and his personal struggle for salvation.

But among the orthodox in eighteenth century New England, no simple transition toward a romantic cult of mourning hinged on the Great Awakening.[60] Rather, many of the qualities of Ariès's "medieval" attitude toward death actually seem to reappear at the end of the seventeenth century: collective ritual, association with an established and inclusive church polity, and the development of a repertoire of dramatic material symbols. If this revived medievalism was challenged by the sectarian dissenters, it was accepted and elaborated in an involutionary fashion among the orthodox—both gentry and yeomen—down to the end of the eighteenth century. Only in the radically transformed context of the new nation did the orthodox follow the path set by the dissenters.

As Congregational townspeople became evangelical citizens of a nation-state, the graven images of the dead were replaced by the ancient, classical symbols of the urn and willow; indeed, recent studies suggest that the political thought of eighteenth-century America was also shaped by surprisingly archaic categories.[61] Perhaps, then, the archaic qualities of orthodox New England's public culture of death are another dimension of what might be called the *ancien régime* of eighteenth-century America.

Notes

Versions of this paper have been presented at the Annual Conference of the Institute for Early American History and Culture, the Association for Gravestone Studies, and the Boston University Early American History Seminar. The author would like to thank Richard Beeman, Harry Stout, John Murrin, Robert Gross, Howard Solomon, David Hall, James Henretta, and especially Michael Zuckerman for their comments, criticisms, and encouragement.
1. Benjamin Gilbert, *A Citizen-Soldier in the American Revolution: The Diary of Benjamin Gilbert in Massachusetts and New York*, ed. Rebecca D. Symmes (Cooperstown, N.Y., 1980), 23, 26, 27, 63–75. While Gilbert was a member of a gentry family, many of the people he visited with were simple yeomen. On balance, Gilbert's visiting behavior was probably typical of most of the young men of his parish. For Gilbert's family, see Josiah H. Temple, *History of North*

Brookfield, Massachusetts . . . (North Brookfield, Mass., 1887), 600–601.

2. Ian R. Tyrrell, *Sobering Up: From Temperance to Prohibition in Antebellum America, 1800–1860* (Westport, Conn., 1979), 16–32.

3. The historical literature on death is large and growing. See, in particular, Philippe Ariès, *Western Attitudes toward Death from the Middle Ages to the Present* (Baltimore, 1974); Ariès, *The Hour of Our Death* (New York, 1981); Peter Benes, *The Masks of Orthodoxy: Folk Gravestone Carving in Plymouth County, Massachusetts, 1689–1805* (Amherst, Mass., 1977); Edwin N. Dethlefsen and James Deetz, "Death's Heads, Cherubs, and Willow Trees: Experimental Archaeology in Colonial Cemeteries," *American Antiquity* 31 (1966): 502–10; Gordon Geddes, "Welcome Joy: Death in Puritan New England, 1630–1730" (Ph.D. diss., University of California, Riverside, 1976); Allan I. Ludwig, *Graven Images: New England Stonecarving and Its Symbols, 1650–1815* (Middletown, Conn., 1966); John McMasters, *Death and the Enlightenment: Changing Attitudes toward Death among Christians and Unbelievers in Eighteenth-Century France* (New York, 1981); David E. Stannard, *The Puritan Way of Death: A Study in Religion, Culture, and Social Change* (New York, 1977); Dickran Tashjian and Ann Tashjian, *Memorials for Children of Change: The Art of Early New England Gravestone Carving* (Middletown, Conn., 1974); and David H. Watters, *"With Bodilie Eyes": Eschatological Themes in Puritan Literature and Gravestone Art* (Ann Arbor, Mich., 1981). Recent works that explore the relationships among death, the family, community, and religion include John Bossy, "Blood and Baptism: Kinship, Community and Christianity in Western Europe from the Fourteenth to the Seventeenth Centuries," *Studies in Church History* 10 (1973): 129–43; Natalie Z. Davis, "Ghosts, Kin, and Progeny: Some Features of Family Life in Early Modern France," *Daedalus* 106 (1977): 87–114; Emmanuel Le Roy Ladurie, *Love, Death, and Money in the Pays d'Oc* (New York, 1982); Gerald F. Moran and Maris A. Vinovskis, "The Puritan Family and Religion: A Critical Appraisal," *William and Mary Quarterly*, 3d ser., 39 (1982): 29–63; and Robert Blair St. George, "A Retreat from the Wilderness: Pattern in the Domestic Environments of Southeastern New England, 1630–1730" (Ph.D. diss., University of Pennsylvania, 1982), 305–59.

4. Perry Miller, *The New England Mind: From Colony to Province* (Boston, 1965).

5. These terms are borrowed from Margaret Spufford, *Contrasting Communities: English Villagers in the Sixteenth and Seventeenth Centuries* (Cambridge, 1974), and Robert Zemsky, *Merchants, Farmers and River Gods: An Essay on Eighteenth-Century American Politics* (New York, 1971), 262–63.

6. My discussion of the nature of religious change in late seventeenth-century New England draws on Miller, *New England Mind*; Robert G. Pope, *The Half-Way Covenant: Church Membership in Puritan New England* (Princeton, N.J., 1969); David D. Hall, *The Faithful Shepherd: A History of the New England Clergy in the Seventeenth Cen-* *tury* (New York, 1971); E. Brooks Holifield, *The Covenant Sealed: The Development of Puritan Sacramental Theology in Old and New England* (New Haven, Conn., 1974); and Charles E. Hambrick-Stowe, *The Practice of Piety: Puritan Devotional Disciplines in Seventeenth-Century New England* (Chapel Hill, N.C., 1982).

7. "Essay on the Laying Out of Towns, &c," *Collections of the Massachusetts Historical Society*, 5th ser., 1 (1871): 474–80; Edward Johnson, *Johnson's Wonderworking Providence, 1628–1651*, ed. J. Franklin Jameson (New York, 1910), 68–74, 96, 110, 116, 190; Perry Miller, *Errand into the Wilderness* (Cambridge, 1956; reprint ed., 1964), 1–16; Sumner C. Powell, *Puritan Village: The Formation of a New England Town* (Middletown, Conn., 1963), 74–115, 135; Richard L. Bushman, *From Puritan to Yankee: Character and Social Order in Connecticut, 1690–1765* (Cambridge, Mass., 1967), 54–77; Kenneth A. Lockridge, *A New England Town: The First Hundred Years, Dedham, Massachusetts, 1636–1736* (New York, 1970), 82, 94; Phillip J. Greven, *Four Generations: Population, Land, and Family in Colonial Andover, Massachusetts* (Ithaca, N.Y., 1970), 41–71; Timothy H. Breen, "Persistent Localism: English Social Change and the Shaping of New England Institutions," *William and Mary Quarterly*, 3d ser., 32 (1975): 3–28; David Grayson Allen, *In English Ways: The Movement of Societies and the Transferal of English Local Law and Custom to Massachusetts Bay in the Seventeenth Century* (Chapel Hill, N.C., 1981), 19–21, 232n., and passim; Allen, "'Vacuum Domicilium': The Social and Cultural Landscape of Seventeenth-Century New England," in *New England Begins: The Seventeenth Century*, ed. Jonathan L. Fairbanks and Robert F. Trent, 3 vols. (Boston, 1982), 1:1–52; and John W. Larkin, "Scattered Plantations and Decent Villages: Settlement Pattern and Community in Rural Massachusetts: A Preliminary Proposal" (typescript, n.d.).

8. Michael Zuckerman, *Peaceable Kingdoms: New England Towns in the Eighteenth Century* (New York, 1970), 46–122.

9. This generalization is based on a systematic survey of the regional origins of families settling in eleven towns in southwest Worcester County in the eighteenth century. Sources are available on request.

10. D. H. Chamberlain, "Old Brookfield and West Brookfield," *New England Magazine*, n.s., 21 (1899–1900): 503; Joseph I. Foot, *An Historical Discourse Delivered at Brookfield, Massachusetts, Nov. 27, 1828* (Brookfield, Mass., 1829), 42.

11. Frederick Burgess, *English Churchyard Memorials* (London, 1963), 28–29; Ernest R. Suffling, *English Church Brasses from the Thirteenth to the Seventeenth Century* (London, 1910; reprint ed., 1970), 17–20; K. A. Steer and J. W. M. Bannerman, *Late Medieval Monumental Sculpture in the West Highlands* (Edinburgh, 1971), 82ff.; A. Graham, "Headstones in Post-Reformation Scotland," *Proceedings of the Society of Antiquaries of Scotland* 81 (1957–58): 1–9; Keith Thomas, *Religion and the Decline of Magic* (New York, 1971), 32–33; Stannard, *Puritan Way of Death*, 103–8;

Ludwig, *Graven Images*, 43ff.; Geddes, "Welcome Joy," 190ff.

12. For Marlborough, see Samuel Adams Drake, *History of Middlesex County, Massachusetts . . . ,* 2 vols. (Boston, 1880), 2:142–43; for other towns, see Caleb Butler, *History of the Town of Groton . . .* (Boston, 1848), 139–42, 263; Lilley Eaton, *Genealogical History of the Town of Reading, Mass., . . .* (Boston, 1874), 203, 567–68; and Lucius R. Paige, *History of Cambridge, Massachusetts, 1630–1877* (Boston, 1877), 232–33, 247. Watertown might be included in this group; see Drake, *History of Middlesex County*, 2:448–53.

13. Drake, *History of Middlesex County*, 2:410–11, 453, 490.

14. In fact, the procession "to the Grave in the South parish" described by Benjamin Gilbert was somewhat atypical on the eighteenth-century Near Frontier. Complex land titles dating back to the 1665 settlement meant that none of the parishes in Brookfield had meetinghouses adjacent to graveyards, and when parish division had broken up the center of the old town, the Hinckley family and others maintained rights in the old burial ground in the South Parish while attending meeting in the North Parish. See Temple, *History of North Brookfield*, 262–63. For Southborough, Athol, and Spencer, see *History of Worcester County, Massachusetts*, 2 vols. (Boston, 1879), 1:218; 2:289, 329. For other examples of proprietary committee decisions, see *History of Worcester County*, 1:528, 562; 2:21, 364, 392, 515.

15. *History of Worcester County*, 2:120, 159.

16. This characterization draws on the concept of "dramaturgy" as developed in the work of Rhys Isaac, most notably in *The Transformation of Virginia, 1740–1790* (Chapel Hill, N.C., 1982); see also Isaac's essay in this volume.

17. Peter Benes, "Additional Light on Wooden Grave Markers," *Essex Institute Historical Collections* 111 (1975): 53–64; Benes, *Masks of Orthodoxy*, 42–43; Ludwig, *Graven Images*, 238ff.; Burgess, *English Churchyard Memorials*, 117–18.

18. Hambrick-Stowe, *Practice of Piety*, 29–30, 197–277; David D. Hall, "The Gravestone Image as a Puritan Cultural Code," *Annual Proceedings of the Dublin Seminar for New England Folklife: Puritan Gravestone Art* (1976): 23–32; Ludwig, *Graven Images*, 58ff.; Stannard, *Puritan Way of Death*, 112–15; Geddes, "Welcome Joy," 254ff.

19. "Thomas Dudley (Ah! Old Must Die)," in Kenneth Silverman, ed., *Colonial American Poetry* (New York, 1968), 132–33, quoted in Tashjian and Tashjian, *Memorials for Children of Change*, 40; Cotton Mather, *Death Made Easy and Happy* (London, 1701), 94, quoted in David Stannard, "Death and Dying in Puritan New England," *American Historical Review* 78 (1973): 1314.

20. For the transformation of carving idioms in the eighteenth century, see James Deetz and Edwin N. Dethlefsen, "Some Social Aspects of New England Colonial Mortuary Art," *American Antiquity* 36 (1971): 30–38; Dethlefsen and Deetz, "Death's Heads, Cherubs, and Willow Trees"; Ludwig, *Graven Images*, 33–52; Benes, *The Masks of Ortho-*

doxy; and Watters, *"With Bodilie Eyes."* It should be emphasized that I disagree with their interpretation that the Great Awakening specifically, and the evangelical impulse more generally, was the most significant influence on eighteenth-century gravestone carving. In fact, if anything, Old Light rather than New Light beliefs were the more significant influence. For criticisms of the "Great Awakening hypothesis," see Hall, "Gravestone Image as Cultural Code"; Lance R. Mayer, "An Alternative to Panofskyism: New England Grave Stones and the European Folk Art Tradition," *Annual Proceedings of the Dublin Seminar for New England Folklife: Puritan Gravestone Art II* (1978): 5–18; and John L. Brooke, "Society, Revolution, and the Symbolic Uses of the Dead: An Historical Ethnography of the Massachusetts Near Frontier, 1730–1820" (Ph.D. diss., University of Pennsylvania, 1982), 448–50, 450 n. 14. Carvings with the initials of the deceased on either side of the soul effigy are most common in the Connecticut Valley in the second half of the eighteenth century and can be seen in the cemeteries in Hadley, Quabbin Hill, Wales, North Brookfield, Mass., and Windsor, Conn.; see Ludwig, *Graven Images*, plate 83, and Edmund V. Gillon, *Early New England Gravestone Rubbings* (New York, 1966), plate 32.

21. This theme from Hebrews 11:4 was commonly used in funeral sermons to argue that the dead had a continuing moral influence over the living. See Abel Stiles, *Death God's Monitor to the Living* (Providence, R.I., 1768), for a full development of this argument by a Congregational minister in Woodstock, Conn.

22. Samuel Mather, *A Testimony from the Scripture against Idolatry and Superstition . . .* (Cambridge, 1672; reprint ed., 1725), 5, quoted in Tashjian and Tashjian, *Memorials for Children of Change*, 8–9.

23. For discussions of seventeenth-century funerals, see Geddes, "Welcome Joy," 190ff.; Tashjian and Tashjian, *Memorials for Children of Change*, 20ff.; Ludwig, *Graven Images*, 58ff.; Sylvester Judd, *History of Hadley . . .* (Springfield, Mass., 1905), 239ff.; William S. Pattee, *History of Old Braintree and Quincy* (Quincy, Mass., 1878), 111–12; and Williston Walker, *The Creeds and Covenants of Congregationalism* (New York, 1893), 79.

24. The pattern of the eighteenth-century funeral can best be followed in the diaries of Ezra Stiles and William Bentley. See in particular *The Literary Diary of Ezra Stiles*, ed. Franklin B. Dexter, 3 vols. (New Haven, Conn., 1901), 1:437, 529, 543; 3: 27ff., 280ff., 313, 315ff., 318–20, 522–23; *The Diary of William Bentley, D.D.*, 4 vols. (Salem, Mass., 1905–14), 1:106–7. Newspaper obituaries and funeral sermons suggest the wide acceptance of this new funeral route. For these hints, and the persistence of the jeremiad theme, see Solomon Stoddard, *God's Frown in the Death of Usefull Men. Shewed in a Sermon Preached at the Funeral of the Honourable Col. John Pynchon, Esq. . . .* (Boston, 1703); John Phipps, *A Breach in Jerusalem's Walls Deplored. A Sermon at Oxford, May 31st, 1761, on the Death of Reverend John Campbell . . .* (Boston, 1761); and Nathan Fiske, *The Character and Blessedness of a Diligent and*

Faithful Servant. A Sermon Delivered at Brookfield, October 16, 1779, at the Funeral of the Honourable Jedidiah Foster . . . (Providence, R.I., 1779).

25. Walker, *Creeds and Covenants,* 79n; *Literary Diary of Ezra Stiles,* ed. Dexter, 1:565; 3:519.

26. See note 6, above, and Joseph Haroutunian, *Piety vs. Moralism: The Passing of the New England Theology* (New York, 1970), chap. 5; Sacvan Bercovitch, *The Puritan Origins of the American Self* (New Haven, Conn., 1975), chap. 3; Bercovitch, *The American Jeremiad* (Madison, Wis., 1978), chaps. 3, 4; and Norman Pettit, *The Heart Prepared: Grace and Conversion in Puritan Spiritual Life* (New Haven, Conn., 1966), chap. 6. On the particular issue of the admission of the unchurched to the Half-Way Covenant, see Pope, *Half-Way Covenant,* 250–51.

27. Newbury, Hingham, Ipswich, Chelmsford, Sudbury, Beverly, Cambridge, Hampton (N.H.), Salem, Lynn, and Reading all supported an inclusive polity before the 1670s; see the respective references in Pope, *Half-Way Covenant,* 16, 225, 207, 255, 23–24, 25–26, 142, 140, 49, 38, 28, 37, 49, 142–43, 141, 38, and Allen, *In English Ways,* 69, 92–94. In the first six of these towns the meetinghouse and burial ground were established immediately adjacent to each other. For meetinghouse and burial ground locations, see *County Atlas of Middlesex, Massachusetts* (New York, 1875) in combination with Drake, *History of Middlesex County,* 1:370–76; 2:362, 399–404; Paige, *History of Cambridge,* 232–33, 247; John J. Currier, *History of Newbury, Massachusetts, 1635–1902* (Boston, 1902), 59, 61, 654; *History of the Town of Hingham, Massachusetts,* 3 vols. (Hingham, Mass., 1893), 1:358; Joseph B. Felt, *History of Ipswich, Essex, and Hamilton* (Cambridge, Mass., 1834), 194, 243; Felt, *Annals of Salem,* 2 vols. (Salem, Mass., 1845–49), 1:283; Edwin M. Stone, *History of Beverly, Civil and Ecclesiastical, from Its Settlement in 1630 to 1842* (Boston, 1843), 205; *Standard History of Essex County, Massachusetts* (Boston, 1878), 249. For Reading, see Lilley Eaton, *Genealogical History,* 567–68; Chester W. Eaton et al., *Proceedings of the 250th Anniversary of the Ancient Town of Redding . . .* (Reading, Mass., 1896), 235; and Pope, *Half-Way Covenant,* 38, 139–40, 249.

28. Dedham, Roxbury, Boston First Church, Woburn, Dorchester, and Charlestown all opposed extended baptism or delayed its implementation. See respective references in Pope, *Half-Way Covenant,* 20, 141, 32–33, 138–39, 152–84, 25–26, 53, 188, 198, 226–31, 33, 214–19, and Lockridge, *New England Town,* 34–36. For meetinghouse and burial ground locations, see Frank Smith, *A History of Dedham, Mass.* (Dedham, Mass., 1936), 144; Francis S. Drake, *The Town of Roxbury . . .* (Roxbury, Mass., 1878), 95–98; Darrett B. Rutman, *Winthrop's Boston: A Portrait of a Puritan Town, 1630–1649* (Chapel Hill, N.C., 1965), 38; Samuel Sewell, *The History of Woburn, in Middlesex County, Mass.* (Boston, 1878), 77; William R. Cutter and Edward F. Johnson, comps., *Transcripts of Epitaphs in Woburn First and Second Burial-Grounds* (Woburn, Mass., 1890), 3; W. D. Orcutt, *A Narrative History of Good Old Dorchester, 1630–*

1893 (Cambridge, Mass., 1893), 223–24; and Richard Frothingham, Jr., *History of Charlestown, Massachusetts* (Charlestown, Mass., 1845–49), 48n, 94, 95.

29. Benes, *Masks of Orthodoxy,* 27, 196–97; Pope, *Half-Way Covenant,* 200. Evidence for the pattern of adoption of death's head imagery in Massachusetts Bay comes from an ongoing survey by the author. For the "Charlestown carver," see Ludwig, *Graven Images,* 287–96.

30. Emory Washburn, *Historical Sketches of the Town of Leicester, Massachusetts, during the First Century from Its Settlement* (Boston, 1860), 9–10, 127–30; Louis E. Roy, *History of East Brookfield, Massachusetts, 1686–1970* (Worcester, Mass., 1970), 43.

31. John M. Stowe, *The History of Hubbardston, Worcester County, Massachusetts* (Hubbardston, Mass., 1881), 123, 130.

32. Henry Fisk, "The Testimony of a People Inhabiting the Wilderness" (1753), MS in Isaac Backus Papers, Trask Library, Andover-Newton Theological School, Newton, Mass. (hereafter ANTS); "Letters of the Sturbridge Separates," MS in Congregational Library, Boston, quoted in Ola Winslow, *Meetinghouse Hill, 1630–1783* (New York, 1952), 232–35.

33. *History of Worcester County,* 1:334–35; Washburn, *Historical Sketches,* 89; James Draper, *History of Spencer, Massachusetts . . .* (Worcester, Mass., 1860), 92; Mortimer Blake, *A Centennial History of the Mendon Association of Congregational Ministers* (Boston, 1853), 95.

34. For an overview, see Walker, *Creeds and Covenants,* 241–44, 283–87.

35. C. C. Goen, *Revivalism and Separatism in New England, 1740–1800: Strict Congregationalists and Separate Baptists in the Great Awakening* (New Haven, Conn., 1962); William G. McLoughlin, *New England Dissent, 1630–1833: The Baptists and the Separation of Church and State,* 2 vols. (Cambridge, Mass., 1971), 1:pts. 5, 6; and McLoughlin, "The First Calvinist Baptist Association in New England, 1754?–1767," *Church History* 36 (1967): 410–18.

36. Washburn, *Historical Sketches,* 82, 84, 459; Hiram C. Estes, "Historical Discourse," in *The Greenville Baptist Church of Leicester, Mass.* (Worcester, Mass., 1887), 20, 31; Samuel S. Greene, *Genealogical Sketch of Descendants of Thomas Greene of Malden, Mass.* (Boston, 1858), 12–13; Holmes Ammidown, *Historical Collections . . . ,* 2 vols. (New York, 1877), 2:176–78; Temple, *North Brookfield,* 282; *Vital Records* of Leicester, Spencer, Charlton, Sturbridge, and Brookfield.

37. *Vital Records; The Confession of Faith and Covenant of the First Congregational Church in North Brookfield, Mass., with a Catalogue of the Members (1752–1878)* (West Brookfield, Mass., 1878); *Manual for the Use of the Members of the Congregational Church, in Sturbridge, January, 1843* (West Brookfield, Mass., 1843), 26–31; "Membership Book, First Congregational Church of Spencer, Massachusetts" (Manuscript, church vault); Greenville (Leicester, Mass.) Baptist Church Records, vol. 1, ANTS; Ammidown,

Historical Collections, 2:176–79; Temple, *North Brookfield*, 282.

38. For sources, see table 2.

39. Lot maps in Draper, *History of Spencer*; Washburn, *Historical Sketches*; Temple, *North Brookfield*; Roy, *East Brookfield*, 45. Spencer Congregational Pew List (1771) in Draper, *History of Brookfield*, 138–39; North Brookfield Covenant Signers (1754) in Temple, *North Brookfield*, 252–53; Leicester Pew List (1783) in Leicester General Records, 1745–1787 (Leicester Town Hall), 338–40. For Baptists, see note 32, above; Greenville Baptist Church Records, vol. 1; and Temple, *North Brookfield*, 282. For Baptist meetinghouse locations in Worcester County, see Ammidown, *Historical Collections*, 1:facing 58, facing 206, 448ff.; 2: facing 31, 100, 105–6, facing 164, 182; Estes, "Historical Discourse," 34; Joseph Hodges, *Historical Sketch of the Baptist Church in Brookfield* (Brookfield, Mass., 1850), 15; Anna R. Leonard, "The Church on Fisk Hill . . . ," *Quinebaug Historical Society Leaflets* (n.d.): 2, 5, 35; Washburn, *Historical Sketches*, 16, 61, 115, 398; and Joseph S. Clark, *An Historical Sketch of Sturbridge, Mass.* (Brookfield, Mass., 1838), 38. For Baptist meetinghouse (and burial ground) locations in the Hampshire County towns of Ashfield, Granby, Montague, New Salem, South Brimfield, and Wilbraham, see Nathaniel B. Sylvester, ed., *History of the Connecticut Valley in Massachusetts*, 2 vols. (Philadelphia, 1879), 1:743–44, 546, 736–37, 561–62, 669; 2:1070–72, 1013. For Congregational meetinghouse locations, see *History of Worcester County*, 1:347, 349, 352, 363–64, 367, 620; 2:120, 159, 173, 196, 329, 364.

40. Fisk, "Testimony of a People."

41. Gravestones: personal survey of all eighteenth-century stones in southwest Worcester County. Here and below the only stones discussed are those for persons aged sixteen or over. For church members and pewholders, see notes 37 and 39, above; and *Catalogue of the Members of the Congregational Church in West Brookfield, from 1758–1861* (West Brookfield, Mass., 1861); *Rules of Order and Discipline, Articles of Faith and Covenant of the Congregational Church in Brookfield, Mass., with Historical Notes and Names of Officers and Members* (West Brookfield, Mass., 1878); Sturbridge pewholder list (1783), Sturbridge Town Records, vol. 3; and Charlton Congregational pew list, 1773, in D. Hamilton Hurd, ed., *History of Worcester County, Massachusetts, with Biographical Sketches of Many of Its Prominent Men* (Philadelphia, 1889), 750; and Charlton Congregational proprietors, 1798, in Ammidown, *Historical Collections*, 2:172.

42. Thirty-eight of the 83 face-decorated stones in the south and north parishes of Brookfield were for Congregational church members, and 13 of 44 in Spencer. I am endebted to Maris Vinovskis for suggesting this breakdown.

43. Washburn, *Historical Sketches*, 87–88, 162; Anson Titus, "Cemeteries," in *Charlton Historical Sketches* (Southbridge, Mass., 1877), 3–4, 10–13; *Vital Records* for Dudley and Sutton. For Hampshire County towns, see n. 39, above.

44. These tables indicate the number of male church members who can be identified on the 1783 valuation, as well as the number of members for whom a face-decorated gravestone can be found for themselves, their wives, their parents, or their dependent children who had reached the age of sixteen. In each case the link with a gravestone is made only once and with the wealthiest of the possible candidates.

45. McLoughlin, *Isaac Backus and the American Pietistic Tradition* (Boston, 1967), 74–76.

46. For a discussion of this debate in the eighteenth century, see Haroutunian, *From Piety to Moralism*, 97ff. The sixteenth- and seventeenth-century background is discussed in Holifield, *Covenant Sealed*, 1–108, 139–96; and McLoughlin, *New England Dissent*, 1:26–48.

47. For examples of the Congregational position, see Elisha Fish, *Japheth Dwelling in the Tents of Shem; or, Infant Baptism Vindicated* (Boston, 1772), and Nathan Fiske, "The Importance of Baptism," in *Twenty-Two Sermons on Various and Important Subjects; Chiefly Practical* (Worcester, Mass., 1794). For the Baptist position, see Fisk, "Testimony of a People"; Benjamin Foster, *God Dwelling in the Tents of Shem; or, Believers Baptism Vindicated . . .* (Worcester, Mass., 1775), and Foster, *Primitive Baptism Defended in a Letter to the Rev. John Cleaveland* (Salem, Mass., 1784).

48. The category of "estimated procreating families" used in table 5 was calculated using the enumerated aggregates of polls and families recorded for each town in the 1764 census and by extrapolating from census figures from the 1800 U.S. Census for New York State. The assumptions here are that the number of men over 45 years of age would roughly correspond to the number of nonprocreating families and that census figures for frontier counties in New York in 1800 could be extrapolated to Worcester County in the 1760s. The counties of Oneida, Rensselaer, Schoharie, and Montgomery each had a ratio of between 91 and 97.3 males over 16 to males under 16 in 1800; Worcester County in 1764 had a ratio of 95.8. Assuming that other characteristics of the male age structure were roughly the same, the combined totals of 4,084 males over 45 and 20,738 polls in these four counties were used to derive a percentage of 19.7—rounded to 20.%—to apply to the Worcester County data for 1764. Thus: "estimated procreating families" equals total families minus 20% of polls.

49. Tables 6 and 7 include people admitted by profession to the three parishes of Brookfield and the Sturbridge Baptist Church, and by profession and letter to the Sturbridge and Spencer Congregational churches and to the Charlton and Leicester Baptist churches, since the records for the latter group do not distinguish between the two modes of admission. Wives of men joining the Leicester Baptist Church cannot be indicated due to fragmentary records of female admission. This analysis does not include 309 people entered as members of the Congregational Church in the North Parish of Brookfield in 1774–76, 1793–95, and 1798 but without dates or "manner of admission." These were periods when the church was without a minister, and these people were probably admitted in some form of consensus-

building covenant renewal. Counting both admissions by letter and profession, the five Congregational churches admitted 893 people in the years covered: 330 men (37%), 212 women at the same time as their husbands (24%), and 351 other married and unmarried women (39%). The Baptist churches in Charlton and Sturbridge admitted 306 people: 124 men (41%), 37 women with their husbands (12%), and 145 other women (47%). Thus these tables account for roughly 60% of Congregational admissions and 50% of Baptist admissions. No systematic attempt has been made to analyse the 496 women who did not join with their husbands. The impression from scanning the Congregational records is that greater numbers of married women joined alone in the earlier decades, with increasing numbers of unmarried women joining in the 1780s and 1790s. The focus here is on male behavior because it is well established that men were less likely to become church members for purely religious or evangelical motives. See Nancy F. Cott, *The Bonds of Womanhood: "Women's Sphere" in New England, 1780–1835* (New Haven, Conn., 1977), and Lonna Malsheimer, "New England Funeral Sermons and Changing Attitudes toward Women" (Ph.D. diss., University of Minnesota, 1976). For an indication of the importance of generational motives for church membership, see the Congregational covenant relations from the 1750s and 1760s recorded in Haynes, *Historical Sketch*, 39–42.

50. Daniel Foster, *Consolation in Adversity and Hope in Death. A Sermon Preached on the Death of Jeduthan Baldwin* . . . (Worcester, Mass., 1789), 12.

51. Daniel Foster, *Consolation*, 15.

52. Benjamin Foster, *Primitive Baptism Defended*, 25–26, emphasis in original.

53. Benjamin Foster, *The Washing of Regeneration; or, The Divine Right of Immersion* . . . (Boston, 1779), 29.

54. Thomas Green, *A Sermon Delivered October 24, 1790; to the Baptist Church and Congregation in Cambridge. At the Administration of the Ordinance of Baptism* (Boston, 1790), 20.

55. Isaac Backus, *A History of New England, with Particular Reference to the Denomination of Christians Called Baptists*, 2d ed., 2 vols. (Newton, Mass., 1871), 2:222.

56. Joshua Eaton, "The Frailty of the Creature," in Eli Forbes, ed., *Some Short Account of the Life and Character of the Reverend Joshua Eaton, to which are Appended Seven Sermons* (Boston, 1773), 28.

57. Letters to the Warren Association, quoted in Backus, *History*, 1:278–79.

58. For discussions of the relationship between awakened, sectarian Protestantism and an increasingly instrumental economic mentality and behavior, see the classic formulation in Max Weber, *The Protestant Ethic and the Spirit of Capitalism* (New York, 1958), 144–54, passim; J. E. Crowley, *This Sheba, SELF: The Conceptualization of Economic Life in Eighteenth-Century America* (Baltimore, 1974), 50–75; and Bushman, *From Puritan to Yankee*, 135–43, 267–88. My interpretation of the relationship between the Great Awakening and economic behavior parallels that of Bushman, but with one critical qualification. Where Bushman

finds the Great Awakening sweeping an entire society driven by "covetousness," I argue that New Light sentiments—and their cultural and structural consequences—struck selectively among particular groups, leaving the majority relatively untouched, still bound by the restraints of a moral economy. For an important discussion of the limited impact of the Great Awakening, see Jon Butler, "Enthusiasm Described and Decried: The Great Awakening as Interpretive Fiction," *Journal of American History* 69 (1982): 305–25.

59. Lawrence Stone, "Death and Its History," review of *Western Attitudes toward Death: The Hour of Our Death*, by Philippe Ariès, *New York Review of Books*, Oct. 12, 1978, 22–32.

60. Stannard, *Puritan Way of Death*. 135–63. In his final study, Ariès has qualified the sharp edges of his sequence by discussing briefly "the persistence of tamed death" (*Hour of Our Death*, 201).

61. For a full discussion, see Brooke, "Society, Revolution," 517–44. On related shifts in political thought, see Bernard Bailyn, *The Ideological Origins of the American Revolution* (Cambridge, Mass., 1967); Gordon S. Wood, *The Creation of the American Republic, 1776–1787* (New York, 1972); and J. G. A. Pocock, *The Machiavellian Moment: Florentine Political Thought and the Atlantic Republican Tradition* (Princeton, N.J., 1975).

The Career of Colonel Pluck: Folk Drama and Popular Protest in Early Nineteenth-Century Philadelphia

In American cities in the eighteenth and nineteenth centuries, working people protested the selfish accumulation of property and inappropriate exercise of power by elites through a series of dramatic public rituals that turned ordinary streets into theaters of moral criticism. In antebellum Philadelphia, citizens took to the streets to express their opposition to the class biases of the Pennsylvania state militia system. In this essay Susan G. Davis explores the uses of street theater as a mode of political communication by focusing on one of its central antimilitia burlesques: the election of John Pluck as leader of the city's 84th foot regiment in 1825. "Colonel Pluck" was hilariously unfit for the job. Neither an upstanding leader of his community nor a model of physical strength and military discipline, he was instead a deformed, bowlegged stable hand. His election marked a symbolic reversal of nineteenth-century urban social order, an inversion that mocked the material prosperity and sense of self-importance that typified heads of militia companies. Bolstered by glowing newspaper accounts, Pluck's popularity was immediate. He not only toured Philadelphia but made triumphant visits to other East coast cities. As a humorous icon of popular sentiment, he poked fun at the ideals of "official" culture.

The militia system was the target of local protest because it was perceived as unfair. As members of "public companies," laboring people with little or no property had no alternative than to participate in required training days. Lack of attendance brought fines they could ill afford. Members of Philadelphia's propertied classes, however, could voluntarily join so-called private companies and either buy exemptions from training or simply pay any fines imposed. Private companies, too, functioned as elite social clubs where captains of local industry and politicians met to discuss common interests. In protest of this two-tiered system, working people first filed petitions for redress and then took their satirical display to the streets. There they put on a series of elections, parades, and burlesques that effectively merged eighteenth-century traditions of English folk drama—mock executions, "skimmingtons," and "rough music"—with the cacophonous, blackfaced fantasy of the nineteenth-century stage. Searching for a form of public discourse, working people successfully adapted earlier forms to the demands of class politics in a stratified urban society.

The processions that followed Colonel Pluck through the streets made the mockery of military discipline explicit by using costume in strategic ways. In response to the stifling "uniformity" they imputed to the militia's role in society, street performers created "anti-uniforms." Soldiers wore fantastical rags, patched pants, oversized hats, and mismatched shoes that mocked the crisp, well-pressed crease lines of militia issue. They carried dead fish instead of polished rifles and wore blackface as a laughable inversion of the dominant Anglo-American heritage of militia leaders. Street parades and processions were symbolically charged theatrical performances aimed not only at undercutting the pretentious airs of posturing elites but also at voicing the discontent of working people concerned that their own material lives were declining in the face of industrial capitalism.

Folk drama, often neglected as quaint festivity, found vigorous and challenging uses as a mode of political communication in early nineteenth-century Philadelphia. In the best recorded and most controversial of these dramas, the city's workingmen recycled older traditions of mock election, charivari, and costumed burlesque to attack Pennsylvania's unpopular militia system. One famous militia burlesquer, Col. John Pluck, stood for decades as the prime symbol of inversion, laughter, and defiance.[1]

In the career of Colonel Pluck in particular and militia burlesques in general, we can trace part of the history of folk drama in the city. This history is a facet of the transformation of older plebeian cultural forms, both rural and urban, in the nineteenth century. Here are keys to the culture and ideology of antebellum workers. Far from meaningless foolery, costumed parades and burlesque protests expressed the shared views of the men who performed them. To untangle and trace their meanings, however, we need to relate militia burlesques to the militia system and to the larger context of politics and society in the city.

The way these folk dramas were viewed by different audiences gives clues to the relationship between culture and class, performance and power, in the industrializing city. Masking and parodies in the streets were often seen by representatives of the propertied—the party press, reformers, and local governmental officials—as wild and irrational, part of the problem of public working-class behavior. Although militia burlesques did take place in disorderly, festive streets, behind officials' concern for order lay uneasiness over the uses of public communication and that foremost medium, the street. The plebeian traditions of street drama posed the problem of the relation between the political and the theatrical. When working-class political protest entered the streets, even in fantastic garb, those with stakes in the established order became uneasy.

*   *   *

Tracing the origins of urban folk dramas is frustrating; evidence is scattered, and documentation of eighteenth-century American popular culture was almost always random or accidental. Burlesques, parodies, and maskings were probably known in Philadelphia and its surrounding countryside from the earliest period of European settlement. After 1800, migrants from the city's hinterland and immigrants from overseas brought a variety of folk dramatic traditions. These older folk traditions interacted with the commercial culture of the stage and press to create a vibrant, local, vernacular culture.

The best known eighteenth-century uses of street theater were the stylized and ritualized actions of Revolutionary crowds and mobs. Philadelphians and other colonial urbanites relied on dramatized actions to voice disaffection, defend popular prerogatives, or threaten justice to wrongdoers. As Alfred Young has shown, colonial traditions of public political ritual were drawn from several sources. Some techniques of crowd justice—for example, hangings in effigy—borrowed from the official theatrical exercises of state power: public whippings, humiliations, and executions. Others, like tarring and feathering, were extrapolated from occupational custom. In this case, Anglo-American sailors recast a maritime punishment into a publicly visible mode of justice, applying it to landlubbers.[2] As the Revolution began in Philadelphia, the populace employed techniques of folk justice against tories, sympathizers, engrossers, and forestallers. Hangings in effigy, burnings of "stamp men," mock funerals for the loss of liberty, and ritualized public humiliation of crown officers were part of local Revolutionary mobilization.[3]

In many eighteenth-century cases, local elites acquiesced, assented to, or collaborated in the production of street dramas. Many crowd actions drew economic and political leaders and the "lower orders" together in revolt. A vivid account of the 1780 procession in "honor" of Benedict Arnold shows the cross-class nature of these street dramas. The traitor's effigy, borne along on a cart,

> was dressed in regimentals, had two faces, emblematic of his traitorous conduct, a mask in his left hand and a letter in his right from Beelzebub. . . . At the back of the figure of the general was the figure of the Devil shaking a purse of money in the General's left ear, and in his right hand a pitchfork ready to drive him into hell as the reward due for the many crimes which his thirst for gold had made him commit.

Arnold's mannikin was surrounded by didactic symbols, explaining his crime and declaring his treachery "held up to public view, for the exposure of his infamy . . . his effigy hanged (for want of his body) as a traitor to his native country and as a Betrayer of the laws of honour." The procession was led by "several gentlemen mounted on horseback," a "line of Continental officers," "sundry gentleman in the line," but also a "Guard of the City Infantry," drawn from among the "lower orders" and "attended by a numerous concourse of people, who after expressing their abhorrence of the Treason and the Traitor, committed him to the flames."[4]

The crowd could also act autonomously and aim their dramatic techniques—and their violence—at local elites and national policies. Rioting broke out in the city in 1779 over the "loyalist" sympathies of local leaders; later, some among the "lower orders" used riots and dramas to demonstrate support for the French Revolution and antagonism to the Jay Treaty and postwar tax policies.[5]

The political uses of impersonation, ridicule, and direct action by the crowd continued in the nineteenth century, but these uses were shaped by shifts in social relations. On one hand, elite support for direct and dramatic action against illegitimate authority waned as local property owners consolidated their own power. At the same time, reformers attacked, modified, and ended the public theatrical exercise of state authority in punishments and executions. Floggings stopped, the stocks disappeared, and public hangings took place inside prison walls.[6]

Even as the official display of power receded from public view, political and economic leaders reorganized public ceremonial roles for themselves. Through patriotic and military ceremony, affluent young men cast themselves in the roles of defenders of the peace and preservers of historical memory.[7] At the same time, those with economic and political power withdrew from participation in plebeian cultural traditions. Despite Quaker suppression of popular culture, affluent Philadelphians had probably understood, if they did not patronize, folk dramatic practices (for example, such Christmas customs as shooting in the New Year).[8] By the early decades of the nineteenth century, educated and propertied classes viewed plebeian dramas and customs as rude and quaint at best; more seriously, they called them barbarous and irrational, an evidence of the degeneration of the lower classes. Samuel Breck, recalling a late eighteenth-century Christmas mummers' play in Boston, commented on this change in attitude. The

mummers burst from the nighttime street into a rich household to perform their antic play and beg a treat in honor of the season. What, Breck wondered, "should we say to such intruders now? Our manners would not brook such usage a moment."[9]

While elites withdrew their tolerance for the old customs, the new commercial theater and popular press reinvigorated folk dramas. Media entrepreneurs conversely drew on the older genres and street culture to build popularity for their novel products.[10] Burlesque, the humorous or mocking exaggeration of traits, burgeoned in Philadelphia's popular theater and street literature, beginning at least as early as John Durang's imitations of Pennsylvania German dialect and manners in his traveling theatricals.[11] In the early decades of the century, caricatures and stereotypes, as well as stock characters, slipped lightly between the stage and street and back again, so that urban working-class life—the most famous example is Mose, the Bowery B'Hoy—was imaged on stages in every Northeastern city. Blackface minstrel characters, Shakespearean staples, and the theater circuit's favored stereotypes all made appearances in street parades.[12]

Parades parodying militia musters opposed the militia system and laws as well as the forced participation in the public militia companies. A widely felt hostility toward the militia laws and officers from the 1820s through the 1840s found expression in political platforms, literature, the theater, and humor—as well as in street parades. This antagonism had its roots in the history and structure of Pennsylvania's militia duties. The militia had always been a two-tiered organization reflecting social divisions and distinctions. Privately organized troops of propertied men had been raised in the mid-eighteenth century. During the Revolution, the radical Committees of Association organized Philadelphia's workers and poor men into public militia companies. After the war, class division persisted in the public-private pattern of military organization.[13] The universal service requirement mandated by federal law in 1792 asserted that defense duty was the right of all eligible men (whites, between eighteen and forty-five years), but Congress left the implementation of local preparedness to the states. While the federal government provided ordnance and supplies, the state governments retained the power to raise, train, and equip men.[14]

In Pennsylvania, perhaps especially in Philadelphia, militia duty weighed unevenly on rich and poor. The state required all eligible men to attend two annual training days and used roll-keeping and fines to enforce participation. Every man had to supply his own uniform and weapon or risk a fine for improper appearance. Workingmen found militia duty an onerous, expensive burden, because muster days deprived them of two or more days of labor annually, because uniforms and shoulder weapons were expensive, and because fines often exceeded a dollar a day. Laborers, mechanics, and artisans viewed militia duties as an unjust burden.[15]

Prosperous artisans, merchants, businessmen, and professionals found easy alternatives to militia duty. With more profitable uses for their time, most men of property paid fines or bought exemptions. The pleasure of belonging to an exclusive, self-regulating, and mainly volunteer militia troop beckoned to others. Although no one has written a social history of the militias in nineteenth-century Philadelphia, it is clear from newspaper accounts and troop histories that volunteer companies served as pivotal social and political organizations. Volunteer militias functioned as the building blocks of local political parties, as networks of influence, opinion, and conviviality. Men who drilled together also ate, drank, did business, and courted together, and a military title was an important prerequisite for election to public office. For men who wished to participate in military activities, the volunteer militia company provided a wide range of personal and social advantages.[16]

The distance between the private and public militia companies grew in the early nineteenth century after the Pennsylvania legislature made a series of decisions to support the volunteers at the expense of the public companies. These decisions were a piecemeal series of militia "reforms," responses to the embarrassments of the War of 1812, the increasing apathy and resistance among public companies, and, most important, to the political influence of the private companies' officers who were themselves political leaders. In 1818, the legislature exempted from further service any man who had belonged to a volunteer company for seven years. This time limitation was a powerful device to encourage volunteer membership. At the same time, lawmakers refused to recognize grievances against public training days and fines. Throughout the early 1820s and 1830s, the legislature rejected petitions to abolish or modify general musters; it stiffened fines and attempted to ensure their collection. In 1824, in the face of increasing demoralization in the public companies, the state restructured the system's funding. Federal monies and revenues from fines were now channeled into the volunteers' coffers.[17] With these new incentives, a plethora of new private companies sprang up, some of them existing only on paper. Yet because volunteer company membership was exclusive and expensive, the militia law had been made no more fair. In fact, reform furthered inequality and spawned continued controversy.

Within this context of antagonism and conflict, working-class members of public militia companies, frustrated with trying to change the militia law through petitions, turned to familiar techniques of folk drama to broadcast their critique of the militia system and its proponents, the officers. In mock elections and burlesque street parades, the opponents ridiculed the "malicious system," trying to end an unjust legal institution, as they put in, by laughing it out of existence.

The best recorded burlesque of a militia muster took place in 1825 in the Northern Liberties (see map of Philadelphia, fig. 5, p. 242). A poor and working-class district clustered around boatyards and docks, with cramped houses adjoining small workrooms, the Northern Liberties had a long history of resistance to unjust authority. Many of the crowd actions against loyalists had drawn personnel from this neighborhood; in the 1820s and 1830s, the adjutant general's militia fines collectors knew that a venture into the Liberties meant risking a pelting with rotten eggs, at the very least.[18]

One day in May 1825, at the election of militia officers, the Liberties' obscure foot regiment, the 84th, nominated and elected as its colonel John Pluck, "a poor, ignorant, stupid fellow," an ostler at a tavern stable.[19] Although the division officers execrated the 84th's choice and invalidated the first polling, a second vote confirmed Pluck by a vast majority.[20]

John Pluck's election was a joke, a slap at the division officers and high state officials. The *Saturday Evening Post* announced: "Pluck has been elected, Governor Schultze not withstanding, and there can be no question but that the gentleman will answer all honest and honorable anticipations. . . . True, it is a little out of his ordinary sphere, but what of that?"[21] A colonelcy was indeed above Pluck's station. As a laborer who cleaned stalls for a living, the new colonel ranked among the lowest of the low, especially compared to the other officers, who were usually lawyers, merchants, and bankers. A manual laborer, Pluck was often filthy, and since he owned no tools and part of his pay was in lodging, his work placed him in the condition of a servant or retainer. He could not even call himself an independent workingman. To elect him regimental colonel inverted all protocol, bringing the smell of the stables into the officers' tents. The *Post* explicated the pranksters' point: "'Honor and Shame from no condition rise: Act well your part and there the honor lies.' . . . If this be the case, Colonel Pluck is to all intents and purposes a right honorable man . . . he acts as well his part whether it is in cleaning out a stable or rubbing down a pony."[22]

The ostler's comrades elected him to show that a servant was a better man with a clearer sense of honor than titled and careering officers, appointed adjutants, and elected officials who time and again thwarted attempts at militia reform. The men of the 84th picked Pluck for more than his occupation and his brave last name. He was severely deformed and, according to several press reports, may have been mentally deficient. "Napoleon is low in stature—Pluck is lower still!" crowed a reporter. "I estimate him at five feet bare."[23] Extremely bowlegged, hunchbacked, and bent over, Pluck with his bulging eyes and huge head had been the object of neighborhood taunts for years.[24]

In electing Pluck, the men of the 84th followed a familiar pattern of social inversion for symbolic purposes. Ritual elevation of the deformed and deficient, common in European folklore, was found in the Feast of Fools of medieval England and the Abbey of Boys of early modern France.[25] Another more recent precedent suggested the mock election. At Garrat, near London, in the late eighteenth century an election spectacle drew both city gentry and rural people to see the investiture of a dwarf or hunchback as mayor, amid a week of festive license. During the political repression of the late eighteenth century, the Garrat election found its way into the literature of the London stage as part of a radical and comic critique of Parliamentary politics and personalities. The implication that the raucous Garrat election was more valid than the serious and corrupt system of repre-

sentation, in which every principal of law could be violated with impunity, connected neatly with radical, democratic sentiments.[26] Even the phrase "a Garrat election" moved into popular speech and glossed a travesty of fair play and established procedure. More broadly, the Garrat election stood as a muffled but unmistakable denunciation of a political system determined to trample the natural rights of ordinary men.[27]

The 84th had invented a novel variation on the Garrat election theme, one with specific local meanings and effects. Pluck was chosen not for a day of reversed role-playing but legally, to hold office for several years. His electors accurately aimed to make their point through inconvenience and embarrassment, as well as through laughter. The 84th pushed the militia burlesque beyond mock elections. To the division officers' chagrin, Pluck's duties included leading his troops through the city streets to muster at the Bush Hill parade ground. As officers could be criticized through the election, so battalion drills, "those vexatious parades," would be lampooned by a comic procession.[28]

The *Post* gives us a description of an addled Pluck and his cheering supporters at the spectacle:

On Wednesday last [May 18] was enacted the Grand Military farce, in which the redoubtable John Pluck made his debut in the character of colonel of the Merry 84th. The sport was not so great as was anticipated by the lovers of frolic and fun, and from the complete indifference with which the Colonel went through his part, apparently unconscious of everything around him, staring with stupid indifference and scarce possessing the spirit to answer occasional questions . . . which, the more plausibly to carry on the joke were put to him by his officers. It is said he once mustered sufficient Pluck to say "he did not know where they were going to march him but would tell them all about it when he got back, if he could remember the way. . . . " which was much applauded as a brave speech by his friends and clamorously encored by the great crowd which had gathered around his quarters.[29]

In the parade, the 84th used two strategies for attacking the militia law. The men simultaneously parodied public battalion days and the uniforms of the officers. The colonel made an outrageous officer, mounted on a spavined white nag and be-hatted with a huge *chapeau-de-bras*, a shoulder-covering woman's bonnet, the bow knotted under his chin. His baggy burlap pants were cinched up with a belt and enormous buckle; spurs half a yard long with murderous rowels and a giant sword parodied ceremonial military dress and made Pluck appear still shorter. The *Post* likely exaggerated Pluck's incapacity; he probably got the joke. It was reported that on taking command he shouted out, "Well, at least I ain't afraid to fight, and that's more than most of them can say!" The mock-muster was purposefully disorderly and topsy-turvy. With hurrahs, the regiment surged through the streets to Bush Hill,

> with the Colonel at their head but so encompassed by horsemen as to be out of sight of those on foot, who were only now and then favored with a glimpse of the little fellow's plume or his long rusty sword as it rose from its extreme length above his cap and served to show the zig-zag course he pursued. His regiment did not wear their uniforms but bore sticks and cornstalks . . . and huddled together in such ungovernable merry mood withall as baffles description, and was in reality "confusion worse confounded."[30]

The parade ground soon exhibited "as motley a collection of figures and as grotesque" as reporters could recall, yet the scene was "more numerously and fashionably attended than any parade of that kind ever witnessed."[31] Militia men with cornstalks and brooms were a familiar sight to Philadelphians: poor men had to carry mock weapons at Muster Day because they rarely owned shoulder arms. But men who objected to militia duties elaborated on this disadvantage, parodying themselves.[32]

Pluck's fame spread quickly. "No one talks of anything else," wrote the *Democratic Press*.[33] A few days later, theater crowds were shouting for Pluck, and he was in demand at the circus. For weeks, editorials complained of the spectacle and decried its effects. Letter writers defended Pluck in the papers; poetasters composed odes to his bravery; amateur historians proposed biographies; collectors saved "Pluckiana"; and the lettered linked his name with Butler's Hudibras and Jonson's Bobadil. New York and Boston papers picked up Pluck's story, and, catching the strains of popular antagonism to the militia system, the papers reprinted sarcastic descriptions of his activities,

Fig. 1. "Col Pluck's Toast at Morse's Hotel," lithograph, ca. 1828. This anonymous caricature of Pluck parodied contemporary heroic images of Andrew Jackson. (Photograph courtesy of the New-York Historical Society.)

to the delight of their readers. The ostler had become a phenomenon in commercial popular culture.[34]

The following spring Pluck led the "Bloody 84th" again, not only through the Liberties but around the city center and throughout the southern district of Southwark (see map, p. 242). He was joined by "fantastical corn toppers" and hailed by crowds of thousands. At the solicitation of New York newspaper editors, Col. William Stone and Maj. Mordecai Noah, Pluck made a tour (fig. 1). At New York City, he was "introduced," "armed and equipped in most ludicrous manner." Drunk, he "exhibited himself in his hotel room for 12½ cents to each visitor."[35]

A national sensation thanks to Stone and Noah, Pluck visited Albany, where he was "nominated for vice-president," toured Providence and Boston (fig. 2), where the police offered to arrest him as a vagabond, and moved on to Richmond, which made him the toast of the town.[36] By October 1826 he was back in Philadelphia long enough for a court-martial to attempt to end the farce. Pluck was pronounced incapable of holding office for seven years and cashiered.[37]

The hilarity that met Pluck's meteoric rise and his

Fig. 2. "Colonel Pluck," lithograph, 1826, by Pendleton of Boston. (Photograph courtesy of the American Antiquarian Society.)

subsequent and abrupt fall into obscurity might tempt us to dismiss him as an amusing oddity of popular culture. But Pluck's career deserves to be taken seriously; his contemporaries took the joke seriously, even while they laughed. Why else court-martial a poor, deficient laborer? Militia advocates argued that the burlesque exposed the militia system to contempt, but contempt had been long simmering and widely shared among workingmen. Pluck's parades and his transformation into an icon of popular culture concentrated this contempt, made a joke of it, and presented it publicly. The militia burlesque did not give the state a bad reputation; it made that reputation impossible to deny.

The press revealed and responded to the offense taken by military leaders. Outraged correspondents declared that Pluck had shamed the entire state; the system had sustained "a death blow." Some officers suggested that the legislature make it a misdemeanor in office for a person to parade in a borrowed uniform.[38] Still others thought that "something should be done to prevent the recurrence of such disgusting scenes." Irreverence for military authority attracted "many of the depraved part of the crowd"; "we saw everywhere surrounding us something filthy or debasing," reported the *Democratic Press*.[39]

For others, Pluck's election and parades were "a declaration of public opinion" about the way the militia law operated. As the *Saturday Evening Post* wrote of his election, "the friends of free suffrage and republican simplicity have eminent cause for congratulation. . . . And as to throwing up the commissions of the militia and the reputation of the state, why, who cares?"[40] A working-class public had made Pluck its symbol of thickheadedness in high places.

But corruption, more than ignorance, characterized Pennsylvania's office holders; the burlesque stood for "the recent election of the most illiterate and unfit candidates" and "the disrepute into which the system has sunk."[41] One "Colonel Washington" wrote:

It is the disgust with which I have seen so many of our offices filled by ignorance and imbecility that induces me to intrude. . . . Why should Pluck be the butt of aspersion when he is only the latest of a long list? . . . The question has long since ceased to be whether the candidate for an epaullette is acquainted with the duty to which he aspires, and the man who would propose such an enquiry on the election ground in Pennsylvania would be looked upon as a mere novice.

In fact, "Washington" alleged, the burlesque's message applied to political realms beyond the militia. Corruption had seeped into every state office.

Those gentlemen who are so tender of the reputation of our state [might] open their eyes a little wider. . . . [They] may open a much more important field of inquiry about our civil department . . . may commence at the very head and also through every branch. . . . [T]heir investigation will afford them numerous and much more interesting opportunities to complain that merit and qualification are not guarantees of office in Pennsylvania. . . . [S]ome of their objects would not be able to defend themselves as well as John Pluck who called himself an 'honest man.'[42]

Pluck's burlesque drew knowing nods as well as laughter. Using inversion, the elevation of the low and the investiture of responsibility in one who seemed an idiot, the mock militia men pointed the accusation of stupidity, self-interest, and dishonesty at public officials.

Pluck's popularity, accomplished through street performance, media accounts, and his tour, rested on widespread antagonism to the militia system and laws, an antagonism that sprang from the city's class divisions. Workingmen clearly had reasons to resent the law and disdain the officers—their hostility toward the unequal burden and the rise of "distinction" gave the joke its bite and force. Yet some among the educated, the propertied, and respectable saw the burlesque's humor, but saw it for different reasons and from a different point of view. For Philadelphians who felt uneasy about Jacksonian social and political change, especially the broadening of political activity and electoral participation, the elevation of a booby could symbolize all they feared from democracy. If militia troops functioned as proto-parties for artisans and mechanics as well as for elites, which we might suspect they did, Pluck's election could be read as labeling the leaders of ordinary men as illegitimate and unqualified. Indeed, this was a thrust of "Washington's" letter. The colonel and his crew might have let militia advocates and reformers laugh at the martial performance of the poorly clothed public companies. The men least able to laugh were the high division officers, charged by law with maintaining the unwieldy, unpopular system.

Evidently Philadelphia's drama was cycled through commercial culture, popularized by Pluck's grand tour, to be taken up in the countryside and in other cities. Opposition to the militia system persisted through the 1820s, 1830s, and 1840s, ending only with the abolition of public musters in 1858. The burlesques helped keep opposition alive and visible. Corntoppers became familiar at annual battalion drills in rural Pennsylvania, New York, and New England. In the spring of 1829, men at Pennsylvania training days substituted canes and cornstalks for muskets, prompting an editor to observe that "ordinary musterings are absurd," for "they only give a parcel of silly ones high titles" and "a little brief authority and a chance to strut their hour in regimentals."[43]

Albany and New York City witnessed large fantastical processions in 1831 and again in 1833. In Albany, "fusileers" and "invincibles" protested the state law dressed in wild costumes, women's curls, and enormous whiskers. One newspaper took up the theme typographically, printing its account of the "Grand Fantastical Procession" in jumbled, mismatched typefaces. In New York City, the Grand Processions were recorded in press reports, Mayor Philip Hone's private diary, and etchings.[44] One graphic artist registered the parades' protest against illegitimate authority and illustrated the connections between transatlantic cultural experiences by using the pseudonym "Hassan Straightshanks" (fig. 3), in a direct reference to the popular cartoons of the radical English artist George Cruikshank.

In Philadelphia, as the Workingmen's party and then the Democratic party took up the cause of militia reform, burlesquers continued their performances.[45] In May 1833 the men of the Northern Liberties revitalized the memory of Pluck. One Col. Peter Albright, a young man active in the Democratic party, allowed his company of the 84th to appear in "fantastical dress," calling themselves the "Hollow Guards." Albright's men marched

> to the music of a penny whistle . . . in no uniformity of uniform. . . . [Each] had endeavored to exceed the other in grotesqueness, and every variety of apparel and decoration was brought into this requisition. . . . The orderly sergeant bore on his right hand a wooden staff shaped like a sword on which was painted "defender of the laws". . . . The adjutant was . . . most ludicrously decorated with ribbons and patches of red flannel; his cap measured at least five feet in circumference. The standard bearer had one leg of his pantaloons red, the other white, and wore for covering an old fire bucket, with a painted rice fan for a cockade; on the seat of honor was lashed a knapsack with "The Bloody 84th" painted upon it. . . . The banner he carried bore on one side—Life Guards of Pennsylvania Senators. On the other, a sketch of Senator Rodgers of Bucks County. . . . Some of the privates were in calico frocks and some in small clothes [knee breeches]. One carried a fish for a weapon, another an old broom . . . a fourth was embellished with the figure of a heart placed conspicuously on his back [as if for target practice].

After this detachment came another "still more singularly attired."

Albright addressed the troops "with martial words," and as the solemn column of men took up the march, they were followed "promiscuously by

Fig. 3. "Grand Fantastical Parade, New-York," lithograph, December 2, 1833, by "Hassan Straightshanks." In this rare visual record of a militia burlesque, many traditional elements appear—antimilitia banners, men in blackface (or perhaps black), wild costumes, and a Pluck-like commander. (Photograph courtesy of the Prints and Photographs Division, Library of Congress.)

ununiformed members with umbrellas, broomhandles and sticks." These men trooped helter-skelter through all the principal streets, to the amusement of the downtown. "At every street corner they gained additional force," and the "thousands who followed entirely blocked up the streets."[46]

Again the press pointed to the explicitly political purposes of the enactment: "To all intents and purposes they looked as ridiculous as ridiculous could be and the object in view—that of establishing the folly and absurdity of our ordinary militia parades was most fully obtained." "Since the militia laws are clearly a farce, none should complain about this. . . . [T]herefore, let [the militia system] be ridiculed until those in authority either amend it or abolish it altogether."[47]

The militia officers, themselves experts at creating imagery through street ritual, did not appreciate

being made the butt of public jokes. Rather than allow the farce to grow into a spectacle à la Pluck, they arrested Peter Albright and prepared to court-martial him "for permitting unsoldier-like conduct." Although some newspapers favored Albright as "a martyr in the cause of the picturesque,"[48] he and his company had trod on important toes. State senator Rogers, whose portrait adorned the banner, was a militia general, editor of the *Doylestown Democrat*, and chair of the legislature's committee on the militia. Albright's parade was a response to Rogers's committee's decision to reject a report recommending the abolition of public trainings and the restructuring of fines. The committee, the press claimed, reported against the bill despite vigorous efforts by city delegates and unanimous support in the house, because Rogers and his friends were unwilling to abolish their own titles and commands.[49] As embarrassing as the display of the general's mug in a tatterdemalion street parade, the burlesque preceded an election for brigadier general by only a few weeks. Resurrecting the memory of Pluck and drawing on all the strains of antagonistic laughter at the pretensions of officers and uniformed militia men, the Hollow Guards threatened the legitimacy of command at a crucial moment, the time of the transfer and confirmation of power.

Far from dampening the guards' enthusiasm, Albright's arrest spurred them on. In the fall, they celebrated the colonel's acquittal with still more theatrical and incongruous costumes—and now, music. Again, they used anti-uniformity: "no two dresses bore the least resemblance to each other." As before, they borrowed images and costumes from the popular theater, "knights clad in armor, a cavalier clad in a bearskin with an iron charm around his middle, Indians, clowns etc." Beards and paint hid faces, and exaggeration had free rein. "Swords under the length of six feet in the blade were 'quite despisable'. Twelve feet was the regulation length of their muskets." In a jab at the serious ceremonialism of the volunteer militias, banners displayed random slogans like "Dinners baked here at the shortest notice." Banners also reminded the audience of the problems of office, merit, and authority, making use of such slogans as "Honor to whom honor is due."[50]

The burlesque continued, celebrating the guards' moral victory and opposing Albright's persecution. Each "exceeded in splendor all former exhibitions," and featured "three to five hundred men," "fully accoutred."[51] In late October, Albright appeared as a Revolutionary soldier. In a powdered wig, his face floured white and his nose generously smeared with "Spanish Brown" shoe polish, he bowed graciously to the crowd. By his Revolutionary garb, gentleman's wig, and brown bedaubed nose, Albright showed he had lost none of his nerve. His costume pointed to the disgrace brought on the militia system by the inequality of burdens and the machinations of self-interested leaders: the makeup literally called the officers a lot of "brown noses." Personal and political antagonism also blended as an effigy of William Hurlick, the city's despised fines collector, swung from a pole.[52]

The antimilitia protests continued in Pennsylvania and New England. In New Haven an "awful battalion" formed under the command of "Timothy Tremendous" to "shame all scarecrows." Their standard showed "a bull rampant," with a Revolutionary veteran "in reverse order [seated backwards] on his back and holding on by the tail," surmounted by the punning motto "The Bull-Work of Our Country." "Music was by callithumpian masters," a band wreaking havoc with broken pots and pans: "the very cats were

dumbfounded by it." A working-class ward in Easton, Pennsylvania, celebrated Jackson Day in 1834 with the election of a Pluck-like "Redoubtable Colonel Scheffler" and planned processions for training days. At Chambersburg, the *Repository* recorded a vast mock battalion in June 1835 with young men in blackface and patched and scavenged clothes. Wild weapons, rough music, and deformed horses were highlights of the parade. "So much for the useless militia system, which excites such indignation," and so much for training days, worse than useless "when men are trained for no other purpose than to make them weary."[53] These were only nearby variations on the mock militias; records of similar burlesque parades can be found from Maine to Georgia, and for later dates in the Midwest.[54]

In Philadelphia, burlesquers harassed militia officers for at least another decade. Colonel Thomas Duffield, long a commander in the Spring Garden district, addressed a volunteer militia convention in Harrisburg in 1842

> with a view to bringing to the notice of the officers present the extraordinary difficulties which they had to encounter in some portions of the county of Philadelphia in attempting to carry out the militia law. . . . [T]here were a large number of persons there opposed to military trainings, and they took every means in their power to bring the military into disrepute and cast ridicule upon them. . . . [They] appeared on parade grounds, dressed in fantastical dresses, and when officers attempted to make them do their duty, they raised riots and mobs.

Duffield reported that resistance spread beyond the parade ground. "When they attempted to collect fines from these persons, they would permit their property to be sold for fines and then bring suits against the officers."[55]

*   *   *

The political use of disguise and burlesque generally and fantastical militias in particular did not originate in Philadelphia; the notion of comic costumed street processions was borrowed from the charivari, or rough music. Violet Alford and Edward P. Thompson have documented and analyzed the uses of rough music, or "skimmington riding," in nineteenth-century England; Bryan Palmer has traced the survival and transformation of this method of folk justice in Canada and the United States.[56] The Philadelphia (and Chambersburg, Easton, New York City, Albany, and New Haven) mock militia parades shared much with European and American charivaris. The use of pots, pans, chamber pots, and household utensils as musical instruments; the elements of inversion, such as backwards seating on an ass, horse, goat, or bull were typical devices of rough musics. Singling out and mocking a transgressor—whether officers, a senator, or the fines collector—preserved the core of folk justice.

The charivari's older use was tied to the control of sexual mores and excess: newlyweds, partners in marriages deemed unnatural because of age disparity or the too-recent death of a spouse, adulterers, wife-beaters, husband-beaters, or others who overstepped the usual bounds of relations between the sexes and generations became targets of mocking, sometimes violent, processions. Palmer and Thompson argue that the charivari found its way into social criticism in the nineteenth century. In England, the skimmington became a community weapon against speculating landlords and other disrupters of older economic relations. Palmer cites an early nineteenth-century American "shivaree" aimed at a wedding celebration, not to tease the bride and groom, but to upbraid the family for using the party to distinguish themselves from their neighbors. The rough musicians directed their scorn at "d——d aristocratical and powerful grand big-bug doins."[57] Political uses of the charivari were thus local, aimed at known violators of social relations that, while not egalitarian, were seen as protected by the shared mores and expectations Thompson has called "moral economy."[58] Contempt for new sources of law and order or hostility to legal and political transformation also found expression in Canadian rough musics: charivari-ists violently protested the confederation of Canada in the 1830s.[59] There was also an earlier and continuing North American precedent; in the Helderberg region of New York State, tenants opposing their landlords' encroachments used calico dresses and tin-horned masks in their nighttime raids.[60]

Links between political protest and the charivari are also found in etymological evidence. In Pennsylvania, both charivari musicians and the bands accompanying mock-militias called themselves "callithumpians." This obscure dialect word was used in

the west of England to designate Jacobins, radical reformers, and "disturbers of order at Parliamentary elections."[61]

Although the connections are difficult to prove conclusively, other sources of the tradition seem to exist in the costumes and dramas of the Luddites, the secret society called the Scotch Cattle, and the Rebecca rioters in the British Isles. These protests by agricultural and rural industrial laborers relied on secret organization, disguised nighttime raids, anonymous threats, and the destruction of offending machines or of obstacles (turnpike gates in the case of the Rebecca riots, knitting frames in the case of the Luddites). Norman Simms argues that the use of folk dramatic techniques—disguises, secret cries, and mythical leaders—is evidence that the Luddites and their like saw themselves as defenders of community, the same community created by less antagonistic dramas, such as Christmas maskings.[62] Certainly Philadelphians heard, whether through the press or by word of mouth from recent immigrants, of the panic the Luddites caused in the English government and the complicity and support that people in textile districts gave the machine breakers.

*   *   *

Mock militias took a familiar form of folk justice and altered it to fit their specific local purposes. That cornstalk militia parades diffused and persisted shows that the issue they addressed was prevalent beyond Philadelphia. The popularity of the burlesques reveals the ease with which older British and European folk dramas could still express dissent, even in the very different, much less repressive political climate of the United States. The charivari had been used to regulate conduct among neighbors or to attack persons who threatened community norms. In the case of the fantastical militias, offenders were known, sometimes personally known to protestors, and their transgression affected the economic well-being of mechanics and artisans and offended their notions about social relations.

Pluck's burlesques and the workingmen's charivaris pushed folk dramatic protest beyond the immediate issue of the odious company drills. The militia system stood for a larger problem of social relations, which workingmen called "distinction." In the drills and conduct of officers, workingmen saw power—symbolized in titles and rank—exaggerated by an unrepublican fondness for prestige and self-differen-tiation. Distinction itself was becoming the basis for power and social authority. The private volunteer companies, which only the most prosperous master artisans could afford to join, were dominated by law-yers, bankers, merchants, and "gentlemen." The vol-unteers provided the militia system with most of its field and division officers. In turn, militia title and rank were concomitants of government officeholding and acknowledged as necessary for entrance into bourgeois "good society." As the burlesquers pointed out, uniform, office, and title were hollow proofs of merit in a frankly unequal system.

In militia elections and commands, workingmen located a means by which businessmen and profes-sionals improved their social image and tried to foist "aristocracy" on ordinary citizens. While these petty tyrants climbed over social equals, they went out of their way to deny their common origins. Military jokes abounded in newspapers and comic periodicals, pointing to the effects of "military pride." "A farmer who was elected to a corporalship in a militia com-pany, his wife after discoursing with him for some time on the advantage which his family would derive from his exaltation, inquired in a doubting tone, 'Husband, will it be proper for us to let our children play with the neighbor's now [?]'"[63] Other slurs com-pared militia officers with drunken blacks and con-cluded that the latter were the more honorable sort of human being.[64] These insults were of a piece with Pe-ter Albright's brown-smeared nose, pointing to the character, motivations, and morals of the officers as corrupt and self-serving.

The same attitude toward officership and the con-struction of social authority through appearance un-derlay the use of fantastical disguises and costumes. The term *fantastical* bore a derogatory implication: it meant anyone in burlesque dress, but "more in rags than ribbands."[65] Like the harlequin, whose diamond-patterned suit was an abstraction of the beggar's rags and patches, and like the English Christ-mas mummer dressed in straw, rags, or paper, the fantastical may have been raggedy as much in imita-tion of the rural poor as because of his own origins.[66] American fantasticals imitating militia troops drew on this double-edged mockery. Appearing in wild anti-uniformity, they at once made fun of the militia's stress on elaborate and uniform dress, brought the of-ficers into contempt with the crazy parodies of their

costumes, and laughed at their own public com-pany's lack of style and prestige. Anti-uniformity was carried to the extreme, in varicolored pants legs, oddly formed hats, and mismatched shoes. Over and over reporters noticed that no two performers looked in any way the same. Similarly, the officers' and vol-unteers' love of equipment was lampooned by carry-ing dead fish or deer legs instead of guns, using rusty culverts for field pieces, and wearing impossibly large swords and bayonets. Pride could be undercut with random banners and broken-down horses—references to the volunteers' satins and fine animals. Another edge of the same laughing mockery was blackface, which injected the raucous laughter of the popular theater into military burlesque.

Commentary on the mock militias affirmed a gen-eralized hostility to pretension and self-aggran-dizement, but critics also drew parallels to concrete and immediate problems in social relations. The most important of these was the hostility between mechanics, craftsmen, and employers that resulted from the crumbling of older crafts and trades.[67] New work routines, the devaluation of skill, the disinte-gration of apprenticeship, gross exploitation of fac-tory, sweatshop, and outworkers—all features of the transformation of the urban economy—caused men to translate the misery caused by these changes into personal antagonism against masters and employers. Feelings quite similar to those expressed about "mili-tary pride" found their way into descriptions of the employers' social style as well as their economic practices. The *Mechanic's Free Press* relentlessly jabbed at the growing tendency to judge men by ex-ternal attributes yet angrily acknowledged that in the modern world, money made the man. The *Press* saw the use of carriages, fine clothes, and titles and the elegance and exclusivity of social events as tools in the construction of inequality.

Radical artisans argued that "The many opportuni-ties that gave men the means and ready access to for-tune . . . have pushed men into good society who pos-itively disgrace bad. . . . [S]uch men . . . are now dictating monarchical principles to us . . . and little kingly notions have crept into our institutions." Part of this project was the creation of "visible lines of distinction."[68]

New inequalities arose from economic practices, but social style was being used to legitimate distinc-tions. "We have men in power," wrote "Peter Single," "who originally were without character and of course without friends. . . . [T]hey succeeded by nefarious means in amassing a small sum, by speculating in human misery, grinding down some poor illiterate being . . . and now ride in their carriage, give balls and act the rich nabob." Single specified men who rose to the status of master artisans and then denied responsibility to their fellows. "When they drain all they can from his labor [they] despise [the workingman] as much as they do the reptile which crawls upon the ground."[69]

For critics like Single and the men of the 84th, militia musters and the militia system could be seen as part of this process of exploitation and legitimation. The *Mechanic's Free Press* described musters as "worse than useless military show," because they forced men to "submit to the degradation of being an instrument for transforming men into peacocks."[70] That is, they provided yet another occasion for men who thought they were better than workingmen to "accumulate popularity" by dressing up, mounting a horse, and ordering a regiment around. The tone of artisan criticism of the militia system shows that many workingmen viewed regimental officers and employers as this kind of accumulating person.

The mock election and burlesque militia parades combined general social criticism, specific political protest, and personal satire of known individuals. Their flexibility in accomplishing all these tasks at once and in accommodating a variety of understandings of social relations testifies to the vibrancy of folk dramatic traditions in the early nineteenth century. That militia burlesques provoked complaint, denunciation, and courts-martial shows that they hit their mark and that mockery could not be shrugged off easily. For Philadelphia's workingmen, older folk traditions could become powerful, public means to attack the legitimacy of distinction, authority, and inequity.

Notes

I wish to thank the Philadelphia Center for Early American Studies, Henry Glassie, and Don Yoder for their support of my research on urban folk culture.

1. The term *folk drama* in folklore scholarship refers to a collection of dramatic genres and practices studied by folklorists, mainly among European peoples. Folk dramas have been defined by their community locus and focus and by their noncommercial production, often but not exclusively by male age cohorts. Broadly, these dramatic traditions are calendrical and festive, and in some of their forms they include rhymes or plays. Folk dramatic customs also comprise processing, begging, and dancing, mimings and maskings. Two major themes of European folk dramas have been discerned: folk "plays" on themes of life, death, and regeneration and the use of processional performances to constitute, outline, and reconstruct communal bonds and boundaries, often at critical times of the year.

Although most scholarship on folklore has remained focused on the integrative, cohesion-promoting uses of traditional dramas, folk dramas have often been turned by the rural poor to contest, protest, and aggressively defend community. Such was the case with the charivari, or rough music, in England: E. P. Thompson, "'Rough Music': le Charivari Anglais," *Annales: Économies, sociétés, civilisations* 27 (1972): 285–315; Violet Alford provides a detailed folkloristic description of the English charivari in "Rough Music," *Folk-lore* 70 (1959): 505–18. Arguments about the political uses of folk drama are extended by Norman Simms in "Ned Ludd's Mummers Play," *Folk-lore* 89 (1978): 166–78.

2. Alfred F. Young, "Pope's Day, Tarring and Feathering, and Cornet Joyce, Jun.: From Ritual to Rebellion in Boston, 1745–1775," paper presented to the Anglo-American Conference on Comparative Labor History, Rutgers University, Apr. 26–28, 1973; Young, "English Plebeian Culture and Eighteenth-Century American Radicalism," in *The Origins of Anglo-American Radicalism*, ed. Margaret Jacob and James Jacob (New York, 1983), 185–212; Dirk Hoerder, "Boston Leaders and Boston Crowds, 1765–1776," in *The American Revolution: Explorations in the History of American Radicalism*, ed. Young (DeKalb, Ill., 1976), 233–71; Edward Countryman, "'Out of the Bounds of the Law': Northern Land Rioters in the Eighteenth Century," in *American Revolution*, ed. Young, 37–69.

3. Steven J. Rosswurm, "Arms, Culture and Class: The Philadelphia Militia and the 'Lower Orders' in the American Revolution" (Ph.D. diss., Northern Illinois University, 1977), 84–106.

4. *Pennsylvania Packet* (Philadelphia), Sept. 30, 1780. Another use of ritual shaming by the crowd occurred on the July Fourth after General Howe's evacuation of the city: a procession bore a prostitute dressed in a high British headdress through the streets, cheering and banging drums. Ridicule of the British turned on the social and sexual "filth" of the woman. Henry D. Biddle, ed., *Extracts from the Journal of Elizabeth Drinker, from 1759–1807, A.D.* (Philadelphia, 1889), 107.

5. Alfred F. Young, "Afterword," in *American Révolution*, ed. Young, 449–61, 458; Thomas Slaughter, "Crowds and Mobs, Riots and Brawls: Public Disorder in the Era of the Constitution," paper presented to the Conference on the Creation of the American Constitution, sponsored by the Philadelphia Center for Early American Studies, Oct. 20, 1984.

6. Michael Meranze, "The Penitential Ideal in Late Eighteenth-Century Philadelphia," *Pennsylvania Magazine of History and Biography* 108 (October 1984): 419–50.

7. Susan G. Davis, *Parades and Power: Street Theatre in Nineteenth-Century Philadelphia* (Philadelphia: Temple University Press, 1985), 49–72.

8. Peter Burke, *Popular Culture in Early Modern Europe* (London, 1978), 207–86. Cf. Peter Buckley, "'A Privileged Place': New York Theatre Riots, 1817–1849," paper presented at the annual meeting of the Organization of American Historians, Apr. 1, 1980, Philadelphia.

9. H. E. Scudder, ed., *The Recollections of Samuel Breck* (Philadelphia, 1877), quoted in William Wells Newell, "Christmas Maskings in Boston," *Journal of American Folklore* 9 (1896): 178.

10. Raymond Williams, "The Press and Popular Culture: An Historical Perspective," in *Newspaper History: From the Seventeenth Century to the Present Day*, ed. George Boyce, James Curran, and Pauline Wingate (London, 1978), 41–50; Dan Schiller, *Objectivity and the News: The Penny Press and the Rise of Commercial Journalism* (Philadelphia, 1980); Peter Buckley, "An Essay on New York Publics," paper presented to the Social Science Research Council, New York City Working Group, Nov. 18, 1983.

11. Elizabeth C. Keiffer, "John Durang, the First Native American Dancer," *Pennsylvania Dutchman* 6 (1954): 26–38; Alfred Shoemaker, "Stoffle Rilbp's Epistle," *Pennsylvania Dutchman* 6 (1954): 39.

12. Richard M. Dorson, "Mose The Far Famed and World Reknowned," *American Literature* 15 (1943): 288–300; Francis Hodge, *Yankee Theatre: The Image of America on Stage* (Austin, Tex., 1964).

13. Rosswurm, "Arms, Culture and Class," 112–73.

14. Paul T. Smith, "Militia of the United States from 1846–1860," *Indiana Magazine of History* 15 (1919): 21–47; John K. Mahon, *History of the Militia and National Guard* (New York, 1983), 49–96.

15. Mahon, *Militia and National Guard*, 46–96; John J. Holmes, "The Decline of the Pennsylvania Militia, 1815–1870," *Western Pennsylvania Magazine of History* 57 (1974): 199–217.

16. Davis, *Parades and Power*, 49–72; Philip S. Klein, *Pennsylvania Politics, 1817–1832: A Game without Rules* (Philadelphia, 1940), 13–14, 32–34.

17. Holmes, "Pennsylvania Militia."

18. *Niles' Weekly Register* (Baltimore), Apr. 4, 1835, 76; July 20, 1833, 344; Sept. 14, 1833, 47.

19. *Niles' Weekly Register*, May 14, 1825, 176.

20. *Saturday Evening Post* (Philadelphia), May 7, 1825.

21. *Saturday Evening Post*, May 7, 1825.

22. *Saturday Evening Post*, May 7, 1825.

23. *Democratic Press* (Philadelphia), May 9, 1825.

24. *Democratic Press*, May 9, 1825; *Saturday Evening Post*, May 15, 1825.

25. Natalie Z. Davis, *Society and Culture in Early Modern France* (Stanford, Calif., 1975), 97–123; Burke, *Popular Culture in Early Modern Europe*, 178–204; Roger D. Abrahams and Richard Bauman, "Ranges of Festival Behavior," in *The Reversible World: Symbolic Inversion in Art and Society*, ed. Barbara Babcock (Ithaca, N.Y., 1978), 193–208.

26. John Brewer, "Theatre and Counter-Theatre in Georgian Politics: The Mock Election at Garrat," *Radical History Review* 22 (Winter 1979–80): 7–40; cf. Thomas W. Lacquer, "The Queen Caroline Affair: Politics as Art in the Reign of George IV," *Journal of Modern History* 54 (1982): 417–66.

27. Francis Grose, *A Classical Dictionary of the Vulgar Tongue* (London, 1796), 161.

28. *Saturday Evening Post*, May 15, 1825.

29. *Saturday Evening Post*, May 21, 1825.

30. *Saturday Evening Post*, May 21, 1825.

31. *United States Gazette* (Philadelphia), May 20, 1825.

32. John F. Watson cited a "corn toppers" parade (the date is unclear): *The Annals of Philadelphia in the Olden Time*, 3 vols. (Philadelphia, 1830; rev. ed. Philadelphia, 1900), 3:363–64.

33. *Democratic Press*, May 26, 1825.

34. Press reception of the burlesque varied with newspapers' militia allegiances. *The Democratic Press*, for example, was hostile to Pluck and his comrades after an initial burst of enthusiasm. Its editor, John Binns, was an active militia volunteer. *The United States Gazette* took a similar position, calling for an end to the spectacles. The *Post* was generally sympathetic. Unfortunately, no labor or workingmen's paper is available for these years in Philadelphia, which limits our ability to understand Pluck's local reception. *United States Gazette*, June 1, 1825; *Democratic Press*, May 19, 24, 1825; *Democratic Press*, May 18, 1826.

35. *Niles' Weekly Register*, Aug. 12, 1826, 413, and Sept. 16, 1826, 48; *Saturday Evening Post*, Sept. 9, 23, 1826.

36. *Niles' Weekly Register*, August 12, 1826, 413, and Sept. 16, 1826, 48; *Saturday Evening Post*, Sept. 9, 23, 1826.

37. *Niles' Weekly Register*, Oct. 28, 1826. The rest of John Pluck's career was truly obscure. A pauper, he was in and out of Blockley almshouse for the rest of his life. He died in Blockley, apparently without family, and was buried in the poorhouse ground in 1839 (*United States Gazette*, Sept. 26, 1839).

38. *United States Gazette*, June 1, 1825.

39. *Democratic Press*, May 19, 1825.

40. *Saturday Evening Post*, May 7, 1825.

41. *United States Gazette*, June 1, 1825.

42. *United States Gazette*, June 1, 1825.

43. *Niles' Weekly Register*, June 27, 1829, 284.

44. *Workingman's Advocate* (New York), May 4, Oct 5, 7, 14, 21, 26, 29, 1831; for New England, Anthony J. Marro, "Vermont's Local Militia Units, 1815–1860," *Vermont History* 40 (1972): 28–42; Telfer Mook, "Training Day in New England," *New England Quarterly* 11 (1938): 675–97; Charles W. Burpee, *The Military History of Waterbury, New Hampshire* (Connecticut, 1891), 31; Marcus Cunliffe, *Soldier and Civilian: The Martial Spirit in America, 1775–1865* (Boston, 1968), 190; and Philip Hone, diary, New-York Historical Society, New York City.

45. We have no social history of the militia reform campaigns in Philadelphia, but see Walter J. Hugins, *Jacksonian*

Democracy and the Working Class: A Study of the New York Workingmen's Movement, 1829–1837 (Stanford, Calif., 1960), 33, 138; Philip S. Foner, History of the American Labor Movement, vol. 1: From Colonial Times to the Founding of the American Federation of Labor, rev. ed. (New York, 1975), 123–24, 467–68, 473–74.

46. Pennsylvania Gazette (Philadelphia), May 21, 1833.

47. Pennsylvania Gazette, May 21, 1833.

48. Pennsylvanian (Philadelphia), Sept. 17, 1833.

49. Pennsylvania Gazette, May 22, 28, 1833.

50. Pennsylvanian, Oct. 29, 1833.

51. Pennsylvanian, Oct. 29, 1833.

52. Pennsylvanian, Oct. 29, 1833.

53. New Haven Standard, quoted in Pennsylvania Gazette, June 6, 1833; Easton Sentinel, Jan. 10, 1834; Ethan Allen Weaver, Local Historical and Biographical Sketches (Germantown, Pa., 1906), 90–91; Niles' Weekly Register, June 6, 1835, 234 (quoting the Chambersburg Repository).

54. Augustus B. Longstreet, Georgia Scenes (New York, 1840), 145; Cunliffe, Soldier and Civilian, 190–92; Theodore Gromert, "The First National Pastime in the Middle West," Indiana Magazine of History 29 (1933): 171–75; Richard Walser, "Don Quixote Invincibles," North Carolina Folklore 24 (1976): 95–100.

55. Military Magazine and Record of the Volunteers of the City and County of Philadelphia (Philadelphia) 3 (1842): 11.

56. Alford, "Rough Music"; Thompson, "Le Charivari Anglais"; Bryan D. Palmer, "Discordant Music: Charivaris and White Capping in Nineteenth-Century America," Labour/La Travailleur 3 (September 1973): 5–62.

57. Thompson, "Le Charivari Anglais"; Palmer, "Discordant Music," 24.

58. E. P. Thompson, "The Moral Economy of the English Crowd in the Eighteenth Century," Past and Present 50 (1971): 76–136; Countryman, "Northern Land Rioters."

59. Palmer, "Discordant Music," 26–33; cf. George M. Story, "Mummers in Newfoundland History: A Survey of the Printed Record," in Christmas Mumming in Newfoundland: Essays in Anthropology, Folklore and History, ed. Herbert Halpert and G. M. Story (Toronto, 1969), 35–61.

60. Henry Christman, Tin Horns and Calico (New York, 1945); David Maldwyn Ellis, Landlords and Farmers in the Hudson-Mohawk Region, 1790–1850 (Ithaca, N.Y., 1946), 225–67. Disguised rent rioters were known in the Helderberg region from at least the 1790s, according to Ellis (p. 242).

61. Hans Kurath, A Word Geography of the Eastern Unites States (Ann Arbor, Mich., 1949), 78; Joseph Wright, The English Dialect Dictionary, 6 vols. (London, 1898–1905), 2:543.

62. Simms, "Ned Ludd's Mummers Play"; cf. David Jones, Before Rebecca (London, 1973).

63. Mechanic's Free Press, Sept. 20, 1828.

64. Philadelphia Comic Almanac for 1835 (Philadelphia, 1835), n.p. This almanac contains a small woodcut of Colonel Pluck.

65. Grose, Classical Dictionary of the Vulgar Tongue, 140.

66. Thelma Niklaus, Harlequin; or, The Rise of the Bergamask Rogue (New York, 1956), 22–34; Simon Lichman, "The Gardener's Story and What Came Next: A Contextual Analysis of the Marshfield Paper Boys' Mumming Play" (Ph.D. diss., University of Pennsylvania, 1981), 254–63.

67. Bruce Laurie, Working People of Philadelphia, 1800–1850 (Philadelphia, 1980), 5–6, 77–78; Richard A. McLeod, "Philadelphia Artisans, 1828–1850" (Ph.D. diss., University of Missouri, 1971), 59–74; Sean Wilentz, Chants Democratic: New York City and the Rise of the American Working Class, 1788–1850 (New York, 1984), 107–42.

68. Mechanic's Free Press, Sept. 6, 1828.

69. Mechanic's Free Press, Apr. 19, 1828; see also Mechanic's Free Press, Oct. 18, 1828.

70. Mechanic's Free Press, Jan. 9, 1830.

Part Six: Reforming the Environment

The "Rural" Cemetery Movement: Urban Travail and the Appeal of Nature

In 1831 America's "rural" cemetery began with the official opening of Mount Auburn Cemetery in Cambridge, Massachusetts. Mount Auburn was different from older colonial burial grounds; it seemed less like a graveyard than a park, more a place for the living to stroll than the dead to sleep. Rather than being hemmed in by narrow streets and crowded tenements, it occupied rolling acreage near the Charles River several miles west of Boston. To contemporaries it seemed an arcadian vale ideal for contemplating the beauty of nature. Between 1830 and the Civil War others like it opened near New York, Philadelphia, New Haven, and elsewhere. Why did these rural retreats become so popular? In the following essay, Thomas Bender links the rural cemetery movement to the emergence of urban industrial centers in the mid-nineteenth century and to the rise of an ideology that stressed the opposition of city and country.

Bender explores this "counterpoint" ideology in Lowell, Massachusetts, an industrial center that grew from farming village to crowded city between 1820 and 1840. First planned as a textile town in a rural setting, Lowell grew so fast and its impact on local forests and fields was so severe that hopes of its remaining a pastoral "middle landscape" were quickly dashed. The failure was due in part to the dangerous power of the machine and how quickly its force could alter the ecological balance of land, rivers, and vegetation. But the industrial discipline that mechanization brought changed local social relations just as profoundly; "distress," alienation, and a distrust of industry's artificiality seemed to threaten the moral basis of society itself. By 1850 the rural cemetery provided a counterpoint to the perceived destructive forces of urban existence, a life described by those experiencing it as a "din," a "city of strangers" that could only be tolerated if one had ready recourse to a romantic, sylvan glade where

meadows silenced the clatter of machines, where soft sunlight opened new sights to eyes hardened by the factory's darkness, where new varieties of plant and animal life broke the grinding monotony of clock time.

The rural cemetery offered a landscape whose soothing contours stood in stark opposition to urban "encroachment" on the human spirit. Perhaps, too, it provided a momentary release that made the inner life of cities—whether in Lowell's mills, Boston's South End, New York's Five Points, or Philadelphia's Southwark—and the regimen of emergent working-class life bearable. For beneath the clarity of Bender's "counterpoint" ideology, as with all ideologies, lay an essentially ambivalent process of shaping ideas about nature and work, a process blurred by the practical routines of class relations. Rural cemeteries certainly enabled America's dead to rest undisturbed by the continual pressures of urban development and rebuilding and helped ease the inevitable overcrowding of older urban graveyards. Yet at the same time the praises of rural cemeteries were sung loudest by captains of urban business and mechanized industry—men like Oliver M. Whipple, Joseph Story, and Nathan Appleton—whose drive for economic growth, territorial expansion, and profit had helped to create the very conditions people sought to escape. They were joined by evangelical ministers who saw in rural cemeteries an opportunity to moralize the landscape and to connect it with the church as another form of escape. As reformed environments, then, rural cemeteries were symbolic texts whose mythic power derived from the tension of the double message they contained.

The rural cemetery movement was a widespread cultural phenomenon in mid-nineteenth-century America.[1] Literally a misnomer, *rural cemetery* de-

The "Rural" Cemetery Movement   BENDER   505

noted a burial ground located on the outskirts of a city that was designed according to the romantic conventions of English landscape gardening. Although historians have noted the development of these cemeteries, they have ignored their ideological background and their place in the emerging urban culture.[2]

In *The Making of Urban America*, John W. Reps expresses surprise that the cemeteries were used more as pleasure grounds than as places for burial and concludes that this "must have astounded and perhaps horrified their sponsors."[3] On the contrary, this phenomenon neither surprised nor outraged anyone. A visit to the local cemetery was considered de rigueur for the tourist, and the popular press carried numerous articles on these romantic burial grounds. Many accounts and engravings depict middle-class Americans resorting for pleasure to these parklike cemeteries, empty or nearly empty of graves for many years. America's rural cemeteries were explicitly designed both for the living and for the dead, and the assumptions underlying their widespread popularity were central to mid-nineteenth-century American ideas about the relation of cityscape and landscape in an urbanizing society.

America's first rural cemetery was Mount Auburn, outside Boston. Dr. Jacob Bigelow was the driving force behind its establishment, and many of Boston's elite supported his five-year campaign, which culminated with the opening of Mount Auburn in 1831. Bigelow's motives are not entirely clear. His familiarity with European medical literature probably alerted him to the potential menace to public health of cemeteries in the center of densely populated cities. He was also moved by a traditional desire to express respect for the dead through an appropriately serene burial site.[4]

Whatever Bigelow's motives, consecration addresses and other commentary on the cemeteries reveal that rural cemeteries were intended to offer far more than resting places for the dead. Mount Auburn and its imitators were expected, from the beginning, to serve the needs of the living. A month after the consecration of Mount Auburn, Henry Bellows, in his oration at the Harvard Exhibition on October 18, 1831, declared that rural cemeteries "are not for the dead. They are for the living."[5] Writing in 1849, Andrew Jackson Downing asserted that thirty thousand persons visited Mount Auburn in a single season.[6]

Clearly, rural cemeteries had some larger significance for midcentury Americans. But what is the relationship between the cemetery movement and more general changes in American society? How was the American attitude toward the rural cemetery related to thought and feeling about America's increasingly urban environment?

The consecration address delivered by Joseph Story at Mount Auburn suggests the nature of these relationships. After explaining that the "magnificence of nature" in the rural cemetery would be more comforting to the mourner than the "noisy press of business" surrounding a city churchyard, Story made broader claims for the significance of Mount Auburn.[7] "All around us," he observed, "there breathes a solemn calm, as if we were in the bosom of a wilderness." Yet "ascend but a few steps, and what a change of scenery to surprise and delight us. . . . In the distance, the City—at once the object of our admiration and our love—rears its proud eminences, its glittering spires, its lofty towers, its graceful mansions, its curling smoke, its crowded haunts of business and pleasure" (fig. 1). Story then proceeded to refine these images of cityscape and landscape into counterpoints: "There is, therefore, within our reach, every variety of natural and artificial scenery. . . . We stand, as it were, upon the borders of two worlds; and as the mood of our minds may be, we may gather lessons of profound wisdom by contrasting the one with the other."[8] A view of the city, Story continued, encourages us to "indulge in the dreams and hope of ambition." The influence of the cemetery's natural landscape, however, will serve as a counterbalance. "The rivalries of the world will here drop from the heart; the spirit of forgiveness will gather new impulses; the selfishness of avarice will be checked; the restlessness of ambition will be rebuked."[9] Story was suggesting that the influence of the rural cemetery could purify the city without compromising its urbanity.

Mount Auburn's attraction for the living encouraged imitators. Following the Boston example, Philadelphia established Laurel Hill Cemetery in 1836, and New York City opened Greenwood in 1838.[10] By 1842 New England had several rural cemeteries, including the one opened in Lowell, Massachusetts, in 1841.[11]

The popular image of Lowell, America's first industrial city, illustrates the pertinence of rural ceme-

Fig. 1. James Smillie, *View from Mt. Auburn (near Boston)*.
Lithograph, 1847. (Reprinted from Cornelia W. Walter,
*Mount Auburn: Illustrated in a Series of Views from Draw-
ings by James Smillie* [New York, 1847], facing p. 112; photograph courtesy of Winterthur Museum Libraries.)

teries to the mid-century American concern about
the relationship of the natural and artificial elements
of the urbanizing environment. Although it was
merely the site of a dozen small farms in 1820, only
twenty years later Lowell was acknowledged as "the
American Manchester" (cf. figs. 2, 3). Because the
landscape was altered so rapidly by urbanization, and
because the city was a self-conscious and highly visible pioneer of American industrialism, Lowell provides an excellent example for this study.

When Lowell was founded in 1821, the dominant
concept of the American landscape was that of "an
immense wilderness [turned] into a fruitful field."[12]
Art and Nature were blended to define the landscape.
Americans assumed that something artificial could
be "introduced into the natural order [showing] that
man has interposed in some way to improve the pro-

cesses of nature." However, an extreme departure
from nature could not be accommodated within this
ideology without upsetting the balance by shifting
from the "cultivated" and the good to the "dissipated
and corrupt."[13]

Lowell and other early factory towns were merged
within this framework through the use of a factory-
in-the-forest image. In 1825, the editor of the *Essex
Gazette* emphasized the harmony between the factories and the natural landscape at Lowell. "It seemed,"
he wrote, "to be a song of triumph and exultation at
the successful union of nature with the art of man, in
order to make her contribute to the wants and happiness of the human family."[14] After two decades of urban growth, however, it appeared that instead of
blending with nature, the city was about to overwhelm it. In 1841, a mill-girl poet wrote: "Who hath
not sought some sylvan spot / Where art, the spoiler,
ventures not."[15]

When midcentury Lowellians, and Americans in
general, abandoned the inadequate imagery of a fac-

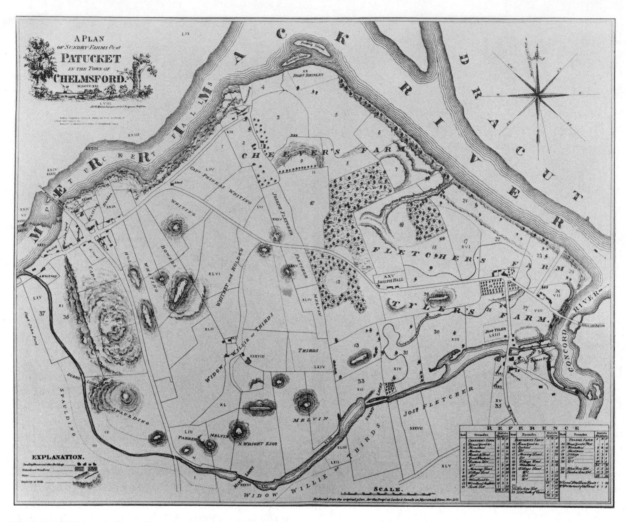

Fig. 2. J. G. Hales, *A Plan of Sundry Farms &c. at Patucket in the Town of Chelmsford,* 1821. (Photograph courtesy of the Lowell Historical Society.)

tory in the forest, they began to visualize the cityscape and natural landscape in terms of the imagery adumbrated by Story. Instead of trying to blend city and country, Americans granted cities their essential urbanity but insisted on easy periodic access to nature. In place of a continuous middle landscape, the American landscape would be defined as a counterpoint between Art and Nature, city and country. The rural cemetery movement provides the earliest and most revealing insight into this new ideology in Lowell and in America.

Oliver M. Whipple, the self-made gunpowder manufacturer and civic leader, was the leading spirit in founding Lowell's rural cemetery. The Proprietors were incorporated on January 23, 1841, and through Whipple's generosity, a scenic forty-five-acre site on the outskirts of the city was acquired.[16]

The cemetery was laid out in the romantic style by George P. Worcester (fig. 4).[17] He had been influenced by the famous French cemetery Père-Lachaise, and some commentators believed that Lowell Cemetery, as well as Mount Auburn, were imitations of it. The American cemeteries had indeed imitated the French one to a certain extent, but there was an important difference in their relationship to nature. Père-Lachaise was an old garden dedicated to a new purpose when it was opened as a cemetery. Mount Auburn and Lowell Cemetery, however, were estab-

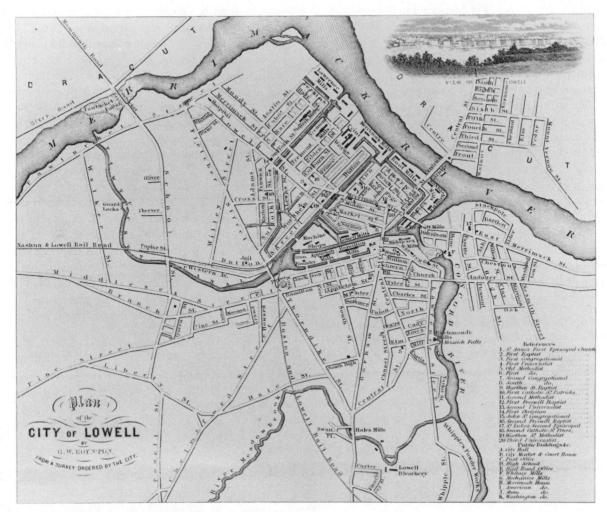

Fig. 3. G. W. Boynton, *Plan of the City of Lowell by G. W. Boynton,* 1845. (Photograph courtesy of the Lowell Historical Society.)

lished on sites of natural beauty with the intention of conserving their original aspect.[18] Mount Auburn and Lowell Cemetery were to be enclaves of natural beauty adjoining the artificial urban environment.

The Reverend Amos Blanchard's consecration address on June 20, 1841, at Lowell reveals the significance of a rural cemetery in an urban society. Although he touched on such themes as the need for a new burial place in rapidly growing Lowell and the respect that should be shown for the dead by making burial places beautiful, Blanchard also addressed himself to larger questions. Midway, he began to explain the role of rural cemeteries in enhancing the ur-

ban environment. The thrust of his remarks was that America's rapidly growing cities, marked by visual monotony and social chaos, generated distress that could be assuaged through the influence of romantically designed cemeteries.

Blanchard characterized Lowell and, by implication, other American cities as "cities of strangers."[19] Life in the city was impersonal, ever in flux, and more concerned with the next commercial opportunity than with a proper attention to the permanent roots of community life. Urban living seemed more like hotel life than the traditional community of fond memory. Blanchard and his generation were jarred by the discovery that even the bones of the dead, man's sacred link with his communal past, were not safe from the next wave of residential and industrial expansion or financial promotion. He informed his audience that "a tomb-stone, in one of our large cities, was lately seen covered with gairish handbills, announcing schemes of business, and of the idlest of fashionable amusements and follies."[20]

The physical removal of burial places from downtown locations to rural cemeteries would reduce the risk of such desecration. Blanchard further hoped that "the aspirations of vanity, and the pride of distinction in place, wealth, and power [would] here receive an effectual rebuke."[21] Possibly a rural cemetery would remind a society uprooting itself, conquering a continent, and covering it with cities that the past could not be entirely ignored. He also revealed his "secret wish that when death shall have torn his beloved ones from his embrace, and when he himself shall have died, they might repose together, where they

should never be disturbed by the encroachments of a crowded and swelling population of the living." In a dynamic society, the rural cemetery could plausibly serve as a focus for the "cultivation of home attachments towards the city of our abode." Six months after Blanchard's address, the Lowell *Courier* echoed this sentiment, assuring its readers that the cemetery will provide "a new and more sacred and binding tie to this city as our home."[22] In this sense, the rural cemetery movement reflected an anxious search for a sanctuary from the "go a-head" spirit of the age.

But the attraction of the rural cemetery went beyond the conflict between memory and desire in an age of progress. Blanchard explicitly linked the rural cemetery to a complex of beliefs emerging in the middle of the nineteenth century in response to increasing urbanization. The key elements of this ideology were expressed three months before Blanchard's consecration address in a poem entitled "Alone With Nature," written by a Lowell mill girl who signed herself "Adelaide."

Fig. 4. *Plan of Lowell Cemetery, Surveyed & Drawn by Butterfield & Clark, Civil Engineers*, 1850. (Photograph courtesy of the Lowell Historical Society.)

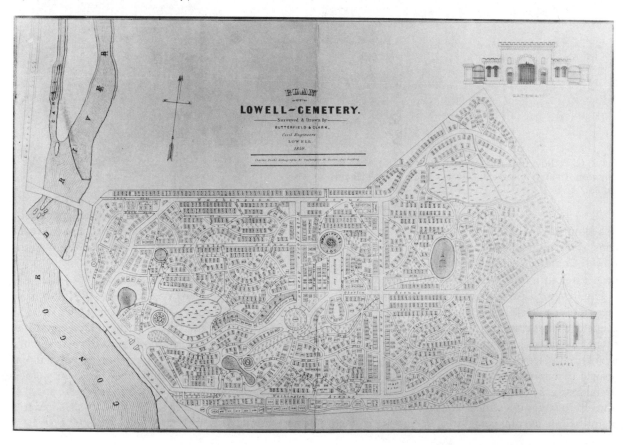

> Alone with nature—will not ye
> Who all her beauty daily see,
> Beneath your native, 'house-hold tree,'
>   Enjoy them for the roving stranger!
> I can not relish half her sweets
> Till taught by bustling, crowded streets,
> To sigh for nature's calm retreats,
>   Then task them for the city-ranger.[23]

In the poem, and in the midcentury American mind, the city is sharply distinguished from the natural landscape, and natural beauty is held to be more necessary for urbanites than for rural dwellers.

As the nation became increasingly urban, Americans who had moved from the country to the city tended to romanticize nature. Only an urban society can afford such romanticizing: in a frontier society trees are not scenic; they are potential houses. Roderick Nash argues that the urban "literary gentleman wielding a pen, not the pioneer with his axe," idealized nature.[24] The example of "Adelaide," the pen-wielding mill girl, suggests that the urge to romanticize nature came from more than heavy draughts of Byron and Wordsworth in a library. An intensely felt need was causing gentleman and mill girl alike to turn to the conventions of romanticism to cope with the emergent city. As the urban environment became paved over, more hurried, and commercial, a change of scenery reminiscent of the rural past, a readily accessible natural sanctuary within close proximity to the city, became necessary. A romantic landscape was sought as a counterbalance to the disturbing aspects of the cityscape. This was the attraction of the rural cemeteries on the outskirts of most American cities.[25] Blanchard understood this when he said that Lowell Cemetery is "accessible at all times, yet so remote from the marts of business as not to be liable to be encroached upon by the spreading abodes of the living: sequestered from the din and bustle of active life."[26]

Throughout his address Blanchard endeavored to set off the solitude and romantic beauty of the rural cemetery against the bustle and aesthetic barrenness of the city. He contrasted the praiseworthy Roman custom of burials along country highways with the modern notions that until very recent times preferred the location of cemeteries "by the city church-yard, crowded, noisy, and grassless, . . . and never visited by the dew, and the sunshine, and the showers of

heaven."[27] This imagery was noted by the editor of Lowell's liveliest nineteenth-century newspaper, the *Vox Populi*. He found the passage in the printed version of Blanchard's address so striking that he checked his copy of Wordsworth's "Essay on Epitaphs," where he found remarkable parallelism, if not outright plagiarism. The editor noted that numerous other expressions in Blanchard's address were nearly identical with passages in the standard romantic authors. Blanchard explained the instances of parallelism by asserting that the boy who had set the type for the printed text must have omitted the quotation marks.[28] The incident illustrates the manner in which urban Americans like Blanchard turned to a corpus of romantic writings, largely British, borrowed the vocabulary of romantic nature, and used it to cope with American problems.[29]

Americans had been using European romantic conventions to celebrate nature for nearly a half-century, but by 1850 they were using them with a significant difference.[30] Formerly, they had used these conventions to identify America as a rural republic, but now they located the American identity within a counterpoint of romantic nature and the city. The American landscape was no longer visualized as of a piece. For midcentury city dwellers, there was an urban "inside" (fig. 5) and a rural "outside." They had developed an adaptive mechanism that would allow them to retain a commitment to nature in an urban and industrial nation. Americans thus avoided an unpalatable choice between city and country. As Frederick Law Olmsted put it, "no broad question of country life in comparison with city life is involved; it is confessedly a question of delicate adjustment" between the natural and the artificial.[31]

A visitor to Lowell in 1843 used the cemetery to describe the city within this new vocabulary. From the city's "busy streets," he passed "through romantic woods" (fig. 6) into the cemetery grounds, where he was filled with "deep peace." "You stand as it were, beyond the world, beyond its cares, its strifes, its false, *ignis fatuus* hopes, and its griefs. You have entered a realm of quietude, melody and beauty."[32]

Two years later, John Greenleaf Whittier expressed his feelings about the American Manchester's rural cemetery. Whittier, who lived in Lowell for nearly a year as editor of the antislavery *Middlesex Standard*, recorded his impressions of the city in *The Stranger in Lowell* (1845). Lowell stretched "far and wide its chaos of brick masonry and painted shingles." It is the home of the "wizard of mechanism," and "WORK is here the Patron Saint." Everywhere the slogan "WORK OR DIE!" glared at the population.[33] After thus describing his first impressions, he wrote of his visit to Lowell's rural cemetery. It is "a quiet, peaceful spot; the city, with its crowded mills, its busy streets and teeming life, is hidden from view. . . . All is still and solemn." The cemetery, he further observed, is not the resort of only the "aged and the sad of heart" but also of "the young, the buoyant," who relax under its "soothing influence."[34]

Twenty years later, J. W. Meader similarly portrayed the romantic cemetery as a sanctuary within an urban-industrial society. The cemetery, he wrote, is "a symbol of the solitude, though now adorned and beautiful, which covered all this realm around the fine falls of Concord, when it was invaded by the all-subduing and all-conquering Divinity of Mechanism."[35] Meader's use of "invaded" and "all-conquering" suggests the defensive nature of the counterpoint concept as manifested in the rural cemetery and later park movement. In the early stages of the introduction of the machine into the forest, Americans regarded it as a sort of technological sublime. Both nature and the machine benefited from the blending of the two. By mid-century, however, the dynamic of the machine and the city's power to obliterate the landscape (fig. 7) prompted Americans increasingly to use metaphors suggesting conquest instead of conciliation to describe the machine in the garden. Nevertheless, the counterpoint strategy was not developed to roll back technology, or even to prevent further progress; it was designed only to prevent total victory by the "wizard of mechanism." Midcen-

Fig. 5. *Middlesex Company Woolen Mill*, Lowell, Massachusetts, ca. 1848. Oil on canvas, 23″ × 30″. In this rare view of the inside of an "urban" mill yard, mill girls enter the Middlesex Mills while a company agent or inspector looks over bags of wool. Like most larger mill buildings in northern New England during the mid-nineteenth century, the Middlesex mill is brick with a projecting stair tower, a bell cupola, and fire ladders hanging on the roof. (Photograph courtesy of the Museum of American Textile History.)

Fig. 6. James Smillie, *Forest Pond, Mount Auburn Cemetery*. Lithograph, 1847. Like Lowell Cemetery, Mount Auburn offered the visitor picturesque views punctuated by moments of quiet reflection and pastoral beauty near a pond surrounded by tall trees and dense shrubbery. (Reprinted from Cornelia W. Walter, *Mount Auburn: Illustrated in a Series of Views from Drawings by James Smillie* [New York, 1847], facing p. 94; photograph courtesy Winterthur Museum Libraries.)

tury Americans attempted to preserve as much of nature as was possible in a nation of cities and machines.

The counterpoint ideology quickly expanded beyond its connection with the rural cemetery and became the foundation of the American park movement. Dr. Elisha Huntington, several times mayor of Lowell, realized what increasing numbers of Americans were recognizing: the attractions of cemeteries for the living could be provided in the form of a public park.[36] In his annual address for 1845, Huntington declared: "We have grown up to a city of twenty-six or seven thousand inhabitants, and with a fair prospect of increasing numbers—we are being hemmed in by walls of brick and mortar, shutting out the pure air of heaven." It is possible, he observed, to walk out of the city "and seek the green, shady fields on our outskirts," but too often one is met with a sign reading "No Trespassers Allowed." The situation demands the establishment of a "public mall or promenade" near the central part of the city. "The value of such, I will not say luxury, but such a necessary of life, as free, open public grounds, is incalculable; we cannot estimate it."[37]

A month later the city council responded by authorizing the purchase of land at each end of the city where North and South Commons, parks of nine and twenty acres, respectively, were subsequently established.[38] The idea of a common, going back to the seventeenth century, took on an added dimension in the mid-nineteenth century. No longer simply the physical and symbolic center of the community, the common now served as a counterpoise to the visual monotony and social routine of emerging forms of urban life.

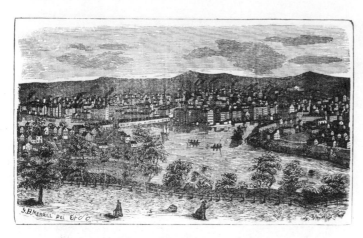

Fig. 7. *View of Lowell*, ca. 1860–65. (Reprinted from Charles Cowley, *A History of Lowell* [Boston, 1868], frontispiece; photograph courtesy of the Hagley Museum and Eleutherian Mills Library.)

Faced with the reality of urbanization, Lowellians turned away from the strategy of blurring city and country; they now defined them as distinct entities counterbalancing each other. In the 1820s and 1830s the machine, or factory, in the forest seemed like a benign development. What Leo Marx has called the "middle landscape" was preserved, even enhanced.[39] But as machines increasingly dominated life and the cityscape threatened to annihilate nature rather than reciprocate with it, Americans began to wonder where progress might end. The counterpoint ideology enabled them to draw a line that would not necessarily arrest further development but would simultaneously ensure an easily accessible natural sanctuary within the larger urban environment. This ideology seems to have taken hold at mid-century and enjoyed success not only in Lowell, but throughout America—most notably in Frederick Law Olmsted's Central Park in New York City.[40]

The midcentury pattern of visualizing the urban environment as a counterpoint of the urban "inside" and the nonurban "outside" began to break down with the approach of the twentieth century. It is clear that by 1893, when James Bayles wrote about contemporary Lowell, the role of the cemetery as a contrast to urban life had been abandoned. He made no mention of "picturesqueness" or the lack of it in his description of Lowell's burial places. In fact, his praise for the cemetery that Blanchard had conse-

Fig. 8. James Smillie, *Plan of Mount Auburn Cemetery, with Monument of Judge [Joseph] Story.* Lithograph, 1847. (Reprinted from Cornelia W. Walter, *Mount Auburn: Illustrated in a Series of Views from Drawings by James Smillie* [New York, 1847], frontispiece; photograph courtesy of Winterthur Museum Libraries.) ▶

crated as a counterbalance to urban materialism focused on "the evidence of the expenditure of vast amounts of wealth" to be found there.[41]

As Americans became more engrossed in the idea of a civilization of machines and as suburban expansion obscured the divisions between city and country, the vitality of the counterpoint perspective was sapped. It had arisen partly in response to a fear that the city and the machine would overwhelm man and nature, but for a generation that often used machine metaphors to describe the good society, this motive was lacking.[42] Further, for this interpretation of the American landscape, city and country had to be distinct. But in 1906, Frederick W. Coburn, an art critic and the historian of Lowell, noted that city and country were being blurred in suburbia. He observed that since the advent of the streetcar and the automobile, the region stretching from Washington, D.C., to Portland, Maine, was becoming one "five-hundred-mile city," essentially urban in character with ubiquitous reminders to suburbanites that they had "not left the city universal behind."[43] America was again becoming a middle landscape, but this one was primarily urban, whereas the earlier one had been essentially arcadian.[44]

In his study of urban planning in America, John W. Reps wondered "why it did not occur to some daring mind that the picturesque curving lines of the local cemetery might serve as a pattern for a successful residential subdivision."[45] The rural cemetery example undoubtedly influenced the romantic suburb movement that began with A. J. Davis's Llewellyn Park (1852) (cf. figs. 8, 9) and ended with Riverside (1869), designed by Frederick Law Olmsted and Calvert Vaux.[46] Later suburban development, however, is another matter. Given the nature of late-nineteenth- and twentieth-century suburban expansion, the rural

Fig. 9. Alexander Jackson Davis, *Map of Llewellyn Park and Villa Sites, on Eagle Ridge in Orange & West Bloomfield (New Jersey)*, 1857, lithograph, 15⅞" × 24¼". (Photograph courtesy of The Metropolitan Museum of Art, Harris Dick Brisbane Fund, 1924.) ▶

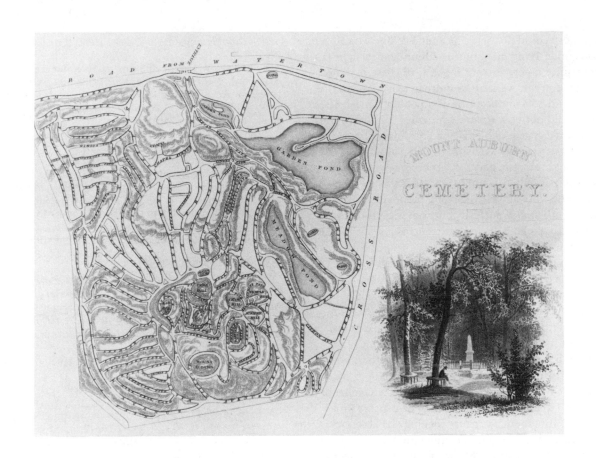

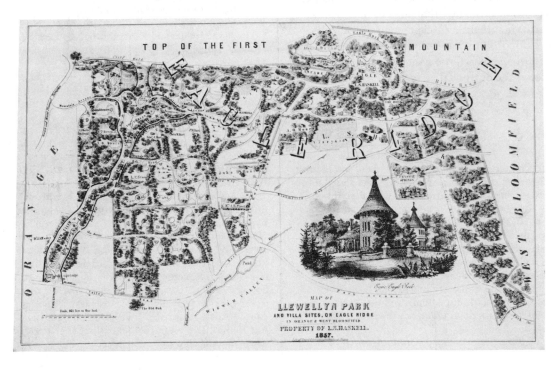

cemetery could not serve as a model. The assumptions underlying most of this suburban development were quite different from those at the base of the rural cemetery movement. Suburban expansion in the 1880s and 1890s was spurred by population densities that could not be humanely provided for within the compact city through existing building technology.[47] The result was an extension of the city, whereas the rural cemetery, the park, and the romantic suburb had been designed as counterbalances to the city. The parks and suburban developments in the late-nineteenth and twentieth centuries, despite an occasional curved lane, have been as artificial as the cities of which they are a part.

When the counterpoint scheme lost its force, a new idea emerged. A rural-urban continuum was now thought to provide optimum living conditions, a concept resulting in a homogenization of the landscape. With the muting of differences, the city lost some of its urbanity and the landscape some of its natural beauty. There is no longer any natural sanctuary abutting the city where one might ease the social, psychological, and visual tensions engendered by urban life. To cope with this twentieth-century problem, the nineteenth-century ideology has been reworked, and it now provides the rationale for the wilderness movement.[48] Since there are no longer enclaves within or near the urban area to obtain an alternative to the urban landscape, men periodically leave megalopolis entirely and seek out primitive areas. Suburban sprawl, the bane of social critics, is lost between the antipodal attractions of the city and the wilderness.

Notes

1. Rural cemeteries were built in every major and in most minor nineteenth-century American cities. For a partial list of the more important cemeteries, with brief descriptions, see *Spring Grove Cemetery: Its History and Improvements* . . . (Cincinnati, Ohio, 1869), 129–33.
2. Neil Harris's *The Artist in American Society: The Formative Years, 1790–1860* (New York, 1966), 200–208, 377–80, is a notable exception. For another useful discussion of the cultural significance of rural cemeteries, see Stanley French, "The Cemetery as Cultural Institution: The Establishment of Mount Auburn and the 'Rural Cemetery' Movement," *American Quarterly* 26, no. 1 (1974): 37–59.
3. John W. Reps, *The Making of Urban America: A His-*

tory of City Planning in the United States (Princeton, N.J., 1965), 326.
4. On Bigelow, Mount Auburn, and its influence, see Hans Huth, *Nature and the American* (Berkeley, Calif., 1957), 66–69, and Cornelia W. Walter, *Mount Auburn* (New York, 1847). At pages 33–35, Walter reprints a lecture that Bigelow used to promote Mount Auburn.

If the rural cemetery was a key element in the mid-nineteenth-century American effort to develop an ideology that would give meaning, coherence, and some comfort in a rapidly urbanizing and industrializing society, the role of Bigelow is suggestive. According to Perry Miller, Bigelow coined the word *technology* and, along with Joseph Story, who was also involved in the establishment of Mount Auburn, was a leader in accommodating the American mind to the values of a civilization of machines. (Perry Miller, *The Life of the Mind in America* [New York, 1965], 289–93, 298.)
5. Quoted by Harris, *Artist in American Society*, 201. At the time of the consecration, the Boston *Courier* predicted that Mount Auburn "will soon be a place of more general resort." (Reprinted in Joseph Story, *An Address Delivered on the Dedication of the Cemetery at Mount Auburn, September 24, 1831* [Boston, 1831], 27.)
6. [Andrew Jackson Downing], "Public Cemeteries and Public Gardens," *The Horticulturist* 4 (July 1849): 10.
7. Story, *Address*, 8, 12. Cf. [Edward Ruggles], *A Picture of New York* (New York, 1848), 163.
8. Story, *Address*, 17–18.
9. Story, *Address*, 20.
10. Reps, *Making of Urban America*, 326; Walter, *Mount Auburn*, 11.
11. In 1842 there were also rural cemeteries in Salem, Worcester, Springfield, and Plymouth, Mass., New Haven, Conn., and Nashua and Portsmouth, N.H. See [J. Brazer], "Rural Cemeteries," *North American Review* 53 (October 1841): 390.
12. Timothy Dwight, *Travels in New-England and New-York*, 4 vols. (New Haven, Conn., 1821–22), 4:516.
13. John William Ward, *Andrew Jackson: Symbol for an Age* (New York, 1955), 33, 36.
14. *Essex Gazette*, Aug. 12, 1825, quoted in John O. Green, "Historical Reminiscences," *Proceedings in the City of Lowell at the Semi-Centennial Celebration of the Incorporation of the Town of Lowell, March 1, 1876* (Lowell, Mass., 1876), 67–68.
15. Adelaide, "Alone With Nature," *Operatives Magazine* (June 1841): 37. According to Harriet Robinson, the pseudonym "Adelaide" was used in the *Lowell Offering* by Lydia S. Hall. (Robinson, *Names and Noms De Plume of Writers in the Lowell Offering* [Lowell, Mass., 1902], ii.) Since it is known that Lydia S. Hall was associated with the *Operatives Magazine*, she was probably "Adelaide" in this case. See also Anon., "Lowell" [a poem], *Mercury* (Lowell), Sept. 5, 1834; F., "Lowell as it was, and as it is," *Courier* (Lowell), Apr. 14, 1840; A. R. A., "Pawtucket Falls," *Literary Repository* (Lowell), 1 (1840): 128; and Ella, "The Window Darkened," *Lowell Offering* 5 (December 1845): 265–67.

16. C. C. Chase, "Brief Biographical Notices of Prominent Citizens of the Town of Lowell—1826–1836," *Contributions of the Old Residents' Historical Association* 4 (1891): 299; Frank P. Hill, *Lowell Illustrated* (Lowell, Mass., 1884), 9; Amos Blanchard, *An Address Delivered at the Consecration of the Lowell Cemetery, June 20, 1841* (Lowell, Mass., 1841), 8.

17. Charles Cowley, *Illustrated History of Lowell* (Boston, 1868), 123.

18. Hans Huth, in *Nature and the American*, 67, makes this point about Mount Auburn.

19. Blanchard, *Address*, 7.

20. Blanchard, *Address*, 15. This issue is prominent in nearly all the rural cemetery commentary of the time. See Story, *Address*, 12; F. W. S. [Rev. Frederick William Shelton], "Rural Cemeteries," *Knickerbocker* 12 (December 1838): 538; and Anon., *The Cincinnati Cemetery of Spring Grove*, enlarged ed. (Cincinnati, Ohio, 1862), 45.

21. Blanchard, *Address*, 19.

22. Blanchard, *Address*, 8; *Courier*, Dec. 9, 1841. See also Blanchard, *Address*, 6. For more general comments on this point, see Story, *Address*, 5; N. P. Willis, *Rural Letters and Other Records of Thought at Leisure* (New York, 1849), 154; Theodore Dwight, *Travels in America* (Glasgow, 1848), 144–46; [Andrew Jackson Downing], rev. of *Designs for Monuments and Rural Tablets . . .* , by J. J. Smith, in *Horticulturist* 1 (January 1847): 329–30; and Harris, *Artist in American Society*, 205–6.

23. *Operatives Magazine* (June 1841), 37. For identification of the author, see n. 15, above.

24. Roderick Nash, *Wilderness and the American Mind* (New Haven, Conn., 1967), 44. For a perceptive treatment of one of these intellectuals and the problem of city and country in America, see Michael H. Cowan, *City of the West: Emerson, America, and Urban Metaphor* (New Haven, Conn., 1967).

25. Andrew Jackson Downing makes this point in his "Public Cemeteries and Public Gardens," 9–10.

26. Blanchard, *Address*, 8. For similar expressions with reference to Mount Auburn, see Dwight, *Travels in America*, 198, and Story, *Address*, 12–16, 20. All of the consecration addresses that I have been able to read stress this point. Readily available samples may be found in the excerpts reprinted in Brazer's review of several of them in his "Rural Cemeteries," 385–412.

27. Blanchard, *Address*, 13–14.

28. *Vox Populi* (Lowell), July 17, 24, 1841. The expressions Blanchard borrowed from Wordsworth can be found in Alexander B. Grosart, ed., *The Prose Works of William Wordsworth*, 3 vols. (London, 1876), 2:25–40. The lines here at issue appear on 32–33.

29. For comments on this "borrowing" tendency in American intellectual history, see Ward, *Andrew Jackson*, 30, 225n, and Nash, *Wilderness and the American Mind*, 44, 50.

30. On the problem of nature, nationalism, and urbanization, see Perry Miller's essay, "Nature and the National Ego," in *Errand into the Wilderness* (New York, 1964), 204–

16, but especially 215–16. Also important are Miller, *The Raven and the Whale: The War of Words and Wits in the Era of Poe and Melville* (New York, 1956), and Harris, *Artist in American Society*.

31. Frederick Law Olmsted and Calvert Vaux, *Report of the Landscape Architects and Superintendents to the President of the Board of Commissioners of Prospect Park, Brooklyn* (1868), reprinted in *Landscape into Cityscape: Frederick Law Olmsted's Plans for a Greater New York City*, ed. Albert Fein (Ithaca, N.Y., 1967), 160.

32. L. J. B. C., "Lowell Cemetery," *Eastern Argus*, reprinted in the *Patriot* (Lowell), Jan. 25, 1844.

33. John Greenleaf Whittier, *The Stranger in Lowell* (Boston, 1845), 9–10. Most of the essays collected in this volume first appeared in the *Middlesex Standard*.

34. Whittier, *Stranger in Lowell*, 42–43.

35. J. W. Meader, *The Merrimack* (Boston, 1869), 274–75.

36. For example, see Downing, "Public Cemeteries and Public Gardens," 11.

37. Elisha Huntington, *Address of the Mayor of the City of Lowell, on the Organization of the Government, April 7, 1845* (Lowell, 1845), 14–16, quotations from 14–15. This portion of the address is reprinted and accompanied by a favorable editorial in the *Vox Populi*, Apr. 11, 1845.

38. Hill, *Lowell Illustrated*, 10, and *A Handbook for the Visitor*, 33. North and South Commons were located at what were then considered the northern and southern ends of the city. They are shown on H. S. Bradley's map of Lowell (1848), which is printed in F. Hedge, *Pictorial Lowell Almanac* (Lowell, Mass., 1849).

39. Leo Marx, *The Machine in the Garden* (New York, 1964), is an extended essay in definition of this term; brief explanations of it can be found on 23, 138–140, 226.

40. For a broader discussion of this ideology and Olmsted's relation to it, see Thomas Bender, *Toward an Urban Vision: Ideas and Institutions in Nineteenth-Century America* (Lexington, Mass., 1975).

41. James Bayles, *Lowell, Chelmsford, Graniteville, Forge Village, Dracut, Collinsville of To-Day . . .* (Lowell, Mass., 1893), 104–10, quotation from 108. In his apparent abandonment of the older role for the rural cemetery, Bayles went farther than most professional cemetery planners of his generation. This professional literature at the turn of the century reveals a tendency at least to give lip service to the older ideal (it was within this tradition that the profession had developed) while emphasizing ideas of keeping cemeteries away from areas of potential industrial expansion, economical land use, and efficient disposal of the dead. These men, while using a lingering rhetoric, saw their task as planners of cemeteries for the dead, not the living. For example, see Alfred Farmar, "The Modern Cemetery," *Overland Monthly*, n.s., 29 (April 1897): 443; Howard E. Weed, *Modern Park Cemeteries* (Chicago, 1912), 15, 25, 94–95, 119–22; Louis Windmuller, "Disposal of the Dead in Cities," *Municipal Affairs* 6 (Fall 1902): 473–77; O. C. Simonds, "Landscape Cemeteries," in *The Standard Cyclopedia of Horticulture*, ed. Liberty Hyde Bailey, 3 vols., continuously paged (New York, 1925), 3:1807–11; and W. D.

Cromarty, "Cemeteries of Yesterday and Today: Their Location and Layout in Relation to the City Plan," *Park and Cemetery* 30 (February 1921): 320–21.

42. For example, see Edward Bellamy's image of the ideal urban society functioning like the machinery in a New England textile factory in his *Looking Backward, 2000–1887* (New York, 1960), 164–65. John William Ward has linked Frederick W. Taylor's scientific management principles to this theme in his essay "The Politics of Design," in *Who Designs America?*, ed. Laurence B. Holland (New York, 1966), 51–85. For more general statements, see Samuel Haber, *Efficiency and Uplift: Scientific Management in the Progressive Era, 1890–1920* (Chicago, 1964); James Weinstein, *The Corporate Ideal in the Liberal State, 1900–1918* (Boston, 1969), chap. 4; Samuel P. Hays, "The Politics of Reform in Municipal Government in the Progressive Era," *Pacific Northwest Quarterly* 55 (October 1964): 157–69; Robert H. Wiebe, *The Search for Order, 1877–1920* (New York, 1967), chap. 6; and Joel H. Spring, *Education and the Rise of the Corporate State* (Boston, 1972), chaps. 1–3.

43. Frederick W. Coburn, "The Five-Hundred-Mile City," *World To-Day* 11 (December 1906): 1251–60. See also Frederick W. Coburn, *History of Lowell and Its People*, 3 vols. (New York, 1920), 1:371.

44. For a discussion of the suburbanization of the American landscape and the consequent problem of environmental symbolism, see Anselm Strauss, "The Changing Imagery of City and Suburb," *Sociological Quarterly* 1 (January 1960): 15–24.

45. Reps, *Making of Urban America*, 326–30.

46. On this movement, see Christopher Tunnard, "The Romantic Suburb in America," *Magazine of Art* 40 (1947): 184–87. In his *The City of Man* (New York, 1953), 195, Christopher Tunnard designates Riverside as the last of the "romantic" suburbs.

47. See Sam Bass Warner, Jr., *Streetcar Suburbs: The Process of Growth in Boston, 1870–1900* (Cambridge, Mass., 1962).

48. Roderick Nash does not explicitly make this argument, but the evidence he presents in *Wilderness and the American Mind* would support it. See also George Butler, "Change in the City Park," *Landscape* 8 (Winter 1958–59): 10–13, and Sigurd Olson, "The Meaning of Wilderness for Modern Man," *Carleton Miscellany* 3 (Spring 1962): 99–113.

Culture and Cultivation: Agriculture and Society in Thoreau's Concord

ROBERT A. GROSS

Too often our understanding of transformations in American material life during the nineteenth century begins and ends with descriptions of urbanism. After all, port towns saw an impressive increase in mercantile trade, sustained the pressures of rapid demographic influx, and witnessed the emergence of radical labor movements. Our focus on urban experience may result also from a prevailing nostalgia that urges us to see the countryside as a static foil against which the dynamic profile of the cityscape took shape. Such a view of life in "rural" towns could hardly be more misleading. Changes in the city were inextricably linked to changes of equal—perhaps greater—magnitude in hinterland communities. The centralizing force of urban industrial capitalism had a parallel in the quiet arrival of agricultural capitalism in farming towns.

As he describes the impact of agricultural "improvement" on husbandmen in Concord, Massachusetts—Revere's destination, Thoreau's town—Robert A. Gross offers complex answers to deceptively simple questions. What did this agricultural "revolution" actually mean to local farmers? How did it affect their material well-being? In exploring the quality and speed of changes in agrarian life, Gross draws on local tax lists and the U.S. agricultural census of 1850. Here, for the first time, we learn in concrete terms whether farm families were making it or losing ground and what they were raising, buying, and selling at ground level. Paradoxically, profound structural change came masked in apparent continuity. Between 1775 and 1860 the number and average acreage of Concord's farms remained consistent as parents balanced family size against limited land resources. Mixed husbandry—cereals, grasses, and cattle—dominated throughout the period. So, too, did a local economy that found families more often interdependent than self-sufficient. Yet the lure of agricultural markets centered in

nearby Boston increasingly shaped farmers' efforts in response to outside demands. Acres of reserved woodlands fell to the ax to provide more acreage for the profitable cultivation of English hay. As better roads made transport quicker and more reliable between 1800 and 1840, a local dairy industry developed. Gross demonstrates that agribusiness was firmly in place before the railroad—that same juggernaut whose tracks were Thoreau's morning footpath into Concord Center each day—arrived in town in 1844.

The pace of rural reform quickened with the train's arrival. Ready access to Boston and the world beyond meant that Concord's farmers could step up production with guaranteed profits. By 1850 the countryman's curse was apparent. Living in two worlds, he now worked twice as hard as his grandfather had, since he continued to labor for a household sufficiency as well as producing for urban markets. As the Concord farmer struggled to mediate the different relations of production of household and market, his consciousness was informed by the ideas and goals of agricultural reformers, literary theorists whose published tracts circulated widely. Their jeremiad extolled the virtues of a systematic approach to time, work, and money as the righteous path to increased profits. Although Thoreau's romantic radicalism may have softened the rigors of preindustrial farm work in eighteenth-century New England, his anguished outcry against the mechanical progress of agrarian reform was nonetheless precise.

The town of Concord, Massachusetts, is usually thought of as the home of minutemen and transcendentalists—the place where "the embattled farmers" launched America's war for political independence on April 19, 1775, and where Ralph Waldo Emerson and Henry David Thoreau, more than a half-century later, waged their own struggles for intellectual independence, both for themselves as writers and for American culture as a whole. But in the late nineteenth century, Concord acquired a distinction it never possessed in the years when it was seedbed of revolutionary scholars and soldiers. It became a leading center of agricultural improvement. Thanks to the coming of the railroad in 1844, Concord farmers played milkmen to the metropolis and branched out into market gardening and fruit raising as well. Concord was nursery to a popular new variety of grape, developed by a retired mechanic-turned-horticulturist named Ephraim Bull. And to crown its reputation, the town called the cultural capital of antebellum America by Stanley Elkins became the asparagus capital of the Gilded Age. Concord was, in short, a full participant in yet another revolution: the agricultural revolution that transformed the countryside of New England in the middle decades of the nineteenth century.[1]

The progress of that agricultural revolution forms my central theme. The minutemen of 1775 inhabited a radically different world from that of their grandchildren and great-grandchildren on the eve of the Civil War. We know the general outlines of how things changed—that farmers gradually abandoned producing their own food, clothing, and tools and turned to supplying specialized, urban markets for a living. In the process, they rationalized their methods and altered the ways they thought about their work. Theirs was a new world in which modern science was wedded to agricultural capitalism. But the process by which that world came into being is little known. Historians have given their attention chiefly to more dramatic events—to the rise of cities and factories, to the story of Boston and Lowell. No less important was the revolution in the countryside. Without it, the creation of an urban-industrial society would have been impossible.

Together, the city and the country underwent a great transformation. The years from around 1800 to 1860 comprise what Emerson called an "age of Revolution"—a time "when the old and the new stand side by side and admit of being compared; when the energies of all men are searched by fear and by hope; when the historic glories of the old can be compen-sated by the rich possibilities of the new era." What could be a better time to be alive, Emerson asked. That is essentially the inquiry I am undertaking—an inquiry into what it was like to make and to experience the great transition to modern agricultural capitalism in Concord.[2]

This investigation represents an early effort to gather together the evidence of agricultural change in Concord and to suggest its implications for the lives of farming people in the middle decades of the nineteenth century. The principal sources have been town valuations and assessment lists and the United States agricultural census of 1850.[3] These enumerations of land, livestock, and crops, among other goods, cover more than a century of Concord history, from the mid-eighteenth century to the eve of the Civil War. They allow us to view the agricultural changes of the antebellum era in long perspective—to date the beginning of fundamental breaks in the old way of life, to observe the parallel decay of the old and the rise of the new, and to pinpoint just when the adoption of new practices decisively accelerated and culminated in the triumph of a new agricultural regime. For the agricultural revolution did not come suddenly in an irresistible wave of change. The process was a slow and uneven one, proceeding by fits and starts and sometimes encountering setbacks along the way. Some things never really changed at all, and not until the end of the period, with the coming of the railroad, had a new world truly been born.

All of this, of course, can be said only with the historian's benefit of hindsight. To the participants in the process, who did not know the outcomes, the transition must have been at times a deeply unsettling experience. It challenged old habits and practices, demanded new responses while promising only uncertain rewards, and swept up those who wanted only to be left alone, comfortably carrying on their fathers' ways. Even those farmers and entrepreneurs who successfully rode the tide must have had their doubts. Those who resisted or just plain failed said little about their fate, succumbing to what Thoreau saw as lives of "quiet desperation." In the effort to reconstruct the experience of the transition, Thoreau's observations bear close reading. Thoreau was the most powerful and articulate critic of agricultural capitalism that America produced in the decades before the Civil War.

Had a visitor come to Concord around 1800 and

Table 1. Distribution of Land in Concord, 1749–1850

	1749	1771	1801	1826	1840	1850
Number of taxpayers	270[a]	273[c]	368	456[e]	520	611
owners	194[a]	204[c]	212	201[e]	213	192
landless	76[a]	69[c]	156	255[e]	307	419
Percent landless	28	25	42	56[e]	59	69
Average size of landholding in acres	56[b]	57[d]	61	60[e]	60	59
Measures of the distribution of land among owners:						
Share of top 20 percent	44.0	40.4	47.1	48.6	50.8	47.4
Gini ratio	.39	.34	.44	.46	.52	.47

Sources: See note 3. The 1850 data were derived from the 1850 Town Assessment List.

[a]In 1749 Concord included parts of the towns of Lincoln and Carlisle. When Lincoln was set off in 1754, Concord lost 20% of its taxpaying population. The number of taxpayers, owners, and landless have been reduced by 20% to reflect this change. No adjustments have been made to compensate for residents of Carlisle because the 24 missing cases on the valuation were concentrated within that area; in effect, the assessors who compiled the valuation and omitted the taxpayers in the north part of town made the adjustment. In 1780 when Carlisle was set off Concord lost 10% of its population; the 24 missing cases represented about 7% of the town. The average size of landholding and the measures of the distribution of land among owners are based on the original valuation, with no adjustments for Lincoln or Carlisle.

[b]The 1749 valuation lists only improved land, not total landholdings. The average holding in improved acres was doubled to estimate average holding of all lands. See Gross, *Minutemen and Their World*, 210n.

[c]The 1771 valuation includes parts of Carlisle separated from Concord in 1780. The number of taxpayers, owners, and landless have been reduced by 10% to adjust for residents of Carlisle. The average size of landholding and the measures of distribution of land among owners have not been adjusted to compensate for Carlisle.

[d]The 1771 valuation assessed only improved land, which has been estimated to be approximately 60% of all land in the town. See Gross, *Minutemen and Their World*, 213n. The average size of landholding has been adjusted on this basis to represent all lands.

[e]The 1826 assessment omits 22 estates listed in 1825 and 1827. These have been included in the data above. If they had been omitted the percentage of landless would have been 57% and the average size of landholding 55 acres. See Town Assessment List for 1825, 1825 file, box A-4, Concord Archives; Town Assessment List for 1827, Town Treasurer's Office (Town Hall, Concord, Mass.). The 22 estates were not used in calculating the measures of distribution of land among owners.

lived through the 1850s, he or she would certainly have been unprepared for the way things changed. At the opening of a new century, the agricultural economy was very much tied to the past. In the size of their farms, in the crops and livestock they raised, in the ways they used the land, farmers still carried on as their fathers had.

For one thing, the number of farms was the same in 1800 as it had been in 1750 and 1771: about two hundred. And the average size of a farm was no bigger in 1800 than it had been before: around sixty acres. These were unchanging facts of life in eighteenth-century Concord; nothing—not even revolution, war, and depression—would alter them in the slightest (see table 1).

This fundamental stability in the number and size of farms was no accident, no haphazard outcome of social evolution. It was a deliberate creation, a rational adaptation to the conditions of farming and family life in the preindustrial, household economy. This arrangement of farms on the landscape arose in response to a basic dilemma Concord began to encounter as early as the 1720s: there were too many young people in town and not enough land for them all—not enough, at least, for them to support families in the usual way. Markets did not exist to sustain comfortable livings on very small farms. Nor would the farming methods of the day have enabled the yeomen of Concord to produce substantial surpluses had the demand for them suddenly appeared. As a result, so long as families continued to be fruitful and multiply as successfully as they did and so long as death continued to stalk New Englanders less relentlessly than it did people in the Old World, the people of Concord would have to face up to the inevitable outcome. There was a fundamental imbalance between numbers and resources. Something would have to give.[4]

As it turned out, what gave was the aspiration of colonial patriarchs to settle all their sons close by on family lands. As early as the 1720s, it was becoming clear that some estates in Concord could not be split up "without Spoiling the Whole." Instead, increasingly, one son—often, but not invariably, the eldest—would inherit the homestead intact. The other children would have to go into trade, take portions and dowries in cash, or, in what was commonly the case, move away and settle on frontier lands. In effect, a continuing exodus of young people to new lands underwrote the stability of Concord's farms. Emigration was the key to the future, to ensuring that old patterns would go on unchanged. That mechanism worked so successfully that the colonial framework of farming in Concord—some two hundred farms of about sixty acres on the average—survived intact not just until 1800 but until the eve of the Civil War. No matter how much things changed, young people growing up on farms in nineteenth-century Concord had in common with their eighteenth-century forebears the expectation that most would move away and make new lives in other towns.[5]

For those who stayed behind on the homesteads around 1800, farming went on in traditional ways. In the household economy of Concord the needs of the family and the labor it supplied largely determined what was produced and in what amounts. This does not mean that farms were self-sufficient. Farmers normally strove to obtain a surplus of goods to exchange with neighbors and to enter into the stream of trade. Given the limited markets and the constraints on production in the eighteenth century, surpluses were necessarily small. Most farmers lacked the incentive or the capacity to participate extensively in trade.

Indeed, most farmers even lacked the ability to be fully self-sufficient. Historians have been led astray by the image of the independent yeoman, wholly dependent on his own resources, that eighteenth-century writers like J. Hector St. John de Crèvecoeur have handed down to us. What we would think of as the basic necessities of colonial husbandry—plows, oxen, pastures, sheep—were absent on a great many farms. A third of Concord's farmers did not own oxen, and if they were like the farmers in the towns of Groton, Marlborough, and Dedham, whose inventories have been examined by Winifred Rothenberg, half of them did not possess a plow and three-

quarters (72 percent) had no harrow (this was the case down to 1840).[6] Nor were farmers in Concord any more self-sufficient in the production of textiles. Almost half had no sheep in 1771, and in 1750 some 56 percent raised no flax at all (see table 2).[7]

What did people do, then, for basic necessities? They borrowed from neighbors or kin, exchanged goods or labor with others, or resorted to the store. Perhaps most often, they made do with what they had. This was a world of scarcity in which expectations were modest and always circumscribed. People had to accept the fact that labor and capital were required to supply all one's necessities "from within." It was the rich—the large landholders and the men who combined farming with a profitable trade—who could aspire to independence. It was they who produced most of the flax in Concord in 1750, planting about one-fourth to one-half an acre on the average, which is what the books say the ordinary farmer usually had. And it was they who could provide a wide variety of their own foods. The wealthy were able to take care of these needs precisely because they were engaged in trade, thereby acquiring the resources to hire labor and diversify livestock and crops. Market participation and self-sufficiency were not at opposite ends of a spectrum. Rather, market dependence without facilitated independence within. So when we read about the self-sufficient farmer, we should be skeptical: he was the exceptional man, uniquely favored by fortune. The editor of the *Old Farmer's Almanack*, Robert Bailey Thomas, spoke for a good many readers when he remarked that "there is a great satisfaction derived from living as much as possible upon the produce of one's own farm." But it was a satisfaction that only a few farmers ever enjoyed. Although independence was the general ambition, interdependence was the inescapable fact of life.[8]

The world of trade, then, offered a way out of the pervasive dependency of farmers on one another—out of the constant borrowing back and forth, the necessity of exchanging work, the endless keeping of accounts to ascertain one's standing in the community-wide network of credits and debts. And trade in agricultural surpluses played an important role in colonial Concord, shaping the principal uses to which people put their lands. In 1774, not long after he fled the fury of revolution for sanctuary in England, Massachusetts governor Thomas Hutchinson was received by George III. One might think that the king

Reforming the Environment

Table 2. Livestock Ownership in Concord, 1749–1850: Distribution and Average Size of Holdings

	1749	1771	1801	1826	1840	1850[a]
Horses						
Percent of taxpayers owning item	53	60	42	26	27	24
Percent of farmers[b] owning item	72	78	76	n.a.	65	n.a.
Average size of holding	1.2	1.2	1.2	1.3	1.3	1.3
Percent of owners with 3 or more	2.2	2.8	1.9	6.5	6.5	4.6
Oxen						
Percent of taxpayers owning item	46	51	36	24	20	15
Percent of farmers[b] owning item	64	68	66	n.a.	60	n.a.
Average size of holding	2.7	2.9	2.8	3.2	3.8	4.1
Percent of owners with 5 or more	5.7	5.9	8.3	14.8	18.3	14.7
Cows						
Percent of taxpayers owning item	70	74	57	43	32	26
Percent of farmers[b] owning item	93	96	93	n.a.	86	n.a.
Average size of holding	3.8	4.3	4.5	3.3	5.2	6.0
Percent of owners with 10 or more	3.3	4.9	11.0	2.7	9.6	21.9
Pigs						
Percent of taxpayers owning item	37	64	46	33	31	17
Percent of farmers[b] owning item	52	84	81	n.a.	80	n.a.
Average size of holding	2.3	2.0	1.7	1.9	2.2	1.8
Percent of owners with 4 or more	14.2	5.2	2.9	9.3	15.5	3.8
Sheep						
Percent of taxpayers owning item	46	39	n.a.	n.a.	3	n.a.
Percent of farmers[b] owning item	62	53	n.a.	n.a.	11	n.a.
Average size of holding	9.0	6.1	n.a.	n.a.	4.0	n.a.
Percent of owners with 15 or more	16.6	3.4	n.a.	n.a.	0.0	n.a.

Sources: see note 3.
[a]Calculated from 1850 Town Assessment List.
[b]A farmer is defined as a male taxpayer reporting crops and livestock on the province or state valuation.

would have examined Hutchinson closely about the political situation in the colony. But no; George III was famous not only for losing an empire but also for promoting the cause of agriculture, and he wanted to know about farming in Massachusetts. "To what produce is your climate best adapted?" asked the king. "To grazing, Sir," Hutchinson replied. "Your Majesty has not a finer Colony for grass in all your dominions: and nothing is more profitable in America than pasture, because labour is very dear."[9]

Hutchinson may have misjudged the political temper of the countryside, but he knew the lay of the land. Throughout the second half of the eighteenth century, farmers in Concord and elsewhere in eastern Massachusetts kept most of their improved land in grass. In Ipswich, over 90 percent of the improved land in 1771 was in meadows and pasture; in Concord that year, 80 percent (see table 3). In a sense,

farmers were doing what came naturally; as Hutchinson said, the soil was well suited to raising grass. But it was the pull of urban markets that prompted farmers to emphasize their mowing and grazing lands. Concord was beef country in the late colonial era. The agricultural economy was based on cereals—mainly rye and corn—for home consumption and beef for market.[10]

This was an extensive agricultural regime, where farmers saved on labor by exploiting land. The trouble was that by the eve of the Revolution, the land was losing its capacity to support livestock. Between 1749 and 1771, cattle holdings increased by a fifth, but to feed them farmers had to expand their pasturage by 84 percent, even though sheep raising was declining sharply.[11] Concord was starting to experience a serious agricultural decline. Indeed, so poor was the town's farming reputation that it

Table 3. Use of Improved Land in Selected Massachusetts Towns, 1771: Percentage Distribution

Town	Tillage	English and Upland Meadow	Fresh Meadow	Salt Marsh	Pasture	Total
		Percentages of Improved Acreage:				
Ipswich	8.9	7.3	7.6	22.7	53.4	100.0
Concord	20.2	12.9	27.4	0.0	39.4	99.9
Acton	22.8	12.3	28.1	0.0	36.8	100.0
Groton	30.1	15.9	22.2	0.0	31.7	99.9
Connecticut Valley towns	49.5	14.9	22.6	0.0	13.0	100.0

Sources: Arlin Ira Ginsburg, "Ipswich, Massachusetts, during the American Revolution, 1763–1791" (Ph.D. diss., University of California, Riverside, 1972), 241; 1771 Province Valuation List, Concord, Massachusetts, State Archives, 132: 199–211; 1771 Province Valuation List, Acton, Massachusetts, State Archives, 132: 49–52; 1771 Province Valuation List, Groton, Massachusetts, State Archives, 133: 1; Sylvester Judd, *History of Hadley: Including the Early History of Hatfield, South Hadley, Amherst and Granby, Massachusetts* (Springfield, Mass., 1905), 385.

Table 4. Land Use in Concord, 1781–1850: Percentage Distribution

Type of Land	1781	1786	1791	1801	1811	1821	1831	1840	1850
					Year of Valuation				
Improved:	64.8	59.2	64.3	60.1	54.8	58.1	56.5	57.8	58.8
Tillage	10.8	9.5	8.5	8.4	8.7	7.9	7.3	7.9	7.3
Grassland	54.0	49.7	55.8	51.7	46.1	50.2	49.2	49.9	51.5
Pasture	28.2	28.8	35.3	28.6	22.5	26.8	26.9	25.8	26.2
Meadow	25.8	20.9	20.5	23.1	23.6	23.4	22.3	24.1	25.3
English meadow	6.8	5.2	5.8	6.3	7.5	8.4	8.3	10.6	15.1
Fresh meadow	19.0	15.7	14.7	16.8	16.1	15.0	14.0	13.5	10.2
Woodland and unimproved:	35.2	36.7	35.6	37.0	38.7	32.4	32.4	33.9	36.2
Woodland	—	27.8	—	27.4	25.6	22.7	13.6	12.9	10.5
Unimproved	—	8.9	—	9.6	13.1	9.7	18.8	21.0	25.7
Unimprovable:	—	4.0	—	2.9	6.5	9.6	11.0	8.1	4.9
TOTAL:	100.0	99.9	99.9	100.0	100.0	100.1	99.9	99.8	99.9
N (in acres)	11,007	12,235	12,447	13,290	13,242	14,377	15,069	15,461	14,582

Sources: Shattuck, *History of the Town of Concord*, 213; Evaluation 1784/6, Massachusetts State Archives, 163: 51; Massachusetts General Court, Valuation Committee, Aggregates of Value, 1791, vol. 1, Archives of the Massachusetts State Library (Massachusetts State Library, Boston); 1801 Town Valuations, Massachusetts State Archives, 1: 34; Massachusetts General Court, Valuation Committee, Valuation of Massachusetts, 1831, Archives of the Massachusetts State Library; Massachusetts General Court, Report of the Valuation Committee as Corrected in the Legislature, 1841, p. 42, Archives of the Massachusetts State Library; Massachusetts General Court, Valuation Committee, Report of the Committee Appointed to Make a Valuation of the Polls and Property of the Commonwealth of Massachusetts, 1850, p. 46, Archives of the Massachusetts State Library.

blighted the marriage prospects of a young cabinet-maker and farmer named Joseph Hosmer. It is said that when he asked for the hand of a wealthy farmer's daughter in Marlborough, Massachusetts, in 1759, he was rejected out of hand. "Concord plains are sandy," complained the father. "Concord soil is poor; you have miserable farms there, and no fruit. There is little hope that you will ever do better than your father, for you have both farm and shop to attend to, *and two trades spoil one*. Lucy shall marry her cousin John; he owns the best farm in Marlboro', and you must marry a Concord girl, who cannot tell good land from poor." Joseph Hosmer ultimately won the girl, but he had to pasture his cattle outside of Con-

Table 5. Percentage Changes in Concord Grain Production by Decade, 1801–1850

Type of Grain	1801–11	1811–21	1821–31	1831–40	1840–50	1801–50
Rye	−37.9	8.2	−21.4	−2.6	−40.1	−71.3
Oats	5.4	62.1	81.7	68.4	−19.6	320.7
Indian corn	−5.3	13.2	0.6	−21.8	18.6	1.0
Barley[a]	—	—	—	—	—	−10.0
Total grains	−13.9	17.1	6.8	7.0	−7.6	6.4
Grains per acre tillage	−17.2	19.2	10.1	−4.3	6.4	10.6

Sources: see table 4.

[a]Values for barley are too small for calculation of significant percentage changes.

cord—in Rutland and Princeton, Massachusetts.[12]

By 1801, though still very much bound to the past, Concord was beginning to feel the stirrings of agricultural change. Markets were opening up everywhere for farmers, thanks to the extraordinary prosperity the United States enjoyed during the era of the Napoleonic wars. The port cities—merchants to the world in the 1790s and early 1800s—boomed, and so, in turn, did their hinterlands. Concord farmers began to raise substantial surpluses of rye, wood, and hay for the markets. They met the needs not only of Boston and Charlestown but also of the rapidly growing nonfarming population at home. Between 1771 and 1801, the share of Concord's population engaged in crafts and trade doubled, from 15 percent to 33 percent.[13]

The agricultural economy remained essentially what it had been: an economy based on cereals, grasses, and cattle. It would stay that way up through 1840. That year 86 percent of the improved land lay in meadows and pasture (see table 4). But within that framework, farmers steadily devoted more and more of their energies to producing for market. They raised three principal commodities for sale: oats, hay, and wood. The production of oats was clearly geared to city markets; it far outstripped the growth in the numbers of horses in Concord, and it clearly paralleled the periods of most rapid increase for Boston and Lowell (see tables 2 and 5). Expanded hay production came as a result of the increasing conversion of pastures and unimproved land to what were called "English and upland meadows," land plowed and seeded with clover, timothy, and herd's-grass. Adoption of English hay was the major agricultural improvement of the era, and Concord farmers took it up

with zeal. They cultivated meadowlands for cash, while relying on the natural river meadows of the Concord and Assabet rivers to feed their own livestock. As a result, the average farmer doubled his production of English hay from 4 to 8 tons between 1801 and 1840, while his output of fresh meadow hay barely increased from about 8 to 8½ tons. For the most part, the land converted to English hay was made available by the clearing of vast woodlands for market (see tables 6 and 7).

At the same time as farmers were concentrating on these staples, they also sought out new crops. They experimented with teasel, broomcorn, and silk, none of which worked. They added potatoes for both family use and sale. A few wealthy farmers engaged in commercial wool growing on a large scale, raising flocks of one thousand or so sheep before the entire business collapsed in the 1830s from cheap western competition.[14] Far more typical were the small-scale efforts of men like "Uncle Ben" Hosmer—Joseph's younger brother—to assemble surpluses for sale.

The story is told that in the 1790s, Ben Hosmer began taking butter, eggs, and other goods to the Cambridge market. He lacked a wagon, as did most farmers in those days; so he had to sling baskets full of butter and eggs across the "old mare's" back and ride her into town. One day Ben Hosmer, who was notoriously impulsive, suddenly decided to pack up the horse and go to market. He was feeling "grand poorly," he declared, and was almost out of "blackstrap." Besides, there was no West India rum in the house to serve if Parson Ripley stopped by. "It was a hot dog-day morning in August," we are told, and by the time Ben Hosmer got going, he was in quite a hurry. He pushed the old mare over the hills to Lex-

Table 6. Land Use in Concord, 1791–1850: Percentage Changes by Decade

Type of Land	1791–1801	1801–11	1811–21	1821–31	1831–40	1840–50
Improved land	−0.3	−9.1	15.0	2.2	4.9	−4.0
Tillage	4.6	4.0	−1.6	−3.1	11.5	−13.1
Grassland	−1.0	−11.2	18.1	3.1	3.9	−2.6
Pasture	−13.6	−21.5	29.2	5.4	−1.6	−4.2
Meadow	20.7	1.5	7.5	0.4	10.7	−0.8
English meadow	16.5	18.0	21.5	4.6	30.5	34.2
Fresh meadow	22.4	−4.7	1.0	−1.9	−1.1	−28.4
Woodland and unimproved	10.8	4.1	−9.1	4.9	7.5	0.6
Woodland	8.2	−6.8	−3.7	−37.2	−2.7	−23.0
Unimproved	18.9	35.1	−19.6	103.6	14.9	15.0
Unimprovable	−21.3	1.6	1.3	55.0	−67.6	−46.6
All lands	6.8	−0.4	8.6	4.8	2.6	−5.7

Sources: see table 4.

Table 7. Crop Production in Concord, 1749–1850: Average per Producer

Type of Crop	*(Number of Producers in Parentheses)*				
	1749	1771	1801	1840	1850[d]
Grain (bushels)	87.7 (230)	90.8 (219)	85.5 (164)[c]	130.9 (159)	132.7 (107)
Rye (bushels)	17.9[a]	23.2[b]	29.6 (139)[c]	20.2 (109)	22.5 (57)
Corn (bushels)	66.3[a]	64.1[b]	55.1 (184)	70.9 (150)	82.7 (105)
Oats (bushels)	0.0[a]	2.1[b]	17.4 (83)	67.6 (118)	65.2 (65)
All hay (tons)	11.5 (221)	10.6 (218)	11.4 (183)	15.1 (171)	27.7 (108)
English hay (tons)	2.8 (137)	3.7 (183)	4.3 (168)	8.0 (165)	—
Meadow hay (tons)	9.9 (219)	7.7 (214)	7.7 (175)	8.5 (148)	—
Cider (barrels)	12.0 (168)	7.9 (167)	10.1 (134)	—	—
Flax (pounds)	39.9 (103)	—	—	—	—

Sources: see note 3.

[a]Calculated by applying distribution of grains in inventoried estates, 1738–1754, to average output of all grains per producer on the 1749 valuation. "Grain" includes wheat. See Middlesex County Probate Records, first series.

[b]Calculated by applying distribution of grains in inventoried estates, 1755–1770, to average output of all grains per producer on the 1771 valuation. "Grain" includes wheat. See Middlesex County Probate Records, first series.

[c]There were 23 missing values for rye in 1801, thereby preventing calculation of total grains in those cases; i.e., there were 187 producers of grain in all.

[d]Calculated from 1850 U.S. manuscript census of agriculture; the 108 farmers listed in the census owned considerably more land than the 192 landholders whose holdings are reported on the 1850 town assessment: 92 acres, compared to 59.

ington so fiercely—his cane was four feet long and an inch in diameter—that she was sweating "profusely" by the time they stopped for rest at a brook in East Lexington. He intended only for her to take a cool drink, but once that mare felt the refreshing waters of the brook, she would have nothing less than a bath. With the panniers full of butter and eggs still on, the mare rolled over and over in the brook.

"To say that Uncle Ben was surprised and aston-ished," it is said, "would be to draw it very mild; nay, he was dumb founded. He had a tremendous voice, and at once opened up the bottom scale." By the time people had rushed to his aid, he was in greater lather than the horse; it was all he could do to sputter curses at her. "Don't you know any better than to lie down in the brook with Dinah's butter and eggs on your condemned back?" The horse had no answer. Soon Ben Hosmer was pounding the poor animal se-

Table 8. Grain Production in Concord, 1801–1855: Percentage Distribution

| Type of Grain | Year of Valuation or Census | | | | | | | |
	1801	1811	1821	1831	1840	1845	1850	1855
Wheat	—	—	—	—	0.6	0.1	0.3	0.4
Rye	28.2	20.4	18.8	12.9	11.7	12.0	7.6	6.3
Oats	8.3	10.1	14.0	23.8	37.5	33.1	32.7	17.1
Indian corn	62.6	69.5	67.2	63.3	46.3	54.7	59.4	75.8
Barley	0.3	—	—	—	3.9	—	0.2	0.4
Peas and beans	0.6	—	—	—	—	—	—	—
Total	100.0	100.0	100.0	100.0	100.0	99.9	100.2	100.0
Grains produced (bushels)	16,791	14,457	16,930	18,080	19,339	16,680	17,868	21,371
Acres tillage	1,112	1,156	1,137	1,102	1,229	1,148[a]	1,068	1,134
Grains per acre								
tillage (bushels)	15.1	12.5	14.9	16.4	15.7	14.5	16.7	18.8

Sources: 1801 Town Valuations, Massachusetts State Archives, 1:34; Shattuck, *History of the Town of Concord*, 213; Massachusetts General Court, Valuation Committee, Valuation of Massachusetts, 1831; Massachusetts General Court, Report of the Valuation Committee as Corrected in the Legislature, 1841, p. 42; Palfrey, *Statistics of Industry in Massachusetts, 1845*, 50; Massachusetts General Court, Valuation Committee, Report of the Committee Appointed to Make a Valuation of the Polls and Property of the Commonwealth of Massachusetts, 1850, p. 46; Francis DeWitt, *Statistical Information Relating to Certain Branches of Industry in Massachusetts, For the Year Ending June 1, 1855* (Boston, 1856), 302–4.

[a]Computed as the average of acres of tillage for 1840 and 1850.

verely. A crowd gathered round, and when he had finally worked off his rage, one latecomer asked him politely if the mare really had lain down in the brook with the butter and eggs. "Don't you see the yolks running all down the ole mare's belly, and the butter is fit for nothing more than grease!"[15]

Ben Hosmer's adventures may seem comical now—they probably did then—but they illustrate the difficulties and risks of carrying foods like butter and eggs to market in the early days of the new republic. By 1840 wagons and roads had so improved that a good deal of butter was being made and sold in Concord. But it was not until the coming of the railroad that large-scale production of milk, eggs, fruits, and garden vegetables became truly profitable in Concord.[16] Before then, small farmers like Ben Hosmer had to concentrate on bulky goods—oats, hay, and wood—supplemented by whatever other surpluses they could get. And note that it was Dinah Hosmer, not Ben, who put up the butter and eggs.

In these circumstances, it is not surprising that farmers continued the effort to supply their own necessities, even as they sought new products for market. To be sure, they were quick to abandon raising their own cloth when cheap textiles started streaming out of the new mills. But a great many farmers never had been able to furnish their own linen or wool. When it came to foodstuffs, they still did as much as they could for themselves. Rye steadily declined in relative importance from 1800 to 1840, but even in 1840 three-quarters of the farmers in town still raised enough for their bread (see table 8). The same holds true for fodder crops. English hay went to market; the fresh meadows fed livestock at home.[17]

This combination of production for both markets and home use meant, in practice, that farmers were adding greatly to the burdens of their work. One crop was not substituted for another. Farmers simply exploited themselves more intensively than ever. Once they had spread their labor over the land, plowing shallowly, manuring thinly, and cultivating infrequently, with the result that yields were low. That was acceptable when farmers chiefly raised grain crops for family use and the profits came from grazing livestock. But now farmers depended for a living on far more intensive work: chopping wood, reclaiming land for English hay, digging potatoes, making butter, and occasionally even nursing mulberry bushes.

Farmers not only labored more intensively than ever. They did so in a radically new setting. By the mid-1820s, the evidence strongly suggests that hired

Table 9. Commerce and Manufacturing in Concord, 1791–1850: Shops, Stores, Mills, and Manufactories

	1791	*1801*	*1831*	*1840*	*1850*
Number of shops	21	47½	41	54	53
Adjacent	—	9	4	9	13
Separate	—	38½	37	45	40
Number of tan and slaughterhouses	6	17	1	0	0
Tan houses	5	6	1	0	0
Slaughterhouses	1	11	0	0	0
Number of stores and warehouses	4	6	6½	8	8
Number of mills	6	6	6	6	5
Grist mills	—	—	2	2	2
Saw mills	—	—	2	2	2
Other mills	2	2	2	2	1
Number of other buildings	47	104	79½	94	111½
Total buildings	84	180½	134	162	177½

Sources: see table 4.

labor had come to supplant family labor on the farm. Between 1801 and 1826 the ranks of landless men in Concord expanded from around 150 to 250, even as opportunities in crafts and trade stagnated and the number of farms remained unchanged (see tables 1 and 9). Those laborers must have been doing something for a living. Since farmers' sons were continuing the exodus out of Concord—but at an earlier age and to lands farther and farther from home—it is likely the laborers were taking their place. The hired hand had become a commonplace figure on the farm as early as 1815. Thomas's "Farmer's Calendar" for May of that year assumed that farmers had already "hired a man for a few months, to help along with your work," and it offered this advice: "If you have a good faithful one, then set store by him and treat him well, and, mind me now, don't you fret.—*Steady, boys, steady*, is the song for a farmer—If you get yourself into a habit of continually fretting, as some do, then it is ten to one if you can get good men to work for you. But some prefer a dull, lazy lubber, because he is cheap! but these *cheap* fellows I never want on my farm."[18]

Thomas's comments suggest that a calculating, even suspicious spirit dominated the relations between farmers and their help. Where once farm boys had labored for their fathers out of duty, love, and an expectation that they would inherit land of their own someday, now it was money—and money alone—

that kept help working on the farm. The social relations of production were imbued with the ethos of agricultural capitalism.

The same rationalizing, economizing impulse transformed the work customs of the community. As late as 1840, many farmers still lacked basic resources to do their work, even as they added to the demands on themselves. Nonetheless, they gave up cooperative practices like the huskings and apple bees of old. These were now condemned as uneconomical and wasteful "frolics," given over to heavy drinking and coarse entertainment. When one writer in the *Concord Gazette* of 1825 wistfully lamented the disappearance of bundling, country dances, and "the joyous huskings" of the past, he was roundly denounced by another for peddling immorality in the press. Neighborly sharing and cooperation probably diminished in another way as well. Agricultural reformers urged farmers to be as sparing as possible in "changing works." Again the *Old Farmer's Almanack* tells the changing sentiment. "There are some," Thomas complained in 1821, "who cannot bear to work alone. If they have a yard of cabbages to hoe, they must call in a neighbour to change work. Now this is very pleasant, but it tends to lounging and idleness, and neglect of business; for we cannot always have our neighbours at work with us." Concord farmers likely took such advice; in *Walden*, Thoreau assumes that the farmer characteristically works alone and is starved for company by the time he comes back from the fields. An era had come to an end; farmers now relied on the claims of cash rather than the chain of community to do their work.[19]

Edward Jarvis, a prominent nineteenth-century medical reformer who grew up in Concord, celebrated this development as a positive force in social life.

> The people of Concord are none the less kind, sympathetic and generous than their fathers, but they are stronger in body and in beast. They are more self-sustaining, and it is better that each should do his own work, with his own hands or by such aid as he can compensate in the ordinary way. . . . The world's work is now as well and completely done as ever and people both individually and socially are as happy and more prosperous, and are loving, generous and ready to aid in distress, poverty, and sickness, wherever these shall present themselves, in any family or neighborhood.[20]

Jarvis wrote in 1878, at the end of the long transition, and he summarized as progress what small farmers at the time may have experienced as a very mixed blessing. Huskings may have wasted corn; changing works may have been a bother; and the exchange of goods and labor among farmers could sometimes end up in hard feelings and lawsuits on both sides. Still, the farmer who lacked money to hire all the help he needed had no alternative but to depend on his neighbors or exploit himself to the hilt.

It is possible, of course, that improvements in farm tools let people do more work in less time. There were certainly people in Concord who were alert to the latest innovations. One of them was the first to use a cast-iron plow at the annual plowing match in Brighton, sponsored by the Massachusetts Society for Promoting Agriculture. Moreover, about a third of Concord's farmers in the mid-nineteenth century belonged to the Middlesex Agricultural Society. But from the absence of plows and harrows from inventories as late as 1840 and from the fact that 40 percent of Concord farmers still had no oxen even then, it appears that labor-saving inventions did not have widespread impact until after the coming of the railroad.[21]

We may gain some clues, too, from the agricultural reform literature of the day. It is full of complaints that boys no longer want to follow their fathers on the farm. Even more to the point, the central theme of that literature—the overwhelming burden of the many pieces on crop rotations, saving manure, raising turnips, and storing tools, among other subjects—is the absolute necessity for system in farm work. The trouble with farming, complained one observer after another, is that men do everything "by halves"—"half fencing, half tilling, and half manuring"—and without any forethought or plan. They labor hard, far harder than they ought, but "to no kind of good purpose." "Their work hurries them on," a New Hampshire writer observed, "and they have not time to make the necessary retrenchments and improvements: but continue (to use the common expression) 'slashing on, heels over head,' without consideration—zeal without improvement; thus they make perfect slaves of themselves, and never reform, pass through the world without enjoying the sweets of living—they follow their fathers' paths and swerve not."[22]

Even before the railroad era, then, Concord farmers had entered the world of modern capitalism, with its characteristic institutions of money and markets. Producing for market had not, however, wholly displaced traditional activities on the farm; men still tried to furnish their food from within. This attempt to combine new demands with old ones added significantly to the burden of farm work; it amounted to a speed-up: more output in less time.

The intensification of farm work accelerated even more sharply after the railroad linked Concord more tightly and speedily to the Boston market. The goods that the city demanded were those that required long hours of unremitting toil. Dairying was probably to become the most important. Between 1800 and 1840, as farmers turned to making butter for sale, the average herd of cows on a farm rose slightly from 4½ to 5. The next decade saw that figure increase again to 6. More dramatically, the proportion of men owning ten cows or more doubled from 11 to 22 percent (see table 2). It was in the 1840s, too, that farmers began on a large scale to reclaim the many acres of boggy meadow in town for English hay. This was immensely costly and labor-intensive work. Those who could afford it hired Irish laborers to do the job; increasingly, cheap foreign labor displaced native help. Finally, the demand for wood boomed in these years; so vigorously did farmers respond to the market that by 1850 they had reduced the forests of Concord to a mere tenth of the town. Some people were already alarmed at the prospect of timber running out.[23] In short, the steady chopping of the ax; the bustle of men spading up meadows, hauling gravel, and raking hay; the clanging of milk pails—these were the dominant sounds on Concord's farms in the 1840s. These sounds reverberate through *Walden*, and all of them finally were orchestrated to the movements of that locomotive whose piercing whistle as it swept into town announced the triumph of a new order (see tables 4 and 5).

It was, of course, precisely that new system of agricultural capitalism that Thoreau assailed so incisively, so unrelentingly. We tend to forget that Thoreau addressed *Walden* first of all to his neighbors, in the faint hope of waking them up, and he invariably drew his evidence of the false "economy" of his time from the life immediately around him. It was the farmers of Concord who plowed their manhood into the soil and pushed barns and lands before them as they crept down the road of life. It was they who were the slavemasters of themselves. Behind these strictures lay a deeper critique of what small farmers were doing to themselves as they tried to keep up with the market. Thoreau's attack was remarkably comprehensive. It emphasized:

1. The extending division of labor in society. People were becoming tools of their tools, individuals reduced to functions.
2. The intensification of work, which meant a tight constriction of individual autonomy. People rationalized their work and harnessed their lives to the clock. There was little in the way of true leisure.
3. The commercialization of life and dominance of commodities over men. Things were in the saddle and rode mankind. People spent their lives accumulating goods they would never enjoy.
4. The inequality of the results: the vast disparity in living standards between different levels of society. Luxuries, Thoreau thought, were built on exploitation of the many by the few.
5. Most important of all, a decay of the spirit. Farmers treated nature not as a medium of spiritual growth but merely as a commodity, as a means for turning crops and livestock into money. And that narrow materialism extended

into all their lives. The farmers and merchants would spend for barns and lands and imposing town halls. But they stinted the lyceum and did too little for the libraries and schools. There was no true culture in Concord.[24]

Yet Thoreau's critique was flawed by his idealization of the preindustrial order. In his travels through Concord he talked to old-timers about what life used to be like and came away romanticizing their picture of independence and self-sufficiency on the farm— a world that hardly ever was. The real world of eighteenth-century farming demanded interdependence and mutual cooperation among households that would never have suited one who marched to a different drummer. Thoreau was too much a part of his own time ever to approve of the more leisurely ways of the eighteenth century. He may have looked suspiciously idle to his neighbors as he wandered off into the woods, but the prescription he offered in *Walden* was close in spirit to the advice of agricultural reformers. People, he said, needed to systematize, to rationalize their lives so that they might cultivate their higher selves in the very process of getting a living. But in giving this counsel and holding up his own experience at Walden Pond, Thoreau inverted the values of the agricultural writers, subjecting them to his highly individualistic, transcendental purposes. By paring back their material needs, providing as much—one might say, as little—as possible for themselves, and keeping their purchases to a minimum, people would be liberated from the grip of economic necessity and into lives of true leisure.

That solution, of course, required enormous self-discipline, parents nearby, and a bachelor's solitary existence. Even then, Thoreau wearied of growing beans and preferred a hunter-gatherer's life. In the end, the critique proved far more powerful than the alternative. There was little the small farmer could do to survive but move to cheaper lands farther west or adapt as best he could to the market, specializing ever more in profitable crops, buying ever more of his necessities at the store, intensifying ever more his exploitation of himself and/or his laborers. Perhaps only those with access to substantial capital or with unenviable capacities for restricting their own wants would come to enjoy the new world of agricultural capitalism. A great many more farming families would be lost in the transition. Theirs was an experience unvarnished with the trappings of a successful middle-class culture. Recovering that experience is the key to understanding what was lost as well as gained in America's "age of Revolution."

Notes

The author acknowledges the support of the Charles Warren Center in American History, the Amherst College Trustees, and the John Simon Guggenheim Memorial Foundation.

1. Stanley M. Elkins, *Slavery: A Problem in American Intellectual and Institutional Life* (Chicago, 1959), 141–42; Edward Ackerman, "Sequent Occupance of a Boston Suburban Community," *Economic Geography* 17 (January 1941): 61–74; Ruth R. Wheeler, *Concord: Climate for Freedom* (Concord, Mass., 1967), 174–75.

2. Ralph Waldo Emerson, "The American Scholar," in *Selections from Ralph Waldo Emerson: An Organic Anthology*, ed. Stephen E. Whicher (Boston, 1957), 77.

3. The assessments and valuations on which I have drawn for my analysis of individual propertyholdings are: 1749 Province Valuation List, box 1, Concord Archives (Special Collections, Concord Free Public Library, Concord, Mass.); 1771 Province Valuation List, Concord, Massachusetts State Archives (State House, Boston), 132:199–210; 1795 Town Assessment List, Town Treasurer's Office (Town Hall, Concord, Mass.); 1798 U.S. Direct Tax (New England Historic Genealogical Society, Boston); 1801 State Valuation, box A-2, Concord Archives; 1826 Town Assessment List, Town Treasurer's Office (Town Hall, Concord, Mass.); 1840 State Valuation, Town Treasurer's Office; 1850 Town Assessment List, Town Treasurer's Office; 1850 U.S. Manuscript Census of Agriculture, Massachusetts State Archives. The 1771 Concord valuation is now more readily available in Bettye Hobbs Pruitt, ed., *The Massachusetts Tax Valuation List of 1771* (Boston, 1978), 194–200.

4. For the story of how people in Concord struggled with the problem of population pressures on land, see Robert A. Gross, *The Minutemen and Their World* (New York, 1976), 68–108, and Gross, "The Problem of Agricultural Crisis in Eighteenth-Century New England: Concord, Massachusetts, as a Test Case" (typescript, Dec. 29, 1975, Concord Free Public Library).

5. The evidence on inheritance practices is drawn from probate records on intestate estates. By the 1740s, most estates were not broken up. Some 61% of inventoried estates between 1738 and 1775 went undivided to a single heir; a quarter of all inventoried estates passed intact to the eldest son. Those estates that were split up by the probate court averaged 142 acres; the estates that were kept intact, by contrast, were nearly half that size, 80 acres, on average. See Middlesex County Probate Records, 1st ser. (Middlesex County Registry of Probate, East Cambridge, Mass.). For a fuller discussion of this matter, see Gross, "Problem of Agricultural Crisis," 5–11. These findings are supported by Christopher M. Jedrey's recent study of inheritance customs in Chebacco parish of Ipswich, Mass., in the eighteenth century. See Christopher M. Jedrey, *The World of John Cleaveland: Family and Community in Eighteenth-Century New England* (New York, 1979), 58–94.

6. Winifred B. Rothenberg, "'Ye Sons of Freemen! Venerate the Plough!' Agricultural Productivity in Three Massachusetts Towns before 1840" (typescript, Brandeis University, 1975), 40–45. James Kimenker found few plows and harrows recorded in Concord estates inventoried in the periods 1750–60 and 1799–1802. See James Kimenker, "The Concord Farmer" (Senior honors thesis, Brandeis University, 1973).

7. That a majority of farmers in 1749 reported no flax at all seems, at first glance, incredible. The conventional wisdom is that the typical Yankee farmer in the eighteenth century regularly supplied the linen fiber for homespun clothes. Following that assumption, I hypothesized that only the big commercial producers of flax reported their output on the 1749 valuation. That expectation proved wrong. By applying an estimate of flax yields from the early 1800s to the 1749 data—150 pounds to an acre—I found that most flax producers devoted a half-acre or less to the crop; this is the usual estimate of land in flax on relatively self-sufficient farms. Another attempt to explain away my surprising findings also failed. Flax is a land-exhausting crop that might have been grown only once every few years, in order to rest the soil. In that case, only a minority of farmers at any one time would have been raising the crop. To test this possibility, I presumed that nature was not biased in favor of the rich; that is, at any single moment a cross-section of the farming population should have been growing flax. Again, the hypothesis did not work. As the table below shows, it was clearly the wealthy farmers who raised flax.

| | Deciles of Farmers[a] Ranked by Acreage of Improved Land | | | | | | | | | | |
| | Poorest | | | | | | | | | Richest | |
	0–9%	10–19%	20–29%	30–39%	40–49%	50–59%	60–69%	70–79%	80–89%	90–100%	Total
Number in decile owning improved land	0	0	5	29	33	31	32	34	33	34	231
Percent producing flax among owners of improved land	—	—	0.0	6.9	24.3	38.7	40.6	52.9	69.7	73.5	43.7

[a]A farmer is defined as a male producer of a crop.

A chi square test on the eight nonempty deciles shows the relationship between flax production and economic status to be significant at less than the .001 level with seven degrees of freedom. The discussion of flax is based on the following sources: Henry Bass Hall, "A Description of Rural Life and Labor in Massachusetts at Four Periods" (Ph.D. diss., Harvard University, 1917), 14–28; Percy Wells Bidwell, "Rural Economy in New England at the Beginning of the Nineteenth Century," *Transactions of the Connecticut Academy of Arts and Sciences* 20 (April 1916): 322–25; and Massachusetts Society for Promoting Agriculture, *Papers; Consisting of Communications Made to the Massachusetts Society for Promoting Agriculture, and Extracts* (Boston, 1807), 41–42.

8. See Richard L. Bushman, "Family Security in the Transition from Farm to City, 1750–1850," *Working Papers of the Regional Economic History Research Center* 4 (1981): 28–32. On flax production, see n. 7, above; for the ample, diverse food supplies found in estates of the wealthy, see Sarah F. McMahon, "'Provisions laid up for the family': Toward a History of Diet in New England, 1650–1850" (typescript, Nov. 2, 1979 [copy in possession of Robert Gross]), 28. The quotation from Robert Bailey Thomas is taken from George Lyman Kittredge, *The Old Farmer and His Almanack* (Boston, 1904), 122. It was not only flax production that was concentrated among the rich. Kimenker finds a similar, though less pronounced, inequality in cider production on colonial Concord's farms. The Gini ratio calculated from the distribution of cider production was a relatively high .43. The biggest cider producers were chiefly the richest farmers; Kimenker, "Concord Farmer," 53.

9. Peter Orlando Hutchinson, comp., *The Diary and Letters of His Excellency Thomas Hutchinson, Esq.*, 2 vols. (Boston, 1884–86), 1:171.

10. Boston imported 3,272 barrels of beef per year during the period 1768–73. The presence of one slaughterhouse and two tanhouses in Concord by 1771 suggests that some cattle raising was being done for the Boston market. See Max George Schumacher, *The Northern Farmer and His Markets during the Late Colonial Period* (New York, 1975), 24–26, and 1771 Province Valuation List, Concord.

11. Between 1749 and 1771, the number of oxen in Concord increased by 21%, the number of cows by 20% (these ratios of change have been calculated after adjusting for the separation of Lincoln in 1754). At the same time, holdings of sheep fell by 40%. Notwithstanding the fact that fewer sheep should have meant more grazing land for cattle, Concord farmers expanded their land in pasture during 1749–71 by 84%. This extensive conversion of land into pasture was the dominant change in land use in the late colonial period. The increase in tillage and meadowland, by contrast, merely kept up with the growth in cattle holdings. Acres in tillage rose by 22% over 1749–71, acres in meadow by 21%. See 1749 Province Valuation List; 1771 Province Valuation List, Concord.

12. Josephine Hosmer, "Memoir of Joseph Hosmer," in *The Centennial of the Social Circle in Concord, March 21, 1882* (Cambridge, Mass., 1882), 115–16, and Josephine Hos-

mer, "Life of Major Joseph Hosmer," Nov. 1869, folder D 1186.1, Concord Antiquarian Society Papers (Concord Free Public Library).

13. On the economic boom in Concord during the 1790s and early 1800s, see Gross, *Minutemen and Their World*, 171–73. The estimate of the nonfarming population is based on the occupations of decedents whose estates were inventoried in Middlesex County in the periods 1750–60 and 1798–1802. See Kimenker, "Concord Farmer," 99–102.

14. For the efforts at silk production, see the reports of Anthony Wright's experiments with silkworms and mulberry trees in the *Concord Yeoman's Gazette*, July 12, 19, 26, 1828. The wool-growing ventures of Joseph Barrett and a few others are documented in Lemuel Shattuck, *A History of the Town of Concord* (Boston, 1835), 217, and J. Fay Barrett, "Memoir of Joseph Barrett," in *Memoirs of Members of the Social Circle in Concord, Second Series: From 1795 to 1840* (Cambridge, Mass., 1888), 91–92.

15. Joseph Hosmer, "Concord in Ye Olden Time," 1889, Adams Tolman Newspaper Scrapbook Collection (Special Collections, Concord Free Public Library).

16. In 1840 the value of "products of the dairy" (including butter and milk) reported for Concord was $6,290. By 1845—one year after the railroad linked Concord to Boston and made possible regular milk sales to the metropolis—farmers produced butter worth $4,345 and sold $3,725 in fluid milk for a total of $8,070. See F. R. Gourgas, Schedule of Mines, Agriculture, Commerce, Manufactures, Middlesex County, Mass., 1840, Records of the Bureau of the Census, RG 29 (National Archives); and John G. Palfrey, *Statistics of the Condition and Products of Certain Branches of Industry in Massachusetts, for the Year Ending April 1, 1845* (Boston, 1846), 50.

17. During the first decades of the nineteenth century, farmers depended on the natural meadows along the Concord River to feed their own livestock, while they raised English hay on upland meadows for sale in the market. This arrangement of hay production became increasingly untenable from the 1820s to the eve of the Civil War as a result of the mounting flowage problem on the Concord and Sudbury rivers. According to Concord-area farmers, in the early 1800s the Middlesex Canal Company began illegally raising the height of a downstream dam it owned at Billerica. When the canal company sold its rights to a textile manufacturing corporation, the dam was elevated still higher. The result was a flooding of the river meadows upstream from the dam; no longer could farmers team wood by the river in winter or depend chiefly on the meadows for river hay. The pressures on the river meadows mounted in the 1840s; by the late 1850s, they had reached a crisis point and set off a political contest between farmers and manufacturers over the settlement of the problem. The state legislature appointed a special commission to inquire into the problem and heard testimony from Concord-area farmers about how the flowage problem had damaged their lands. In the end, the farmers got no satisfaction in the matter. As Morton J. Horwitz has demonstrated, prodevelopment sentiments dominated riverine law in this era; manufacturing corpora-

tions were exempted from liability for damages when their exploitation of waterpower resulted in the flooding of lands owned by farmers, whether upstream or downstream from the mills. See [Commonwealth of Massachusetts, General Court], *Report of the Joint Special Committee upon the Subject of the Flowage of Meadows on Concord and Sudbury Rivers. January 28, 1860* (Boston, 1860); Henry D. Thoreau, *A Week on the Concord and Merrimack Rivers*, ed. Carl F. Hovde, William L. Howarth, and Elizabeth Hall Witherell (Princeton, N.J., 1980), 6, 38; Morton J. Horwitz, *The Transformation of American Law, 1780–1860* (Cambridge, Mass., 1977), 33–53.

18. Kittredge, *Old Farmer*, 85–86.

19. *Concord Gazette and Middlesex Yeoman*, Dec. 31, 1825, Jan. 28, 1826; Kittredge, *Old Farmer*, 179; Henry D. Thoreau, *Walden*, ed. J. Lyndon Shanley (Princeton, N.J., 1971), 135–36.

20. Edward Jarvis, "Traditions and Reminiscences of Concord, Massachusetts; or, A Contribution to the Social and Domestic History of the Town, 1779 to 1877" (manuscript, 1878, Concord Free Public Library), 40.

21. *Concord Yeoman's Gazette*, Oct. 22, 1825, Nov. 4, 1826; Kimenker, "Concord Farmer," 90–91, 108–9.

22. This analysis of agricultural reform literature is based principally on a reading of the farming items, chiefly reprints from the agricultural press, that appeared in Concord newspapers, 1817–30, of speeches before the Middlesex Agricultural Society, and of prominent works by agricultural reformers in the period. See *Middlesex Gazette*, Nov. 2, 1816–Sept. 1, 1821; *Middlesex Observer*, June 22–Dec. 28, 1822, Jan. 4–June 14, 1823; *Concord Gazette and Middlesex Yeoman*, Nov. 29, 1823–Mar. 4, 1826; *Concord Yeoman's Gazette*, Mar. 11, 1826–Dec. 26, 1829; Thomas G. Fessenden, "Address," *New England Farmer* 1 (Oct. 19, 1822): 89–92; Josiah Adams, *An Address to the Society of Middlesex Husbandmen and Manufacturers, on Their Anniversary at Concord, October 2, 1823* (Concord, Mass., 1823); Charles Briggs, *Discourse Delivered at Concord, October the Fifth, 1825* (Concord, Mass., 1825); John M. Cheney, *An Address Delivered before the Society of Middlesex Husbandmen and Manufacturers, at Concord, Mass., Oct. 5, 1831* (Concord, Mass., 1831). Two later works by prominent agricultural writers summarize the critique expressed by writers and speakers in Concord. See Henry Colman, *Fourth Report of the Agriculture of Massachusetts: Counties of Franklin and Middlesex* (Boston, 1841), and Horace Bushnell, "Agriculture at the East," in Bushnell, *Work and Play, or Literary Varieties* (New York, 1864), 227–61. Quotations are from *Middlesex Gazette*, Aug. 1, 1818.

23. The *Middlesex Gazette* drew attention to a report from New Jersey that "clearing of forests has been so rapid that within a few years, timber and wood will be lacking for necessary purposes" and found that it was "particularly applicable to many parts of this vicinity and richly merits attention." See *Middlesex Gazette*, Dec. 25, 1820. For an overview of the timber problem, see Kathryn Whitford, "Thoreau and the Woodlots of Concord," *New England Quarterly* 23 (Sept. 1950): 291–306. In 1855 almost 20% of the population of Concord was foreign-born, and Irish natives were 86% of the foreign-born population. See Francis DeWitt, *Abstract of the Census of the Commonwealth of Massachusetts, Taken with Reference to Facts Existing on the First Day of June, 1855, with Remarks on the Same* (Boston, 1857), 116.

24. For an extended analysis of Henry David Thoreau's critique of agriculture and society in Concord, see Robert A. Gross, "'The Most Estimable Place in All the World': A Debate on Progress in Nineteenth-Century Concord," *Studies in the American Renaissance* 2 (1978): 1–15.

Domestic Architecture as an Index to Social History: The Romantic Revival and the Cult of Domesticity in America, 1840–1870

CLIFFORD E. CLARK, JR.

In the mid-nineteenth century the form and decoration of America's middle-class domestic architecture changed. The shift in taste was evident in a new spate of published design manuals and in the houses actually built between 1840 and the Civil War. While the landscape of Federal and Jacksonian America had been dominated by classical houses whose sturdy columns and restrained facades invoked Republican virtue, the gothic, Italian, and bracketed styles of the 1840s represented a new attempt to use architecture to promote a series of reforms that centered on Christian family life as the basis of a new social order. In this essay Clifford E. Clark, Jr., examines the intersection of architectural change and related developments in evangelical Protestantism, in aesthetic theory, and in how nineteenth-century people viewed nature.

Consider the dominant new styles themselves. Gothic cottages, marked by pointed arches, vertical board-and-batten siding, and stained-glass windows, represented a symbolic transference of ecclesiastical imagery from the parish church to the single-family home. At the same time, earthen colors and idealized rural settings suggest the home's place in a romanticized, morally uplifting nature. Italianate and bracketed houses were suitable for warm climates but were also, as Clark observes, seen as a "link between town and country." Together these three styles provided a focus for the contrast of technological progress and sentimental historicism, practicality and spirituality, rural retreat and urban bustle. By the early 1850s, their mediating quality was further enhanced by the establishment of picturesque suburban enclaves within an easy train ride of urban workplaces. In keeping with contemporary shifts in aesthetic theory, these houses allowed for the moral improvement of the individual qua individual; they were at once both aesthetically and ethically instructive. Not only applied bric-a-brac argued for social change. Floor plans were equally influential, offering new rooms for specific functions: nurseries, dining rooms, libraries, and separate bedrooms for children. As they split kitchens and domestic work spaces to the rear of the house, these structures also proclaimed a radical new disjunction between public and private space.

This was the house that became under the watchful eyes of Protestant ministers the stage for the domesticity movement. What A. J. Downing was to wood and stone, Horace Bushnell was to family worship. The title of his best-seller, Christian Nurture (1847), reveals the importance of the domestic environment to social reformers. Rather than focusing on conversion as the key to Christian faith, Bushnell argued that the education of Christians should begin in the home. As middle-class women gained new prominence in their narrowed roles as child rearers, moral guides, and homemakers, houses literally adopted "cross-plans" and stoves became miniature altars of domestic worship. Although these mid-nineteenth century cottages and villas are today preserved with loving care, they are artifacts of a reform movement that made individual character a detached focus of education, self-control a necessary virtue, and the separation of public and private selves a key to social success.

In the middle decades of the nineteenth century, a major change took place in American domestic architecture. Classical revival homes, long associated with the virtuous republicanism of the American Revolution, were replaced by picturesque gothic revival cottages and Italianate villas.[1] The shift in style from classical to romantic was not fortuitous; it represented the fruits of an intense crusade that, in terms of its social significance, deserves to rank with temperance and abolitionism as a major reform movement of the time.[2] Basing their arguments on the new needs created by the changing attitudes toward nature, religion, technology, and the family, the advocates of domestic architectural reform in less than three decades transformed the housing standards of the nation.

Although many historians have recognized the shift in domestic architectural styles at mid-century, few have tried to compare the housing crusade to other reform movements or to understand the broader social forces behind the changes.[3] Why was the crusade for new forms of domestic architecture so popular after 1840? In what ways did the changes in architecture reflect changing attitudes toward religion and the family? To what extent did the rationalization and specialization of function, so integral to the process of modernization, find an expression in the design of the house floor plans?[4] What, in short, are the kinds of insights into American social history that can be gained by the study of domestic architecture? These questions can be answered by examining the vast literature about home design that was published in popular magazines and "House Pattern Books" and comparing that literature to the houses that were actually built. Although statistical data on house construction are incomplete, sufficient state studies and local histories are available to make comparisons possible. By contrasting the values and assumptions expressed in the reform literature with the plans of houses now in existence, some idea may be gained about the discrepancies between the ideals of the reformers and what happened in practice.[5]

Although gothic and other forms of romantic architecture were built in America as early as the turn of the nineteenth century, the crusade for a new domestic architectural style did not find a mass following until the 1840s. In that decade, Andrew Jackson Downing crystallized public opinion by publishing his *Treatise on the Theory and Practice of Landscape Gardening . . . With remarks on rural architecture . . .* (New York, 1841) and *Cottage Residences; or, A Series of Designs for Rural Cottages and Cottage Villas . . .* (New York, 1842). These two works, which went through more than twenty editions in the next thirty years, codified the aesthetic theory of the new movement and provided examples of the different kinds of revival houses that could be built. The new interest in architectural reform, stimulated by Downing's writings, was reflected in the number of building guide books published after 1840. Between 1800 and 1840, twenty editions of builders' guides were printed. In the two decades after 1840, this number tripled, and, in the 1870s, an additional fifty-eight editions came out. These books, which contained architectural drawings of house plans with extensive discussions of the theories behind the designs, were used by local carpenters to construct the latest housing styles. After the 1870s, the number of builders' books declined as professional architects began to control more of the design of private residences.[6]

At the height of the early romantic revival, three basic house styles competed for the position of being the most popular. The first, the "gothic" revival home, was described by one contemporary as "a building, the character of whose architecture is distinguished by the upward direction of its leading lines, and by such curves as may be introduced meeting, or having a tendency to meet in a point."[7] In its most popular form as a rural cottage, the gothic style emphasized verticality by its steeply pitched roofs, board-and-batten siding, sharply pointed dormers, and ornamentation on the gables (see fig. 1). The rural gothic revival style not only harmonized well with natural surroundings, but because of its origin in a more religious age, was also thought to symbolize an eminently Christian form of private dwelling. In such a rural home, isolated from the vices of city life, the Christian family could "worship God, with none to molest or make us afraid."[8] The early gothic revival reached its peak in the 1840s and 1850s, although there was a second revival of the style in the 1880s, largely resulting from the writings of the English critic John Ruskin. In the second revival, gothic was used primarily in the design of large civic and educational buildings.

Even more popular than the gothic revival was the Italianate style, inspired by the villas of Tuscany and

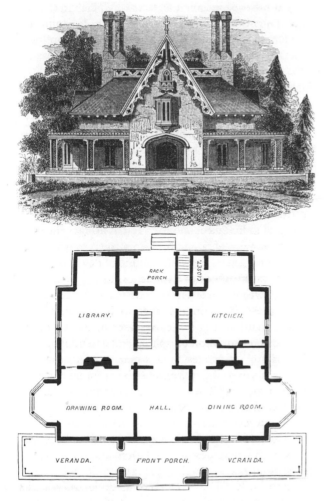

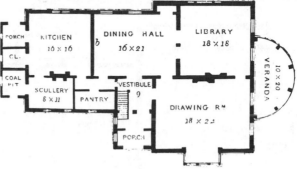

Fig. 2. Villa in the Italian style. Villas in the Italian style were known for their asymmetrical grouping of forms and the use of a tower to provide a view of the surrounding countryside. (Reprinted from Andrew Jackson Downing, *The Architecture of Country Houses* [New York, 1850], 289.)

Fig. 1. Gothic-style cottage-villa. This house was built for an upper-class man of wealth. Downing in his first writings preferred that such houses be built of stone, following the example of the English gentry. (Reprinted from Andrew Jackson Downing, *The Architecture of Country Houses* [New York, 1850], 296–97.)

known by its asymmetrical grouping of forms. The Italianate style could most easily be recognized by its flat-roofed tower and broad veranda, or porch, which was thought to "convey at once an expression of beauty arising from a superior comfort or refinement of the mode of living" (see fig. 2). Contemporaries recommended this style for the rectangular suburban lot. As one architect wrote, "Its form possesses sufficient regularity to harmonize with the buildings in the city, whilst its character shows it to be a link between town and country."[9]

The third basic style was known as "bracketed" because of the heavy brackets under the projecting eaves (see fig. 3).[10] Similar in some respects to the Italianate style, it became enormously popular in part because it was a modification of the earlier classical rectangular shape and in part because it appeared to be highly functional. As one architect wrote, "the coolness and dryness of the upper story, afforded by the almost veranda-like roof, will render this a delightful feature in all parts of our country where the summers are hot." The ease of construction and the picturesqueness achieved by modifying the windows and the porch made the "bracketed" style the most popular building form at midcentury.[11]

Mid-Victorian Americans appear to have chosen the gothic, Italianate, and bracketed forms more often than the other historical revival styles because

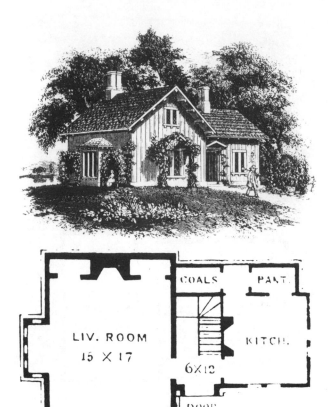

Fig. 3. Bracketed-style cottage. This modest house, with its board-and-batten siding that stressed verticality, was designed for middle-class families. (Reprinted from Andrew Jackson Downing, *The Architecture of Country Houses* [New York, 1850], 79.)

these three forms best combined the latest technology (in terms of heating, ventilation, and sanitation) with the more significant historical associations. If the gothic were popular because it was the ultimate symbol of the "Christian home," the Italianate and the bracketed styles with their towers and overhanging roofs were adopted for their functionality—cooling in summer as well as providing the vistas of the natural world that were considered at the time as being so important for the mental health of the public. The combination of significant historical associations with relative ease of construction and functionality appealed to a middle-class public that wanted to blend the best of the past with the needs of the present.[12]

The interest in the gothic, Italianate, and bracketed house styles after 1840 was supported and intensified by a number of social changes taking place in the period. The new concern for a proper form for domestic residences was reinforced by what the historian John Higham has called the movement from boundlessness to consolidation, a reaction against the hectic economic growth and rapid mobility that were fueled by the expansion of cities, the westward movement, and the beginnings of industrialization. "These frequent changes of residence," wrote one observer, "are destructive of much of that home-feeling which is essential to the education of the affections and moral sentiments." Others complained that "a constant moving from house to house causes one to acquire thriftless habits, and is opposed to the practice of a wise and judicious economy." To counteract the restless movement of population from town to town, the housing reformers urged the public to develop a deeper commitment to a single dwelling place. "Thus," wrote one observer, "the man who has a home, presenting comfort allied to taste, feels a love for it, a thankfulness for its possession, and a proportionate determination to uphold and defend it against all invading influences. Such a man is, of necessity— we might say selfishly, a good citizen; for he has a stake in society." The home thus became an island of stability in an increasingly restless society.[13]

The interest in new housing styles in the 1840s was also stimulated by the expansion of the housing market, the increases in population, and the development of railroads, which made it possible to commute to work. The expansion of urban areas created a need for entirely new communities. To meet the demand for new residences, the housing advocates placed a great deal of emphasis on creating a distinctly "suburban" style. Building in the suburbs allowed an individual to combine "urban conveniences" (new forms of heating and plumbing) with "the substantial advantages of rural conditions of life." These included not only direct access to nature, which was thought of as a source of truth and beauty, but also a defense against the ruinous rents and vices of city life. In the city, with the proximity to intemperance and open vice, wrote one reformer, there could be "no feeling of privacy, no security from intrusion." The suburb, by contrast, was a protected retreat where the family would be safe. "The essential qualification of a suburb is domesticity," wrote Frederick Law Olmsted, the landscape architect. "The fact that the families dwelling within a suburb enjoy much in common, and all the more enjoy it because it is in common . . . should be everywhere manifest in the completeness, and choiceness, and the beauty of the means they possess of coming together . . . and especially of recreating and enjoying them together on common ground."[14]

Yet another influence on the new housing styles was the shift in attitudes toward the conceptions of taste and beauty that grew out of the romantic movement in the 1830s. Classical revival architecture associated with Thomas Jefferson and Benjamin Henry Latrobe had rested on the theory that forms were beautiful in themselves and that architecture should display the principles of simplicity, harmony, and proportion; the romantics, borrowing from British aesthetic theorists like Archibald Alison, now argued that structural forms were beautiful only in terms of the thoughts that they raised in the mind of the viewer. Thus gothic architecture, which was popularized in the works of Byron and Sir Walter Scott, became emblematic of the ideals of an earlier Christian age. "The sublime, the glorious Gothic," wrote one reformer, was "the architecture of Christianity."[15]

To an aesthetic theory that associated architectural forms and spiritual ideals, American reformers added an ethical dimension. Taste and the perception of beauty were inextricably related to the moral development of the individual. Searching for a proper justification for their position, New York architectural reformers Henry Cleveland and William Backus quoted the words of federalist Timothy Dwight of Yale, who argued that "the first thing powerfully operated on, and, in its turn, proportionally operative, is the taste. The perception of beauty and deformity, of refinement and grossness, of decency and vulgarity, of propriety and indecorum, is the first thing which influences man to escape from a grovelling, brutish character. . . . In most persons, this perception is awakened by what may be called the exterior of society, particularly by the mode of building." It followed from this theory that the environment that surrounded the individual was a crucial force in shaping his or her personality. The morals, civilization, and refinement of the nation, according to the housing reformers, depended on the construction of a proper domestic national architecture.[16]

The choice of a quotation from Dwight to justify their position is significant, for it reveals both the continuities with and the differences between the ideals of the reformers and the objectives of the sponsors of the earlier Greek revival. When earlier neoclassical reformers like Dwight spoke of the importance of "the exterior of society," they meant to emphasize that the exterior of the buildings should mirror a public order of balance and equilibrium. The very placement and arrangement of public buildings—as, for example, in the planned layout of Washington, D.C.—was seen as exemplifying in a geographical manner the precise divisions that were embodied in the Constitution in terms of checks and balances.[17] Although the new reformers shared the earlier Federalist interest in creating an environment that would symbolize important ideals, their major concern was not with *public* buildings but rather with *private* behavior. What reformers like Cleveland and Backus wanted to do was to take that part of the aesthetic theory that had supported the earlier revival of neoclassical styles and turn it into a justification for the creation of a new, private, domestic lifestyle for the middle class. Instead of emphasizing public order and republican virtues, they wanted to stress the importance of private discipline and self-control.

By the 1840s, then, the shift toward consolidation with its emphasis on social stability, the need for new housing, the growth of suburbs, and the acceptance of the romantic criteria for beauty and taste all served to inspire a new interest in the gothic, Italianate, and bracketed styles of housing. But before that interest reached the intensity of a major reform crusade, it needed further support. This it gained from the changes in Protestantism and the reform movements of the times.

*   *   *

The outlook of American Protestants began to shift in the 1840s. In the previous two decades, Protestant theology had been strongly shaped by the massive revivals that had occurred during the Second Great Awakening. Led by Charles Grandison Finney, Lyman Beecher, and others, the revivalists had placed an emphasis on individual conversion. Save the individual, Finney urged, and persuade him to dedicate his life to Christ, and that individual would observe the Sabbath, free the slave, and banish alcohol from the world. Although Finney's arguments, known to his contemporaries as "moral suasion," were persuasive at the time, by the 1840s they had become out of date. For the aggressive reformer who hoped to wipe out sin and perfect the individual, moral suasion seemed weak. Too many professed Christians continued to go about their sinful ways. The revivals, moreover, had proved to be an enormously disruptive force in communities. By inspiring individuals to make their own peace with God, they made individuals distrust the settled churches. As a result, sects and denominations broke apart and the churches began to squabble among themselves.[18]

By the 1840s a major reaction had begun to develop in the eastern churches against revivalism. It was led by Horace Bushnell, a Hartford minister, who published his views in 1847 in a book entitled *Christian Nurture*. The true approach to Christianity, Bushnell argued, was that the child should "grow up a Christian, and never know himself as being otherwise." How could this be accomplished? Simply place the child in a Christian home and surround him with Christian parents who would set the proper example. In a sermon entitled "The Organic Unity of the Family," Bushnell argued that the child "breathes the atmosphere of the house. He sees the world through his parent's eyes. Their objects become his. Their life and spirit mold him."[19]

Housing reformers were quick to take this religious argument and turn it to their own ends. "We are in no little danger of losing sight of the importance which God has attached to the family relation," wrote one architect. Those who are wise should recognize the importance of the nursery. "There is so intimate a connection between taste and morals, aesthetics and Christianity," wrote another, "that they in each instance, mutually modify each other; hence whatever serves to cultivate the taste of the community . . . will give to Christianity increased opportunity and means of charming the heart and governing the life."[20]

Having agreed with Bushnell that the home was a crucially important influence in shaping the religion of the child, the housing reformers set out to design as Christian a home as possible. The result was the conception of the house as a church, which reached its fullest development in the gothic revival style. No efforts were spared in providing the house with the proper associations. One of the most heavily used symbols was the cross. The house was often designed on a cross plan, and crosses were usually attached to the tops of the gables. One building pattern book even supplied a full page with twenty different designs of crosses that might be used. In addition to the crosses, stained glass became popular for providing accents in the windows, and some of the guide books suggested that three primary colors be used to symbolize the Trinity. For the front parlor, a pump organ could be purchased upon which the family's favorite hymns could be played. Even stoves and bedroom furniture could be designed following gothic standards. All in all, the rural gothic house became the perfect place for Christian nurture.[21]

If the shifting outlook of Protestantism stimulated an interest in housing reform, so, too, did the new approach that was becoming evident in the temperance and abolitionist crusades. Like the revivalists, the antislavery and temperance men had at first placed their emphasis on reforming the individual. By the 1840s it had also become evident to them that their tactics were not working. Individual commitments had to be strengthened by institutions. Turning away from their earlier belief in moral suasion, the abolitionists both sought support in the political arena and stressed the importance of the family as a new instrument of social reform. As one popular abolitionist argued, "a few usages maintained, a few rights guaranteed to the slaves, and the system is vitally wounded. The right of chastity in the woman, the unblemished household love, the right of parents in their children—on these three elements stands the whole weight of society." Significantly, too, when Abraham Lincoln tried to explain the Republican party's attitude toward property to the lower classes, he did it by making an analogy to the ownership of a home. "Let not him who is houseless," Lincoln argued, "pull down the house of another; but let him labor diligently and build one for himself, thus by example assuring that his own shall be safe from violence when built." In a similar manner, as the temperance leaders shifted from an emphasis on moral suasion and began to seek legal sanctions, they, too, stressed the harmful influence of alcohol on the family.[22]

The intensive propaganda campaigns waged by the temperance and abolitionist crusaders with their stress on the family strengthened the program of the housing reformers. "Nothing has more to do with the morals, the civilization, and refinement of a nation, than its prevailing Architecture," wrote one architect. "Virtue and Beauty are twin sisters; while Vice and Deformity are in constant association. The moral and refined seek a home where the virtuous influences that are reflected from Beauty and Order, are congenial to their cultivated minds and moral constitutions." Other reformers went even further. Improvements in domestic architecture would not only cure the vices of the individual, they would reform and uplift society itself. As one crusader wrote:

> No man, we think, could live just the life in a well-proportioned and truely beautiful dwelling that he would in a mud shanty or rude log cabin. Certain elevating influences would steal into him unawares . . . that would lift his life above its otherwise lower level. It would be made, unconsciously perhaps, more human, more dignified and tasteful. . . . And so, too, this power of the tasteful is seen very often in the influence which a single dwelling will exert upon almost all in its neighborhood.

The man who improved the dwelling houses of the people would make a lasting reform in the foundations of society.[23]

In addition to stressing the effectiveness of housing reform as an instrument of social change, the advocates of the romantic revival broadened their social outlook in the 1850s. In the previous decades the movement had been dominated by Calvert Vaux and Gervase Wheeler, English architects who had helped to popularize the ideas of Downing. These men were deeply aristocratic in their outlook. Houses were important because they rooted the individual to the land. They also advocated a strict class system of housing with villas for the rich, cottages for the middle class, and farmhouses for the laborers. The worst sin a man could commit in the eyes of these architects was to aspire to a house above his social status.[24]

By the 1850s the elitism of the early landscape architects was beginning to come under attack. As in the antislavery and temperance crusades, the reform movements developed a more democratic appeal as they became more popular and tried to reach a larger audience. Some advocates of the romantic revival were quick to point out the inadequacies of the "foreign architects, settling in our midst." These men, asserted one reformer, had "written with reference to the wants of the wealthy only. . . . When treating of the improvements of landscape in this country," the critic continued, "one should write for the masses, for men who are either poor, or only moderately wealthy." Thereafter numerous "House Pattern Books" appeared designed for those with limited means.[25]

Thus, by the 1840s the influence of the temperance and antislavery movements together with the new outlook of Protestantism, the reaction against the pace of social change, the need for new housing, the expansion of the cities, and the vogue of romanticism all served to give the advocates of domestic housing reform an unprecedented influence on the American public. Although no precise statistics exist on the number of revival houses actually built, almost every town of moderate size had its gothic, Italianate, and bracketed houses.[26]

* * *

Another way to analyze the significance of the housing reform movement is to look at it in terms of the social science concept of modernization. As Richard D. Brown has defined it:

> The core of its meaning expresses two ideas; economic development as measured by per capita output; and social and political change in the direction of rational, complex, integrated structures. The economic side of modernization is commonly associated with the enshrinement of the productive ideal and its concomitants; rationalized production, mobilization of resources, increasing specialization of economic functions, and an increasing scale and integration of economic operation.[27]

This definition is particularly helpful when we focus on the changing roles of architects and women and their relationship to the home.

Architects, like doctors and lawyers in the early decades of the nineteenth century, were not well organized as a profession. Just as the doctor was forced to compete with the midwife, the barber-surgeon, and the quack, those who aspired to the status of "architect" were threatened by existing ranks of local carpenters and village mechanics. To improve their own position and undermine the competition in the 1840s, these self-styled architects used two arguments. Drawing on British aesthetic theory, they insisted that specially trained architects were needed because only they could design the kind of house that had the proper associations for the Christian family. Pointing with disdain at the crude mistakes made by country carpenters, such as the use of classical columns to hold up the porch on a gothic house, they argued that only they had knowledge of the true historical styles. Even more important than their knowledge of the past was their command of the latest techniques in the sciences of heating, plumbing, and construction. As one of them bluntly put it, "If there are such intimate relations between esthetic beauty and moral excellence, why not employ more tact and talent in marrying the useful and beautiful together here?" The "House Pattern Books" thus placed a strong emphasis on the functionality of the dwelling. "In arranging the apartments," wrote one architect, "special attention should be given to the saving of needless labor." In the period that first saw the widespread use of interior plumbing, central heating, lighting (with gas), refrigeration, and sewers, the architect established himself as the specialist in these areas and wrote books on the latest developments in each field.[28]

Another theme contained in all the "House Pattern Books" was the necessity of using an architect to ensure that the design would be "honest" and "truthful." Buildings were constructed for particular purposes that should be evident in their structure. "Without this qualification," wrote one reformer, "it can have neither true value nor real beauty." A house should look like a house and not like a Greek temple, wrote another. Nothing was more absurd than a "Grecian temple in clapboards with its kitchen and cooking apparatus at one end and its prim fluted columns at the other! A temple of Minerva with its sauce-pans and pianos!" The continual emphasis on honesty and truthfulness in architectural design reflected the mid-Victorian preoccupation with appearances. In a mass society with an increasing number of aliens and immigrants, it was particularly important to be able to recognize differences in social status.[29]

In their concern for drumming up more business, cutting out the competition, and establishing architectural design as a profession, the architects themselves became the major spokesmen in the crusade for new housing standards. They thereby helped to popularize their own position and eventually succeeded in establishing their profession on a firm footing. The irony is that one of the major agents of their success, the "House Pattern Book," had the drawback of undermining their business; for if the man in the street could buy a book on the latest developments in central heating, he could dispense with the services of the architect.[30]

In a similar fashion, the role of women in the middle decades of the nineteenth century became increasingly specialized, and that specialization was reflected in the design of the houses. The beginnings of industrialization during the age of Jackson had divided women's roles into two different categories according to their social class. The influx of large numbers of lower-class women into the textile mills had identified low-skill industrial work as "women's work." At the same time, middle- and upper-class women were excluded from such fields as medicine where they had served as midwives and occasionally as "doctoresses."[31] In part as a reaction to this exclusion, middle-class women had begun to develop their own specialty—the care of children and the home.

The process of specialization within the home could clearly be seen in the floor plans of the houses. The usual layout consisted, on the first floor, of a front porch and an entrance hall and stairs, a front parlor or drawing room for the entertainment of guests, a family room (sitting room), a dining room, and often a bedroom for "age and sickness." Further toward the back of the house was the kitchen, usually followed by a wash house or a summer kitchen. If the family had some wealth, the house would also have a library, often with a side door leading to the garden. On the second floor would usually be three or four bedrooms, a nursery, and a bath.

Each room was seen as having a special function. As one reformer put it, "merchants find the classification of their goods indispensable, or separate rooms for different classes of things. And why [is] not this principle equally requisite in a complete house?" The library, usually located near the back in a more quiet part of the house, was for the gentleman who "has either professional occupations, or literary taste." It had its own side entrance so that his comings and goings would not disturb the rest of the family. There were also specialized rooms for the children. A separate room was designated as the nursery, indicating both the importance placed on the early years of life and the desire not to be awakened in the night by the crying of children. Each child had a separate bedroom. As one reformer argued, "satisfying this home-feeling will also contribute immeasurably to their [the children's] love of the homestead. Without it, it is only their *father's* home, not theirs . . . But, by giving them their own apartment, they themselves become personally identified with it, and hence love to adorn and perfect all parts."[32]

The greatest emphasis, however, was placed on designing the rooms to fit the needs of the woman in the family. Here a careful separation was made between those parts of the house that were public and those that were private. It was important, said the advocates of housing reform, that the kitchen and other service aspects of the house be hidden from the eyes of any visitors. Kitchens were often placed in the basement. If servants were hired, a back staircase was put in to give them access to the kitchen and keep them out of sight. Vast efforts were also made to organize the preparation of food in order to make the process of feeding the family both more efficient and more sanitary. Special stoves were designed and a new emphasis was placed on uniting convenience with economy.[33]

In addition to rationalizing the use of the kitchen and service aspects of the house, the architects of the time stressed the importance of giving the young girls and women their "own-room upstairs." As one reformer warned, "the young girl that, finding no intrinsic pleasure at home, nor regarding it otherwise than as the sphere of her domestic duties, would seek away from its shelter, and with other companions . . . [find] pleasure and excitements neither so wholesome or refining as a fond parent would wish." Ladies needed their own rooms where they could relax and follow their own artistic or literary inclinations.[34]

If the house were designed so that each individual could have his or her own private room, rooms were also designated where the family could come together. One of these was the front parlor, which was supposed to be "accessible to visitors" and to display "elegance and the appearance of lady habitancy." Equal in importance to the front parlor was the dining room. As one architect wrote, "it is in this apartment that the different members of the family are sure to assemble . . . and it is highly desirable that such a room should fitly and cheerfully express its purpose, . . . so as to heighten this constant and familiar reunion as much as possible."[35]

*   *   *

What does the specialization of function in the different rooms of the house tell us about the social changes taking place in the period? Since the changes in attitudes and social roles are difficult to trace, care must be taken to distinguish between questions about which there is reasonable information and those that need further work.[36] If one starts with the floor plans, it is clear that a major preoccupation of the housing reformers was to separate the "public" from the "private" sides of life. This concern could be seen both in the comments, mentioned earlier, about setting aside special rooms for women and children and in the actual placement of the front entrance hall, the stairs, and the parlor. By putting the stairs to the second floor, for example, in an unobtrusive position at the side of the house rather than in a central entrance hall as in the earlier classical revival homes, the reformers clearly implied that visitors were not welcome upstairs.

This continual attempt to separate public from private in all aspects of the design of the house reveals important mid-Victorian assumptions about permissible behavior. Downstairs, the location of the front parlor and the elaborate suggestions made about its furnishings implied that the parlor was to be a space for social interaction rather than for relaxation.[37] Relations with individuals outside the family would have to take place according to elaborate social conventions in a specially designed environment. These social rules were spelled out in considerable detail in the "House Pattern Books" and etiquette manuals. The front parlor thus helped to fill the need for a more controlled social environment and a more formal set of social relationships that were created by the growing complexity of industrial America.

Similarly, the design of the second floor, with its emphasis on creating a separate space for each member of the family, reveals certain underlying assumptions about family life. It implies that the family was not an organic unit but rather was made up of separate, unique individuals who each had a specific role to play. Interaction within the family, like the public interaction with guests, was to take place primarily in specifically designated areas—the dining room, porch, and back parlor (family room). In these areas, family interaction often became organized around certain rituals—meals, musical events, and games—which were increasingly governed by elaborate codes of behavior, such as dinner table rules. One has only to look at the formal portraits of families that were painted during this period to see the ways in which personal interaction became stylized (fig. 4). The design of the house thus implied that the family was an organization that was not an end in itself but rather a vehicle for promoting the development of each of its members.

When the pattern of specialized behavior that is implicit in the layout of the house is compared to the popular conception of the family found in the advice books of the time, there seems to be a disparity between the ideal and actual practice. If the ideal emphasized the organic unity of the family that would protect it against the dangers of the outside world, the reality seemed more to be a group of atomistic individuals who came together only on such special occasions as mealtimes. What seems apparent is that mid-Victorian Americans were trying to combine an older communalism, drawn from their experience in simple colonial homes where there were few rooms, with a new emphasis on specialization. What held the two ideas together was the notion that the informed private conscience, in its proper setting of Christian nurture (literally from below—from the kitchen or dining room up to the children's bedrooms), could be trusted with establishing proper

Fig. 4. Eastman Johnson, *The Hatch Family*, 1871. Oil on canvas, 48" × 73⅜". This painting shows Alfrederic Smith Hatch, a prominent Wall Street banker, relaxing with his family in the library of their New York City residence at Park Avenue and Thirty-seventh Street. (Photograph courtesy of The Metropolitan Museum of Art, Gift of Frederick H. Hatch.)

habits that would later protect the children in the outside world. It was a fragile combination that, in its attempt to reconcile private concerns with public duties, appears often to have placed contradictory pressures on the individual.

At the same time that family roles were becoming more specialized and the limits of personal behavior in social situations were becoming more codified, there was also an attempt to enlarge the limits of private freedom. Boundaries were deliberately drawn between public and private, downstairs and upstairs, in order to allow even greater freedom in certain areas. By assigning each child a separate room, mid-Victorian Americans sought to encourage a greater degree of individualism, albeit within specifically designated limits. The emphasis on the moral education of the child, with its stress on developing a sense of taste and beauty, encouraged curiosity and speculation. The hope was that by establishing certain carefully defined limits, freedom and social control could be combined. By creating a controlled setting and encouraging specific forms of behavior, the individual would be encouraged to develop his or her potential to its furthest limits.

Although more study of etiquette manuals and diaries is necessary before further extrapolations can be drawn from the evidence about specialization within the house and within the family, an examination of the house designs may well provide more clues to other important questions. Take, for example, the introduction in this period of bathrooms with toilets. The literature on house design is curiously silent about these rooms. Why is this so? What regulations were set on behavior within the bathroom? What did these regulations imply about attitudes toward dirt and cleanliness? To answer these questions further analyses must be made of housing designs and health and childcare manuals.

*   *   *

How successful were the advocates of housing reform in establishing new standards for family dwellings? Judged by the construction that took place, there is no doubt that they created a distinctly American housing style, somewhere between the English villa and the English cottage in size, that became a common feature of the landscape. From studies by Stephan Thernstrom and Sam Bass Warner, we also know that the ownership of a house became increasingly important for mid-Victorian Americans. Since home ownership required a fair amount of income and a steady job, it became one of the distinctive marks of having gained economic security.[38] Yet, when judged by the standards that the architects themselves set, they were less successful. Where the reformers had pleaded for integrity of design and the appropriateness of different styles for different physical settings, the public built houses like the so-called Wedding-Cake House in Kennebunk, Maine, which applied gothic veneer to an older classical revival form (fig. 5), or placed gothic and Italianate homes next to one another, as in Watertown, Connecticut. Instead of being a dwelling with a simple, functional design, the house became a status object, with the "habitable parts of the house . . . either in the rear or the basement, and . . . the main portions facing on the street . . . devoted to the show-rooms, which are kept closed except on rare occasions." Thus, by the 1870s, the vogue of the French mansard roof and the search for ever more complicated and elaborate designs revealed a decline in interest in gothic, Italianate, and bracketed houses. In their place, Americans increasingly chose the new French, "Queen Anne," and "shingle" styles.[39]

The decline of public interest in the three early styles was matched by a decline in the influence of the earlier generation of architectural reformers. Paradoxically, the loss of influence was in part a consequence of the success of the housing crusade. So convinced was the public of the necessity of owning

Fig. 5. The Wedding-Cake House (George W. Bourne House), Kennebunkport, Maine, 1826, with alterations of ca. 1855. The underlying Federal-style brick house was built for shipbuilder George W. Bourne; in the mid-1850s he added an overlay of gothic trim and board-and-batten siding to his barn and connecting ell, to his latticed porch (now removed), and to the front and sides of his house, and he built a gothic fence (taken down in 1962). (Photograph courtesy of the Brick Store Museum.)

one's house that the case for the possession of a home no longer needed to be made. But, to a larger extent, the architects were themselves responsible for their loss of control over the housing reform movement. The root of the problem lay in the architectural ideals themselves. Since the home was seen as standing for certain spiritual values, it was not long before it became identified with the distinctive personality of its owner. If, as Downing wrote, "every thing in architecture that can suggest or be made a symbol of social and domestic virtues, adds to its beauty," and if "the highest beauty of which Domestic Architecture is capable is that of individual expression," then it was inevitable that more ornate and elaborate forms would be developed to prove the superiority of one man to another. In a reaction against the conformity of styles that had resulted from their popularization in newspapers, magazines, and "House Pattern Books," and the application of machine technology to the mass production of ornate woodwork, many individuals turned to a random eclecticism of styles (see fig. 6).[40]

Even more difficult for the architect at mid-century than his attempt to confine individual expression within a specified set of artistic standards was his attempt to draw the precise boundaries between what was public and what was private. When he followed

Fig. 6. Late nineteenth-century eclecticism: Hermosa Vista, Redlands, California, 1890. By the end of the nineteenth century, the search for appropriate historical styles had reached a degree of absurdity, as seen in this house built by orange grower David A. Morey, which combined a French mansard roof, a so-called "Turkish" onion dome, brackets, an Italianate tower, and a railing in the Chinese taste. (Photograph from *Redlands Daily Facts* [1890s], reprinted from John Maass, *The Victorian Home in America* [New York, 1972], 161.)

the trend toward specialization of function found in other sectors of society and tried to identify the wife and children with their own parts of the house, the result was that contradictory demands were often placed on all parties. The woman was supposed to be a lively conversationalist in the front parlor and a specialist in the back kitchen at the same time. The children were supposed to be creative, but out of sight and confined in areas where they would have little contact with the outside world to stimulate their curiosity.

Ironically, the greatest success for the architects came not when they were erecting barriers but when they were breaking them down. By using wide porches and rural settings for their houses, the reformers overcame the rigid separation of the house from nature that had been one of the hallmarks of the earlier classical revival. Just as Olmsted designed his park systems in such a way that they combined glorious vistas with the accommodation (out of sight) of large numbers of people, the architects created a middle landscape where the individual could enjoy the more pleasant aspects of nature while avoiding its rigors.[41]

The success of the house reformers can be seen ultimately in the way in which the family home came to be the major symbol of middle-class values at mid-century. It stood for the individual's taste and virtues, for dedication to family and belief in the ideals of efficiency, order, sobriety, and domesticity. As one male convert to the movement wrote in the 1850s, "a house is the shape which a man's thoughts take when he imagines how he should like to live. Its interior is the measure of his social and domestic nature; its exterior, of his esthetic and artistic nature. It interprets, in material form, his ideas of home, of friendship, and of comfort."[42]

Notes

The author wishes to acknowledge a grant from the National Endowment for the Humanities and the research assistance of Nancy Hoyt.

1. James Early calls this change an "architectural revolution." *Romanticism and American Architecture* (New York, 1965), 67. Because the crusade for a new kind of domestic architecture was not political and because it was overshadowed by the Civil War, its social importance has been overlooked by most historians. The major exception to this statement is Neil Harris, *The Artist in American Society* (New York, 1966), chap. 8. Harris provides the best introduction to this subject, but he tends to overemphasize the elitism of the broader social movement because he concentrates on Andrew Jackson Downing and his upper-class clients; a different but important perspective on the conservative values attached to the discussion of houses in American literature is Allen Guttman's *The Conservative Tradition in America* (New York, 1967), chap. 2.

2. It should be noted that the argument here is not that the housing crusade was as organized or had as large a membership as did the temperance movement or the abolitionist crusade, but rather that it shared similar values and priorities, particularly the vision of a middle-class suburban society. It is further asserted that the housing crusade's indirect influence on behavior by encouraging the construction of a different kind of house was as great as that of the other reform movements whose goal was also the modification of behavior. Thus, although the housing crusade does not fit the usual definition of a social movement (see Rudolf Heberle, "Types and Functions of Social Movements," *International Encyclopedia of the Social Sciences*, vol. 14 [New York, 1968], 438–44), I would argue that its social impact was just as great.

3. The best studies of mid-Victorian American architecture are Vincent J. Scully, Jr., "Romantic Rationalism and the Expression of Structure in Wood: Downing, Wheeler, Gardner, and the 'Stick Style,' 1840–1876," *Art Bulletin* 35 (1953): 121–43; Edna Donnell, "A. J. Davis and the Gothic Revival," *Metropolitan Museum Studies* 5, pt. 2 (1936); John Maass, *The Gingerbread Age* (New York, 1957); Maass, *The Victorian Home in America* (New York, 1972); Alan Gowans, *Images of American Living* (Philadelphia, 1964); and James M. Fitch, *Architecture and the Esthetics of Plenty* (New York, 1961).

4. A good example of the usefulness of applying the concept of modernization to social history is Richard D. Brown, "Modernization and the Modern Personality in Early America, 1600–1865: A Sketch of a Synthesis," *Journal of Interdisciplinary History* 2 (1972): 201–28.

5. For "House Pattern Books," see Henry-Russell Hitchcock, *American Architectural Books*, 2d ed. (Minneapolis, Minn., 1962); for magazine articles to 1851, see Talbot Hamlin, *Greek Revival Architecture in America* (New York, 1944), appendix B. A central problem in the study of cultural history is to avoid viewing the past only through the eyes of contemporary reformers. For a useful discussion of this problem, see Robert J. Berkhofer, "Clio and the Culture Concept: Some Impressions of a Changing Relationship in American Historiography," *Social Science Quarterly* 53 (1972): 314. The best studies of domestic architecture in America are: Roger Kennedy, *Minnesota Houses* (Minneapolis, Minn., 1967); Wilbur D. Peat, *Indiana Houses of the Nineteenth Century* (Indianapolis, Ind., 1962); Bainbridge Bunting, *Houses of Boston's Back Bay; an Architectural History, 1840–1917* (Cambridge, Mass., 1967); Charles Lockwood, *Bricks and Brownstone: The New York Row House, 1783–1929* (New York, 1972); I. T. Frary, *Early*

Homes of Ohio (New York, 1936); Antoinette F. Downing and Vincent J. Scully, Jr., *The Architectural Heritage of Newport, Rhode Island, 1640–1915* (Cambridge, Mass., 1952); Dutchess County Planning Board, *Landmarks of Dutchess County, 1683–1867* (New York, 1969); Bernard Foerster, *Architecture Worth Saving in Rensselaer County, New York* (Troy, N.Y., 1965); and New York State Council on the Arts, *Architecture Worth Saving in Onondaga County* (Syracuse, N.Y., 1964).

6. These totals, which were drawn from Hitchcock, *American Architectural Books*, were tabulated by counting both the original edition and the subsequent reprintings. A good estimate of the popularity of the different revival styles, as published in *Godey's Ladies Magazine*, can be found in George L. Hersey, "Godey's Choice," *Society of Architectural Historians Journal* 18 (1959): 110. Interestingly, most of the "House Pattern Books" between 1840 and 1870 were written by architects who hoped thereby both to give their professions more status and to stir up more business for themselves. For the latter, see J. Riddell, *Architectural Designs for Country Residences* (Philadelphia, 1861), preface.

7. Gervase Wheeler, *Rural Homes . . .* (New York, 1851), 32. There were numerous other competing styles, such as the "Swiss" and "Romanesque." In 1867, Alexander Jackson Davis listed in his diary fourteen different styles for homes.

8. Sereno E. Todd, *Todd's Country Homes . . .* (New York, 1870), 33.

9. Andrew Jackson Downing, *The Architecture of Country Houses* (New York, 1850), 109–10; Gervase Wheeler, *Homes for the People, in Suburb and Country . . .* (New York, 1855), 44.

10. Although the "bracketed mode," as it was called by contemporaries, was a label that was often applied to the first two revival types (i.e., there were "gothic cottages in the bracketed style"), in the eclectic sampling at mid-century, I would argue that it achieved a status of its own. For a contemporary view supporting my own, see *The Architectural Review and American Builders' Journal* (November 1868) as quoted in Peat, *Indiana Houses*, 96.

11. Downing, *Cottage Residences . . .* (New York, 1842), 99. It is difficult to judge the number of houses actually built in each style. Since the romantic revival homes are not now as popular as their classical predecessors, the revival homes have often been torn down. Those that survive are often in disrepair. See the "Gothic house," Watertown, Conn.

12. For the significance that Victorians placed on historical associations, see Peter Conrad, *The Victorian Treasure-House* (London, 1973).

13. John Higham, *From Boundlessness to Consolidation: The Transformation of American Culture, 1848–1860* (Ann Arbor, Mich., 1969), 1–28; *Harper's New Monthly Magazine* 30 (1865): 740; J. H. Hammond, *The Farmer's and Mechanic's Practical Architect* (Boston, 1858), 27; Samuel Sloan, *City Homes, Country Homes, and Church Architecture* (Philadelphia, 1871), 746–47.

14. See Kirk Jeffrey, "The Family as Utopian Retreat from the City: The Nineteenth-Century Contribution," *Soundings* 55 (1972): 21–41; F. L. Olmsted, Vaux & Co., "Preliminary Report Upon the Proposed Suburban Village at Riverside, near Chicago" (New York, 1868), 7, 26–27; see also William B. Lang, *Views, with Ground Plans, of the Highland Cottages at Roxbury . . .* (Boston, 1845).

15. For the aesthetic theory of the romantic revival, see James Early, *Romanticism and American Architecture*, 34–35; Walter J. Hipple, Jr., *The Beautiful, the Sublime, and the Picturesque in Eighteenth-Century British Aesthetic Theory* (Carbondale, Ill., 1957); Henry Cleveland, "American Architecture," *North American Review* 43 (1836): 380.

16. President Timothy Dwight, as quoted in Henry Cleveland and William and Samuel Backus, *Village and Farm Cottages . . .* (New York, 1856), 47.

17. James S. Young, *The Washington Community, 1800–1826* (New York, 1966), chap. 1.

18. Perry Miller, *The Life of the Mind in America* (New York, 1965), pt. 1; William G. McLoughlin, *Modern Revivalism* (New York, 1959).

19. Horace Bushnell, *Christian Nurture* (New York, 1900), 106–7; the other forces behind the shift from revivalism to liberal Protestantism are too complex to go into here. See McLoughlin, *The Meaning of Henry Ward Beecher* (New York, 1970); and Sydney Ahlstrom, *A Religious History of the American People* (New Haven, Conn., 1972), chaps. 36, 46.

20. *New Englander* 8 (1850): 432; William H. Ranlett, *The Architect . . .* (New York, 1847), 3. There is a growing literature on children and the family; see Bernard W. Wishy, *The Child and the Republic* (Philadelphia, 1967), and Edward N. Saveth, "The Problem of American Family History," *American Quarterly* 21 (1969): 311–29.

21. Thomas U. Walter and John J. Smith, *Two Hundred Designs for Cottages and Villas, . . .* (Philadelphia, 1847), plate 33; for furniture, see John Maass, *The Gingerbread Age* (New York, 1957), 88; for stained glass, see Sloan, *City Homes*, 57. On the symbolism in gothic architecture, see Donnell, "A. J. Davis and the Gothic Revival," 187.

22. Henry Ward Beecher, "The Nation's Duty to Slavery," in *Patriotic Addresses in America and England*, ed. John R. Howard (New York, 1891), 220; Aileen S. Kraditor, *Means and Ends in American Abolitionism* (New York, 1967), chaps. 5–6; Joseph R. Gusfield, *Symbolic Crusade* (Urbana, Ill., 1963), chap. 2; Lincoln, *Works*, as quoted in Eric Foner, *Free Soil, Free Labor, Free Men* (New York, 1970), 20.

23. Oliver P. Smith, *The Domestic Architect* (Buffalo, 1852), iii; *New Englander* 9 (1851): 61; Cleveland and Backus, *Village and Farm Cottages*, 4.

24. Harris, *Artist in American Society*, 210; Wheeler, *Homes for the People, in Suburb and Country*, 94.

25. Sloan, *City Homes*, 334–35, 746–47; J. H. Hammond, *Farmer's and Mechanic's Practical Architect*, 94; Charles P. Dwyer, *The Economic Cottage Builder . . .* (New York, 1856); T. Thomas, Jr., *The Workingman's Cottage Architecture* (New York, 1848); Orson S. Fowler, *A Home for All* (New York, 1856).

26. See, for example, Peat, *Indiana Houses.*

27. Brown, "Modernization and the Modern Personality," 33.

28. Daniel T. Atwood, *Atwood's Country and Suburban Houses* (New York, 1871), 143; Cleveland and Backus, *Village and Farm Cottages,* 43. On the technological innovations in building, see James M. Fitch, *American Building,* 2d ed. (Cambridge, 1966), chap. 4.

29. Atwood, *Atwood's Country and Suburban Houses,* 143; Cleveland and Backus, *Village and Farm Cottages,* 42–43; *New Englander* 8 (1850): 421.

30. The American Institute of Architects was formed in 1857 and the first professional school of architecture opened in 1866.

31. Gerda Lerner, "The Lady and the Mill Girl: Changes in the Status of Women in the Age of Jackson," *American Studies Journal* 10 (1969): 7–8; Ronald G. Walters, "The Family and Ante-bellum Reform: An Interpretation," *Societas* 3 (1973): 221–31.

32. Fowler, *A Home for All,* 63. Merchants usually came home by 3 P.M. when they had their dinner. They stayed home for the rest of the afternoon, often working on their accounts in their library (Bunting, *Houses of Boston's Back Bay,* 129).

33. See Catharine Beecher and Harriet Beecher Stowe, *The American Woman's Home* (New York, 1869). The best discussion of specialization within the home from the perspective of changing technology is Fitch, *Architecture and the Esthetics of Plenty,* chap. 5.

34. Wheeler, *Rural Homes,* 277.

35. Calvert Vaux, *Villas and Cottages . . .* (New York, 1857), 44; Barbara Cross, ed., *The Educated Woman in America* (New York, 1965), 1–13.

36. On the use of art and architecture as historical evidence, see Theodore K. Rabb, "The Historian and the Art Historian," *Journal of Interdisciplinary History* 4 (1973): 107–17. On the study of roles, see Charles E. Rosenberg, "Sexuality, Class, and Role in Nineteenth-Century America," *American Quarterly* 25 (1973): 131–53. Recent essays in European history that point up the uses to which the study of domestic housing might be put are Richard A. Goldthwaite's "The Florentine Palace as Domestic Architecture," *American Historical Review* 77 (1972): 967–1012, and Eric Mercer, "The Houses of the Gentry," *Past and Present* 5 (1954): 11–32.

37. George W. Harvey, *The Principles of Courtesy* (New York, 1852), 213; David H. Arnot, *Gothic Architecture Applied to Modern Residences* (New York, 1849), 32.

38. Sam Bass Warner, Jr., *Streetcar Suburbs: The Process of Growth in Boston, 1870–1900* (Cambridge, Mass., 1962), 6–11; Stephan Thernstrom, *Poverty and Progress* (Cambridge, Mass., 1964), 28, 115–20.

39. Hersey, "Godey's Choice," 105; *Harper's New Monthly Magazine* 30 (1865): 739; Vincent Scully, Jr., *The Shingle Style* (New Haven, Conn., 1955).

40. A. J. Downing, *The Architecture of Country Houses,* 23. For an interesting explanation of the process of standardization in house styles, see Warner, *Streetcar Suburbs.*

41. Olmsted and Vaux, "Preliminary Report to the Commissioners for Laying Out a Park in Brooklyn, New York . . . ," in *Landscape into Cityscape,* ed. Albert Fein (Ithaca, N.Y., 1967), 89–95; John William Ward, *Red, White, and Blue* (New York, 1969), 292.

42. H. W. Beecher, "Building a House," in *Star Papers* (New York, 1859), 285–92.

Notes on the Contributors

Norman F. Barka holds a Ph.D. in anthropology from Harvard University. He is currently Professor of Anthropology at the College of William and Mary in Williamsburg, Virginia. He has engaged in a variety of historical archaeological research in eastern Virginia for the past twenty years, including the excavation of the well-preserved remains of the pottery factory of the "poor Potter" of Yorktown. His current research interests are in the Caribbean, where for the past seven years he has studied Dutch and English cultural adaptations and settlement patterns on the island of St. Eustatius. Dr. Barka is a past president of the Society for Historical Archaeology and since 1982 has been Editor of the Society's *Newsletter*.

Thomas Bender is a cultural historian with a particular interest in cities. He received his Ph.D. at the University of California at Davis in 1971. Since 1974 he has taught at New York University, where he is presently University Professor of the Humanities and Professor of History. His books include *Toward an Urban Vision* (1975), which won the Frederick Jackson Turner Prize of the Organization of American Historians, *Community and Social Change in America* (1978), and *New York Intellect: A History of Intellectual Life in New York City, from 1750 to the Beginnings of Our Own Time* (1987).

Betsy Blackmar teaches in the History Department at Columbia University. A graduate of Smith College, she received her Ph.D. in history from Harvard University in 1981. She taught previously in the American Studies Program at Yale University. A coeditor of *Visions of History* (1983), Blackmar has also worked on the Radical History Collective. She is currently writing with Roy Rosenzweig a social history of Central Park, a project that extends the range of material covered in her book, *The Quality of Rents: Property and Housing Relations in New York City, 1785–1850* (forthcoming, 1988).

John L. Brooke has been Assistant Professor of History at Tufts University in Medford, Massachusetts,

since 1983. He received a B.A. from Cornell University in 1975 and his M.A. and Ph.D. in history from the University of Pennsylvania in 1977 and 1982. He taught previously at Franklin and Marshall College and at Amherst College. In addition to teaching, he has also served as an Associate Editor of *Markers: The Journal of Gravestone Studies*. A recipient of NEH and Charles Warren Center Fellowships in 1986–87, his works-in-progress include "Peoples on a Middle Landscape: Society and Political Culture in Central New England, 1713–1861," and "Joseph Smith, Early American Occult Traditions, and the Origins of Mormonism."

Lois Green Carr has been the Historian for Historic St. Mary's City—an outdoor museum of Maryland history and archaeology on the site of Maryland's seventeenth-century capital—since 1967 and Adjunct Professor of History at the University of Maryland, College Park, since 1982. She received her Ph.D. in history from Harvard University in 1968. Since the 1970s she has been cooperating with several others (including Lorena S. Walsh and Russell R. Menard) on a study of colonial Chesapeake probate records for what they reveal about social and economic change and continuity. She has authored and coauthored numerous articles published in scholarly journals and collections, among them "The Planter's Wife: The Experience of White Women in Seventeenth-Century Maryland" for the *William and Mary Quarterly* (3d ser., 34 [1977]), and most recently, she and Lorena S. Walsh contributed "Consumer Behavior in the Colonial Chesapeake" to *Of Consuming Interests: The Style of Life in the Eighteenth-Century* (ed. Cary Carson, Ronald Hoffman, and Peter Albert; forthcoming).

Cary Carson is Director of Historical Research at The Colonial Williamsburg Foundation. A graduate of Carleton College and the Winterthur Program in Early American Culture, he received his Ph.D. in history from Harvard University in 1974. Before arriving in Williamsburg in 1976, he had served as Coordinator of Research at St. Mary's City, Maryland, and had been a Research Associate at the Smithsonian Institution. Carson has also taught courses in social history and material culture at Yale University, Carleton College, and the College of William and Mary. His published work includes "Doing History with Material Culture," in *Material Culture and the Study of American Life* (1978), "Living Museums of Everyman's History," in *Harvard Magazine* (1981), and articles in such journals as *History News, Maryland Historical Magazine*, and *Vernacular Architecture*. As coauthor of *Teaching History at Colonial Williamsburg*, he continues to be interested in how historical learning happens in exhibit galleries, period rooms, and outdoor history museums. He is currently studying the "changing contours of early American material life," by which he means a history of social relations as they became ever more dependent on the intervening agency of consumer goods.

Clifford E. Clark, Jr., received his B.A from Yale University in 1963 and his Ph.D. from Harvard University in 1968. He has taught at Harvard, Amherst College, and Carleton College, where he is now Chair of the History Department and the American Studies Program and is the M. A. and A. D. Hulings Professor of American Studies. He is author of *Henry Ward Beecher: Spokesman for a Middle-Class America* (1978) and *The American Family Home, 1800–1960* (1986). Interested in nineteenth- and twentieth-century material culture and social history, Clark has explored the relationship between domestic architecture and the ideals of middle-class family life in his most recent writings. He is currently editing a book on Minnesota history in the twentieth century and is also writing part of a book on society and cultural values in late nineteenth-century America.

Susan G. Davis teaches folklore, communication, and the history of vernacular culture in the Department of Communication at the University of California at San Diego. A folklorist, she received her M.A. from the Cooperstown Graduate Program and her Ph.D. from the University of Pennsylvania. She is the author of *Parades and Power: Street Theatre in Nineteenth-Century Philadelphia* (1985) as well as numerous articles on working-class culture, oral history, folk drama, and street parades. Davis's current

research explores the history of American traditions of public spectacle and the relationships between festivals, spectacles, and corporate public relations.

Robert J. Dinkin has been teaching history at California State University at Fresno since 1968. He received his graduate training at Columbia University. "Seating the Meetinghouse in Early Massachusetts" first appeared as a chapter in his Ph.D. dissertation, "Provincial Massachusetts: A Deferential or a Democratic Society?" (1968). He is the author of *Voting in Provincial America: A Study of Elections in the Thirteen Colonies, 1689–1776* (1977) and *Voting in Revolutionary America: A Study of Elections in the Original Thirteen States, 1776–1789* (1982). He has just finished a book-length manuscript on electioneering in American history and is currently doing research for a history of women in American politics.

Henry Glassie received his M.A. from the Cooperstown Graduate Program and his Ph.D. in folklore from the University of Pennsylvania. He has served as Assistant Director of the Folklore Institute at Indiana University and as Chairman of the Department of Folklore and Folklife at the University of Pennsylvania, where he is currently Professor of Folklore and American Civilization and a member of the graduate faculties in Architecture, Historic Preservation, and City Planning. His major books include *Pattern in the Material Folk Culture of the Eastern United States* (1968), in which he combined lessons learned from the geographer Fred Kniffen and from his teachers in folklore to call folklorists to the study of material culture; *Folk Housing in Middle Virginia* (1975), in which he developed an interpretive framework for vernacular architecture out of structuralist theory; *All Silver and No Brass* (1975), a study of folk drama; *Passing the Time in Ballymenone* (1982), in which he brought together his interests in oral literature and material culture in an ethnographic account of life in an Ulster community; and *Irish Folktales* (1985). Since 1982, while continuing to teach courses in American architecture, furniture, and folk art, he has concentrated his attention on Turkey. During six visits, one lasting eight months, he has conducted fieldwork on the full range of the vital traditions of Turkish material culture, focusing on woodworking, ceramics, and textiles.

Robert A. Gross is currently Professor of History and

American Studies at Amherst College. He earned his B.A. in American studies from the University of Pennsylvania and received his Ph.D. in history from Columbia University in 1976. He has been Visiting Professor at Smith College, Mount Holyoke College, and Brandeis University, and was Chair of American Studies at Sussex University in 1982–83. His sustained interest in the social history of experience in American communities has resulted in *The Minutemen and Their World* (1976) and numerous articles on Henry D. Thoreau, Emily Dickinson, Shays' Rebellion, and most recently, an introductory essay in Northeastern University Press's 1986 reprint of Francis Underwood's classic, *Quabbin*. In addition to teaching such seminars as "The Embodied Self in American Culture" and "The History of the Book in American Society," he is currently working on two books. *The Transcendentalists and Their World* is a sequel to his first book that views the ideas of Emerson and Thoreau in the context of changes in Concord's material life during the nineteenth century. His second project, a study of the meaning of books, is called *The Authority of the Word: Books, Culture, and Society in America.*

Sam Bowers Hilliard was born and grew up in Bowersville, a small town in northern Georgia. Currently Alumni Professor of Geography and Anthropology at Louisiana State University at Baton Rouge, he earned his A.B. and M.A. Degrees from the University of Georgia at Athens, and his M.S. and Ph.D. degrees from the University of Wisconsin at Madison. He has previously taught at the University of Wisconsin at Milwaukee and Southern Illinois University at Carbondale. A specialist in historical geography, Hilliard has published widely on southern culture during the antebellum period. In addition to articles in the *Annals of the Association of American Geographers*, *Geographical Review*, and *Technology and Culture*, he is the author of *Hog Meat and Hoecake: Food Supply in the Old South, 1840-1860* (1972), *Man and Environment in the Lower Mississippi Valley* (1978), the *Atlas of Antebellum Southern Agriculture* (1984), and, most recently, *Louisiana: Its Land and People* (1987).

Rhys Isaac teaches at La Trobe University in Melbourne, Australia. In 1983 his book, *The Transformation of Virginia, 1740–1790* (1982), was awarded the Pulitzer Prize for History. He is currently working on

a fuller in-depth study of the world of the Virginia squire whose diary is featured in the essay in this volume. In the process, he is discovering the paradox of inverse scale—the more particular the subject (if it is to be dealt with intensively), the more varied and extensive the research. In this case not just local knowledge but wider eighteenth-century systems of natural philosophy, medicine, law, and literary convention must be studied. Parallel with this, Isaac is undertaking a further venture in ethnographic methodology, an attempt to review systematically as "performance" the range of genres of material survivals—including those verbal artifacts we call "documents"—from which the historian may attempt to reconstruct past worlds.

William M. Kelso is Director of Archaeology at Monticello, the Thomas Jefferson Memorial Foundation. A graduate of Baldwin-Wallace College and the College of William and Mary, he received his Ph.D. from Emory University in 1971. Currently also a Lecturer in the School of Architecture at the University of Virginia, he has previously served as Commissioner of Archaeology on the Virginia Historic Landmarks Commission. The author of *Kingsmill Plantation, 1619–1800* (1984), he has also published articles in the *Journal of New World Archaeology* and the *World Book Yearbook* (1985). His current research interests include the material culture of British colonial life in North America and the Caribbean, the growth and development of the plantation system in the American South, the Afro-American tradition in the decorative arts, and early American landscape design.

Gary Kulik is Chairman of the Department of Social and Cultural History at the Smithsonian Institution's National Museum of American History. He received his Ph.D. in American civilization from Brown University and has previously been Curator of the Slater Mill National Historic Site in Pawtucket, Rhode Island. In addition to numerous essays and journal articles, he has edited *Rhode Island: An Inventory of Historical and Engineering Sites* (1978) and (with Roger Parks and Theodore Z. Penn) *The New England Mill Village, 1790–1860* (1982). Now primarily engaged in the conceptual development of the museum's major interpretive exhibits in social and cultural history, he continues to research and write on early industrial history, on the history of history museums, and on conceptions of the New England past in the late nineteenth and twentieth centuries.

Russell R. Menard is Professor and Chair of the Department of History at the University of Minnesota. He received his Ph.D. from the University of Iowa in 1975 and was a fellow of the Institute of Early American History and Culture before moving to Minnesota. He is the author of *The Economy of British America, 1607–1790* (1985), *Economy and Society in Early Colonial Maryland* (1985), and numerous articles in such journals as the *William and Mary Quarterly, Maryland Historical Magazine, Journal of Economic History, Southern Studies, Virginia Magazine of History and Biography*, and *Explorations in Economic History.* His current research projects include studies of the transition to slavery in the Americas, the rise of plantation regime in the Carolina lowcountry, and the role of long-range trade in the early modern period.

James H. Merrell is Assistant Professor of History at Vassar College. He was educated at Lawrence University, Oxford University, and Johns Hopkins University before receiving fellowships at the Newberry Library's D'Arcy McNickle Center for the History of the American Indian and the Institute of Early American History and Culture. He is the author of several articles on Indians in early America and is currently completing a book on the Catawbas before the age of Indian Removal. He has coedited (with Daniel K. Richter) *Beyond the Covenant Chain: The Iroquois and Their Neighbors in Native North America, 1600–1800* (1987).

Philip D. Morgan is currently Editor of Publications at the Institute of Early American History and Culture in Williamsburg, Virginia. He received his doctorate from University College, London, and has taught at the University of California at Berkeley. He has written a number of essays on aspects of slavery in South Carolina and Virginia and has a book in press entitled *Slave Counterpoint: Black Culture in the Eighteenth-Century Chesapeake and Lowcountry.* He is presently working on a study of the world of Thomas Thistlewood, an overseer and planter who lived in southwestern Jamaica in the latter half of the eighteenth century. Thistlewood's extensive diaries, when combined with local sources, provide one of

the richest inside perspectives on daily life in a slave society.

Jules David Prown is Paul Mellon Professor of the History of Art at Yale University. His publications include a two-volume monograph, *John Singleton Copley* (1966), *American Painting from Its Beginnings to the Armory Show* (1969), *The Architecture of the Yale Center for British Art* (1977), and numerous other writings. A graduate of Lafayette College, he holds an M.A. from the Winterthur Program in Early American Culture at the University of Delaware and took his Ph.D. in fine arts at Harvard University. In addition to teaching at Yale for over twenty-five years, he has served as Curator of American Art at the Yale University Art Gallery and Director of the Yale Center for British Art. He has become increasingly interested in material culture in recent years, teaching a regular graduate seminar at Yale, "American Art and Artifacts: The Interpretation of Objects." Currently he is vexed by the question of the extent to which the aesthetic aspects of objects affect their value as cultural evidence, and he is interested in learning more about anthropological approaches to aesthetics.

A. G. Roeber is a graduate of the University of Denver and Brown University, where he received his Ph.D. in history in 1977. Currently Associate Professor of History at the University of Illinois, he has also taught at Princeton and Lawrence universities. The author of *Faithful Magistrates and Republican Lawyers: Creators of Virginia Legal Culture, 1680–1810* (1981), he has also written numerous articles on eighteenth-century American law and society. At present he is working on a book that examines the relationships between law, ideology, and religion among German-Americans between 1727 and 1817.

Rodris Roth is a Curator at the Smithsonian Institution's National Museum of American History. A graduate of the University of Minnesota, she received an M.A. as a fellow in the Winterthur Program in Early American Culture at the University of Delaware in 1965. She has written on a wide range of topics; among her publications are *Floor Coverings in Eighteenth-Century America* (1967) and articles on the Colonial Revival, furniture at the Centennial, the kitchen, and patented furniture. She has worked on a number of major exhibitions and installations at the

Smithsonian, including the "Hall of Everyday Life in the American Past," "1876: A Centennial Exhibition," a special display entitled "Going to Housekeeping" in conjunction with the acquisition of a portion of a balloon-frame house, and, most recently, a temporary exhibition, "New and Different: Home Interiors in Eighteenth-Century America." These and related topics remain the focus of her research with particular emphasis on objects and their significance in the domestic setting.

Robert Blair St. George is Assistant Professor of American Studies and History at Boston University. A graduate of Hamilton College and the Winterthur Program in Early American Culture at the University of Delaware, he received his Ph.D. in folklore from the University of Pennsylvania in 1982. He previously taught at Rutgers University (Newark), the Winterthur Program, and the University of Pennsylvania. His published work on different aspects of expressive culture in early America includes *The Wrought Covenant: Source Materials for the Study of Craftsmen and Community in Southeastern New England, 1620–1700* (1979) and "'Heated Speech' and Literacy in Seventeenth-Century New England," in *Seventeenth-Century New England*, ed. David G. Allen and David D. Hall (1984). He is currently writing a book about property and popular culture in early New England.

Marylynn Salmon, Associate Professor of History at the University of Maryland, Baltimore County, received her Ph.D. from Bryn Mawr College in 1980. One of the early contributors to the new field of women's legal history, she is the author of *Women and the Law of Property in Early America* (1986) and coauthor (with Carole Shammas and Michel Dahlin) of *Inheritance in America: From Colonial Times to the Present* (1987). Currently she is exploring the intersection of religion and law in the lives of early American women.

Billy G. Smith completed his Ph.D. at UCLA in 1981. While writing his doctoral dissertation he developed methods of analyzing primary sources as a computer programmer and research associate at the St. Mary's City Commission, working on a project to reconstruct the history of the early Chesapeake Bay region. He has published articles in the *William and Mary Quarterly, Labor History, Social Forces*, and

the *Journal of Economic History.* Currently he is involved in three projects. First, he is completing a book on the lives of laboring Philadelphians between 1750 and 1800. He is also editing a series of historical documents bearing on life in the Quaker City during the Constitutional and Early National periods. Finally, he is analyzing newspaper advertisements for runaway slaves in the mid-Atlantic region during the second half of the eighteenth century.

Garry Wheeler Stone is currently Special Assistant for Historical Development in the Natural Resource Group of the New Jersey Department of Environmental Protection. Previously the Chief Archaeologist and Director of Research at Historic St. Mary's City, Stone received his Ph.D. in 1982 from the Department of American Civilization at the University of Pennsylvania. His publications on early American material culture and social history have appeared in *Historical Archaeology*, the *Papers* of the Conference on Historic Site Archaeology, *Maryland Historical Magazine*, and elsewhere. Presently, he is writing an article on the archaeological evolution of the Virginia House.

Kevin M. Sweeney is Director of Academic Programs at Historic Deerfield, Inc., in Deerfield, Massachusetts, and Five College Assistant Professor of American Studies at Smith College. He received his Ph.D. in history from Yale University, where his dissertation won the 1987 Jamestown Prize from the Institute of Early American History and Culture. He has previously taught at the Westover School, the University of Hartford, Trinity College, and the Winterthur Program in Early American Culture at the University of Delaware. Research for this article began while he was Administrator-Curator of the Webb-Deane-Stevens Museum in Wethersfield, Connecticut. This essay and related papers that have appeared in *Antiques, Proceedings of the Dublin Seminar for New England Folklife, Markers III, Winterthur Portfolio*, and *The Great River: Art and Society of the Connecticut Valley, 1635–1820*, are parts of a larger, ongoing study of preindustrial material life and cultural change in the Connecticut River Valley.

Dell Upton is Associate Professor of Architectural History in the Department of Architecture at the University of California at Berkeley. A graduate of Colgate University, he received his Ph.D. in American civilization from Brown University. A founding member of the Vernacular Architecture Forum, he is also editor of its *Newsletter*. He is the author of *Holy Things and Profane: Anglican Parish Churches in Eighteenth-Century Virginia* (1986) and the editor (with John Michael Vlach) of *Common Places: Readings in American Vernacular Architecture* (1986) and of *America's Architectural Roots: Ethnic Groups that Built America* (1986). Upton is currently completing a bibliography of North American vernacular architecture and cultural landscape studies and beginning to investigate the commercialization of Anglo-American architecture, 1750–1850, through a study of the development of the architectural profession, the promotion of architectural fashions, and the commodification of space.

Melvin Wade is president of the Texas Association for the Study of Afro-American Life and History, Inc. He has taught at the University of California at Santa Barbara, the University of Nebraska at Omaha, Vassar College, and the University of Texas at Austin. Holder of B.A. and M.A. degrees in speech communication from Oklahoma State University, he is currently completing his Ph.D. in folklore and anthropology at the University of Texas at Austin. His doctoral dissertation is entitled "Juneteenth in Austin, Texas: The History of An Afro-American Emancipation, 1867–1920." His recent research interests focus on the evolution of Afro-American communities and communal celebrations. His recent publications include "'Justin' to the Change: Traditional Agricultural Practices among Black Freed Farmers in East Texas, 1865–1900," in *Texana II: Cultural Heritage of the Plantation South*, ed. Lee Johnson (1985), and "Juneteenth in Texas," in *The Texas Experience*, ed. Archie McDonald (1986).

Lorena S. Walsh has been a Research Fellow at the Colonial Williamsburg Foundation since 1980. She received her Ph.D. from Michigan State University in 1977. In collaboration with Lois Carr, Russell Menard, and P. M. G. Harris, she has worked on a long-term study of the economy and society of the colonial Chesapeake based on probate records. Her publications include essays on women, family, community history, demography, consumer behavior, work patterns, and agriculture in such journals as the *William and Mary Quarterly*, *Historical Methods*, and the *Journal of Economic History*. She is currently

writing a history of agriculture and of plantation management in Virginia and Maryland from 1620 to 1820, based on account books. She is also co-director of a prosopographical study of York County, Virginia, sponsored by the Colonial Williamsburg Foundation.

Joseph S. Wood teaches cultural geography at the University of Nebraska at Omaha. He studied geography at Middlebury College, the University of Vermont, and Pennsylvania State University, where he received his Ph.D. in 1978. His interest in the evolution of settlement landscapes extends from New England villages to modern subdivisions. He is presently investigating the suburbanization of central cities and the conversion of warehouse districts into entertainment places. He also has a developing interest in the cultural landscape of post-Mao China, especially in the contradictions inherent in the material culture of special economic zones. A study of the nineteenth-century New England village as a vernacular form was published in *Perspectives in Vernacular Architecture II* (1986).

Index

Abolition, 536, 540, 541

Account books, as historical sources, 188, 208, 237

Action: collective, 160, 400; crowd, 488; as ritual, 422, 428; social, 48, 67, 420; as statements, 40–41; as text, 434n6. *See also* Culture; Drama; Performance; Ritual

Adams, Charles, 415

Adams, John, 69, 287, 339, 346, 348

"Aesthetic dilemma," 29–30

Aesthetics: and criticism, 29–30; and cultural values, 20, 29; and exchange, 7; and experience, 29; and gratification, 22; and standards, 337; and theory, 539, 541–42

Affecting contact, 21

Affecting presence, 10, 86

Affective individualism, 149

Africa, 177, 179–80

African heritage, 69, 96, 97, 99, 100, 144, 172; and ancestors, 174; consciousness of, 175, 177; and foodways, 324; and origins of lowcountry slaves, 226n17. *See also* Afro-American(s); Slavery; Slaves

African Union Meeting House, 172

African Union School, 172

Afro-American(s), 46, 54, 79, 105, 431, 432; and foodways, 208; and music, 57–58, 361; and patriarchy in family and society, 180–81; survival strategy of, 106, 107. *See also* Africa, Slavery, Slaves, Work

Agrarian society (premodern), 57

Agricultural reform, 12, 351, 519–31 passim

Agriculture: commercial, 276; and displacement of Indians from land, 96; and enclosure, 377; English, 163; and farming regions in the Chesapeake region, *146*, 148; and markets,

196; mixed, 145–48, 186; and persistence of open fields, 163, 346; and progress in South and food supply, 312–13; specialization in, 338, 342

Aimes, Hubert H. S., 172, 181n16

Alabama, 312, 313, 318, 320, 324, 327

Albany, New York, 442, 453, 463, 491, 494, 498

Alexander, John K., 234

Alford, Violet, 496

Algonkians, 469. *See also* American Indians

Alison, Archibald, 539

Almy, William, 388

Altamaha River, 317

American Indians, 11, 412, 469; and history, 96; of the southern piedmont region, *96*; wampum and, 7; wigwams of, 117, 119; woodlore of, 133. *See also* Catawba Nation; Culture

American Studies, 3, 9, 71, 74

Anburey, Thomas, 345, 348, 362, 366

Andover, Massachusetts, 162, 409

Annales: Economies, Sociétés, Civilisations, 7

Annales "paradigm," 6. *See also* Bloch, Marc; Braudel, Fernand; Febvre, Lucien

Annapolis, Maryland, 114, 186

Anthropology, and historians, 40

Antigua, 233

Apo festival, 176

Applied arts, 30–31, 34n23. *See also* Furnishings; Furniture; Morris, William

Apprentices, 250, 254, 373, 390

Apprenticeship, 350; decline in, 376, 498

Appropriations: of Afro-American dance and music by Virginia gentry, 57–58; of American Indian wigwam by English settlers, 117; of American Indian woodlore by English settlers, 133; of Anglo-American land laws by Catawba Nation, 104; of

black performance styles by white parades, 174, 177; of Catawba Nation lands by whites, 102–4; of courtly customs by Afro-American satirists, 58; as cultural "borrowing," 174; of labor by capitalists, 361; of white election-day forms by blacks, 172, 174

Archaeology, 23, 27–29, 114–50 passim; in England, 114–15. *See* Binford, Lewis. *See also* Plantations: Flowerdew Hundred, Kingsmill, St. John's, Wolstenholmtown

Architects, 538, 541–42, 543, 545–47

Architectural theory, 539

Architecture, 24, 30, 76, 348; American, 54, 144–45, *146*; American Indian, 117; and building, 33n2, 117, 125; and class structure, 340–41, 346–47, 378–82, 389–90; as coded nonverbal statement, 54, *55*, 84; domestic, 266, 337, 347, 536–47 passim; and domestic furniture, 263, 264; English, 54, 116, 117, 133; high-style, 239, *241*; impermanent, 114–50; military, *126*; and moral reform, 535–47 passim; Palladian, 53–56; and privacy, 286–87; and protest, 346, 390; rebuildings of, 145, 148, 197; social experience of, 357; and social structure, 341; vernacular, 114–50 passim, 237, 239, *240–41*, 357–68 passim. *See also* Churches; Courthouses; Dendrochronology; Doorways; Earthfast construction, House, Palladio; Room use; Technology; Timber framing; Vernacular threshold

Ariès, Philipe, 480

Armstrong, Robert Plant, 13n26, 86. *See also* Affecting presence; Phenomenology

Arnold, Benedict, 488–89

Arson, against mill owners, 397–98

Art, 6, 7, 29–30, 31, 68, 72, 74, 508; and affecting presence, 10; and econ-

A page number in italic indicates an illustration relating to the subject.

omy, 9–11; folk, 10, 84, 85; history of, 18, 23, 27–29; as inverse of money, 10; as landscape, 83; as metaphoric power, 10; tea-drinking as, 446

Artisans, 172, 239, 241, 270, 273, 288, 297, 345, 349, 350, 372, 375, 376, 387, 388, 389, 390, 391, 471, 490, 494, 497, 541; barn-builders, 133; blacksmiths, 166; cabinetmakers, 276, 278, 284, 287; carpenters, 123, 133–34, 194, 216, 219, 340–41, 377, 541; chairmakers, 276; clockmakers, 28; coopers, 194; high cost of, 142; houses of, *377, 379, 390;* house-wrights, 118, 131, 133; joiners, 267, 268, 276; masons, 377; in Philadel-phia, 233–54 passim; silversmiths, 241, *342;* weavers, 385–401 passim; women as, 247. *See also* Labor; Shoemakers, Tailors; Wages; Work

Artist, isolation of, 71

Ashanti people, 172, 174, 175, 176; chief of, 180

Athens, Georgia, 320

Atherton, Lewis, 320

Auctions, of meetinghouse seats, 414

Authenticity, 23, 65; artist's search for, 74; and culture, 73

Authority, 41–42, 340, 349, 420, 422, 427, 429, 430, 432, 476, 489, 497; aesthetic, 345; African ancestors and, 172; division of in marriage settlement, 298–99; and New En-gland town government, 161; and patriarchy, 51, 53; social, 48, 338–39. *See also* Father; Patriarchy; Power

Autonomy: as economic goal, 222–23; of women in marriage, 299

Backus, Isaac, 479

Backus, William, 539

Ballads, 71, 75–76, 78, 81–82

Baptism, 469, 470, 478, 479, 480

Baptists, 389, 392, 393, 437n43, 464, 471–73, 476, 477–80

Barbados, 205

Barbecues, 58, 315, 323

Barka, Norman F., 551

Barns, 8, 118; "pole" type, 129; raising of, 117; similarity of houses to, 124, 130, 131, 136, 149; similarity of meetinghouses to, 410

Barter, 7, 100, 104; among slaves, 220. *See also* Exchange; Self-sufficiency

Bartram, William, 208

Base and superstructure, in Marxist theory; *see* Structure

Beard, Mary R., 292, 293

Beaufort County, South Carolina, 221, 223

Beckett, Samuel, 67–69, 87

Beecher, Lyman, 539

Belief(s), 7, 31, 510–11; of New En-gland blacks in transmigration of souls after death, 179; patterns of, 22–23; in posterity, 144; and rural culture, 387. *See also* Culture; Folk-lore; Religion

Bender, Thomas, 12, 551

Bercovitch, Sacvan, 71

Berlin, Massachusetts, meetinghouse in, 415, *416*

Beverages, consumed in South, 319–20. *See also* Chocolate; Coffee; Dairy products

Beverly, Robert, 56–57, 136, 144. *See also* Plantations: Blandfield

Beverly, Massachusetts, 162, 410

Bezanson, Anne, 235, 250

Bidwell, Percy Wells, 196

Bigelow, Dr. Jacob, 506

Billerica, Massachusetts, 161, *163*

Binford, Lewis, 80

Biography, 67, 78; as frame of history, 65

Black community; *see* Community

Black coronation festivals, 171–82. *See also* African heritage; Afro-American(s); Ritual

Blackmar, Betsy, 11, 551

Blackstone River, 387, 391, 394

Blanchard, Rev. Amos, 509–10, 511, 514

Bloch, Marc, 6

Boarding, as residential pattern, 378

Boas, Franz, 8

Body, human, 338; as metaphor of so-cial order, 53–55, 429; symmetry of, 344–45. *See also* Architecture; Dis-ease

Bolzius, Johann, 205

Boston, Massachusetts, 11, 41, 336, 338, 342, 348, 408, *409, 411,* 412, 441, 442, 444, 447, 450, 456, 489, 491, 506, 520, 525, 529

Boston News-Letter, 457

Boston Tea Party, 442

Boundary maintenance, in black coro-nation festivals, 172, 173–74

Bourgeoisie, 376

Brattle Street Church, Cambridge, Massachusetts, 412

Braudel, Fernand, 3–7, 10, 12

Bread, 318–19, 442. *See also* Corn-bread; Wheat

Brecht, Bertolt, 204

Breck, Samuel, 489

Bridenbaugh, Carl, 234, 235

Brigden, Thomas and Michael, 284, 287

Brooke, John L., 12, 551

Brook Farm, as movement, 70

Brookfield, Massachusetts, 463, 466, 470, 476–77, 478

Brown, Moses, 388, 389

Brown, Richard D., 541

Brown, Robert E., 408

Brownson, Orestes, 74, 75

Building industry, 372, 381. *See also* Architecture; Artisans: carpenters, housewrights; Laborers

Burial, 464, 474, 476, 478

Burial grounds, 12, 466, 506

Burke, Kenneth, 61, 66, 69

Burlesque, 488, 492, 495; political uses of, 496–97

Bushnell, Horace, 540

Busia, Kofi A., 175

Byrd, William, II, 98

Byron, George Gordon, 511, 559

Callithumpians, 497

Calvinism, 474

Canton, China, 452

Capital, 348, 349, 373, 375, 376; fruits of merchant, 343; and investment, 377

Capitalism, 3, 4, 5; agrarian, 337–40, 353n13, 520–31 passim; conflict of with Christian values, 75–76; indus-trial, 350, 387, 398; resistance to, 391. *See also* Hegemony; Labor; Marx, Karl; Paternalism; Power

Capitalists, 336; merchants as, 337; in textile industry, 389, 398

Caribbean: plantations in, 206–7; slav-ery in, 223; society in, 204, 223, 271

Carolinas, 97, 100, 101, 103, 117, 137, 317. *See also* North Carolina; South Carolina

Carr, Lois Green, 11, 551

Carson, Cary, 9, 11, 422, 551–52

Carter, Landon, 42, 48, 50, 53, 54, 359, 362, 367, 421, 430. *See also* Planta-tions: Sabine Hall

Carter, Robert, 362, 430, 442

Casco Bay, Maine, fort at, *126*

Catawba Nation, 95–107 passim; adoption of English technology by, 100; alcoholism among, 100, 103; colonists' perceptions of, 98; con-

Lord, Albert, 80
Louisiana, 312, 316, 319, 320; techniques of butchering among French in, 315
Lovell, Margaretta, 32
Lowcountry (coastal Georgia and South Carolina), 204–25 passim, 316. *See also* Georgia; Rice; South Carolina
Lowell, Massachusetts, 74, 391, 395, 506–16 passim, 520
Lowell Cemetery; *see* Cemeteries
Lowell factory girl, 74, 510–11 ("Adelaide")
Lowenthal, David, 167
Lowie, Robert, 8
Lowndes' Trustee v. Champney's Executors (1821), 301, 305
Luddites, 497
Lynn, Massachusetts, 161, 173, 174, 176, 393

McCusker, John J., 234
Main, Jackson Turner, 234, 237, 243, 255n10, 412
Maine, 126, 496, 545
Manchester, Massachusetts, 162, 414
Manhattan; *see* New York
Manheim, Pennsylvania, 454
Manley, William, 278
Manufacturers' and Farmers' Journal, 396–97
Marginality, 173
Mariners, 263, 297, 304; in Philadelphia, 235, 239, 245, 248–50
Market, 375, 521; expansion of, 144–45, 147, 196, 525; export, 193, 196, 252, 276; housing, 372, 377; import, 252; and Indians, 96; investment, 376; labor, 396; limited engagement with, 222; real estate, 11, 372, 376; society, 378; tobacco, 142–43, 193, 428; urban, 268, 522, 525. *See also* Capitalism; Commerce; Economy; Exchange; Property; Trade
Marriage: division of authority within, 298–301; as gender ritual, 56–57; as property relation, 11, 292–95; settlements, 291–306 passim; and tea ritual, 445. *See also* Family; Law; Property; Ritual
Marx, Karl, 4, 21, 26, 61
Marx, Leo, 514
Marxism, 35–36 (readings); and language, 4
Maryland, 114, *115, 122,* 124, 129, *130,* 131, 137, 145–47; Robert Cole's plantation in, 185–97 passim

Massachusetts, 117, 123, 125, 131, 135, 161–62, 166–67, 172, 173, 178, 179, 263, 279, 338, 339, 387, 394, 399, 408–17 passim, 463–80 passim, 519–31 passim
Massachusetts Society for Promoting Agriculture, 529. *See also* Reform
Material, 18–19, 376; choice of for building, 133; decay-resistant, 133. *See also* Earthfast construction; Timber framing; Woods
Material culture, 3, 6, 8, 17, 18–19, 22, 27, 31, 83, 144, 148, 165; bibliography of works on, 34–37, 91–92; classification of, 19, 30–31; and cultural confrontation, 100–102; of death, 472, 479; definition of, 18–19, 22, 31; as methodology, 21, 23–27; as university subject, 8, 18. *See also* Architecture; Art; Culture; Furniture; Landscape; Language; Property
Material history, 3
Materialism, 514
Material life, 3–12 passim; definition of, 3–4, 5, 10; level of among Catawbas, 106; in New World, 117; standards of among laboring Philadelphians, 233–54; in Wethersfield, Connecticut, 263. *See also* Art; Braudel, Fernand; Economy; Exchange; Market; Property; Standard of living
Mather, Cotton, 347, 411, 467
Mather, Samuel, 468
Mathewes and others v. The Executors of Mathewes et al. (1762), 301
Mauss, Marcel, 6, 348
Mead, Margaret, 8
Meaning, 41, 64–65, 83, 85, 88; contested, 52; and landscape, 358, 372; of law, 432; of village, 163. *See also* Communication; Exchange; Myth; Structuralism; Structure; Value(s)
Meat, 319, 321, 327; distribution of, 322; packing of, 338; preparation of, 314, 315, 338; seasonal consumption of, 315; types of available (beef), 315–16, 323, 325, 523; (fish, foul, game), 317; (mutton), 316, 323; (pork), 313, 314–15, 321–23, 325, 328; (poultry), 316. *See also* Foodstuffs, Livestock
Meetinghouses, 12, 160, 162, *166,* 167, 346, 408–17, 466, 468, 469, 471
Memory: and architecture, 358; collective, 97; historical, 489; material environment and, 7
Memphis, Tennessee, 315

Menard, Russell R., 11, 554
Mentalité, 7; peasant, 149; of property-owning slaves, 221–22
Merchants, 248, 271, 276, 284, 285, 286, 296–97, 300, 304, 338, 339, 340, 342, 346, 348, 353n13, 372, 376, 442, 490, 497; and brick houses, 146; and credit, 294–95; as capitalist class, 377; impact on wealth structure, 5; as mediators of scarce resources, 10, 186; as owners of textile mills, 388, 389; in Salem, Massachusetts, 162; use of material environment by, 267, 270, 273. *See also* Capitalism; Economy; Landscape; Market; Power
Meriden, Connecticut, *166*
Merrell, James, 11, 554
Merrill, Michael, 393
Merrimack River, 389
Metaphor, 4, 28, 59n9; and art, 10, 85–88; biography as historical, 65; courtroom as, 49, 423–25; definition of, 52; doorways as, *344–45;* and ethnography, 53; interchangeability of, 52–53; of patriarchy, 50; sources of, 53; of village, 362. *See also* Body, human; Performance; Value(s)
Metonymy, 42
Middlesex Agricultural Society, 529
Middlesex County, Massachusetts, 465, 466, 469
Middletown, Connecticut, 287, 338, 340, 341, 348, 350
Militias, 188, 338, 339, 488–99 passim; drilling of, 176; training day of, 172
Miller, Amelia, 337
Mills: architecture of, 397; owners of, 385–400 passim; textile, 12, 74, 222, 335, 385–401 passim, *512, 514,* 527; workers in, 222, 385–401 passim. *See also* Capitalism: industrial; Paternalism; Strikes; Wages
Mind, 20, 64–65, 66; as culture, 9, 23, 29; primitive, 6; relativism of, 79; syntactic, 85; universal, 88; and vernacular threshold, 148. *See also* Culture; Lévi-Strauss, Claude; Myth; Structuralism
Ministers, 268, 339, 468, 474, 476. *See also* Beecher, Lyman; Bushnell, Horace; Finney, Charles Grandison; Mather, Cotton; Mather, Samuel; Stoddard, Solomon; Taylor, Edward; Whitefield, George; Willard, Samuel; Williams, Stephen
Mintz, Sidney, 225

Index

Reps, John W., 506, 514
Republican Party, 540
Revivalism, 540. *See also* Religion
Revolution: American, 69, 103, 105,
209–10, 234, 237, 239, 243, 247, 248,
250, 252, 254, 282, 298, 303, 342,
375, 376, 390, 394, 414, 442, 448,
456, 464, 488, 523; consumer, 3,
288, 336, 337; French, 489
Rhode Island, 135–36, 171, 172, 174,
178, *386*, 385–401 passim
Rice, 204–225 passim, 316; consumption of in South, 319
Riegl, Alois, 25, 34n15
Rippon v. Dawding (1769), 293–94
Rites of passage, 474
Ritual: baptism, 31, 472; confession,
430; cycle, 41; death, 464–80 passim; disruption of, 97; eucharist, 10;
function of, 176; gender and, 56–57;
of gentility, 277, 288; hospitality as,
364; of moral identification, 338;
New Year's, 178, 489; official, 173;
order of landscape, 98–99; of patriarchy, 175–77, 180; protests, 5; of purification, 175; sacred and secular,
42, 464; of social authority, 56–57,
429–33; of social inversion, 4, 491;
tea-drinking as, 440, 446. *See also*
Communitas; Inversion; Meaning;
Performance
Roads, 166
Roeber, A. G., 12, 364, 554
Romanticism, 74, 511, 530, 541
Romantic revival, 536, 541. *See also*
Morris, William; Nature; Style
Room use: cellars, 278; chambers, 265,
268, 276, 279, 281, 282, 283, 285,
286; closets, 278–79; dining rooms,
264, 277, 286, 364, 366, 543; garrets,
281; halls, 265, 275, 276, 282, 346,
542; kitchens, 265, 276, 278, 324,
360, 542–43; lean-tos, 265; libraries,
542; nurseries, 542; parlors, 264–65,
268, 273, 275, 281, 283, 285, 287,
288, 366, 542, 543; patterns in, 264,
359–60; placement of furniture and,
275; and room nomenclature, 287;
and sets of chairs, 279; specialization of in nineteenth century, 543.
See also Architecture; Furniture;
House(s); Inventories, probate
Roth, Rodris, 9, 12, 277, 554–55
Rothenberg, Winifred, 522
Roxbury, Massachusetts, 166
Ruskin, John, 87, 89, 536
Rutgers, Henry, *374, 376*
Rutman, Darrett, 408

St. Clement's Manor, St. Mary's
County, Maryland, 186
St. George, Robert Blair, 9, 11, 554
St. Helena Island, South Carolina, *225*
Salem, Massachusetts, 161, 173, 177
Salem Village (now Danvers), Massa-
chusetts, 162
Salmon, Marylynn, 11, 554
Sapelo Island, Georgia, *224*
Saponi Indians, migration of, 98
Sartre, Jean-Paul, 6, 66, 86, 87
Savannah, Georgia, 320
Schaats, Bartholomew, *342*
Schutz, Alfred, 61
Scituate, Massachusetts, 125
Seating, of meetinghouses in New En-
gland, 408–17
Second Great Awakening, 539. *See*
also Revivalism
Self-referentiality, 32. *See also* Art
Self-sufficiency, 191–92, 522
Semiotics, 22, 28, 32, 35 (readings), 84,
337, 352n5. *See also* Communica-
tion; Culture; Metaphor; Symbol-
ism
Sermons, 467, 468, 478
Servants, 118, 144, 172, 195, 250, 373,
412, 542; and courts, 430–32; inden-
tured, 193; male, 188–89. *See also*
Apprentices; Labor; Slaves
Settings, 54–55; of Virginia society,
358–68 passim
Settlements: dispersed, 161–62, *163*,
165, 166; and factionalism, 48;
linear form of, 163; marriage, 11,
292–306; nucleated, 163–65, 168n8,
346–47; patterns of in New England
villages, 159–66; patterns of Virginia
plantations as, 362. *See also* Land-
scape; Plantation(s); Towns; Trusts;
Villages; Widows
Sewall, Samuel, 441
Seymour, Connecticut, 175
Shame, ritual use of, 430, 431. *See also*
Gossip; Ritual
Sharecropping, 224, 327, 332n142
Shaw, Major Samuel, 452
Shays' Rebellion, 346. *See also* Protest,
popular
Shenandoah Valley, 360–61
Shippen, Nancy, 444, 445, 448
Shoemakers, 267, 276, 390; household
budget of, 250; in Philadelphia, 235,
239, 250–52; and poor relief, 251–
52. *See also* Artisans; Journeymen;
Labor
Shoes, 193, 252; domestic production
of, 197; price index of, 239, 243,

250–51, 259n99. *See also* Lynn,
Massachusetts
Simms, Norman, 497
Situation, definition of, 50, 52
Skill, as basis of power, 350; devaluation of, 498. *See also* Artisans
Slater, Samuel, 387, 389, 392, 393,
394; house of, *389*
Slater Mill, *388*, 391, 392, 397
Slavery, 11, 77, 99, 106; flexibility of
task system, 217; gang system in,
204–7, 209, 216; task system in,
203–25
Slaves, 42, 43, 48, 50, 100, 103, 144,
212, 213, 214, 215, 250, 295, 296,
304, 314, 316, 319, 341, 373, 426,
432; attitudes of, 220–21; Caribbean, 223; and church attendance,
55, 222, 366; and courts, 430–32;
driver, *212, 213*, 216; economic activities of, 208; emancipation of,
217, 223, 328; foodways of, 208,
321–25, 328, 361; gardens of, 323,
361; housing, *358, 359, 360, 367*; internal economy of, 220–21; and labor system, 204; landscape of, 364–
67; and property ownership in lowcountry, 218–22; religion of, 51. *See*
also African heritage; Afro-Amer-
ican(s); House(s): slave; Labor; Property; Servants
Slums, *379*. *See also* Tenements
Slye, Robert, 186
Smith, Adam, 194
Smith, Billy G., 11, 555
Smith, John, 95, 106, 130, 131, 149
Socialization process, in black coronation festivals, 172, 176–77
Society, 22, 72–73; on Caribbean plantations, 204; definition of, 22, 72; as
dynamic product, 40; in early Chesapeake region, 143, 196; English
aristocratic, 292; imperfection of,
74–75; rank, 408. *See also* Class;
Culture
Society of the Cincinnati, 452
Soil: in Concord, Massachusetts, 523,
524; quality of in early Maryland,
186–87
South, American: as cultural region,
312; foodways of before Civil War,
312–28. *See also* Regional Culture
South Carolina, 11, 69, 97, 102, 105,
118, 204–225 passim, 293–306 passim, 312, 317, 319; aristocracy of,
297
South Carolina Court of Chancery, 294
Southern Claims Commission, 219

Towns, 159–60, 168n24; planning of, 30; secular centers of, 347; system in New England, 161
Townshend, Dr. David, 452
Townshend Acts, 442
Trade, 4, 522; as basis of material prosperity, 276; effects of on Catawba–white relations, 105–6; financial risks of, 297–98; foreign, 191, 440; fur-, 338; goods, 100; of horses among slaves, 213–14; importance of salt in pre-contact American Indian trade, 107n53; as indication of social position, 297; itinerant, with slaves, 208; relationships in New England towns, 165; between slaves and freemen, 208. *See also* Communication; Economy; Exchange; Market; Merchants
Tradition, 12, 105; in African food production, 208, 324; coercive use of, 347–48; as determinant of furniture usage, 264; folk, 164, 180; moral reformation of, 5; oppositional, 387; oral, 8; tea-drinking as, 440. *See also* Communication; Performance; Style
Traditional foodways, 11, 208, 312–28 passim
Traditional forms, persistence of in culture, 275, 287
Traditional knowledge, 4
Traditional moral code, 351
Transformation: of Chesapeake society, 117; of culture, 6; in ritual, 173. *See also* Metaphor; Structuralism
Translation, 40. *See also* Ethnography; Fieldwork
Transportation of produce, 527. *See also* Foodstuffs; Railroad
Trinity Church Farm, New York, 373, *374, 376, 379*
Trustees, power of in controlling property, 298
Trusts, to protect inheritance, 292, 294, 296, 300
Tunno v. Trezevant (1804), 294–95, 297
Tylor, E. B., 6
Typification, 53
Tyrrel v. Hope (1743), 300–301

University professors, 8
University programs in material culture study, 8, 18
Upton, Dell, 9, 11, 555–56
Urban society, 234–55 passim, 326, 371–82 passim, 509–16 passim

Utopia Leasehold, James City County, Virginia, 124, *132*

Value(s): acceleration and intensification of, 9–10; aesthetic, 20, 33n2; appraised, 263; asserted by artifacts, 337; community, 346; conflicting, 350; cultural, 64, 353n6, 420, 536; of estate and buildings, 149; of estates, 195; iconic or associational, 20; inherent and attached, 19–20; labor, 375; of land, 198n12, 376; of Maryland plantation assets, 195; middle-class, 547; preindustrial, 387; of tobacco as currency, 190, 198n10; use, 20, 375. *See also* Beliefs; Culture; Myth; Structure
Vance, James, 376
Vaux, Calvin, 514, 541
Vegetables, consumed in South, 319, 321, 323–25
Veracity of evidence, in artifact analysis, 20–21
Vermont, 337
Vernacular architecture; *see* Architecture; Churches; Courthouses; Furniture; House(s); Meetinghouses
Vernacular objects, 20
Vernacular threshold: in architecture, 134, 135, 148; in mind, 148
Villages, 159, 160, *162,* 164, 167; definition of, 160; establishment of: (Beverly, Billerica, Lynn, Manchester, Salem, Massachusetts), 161–62; (East Haven, Connecticut), 163–64; 166; mill, 400; nucleated, 346, 464–65; southern plantations as, 362. *See also* Community; Settlements; Towns
Virginia, 54, 100, 101, 114, *115,* 123–24, 131, 136, 145, 147, 312, 313, 318, 321, 357–68 passim, 419–33 passim, 442, 446
Virginia Gazette, 420

Wade, Melvin, 11, 556
Wages, 194, 217, 222, 234–35, 243–54 passim, 376, 377, 379, 392, 395–98; regulation of, 389. *See also* Money; Labor; Strikes; Women
"Walking city," 372, 379
Wallingford, Connecticut, 163
Walsh, Lorena S., 9, 11, 556
Wampum, functions of, 7
Warhol, Andy, 68
Warner, Sam Bass, 234, 372, 544
War of 1812, 396, 490
Washington, Booker T., 360

Washington, George, 187, 362, 444
Water, symbolic meaning of, 479. *See also* Baptism
Water rights, 387, 394
Watertown, Connecticut, 545
Watertown, Massachusetts, 161, 410, 414, 466
Webb, Joseph, Jr., 262, 340–41, 342
Weddings, celebrations of in South, 323. *See also* Family; Marriage; Settlements
Wenham, Massachusetts, 414
West Indies: gang system of slave labor in, 216; sugar plantations in, 205, 206–7, 319. *See also* Slavery; Slaves
Westmoreland County, Virginia, 427, 429
Wethersfield, Connecticut, 175, 261–88 passim, 338, 340–41, 346
Wheat: advantages of, 147–48; cultivation of in early Chesapeake, 146–47; use of in southern foodways, 318. *See also* Bread
Wheeler, Gervase, 541
Whipple, Oliver M., 508
Whitefield, George, 470
Whitman, Walt, 66, 67, 71, 79
Whittier, John Greenleaf, 512–13
Widows, 143, 236, 248, 281, 303, 304, 305, 306, 372–73, 378; and probate, 262; and property, 292. *See also* Gender; Settlements; Women
Wigwam, 117, 119
Wilkinson, Oziel, 388, 389, 390, 392
Wilkinson Mill, Pawtucket, Rhode Island, *388*
Willard, Samuel, 343
Williams, Israel, 339, 346, 414
Williams, Raymond, 337
Williams, Stephen, 346, 349
Williamsburg, Virginia, 365, 420, 421, 431
Willis, Edmund, 376
Wills, inability of *femes covert* to write, 292, 302, 303. *See also* Settlements; Women
Wilson, Dr. John S., 314
Wilton, Connecticut, 164
Winterthur Portfolio, 18
Winthrop, John, 161, 338, 346, 347
Wolcott, Roger, 341, 348
Women, 173, 174, 339, 378; in Afro-American society, 180; attitudes of toward property control, 304; ballad singer, 78; boycotting tea, *443;* in business, 298–99, 304, 306; changing status of, 307n9; clothing of in Philadelphia, 205; in cloth-making